C++Builder™ 5 Developer's Guide

Jarrod Hollingworth
Dan Butterfield
Bob Swart
Jamie Allsop

201 West 103rd St., Indianapolis, Indiana, 46290 USA

C++Builder™ 5 Developer's Guide

Copyright © 2001 by Sams Publishing

International Standard Book Number: 0-672-31972-1

Library of Congress Catalog Card Number: 00-102818

Printed in the United States of America

First Printing: November 2000

03 02 01 00   4   3   2   1

Trademarks

Warning and Disclaimer

ASSOCIATE PUBLISHER
Michael Stephens

ACQUISITIONS EDITOR
Carol Ackerman

DEVELOPMENT EDITOR
Robyn Thomas

MANAGING EDITOR
Matt Purcell

PROJECT EDITOR
Andrew Beaster

INDEXERS
Sandy Henselmeier
Eric Schroeder

PROOFREADERS
Candice Hightower
Jessica McCarty

TECHNICAL EDITORS
Peter Nunn
Paul Strickland
John Thomas
Eamonn Wallace

TEAM COORDINATOR
Pamalee Nelson

MEDIA DEVELOPERS
William Eland
Matt Bates

INTERIOR DESIGNER
Ann Jones

COVER DESIGNER
Ann Jones

LAYOUT TECHNICIANS
Ayanna Lacey
Heather Hiatt Miller
Stacey Richwine-DeRome

Overview

Contents

About the Authors

Major Authors

Jarrod Hollingworth

Jarrod has been professionally programming since 1993. He is now running his own business, Backslash (http://www.backslash.com.au), developing software applications for the Internet and key business sectors and working as a software development consultant. He has a solid background in C/C++ programming in the telecommunications industry and assisted in the development of the world's first live operator–answered GSM (digital mobile) short-messaging system.

Starting in 1985 as a self-taught hobbyist programmer in BASIC and Assembly, he moved to Pascal and C/C++ through completion of a bachelor of science degree in computing at Deakin University in Australia. His professional roles in software development have ranged from programmer to software department manager.

With several years of experience in C++Builder and Delphi and having worked on project teams using Microsoft Visual C++, he believes that with few exceptions C++Builder is the best tool for developing Windows applications.

Jarrod lives in Melbourne, Australia, with his wife, Linda. His other major interests include traveling and cycling. Jarrod can be contacted at jarrod@backslash.com.au.

Dan Butterfield

Dan is currently writing mathematical modeling and geographical information system (GIS) software for environmental applications in the Aquatic Environments Research Centre (AERC) at the University of Reading in the UK. As sole software developer for the research center, Dan works closely with colleagues to provide implementations of ground-breaking water quality modeling and data visualization software. INCA (Integrated Nitrogen in Catchments), the latest incarnation of an original nitrogen model, is in use worldwide and is undergoing continual development. Dan started programming in BASIC at age 12 and has programmed professionally in REXX, Fortran, Pascal, C, and now C++. All of Dan's development work over the past two years has been exclusively with Borland C++Builder.

Bob Swart

Bob Swart (*aka* Dr. Bob—http://www.drbob42.com) is a senior technical consultant using Delphi, C++Builder, and JBuilder (and soon Kylix) for TAS Advanced Technologies (http://www.tas-at.com) in Best, The Netherlands. Bob is a freelance technical author for

The Delphi Magazine, Delphi Developer, UK-BUG NewsLetter, and *SDGN Magazine*. He is a coauthor of *The Revolutionary Guide to Delphi 2, Delphi 4 Unleashed,* and *C++Builder 4 Unleashed*. Bob has spoken at Borland conferences all over the world.

Jamie Allsop

Jamie lives in Northern Ireland. Mostly self-taught, he has used a variety of languages, but C++ is his language of choice. He has used C++Builder since it was first released, and it is his preferred development tool. He has a degree in electronic engineering and is currently doing research. He also runs his own software company, Shiying, with his wife and has developed components for communication and real-time DSP applications. Other interests include football (the using-feet kind) and badminton.

Contributing Authors

Rob Allen

Rob lives in London, UK. He has a degree in electronic engineering but has spent the last five years programming with Borland C++ 4.5 and 5 and C++Builder 3. Rob has experience writing test and measurement tools for the mobile phone industry.

Khalid Almannai

Khalid lives in Bahrain. He started programming with Borland C++ 4.5, and his knowledge of programming languages includes C, C++, BASIC, and Delphi. He has two years of experience with C++Builder.

Drew Avis

Drew Avis is a technical writer specializing in online documentation. He lives in Merrickville, Ontario, and currently works for Nortel Networks. Drew has worked for small and large software companies, and he has developed and taught a technical writing course for engineers at the University of Calgary. In his spare time Drew brews beer, plays hockey, and works on his homebrew recipe software StrangeBrew.

Jay Banks

Jay lives in the UK. He has been a programming enthusiast since he was 11 and has programming experience in a number of areas, including accounting, machine control, security, components, games, educational, and databases. His C++Builder experience is varied.

Eduardo Bezerra

Eduardo lives in Rio de Janeiro, Brazil. He has been programming for 19 years and has extensive experience in C++ development. Eduardo started programming with Borland Turbo C and has worked with all Borland C/C++ compilers up to C++Builder. He owns a small company specializing in consulting services and development for business areas such as the Internet and telecommunications. He has been working with COM for four years, integrating systems and creating solutions for distributed environments.

Phillip H. Blanton II

Phillip attended the University of Northern Colorado, where he studied physics and computer science. He has been programming personal computers with Borland tools since 1987. Over the past 13 years he has worked in a number of technical roles, including network administrator, IS department director, database application developer, and network security specialist. He is currently a senior software engineer with TurboPower Software in Colorado Springs. He lives in the mountains surrounding Woodland Park, Colorado, with his wife Mary Ann, two daughters Daly and Sydney, and Harley the Wonder Dog. You can reach him via email at phillipb@turbopower.com.

Joe Bonavita

Joe lives in Connecticut and has been programming for 14 years, three of those years in C++Builder. Joe started programming when he was 14 on a Commodore 64 and is a self-taught programmer. He graduated to the PC, then to BASIC, Assembler, and C++. Joe started using C++Builder beginning with version 1. Thanks to his wife, who gives him the support needed to keep moving forward in the ever-changing field of programming, he is learning other languages and contributing to books such as this one. Joe believes that books like this are very beneficial to self-starters.

J. Alan Brogan

Alan lives in Kerry, Ireland. He has been programming and teaching for more than 10 years and is currently leading a team developing software within the telecommunications industry. Alan has used other languages but prefers the simplicity and elegance of C and C++. He has always preferred Borland's IDEs and still uses Turbo C, but he spends most of his programming day with C++Builder.

Mark Cashman

Mark is a professional software developer with experience in a variety of industries, ranging from insurance to manufacturing, to geographic information systems for bulk product delivery. His specialties include computer/human interaction, relational databases, component-based software, object-oriented development, and Web site/Web software development, including his own site, The Temporal Doorway, whose C++Builder section can be found at `http://www.temporaldoorway.com/programming/index.htm`. He has been a methodology consultant, a developer, and a manager and is currently Senior Software Developer for V-Technologies, LLC, a vendor of shipping-oriented middleware. Mark is a member of Borland TeamB, an association of official but unpaid newsgroup support people, selected for their knowledge of Borland products and willingness to help other developers. He is also an award-winning artist, a published author of science fiction (currently working on his third novel) and nonfiction (including several articles for *C++Builder Developer's Journal*), a composer of computer-based fusion music, and a rock climber with several first ascents to his credit.

Damon Chandler

Damon has been programming for more than 15 years. Mostly self-taught, he followed a common path to C++ programming: GW-BASIC, Pascal, then C++. Damon is an engineer by trade and a programmer at heart. He is currently working in the Visual Communications Lab at Cornell University, where his research primarily centers around wavelet image compression. C++Builder is his tool of choice, and he has recently been made a member of TeamB.

Jeppe Cramon

Jeppe lives in Copenhagen, Denmark. He has been programming for seven years, starting out on Pascal, then moving on to C++, Visual Basic, Java, and C#. Jeppe has been using C++Builder the last four years and has recently started working with XML, ASP, DHTML, COM, and .NET programming. Jeppe holds an engineering degree in electronics and computer science. Besides running a small consulting firm, Jeppe also contributes to the Bytamin-C Web site (`http://www.bytamin-c.com`) and has developed a free WinZip clone—Jzip—and an arcade game—B.U.G.S.—for OS/2 and Windows. Jeppe is also an enthusiastic skier and drummer in his sparse spare time.

Mark Davey

Mark lives in Hampshire, England. He has been writing software professionally since his teens and has been using C++Builder for two years. He has been mostly involved in writing real-time embedded control systems for broadcasting applications with leading UK broadcast engineering companies and is currently developing radio communication systems. Mark also has a private enterprise in data logging systems for the motorsport industry, developing exclusively with C++Builder. He is deeply interested in music, art, and technology. He is shortly to be married to Sarah.

Paul Gustavson

Paul lives in Virginia and is a senior systems engineer for Synetics, Inc. (http://www.synetics.com), a U.S.-based company providing knowledge management, systems engineering, and enterprise management services. Paul supports a wide variety of advanced distributive simulation efforts within the DoD community and is an experienced software developer specializing in C++Builder. He also is a partner in SimVentions (http://www.simventions.com), an upstart company developing and leveraging existing technologies and techniques to create innovative applications and solutions that engage the mind and further knowledge. Paul has been developing applications for the Windows environment since the introduction of Windows 3.1 (1993), and he has published and presented over a dozen technical papers for the Simulation Interoperability Standards Organization (http://www.sisostds.org).

John MacSween

John graduated from Glasgow University with an honours degree in naval architecture and ocean engineering. He presently works for Henry Abram & Sons Ltd, a project cargo and heavy lift shipping company in Glasgow, Scotland. John has been programming since the age of 14 and has used BASIC, Fortran, and C++. He has been programming in C++Builder for approximately one and a half years and uses it to create various in-house engineering applications. John may be contacted at j.a.macsween@henryabram.co.uk or http://www.redrival.com/mandtsoftware/.

Stéphane Mahaux

Stéphane runs his own software consulting company, Hyperian Development Solutions (http://www.hyperian.ab.ca), in Edmonton, Canada. He started programming before the Windows 3 era and has been programming professionally for more than 10 years. He has been using C++Builder since version 1. Stéphane also has lived in France, where he managed a business specializing in database tools. He wrote a monthly column in *Point DBF* magazine about database programming in various development tools.

William Morrison

Hooked on Borland products since being introduced to Turbo Pascal 7 in high school, Bill has been programming professionally with C++Builder and Delphi for more than three years. Bill has written predictive dialers and standard business applications using C++Builder and is experienced with ISAPIs, APIs, and C/S database design. He assists new C++Builder and Delphi users through the Undernet IRC help channels and can be seen occasionally contributing on the various Borland Usenet groups. Bill is currently vice president of Software Development for CXC Consulting (http://www.cxcca.com), located in sunny Southern California. Bill wishes to thank Jason Wharton (IBObjects) and Jeff Overcash (IBX) for their assistance with the InterBase sections in this book, showing just what a great group of programmers InterBase has supporting it.

Ionel Munoz

Ionel lives in Quebec. His current occupation is as a senior software analyst at EXFO, a leading manufacturer of fiber optics test equipment. His job involves developing architectures and frameworks, most of them based on COM/DCOM. Ionel started programming in Turbo Pascal in 1990 and C++ in 1992, and he has used C++Builder since version 1. He has developed applications in many areas, including games, components, Java applets, client/server databases, data acquisition systems, and multimedia. He has been developing with COM since 1995 and is experienced in using ATL in both VC++ and C++Builder. He has contributed to Borland's CodeCentral source code database, with several COM-related examples. His interests beyond computer science are traditional karate, books, and music. Ionel has a wife, Sylvia, and a daughter, Marietta.

Jean Pariseau

Jean works as a chef at a prestigious New England country club while attending college at the Community College of Rhode Island, where he's about to receive his associates degree in engineering. Jean has been programming for about 14 years, starting on a Commodore 64 and working up through the Amiga platform and now Windows-based machines. Mostly self taught, Jean works with C++, Pascal/Delphi, Assembler, Lisp, and Java. Jean's programming interests revolve around computer algebra, numerical methods, computational fluid dynamics, and compiler design.

Pete Pedersen

Pete lives in Logan, Utah, and has been programming professionally for over 30 years. He has used Borland's tools for about eight years, and C++Builder since version 1. During his career, he has been an international consultant and the founder of a software company (BlueLine Software) and has written articles for trade publications. He is currently employed by Spiricon, a leader in laser diagnostics. When not working, he enjoys spending time with his family. He and his nine-year-old son, Cameron, are collaborating on a programming book for kids, using C++Builder.

Ruurd F. Pels

Ruurd works in the Netherlands as an IT consultant for TAS Advanced Technologies B.V. His main area of expertise is software engineering, particularly in C++. He is a regular contributor to Dr. Bob's C++Builder Gate (http://www.drbob42.com/Cbuilder/) and occasionally publishes reviews and articles. He can be reached at ruurd@worldonline.nl. Ruurd is married to Angelien and the father of two sons, Ruben and Daniël.

Sean Rock

Sean lives in Bolton, UK. He is originally from San Diego, California, but has lived in the UK for the past five and a half years. Sean started programming in college using Pascal and has taught himself Delphi and C/C++. Sean uses computer programming primarily as a hobby but does take on freelance work for local companies. He has been using C++Builder for about two years and just recently started the Component Writer's Guide Web site, dedicated to writing VCL components, which can be found at http://www.componentwriter.co.uk.

Simon Rutley-Frayne

Simon lives in Devon, UK. He began programming with C++Builder just over two years ago and soon after started Casimo Software (http://www.casimosoftware.co.uk), developing shareware software and components. Simon runs his own computer consultancy business and is the Components/Applications and Books editor of TheBits (http://www.thebits.org), where he is responsible for component and book reviews and updates.

Vikash Shah

Vikash lives in Middlesex, England. Since earning his degree in mathematics and computer science, he has gained three years professional C++ experience, including two years with C++Builder.

Malcolm Smith

Malcolm lives in Australia. He is a self-taught programmer working as an analyst programmer, developing customized MIS solutions for the printing industry, and device drivers for monitoring and surveillance equipment in the security industry. He also runs his own business, MJ Freelancing, developing encryption, anti-piracy, and other tools and components.

Keith Turnbull II

A graduate of Michigan State University, Keith has been in network programming since 1991. He has worked on a range of products, from online games to insurance enrollment software. He is currently the vice president of client/server development for Intercanvas Design, Inc. Keith lives in Des Moines, Iowa, with his wife, two dogs, three cats, and four computers.

Chris Winters

Chris lives in Richmond, Virginia. He has been programming for six years, two years professionally. Although fluent in C/C++, Chris has used BASIC, HTML, Java, Assembly, MS Access, and Delphi. He started with Turbo C++ (DOS) and has been using C++Builder since version 1. Chris currently works for PSINet, one of the world's largest and most experienced providers of IP-based communications services for business. He has two kids, Lauren Ashley and Collin Mason. He also writes system utilities and shareware programs and experiments with new Win32 APIs. You can visit him at http://www.encomsysware.com.

William Woodbury

Bill has been programming since he was 12. He has used a variety of languages, including ADA, BASIC, Pascal, Java, C/C++, and Assembly, and he currently uses C++Builder. He has written graphics applications, games, and networking applications.

Siu-Fan Wu

Siu-Fan obtained his bachelor of science degree in physics and his Ph.D. in electronic and electrical engineering from the Univerity of Surrey in the UK. He worked for the Canon Research Centre (UK) as a research scientist on sound field visualization and then as a lecturer at Singapore Polytechnic. Currently he is a lecturer at the Hong Kong Institute of Vocational Education, teaching mainly microprocessors and instrumentation. His research interests include image processing, compression, and retrieval. He has been programming with Borland C and C++Builder for about nine years.

Yoto Yotov

Yoto Yotov is currently studying in Montreal. Often working with C++Builder, he has continuously explored it since its first appearance. He has published articles in various technical journals and Web sites.

Zexiang Wu

Zexiang Wu has been programming with Borland C++ for ten years. Her recent work has focused on interface programming. Away from work, she enjoys backpacking, classical and folk dancing, and she especially enjoys sampling food from different countries; her favorites are from southern China where she originates.

Dedications

Jarrod Hollingworth

I dedicate this book to my wife, Linda. Throughout the many long days and late nights, her love, support, understanding, and acceptance of my constant phrase "another 15 minutes" (an hour and a half in the real world) have made this book possible.

Dan Butterfield

To my family.

Bob Swart

For Yvonne, Erik, and Natasha.

Jamie Allsop

To Wenmay (Wu Ze Xiang), who never lost faith.

Acknowledgments

Jarrod Hollingworth

First I'd like to thank Dan Butterfield. From concept to completion, Dan shared the author-side organizational tasks with me. With more than 30 contributing authors, these tasks were very demanding, and the time and effort that Dan invested in them is extremely appreciated. I'm sure that Dan would agree that it was quite a challenge!

This book has opened my eyes to the fact that the publishing process is very involved indeed. As the acquisitions editor, Carol Ackerman took the book onboard and managed the manuscript submissions and the overall schedule. Robyn Thomas was the development editor for this book. Her eagle eye for quality and content-related issues ensured that the book as a whole is more than the sum of its parts. It was a pleasure working with both Carol and Robyn. I'd also like to thank technical editors Paul Strickland, John Thomas, Peter Nunn, and Eamonn Wallace for their attention to detail, copy editors Gene Redding and Pat Kinyon (who, with their superior knowledge of English, improved the grammar in just about every paragraph), project editor Andrew Beaster, and all other staff at Macmillan.

For their assistance with various issues in writing my topics, I'd like to thank Charlie Calvert, Michael Swindell, Tim Del Chiaro, John Wiegley, Lee Cantey, Maurice Barnum, David Marancik, Karen Giles, John Kaster, and David Intersimone at Borland and Kent Reisdorph and Per Larsen at Turbopower Software Company.

Finally I'd like to thank each and every author in this book, but in particular Bob Swart, Jamie Allsop, Ionel Munoz, and Vikash Shah, who showed exceptional commitment and enthusiasm. With such a large breadth of experience, each author has donated a piece of his knowledge to make this book an invaluable resource for C++Builder developers.

Dan Butterfield

I would like to thank (in no particular order):

The directors of the AERC, Professor Paul Whitehead and Dr. Penny Johnes, for their patience and understanding on those occasions when book deadlines interfered with my day job. My colleagues and friends, for their interest and support, but especially Brian Cox, Andrew Wade, Hannah Prior, Steve Gurney and of course Cam Sans, who helped keep me sane. Matt Roberts and Andrew Burns for invaluable Web site help and advice. Erika Meller and Heather Browning for their image manipulation and graphic design skills. Nicola Tuson and Joan Bachelor for helping out with online chat transcriptions.

Everyone at Macmillan, but especially Carol Ackerman, Robyn Thomas, Andrew Beaster, and Paul Strickland, who all had to work incredibly hard to make this book a reality.

Finally, a huge thank you to Jarrod for getting this whole thing started (and for all those late night/early morning Internet chats ;o), and to all the authors involved—your commitment and patience astounded me daily. Thanks guys!

Bob Swart

I need to thank Yvonne for putting up with me writing yet another set of chapters. The phrase "almost done" slowly lost its meaning to her.

Also, thanks to Jarrod and Dan for putting this book together—without you, it wouldn't be the same.

Jamie Allsop

It goes without saying that I am eternally grateful to both Jarrod and Dan. I want to thank you for taking on a task that few can comprehend the enormity of. Because you believed that a book could be written, I (and the other authors) also believed it could be done. I would also like to thank you for your continued encouragement throughout the project; it made the long hours I spent writing and coding worth it and even helped get some chapters finished. Thank you for helping me realize a dream.

I want to thank all the authors of the book; if any one of you had not written the sections you did, the book would never have made it to maturity.

I would like to thank all the editors at Sams for the excellent work that they put into the book to ensure it is of high quality. I especially would like to thank development editor Robyn Thomas for all her heading suggestions and comments that greatly helped to shape the sections that I wrote. I would also like to thank Paul E. Strickland, one of the technical editors, for his comments and suggestions. Gene Redding and Pat Kinyon also deserve a mention for the excellent work they put into copy editing the chapters I was involved with. Your attention to detail is incredible.

I would like to thank my family and friends for their support, patience, and understanding throughout the time I have been involved in the book, notably my twin brother Kristin, my mum Norah, my dad Terry, and my friends Hong and Kendo.

Finally, and most importantly, I would like to thank my wife, Wenmay, who supported and cared for me throughout the writing of the book. She continually encouraged me and didn't mind when I had to put the book first; believe me, that happened very often! Without her, my contribution would surely have been much smaller.

Tell Us What You Think!

As the reader of this book, *you* are our most important critic and commentator. We value your opinion and want to know what we're doing right, what we could do better, what areas you'd like to see us publish in, and any other words of wisdom you're willing to pass our way.

As an Associate publisher for Sams, I welcome your comments. You can fax, email, or write me directly to let me know what you did or didn't like about this book—as well as what we can do to make our books stronger.

Please note that I cannot help you with technical problems related to the topic of this book, and that due to the high volume of mail I receive, I might not be able to reply to every message.

When you write, please be sure to include this book's title and author as well as your name and phone or fax number. I will carefully review your comments and share them with the author and editors who worked on the book.

Fax: (317) 581-4770

Email: samsfeedback@macmillanusa.com

Mail: Michael Stephens
       Sams Publishing
       201 West 103rd Street
       Indianapolis, IN 46290 USA

Introduction

This has been an extremely interesting project on which to work. Our goal seemed simple—to produce a new book for C++Builder 5 that covered not only material new to version 5, but also techniques and topics not covered anywhere else.

The book was born on "The Bits" (http://www.thebits.org) C++Builder technical discussion list with an email from Jarrod Hollingworth in mid-November 1999:

> Well I've just returned from the Australia & New Zealand BorCon99 and it was fantastic. They showed a lot of great enhancements to all products and the tutorials and sessions were very informative…great stuff. I don't think that it's likely that there will be a C++*Builder 5 Unleashed* book…

This revelation was a disappointment to everyone subscribed to The Bits list because not only have the *Unleashed* books proved invaluable resources, but they are often the only readily available C++Builder reference books (the bundled Borland "Teach Yourself …" and "Developer's Guide" manuals aside).

It gradually became clear that several list subscribers had been considering writing articles on their particular areas of expertise, and so the project was born. Our first task was to decide what kind of book we should write and what topics the C++Builder community would like to see in it. To this end, the original Web site (dubbed "The C++Builder Book Writers' Guild") was set up, complete with online survey. We advertised the survey on the most active C++Builder discussion lists and newsgroups. The results from this survey and from online discussions (which can be found on the book's Web site at http://www.bcb5book.force9.co.uk) helped shape the book.

So, here we are with the final product. The book has been written by 34 authors from all over the world, in countries including Australia, Bahrain, Brazil, Canada, Denmark, Hong Kong, Ireland, the Netherlands, the UK, and the U.S. Each author contributed topics in his area of expertise and managed this task using email, online chats, and the Web site (and the occasional telephone call). All of the authors have full professional and personal lives and have somehow managed to work on the book in the little spare time that they have. The majority of the authors have little or no professional writing experience, though you may recognize the names of several authors from other C++Builder and Delphi books, as TeamB newsgroup members, or hosts of C++Builder-related Web sites.

It has, of course, been very hard work. At the time of writing, the project organizers have collectively spent well over 600 hours, sent over 2,000 emails, and received over 3,500 emails on organizational matters alone. It has been an incredibly rewarding experience, and hopefully, the brief history of the project given here will persuade you that there is nothing magical about technical book writing—you can do it, too. We hope that we have created a book that users of all versions of C++Builder will find useful in the development of all types of applications. We have worked hard to include topics and techniques not covered in any other book and have done our best to cover the majority of features new to C++Builder 5. Above all, we hope that, through the unique way in which the book has been written, we have adhered to the C++Builder/Delphi ethos: sharing of knowledge.

Important Things to Note

Because of the way this book was written, with so many authors and over a relatively short time period, there are bound to be differences in writing styles between, and perhaps even within, chapters. We (the authors and a team of editors at Sams) have all worked hard to reduce the impact of this, but it is bound to be obvious in places.

As with all technical books, and despite our best efforts, it is inevitable that there will be the occasional error in the text and accompanying program code. In light of this, we shall maintain a list of errata on the book Web site at http://www.bcb5book.force9.co.uk and on the Sams Web site at http://www.samspublishing.com. You can also email bug reports and general queries/comments to feedback@bcb5book.f9.co.uk.

The Companion CD-ROM

The companion CD-ROM contains all of the example code and C++Builder projects from the book. The code is organized by chapter and can be accessed from a custom-built interface. Some of the chapter folders also contain README.TXT files that provide important information about the projects in that chapter. These include chapters 13, 15, 16, 18, and 19.

There are also many freeware, shareware, demo and trial components, and applications that should be of interest to C++Builder users. These may also be viewed from the interface to the CD-ROM. To ensure that the CD-ROM list of contents is up to date, it is supplied as a README.TXT file in the CD-ROM's root directory.

A Word of Thanks

During the course of the project, the list of contributing authors changed regularly as other commitments took priority and topics were added or altered. We'd like to take this opportunity to thank everyone who volunteered to help but were unable to see the book through to completion. We are particularly grateful to Rick Malik, the creator (and host) of the original book Web site, who put in a lot of time and effort during the initial stages of the project.

Who Should Read This Book?

This book is not a C++ primer, nor is it a tutorial on using C++Builder, the application. Rather, it is a guide to using C++Builder to create better, larger, more complex applications, to help expand your current C++Builder skills, and to investigate the features new to C++Builder 5.

If you already have experience developing applications with C++Builder, are looking to upgrade from version 4 to version 5, or want to build on your current knowledge, this book is for you. That said, there is a natural, rapid progression through most of the chapters and through the book as a whole. This should even make the book useful to C++Builder beginners as, although the book was originally intended to be for intermediate/advanced readers only, the final product has proved to be accessible to readers of all levels despite the advanced nature of the topics.

C++Builder System Requirements

C++Builder 5 Developer's Guide is written, for the most part, for users of C++Builder version 5. Most of the text and example code, however, is applicable to C++Builder version 4 as well. Table I.1 shows the applicability of various versions of C++Builder.

TABLE I.1 Percentage of This Book That Is Applicable to Different Versions of C++Builder

C++Builder Version	Applicability
C++Builder 5 Enterprise	100%
C++Builder 5 Professional	94%
C++Builder 5 Standard	77%
C++Builder 4 Enterprise	84%
C++Builder 4 Professional	79%

Although most of the code in the book should work with C++Builder version 4 (except version 5 specifics, of course), a lot of the C++Builder project files on the CD-ROM that accompanies this book will be in version 5 format. Because this format is incompatible with C++Builder version 4, it will be necessary for version 4 users to create new projects, insert code from the companion CD-ROM, and add forms and properties as appropriate.

The minimum system requirements for C++Builder 5 Enterprise are as follows:

- Intel Pentium 90 or higher (P166 recommended)
- Microsoft Windows 2000, Windows 95, 98, or NT4.0 with Service Pack 3 or later

- 32MB RAM (64MB recommended)
- Hard disk space: 253MB for compact install, 388MB for full install
- CD-ROM drive
- VGA or higher resolution monitor
- Mouse or other pointing device

How This Book Is Organized

This book is organized into seven parts. The first five parts have been arranged with natural progression in mind. These cover topics ranging from C++Builder and C++ techniques through communications, database, Web and distributed programming, to advanced, more general programming topics such as OpenGL programming and software installation/distribution. The last two parts contain C++Builder hints, tips, how-tos, an example real-world application, and other recommended sources of C++Builder information.

The parts of the book are as follows:

- **Part I: "C++Builder 5 Essentials"**—This part, consisting of Chapters 1–11, contains everything you need to know to make the best use of C++Builder 5 when developing applications. This includes an introduction to C++Builder and the Integrated Development Environment (Chapters 1 and 2); advice on C++ programming and software development with C++Builder (Chapters 3–5); compiling, optimizing, and debugging considerations (Chapters 6 and 7); and comprehensive information on using and writing VCL components (Chapters 8–11).

- **Part II: "Communications, Database, and Web Programming"**—This part, consisting of Chapters 12–14, covers many aspects of communications, database, and Web programming. This includes serial communications and Internet protocols (Chapter 12); WebBroker, InternetExpress, and XML programming (Chapter 13); and database programming, particularly ADO Express, InterBase Express, the new Data Module Designer, and a discussion of database architecture options (Chapter 14).

- **Part III: "Interfaces and Distributed Computing"**—This part, consisting of Chapters 15–22, provides detailed information on all aspects of interfaces and distributed computing. This includes using and writing DLLs, C++Builder packages, and plug-ins (Chapter 15); COM, DCOM, and COM+ programming (Chapters 16–18); MIDAS 3 (Chapter 19); CORBA (Chapter 20); integration with Microsoft Office, particularly Word and Excel (Chapter 21); and ActiveX programming (Chapter 22).

- **Part IV: "Advanced Topics"**—This part, consisting of Chapters 23–26, covers advanced topics generally not found in C++Builder reference books. These include advanced printing and data presentation techniques (Chapter 23); a comprehensive look at the use of the Win32 API (Chapter 24); image processing, graphics (GDI, GIFs, JPEGs, and so on), and sound (WAV, MP3, and so on) with C++Builder (Chapter 25); and a look at advanced graphics programming with DirectX and OpenGL (Chapter 26).

- **Part V: "C++Builder Application Deployment"**—This part, consisting of Chapters 27–29, contains more information not generally found in C++Builder books. This includes techniques and advice for creating standard Windows and HTML help files (Chapter 27); software distribution considerations, with a particular emphasis on shareware (Chapter 28); and techniques for software installation and updates, including version control with TeamSource (Chapter 29).

- **Part VI: "Knowledge Base"**—This part, Chapters 30 and 31, contains a set of C++Builder hints, tips, and how-tos (Chapter 30); and an example real-world application (Chapter 31).

- **Part VII: "Appendix"**—This appendix contains a comprehensive list of C++Builder resources, including Web sites (especially the Borland community Web site and CodeCentral), newsgroups, discussion lists, forums, books, magazines, and user groups.

Conventions Used in This Book

This section describes the important typographic terminology and command conventions used in this book. Features in this book include the following:

NOTE

Notes give you comments and asides about the topic at hand, as well as full explanations of certain topics.

TIP

Tips provide great shortcuts and hints on how to use C++Builder 5 more effectively.

CAUTION

These warn you against making your life miserable and tell you how to avoid the pitfalls in programming.

In addition, you'll find various typographic conventions throughout this book:

- Commands, variables, directories, and files appear in text in a special `monospaced font`.
- Placeholders in syntax descriptions appear in a *`monospaced italic`* typeface. This indicates that you will replace the placeholder with the actual filename, parameter, or other element that it represents.

C++Builder 5 Essentials

IN THIS PART

Introduction to C++Builder

Chris Winters
Khalid Almannai
Jarrod Hollingworth
Vikash Shah

CHAPTER

1

IN THIS CHAPTER

- **C++Builder Basics**
- **What's New in C++Builder 5**
- **Upgrading and Compatibility Issues**
- **Migration from Delphi**
- **Advantages and Disadvantages of C++Builder 5**
- **Preparation for Kylix**

Throughout this chapter we will introduce you to Borland C++Builder, one of the leading development environments for creating Internet, desktop, client/server, and distributed applications. It combines the ease of a RAD environment with the power and performance of ANSI C++.

C++Builder is the tool of choice for hobbyist programmers, development teams in small and medium-size companies, and large teams in major corporations alike.

> **NOTE**
>
> For more information on the features and benefits of C++Builder, see the "Features & Benefits" and "New C++Builder Users" links on the C++Builder Web site at `http://www.borland.com/bcppbuilder/`.

Seasoned C++Builder 5 programmers might choose to skip this chapter. For the rest of you, we will show the basics of C++Builder, migrating to C++Builder from other development environments, the advantages and disadvantages of C++Builder in comparison with other development environments, and an overview of what's new in version 5 of C++Builder.

On a slightly different note, we introduce you to *Kylix*, the code name for Borland's upcoming development environment for the Linux operating system, one of the most anticipated development products in recent years. Kylix is basically C++Builder and Delphi for Linux, allowing you to create Linux applications as easily as you can create Windows applications with C++Builder and Delphi. Most of what you have learned and will learn with C++Builder and much of your existing code can be applied to Kylix.

C++Builder Basics

In this section we will describe the basics of C++Builder and develop a simple application. By reading over the basics, you will see that C++Builder is quite easy to use.

Hello World! A Basic Start

You just opened up your copy of C++Builder, threw the manuals aside, installed it, and are ready to go—right? We will go through the basics of C++Builder, projects, the VCL (Visual Component Library), Object Inspector, and more. If you are a beginner and need to learn really quickly, this chapter is for you! If you are an advanced developer and you are ready to burn more knowledge into your head, skip this chapter and move on to the real meat-and-potatoes.

Developers used to do command-line programming using great products such as Turbo C++. Since Windows dominated the operating system market, compilers moved very quickly toward

Windows programming. When Borland introduced Borland C++ Compiler 3.1, the world started moving into Windows development. However, it was still hard to grasp, and you still had to do all the hard work. Sometimes it would take three to five pages just to display a window, because of all the code to catch the messages to manipulate the window, draw the window, and perform other techniques within the Windows environment.

With the introduction of OWL (ObjectWindows Library), things started getting easier. OWL contained all the programming headaches and made it easier to develop applications. The Borland C++ 3.1 compiler contained OWL, and Windows development started getting a little easier. After some time, Borland introduced Borland 5.0 compiler, which OWL and the IDE improved.

Shortly after the success of Borland C++ 5.0, Delphi appeared on the market. Delphi was the visual Pascal language. Soon after the release, Borland released C++Builder, which was developed from Delphi. C++Builder used the same technology and from that point, Windows development became a lot easier than before. Delphi contained advanced RAD (Rapid Application Development) technologies, and C++Builder inherited this technology and became one of the best compilers in the world today. Compared to Visual C++, developing applications is faster and can be easily ported to other platforms.

For the end user and the future developer, C++Builder has become one of the most popular compilers in the world. It is easy to use, and you can quickly learn how to navigate. Visual Basic developers will see that Visual Basic's component manipulation is similar to C++Builder's. Also, the IDE is somewhat similar and easy to navigate around.

You *do* have to learn C++, which takes several years to master. However, Borland C++Builder can aid in that learning. Borland/Inprise has made it easy—the VCL and its class functions do the hard work for you. If you want to move to the fast-paced world of RAD development, C++Builder is the way to go.

OK, let's get started. First, consult your manuals and make sure C++Builder is installed properly on your system. Then, go ahead and start it up.

> **NOTE**
>
> I will not go into great detail about each part of C++Builder, because that's a whole book in itself! Plus, you can access the manuals or online help for installation and operation. What I will do is explain some basics to get you started building simple applications.

When C++Builder has fully loaded, you will see the three main windows for the programming environment. This is called the *Integrated Development Environment* (IDE). The IDE has everything you need in one place, as you can see in Figure 1.1. The IDE is the programming work area for your project. Here you will manipulate controls or components, type in code, configure C++Builder, and maybe set properties of the project.

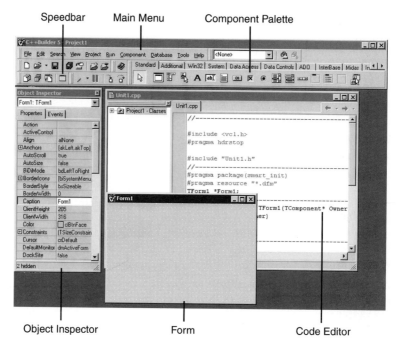

FIGURE 1.1
The C++Builder IDE.

The VCL, Forms, and Components

The Visual Component Library (VCL) is a repository of the components used to create C++Builder applications. A component is an object you use to make up the program, such as a check box, a drive combo box, or a graphical image. These components are chosen by left-clicking and placing them in your work area. VCL components are code that is compiled to perform certain operations, eliminating even more code that you might have to type.

You can also add or write your own components, which is discussed in upcoming chapters. The components that make up the VCL remove most of the hard work for you. These components are located in the Component Palette. See the section "The Component Palette," later in this chapter.

All components have properties, which can be manipulated by code or C++Builder. A component's properties determine how it performs, how it looks, what functionalities it has, and so forth. You can modify the properties of a component with the Object Inspector, which is the panel at the left of the screen under the main menu when the Properties tab is selected (refer to Figure 1.1). You can also change property settings in code, but I would not recommend that unless you get really familiar with C++Builder and the VCL.

The Object Inspector also has an Events tab, where you can create events to indicate user interaction with the component. These events perform other actions that you define.

The Form

A form is a visible window that is, in most instances, the user interface of your application. When you create a new application in C++Builder, a blank form is created automatically. To build the user interface you simply add visual components to the form, then position and size them accordingly. You can also add non-visual components to a form, such as timers. These appear as a simple component icon at designtime but are not visible at runtime.

By default, when a user runs your application the form will be displayed in the center of the screen. You can alter the initial position of the form and other settings by changing the form properties in the Object Inspector.

The Speedbar

The Speedbar provides quick access to the menu functions most commonly used within C++Builder, such as Run, Step Through, View Unit, View Form, and Add to Project. You can customize the Speedbar to your liking by adding the functions you prefer and removing those you don't use.

Customizing the IDE Toolbars

One of the main features of the IDE is its capability to be customized. You can add or remove any speed button to or from any toolbar except for the Component Palette, which contains components, not commands. The C++Builder toolbars are as follows:

- Standard
- View
- Debug
- Custom
- Component Palette

To customize a C++Builder toolbar, follow these steps:

1. Right-click anywhere on the toolbar.
2. Choose Customize.

3. The Toolbars Customize dialog will be displayed, as shown in Figure 1.2.

4. Click on the Commands page.

5. Now you can drag and drop any command you want to the toolbar.

6. To remove any speed button from the toolbar, just drag it outside the toolbar.

FIGURE 1.2

The Toolbars Customize dialog.

The Component Palette

The Component Palette, located under the main menu, is an inventory of all the components in the VCL. These components are grouped by categories, the names of which are displayed on the tabs above the components. To pick a component, click it with your left mouse button, then click again on the form to place the component where you want it. As indicated previously, you can modify the component's properties with the Object Inspector or by changing the code.

Events and Event Handlers

In your first lesson in learning C++Builder, we will place a simple button on the form, set an event for the button, and run the program.

You see buttons on almost every Windows application. It is a simple object that enables a user to trigger an event.

The Button component is located under the Standard tab of the Component Palette. Its icon looks like a standard button with OK in the middle. To place a Button component on the form, left-click the icon one time; then, left-click again on the center of the form. Figure 1.3 shows the form with the button.

Voila! You now have placed a button on the form, and C++Builder has created an instance of that button within the code. At the moment the button isn't very useful because it doesn't do anything. If you were to compile and run the application nothing would happen when you click on the button. Typically though, when a user presses the button you want to perform some action, such as saving information that the user may have entered, displaying a message to the user, and so on.

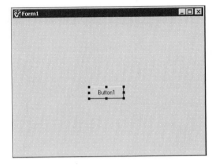

FIGURE 1.3
A Button *component added to the form.*

When the button is clicked at runtime, an event is generated. For your application to respond to this event you need to create an event handler. An event handler is simply a function that is automatically called when its event occurs. C++Builder creates the outline for the OnClick event handler, the event that occurs when the user clicks the button, when you double-click on the Button component at designtime. You can do the same thing by selecting the Button and then double-clicking in the OnClick field on the Events tab in the Object Inspector. Once the outline for the event handler is created, you can then add code to perform the necessary action that should occur when the button is clicked.

The outline for the OnClick event handler is shown in the following code.

```
void __fastcall TForm1::Button1Click(TObject *Sender)
{
}
```

If you right-click with the mouse in the Code Editor and choose Open Source/Header File, you will see the following code:

```
//--------------------------------------------------------------
--------------
#ifndef Unit1
#define Unit1
//--------------------------------------------------------------
--------------
#include <Classes.hpp>
#include <Controls.hpp>
#include <StdCtrls.hpp>
#include <Forms.hpp>
//--------------------------------------------------------------
--------------
class TForm1 : public TForm
```

```
{
__published:      // IDE-managed Components
        TButton *Button1;
        void __fastcall Button1Click(TObject *Sender);
private:     // User declarations
public:          // User declarations
        __fastcall TForm1(TComponent* Owner);
};
//-------------------------------------------------------------------
---------------
extern PACKAGE TForm1 *Form1;
//-------------------------------------------------------------------
------------
#endif
```

This code is generated automatically within C++Builder. I put it here for clarity to show you what C++Builder can do for you automatically.

Now we'll add code to display a message when the button is clicked, that the program is going to end, and then we'll terminate the program. In the code editor, click on Unit1.cpp to move back to the Button component's event. Type the following code inside the event that you just created:

```
void __fastcall TForm1::Button1Click(TObject *Sender)
{
    ShowMessage("Hello world! This is a test application! Press OK");
    Close();
}
```

This code can probably be understood even by a beginner. When the program runs, the user clicks on the button and an event is triggered. Our OnClick event handler will display a dialog box with our friendly message. When the user closes the dialog box our program then terminates due to the Close() method that we called.

Let's Run It and See!

From the Speedbar, click the green arrow that looks like the Play button of a tape player. On the main menu, click Run and choose Run. (As a shortcut, you could press F9 instead.) When you press the Run button, C++Builder will start to compile and execute the program. It then waits until you press the button. When you do so, the dialog appears revealing the message. The program exits when you press OK.

After viewing your program, let's close out our current project. From the main menu, choose File, New Application. C++Builder will ask if you want to save the application project; answer No. Let's write a real program that can do something.

Your First Real Program

Choose File, New Application from the main menu. C++Builder will create a new project and generate code to create an empty form. Now we're ready to create an application with as little code as possible.

On the Component Palette, select the Additional tab and then the Image component. If you aren't sure, its icon has the sky, a hill, and water at the foot of the hill. If you put your mouse over each icon, a helper will tell you what it is.

After selecting the Image component by clicking it, move your mouse to the form and click one time to place the component on the form. You will not see much, but a square outline will appear. This component displays graphical images.

Under the Properties tab in the Object Inspector, go to the stretch attribute and select True.

From the Component Palette, go to the Dialogs tab and choose the OpenDialog component. If necessary, scroll through the Component Palette with the left and right arrows. The OpenDialog component looks like an open yellow folder. Select it with your left mouse button and place it anywhere in the top right corner of the form. The component now is part of your form and is used for displaying a dialog box in which you can choose files. It can also open the files that you pick.

Now we want to set an attribute to this component. Go to the Object Inspector and look for the attribute named Filter, located under the Properties tab. Enter the following text into the edit box for that attribute:

```
BMP files|*.bmp
```

From the Standard tab of the Component Palette, select two Button components. Instead of placing one Button component at a time, you can place multiple Button components by holding down the Shift key and pressing the Button icon from the Component Palette.

Click on the form and a Button component appears. Click on the form again and another Button component appears.

Now select the white arrow on the left side of the Component Palette. This is the Object Selector in which you can navigate and select your components or objects on your form. Because we are done placing buttons, we now want to be able to select other components.

Click one time on the Button1 component on the form. This selects the button itself. We now want to modify the attributes of that particular component. In the Object Inspector, click inside the Caption attribute and replace the existing text with the words Get Picture. The Caption attribute is where the button displays information to the user. Delete the existing text if needed. This gives your button a new caption to users.

Go to the Win32 tab in the Component Palette and select the status bar. It looks like a gray bar with a grip. Hold your mouse over the components a couple of seconds to find the component named StatusBar. A status bar is usually located at the bottom of most Windows applications and displays the status of an application.

Place this on the form. You will see that the component falls to the bottom of the form.

Now double-click on the Button component on the form (Object Inspector will display Button1) to set an event. Enter the following code:

```
void __fastcall TForm1::Button1Click(TObject *Sender)
{
   if(OpenDialog1->Execute())
   Image1->Picture->LoadFromFile(OpenDialog1->FileName);
    StatusBar1->SimpleText = OpenDialog1->FileName;
}
```

Let's pause to explain what's going on. The window you now see is the Source Code window. It can always be accessed by the Project Manager or by the Object Inspector. The Source Code Edit window is where you will type in source code for your program.

Now let's set focus on our form. To access our form, we can use the Speedbar tool button named Toggle Form/Unit. It looks like a form and a piece of paper with arrows pointing toward the form on both sides. If you hold your cursor over this button, it will display Toggle Form/Unit (F12). Another way to toggle between forms and code is with the F12 key. Press F12 now to set focus on the form.

Click one time on Button2 (Object Inspector will display Button2) on the form and set the caption to Close. Double-click on that button and enter the following code:

```
void __fastcall TForm1::Button2Click(TObject *Sender)
{
    Close();
}
```

Now focus on your form again by moving the source code editor out of the way and clicking on your form. Doesn't look like much, does it? Soon you will see how much C++Builder has done for you with a little bit of code!

Before running this application, arrange your buttons and other components nicely to give a clean look. Use the white arrow selector on the left side of the Component Palette to select any component. You will not be able to move the StatusBar component at the bottom of the form, so you can skip that one.

Press the green Run arrow, or choose Run, Run from the main menu. C++Builder should compile the program if you did not have any typos. Your program should appear with two buttons with the captions Get Picture and Close. Choose the Get Picture button.

An Open dialog box will appear asking for a file with the .BMP extension. Go to your Windows directory under your C: drive and select SETUP.BMP or another file that has a .BMP extension.

After selecting the file, press OK. You should see a picture of the Windows Setup bitmap. At the bottom of the form, the name of the file will be in the status bar. You have written your first application that really works, and with as little code as possible! Let's explain what really happened, so that you can get a feel for the components.

First you placed an Image component on the form. This component enables you to display .BMP files within your program. With this component, C++Builder takes all the grunt work out for you.

If you wanted to display a graphic file in Windows, you would first need pages and pages of code just to load the palette of colors the BMP has. You would also have to perform error checking against the BMP structure it fills in, error check to make sure it's a .BMP file, set the resolution, and much more, just to display the picture itself. C++Builder has already done this for you. All you have to do is drop the component on the form and set its properties. You then set the stretch property, which stretches the picture to match the size of the component you placed on the form. For larger pictures, resize the component using your mouse.

After dropping the Image component on the form, you also placed an OpenDialog box. The OpenDialog component lets the user select a file to open under a directory. In this case, we used the OpenDialog component to select the filename of the image to open. The Image component determines if it is a graphic file, reads it in, and displays its contents. We set the Filter property on this component to find all files that end in the .BMP extension, which describes the file type we are opening. It will also display this file type in the OpenDialog box as the type to open. The | is a separator to tell C++Builder there's another parameter coming for this type of property. *.BMP tells the OpenDialog box to open only files that end in .BMP.

If you want to see how this looks or change the filter settings during designtime, go to Form1 and select the OpenDialog component by clicking it. Then go to the Object Inspector. In the Filter section, double-click within the text area and a table will come up that displays what I just described.

After that you placed two Button components. We also set the captions of the Button components, which identifies what the buttons do. Then we set events for the Button components. You can also set other events with the Object Inspector. The Object Inspector has an Events tab that lists the events a component has. To set off a particular event, simply double-click in the text area of that event.

If you were to write this whole program using barebones code, you would produce at least 20 pages of code. The idea of this chapter is to show you the basics and to demonstrate how quickly you can use C++Builder.

Let's write another program using different components. This will give another example of RAD technology within C++Builder.

From the main menu, select File, New Application. A new project will be created. Let's save this project by selecting File, Save Project As from the main menu.

Give the form's source code a name. Change the default `Unit1.cpp` to `Mainfrm.cpp`.

After saving the form's source code, the project source code will appear. By default, it is `Project1.pbr`. Name it `Proj.bpr`.

Place two `ListBox` components on the form. The list boxes are in the Standard tab in the Component Palette. Don't worry about placing them in a specified location, but do align them next to each other. C++Builder creates them as `ListBox1` and `ListBox2`.

Drop an `EditBox` and two `Buttons` below the list boxes. They are also located in the Standard tab in the Component Palette. Align them any way you want. C++Builder creates the buttons as `Button1` and `Button2`. It also creates an `Editbox` named `Edit1`.

Select `Button1`. In the Object Inspector, select the `Caption` property. Change the caption to **ADD**.

Select `Button2`. In the Object Inspector, select the `Caption` property. Change the caption to **REMOVE**.

Select `Edit1`. In the Object Inspector, select the `Text` property. Remove the string within the `Text` property.

Drop a `Label` component under the `Edit1` edit box. In the Object Inspector, select the `Caption` property. Enter **Friends' Names**.

To select the form itself, click anywhere on the form, but not on any component. You can also do this inside the Object Inspector by selecting `Form1` in the drop-down box. Select the Events tab in the Object Inspector and look for the `OnCreate` event. Double-click inside the property setting for this event. C++Builder will now create the following code for the event handler:

```
void __fastcall TForm1::FormCreate(TObject *Sender)
{
}
```

You need to place code inside this event. It is triggered when the form is created at runtime. This means that when you run this program, Windows will create the form and execute any code within the event. Type the following inside the event handler:

```cpp
void __fastcall TForm1::FormCreate(TObject *Sender)
{
    ListBox1->Items->Add("David Sexton");
    ListBox1->Items->Add("Randy Kelly");
    ListBox1->Items->Add("John Kirksey");
    ListBox1->Items->Add("Bob Martling");
}
```

Switch back to the form and double-click on Button1. This is the button with the Add caption. An event will be created. Type the following inside the event handler:

```cpp
void __fastcall TForm1::Button1Click(TObject *Sender)
{
    String GetListItem = ListBox1->Items->Strings[ListBox1->ItemIndex];
    ListBox2->Items->Add(GetListItem);
}
```

Switch back to the form, and double-click on Button2. This is the button with the Remove caption. C++Builder will create an event. Type the following inside the event handler:

```cpp
void __fastcall TForm1::Button2Click(TObject *Sender)
{
    ListBox2->Items->Delete(ListBox2->ItemIndex);
}
```

Switch back to the form and select the Edit1 edit box. From the Object Inspector, choose the Events tab. Find the OnKeyPress event. Double-click in the empty area for this event, and the event handler will be created by C++Builder. Type the following code in the event handler:

```cpp
void __fastcall TForm1::Edit1KeyPress(TObject *Sender, char &Key)
{
    if (Key==13)
    {
        ListBox2->Items->Add(Edit1->Text);
        ListBox1->Items->Add(Edit1->Text);
    }
}
```

Now let's save the project we are working on. Remember to always save your work! Select File, Save All from the main menu. After saving the project, let's make the project. Press Ctrl+F9 or choose Project, Make Proj.exe. This will create the executable. If there are any errors, check for typos.

Let's run it and see what happens. Press the green arrow to run the application we just created. You can also choose Run from the main menu as well. I will explain how the code works in a minute.

The application should appear as a regular window with two list boxes with names in them. There should also be two buttons on the form.

The edit box (which is our Edit1 component) will have the cursor in it ready for us to type. Enter your friends' names.

As soon as you press Enter, each name will be added not only to the first list box but also to the second list box.

Select one of the names and press the Add button. The name you selected will appear in the next list box beside it. If you press Remove, the name will disappear from the second list box only. Select the names and add them to the other list box. Then remove the names.

As you see, we added an event for FormCreate. This event executes after the form's creation. In this event you will see that there are some strings to be added inside ListBox1. The strings are added to the items of the list box.

The next event we set is under Button1. We created a string from the String class named GetListItem, which equals the item that was selected by the user. How did this event know that the item was selected? It didn't. It read the item's index. If there was no selection, it would be null. The next line adds the string from the index of ListBox1.

Button2's event is smaller than the first. It gets the index of the item inside ListBox2 and deletes it.

For our third event, we used an OnKeyPress for the Edit1 edit box. When a user enters data and presses a key, the event is triggered, executing code inside it. This particular event scans for the Enter key, which is equal to 13. Of course, we could have used the VK_ENTER value that C++Builder defines as the Enter key. The if statement checks the passed parameter of Key to see if this is true. If it is, the code inside the if statement executes and adds the string within the edit box to both list boxes.

We created three events, and the code is pretty small. We also put several components on the form without any code at all. We have a working program with minimal code.

As you can see, you built this application in just a few minutes. Once you get used to the Component Palette, the Object Inspector, and some operations within the IDE, you'll be on your way to learning the ins and outs of C++Builder. If you compare the time required to develop applications using other compilers, such as Visual C++ or Microsoft Foundation Classes (MFC), you will see that C++Builder is far superior to the others.

Explore the menu items under C++Builder. The online help will also guide you through the menu items, Object Inspector, and some other options within the IDE.

How to Get Around

This section gives the answers to some commonly asked questions about the C++Builder compiler.

- How do I look at a project's source code and other source code for each form?

  You can do this by using the Project Manager and the Project menu item in the main menu. Project, View Source will display the main entry source for the starting application. If you want to view source files from other forms, includes, or resource files, use the Project Manager. To bring up the Project Manager, select View, Project Manager or press Ctrl+Alt+F11.

- How do I change properties on a component?

  You can do this with the Object Inspector. To bring it up, press F11 or choose View, Object Inspector. In the Object Inspector, select your component and the properties will be loaded within the Object Inspector. From there you can set events and change properties.

- I am trying to arrange my components precisely, but I am having difficulty. Can I have more control over the alignment?

  To move a component to the exact location you want, press Control and use the arrow keys to move the component. This will give you the exact pixel alignment you need within C++Builder.

- I just compiled and ran my application, but now it seems to be locked up. A bunch of weird windows popped up and I do not know what to do. How can I stop this madness?

  You can get C++Builder to reset the program. Press Ctrl+F2 or select Run, Program Reset. This will kill your program completely and take away those nasty whatever-they-are-windows, and you'll be back to your code.

- I compiled my first program, but I want to create my own icon and include it in my program. How do I do this?

  First, use the trusty and wonderful Image Editor. Open it by selecting Tools, Image Editor in the main menu. Simply create a new icon from there and save it. Then, select Project, Options. The Project Options dialog will appear. Select the Application tab and press the Load Icon button. Locate your icon and press OK. Then you will have to rebuild your project. Compiling or making your project will not do it. You will have to rebuild all by choosing Project, Build All Projects from the main menu. After that, your application will contain your new icon!

- Every time I compile an application, my form has the name Form1. How do I change this?

    Remember the Object Inspector? We talked about this for setting properties for components. You can also use it to set properties for your forms. Use the Caption property attribute to change a form's title. Try experimenting with the Object Inspector for different results!

- I am tired of choosing the menu items for something simple. Isn't there an easier way?

    Yes—it's called the Speedbar, and it is located right above the Object Inspector (by default). If you want, for example, to create a new application object, press the button with the image of a white piece of paper. If you do not know what those buttons are, hold your cursor over one for a couple of seconds, and a helper will appear to tell you what the button is.

- I have all my components in place and do not want to move them. Sometimes I accidentally move them by mistake. Is there a way I can keep these components still?

    Yes, you can do this by choosing Edit, Lock Controls from the main menu. This will lock all controls on the form.

What's New in C++Builder 5

As with the staggered releases of new versions of Borland C++Builder and Borland Delphi in the past, C++Builder 5 introduces new features first seen in Delphi 5 and then adds some more. There are many new features and enhancements in the areas of Web programming, distributed application development, team development, application localization, debugging, database application development, and developer productivity, among others. Most of the new features and enhancements are covered in more detail throughout this book.

C++Builder 5 is available in three versions: Standard (Std), Professional (Pro) , and Enterprise (Ent). Standard has the fewest features but is still a powerful development environment for Windows programming and includes over 85 components for RAD programming, the award-winning compiler, advanced debugger, and more. The Professional version has over 150 components and adds features including the new CodeGuard™ tool, multiprocess debugging, and standard database functionality. The Enterprise version has over 200 components, including Internet Express, CORBA development, Microsoft SQL Server 7 and Oracle 8i support, MIDAS development, a full suite of internationalization tools, TeamSource version control manager, and more.

Missing from C++Builder 5 is Merant (formerly Intersolv) PVCS Version Control.

> **NOTE**
>
> The full-feature matrix highlighting all of the new features in each version (Standard, Professional, Enterprise) of C++Builder 5 is available from the "Feature List" link on the C++Builder Web site at http://www.borland.com/bcppbuilder/.
>
> You can also see information on the new features in the "What's New" section of the C++Builder online help.

The features listed in the following sections are available in the Professional and Enterprise versions of C++Builder 5 and not in the Standard version, except where noted. In the remainder of the book, we will not make a distinction of which versions of C++Builder the new features apply to. Consult the full-feature matrix if necessary.

Web Programming

Most people know that one of C++Builder's strengths is in developing Web and Internet applications. In C++Builder 5, Borland has added the Active Server Page (ASP) Application Wizard, Internet Express (Ent), a new Web browser component, and WebBroker enhancements.

The new Internet Express (Ent) allows you to build "thin" clients for the Web by presenting data from MIDAS servers and back-end databases using XML and HTML 4. Thin clients are smaller in size than regular (or "fat") clients. They do not access the database directly and therefore do not require the Borland Database Engine (BDE) to be installed on the client machine.

WebBroker is now available in the Professional version of C++Builder 5 (previously Enterprise only) and is now able to preview with HTML 4 support. The last main Web programming addition to C++Builder 5 is the new Web browser component, which allows you to integrate HTML browsing into your applications. This seemingly simple feature can be used in many ways, such as to

- Create your own customized Web browser. For instance, develop one for your company that allows users to view Web pages only within the company's intranet.
- Create the user interface for your program in HTML. This has several benefits. The user interface can now be created by nonprogrammers. If there are Web page developers in your organization, they can assist in application development. Additionally, you can dynamically customize the user interface for a particular user's level of experience simply by loading a different HTML file. The user interface can also be customized for a particular client. Shipping a new version of the user interface is as easy as downloading an HTML file, something that browsers do extremely well.

C++Builder 5 Essentials

- Integrate your help files using HTML, making the creation of help files as simple as creating Web pages.

Several products, such as Microsoft Encarta and Microsoft Office 2000, use a Web browser control in these ways. America Online (AOL) and CompuServe use Web browser controls to create their customized browser applications.

Distributed Applications

CORBA (Ent) now supports the VisiBroker ORB v4.00 and CORBA 2.3–compliant clients and servers. Other new CORBA features include the Portable Object Adapter and Objects By Value. There are enhancements to the Visual TypeLibrary Editor, Interface Repository, CORBA Wizards, and more.

MIDAS (Ent) now has XML data packet support, a stateless DataBroker, a new Web Connection component, server object pooling, and provider options.

Team Development

A great new feature in C++Builder 5 is TeamSource. It is included in the Enterprise version and can be purchased separately for the Professional version.

TeamSource is a front-end version control manager that allows parallel development of projects. Developers work on their own local copies of the project. In most cases, TeamSource automatically handles the merging of changes. A visual compare utility simplifies the task of resolving conflicts. TeamSource tracks version history and allows a particular state of the project to be bookmarked.

The actual back-end file versioning is performed by separate version control software. C++Builder 5 (Ent) includes the Borland ZLib back-end version control software and also supports an interface to Merant PVCS (purchased separately). Plug-ins can be written for TeamSource to support other back-end version control software.

Application Localization

New to C++Builder 5 Enterprise are the Translation Suite, Translation Repository, RC Translator, and DFM Translator. These features can also be purchased separately for C++Builder Professional. They allow you to internationalize or localize your applications for new languages and cultures, simultaneously developing your application for multiple locales.

The Resource DLL Wizard has been enhanced to allow you to translate your applications to new languages easily.

Debugging

Perhaps one of the best new features that most C++Builder programmers can benefit from is CodeGuard. CodeGuard is a runtime error-detection tool that can locate and diagnose memory and resource leaks. In addition, some other new debugging features are an FPU/MMX View and breakpoint actions (all versions) and groups (all) for programmable breakpoint control and managing multiple breakpoints at once.

Database Application Development

There are several new database features in C++Builder 5, including the DataModule Designer, InterBase Express, and ADO Express.

The DataModule Designer, first seen in Delphi 5, allows you to see and design the parent-child relationships among data-access components in the tree view and entity relationship dependencies (including master-detail) in the Data Diagram view.

With InterBase Express, you can develop high-performance database applications using InterBase that don't require the Borland Database Engine (BDE). It comes with the new SQL monitor for advanced data access debugging.

ADOExpress is a new set of components that allows you to access relational and non-relational databases using Microsoft's ActiveX Data Object (ADO) and OLEDB technology. Using ADO, you can access standard databases, email, file systems, spreadsheets, and other information. ADOExpress applications don't require the BDE.

In addition to these new features, C++Builder 5 now has InterBase 5.6, MS SQL Server 7, and Oracle 8i support.

Developer Productivity

There are some great new features in the area of developer productivity. Multithreaded background compilation (all) allows you to continue working while the compiler is doing its stuff. Custom Desktop Settings (all), with auto-debug mode switching, allows you to arrange and save different IDE desktops just the way you want. You can set a separate layout for debugging applications and, as you switch in and out of debugging, the desktop changes your layout automatically.

An integrated to-do list manager lets you add simple task reminders with a comment and priority to your projects. A to-do item can appear in your code as a reminder to come back to something that needs to be finished. There's a new to-do list view to manage those items.

Several wizards have been added, including a Windows 2000 Client Logo Application Wizard (all), Console Application Wizard (all), Control Panel Applet Wizard, and simple C and C++ Application Wizards (all).

There is also enhanced Microsoft Visual C++ support, including Visual C++ 6.0 projects, Microsoft Foundation Class (MFC) 6.0, and Active Template Library (ATL) 3.0 support.

There are many more developer-productivity features and enhancements new to C++Builder 5, including per-file project options override (all), property categories (all), and property images (all) in the Object Inspector; programmable code editor key mappings (all); new components (all); and the capability to import automation servers as components.

Companion Tools CD-ROM

The C++Builder 5 companion tools CD-ROM (Pro/Ent) contains more than 40 useful third-party tools. Some are full versions, and some are shareware and trial versions. Some of the full and free tool highlights are

- Debug Server 1.1 from Elitedevelopments is a COM/DCOM-based debugging output manager that lets you centrally collect, manage, and display debug messages from your applications.
- Morfit's 3D Engine SDK 3.0 and WorldBuilder 3.1 allow you to incorporate 3D graphics into your applications and develop arcade-quality games.
- GExperts is an open-source product that contains dozens of IDE enhancements to speed development. Several "Experts" are included to navigate, search, and transform your code. GExperts also provides shortcuts for common programming tasks, quick access to information relevant to C++Builder developers, and extensive customizing of the IDE.

Upgrading and Compatibility Issues

C++Builder 5 was officially released on March 22, 2000. At the time of the writing of this book, there are several known compatibility problems in C++Builder 5 with existing projects and third-party tools, and there are unresolved bugs. An update (patch) is not yet available. The C++Builder 5 bug list can be found on the Borland C++Builder Web site via the "Updates and Patches" and then "Investigate Bugs" links at http://www.borland.com/bcppbuilder/.

Sign up for the C++Builder tech alert from the Borland Web site to get the latest information on known issues and update releases. You should also read the README.TXT files in the root folder of the C++Builder installation CD-ROM for known issues at the time of release.

Upgrading C++Builder from an Earlier Version

C++Builder 5 can coexist with earlier versions of C++Builder on your machine, but shared applications such as the BDE will be upgraded to the latest version. C++Builder 5 can also coexist with Delphi installations. The same general rules apply.

If you have no use for the previous version of C++Builder, then you should uninstall the previous version before installing C++Builder 5. You should also read the INSTALL.TXT and README.TXT files in the root folder of the installation CD-ROM for further installation and upgrading notes.

Using Existing Projects in C++Builder 5

When you load a project created in a previous version of C++Builder, the project is automatically converted to work with C++Builder 5. The project file is updated to XML format, and the earlier VCL library versions listed in it are updated to list C++Builder 5 libraries. Some slight changes to the USE* clauses in the main project file source are also made.

You may have written version-specific code into your projects or used third-party components that do. Changes to properties and methods in the VCL between different C++Builder versions have typically necessitated the use of #ifdef VERXXX clauses to compile the correct usage. If any of the version-specific code is testing explicitly for C++Builder 4 or earlier versions without a "catch-all" for forward compatibility, you may need to update the clauses.

For example, if the code tested #ifdef VER125 for C++Builder 4–specific code, you will need to add either an #ifdef VER130/#endif or an #else catch-all to specify the C++Builder 5–specific code.

If you don't have the source code, usually because it is a third-party component or package, then you will need to contact the vendor to get an update.

Creating Projects Compatible with Previous Versions of C++Builder

If you need to create projects that can be used with earlier versions of C++Builder, there are several areas in which care must be taken. In particular, you cannot use new features in forms and project source code, such as new properties, methods, or events. There are several new project, compiler, and linker options that should not be used. The help file contains detailed information on the new features added to C++Builder 5.

In C++Builder 5, form files are stored as text rather than binary as in previous versions. To save a form as binary, right-click on the form and uncheck Text DFM. If you want all forms created in the future to be saved as binary, uncheck the New Forms as Text option on the Preferences page of Tools, Environment Options.

As shown in detail in Chapter 2, "C++Builder Projects and More on the IDE," project files are now saved in XML format. The project file in previous versions of C++Builder used a makefile format. You can export a makefile format project file by using the Project, Export Makefile option. You will need to rename the makefile with a .bpr extension and make several changes to the options listed in the file, including the C++Builder version number, set in the VERSION option, and VCL file versions listed in the LIBRARIES, SPARELIBS, PACKAGES, and CFLAG1 options. Converting the project file to previous versions is a bit involved; there are other changes that may be necessary.

The to-do list is a new feature in C++Builder 5. However, the in-source to-do list items and global project to-do file require no changes for support in previous versions.

If you see the message Error reading symbol file when opening a C++Builder 4 project, you should rebuild the application. C++Builder 4 symbol files are not compatible with C++Builder 5.

Solving Other Project Upgrading Issues

There are several new method parameters, data values, classes, and VCL behaviors in C++Builder 5 that you should be aware of. Some of the main changes are listed here.

- **TPoint** TPoint is no longer a structure. The initialization syntax has changed from using braces ({ and }) to formally typecasting two coordinates as a TPoint. See "TPoint, compatibility issues" in the online help.

- **TPropertyEditor** The parameter list for the TPropertyEditor constructor has changed to TPropertyEditor(const di_IFormDesigner ADesigner, int AropCount.

- **TComponentList** There is a new class named TComponentList to store and maintain a list of components. It is defined in the include file cntnrs.hpp. See the online help for information on how to use TComponentList.

- **AnsiString sprintf** The sprintf() method of the AnsiString class now overwrites the current contents of the string rather than append to the existing string. A new cat_sprintf() method provides the old behavior.

- **TCppWebBrowser** and **THTML** The TCppWebBrowser component on the Internet page replaces the THTML component from Netmasters. See the online help for upgrading notes.

- **MIDAS** Several changes have been made to MIDAS. See the online help for additional information.

There are many more upgrading issues in C++Builder 5. The "Upgrading to Borland C++Builder 5" book on the Contents tab of the online help contains detailed information.

Migration from Delphi

This section is not to teach you C++, but to get you started with programming in C++Builder, if you know how to program in Delphi. The first thing you should note when programming in C++Builder is that it is case sensitive. It may look like a hard thing to do if you have been programming in Delphi for a long time, but you will get used to it.

> **CAUTION**
>
> Unlike Delphi, the code in C++ is case sensitive.

Here we will compare Delphi and C++Builder in the major programming areas. At the end of this discussion, you should be able to translate most of your Delphi code to C++Builder without any trouble.

Comments

The first thing you need to know is how to enter comments in C++Builder. Table 1.1 compares Delphi to the C++Builder way of creating comments.

TABLE 1.1 Delphi-to-C++Builder Comments Comparison

Delphi	C++Builder
`{ My comments in Delphi }`	`/* My comments in C++Builder */`
`(* Another comment in Delphi *)`	
`// One line of comments`	`// One line of comments`

Variables

As in Delphi, in C++Builder you must declare the variable type before you can use it. Table 1.2 compares Delphi variables with those of C++Builder. The table also shows the number of bytes that each type requires.

TABLE 1.2 Delphi-to-C++Builder Variables Comparison

Type	Size (bytes)	Delphi	C++Builder
Signed integer	1	`ShortInt`	`char`
	2	`SmallInt`	`short, short int`
	4	`Integer, LongInt`	`int, long`
	8	`Int64`	`__int64`

TABLE 1.2 Continued

Type	Size (bytes)	Delphi	C++Builder
Unsigned integer	1	Byte	BYTE, unsigned short
	2	Word	unsigned short
	4	Cardinal, LongWord	unsigned long
Floating point	4	Single	float
	8	Double	double
	10	Extended	long double
Variant	16	Variant, OleVariant, TVarData	Variant, OleVariant, VARIANT
Character	1	Char	char
	2	WideChar	WCHAR
Dynamic string	-	AnsiString	AnsiString
Null-terminated string	-	PChar	char *
Null-terminated wide string	-	PWideChar	LPCWSTR
Dynamic 2-byte string	-	WideString	WideString
Pointer	8	Pointer	Void *
Boolean	1	Boolean	bool

The table covers most variables. For more information, refer to the C++Builder help.

Constants

There are two ways to declare a constant in C++Builder. The old way is to use the preprocessor directive #define like this:

```
#define myconstant   100
```

The new and safer way of defining constants is by using the const keyword, as follows:

```
const int myconstant = 100;
```

myconstant is again declared as a constant, but this time it's declared as an integer.

Operators

This section explains C++Builder operators, and how you can convert Delphi operators to C++Builder. Table 1.3 lists operators types in Delphi and their counterparts in C++Builder.

TABLE 1.3 Delphi-to-C++Builder Assignment Operators Comparison

Operator	Operator Type	Delphi	C++Builder
Assignment	Assign	:=	=
	Add then Assign	None	+=
	Subtract then Assign	None	-=
	Multiply then Assign	None	*=
	Divide then Assign	None	/=
	Modulus then Assign	None	%=
	Bitwise And then Assign	None	&=
	Bitwise Or then Assign	None	|=
	Bitwise Xor then Assign	None	^=
	Bitwise Shl then Assign	None	<<=
	Bitwise Shr then Assign	None	>>=
Comparison	Equal	=	==
	Not equal	<>	!=
	Greater than	>	>
	Greater than or equal to	>=	>=
	Less than	<	<
	Less than or equal to	<=	<=
Arithmetic	Add	+	+
	Subtract	-	-
	Multiply	*	*
	Divide float values	/	/
	Divide integer values	div	/
	Modulus	mod	%
Logical	And	and	&&
	Or	or	||
	Not	not	!

TABLE 1.3   Continued

Operator	Operator Type	Delphi	C++Builder
Bitwise	and	And	&
	or	Or		
	xor	Xor	^
	not	Not	~
	Shift to the left	Shl	<<
	Shift to the right	Shr	>>
Pointers	Deceleration	^Type	Type*
	Dereferencing	pointer^	*Pointer
	Address of variable	@Variable	&Variable
	References	var	Type&
Class	Class declaration	class	class
	Structure declaration	record	struct
	Scope resolution	.	::
	Direct access	.	.
	Indirect access	None	->
Others	Increment	Inc()	++
	Decrement	Dec()	--
	String quoting	'	"

Assignment Operators

In C++ you can combine different operators with the assign operator (+=). For example, the following

```
x = x + 2;
```

can be written as follows:

```
x += 2;
```

Increment and Decrement Operators

In C++ you can increment or decrement variables using prefix or postfix methods. The following is an example of how to use both:

```
x = ++y; // prefix
```

```
x = y++; // postfix
```

The first statement tells the compiler to increment y first, then assign x to the new incremented value of y. The second statement is the opposite. It first assigns x to y then increments y. The following example should clarify:

```
int x=5, y=5;
x = ++y;
// at this point x=y=6
// … later on
x = y++;
// now x=6 and y=7
```

Conditional Operators

The conditional operator (?:) is the only operator in C++ that takes three expressions and returns a value. It is written as follows:

```
(expression1) ? (expression2) = (expression3)
```

The operator returns expression2 as a value when expression1 is true. Otherwise it returns expression3. For example

```
return ((a >b)? c : d);
```

This can be written using an if-else statement as follows:

```
if (a>b) return (c);
else return  (d);
```

Pointer Operators

The indirection (*) operator is used to declare pointers. The same symbol is also used to dereference a pointer, and in this case it's called a *dereference operator*. Dereferencing a pointer is the way to retrieve the value it is pointing to. The compiler is clever enough to tell the difference. Look at the following example:

```
int x, y = 8;
int* ptr = &y; // ptr declared and initialized to hold the address of y
x = *ptr;      // dereferencing ptr.
```

Here is how you used to do the same thing in Delphi:

```
var
x,y : Integer;
ptr : ^Integer;
begin
y:=8;
ptr := @y;
x := ptr^;
end;
```

The (*) and (&) operators in C++ are equivalent to the (^) and (@) operators in Delphi, respectively. The (&) is called the *address-of* operator; it is used to retrieve the address of a variable in memory.

The (&) operator is also used to declare *references*. A reference is just a special case of a pointer, and you can treat it as a regular object. References are very useful when used to pass parameters to functions. In Delphi, parameters passed by reference are also called *variable parameters*. In this case, the (&) reference operator in C++ is equivalent to the var keyword in Delphi.

The new and delete Operators

You can always declare variables like this:

```
char buffer[255];
```

buffer is now allocated on the stack, and this type of variable is called a *local variable*. There are two problems with local variables. First, they are destroyed when the function returns. Second, the memory size that can be allocated on the stack is limited.

You can solve these problems by allocating memory from the heap, as follows:

```
char* buffer;
buffer = new char;
```

Or you can write it in one line, such as

```
char* buffer = new char;
```

Now you have a variable that can be used everywhere in your program with the size you want. The only thing you need to remember is that any memory allocated needs to be freed. This is done with the delete operator, as follows:

```
delete buffer;
```

Class Operators

There are two ways to access data members and member functions of a class, by using direct or indirect access. See the "Classes" section, later in this chapter, for more detail.

Controlling Program Flow

As in Delphi, C++Builder has several structures for conditional branching and looping. These structures are

- if-else statements
- switch statements

- for loops
- while and do-while loops

C++Builder also has break and continue commands, which are quite similar to the ones in Delphi to break or continue the flow of execution. Table 1.4 shows examples of how to use conditional branching and looping structures in Delphi and their counterparts in C++Builder.

TABLE 1.4 Delphi-to-C++Builder Conditional and Loop Statement Comparison

Statement	Delphi	C++Builder
if-else	if (i = val) then	if (i == val)
	begin statement1; ...; end;	{ statement1; ...;}
	if (i = val1) then	if (i == val1)
	begin statement1; ...; end	{ statement1; ...;}
	else if (i = val2) then	else if (i == val2)
	begin statement1; ...; end	{ statement1; ...;}
	else	else
	begin statement1; ...; end;	{ statement1; ...;}
switch	case \<Expression\> of	switch (\<Expression\>){
	val1 :	case Val1:
	statement;	statement; break;
	val2 :	case Val2:
	statement;	statement; break;
	...	...
	else statement;	default : statement;
	end; // end case	} // end switch
for	for i := val1 to val2 do	for(i=val1;i<=val2;i+=inc)
	begin statement1; ...; end;	{ statement1; ...;}
	// Increment by 1 only.	// Increment by any value
		// depends on inc value.
	for i:=val1 downto val2 do	for(i=val1;i>=val2;i-=dec)
	begin statement1; ...; end;	{ statement1; ...;}
	// Decrement by 1 only.	// Decrement by any value
		// depends on dec value.

TABLE 1.4 Continued

Statement	Delphi	C++Builder
`while`	`while i = val do`	`while (i == val)`
	`begin statement1; ...; end;`	`{ statement1; ...; }`
`do-while`	`repeat`	`do`
	`statement1;`	`{`
	`...`	`statement1;`
	`...`	`...`
	`until (i = val)`	`} while (i != val);`

The following are some tips on how to use these statements and commands:

- You need to place a `break` keyword at the end of each `case` statement to stop execution. Failing to do so will cause the execution of the statements that come under later `case` statements until it reaches the `break` statement or the end of `switch`. This seems odd, but it has its usefulness sometimes.

- The selector expression in the `switch` statement won't accept non-ordinal types such as strings.

- The `for(;;)` loop is equivalent to a `while(true)` or `while(1)` loop. All are infinite loops. To quit such loops, use the `break` keyword.

Functions and Procedures

As in Delphi, a function in C++Builder must be declared (*prototyped*) before it can be used. Unlike Delphi, C++Builder has no special keywords that are used to declare functions such as `function` and `procedure`. Table 1.5 shows examples of function declarations in both Delphi and C++Builder.

TABLE 1.5 Delphi-to-C++Builder Function Declaration Comparison

Delphi	C++Builder
`procedure Add;`	`void Add();`
`procedure Add(x, y: Integer);`	`void Add(int x, y);`
`function Add: Integer;`	`int Add();`
`function Add (x, y: Integer): Integer;`	`int Add (int x, y);`

Any C or C++ program must have a `main()` function that will be the entry point of the program. For GUI applications it is called `WinMain()`. `main()` functions just like any other function: It takes parameters and returns values. Figure 1.4 shows the `main()` function when you create a new console application. Note that you can create a console application by choosing File, New, Console Wizard.

The `main()` function takes two parameters, `argc` and `argv`, and returns an integer value. It is unlike other functions in that it can't be called directly; it is called automatically when the program starts running.

Functions in C++ use an opening brace (`{`) to begin and a closing brace (`}`) to end. These braces are equivalent to Delphi `begin` and `end` keywords.

In Figure 1.4 you can see that C++Builder uses the `return` keyword to return values. It will also cause the termination of the called function (`main()` in this case). You need to be careful here. Unlike Delphi's `Result` keyword, `return` will terminate the function immediately, so any statements coming after it will be ignored.

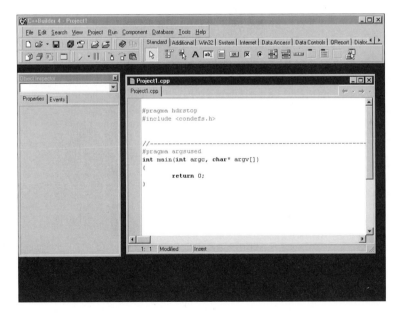

FIGURE 1.4
The C++Builder code editor window for a new console application.

Classes

Delphi and C++Builder have the same way of controlling the access of functions. They hide these functions in structures called *classes*. Collecting functions in a class to accomplish a specific task is called *encapsulation*.

From C, C++ inherited the struct keyword, which is almost identical to class. The only difference between structures and classes is that structure data members and member functions are public by default, whereas a class's default is private.

As in Delphi, a class in C++Builder has the following features:

- Constructors and destructors
- Access control to data members and member functions
- A pointer called this, which is equivalent to self in Delphi

One of the most powerful features of classes in C++ is that they can be built using *multiple inheritance*. Multiple inheritance is when a class is derived from two or more base classes. In Delphi (actually Pascal), classes are derived from a single base class.

Let's look at some of the class syntax for various types of inheritance:

- No inheritance
  ```
  class MyClass {  // no inheritance.
  // Private by default so anything declared here is private.
  private:
  // Private declaration
  protected:
  // Protected declaration
  public:
  // Public declaration
  };  // MyClass is terminated by semicolon.
  ```
- Single inheritance
  ```
  class MyClass: BaseClass1
  {...};
  ```
- Multiple inheritance
  ```
  class MyClass: BaseClass1, BaseClass2,  BaseClass3
  {...};
  ```

Constructors and Destructors

Every class has a constructor and a destructor. If the programmer does not write a specific constructor or destructor for the class, the compiler will create default ones.

The constructor's main purpose is to allocate space for the class and to initialize class data members. The destructor's job is to free the allocated memory.

A class can have more than one constructor, but it has only one destructor. Constructors and destructors are just like any other member functions of the class, but they have some special features:

- They don't return values (not even void).
- The constructor takes the name of the class, and the destructor takes the name of the class preceded by the ~ symbol. For example

```
class A {
Public:
A();  // Constructor
~A(); // Destructor
}
```

- Constructors can take parameters as n
- They can't be called as a norma

Accessing Data Members and

Assume you have the following simple cl

```
class Rabbit {
Private
int speed=20;
};
```

Later, you can declare it in your program using

```
Rabbit Rabbit1;
Rabbit* Rabbit2 = new Rabbit;
```

Rabbit1 is created on the stack, and Rabbit2 is create   the speed data member for both of them using the direct access o

```
Rabbit1.speed=30;
```

```
(*Rabbit2).speed=30;
```

To make it easier to access data members of classes such as Rabbit2, C++ introduced the arrow operator (->). The above statement can be written as

```
Rabbit2->speed=30;
```

The this Pointer

Like the self pointer in Delphi, this is a hidden data member in all C++Builder classes. The following is an example of how to use the this pointer:

```
__fastcall TForm1::TForm1(TComponent* Owner) : TForm(Owner)
{
TLabel *Label1 = new TLabel(this);
Label1->Parent = this;
Label1->Caption = this->Width;  // which is equivalent to Form1->Width;
}
```

Preprocessor Directives

Preprocessor directives are special instructions for the compiler. They are specified on a line that starts with the # symbol. Preprocessor directives are usually placed at the beginning of a unit. Many directives can be placed just about anywhere in the unit, but certain directives must be placed at a particular position within the unit, such as the #pragma argsused directive, which must be placed before the definition of the function to which it applies. We will look at the #define and #include preprocessor directives.

The #define Directive

As shown in the "Constants" section, earlier in this chapter, the preprocessor command #define can be used to declare constants.

The #define command is also used to create macros. Macros are just like any other function and can have parameters as follows:

```
#define MAX(A,B) ((A)>(B)?(A): (B)
#define MIN(A,B) ((A)>(B)?(B): (A)
```

You use them as follows:

```
int x, y, max ;
x = 5;
y = 6;
max = MAX(x,y); // Remember that C++Builder is case sensitive.
```

The #include Directive

Before we discuss the #include directive, you need to know the use of a header file. C++ uses a header file as an interface to source code files.

Most of the time all declarations of constants, variables, and functions should be placed in the header files, and only the implementation part should be kept in the .CPP source file.

During compilation, the #include directives will be replaced with the header file to which the directive is pointing. The syntax can take one of the following forms:

```
#include <headerfile.hpp>
#include "headerfile.hpp"
```

The first statement tells the compiler to search for the headers only in the include files, which are set in Project, Options, Directories/Conditionals. In the second statement, the compiler will start searching for the headers in the current directory. Then it will continue searching in the include files.

Types of Files

Table 1.6 compares Delphi file types to those in C++Builder.

TABLE 1.6 Delphi-to-C++Builder File Type Comparison

Delphi	C++Builder	Description
DPR	BPR	The Builder project.
PAS	CPP	Each unit has a source code file plus one main project file.
DFM	DFM	A binary file that describes the form and all its components.
PAS	H or HPP	A header file.
RES	RES	A compiled binary resource file.
DCU	OBJ	Compiled binary object.
BPG	BPG	Combination of projects in one group file.
DPK	BPK	Source file listing the units used in the package.
None	BPI	Import library file created for each package file.
BPL	BPL	The runtime library. It's like Windows DLL with special Builder features.
None	LIB	Static library files.
~*	~*	Backup files.
None	MAK	A text file that contains information for which files the Builder needs to compile and link for this project.
MAP	MAP	A text file that contains information used to perform low-level debugging tasks.
None	TDS	Turbo Debugger Symbol—contains debugging information.

The following points should help to clarify the file type comparisons in Table 1.6.

- The first five types are created on the first Save of the project.
- The CPP and HPP files are equivalent to the implementation and interface sections, respectively, of the PAS file.

- The OBJ files are created when selecting Project, Compile Unit. The same type of file will be created when compiling a package.
- The BPK file will be created when you save a package file.
- BPI, BPL, and LIB files are created when a package is compiled or installed.
- In C++Builder 4 and C++Builder 5, MAK has been replaced by BPR. If you try to open MAK file in C++Builder 4 or higher, the IDE will convert it to a BPR file.
- The TDS file contains debugging information. This file will get larger when the Project, Options, Compiler, Debug Information menu item is enabled.

Advantages and Disadvantages of C++Builder 5

In this section, we discuss some of the features of C++Builder that could affect a software engineering project. It would be fair to assume that the majority of this book's readers will have settled upon C++Builder as their chosen development platform. The intention here is to highlight some of those features that make C++Builder such a useful tool, while bringing the reader's attention to other issues that could cause difficulties.

Visual Reality: True Rapid Application Development

For C++ programmers who require a truly visual environment for designing applications with rich, professional-looking user interfaces, the C++Builder IDE with the accompanying Visual Component Library is the only comprehensive, integrated solution. C++Builder's array of project templates helps get a new program up and running in under a minute, and there is no faster way to start Windows programming in C++. The Object Repository provides an invaluable way to reuse code for productivity and consistency. Even a moderately experienced user will be able to create a simple multifile text editor with menus, toolbars (that can dock or float), and other basic features, all in half an hour. Not only is this astoundingly productive, it can be lots of fun. Being able to see how your application looks while you are designing it reduces the need for trial and error.

C++Builder 5 adds some new features to those seen in previous versions that make visual development even easier. For example, the TFrame component allows you to work with independent, reusable form-like windows that can then be placed within forms or even on the Component Palette for later use. Improvements to the Object Inspector include enhanced editors for TColor and TCursor properties, as well as property and event lists that are now categorized to allow infrequently used sets of items to be hidden. This makes it easier to find what you are looking for.

On the left side of Figure 1.5, the TCursor property editor in the Object Inspector is shown at work in a project containing two frames that are being used within the main form.

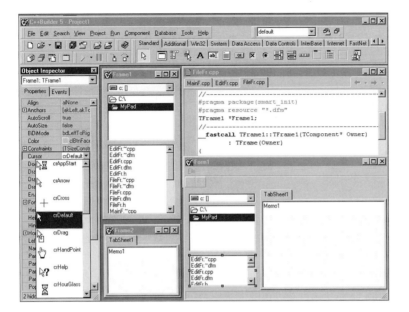

FIGURE 1.5
Some of the new visual development enhancements in C++Builder 5.

Microsoft's Visual C++, although "visual" in name, does not offer this WYSIWYG method of development. This is perhaps the most significant advantage of C++Builder over Visual C++.

Visual C++ users have two realistic alternatives for Windows application development. One is to develop programs with the supplied resource editor and the Microsoft Foundation Classes (MFC) library. The other is to develop back-end code as a dynamic link library (DLL) to be used by a graphical user interface (GUI) created in another development environment better suited to visual programming, for example Microsoft's own Visual Basic language.

The first option does not offer a great deal of visual interaction. While the use of the resource editor allows dialog boxes to be laid out in a way similar to C++Builder's form designer, the variety of ways in which controls can be manipulated at designtime in C++Builder is far more powerful. In fact, C++Builder also comes with the MFC, which is included for those rare times when it would be preferred, though the main reason for its inclusion is for compatibility with existing MFC code. (Visual C++ does not provide a migration path from C++Builder.)

Furthermore, only standard controls are catered to by the resource editor, while C++Builder's system can support the thousands of additional VCL components that are available. The MFC is a very "thin" wrapper around the Windows Application Programming Interface (API) and, although it is more complete in its coverage of the API than the VCL, it does not provide the same high level of built-in functionality and places the burden on the programmer.

The other option actually does present certain benefits in that, from an architectural point of view, the separation of an application's "engine" from its user interface can provide flexibility and expandability. Nevertheless, the capability of C++Builder to serve well as both a C++ compiler and a visual GUI designer supports its claim to be the most productive of the two systems. A well-engineered program written in C++Builder can support the GUI separation idea equally well.

Keeping Up with the Joneses: The C++ Standard

For many years now, Borland has been several strides ahead of the pack in ensuring that its compiler is up to date with the latest ANSI/ISO standards. C++Builder 5—built upon the version 5.5 model of the Borland 32-bit C++ compiler (BCC32)—is no exception. The current details of the language are formalized in the latest ANSI/ISO specification. It differs from the previous version of the standard in several respects, notably in the areas of C++ templates and namespaces.

This may not mean a great deal in small, monolithic applications developed prototypically and largely within the confines of the form designer. However, for a serious application that has been designed with scalability in mind, a compiler as rigorous and standard-compliant as BCC32 is crucial to the long-term success of a project.

As a consequence of Borland's policy on the issue of continual improvements to its back-end compiler, however, some developers will find that existing programs that correctly compile under previous versions of C++Builder will fail to do so under version 5. This problem is likely to manifest itself only in cases where heavy use is made of a feature whose treatment by the compiler has undergone a particularly major change, such as templates.

I speak from first-hand experience, having spent time converting such an application created in C++Builder 3 to run under version 4 and then again to version 5. Although this particular application has been exposed as being badly written in some places—a good thing to be aware of as a developer and certainly food for thought—it did set my project back. As a keen software engineer and one who is learning all the time, I found the experience to be a positive one. Unfortunately, in such circumstances, project management and the all-important customer may not be quite so enthused. The moral of this story is that the long-term benefits of the compiler can be greatly appreciated, but one cautious eye needs to stay on the here and now.

C++Builder also extends the compiler to support proprietary (that is, non-portable) extensions to the C++ language in order to support the VCL. While in many circumstances you may choose to avoid them for reasons of portability, this is another string in the bow of the compiler. For example, the __closure keyword, which supports the concept of a member-function pointer for an instance and not a class, can be useful, because there is no clean way to achieve a similar effect within the scope of the current C++ specification. See the "keyword extensions" reference on the "__closure" page in the online help for more information.

Choosing the Right Development Environment

Whatever claims are made by compiler vendors, no one platform is perfect. There will always be supporters who back one side and find only fault with the other. As a piece of software evolves over time, it is inevitable that problems will arise that will reveal flaws in the chosen development tool. This is a fact of life for a developer.

C++Builder 5 is a development tool, not a panacea for all our programming troubles. Of course, this is not exclusive to C++Builder, and there are areas of software development to which it is ideally suited and superior to its competitors and other to which it is not.

Having said this, there is no disputing that C++Builder 5 is a robust and intuitive development environment that can be an immensely powerful and productive solution. For those developers who go the Microsoft route, there may be very pressing reasons for doing so—or the dominant reason may simply be that Borland is not Microsoft.

By the time you read this, it is expected that Borland will have ported C++Builder to run under the Linux operating system. The potential to write multiplatform applications is sure to interest many people and sway them toward the product. See the section "Preparation for Kylix," later in this chapter.

C++Builder Advantages and Disadvantages Conclusion

It is possible to draw some useful conclusions from this discussion. While the following lists are by no means exhaustive, we can identify some particular advantages and disadvantages to C++Builder. We have not focused on database or Internet features, which are also key selling points of C++Builder, but they do appear in the following list.

A summary of the advantages of C++Builder 5 is provided in the following list:

- It is a powerful form designer.
- It is suitable for both traditional C++ programming and rapid user interface development, because it integrates an ANSI/ISO–compliant compiler with a truly visual development environment.
- Its comprehensive Visual Component Library can be supplemented through acquisition of third-party components (including Delphi components) and by creating your own.
- Proprietary C++ extensions support additional programming constructs.
- Project templates and the Object Repository allow for quick project setup and reuse.
- Easy-to-use database support is provided through data-aware components and the Borland Database Engine.
- It provides powerful support for Internet development.

- Migration from Visual C++ to C++Builder is relatively straightforward.
- It provides a possible route for porting applications to Linux.

A summary of the disadvantages of C++Builder 5 is provided in the following list:

- The form designer's ease of use can encourage a haphazard program structure if its design is not in place early on.
- Due to changes in the compiler, it might not be worth upgrading from earlier versions if a program is going to require major changes to compile under version 5.
- Migration from C++Builder to Visual C++ is usually very difficult.
- Choosing a Borland product over Microsoft may have long-term consequences due to Microsoft's general domination of the industry.

Preparation for Kylix

Kylix is the internal code name for Borland's development environment for the Linux operating system. (The official product name has not yet been announced at the time this is being written.) In basic terms, it is "Delphi and C++Builder for Linux." With Kylix you can develop applications for Linux systems as easily as you can currently develop Windows applications with C++Builder. It will be possible to port many of your existing C++Builder applications to Linux.

There are many similarities between Kylix and C++Builder (and Delphi), but there are also some important differences, mostly brought about by the differences between the Windows operating system and the Linux operating system. We'll take a look at some of these to alert you to new possibilities with C++Builder. If you are considering porting your applications to Linux, you should be aware of the similarities and differences between Kylix and C++Builder.

When I was in the Boy Scouts, we had a simple motto: "Be Prepared!" I still think that it is a great motto, and in the game of software development it's something that we should keep in mind.

Note that what is presented in the remainder of this section is based on information from public announcements and discussions of Kylix available at the time of writing this book. The information here should be considered speculative, because the product is not yet complete, and most of the features and specific details have not been publicly released.

Similarities Between Kylix and C++Builder

The basic framework for Kylix will be very similar to C++Builder in most respects. Apart from the general differences between the Windows user interface and the various Linux user interfaces available, the IDE in both products will be almost identical. There will be the Object

Inspector, a class browser, various component tabs in the Component Palette, and a code editor.
You will be able to reuse what you've already learned with C++Builder. Figure 1.6 is a very
early (pre-release) screenshot of a Delphi project loaded into Kylix. The K Desktop
Environment (KDE) of Linux is being used. Note the similarities to the C++Builder IDE.

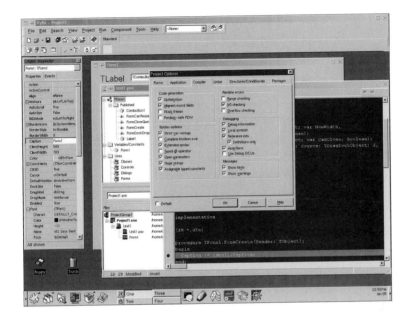

FIGURE 1.6
The Kylix IDE, displayed in Linux using the K Desktop Environment.

Just as C++Builder shares a lot of common functionality and look-and-feel with Delphi, my
guess is that the addition of Kylix into the pool will result in common core features being
shared among all three products. As new features are implemented in any one of the products,
those features will be available in the others in the next release.

In the C++Builder version of Kylix, you'll still be writing C++ code just as you do today.
You'll hardly notice the difference. After all, C++ is C++.

Differences Between Kylix and C++Builder

Because Linux is not Windows, there are some features in C++Builder that we won't see in
Kylix, at least initially. These Windows-specific technologies include COM, DCOM, COM+,
ActiveX, and Win32 API calls. A few years ago, Microsoft, Digital, and another large company
were developing DCOM for UNIX servers. If it's not available already, then it's only a matter

of time before it is. It is possible that SOAP (Simple Object Access Protocol) support will be included at some stage.

I'm guessing that many of the Win32 API calls will have an equivalent in Linux, either transparently using a system API layer or specific to Linux. The latter would make porting of applications between the two more difficult.

The VCL for Linux will be named the Borland Component Library for Cross Platform (CLX for short, pronounced "clicks"). The various CLX components will be grouped into logical units such as visual components, data access components, and so on. The GUI components will be built on TrollTech's Qt framework. Qt is a cross-platform C++ GUI application framework that was selected by Borland as the most suitable framework to use in the Linux environment. Qt is installed with the KDE but must be installed separately when using Gnome or other Linux desktops. CLX will appear in the Windows versions of C++Builder and Delphi to facilitate easier porting of applications between Linux and Windows. However, for performance reasons, the VCL should still be used if the target operating system for the application is Windows.

Kylix will include a new thin database access layer, likely to be called DBExpress, as a replacement for the Borland Database Engine (BDE). The current discussion suggests that it will support a limited set of underlying databases and require only a single DLL to be installed with the client.

Porting C++Builder Projects to Kylix

Porting C++Builder projects to Kylix will depend on the features that are implemented in Kylix. The previous sections should give a general feel of the types of porting issues you're likely to find.

Porting most applications will definitely be possible. It would be great if it were possible without source code modifications but, realistically, many applications will require at least some basic tweaking.

So When?

Based on current discussions, the Delphi version of Kylix will be released in late 2000. By the time you're reading this, it may already be released, and you will know more about it than I do!

The C++Builder version? Current discussions put that at early 2001.

Summary

In this chapter, you learned the basics of C++Builder for beginners and those moving from Delphi. If this was your first look at C++Builder, you should now be able to see its enormous potential for developing Windows applications. You were also introduced to some of the new features and enhancements in C++Builder 5 and some of the upgrading and compatibility issues when migrating existing projects and third-party tools. Finally, you learned a little about Kylix, Borland's upcoming product for software development on the Linux platform.

Several of the concepts discussed in this chapter will be covered in detail in the following chapters, and many new concepts will be introduced.

C++Builder Projects and More on the IDE

Jamie Allsop
Yoto Yotov
Jarrod Hollingworth
Khalid Almannai
Dan Butterfield

IN THIS CHAPTER

- **Understanding C++Builder Projects**

- **Using the Object Repository**

- **Understanding and Using Packages**

- **Introducing New IDE Features in C++Builder 5**

The complete text for this chapter appears on the CD-ROM.

Programming in C++Builder

Jamie Allsop

IN THIS CHAPTER

- Coding Style to Improve Readability
- Better Programming Practices in C++Builder
- Further Reading

This chapter introduces important concepts concerned with how code is written in C++Builder.

The first section concentrates on how the readability of code may be improved. Optimizing the readability of code is very important. More readable code is easier to understand and maintain, and this can have a big effect on the cost of a software project. It is more than just making code look pretty on a page; it is about augmenting the code's description such that its purpose, intent, and behavior are adequately reflected.

Adopting a coding style and applying it consistently is probably the easiest way to achieve more readable code. However, some styles offer greater improvement than others, and this section looks at a variety of approaches to several considerations in an effort to give the reader some insight into which styles they should adopt. More importantly, it offers suggestions as to why certain styles are possibly more effective than others as well as warnings on the application of certain styles. Some techniques in moderation are very effective but when overused will decrease readability. Situations such as this are highlighted. The fundamental elements of coding style are examined in turn, and guidelines are presented on how each element can affect readability, along with suggestions on how each element can be used to best effect. Where appropriate, effective use of the IDE is also covered.

The second section covers a variety of topics concerning the writing of C++ code in C++Builder applications. A wide range of topics is covered, from the use of new and delete to the use of const in programs. The main purpose of the section is to highlight areas of coding that are often misunderstood or misused. Often, certain concepts are not fully appreciated, particularly by programmers whose background is not in C++. However, the main target audience is those whose background is in C++. They will find explanations of specific issues concerning the use of C++ in C++Builder and should therefore benefit from the topics covered. Some topics begin with more straightforward material before moving the discussion to advanced concepts. Also, many of the topics address issues that arise as a result of the Object Pascal heritage of the VCL (Visual Component Library).

Finally, the last section, "Further Reading," lists the references that appear throughout the chapter, along with a brief description of the reference itself. You are encouraged to seek out these references; reading them should prove very beneficial.

Coding Style to Improve Readability

This section looks at some of the issues in improving the readability of code and offers possible methods of achieving this. Regardless of which styles and methods are chosen, the one thing that should be remembered is that you must be consistent. Consistency is very important (note that code in this section is written in different styles to illustrate points in the text).

The Use of Short and Simple Code

It may be obvious, but always try to keep any given block of code short and simple. This achieves two things.

First, it means that your code is ultimately the culmination of many smaller pieces of code, each of which serves a specific and understandable role. This means that at different parts of the code the complexity of the code is governed only by the level of abstraction, not by the amount of code present. Consider the two functions in Listing 3.1.

LISTING 3.1   Code Complexity and Level of Abstraction

```cpp
#include <vector>

double GetMaximumValue(const std::vector<double>& Vector)
                        throw(std::out_of_range)
{
    double Maximum = Vector.at(0);

    for(int i=0; i<Vector.size(); ++i)
    {
        if(Vector[i] > Maximum)
        {
            Maximum = Vector[i];
        }
    }

    return Maximum;
}

void NormalizeVector(std::vector<double>& Vector)
{
    if(!Vector.empty())
    {
        double Maximum = GetMaximumValue(Vector);

        for(int i=0; i<Vector.size(); ++i)
        {
            Vector[i] -= Maximum;
        }
    }
}
```

Both of the above functions are similar in terms of the complexity of the code that they contain, but the second function, `NormalizeVector`, performs in total a more complex task, because the level of abstraction is higher.

> **TIP**
>
> Use the pre-increment operator instead of the post-increment operator—for example, in Listing 3.1, ++i is used in preference to i++. Using either of the increment operators will increment i, but the post-increment version will return the old value of i. Since this is not required, the extra processing time is wasted. Typically, the post-increment operator is implemented in terms of the pre-increment operator. The pre-increment operator is therefore faster than the post-increment operator.
>
> For built-in types such as int, there is little difference in speed, but for user-defined types this may not be the case. Regardless, if the post-increment operator is repeatedly used unnecessarily, there will be a cost in terms of performance.

Second, it means that when you are reading code you are never too far away from local variable declarations and function parameters (which contain type information). To this end, if you find yourself writing large pieces of code that perform several tasks, consider how the code could be separated into smaller conceptual blocks and rewritten accordingly.

The Use of Code Layout

The easiest way to improve the layout of your code is to make sure that braces ({}) are placed on their own line and that matching pairs line up. Code inside braces should then be indented by a predetermined amount that is used consistently throughout the program. Typically, two to four spaces are used as a suitable indent, though some use more and some use only one. (Beware of too many spaces; this can actually degrade readability.)

> **TIP**
>
> Make sure the Use Tab Character setting on the General tab in Tools, Editor Options is unchecked. This ensures that spaces are inserted for tabs. In general, avoid using Tab; use spaces instead.

Why is this so helpful? First, it allows fast visual scanning of the code. The code can be broken quickly into its constituent functional blocks, and each block's nature can be seen from the line starting the block. Second, the scope of the code is very clear. It is obvious which variables are in or out of scope at any given time, and this can be helpful in tracking down problem code. This is an important feature of this approach. Remember that the scope of any given block *includes* the block header statement (such as a for statement or a function header), and the functional part of the block is the code *contained* by the braces. Aligning the braces with the block header statement and indenting the functional code show this logical relationship explicitly.

The reason this layout style is so effective is that it is easier to match a pair of braces than it is to match an end brace with a keyword (or other permutations), due to the lack of symbolic similarity. It is also easy to maintain, because each opening brace must have a corresponding ending brace in the same column.

> **TIP**
>
> The IDE allows you to indent and unindent selected blocks of code using, respectively, CTRL+SHIFT+I and CTRL+SHIFT+U. The number of spaces that the editor indents or unindents the selected code is determined by the value of the Block indent setting on the General tab in Tools, Editor Options. Setting this value to 1 (one) offers the greatest flexibility.

Indenting both the braces and the code contained in them together is not as effective, because the braces are hard to pick out in the code. For single blocks of code this is not such a problem, but for nested blocks it can become confusing. That said, some still prefer this approach. For an alternative discussion of this, please refer to *A Practical Handbook of Software Construction* by McConnell, 1993, p. 399. Be aware that most of the discussion presented in the book refers to languages that use keywords to show control block structures, such as begin and end, and the considerations involved are therefore somewhat different, though the distinction is not considered by the text. Tread cautiously.

When code is laid out as previously described—braces on their own line, matching pairs of braces lined up, and code within the braces indented—it can be read easily. Loop constructs can be marked as blocks, and nested constructs become very clear. No room is left for ambiguity. One instance in which this can be particularly useful is in the use of nested if-else statements. The following code is unclear:

```cpp
#include <ostream>

// We have : int A <= int B <= int C

if(A + B > C)
   if((A==B) || (B==C))
   if((A==B) && (B==C)) std::cout << "This is an EQUILATERAL triangle";
   else
   if( (A*A + B*B) == C*C )
        std::cout << "This is a RIGHT-ANGLED ISOCELES triangle";
     else std::cout << "This is an ISOCELES triangle";
   else
      if( (A*A + B*B) == C*C )std::cout << "This is a RIGHT-ANGLED triangle";
     else std::cout << "This is a TRIANGLE";
     else std::cout << "This is NOT triangle";
```

Its meaning is straightforward when written as follows:

```cpp
#include <ostream>

// We have : int A <= int B <= int C

if(A + B > C)
{
    if((A==B) || (B==C))
    {
        if((A==B) && (B==C))
        {
            std::cout << "This is an EQUILATERAL triangle";
        }
        else if( (A*A + B*B) == C*C )
        {
            std::cout << "This is a RIGHT-ANGLED ISOCELES triangle";
        }
        else
        {
            std::cout << "This is an ISOCELES triangle";
        }
    }
    else if( (A*A + B*B) == C*C )
    {
        std::cout << "This is a RIGHT-ANGLED ISOCELES triangle";
    }
    else std::cout << "This is a TRIANGLE";
}
else std::cout << "This is NOT triangle";
```

Always consider if there is a better, clearer way to write code, especially if you find yourself writing large nested if and if-else statements. If you are writing a large if-else block, consider replacing it with a switch statement. This may not always be possible. In the case of large nested if statements, try restructuring the code into consecutive if-else statements.

In a similar vein, try to keep lines of code short. This makes it easier to read in the editor window and also makes it easier to print out.

TIP

Often when code is printed, some code lines are too long for the page onto which they are printed. When this occurs, one of two things happens: The lines are wrapped to the start of the next line or the lines are simply truncated. Both are unsatisfactory and degrade the readability of the code.

The best way to prevent this is to ensure that excessively long lines of code either are avoided or that they are carefully broken to multiple lines. When you are writing code in the Code Editor, the right margin can be used as a guide to the width of the printable page that you use. Change the right margin setting on the Display tab in the Tools, Editor Options menu so that the value represents the absolute printable right margin. In other words, set it so that characters that appear after this margin either are not printed or are wrapped to the next line (if Wrap Lines is checked in the File, Print menu). This will depend on the page size used and the value of the left margin setting (also in the File, Print menu).

For A4 paper and a left margin setting of 0, the right margin should be set to 94. This means that code lines that extend past this line will not be printed as they appear on the screen. To ensure that the right margin is visible in the Code Editor, make sure that the Visible Right Margin setting on the Display tab in the Tools, Editor Options menu is also checked.

Common reasons why code lines can become excessively long include heavily nested loops or selection constructs, use of `switch` statements with complex code inside, trying to write `for` and `if` statements on the same line, long function parameter lists, long Boolean expressions inside `if` statements, and string concatenation using the + operator.

For heavily nested loops or selection constructs, decrease your indent size if it is large or redesign the code so that some of the work is carried out by functions.

`switch` statements can be written differently. For example

```
switch(Key)
{
  case 'a' : // a very long line of code that disappears ...
          break;
  case 'b' : // another very long piece of code ...
          break;
  default  : // Value not required - default processing
          break;
}
```

This can be rewritten as

```
switch(Key)
{
  case 'a'

  : // a very long line of code that can now all be seen
    break;

  case 'b'
```

```
   : // another very long piece of code that can also be seen
     break;

  default

   : // Value not required - default processing
     break;
}
```

With `for` and `if` statements all on one line, place the code executable part of the statement on a separate line. For example

```
for(int i=0; i<10; ++i) // long code that disappears ...
```

This can be replaced by the following:

```
for(int i=0; i<10; ++i)
{
  // long piece of code that no longer disappears
}
```

The `if` statement can be similarly written. For example

```
if( Key == 'a' || Key == 'A' ) // long code that disappears ...
```

This can be replaced with

```
if( Key == 'a' || Key == 'A' )
{
  // long piece of code that no longer disappears
}
```

In fact, it is better practice to write such one-line statements in this way, because it allows the debugger to trace into the line of code that is to be executed.

Long Boolean expressions inside `if` statements should be written on several lines, such as in the following:

```
if(Key == VK_UP || Key == VK_DOWN || Key == VK_LEFT...
{
  // Code here
}
```

This is better written as follows:

```
if(Key == VK_UP
    || Key == VK_DOWN
    || Key == VK_LEFT
    || Key == VK_RIGHT
    || Key == VK_HOME
    || Key == VK_END)
{
```

```
  // Code here
}
```

This code raises an important point concerning the placement of the || or similar operator. The reason for placing it on the left side of each line is that we read from left to right. Placing it on the right makes the reading both slower and less natural, and it distorts the emphasis of the expression. Placing the operator on the right side of each line in the expression to show that there is more after the line is unnecessary, because people tend to read code by scanning blocks, not by reading individual lines as a computer does.

Long function parameter lists can be dealt with similarly, by placing each parameter on a new line. For example

```
void DrawBoxWithMessage(const AnsiString &Message, int...
```

This can be rewritten as shown in Listing 3.2.

LISTING 3.2   Writing Long Function Parameter Lists

```
void DrawBoxWithMessage(const AnsiString &Message,
                        int Top,
                        int Left,
                        int Height,
                        int Width);
```

It is important to place the comma at the end of each line. Placing the comma at the start of each line makes the code more difficult to read, because you would not expect to encounter a comma in this position in normal written text. The comma is for the compiler to separate the parameters and has no other meaning; its use should not unduly confuse someone reading the program. Note that the positioning of the comma is in contrast to the previous discussion of operator placement.

The same approach can be taken with long string concatenations:

```
AnsiString FilePath = "";
AnsiString FileName = "TestFile";

FilePath = "C:\\RootDirectory" + "\\" + "Branch\\Leaf" + ...
```

This can be rewritten as shown in Listing 3.3.

LISTING 3.3   Writing Long String Concatenations

```
AnsiString FilePath = "";
AnsiString FileName = "TestFile";

FilePath = "C:\\RootDirectory"
         + "\\"
```

Listing 3.3   Continued

```
       + "Branch\\Leaf"
       + FileName
       + ".txt";
```

The code in Listing 3.2 and Listing 3.3 is very clear, but it may not be very easy to maintain due to the amount of indentation required. For those who find adding lots of spaces difficult (some people really do!), an alternative approach is to use the standard indent for each of the following lines in such an expression. For example, if you are using a three-space indent, then the code from Listing 3.2 would become

```
void DrawBoxWithMessage(const AnsiString &Message,
   int Top,
   int Left,
   int Height,
   int Width);
```

This degrades readability but results in code that is easier to maintain, a rather dubious trade-off, but sometimes a reasonable one.

Tip

You can save time writing code by using the code templates. These are accessed from the editor by pressing Ctrl+J and then using the up and down arrow keys or the mouse to select a template. However, remember that in order to maintain consistency with your own coding style and to get the best use of code templates, you should customize the templates that C++Builder provides. To edit code templates, go to Tools, Editor Options and select the Code Insight tab. Note that the | character is used to indicate where the cursor will be placed initially when the template is pasted into the editor. Code templates can also be edited manually in the `$(BCB)\Bin\Bcb.dci` file (where `$(BCB)` is the C++Builder 5 installation directory).

The Use of Sensible Naming

One of the best ways to improve the readability of code is to use sensible naming for variables, types, and functions. *Type names* include those used for naming actual types; for example `int` is the type name for an integer, `TFont` is the type name for the VCL's font class. *Variable names* are the names of variables that are declared to be of a specific type, for example, in the code

```
int NumberOfPages;
```

`NumberOfPages` is the name of a variable of type `int`.

Function names are given to functions to describe what they do. We'll consider variable names first, though most of what is said about variable names applies equally to type names and function names.

Choosing Variable Names to Indicate Purpose

Generally, you want to choose a name that reflects a variable's nature and purpose. If possible, it should also suggest what type the variable is. For example, `String EmployeeName;` is better than `String S;`.

When the variable pops up later in code, you will have no idea what `S` is for. For example, is it the number of pages in a book or a string representing a person's name? You also won't know what it is—for example, an `int`, a `double`, a `String`? `EmployeeName` is obvious: It is a variable that holds the name of an employee, and it is most likely a string.

Using descriptive names such as this is easy to do and makes everyone's life much easier when the code is read at a later date. Every time a new variable is declared, ask the question, "What is the variable's purpose?" Summarize the answer to the question and you have a sensible variable name.

When naming a variable, a word or short phrase is often used. Using a capital letter to start each word in the variable name is a popular method of making the name clear and easy to read. Others prefer all lowercase with underscores to separate words and, still others, a mixture of both. To illustrate, the previous declaration could be written as any of the following:

```
String EmployeeName;
String employee_name;
String Employee_Name;
String employeeName;
```

A disadvantage of using underscores is that variable names can quickly become very long. These are okay technically, but they start to make code look cluttered and also increase the symbolic appearance of variable names. Some suggest that all variable names should start with a lowercase letter, such as the `employeeName` example. This is often done to separate variable names from type names, which would typically start with a capital letter. Others start a variable name with a lowercase letter only when it is a temporary variable, such as a `temp` variable in a `swap` function. A compromise should be found so that a variable name is meaningful but also concise. That said, the meaningfulness of a variable name is most important.

Modifying Variable Names to Indicate Type

In general, knowing the purpose of a variable is often more important to the understanding of a piece of code than knowing what type the variable is. However, there are times when you may want to remind yourself of the variable type because special rules might apply. A simple example to illustrate this is given in Listing 3.4.

LISTING 3.4   Illustrating the Need to Be Aware of a Variable's Type

```cpp
int Sum = 0;
int* Numbers = new int[20];

for(int i=0; i<20; ++i)
{
    Numbers[i] = i*i;
    Sum += Numbers[i];
}

double Average = Sum/20; // Sum is an int, needs cast as a double
```

The answer to the code in Listing 3.4 should be 123.5, but the value in Average will be 123. This is because Sum is an int, and when you divide by 20 (treated as an int), you get an int result that is assigned to Average.

> **TIP**
>
> Try to declare variables just before they are used; this helps ensure that variables are created only if they are actually needed. If code contains conditional statements (or throws an exception), it may be that some of the variables declared are not used. It is sensible not to incur the cost of creating and destroying such variables unless they are used. Be wary, though, of placing declarations inside loops, unless that is what is intended. It is also a good idea to initialize variables when they are declared. On a similar note, never mix pointer and non-pointer declarations on the same line. Doing so is confusing at best.
>
> It is preferable to have variables declared as
>
> `Type VariableName;`.
>
> Hence, a pointer to an int should be written as
>
> `int* pointerToInt;`
>
> But if we write
>
> `int* pointerToInt, isThisAPointerToInt;`
>
> then PointerToInt is a pointer to an int and isThisAPointerToInt is not a *pointer* to an int, it *is* an int. Actually, this is what the declaration is saying:
>
> `int *pointerToInt, notPointerToInt;`
>
> This is still not clear, and the declaration is no longer written in the Type VariableName format. The solution is to write the declarations on separate lines. The ambiguity then disappears.
>
> `int* pointerToInt = 0;`
> `int  notPointerToInt;`

You should ensure that pointers are explicitly initialized either to NULL (0) or to some valid memory location. This prevents the accidental use of wild pointers (those that point to an undefined memory location).

To obtain the expected result of 123.5 for Average in Listing 3.4, the last line of the code snippet should be as follows:

```
double Average = static_cast<double>(Sum)/20; // Performs as expected
```

This results in Sum being cast as a double before being divided by 20 (treated as a double). Average is now assigned the double value 123.5.

TIP

Make sure you are familiar with the four types of C++ casts, and always use C++-style casting in preference to C-style casting. C++-style casts are more visible in code and give an indication of the nature of the cast taking place.

This example is somewhat trivial, and adding type information to the variable name would be a bit like using a sledgehammer to crack a nut. A more sensible solution is probably to declare Sum as a double.

Sometimes type information may be required. One method of adding type information to a variable name is to use a letter (or letters) as a symbol at the start or at the end of each variable name. For example, you might use b for bool, s for a string, and so on. A problem with this approach is that type information can be added unnecessarily to too many different types of variables. The emphasis is then invariably placed on the type information and not on the variable's purpose. Also, there are many more possible types for a variable than there are letters of the alphabet. As a result, such symbols can themselves become confusing and complex. An infamous example of such a convention is the Hungarian Notation commonly seen in Win32 API code.

NOTE

The Hungarian Notation has its roots in Win API programming and advocates adding symbols to all variables to indicate their type. Since there aren't enough letters for all types, oddities in the notation are common. For example, Boolean variables are prefixed with an f, strings with an sz, pointers with p, and so on. A complete list is not appropriate here. The notation is infamous because many feel it creates more problems than it solves. These arise mostly from inconsistencies (such as the variable wParam being a 32-bit unsigned integer, not a 16-bit unsigned integer as the prefix implies) and names that are difficult to read. A perusal of the Win32 API help files should reveal some examples of the notation. Heavily typed notations are dangerous because they place the emphasis of a variable name on the variable's type, which often does not tell you much about the variable.

When reading such code, it is not always easy for the reader to mentally strip away the type codes, and this can decrease the code's overall readability. If you want prefixed (or even appended) type symbols, a compromise is to restrict the use of added symbols to only a few specific types.

Modifying Variable Names to Indicate Characteristics or Restrictions

A variable's name can also be used to convey information regarding some characteristic that a variable may have or to point out some restriction that may be applicable. It is important to know when a variable is a pointer, because pointers can easily wreak havoc in a program. For example, if you have a pointer to an int and accidentally add 5 to it without dereferencing it first, you have a problem. It is good practice to use a pointer only when no other type can be used, such as a reference (which are implicitly dereferenced).

It is also sometimes important to know when a variable is static, when a variable is a class data member, or when a variable is a function parameter. Suitable symbols that could be prefixed would be p_ for a pointer, s_ for a static variable, d_ or m_ for a class data member, and a_ for a function parameter. (An a_ symbol is used to differentiate a function parameter from a pointer and should be read as "where the parameter a_x represents the argument passed to the function." The use of a_ then becomes reasonable.)

An underscore is often used to separate a prefix from the variable name proper. This makes it easier to strip away the prefix when reading the code. If a separating underscore is used with an information symbol, then it is possible to append the symbol to the end of the variable name. This has the advantage of allowing the variable name to be read more naturally. For example, when reading s_NumberOfObjects, you would probably say "this is a static variable that holds the number of objects," whereas reading NumberOfObjects_s, you might say "this variable holds the number of objects and is static." This places the emphasis on the purpose of the variable (to store the number of objects). Which you prefer is probably a matter of personal choice. A problem with all such symbols occurs when more than one is applicable; then the syntax is not so tidy. Solutions such as always *prefixing* p_ for pointers and *appending* the other symbols can solve most of these problems, but not all.

Another common situation that often receives special attention is the naming of variables whose values do not change, in other words *constants*. Such variables are often named using all capital letters.

When you declare variables of certain classes, it is often sensible to include the class name (without any prefixed letter, for example T or C, if it is present; this is explained shortly) as part of the variable name. This is often done by prefixing some additional information to the name, or it can be as crude as appending a number to the class name as the C++Builder IDE does, though generally a little more consideration should be applied. For example, consider the following variable declarations.

```
TComboBox* CountryComboBox;
TLabel* NameLabel;
String BookTitle;
```

In the case of TComboBox and TLabel, it is appropriate to include the class name as part of the variable name. However, in the case of BookTitle, it is fairly obvious that it is a string, and adding the word String to the variable name perhaps does more harm than good.

Of special note in C++Builder is the naming of private member variables, which have a corresponding __property declaration. By convention, such variables are prefixed with the letter F (for *Field*). You should follow this convention and avoid using a capital F prefix for other purposes. The purpose of a prefix in this case is to allow the property name to be used unchanged (it is not necessary to think of a similar-sounding variant name).

Choosing Type Names

As was mentioned earlier, the naming of types should be approached in a fashion similar to the naming of variables. However, some conventions need to be considered.

For classes, convention says that if the class derives from TObject, then the class name should be prefixed with the letter T. This lets the user of the class know that it is a VCL-style class, and it is consistent with the naming of other VCL classes. This has a beneficial side effect. Variables declared of the class can use the class name without the prefix, making it obvious what the variable is. Non-VCL (that is, *normal* C++) classes can also use a prefix, but it is wise perhaps to use a prefix other than T, such as C to indicate that the normal C++ object model applies and reinforce that the class does not descend from TObject. This distinction can be important: VCL-style classes must be created dynamically; non-VCL classes do not have this restriction.

The naming of other types, such as enums, Sets, structs, and unions, can be handled in a similar fashion. By convention, C++Builder prefixes a T to enumeration and Set names, though some may prefer not to follow this convention, which has no specific meaning. Avoid using an E as a prefix; C++Builder uses this for its exception classes.

Because enums and Sets are commonly used in C++Builder, it is worth mentioning some points specifically related to their naming. A Set is a template class declared in $(BCB)\Include\VCL\sysset.h as

```
template<class T, unsigned char minEl, unsigned char maxEl>
➥ class RTL_DELPHIRETURN Set;
```

Ignoring RTL_DELPHIRETURN, which is present for VCL compatibility, we can see that a Set template takes three parameters: a type parameter and two range-bounding parameters. Hence, a Set could be declared as

```
Set<char, 'A', 'Z'> CapitalLetterMask;
```

If a Set is to be used more than once, a typedef is normally used to simplify its representation, as seen here:

```
typedef Set<char, 'A', 'Z'> TCapitalLetterMask;
// Later in the code
TCapitalLetterMask CapitalLetterMask;
```

Sets are often used to implement masks (as in this case), hence the use of the word Mask in the names used in the previous code. An enumeration is typically used to implement the contents of a Set. For example, the following definitions can be found in $(BCB)\Include\VCL\graphics.hpp:

```
enum TFontStyle { fsBold, fsItalic, fsUnderline, fsStrikeOut };

typedef Set<TFontStyle, fsBold, fsStrikeOut> TFontStyles;
```

Most enums used by the VCL are to facilitate the use of Sets. For convenience they are declared at file scope. Simply including the file allows easy access to the Set. This means that the potential for a name collision is high. To avoid such collisions, the "initials" of the enum name are prefixed to each of the values that the enum can take. This minimizes the chance of a name collision. This is good practice and should be used in your own code. For example, the initials of TFontStyle (excluding the T) are fs, which is prefixed to each of the enums. Another method that can be used to prevent name collisions is to place enums and typedefs inside the class definitions that use them. This means that such enums and typedefs, when called from outside the class, must be qualified by the class namespace. The same can be applied to const values.

Using a typedef in certain situations (such as this one) can improve readability. A typedef can also improve readability in the declaration of function pointers (and particularly __closures, i.e. events, discussed in Chapter 9, "Creating Custom Components"). Beyond situations such as these, typedefs should be used sparingly because you are actually hiding the type of the variable. Using typedefs too much will result in confusion.

Choosing Function Names

Function names should be precise and describe what the function does. If it is not possible to describe precisely what a function does, then perhaps the function itself should be changed. Different kinds of functions should be named in slightly different ways.

A function that does not return a value (a `void` function) or returns only function success information—in other words, those that return no data—should generally be named using an *object verb* name, such as `CreateForm()`, `DisplayBitmap()`, and `OpenCommPort()`. A member function of this type often does not require a qualifying object, because the object that calls the function generally can fulfill that role.

If a function does return a data value, then the function should be named to reflect the nature of the return value, such as `GetAverage()`, `log10()`, and `ReadIntervalTimeOut()`.

Some prefer to make the first word in a function name lowercase. This is a matter of personal preference, but consistency should be maintained.

In general, function names can be longer than variable names, and if you need to write a long function name, you should not be overly concerned. However, take care to ensure that a long function name is not the product of a poorly designed function that tries to perform too many poorly related operations. In fact, you should endeavor to write functions that perform a single well-defined task, and the name of the function should reflect that. If you must write a function that does more than one thing, the name should make that obvious.

Adhering to Naming Conventions

How variables, types, and functions are named is an extensive topic, encompassing a myriad of concerns. Mentioning every convention that could be used is impossible. That being the case, you should endeavor to adhere to the following guidelines:

- Name a variable or a function such that its purpose is obvious. If this means more typing, then so be it.

- Name a type so that its intended use is obvious. Try not to use a name that is an obvious choice for a variable of the type. Prefixing a letter symbol can help.

- Be consistent! With practice, even the most obscure naming system can be understood if it is consistently applied.

The Use of Code Constructs

One of the best ways to improve the readability of code is through the appropriate use of code constructs—using the right tool at the right time for the right job. Therefore it is important to understand when to use `const` (and when not to), when to use references instead of pointers, which `loop` statement is most appropriate, whether to use multiple `if-else` statements or a single `switch` statement, when to represent something with a class and when not to, when to throw an exception and when to catch it, how to write an exception specification, and so on.

Most of these are design issues, but some are simple to add to code and can improve not only readability but also robustness. The use of const and references (along with other coding issues) is discussed in the next section. This is an area of programming in which you can continually improve.

The bottom line is this: If you know what you are doing when you write code, and you are doing it for the right reasons and in the right way, then your code will be easier to follow. This is because what the reader expects to happen will happen. If it doesn't, the reader will become confused by the code, which is to be avoided.

The Use of Comments

The main purpose of comments is to allow the annotation of the code to improve readability. Judicious use of comments does just that, but care needs to be taken not to make the code untidy by putting comments here and there without any real strategy.

Comments can be applied throughout implementation code to annotate specific areas where confusion might arise. If you do this, use only C++-style comments beginning with //. This prevents comments from being finished prematurely by the unexpected occurrence of a C-style comment end, */.

Using Comments to Document Code

How comments are added to implementation code is important. If it is done poorly, the effect can be to make code even more unclear. If a few guidelines are followed, comments can improve the readability of code.

It is important not to interrupt the layout of the code. Comments should be separated from the code, either with space or a differing style (such as italic) or by using a different color. A comment should be indented when code is indented. This is particularly important if the comments discuss the code's functionality. Comments written in this way can be scanned independently from the code, and the code can be scanned independently from the comments. Some programmers prefer not to separate a comment line from a code line, because they feel that use of color and style is sufficient to separate the comments from the code.

> **TIP**
>
> By modifying the settings on the Colors tab in the Tools, Editor Options menu, it is possible to remove or highlight comments as required. To hide a comment from view in the editor window, simply change the color of the comment so that it matches the editor window background color; in the Defaults setting this is white. To highlight a comment, try changing the background color to blue and setting the foreground color to white. You can experiment to see what you like most.

If a comment is specifically related to a single line of code and room permits, it is better to add the comment on the same line following the code. If several lines require such comments, an effort should be made to ensure that each comment starts at the same column in the editor. The advantage of such comments is that they do not interfere with the code's layout. For example, code could be commented as follows:

```
double GetMaximumValue(const std::vector<double>& Vector)
➥              throw(std::out_of_range)
{
    // Initialize Maximum, if the vector is empty an
    // std::out_of_range exception will be thrown

    double Maximum = Vector.at(0);

    for(int i=0; i<Vector.size(); ++i)
    {
        if(Vector[i] > Maximum)        // If the ith element is greater
        {                              // than the current value in
            Maximum = Vector[i];       // Maximum then set Maximum equal
        }                              // to its value
    }

    return Maximum;
}
```

The comments for the if statement are superfluous, but they have been added to illustrate how comments can be laid out. Comments can also be appended to the closing brace of loop and selection statements:

```
}//end if
}//end for
}// ! for
}//end for(int i=0; i<Vector.size(); ++i)
```

The last example might be too much sometimes, but it can be useful when writing code or when a loop or selection construct spans more than one page.

Comments are very useful when documenting code. They are particularly useful for summarizing important information about a function's operational characteristics. There are many ways to present such information, but the important thing is to use one method consistently. If there is something important to say about a function, the information should appear in the header file that declares it and in the implementation file that implements it. Whoever maintains the code needs as much information as the user of the code. You should always have a brief summary of a function's purpose above the function implementation and at the function's declaration. You should also list any requirements that must be met for the function to operate as expected (sometimes referred to as *preconditions*) and any promises that the function makes to the user (sometimes referred to as *postconditions*). Any condition that results in undefined behavior should be explicitly stated and included in any list of requirements. Information pre-sented in this way can be thought of as a contract for the function—if you do this, then the function promises to do that.

Only enough information as is necessary needs to be documented. For short, simple functions, little needs to be written. Conversely, large complex functions may require more lengthy com-ments. If this is so, two considerations must be kept in mind. Users of a function don't need to know of implementation issues internal to the function or how a function affects any private or protected data (assuming the function is a class member function). Such information should not appear in a header file. Also remember that comments are most useful when they are close to where they are directed in the implementation. It may be that some of the description is too detailed and some of the information given would be better placed elsewhere. An example of commenting a function in the implementation file would be as follows:

```
//----------------------------------------------------------//
//
// PURPOSE  : Returns the maximum value present in a vector
//            of doubles
//
// REQUIRES : The vector passed is not empty
//
// PROMISE  : The function will return the value of the
//            largest element
//
//----------------------------------------------------------//

double GetMaximumValue(const std::vector<double>& Vector)
                  throw(std::out_of_range)
{
   double Maximum = Vector.at(0);

   for(int i=0; i<Vector.size(); ++i)
   {
      if(Vector[i] > Maximum)
      {
         Maximum = Vector[i];
      }
   }

   return Maximum;
}
```

Similarly, the header file could look like this:

```
double GetMaximumValue(const std::vector<double>& Vector)
                  throw(std::out_of_range)
   // PURPOSE  : Returns the maximum value in a vector of doubles
```

```
// REQUIRES : The vector passed is not empty
// PROMISE  : Returns the value of the largest element
```

Remember that the header files in a program are often the only up-to-date documentation available for an interface, and as such they should be clear and accurately maintained (kept up-to-date). If this is not done, comments can quickly become useless. If code is changed, then always change any comments that relate to that code.

If you find yourself having to write extensive comments to explain a particularly tricky piece of code, it may be that the code itself should be changed.

Using Comments to Ignore Code

Another use of comments of particular note to C++Builder is the commenting out of the names of unused parameters in IDE-generated event handlers. It is common that some or all of the parameters are not used by the function. Commenting out the parameter names does not alter the function signature, but it does show explicitly which of the parameters are actually used. If parameters are written on the same line, then C-style comments must be used to achieve this. The parameter list can be rearranged to allow commenting with C++-style comments, but the result looks untidy. Therefore, caution must be exercised. The following code snippet of an event handler for a TButton MouseUp event is shown for illustration:

```cpp
void __fastcall TMainForm::Button1MouseUp(TObject* /*Sender*/,
                                          TMouseButton /*Button*/,
                                          TShiftState /*Shift*/,
                                          int X,
                                          int Y)
{
    // Display the cursor position within Button1
    Label1->Caption.sprintf("%d,%d", X, Y);
}
```

> **TIP**
>
> The MouseUp event handler uses the sprintf() AnsiString member function to modify the Caption property of Label1. This works because the sprintf() member function returns the AnsiString (*this) by reference. In general, however, a property should be modified only by assigning a new value to it using the assignment operator.

It is possible to delete the unused parameter names, but this can make the function header confusing, especially if you decide to use one of the parameters at a later date. A solution is to comment out the parameter name and then replace the commented out comma or closing bracket *before* the comment, as follows:

```
void __fastcall TMainForm::Button1MouseUp(TObject* ,//Sender,
                                          TMouseButton ,//Button,
                                          TShiftState ,//Shift,
                                          int X,
                                          int Y)
{
    // Display the cursor position within Button1
    Label1->Caption.sprintf("%d,%d", X, Y);
}
```

This is effective and easily maintainable. If you want to use the parameter later, simply delete the // and the extra comma or extra closing bracket. An alternative is as follows:

```
void __fastcall TMainForm::Button1MouseUp(TObject* ,//Sender
                                          TMouseButton ,//Button
                                          TShiftState ,//Shift
                                          int X,
                                          int Y)
{
    // Display the cursor position within Button1
    Label1->Caption.sprintf("%d,%d", X, Y);
}
```

This differs only in the removal of the redundant commas from the end of each comment. You may find this is an improvement, because a comma (or bracket) at the end of a comment could be a distraction.

Using Comments to Improve Appearance

A final use of comments is to help improve the overall appearance of the code as it appears on the screen or when it is printed. This is done by placing boxes around headings, placing divider lines between functions, and so on. When using comments in this way, care should be taken not to obscure the code within a forest of * characters or other such symbols. You must also be consistent for this to be useful.

C++Builder automatically places a divider line between blocks of code that it generates. This helps improve the appearance of the code, because there is additional visual separation. It is good practice to do this with your own code.

TIP

C++Builder 5 lets you change the default divider line that it places between sections of code that it generates. You can do so by editing the following entry in the BCB.BCF file in the $(BCB)\BIN folder. If the entry does not exist, you will have to create it. As you can see, the format is similar to an *.ini file.

```
[Code Formatting]
Divider Line=//---- My Custom Divider Line ----//
```

The divider line should begin as a comment line, with //. A good method of adding the line you want is to first write it in the Code Editor, then cut and paste it to the BCB.BCF file. That way you know exactly what it will look like. This helps IDE-generated code look consistent with your own code. It is a good idea to add this divider line to your code templates.

A Final Note on Improving the Readability of Code

Ultimately, the best descriptor of the code's purpose and how it operates is the code itself. By improving the code's readability, you enhance this description.

Better Programming Practices in C++Builder

This section looks at some ways to improve how you write C++ code in C++Builder. Entire books are devoted to better C++ programming, and you are encouraged to read such texts to deepen your understanding of C++. A list of suggested reading is given at the end of this chapter. The topics discussed here are those that have particular relevance to C++Builder and those that are often misunderstood or misused by those new to C++Builder.

Use a String Class Instead of char*

Say goodbye to char* for string manipulation. Use either the string class provided by the C++ Standard Library or the VCL's native string class AnsiString (which has been conveniently typedefed to String). You also could use both. You can access the C++ Standard Library's string class by including the statement

```
#include <string>
```

at the top of your code. If portability is a goal, this is the string class to use. Otherwise, use AnsiString, which has the advantage that it is the string representation used throughout the VCL. This allows your code to work seamlessly with the VCL. You should endeavor to become familiar with the methods that AnsiString offers. Because strings are required so often, this will pay itself back in terms of improved use and efficiency.

For circumstances in which an old-style char* string is required, such as to pass a parameter to a Win32 API call, both string classes offer the c_str() member function, which returns such a string. In addition, the AnsiString class also offers the popular old-style sprintf() and printf() functions (for concatenating strings) as member functions. It offers two varieties of each: a standard version and a cat_ version. The versions differ in that the cat_ version adds the concatenated string to the existing AnsiString, and the standard version replaces any existing contents of the AnsiString. The difference between the sprintf() and printf() member functions is that `sprintf()` returns a reference to the `AnsiString`, and `printf()` returns the length of the final formatted string (or the length of the appended string, in the case of `cat_printf`). The function declarations are

```
int __cdecl printf(const char* format, ...);
int __cdecl cat_printf(const char* format, ...);
AnsiString& __cdecl sprintf(const char* format, ...);
AnsiString& __cdecl cat_sprintf(const char* format, ...);
```

These member functions ultimately call `vprintf()` and `cat_vprintf()` in their implementation. These member functions take a `va_list` as their second parameter, as opposed to a variable argument list. This would require the addition of the `#include <stdarg.h>` statement in your code. The function declarations are

```
int __cdecl vprintf(const char* format, va_list paramList);
int __cdecl cat_vprintf(const char* format, va_list paramList);
```

The respective `printf()` and `sprintf()` functions perform the same task, differing only in their return types. As a result, this is the only criterion that is required when deciding which of the two to use.

CAUTION

Note that the `printf()` and `sprintf()` AnsiString member functions in C++Builder version 4 are the same as the `cat_printf()` and `cat_sprintf()` functions in version 5, *not* the `printf()` and `sprintf()` AnsiString member functions. Care should be taken when converting code between the two versions.

Understand References and Use Them Where Appropriate

References are often misunderstood and therefore are not used as often as they should be. Often it is possible to replace pointers with references, making the code more intuitive and easier to maintain. This section looks at some of the features of references and when they are most appropriately used. The reason for the abundance of pointer parameters in the VCL in C++Builder is also discussed.

A reference always refers to only one object, its *referent*, and it cannot be re-bound to refer to a different object ("object" in this context includes all types). A reference must be initialized on creation, and a reference cannot refer to nothing (NULL). Pointers, on the other hand, can point to nothing (NULL), can be re-bound, and do not require initialization on creation. A reference should be considered an alternative name for an object, whereas a pointer should be considered an object in itself. Anything that is done to a reference is also done to its referent and vice versa. This is because a reference is just an alternative name for the referent; they are the same thing. We can see therefore that references, unlike pointers, are implicitly dereferenced.

The following code shows how a reference can be declared:

```
int X = 12; // Declare and initialize int X to 12

int& Y = X; // Declare a reference to an int, i.e. Y, and
            // initialize it to refer to X
```

If we change the value of Y or X, we also change the value of X or Y, respectively, because X and Y are two names for the same thing. Another example of declaring a reference to a dynamically allocated variable is

```
TBook* Book1 = new TBook(); // Declare and create a TBook object

TBook& Book2 = *Book1;      // Declare a TBook reference,
                            // i.e. Book2, and initialize it
                            // to refer to the object pointed
                            // by Book1
```

The object pointed to by Book1 is the referent of the reference Book2.

One of the most important uses for references is the passing of user-defined types as parameters to functions. A parameter to a function can be passed by reference by making the parameter a reference and calling the function as if it were passed by value. For example, the following function is the typical swap function for two ints:

```
void swap(int& X, int& Y)
{
   int temp;
   temp = X;
   X = Y;
   Y = temp;
}
```

This function would be called as follows:

```
int Number1 = 12;
int Number2 = 68;

Swap(Number1, Number2);

// Number1 == 68 and Number2 == 12
```

Number1 and Number2 are passed by reference to swap, and therefore X and Y become alternative names for Number1 and Number2, respectively, within the function. What happens to X also happens to Number1 and what happens to Y also happens to Number2. A predefined type such as an int should be passed by reference only when the purpose is to change its value; otherwise, it is generally more efficient to pass by value. The same cannot be said for user-defined types (classes, structs, and so on). Rather than pass such types to functions by value, it is more efficient to pass such types by const reference or, if the type is to be changed, then by non-const reference or pointer. For example:

```
void DisplayMessage(const AnsiString& message)
{
    //Display message.
    // message is an alias for the AnsiString argument passed
    // to the function. No copy is made and the const qualifier
    // states that the function will not (cannot) modify message
}
```

is better than:

```
void DisplayMessage(AnsiString message)
{
    //Display message.
    // message is a copy of the AnsiString argument passed
}
```

The first function is better for two reasons. First, the `AnsiString` parameter is passed by reference. This means that when the function is called, the `AnsiString` used as the calling argument is used, because only a reference is used by the function. The copy constructor of `AnsiString` does not need to be invoked (as it would be on entering the second function), and neither does the destructor, as it would be at the end of the second function when `message` goes out of scope. Second, the `const` keyword is used in the first function to signify that the function will not modify `message` through `message`. Both functions are called in the same way:

```
AnsiString Message = "Hello!";

DisplayMessage(Message);
```

However, the first is safer and faster. Note that the calling code need not be directly affected.

Functions can also return references, which has the side effect of the function becoming an *lvalue* (a value that can appear on the left side of an expression) for the referent. This also allows operators to be written that appear on the left side of an expression, such as the subscript operator. For example, given the `Book` class, an `ArrayOfBooks` class can be defined as follows:

```
class Book
{
    public:
            Book();
            int NumberOfPages;
};

class ArrayOfBooks
{
  private:
            static const unsigned NumberOfBooks = 100;
  public:
```

```
        Book&  operator[] (unsigned i);
};
```

In this case, an instance of `ArrayOfBooks` can be used just like a normal array. Elements accessed using the subscript operator can be assigned to and read from, such as in the following:

```
ArrayOfBooks ShelfOfBooks;
unsigned PageCount = 0;

ShelfOfBooks[0].NumberOfPages = 45;          // A short book!
PageCount += ShelfOfBooks[0].NumberOfPages; //PageCount = 45
```

This is possible because the value returned by the operator is the actual referent, not a copy of the referent.

Generally we can say that references are preferred to pointers because they are safer (they can't be re-bound and don't require testing for `NULL` because they must refer to something). Also, they don't require explicit dereferencing, making code more intuitive.

What then of the pointers used in C++Builder's VCL? The reason behind the extensive use of pointers in the VCL is that the VCL is written in Object Pascal, which uses Object Pascal references. An Object Pascal reference is closer to a C++ pointer than a C++ reference. This has the side effect that, when the VCL is used with C++, pointers have to be used as replacements for Object Pascal references. This is because an Object Pascal reference (unlike a C++ reference) *can* be set to `NULL` and *can* be re-bound. In some cases it is possible to use reference parameters instead of pointer parameters, but because all VCL-based objects are dynamically allocated on free store and therefore are referred to through pointers, the pointers must be dereferenced first. Because the VCL relies on some of the features of Object Pascal references, pointers are used for object parameter passing and returning. Remember that a pointer parameter is passed by value, so the passed pointer will not be affected by the function. You can prevent modification of the object pointed to by using the `const` modifier.

Avoid Using Global Variables

Unless it is absolutely necessary, don't use global variables in your code. Apart from polluting the global namespace (and increasing the chance of a name collision), it increases the dependencies between translation units that use the variables. This makes code difficult to maintain and minimizes the ease with which translation units can be used in other programs. The fact that variables are declared elsewhere also makes code difficult to understand.

One of the first things any astute C++Builder programmer will notice is the global form pointers present in every form unit. This might give the impression that using global variables is OK; after all, C++Builder does it. However, C++Builder does this for a reason, which we will discuss at the end of this section. For now, we will examine some of the alternatives to declaring global variables.

3

**PROGRAMMING IN
C++BUILDER**

Let's assume that global variables are a must. How can we use global variables without incurring some of the side effects that they produce? The answer is that we use something that *acts* like a global variable but is not one. We use a class with a member function that returns a value of or reference to (whichever is appropriate) a static variable that represents our global variable. Depending on the purpose of our global variables (for example, global to a program or global to a library), we may or may not need access to the variables through static member functions. In other words, it may be possible to instantiate an object of the class that contains the static variables when they are required. We consider first the case where we do require access to the static variables (representing our global variables) through static member functions. We commonly refer to this kind of class as a *module*.

With a module of global variables, we improve our representation of the variables by placing them into a class, making them private static variables, and using static getters and setters to access them (for more information, see *Large-Scale C++ Software Design* by Lakos, 1996, p. 69). This prevents pollution of the global namespace and gives a certain degree of control over how the global variables are accessed. Typically, the class would be named Global. Hence, two global variables declared as

```
int Number;
double Average;
```

could be replaced by

```
class Global
{
 private:
    static int Number;
    static double Average;

    //PRIVATE CONSTRUCTOR
    Global(); //not implemented, instantiation not possible

  public:
    // SETTERS
    static void setNumber(int NewNumber) { Number = NewNumber; }
    static void setAverage(double NewAverage) { Average = NewAverage; }

    // GETTERS
    static int getNumber() { return Number; }
    static double getAverage() { return Average; }
};
```

Accessing Number is now done through Global::getNumber() and Global::setNumber(). Average is accessed similarly. The class Global is effectively a module that can be accessed throughout the program and does not need to be instantiated (because the member data and functions are static).

Often such an implementation is not required, and it is possible to create a class with a global point of access that is constructed only when first accessed. This has the benefit of allowing control over the order of initialization of the variables (objects must be constructed before first use). The method used is to place the required variables inside a class that cannot be directly instantiated, but accessed only through a static member function that returns a reference to the class. This ensures that the class containing the variables is constructed on first use and is constructed only once.

This approach is often referred to as the *Singleton pattern* (for more information, see *Design Patterns: Elements of Reusable Object-Orientated Software* by Gamma *et al.*, 1995, p. 127). Patterns are a way of representing recurring problems and their solutions in object-based programs. For more on patterns, see Chapter 4, "Advanced Programming with C++Builder."

The basic code required to create a Singleton (as such a class is commonly referred to) is as follows:

```
class Singleton
{
    public:
            static Singleton& Instance();

  protected:
            Singleton(); // Not Implemented, Instantiation not possible
};
```

An implementation of `Instance` is

```
Singleton& Singleton::Instance()
{
    static Singleton* NewSingleton = new Singleton();
    return *NewSingleton;
}
```

The initial call to `Instance` will create a new Singleton and return a reference to it. Subsequent calls will simply return a reference. However, the destructor of the Singleton will not be called; the object is simply abandoned on free store. If there is important processing that must be executed in the destructor, then the following implementation will ensure that the Singleton is destructed:

```
Singleton& Singleton::Instance()
{
    static Singleton NewSingleton;
    return NewSingleton;
}
```

This implementation causes its own problem. It is possible for another static object to access the Singleton after it has been destroyed. One solution to this problem is the *nifty counter technique* (for more information, see *C++ FAQs* Second Edition, Cline *et al.*, 1999, p. 235, and

Large-Scale C++ Software Design, Lakos, 1996, p. 537), in which a static counter is used to control when each object is created and destroyed. If you find the need for this technique, perhaps a re-think of the code would also be helpful. It may be that a slight redesign could remove the dependency.

It should now be clear that static variables are like global variables and can almost always be used in place of global variables. Remember, though, that ultimately global variables should be avoided.

Understand How C++Builder Uses Global Variables

What then of the global form pointer variables in C++Builder? Essentially, global form pointer variables are present to allow the use of non-modal forms. Such forms require a global point of access for as long as the form exists, and it is convenient for the IDE to automatically create one when the form is made. The default operation of the IDE is to add newly created forms to the auto-create list, which adds the line

```
Application->CreateForm(__classid(TFormX), &FormX);
```

(where *X* is a number) to the WinMain function in the project .cpp file. Modal forms do not require this, because the ShowModal() method returns *after* the forms are closed, making it possible to delete them in the same scope as they were created in. General guidelines on the use of forms can therefore be given.

> **TIP**
>
> You can uncheck the Auto Create Forms option on the Forms property page in the Tools, Environment Options menu to change the behavior of the IDE so that forms are not automatically added to the auto-create list. When this is done, forms are instead added to the available list.

First, determine if a form is to be a Modal form or a Non-Modal form.

If the form is Modal, then it is possible to create and destroy the form in the same scope. This being the case, the global form pointer variable is not required, and the form should not be auto-created. Remove the Application->CreateForm entry from WinMain either by deleting it or by removing it from the auto-create list on the Forms page in the Project, Options menu. Next, either delete or comment out the form pointer variable from the .h and .cpp files, and state explicitly in the header file that the form is Modal and should be used only with the ShowModal() method. That is, in the .cpp file remove

```
TFormX* FormX;
```

and from the .h file, remove

```
extern PACKAGE TFormX* FormX;
```

Add a comment such as the following:

```
// This form is MODAL and should only called with the ShowModal() method.
```

To use the form, simply write

```
TFormX* FormX = new TFormX(0);
try
{
   FormX->ShowModal();
}
__finally
{
   delete FormX;
}
```

Because you most likely do not want the form pointer to point elsewhere, you could declare the pointer as const:

```
TFormX* const FormX = new TFormX(0);
try
{
   FormX->ShowModal();
}
__finally
{
   delete FormX;
}
TFormX(this);
FormX->ShowModal();
delete FormX;
```

The use of a try/__finally block ensures that the code is exception-safe. An alternative to these examples is to use the Standard Library's auto_ptr class template:

```
auto_ptr<TFormX> FormX(new TFormX(0));
FormX->ShowModal();
```

Whichever technique you use, you are guaranteed that if the code terminates prematurely because an exception is thrown, FormX will be destructed automatically. With the first technique this happens in the __finally block; with the second it occurs when auto_ptr goes out of scope. The second technique can be further enhanced by making the auto_ptr const, since generally it is not required that the auto_ptr lose ownership of the pointer, as in the following code. (For more information, see *Exceptional C++: 47 Engineering Puzzles, Programming Problems, and Solutions* by Sutter, 2000, p. 158.)

```
const auto_ptr<TFormX> FormX(new TFormX(0));
FormX->ShowModal();
```

Of particular note in the code snippets is that 0 (NULL) is passed as the argument to the AOwner parameter of FormX. This is because we handle the destruction of the form ourselves.

> **TIP**
>
> Using auto_ptr is an effective way of managing the memory of VCL-based objects. It is exception-safe and easy to use. For a VCL object that takes an owner parameter in its constructor, you can simply pass 0, because you know that the object will be deleted when the auto_ptr goes out of scope.

If the form is Non-Modal, you must decide only whether or not you want it auto-created. If you don't, you must ensure that it is removed from WinMain. When you want it created later, you can use the form's global pointer and the new operator. Show the form using the Show() method. Remember that you cannot delete Modal forms, because Show() returns when the form is shown, not when it is closed. Therefore, it may still be in use. For example, if the form is auto-created, write

```
FormX->Show();
```

Otherwise create and show it this way:

```
FormX = new TFormX(this);
FormX->Show();
```

It is important not to create the form again after it has been auto-created, because this will overwrite the reference to the auto-created form. This means that the auto-created instance can no longer be accessed by the application and can result in the application crashing when an attempt to dereference the global pointer is made. It is advisable therefore to check the value of the pointer for equality with NULL (0) before creation:

```
if(FormX == 0) FormX = new TFormX(this);
FormX->Show();
```

This is possible because the form pointer is a global variable that is guaranteed to be initialized to zero. Using this technique ensures that the global pointer will always point to a valid location and will not be overwritten.

As an aside to this topic, the practice of declaring variables or functions as static so that they have scope only within the translation unit in which they are declared is deprecated. Instead, such variables and functions should be placed in an *unnamed* namespace. (For more information, see *ANSI/ISO C++ Professional Programmer's Handbook: The Complete Language* by Kalev, 1999, p. 157.)

Understand and Use const in Your Code

The const keyword should be used as a matter of course, not as an optional extra. Declaring a variable const allows attempted changes to the variable to be detected at compile time (resulting in an error) and also indicates the programmer's intention not to modify the given variable. Moreover, not using the const keyword indicates the programmer's intention to modify a given variable. The const keyword can be used in a variety of ways.

First, it can be used to declare a variable as a constant:

```
const double PI = 3.141592654;
```

This is the C++ way to declare constant variables. Do not use #define statements. Note that const variables must be initialized. The following shows the possible permutations for declaring const variables. Pointer and reference declarations are read from right to left, as the following examples show:

```
int Y = 12;
const int X = Y;        // X equals Y which equals 12, therefore X = 12
                        // X cannot be changed, but Y can

// In the next declaration the pointer itself is constant

int* const P = &Y;      // The int pointed to by P, i.e. Y can be
                        // changed through P but P itself cannot change

// The next two declarations are the same:

const int* P = &Y;      // The int pointed to by P, i.e.
int const* P = &Y;      // Y cannot be changed through P


// The next two declarations are the same:

const int* const P = &Y;   // Neither P, nor what it points to,
P
int const* const P = &Y;   // i.e. Y can be changed through P

// The next two declarations are the same:

const int& R = Y           // The int referred to by R, i.e.
R
int const& R = Y           // Y cannot be changed through R
```

After reviewing the previous examples, it is helpful to reiterate how const is used with pointer declarations. As stated previously, a pointer declaration is read from right to left, so that in int * const the const refers to the *. Hence, the pointer is constant, though the int it points to can be changed. With int const * the const refers to the int. In this case the int itself is constant, though the pointer to it is not. Finally, with int const * const, both the int and

the * are constant. Also remember that int const and const int are the same, so const int
* const is the same as int cosnt * const.

If you want to declare a literal string of chars, declare it as one of the following:

```
const char* const LiteralString = "Hello World";
char const * const LiteralString = "Hello World";
```

Both of the previous strings and the pointers to them are constant.

Function parameters should be declared as const in this fashion when it is appropriate, such as
when the intention of the function is not to modify the argument that is passed to the function.
For example, the following function states that it will not modify the arguments passed to it:

```
double GetAverage(const double* ArrayOfDouble, int LengthOfArray)
{
    double Sum = 0;

    for(int i=0; i<LengthOfArray; ++i)
    {
        Sum += ArrayOfDouble[i];
    }

    double Average = Sum/LengthOfArray;
    return Average;
}
```

Another way of thinking about this is to assume that if the const keyword is not used for a
parameter, then it must be the intention of the function to modify that parameter's argument,
unless the parameter is pass-by-value (a copy of the parameter is used, not the parameter
itself). Notice that declaring int LengthOfArray as a const is inappropriate, because this is
pass-by-value. LengthOfArray is a copy, and declaring it as a const has no effect on the argument passed to the function. Similarly, ArrayOfDouble is declared as follows:

```
const double* ArrayOfDouble
```

not

```
const double* const ArrayOfDouble
```

Because the pointer itself is a copy, only the data that it points to needs to be made const.

The return type of a function can also be const. Generally it is not appropriate to declare types
returned by value as const, except in the case of requiring the call of a const-overloaded
member function. Reference and pointer return types are suitable for returning as consts.

Member functions can be declared const. A const member function is one that does not modify the this object (*this). Hence, it can call other member functions inside its function body
only if they are also const. To declare a member function const, place the const keyword at

the end of the function declaration and in the function definition at the same place. Generally, all getter member functions should be const, because they do not modify *this. For example

```
class Book
{
    private:
            int NumberOfPages;
     public:
            Book();
            int GetNumberOfPages() const;
};
```

The definition of GetNumberOfPages() could be

```
int Book::GetNumberOfPages() const
{
    return NumberOfPages;
}
```

The final area in which const is commonly encountered is when operators are overloaded by a class and access to both const and non-const variables is required. For example, if a class ArrayOfBooks is created to contain Book objects, it is sensible to assume that the [] operator will be overloaded (so that the class acts like an array). However, the question of whether or not the [] operator will be used with const or non-const objects must be considered. The solution is to const-overload the operator, as the following code indicates:

```
class ArrayOfBooks
{
    public:
            Book&       operator[] (unsigned i);
            const Book& operator[] (unsigned i) const;
};
```

The ArrayOfBooks class can use the [] operator on both const and non-const Books. For example, if an ArrayOfBooks object is passed to a function by reference to const, it would be illegal for the array to be assigned to using the [] operator. This is because the value indexed by i would be a const reference, and the const state of the passed array would be preserved.

Remember, know what const is and use it whenever you can.

Be Familiar with the Principles of Exceptions

An exception is a mechanism for handling runtime errors in a program. There are several approaches that can be taken to handling runtime errors, such as returning error codes, setting global error flags, and exiting the program. In many circumstances, an exception is the only appropriate method that can be employed effectively, such as when an error occurs in a constructor. (For more information, see *ANSI/ISO C++ Professional Programmer's Handbook: The Complete Language* by Kalev, 1999, p. 113.)

3

PROGRAMMING IN
C++BUILDER

Exceptions will commonly be encountered in two forms in C++Builder programs: C++ exceptions and VCL exceptions. Generally the principles involved with both are the same, though there are some differences.

C++ uses three keywords to support exceptions; `try`, `catch`, and `throw`. C++Builder extends its exception support to include the `__finally` keyword.

The `try`, `catch`, and `__finally` keywords are used as headers to blocks of code (that is, code that is enclosed between braces). Also, for every `try` block there must *always* be one or more `catch` blocks *or* a single `__finally` block.

The `try` Keyword

The `try` keyword is used in one of two possible ways. The first and simplest is as a simple block header, to create a `try` block within a function. The second is as a function block header, to create a *function* `try` block, either by placing the `try` keyword in front of the function's first opening brace or, in the case of constructors, in front of the colon that signifies the start of the initializer list.

> **NOTE**
>
> C++Builder does not currently support function `try` blocks. However, because it makes a real difference only with constructors and even then has little impact on their use, it is unlikely that its omission will have any effect. For those who are interested, it will be supported in version 6 of the compiler.

The `catch` Keyword

Normally, at least one `catch` block will immediately follow any `try` block (or function `try` block). A `catch` block will always appear as the `catch` keyword followed by parentheses containing a single exception type specification with an optional variable name. Such a `catch` block (commonly referred to as an *exception handler*) can catch only an exception whose type *exactly* matches the exception type specified by the `catch` block. However, a `catch` block can be specified to catch *all* exceptions by using the *catch all* ellipses exception type specifier, `catch(...)`.

A typical try/catch scenario is as follows:

```
try
{
    // Code that may throw an exception
}
catch(exception1& e)
{
    // Handler code for exception1 type exceptions
```

```
}
catch(exception2& e)
{
    // Handler code for exception2 type exceptions
}
catch(...)
{
    // Handler code for any exception not already caught
}
```

The __finally Keyword

The last of these, __finally, has been added to allow the possibility of performing cleanup operations or ensuring certain code is executed regardless of whether an exception is thrown. This works because code placed inside a __finally block will always execute, even when an exception is thrown in the corresponding try block. This allows code to be written that is exception-safe and will work properly in the presence of exceptions. A typical try/__finally scenario is

```
try
{
    // Code that may throw an exception
}
__finally
{
    // Code here is always executed, even if
    // an exception is thrown in the preceding
    // try block
}
```

It should be noted that try/catch and try/__finally constructs can be nested inside other try/catch and try/__finally constructs.

The throw Keyword

The throw keyword is used in one of two ways. The first is to throw (or rethrow) an exception, and the second is to allow the specification of the type of exceptions that a function may throw. In the first case (to throw or rethrow an exception), the throw keyword is followed optionally by parentheses containing a single exception variable (often an object) or simply the single exception variable after a space, similar to a return statement. When no such exception variable is used, the throw keyword stands on its own. Then its behavior depends on its placement. When placed inside a catch block, the throw statement rethrows the exception currently being handled. When placed elsewhere, such as when there is no exception to rethrow, it causes terminate() to be called, ultimately ending the program. It is not possible to use throw to rethrow an exception in VCL code. The second use of the throw keyword is to allow the specification of the exceptions that a function may throw. The syntax for the keyword is

```
throw(<exception_type_list>)
```

The *exception_type_list* is optional and when excluded indicates that the function will not throw any exceptions. When included, it takes the form of one or more exception types separated by commas. The exception types listed are the only exceptions the function may throw.

Unhandled and Unexpected Exceptions

In addition to the three keywords described, C++ offers mechanisms to deal with thrown exceptions that are not handled by the program and exceptions that are thrown but are not expected. This might include an exception that is thrown inside a function with an incompatible exception specification.

When an exception is thrown but not handled, `terminate()` is called. This calls the default terminate handler function, which by default calls `abort()`. This default behavior should be avoided because `abort()` does not ensure that local object destructors are called. To prevent `terminate()` being called as a result of an uncaught exception, the entire program can be wrapped inside a `try/catch(...)` block in `WinMain()` (or `main()` for command-line programs). This ensures that any exception will eventually be caught. If `terminate()` is called, you can modify its default behavior by specifying your own terminate handler function. Simply pass the name of your terminate handler function as an argument to the `std::set_terminate()` function. The `<stdexcept>` header file must be included. For example, given a function declared as

```
void TerminateHandler();
```

The code required to ensure that this handler is called in place of the basic `terminate()` handler is

```
#include <stdexcept>

std::set_terminate(TerminateHandler);
```

When an exception is thrown that is not expected, then `unexpected()` is called. Its default behavior is to call `terminate()`. Again, the opportunity exists to define your own function to handle this occurrence. To do so, call `std::set_unexpected()`, passing the function handler name as an argument. The `<stdexcept>` header file must be included.

Using Exceptions

This brings the discussion to consideration of the exceptions that can and should be thrown by a function and where such exceptions should be caught. This should be decided when you are designing your code, not after it has already been written. To this end, you must consider several things when you write a piece of code. Some of the topics are very complex, and it is beyond the scope of this book to cover all the issues involved. Instead, check the "Further Reading" section at the end of this chapter for more information.

You must consider if the code you have written could throw one or more exceptions. If so, you must then consider if it is appropriate to catch one or more of the exceptions in the current scope or let one or more of them propagate to an exception handler outside the current scope. If you do not want one or more of the exceptions to propagate outside the current scope, then you must place the code in a `try` block and follow it with the one or more appropriate `catch` blocks to catch any desired exceptions (or all exceptions, using a catch-all block). To this end, you should be aware of the exceptions built into the language itself, the C++ Standard Library, and the VCL and be aware of when they may be thrown. For example, if `new` fails to allocate enough memory, `std::bad_alloc` is thrown.

Throw an exception in a function only when it is appropriate to do so, when the function cannot meet its promise. (See the section "The Use of Comments," earlier in this chapter, for a discussion of a function's promise. Also see *C++ FAQs*, Second Edition, Cline *et al.*, 1999, p. 137.)

You should catch an exception only when you know what to do with it, and you should always catch an exception by reference. (For more information, see *More Effective C++: 35 New Ways to Improve Your Programs and Designs* by Meyers, 1996, p. 68.) VCL exceptions *cannot* be caught by value. Also, it may not be possible to fully recover from an exception, in which case the handler should perform any possible cleanup and then rethrow the exception.

You should understand when and how to use exception specifications for functions and be wary of the possibility of writing an incorrect specification. This will result in `unexpected()` being called if an unspecified exception is thrown inside a function and it is not handled within that function.

You should ensure that you write exception-safe code that works properly in the presence of exceptions. For example, simple code such as this is not exception safe:

```
TFormX* const FormX = new TFormX(0);
FormX->ShowModal();
delete FormX;
```

If an exception is thrown between the creation and deletion of the form, the form will never be deleted, so the code does not work properly in the presence of exceptions. For an exception-safe alternative, see the section "Avoid Global Variables," earlier in this chapter.

If you are writing container classes, endeavor to write code that is *exception-neutral*—code that propagates all exceptions to the caller of the function that contains the code. (For more information, see *Exceptional C++: 47 Engineering Puzzles, Programming Problems, and Solutions* by Sutter, 2000, p. 25.)

Never throw an exception from a destructor, because the destructor may have been called as a result of stack unwinding after a previous exception was called. This calls `terminate()`. Destructors should have an exception specification of `throw()`.

3

PROGRAMMING IN
C++BUILDER

A Final Note on Exceptions

Finally, you should appreciate the differences between VCL and C++ exceptions. VCL exceptions allow operating system exceptions to be handled as well as exceptions generated from within the program. Such exceptions must be caught by reference. VCL exceptions generated from within the program cannot be caught by value. An advantage of VCL exceptions is that they can be thrown and caught within the IDE.

Use `new` and `delete` to Manage Memory

The VCL requires that all classes that inherit from `TObject` are created dynamically in free store. Free store is often referred to as the heap, but free store is the correct term when applied to memory allocated and deallocated by `new` and `delete`. The term *heap* should be reserved for the memory allocated and deallocated by `malloc()` and `free()`. (For more information, see *Exceptional C++: 47 Engineering Puzzles, Programming Problems, and Solutions* by Sutter, 2000, p. 142.) This means a lot of calls to `new` and `delete` in C++Builder programs, so it is important to understand a few things about how `new` and `delete` work.

> **CAUTION**
>
> A Non-Plain Old Data (Non-POD) object is essentially any but the most trivial of classes. Such objects must have their memory allocated by using `new`; the C equivalent `malloc()` will not suffice (its behavior is undefined) and be subsequently deallocated with `delete`, not `free()`. The `new` and `delete` operators ensure that, in addition to the allocation/deallocation of memory, the object's constructor and destructor, respectively, are called.
>
> The `new` operator also returns a pointer that is suitable to the object created, not merely a `void` pointer that must be cast to the required type. `new` and `delete` call operator `new`/operator `delete`, respectively, to allocate/deallocate memory, and these can be overloaded for specific classes. This allows the customization of memory allocation/deallocation behavior. This is not possible with `malloc()` and `free()`.
>
> (For more information, see *ANSI/ISO C++ Professional Programmer's Handbook: The Complete Language* by Kalev, 1999, p. 221.)

A successful call to `new` allocates sufficient memory in free store (using `operator new`) calls the object's constructor and returns a pointer of the type pointer-to-the-object-type-created. A correctly initialized object is the result. Subsequently calling `delete` calls the object's destructor and deallocates the memory obtained previously by calling `new`.

> **CAUTION**
>
> Never call a VCL object's `Free()` method to destroy a VCL object. Always use `delete`. This ensures that the object's destructor is called and that the memory allocated previously with `new` is freed. `Free()` does not guarantee this, and it is bad practice to use it.

If the call to `new` is unsuccessful, a `std::bad_alloc` exception is thrown. Note that the `bad_alloc` exception is defined in the standard library file `<new>`. Hence, you must include `#include <new>` in your program, and it is in the `std` namespace. It does not return `NULL`. Therefore, you should not check the return pointer for equality with `NULL`. The program should be prepared to catch the `std::bad_alloc` exception and, if the function that calls `new` does not catch the exception, it should pass the exception outside the function, so that calling code has the opportunity to catch it. Either of the following would be appropriate:

```
void CreateObject(TMyObject* MyObject) throw()
{
   try
   {
      MyObject = new TMyObject();
   }
   catch(std::bad_alloc)
   {
      //Print a message "Not enough memory for MyObject";
      // Deal with the problem
      // or exit gracefully
   }
}
```

or

```
void CreateObject(TMyObject* MyObject) throw(std::bad_alloc)
{
   MyObject = new TMyObject();
}
```

The use of exceptions allows the code that handles the error to be centralized, which leads to safer code that is more intuitive. The `throw` keyword added to the function header is called an *exception specification*. The effect of its inclusion in the function header is to specify which exceptions the function may throw. For more explanation refer to the section "Be Familiar with the Principles of Exceptions," earlier in this chapter. In the case of the first `CreateObject()` function, a `throw()` exception specifier is used to indicate that no exception will be thrown by the function. This is acceptable, because the only exception that may be thrown, `std::bad_alloc`, is caught and dealt with by the function itself. In the case of the second implementation of `CreateObject()`, the exception specifier `throw(std::bad_alloc)` is used

3

PROGRAMMING IN
C++BUILDER

to indicate that the only exception that the function can throw is `std::bad_alloc`. This should be caught and handled by one of the calling routines.

There is also the possibility of writing your own out-of-memory function handler to deal with failed memory allocation. To set a function as a handler for out-of-memory conditions when using new, call the `set_new_handler()` function (also defined in <new>), passing as a parameter the name of the function you will use as the out-of-memory handler. For example, if you write a function (non-member or `static` member) called `OutOfMemory` to handle such occurrences, the necessary code would be

```
#include <new>

void OutOfMemory()
{
    // Try to free some memory
    // if there is now enough memory then this
    // function will NOT be called next time
    // else either install a new handler or throw an exception
}

// Somewhere in the main code, near the start write:
std::set_new_handler(OutOfMemory);
```

This code requires some explanation, because the sequence of events that occurs when new fails dictates how the `OutOfMemory` function should be written. If new fails to allocate enough memory, then `OutOfMemory` is called. `OutOfMemory` tries to free some memory (how this is done will be discussed later); new will then try again to allocate the required memory. If it is successful, we are finished. If it is unsuccessful, the process just described will be repeated. In fact, it will repeat infinitely until either enough memory is allocated or the `OutOfMemory` function terminates the process.

To terminate the process, the `OutOfMemory` function can do several things. It can throw an exception (such as `std::bad_alloc()`), it can install a different memory handler that can then try to make more memory available, it can assign NULL to set_new_handler (`std::set_new_handler(0)`), or it can exit the program (not recommended). If a new handler is installed, then this series of events will occur for the new handler (which is called on the subsequent failed attempt). If the handler is set to NULL (0), then no handler will be called, and the exception `std::bad_alloc()` will be thrown.

Making more memory available is dependent on the design of the program and where the memory shortage arises from. If the program keeps a lot of memory tied up for performance reasons but does not always require it to be available at all times, then such memory can be freed if a shortage occurs. Identifying such memory is the difficult part. If there is no such memory usage in the program, then the shortage will be a result of factors external to the program, such as other memory-intensive software or physical limitations. There is nothing that can be done about physical limitations, but it is possible to warn the user of a memory shortage so that memory-intensive software can be shut down, thereby freeing additional memory.

The trick is to give an advance warning before all the memory is used up. One approach is to pre-allocate a quantity of memory at the beginning of the program. If new fails to allocate enough memory, then this memory can be freed. The user is warned that memory is low and told to try to free more memory for the application. Assuming that the pre-allocated block was large enough, the program should be able to continue operating as normal if the user has freed additional memory. This preemptive approach is simple to implement and reasonably effective. There are other approaches, and the reader is directed to the books in the "Further Reading" section for more information.

It is important to note that if you want to allocate raw memory only, then operator new and operator delete should be used instead of the new and delete operators. (For more information, see *More Effective C++: 35 New Ways to Improve Your Programs and Designs* by Meyers, 1996, p. 38.) This is useful for situations in which, for example, a structure needs to be allocated dynamically, and the size of the structure is determined through a function call before the dynamic allocation. This is a common occurrence in Win32 API programming:

```
DWORD StructureSize = APIFunctionToGetSize(SomeParameter);

WIN32STRUCTURE* PointerToStructure;
PointerToStructure = static_cast<WIN32STRUCTURE*>(operator new(StructureSize));
// Do something with the structure
operator delete(PointerToStructure);
```

It is clear that the use of malloc() and free() should not be required.

Finally, we will discuss the use of new and delete in dynamically allocating and deallocating arrays. Arrays are allocated and deallocated using operator new[] and operator delete[], respectively. They are separate operators from operator new and operator delete. When new is used to create an array of objects, it first allocates the memory for the objects (using operator new[]) and then each object is initialized by calling its *default constructor*. Deleting an array using delete performs the opposite task: It calls the destructor for each object and then deallocates the memory (using operator delete[]) for the array. So that delete knows to call operator delete[] instead of operator delete, a [] is placed between the delete keyword and the pointer to the array to be deleted:

```
delete [] SomeArray;
```

Allocating a single-dimensional array is straightforward. The following format is used:

```
TBook* ArrayOfBooks = new TBook[NumberOfBooks];
```

Deleting such an array is also straightforward. However, remember that the correct form of delete must be used—delete []. For example

3

PROGRAMMING IN
C++BUILDER

```
delete [] ArrayOfBooks;
```

Remember that [] tells the compiler that the pointer is to an array, as opposed to simply a pointer to a single element of a given type. If an array is to be deleted, it is essential that delete [] be used, not delete. If delete is used erroneously, then at best only the first element of the array will be deleted. We know that when an array of objects is created, the default constructor is used. This means that you will want to ensure that you have defined the default constructor to suit your needs. Remember that a compiler-generated default constructor does not initialize the classes' data members. Also, you will probably want to overload the assignment operator (=) so that you can safely assign object values to the array objects. A two-dimensional array can be created using code such as the following:

```
TBook** ShelvesOfBooks = new TBook*[NumberOfShelves];

for(int i=0; i<NumberOfShelves; ++i)
{
    ShelvesOfBooks[i] = new TBook[NumberOfBooks];
}
```

To delete such an array use the following:

```
for(int i=0; i<NumberofShelves; ++i)
{
    delete [] ShelvesOfBooks[i];
}

delete [] ShelvesOfBooks;
```

One thing remains unsaid: If you want to have an array of objects, a better approach is to create a vector of objects using the vector template from the STL. It allows any constructor to be used and also handles memory allocation and deallocation automatically. It will also reallocate memory if there is a memory shortage. This means that the use of the C library function realloc() is also no longer required. For more information on the vector template class, refer to the "Introduction to the Standard C++ Library and Templates" section in Chapter 4.

Placement new (allocation at a predetermined memory location) and nothrow new (does not throw an exception on failure, returns NULL instead) have not been discussed, because they are beyond the scope of this section. However, if more information is required on either of these, please refer to the "Further Reading" section.

Understand and Use C++-Style Casts

There are four C++ casts. They are outlined in Table 3.1.

TABLE 3.1   C++-Style Casts

Cast	General Purpose
static_cast<T>(exp)	Used to perform casts such as an int to a double.
	T and exp may be a pointer, a reference, an arithmetic type (such as int), or an enum type. You cannot cast from one type to another, such as from a pointer to an arithmetic.
dynamic_cast<T>(exp)	Used to perform casting down or across an inheritance hierarchy. For example, if class X inherits from class O, then a pointer to class O can be cast to a pointer to class X, provided the conversion is valid.
	T may be a pointer or a reference to a defined class type or void*.
	exp may be a pointer or a reference. For a conversion from a base class to a derived class to be possible, the base class must contain at least one virtual function; in other words, it must be polymorphic. One important feature of dynamic_cast is that if a conversion between pointers is not possible, a NULL pointer is returned; if a conversion between references is not possible, a std::bad_cast exception is thrown (include the header file <typeinfo>). As a result, the conversion can be checked for success.
const_cast<T>(exp)	This is the only cast that can affect the const or volatile nature of an expression. It can be either cast off or cast on. This is the only thing const_cast is used for.
	For example, if you want to pass a pointer to const data to a functionthat only takes a pointer to non-const data, and you know the data will not be modified, you could pass the pointer by const_casting it.
	T and exp must be of the same type except for their const or volatile factors.
reinterpret_cast<T>(exp)	Used to perform unsafe orimplmentation-dependent casts. This cast should be used only when nothing else will do. This is because it allows you to re-interpret the expression as a completely different type, such as to cast a float* to an int*. It is commonly used to cast between function pointers. If you find yourself needing to use

3

PROGRAMMING IN C++BUILDER

TABLE 3.1 Continued

Cast	*General Purpose*
	reinterpret_cast, decide carefully if the approach you are taking is the right one, and remember to document clearly your intention (and possibly your reasons for this approach).
	T must be a pointer, a reference, an arithmetic type, a pointer to a function, or a pointer to a member function. A pointer can be cast to an integral type and vice versa.

The casts most likely to be of use are static_cast (for trivial type conversions such as int to double) and dynamic_cast.

An example of using static_cast can be found in the last line of the following code:

```
int Sum = 0;
int* Numbers = new int[20];

for(int i=0; i<20; ++i)
{
    Numbers[i] = i*i;
    Sum += Numbers[i];
}

double Average = static_cast<double>(Sum)/20;
```

The astute among you will recognize this as the code from Listing 3.4 earlier in this chapter.

One of the times when dynamic_cast is commonly used in C++Builder is to dynamic_cast TObject* Sender or TComponent* Owner, to ensure that Sender or Owner is of a desired class, such as TForm. For example, if a component is placed on a form, it may be necessary to distinguish if it was placed directly or was perhaps placed on a Panel component. To carry out such a test, the following code is required:

```
TForm* OwnerForm = dynamic_cast<TForm*>(Owner);
if(OwnerForm)
{
    //Perform processing since OwnerForm != NULL, i.e. 0
}
```

First a pointer of the required type is declared, and then it is set equal to the result of the dynamic_cast. If the cast is unsuccessful, the pointer will point to the required type and can be used for accessing that type. If it fails, it will point to NULL, and hence can be used to evaluate a Boolean expression. Sender can be similarly used. The situations that require such casting are many and varied. What is important is to understand what it is that you want to achieve and make your intention and reasoning clear.

Each of the C++ casts performs a specific task and should be restricted for use only where appropriate. The C++ casts are also easily seen in code, making it more readable.

Know When to Use the Preprocessor

It is not appropriate to use the preprocessor for defining constants or for creating function macros. Instead, you should use `const` variables or `enum` types for constants and use an `inline` function (or `inline` template function) to replace a function macro. Consider also that a function macro may not be appropriate anyway (in which case the `inline` equivalent would not be required).

For example, the constant π can be defined as

```
const double PI = 3.141592654;
```

If you wanted to place this inside a class definition, then you would write

```
class Circle
{
    public:
            static const double PI; // This is only a declaration
};
```

In the implementation (`*.cpp`) file, you would define and initialize the constant by writing

```
const double Circle::PI = 3.141592654;
// This is the constant definition
                                // and initialization
```

Note that the class constant is made `static` so that only one copy of the constant exists for the class. Also notice that the constant is initialized in the implementation file (typically after the `include` directive for the header file that contains the class definition). The exception to this is the initialization of integral types, `char`, `short`, `long`, `unsigned`, and `int`. These can be initialized directly in the class definition. When a group of related constants is required, an `enum` is a sensible choice:

```
enum LanguagesSupported { English, Chinese, Japanese, French };
```

Sometimes an `enum` is used to declare an integer constant on its own:

```
enum { LENGTH = 255 };
```

Such declarations are sometimes seen inside class definitions. A `static const` variable declaration (like that for `PI`) is a more correct approach.

Replacing a function macro is also easily achieved. Given the macro

```
#define cubeX(x) ( (x)*(x)*(x) )
```

the following `inline` function equivalent can be written:

```
inline double cubeX(double x) { return x*x*x; }
```

Notice that this function takes a double as an argument. If an int were passed as a parameter, it would have to be cast to a double. Because we want the behavior of the function to be similar to that of the macro, we should avoid this necessity. This can be achieved in one of two ways: Either overload the function or make it a function template. In this case, overloading the function is the better of the two choices, because a function template would imply that the function could be used for classes as well, which would most likely be inappropriate. Therefore, an int version of the inline function could be written as

```
inline int cubeX(int x) { return x*x*x; }
```

Generally, we want to avoid using #define for constants and function macros. #define should be used when writing include guards. Remember that include guards are written in the header file to ensure that a header already included is not included again. For example, a typical header file in C++Builder will look like this:

```
#ifndef Unit1H  // Is Unit1H not already defined?
#define Unit1H  // If not then we reach this line and define it

// Header file code placed here...

#endif          // End of if Unit1H not defined
```

This code ensures that the code between #ifndef and #endif will be included only once. It is a good idea to follow some convention when choosing suitable defines for header files. C++Builder uses an uppercase H after the header filename. If you write your own translation units, you should follow this convention. Of course, you can use a different naming convention, such as pre-pending INCLUDED_ to the header filename, but you should be consistent throughout a project. Using include guards prevents a header file from being included more than once, but it must still be processed to see if it is to be included.

TIP

When you follow the IDE naming convention for include guards (appending an 'H' to the end of the header filename), the IDE treats the translation unit as a set, and it will appear as such in the Project Manager. If you do not want your .cpp and .h files to be treated in this way, do not use IDE-style include guards.

It has been shown that for very large projects (or more generally, projects with large, dense include graphs), this can have a significant effect on compile times. (For more information, see *Large-Scale C++ Software Design* by Lakos, 1996, p. 82.) Therefore, it is worth wrapping all include statements in an include guard to prevent the unnecessary inclusion of a file that has been already defined. For example, if Unit1 from the previous code snippet also included

ModalUnit1, ModalUnit2, and ModalUnit3, which are dialog forms used by other parts of the program, their include statements could be wrapped inside an include guard as follows:

```
#ifndef Unit1H  // Is Unit1H not already defined?
#define Unit1H  // If not then we reach this line and define it

#ifndef ModalUnit1H       // Is ModalUnit1H not already defined?
#include "ModalUnit1.h"   // No then include it
#endif                    // End of if Unit1H not defined

#ifndef ModalUnit2H
#include "ModalUnit2.h"
#endif

#ifndef ModalUnit3H
#include "ModalUnit3.h"
#endif


// Header file code placed here...

#endif            // End of if Unit1H not defined
```

This is not pretty but it is effective. Remember that you must ensure that the names you define for include guards must not match any name that appears elsewhere in your program. The define statement will ensure that it is replaced with nothing, which could cause havoc. That is why a naming convention must be agreed upon and adhered to.

3

PROGRAMMING IN
C++BUILDER

TIP

Note that the Project Manager in C++Builder 5 has been improved to include an expandable list of header file dependencies for each source file included in a project. Simply click on the node beside the source filename to either expand or collapse the list. Note that the header file dependency lists are based on the source file's .obj file, hence the file must be compiled at least once to use this feature. Also note that the list could be out of date if changes are made without recompilation.

Know when using the preprocessor will benefit the program and when it won't. Use it carefully and only when necessary.

Learn About and Use the C++ Standard Library

The C++ Standard Library, including the Standard Template Library (STL), is a constituent part of ANSI/ISO C++, just as the definition for bool is. You can save a lot of unnecessary coding by learning to use its features in your programs. The Standard Library has an advantage over homegrown code in that it has been thoroughly tested and is fast, and it *is* the standard, so portability is a big bonus. Standard Library features are summarized in the following list:

- Exceptions, such as `bad_alloc`, `bad_cast`, `bad_typeid`, and `bad_exception`
- Utilities, such as `min()`, `max()`, `auto_ptr<T>`, and `numeric_limits<T>`
- Input and output streams, such as `istream` and `ostream`
- Containers, such as `vector<T>`
- Algorithms, such as `sort()`
- Function objects (functors), such as `equal_to<T>()`
- Iterators
- Strings, such as `string`
- Numerics, such as `complex<T>`
- Special containers, such as `queue<T>` and `stack<T>`
- Internationalization support

Nearly everything in the Standard Library is a template, and most of the library consists of the STL, so it is very flexible. For example, the `vector` template class can be used to store any kind of data of the same type. As a result, it is a direct replacement for arrays in C++ and should be used in preference to arrays whenever possible. For more information about the STL, refer to the "Introduction to the Standard C++ Library and Templates" section in Chapter 4.

Further Reading

This section lists some texts that cover the material presented in this chapter much more thoroughly, and they should be a first source for more information about C++ programming. The books are listed in alphabetical order according to the author's name. A brief summary of the contents of each book is also given.

- Cline, M., Lomow, G., and Girou, M. (1999). *C++ FAQs* Second Edition. Addison-Wesley Longman, Inc.

  This text is based on the online C++ FAQ at `http://www.cerfnet.com/~mpcline/c++-faq-lite/`, but it offers much more than the online FAQ. It covers topics from basic to very advanced and is well written, having evolved over several years. This book offers very good value and makes an excellent reference, a great choice for a second book on C++.

- Gamma, E., Helm, R., Johnson, R., and Vlissides, J. (1995). *Design Patterns: Elements of Reusable Object-Orientated Software*. Addison-Wesley Longman, Inc.

This is the pioneering text on design patterns. Examples are given in C++ (and Smalltalk), making it particularly useful. This book should help you to approach object-based programming in a different way.

- Horton, I. (1998). *Beginning C++: The Complete Language*. Wrox Press.

  This text has complete coverage of ANSI/ISO C++. It is not compiler specific and is very up to date. It is precise and includes information not found in other books. It makes a very good first book on C++.

- Kalev, D. (1999). *ANSI/ISO C++ Professional Programmer's Handbook: The Complete Language*. Que Corporation.

  This is a relatively recent text with many interesting insights into the C++ standard. It is a handy reference for many of the more advanced topics in C++. It focuses a lot on *why* certain features are present, offering an insight rarely found in many similar books.

- Lakos, J. (1996). *Large-Scale C++ Software Design*. Addison-Wesley Longman, Inc.

  Despite the title, this text is essential reading for anyone involved in any but the most trivial C++ projects. Divided into three parts covering basics, physical design, and logical design, the book has many guidelines and principles scattered throughout (collated at the end for ease of reference) that make reading it instantly productive.

- McConnell, S. C. (1993). *Code Complete: A Practical Handbook of Software Construction*. Microsoft Press.

  This text offers a very thorough treatment of how code is written. It is a definitive guide to this subject and should be read by anyone who really wants to examine and understand the merits of the different ways code is written. It does not present one particular method of writing code but rather comments on a variety of techniques.

- Meyers, S. (1998). *Effective C++ Second Edition: 50 Specific Ways to Improve Your Programs and Designs*. Addison-Wesley Longman, Inc.

  Perhaps one of the most famous C++ books, it is written in an easy-to-read style, its size belies the great wealth of information it contains.

- Meyers, S. (1996). *More Effective C++: 35 New Ways to Improve Your Programs and Designs*. Addison-Wesley Longman, Inc.

  The follow-up text to *Effective C++* offers more pearls of wisdom to be digested by the avid programmer. Meyers' books are definitely a must read.

- Sutter, H. (2000). *Exceptional C++: 47 Engineering Puzzles, Programming Problems, and Solutions*. Addison-Wesley Longman, Inc.

  As the title suggests, this is an advanced text based on the "C++ Guru of the Week" series, which can be found on the `comp.lang.c++.moderated` newsgroup. It covers many topics and is highly informative. Once several of the previous texts have been digested, thisbook's true value can be appreciated.

3

PROGRAMMING IN C++BUILDER

Summary

This chapter has covered a lot of ground. The main points to remember from the chapter are as follows:

- Use a definite style when writing code and apply it consistently. This makes the code clearer and more maintainable.
- Ensure that commenting in code is up to date and of suitable detail.
- Try to understand why code is written the way it is and what consequences might arise from other approaches.
- Try to improve your knowledge of C++ and the C++Builder IDE. Both will greatly improve your productivity.

Advanced Programming with C++Builder

Stéphane Mahaux
Yoto Yotov
Vikash Shah

IN THIS CHAPTER

- Introducing the Standard C++ Library and Templates
- Using Smart Pointers and Strong Containers
- Implementing an Advanced Exception Handler
- Creating Multithreaded Applications
- Introducing Design Patterns

The complete text for this chapter appears on the CD-ROM.

User Interface Principles and Techniques

Jamie Allsop
Zexiang Wu

IN THIS CHAPTER

One of C++Builder's greatest strengths is its capability to allow visual development of an application's user interface (UI). To make sure your interface meets the user's expectations and requirements, you should adhere to some basic principles and guidelines. Coupled with the knowledge of how to implement the interface to meet these requirements, this should be enough to help you create intuitive, easy-to-use applications.

The first section of this chapter looks at some principles of UI design and offers guidelines as to how to meet such principles. The remainder of the chapter builds on the first by offering implementation advice and suggestions in relation to each of the guidelines presented in the first section. A sample application is presented and used as a focus for the discussion of a variety of techniques related to UI creation and design. Not all of the topics covered are directly relevant to the sample application, and alternative examples are used in those cases.

User Interface Guidelines

When designing a user interface, there are some basic principles and guidelines that you should adhere to. Most of these are common sense, but some may not be so obvious. The following list summarizes the main guidelines to be aware of. Note that these are not presented in any particular order.

- Meet the user's expectations—An application that enables a user to perform a specific task should function the way the user would expect. If you meet the user's expectations, he will be comfortable using the interface.

- Keep the interface clear and simple—An interface's appearance should convey its function in an obvious manner and allow easy navigation from one part of the interface to another. Simple and clear interfaces don't distract the user's attention from key tasks. Group related controls together but avoid areas with a high density of controls. Also, ensure that controls that receive mouse input are of a reasonable size; this encourages error-free navigation. Similarly, don't have very large distances between frequently used controls. Both situations will make the user tired, the first because excessive concentration is required and the second because excessive mouse movement is required.

- Make the interface intuitive and familiar to use—Try to make it possible for users to figure out how to perform a task without having to be taught. Few users will be totally familiar with your interface, so you are guaranteed that at some time they will come across something unfamiliar. If this happens early in the learning process and the user cannot overcome his lack of knowledge, he may choose not to use your application. On the other hand, if you provide users with an intuitive interface, they will learn how to use it in less time and experience the more advanced capabilities of your application sooner. This is important when a user is trying to identify how powerful your application is and whether or not it is suitable for his needs. An additional consideration is to ensure that tasks in your interface are logically sequenced; in other words, your interface should function in an order that makes sense to the user. This will help make the user feel comfortable with your application.

- Keep the interface friendly—If you provide the user with a friendly interface, he won't mind spending time learning and using it. If the user spends more time doing something, he will become more accomplished at it. A willingness to spend time using an interface that is familiar and intuitive will affect the learning curve of your application, allowing productive use in as short a time as possible.

- Provide the user with feedback—Providing feedback to the user can help build his confidence and reassure him of what he is doing. It can also help keep the user's interest when mundane or long tasks are being carried out. This is a very important facet of any interface, and you should endeavor to provide feedback that is as useful and accurate as possible. Feedback can take many forms, some of which are taken for granted, such as a button that looks pressed when it is clicked. Details such as these should not be considered optional. At a more fundamental level, your whole interface is feedback for the user. By adding extra feedback, you simply enhance what the user already experiences. In some cases, additional feedback may be essential, such as when the user has some form of disability (the subject of the next point).

- Make your interface as accessible as possible—This means providing varied types of feedback and varied forms of input to meet the needs of users who may have difficulty with normal approaches. For example, you could provide additional audio feedback for users with impaired sight, or you could provide speech recognition–driven input for users who have difficulty manipulating the standard input devices.

- Provide help—Sometimes a user will get stuck. To cope with this, you can do two things: Provide useful documentation and provide support. You should always provide some form of documentation, as either online help or printed documentation. Chapter 27, "Creating Help Files and Documentation," is devoted to the creation of documentation support for your applications. If possible, you should also provide some form of support. The kind of support you provide can range from simple email-based support to 24-hour manned support, either telephone-based or on-site. Providing at least email-based support should be considered mandatory.

- Allow customization—Let the user customize the interface to his liking. Simple things such as choice of color can have a significant effect on whether a user likes an interface. The use of system colors, such as clMenu (for menus), can help your interface take on an appearance the user likes. But customization is not just letting the user move things around so the interface looks good. It is about allowing the user to access functionality that he uses frequently in a way that is most convenient for him. Not everyone will use your application in the same way. Allowing a user to modify the interface to reflect his normal usage patterns can help make your application become the user's preferred tool.

- Provide an escape route for the user—Even the most experienced user will take a misstep. Provide some form of escape to let him backtrack. In its most common form, this means providing an undo function, which is now almost a standard feature of all editing-type interfaces.

- Inform the user of errors in an understandable way—No matter how foolproof you might think your interface is, some user somewhere will cause an error to occur. When that happens, the normal response is to display a message box to the user indicating what the error is and how to avoid it. Sometimes you may even give the user a second chance to complete the operation that caused the error. One of the single most annoying things to do in this situation is to display a message box that provides only a cryptic message that even the developer may not understand. From the user's point of view, the interface will appear broken, and this is certainly not a comfortable feeling. You should therefore endeavor to provide constructive information regarding any errors that may arise. In fact, if possible, try to prevent the error from affecting the user at all by catching it when it occurs. A problem with all this is that it is very difficult to identify all possible sources of errors and either insulate the user from the error or provide constructive feedback about the error. Good error handling in an interface is often an area of continual improvement.

- Use symbols, images, and color to make the interface more interesting and easier to navigate—Symbols make an interface quicker to navigate because it is quicker to recognize a symbol than it is to read text. A common approach to using symbols is to provide them alongside text. Users will initially rely on the text descriptions to aid navigation, but as familiarity with the related symbols grows, the user can use them instead. Symbols must be consistent throughout an interface to achieve the maximum benefit, and they should also be carefully designed so that their meaning is obvious. Images can also be used to enhance an interface, either as graphical elements that provide a function or simply to make the interface interesting. Careful thought is required when adding images. Color can be used to group related controls, provide visual separation, or carry additional information, such as syntax highlighting in an IDE.

- Make use of all input devices—Different users like to do things in different ways. Some find different methods of input more convenient than others. Your interface should respond to both pointing input (such as the mouse) and keyboard input. You should also try to adhere to common conventions. For example, if your interface provides a copy function, a user will assume that he can use the keyboard to perform the copy and will expect that the keyboard shortcut is Ctrl+C.

As was said at the beginning, most of these guidelines are common sense, but it doesn't hurt to list them. When you're under a pile of printed code or slaving over a hot debugger, it is sometimes easy to forget that someone somewhere who doesn't even speak your language or know where your country is may end up using your program, and he will have very definite ideas about what it should do.

It is often worthwhile to review interfaces you create to see if they adhere to the guidelines presented or, better still, have them tested and reviewed by a third party. It can also be helpful to review other interfaces you are familiar with to help pinpoint interface designs that you like or don't like. Sometimes studying what is bad about an interface can be just as instructive as considering what is good about an interface. You may want to identify aspects of interface design that are considered not good to help avoid repeating such mistakes in your own design.

The Example Projects Used in This Chapter

The remainder of this chapter is broken into sections that deal with specific issues that arise when implementing the user interface for applications. Each section discusses a specific topic. Throughout most of these sections, reference will be made to the MiniCalculator application that has been developed to illustrate most of the topics discussed in this chapter. This application, along with full source code and all images, is available on the CD-ROM. There is also an executable version available (`MiniCalulator.exe`). It is useful to run this program and play with it. In those sections that are not directly relevant to the MiniCalculator project, other example projects are used. These are shown in Table 5.1, along with the titles of the sections in which they appear. For projects that appear in more than one section, the sections are ordered as they appear in this chapter.

TABLE 5.1   Projects Other than MiniCalculator Used in This Chapter

Project	Section(s)
`Focus.bpr`	"Moving Input Focus"
`MDIProject.bpr`	"Customizing the Client Area of an MDI Parent Form" "Using Action Lists"
`Panels.bpr`	"Using `Align`" "Using `Anchors`" "Using `Constraints`"
`ProgressCursor.bpr`	"Using `TProgressBar` and `TCGauge`" "Using the Cursor"
`ScreenInfo.bpr`	"Coping with Differing Screen Conditions"

Of the projects listed in Table 5.1, the MDIProject is notably different. It is a multiple-document interface (MDI) application. All the rest are single-document interface (SDI) applications. SDI applications typically have a single main form, and other forms are shown as required, either modally (such as dialog boxes) or non-modally, but they are not child windows of the main form. With an MDI application, some of the forms that are created are designated as child windows of the main (MDI parent) form. Such forms are confined to the client region of the MDI parent form. Essentially, the MDI parent form acts as a visual container of the child forms. Child forms are shown non-modally. This allows you to switch between child windows within the parent form. MDI applications generally offer certain common functionality, such as the capability to arrange child windows, merge menus, and open different kinds of child windows. To see how this done in practice, you can examine the `MDIProject.bpr` project.

Introducing the MiniCalculator Project

The MiniCalculator program provides the basic functionality of a simple calculator. The interface has been designed to be similar to that of a real calculator, with additional features that a user would expect a Windows application to provide. This is an important point. Simply creating an interface that mimics a real calculator offers the user a familiar interface, but it also introduces all the restrictions that a real calculator has. What we want to achieve is an interface that, while familiar because of its similarity to a real calculator, does not have its usability and functionality constrained by that similarity. This is a topic we will visit again in the section, "Enhancing Usability Through Appearance."

Figure 5.1 shows a screenshot of MiniCalculator. As you can see, it has a highly graphical interface and looks like a calculator. Anyone with experience using a calculator should find it very simple to access the basic calculator functionality that MiniCalculator offers. In addition, anyone with experience with any basic Windows application will be able to access the additional functionality that we have been able to provide as a result of MiniCalculator being such an application.

FIGURE 5.1
The MiniCalculator.

It should be noted that only the components that come with C++Builder have been used to create the MiniCalculator application. No custom or third-party components have been employed. This should give you an idea of what is possible with C++Builder. The components that comprise the MiniCalculator program are listed in Table 5.2 under the tab on which they appear on the Component Palette.

TABLE 5.2   Components Used in the MiniCalculator Project

Component Palette Tab	Component(s)
Standard	TActionList
	TMainMenu
	TPanel
	TPopupMenu
Additional	TApplicationEvents
	TBevel
	TBitBtn
	TControlBar
	TImage
	TSpeedButton
Win32	TImageList
	TStatusBar
Dialog	TColorDialog

Much of the time spent creating the MiniCalculator program was in designing the layout and creating the images (such as the buttons). All the images used in MiniCalculator were created using JASC's Paint Shop Pro package. A trial version of Paint Shop Pro is available on the accompanying CD-ROM.

Enhancing Usability by Providing Feedback to the User

Giving the user of an application continual feedback is a good way to enhance the usability of the application's interface. There are several standard approaches that are commonly employed. You can use a status bar to provide additional status information about the application, such as the cursor position. You can use hints to provide clues for the user. You can use progress indicators such as a progress bar to indicate the progress of long operations, and you can use the cursor shape to indicate the current mouse function, if any is possible. For example, an hourglass cursor is often used to indicate that no mouse action (other than moving) is possible, and a hand cursor is often used to indicate that a control is hyperlinked.

This section looks at using each of these methods to provide feedback to the user and illustrates implementation techniques that are commonly required.

Using TProgressBar and TCGauge

A progress bar is a good method of indicating the progress of a long operation. It reassures the user that the program is still functioning and carrying out the task requested of it. There are two progress components in C++Builder that can be used with a minimum of effort. These are TProgressBar and TCGauge.

TProgressBar is found on the Win32 tab of the Component Palette, and TCGauge is found on the Samples tab of the Component Palette. The ProgressCursor.bpr project on the CD-ROM that accompanies this book shows the two controls in a variety of configurations. Of the two controls, TCGauge is in many ways superior. It is obvious what information TCGauge is providing, and the progress indicated is easily quantified.

In this way TProgressBar is not so good. The use of segmentation in TProgressBar is one of the reasons that it does not perform its task well. The segmentation bears no relation to the amount of progress being made. Therefore, the user can only guess at how much progress has been made. Still, it is one of the Win32 standard controls, and users are familiar with it. When an accurate estimate of progress is not required, it is adequate. TCGauge is also not perfect, but with the source in the cgauges.cpp file in the $(BCB)\Examples\Controls\Source directory, you can always change it to suit your needs.

The operation of TProgressBar and TCGauge is similar. Given a TProgressBar called ProgressBar and a TCGauge called CGauge, we can set the minimum, maximum, and start position as follows:

```
//Minimum
ProgressBar->Min = 0;
CGauge->MinValue = 0;

//Maximum
ProgressBar->Max = 100;
CGauge->MaxValue = 100;

//Current Position
ProgressBar->Position = 0;
CGauge->Progress = 0;
```

We can increment the current position for each control by 1 as follows:

```
//Increment by one
ProgressBar->Position = ProgressBar->Position + 1;
CGauge->Progress = CGauge->Progress + 1;
```

For both controls, trying to increment past the maximum value for the control has no effect. However, TProgressBar also provides the StepIt() and StepBy() methods. StepIt() increments the Position of TProgressBar by the value of its Step property. StepBy() increments the Position of TProgressBar by the amount specified in the single int argument that you pass to the method. Incrementing Position using these two methods does not cause Position to stop at Max when it is reached. Instead, Position resets to 0 and continues to be incremented. You can see this in practice in the ProgressCursor.bpr project.

The choice of progress indicator is up to you, but for long operations, you should always use an indicator of some kind, even if it's only to let the user know that the program still functions.

Using the Cursor

Changing the cursor image to provide feedback to the user or to provide additional information to the user is a common technique in interface programming. In C++Builder, handling the cursor is easy. You can access the cursor in one of two ways.

You can set the TCursor properties of a control, such as the Cursor and DragCursor properties. These affect how the cursor appears when it is over the control under different circumstances. For example, the cursor specified in the DragCursor property is the one displayed when dragging the control. The cursor specified in the Cursor property is the one displayed when the cursor enters the control. Note that these are effective only when the Screen-> Cursor property is crDefault.

You also can access the global cursor through the Cursor property of the global Screen variable. When you change the value of Screen's Cursor property, you should always make a copy of the original cursor so that it can be restored when you have finished with the cursor. The structure you should use is

```
TCursor OriginalCursor = Screen->Cursor;
Screen->Cursor = crXXXX; // Assign the new cursor
try
{
    // Do what you want to do
}
__finally
{
    // Restore the original cursor
    Screen->Cursor = OriginalCursor;
}
```

The ProgressCursor.bpr project on the CD-ROM that accompanies this book shows both methods of changing the cursor.

Using Custom Cursors

To use a custom cursor you must first assign your cursor to the global Screen variable's Cursors array property. For custom cursors you can use any positive index. The stock cursors use -22 (crSizeAll) to 0 (crDefault). To obtain an HCURSOR to assign to the array use the WinAPI LoadCursor() or LoadCursorFromFile() function. To load animated cursors use the LoadCursorFromFile() function. For example in the ProgressCursor.bpr project we load the "Face" animated cursor as follows:

```
Screen->Cursors[crFaceAnimatedCursor] = LoadCursorFromFile("Face.ani");
```

Face.ani is the file containing the animated cursor. crFaceAnimatedCursor is a constant set equal to 1 in the initialization list of Form1's constructor. This helps keep code more readable. We use this index when we assign the custom cursor to the global Screen variable's Cursor property later in the program, as follows:

```
Screen->Cursor = crFaceAnimatedCursor;
```

Incidentally, the looping motion of the Face animated cursor was created by moving the cursor hotspot for each frame of the animation.

The LoadCursor() function loads a cursor from a resource. In ProgressCursor.bpr we use this to load the Eye cursor. First we create a resource file (.rc) with these contents:

```
EyeCursor CURSOR Eye.cur
```

Then we use LoadCursor() to assign the HCURSOR to Screen->Cursors as follows:

```
Screen->Cursors[crCustomEyeCursor] = LoadCursor(HInstance, "EyeCursor");
```

Again, crCustomEyeCursor is a constant that keeps the code readable when we later assign the cursor to the Cursor property of CustomCursorCheckBox:

```
CustomCursorCheckBox->Cursor = crCustomEyeCursor;
```

Using custom cursors is easy. The difficulty arises in creating the custom cursors. A good cursor editing tool is a must. For more information on using resources in your applications, refer to the "Using Predefined Images in Custom Property and Component Editors" section in Chapter 10, "Creating Property and Component Editors." This section discusses resources in property and component editors, but the information is equally applicable here.

Using TStatusBar

TStatusBar (found on the Win32 tab of the Component Palette) provides an excellent mechanism for providing feedback and additional information to the user of an application. It can even provide additional control to the user by responding to the mouse. In its simplest form, TStatusBar is a single panel (SimplePanel = true) displaying only text information, as determined by the value of the SimpleText property.

For many applications this is sufficient; however, `TStatusBar` can offer much more than this. `TStatusBar` can also have multiple panels, and each of these can be owner-drawn if required (set the `Style` property to `psOwnerDraw`). Each panel in a status bar is encapsulated by a `TStatusPanel` object. Table 5.3 shows the properties of `TStatusPanel` most often used.

TABLE 5.3 `TStatusPanel` Properties Most Commonly Used

Property	Use
Alignment	Determines how the `AnsiString` text contained in the `Text` property should be aligned within the status panel. It can take the value `taLeftJustify`, `taCenter`, or `taRightJustify`.
Bevel	Determines the appearance of the bevel drawn around the edge of the status panel. It can take the value `pbNone`, `pbLowered`, or `pbRaised`. If `Bevel` is set to `pbNone`, then the panel has no bevel and it is indistinguishable from the rest of the status bar (unless it is owner drawn to appear differently).
Index	A read-only property inherited from `TCollectionItem` that indicates the index (0-based) of the panel within the status bar. It is used with the `Items` and `Count` property of `TStatusBar`'s `Panels` property. The `Panels` property is of type `TStatusPanels`. `Items` is an array of `TStatusPanel` objects. The `Index` property of a `TStatusPanel` indicates the index in the `Items` array. Use `Panels->Count` to iterate through the panels (`Panels->Items`) of a status bar.
Style	Determines how the panel is displayed. It can be either `psText` or `psOwnerDraw`. `psText` is the default and indicates that the string in the `Text` property is displayed using the status bar font with the alignment specified by the panel's `Alignment` property. If `Style` is `psOwnerDraw`, then you must supply the necessary code to render the panel onto the status bar's `Canvas` in the status panel's `OnDrawPanel` event.
Text	Determines the string that will be displayed in the panel if the panel's `Style` is `psText`. Even if the `Style` is `psOwnerDraw`, this value can still be used to store the string value to be rendered.
Width	Determines the width of the panel. The height of every panel is the same and can be determined by reading the `ClientHeight` property of the status bar that contains the panel. Note that `TStatusPanel` has no `Visible` property. If you want to hide a status panel from view, you can do so by setting its `Width` property to `0`.

To access the status panels of a status bar, you must use the Items property of TStatusBar's Panels property. For example, to assign the string "This is Panel 0" to the Text property of the first panel (Index == 0) in a multipanel status bar (called StatusBar1), you would use the following code:

```
StatusBar1->Panels->Items[0]->Text = "This is Panel 0";
```

As mentioned in the Index entry of Table 5.3, TStatusBar's Panels property is of type TStatusPanels, a TCollection descendant. As such, its Count property can be used to determine how many panels are present in the status bar.

The MiniCalculator example program uses a TStatusBar with three panels. The first and third panels are owner drawn (Style = psOwnerDraw), and the second panel simply displays text assigned to its Text property (more about this in the next section, "Using Hints").

We will now look at the first owner-drawn panel. The MiniCalculator program can respond to input from the keyboard. This allows the user to use the application as if it were a real calculator, with the keyboard (mainly the numeric keyboard) acting as the calculator's keys. By default this is enabled, but the user can disable it if he wants. In addition, there are times when the application cannot respond to keyboard input. This will occur when the main form of the application loses focus. In the MiniCalculator program, the first panel (0) is responsible for showing the user the status of the keyboard input and also for allowing the user to enable or disable keyboard input as he prefers. To indicate the status of keyboard input, three images are used: one to indicate that keyboard input is enabled and the main form has focus; one to indicate that the keyboard is enabled but that the main form does not have focus; and one to indicate that keyboard input is disabled. These are stored in three TImage components: HasKeyboardFocusImage, HasNoKeyboardFocusImage, and DisableKeyboardImage. To draw the image onto the status bar, we must implement TStatusBar's OnDrawPanel event. The OnDrawPanel event has three parameters:

```
TStatusBar*    StatusBar,
TStatusPanel*  Panel,
const TRect&   Rect
```

These three parameters are a pointer to the status bar that triggered the event, a pointer to the panel the event is for, and a const TRect structure to indicate the region to be drawn. To draw on the panel, you use the Rect parameter to set the bounds of the image you are using and use the Canvas property of the StatusBar parameter to do the actual drawing.

Listing 5.1 shows how this was done for the MiniCalculator program. Note that the code required to draw the other owner-drawn panel, with Panel->Index == 2, has been omitted for clarity. The code for this panel is shown in Listing 5.4.

LISTING 5.1   Implementing `TStatusBar`'s `OnDrawPanel` Event—Part 1

```cpp
void __fastcall TMainForm::StatusBar1DrawPanel(TStatusBar* StatusBar,
                                               TStatusPanel* Panel,
                                               const TRect& Rect)
{
    if(Panel->Index == 0)
    {
        if(EnableKeyboardInput)
        {
            if(CanUseKeyboard)
            {
                // Paint the Keyboard image onto the panel
                StatusBar->Canvas->Draw(Rect.Left,
                                        Rect.Top,
                                        HasKeyboardFocusImage->Picture->Bitmap);
            }
            else
            {
                StatusBar->Canvas->Draw(Rect.Left,
                                        Rect.Top,
                                        HasNoKeyboardFocusImage->Picture->Bitmap);
            }
        }
        else
        {
            StatusBar->Canvas->Draw(Rect.Left,
                                    Rect.Top,
                                    DisableKeyboardImage->Picture->Bitmap);
        }
    }
    // if(Panel->Index == 2) Omitted - see Listing 5.2
}
```

The code in Listing 5.1 is straightforward. First we make sure that `Panel` is the first panel. We do this by checking that its `Index` property is equal to `0`. To decide which image to draw, we check the value of two variables:

- `EnableKeyboardInput`   If `true`, then keyboard input is enabled; `false` otherwise.
- `CanUseKeyboard`   If `true`, the main form has focus and keyboard input is possible (if enabled); `false` otherwise.

These are `bool` properties, not variables, and help simplify the coding required for the status bar and the application as a whole. This is discussed again later in this section.

Regardless of which image is used, the method of drawing is the same. The `Draw()` method of `StatusBar`'s `Canvas` property is used. This takes as its parameters the coordinates of the left-top corner of the region on which you want to render your image and a pointer to a `TGraphic`-derived object, such as a `TBitmap` object, as in this case. In the MiniCalculator program, the `Height` of the status bar is `30`, and the `Width` of the first panel is `72`. The panel width includes a one-pixel bevel, even if the `Bevel` property is set to `pbNone`; setting `Bevel` to `pbNone` simply means that the bevel will not be drawn. In addition to the one-pixel bevel, enclosing the panel there is a two-pixel strip across the top of the status bar. Therefore, to calculate the dimensions the `Rect` parameter will have, you can use the following:

```
UseablePanelHeight = StatusBar->Height - 4 - 2*StatusBar->BorderWidth;
UseablePanelWidth  = Panel->Width - 2;
```

This indicates that the available space in the first panel is 70 pixels by 26 pixels. This is the size of the images that we want to display in the panel; the status bar's height and the panel's width were deliberately chosen so that this would be the case. Figure 5.2 illustrates this.

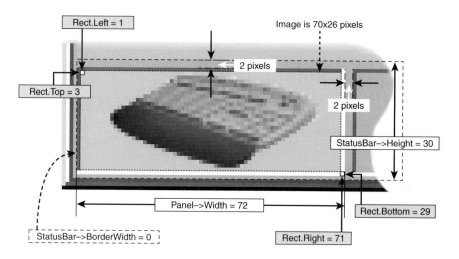

FIGURE 5.2

An owner-drawn status bar.

The status bar in the MiniCalculator program also responds to user input from the mouse. When the left mouse button is pressed in the first panel of the status bar, the `EnableKeyboardInput` property is toggled, either enabling or disabling keyboard input. To do this we must implement `TStatusBar`'s `OnMouseDown` event. In the `OnMouseDown` event handler, we check to see if the mouse is over the first panel of the status bar when the event is fired. If it is, we toggle the `EnableKeyboardInput` property. Listing 5.2 shows the code.

LISTING 5.2   Implementing `TStatusBar`'s `OnMouseDown` Event

```
void __fastcall TMainForm::StatusBar1MouseDown(TObject* Sender,
                                               TMouseButton Button,
                                               TShiftState Shift,
                                               int X,
                                               int Y)
{
   if(Button == mbLeft)
   {
      // Is the mouse inside the first panel ???
      // and inside the panel's bevel ???
      if(   X > 1
         && X < (StatusBar1->Panels->Items[0]->Width - 1)
         && Y > 3
         && Y < (StatusBar1->Height - 1) )
      {
         // If yes then toggle the keyboard input
         if(EnableKeyboardInput) EnableKeyboardInput = false;
         else EnableKeyboardInput = true;
      }
   }
}
```

Referring to Figure 5.2 should help make this code more clear. When the value of the
`EnableKeyboardInput` property is changed, its set method is called. The code for this is shown
in Listing 5.3.

LISTING 5.3   The `EnableKeyboardInput` Set Method

```
void __fastcall TMainForm::SetEnableKeyboardInput(bool NewEnableKeyboardInput)
{
   if(EnableKeyboardInput != NewEnableKeyboardInput)
   {
      FEnableKeyboardInput = NewEnableKeyboardInput;
      if(EnableKeyboardInput)
      {
         OnKeyDown = CalculatorKeyDown;
         OnKeyUp   = CalculatorKeyUp;
         StatusBar1->Panels->Items[1]->Width = 60;
      }
      else
      {
         OnKeyDown = 0;
         OnKeyUp   = 0;
```

LISTING 5.3   Continued

```
        StatusBar1->Panels->Items[1]->Width = 0;
    }
    StatusBar1->Invalidate();
  }
}
```

Of note in Listing 5.3 is that, when we change the value of FEnableKeyboardInput, the status bar's Invalidate() method is called to force the control to repaint and therefore fire the OnDrawPanel event, which allows the image in panel 0 to be updated. Also, you can see that the main form's OnKeyDown and OnKeyUp events are set. When they are set to 0, MiniCalculator will not respond to keyboard input. When they are set to the CalculatorKeyDown() and CalculatorKeyUp() methods, keyboard input is handled.

It is possible to make the panel look and act just like an ordinary button. To do this, set the Bevel property to bpRaised. When the OnMouseDown event is fired, change the Bevel property to bpLowered; then when the OnMouseUp event occurs change the Bevel property back to bpRaised. In addition, you should check to see if OnMouseUp occurred inside the panel. If it did, then you can consider that the panel has been clicked and can act accordingly.

We shall consider the third status bar panel in the MiniCalculator program. It is also owner drawn. This panel displays a description of a button's function if appropriate. It is highly likely that this description will be larger than the space available to display it. If this is so, then it is preferable to truncate the description and add an ellipsis (...) to the end of the string. This makes it clear that the remainder of the string is hidden, and it also looks more tidy than having text simply chopped off at the end. To display a string in this way, we use the WinAPI DrawText()function. We will use this function throughout this chapter, so we will describe its capabilities briefly here.

DrawText() is declared as

```
int DrawText(
    HDC      hDC,        // Pass Canvas->Handle
    LPCTSTR  lpString,   // Pass string.c_str(), where string is an AnsiString
    int      nCount,     // -1 for NULL terminated string, otherwise length
    LPRECT   lpRect,     // Pointer to TRect structure with dimensions
    UINT     uFormat     // Text-drawing flags
        );
```

DrawText() returns the text height when successful. It is the formatting flags that you can use with this function that make it so versatile. These are listed in Table 5.4. Note that in Table 5.4 the entries are not arranged alphabetically. They are arranged in related groups.

TABLE 5.4 The WinAPI `DrawText()` Function Formatting Flags

Flag	Use
DT_CALCRECT	No text is drawn; the TRect pointed to by the lpRect parameter is modified to bound the formatted text.
DT_LEFT	Justifies the text to the left of the TRect pointed to by the lpRect parameter.
DT_CENTER	Justifies text to the center of the TRect pointed to by the lpRect parameter.
DT_RIGHT	Justifies the text to the right of the TRect pointed to by the lpRect parameter.
DT_BOTTOM	Aligns text to the bottom of the TRect pointed to by the lpRect parameter. Must be called with DT_SINGLELINE.
DT_VCENTER	Aligns text (vertically) to the center of the TRect pointed to by the lpRect parameter. Must be called with DT_SINGLELINE.
DT_TOP	Aligns text to the top of the TRect pointed to by the lpRect parameter. Must be called with DT_SINGLELINE.
DT_SINGLELINE	Displays text on a single line; line feeds and carriage returns do not break the line.
DT_END_ELLIPSIS	If the text won't fit in the TRect pointed to by the lpRect parameter then the text is truncated and an ellipsis (…) is appended. If DT_MODIFYSTRING is specified, the given string is also modified.
DT_PATH_ELLIPSIS	Similar to DT_END_ELLIPSIS, but for paths with the backslash (\) character. Text before the backslash or between pairs is replaced by an ellipsis (…) if the text is too long. If DT_MODIFYSTRING is specified, the given string is also modified.
DT_MODIFYSTRING	If set and DT_END_ELLIPSIS or DT_PATH_ELLIPSIS is also specified, the text will be modified to reflect the text drawn. Has no effect otherwise.
DT_EDITCONTROL	The text is displayed as if it were in a multiline edit control. Partially visible last lines are not displayed, and the average character width is calculated.
DT_EXPANDTABS	Tabs are expanded. The default tab size is eight characters.
DT_EXTERNALLEADING	The external leading height of the font (the space that should appear between lines) is displayed.
DT_NOCLIP	Draws text without clipping. The operation is faster with this flag set.

5

USER INTERFACE PRINCIPLES AND TECHNIQUES

TABLE 5.4 Continued

Flag	Use
DT_NOPREFIX	If this flag is included, prefix characters are not processed. For example, an ampersand (&) is drawn as an &. Normally this would be drawn as an accelerator key by drawing a line under the following character, as in menus.
DT_RTLREADING	Draws the text in right-to-left order for bidirectional support.
DT_TABSTOP	Sets the tab size. The default is eight characters. Places the new value in bits 8–15 of the uFormat parameter.
DT_WORDBREAK	If the text is too long to be displayed in the TRect pointed to by the lpRect parameter, the line is broken to the next line. Linefeed/carriage returns also break the line.

Listing 5.4 shows the code required to render text onto the status bar's Canvas. This is the same event handler as that shown in Listing 5.1. However, the owner-drawing code for Panel->Index == 0 has been omitted, and the code for Panel->Index == 2 is shown.

LISTING 5.4 Implementing TStatusBar's OnDrawPanel Event—Part 2

```
void __fastcall TMainForm::StatusBar1DrawPanel(TStatusBar* StatusBar,
                                               TStatusPanel* Panel,
                                               const TRect& Rect)
{
   if(Panel->Index == 0)
   {
      // Omitted for clarity - see Listing 5.1
   }
   else if(Panel->Index == 2)
   {
      TFontStyles FontStyle;

      TColor OldBrushColor = StatusBar->Canvas->Brush->Color;
      TFontStyles OldFontStyle = StatusBar->Canvas->Font->Style;

      StatusBar->Canvas->Font->Style = FontStyle;
      StatusBar->Canvas->Brush->Color = clSilver;
      StatusBar->Canvas->FillRect(Rect);

      TRect PanelRect = Rect;
      PanelRect.Left   += 2;
      PanelRect.Right  -= 2,
```

LISTING 5.4   Continued

```
DrawText( StatusBar->Canvas->Handle,
          Panel->Text.c_str(),
          -1,
          &PanelRect,
          DT_LEFT
          |DT_NOPREFIX
          |DT_END_ELLIPSIS
          |DT_SINGLELINE
          |DT_VCENTER
          |DrawTextBiDiModeFlagsReadingOnly() );

    StatusBar->Canvas->Font->Style = OldFontStyle;
    StatusBar->Canvas->Brush->Color = OldBrushColor;
  }
}
```

In Listing 5.4 we can see that the rendering of the button description into the third
(`Panel->Index == 2`) status bar panel involves four steps:

1. First we save the current `StatusBar->Canvas` properties that we are going to change, and
   then we assign the values to the `StatusBar->Canvas` that we require.

2. We modify the `Rect` representing the panel's region so that we have a 2-pixel border on
   both sides of the panel.

3. We draw the `Panel->Text` onto `StatusBar->Canvas` using the `DrawRect()` function. We
   align it to the left (`DT_LEFT`) and center it vertically (`DT_VCENTER`) within the `PanelRect`. In
   addition, we specify that `Panel->Text` should be drawn as a single line (`DT_SINGLELINE`)
   and that an ellipsis should be displayed if there is not enough room to draw the whole
   string (`DT_END_ELLIPSIS`). We also turn off the processing of prefix characters
   (`DT_NOPREFIX`) and use the `TControl`'s `DrawTextBiDiModeFlagsReadingOnly()` function
   to see if the `DT_RTLREADING` flag should be set.

4. Finally, we reset the `StatusBar->Canvas` properties that we modified to their original
   values.

The `DrawText()` function is a powerful tool for rendering text onto a destination `Canvas`, and
the formatting flags make it easy to customize how the text will appear. We use this function
several times throughout the chapter, so it is worthwhile to familiarize yourself with it.

Using Hints

Hints are a good way to augment your interface and provide additional information or prompts
to the user. The `ShowHint` property of a control determines whether or not the string in the control's `Hint` property will appear when the mouse is paused over the control. Optionally, you

can pass this responsibility to the control's parent by setting `ParentShowHint` to `true`. The control's hint will be shown only if the parent allows hints to appear. This can sometimes make coding simpler and also makes it easy to turn hints on or off globally. Using a hint that pops up when the mouse is paused over a control is perhaps the most common form of displaying hints.

A hint can consist of a short hint, a long hint, or both. To create a hint that contains both a short hint and a long hint, use the vertical bar character (|) in the hint text to separate the short hint from the long hint, with the short hint appearing first. For example

```
AnsiString MyHint = "Short Hint|This is a Long Hint";
```

Note that the terms *Short Hint* and *Long Hint* indicate the position of the hint within the whole hint string and do not refer to their lengths. The terms originate from the their use. The short hint is the first part of a hint and normally is used in a pop-up hint. The second part of the hint, the long hint, is normally more descriptive and displayed in a status bar. Because of these uses, the short hint will generally be short and the long hint will generally be longer.

Only the short hint is shown when a pop-up hint is displayed. The long hint is passed to `TApplication`'s `OnHint` event. From there it is possible to assign the long hint to another control for display, for example to a status bar. To have *only* a short hint, include the | character at the end of the string; otherwise, the short hint will also be used as a long hint. To have only a long hint, start your string with the | character. To retrieve the short hint or long hint from a hint string, use the global `GetShortHint()` and `GetLongHint()` functions, respectively, passing your hint as the single argument.

`TApplication` has several properties that allow you to customize how hints appear in your application, how long they take to appear, and how long they appear. The properties of interest are shown in Table 5.5.

TABLE 5.5   `TApplication` Properties for Hints

Property	Use
Hint	Contains the long hint of a control when the mouse passes over it.
HintColor	Specifies the color of the hint box. By default this is the system color `clInfoBk` (typically a pale yellow color), but you may assign any color to it.
HintHidePause	Specifies how long a pop-up hint will stay visible, provided the mouse remains over the control. The default is 2500 milliseconds. You can assign a different value, also in milliseconds.

TABLE 5.5   Continued

Property	Use
HintPause	Specifies the time that must elapse before a control's hint is displayed when the mouse is stationary above the control. The default is 500 milliseconds. You can assign a different value, also in milliseconds.
HintShortCuts	Specifies whether or not shortcut information in a TCustomAction-derived object (an action object) is displayed in parentheses after the string specified in the action's Hint property. For example, if an action called TCopyAction had a hint of "Copy" and a ShortCut of Ctrl+C, then the hint for the action would be displayed as "Copy (Ctrl+C)".
HintShortPause	Specifies the time to wait before activating another hint if a hint has already been shown. The default is 500 milliseconds. You may assign a different value, also in milliseconds.
ShowHint	Specifies whether or not hints are enabled for the entire application. If false, no hints will be shown. The default is true.

In addition to the properties shown in Table 5.5, TApplication also provides the
ActivateHint() method to force a hint to be displayed. It is declared in
$(BCB)\Include\Vcl\Forms.hpp as

```
void __fastcall ActivateHint(const Windows::TPoint& CursorPos);
```

To use the function, simply pass the current position of the mouse cursor using the global
Mouse object's CursorPos property. TApplication then shows the hint for the control under
the cursor. For example, you would write

```
Application->ActivateHint(Mouse->CursorPos);
```

TScreen provides the HintFont property that allows you to customize the font used to display
pop-up hints. It should be apparent then that you can be reasonably flexible with hints in your
application.

Using Hints Manually

In the MiniCalculator program, a separate hint is shown for each panel in the status bar. This
presents two problems. TStatusPanels do not have their own Hint properties because they
represent only a region on the Canvas of TStatusBar. Only TStatusBar itself has a hint. To

display a different hint for each panel, the position of the mouse cursor within TStatusBar must be determined and the Hint property of TStatusBar set appropriately. Additionally, when a hint is shown for a control, it is not shown again until the mouse leaves and then re-enters the control. This means that if the mouse enters the status bar on the first panel and a hint is displayed, moving the mouse so that it is over the second panel will not result in a hint being displayed. The mouse must be first moved out of the status bar and then back into the status bar at the required panel. If we want a hint to be shown for each panel without leaving the panel, we must force the hint of TStatusBar to be reshown.

In the MiniCalculator program, we do this by implementing the TStatusBar's OnMouseMove event. Listing 5.5 shows one possible implementation.

LISTING 5.5   Implementing TStatusBar's OnMouseMove Event to Allow Separate Hints for Each Status Bar Panel

```
void __fastcall TMainForm::StatusBar1MouseMove(TObject* Sender,
                                               TShiftState Shift,
                                               int X,
                                               int Y)
{
    int BorderWidth = StatusBar1->BorderWidth;

    TRect Panel0(StatusBar1->ClientOrigin.x + BorderWidth + 1, // Left

               StatusBar1->ClientOrigin.y + 3 + BorderWidth, // Top

               StatusBar1->ClientOrigin.x + BorderWidth       // Right
               + StatusBar1->Panels->Items[0]->Width - 1,

               StatusBar1->ClientOrigin.y + 3                 // Bottom
               + StatusBar1->Height - 1);

    TRect Panel1(Panel0.Right + 2 + 1,                        // Left
               Panel0.Top,                                    // Top  is same
               Panel0.Right + 2
               + StatusBar1->Panels->Items[1]->Width - 1,     // Right
               Panel0.Bottom);                                // Bottom is same

    TRect Panel2(Panel1.Right + 2 + 1,                        // Left
               Panel0.Top,                                    // Top is same
               Panel1.Right + 2
               + StatusBar1->Panels->Items[2]->Width - 1,     // Right
               Panel0.Bottom);                                // Bottom is same
```

LISTING 5.5   Continued

```
// See where the mouse is and then show the correct hint :-)

// Use the WinAPI function to see if the cursor is in any of our Rects.
// If it is, set the appropriate hint. Otherwise StatusBar1->Hint = ""

//BOOL PtInRect(
//   CONST RECT *lprc,    // address of structure with rectangle
//   POINT pt             // structure with point
//            );

if(PtInRect(&Panel0, Mouse->CursorPos))
{
   if(EnableKeyboardInput)
   {
      StatusBar1->Hint = "Click to Disable Keyboard Intput|";
   }
   else
   {
      StatusBar1->Hint = "Click to Enable Keyboard Input|";
   }
   if(StatusBar1->Tag != 0)
   {
      StatusBar1->Tag = 0;
      Application->ActivateHint();
   }
}
else if(PtInRect(&Panel1, Mouse->CursorPos))
{
   StatusBar1->Hint = "Keyboard Short Cut|";
   if(StatusBar1->Tag != 1)
   {
      StatusBar1->Tag = 1;
      Application->ActivateHint();
   }
}
else if(PtInRect(&Panel2, Mouse->CursorPos))
{
   StatusBar1->Hint = "Button Function|";
   if(StatusBar1->Tag != 2)
   {
      StatusBar1->Tag = 2;
      Application->ActivateHint();
   }
```

LISTING 5.5 Continued

```
      }
      else
      {
         // No Hint
         StatusBar1->Tag = StatusBar1->Panels->Count;
         StatusBar1->Hint = "|";
      }
}
```

Of note in Listing 5.5 is the creation of a TRect structure to represent each region for the status bar panels. For each region, we include only the area within each panel's bevel (we don't include the bevel) and do not include the 2-pixel spacing between the panels. To refresh your memory regarding the regions of a status panel, it may be helpful to look again at Figure 5.2. We then use the WinAPI PtInRect() function to see if the mouse cursor is in any of the panels. PtInRect() is declared as

```
BOOL PtInRect(
      CONST RECT *lprc,    // The address of a TRect structure
      POINT pt             // A TPoint structure
               );
```

You simply pass the address of the TRect that you want to see if the mouse is in and pass the mouse position as a TPoint structure. If the mouse is in the TRect representing the panel, and this is the first time that the mouse has moved into the panel, StatusBar1's Hint property is set to the correct string and TApplication's ActivateHint() method is called to display the hint. Calling ActivateHint() forces an immediate display of the hint. This means there is no pause as there would be for normal hints. In some situations this is what you require, but in our case a pause before displaying the hint would be more appropriate. We need to implement some helper functions to allow us to do this.

First it is important to point out the use of TStatusBar's Tag property in determining whether a hint has already been displayed for a given panel. When an OnMouseMove event occurs inside a panel's region, a hint is forced only if this is the first OnMouseMove event in that panel. This ensures correct behavior; a hint is displayed only once for a control when the mouse remains in that control. To show the hint again, the mouse must first leave the control. In this case, the mouse must only leave the panel. This will result in a different value being assigned to the StatusBar1's Tag property. The index of each panel is assigned to StatusBar1's Tag property on the first call to the OnMouseMove handler. When the mouse leaves the status bar control and then re-enters, the value of the Tag property is immaterial, because in this case we do not need to force a hint to be displayed. On entering the control and there being a hint to display, the current hint will be shown. It is therefore important to ensure that the Hint property of TStatusBar is set to "" or "|". Both symbolize empty hint strings. Note also that if an OnMouseMove event occurs on the status bar but not in any of the panels' hint regions, the Tag property is set to the number of panels in the status bar. There definitely will not be a panel with this index. This allows the hint to be redisplayed if the mouse leaves the panel but not the status bar and does not enter any other panels. If the BorderWidth property of the status bar is large, leaving and re-entering a panel in this way will be noticeable.

Displaying a hint after a pause, as is normally done, is more complex. To do this we use the WinAPI SetTimer() function to install a callback function that lets us know when the desired time period has elapsed. When it has, the hint is displayed. Several functions are required. The additional declarations needed in the form's header file are shown in Listing 5.6.

LISTING 5.6   Additional Declarations Required to Allow Delayed Manual Hint Display

```
UINT HintTimerHandle;
static void CALLBACK HintTimerCallback(HWND Wnd,
                                       UINT Msg,
                                       UINT TimerID,
                                       DWORD Time);
void __fastcall    HintTimerExpired();
void __fastcall    DisplayHint(int Pause);
void __fastcall    StopHintTimer();
```

The callback function, HintTimerCallback(), is made a static function in the form's class declaration. This is because a pointer to this function will be passed to the WinAPI SetTimer() method, and it expects a normal function pointer. A variable HintTimerHandle is also declared to store the handle returned from the SetTimer() function so that the timer can be stopped when it is not needed. The implementation of these functions is shown in Listing 5.7.

LISTING 5.7   Implementation of Manual Delayed Hint Helper Functions

```
//-----------------------------------------------------------------//
void CALLBACK TMainForm::HintTimerCallback(HWND Wnd,
                                           UINT Msg,
                                           UINT TimerID,
                                           DWORD Time)
{
    // Add a bit of type safety
    TObject* VCLObject  = reinterpret_cast<TObject*>(Wnd);
    TForm1*  Form1Object = dynamic_cast<TForm1*>(VCLObject);
    if(Form1Object) Form1Object->HintTimerExpired();
```

LISTING 5.7   Continued

```
}
//----------------------------------------------------------------------//
void __fastcall TMainForm::HintTimerExpired()
{
    StopHintTimer();
    Application->ActivateHint(Mouse->CursorPos);
}
//----------------------------------------------------------------------//
void __fastcall TMainForm::DisplayHint(int Pause)
{
    StopHintTimer();
    HintTimerHandle = SetTimer(this,
                               0,
                               Pause,
                               reinterpret_cast<TIMERPROC>(HintTimerCallback));
    if(HintTimerHandle == 0) Application->CancelHint();
}
//----------------------------------------------------------------------//
void __fastcall TMainForm::StopHintTimer()
{
    if(HintTimerHandle != 0)
    {
        KillTimer(this, HintTimerHandle);
        HintTimerHandle = 0;
    }
}
//----------------------------------------------------------------------//
```

The DisplayHint() function is where it all starts. This is called in the OnMouseDown event handler instead of Application->ActivateHint(), with Application->HintPause passed as the single argument. All the lines in Listing 5.5 that are as follows

```
Application->ActivateHint();
```

should be replaced by

```
DisplayHint(Application->HintPause);
```

We use Application->HintPause to retrieve the current delay used by the application. This ensures consistency with other hints. In some cases, though, you may want to pass a different value.

When `DisplayHint()` is called, it first stops any previous timer that is in use. It then sets a new timer, passing as arguments the `this` pointer, so that the `HintTimerExpired()`function can be called from the `static` callback function; the required delay in milliseconds (`Pause`); and a pointer to the callback function to receive the message that the timer has finished. Notice that the callback function pointer needs to be cast to `TIMERPROC`. We use `reinterpret_cast` for this because we are dealing with function pointers. If we are unsuccessful in setting the timer (that is, `SetTimer()` returns 0), then we cancel any current hint by calling `Application->CancelHint()`. Without this, we cannot display our new hint.

When the timer expires, our callback function is called. It has four parameters, but we are interested in only the first, the `HWND Wnd` parameter. This is where we stored our `this` pointer in the call to `SetTimer()`. With this we can call the `HintTimerExpired()` function to actually display the hint. Because the `Wnd` is not a pointer, we first cast it to a `TObject*` using `reinterpret_cast`. Then we try to `dynamic_cast` the `TObject*` to a `TForm1*`. This gives us a chance to check if the pointer is valid before we dereference it. Dereferencing an invalid pointer is an access violation and something we would like to avoid.

Finally, the `HintTimerExpired()` function stops the current hint timer by calling `StopHintTimer()` and then displays the hint using `Application->ActivateHint()`. The `StopHintTimer()` function simply checks that there is a timer to stop (by checking the `FHintTimerHandle` variable). If so, it stops it with the WinAPI function `KillTimer()`. It then sets the `FHintTimerHandle` variable to 0.

When the mouse passes over the panels of the status panel, the hints for each panel appear just as ordinary hints do.

Using Customized Hints

Sometimes you will want to display custom hints to the user. In the MiniCalculator program, a pop-up hint is displayed when the mouse moves over the Memory Recall button. The hint displays the contents of the memory. We want this hint to look like the main display of the calculator (refer to Figure 5.1 to see the MiniCalculator interface).

To create a custom hint, you must derive a new hint window class from `THintWindow`. You must then assign the `TMetaClass*` of the class type (using the `__classid` operator) to the global `HintWindowClass TMetaClass*` variable.

First we will look at creating a `THintWindow`-derived class. Table 5.6 shows the `virtual` methods provided by `THintWindow` and gives the purpose of each. For convenience, the first line in each entry in the Purpose column shows the function's return type and parameter list.

TABLE 5.6   The virtual Methods of THintWindow

Method	Purpose
CreateParams()	void CreateParams(TCreateParams& Params)
	Override this method to control the type of window created to represent the hint.
Paint()	void Paint(void)
	Override this method to control how the hint is rendered to the screen. Use the hint window's ClientRect property to get the bounds of the area to be painted and the hint window's Canvas property to perform the rendering.
CalcHintRect()	Windows::TRect CalcHintRect(int MaxWidth, const AnsiString AHint, void* AData)
	Override this method to set the desired size of the hint to be displayed. The three parameters can be used to make any required calculations. The TRect structure returned by this method indicates the size of the client area of the hint window.
ActivateHint()	void ActivateHint(const Windows::TRect& Rect, const AnsiString AHint)
	Override this method to control where on the screen the hint is displayed. As implemented in THintWindow, ActivateHint() displays the hint window at the coordinates provided by the Rect parameter if it appears on the screen. Otherwise, Rect is modified so that the nearest onscreen position is used. The ActivateHint() method also sets the Caption property of THintWindow. The Caption property is used in the CalcHintRect() method to determine how big the hint window needs to be and is used in the Paint() method to render the hint text (Caption) onto the hint window.

TABLE 5.6   Continued

Method	Purpose

ActivateHintData()	void ActivateHintData(const Windows::TRect& Rect,
	
	                                            const AnsiString AHint,
	
	                                            void* AData)
	
	Override this method to use the additional void* parameter AData. Otherwise, this method is similar to the ActivateHint() method. As implemented in THintWindow, the AData parameter is ignored.

IsHintMsg()	bool IsHintMsg(tagMSG& Msg) Override this method to specify any messages that require the hint window to be hidden. As implemented in THintWindow, this occurs for all mouse, keyboard, command, and activation messages. The global Application object calls IsHintMsg() to check messages while the hint window is being displayed. If it returns true, the hint window is hidden.

By overriding the virtual methods inherited from THintWindow, we can customize the appearance of our hint class. The definition for the THintWindow-derived class used in the MiniCalculator program is shown in Listing 5.8. The class is called TCalculatorHintWindow.

LISTING 5.8   Class Definition for TCalculatorHintWindow

```
class TCalculatorHintWindow : public THintWindow
{
    typedef THintWindow inherited;
protected:
    virtual void __fastcall Paint(void);
    virtual void __fastcall CreateParams(TCreateParams &Params);
public:
    __fastcall virtual TCalculatorHintWindow(Classes::TComponent* AOwner);

    virtual void __fastcall ActivateHint(const Windows::TRect& Rect,
                                         const AnsiString AHint);

    virtual void __fastcall ActivateHintData(const Windows::TRect& Rect,
                                             const AnsiString AHint,
```

Listing 5.8   Continued

```
                                                void* AData);

    virtual Windows::TRect __fastcall CalcHintRect(int MaxWidth,
                                           const AnsiString AHint,
                                           void* AData);

    virtual bool __fastcall IsHintMsg(tagMSG& Msg);

    __property BiDiMode ;
    __property Caption ;
    __property Color ;
    __property Canvas ;
    __property Font ;
public:
    inline __fastcall virtual ~TCalculatorHintWindow(void)
    { }

public:
    inline __fastcall TCalculatorHintWindow(HWND ParentWindow)
                    : THintWindow(ParentWindow)
    { }
};
```

Of the methods shown in the declaration, only CreateParams(), Paint(), and
CalcHintRect() are modified from the inherited methods. The remainder simply call the
inherited THintWindow methods in their implementations. Listing 5.9 shows the implementation of the TCalculatorHintWindow class.

Listing 5.9   Implementation of TCalculatorHintWindow

```
//--------------------------------------------------------------//
//                        CONSTRUCTOR                           //
//--------------------------------------------------------------//
__fastcall
TCalculatorHintWindow::TCalculatorHintWindow(Classes::TComponent* AOwner)
                                        : THintWindow(AOwner)
{
    Canvas->Font->Name = "Arial";
    Canvas->Font->Color = clBlack;
}
```

LISTING 5.9 Continued

```
//-------------------------------------------------------------------//
//   CreateParams                                                    //
//-------------------------------------------------------------------//
void __fastcall TCalculatorHintWindow::CreateParams(TCreateParams &Params)
{
  inherited::CreateParams(Params);

  Params.Style = WS_POPUP;
  Params.WindowClass.style = Params.WindowClass.style | CS_SAVEBITS;

  if(NewStyleControls) // Check the global NewStyleControls variable
  {
    Params.ExStyle = WS_EX_TOOLWINDOW;   // Hint window is a Tool window
    AddBiDiModeExStyle(Params.ExStyle);
  }
}


//-------------------------------------------------------------------//
//   Paint                                                           //
//-------------------------------------------------------------------//
void __fastcall TCalculatorHintWindow::Paint(void)
{
  TRect Rect = ClientRect;

  Canvas->Brush->Color = clBlack;
  Canvas->FillRect(Rect);

  Rect.Left += 4;
  Rect.Top   += 4;
  Rect.Right -= 4;
  Rect.Bottom -= 4;

  Frame3D(Canvas, Rect, clBtnShadow, clBtnHighlight, 1);

  Canvas->Brush->Color = TColor(0xB4CDBB);
  Canvas->FillRect(Rect);

  Rect.Left += 1;
  Rect.Top   += 5;
  Rect.Right -= 1;
  Rect.Bottom -= 1;
```

5

**USER INTERFACE
PRINCIPLES AND
TECHNIQUES**

LISTING 5.9   Continued

```
    DrawText( Canvas->Handle,
              Caption.c_str(),
              -1,
              &Rect,
              DT_RIGHT
              |DT_NOPREFIX
              |DT_SINGLELINE
              |DrawTextBiDiModeFlagsReadingOnly() );
}


//----------------------------------------------------------------------------//
// CalcHintRect                                                               //
//----------------------------------------------------------------------------//
Windows::TRect __fastcall
TCalculatorHintWindow::CalcHintRect(int MaxWidth,
                                    const AnsiString AHint,
                                    void* AData)
{
    TRect Rect(0, 0, MaxWidth, 0);
    DrawText( Canvas->Handle,
              AHint.c_str(),
              -1,
              &Rect,
              DT_CALCRECT
              |DT_SINGLELINE
              |DT_NOPREFIX
              |DrawTextBiDiModeFlagsReadingOnly() );

    // We want a minimum width for our hint: at least 3 times the height.
    if((Rect.Right - Rect.Left) < 3*(Rect.Bottom - Rect.Top))
    {
        Rect.Right = Rect.Left + 3*(Rect.Bottom - Rect.Top);
    }

    Rect.Right  += 20;
    Rect.Bottom += 12;

    return Rect;
}


//----------------------------------------------------------------------------//
// ActivateHint                                                               //
//----------------------------------------------------------------------------//
```

LISTING 5.9 Continued

```
//------------------------------------------------------------------------//
void __fastcall TCalculatorHintWindow::ActivateHint(const Windows::TRect& Rect,
                                                    const AnsiString AHint)
{
    inherited::ActivateHint(Rect, AHint);
}


//------------------------------------------------------------------------//
// ActivateHintData                                                       //
//------------------------------------------------------------------------//
void __fastcall
TCalculatorHintWindow::ActivateHintData(const Windows::TRect& Rect,
                                        const AnsiString AHint,
                                        void* AData)
{
    inherited::ActivateHintData(Rect, AHint, AData);
}


//------------------------------------------------------------------------//
// IsHintMsg                                                              //
//------------------------------------------------------------------------//
bool __fastcall TCalculatorHintWindow::IsHintMsg(tagMSG& Msg)
{
    return inherited::IsHintMsg(Msg);
}
//------------------------------------------------------------------//
```

We will now take a more detailed look at some of the implementation issues of the code presented in Listing 5.9. We begin with the constructor.

The constructor is straightforward. We simply set the font style to Arial and the font color to clBlack. This makes the hint window font the same as that of MiniCalculator's main display.

The overridden CreateParams() method is almost the same as THintWindow's CreateParams() method. The only difference is that we make the window style WS_POPUP only. THintWindow also adds WS_BORDER to the style. We do not want a border around our window, so we use only WS_POPUP. The remainder of the code is straightforward. The CS_SAVEBITS flag added to the WindowClass.style field of Params indicates that Windows should save the area of screen obscured by the hint as a bitmap and then draw it back when the hint disappears. This means that no WM_PAINT messages need to be sent to any windows

5

covered by the hint. With small windows such as hints, this is practical. Finally, we check the value of the global NewStyleControls variable. If it is true (for Win9x and above it is), then we add the necessary extended styles, WS_EX_TOOLWINDOW to indicate that the hint window will be a tool window, and the necessary flags for bidirectional support, using the member function AddBiDiModeExStyle(). For more information about this function, refer to the C++Builder online help.

The real work of the class is carried out in the CalcHintRect() and Paint() methods. In the CalcHintRect() method we first create a TRect variable, called Rect, setting its Right property to the value of the MaxWidth parameter. We then pass the address of Rect to the WinAPI DrawText() function, along with the AHint string and the Handle of our window's Canvas. The function call is

```
DrawText( Canvas->Handle,      // Our Canvas Handle
          AHint.c_str(),       // Returns a NULL terminated version of AHint
          -1,                  // Indicates the string is NULL terminated
          &Rect,               // The TRect we want to determine the size of
          DT_CALCRECT          // Function call calculates the TRect required
          |DT_SINGLELINE       // We want a single line
          |DT_NOPREFIX         // Don't process prefix characters (such as &)
          |DrawTextBiDiModeFlagsReadingOnly() );
```

The DT_CALCRECT flag indicates that no text is actually drawn. Rather, the TRect required to accommodate the text is defined, based on the MaxWidth, the AHint string, and the Canvas->Handle.

Once the TRect required to accommodate the hint has been calculated, we check to see if it has the correct aspect ratio. We want the hint to appear as a smaller version of the main display, so we want the width to be at least three times the height. In addition, we want extra room to the left side of and above the text. We therefore add a constant to the Bottom and Right of the TRect before returning the value. This will allow us to offset the text to the right and down within the hint window. The code is

```
if((Rect.Right - Rect.Left) < 3*(Rect.Bottom - Rect.Top))
{
    Rect.Right = Rect.Left + 3*(Rect.Bottom - Rect.Top);
}

Rect.Right  += 20;
Rect.Bottom += 12;

return Rect;
```

The ratio and constant values are arbitrary and are based on what looks right.

Finally, we paint our hint window in the overridden `Paint()` method. The functionality of this method can be broken into two parts. The first part draws the background for the hint window, and the second renders the hint text. The code for the first part is

```
TRect Rect = ClientRect;

Canvas->Brush->Color = clBlack;
Canvas->FillRect(Rect);

Rect.Left   += 4;
Rect.Top    += 4;
Rect.Right  -= 4;
Rect.Bottom -= 4;

Frame3D(Canvas, Rect, clBtnShadow, clBtnHighlight, 1);

Canvas->Brush->Color = TColor(0xB4CDBB);
Canvas->FillRect(Rect);
```

First we retrieve the `TRect` that bounds the area we can draw on. We paint it black, then 4 pixels in from the edge we use the VCL `Frame3D()` utility function to draw a lowered bevel. We then fill the area enclosed by the frame with a color to match MiniCalculator's main display. Finally, we draw the text onto the hint window using this code:

```
Rect.Left   += 1;
Rect.Top    += 5;
Rect.Right  -= 1;
Rect.Bottom -= 1;

DrawText( Canvas->Handle,
          Caption.c_str(),
          -1,
          &Rect,
          DT_RIGHT          // Right align the text
          |DT_NOPREFIX      // No prefixes
          |DT_SINGLELINE    // Single line
          |DrawTextBiDiModeFlagsReadingOnly() );
```

We specify the `Rect` variable that the text will drawn into. We leave a 1-pixel border on the left, right, and bottom and a 5-pixel border at the top. We then use the WinAPI `DrawText()` function to draw the text on the hint window's `Canvas`. We use the same flags as we did for the

CalcHintRect() method, except that we have removed the DT_CALCRECT flag (we are not calculating, we are drawing), and we have added the DT_RIGHT flag to align the text to the right of Rect. Figure 5.3 shows what the hint window looks like in use. Incidentally, the number displayed in the hint window in Figure 5.3 is not π but rather 22 divided by 7, often used as a rough approximation for π.

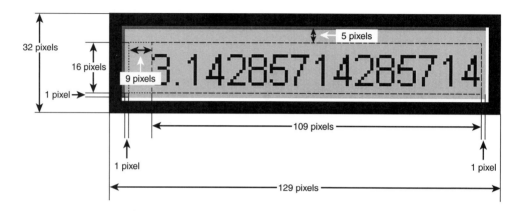

FIGURE 5.3
The TCalculatorHintWindow *custom hint window.*

To use the TCalculatorWindow hint window class we must assign its type to the global HintWindowClass variable as follows:

```
HintWindowClass = __classid(TCalculatorHintWindow);
```

This is discussed in the next section.

Using TApplication's OnHint Event

The TApplicationEvents component (found on the Additional tab of the Component Palette) makes it easy to respond to TApplication events and notably to TApplication's OnHint event.

When TApplication's OnHint event is fired, TApplication's Hint property contains the long hint string of the Hint property of the control that caused the event to be fired. Remember that if no | character is used to separate the hint into a short hint and a long hint, then the string representing the control's hint will be used for both. When implementing TApplication's OnHint event handler, reading the value of this long hint is straightforward. You simply read the value of the global Application object's Hint property, for example

```
AnsiString CurrentLongHint = Application->Hint;
```

In the MiniCalculator program, hint handling is centralized in the TApplication's OnHint event. Of particular note in the MiniCalculator program is that we want to be able to display two pieces of information in our status bar, and we want to use a different hint window class for some of the pop-up hints.

First we look at the need to display information in more than one panel of the status bar. To do this we need to separate the long hint we obtain from Application->Hint into two strings. The first string should contain the keyboard shortcut for each button in the calculator, and the second string should contain a description of the button. We have already seen how the | character can be used to separate short and long hints. We can also use this to separate the long hint into two halves. We simply add a | to the long hint at the position we want the string split. For example, the = key of MiniCalculator has no short hint, but its long hint is in two parts; "Enter" and "Equals". "Enter" signifies the keyboard shortcut for the button, and "Equals" is the button's description. The Hint property for this button is

```
"|Enter|Equals"
```

This is of the format "ShortHint|LongHint1|LongHint2". Only the string "Enter|Equals" will appear in the Application->Hint property. We can therefore use the GetShortHint() global function to retrieve the first long hint and the GetLongHint() global function to retrieve the second long hint. If you do not want either a first long hint or a second long hint, it is important to add a | character to the string to signify this. This is because GetShortHint() and GetLongHint() will return the whole string if the | character is not found. For example, the following string

```
"||LastLongHint"
```

will result in Application->Hint containing "|LastLongHint". In turn, when we call GetShortHint() the result is "", and when we call GetLongHint() the result is "LastLongHint". Similarly, if you want to have only a first long hint, you must write your hint string in the format "|FirstLongHint|".

To place the first long hint in the second status bar panel and place the last long hint in the third status bar panel requires the following code in the Application->OnHint handler:

```
StatusBar1->Panels->Items[1]->Text = GetShortHint(Application->Hint);
StatusBar1->Panels->Items[2]->Text = GetLongHint(Application->Hint);
```

We now turn our attention to the need to display different pop-up hint windows for different controls in the MiniCalculator program. In the previous section, "Using Customized Hints," we saw how to develop our own hint windows. We also saw how to assign our hint window class to the global HintWindowClass variable using the __classid operator. To switch between hint window classes for different hints, we simply read the value of `Application->Hint` in the `Application->OnHint` handler and assign the `HintWindowClass` variable accordingly. Listing 5.10, the full implementation of the `Application->OnHint` handler as it appears in the MiniCalculator program, shows this.

LISTING 5.10   Implementation of `Application->OnHint` Using `TApplicationEvents->OnHint`

```
void __fastcall TMainForm::ApplicationEvents1Hint(TObject *Sender)
{
   if(Application->Hint=="Ctrl+V|Memory Recall" || Application->Hint=="LCD")
   {
      Application->HintHidePause = 10000;  // 10 seconds delay
      HintWindowClass = __classid(TCalculatorHintWindow);
   }
   else
   {
      Application->HintHidePause = HintDisplayTime; // Set in constructor
      HintWindowClass = __classid(THintWindow);
   }

   if(Application->Hint != "LCD")
   {
      StatusBar1->Panels->Items[1]->Text = GetShortHint(Application->Hint);
      StatusBar1->Panels->Items[2]->Text = GetLongHint(Application->Hint);
   }
}
```

We want to show our custom hint window when the user pauses over either the Memory Recall button (`SpeedButtonMemoryRecall`) or the LCD screen display (`LCDScreen`). We also want a longer delay to allow the reader to read the number that the hint will contain, because it may be rather complex. We use the long hint of the controls to see which control generated the hint. In the case of `LCDScreen`, we do not want this long hint displayed, so we do not assign the hint to the status panel if the hint is equal to `"LCD"`, the long hint of the `LCDScreen` `TLabel` control.

The `HintDisplayTime` variable is set in the constructor to the `Application`'s `HintHidePause` value. This allows `Application->HintHidePause` to be restored to its original value when the standard hint window is displayed.

Finally, we will look at how the short hints are assigned to the `Hint` property of these two controls. The method for both is similar, so we will look at only the `Hint` property of `LCDScreen`. We want to show a pop-up hint only if the width of the number being displayed is greater than the width of `LCDScreen`. We check every time `LCDScreen` is updated. This occurs in the `UpdateLCDScreen()` member function. Listing 5.11 shows the implementation.

LISTING 5.11 Implementation of UpdateLCDScreen()

```
void __fastcall TMainForm::UpdateLCDScreen(const AnsiString& NewNumber)
{
    int NumberWidth = LCDScreen->Canvas->TextWidth(NewNumber);

    if(Operation == coComplete)
    {
        if(    (NumberWidth >= LCDScreen->Width)
            && (LCDScreen->Alignment == taRightJustify) )
        {
            LCDScreen->Alignment = taLeftJustify;
        }
        else if(    (NumberWidth < LCDScreen->Width)
                 && (LCDScreen->Alignment != taRightJustify) )
        {
            LCDScreen->Alignment = taRightJustify;
        }
    }
    else if(LCDScreen->Alignment != taRightJustify)
    {
        LCDScreen->Alignment = taRightJustify;
    }

    LCDScreen->Caption = NewNumber;

    int pos    = LCDScreen->Hint.Pos("|");
    int length = LCDScreen->Hint.Length();

    AnsiString LCDScreenHint
            = LCDScreen->Hint.SubString(pos, length-pos+1);
    LCDScreen->Hint = NewNumber + LCDScreenHint;

    if(NumberWidth >= LCDScreen->Width) LCDScreen->ShowHint = true;
    else LCDScreen->ShowHint = false;
}
```

UpdateLCDScreen() is called each time we want to change the value being displayed on the screen, with the new number required (as an AnsiString) being passed by const reference. We first determine the width in pixels that the new number will require when drawn onto the LCDScreen's Canvas. Based on this information, the current operation being performed by the calculator, and the current LCDScreen->Width, we set the required justification. We then assign the NewNumber to the Caption property of LCDScreen. The remainder of the code does two things. First it prepends the new number to the Hint property of LCDScreen so that Hint becomes

```
"NewNumber|LCD"
```

Finally, depending on the width of the new number and the width of LCDScreen, we set LCDScreen's ShowHint property. If the new number is wider than LCDScreen, we set LCDScreen->ShowHint to true; otherwise we suppress the display of a hint by setting LCDScreen->ShowHint to false.

Enhancing Usability Through Input Focus Control

Sensible control of user input and input focus is one way to ensure that your program is as easy to use as possible. *Input focus* determines which user interface control receives attention from the standard input devices. Input received from serial and parallel devices that are not keyboards, mice, or other pointing devices is not included. While such devices can be associated with input focus, this is not the norm for user interface controls. A control is said to have input focus if it can respond to being manipulated by one of the standard input devices.

You can do two things when a control has input focus: respond to the input or move the focus to another control that can respond to the input. We will briefly look at and give an example of each situation.

Responding to Input

The MiniCalculator program responds to the keyboard and to the mouse. This functionality can be switched on or off by the user. The program also gives feedback to the user to indicate when the program can respond to keyboard input. To respond to input from the keyboard, the MainForm's OnKeyDown and OnKeyUp events are handled. Two functions, CalculatorKeyDown() and CalculatorKeyUp(), are used for the implementation of the respective OnKeyDown and OnKeyUp events. These functions are assigned to MainForm's events in the set method of the EnableKeyboardInput property. When MainForm is created, EnableKeyboardInput is set to true, which calls the SetEnableKeyboardInput() method. The implementation is shown in Listing 5.12, which is the same as that shown previously as Listing 5.3 and is repeated here for convenience.

LISTING 5.12   Implementation of SetEnableKeyboardInput()

```cpp
void __fastcall TMainForm::SetEnableKeyboardInput(bool NewEnableKeyboardInput)
{
    if(EnableKeyboardInput != NewEnableKeyboardInput)
    {
        FEnableKeyboardInput = NewEnableKeyboardInput;
        if(EnableKeyboardInput)
        {
            OnKeyDown = CalculatorKeyDown;
```

LISTING 5.12   Continued

```
         OnKeyUp   = CalculatorKeyUp;
         StatusBar1->Panels->Items[1]->Width = 60;
      }
      else
      {
         OnKeyDown = 0;
         OnKeyUp   = 0;
         StatusBar1->Panels->Items[1]->Width = 0;
      }
      StatusBar1->Invalidate();
   }
}
```

FEnableKeyboardInput is initialized to false, ensuring that the body of the first if statement is executed. The lines of interest are

```
OnKeyDown = CalculatorKeyDown;
OnKeyUp   = CalculatorKeyUp;
```

Here the events are assigned to the functions that will handle the events.

The CalculatorKeyDown() method is shown in Listing 5.13.

LISTING 5.13   Implementation of CalculatorKeyDown()

```
void __fastcall TMainForm::CalculatorKeyDown(TObject* Sender,
                                             WORD& Key,
                                             TShiftState Shift)
{
   switch(Key)
   {
      case VK_NUMPAD1 :
      case '1'          : ButtonDown(cb1);
                          ButtonPressNumber(cb1);
                          break;
      case VK_NUMPAD2 :
      case '2'          : ButtonDown(cb2);
                          ButtonPressNumber(cb2);
                          break;
      case VK_NUMPAD3 :
      case '3'          : ButtonDown(cb3);
                          ButtonPressNumber(cb3);
                          break;
      case VK_NUMPAD4 :
```

LISTING 5.13   Continued

```
        case '4'        : ButtonDown(cb4);
                          ButtonPressNumber(cb4);
                          break;
        case VK_NUMPAD5 :
        case '5'        : ButtonDown(cb5);
                          ButtonPressNumber(cb5);
                          break;
        case VK_NUMPAD6 :
        case '6'        : ButtonDown(cb6);
                          ButtonPressNumber(cb6);
                          break;
        case VK_NUMPAD7 :
        case '7'        : ButtonDown(cb7);
                          ButtonPressNumber(cb7);
                          break;
        case VK_NUMPAD8 :
        case '8'        : ButtonDown(cb8);
                          ButtonPressNumber(cb8);
                          break;
        case VK_NUMPAD9 :
        case '9'        : ButtonDown(cb9);
                          ButtonPressNumber(cb9);
                          break;
        case VK_NUMPAD0 :
        case '0'        : ButtonDown(cb0);
                          ButtonPress0();
                          break;

        case VK_DECIMAL : ButtonDown(cbPoint);
                          ButtonPressPoint();
                          break;

        case VK_PRIOR   : ButtonDown(cbExponent);
                          ButtonPressExponent();
                          break;

        case VK_ADD      : ButtonDown(cbAdd);
                          ButtonPressOperation(coAdd);
                          break;
        case VK_SUBTRACT : ButtonDown(cbSubtract);
                          ButtonPressOperation(coSubtract);
                          break;
        case VK_MULTIPLY : ButtonDown(cbMultiply);
                          ButtonPressOperation(coMultiply);
```

LISTING 5.13   Continued

```
                       break;
        case VK_DIVIDE    : ButtonDown(cbDivide);
                            ButtonPressOperation(coDivide);
                            break;

        case VK_RETURN    : ButtonDown(cbEquals);
                            ButtonPressEquals();
                            break;
        case VK_BACK      : ButtonDown(cbBackspace);
                            ButtonPressBackspace();
                            break;
        case VK_DELETE    : if(Shift.Contains(ssCtrl))
                            {
                                ButtonDown(cbAllClear);
                                ButtonPressAllClear();
                            }
                            else
                            {
                                ButtonDown(cbClear);
                                ButtonPressClear();
                            }
                            break;

        case 'C' : if(Shift.Contains(ssCtrl))
                   {
                       ButtonDown(cbMemoryAdd);
                       ButtonPressMemoryAdd();
                   }
                   break;
        case 'V' : if(Shift.Contains(ssCtrl))
                   {
                       ButtonDown(cbMemoryRecall);
                       ButtonPressMemoryRecall();
                   }
                   break;
    }
}
```

Like most key down handlers, `CalculatorKeyDown()` consists of a large `switch` statement that delegates each key occurrence to a function that deals with the actual processing. First the `ButtonDown()` method is called, which changes the appropriate button's `Down` property to `true`. This provides the user with visual confirmation of the button he just pressed. Next a function that encapsulates the button's actual function is called to perform the required processing. The

CalculatorKeyUp() method is nearly identical to the CalculatorKeyDown() method, with a couple of notable differences. Listing 5.14 shows the implementation of CalculatorKeyUp().

LISTING 5.14   Implementation of CalculatorKeyUp()

```
void __fastcall TMainForm::CalculatorKeyUp(TObject *Sender, WORD &Key,
    TShiftState Shift)
{
  switch(Key)
  {
    case VK_NUMPAD1 :
    case '1'        : ButtonUp(cb1);
                      break;
    case VK_NUMPAD2 :
    case '2'        : ButtonUp(cb2);
                      break;
    case VK_NUMPAD3 :
    case '3'        : ButtonUp(cb3);
                      break;
    case VK_NUMPAD4 :
    case '4'        : ButtonUp(cb4);
                      break;
    case VK_NUMPAD5 :
    case '5'        : ButtonUp(cb5);
                      break;
    case VK_NUMPAD6 :
    case '6'        : ButtonUp(cb6);
                      break;
    case VK_NUMPAD7 :
    case '7'        : ButtonUp(cb7);
                      break;
    case VK_NUMPAD8 :
    case '8'        : ButtonUp(cb8);
                      break;
    case VK_NUMPAD9 :
    case '9'        : ButtonUp(cb9);
                      break;
    case VK_NUMPAD0 :
    case '0'        : ButtonUp(cb0);
                      break;
    case VK_DECIMAL : ButtonUp(cbPoint);
                      break;

    case VK_PRIOR   : // PageUp for Exponent
                      // Button toggles so KeyUp not required
                      break;
```

LISTING 5.14 Continued

```
    case VK_ADD       : ButtonUp(cbAdd);
                        break;
    case VK_SUBTRACT  : ButtonUp(cbSubtract);
                        break;
    case VK_MULTIPLY  : ButtonUp(cbMultiply);
                        break;
    case VK_DIVIDE    : ButtonUp(cbDivide);
                        break;

    case VK_RETURN    : ButtonUp(cbEquals);
                        break;
    case VK_BACK      : ButtonUp(cbBackspace);
                        break;
    case VK_DELETE    : if(SpeedButtonAllClear->Down)
                        {
                            ButtonUp(cbAllClear);
                        }
                        else
                        {
                            ButtonUp(cbClear);
                        }
                        break;

  case 'C' : ButtonUp(cbMemoryAdd);
             break;
  case 'V' : ButtonUp(cbMemoryRecall);
             break;
  }
}
```

The first thing to notice is that there is no key up handler for VK_PRIOR (the Page Up key) for the Exponent button. This is because pressing the Exponent button toggles its up/down state. Therefore, we need only handle the key down event, which calls the ButtonPressExponent() method and sets the state of the button according to its current state.

Also worth noting is that the key down handler for Ctrl+C (see Listing 5.13) checks whether ssCtrl is contained in the Shift set parameter. However, the key up handler in Listing 5.14 does not. This is because we are interested only in whether or not Ctrl was pressed when C is pressed, not when C is released. Including the check for the key up occurrence can result in the Memory Add button remaining pressed if Ctrl is released before C is released. Obviously this is not desirable.

Finally, we should note that the code used in the key down handler for VK_DELETE (the Delete key)—that is, for the SpeedButtonClear and SpeedButtonAllClear buttons—is distinguished by the presence of the ssCtrl in the Shift parameter (see Listing 5.13). However, in the key up handler (see Listing 5.14), no check is made for the Ctrl key. Instead, the Down property of the SpeedButtonAllClear button is checked to see if it is pressed. If so, it is released; otherwise, the SpeedButtonClear must be Down, in which case it is released.

Moving Input Focus

In the MiniCalculator program, the main form (MainForm) must have input focus in order to respond to input from the keyboard. However, in certain situations, input focus can leave the main form. We detect these situations and then return input focus to the main form. Input focus can leave the main form in two circumstances. The first is when the application itself loses focus. We are not concerned about this situation because obviously the main form should lose input focus at this time. The second time the main form can lose focus is when an undocked control gains focus. This will occur when we click, drag, or resize an undocked control. The control, LCDPanel, can be undocked from the main form. Therefore, in the MiniCalculator program, we detect times when LCDPanel is undocked (LCDPanel->Floating == true) and receives input focus. We then call MainForm's SetFocus() method to return focus to it. For example, if LCDPanel is resized when it is undocked, the main form loses focus. Therefore, in LCDPanel's OnResize event we write

```
if(LCDPanel->Floating) SetFocus();
```

to return focus to the main form. We have already seen how we monitor the state of the main form's input focus in the section, "Using TStatusBar," earlier in this chapter.

A common technique often used in interfaces is to lead the user to complete edit boxes in order. When one is completed, focus is automatically moved to the next one. This makes completing such edit boxes easy. The FromToForm of the FromToUnit in the Focus.bpr project on the CD-ROM that accompanies this book illustrates how this is done. All that is required is that you implement each edit box's OnKeyUp event. In this example we want the user to enter two 4-digit numbers, one in each edit box. When the first edit box is complete, input focus is moved to the second box. When it is complete, input focus is moved to the OK button. If the second edit box is complete but the first is not, then input focus goes back to the first edit box. The implementation for edit box 1 (Edit1) and edit box 2 (Edit2) is shown in Listings 5.15 and 5.16, respectively.

LISTING 5.15   Implementation of Edit1KeyUp()

```
void __fastcall TFromToForm::Edit1KeyUp(TObject* Sender,
                            WORD& Key,
```

LISTING 5.15   Continued

```
                                     TShiftState Shift)
{
   if(Edit1->Text.Length() == Edit1->MaxLength)
   {
      FinishNumberComplete = true;
      if(StartNumberComplete)
      {
         BitBtnOK->Enabled = true;
         BitBtnOK->SetFocus();
      }
      else Edit2->SetFocus();
   }
   else
   {
      FinishNumberComplete = false;
      BitBtnOK->Enabled = false;
   }
}
```

LISTING 5.16   Implementation of Edit2KeyUp()

```
void __fastcall TFromToForm::Edit2KeyUp(TObject* Sender,
                                    WORD& Key,
                                    TShiftState Shift)
{
   if(Edit2->Text.Length() == Edit2->MaxLength)
   {
      StartNumberComplete = true;
      if(FinishNumberComplete)
      {
         BitBtnOK->Enabled = true;
         BitBtnOK->SetFocus();
      }
      else Edit1->SetFocus();
   }
   else
   {
      StartNumberComplete = false;
      BitBtnOK->Enabled = false;
   }
}
```

To ensure that the first edit box (Edit1) has focus when FromToForm is first displayed, we set its TabOrder property to 0. We set Edit2's TabOrder property to 1, BitBtnOK's TabOrder to 2, and BitBtnCancel's TabOrder to 3. The TabOrder property makes it easy to control the tab order in groups of controls, and it is worth thinking carefully about what order you use in your interface if tabbing through controls is appropriate. You should run the Focus project and see it working. One thing that should be noted about this simple example is that any character can be input to the edit boxes. We could write code that filters out all characters that are not numbers, but this is not the purpose of this example. An even better solution is to use an edit component that allows you to specify a string of characters that can be filtered in or filtered out of the edit box. Such a component is presented in the "Overriding DYNAMIC Functions" section of Chapter 11, "More Custom Component Techniques."

Enhancing Usability Through Appearance

One of the best ways to improve your user interface is to improve its appearance. This is more than just making your interface pleasant to look at; it is about conveying additional information through the use of symbols, color, layout, and shape. By optimizing the appearance of the user interface for your application, you help make the interface more intuitive and familiar. This has a twofold effect. First, users need less time to learn the interface, both because it is familiar and because unfamiliar elements can be guessed. Second, not only do users need less time to learn the interface, they also are prepared to spend more time using the interface. Coupling these benefits clearly improves the usefulness of your application dramatically.

How do you decide on the best way to present the interface of your application to the user? That depends on the type of application you are developing. If you are developing an application that performs the task of a real-world equivalent that is widely used and understood, then your best bet is to use that equivalent as a guide for how your interface should look and act. If there is no obvious real-world equivalent, then you should still try to make your interface as familiar as possible. This usually means that you should make your interface appear as other well-known applications appear. Particular attention should be paid to those applications that perform a similar task or similar kind of task.

Consider an example of creating a phone dialer application. How should the interface be designed? For maximum user familiarity, the best approach is to model the interface after a real phone. More users are more likely to be familiar with a phone interface than with an edit box that you simply type a number into. However, the choice is not so simple. You must remember the context in which the user meets the phone interface (that of being a computer application) and the task it is expected to carry out. Your application is a computer program, and in that sense the user will expect certain behavior. For example, when the user clicks on a button, he will expect it to look clicked. No matter how nice an interface is, if it doesn't act like an interface, it is a waste of time. Also, you must be careful when copying real-world equivalents so that you do not introduce their limitations to your application. For example, creating an interface that looks like a telephone handset is very nice, but if users must use the mouse to click each button to enter a number, they will soon become very frustrated. It is quicker and easier to use the keyboard to input numbers, so you must provide this facility.

The task of the interface is equally important to deciding the appearance. In the case of a phone dialer application, we must consider that the capability to make phone calls may be secondary to the application's true purpose. For example, it may be used primarily for sending and receiving faxes, with the capability to edit faxes a major element. In that case, an interface based on a real-world phone may be inappropriate. A traditional multiple document interface (MDI) file-based user interface may be more familiar and comfortable for users.

If you opt for a file-based MDI interface, then other factors regarding appearance must be considered. For example, the first menu people will expect to see is the File menu; they will also expect a Window menu and so on. You can see then that how your interface appears to the user is a difficult decision with many factors that must be considered.

Designing the appearance of an interface is linked to how the interface should function, and such a design can take a long time to develop. In the MiniCalculator program it was decided that the appearance of the interface should mirror that of a real-world calculator (though the functionality has not been restricted to that of a real-world calculator). This meant making the buttons symbolic rather than simple text buttons. As a result, the interface is highly graphical, consisting almost entirely of button images. Using symbols on buttons instead of text has the advantage that no separate resources for the buttons need be supplied for different locales. Of course this is not the case with text strings, such as the description strings that appear in the third panel of MiniCalculator's status bar.

In general it is preferable always to provide a symbol representing each button or menu item, even if text is used. The user will read the text and associate the symbols with the text. Later, when the user is familiar with the symbols, the text may no longer be required. In some situations it may be appropriate to allow the user to remove text descriptions from controls if they are no longer required. This can be of great benefit to the application, because it frees available screen space. This is particularly noticeable in the toolbars and coolbars of MDI applications, where it is desirable to have as large a space as possible within the parent window to allow child windows to be edited. Allowing the user to reposition text labels also can help.

This section looks at how symbols can be used on their own and with text to improve interface appearance.

Using Symbols on Their Own with Buttons

If you want to provide buttons that do not have text, or the text forms part of the button's symbol, then TSpeedButton is a good choice. The advantage of TSpeedButton is that no focus rectangle is drawn on the button when it is clicked or receives focus, so your well-designed buttons won't be disfigured. Additionally, TSpeedButton has a Down property, which gives you one extra state. The GroupIndex property is also helpful in controlling buttons as groups and saves you a lot of coding. A disadvantage of TSpeedButton is that it doesn't have a window handle and some of the events that TBitBtn has. This is because it derives from TGraphicControl and not TWinControl. Apart from that, the choice is yours. The information presented here can be applied to either button. Normally TButton should not be used unless you definitely don't want an image on your buttons.

You can cover a button entirely with your own image. The buttons in MiniCalculator were created in this way. The main concern is that you must size both your bitmap and your button correctly. Figure 5.4 shows the bitmap for the plus (+) button.

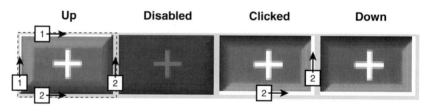

FIGURE 5.4

Glyph layout for TSpeedButton *and* TBitBtn.

Each image in the bitmap represents a state for the button. Normally, the Clicked and Down states will be the same, though not always. The method for sizing your button and bitmap is straightforward. Set the size of the button equal to the size of the image you are going to use to cover the button. Then add a 1-pixel border to the top and left side of your image and a 2-pixel border to the bottom and right side of your button. This is shown in Figure 5.4. Note that the Clicked and Down images will be automatically offset to the bottom and right. Therefore, the size of the image will be smaller. You should allow for this by placing a white or (preferably) transparent 2-pixel border to the bottom and right of each image. White has been used for clarity in Figure 5.4. To use the image for your button, save the button glyph as a bitmap and assign it to the Glyph property at designtime. Don't forget to set the NumGlyphs property to the appropriate value. One thing to bear in mind when designing your buttons' images is that when your button is depressed, it will have a black border on the left and top and a white border on the right and bottom. You should create your images with this in mind; otherwise your buttons might look strange.

You should note that the two memory buttons in MiniCalculator use M+ and MR as their symbols. This is something that you should avoid. These are not truly symbolic; they are the initials of each button's function. A better choice would be something similar to a copy symbol for the memory add (M+) button and a paste symbol for the memory recall (MR) button. We leave the creation of such symbols as an exercise for you.

Using `TSpeedButton`'s `GroupIndex` Property

The MiniCalculator makes extensive use of `TSpeedButton`'s `GroupIndex` property to help control the behavior of the buttons used in the interface. Examples include the three number-base buttons: octal, decimal, and hexadecimal all share the same `GroupIndex` of 2, and the `AllowAllUp` property is `false`. No other buttons in the interface have this `GroupIndex`. This means that only one of the number-base buttons may be depressed at any one time, and at least one of them must be depressed. We do not need to write any code to achieve this. Simply setting the `GroupIndex` property is enough. Similarly, the Exponent button (`SpeedButtonExponent`) has its own `GroupIndex` of 3, allowing it to be pressed or released regardless of the state of any other button in the interface. The remaining buttons in the interface all share the same `GroupIndex` of 1, with the `AllowAllUp` property set to `true`. This means all the buttons can be up at the same time, but only one may be depressed at any one time. Again, all this is achieved without having to write any code, making the `GroupIndex` property of `TSpeedButton` a useful tool when creating an interface.

A Note About Flicker

To help reduce flickering when moving the control bar bands that contain the speed buttons in MiniCalculator, their `ControlStyle` properties have `csOpaque` added to them in the constructor of `MainForm`. `csOpaque` indicates that the control fills its client rectangle entirely, and therefore controls beneath the control do need repainting as they are obscured by the control. To see the difference this flag makes, comment out the code in `MainForm`'s constructor that adds the `csOpaque` flags and run the program.

Using Symbols in Addition to Text

In the MiniCalculator program, symbols were used in addition to text in the drop-down and pop-up menus. At its simplest level of use, `TMenuItem` allows you to add an image through its `Bitmap` property. If you are not going to disable the menu item, and you do not mind being limited to an image of 16×16 pixels, this provides a convenient and easy way to add an image to the menu item in question. However, if you are going to disable the menu item, using the `Bitmap` property is not so satisfactory. This is because the image used for the disabled menu item will be generated from the image you supply. In many cases the generated image will look fine, but if it doesn't you will need to generate your own disabled image and owner-draw the menu item. Likewise, if you want an image of a size other than 16×16, then owner-drawing the menu item is the way to achieve that.

In the MiniCalculator program, the ControlBarPopup menu uses the Bitmap property to add images to the menu items, but the View menu in MainMenu is owner drawn to provide images in the menu items. Owner-drawing a menu item is easier than you may think. To owner-draw a menu item, you must have either a non-NULL Images property in the parent menu or have its OwnerDraw property set to true. You must then write a handler for either the OnDrawItem event or the OnAdvancedDrawItem event. The OnAdvancedDrawItem event provides more information about the state of the menu item and is therefore preferable. A single event handler for all of the menu items in MainMenu's View menu is shared between all the menu items. The Tag property of the menu item is used to determine which image should be displayed by the handler. The handler is called ViewMenuItemsAdvancedDrawItem() and is assigned to the OnAdvancedDrawItem events of the menu items in MainForm's constructor. For example, for the menu item ViewDisplay, we write

ViewDisplay->OnAdvancedDrawItem = ViewMenuItemsAdvancedDrawItem;

Listing 5.17 shows the implementation of ViewMenuItemsAdvancedDrawItem().

LISTING 5.17   Implementation of ViewMenuItemsAdvancedDrawItem()

```
void __fastcall TMainForm::ViewMenuItemsAdvancedDrawItem(TObject* Sender,
                                                         TCanvas* ACanvas,
                                                         const TRect& ARect,
                                                         TOwnerDrawState State)
{
    TMenuItem* MenuItem = dynamic_cast<TMenuItem*>(Sender);

    if(MenuItem)
    {
        // Step 1 - Save ACanvas properties that we are going to change
        TColor OldFontColor  = ACanvas->Font->Color;
        TColor OldBrushColor = ACanvas->Brush->Color;

        int TextOffset = ARect.Left+1;

        try
        {
            // Step 2 -  Draw the check region and the image. The images used
            //           depends on whether the item is selected and whether
            //           it is checked...

            std::auto_ptr<Graphics::TBitmap> CheckedImage(new Graphics::TBitmap());
            std::auto_ptr<Graphics::TBitmap> ToolbarImage(new Graphics::TBitmap());

            // Step 3
```

LISTING 5.17   Continued

```
    ViewMenuImageList->GetBitmap(MenuItem->Tag, ToolbarImage.get());
    ToolbarImage.get()->Transparent = true;

    // Step 4
    if(State.Contains(odChecked))
    {
        if(State.Contains(odSelected))
        {
            MenuCheckImageList->GetBitmap(1, CheckedImage.get());
        }
        else
        {
            MenuCheckImageList->GetBitmap(0, CheckedImage.get());
        }

        ACanvas->Draw(ARect.Left+1,
                      ARect.Top+2,
                      CheckedImage.get());
    }

    // Step 5
    ACanvas->Draw(ARect.Left+21,
                  ARect.Top+2,
                  ToolbarImage.get());

    TextOffset = ARect.Left + 60;
}
__finally
{
    // Step 6
    if(State.Contains(odSelected))
    {
        ACanvas->Font->Color = clHighlightText;
        ACanvas->Brush->Color = clHighlight;
    }
    else
    {
        ACanvas->Font->Color = clWindowText;
        ACanvas->Brush->Color = clMenu;
    }

    ACanvas->FillRect( Rect( TextOffset,
                             ARect.Top,
                             ARect.Right,
```

LISTING 5.17 Continued

```
                                ARect.Bottom ) );

        // Now draw the text :@)
        // Use the WinAPI function DrawText as it
        // draws the underscores correctly :-)

        DrawText( ACanvas->Handle,
                MenuItem->Caption.c_str(),
                MenuItem->Caption.Length(),
                &Rect(TextOffset+2, ARect.Top+2, ARect.Right,  ARect.Bottom),
                DT_EXPANDTABS|DT_SINGLELINE|DT_LEFT );

        // Step 7
        ACanvas->Font->Color = OldFontColor;
        ACanvas->Brush->Color = OldBrushColor;
    }
  }
}
```

The code in `ViewMenuItemsAdvancedDrawItem()` draws three things. First it draws a check mark for the menu item, either up or down. Then it draws a 36-pixel wide and 18-pixel high image representing the panel whose visibility is to be changed. Finally, it renders the text description of the panel, with the correct accelerator key underlined. To do this we use the WinAPI `DrawText()` function that was described earlier, in the "Using `TStatusBar`" section. The images that are displayed are stored in the image list `ViewMenuImageList`, and the index for each image corresponds to the `Tag` property of the menu item that fired the event. We retrieve a pointer to the menu item that fired the event by `dynamic_casting` `Sender` to a `TMenuItem*`. The remainder of the function can be described as follows:

1. We save the `ACanvas` properties that we are going to change.

2. We create two bitmaps: one to hold the check mark image and one to hold the panel image. We use the C++ Standard Library's `auto_ptr<>` template class to hold the pointer to the `TBitmap` image so that it will automatically be destroyed even if an exception is thrown. We perform this and all steps up to step 5 inside a `try` block. Step 6 is performed inside a `__finally` block. This is where the text is rendered. If an exception is thrown when drawing the images on the menu item, the `try/__finally` construct ensures that the code to render the text is always executed.

3. We retrieve the image for the panel based on the menu item's `Tag` property from the image list `ViewMenuImageList`. We then set the bitmap's `Transparent` property to `true`. Note how we use `auto_ptr`'s `get()` method to retrieve the `TBitmap` pointer.

4. If the `State` parameter contains the `odChecked` flag, then we draw a check mark image. Which one we draw depends on whether or not the `State` parameter also contains the `odSelected` flag. If we require a check mark image, we retrieve the appropriate one from the `MenuCheckImageList`.

5. We then draw the panel image and set the `TextOffset` variable to `60` to allow for the check mark space and panel image. We use this value to determine where we should begin drawing the menu item description text.

6. We now draw the menu item text description. We offset the text by the amount specified in the `TextOffset` variable. If an exception was thrown in the previous `try` block, this value will be `0`; otherwise it will be `60` to allow for the images that have been drawn on the menu item. First we set text and background color based on whether the `State` parameter contains the `odSelected` flag. Next we fill the background using the current `Brush->Color`; finally, we draw the text using the WinAPI `DrawText()` function and the current `Font->Color`.

7. Now that we have finished drawing the menu item, we reset the old `ACanvas` properties that we changed.

Having provided an implementation for the `OnAdvancedDrawItem` event, one thing remains. We must implement the `OnMeasureItem` event for each menu item to ensure there is enough space for our custom drawing. Again, as for the `OnAdvancedDrawItem` event, we write one implementation and share it with all menu items by setting each menu item's `OnMeasureItem` event equal to the function in `MainForm`'s constructor. The function we use is called `ViewMenuItemsMeasureItem()`, and its implementation is shown in Listing 5.18.

LISTING 5.18   Implementation of `ViewMenuItemsMeasureItem()`

```
void __fastcall TMainForm::ViewMenuItemsMeasureItem(TObject* Sender,
                                                    TCanvas* ACanvas,
                                                    int& Width,
                                                    int& Height)
{
   TMenuItem* MenuItem = dynamic_cast<TMenuItem*>(Sender);

   if(MenuItem)
   {
      Height = 22;
      Width = ACanvas->TextWidth(MenuItem->Caption) + 62;
   }
}
```

To determine who fired the event, we `dynamic_cast` Sender to a `TMenuItem` pointer. If successful, we set the `Height` parameter to 22 pixels to allow for the height of the panel images plus a 2-pixel border above and below each image. The `Width` parameter is set to the width, in pixels, that will be occupied by the `Caption` property of the menu item using the current `Canvas` of the menu item, as specified by the `ACanvas` parameter. The `TextWidth` method is used to obtain this information. To this we add 62 to allow for the width of the check mark image (18 pixels) and the panel image (36 pixels) and borders between them, the edge of the menu item, and the text description (from the `Caption` property).

As you can see, owner-drawing menu items is not too difficult, but it can make a big difference to your menus, improving both their appearance and flexibility. By sharing the event handlers for groups of menu items, you can minimize the amount of code, making the use of owner-drawn menus even more attractive.

Using Color to Provide Visual Clues

Using color is an easy and effective way to improve the clarity and intuitiveness of your interface. You can see how the color of the buttons in the MiniCalculator program has been used to group buttons according to their purpose. Teal buttons are for performing operations, black buttons are for inputting values, orange buttons are for editing or clearing values, blue buttons are memory functions, and green buttons are for changing the number base. Using color in this way helps make it easy to associate functionality with controls even if that functionality is not known. Much time can be spent on choosing appropriate colors or selecting colors that most people will find easy to differentiate, such as those who are color-blind. How you use color to improve the appearance and usefulness of your interfaces depends on many factors, but using color to create groups is a simple and effective method that can be easily employed in many situations. Other uses will also become apparent, depending on the application.

Using Shaped Controls

A common desire in interface programming is to be released from the confines of the rectangular Windows world and embrace the artistic freedom that comes from using non-rectangular controls. There is more than one way to achieve this, but we will present one simple approach that can find a multitude of uses.

To create a non-rectangular windowed control (a `TWinControl` descendant), use one of the WinAPI region functions to create a region and then assign it to the control. The region functions are used to describe a region of a device surface. They can be rectangular, elliptical, polygonal, or a combination of shapes. Regions can be filled, painted, inverted, and framed and can be used to test for the presence of the mouse cursor. Because regions can be of irregular shape, you can use them to create irregularly shaped buttons. A region is a graphics device interface (GDI) object and must therefore be created. To create a region, use one of the many WinAPI functions designed for doing so. These are listed in Table 5.7.

TABLE 5.7 Region-Creation Functions

Function	Description
CreateEllipticRgn()	Creates an elliptical region given the left-top and right-bottom coordinates of the bounding rectangle.
CreateEllipticRgnIndirect()	Creates an elliptical region given the bounding rectangle as a pointer to a TRect structure.
CreatePolygonRgn()	Creates a polygonal region given an array of points that defines the region and a fill mode that determines which parts of the polygon are filled.
CreatePolyPolygonRgn()	Creates one or more polygonal regions given an array of arrays of points. A fill mode is specified to determine which parts of each polygon are filled.
CreateRectRgn()	Creates a rectangular region given the left-top and right-bottom coordinates of the bounding rectangle.
CreateRectRgnIndirect()	Creates a rectangular region given the bounding rectangle as a pointer to a TRect structure.
CreateRoundRectRgn()	Creates a rounded rectangular region given the left-top and right-bottom coordinates of the bounding rectangle and the width and height of the ellipse that is used to form the rectangle's corners.
ExtCreateRegion()	Creates a region based on the transformation of an existing region.
CombineRgn()	Creates a region based on the combination of two other regions, given a mode that specifies how the two regions should be combined.

To learn more about the region creation functions listed in Table 5.7, refer to the Win32 SDK online help. Another good source of information for this topic and all Win32 GUI issues is the excellent book, *Win32 Programming*, by Rector and Newcomer, published by Addison-Wesley (1997).

Once you have created your region, you use the WinAPI SetWindowRgn() function to assign the region to a windowed control. The SetWindowRgn() function is declared as

```
int SetWindowRgn(
    HWND hWnd,      // handle to window whose window region is to be set
    HRGN hRgn,      // handle to region
    BOOL bRedraw    // window redraw flag - normally TRUE for visible controls
                );
```

The return value is non-zero to indicate success. As an example of how to use regions to create non-rectangular controls, the MiniCalculator program has a panel of buttons representing constant values, such as π. These are TBitBtn components set as rounded rectangular regions. To illustrate the code required, Listing 5.19 shows a snippet of the code that appears in MainForm's constructor to create the rounded rectangular π button (called ConstantPieBitBtn).

LISTING 5.19 Creating a Rounded Rectangular Button

```
// Step 1 - Create the region
HRGN hRoundRectRegion1
       = CreateRoundRectRgn( 0,                          // Left
                             0,                          // Top
                             ConstantPieBitBtn->Width+1,  // Right
                             ConstantPieBitBtn->Height+1, // Bottom
                             14,                          // Ellipse Width
                             14 );                        // Ellipse Height


// Step 2 - Assign the region to the button
SetWindowRgn( ConstantPieBitBtn->Handle, hRoundRectRegion1,  TRUE );
```

Normally when you are finished with a region, you delete it using the DeleteRgn() macro, passing the region handle as the single argument. However, when you assign a region handle using the SetWindowRgn() function, the operating system gains ownership of the region. You should not perform any further function calls using the region handle, and in particular you should not delete it.

Creating the images for a non-rectangular button requires a bit of experimentation, but it is not too difficult. For rounded edges you will want to use some form of antialiasing to reduce the pixilated look of the edges. The effectiveness of this depends on careful choice of color so that the button edges blend into the background. You can see how this was achieved by examining the images used for the MiniCalculator program.

One thing to note is that, if you want to be successful with non-rectangular buttons, you will probably have to derive your own button component and override the `OnPaint()` method so that you have total control over how the button is rendered. Using `TBitBtn` as it stands is not satisfactory. The focus rectangle and default click behavior make it almost unusable for non-rectangular buttons. However, creating your own button component is not too difficult. Chapter 9, "Creating Custom Components," should set you on the right track.

Enhancing Usability by Allowing Customization of the User Interface

A good way to improve the usability of your interface is to allow the user to customize its appearance. This can be as simple as changing the color of different elements of the interface, or it can be as complex as allowing the user to undock parts of the interface or rearrange others. The capability to resize an interface is important, as is the capability to make only certain parts of the interface visible at any given time. Of all these, using color is probably the simplest. All you need to do is give the user access to the `Color` properties of the controls you use to create the interface. In some cases this may not be appropriate, such as when the interface is highly graphical, because there may only be small areas of the interface suitable for such customization. The MiniCalculator program is an example of this. A good way to meet the user's expectations in terms of color is to use the system colors when possible. The system colors are shown in Table 5.8 along with a brief description of what they are for.

TABLE 5.8   System Colors

System Color	Description
clBackground	Current background color of the Windows desktop
clActiveCaption	Current color of the title bar of the active window
clInactiveCaption	Current color of the title bar of inactive windows
clMenu	Current background color of menus
clWindow	Current background color of windows
clWindowFrame	Current color of window frames
clMenuText	Current color of text on menus
clWindowText	Current color of text in windows
clCaptionText	Current color of the text on the title bar of the active window
clActiveBorder	Current border color of the active window

TABLE 5.8   Continued

System Color	Description
clInactiveBorder	Current border color of inactive windows
clAppWorkSpace	Current color of the application workspace
clHighlight	Current background color of selected text
clHighlightText	Current color of selected text
clBtnFace	Current color of a button face
clBtnShadow	Current color of a shadow cast by a button
clGrayText	Current color of text that is dimmed
clBtnText	Current color of text on a button
clInactiveCaptionText	Current color of the text on the title bar of an inactive window
clBtnHighlight	Current color of the highlighting on a button
cl3DDkShadow	Dark shadow for three-dimensional display elements
cl3DLight	Light color for three-dimensional display elements (for edges facing the light source)
clInfoText	Text color for ToolTip controls
clInfoBk	Background color for ToolTip controls

For example, when displaying text in a window, use the clWindowText color. If the text is highlighted, use clHighlightText. These colors will already be specified to the user's preference and should therefore be a good choice for the interface. This section concentrates on the resizing, aligning, visibility, and docking capabilities of a user interface. The MiniCalculator provides all these features, and so it is used as an example. The remainder of this section is broken into subsections, each giving an example of a particular technique.

Docking

In the MiniCalculator program, the main display can be undocked from the rest of the interface and then positioned and resized independently. The main display is a TPanel called LCDPanel. To make it possible to undock this panel from the main form, we must do three things:

1. Set LCDPanel->DragKind to dkDock.
2. Set LCDPanel->DragMode to dmAutomatic.
3. Set MainForm->DockSite to true.

We can do all this at designtime using the Object Inspector. This is all that is required to make the `LCDPanel` dockable, but to make it work well, a little more work is required.

We must consider what changes, if any, we need to make when `LCDPanel` is undocked from `MainForm`. This is not as simple as it first appears. Our first thought probably is to write a handler for the `MainForm->OnUnDock` event. However, this is not suitable because there is a bug in the VCL that results in `OnUnDock` not being fired the first time a control is undocked. If you require any resizing, then clearly it will not work as you expect. A better approach is to write a handler for `LCDPanel`'s `OnDockEnd` event and check the value of the `Floating` property of the panel. If `Floating` is `true` and this is the first call to `OnDockEnd`, then the control has been undocked. This event occurs at the same time as the `OnUnDock` event, so there is no perceptible difference to the user. The only additional requirement of using this method is that we must use a variable to indicate whether the call to `OnEndDock` is the first call in the docking action. This is because `OnEndDock` is called at the end of every move made by a docking control. We will use a `bool` variable, `FirstLCDPanelEndDock`, to indicate if the `OnEndDock` event is the first in the current docking sequence. We therefore add the line

```
bool FirstLCDPanelEndDock;
```

to `MainForm`'s class definition and initialize it to `true` in `MainForm`'s constructor:

```
FirstLCDPanelEndDock = true;
```

The code required in `LCDPanel`'s `OnEndDock` event is shown in Listing 5.20.

LISTING 5.20   Implementation of `LCDPanel->OnEndDock`

```
void __fastcall TMainForm::LCDPanelEndDock(TObject *Sender,
                                           TObject *Target,
                                           int X,
                                           int Y)
{
   if(LCDPanel->Floating)
   {
      SetFocus();
   }
   if(FirstLCDPanelEndDock)
   {
      if(LCDPanel->Floating) FirstLCDPanelEndDock = false;
      Height = Height - LCDPanel->Height;
   }
}
```

5

USER INTERFACE PRINCIPLES AND TECHNIQUES

If this is the first time that LCDPanel's OnEndDock event is fired in the current docking sequence (that is, LCDPanel has just been undocked and FirstLCDPanelEndDock is true), then we resize MainForm by subtracting the Height of LCDPanel from MainForm's current Height. We do this even if the control is not floating, because we add the Height of LCDPanel back to MainForm in MainForm's OnDockDrop event, which will be fired if LCDPanel is not Floating. This can occur the very first time we try to undock LCDPanel where it is possible to undock and dock LCDPanel in the same docking action.

We do not need to reposition the remaining two controls that are directly on MainForm—ButtonsControlBar and StatusBar1—because their Align properties are alClient and alBottom, respectively. We can now undock LCDPanel, and MainForm will be automatically resized appropriately. Notice that before we resize MainForm we first reset the FirstLCDPanelEndDock to false, but only if LCDPanel is Floating. Again, this is because the first time you undock the panel it is possible to undock and dock in the same action. LCDPanel may not be Floating, and setting FirstLCDPanelUnDock to false would mean that this code would not be executed the next time the panel is actually undocked.

Note that every time LCDPanelEndDock() is called and LCDPanel->Floating is true, we call SetFocus() for the MainForm. This ensures that MainForm never loses input focus from the keyboard. This was discussed in more detail in the section "Enhancing Usability Through Input Focus Control."

Docking LCDPanel back onto MainForm is a bit more complicated than undocking it. First we must implement MainForm's OnGetSiteInfo event handler. This event passes a TRect parameter, InfluenceRect, by reference. This TRect specifies where on the form docking will be activated if a dockable control is released over it. This allows you to specify docking regions on a control for specific controls. In the MiniCalculator program we specify a dockable region equal to the Height of LCDPanel and the ClientWidth of MainForm starting at the top of the main form. The event handler is shown in Listing 5.21.

LISTING 5.21   Implementation of MainForm->OnGetSiteInfo

```
void __fastcall TMainForm::FormGetSiteInfo(TObject* Sender,
                                           TControl* DockClient,
                                           TRect& InfluenceRect,
                                           TPoint& MousePos,
                                           bool& CanDock)
{
    if(DockClient->Name == "LCDPanel")
    {
        InfluenceRect.Left   = ClientOrigin.x;
        InfluenceRect.Top    = ClientOrigin.y;
        InfluenceRect.Right  = ClientOrigin.x + ClientWidth;
```

LISTING 5.21   Continued

```
        InfluenceRect.Bottom = ClientOrigin.y + DockClient->Height;
    }
}
```

The first thing we do inside `FormGetSiteInfo()` is check to see if the `DockClient`—the
`TControl` pointer to the object that caused the event to be fired—is `LCDPanel`. If it is, then we
define the docking site above which `LCDPanel` may be dropped by specifying suitable values
for the `InfluenceRect` parameter. We do not use the remaining parameters: `MousePos` and
`CanDock`. `MousePos` is a reference to the current cursor position, and `CanDock` is used to determine if the dock is allowed. With `CanDock` set to `false`, the `DockClient` cannot dock.

We must now implement `MainForm`'s `OnDockOver` event. This event enables us to provide
visual feedback to the user as to where the control will be docked if the control is currently
over a dock site (the mouse is inside `InfluenceRect`) and the control is dockable (`CanDock`
`== true`). We use the `DockRect` property of the `Source` parameter, a `TDragDropObject`
pointer, to define the docking rectangle that appears to the user. The implementation of
`MainForm->OnDockOver` is shown in Listing 5.22.

LISTING 5.22   Implementation of `MainForm->OnDockOver`

```
void __fastcall TMainForm::FormDockOver(TObject* Sender,
                                        TDragDockObject* Source,
                                        int X,
                                        int Y,
                                        TDragState State,
                                        bool& Accept)
{
    if(Source->Control->Name == "LCDPanel")
    {
        TRect DockingRect( ClientOrigin.x,
                           ClientOrigin.y,
                           ClientOrigin.x + ClientWidth,
                           ClientOrigin.y + Source->Control->Height );

        Source->DockRect = DockingRect;
    }
}
```

When the docking control moves over its `InfluenceRect` (as defined in `OnGetSiteInfo`), the
outline rectangle that signifies the control's position is snapped to the `Source->DockRect`
defined in `OnDockOver`. This gives the user visual confirmation of where the docking control
will be docked if he releases the control. In this case, `Source->DockRect` is set equal to the

Height of the control and the `ClientWidth` of the main form, with `TRect` starting at `ClientOrigin`. In fact, this is the same as the `InfluenceRect` specified in `OnGetsiteInfo`.

The remaining parameters are not used: `X`, the horizontal cursor position; `Y` the vertical cursor position; `State`, of type `TDragState`, the movement state of the mouse in relation to the control; and `Accept`. Setting `Accept` to `false` prevents the control from docking.

Finally, we implement `MainForm->OnDockDrop`. This event allows us to resize the control to fit the `DockRect` specified in the `OnDockOver` handler. It also allows us to perform any other processing that is needed, such as resizing the form or resetting the `Anchors` or `Align` property. The implementation for `MainForm->OnDockDrop` is shown in Listing 5.23.

LISTING 5.23   Implementation of `MainForm->OnDockDrop`

```cpp
void __fastcall TMainForm::FormDockDrop(TObject* Sender,
                                        TDragDockObject* Source,
                                        int X,
                                        int Y)
{
   if(Source->Control->Name == "LCDPanel")
   {
      Source->Control->Top = 0;
      Source->Control->Left = 0;
      Source->Control->Width = ClientWidth;

      // Allow space...
      Height = Height + Source->Control->Height;

      // Must reset the Align of LCDPanel
      Source->Control->Align = alTop;

      // Reset the FirstLCDPanelEndDock flag
      FirstLCDPanelEndDock = true;
   }
}
```

The implementation of `FormDockDrop()` as shown in Listing 5.23 is not as simple as it first appears. First we resize `LCDPanel` to fit the top of the form. We then allow space for the docked panel by increasing the `Height` of `MainForm` by the `Height` of `LCDPanel`. Next reset `LCDPanel->Align` to `alTop`. We must do this as the `Align` property is set to `alNone` when `LCDPanel` is undocked. Finally, we reset `FirstLCDPanelEndDock` to `true` in readiness for the next time `LCDPanel` is undocked.

There are two things of note. First, we must adjust the `Height` of `MainForm` *before* we reset the `Align` property of `LCDPanel` to `alTop`. If `LCDPanel->Align` is set to `alTop` before `MainForm`'s `Height` is adjusted, `MainForm`'s `Height` may be adjusted twice. This is because `MainForm` will be automatically resized to accommodate `LCDPanel` if `LCDPanel->Align` is `alTop` and there is not sufficient room. Subsequently changing `MainForm`'s `Height` manually results in twice as much extra height as was needed. Changing the `Height` of `MainForm` first circumvents this problem because there will always be enough room for `LCDPanel`. When its `Align` property is set to `alTop`, no automatic resizing is required.

Second, we do not need to perform any repositioning of the other controls on `MainForm`. This is because there are only two other controls directly placed on `MainForm`, and both have their `Align` properties set to a value other than `alNone`. The two controls are `ButtonsControlBar` (a `TControlBar`) and `StatusBar1` (a `TStatusBar`). `StatusBar1->Align` is `alBottom`, and `ButtonsControlBar->Align` is `alClient`. By providing the extra height on the form, these controls are automatically repositioned.

In many ways, the docking capabilities of MiniCalculator are small, but they are sufficient. For a more involved example of docking in C++Builder, you should study the example project `dockex.bpr` in the `$(BCB)\Examples\Docking` folder of your C++Builder 5 installation.

Resizing

To cope with resizing, you can handle both the `OnResize` and `OnConstrainedResize` events; which one depends on what you want to achieve. In the MiniCalculator program, there is an example of each: When `LCDPanel` is resized, we must update the justification of the labels within the panel in `OnResize`, and when `ButtonsControlBar` is resized, we must prevent the control from being made smaller than the control bands it contains in `OnConstrainedResize`. You can also control resizing more generally by setting the `Align`, `Anchors`, `AutoSize`, `Constraints`, `Height`, `Left`, `Top`, and `Width` properties of controls. There are examples of all but the `AutoSize` property in the MiniCalculator program. By default, `AutoSize` is `false`. Setting it to `true` causes the control to resize automatically to accommodate its contents.

Using `Align`

The `Align` property can be used to create regions on a control, typically a form, that resize according to specific rules. To create areas that can be resized beside areas that cannot, use a combination of nested panels and set their `Align` properties to create the desired effect. There is an infinite number of possible layouts, and experimentation is useful. By combining the use of aligned panel components with `Constraints` carefully set, very clever resizing interfaces can be developed with a minimum of work.

The sample project, Panels.bpr, contained on the CD-ROM that accompanies this book, illustrates simple use of panel components to create a resizing interface. The panels each have their Align properties variously set so that each panel exhibits different qualities when the main form, Form1, is resized. The Constraints of Panel1 and Panel2 are set so as to make the interface more robust by preventing the interface from being resized too small.

In the MiniCalculator program, the interface is divided into three control regions. At the top is an alTop Aligned TPanel called LCDPanel. In the middle is an alClient Aligned TControlBar called ButtonsControlBar, and at the bottom is an alBottom Aligned TStatusBar called StatusBar1. The MinHeight and MaxHeight Constraints of LCDPanel and StatusBar1 are set to their actual Heights, which therefore cannot be modified. Figure 5.5 shows this layout.

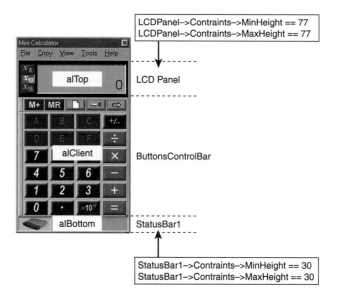

FIGURE 5.5

The Align layout of MiniCalculator.

When MiniCalculator is resized, only the widths of LCDPanel and StatusBar1 can be changed, whereas both the height and width of ButtonsControlBar can be changed.

Using Anchors

The Anchors is similar to the Align property but allows an extra degree of control. The use of anchors is essential to the correct layout of the LCD display at the top of MiniCalculator. The LCD display was created using two TPanel components, three TLabel components, and three TSpeedButton components. All the components are placed on a TPanel component called LCDPanel. LCDPanel has its Constraints->MinWidth property set to 227 pixels and its

`Constraints->MinHeight` and `Constraints->MaxHeight` properties both set to 77 pixels (as shown in Figure 5.5). Its height cannot be changed, and its width cannot be less than 227 pixels.

Another `TPanel` component, `BackgroundDisplay`, is placed on top of `LCDPanel` and anchored to it by the anchors `akLeft`, `akRight`, `akTop`, and `akBottom`. This ensures that `BackgroundPanel` is resized when `LCDPanel` is resized, but with the border size maintained. Because the height of `LCDPanel` will not vary at runtime, the anchors `akTop` and `akBottom` are not required, but including them makes it easy to resize the height of `LCDPanel` at designtime.

Figure 5.6 shows the anchors used by the three `TLabel` components that are placed on `BackgroundPanel`. This can be referred to when each of the labels is discussed.

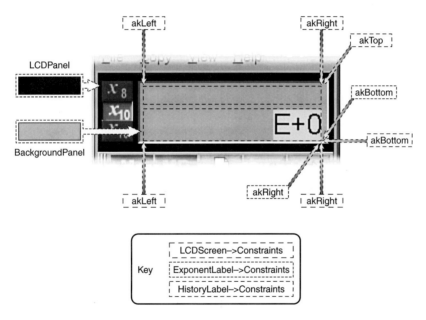

FIGURE 5.6
The anchors used by the three `TLabel` components in MiniCalculator's display.

`LCDScreen`, a `TLabel` component, is anchored to the `BackgroundDisplay` `TPanel` component by the anchors `akLeft`, `akRight`, and `akBottom`. We could have included `akTop`, but we did not want the height of `LCDScreen` modified during designtime if we modified the height of either `BackgroundPanel` or `LCDPanel`. In a similar fashion to `BackgroundDisplay`, `LCDScreen` is anchored to `akBottom` unnecessarily at runtime but conveniently at designtime. If `LCDPanel`'s height is changed at designtime, `BackgroundPanel`'s height will also change. The height of `LCDScreen` will not be affected, but it will move to maintain its gap with the bottom of `BackgroundPanel`. The `akLeft` and `akRight` anchors ensure that the same left and right borders are maintained at both designtime and runtime.

The `HistoryLabel` component is anchored to `BackgroundPanel` in almost the same way as `LCDScreen`; its `Anchors` property contains `akLeft` and `akRight` but, instead of `akBottom`, `akTop` is included. Again, as for `LCDScreen`, only `akLeft` and `akRight` are required, but including `akBottom` makes it easier to manipulate `HistoryLabel` at designtime. If the height of `LCDPanel` is changed at designtime, the distance of `HistoryLabel` from the edge of `BackgroundPanel` will remain constant. Therefore only the gap between `HistoryPanel` and `LCDScreen` will change.

Finally, the `ExponentLabel` component is anchored to `BackgroundPanel`, using `akRight` and `akBottom`. The position of these anchors is the same as the `akRight` and `akBottom` anchors of `LCDScreen`. Also, as for `LCDScreen`, the `akBottom` anchor is not required at runtime, but including it makes it easier to manipulate the label at designtime.

It is important to note that you can change the position of an anchor at runtime without having to re-anchor to that position. This is done with the `LCDScreen` component when an exponent is being edited. When `SpeedButtonExponent` is pressed, the `LCDScreen` label must be shrunk and moved away from above `ExponentLabel`. This is done so that when `ExponentLabel` is made visible, the user can see both it and `LCDScreen`. The code to reposition and resize `LCDScreen` to allow for the now visible `ExponentLabel` is as follows:

```
int LCDScreenLeft = LCDScreen->Left;
LCDScreen->Width = LCDScreen->Width - ExponentLabel->Width;
LCDScreen->Left = LCDScreenLeft;
```

By changing the width of `LCDScreen`, either the left or right anchor must be moved. Which is moved depends on the value of `LCDScreen`'s `Alignment` property. If it is `taRightJustify`, then the left anchor will be moved. If it is `taLeftJustify`, then the right anchor will be moved, and if it is `taCenter`, both anchors will be moved. Referring to the previous code snippet, we can see that if we change the width of `LCDScreen`, whose `Alignment` will be `taRightJustify`, then the left anchor will be moved. Because the right anchor remains unchanged, the effect is to decrease the width of `LCDScreen` without moving it from behind `ExponentLabel`, which is now visible. We adjust the `Left` property of `LCDScreen` so that it has its old value, thereby shifting `LCDScreen` to the left as we desire. There is an alternative approach, and that is to change the alignment of `LCDScreen` to `taLeftJustify` before changing `LCDScreen`'s `Width`. After the width is changed, we simply change `Alignment` back to `taRightJustify` to restore the original setting. The following code is therefore equivalent to the previous code snippet:

```
LCDScreen->Alignment = taLeftJustify;
LCDScreen->Width = LCDScreen->Width - ExponentLabel->Width;
LCDScreen->Alignment = taRightJustify;
```

The `Anchors` property is a very useful tool to help control the layout of an interface. A particularly common use is to anchor buttons on resizable dialog boxes. The sample project,

`Panels.bpr`, on the accompanying CD-ROM, shows two `TBitBtn` components on `Panel5` (the `clRed` panel). When the form is resized, the buttons maintain their distance from the right edge of the form. The same effect can be achieved by placing the buttons directly onto the form the required distance from the right edge and setting the right anchor for each button (`akRight == true`).

Using `Constraints`

`Constraints` provide an excellent mechanism for constraining the size of a control. The main thing to remember about `Constraints` is that a control cannot be resized to a size outside the `Constraints` of itself and cannot be resized to violate the `Constraints` of any visible control that it contains.

The sample project, `Panels.bpr`, uses `Constraints` to prevent the main form from being made too small. `Panel1`'s `Constraints->MinHeight` property is set to `300`, and `Panel2`'s `Constraints->MinWidth` property is also set to `300`. This means that the client area of `Form1` (the main form) cannot be less than 300×300. We could alternatively set the `MinHeight` and `MinWidth` `Constraints` of `Form1`, but to achieve the same value of 300×300 we need to take into account the difference between the form's `Height` and its `ClientHeight` and the form's `Width` and its `ClientWidth`.

MiniCalculator also uses `Constraints`. The main form, `MainForm`, has `Constraints->MinHeight` set to `52` pixels, and `Constraints->MinWidth` is set to `248` to ensure that the main menu is always visible. This also ensures that `StatusBar1` remains visible because only its `MinHeight` and `MaxHeight` `Constraints` are set (both equal `30`, the `Height` of `StatusBar1`). `LCDPanel` has its own `MinWidth` `Constraint` because it is dockable and can therefore be resized independently of `MainForm`. `LCDPanel`'s `MinHeight` and `MaxHeight` `Constraints` are both set to `77`, the `Height` of `LCDPanel`. `LCDPanel`'s height therefore cannot be changed. `ButtonsControlBar` has its `Constraints` determined dynamically at runtime so that they always accommodate the controls it contains, regardless of their position within the control bar. To do this we must implement `ButtonsControlBar`'s `OnConstrainedResize` event.

Using `OnConstrainedResize`

Use `OnConstrainedResize` to update acontrol's `Constraints` when the control is resized. As was mentioned in the last section the MiniCalculator program dynamically updates the `Constraints` of the `TControlBar` component, `ButtonsControlBar`. The purpose of this is to constrain the minimum height and width of the control bar so that it will always accommodate the controls it contains, no matter where they are positioned within the control bar. The implementation of `ButtonsControlBar->OnConstrainedResize` is shown in Listing 5.24.

LISTING 5.24   Implementation of `ButtonsControlBar->OnConstrainedResize`

```
void __fastcall TMainForm::ButtonsControlBarConstrainedResize(TObject* Sender,
                                                        int& MinWidth,
                                                        int& MinHeight,
                                                        int& MaxWidth,
                                                        int& MaxHeight)
{
    GetControlBarMinWidthAndHeight(ButtonsControlBar, MinWidth,  MinHeight);
}
```

The `OnConstrainedResize` event has four parameters, each of which corresponds to one of the `Constraints` of the control for which the event is fired: `MinWidth`, `MinHeight`, `MaxWidth`, and `MaxHeight`.

`ButtonsControlBarConstrainedResize()` in itself doesn't do very much. However, it does call the descriptively named `GetControlBarMinWidthAndHeight()`, passing as arguments a pointer to the control bar we are interested in and the `MinWidth` and `MinHeight` parameters so that their new values can be calculated and assigned. `GetControlBarMinWidthAndHeight()` is declared as follows:

```
void __fastcall GetControlBarMinWidthAndHeight(TCustomControlBar* ControlBar,
                                               int& MinWidth,
                                               int& MinHeight);
```

Both the `int` parameters of `GetControlBarMinWidthAndHeight()` are passed by non-const reference, allowing us to modify the values passed. The implementation of `GetControlBarMinWidthAndHeight()` is shown in Listing 5.25.

LISTING 5.25   Implementation of `GetControlBarMinWidthAndHeight()`

```
void __fastcall
TMainForm::GetControlBarMinWidthAndHeight(TCustomControlBar* ControlBar,
                                          int& MinWidth,
                                          int& MinHeight)
{
    int MinLeft   = 0;
    int MinTop    = 0;
    int MaxRight  = 0;
    int MaxBottom = 0;

    bool FirstVisible = true;

    for(int i=0; i<ControlBar->ControlCount; ++i)
    {
```

LISTING 5.25 Continued

```
        if(ControlBar->Controls[i]->Visible)
        {
            if(FirstVisible)
            {
                MinLeft   = ControlBar->Controls[i]->Left-11;
                MinTop    = ControlBar->Controls[i]->Top-2;
                MaxRight  = ControlBar->Controls[i]->Left
                            + ControlBar->Controls[i]->Width + 2;
                MaxBottom = ControlBar->Controls[i]->Top
                            + ControlBar->Controls[i]->Height + 2;
                FirstVisible = false;
            }
            else
            {
                if((ControlBar->Controls[i]->Left-11) < MinLeft)
                {
                    MinLeft = ControlBar->Controls[i]->Left-11;
                }
                if((ControlBar->Controls[i]->Top-2)  < MinTop)
                {
                    MinTop  = ControlBar->Controls[i]->Top-2;
                }
                if( (ControlBar->Controls[i]->Left
                     + ControlBar->Controls[i]->Width + 2) > MaxRight)
                {
                    MaxRight = ControlBar->Controls[i]->Left
                            + ControlBar->Controls[i]->Width + 2;
                }
                if( (ControlBar->Controls[i]->Top
                     + ControlBar->Controls[i]->Height + 2) > MaxBottom)
                {
                    MaxBottom = ControlBar->Controls[i]->Top
                            + ControlBar->Controls[i]->Height + 2;
                }
            }
        }
    }
    MinWidth  = (MaxRight - MinLeft);
    MinHeight = (MaxBottom - MinTop);
}
```

The operation of GetControlBarMinWidthAndHeight() is quite simple. For each visible control in the control bar, we calculate a value to represent the left, right, top, and bottom of the control, including the control band border around the control. The control band border includes the handle of the band that is used for moving the control within the control bar. In this case there is an 11-pixel border on the left side and a 2-pixel border on the remaining sides. We then check each value against MinLeft, MaxRight, MinTop, and MaxBottom. If smaller or larger, as appropriate, we update the appropriate value. Finally, we calculate the required value for MinWidth and MinHeight as

```
MinWidth  = (MaxRight - MinLeft);
MinHeight = (MaxBottom - MinTop);
```

These are now the new values of the MinWidth and MinHeight Constraints of ButtonsControlBar.

Using OnResize

Use OnResize to update a control's appearance or perform other necessary tasks when the control is resized. OnResize is called after the control has been resized. Do not use OnResize to update values in the Constraints property; use OnConstrainedResize instead. The reason is that the calling sequence for OnResize and OnConstrainedResize is OnResize→OnConstrainedResize[→OnResize]. If the values in the Constraints property are changed in OnConstrainedResize, OnResize is called a second time to allow any additional resizing to be handled. If you update Constraints in OnResize, your code will be executed twice.

In MiniCalculator, the OnResize event for LCDPanel is implemented to ensure that the correct justification of the label components it contains is maintained. The implementation of the OnResize handler is shown in Listing 5.26.

LISTING 5.26 Implementation of LCDPanel->OnResize

```
void __fastcall TMainForm::LCDPanelResize(TObject *Sender)
{
    UpdateLCDScreen(LCDScreen->Caption);
    UpdateHistoryLabel(HistoryLabel->Caption);
    if(LCDPanel->Floating && MainForm->Visible) SetFocus();
}
```

The OnResize handler does three things. It updates the LCDScreen label, then it updates the HistoryLabel label, and finally it resets input focus to the main form if the panel is Floating (that is, it has been undocked from the main form). Note that it only calls SetFocus() if the main form is visible. This check is made because the OnResize event may occur before the main form is shown initially, such as when the panel is resized to match some previous setting. Refer to the section "Enhancing Usability by Remembering the User's Preferences," later in this chapter, for more information.

When we call UpdateLCDScreen(), we pass the current LCDScreen->Caption as the single argument. Essentially we then pass the current Caption and see if we need to adjust how the Caption is displayed based on the new size of LCDPanel.

We saw the implementation of UpdateLCDScreen() in Listing 5.11, but we will repeat it in Listing 5.27 for convenience.

LISTING 5.27   Implementation of UpdateLCDScreen()

```
void __fastcall TMainForm::UpdateLCDScreen(const AnsiString& NewNumber)
{
   int NumberWidth = LCDScreen->Canvas->TextWidth(NewNumber);

   if(Operation == coComplete)
   {
      if(   (NumberWidth >= LCDScreen->Width)
         && (LCDScreen->Alignment == taRightJustify) )
      {
         LCDScreen->Alignment = taLeftJustify;
      }
      else if(   (NumberWidth < LCDScreen->Width)
              && (LCDScreen->Alignment != taRightJustify) )
      {
         LCDScreen->Alignment = taRightJustify;
      }
   }
   else if(LCDScreen->Alignment != taRightJustify)
   {
      LCDScreen->Alignment = taRightJustify;
   }

   LCDScreen->Caption = NewNumber;

   int pos = LCDScreen->Hint.Pos("|");
   int length = LCDScreen->Hint.Length();
   AnsiString LCDScreenHint
            = LCDScreen->Hint.SubString(pos, length-pos+1);
   LCDScreen->Hint = NewNumber + LCDScreenHint;

   if(NumberWidth >= LCDScreen->Width) LCDScreen->ShowHint = true;
   else LCDScreen->ShowHint = false;
}
```

The operation of `UpdateLCDScreen()` is broken into three stages.

1. We check the size, in pixels, required to display the `NewNumber` string. (In this case, `NewNumber` is actually the current `Caption` property of `LCDScreen`.) To do this we use the `TextWidth()` method of `TCanvas`.

2. We then set the correct justification (the `Alignment` property of `LCDScreen`), depending on whether an operation has just finished or there is one ongoing. If an operation has just finished, `Operation` is equal to `coComplete`, and `LCDScreen` is not wide enough to display the whole number, then we want to left-justify the label (`LCDScreen->Alignment = taLeftJustify`). `Operation` is `coComplete` when we are displaying the answer of an operation, and therefore it is more important to see the start of the number than the end of the number. If there is enough width to display the number, then we right-justify `LCDScreen`, because this is the preferred justification (`LCDScreen->Alignment = taRightJustify`). Otherwise, if `Operation` is not `coComplete`, then there is an operation ongoing; `LCDScreen` is displaying a value that is currently being edited or is capable of being edited. We want to right-justify (`LCDScreen->Alignment = taRightJustify`) the label `Caption` so that the part of the number that is being edited is always visible.

3. Finally, if `NewNumber` is too wide to be displayed on `LCDScreen`, we prepend `NewNumber` to `LCDScreen`'s `Hint` property. This is discussed at length in the previous section, "Using Customized Hints."

After we call `UpdateLCDScreen()`, we call `UpdateHistoryLabel()`, which performs a task similar to that performed by `UpdateLCDScreen()`. It adjusts the justification of `HistoryLabel` according to the width of the `HistoryLabel->Caption` text. However, unlike `UpdateLCDScreen()`, `UpdateHistoryLabel()` does not need to adjust the size of `HistoryLabel`. As a result, `UpdateHistoryLabel()` is much simpler. The implementation is shown in Listing 5.28.

LISTING 5.28   Implementation of `UpdateHistoryScreen()`

```
void __fastcall TMainForm::UpdateHistoryLabel(const AnsiString& NewHistory)
{
    int HistoryWidth = HistoryLabel->Canvas->TextWidth(NewHistory);

    if(   (HistoryWidth >= HistoryLabel->Width)
       && (HistoryLabel->Alignment == taLeftJustify) )
    {
        HistoryLabel->Alignment = taRightJustify;
    }
    else if(   (HistoryWidth < HistoryLabel->Width)
            && (HistoryLabel->Alignment != taLeftJustify) )
    {
```

LISTING 5.28   Continued

```
        HistoryLabel->Alignment = taLeftJustify;
    }

    HistoryLabel->Caption = NewHistory;
}
```

As for `UpdateLCDScreen()`, we use `TextWidth()` to determine the width in pixels of the `NewHistory AnsiString`. If `NewHistory` is too wide for the whole string to be displayed in `HistoryLabel`, then we right-justify `HistoryLabel` so that the most recent result is shown. Otherwise we left-justify `HistoryLabel`. This gives the appearance of text scrolling left when the right edge of `HistoryLabel` is reached.

Finally, at the end of the `OnResize` handler we check to see if `LCDPanel` is `Floating`, indicating that it has been undocked from the main form (`MainForm`). If so, then `MainForm` will no longer have focus, because the action of resizing `LCDPanel` will have set the focus to the panel. We must therefore reset focus to the main form by calling `SetFocus()`. This ensures that `MainForm` can respond to keyboard input if it is enabled.

Using `TControlBar`

`TControlBar` is normally used as a visual container for `TToolBars`. In fact, it can be used as a visual container for other controls and is not restricted to toolbars; the controls contained by `TControlBar` do not even need to be of the same type. The MiniCalculator program uses `TControlBar` as a visual container for `TPanel` components. We call our `TControlBar` `ButtonsControlBar`; refer to Figure 5.5 for an image. To meet the requirements of our program, we must change some of the properties of `ButtonsControlBar` at designtime. We make the following changes:

- `DockSite = false`

  We are not going to make the controls inside `TControlBar` dockable, and we do not want `LCDPanel` to be able to dock onto the control bar, so we set this property to `false`.

- `RowSize = 31`

  The height of the bands within our control bar are exact multiples of 31. `RowSnap` is also `true`, ensuring the control bar aligns controls to 31 pixel rows.

- `AutoDrag = false`

  We do not want the bands in the control bar to be undocked when they are dragged off the control bar. Instead, we want them to remain inside the control bar. Therefore, we set `AutoDrag` to `false`.

- AutoDock = false

    We do not allow docking on our control bar, and so we do not need the AutoDock facility. We set it to false.

To use the control bar, we place the panels that we want to appear as control bar bands in the control bar at designtime. The control bar control does the rest. It adds the band grip to the left side of the panel (the two vertical lines that are used to drag the control within the control bar) and a frame around the panel. Some slight repositioning may be required.

> **TIP**
>
> When MiniCalculator was being written, it was often necessary to move the buttons to different controls as the interface evolved. Doing this one control at a time is tedious and error prone. However, it is not possible to select the buttons by dragging a rectangle around them without also selecting the control on which they are placed. There is one easy way of selecting a large group of controls without selecting the control on which they are placed. Simply view the form as text (right-click the form and select View as Text from the context menu). Then you can cut and paste the text versions of the controls as you please.

Using a control bar to control how the panels are positioned within MiniCalculator greatly simplifies the code used to write the interface, and it allows the interface to be customized in a way that should be familiar to most users. In its current state, ButtonsControlBar allows reasonable flexibility, but more work is needed to make moving control bands more robust, particularly to prevent controls from overlapping. However, it is still possible to allow a certain degree of customization. Notably, the MiniCalculator provides the capability to left- or right-align individual controls within ButtonsControlBar or all controls at once. It also allows the control bar to snap to the size of the controls that it contains. This functionality is accessed through a pop-up menu. Five choices are available:

1. Snap to Fit

    ButtonsControlBar is resized to fit the controls it contains.

2. Align Left

    The control bar band under the mouse when the pop-up menu is activated is aligned to the left of ButtonsControlBar.

3. Align Right

    The control bar band under the mouse when the pop-up menu is activated is aligned to the right of ButtonsControlBar.

4. Align All Left

   All the control bar bands in `ButtonsControlBar` are aligned to the left.

5. Align All Right

   All the control bar bands in `ButtonsControlBar` are aligned to the right.

Choices 1, 4, and 5 are always available, but choices 2 and 3 are only available if the pop-up menu, called `ControlBarPopupMenu`, is activated above one of the controls inside `ButtonsControlBar`.

Resizing `TControlBar` to Fit Its Contents

First we will look at the code used to resize `ButtonsControlBar` to fit its contents. From the pop-up menu (`ControlBarPopupMenu`), clicking menu item `SnapToFit1` executes its `OnClick` handler. This calls the helper function `FitToControlBar()`, which is declared as

```
void __fastcall FitToControlBar(TCustomControlBar* ControlBar);
```

The single parameter is a pointer to the control bar that we want to fit to its contents. The implementation is shown in Listing 5.29.

LISTING 5.29   Implementation of `FitToControlBar()`

```
void __fastcall TMainForm::FitToControlBar(TCustomControlBar* ControlBar)
{
   int MinWidth  = 0;
   int MinHeight = 0;

   GetControlBarMinWidthAndHeight(ControlBar, MinWidth, MinHeight);

   int WidthDifference  = ButtonsControlBar->Width  - MinWidth;
   int HeightDifference = ButtonsControlBar->Height - MinHeight;

   Width  = Width  - WidthDifference;
   Height = Height - HeightDifference;
}
```

To resize the control bar, we first call `GetControlBarMinWidthAndHeight()`, whose implementation was shown in Listing 5.25. This gives us the minimum width and height of the control. We use these values to calculate the difference between the current width and height and the width and height to which we want to set the control bar. We then subtract these values from the main form's `Width` and `Height` settings. We subtract from the main form's width and height and not from `ButtonsControlBar`'s width and height because `ButtonsControlBar`'s `Align` property is set to `alClient`. It would be automatically resized to fit the form. Changing the form size works because `ButtonsControlBar`'s `Align` property is `alClient`; `ButtonsControlBar` will be automatically resized to fit the form.

Aligning Controls Inside TControlBar

MiniCalculator provides the capability of aligning the controls inside TControlBar either individually or all at once. The controls can be aligned either to the left or to the right. As we have already said, we use a pop-up menu called ControlBarPopupMenu to access this functionality. The functionality offered to the user depends on where in ButtonsControlBar the ControlBarPopupMenu is popped up. If it is activated over one of the controls inside ButtonsControlBar, then the user can align that control by itself or all controls. If ControlBarPopupMenu is activated and it is not over one of the controls inside ButtonsControlBar, then the user can choose only to align all the controls in ButtonsControlBar.

To determine where on ButtonsControlBar the pop-up menu was activated, we implement ButtonsControlBar's OnContextPopup event. This assumes that ButtonsControlBar's PopupMenu property is set to ControlBarPopupMenu, the pop-up menu. ButtonsControlBar's OnContextPopup event handler implementation is shown in Listing 5.30.

LISTING 5.30   Implementation of ButtonsControlBar->OnContextPopup

```
void __fastcall TMainForm::ButtonsControlBarContextPopup(TObject *Sender,
                                                          TPoint &MousePos,
                                                          bool &Handled)
{
    // Determine where on the Control Bar the mouse was clicked,
    // i.e. what control was it in ??
    TRect* ControlRects = new TRect[ButtonsControlBar->ControlCount];

    try
    {
        for(int i=0; i<ButtonsControlBar->ControlCount; ++i)
        {
            if(ButtonsControlBar->Controls[i]->Visible)
            {
                ControlRects[i] = ButtonsControlBar->Controls[i]->BoundsRect;
                ControlRects[i].Left    -= 11;
                ControlRects[i].Top     -= 2;
                ControlRects[i].Right   += 2;
                ControlRects[i].Bottom  += 2;
            }
            else
            {
                ControlRects[i] = TRect(0,0,0,0); // No Rect
            }
        }
```

LISTING 5.30   Continued

```
    for(int i=0; i<ButtonsControlBar->ControlCount; ++i)
    {
        if(PtInRect(&ControlRects[i], MousePos))
        {
            AlignLeft1->Visible   = true;
            AlignRight1->Visible  = true;
            ControlBarPopupMenu->Tag = ButtonsControlBar->Controls[i]->Tag;
            break;
        }
        else
        {
            AlignLeft1->Visible   = false;
            AlignRight1->Visible  = false;
            ControlBarPopupMenu->Tag = cbpNone;
        }
    }
}
__finally
{
    delete [] ControlRects;
}
}
```

To determine whether the menu was activated over one of the visible controls in
ButtonsControlBar, we use an array of TRects to store the boundaries of each control. If the
control is not visible, we use a TRect with no size so that the mouse cannot be inside the control's TRect when the menu pops up. To determine the TRect occupied by a control in
ButtonsControlBar, we read the control's BoundsRect property and then modify it to allow
for the band grip (11 pixels on the left side) and the frame border (2 pixels on the remaining
sides).

Once we have all the TRects for all the controls, we simply iterate through them and use the
WinAPI PtInRect() function to see if the mouse lies inside any of the controls' boundaries. If
it does, we set the Tag property of ControlBarPopupMenu equal to that of the control the
mouse is over. The Tag property is used to store which control the mouse was in when the pop-
up menu was activated. We use this to determine which control to align in
ControlBarPopupMenu's OnClick handler if the user selects to align only a single control. In
addition, if the mouse was in a control when the pop-up menu was activated, we make the
menu items for aligning individual controls visible, namely AlignLeft1 and AlignRight1.
Otherwise we keep them hidden.

Notice the use of the resource protection `try/__finally` blocks to ensure that `ControlRects` is deleted even if an exception is thrown.

Before we continue we should point out how we use the `Tag` property of the controls inside `ButtonsControlBar` to identify each control. Inside the constructor of `MainForm` we assign a value to the tag of each of the panel components used in the control bar. To aid readability we use an enum, `TControlBarPanel`, declared as

```
enum TControlBarPanel { cbpFunctionButtons,
                        cbpNumberButtons,
                        cbpNone };
```

to enumerate the panels that are contained in `ButtonsControlBar`. In `MainForm`'s constructor we write

```
FunctionButtonsPanel->Tag  = cbpFunctionButtons;
NumberButtonsPanel->Tag     = cbpNumberButtons;
```

If we want to add more panels to `ButtonsControlBar`, we simply add an entry to `TControlBarPanel` for the new panel and assign it to its `Tag` in `MainForm`'s constructor. For example, if we add a panel called `ConstantsButtonsPanel`, then we would add `cbpConstantsButtons` to `TControlBarPanel` and write

```
ConstantsButtonsPanel->Tag = cbpConstantsButtons;
```

in `MainForm`'s constructor. The new panel is then ready for use.

We can now look at how we align the controls within `ButtonsControlBar`. There are no properties of `TControlBar` that control the alignment of the bands it contains, so we must perform the alignment manually. The principles behind this are quite simple, though as we shall see the implementation is more involved than may be first thought. To illustrate the main principles, we will use a control called `Panel` as an example.

To align controls to the left of the control bar, we set the `Left` property of the control we want to align to 11. This allows for the band grip at the left side of the control band that contains the control. Doing this sets the control band flush with the left side of the control bar. Hence, we write

```
Panel->Left = 11;
```

When the control bar is resized, the control will remain flush against the left side of the control bar. In fact, this is the default behavior of `TControlBar`, which makes aligning controls to the left easy.

To align a control to the right is a little more complex. If we want to simply align the control to the current right side of the control bar, we set the `Left` property of the control so that the right side of the control is flush with the current right side of the control bar. We write the following:

```
Panel->Left = ButtonsControlBar->ClientWidth - Panel->Width - 2;
```

When the control bar is made smaller than the current width, the control stays right-aligned, but when it is made larger than the current width, the control stays at the position indicated by its `Left` property. To force the control to stay right-aligned, we must set its `Left` property to a value greater than any possible width the control bar can take. We do this by setting the control's `Left` property to the width of the screen:

```
Panel->Left = Screen->Width;
```

Now when the control bar is resized, the control will remain aligned to the right side of the control bar.

Listing 5.31 shows the implementation of the `OnClick` handler for the pop-up menu item that aligns a single control to the left.

LISTING 5.31 Implementation of `AlignLeft1Click()`

```
void __fastcall TMainForm::AlignLeft1Click(TObject *Sender)
{
    ArrangeControlBarBands(ButtonsControlBar,
                     TControlBarPanel(ControlBarPopupMenu->Tag),
                     cbaLeft);
}
```

`AlignLeft1Click()` calls the helper function `ArrangeControlBarBands()` to perform the actual moving of the control. A pointer to the control bar is passed as the first argument, then the `Tag` of the control is passed to identify which control is being aligned. Finally, `cbaLeft` is passed to indicate that we want to align the control to the left. The declaration for `ArrangeControlBarBands()` is

```
void __fastcall ArrangeControlBarBands(TCustomControlBar* ControlBar,
                          TControlBarPanel CurrentBandTag,
                          TControlBarAlignment Alignment);
```

`TControlBarAlignment` is an enum declared as

```
enum TControlBarAlignment { cbaLeft,
                            cbaRight,
                            cbaAllLeft,
                            cbaAllRight };
```

5

It is used by `ArrangeControlBarBands()` to determine what alignment is required. The implementation of `ArrangeControlBarBands()` is quite involved and is shown in Listing 5.32.

LISTING 5.32   Implementation of `ArrangeControlBarBands()`

```
void __fastcall
TMainForm::ArrangeControlBarBands(TControlBar* ControlBar,
                                  TControlBarPanel CurrentBandTag,
                                  TControlBarAlignment Alignment)
{
   // Step 1
   std::list<TControlBandInfo> BandList;

   TControlBandInfo ControlBarBand;

   // Step 2
   for(int i=0; i<ControlBar->ControlCount; ++i)
   {
      if(ControlBar->Controls[i]->Tag == CurrentBandTag)
      {
         ControlBarBand = TControlBandInfo(ControlBar->Controls[i],
                          ControlBar->Controls[i]->Left,
                          ControlBar->Controls[i]->Top,
                          ControlBar->Controls[i]->Height + 2,
                          ControlBar->Controls[i]->Visible);
      }
      BandList.push_back(TControlBandInfo(ControlBar->Controls[i],
                                          ControlBar->Controls[i]->Left,
                                          ControlBar->Controls[i]->Top,
                                          ControlBar->Controls[i]->Height + 2,
                                          ControlBar->Controls[i]->Visible));
   }

   // Step 3
   if(Alignment == cbaLeft)
   {
      // This is the same as BandList.sort();
      BandList.sort(std::less<TControlBandInfo>());
      ControlBarBand.Left = 11;
   }
   else if(Alignment == cbaRight)
   {
      BandList.sort(std::greater<TControlBandInfo>());
      ControlBarBand.Left = Screen->Width;
   }
```

LISTING 5.32   Continued

```cpp
// Step 4
std::list<TControlBandInfo>::iterator pos;

bool NoFreeColumn = false;

for(pos = BandList.begin(); pos != BandList.end(); ++pos)
{
    // Step 5
    if(   CurrentBandTag != pos->Control->Tag
       && pos->Visible )
    {
        // Step 6
        if(   (Alignment == cbaLeft)
           && (pos->Left < (ControlBarBand.Control->Width + 2)))
        {
            NoFreeColumn = true;
        }
        if(   (Alignment == cbaRight)
           && (   (ControlBar->ClientWidth-(pos->Left+pos->Control->Width+2))
                < (ControlBarBand.Control->Width + 2) ) )
        {
            NoFreeColumn = true;
        }

        // Step 7
        if(   ControlBarBand.Top >= pos->Top
           && ControlBarBand.Top < (pos->Top + pos->Height + 2) )
        {
            // No free space move to the next free Row
            if(NoFreeColumn) ControlBarBand.Top = pos->Top + pos->Height + 2;
            else break;
        }
        // Step 8
        else if( ControlBarBand.Top < pos->Top )
        {
            // Free space
            std::list<TControlBandInfo>::iterator pos2;
            int Offset = 0;
            bool FirstVisibleControl = true;

            // Step 9
            for(pos2 = pos; pos2 != BandList.end(); ++pos2)
            {
                if(   pos2->Visible
```

LISTING 5.32   Continued

```
                        && FirstVisibleControl
                        && pos2->Control->Tag != CurrentBandTag)
                  {
                     // First control
                     Offset = 2
                                 + ControlBarBand.Top
                                 + ControlBarBand.Height - pos2->Top;

                     FirstVisibleControl = false;
                  }
                  if(pos2->Visible) pos2->Top = pos2->Top + Offset;
               }
               break;
         }
         NoFreeColumn = false;
      }
   }

   // Step 10
   for(pos = BandList.begin(); pos != BandList.end(); ++pos)
   {
      pos->Control->Visible = false;
      if(pos->Control->Tag == CurrentBandTag)
      {
         pos->Left = ControlBarBand.Left;
         pos->Top  = ControlBarBand.Top;
      }
   }

   // Step 11
   if(Alignment == cbaLeft)
   {
      BandList.sort(std::less<TControlBandInfo>());
   }
   else if(Alignment == cbaRight)
   {
      BandList.sort(std::greater<TControlBandInfo>());
   }

   // Step 12
   for(pos = BandList.begin(); pos != BandList.end(); ++pos)
   {
      pos->Control->Top = pos->Top;
      pos->Control->Left = pos->Left;
```

LISTING 5.32   Continued

```
      pos->Control->Visible = pos->Visible;
   }
}
```

The `ArrangeControlBarBands()` method makes use of the class `TControlBandInfo`. The definition of `TControlBandInfo` is shown in Listing 5.33. Of particular note in Listing 5.33 is the
implementation of `operator <` and `operator >`. These are used to sort a list of
`TControlBandInfo` objects. Both sort the control bands from top to bottom, but where the top
value is the same, `operator <` sorts from left to right and `operator >` sorts from right to left.
This is used to sort control bands when aligning left and when aligning right, respectively. The
rest of the class is straightforward and allows the class to be used with the C++ Standard
Library container classes. For more information, refer to the section "Introducing the Standard
C++ Library and Templates" in Chapter 4, "Advanced Programming with C++Builder."

Referring back to Listing 5.32, we can summarize the operation of
`ArrangeControlBarBands()`. The following steps refer to the steps shown in the listing as
comments; for example, step 1 here refers to `// Step 1`:

1. We create a C++ Standard Library `list<>` of type `TControlBandInfo` called `BandList`
   and a single variable of type `TControlBandInfo` called `ControlBarBand`. This will be
   used to store information of the current band that we want to align. To use `list<>`, we
   must have the include statement `#include <list>` in our implementation file.

2. We then iterate through each of the controls in `ButtonsControlBar` and add a
   `TControlBandInfo` object to our `BandList` with each band's relevant information. While
   iterating through the controls, we check to see if the control is the current control that we
   are aligning. If it is, we make an additional copy of its information in the
   `ControlBarBand` variable.

3. We then sort the list of `TControlBandInfo`s, depending on the alignment we are performing. To align left we use `operator < (std::less<TControlBandInfo>())`, and to align
   right we use `operator > (std::greater<TControlBandInfo>())`. We use the Standard
   Library's `less<>` and `greater<>` function objects to tell the `sort()` member function of
   `list<>` which we want to use. In fact, we do not need to specify if we are using
   `operator <` because this is the default operator used by `sort()`. At this stage we also set
   the `Left` member of `ControlBarBand` to the desired value based on the alignment. To use
   the `less<>` and `greater<>` function objects, we must have the include statement
   `#include <functional>` in our implementation file.

4. We then create an iterator to iterate through our list of TControlBandInfos. For more information about iterators, refer to the section "Introducing the Standard C++ Library and Templates" in Chapter 4.

5. We check that the control we are comparing ControlBarBand with is not ControlBarBand and is Visible.

6. Then, based on the required alignment, we see if there is not enough space on the appropriate side of the current control (NoFreeColumn = true). This will be important if the control occupies the same row or rows as ControlBarBand.

7. If the control that we want to align is occupying the same row as another control, and there is no free space beside the control (NoFreeColumn == true), then we must move it to occupy the row just after that control. If there is free space, we are finished searching and exit the for loop.

8. Otherwise, if we find an unoccupied space, we set the Top member of ControlBarBand to the free top position.

9. We then iterate through the remaining controls that will appear below our control and offset their Tops to allow room for our control.

10. Now that we have calculated the new positions of the control bands, we iterate through them and set their Visible properties to false. When we reach the control that we are aligning, we copy the values from ControlBarBand to the equivalent list entry for the control. We set the visibility of the controls to false so that we can reposition them with ButtonsControlBar, making any changes to the values we assign.

11. Now that the new positions have been stored in our BandList, we sort the list once more to ensure the topmost control is the first.

12. Finally, we iterate through the controls one last time, assigning the new Top and Left values and setting the visibility of the controls back to their original values.

Although less complex than it first appeared, ArrangeControlBarBands() is nevertheless quite involved. However, it is still not perfect and can be improved. The control bar is not broken into columns, so it is possible for a control to be moved unnecessarily. Regardless, it does show the main principles involved.

LISTING 5.33   TControlBandInfo Class Definition

```
class TControlBandInfo
{
public:
    TControl* Control;
    int       Left;
    int       Top;
```

LISTING 5.33   Continued

```
int        Height;
bool       Visible;

// Constructor
inline __fastcall TControlBandInfo() : Control(0),
                                       Left(0),
                                       Top(0),
                                       Height(0),
                                       Visible(false)
{}
// Constructor
inline __fastcall TControlBandInfo(TControl* control,
                                   int left,
                                   int top,
                                   int height,
                                   bool visible) : Control(control),
                                                   Left(left),
                                                   Top(top),
                                                   Height(height),
                                                   Visible(visible)
{}
// Copy Constructor
inline __fastcall TControlBandInfo(const TControlBandInfo& ControlBandInfo)
                : Control(ControlBandInfo.Control),
                  Left(ControlBandInfo.Left),
                  Top(ControlBandInfo.Top),
                  Height(ControlBandInfo.Height),
                  Visible(ControlBandInfo.Visible)
{}
// OPERATOR =
TControlBandInfo& operator=(const TControlBandInfo& ControlBandInfo)
{
   Control = ControlBandInfo.Control;
   Left = ControlBandInfo.Left;
   Top = ControlBandInfo.Top;
   Height = ControlBandInfo.Height;
   Visible = ControlBandInfo.Visible;
   return *this;
}
// OPERATOR ==
bool operator==(const TControlBandInfo& ControlBandInfo) const
{
    if(    Control == ControlBandInfo.Control
       && Left == ControlBandInfo.Left
```

LISTING 5.33   Continued

```cpp
            && Top == ControlBandInfo.Top
            && Height == ControlBandInfo.Height
            && Visible == ControlBandInfo.Visible)
        {
            return true;
        }
        else return false;
    }
    // OPERATOR <
    bool operator<(const TControlBandInfo& ControlBandInfo) const
    {
        if(Top < ControlBandInfo.Top) return true;
        else if(   Top == ControlBandInfo.Top
                && Left < ControlBandInfo.Left) return true;
        else return false;
    }
    // OPERATOR >
    bool operator>(const TControlBandInfo& ControlBandInfo) const
    {
        if(Top < ControlBandInfo.Top) return true;
        else if(   Top == ControlBandInfo.Top
                && Left > ControlBandInfo.Left) return true;
        else return false;
    }
};
```

The only difference between aligning a single control and all controls is that aligning all controls involves calling ArrangeControlBarBands() for all the controls in the control bar. For comparison, Listing 5.34 shows the OnClick event handler for aligning all controls to the right. Note that the controls are arranged in order; a list of TControlBandInfo objects is created and sorted. The TControl* from the sorted list is then used to obtain the Tag for use in the call to ArrangeControlBarBands(). Each control is then aligned to the right. Finally, after sorting, all controls are iterated through once more and their Left properties are set to Screen->Width to ensure right alignment when the control bar is resized.

LISTING 5.34   Implementation of AlignAllRight1Click()

```cpp
void __fastcall TMainForm::AlignAllRight1Click(TObject *Sender)
{
    std::list<TControlBandInfo> BandList;

    for(int i=0; i<ButtonsControlBar->ControlCount; ++i)
```

LISTING 5.34   Continued

```
{
    BandList.push_back(TControlBandInfo(ButtonsControlBar->Controls[i],
                            ButtonsControlBar->Controls[i]->Left,
                            ButtonsControlBar->Controls[i]->Top,
                            ButtonsControlBar->Controls[i]->Height + 2,
                            ButtonsControlBar->Controls[i]->Visible));
}
BandList.sort(std::greater<TControlBandInfo>());

std::list<TControlBandInfo>::iterator pos;
for(pos = BandList.begin(); pos != BandList.end(); ++pos)
{
    ArrangeControlBarBands(ButtonsControlBar,
                            TControlBarPanel(pos->Control->Tag),
                            cbaRight);
}

BandList.sort(std::greater<TControlBandInfo>());
for(pos = BandList.begin(); pos != BandList.end(); ++pos)
{
    pos->Control->Left = Screen->Width;
}
}
```

Using the methods previously described ensures reasonably predictable aligning behavior; a newly aligning control will not displace an existing aligned control if it shares the same row. Having said that, inconsistency still arises. Nevertheless, the current behavior gives adequate control over the interface.

Controlling Visibility

Offering users the ability to show or hide parts of the interface is a relatively easy way to allow user customization. By simply changing the Visible property of a control, you can control whether or not the control appears in the interface. This allows you to provide functionality that some users want but that others may find a nuisance. Those that need the functionality can make the required controls visible, and those that don't want it can hide the controls. The main consideration with showing and hiding controls is that you must ensure that the appearance of the interface remains acceptable. In other words, hiding a control should not leave a large gap in the interface, and showing a control should not affect the current layout any more than necessary.

5

USER INTERFACE
PRINCIPLES AND
TECHNIQUES

The MiniCalculator program gives you the option of showing or hiding any of the controls in ButtonsControlBar as well as the ability to show or hide either the main display (LCDPanel) or the status bar (StatusBar1). This functionality is accessed from the View menu of the program's main menu. We have already looked at this menu in the previous section, "Using Symbols in Addition to Text." Here we look at what the menu actually does. When View is clicked and the menu is displayed, the controls whose visibility can be changed are examined one-by-one in the OnClick handler for the View menu item (called View1). This is done to see which are visible and which are not. The implementation is straightforward and is shown in Listing 5.35.

LISTING 5.35   Implementation of View1Click()

```
void __fastcall TMainForm::View1Click(TObject *Sender)
{
   if(LCDPanel->Visible) ViewDisplay->Checked = true;
   else ViewDisplay->Checked = false;

   if(NumberButtonsPanel->Visible) ViewNumberButtons->Checked = true;
   else ViewNumberButtons->Checked = false;

   if(FunctionButtonsPanel->Visible) ViewFunctionButtons->Checked = true;
   else ViewFunctionButtons->Checked = false;

   if(StatusBar1->Visible) ViewStatusBar->Checked = true;
   else ViewStatusBar->Checked = false;
}
```

Hiding the main display (LCDPanel) is of dubious value, but we need the ability to reshow the panel because it may be hidden when the panel is undocked form the main form and is floating. Hence, we still need a menu entry for this panel. When the ViewDisplay menu item is clicked, LCDPanel is either shown or hidden, depending on its current visibility. The OnClick handler for ViewDisplay is shown in Listing 5. 36.

LISTING 5.36   Implementation of ViewDisplayClick()

```
void __fastcall TMainForm::ViewDisplayClick(TObject *Sender)
{
   if(ViewDisplay->Checked)
   {
      LCDPanel->Visible = false;
      ViewDisplay->Checked = false;
      if(!LCDPanel->Floating)
      {
```

LISTING 5.36   Continued

```
            // Set the size of the form...
            Height = Height - LCDPanel->Height;
        }
    }
    else
    {
        if(!LCDPanel->Floating)
        {
            // Set the size of the form...
            Height = Height + LCDPanel->Height;
        }

        LCDPanel->Visible = true;
        ViewDisplay->Checked = true;

        if(LCDPanel->Floating)
        {
            SetFocus();
        }

        //Reset the StatusBar to the bottom
        if(StatusBar1->Visible) StatusBar1->Align = alBottom;
    }
}
```

Of all the controls, changing the visibility of LCDPanel is the most involved, because it may be undocked from the main form. However, it is still a reasonably simple operation.

If LCDPanel is visible (ViewDisplay->Checked == true), then we hide it (LCDPanel->Visible = false) and uncheck the menu item (ViewDisplay->Checked = false). Then, if LCDPanel is currently docked on the main form (!LCDPanel->Floating), we adjust the height of MainForm to account for the panel no longer being visible.

If LCDPanel is not visible, we first check to see if it is currently docked to the main form (LCDPanel->Floating == false). If it is, we adjust the height of MainForm to accommodate the panel. We then make it visible and check the ViewDisplay menu item. If LCDPanel was undocked from MainForm, making it visible sets input focus to it. If this is the case, then we must reset input focus to the main form using SetFocus(). Finally, if StatusBar1 is visible, we realign it to the bottom of MainForm.

Changing the visibility of StatusBar1 is much more straightforward. The only thing we must remember to do is to change the height of MainForm to account for the change. Listing 5.37 shows this.

LISTING 5.37   Implementation of `ViewStatusBarClick()`

```cpp
void __fastcall TMainForm::ViewStatusBarClick(TObject *Sender)
{
    if(ViewStatusBar->Checked)
    {
        StatusBar1->Visible = false;
        ViewStatusBar->Checked = false;
        Height = Height - StatusBar1->Height;
    }
    else
    {
        Height = Height + StatusBar1->Height;
        StatusBar1->Visible = true;
        ViewStatusBar->Checked = true;
    }
}
```

Finally, we change the visibility of the control bands inside `ButtonsControlBar`. The code for all bands is similar, so we shall only look at one, the one used to change the visibility of `NumberButtonsPanel`. Listing 5.38 shows the code.

LISTING 5.38   Implementation of `ViewNumberButtonsClick()`

```cpp
void __fastcall TMainForm::ViewNumberButtonsClick(TObject *Sender)
{
    if(ViewNumberButtons->Checked)
    {
        NumberButtonsPanel->Visible = false;
        ViewNumberButtons->Checked = false;
        if(AutoFit->Checked) FitToControlBar(ButtonsControlBar);
    }
    else
    {
        NumberButtonsPanel->Visible = true;
        ViewNumberButtons->Checked = true;
        //Reset the StatusBar to the bottom
        if(StatusBar1->Visible) StatusBar1->Align = alBottom;
    }
}
```

When hiding `NumberButtonsPanel`, we uncheck the related menu item and set `NumberButtonsPanel->Visible` to `false`. Then if the `AutoFit` menu item on the Tools, Options menu is checked, we call the `FitToControlBar()` helper function to resize `ButtonsControlBar` to fit the remaining visible controls. If there are no remaining controls, `ButtonsControlBar` will disappear as its `Height` becomes 0.

When reshowing `NumberButtonsPanel`, we check the related menu item and set `NumberButtonsPanel->Visible` to true. We do not need to resize `ButtonsControlBar` because that will be done automatically to accommodate the newly visible control. Finally, if `StatusBar1` is visible, we realign `StatusBar1` to the bottom of `MainForm`.

Customizing the Client Area of an MDI Parent Form

Allowing the user to customize the background of an MDI parent form, typically by adding an image to it, is not as easy as it first appears and therefore deserves a special mention. To do this, you must subclass the window procedure of the client window of the parent form. (For more information about subclassing, refer to the "Using Non-Visual Components to Respond to Messages Sent to Other Components" section in Chapter 11, "More Custom Component Techniques.") This is because the client window of the parent form is the background for the MDI child windows. You must draw on the client window, not the form itself. For more information about this, refer to the Win32 SDK online help under "Frame, Client, and Child Windows." To access the client window, use the form's `ClientHandle` property. To draw on the client window, you must respond to the `WM_ERASEBKGND` message. The `MDIProject.bpr` on the CD-ROM contains the code required to display an image on the background of an MDI parent form. The image may be centered, tiled, or stretched. When you are reading the code, you should note two things. First, we draw onto an offscreen bitmap, and then we use either the WinAPI `BitBlt()` or `StretchBlt()` function to draw the image onto the client window. This minimizes flicker. Second, we use the `Draw()` method to draw our image onto the `Canvas` of the offscreen bitmap. We do this rather than use `BitBlt()` because we want to support JPEG images. `TJPEGImage` derives from `TGraphic` and so implements the `Draw()` method, but `TJPEGImage` does not have a `Canvas` and so cannot be used with `BitBlt()`.

Enhancing Usability by Remembering the User's Preferences

The easiest way to remember a user's preferences is to store them in the Registry. C++Builder makes its easy to store and retrieve values to and from the Registry by making available two VCL classes designed for the purpose. These are `TRegistry` and `TRegIniFile`. Of these, `TRegistry` is given a cursory mention in the Developer's Guide that ships with C++Builder, and we will not expand further on `TRegistry` here. We are more interested in the `TRegIniFile` class. The `TRegIniFile` class makes using the Registry very easy indeed, and you should use it in preference to `TRegistry`. `TRegIniFile` descends from `TRegistry` and offers greater functionality at a higher level of abstraction. To access either `TRegistry` or `TRegIniFile` you must add the following include statement to your unit.

```
#include <Registry.hpp>
```

The properties and methods of TRegIniFile that you are most likely to need are shown in Table 5.9.

TABLE 5.9   The Properties and Methods of TRegIniFile

Property or Method	Description
FileName	Read-only. Returns, as an AnsiString, the Registry path specified when the TRegIniFile object is created.
RootKey	Specifies the root key of the TRegIniFile object. By default this is HKEY_CURRENT_USER. You can change this if this is not the root key you want.
ReadBool()	Reads a bool value from a specified data value in a key. A default value can be supplied and is used if the entry does not exist.
ReadInteger()	Reads an int value from a specified data value in a key. A default value can be supplied and is used if the entry does not exist.
ReadString()	Reads an AnsiString value from a specified data value in a key. A default value can be supplied and is used if the entry does not exist.
WriteBool()	Writes a bool value to a specified data value in a key. If no such entry exists, it is created.
WriteInteger()	Writes an int value to a specified data value in a key. If no such entry exists, it is created.
WriteString()	Writes an AnsiString value to a specified data value in a key. If no such entry exists, it is created.

An important feature of TRegIniFile is that reading from or writing to a Registry entry that does not exist does not result in an error. An alternative default value that you supply is used instead of the missing entry value. When writing, the missing Registry entry is created. This makes using TRegIniFile very simple.

TRegIniFile is used in the MiniCalculator program to store and read the user's preferences. Registry entries are written on two occasions. If the user clicks the Save Current Configuration menu item on the Tools menu, then all the current settings for MiniCalculator are stored. Alternatively, if the user has checked the Auto Save Configuration option on the Option sub-menu of the Tools menu, then the configuration of MiniCalculator is written to the Registry when MiniCalculator is closed. We will look at the code for the first possibility, shown in Listing 5.39.

LISTING 5.39 Implementation of `SaveCurrentLayout1Click()`

```
void __fastcall TMainForm::SaveCurrentLayout1Click(TObject *Sender)
{
    std::auto_ptr<TRegIniFile>
                    Registry(new TRegIniFile("Software\\MiniCalculator"));

    // Save the option settings to the Registry
    Registry->WriteBool("Options","AutoSaveLayout",AutoSaveLayout->Checked);
    Registry->WriteBool("Options","AutoFit",AutoFit->Checked);

    // Now save all the settings
    WriteSettingsToRegistry (Registry);
}
```

The first thing we do is create a new `TRegIniFile` object. We use the C++ Standard Library's `auto_ptr<>` to ensure that it is destroyed when the `auto_ptr<>` goes out of scope, as would happen if an exception were thrown. In the constructor, we pass the sub-entry that we want to access in the Registry. The root key is automatically initialized to `HKEY_CURRENT_USER`, so the total path is

`HKEY_CURRENT_USER\Software\MiniCalculator`

All our future read and write operations will take place inside this Registry entry.

Next we use the `WriteBool()` method to write the options. The first parameter specifies the key and the second parameter the data name. The final parameter indicates the value of the data:

`Registry->WriteBool("Options","AutoFit",AutoFit->Checked);`

Either parameter updates or creates a new entry of

`HKEY_CURRENT_USER\Software\MiniCalculator\Options: Name = AutoFit | Data = ?`

If `AutoFit->Checked` is true, then the data value will be 1. Otherwise it will be 0.

We then call `WriteSettingsToRegistry()` to write all the settings of MiniCalculator to the Registry. Listing 5.40 shows the code.

LISTING 5.40 Implementation of `WriteSettingsToRegistry()`

```
void __fastcall
TMainForm::WriteSettingsToRegistry(const std::auto_ptr<TRegIniFile>& Registry)
{
    // The LCDPanel
```

LISTING 5.40   Continued

```
// - Color
Registry->WriteInteger("Settings\\Display\\Color",
                       "SurroundColor",
                       LCDPanel->Color);

Registry->WriteInteger("Settings\\Display\\Color",
                       "BackgroundColor",
                       BackgroundPanel->Color);

Registry->WriteInteger("Settings\\Display\\Color",
                       "ExponentColor",
                       ExponentEditColor);

// - Docking
Registry->WriteBool("Settings\\Display",
                    "Floating",
                    LCDPanel->Floating);

Registry->WriteInteger("Settings\\Display",
                       "UndockWidth",
                       LCDPanel->UndockWidth);

Registry->WriteInteger("Settings\\Display",
                       "UndockHeight",
                       LCDPanel->UndockHeight);

if(LCDPanel->Floating)
{
   TRect UndockedRect;
   if(GetWindowRect(LCDPanel->HostDockSite->Handle, &UndockedRect))
   {
      Registry->WriteInteger("Settings\\Display",
                             "UndockLeft",
                             UndockedRect.Left);

      Registry->WriteInteger("Settings\\Display",
                             "UndockTop",
                             UndockedRect.Top);

      Registry->WriteInteger("Settings\\Display",
                             "UndockRight",
                             UndockedRect.Right);

      Registry->WriteInteger("Settings\\Display",
```

LISTING 5.40   Continued

```
                                    "UndockBottom",
                                    UndockedRect.Bottom);
    }
}

// The Main Form
Registry->WriteInteger("Settings\\Position","MainFormTop",Top);
Registry->WriteInteger("Settings\\Position","MainFormLeft",Left);
Registry->WriteInteger("Settings\\Size","MainFormHeight",Height);
Registry->WriteInteger("Settings\\Size","MainFormWidth",Width);

// The Status Bar
Registry->WriteBool("Settings\\StatusBar","Visible",StatusBar1->Visible);
Registry->WriteBool("Settings","EnableKeyboard",EnableKeyboardInput);

// The Control Bar settings
for(int i=0; i<ButtonsControlBar->ControlCount; ++i)
{
    AnsiString ControlPath = "Settings\\ControlBar\\";
    ControlPath += ButtonsControlBar->Controls[i]->Name;

    Registry->WriteInteger(ControlPath,
                        "Left",
                        ButtonsControlBar->Controls[i]->Left);

    Registry->WriteInteger(ControlPath,
                        "Top",
                        ButtonsControlBar->Controls[i]->Top);
    Registry->WriteInteger(ControlPath,
                        "Height",
                        ButtonsControlBar->Controls[i]->Height+2);
    Registry->WriteBool(ControlPath,
                        "Visible",
                        ButtonsControlBar->Controls[i]->Visible);
    }
}
```

The code to write values to the Registry is pretty straightforward. The hardest decision is what to write to the Registry. The only thing of particular note in this regard is the coordinates of the LCDPanel if it is undocked from the main form (Floating). If LCDPanel is undocked from the main form, it will be contained by an object of type FloatingDockSiteClass. The default type paints a border and title bar around the floating control. We need the bounding rectangle of the control's docking host to accurately redisplay the panel in the same position. To access the docking host, we read the `HostDockSite` property. To get the bounding rectangle of the host dock site, we pass its window handle to the WinAPI function `GetWindowRect()` along with the address of a `TRect` to hold the boundary values, as follows:

```
TRect UndockedRect;
if(GetWindowRect(LCDPanel->HostDockSite->Handle, &UndockedRect))
{
   ... // code removed for clarity
}
```

For `ButtonsControlBar` we iterate through all the controls and write the necessary values of each to a key equal to the control's name. This will allow us to distinguish which entries are for which control when we read the Registry entries later.

As you can see, writing to the Registry couldn't really be any easier. The tricky part is knowing what to do with the information when you read it back in from the Registry. We will look at this now.

Whenever MiniCalculator is executed and the constructor of `MainForm` is called, we call the function `ReadAllValuesFromRegistry()` to read in all the values we have stored there. The first time we do this there will be no Registry entries, but that doesn't matter. The default values that we supply for each option or the settings that we want to read are used instead. Listing 5.41 shows the implementation of `ReadAllValuesFromRegistry()`.

LISTING 5.41   Implementation of `ReadAllValuesFromRegistry()`

```
void __fastcall TMainForm::ReadAllValuesFromRegistry()
{
   //Try to read the required setup values from the Registry
   //If this is the first time the program has been executed
   //then there will be no Registry keys

   std::auto_ptr<TRegIniFile>
               Registry(new TRegIniFile("SOFTWARE\\MiniCalculator"));

   // Read the options
   AutoSaveLayout->Checked
     = Registry->ReadBool("Options","AutoSaveLayout",AutoSaveLayout->Checked);

   AutoFit->Checked
     = Registry->ReadBool("Options","AutoFit",AutoFit->Checked);

   // Now read the settings
   ReadSettingsFromRegistry (Registry);
}
```

The code in `ReadAllValuesFromRegistry()` is pretty simple. We read the two options values and then read the rest of the settings by calling the function `ReadSettingsFromRegistry()`. Notice how we use the current value of each option as the default value (the third argument). This ensures that the absence of a Registry entry has no effect. The option is simply assigned its current value. You will notice this throughout Listing 5.42, which shows the implementation of the `ReadSettingsFromRegistry()` function.

LISTING 5.42   Implementation of `ReadSettingsFromRegistry()`

```
void __fastcall
TMainForm::ReadSettingsFromRegistry(const std::auto_ptr<TRegIniFile>& Registry)
{
  // The LCDPanel

  // - Color
  LCDPanel->Color = Registry->ReadInteger("Settings\\Display\\Color",
                                    "SurroundColor",
                                    LCDPanel->Color);
  BackgroundPanel->Color = Registry->ReadInteger("Settings\\Display\\Color",
                                    "BackgroundColor",
                                    BackgroundPanel->Color);
  ExponentViewColor = BackgroundPanel->Color;
  ExponentEditColor = Registry->ReadInteger("Settings\\Display\\Color",
                                    "ExponentColor",
                                    ExponentEditColor);


  // - Docking
  LCDPanel->UndockWidth = Registry->ReadInteger("Settings\\Display",
                                    "UndockWidth",
                                    LCDPanel->UndockWidth);

  if(LCDPanel->UndockWidth > Screen->Width)
  {
    LCDPanel->UndockWidth = Screen->Width;
  }

  LCDPanel->UndockHeight = Registry->ReadInteger("Settings\\Display",
                                    "UndockHeight",
                                    LCDPanel->UndockHeight);

  bool Floating = Registry->ReadBool("Settings\\Display",
                                    "Floating",
                                    LCDPanel->Floating);
```

LISTING 5.42   Continued

```
if(Floating)
{
   int UndockLeft = Registry->ReadInteger("Settings\\Display",
                                      "UndockLeft",
                                      LCDPanel->Left);
   int UndockTop  = Registry->ReadInteger("Settings\\Display",
                                      "UndockTop",
                                      LCDPanel->Top);
   TRect UndockedRect(UndockLeft,
                   UndockTop,
                   UndockLeft + LCDPanel->UndockWidth,
                   UndockTop + LCDPanel->UndockHeight);

   int UndockRight = Registry->ReadInteger("Settings\\Display",
                                      "UndockRight",
                                      UndockedRect.Right);

   int UndockBottom = Registry->ReadInteger("Settings\\Display",
                                      "UndockBottom",
                                      UndockedRect.Bottom);

   if(UndockRight > Screen->Width)
   {
      int Offset = UndockRight - Screen->Width;
      UndockedRect.Right -= Offset;
      UndockedRect.Left  -= Offset;
      if(UndockedRect.Left < 0) UndockedRect.Left = 0;
   }
   if(UndockBottom > Screen->Height)
   {
      int Offset = UndockBottom - Screen->Height;
      UndockedRect.Bottom -= Offset;
      UndockedRect.Top    -= Offset;
      if(UndockedRect.Top < 0)
      {
         Offset = 0 - UndockedRect.Top;
         UndockedRect.Top = 0;
         UndockedRect.Bottom += Offset;
      }
   }

   LCDPanel->ManualFloat(UndockedRect);
}
```

LISTING 5.42 Continued

```cpp
// The Main Form
 int top, left, height, width;

top    = Registry->ReadInteger("Settings\\Position","MainFormTop",Top);
left   = Registry->ReadInteger("Settings\\Position","MainFormLeft",Left);
height = Registry->ReadInteger("Settings\\Size","MainFormHeight",Height);
width  = Registry->ReadInteger("Settings\\Size","MainFormWidth",Width);

if(width > Screen->Width) width = Screen->Width; // disaster!
if(left+width > Screen->Width)
{
   left -= (left+width) - Screen->Width;
}
if(height > Screen->Height) height = Screen->Height; // disaster!
if(top+height > Screen->Height)
{
   top -= (top+height) - Screen->Height;
}

Top = top;
Left = left;
Height = height;
Width = width;


// The Status Bar
StatusBar1->Visible = Registry->ReadBool("Settings\\StatusBar",
                                         "Visible",
                                         StatusBar1->Visible);
//if(!StatusBar1->Visible) Height -= StatusBar1->Height;

EnableKeyboardInput = Registry->ReadBool("Settings",
                                         "EnableKeyboard",
                                         EnableKeyboardInput);

// The Control Bar
std::list<TControlBandInfo> BandList;

for(int i=0; i<ButtonsControlBar->ControlCount; ++i)
{
   AnsiString ControlPath = "Settings\\ControlBar\\";
   ControlPath += ButtonsControlBar->Controls[i]->Name;

   int ControlLeft
```

LISTING 5.42   Continued

```
                       = Registry->ReadInteger(ControlPath,
                                        "Left",
                                        ButtonsControlBar->Controls[i]->Left);
            int ControlTop
                = Registry->ReadInteger(ControlPath,
                                        "Top",
                                        ButtonsControlBar->Controls[i]->Top);
            int ControlHeight
                = Registry->ReadInteger(ControlPath,
                                        "Height",
                                        ButtonsControlBar->Controls[i]->Height+2);
            bool ControlVisible
                 = Registry->ReadBool(ControlPath,
                                        "Visible",
                                        ButtonsControlBar->Controls[i]->Visible);

            BandList.push_back(TControlBandInfo(ButtonsControlBar->Controls[i],
                                        ControlLeft,
                                        ControlTop,
                                        ControlHeight,
                                        ControlVisible));
    }
    BandList.sort();

    std::list<TControlBandInfo>::iterator pos;

    for(pos = BandList.begin(); pos != BandList.end(); ++pos)
    {
        pos->Control->Visible = false;
    }

    for(pos = BandList.begin(); pos != BandList.end(); ++pos)
    {
        pos->Control->Top = pos->Top;
        pos->Control->Left = pos->Left;
        pos->Control->Visible = pos->Visible;
    }

    // Reset any size adjustments made by ButtonsControlBar
    Top = top;
    Left = left;
    Height = height;
    Width = width;
}
```

As was stated earlier, writing to the Registry is easy. Reading from the Registry is equally easy. Deciding what to do with the data is slightly more complex, as you can see from Listing 5.42. Much of Listing 5.42 is self-explanatory but the handling of the LCDPanel data and the ButtonsControlBar data requires further explanation.

If LCDPanel is floating, then we need to use the ManualFloat() method to undock the control. For this we need a TRect variable containing the correct region in which the panel should be displayed. We already stored this information in the UndockLeft, UndockTop, UndockRight, and UndockBottom Registry values. We also stored LCDPanel's UndockWidth and UndockHeight. Your first thought will probably be to use the four UndockXXX coordinates to create a suitable TRect and then use this in the call to ManualFloat. This is not correct. A quirk of the implementation of ManualFloat is that it doesn't use the TRect you pass in the manner you expect. The Left and Top properties represent the Left and Top of the floating docking host (*not* the LCDPanel), but the Right and Bottom properties do not represent the Right and Bottom of the floating docking host. Instead, the Right and Bottom properties are used to calculate the Width and Height of LCDPanel. Therefore, we must create our TRect as follows:

```
TRect UndockedRect(UndockLeft,
                   UndockTop,
                   UndockLeft + LCDPanel->UndockWidth,
                   UndockTop + LCDPanel->UndockHeight);
```

The remainder of the code for LCDPanel is concerned with repositioning the floating panel if it appears off the screen at lower resolutions.

The interpretation of the Registry entries for ButtonsControlBar is also problematic. We must sort the controls into order of increasing Top properties, and we must then draw each control onto the control bar. We need to draw the topmost controls first because TControlBar automatically aligns controls either to the top or to just below an existing control. If we put the bottom-most controls on first, they would be moved to the top, and we do not want this to happen. The code used to sort controls is the same as that used in the ArrangeControlBarBands() method in Listing 5.32 and described in the section, "Aligning Controls Inside TControlBar," earlier in this chapter. We create a list of TControlBandInfo objects, sort the list, make all the controls invisible (Visible = false), and then replace each visible control one by one, starting with the topmost. The TControlBandInfo class is shown in Listing 5.33 and also is described in the earlier section, "Aligning Controls Inside TControlBar."

Notice that we reposition and resize the main form if the resolution causes the main form to be either too large or moved off the screen. This is an example of how to make your programs capable of handling varying screen conditions. This is the subject of the next section.

Coping with Differing Screen Conditions

This section looks at how to detect varying screen conditions so that you can display your interface consistently on different computers with different screen settings. There are three that should always be thought of: screen resolution, font sizes, and color depths. Of these three, resolution and font size are the most important. Limited color depth is not normally a major concern unless you design an interface that requires true color depth.

Coping with Different Screen Resolutions

To determine the urrent resolution of the screen, read the global `Screen` variable's `Width` and `Height` properties. You can then use each control's `ScaleBy` property to scale each control so that the interface has the same apparent size at different screen resolutions. It is important to realize that there are limits to this. If you have designed an interface that is quite large, you may not be able to scale it down for lower resolutions; you may have to simply make it smaller. By noting the screen resolution at which the application is developed, you can calculate the size difference ratio by dividing the screen height at development time by the screen height at runtime. You can use this when setting the `ScaleBy` property. This technique is outlined in the Developer's Guide that ships with C++Builder, and you should refer there for more information.

Coping with Different Font Sizes

When you create an application, the `PixelsPerInch` property of the forms you use indicates the font size used during development. By default, `TForm`'s `Scaled` property is set to `true`. This means that your form and the controls on them will be automatically resized when the font size changes. In many cases, such as in the MiniCalculator program, you do not want this to happen. To prevent this automatic scaling, set `Scaled` to `false`. To determine the font size at runtime, simply read the `PixelsPerInch` property of the global `Screen` variable.

Coping with Different Color Depths

The need to cope with different color depths arises when you develop an application on a machine at a higher color depth than that provided by the current machine running the application. If your application makes use of colors outside those available at the lower color depth, the operating system will display the application using the closest match for each color. This can sometimes turn a nice interface into an awful one. If this is a possibility with your application, then you should take steps to avoid it.

There are two approaches. The first and simplest is to limit the colors used in the interface to those of the lowest color depth at which your application will be used. This will typically be

16-bit color and is more than adequate for most purposes. The second is to determine the color depth at runtime and supply different images for the interface according to the color depth available.

To determine the current color depth of the screen at runtime, use the WinAPI `GetDeviceCaps()` function, passing the `Canvas->Handle` of one of your visual controls, such as the main form. The code required is

```
int ColorDepth = 0;

if(GetDeviceCaps(Canvas->Handle, RASTERCAPS) & RC_PALETTE)
{
    ColorDepth = GetDeviceCaps(Canvas->Handle, COLORRES);
}
else
{
    ColorDepth = GetDeviceCaps(Canvas->Handle, BITSPIXEL)
                 * GetDeviceCaps(Canvas->Handle, PLANES);
}
```

The sample project on the CD-ROM that accompanies this book, `ScreenInfo.bpr`, displays the color depth, font size, and screen resolution to illustrate determining these values at runtime.

Coping with Complexity in the Implementation of the User Interface

Programming the interface of an application is a very difficult task. Taking the MiniCalculator program as an example, you will probably agree that it doesn't do anything startling; in fact, the code required to make it add, subtract, multiply, and divide is very short, approximately 10 to 20 lines. A few hundred lines of code is used to allow conversions between number bases and so on, but the remaining 2,500 or so lines are devoted exclusively to the interface. Even with that, the interface is far from complete. Any techniques or tools that can help keep the complexity of the interface code to a minimum are therefore of great benefit. We look briefly at two that were used in the MiniCalculator program.

Using Action Lists

An action list's sole purpose in life is to help make interface programming easier. It does this by centralizing code. Using action lists and the theory behind them is explained reasonably well in the Developer's Guide (and online help) that ships with C++Builder 5, but it doesn't hurt to show a practical example.

In MiniCalculator, an action list called `ActionList1` is used to centralize the copying action performed by the menu items in `MainMenu`'s Copy menu and also the copying action performed by the menu items in `CopyPopupMenu`. The MiniCalculator program allows a copy to be made of the current history, the current number being displayed, or the current number in the memory. An action is created for each: `CopyHistoryAction`, `CopyNumberAction`, and `CopyMemoryAction`. Each action has its own keyboard shortcut, which we specify by setting the action's `ShortCut` property. `CopyHistoryAction` uses Ctrl+H, `CopyNumberAction` uses Ctrl+N, and `CopyMemoryAction` uses Ctrl+M. Finally, all that remains is to implement each action's `OnExecute` event. Listing 5.43 shows the implementation of each.

LISTING 5.43   Implementation of `OnExecute` for the actions `CopyHistoryAction`, `CopyNumberAction`, and `CopyMemoryAction`

```
//------------------------------------------------------------------------//

void __fastcall TMainForm::CopyHistoryActionExecute(TObject *Sender)
{
   AnsiString HistoryString = HistoryLabel->Caption;
   Clipboard()->AsText = HistoryString;
}
//------------------------------------------------------------------------//

void __fastcall TMainForm::CopyNumberActionExecute(TObject *Sender)
{
   AnsiString NumberString = LCDScreen->Caption;
   if(ExponentLabel->Caption != "E+0" && ExponentLabel->Caption != "E-0")
   {
      NumberString += ExponentLabel->Caption;
   }
   Clipboard()->AsText = NumberString;
}
//------------------------------------------------------------------------//

void __fastcall TMainForm::CopyMemoryActionExecute(TObject *Sender)
{
   Clipboard()->AsText = MemoryString;
}
//------------------------------------------------------------------------//
```

Now that we have our actions defined, to use them with our menus we simply set the `Action` property of each menu item to the correct action. For example, in `CopyPopupMenu`, we set the `Action` property of the menu item called `CopyHistory1` to `CopyHistoryAction`. We also set the `Action` property of the `History1` menu item of the Copy menu in `MainMenu` to

CopyHistoryAction. For both menu items, the ShortCut properties, ImageIndex properties, and Caption properties are all changed to reflect those in CopyHistoryAction. In addition, their OnClick events are set equal to CopyHistoryAction's OnExecute event. Hence, the action is executed when the item is clicked.

The example presented here, while simple, still benefits from the ease of coding that actions bring. When designing an interface with many menus and toolbars, actions can be indispensable.

Another example of using actions can be found in the MDIProject.bpr project on the accompanying CD-ROM. As the name suggests, this is an MDI project and, like most MDI applications, it has a Windows menu that allows the user to arrange the child windows in various ways: tiling horizontally, tiling vertically, and cascading. To do this, we add one each of the standard actions TWindowTileHorizontal, TWindowTileVertical, and TWindowCascade to a TActionList. We do not need to write any code; all we do is assign the Action properties of the appropriate menu items to each standard action in the action list. If we provide a TImageList component and set the Images property of the action list to the image list, an image for each of the standard actions will be automatically added to the image list when the action is added to the action list. If we also assign the SubMenuImages property of the Windows menu item (called Window1) to the same image list, the images will automatically appear in the menu for each menu item as appropriate. In MDIProject.bpr, custom images are used.

Sharing Event Handlers

We've already seen an example of sharing event handlers earlier in this chapter, in the section "Using Symbols in Addition to Text." We will now examine the technique a little more closely and see how it can be used to reduce the complexity of user interface–related code.

When designing user interfaces, particularly those for data entry, it is common to create an interface consisting of several instances of one control to a form. Controls used in this way will generally perform very similar functions, or at least interpret the data entered to them in a similar way. For example, if you created a data entry form consisting of multiple TEdit components, you may want to use each TEdit component's OnExit event to place the contents of each TEdit control into a structure or array for use elsewhere in the program. If such a form contained 10 TEdit controls, then we'd normally need 10 corresponding OnExit event handlers, one for each control. Because each event handler would perform an essentially similar task, we are duplicating code unnecessarily. For large interfaces this can quickly lead to long and complex code that becomes difficult to maintain. One way to prevent this is for all controls that perform similar tasks to share one event handler.

In MiniCalculator, this technique is employed several times. One such use is the implementation of OnClick events for the number buttons. Because each number button differs only in the number it represents, a single event handler can be shared among them. The `OnClick` event for each button is assigned to our single event handler, `NumberSpeedButtonClick()`, in `MainForm`'s constructor.

> ### TIP
>
> It is possible (and desirable) to perform this assignment at designtime. Move the declaration for `NumberSpeedButtonClick()` to the IDE-managed part of `MainForm`'s header file. This will be the published section of the form's class definition, with the comment
>
> // IDE-managed Components
>
> You can then select the `OnClick` handler by activating the drop-down list for each number button's `OnClick` event in the Object Inspector. This method was used to assign the `OnClick` events of the color panel components used in the `SettingsForm` form.

Using this method means we must have some way of determining which button was clicked. To do this we store an `enum` value representing each button in the button's `Tag` property. The enum we use is declared as

```
enum TCalculatorButton { cb1='1',
                         cb2='2',
                         cb3='3',
                         cb4='4',
                         cb5='5',
                         cb6='6',
                         cb7='7',
                         cb8='8',
                         cb9='9',
                         cbA='A',
                         cbB='B',
                         cbC='C',
                         cbD='D',
                         cbE='E',
                         cbF='F',
                         cb0,
                         cbSign,
                         cbPoint,
                         cbExponent,
                         cbAdd,
                         cbSubtract,
                         cbMultiply,
```

```
        cbDivide,
        cbEquals,
        cbBackspace,
        cbClear,
        cbAllClear,
        cbMemoryAdd,
        cbMemoryRecall };
```

For convenience, we set each of the numbered buttons' enum values equal to the character that represents it. This allows the Tag of each numbered button to be used directly to update the AnsiString that represents the calculator display. What matters here is that the enum value for each calculator button is unique. The appropriate enum for each button is assigned in MainForm's constructor. For example, for the number 1 button we write

```
SpeedButton1->Tag = cb1;
```

Listing 5.44 shows the implementation of NumberSpeedButtonClick().

LISTING 5.44   Implementation of NumberSpeedButtonClick()

```
void __fastcall TMainForm::NumberSpeedButtonClick(TObject *Sender)
{
    TSpeedButton* SpeedButton = dynamic_cast<TSpeedButton*>(Sender);

    if(SpeedButton)
    {
        ButtonPressNumber(static_cast<TCalculatorButton>(SpeedButton->Tag));
        ButtonUp(static_cast<TCalculatorButton>(SpeedButton->Tag));
    }
}
```

The first thing we do in NumberSpeedButtonClick() is dynamic_cast Sender to a TSpeedButton pointer. If successful, we know that a TSpeedButton fired the event, so we proceed. The next step simply calls the function ButtonPressNumber(), which updates the display with the number we pressed. ButtonPressNumber() expects a TCalculatorButton. Even though we assigned a TCalculatorButton to the Tag of each button, Tag is an int by definition. To remove the compiler warning telling us this, we must static_cast our Tag property to the TCalculatorButton enum type. Finally, we call ButtonUp() to make sure the button is released and cast the Tag property to the correct type.

The technique described is simple and effective. There is a problem in assigning numbers only to the Tag property. Code can quickly become difficult to read because numbers on their own have little or no meaning. To maintain readability, MiniCalculator uses several enums to make it clear exactly what is being stored in the Tag property for each control.

Another method of determining which control fired an event is to compare the Sender pointer with that of each control until a match is made. For example

```
if(Sender == SpeedButton1)      { /* code here */ }
else if(Sender == SpeedButton2) { /* code here */ }
else if(Sender == SpeedButton3) { /* code here */ }
else if(Sender == SpeedButton4) { /* code here */ }
// and so on ...
```

This is a simple and effective approach. However, we used the Tag property approach because it offers greater versatility, such as allowing the Tag value to represent something other than simply an identifier. For example, it can represent the value of a button in addition to its identity.

Summary

In this chapter we took an in-depth look at user interface design and implementation. We discussed user interface design philosophy and noted that above all a user interface should meet users' expectations and be intuitive.

Using the example MiniCalculator application, we saw how C++Builder can be employed to create effective, professional-quality user interfaces that give users ready access to all of an application's functionality. We closely examined the use of some of C++Builder's most often-used standard controls, including TStatusBar, TSpeedButton, TLabel, TPanel, and TControlBar. We also saw simple and advanced techniques such as using the cursor, using hints, input focus control, customized buttons, shaped controls, menus, docking, resizing, anchors, and constraints; remembering users' preferences by storing data in the Windows Registry; coping with different screen conditions; and managing user interface code complexity. In fact, we have just scratched the surface! It has been impossible to include or even mention many aspects of interface programming, notably localization and internationalization. This is a large topic that deserves a chapter of its own. For an introduction to the issues involved, refer to the "Language Internationalization and Localization" section of Chapter 28, "Software Distribution."

Creating an effective interface is a real challenge, as you will have gathered from reading this chapter. But it is a rewarding challenge with something concrete to see at the end. You may even want to experiment further with the MiniCalculator program to see if you can turn it into a really useful application; the foundation is there to build on. If you are interested in floating-point number handling, refer to the "Programming Using Floating-Point Numbers" section in Chapter 30, "Tips, Tricks, and How Tos."

This chapter should provide a good foundation. Using the techniques and advice presented here should help you design application user interfaces that not only have visual impact but are also a blessing to use.

Compiling and Optimizing Your Application

Jarrod Hollingworth

IN THIS CHAPTER

- Understanding How the Compiler Works
- Speeding Up Compile Times
- Exploring the C++Builder 5 Compiler and Linker Enhancements
- Optimizing: An Introduction
- Optimizing for Execution Speed
- Optimizing Other Aspects of Your Application

This chapter will explain how the compiler and linker work. You'll see how to get the most speed out of your compiles and applications by using several speed-optimizing techniques. Other optimization aspects will also be discussed.

Compiling and optimizing are interrelated techniques. *Compiling* is the process of taking high-level code and data that programmers can work with and transforming it into low-level code and data that the CPU can use. *Optimizing* is the process of streamlining some aspect of an application, such as speed or size. As we'll see, optimizing at a very low level can involve reordering machine code instructions and choosing the best set of instructions for the job. This is handled automatically to some extent by C++Builder's optimizing compiler.

Compiling and optimizing are processes that all programmers should understand. Compiler knowledge and an understanding of the machine code that the compiler generates will assist your high-level programming skills and help you with debugging. Optimizing should be a priority in your project goals.

Throughout this chapter, the term *compiler* refers to C++Builder's optimizing compiler as a whole. The term *optimizer* refers to the optimization process of the compiler in particular. The optimizer is not a separate utility but rather is integrated with the compiler.

By the end of this chapter you will be more productive, have a better understanding of how applications work, and know how to streamline your applications. This chapter is also recommended as a prerequisite to Chapter 7, "Debugging Your Application."

Understanding How the Compiler Works

The compiler is one of the most commonly used features in C++Builder. It is also one of the most taken-for-granted and cursed features. In any case, the compiler is an integral part of C++Builder, without which most other features are virtually useless!

What goes on when you select Make or Build? You get a running version of your application, bugs aside. Behind the scenes, it is quite a lot more involved than that. To build an application, the C++Builder compiler processes each unit in turn, performing several compilation phases on your code to produce an executable or DLL. These phases are outlined in the following list:

- **Phase 1: Preprocess**   Preprocessor directives are invoked, and macros are expanded throughout the source code. Header files are included.

- **Phase 2: Tokenizing and Parsing**   Output code from the preprocessor is analyzed, including the examination of tokens in the source and the creation of a syntax tree to allow code generation.

- **Phase 3: Code Generation**   Native machine instructions for each statement are generated. The code is optimized, using instruction pairing and other processor-dependent features. Machine code is written to disk in an `.obj` file. Debug information is written to the end of the file if necessary.

- **Phase 4: Link** The linker reads in all segment definitions from each object file and creates a global symbol table. A list of symbols necessary for the executable is generated. The linker then combines the compiled code from the required units, resources, and form files with statically linked libraries and a special startup object file to create the resulting executable or DLL file.

The C++Builder compiler uses what's called the recursive descent model, with infinite lookahead. This basically means that preprocessing, tokenizing, parsing, and code generation are all performed at the same time during compilation in recursive steps, not with multiple passes like some other compilers.

Various optimizations, such as subexpression folding (const math computations, for example), inlining, and integral constant replacements, are performed in the high-level (front-end) compilation phases. The expression tree is also highly compacted. Other optimizations such as scheduling and invariant code optimizations are performed in the low-level (backend) compilation phases. Optimizations are not performed across function boundaries.

With its various optimizations, the compiler already produces fast code, compared to other mainstream compilers, but look for some tweaks to appear in the future, perhaps in C++Builder 6. For more information on compilers and how they work, see the following:

- *Introduction to Compiling Techniques*, by J.P. Bennett, Second Edition, McGraw-Hill 1996, ISBN 0-07-709221-X.
- *Compilers and Compiler Generators*. This is an excellent and comprehensive online book that can also be downloaded as PDF files. `http://www.scifac.ru.ac.za/compilers/`

There are many books available on compilers, how they work, and how to make one. Check your local university library. Transcripts of several university courses covering compilers are also available on the Internet.

Most compiler and linker options can be set from the Compiler, Advanced Compiler, Linker, and Advanced Linker tabs of the Project Options dialog. However, there are a few that can only be set in the project file or used on the command line.

As discussed in Chapter 2, "C++Builder Projects and More on the IDE," C++Builder 5 uses a new project file format based on Extensible Markup Language (XML). To use the remaining compiler and linker options, you need to modify the project file. You can open the project file in the IDE by selecting Project, Edit Option Source. Compiler options are set in the `<OPTIONS>` section of the project file in the `<CFLAG1 value="..."\>` entry, linker flags in `<LFLAGS...\>`, resource compiler options in `<RFLAGS...\>`, Pascal compiler options in `<PFLAGS...\>`, and assembler options in `<AFLAGS...\>`.

> **TIP**
>
> In the Examples folder where C++Builder was installed, you'll find a fantastic program called WinTools. It lists the various command-line options for the compiler and other command-line tools provided with C++Builder, and it has some great built-in functions!

A complete listing of compiler, linker, and other command-line utility options are available in the C++Builder 5 help file.

Speeding Up Compile Times

The C++Builder compiler is fast! It compiles C++ code almost twice as fast as the GNU C++ compiler and is comparable in speed to the Microsoft Visual C++ compiler. If you've used Delphi before, and you think that the C++Builder compiler takes much longer to compile a similar size application, you're right. The relatively slow compilation speed of C++ when compared to Delphi's Object Pascal is due to several reasons:

- C++ allows for header (include) files. Object Pascal does not. Header files can be nested, and this can set up a lot of complex code to be processed. A simple 10-line program may be several hundred thousand lines long because of header file nesting, which takes up most of the compile time.

- C++ has macros. Object Pascal does not. Macros require a preprocessor to parse and expand them.

- C++ has templates. Object Pascal does not. Templates are very complex to analyze.

- C++ semantics must conform to the ANSI standard. The "grammar" of C++ is somewhat more complex than that of Delphi, which is based on Pascal but developed to Borland's standard.

In general, C++ provides more flexibility in program design than Delphi's Object Pascal. However, this comes at the expense of compile time and in some cases code readability. There are several simple methods you can employ to speed up your C++Builder compile times. The most dramatic improvement can be achieved by using precompiled headers. This and other methods are described in the following sections.

Precompiled Headers

Precompiled headers are presented as a set of options on the Compiler tab of the Project Options dialog. When enabled by checking either Use Precompiled Headers or Cache Precompiled Headers, the compiler stores a compiled binary image of header files included in the various units in a disk-based file (vcl50.csm in the C++Builder lib directory by default).

Subsequent use of the same sequence of header files in another unit dramatically speeds up that unit's compile time by using the header files previously compiled. Selecting Cache Pre-Compiled Headers causes the compiler to load the precompiled headers in memory to further speed up the compile process.

The `#pragma hdrstop` directive in a unit causes the compiler to stop generating precompiled headers at that point. It is important to note that the order of the header files before the `#pragma hdrstop` directive in each unit is significant. Changing the order of the header files in two separate units can change the code resulting from those header files in each unit. Therefore, this requires both lists of header files to be compiled and stored separately as pre-compiled header groups.

Header files after the `#pragma hdrstop` directive are processed each time the unit is compiled. Typically, you should include header files common to two or more units before this directive so that they are compiled once only. Include all header files specific to each unit after the directive. By doing this, we are trying to get the most common match between header file lists in each unit to obtain the most benefit from this option.

The IDE automatically inserts the `#pragma hdrstop` directive in new units and places VCL header files included before the directive and unit specific header files after the directive. A good example of header file grouping and order is shown in the top section of the fictional units `LoadPage.cpp` and `ViewOptions.cpp` in Listings 6.1 and 6.2.

LISTING 6.1 Precompiled Header File Group in `LoadPage.cpp`

```
//--------------------------------
----
// LoadPage.cpp

#include <vcl.h>
#include <System.hpp>
#include <Windows.hpp>
#include "SearchMain.h"
#pragma hdrstop

#include "LoadPage.h"
#include "CacheClass.h"
//-------------------------------
----

// Code here...
```

LISTING 6.2 Precompiled Header File Group in `ViewOptions.cpp`

```
//---------------------------------------
-
// ViewOptions.cpp

#include <vcl.h>
#include <System.hpp>
#include <Windows.hpp>
#include "SearchMain.h"
#pragma hdrstop

#include <Graphics.hpp>
#include "ViewOptions.h"
//---------------------------------------
-

// Code here...
```

By effectively grouping header files included in each unit and using precompiled headers, you can often see compile speeds increase up to 10 times!

> **NOTE**
>
> For information on speeding up compile times even further using precompiled headers, there is an excellent article on the BCBDEV Web site at `http://www.bcbdev.com/` under the Articles link.

Other Techniques for Speeding Up Compile Times

There are other techniques that can be used to speed up compile times. They aren't as effective as using correctly grouped precompiled headers, but they are worth considering if compile speed is very important, particularly on large projects.

You should be careful about which header files are included in your units. Compiling unnecessary code is wasteful of precious compile time, so in general you should not include unused header files. However, if you have included an unused header file in a unit to preserve header grouping when using precompiled headers, leave it in. Also, avoid changing header files too often. Each time you change a header file, the precompiled header groups that use this header file must be regenerated.

Use `Make` instead of `Build`. When `Make` is selected, the compiler attempts to detect which source files have been modified since they were last compiled and compiles only those. `Build`, on the other hand, will recompile every source file in the project. Obviously `Build` will take more time than `Make`, but there are times where Build is required.

`Build` is recommended after changing project options and when files are checked out or updated from a version control system. You should also use `Build` when compiling a release version of your application. This could be a debug or beta build going to testers or the final version to ship.

You should uncheck the Don't Generate State Files option on the Linker tab of Project Options. This will speed up subsequent compiles (particularly the first compile when re-opening the project and when working with multiple projects in the IDE) as the linker saves state information in a file.

If you are not in a debugging phase for the project, disable all debugging options by selecting the Release button on the Compiler tab of Project Options and uncheck Use Debug Libraries on the Linker tab. If you do not yet need to compile a release version of the application, set Code Optimization on the Compiler tab of Project Options to None and uncheck Optimization in the Code Generation section on the Pascal tab.

It is important to look at the application structure and consider using packages or DLLs for modular parts, particularly in large projects. Both `Make` and `Build` will be considerably faster.

If you are not using floating-point math in your applications, checking None in the Floating Point group of the Advanced Compiler tab will speed up the link time slightly, because the floating-point libraries will not be linked with your application.

These are things you can do within C++Builder and your code to minimize compile times. However, an important consideration is the computer hardware you are using. A software development system such as C++Builder requires higher-than-average system specs for CPU speed, RAM, and disk speed. Increasing these will yield a faster compile. In general, you should place slower IDE peripherals (such as an older CD-ROM drive) on a separate IDE controller from the hard drive. Defragmenting your hard drive may also improve the compile time slightly.

On multi-processor (SMP) machines you can take advantage of all processors by invoking compilation of several modules simultaneously. The Borland MAKE utility provided does not support this directly, but you can write a script to run individual MAKEs of separate modules simultaneously. Alternatively, you can use the free GNU Make with the `-j [jobs]` command-line switch for parallel execution. You can get GNU Make for Windows from `http://sourceware.cygnus.com/cygwin/`.

Download the full Cygwin distribution, or at least the `cygwin1.dll` and `make.exe` files. For documentation, see `http://www.gnu.org/software/make`. To use GNU Make in C++Builder 5, you'll need to export a makefile, either from the Project menu in the IDE or using the `BPR2MAK.EXE` command-line utility, because the project file is now stored in XML format. See `BPR2MAK.EXE` in the online help index for more information.

Finally, it probably doesn't need to be said that you should close other applications when working with C++Builder, particularly those that are memory or CPU intensive. If you're getting low on memory, things will certainly slow down considerably. I've also found that development on Windows NT and Windows 2000 is more responsive than Windows 95/98 (and provides a better debugging environment).

One additional method of speeding up compile times is discussed in the section "Background Compilation," later in this chapter. See that section for more information.

Now let's look at some of the new enhancements to the compiler and linker in C++Builder 5.

Exploring the C++Builder 5 Compiler and Linker Enhancements

There are several new features and enhancements to the compiler and linker in C++Builder 5. Perhaps the most eagerly anticipated enhancement is background compilation. C++Builder 5 also includes Microsoft Visual C++ compatibility enhancements, new file support, enhanced linker warnings and switches, enhancements to extended error information, and more.

Background Compilation

The new background compilation feature improves productivity by allowing you to keep working within the IDE when compiling your project. The larger and more complex the project, the more time the compilation process takes and the more benefit you will get out of this enhancement.

During a background compile, you can continue editing files and forms in the IDE. As each file in the project is needed by the compiler, it is temporarily marked as read-only. As a result, for a short period of time the source file or form you are editing cannot be changed.

During the background compile, you can also move between different files and forms in the IDE. You must be aware that some of the changes you are making at the time will be included in the compile and others won't, depending on which files the compiler has already processed at the time of the change. Additionally, the compiler may catch incomplete changes and report compiler errors or warnings on these partial changes.

Background compilation has some limitations. It cannot be used with packages, the Make All Projects option, or the Build All Projects option. Also, Code Insight features (code completion, code parameters, and ToolTip symbol insight) do not function during a background compile, and several menu items such as Project, Options are disabled.

TIP

A background compile is up to 25% slower than a foreground compile. Background compilation is performed in a separate thread, and the thread switching, synchronized access to edit buffers, and synchronization with the IDE's main thread are the cause of the speed reduction. When performing a Make or Build that you must wait for, such as when you need to do a test run, you should disable background compilation. Select Tools, Environment Options and go to the Preferences tab. Uncheck Background Compilation in the Compiling group.

The best way to use background compilation is to kick off a compile periodically (usually with Project, Make—Ctrl+F9) and continue working. If the project is being developed by a team, start a background compile after you incorporate their changes (usually after an update action if using a version control system) and continue your work on the project.

When you get to the stage at which you need to do a test run, the compile will most likely happen very quickly. Try not to change header files in that last stage as all units that include the header will require a recompile. This is a compile that you need to wait for.

Miscellaneous Compiler Enhancements

Microsoft Visual C++ compatibility enhancements include two new function modifiers, __msfastcall and __msreturn. These allow you to create functions in DLLs that can be used from Microsoft Visual C++ applications. Two new compiler switches, -VM and -pm, can be used to specify when the __msfastcall function modifier is used.

There are seven new __declspec declarations that fill a variety of roles. The __declspec(naked) declaration causes the compiler to not generate prolog and epilog code (setup and restore code for a function call) for a particular function. The __declspec (noreturn) declaration informs the compiler that the function does not return (for example, an exit function that aborts the application). Previously, use of such a function might have resulted in a compiler warning message.

Extended Error Information is a new option on the Compiler tab of the Project Options dialog. When it is set, additional compiler information is available for compiler warnings and errors, such as the parser context (for example, the name of the function that was being parsed when the compiler found the error). Click the plus symbol (+) next to the warning or error to view the extended error information.

A useful addition for debugging purposes is the new __FUNC__ preprocessor macro. It is expanded to a string literal of the name of the function in which it is contained. The following code would generate the messages Enter(TForm1::Button1Click) and Exit(TForm1::Button1Click) to the debug event log (View, Debug Windows, Event Log):

```
#define DFUNC_ENTRY OutputDebugString("Enter(" __FUNC__ ")")
#define DFUNC_EXIT OutputDebugString("Exit(" __FUNC__ ")")

void __fastcall TForm1::Button1Click(TObject *Sender)
{
    DFUNC_ENTRY;
    ShowMessage("In the middle.");
    // Some code.
    DFUNC_EXIT;
}
```

The __FUNC__ macro also works in class methods declared in the class definition.

New Linker Enhancements

A new Advanced Linker page has been added to the Project Options dialog. From this page, you can access several new and existing linker options, including delay loading selected DLLs. This option causes selected DLLs to be loaded only when an entry point is called, speeding up application startup and reducing memory requirements for DLLs that are infrequently used. This may also help in building modular applications by not requiring the DLLs to be shipped if they are not called when running in "reduced" mode.

Several new linker command-line switches have been added. The new Advanced Linker project options can be used to set some of the new command-line switches. Others include -GF to set advanced link image flags, -GD to generate a Delphi-compatible (.DRC) resource file, and -ad to link to a 32-bit Windows device driver. (You still need to modify the DDK headers and create the proper import libraries.)

Additionally, you now have more control over linker warnings. See "Linker Enhancements" in the C++Builder 5 help file for more information on these and other linker enhancements.

Optimizing: An Introduction

Optimizing is the process of streamlining some aspect of an application such as execution speed, program size, memory requirements, network bandwidth use, or disk access speed. Optimizing has been said to be both a science and an art; it involves both analytical analysis and creative design.

Moore's Law, which states that the number of transistors per square inch on an integrated circuit doubles about every 18 months, has been closely held for over three decades. The current Pentium III processor contains over 28 million transistors. Combined with increasing CPU clock speeds, this is bringing about a similar trend in CPU performance. The performance and specifications of other computer hardware constantly increase also. More RAM, bigger and faster hard drives, faster networks, faster CD-ROMs, faster video cards, and faster modems are appearing all the time. So why aren't we satisfied with our current hardware? Because it's not fast enough or big enough. As fast as hardware specifications increase, software requirements expand even more.

Computer games are partially to blame for the hardware-software race. Modern games, especially those that use complex 3D graphics, push the hardware to the limit. Additionally, operating systems and user interfaces become more complex, and applications software uses more graphics, handles more data, and performs more functions. Non-linear desktop video editing, a relatively new hobby for non-professional enthusiasts, is a prime example. It requires lots of RAM, a fast CPU, and an extremely large, lightning-fast hard drive.

When performance is a problem, you generally have two choices: a hardware solution or a software solution. Hardware solutions are often very limiting in the performance increase that can be achieved and are usually prohibitively expensive. However, they should not be ruled out as a viable solution, because in some cases a hardware solution can be the easiest to implement, particularly if the application is used in-house.

A hardware solution isn't generally optimizing, though. It is possible to configure or substitute hardware to optimize hardware performance, but that falls outside the scope of this book. The remainder of this chapter will look at software optimization.

Compiling and Optimizing Your Application
CHAPTER 6

229

6

COMPILING AND
OPTIMIZING YOUR
APPLICATION

For many desktop applications, performance is not an issue. However, there are certain types of applications and functionality that do require a performance boost. In the majority of cases it's execution speed, program size, or memory usage that needs tuning.

You should only attempt to optimize a working application that has been tested and debugged. Set measurable performance goals for the application. If the application meets those goals, it doesn't need optimizing. You should also avoid over-optimizing. Stop optimizing as soon as you get it to meet the goals you've set.

Make performance goals realistic. It's pointless to set a goal to develop an application to compress one hour of full-screen, full-rate video data to 20:1 in less than a minute (and it's not possible in software on today's computers). When it is difficult to know beforehand what is realistic, discuss it with several developers and make a reasonable guess.

In most cases, performance goals should be at a level that is acceptable to the users and no more. It's equally pointless to squeeze your program into 1MB file size when the user would be happy if it fits on a single 1.44MB floppy disk. When execution speed is the important factor, it may even be enough just to make the user *think* that the application runs fast enough.

Optimization should be targeted only at the parts of the application that need optimizing. To optimize an application, you need to understand how it works and know exactly where it is underachieving. Concentrate your efforts and develop an optimization strategy that will achieve the best results first.

It is also important to realize that optimization often adds complexity to your code. This can have a negative impact on maintainability, testability, and robustness. The more complex the code, the more likely that bugs will be introduced when changes are made to the application in the future. In addition, bugs will be harder to find and fix. Complex code is less comprehensible, and modifications made to the program in the future will require more development time.

Every project should have a set of clearly defined goals. These will vary greatly from project to project. The following objectives should be prioritized and adhered to:

- Speed
- Size
- Maintainability
- Testability
- Reusability
- Robustness
- Scalability
- Portability
- Usability
- Safety

The application design determines the level at which each of the objectives is met, so you need to keep all objectives in mind from the very beginning. Assuming that speed and size are fairly high in the list of priorities, you should make high-level design changes to optimize speed and size early on in the project.

Low-level optimizations should be performed very late in the project. Often, a change in the design at any level can render some low-level optimizations worthless, wasting the time and effort invested. This is particularly true for time spent optimizing at the lowest level, hand-tuning assembly code (a black art today), which you will likely have to repeat if the code changes or higher-level optimizations such as using a different algorithm are performed.

You should document any optimization changes that you make in the application and also if you suspect any areas performing under-par when developing it in the first place.

Optimizing for Execution Speed

Optimizing for execution speed is the most common of all optimization tasks. It often drives the user's overall impression of the application. In addition, with the increased complexity of calculations and branches in some of today's applications and the increased volume of data to be processed, the CPU is still a limiting factor. C++Builder's optimizing compiler produces fast executable code that is similar in performance to code compiled with Delphi, Visual C++, and GNU C++.

> **NOTE**
>
> At the time this book is being written, John Jacobson is conducting Jake's Code Efficiency Challenge to compare the speed of code using C++Builder, Delphi, and Visual C++. It looks at various solutions to specific problems and how fast the resulting code runs. You can find it at `http://home.xnet.com/~johnjac/`.

Each optimizing compiler has its own strengths and weaknesses, so when looking at a comparison of execution speed, a variety of tests is necessary. Tests claiming a difference in speed of five times or more between the code generated by different compilers are likely demonstrating a particular weakness of one compiler and should not be used for a general comparison.

The C++Builder optimizing compiler will likely speed up your code by only 20% to 150% in most cases. There is still a need for much greater improvements in some applications. The most likely applications to require greater speed optimizing are those that

- Perform a lot of complex mathematical calculations. Real-world scientific or engineering models, fractal generators, and applications that use 3D graphics are typical examples.
- Process large amounts of data, such as data compression, sorting, searching, or encryption.

Compiling and Optimizing Your Application

CHAPTER 6

231

6

COMPILING AND
OPTIMIZING YOUR
APPLICATION

- Solve a problem. These often iterate many times and contain complex branch or indexing statements. Event simulators, best-fit determination, and puzzle solvers are all examples.

Sometimes the limiting factor is not the execution speed but something outside the control of the application, such as a slow hard disk, a congested WAN, or even a user who responds slowly to a blocking event. There are many techniques you can employ to optimize an application for speed. The techniques typically fall into the following categories:

- Compiler optimization settings
- Changes to the design and algorithms
- Low-level code changes
- Data changes
- Hand-tuned assembly code
- External optimization
- Hiding execution speed

The last option, while not exactly an optimization technique as such, can be particularly relevant in certain situations. If the task must be finished before the user can continue, then use a progress bar or an animation to show the user that the application is still functioning. If possible, perform the processing in a background thread while the user keeps working.

Some optimization techniques produce better results than others, and some require much more effort to implement. Generally, the best performance gains can be achieved through design and algorithm changes, and the easiest to implement are compiler settings and low-level code changes. Not all optimization techniques may be appropriate for a particular application.

It should be mentioned that several of the techniques for optimizing execution speed increase the size of the executable, going against any program size optimizations. In the following sections, most of the speed optimization techniques that will be discussed will be demonstrated using an example application.

Crozzle Solver Application Example

The example application that we'll use to demonstrate many of the optimization techniques is a "crozzle" solver. This example fits into the third category previously described; it involves complex branches and indexing statements. A description on what it does is necessary for some of the optimization techniques presented.

A crozzle is like a crossword in that it involves interlocking words within a grid, except that you start with an empty grid and are given the list of words to place within the grid. The goal is to interlock the words in one contiguous block in such a way as to achieve the highest score.

Each interlocked word within the crozzle solution is worth 10 points. Interlocking letters are also scored: A–F are 2 points, G–L are 4 points, M–R are 8 points, S–X are 16 points, Y is 32 points, and Z is 64 points. Words can be used only once and are placed horizontally or vertically in a 15×10 grid.

Only complete words are permitted to be formed within the grid, and you cannot score words within words. For example, if SCARE and CAR were in the word list, and the word SCARE is placed, you cannot claim an additional 10 points or interlocking C, A, or R for the inline word CAR. Traditionally, a crozzle uses a word list of about 110 to 120 words of between 3 and 15 letters.

I chose this example because it is somewhat visual and a bit of fun, it takes an extraordinary amount of time to run, and it can be used to demonstrate many of the optimization techniques and difficulties that will be covered. About 12 years ago, I wrote a very crude version of the crozzle solver in BASIC and later in optimized assembly code in an attempt to win a $2000 prize in a magazine. Unfortunately, it wasn't complete enough or optimized enough for the computers back then to produce even partial solutions within the available time.

Through a much-improved algorithm, the version that we'll use here is much more complete in terms of functionality and base speed than those early versions (it could still use a little polishing). It is about 2900 lines of source code contained in 4 units and 3 header files—not a large project but nice. Figure 6.1 shows the Crozzle Solver application that we'll be working with. It is displaying a simple solved crozzle.

FIGURE 6.1

The Crozzle Solver application with a simple solved crozzle.

The initial version of the application is provided in the CrozzleInitial subdirectory on the CD-ROM that accompanies this book. The final version, after applying the optimization techniques discussed later, is provided in the CrozzleFinal subdirectory. Both C++Builder 4 and 5 are supplied for your convenience; they are identical except for the project file and to-do list.

Compiling and Optimizing Your Application

233

CHAPTER 6

6

COMPILING AND
OPTIMIZING YOUR
APPLICATION

The Crozzle Solver application can be used to solve completely from a blank grid or to build on an existing, partially complete user- or computer-generated solution. The word list and crozzle grid are stored together in a CRZ text file. An example of each is provided in the files `ExampleBlank.crz` and `ExampleToFinish.crz`. Simply edit the file and type the words into the grid as required and type the full list of words below the grid, one per line. Leave the words initially placed in the grid in the word list.

The crozzle application can be used to solve words in the whole grid or in a specific portion of the grid. To solve the whole grid, use the Solve Whole button after the crozzle is loaded. To solve a specific area, select the area to solve with the mouse, set either Selection Bounds Words or Selection Bounds Interlocking Letters from the Options menu, and use the Solve Sel button.

The crozzle solver automatically outputs the current highest-scoring crozzle solution to the file `HighScore.crz`, which can be loaded for viewing later. There are several interesting View options. Experiment with them to get an insight into how the Crozzle Solver application goes about its job. Presently, the Save and Save As options are not particularly useful, because it is difficult to save a crozzle during the solve process, and the crozzle ends with the same grid it started with.

Exponential Timings

Through optimization, we'll progressively speed up the crozzle solver in several stages. At each stage, relative speed improvements will be noted. These will be expressed as a percentage speed improvement over the previous timing, and the total number of times faster will be compared to the original timing. All timing and score tests are performed in the C++Builder IDE on a Pentium II 266MHz with 128MB of RAM, running Windows 2000 Professional. The timings listed are an average of three runs.

Two example files, `RunComplete.crz` and `RunPartial.crz`, are provided on the CD-ROM in the same directory as the example applications. `RunComplete.crz` uses a list of 11 words to solve every solution possible in a relatively short period of time and will be used for all speed timings in this chapter. The `RunPartial.crz` example uses a full list of 115 words. Solving every possible solution in this example is simply not achievable with today's hardware, irrespective of how well we optimize the program. Both examples solve from a blank crozzle grid, thus attempting all possible combinations.

A typical user-generated high-scoring solution uses about 35 to 40 words from the complete word list, and the score varies from about 600 to 800 points. You might think that it would be fairly easy to write a program to try all combinations of words to get the best scoring solution. Think again! The number of combinations is phenomenal.

Table 6.1 shows the run time of the initial Crozzle Solver application (compiled without optimization settings) when used to solve the first 5 to 11 words from the `RunComplete.crz` file.

The table also shows the number of word combinations attempted, the number of complete valid solutions found, and the highest score achieved.

TABLE 6.1 Example Run Data for a Word List of 5 to 11 Words

Words	Time (sec)	Word Combinations	Solutions	Highest Score
5	0.0318	3,577	1,492	90
6	0.288	31,257	9,892	102
7	2.96	317,477	101,604	120
8	47.1	4,765,661	1,192,436	146
9	458	44,057,533	11,123,772	164
10	6,294	554,577,981	152,343,008	190
11	79,560	>6,000,000,000	>1,900,000,000	208

The first thing to note from the table is that, even with a list of only 11 words (RunComplete.crz), the run time is over 22 hours! On average, the run time increases by almost 1100% for each extra word. Figure 6.2 shows a graph of the run time from Table 6.1. The table and graph are included in the CrozzleTimings.xls Microsoft Excel spreadsheet on the CD-ROM.

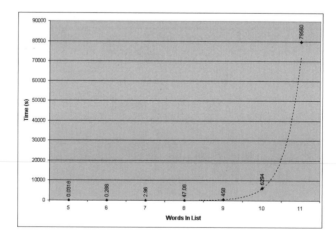

FIGURE 6.2

A graph of the run times for 5 to 11 words from Table 6.1.

From the table data and the run time graph we can conclude that the run time follows an exponential pattern. This is also apparent in a graph of the logarithm of the run time, which produces a linear result. This graph and a graph of the high score are also available in the spreadsheet on the CD-ROM.

By extrapolation we can estimate that, without further optimization, 15 words will take about 50 years to solve, 17 words will take more than 7,000 years, and 20 words more than 10 million! I can't wait for the first 1EHz (Exahertz—one billion GHz) CPU, but even that would take over a hundred million years to completely solve a list of just 30 words.

We would expect both the run time and score to taper off as the number of words in the list exceeds about 40. Most words in a list of 40 could be placed in the grid simultaneously to form a solution. Until this point there has been ample space to place words in the grid, but now there is little space left. It is difficult to place additional words, and hence the number of combinations does not increase at the same rate for each additional word added to the list. In any case, we can see that there is no way to completely solve a list of 115 words, at least not in the life of this universe.

The result for the example crozzle using the unoptimized (baseline) crozzle solver with all compiler optimizations disabled is

Initial Timing: 79,560 seconds for 11 words

Now let's start speeding this thing up a bit!

Project Options for Execution Speed

There are several project options that affect execution speed. They are spread across several tabs of the Project Options dialog. Set the following project options to maximize the speed:

- Compiler tab: Click the Release button. It will set most optimizations for you. Set Code Optimization to Speed, disable all options in the Debugging group, and uncheck Stack Frames in the Compiling group.

- Advanced Compiler tab: Set Instruction Set to Pentium Pro, set Data Alignment to Quad Word, set Calling Convention to Register, set Register Variables to Automatic, set Floating Point to Fast, and uncheck Correct Pentium FDIV flaw.

- C++ tab: If possible with your application, disable exception handling by unchecking the Enable RTTI and Enable Exceptions options in the Exception Handling group. Otherwise, check Fast Exception Prologs. Set Virtual Tables to Smart.

- Pascal tab: In the Code Generation group, check Optimization and Aligned Record Fields and uncheck Stack Frames and Pentium-Safe FDIV. Disable all options in the Runtime Errors and Debugging groups.

- Linker tab: In the Linking group, uncheck Create Debug Information, Use Dynamic RTL, and Use Debug Libraries options. Set Map File to Off. If you are creating DLLs, the image base for all DLLs used by an application should be unique and offset sufficiently to prevent them from overlapping in memory.

- Packages tab: Uncheck Build with Runtime Packages.

- Tasm tab: Set Debug Information to None.
- CodeGuard tab: Uncheck CodeGuard Validation.

> **NOTE**
>
> Enabling compiler and other optimization settings as described here can hinder debugging of your application. The optimizer may rearrange or even remove code and variables. This can stop breakpoints and single stepping in the debugger from functioning as expected. As previously mentioned, you should debug your application first.

For our crozzle application, several of these options will have no effect. However, just by enabling code optimization, we have a significant improvement in speed. With all options set as described, we now have the following:

Current Timing: 51,240 seconds. **Improvement:** 55% (total speedup 1.55 times)

You should be careful when setting the various options listed. The Instruction Set option on the Advanced Compiler tab should be set to the base target machine that you want the application to run on, because processors are not forward compatible. The difference between a 386 and a Pentium Pro for the Crozzle Solver application is negligible.

With the compiler optimization set to Speed, simply setting Register Variables to Automatic rather than None results in a 40% speed increase for the crozzle application.

Remember that C++Builder 5 allows different settings for each unit (node-level options). Use this to your advantage. If all speed-critical code is in one unit, consider aggressive settings for only that unit.

Detecting Bottlenecks

Most of the remaining optimization techniques require you to have a good understanding of the application and specifically to know exactly where your application is spending most of its time. In most applications, between 80% and 90% of the time is spent executing only 10% to 20% of the code, typically in a few loops or a few commonly executed functions.

Using the knowledge of where your program's bottlenecks are, you can achieve the best results with the least effort. There are several techniques for finding bottlenecks:

- Use a profiler
- Manually time sections of code
- Inspect the design and code

Profiling

By far the easiest method of detecting bottlenecks is to use a profiler. A profiler is a tool that tracks the execution time of an application while it is running and provides detailed statistics on which portions of the application run most frequently or consume the most time. Most profilers track the execution time down to the function level. However, some profilers can track execution time down to the line level.

Typically function profilers can monitor your application as they are, but some require changes in the source code. The choice of a function profiler or a line profiler depends on the structure of your application, but generally a function profiler is more than sufficient. Profilers work with multithreaded applications.

There are several profilers available, and a few are specially designed to be used with C++Builder. One is Sleuth StopWatch by TurboPower Software Company. It is part of the Sleuth QA Suite. I'll be using version 1.0, which allows function profiling, to profile the Crozzle Solver application. StopWatch also includes a code disassembly view that displays assembly code instruction pairing information that can assist you with low-level assembly code optimization.

I should point out that at the time this book is being written, Sleuth QA Suite 2.0 is about to be released. It will be a great update and includes new features such as coverage analysis, line profiling, automation support, the capability to export views to HTML, user-defined views, and critical-path analysis.

Sleuth QA Suite also includes Sleuth CodeWatch, a utility that is similar in function to CodeGuard. It detects memory and resource leaks and can filter out VCL leaks. It also catches memory overwrites, detects invalid parameter and return values for Win32 API calls, logs all Win32 API calls, and more. You can get more information and download a trial version of Sleuth QA Suite from `http://www.turbopower.com/`.

Some other profilers of note are

- QTime from Automated QA is available in both a lite and standard version. It works with C++Builder 3 and later. The standard version includes many useful features, including code coverage and code tracing. For more information or to download a trial version, go to `http://www.totalqa.com/`.

- RQ's Profiler is very inexpensive, but it requires you to add macro calls to your source code and link with the Profiler DLL. It has a code editor to assist with this. RQ's Profiler works with C++Builder version 1 through 5. You can get more information and download a shareware trial version from `http://ourworld.compuserve.com/homepages/rq/`.

- Intel's VTune Analyzer includes a sampling profiler, a Code Coach to recommend C++ source level optimizations, call graph profiling, static assembly code analysis to indicate pairing and penalty issues on a variety of processors, and more. However, it does not integrate directly with C++Builder, and I found it difficult to use. It has both function and line profiling. For more information and to download a trial version, go to `http://developer.intel.com/vtune/analyzer/`.

A Profiling Example

When you are profiling, you should stop all non-essential applications that may interfere with the timing. For an accurate view, you should repeat a profile test a few times and average the results.

A problem with all profilers is that they don't handle recursive functions very well. Timings are per function name rather than per invocation of the function, and they include time spent in child functions. This is difficult to interpret. Unfortunately, the Crozzle Solver application uses recursion to generate the crozzle solutions. The `SolveWord()` function is called recursively to build each word in the solution. We're going to profile the Crozzle Solver application using Sleuth StopWatch from TurboPower. To solve the recursion problem, we'll need to perform some code trickery.

We'll need to unroll the recursion to a particular depth. This means creating several copies of the functions in the recursion loop and chaining them together. The Crozzle Solver application has a recursion loop that is three functions wide and one function deep.

This means that function A calls functions B, C, and D. Functions B, C, and D each call function A. In other words, function A fans out to three functions wide, and we can go down one level before returning to the first function. If you had a single function A that called itself, the recursion loop would be one wide and zero deep.

In the Crozzle Solver application, function A is `SolveWord()`, functions B, C, and D are `SolveFirstWord()`, `SolveAdjacent()`, and `SolveStandardWord()`, respectively. `SolveWord()` builds on the current crozzle by placing one additional word using one of the other three specialized functions. `SolveFirstWord()` is used only to place all combinations of each initial word in the grid. `SolveStandardWord()` interlocks another word from the list with the current crozzle.

If a word that is placed in the grid is adjacent to a word in the next row or column, then one or more invalid two-letter words are formed. Words must be placed to run through these squares to form a valid word. `SolveAdjacent()` attempts to do this. You can see this by enabling View, Thinking and View, Pause View to see how words are placed and how adjacent letters are solved. Either a new word is placed through the adjacent squares or the adjacent word is rejected.

Fortunately, the runtime recursion depth of the Crozzle Solver application, which is the number of times that the function-call loop can be cycled, or the stack size if you like, is dependent on the number of words in the word list, which means that we can easily control it. The maximum depth is $N+1$, where N is the number of words in the list. We'll unroll the recursion loop eight times to use a list of seven words.

Compiling and Optimizing Your Application

CHAPTER 6

239

6

COMPILING AND
OPTIMIZING YOUR
APPLICATION

First we copy the `SolveWord()`, `SolveFirstWord()`, `SolveAdjacent()`, and `SolveStandardWord()` functions and paste seven times. Next we modify the function names of the seven copies by adding a 2, 3, 4, and so on to the end of the name. Now we have eight unique copies of each function.

Then we chain them together by changing the call to `SolveWord()` in the original `SolveFirstWord()`, `SolveAdjacent()`, and `SolveStandardWord()` functions to `SolveWord2()`. In `SolveWord2()` we call `SolveFirstWord2()`, `SolveAdjacent2()`, and `SolveStandardWord2()`. We change these functions to call `SolveWord3()` and so on until we finally get `SolveWord8()` to call `SolveFirstWord8()`, `SolveAdjacent8()`, and `SolveStandardWord8()`, at which time we leave these to call the original `SolveWord()`, thus completing the loop.

It's a bit tricky, but if you follow it through carefully you shouldn't have much trouble. All we're really trying to do is extend the loop depth to eight. We also need to add function prototypes for all of the newly created function copies.

From within C++Builder we fire up Sleuth StopWatch from the Tools menu and set the analysis settings for this project by answering a few questions. We'll set Trigger Mode profiling on the `SolveCrozzle()` routine and time all routines with source and time leaf nodes individually. Once the analysis settings are configured, we run the crozzle solver from within StopWatch, load the eight-word crozzle file, solve it completely, and exit the crozzle solver.

StopWatch now displays the profiling information. Figure 6.3 shows the StopWatch profiling results for the Crozzle Solver application after completely solving a word list containing seven words.

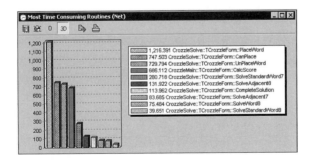

FIGURE 6.3
The profiling results as displayed in Sleuth StopWatch.

To obtain the true stats for the recursive functions, we must total the Times Called, Net Time, and Gross Time values for each of the eight copies of the four functions. From that we recalculated the Net %, Net Average, and Gross Average. The final profiling results are shown in Table 6.2. Note that with non-recursive functions, the whole process of profiling is much simpler than this.

TABLE 6.2 Final Profiling Results for the Crozzle Solver Using a List of Eight Words

Function	Calls	Net Time (ms)	Net %	Net Average (ms)	Gross Time (ms)	Gross Average (ms)
PlaceWord	317462	1216.4	28.78	0.0038	1216.4	0.0038
CanPlace	544926	747.5	17.68	0.0014	747.5	0.0014
UnPlaceWord	317462	729.8	17.27	0.0023	729.8	0.0023
CalcScore	101604	686.1	16.23	0.0068	686.1	0.0068
SolveStandardWord	167474	356.6	8.43	0.002	24029.0	0.1435
SolveAdjacent	149988	253.95	6.01	0.0017	283.4	0.0019
SolveWord	317463	116.7	2.76	0.0004	28663.6	0.0903
CompleteSolution	101604	114.0	2.70	0.0011	803.6	0.0079
SolveFirstWord	1	0.00	0.00	0.00	4224.6	4224.6

From the profiling results we can see that we need to concentrate our efforts on the PlaceWord(), CanPlace(), UnPlaceWord(), and CalcScore() functions. The Crozzle Solver application has a rather broad bottleneck in terms of functions, but overall it is the entire solve algorithm that needs streamlining.

Profiling should be performed at various stages of optimization so that you know what effect each change has on the execution structure and speed. You will probably find changes that actually slow down the application!

Manual Code Timing

Manually timing sections of code involves inserting stopwatch-type timing code into your application at strategic places. With little knowledge of where the time-intensive sections are, you need to start at the top, with loops and individual function calls. You then drill down into the code until you identify the key areas that are consuming the most time. Listing 6.3 demonstrates how you can time a section of code.

LISTING 6.3 Timing a Section of Code

```
#include <time.h>

void TMyClass::SomeFunction()
{
    clock_t StartTime,
            StopTime;

    // Some code here.

    // Start the clock.
```

Compiling and Optimizing Your Application

CHAPTER 6

241

6

COMPILING AND
OPTIMIZING YOUR
APPLICATION

LISTING 6.3 Continued

```
StartTime = clock();

// Code to time in here.

// Stop the clock.
StopTime = clock();
// Report the elapsed time.
ShowMessage("Elapsed time: " +
            FloatToStrF((StopTime-StartTime)/CLK_TCK, ffFixed, 7, 2) +
            " seconds");

// Rest of code here.
}
```

The code that you want to time goes in the center section. If the code is rather fast (executes in under a second), you can add a simple loop around the section of code, unless of course the code has side effects that cause the behavior of the code to change after the first run. You then time the whole lot and divide the elapsed time by the number of loop iterations.

Typically, if the timing code is in a function that is called many times, you wouldn't use `ShowMessage()` to display the elapsed time. Instead, you could write it to the Debug Event log, using `OutputDebugString()` if you're running in the IDE, or to your own file.

Design Inspection

The design inspection method can be used where formalized design documentation exists. Look at the core of the application design and then look for critical points in the data flow or execution path. Analyze pseudo-code, flow charts, dataflow diagrams, and process sections of IPO and N-S diagrams and Warnier-Orr diagrams.

Look for processes that are called from many places and loops, particularly nested loops. This will give you an idea of which areas are frequently called; in most cases, this is where bottlenecks occur.

Code Inspection

The code inspection method involves looking at the source code level for loops, complex branches, indexing statements and pointer arithmetic, or mathematical calculations. Object-oriented code typically contains many small methods and often hides complex pointer arithmetic.

With both the design inspection and code inspection methods, you will still need to time sections of code to verify that you are indeed looking at the troublesome areas. Use the manual timing methods previously described.

With all methods, you need not only to find the bottlenecks but also to decide which bottlenecks are most relevant. A bottleneck in a background thread that has no effect on the user is not likely to be worth tuning.

Optimizing the Design and Algorithms

The biggest gains most often come from optimizing the design, choosing better algorithms, or optimizing the existing algorithms. To optimize the design you need a very good understanding of how the application works. On the other hand, algorithms are usually implemented at a fairly low level, often isolated from the bulk of the application. The code that implements the algorithm is often complex but, if designed and written well, it can still be easy to use.

Making Design Decisions

Optimizing the design requires that you look at the bigger picture, at things such as application architecture and technologies used to implement fundamental features. It is mostly applicable to large applications that are modular or distributed, or that interface with other applications. There are many technical issues that will be faced when designing Windows applications.

A method call to an interface in an in-process COM object will be faster than the same call to an out-of-process COM object, and faster again than the same call to a DCOM object on a remote machine. When scaling a modular application that uses COM as the framework to using DCOM, you need to take this into account. In many cases there are alternative technologies. What about CORBA or a custom TCP/IP socket–based interface?

There are many more alternatives to consider for database applications. C++Builder 5 already includes three methods of database access: the BDE, ADO Express, and InterBase Express. It appears that there is another on the way: DB Express. There are more than 20 third-party BDE alternatives. There are always trade-offs between performance, usability, and features.

In these and other technology decisions, a lot of homework is necessary to find and weigh the advantages and disadvantages of each alternative. Perhaps the best source for this information is the Borland newsgroups. Questions relating to performance and design decisions are often asked and, if you have a specific question in mind, there are experts who are glad to help. Keep your eye out for TeamB members. A complete listing of C++Builder-related Borland and other newsgroups is in Appendix A, "Information Sources."

The following is a list of several overall design optimization techniques:

- Reduce complexity. Don't modularize your application too much. Don't "over-normalize" your database.
- Streamline the execution path. Avoid chaining calls to distributed objects.
- Avoid slow technologies. Choose the best one for the job.
- Use efficient third-party tools for report generation, data compression and encryption, communication, and other needs.
- Minimize graphics and visual controls, particularly if they are updated often. Consider disabling and hiding them during the update and enabling and displaying them again after the update is complete.

- Perform long tasks in a second thread where possible.

- Minimize network traffic and disk access. Consider using client data sets, and read and write data in a few larger chunks instead of many smaller ones. On network or other communications links with a high latency, consider sending multiple requests and subsequent replies at once.

- Design effectively for multiprocessor machines. Spread the workload evenly between each processor and reduce blocking interprocess communication.

- Reduce memory use. Multithreaded applications and those that run in an environment with several simultaneous applications running should be memory conscious to allow the operating system to schedule them efficiently.

There's no one set method for optimizing the design of your application. If in doubt, ask other experienced people in your field. User groups are a haven for serious and hobbyist programmers with varying backgrounds and experience.

The Crozzle Solver application has a rather simple design. Most of the techniques listed don't really apply to it. One design aspect of the crozzle solver that has been optimized in the initial design is TDrawGrid, used to display the crozzle. By default the current state of the crozzle is not updated in TDrawGrid throughout the solve process. However, the user can enable this from the View menu.

One further design optimization that we can perform is to slightly streamline the execution path by restructuring the function hierarchy. Currently, when the Solve button is pressed, SolveCrozzle() is called. It in turn calls SolveWord() to start generating solutions. SolveWord() is a generic function that can be called to start solving a blank crozzle or to build on the initial or current crozzle. In the SolveWord() function, the following code appears:

```
if (WordsPlaced.NumPlaced == 0) {
    SolveFirstWord();
    return(true);
}
```

The call to SolveFirstWord() is only required at the very highest level in recursion, as tested by the if statement (no words placed yet). The SolveWord() function is called recursively from all levels, which means that this if statement is executed every time. We can move the SolveFirstWord() function call outside the recursion loop and place it in the initial calling function, SolveCrozzle(). The simple call to SolveWord() from SolveCrozzle() now becomes this:

```
if (SolveFromBlank) {
    SolveFirstWord();
} else {
    SolveWord();
}
```

We call `SolveFirstWord()` only if we have a blank crozzle; otherwise we still call `SolveWord()` to start building on the initial solution. This keeps the `if` statement from being evaluated in each call to `SolveWord()`—over 6,000,000,000 times in the 11-word example!

Now we have the following results:

Current Timing: 49,525 seconds. **Improvement:** 3.5% (total speedup 1.61 times)

Not a huge result, but it was easy to implement.

Choosing Algorithms

Algorithms usually provide the biggest scope for improving the speed of an application. For any given problem there are many ways to obtain a solution, so choosing an appropriate algorithm is important. For standard problems there are usually several reasonable algorithms publicly available.

An algorithm is a method of solving a problem. It has five primary characteristics:

- Boundedness. It stops at some point.
- Correctness: It finds the correct answer to the problem.
- Predictability: It will always do the same thing if given the same input data.
- Finiteness: It can be described in a finite number of steps.
- Definition: Each step in the algorithm has a well-defined meaning.

The algorithms for a particular problem will often vary dramatically in speed. One example is in games development, where there is fierce competition between various 3D graphics engines. In some cases the speed or the algorithm varies according to the input data.

Another example of speed differences is with various sorting algorithms. Three well-known ones are bubble sort, selection sort, and quick sort. If you compile and run the Threads application from the `Examples` folder installed with C++Builder, you'll see that the three sorting algorithms vary in performance.

The speed of these three sorting algorithms depends both on the number of elements to sort and on the initial order of the elements. Using the random set of 115 elements that the Threads application generates, quick sort is fastest and bubble sort slowest. With fewer than about 10 elements, however, bubble sort is fastest and quick sort slowest. With 115 elements already in sort order, bubble sort is fastest and quick sort slowest, and in reverse order selection sort is fastest and bubble sort slowest.

If the speed of the algorithm in your application varies widely according to the input data, and if the input data varies, consider incorporating two or more algorithms into your application to perform the same task and call the most appropriate one.

Algorithms are often described in big-O notation (asymptotic complexity). Big-O notation can be thought of as shorthand for describing an algorithm's execution time relative to the size of

Compiling and Optimizing Your Application

CHAPTER 6

245

6

COMPILING AND
OPTIMIZING YOUR
APPLICATION

the problem. $O(N)$ describes a linear relationship between the execution time and the problem size. For one to three elements, the time required may be 1, 2, or 3 seconds. With an $O(N^2)$ algorithm, the time required to solve the problem increases with the square of the problem size. For one to three elements the time required may be 1, 4, or 9 seconds. With an $O(2^N)$ algorithm the growth rate is large, and such an algorithm is typically considered infeasible to complete.

The bubble sort is $O(N^2)$ and therefore should be used only for small N. There are better sorting algorithms available for small N. Quicksort is an $O(\log N)$ algorithm and is one of the fastest sorting algorithms for large N. The crozzle solver algorithm is $O(2^N)$, not a good prospect. Sometimes it is possible to replace an $O(N^2)$ algorithm with an $O(N)$ algorithm and an $O(N)$ algorithm with an $O(\log N)$ algorithm.

It is important to note that two different algorithms do not necessarily produce exactly the same result. You may choose a faster algorithm that has less accuracy or an increased error rate. Many years ago I wrote a circle algorithm that was much faster than the standard one available on the system for small to medium-size circles. It used a `sqrt()` function to draw points on the circumference instead of drawing an N-sided polygon. It produced a much better-looking circle, but for large circles it became slower than the standard routine.

Here are several good algorithm references:

- "Numerical Recipes in C" is an online book available in PDF format at `http://www.ulib.org/webRoot/Books/Numerical_Recipes/`.

- The Stony Brook Algorithm Repository has solutions for many different problems and includes source code: `http://www.cs.sunysb.edu/~algorith/`.

- Object-Oriented Numerics (`http://oonumerics.org/`) has Blitz++, a C++ class library for scientific computing. It is a high-performance library using template techniques and provides dense arrays and vectors, random number generators, and small vectors and matrices. It is open source, and there are also many links to other available libraries.

- Three avenues for game and graphics algorithms are `http://www.gamedev.net/`, `http://www.magic-software.com/`, and the Newsgroup `comp.graphics.algorithms`.

- Dr. Dobb's Journal (`http://www.ddj.com/`) contains articles on algorithms from time to time. In particular, see the April 2000 issue, a special on algorithms. You can purchase individual articles online or a CD-ROM of over 11 years of issues for around US$80.

- *Introduction to Algorithms* by Cormen, Leiserson & Rivest. ISBN 0262031418. 1990.

- *Algorithms in C++* by Sedgewick. ISBN 0201510596. 1992.

- *The Art of Computer Programming: Sorting and Searching* by Knuth. ISBN 0201896850. 1998.

There are many algorithms in the areas of sorting, compression, graphics, and data storage that have publicly available source code to drop right into your application.

Improving Algorithms

If an algorithm is non-standard, it's likely that you developed it yourself, and you're more likely to resort to seeking speed improvements in the existing algorithm than to seek a replacement algorithm. It is often possible to improve upon an existing algorithm, particularly if it is complex in nature.

If you're using the Standard Template Library (STL), you'll find templates that provide arrays and sorting functions that have been optimized for specific data types. Containers vary in performance. In the STL documentation, the C++Builder help files contain several optimization hints with the STL.

TIP

A great Web site that contains STL timings and optimizations can be found at http://www.tantalon.com/pete/cppopt/main.htm.

One generic approach to speeding up an algorithm is to use table look-ups or simple value look-ups instead of mathematical or logical calculations. The table or values can sometimes be generated prior to runtime and coded into a static array in source code. Other times they may need to be generated at runtime, before the algorithm is executed, or even within the algorithm itself.

NOTE

Using precalculated tables or values requires memory to store them, and sometimes the size of this data can be very large. You need to weigh the speed against the size and find a happy medium.

When generating the table or values at runtime, you must weigh the time to create them and keep them current against the time saved in the algorithm. A prime example of the table approach is the Cyclic Redundancy Check (CRC) calculation algorithm. CRCs are often used in data transportation to validate that the data received is the same as the data sent. The sender calculates the CRC and appends it to the data. The receiver also calculates the CRC and compares it to the CRC sent with the data. If they match, the data was received correctly.

In a slow CRC-calculation algorithm, the CRC is generated by iterating through each byte of the data and performing polynomial modulo two arithmetic. It sounds long and it takes long. With the *faster table method*, a table of 256 values, one for each ASCII character, is either pre-generated and initialized in the source code or generated at runtime before the CRC algorithm runs. Then in the algorithm a lookup into the table for each character of data avoids the need for a lot of the calculations at each step. Calculations are still required, but they are greatly reduced. It is akin to looking up a large multiplication table rather than doing the math with pencil and paper.

Other candidates for a table of values are a large `switch` statement or numerous `if else` statements. If you are only performing static calculations or calling functions in the various `case` or `if` statements, consider storing the precalculated values or function pointers in a table. Replace a `case` statement with a simple table lookup using the `switch` value. Consider the following simple example:

```
switch(NumSides) {
    case 1: Circle(x, y, r); break;
    case 2: PolyError(x, y, r); break;
    case 3: Triangle(x, y, r); break;
    case 4: Square(x, y, r); break;
    case 5: Pentagon(x, y, r); break;
}
```

This can be replaced by the following:

```
void (*Polyfunctions[5])(int, int, int) = {
    Circle, PolyError, Triangle, Square, Pentagon
};

    // Later in some function.
    PolyFunctions[NumSides](x, y, r);
```

Replace an `if` statement with a simple table lookup using a value to represent each possible combination of the Boolean expressions. In the expression if `(A && B)`, A can be `true` or `false` and B can be `true` or `false`. There are four possible combinations. Using bitwise math, calculate a binary value of `00` when both A and B are `false`, `01` if B is `true`, `10` if A is `true`, or `11` if both A and B are `true`. The binary values are equivalent to decimal 0 to 3. Use this value to index the lookup table.

The baseline crozzle solver algorithm includes several optimizations that store values that would normally require considerable effort to recalculate in tables for reuse. Some of these cases are presented in the following paragraphs.

To place a word in the grid, the crozzle solver goes through each word in the word list. It goes through each letter in each word and determines where that letter appears in the grid (if at all). If it does appear, a series of tests are required to determine if the word can be interlocked at that place and whether the word can be placed horizontally or vertically. There are two optimizations here.

First, an array is used to store the positions at which each letter of the alphabet is placed within the grid. As a word is placed, the position in the grid of each letter in the word is added to the appropriate array. This saves enormous time, because it isn't necessary to scan 10 rows of 15 squares each time we want to search for a place to interlock the current word.

Secondly, as a word is placed in the grid, its orientation is stored in each square that the word occupies. Two simple Boolean values are used for each square: HorizWord and VertWord. In the case of an interlocking square, both can be set to true. This also saves time, because otherwise it is difficult to determine if the word can be placed horizontally or vertically at a particular square. This is easy to do visually, but it's not so easy programmatically because of several square content tests that are involved and grid boundaries that must not be exceeded.

Another stored value optimization is in the calculation of the crozzle score. As profiling showed us, the CalcScore() function is one of the bottlenecks. Rather than scanning the grid testing for interlocking squares and then adding the score of the letter at that square to the total score, the score for each letter square is set at the time the square is interlocked. This is stored with the other square information in the crozzle grid. All that is needed then is to total the score of each square in the grid (limited to the four boundaries of the words in the grid), saving on several value tests. This is as much as 5% faster.

From the profiling that we performed earlier, we know that bottlenecks exist in a variety of functions, namely position searching, placement testing, word placement, and word removal. Later we'll get into code optimizations, but if we could remove the overall workload in these functions, we'd see a great improvement. Let's now apply some further algorithm optimizations to the crozzle solver.

One of the biggest drawbacks with the current crozzle solver algorithm is that it generates duplicate combinations of interlocked words. If the words JAR and ROD are in the word list, then at one point the algorithm places the word JAR horizontally and later intersects the word ROD vertically through the R. Later the algorithm places the word ROD vertically and intersects the word JAR horizontally through the R, producing the same result!

Let's add some duplicate solution detection. This is rather complex to describe, but there are two basic rules, depending on whether we are solving from a partial solution or a blank crozzle:

- Solve from a partial solution: We can only place a word if it intersects with the most recently placed word that is after it in the word list or if it intersects with any word placed after that word. If there is no word already placed that is after it in the word list, then it can intersect with all words. For example, given the word list CAB, BIT, CAT and solving a partial crozzle with the word CAB already placed, the word CAT can intersect the C of CAB. However, then BIT can only intersect with the T of CAT and not the B of BIT, because that combination was previously solved.

- Solve from a blank crozzle: The previous rule applies, and we can further eliminate duplicate combinations. Once the initial word is placed, we cannot place a word that is earlier in the word list. There is no need to do so, because earlier we tried every combination using that word. For example, given the same word list (CAB, BIT, CAT) we can place the word CAB first and then intersect the words BIT and CAT. Later, when we

Compiling and Optimizing Your Application

249

CHAPTER 6

6

COMPILING AND
OPTIMIZING YOUR
APPLICATION

remove the word CAB and place the word BIT first, there is no need to attempt to place the word CAB at any stage because we solved all combinations of this earlier.

To implement this, we need to track the highest word in the word list that appears in the grid, and we need to set an index of which previously placed words we can intersect with. To solve from a blank grid, each time we try to place a word in the grid, we can skip all words in the word list before the first word placed. We can set the word list index of the first word that we can place outside the recursion loop in the `SolveCrozzle()` and `SolveFirstWord()` functions.

The solution to the duplicate combination problem and the testing are both very laborious. Specific test cases were required to ensure that the algorithm still functions correctly by solving all possible combinations.

This new duplicate combination elimination now has the following speed statistics:

Current Timing: 24.33 seconds. **Improvement:** 203600% (total speedup 3270 times)

Wow! Can that be right? You bet. Those duplicate combinations and attempts to place words that weren't necessary were killing us.

There is one other minor algorithm improvement that we'll put in. When placing a standard word and determining whether a square in the grid that contains a letter is an interlocking square (that is, whether it has a horizontal word and a vertical word running through it), the algorithm currently tests the state of both the `HorizWord` and `VertWord` Boolean values for the square. This can be more easily determined simply by testing the score of the square.

The results are now

Current Timing: 23.68 seconds. **Improvement:** 2.7% (total speedup 3360 times)

A final note on improving algorithms: Take a look at the various algorithms that are available (see references in the "Choosing Algorithms" section, earlier in this chapter). See how different algorithms that perform the same task vary in their approach to the problem. Sometimes you need to look outside the square.

Exploring Techniques for Streamlining Code

There are many techniques for speeding up C++ code. Efficient-looking C++ code does not necessarily mean efficient machine code. It is also true that many of the C++ code improvements result in code that is less readable and less maintainable, something you should consider when sticking to project priorities.

The Modern Processor

Modern processors are very complex, and so is the machine code they run. Other than using inline assembly, usually you can't directly affect the machine code that is generated from your C++ code. However, there are a few things that you can do to improve the performance of your code. What those things are varies according to the features of a particular processor.

In the following sections we look at features of Intel's Pentium processor, in particular the Pentium II processor. Most of the features covered apply equally to AMD's K-series processors.

Branch Prediction

The most important optimization for the Pentium II processor is static and dynamic branch prediction. There are three types of branches: unconditional, forward conditional, and backward conditional. In C++, unconditional branches are generated directly from the use of con-tinue, break, and goto statements and indirectly from if, ?: and switch statements. Forward conditional branches are generated directly from if, ?:, switch, and while statements. Backward conditional branches are generated directly from for, while, and do statements.

Take for example the (badly designed) code in Listing 6.4, which can call a different algorithm to optimize the drawing of small circles.

LISTING 6.4   A Bad Example of Branching

```
if (Radius > MaxRadius) {
    return(false);
}

if (Radius < 50 && Filled) {
    CircleSmallAlgorithmFilled(X, Y, Radius);
}

if (Radius < 50 && !Filled) {
    CircleSmallAlgorithmOpen(X, Y, Radius);
}

if (Radius >= 50 && Filled) {
    CircleLargeAlgorithmFilled(X, Y, Radius);
}

if (Radius >= 50 && !Filled) {
    CircleLargeAlgorithmOpen(X, Y, Radius);
}

return (true);
```

The machine code generated by the compiler for the first two if statements is actually similar to that in Listing 6.5.

LISTING 6.5   Compiler-Generated Code for the Bad Branching Example

```
if (Radius <= MaxRadius) {
    goto ifb;
```

LISTING 6.5   Continued

```
}
return(false);

ifb:
if (Radius >= 50) {
    goto ifc;
}

if (!Filled) {
    goto ifc;
}

CircleSmallAlgorithmFilled(X, Y, Radius);

ifc:

// etc. The other three if statements contain similar code.
```

Notice in the compiler-generated code in Listing 6.5 that the `if` statements generate the oppo-site Boolean expression. Each condition in the `if` statement is a forward conditional branch. When `else` statements are used, unconditional branches are required at the end of each `if` or `else` block, except the last, to jump out of the block once all statements in it have been exe-cuted, skipping the code in all following `else` blocks.

In dynamic branch prediction, the processor stores the last four jump or continue directions that each of the previous 512 branches took. From this branch history, the processor guesses which direction a branch will take the next time and pre-fetches the instructions at the target location. It can identify patterns up to four directions in length, such as a branch that jumps every second time or one that jumps twice, continues, jumps, with this pattern repeated.

If the branch is not yet in the history, typically because the code has not been executed before, then static branch prediction comes into play. Unconditional and backward condi-tional branches are predicted to be taken (jump) and forward conditional branches are pre-dicted not to be taken (continue).

Incorrect static and dynamic branch predictions are expensive in time, particularly if they occur within a loop. An incorrect prediction means that the pre-fetched instructions must be flushed from the execution pipeline and the correct target instructions fetched.

There are two primary changes you can make in C++ code to improve branching perfor-mance. First, reduce the number of branches. This reduces the possibility of incorrect predic-tions and also reduces the amount of branch history that must be kept. The second change is to use `if else` statements (and particularly nested `if` statements) instead of multiple `if` state-ments at the same block level.

In our previous circle-drawing code, if `Radius` exceeds `MaxRadius`, then only one forward conditional branch is executed. Otherwise, seven forward conditional branches must be executed to go through each possible combination. Listing 6.6 shows how to change the code to achieve a reduction in branching.

LISTING 6.6   A Much-Improved Branching Design

```
if (Radius > MaxRadius) {
    return(false);
} else if (Radius < 50) {
    if (Filled) {
        CircleSmallAlgorithmFilled(X, Y, Radius);
    } else {
        CircleSmallAlgorithmOpen(X, Y, Radius);
    }
} else {
    if (Filled) {
        CircleLargeAlgorithmFilled(X, Y, Radius);
    } else {
        CircleLargeAlgorithmOpen(X, Y, Radius);
    }
}

return (true);
```

In Listing 6.6, the same single forward conditional branch is executed if `Radius` exceeds `MaxRadius`, but for three of the four combinations only three forward conditional and one unconditional branch are required. The last combination, `Radius >= 50` and `!Filled`, requires just the three forward conditional branches. The unconditional branch is not needed because execution simply falls through to the code following the entire `if else` block. Unfortunately, we don't have this control for the implied `if else` blocks present in `switch` statements.

The other thing that we can do to streamline branches is to improve branch predictability. When executing this code for the first time, static branch prediction comes into play. The first part of the code generated by the compiler is a forward conditional branch. Remember that this is predicted to fall through, to continue.

Suppose that 95% of the circles drawn do not exceed the maximum radius and also, this code is not held in the branch history, because a large number of branches have occurred since the last time the code was executed. Under these circumstances, the branch prediction is incorrect. We would also have bad branch prediction if most of the circles had a radius greater than or equal to 50.

You should order your C++ code so that the most likely condition is executed in the first `if` block, the second most likely in the first `else` block, and so on. Listing 6.7 shows a more efficient piece of code, assuming most circles have a large but valid radius.

Compiling and Optimizing Your Application

CHAPTER 6

253

6

COMPILING AND
OPTIMIZING YOUR
APPLICATION

LISTING 6.7   Restructured Branching to Suit the Most Common Conditions

```
if (Radius <= MaxRadius) {
    if (Radius >= 50) {
        if (Filled) {
            CircleSmallAlgorithmFilled(X, Y, Radius);
        } else {
            CircleSmallAlgorithmOpen(X, Y, Radius);
        }
    } else {
        if (Filled) {
            CircleLargeAlgorithmFilled(X, Y, Radius);
        } else {
            CircleLargeAlgorithmOpen(X, Y, Radius);
        }
    }
} else {
    return(false);
}

return (true);
```

A final possibility for Boolean expressions is to evaluate them using the bitwise operators |
and & instead of || and &&. For example, the code if ((A && B) || C) can be replaced with
if ((A & B) | C). When you use bitwise operators instead of Boolean operators, the expres-
sion turns into one large bitwise calculation, and only one forward conditional branch is
required. In some cases, bitwise operator calculation is faster than multiple branches when
using Boolean operators, but in other cases it is slower. You will need to perform some basic
profiling or timing tests to determine this.

Cache

The processor has 16KB of level-1 cache for code and 16KB of level-1 cache for data. The
level-1 cache is an area of processor memory that is used for all machine code instruction execution and memory access. If either the machine code that must be executed or the data that
must be accessed is not in the cache, then time is required to load it. Loading the code into the
cache often takes longer that it does to execute it.

When programming loops, try to keep them as tight as possible to keep the entire loop in the
code cache. The first time through the loop will be a little slower because of cache loading, but
after that it will run at full speed if it's still in the cache.

Code Tuning

We'll look at many code-tuning techniques using small code snippets along the way. At the
end of this section we'll apply several of these techniques to the Crozzle Solver application.

Four general principles apply:

- Remove redundant code. In large applications, implementation of design and code changes can render some code obsolete. A newer, possibly more efficient function typically can replace an older and slower one. Sometimes the code can be eliminated altogether.

- Don't use the `register` keyword. With register variables set to automatic, the compiler makes very good decisions about which variables should be used with registers.

- Use the `const` keyword for variables, function parameters, and member functions for which the value should not be modified. This allows the compiler to make specific optimizations accordingly.

- Don't defeat the type system. Unnecessarily mixing different data types, such as assigning a `double` to a `long`, causes data conversions that are slow and prevents the compiler from performing certain optimizations.

Now let's look at some specific tuning techniques.

Use Inline Functions

Standard function calls include overhead at the machine code level to pass and return parameters, either by pushing and popping values onto the stack or by priming specific processor registers, and to perform the actual function call and return. For very small functions such as class member access functions, this overhead is more than that of the actual function code.

> **NOTE**
>
> For information on how function calls and stack pointers work at the machine-code level, see Chapter 4, "Procedure Calls, Interrupts, and Exceptions," in Volume 1 of the Intel Architecture Software Developer's Manual. You can download this manual in PDF format from Intel's Web site at `http://developer.intel.com/design/processor/`. Select the appropriate processor, for example the Pentium II, and then enter the Manuals section.

Inline functions can be used to eliminate or reduce function call overhead. An inline function operates programmatically in exactly the same manner as a normal function. However, when the code is compiled, a copy of the function is placed inline at the position of the function call. This also enables the optimizer to work more efficiently.

There are two main drawbacks to inline functions. First, they increase the code size, particularly if the inline function is large and called from many places. Second, if the function call is within a loop, then the increased code size reduces the chance that the entire loop will fit into the code cache (as previously described).

Compiling and Optimizing Your Application

255

CHAPTER 6

6

COMPILING AND
OPTIMIZING YOUR
APPLICATION

Inline functions are defined by explicit use of the `inline` keyword for normal functions and class methods defined outside the class body, and automatically for class methods defined in the class body. Listing 6.8 demonstrates.

LISTING 6.8 An Example of Inline and Normal Functions

```
class TMyClass
{
private:
    int FValue;
public:
    void SetValue(int NewValue) { FValue = NewValue; }
    int  GetValue() const { return(FValue); }
    void DoubleIt();
    void HalveIt();
};

inline void TMyClass::DoubleIt()
{
    FValue *= 2;
}

void TMyClass::HalveIt()
{
    FValue /= 2;
}

inline int Negate(int InitValue)
{
    return(-InitValue);
}

void SomeFunction()
{
TMyClass Abc;
int NegNewVal;

    Abc.SetValue(10);
    Abc.DoubleIt();
    NegNewVal = Negate(Abc.GetValue());
}
```

In Listing 6.8 `TMyClass::SetValue()`, `TMyClass::GetValue()`, `TMyClass::DoubleIt()`, and `Negate()` are all inline functions, but `TMyClass::HalveIt()` and `SomeFunction()` are not.

> **TIP**
>
> If you are experimenting with inline functions, you should note that they are disabled by default when compiling with full debugging options and are called as normal functions. You can override this behavior to see more easily how they work in the CPU view of the debugger by unchecking Disable Inline Expansions on the Compiler tab of Project Options.

To be expanded inline, inline functions must be defined prior to the functions that call them. In Listing 6.8, if Negate() were defined after SomeFunction(), then it would not be expanded inline.

There are some restrictions to which functions can be expanded inline, particularly when exception handling is enabled. A function that has an exception specification, takes a class argument by value, or returns a class with a destructor by value will not be expanded inline.

In the Crozzle Solver application, we must resort to trial and error to see which of the main functions produced a better result when inlined. Only the CanPlace() function produces a faster result.

Current Timing: 23.46 seconds. **Improvement:** 0.9% (total speedup 3391 times)

Despite the large number of function calls involved, other factors come into play, such as the code cache and the fact that we're using the register calling convention by default (compiler options). Inline functions are best suited to small functions.

Eliminate Temporary Objects and Variables

The creation and destruction of temporary objects and variables take time, particularly for an object, which can contain complex constructor and destructor code. This should be reduced or eliminated.

Declare objects, strings, and simple variable types such as int, long, and double in the closest local scope possible. Listing 6.9 creates three temporaries: Obj, Name, and Length.

LISTING 6.9 Three Temporaries Are Created

```
void SomeFunc(bool State)
{
    TComplexObj Obj;
    String Name;
    int Length;

    if (State) {
        Name = "This is a string.";
        Length = Name.Length();
```

LISTING 6.9   Continued

```
        DoSomething(Name, Length);
    } else {
        Obj.Weight = 5.2;
        Obj.Speed = 0;
        Obj.Acceleration = 1.5;
        Obj.DisplayForce();
    }
}
```

We can reduce the time spent on temporary creation by localizing their scope or eliminating them altogether. Listing 6.10 demonstrates this.

LISTING 6.10   Temporaries Moved to Minimal Scope

```
void SomeFunc(bool State)
{
    if (State) {
        String Name;
        Name = "This is a string.";
        DoSomething(Name, Name.Length());
    } else {
        TComplexObj Obj;
        Obj.Weight = 5.2;
        Obj.Speed = 0;
        Obj.Acceleration = 1.5;
        Obj.DisplayForce();
    }
}
```

To speed up the creation of temporaries, initialize objects at declaration by using an initialization or copy constructor. Simply declaring them and then assigning an initial value uses the default constructor followed by the copy constructor. Listing 6.11 shows how Listing 6.10 can be improved with this principle.

LISTING 6.11   Temporaries Initialized at Declaration

```
void SomeFunc(bool State)
{
    if (State) {
        String Name("This is a string.");
        DoSomething(Name, Name.Length());
    } else {
        TComplexObj Obj(5.2, 0, 1.5);
        Obj.DisplayForce();
    }
}
```

When incrementing or decrementing, using the postfix ++ and - - operators, a temporary is created to store the return value, as in the ++ (postfix) operator of MyIntClass used in the expression A++ in Listing 6.12.

LISTING 6.12   A Temporary Created for operator++ to Return Initial Value

```
class TMyIntClass
{
private:
    int FValue;
public:
    TMyIntClass(int Init) { FValue = Init; }
    int GetValue() { return FValue; }
    // Postfix ++ operator.
    int operator++(int) {
        int Tmp = FValue;
        FValue = FValue + 1;
        return(Tmp);
    }
    // Prefix ++ operator.
    int operator++() {
        FValue = FValue + 1;
        return(FValue);
    }
};

void MyFunc()
{
TMyIntClass A(1);

    // A temporary is used.
    A++;

    // The return value of A++ was not required.
    // It is better to use the following because no temporary is used.
    ++A;
}
```

If the return value of the postfix increment or decrement operator is not required, use prefix increment or decrement instead. Then, no temporary is used. In Listing 6.12 we can eliminate the temporary by using ++A instead of A++.

When an object is passed by value to a function, a temporary object is created with the copy constructor for the function to use. It is preferable to pass by const reference instead to eliminate the temporary. For example, a function defined as MyFunc(TMyClass A) should be defined as MyFunc(const TMyClass &A) to eliminate the temporary object. A temporary is also created if a const reference parameter is passed but the types do not match.

Compiling and Optimizing Your Application

CHAPTER 6

259

6

COMPILING AND
OPTIMIZING YOUR
APPLICATION

A final temporary object elimination technique is called *return value optimization*. Where an object or variable is to be returned by value and that value is created only for return, it is much better to build it in-place rather than to create a temporary to hold the value and return the temporary. This is demonstrated in Listing 6.13.

LISTING 6.13   Return Value Optimization

```
TMyClass TmpReturnFunc(bool Something)
{
    TMyClass TmpObj(0, 0);

    if (Something) {
        TMyClass Obj1(1.5, 2.2),
                 Obj2(1.8, 6.1);
        TmpObj = Obj1 + Obj2;
    }
    return(TmpObj);
}

TMyClass FastReturnFunc(bool Something)
{
    if (Something) {
        TMyClass Obj1(1.5, 2.2),
                 Obj2(1.8, 6.1);
        return(Obj1 + Obj2);
    } else {
        return(TMyClass(0, 0));
    }
}

void MyFunc()
{
    TMyClass A;

    A = TmpReturnFunc(AddThem);   // Temp was created in TmpReturnFunc
    A = FastReturnFunc(AddThem);  // Return object built directly in A.
}
```

In the first function, `TmpObj` must be constructed and destructed. In the second function, the return value can be built in the location of assigned object `A`.

Invariant Calculations

Invariant calculations that appear inside a loop should be moved outside the loop. In Listing 6.14, the invariant `if` statement and `x + 5` calculation in the first section of the code are moved outside the loop in the second section. Now they are evaluated once instead of each time through the loop.

LISTING 6.14 Moving Invariant Calculations Outside the Loop

```
// Slow loop.
for (int i = 0 ; i < 10 ; i++) {
    if (InitializeType == Clear) {
        a[i] = 0;
        b[i] = 0;
    } else {
        a[i] = y[i];
        b[i] = x + 5;
    }
}

// Fast loops.
if (InitializeType == Clear) {
    for (int i = 0 ; i < 10 ; i++) {
        a[i] = 0;
        b[i] = 0;
    }
} else {
    int Total = x + 5;
    for (int i = 0 ; i < 10 ; i++) {
        a[i] = y[i];
        b[i] = Total;
    }
}
```

Watch out for any invariant portions of expressions, such as parts of a calculation that are fixed, invariant array index values, and pointer math contained within loops. Move them out, also.

Array Indexing and Pointer Math

If you have an expression that uses complex array indexing or pointer math, and the expression is used several times, it might be better to calculate a pointer to the correct data element or object and reuse that pointer. Consider the sections of code in Listing 6.15 from the crozzle solver algorithm. Because the lines are so long, they have been split into multiple lines.

LISTING 6.15 Complex Array Indexing (Pointer Math)

```
// Complex array index part one from SolveStandardWord().
k = CrozLetterPos[Words[CurrWordNum].Letters[CurrLetterIdx]].NumPositions-1;
while (k >= 0 &&
        CrozLetterPos[Words[CurrWordNum].Letters[
            CurrLetterIdx]].WordPlacedIdx[k] >=
            PlacedIdxLimit) {
    CurrX = CrozLetterPos[Words[CurrWordNum].Letters[
                CurrLetterIdx]].Position[k].x;
```

Compiling and Optimizing Your Application

261

CHAPTER 6

6

COMPILING AND
OPTIMIZING YOUR
APPLICATION

LISTING 6.15   Continued

```
        CurrY = CrozLetterPos[Words[CurrWordNum].Letters[
                    CurrLetterIdx]].Position[k].y;
        // More code here.
    }


    // Complex array index part two from PlaceWord().
    CrozLetterPos[Words[WordNum].Letters[LetterIdx]].Position[
                CrozLetterPos[Words[WordNum].Letters[
                    LetterIdx]].NumPositions].x = CurrX;
    CrozLetterPos[Words[WordNum].Letters[LetterIdx]].Position[
                CrozLetterPos[Words[WordNum].Letters[
                    LetterIdx]].NumPositions].y = StartY;
    CrozLetterPos[Words[WordNum].Letters[LetterIdx]].WordPlacedIdx[
                CrozLetterPos[Words[WordNum].Letters[
                    LetterIdx]].NumPositions] =
                        CrozGrid[StartY][CurrX].HorizPlacedIdx;
    CrozLetterPos[Words[WordNum].Letters[
                    LetterIdx]].NumPositions++;
```

If you can follow that mess, you're doing well! In both sections of code it is better to use a temporary pointer to the correct data item, a TCrozLetterPos structure. Listing 6.16 shows how to change the code to use temporary pointers.

LISTING 6.16   Simplified Array Indexing (Pointer Math)

```
// Simple array index part one from SolveStandardWord().
TCrozLetterPos *TmpPos;

    TmpPos = &CrozLetterPos[Words[CurrWordNum].Letters[CurrLetterIdx]];

    k = TmpPos->NumPositions-1;
    while (k >= 0 && TmpPos->WordPlacedIdx[k] >= PlacedIdxLimit) {
        CurrX = TmpPos->Position[k].x;
        CurrY = TmpPos->Position[k].y;
        // More code here.
    }

// Simple array index part two from PlaceWord().
TCrozLetterPos *TmpPos;

    TmpPos = &CrozLetterPos[Words[WordNum].Letters[LetterIdx]];
    TmpPos->Position[TmpPos->NumPositions].x    = CurrX;
    TmpPos->Position[TmpPos->NumPositions].y    = StartY;
    TmpPos->WordPlacedIdx[TmpPos->NumPositions] =
        CrozGrid[StartY][CurrX].HorizPlacedIdx;
    TmpPos->NumPositions++;
```

The two sections of code are much more readable and perform much better.

Current Timing: 22.28 seconds. **Improvement:** 5.3% (total speedup 3571 times)

That's an improvement of 5% just for these two small parts.

Floating-Point Math

With current processors, the floating-point instructions are very fast. The floating-point functions implemented in C++Builder, such as `cos()` and `exp()`, usually are fast enough. However, to achieve the ultimate floating-point math speed, consider using the new C++Builder 5 `fastmath` functions.

To use them, add `#include <fastmath.h>` to the units that need them. Many standard math routines will be automatically remapped to `fastmath` routines, including `cos()`, `exp()`, `log()`, `sin()`, `atan()`, and `sqrt()`. To turn off the Auto-Remap feature and use the `fastmath` routines, explicitly add `#define _FM_NO_REMAP` before including the header and use `_fm_<function>` instead of `<function>` where applicable. For example, replace `cos()` with `_fm_cos()`. See the online help for more information.

CAUTION

The `fastmath` routines do not check most error conditions. Use them only where speed is a high priority and your application has been thoroughly tested.

One worthwhile floating-point math code tuning technique is the use of floating-point divides in a loop. If you are doing a floating point divide `X = A/B` and the divisor `B` is constant, calculate a temporary variable `T = 1/B` before the loop and change the calculation to `X = A * T`. This is beneficial because floating-point multiplication is slightly faster than a floating-point divide.

Other Code-Tuning Techniques

There are two other techniques that deserve mention but are more specialized for certain applications. They include

- Disable Runtime Type Identification if possible. To do this, you must refrain from using `dynamic_cast` and `typeid`.

- Avoid virtual functions where possible. Each call results in a function table lookup.

- Where graphics are necessary, minimize repainting. Use `InvalidateRect()` to repaint only the portions of the control that are necessary. Use an off-screen surface to draw an object and then copy to the screen in one operation, or hide the control during the procedure using the `Hide()` and `Show()` methods.

Compiling and Optimizing Your Application

CHAPTER 6

263

6

COMPILING AND
OPTIMIZING YOUR
APPLICATION

In the `SolveWord()` function, we periodically call `Application->ProcessMessages()` to handle any user interaction and display updates that are pending. This is necessary because the program is executing code intensely and ignoring other events. If we remove this part of the code, we reduce the run time by 1.5%. We'll deliberately leave it in so that the user can interrupt the solve process and change view options.

That's it for code tuning. We looked at several of the most useful techniques for improving the performance of your application. Now we need to look at a few other tuning aspects.

Techniques for Streamlining Data

Just as there are techniques for streamlining code, there also are techniques for streamlining data. As we saw earlier, the processor has a cache for code and data. It is just as important to keep data in the cache as it is to keep code there.

Sequential memory access is faster than random memory access because a block is transferred to the data cache as each portion of memory is read. The data to the end of that block is accessed within the cache, which is very fast. As a result, linked lists, hash tables, and trees are very inefficient, because the data is not stored sequentially.

> **TIP**
>
> If you use linked lists, use a custom managed-memory pool. Allocate space for several nodes in the linked list and use the nodes for objects that are created and deleted in the list. When an object is deleted, do not free the memory; instead, reuse it for a subsequent object. This enhances location of data and avoids the overhead of allocating and freeing memory for each object.

The use of smaller data types increases the possibility that the required data is in the cache, because more variables and objects will fit in. This is particularly important with the use of structures and objects. When using multidimensional arrays, keep them as small as possible.

It is important when designing data structures that items have a good locality of reference. If you have two arrays, X `A[]` and Y `B[]`, you must decide the best way to structure the data, depending on how it is to be accessed. If the array `A[]` is accessed independently of `B[]`, it is better to declare them separately. If both arrays are accessed at the same time, particularly with the same index, then it is better to group array items together. Listing 6.17 demonstrates both methods.

LISTING 6.17 Separate and Simultaneous Access for Good Locality of Reference

```cpp
// Good for separate sequential access.
X A[100];
Y B[100];

void SepFunc()
{
    int Sum = 0;
    for (int i = 0 ; i < 100 ; i++) {
        Sum += A[i];
    }

    // later in code.
    B[Index] = Q * R;
}

// Good for access to both arrays simultaneously.
struct {
    X A;
    Y B;
} T[100];

void SimFunc()
{
    int AveDiff = 0;
    for (int i = 0 ; i < 100 ; i++) {
        AveDiff += T.B[i] - T.A[i];
    }
    AveDiff /= 100;
}
```

By defining substructures to contain array items, we can modify the Crozzle Solver application to use better locality of reference in the TCrozLetterPos and TUnsolved structures. In doing so, the time actually increases to 22.65 seconds! In optimizing TCrozLetterPos, a 12-byte structure TPlacedLetter was created as the array item. This has stopped the processor from being able to use power of two pointer math in the machine code to calculate the position of the array items. Power of two math is supported within machine code instructions without a performance penalty.

Padding TPlacedLetter with a 4-byte int to bring it to a total of 16 bytes (2 to the power of 4) yields a time of 22.04 seconds. We can do even better by changing the two int values in the TPos structure to 2-byte short values. This makes TPlacedLetter 8 bytes, a power of two, but we now have to pad the less-used TAdjLetter array item to 8 bytes by adding a dummy short value. Now the time is

Current Timing: 21.79 seconds. **Improvement:** 2.2% (total speedup 3651 times)

Compiling and Optimizing Your Application

CHAPTER 6

265

6

COMPILING AND
OPTIMIZING YOUR
APPLICATION

A multidimensional array such as T[5][10] is stored as 5 sets of 10 items of type T. What this means is that the items T[0][0] to T[0][9] are located adjacently in memory, followed by T[1][0] to T[1][9] and so on, right through to T[4][9]. Because of this ordering, there is a slow way and a fast way to access all items of the array in a nested loop. This is shown in Listing 6.18.

LISTING 6.18 Accessing Data in a Multidimensional Array

```
// Slow way to clear the array. Indexing is not sequential.
for (a = 0 ; a < 10 ; a++) {
    for (b = 0 ; b < 5 ; b++) {
        T[b][a] = 0;
    }
}

// Fast way to clear the array. Indexing is sequential.
for (b = 0 ; b < 5 ; b++) {
    for (a = 0 ; a < 10 ; a++) {
        T[b][a]  = 0;
    }
}
```

The crozzle application already reads through the two-dimensional grid in the correct method.

Another technique for streamlining data is to use reference counting to avoid constructing and destructing an object when it is used multiple times. If you dynamically create unchangeable (const) objects, consolidate the multiple instances. Create an instance of the object using new the first time it is required and set a reference count variable to 1. On subsequent instances, simply return a pointer to the same object and increase the reference count. When the object is no longer required and the reference count reaches zero, it can be deleted.

Finally, redundant data is just as bad as redundant code. Find and remove it.

Hand-Tuning Assembly Code

Writing assembly code these days is a black art. The instruction set for the Pentium II processor contains over 200 integer instructions, almost 100 floating-point instructions, and about 30 system instructions. In addition to those "regular" instructions, there's about 60 streaming SIMD extension instructions and around 60 MMX instructions. Throw in the processor nuances such as level-1 and level-2 cache, multiple pipelines that support parallel execution, paging, branch prediction, specific register use, dynamic dataflow analysis, speculative execution, and other detailed features and it all looks a bit too hard.

Despite all that you need to learn to be able to write efficient assembly code, it has one big advantage: ultimate control. You can design code that will outperform an equivalent set of code written in C++ because you can use specific features of the processor and machine code to optimize at the lowest level. The C++ compiler can generate and optimize only the code that you write in C++. One of the main advantages with using a high-level language, and a disadvantage in this case, is that it hides the underlying native machine code.

Teaching and demonstrating x86 (the Pentium processor family) assembly code is beyond the scope of this book. There are many great books out there if you're interested. Some good references available at your fingertips are

- The Art of Assembly Language Programming (`http://webster.cs.ucr.edu/`)   An online book with over 1500 pages, available for download in PDF format or viewable online in HTML.
- Intel Architecture Software Developer's Manual (`http://developer.intel.com/design/processor/`)   This is a three-volume set with just about everything you want to know about the Pentium processors. It is available for download from the Manuals section.
- Iczelion's Win32 Assembly HomePage (`http://win32asm.cjb.net`)   An excellent Win32 assembly site with great tutorials and links.
- Optimizing for Pentium Microprocessors (`http://www.agner.org/assem/`)   Agner Fog's Web site, containing detailed information on optimizing assembly code for Pentium processors.
- The x86 Programming Newsgroup (`comp.lang.asm.x86`).

To get more familiar with assembly code, you should enable all debug options and disable optimizations. Step through your code at the machine-code level via the CPU view in the debugger. Simply add a breakpoint to your code, run your application and, when the breakpoint is hit, bring up the CPU view. Stepping over and into machine code works the same as stepping over and into your C++ code. Examine the C++ code and equivalent assembly code.

TIP

You can generate assembly code listings of your C++ source files by adding the `-B` option to the `CFLAG1` section in the project file and checking Generate Listing and Expanded Listing on the Tasm page of Project Options. Each CPP file will generate an equivalent ASM file when the project is compiled. A separate method is to run `BCC32.EXE -I<Include Path> -S file.cpp` on the command line. C++ code appears as comments; useful comments are also given on registers that contain C++ variables.

In several of the previous sections, I've described some of the processor-specific features such as the instruction and data cache and branch prediction. They are just as applicable to assembly code as they are to C++ code.

Compiling and Optimizing Your Application

CHAPTER 6

267

6

COMPILING AND
OPTIMIZING YOUR
APPLICATION

Writing assembly code is much more difficult than writing C++ code, and it is much easier to introduce bugs. Also, it is much harder to find bugs. Consider maintainability and the skills of other programmers working on the project when deciding whether or not to optimize using inline assembly code.

Assembly code can be added directly in your C++ code using the asm keyword for individual assembly statements or in a block enclosed in braces. A register can be used in C++ code by prefixing it with an underscore, such as _EDX, _ECX, and so on. Listing 6.19 shows C++ code that contains an inline assembly code block to compute the factorial of an integer.

LISTING 6.19 An Example of Inline Assembly Code to Compute a Factorial

```
int Factorial(int Value)
{
    _EDX = Value;
    asm {
        push ebp
        mov  ebp,esp
        push ecx
        push edx
        mov [ebp-0x04],edx
        mov eax,0x00000001
        cmp dword ptr [ebp-0x04],0x02
        jl end
top:
        imul dword ptr [ebp-0x04]
        dec dword ptr [ebp-0x04]
        cmp dword ptr [ebp-0x04],0x02
        jnl top
end:
        pop edx
        pop ecx
        pop ebp
    }
    return (_EAX);
}
```

As you can see, inline assembly code is more complex than C++ code. Here are some tips when writing inline assembly code:

- When writing assembly code, you'll get the most benefit producing it from scratch, forgetting about any C++ deficiencies. It's not a good idea to try to improve on the assembly code produced by the optimizing compiler.

- Break code into small logical pieces, use well-defined interfaces, and document the code well.

- Use instruction pairing wherever possible. Often you will need to write assembly code that executes out of logical order to make best use of parallel execution.

- Reduce dependency chains. Break up statements that rely on the value of the previous statement to make better use of instruction pairing.

- When performing lengthy instructions such as floating-point instructions, make sure that the processor has something else to do during this time. Pair with other code.

- Always match a return (RET) instruction with a call (CALL) instruction to make best use of the return stack buffer (RSB).

- Align data to make best use of space and instruction speed. In particular, align data on 32-byte boundaries to avoid cache-line misses.

- Using inline assembly code affects the compiler optimizations performed to the function as a whole. Unlike some other optimizers, the C++Builder optimizer still performs code optimizations on a function containing inline assembly. You should perform timings to determine whether the improvements in using inline assembly code outweigh the loss in compiler optimizations.

You should note that there are particular register restrictions when using inline assembly code within C++. Register values are not guaranteed to be preserved across separate asm blocks. You must preserve the ECS register with functions using the __fastcall calling convention. You should always preserve the ESP and EBP registers. For other restrictions, see the references previously listed.

Good luck with your hand-tuned assembly code!

Using External Optimization

Apart from the internal application issues, sometimes optimization can be performed externally. We saw earlier that the speed of the various sort algorithms depends on the initial ordering of the data. This is true for other applications as well.

In the Crozzle Solver application, the order of the words in the word list affects the run time. It is better to list the words in order from longest to shortest. Doing so produces the following result:

Current Timing: 17.94 seconds. **Improvement:** 21.5% (total speedup 4435 times)

Although not a speed optimization, with an open-ended solve such as the list of 115 words in the RunPartial.crz file, it would be better to set the word order such that the words most likely to produce the highest score are placed first in the word list. Some trade-off between the letter scores of each word and the length of the word would make an optimal order. Additionally, for the user to get an acceptable result for a long word list, a better approach would be to solve small areas of the grid using selection bounding and build on the solution a piece at a time.

Compiling and Optimizing Your Application

CHAPTER 6

269

6

COMPILING AND
OPTIMIZING YOUR
APPLICATION

Execution Speed Optimization Summary

I've shown you many techniques for optimizing the design, algorithm, code, and data and given an overview of using assembly code and external optimization influences. For the Crozzle Solver application, there are several other optimizations that can be implemented, such as the following:

- Using `const` function parameters where appropriate.
- Merging the Boolean `IsValid`, `IsLetter`, and `IsBlank` values into a single enumeration to save on data space.
- Searching for words based on non-interlocking squares in the grid rather than searching for squares based on the letters in each word.
- Performing a round robin of words to place at each level in recursion rather than always starting at the beginning of the word list. This would not be faster but would more likely produce a higher score in a given amount of time.
- Keeping a record of interlocking squares and using only those when computing the score of the current crozzle.

I'll leave these optimizations up to you. See what else you can come up with.

The initial execution time of the crozzle solver was 79,560 seconds, or 22.1 hours. The final execution time was 17.94 seconds, an improvement of 4435 times.

For $O(2^N)$ algorithms such as the crozzle solver, the level of speed increase shown here is sometimes achievable, though this is fairly rare in general algorithms. As a separate speed measure, solving the `RunPartial.crz` file for a period of five minutes with the initial crozzle solver produced a high score of 402. Using the final crozzle solver, the high score is 484.

Optimizing Other Aspects of Your Application

Besides optimizing for execution speed, there are several other aspects that can be optimized in applications today, such as program size, runtime memory size, disk access speed, and network bandwidth. Each has several overall techniques, some of which are listed briefly in the next two sections.

Optimizing Program Size

Optimizing for program size assumes that smaller is better. This is usually for reasons such as distribution, where floppy and CD-ROM capacities and Internet access speeds are a constraint, and for reduction in system memory used, which is particularly important if there are many applications running on the same machine.

The C++Builder compiler options include a Size Optimization setting. This will produce a better result than disabling optimizations and a slightly better result than the Speed Optimization setting. The other main project settings that affect code size are several debugging options, which should be disabled and Data Alignment set to Byte.

If the shipping size is important, you can build with runtime libraries and packages and ship these in the first release. This will control the size of subsequent updates. Use a modular design and send only the modules that have changed, or use a patch program to apply a small set of changes to a program.

Going somewhat against speed optimizations, you can reduce the program size by using algorithms instead of static data tables. You can also reduce program size by creating the tables dynamically.

If your program uses a lot of graphical or sound data, you can sometimes trade quality for size. Use JPEG for photo pictures and GIF or PNG for simple graphics. Use a higher compression ratio, fewer colors, or smaller images. Reduce the number of bits or the sample rate and consider mono over stereo for sound.

Don't forget the many file compression programs that are available, such as ZIP. Additionally, most installation programs will compress your files. One final consideration is the use of a runtime EXE and DLL decompressor. These have a slower startup time, but your program is always compact.

Final Optimization Aspects

To find out more, make useof the Borland newsgroups and the Web sites devoted to programming.

- **Disk access**   Sequential read and write is fastest because it minimizes disk head movement. Read in large chunks, not a character at a time.
- **Startup time**   Specify a unique and non-overlapping load address for all of your DLLs. Minimize the use of ActiveX controls where they will be visible at startup. Display a splash screen, perhaps with a tip-of-the-day to distract the user.
- **Network latency**   Send multiple packets simultaneously and receive replies in a block.
- **Client/server database access**   Use cached updates. Perform a potentially long query in a thread (such as for an update). The thread can come back with a list of errors to allow the user to return and fix them one at a time. Use SQL Monitor to see what your program is up to. For incremental search fields, use a delay before retrieving the matching data set. For a grid or list box load no more than perhaps two screens of items. Set scrollbar size appropriately. Use ranges instead of filters to restrict the set of records to return.

Remember that these rules apply generally. There will certainly be instances where you will need to go against some of them and cases where the opposite is true.

Summary

In this chapter we looked at how the compiler works, various methods to speed up compile times, and new features in C++Builder 5. We also took an in-depth look at optimization, particularly optimizing for execution speed.

Compiling and optimizing are advanced topics that are important to understand. I have found that knowledge of both from an early stage has assisted me no end in programming and debugging, and I encourage you to examine these topics further through the references provided throughout the chapter and in your own research.

Debugging Your Application

Jarrod Hollingworth

IN THIS CHAPTER

- **Debugging Overview**
- **Basic Debugging Techniques**
- **Using the C++Builder Interactive Debugger**
- **CodeGuard**
- **Advanced Debugging**
- **Testing**

Throughout this chapter we will examine many aspects of debugging applications. The term "applications" is used in a fairly loose sense; many of the principles apply to all types of projects.

Debugging is an advanced topic and an important aspect of programming that is often looked at by developers in only a cursory manner. This chapter is for all readers regardless of experience.

We'll not be covering debugging of specific areas of development such as ISAPI, DirectX, or MIDAS applications, though we will cover briefly debugging DLLs and using remote debugging, both of which can be extended to debugging COM, DCOM, CORBA, and ActiveX servers. We will also cover CodeGuard and several other new features in C++Builder 5, with some notes on testing.

Debugging Overview

Debugging is the process of locating of and correcting software bugs. Admiral Grace Hopper coined the term "bug" on September 9, 1945, when a moth was found to be the cause of a glitch in the Harvard Mark II mainframe computer. This term was readily adopted in software development to mean a programming glitch or error.

So why do we have bugs? Writing bug-free code is very difficult. You may remember the public announcement from Microsoft of the thousands of bugs present in the first consumer release of Windows 2000. In large and complex systems, the number of bugs can be huge.

Bugs can be classified into several categories:

- **Syntactical**   The compiler catch this type of error. The presence of syntactical errors suggests that other less-noticeable bugs may also be present.

- **Build**   Under certain conditions, a compilation might not produce the correct executable. This may be caused by doing a Make instead of a Build after incorporating source code changes from a version control system, using an incorrect library path or include path, or continuing to make software changes while a background compilation is in progress.

- **Semantic**   These include using uninitialized variables, using & instead of &&, and using the wrong variable name. The compiler cannot detect these.

- **Algorithm Logic**   Bugs caused by logic errors are more difficult to find. A simple example would be sorting a list of items by a size property with the largest first instead of the smallest first.

- **Pairing**   Some programming tasks, usually resource-based, require that a second task be performed in response to an initial task. Examples of pairing bugs are memory that is created but not freed, files that are opened but not closed, a stack onto which an item is pushed on but never popped off. A subtler example is a reference count that is incremented when an object is used and not decremented when it is released.

- **Interface**   This is a mismatch in data sent from one application to another, or in the interface definition. It is usually caused by an incorrect protocol or interface version.

- **Side Effects**   By executing some code, you inadvertently cause another part of the system to function incorrectly. Overwriting memory and initializing a variable with the wrong value are examples.

- **Basic Functionality**   Basic functionality bugs are those in which a feature works but not as intended, for example because some part of it was left out or because results are produced for data from an incorrect source.

Most bugs fall under one of these categories. There are other, less specific categories, such as user interface bugs that result in an application that is difficult to use and performance bugs causing the application to be too slow.

The first principle of writing bug-free software is that you can't rely on the compiler to pick up your mistakes. By all means, enable all possible compiler warnings and take notice of them, but as a secondary function only. Of the bug categories listed previously, the compiler can help with only the first one. When you select to Make or Build the project, you should be confident that it will compile and run correctly.

The Code Insight feature in C++Builder contains several features that both increase your productivity and reduce the incidence of bugs. These include code completion, code parameters, code templates, and ToolTip symbol insight. Each of these can help reduce bugs. See the C++Builder online help for further information on these great productivity features.

Project Guidelines

Debugging should be seen as the last resort in the whole software error overview. You should endeavor to minimize bugs from the very beginning and build automatic defense and detection mechanisms into your software.

In the "Optimizing: An Introduction" section of Chapter 6, "Compiling and Optimizing Your Application," the following project objectives were presented:

- Speed
- Size
- Maintainability
- Testability
- Reusability

- Robustness
- Scalability
- Portability
- Usability
- Safety

If maintainability, testability, reusability, robustness, usability, or safety is important to your project, then prevention, detection, and removal of bugs will be a very important process throughout the project.

The saying "a rolling stone gathers no moss" is not true for software and bugs, if you consider the rolling stone to be your evolving application and the moss to be bugs! The more development you do, the more likely it is that bugs will be introduced. Don't spend time developing features that are not likely to be used just because it's fun to do. First, it is time that could be better spent making the product more robust. Secondly, these features can be the cause of unnecessary bugs.

Spend time finding stable third-party components and libraries that you can use in your application. If you don't have to develop it yourself, you're less likely to introduce bugs yourself.

When a new feature is implemented in the application, inform all other project members. This will alert them to the changes or potential conflicts in interfaces and allow them to reuse the new functionality that you have added. This reduces the likelihood of two separate implementations of the same feature and thus reduces development time and the incident of bugs.

Programming Guidelines

Most good programming techniques reduce bugs and the time required locating and fixing them. Chapter 3, "Programming in C++Builder," discusses several coding style issues and good programming practices. Use good object-oriented design and good information and functionality hiding. Each C++ function or class method should have one well-defined task.

A very important factor in all software development is code readability and source-level documentation. Regardless of whether it is just you or a team of programmers developing the application, you should always write code as if other people need to understand it. Comment on particularly tricky sections of code or code that has been programmed a certain way for efficiency or validation purposes.

During development, ask yourself what assumptions you are making. Assumptions can cause problems later, because quite often the normal boundaries in code and data are crossed. You should verify that the assumption is true before continuing, particularly if the assumption is based on user input or input from interfaces to external systems.

If specific functionality or output is mission critical or has an impact on safety, you should ensure that it works correctly. Consider using a second method, such as a different algorithm, to validate the results of the first.

During development, you should step through each line of your source code mentally and then using the debugger as each small part is completed. Nothing will give you a better understanding of how your code works.

You should also be very careful when fixing existing bugs not to introduce others. Don't assume because you've made a quick fix that it will work or that you haven't broken something else. Stick to the rule "if it ain't broke, don't fix it!" Don't pull one nut off each of three wheels to attach the fourth.

Preventative measures in C++ involve checking error return values of functions, throwing exceptions, using exception handlers to catch anticipated and unanticipated exceptions, and using good type checking. Some exception handling information is given in Chapters 3 and 4, "Advanced Programming with C++Builder." Don't forget to test your error handling code, too.

The Debugging Task

When you finally come to the task of debugging, and you always will, there are a few key concepts that you should follow.

When you find a bug, document and prioritize it immediately. You can use the new To-Do list feature of C++Builder 5, detailed in Chapter 2, "C++Builder Projects and More on the IDE," or simply use an ordered text file if you don't have formal bug-tracking software. Once the bug is documented, you should fix it as soon as possible. Don't put it off until the end of the project. This is one of the major reasons for out-of-control bug lists and poor estimation of development time. If you keep to a near-zero bug list, you are doing yourself and the project manager a huge favor.

The bug list is not always bad news, particularly when most of the bugs have been moved to the "fixed" list. Consider making the bug list and fixed list available to your customers (whether they are internal or external). Personally, I'm more confident in a product that is upfront and in which I can see that bugs are being resolved.

Before implementing a bug fix, you should make a backup copy of the source code. Use a version control system or simply save the original source file under another name or in a separate folder.

A fantastic reference for all programmers is the book *Code Complete* by Steve McConnell, published by Microsoft Press (ISBN 1-55615-484-4, 1993). It covers all aspects of software construction and is a great read. I refer to it as "the programmer's bible." It is still my favorite book on software development.

Finally, never allow the same bug to bite you twice. Learn from your own and others' mistakes and prevent them from happening in the future.

Basic Debugging Techniques

In this section, we will examine some basic methods for locating bugs. In later sections, we will see how to locate bugs using the interactive debugger supplied with C++Builder and look at several advanced debugging topics.

Before embarking on a possibly lengthy debugging mission, if you suspect that the problem lies in third-party components or libraries, you should check with the vendor to determine if such a problem is a known issue and if there is an update or patch that will correct it.

The main techniques of locating bugs are

- Manual or programmatic examination of application output as a result of testing.
- Manual or programmatic examination of the execution path and internal data.
- Programmatically trapping invalid conditions using assertions and other checks.
- Programmatically catching exceptions through the implementation of exception handling.

Manual examination relies on stepping through code or outputting information at appropriate places, often using the C++Builder interactive debugger. Using the knowledge of what the input data is and the correct course of action that the application should take, you can determine if it is functioning correctly.

Programmatically trapping invalid conditions and exceptions can tell you exactly where the bug was discovered. The problem is that where the bug is discovered can often be very far from where the bug starts. Use these techniques as a starting point for locating bugs.

Several of the techniques presented here are described in more detail later in this chapter. To track down the specific source of a bug, three main processes can be used, as described in the following list.

- Mentally trace backward from where the bug is detected through the execution path that has occurred, using the knowledge of variable and object states. Examine the call stack to give you clues as to the execution path. Follow the data that could have caused the bug to occur. Use manual or programmatic examination or strategically placed assertions for subsequent runs to narrow the source of the bug.
- From a point in the execution path that is known to be sound, walk through the code, mentally or using the interactive debugger, toward the point where the bug was detected. Use the same techniques as for the trace backward method.

- The third method is called "divide and conquer" and involves a kind of binary search or bracketing to find the bug. The region is refined—typically halved as in a binary search—repeatedly by changing the outer inspection points and narrowing the source of the bug to a small section of code. Again, use the techniques described for the trace backward method.

However you decide to locate the bug, it should be a systematic approach based on correct and reproducible program output or debug information and not some random or sporadic approach. If you cannot reproduce the error reliably, then it is likely that the error is caused by uninitialized data or memory overwrites.

If in a relatively short period of time you have not found the bug, take a short break and then try a different approach or consult another developer for his view. Often, describing the problem to someone else helps you realize where the bug is located. Be especially wary of recently modified code.

When you find a bug, spend the time to find the real cause of the problem and the right solution. Don't use quick fixes, which are likely to miss other error causes or introduce other bugs. Once the fix is implemented, test it thoroughly.

Outputting Debug Information

A basic debugging technique is to output information at one or more places in your application to see what code is being executed and the state of particular objects and variables. Only you can decide what output is appropriate, but you should display input data to verify that it is correct, display parameters passed to key functions, and display execution path information to show you what decisions the application makes at key stages. We'll look at several techniques in this section that can be used to output this information.

A useful new feature in C++Builder 5 is that _DEBUG is defined in the Conditional defines list on the Directories/Conditionals tab of the project options when the Full Debug button on the Compiler tab is pressed. It is defined by default. When the Release button is pressed, _DEBUG is removed from the Conditional defines list. You can change the name of this definition by adding a string value named DebugDefine in the HKEY_CURRENT_USERS\Software\Borland\ C++Builder\5.0\Debugging key in the Windows Registry.

The _DEBUG definition allows you to specify certain sections of code that should be compiled into the application only when it is compiled with Full Debug options by using the #ifdef and #endif preprocessor directives. Users of C++Builder 4 and earlier must manually add and remove _DEBUG or a similar definition to the Conditional defines list or specify it in code with #define _DEBUG. We'll use the _DEBUG definition throughout the remainder of this section.

There are several ways to output debugging information from within your code. The simplest method is to use `printf()` or `cout <<` statements if you are debugging a console application. You must include the `stdio.h` header file when using `printf()` and `iostream.h` when using `cout <<`. Listing 7.1 shows how either of these methods can be used to write a generic debug message output function, `MyDebugOutput()`, and an example of how it might be used from within an application. The text `Debug:` will be displayed at the start of each debug message, to distinguish debug messages from regular application output.

LISTING 7.1   Outputting Debug Messages in Console Applications

```
#include <stdio.h>
#include <iostream.h>

void MyDebugOutput(AnsiString OutputMessage)
{
    // Method 1: Display the debug message using printf().
    printf("Debug: %s\n", OutputMessage.c_str());

    // Method 2: Display the debug message using cout <<.
    cout << "Debug: " << OutputMessage.c_str() << endl;
}

void NormalFunc(int MaxLines)
{
    // Application code here.

    MyDebugOutput("Before loop, MaxLines=" + IntToStr(MaxLines));
    for (int i = 0 ; i < MaxLines ; i++) {
        MyDebugOutput("In loop, i=" + IntToStr(i));

        // More application code here.
    }
}
```

For GUI applications, you can use a label, an edit box, or a memo on a form or use `ShowMessage()` or `MessageDlg()` pop-up dialog boxes. You can even use the Win32 API function `MessageBeep(0xFFFFFFFF)` to make a sound for an audible rather than visual cue. Listing 7.2 shows the `MyDebugOutput()` function from Listing 7.1, rewritten to use these GUI output methods. The `MyDebugBeep()` function in Listing 7.2 can be called anywhere that you need an audio cue in your application.

LISTING 7.2 Outputting Debug Messages in GUI Applications

```cpp
void MyDebugOutput(AnsiString OutputMessage)
{
    // Method 1: Display the debug message to a label, edit box and
    // memo on the main form. Any one of these is probably sufficient.
    MainForm->ErrorLabel->Caption = OutputMessage;
    MainForm->ErrorEdit->Text = OutputMessage;
    MainForm->ErrorMemo->Text = OutputMessage;

    // Method 2: Display the debug message using ShowMessage().
    ShowMessage(OutputMessage);

    // Method 3: Display the debug message using MessageDlg().
    MessageDlg(OutputMessage, mtInformation, TMsgDlgButtons() << mbOK, 0);
}

void MyDebugBeep()
{
    // Make the default Windows beep.
    MessageBeep(0xFFFFFFFF);
}
```

> **TIP**
>
> In a multithreaded application, it is often helpful to also output the thread ID. The current thread ID can be retrieved with the `GetCurrentThreadId()` Win32 API function.

The previous debugging output methods are fine for basic purposes. One problem with the pop-up dialog boxes is that they are difficult to use when debugging a `Paint()` method of a graphical component. The display of the pop-up dialog box can obscure part of the control, causing a `WM_PAINT` message to call the `Paint()` method again.

A better alternative if debugging within the IDE is to use the `OutputDebugString()` Win32 API function. It is a generic function that outputs a given string that can be picked up by a debugger. In our case, the message is output to the C++Builder integrated debugger and sent to the event log. No output is generated if the application is run outside the IDE (outside the debugger).

You can see the event log from View, Debug Windows, Event Log or by pressing Ctrl+Alt+V. Dock the Event Log window below the Code Editor or Class Explorer. The `OutputDebugString()` function takes one parameter, the user-defined message to output of type const char *, giving you total control. All output to the event log is prefixed with ODS: and has a suffix of Process <project>.exe.

Some great features are packed into two macros: TRACE and WARN. They use OutputDebugString()to generate messages but automatically provide file and line number information and support the iostream operators for constructing the user-defined message. To enable these, you must use #define __TRACE and #define __WARN and after them add the statement #include <checks.h>. Then you can use them in your code. TRACE takes one argument, a string stream that is the user-defined message. WARN takes two arguments: a test expression and the user-defined message. It will only output the message if the expression evaluates to true.

Listing 7.3 combines the _DEBUG define and the TRACE and WARN macros to conditionally generate the debug output. While it is okay to leave these compiled in when shipping your application, since the OutputDebugString() messages won't appear anywhere, the application will suffer a very slight performance hit. The TRACEF macro in Listing 7.3 is similar to TRACE, but I've added the function name to the message. The OutputDebugString() function is also demonstrated.

LISTING 7.3   Using TRACE, WARN, and OutputDebugString when Compiled in Debug Mode

```
#ifdef _DEBUG
#define __TRACE
#define __WARN
#endif
#include <checks.h>
#pragma option -w-ccc

#define TRACEF(s) TRACE(__FUNC__ ": " << s)

void MyFunc(AnsiString Title, int *MyArray, int Max)
{
int i,
    Sum = 0;

    TRACE("Simple trace");
    TRACEF("Includes function name");

    for (i = 0 ; i < 10 ; i++) {
        Sum += MyArray[i];
    }

    TRACE("The sum is " << Sum);
    WARN(Sum > Max, "The Sum is too big! The maximum is " << Max);

    OutputDebugString(Title.c_str());
}
```

You'll notice in Listing 7.1 that the -w-ccc compiler option is set using the #pragma option preprocessor directive. TRACE and WARN are actually implemented as a do { } while (0) loop, which results in a Condition is always true compiler warning for each use. This directive disables that warning. Alternatively, you can set the compiler option directly in the project file or disable the warning through the project options by setting Warnings to Selected on the Compiler tab, pressing the Warnings button, and unchecking the Condition is always true... warning, prefixed with W8008 in C++Builder 5.

Often, when outputting debug information, you'll want to display the contents of some variable and include the variable name, such as SomeVar=Value, or display the result of some simple calculation along with the expression that produced it, like A+B=13. This can be difficult to put together in the formulation of the debug string and difficult to change. The # macro directive can alleviate a lot of the difficulties by converting a macro argument to a string literal. The DEBUGEXP macro in Listing 7.4 demonstrates this.

LISTING 7.4   A Simple Expression Log Macro

```
#ifdef _DEBUG
#define __TRACE
#define __WARN
#endif
#include <checks.h>
#pragma option -w-ccc

#define DEBUGEXP(x) TRACE(__FUNC__ ": " #x "=" << (x))

void MyFunc()
{
int A = 6,
    B = 7;

    DEBUGEXP(A);
    DEBUGEXP(A+B);
}
```

You must be aware of possible side effects that can occur from passing certain arguments to all of the macros covered so far, such as function calls, variable assignments, or ++ increment or -- decrement operators. For example, writing DEBUGEXP(++a) will actually increment a, but if _DEBUG is not defined, the statement is not executed, and a will not be incremented.

Generally it is advisable to stay away from macros like DEBUGEXP and implement them as inline functions. However, a macro is required to use the __FUNC__ macro and # (convert to string) macro directive in the previous example.

One last pair of macros is presented in Listing 7.5 for tracing the execution of statements.

LISTING 7.5   Tracing Code Execution

```
#ifdef _DEBUG
#define __TRACE
#define __WARN
#endif
#include <checks.h>
#pragma option -w-ccc

#define DEBUGTRCN(s) TRACE("CMD: " #s); s
#define DEBUGTRCC(s) s; TRACE("CMD: " #s)

void MyFunc()
{
int i,
    Sum;

    DEBUGTRCN(Sum = 0);
    DEBUGTRCN(for (int i = 0 ; i < 10 ; i++) {);
    DEBUGTRCN(Sum += i);
    DEBUGTRCC(});

    DEBUGTRCN(if (Sum > 20) {);
    DEBUGTRCN(ShowMessage("Sum is large"));
    DEBUGTRCC(} else {);
    DEBUGTRCN(ShowMessage("Sum is small"));
    DEBUGTRCC(});
}
```

The DEBUGTRCN and DEBUGTRCC macros in Listing 7.5 expand to two statements each: One displays the statement that is being executed, and the other is the actual statement that executes. DEBUGTRCN is used for most statements, but for statements that include a closing brace (}), you must use DEBUGTRCC, as demonstrated in the example. Because the macros expand into two statements, they cannot be used for statements that must be singular, such as a single statement executed after an if or for statement, without using braces to encompass the statement. There are no side-effect issues with these macros, however.

Using Assertions

An assertion is a means of validating assumptions made in code. It asserts that a particular expression is true. If the statement is not true, then the assertion can display an error message and abort or throw an exception. The WARN macro in the previous section is an example of a basic assertion, except that it uses the reverse logic and only displays some debug output without aborting. Some programmers prefer to implement exception handling instead of assertions. We'll look at that briefly in the next section, "Implementing a Global Exception Handler."

Adding the appropriate assertions to your code can be a lengthy process. It is best to add them as you code, so that the assumptions you're making are fresh in your mind. Assertions are usually added to the start of a function call or class method but can be used anywhere in your code.

Assertions are usually included only in a debug or test release and rarely in a final shipping release. However, the assertion statements should be left in the source code and compiled out with the use of #ifdef preprocessor directives. This allows you to use them to perform more testing in the future, after new features are added to the application, for example. Most assertions have the compile-out functionality built in.

To use the built-in assertions in C++Builder, you must include the assert.h header file by adding #include <assert.h> to your code. Then, anywhere in your code that you want to make an assertion, simply enter assert(expression). Remember that, unlike the WARN macro, the expression should evaluate to true for normal operation and false if the assumption is incorrect.

Listing 7.6 demonstrates the use of assertions for validating function parameters for range and validity and for general conditions.

7

DEBUGGING YOUR
APPLICATION

LISTING 7.6   Using Assertions

```
// Standard header files above this.
#include <assert.h>

// Functions start here.
void MyFunc(int Width)
{
int Length;

    // Width can't be zero.
    assert(Width != 0);

    Length = Area/Width;

    // Length should be less than MaxLength
    assert(Length < MaxLength);

    // Everything ok, continue.
```

LISTING 7.6   Continued

```
}

void DisplayNode(TNode *Node)
{
    // Make sure that the node is valid.
    assert(Node != (TNode *)NULL);

    // Everything ok,  continue.
}
```

When an assertion fails in a console application, the message Assertion failed:, followed by the assertion expression, the unit filename, and the line number of the assertion statement, is output to stderr. In a GUI application, a dialog box is displayed that contains the assertion expression, the unit filename, and the line number of the assertion statement. Figure 7.1 shows the error message that would appear in a GUI application if zero were passed in the argument to MyFunc() in the previous example.

FIGURE 7.1

This assertion dialog box appears when an assertion is fired.

Assertions can be removed from your code at compile time by defining NDEBUG. This can be done in the Conditional defines list on the Directories/Conditionals tab of the project options or by adding #define NDEBUG before the #include <assert.h> if _DEBUG is not defined to tie all debug code to a single definition. As stated previously, assertion statements should be left in your code.

Because assertions can be compiled out, the assertion statements should not contain any assignment statements, variable increments or decrements, or calls to functions that may create side effects. Going against this rule will create inconsistencies between debug and release versions of your application. Remember to document any assumptions that are unclear in the source code.

Implementing a Global Exception Handler

An alternative or an addition to using assertions is to use good exception handling. In particular, implement a global exception handler to catch all unhandled exceptions.

A global exception handler can report what the exception is and where it occurred and possibly the current state of the application. An advanced global exception handler that logs the application state to a file is covered in detail in the "Implementing an Advanced Exception Handler" section in Chapter 4.

A simple alternative to the method described in Chapter 4 is to compile with exception location information by checking Enable Exceptions and Location Information on the C++ tab of the project options or by setting the -xp compiler command-line option. By adding #include <except.h>, you have access to three important functions:

- __ThrowExceptionName(): Returns a (char *) pointer to the name of the thrown exception.

- __ThrowFileName(): Returns a (char *) pointer to the name of the file in which the exception occurred.

- __ThrowLineNumber(): Returns an unsigned int containing the line number of the source file in which the exception occurred.

A simple global exception handler is demonstrated in the following code:

```
#include <except.h>

  // In the main function for the application.
    try {
        // Do the main work here (call functions etc.)
    }
    catch ( Exception &e ) {
        ShowMessage(e.Message + "\nType: " + __ThrowExceptionName() +
                    "\nFile: " + __ThrowFileName() + "\nLine: " +
                    AnsiString(__ThrowLineNumber()));
    }
```

Of course you can build a more elaborate version, for example one that could write the information to a file, so that you could ask the user to email the file to your help desk.

Other Basic Debugging Issues

There are a few nuances of C++ that can make it hard to find a bug when eyeballing the code. Some of them are given in the following list:

- Be aware that numbers starting with 0 (zero) are octal values. The number 010 is octal 10 (8 in decimal).

- Be careful not to confuse the number *0* (zero) with the letter O (oh), when setting up input data and performing string or character comparisons.

- Watch out for expressions that use the bitwise operators &, |, or ~ instead of the Boolean operators &&, ||, or ! unless it is intentional, such as for optimization reasons.

- Enclose macro expressions in parentheses. A macro MAX(a,b) defined as a>=b?a:b will not work with Z = Y + MAX(A,B). Define it in parentheses, as (a>=b?a:b) instead.

- Beware of side effects when using macros. If MAX(a,b) is defined as (a>=b?a:b), then the expression Z = MAX(A++,B) will cause A to be incremented twice, but Z will contain the value as if A were incremented once.

- Warn other programmers that a macro is a macro and not a function by using uppercase names, and use inline functions instead of macros where possible.

- Avoid tricky functions such as strncpy(s1, s2, length), which may or may not append a trailing NULL character to string s1 when copying string s2, depending on the value of the length argument and the length of s2.

In the following sections, we move to more advanced debugging techniques.

Using the C++Builder Interactive Debugger

C++Builder's interactive debugger contains many advanced features, including expression evaluation, data setting, object inspection, complex breakpoints, a machine code disassembly view, an FPU and MMX register view, cross-process debugging, remote debugging, attaching to a running process, watching expression results, call stack viewing, the ability to single-step through code, and more. During development you will spend a lot of time using it, or at least you should!

The debugger is not just for finding bugs; it is also a general development tool that can give you great insight into how your application works at a low level.

To use the debugger effectively, you must first disable compiler optimizations. When compiler optimizations are enabled, the optimizer will do everything in its power to speed up or reduce the size of your code, including removing, rearranging, and grouping sections of code. This makes it very difficult to step through your code and to match up source code with machine code in the CPU view. If you set a breakpoint on a line and it is not hit when you are confident that the line was executed, it is probably because you have optimizations enabled.

Screen real estate becomes a problem with the many debug views that you're likely to need during a debugging session. In C++Builder 5, make use of the desktop settings to create a layout appropriate for programming and a separate layout for debugging.

My typical desktop layout for debugging is shown in Figure 7.2. You can see: (A) The Call Stack, Watches, and Local Variables views docked together vertically and placed on the left of the screen. (B) The Code Editor placed center to upper-right and occupying most of the screen.

(C) The CPU view placed below the Code Editor window at the bottom right of the screen. From time to time during debugging, I display the Debug Inspector window and superimpose it over (A) and dock the Event Log below the Code Editor when the CPU view is not needed. For a layout such as this, a large monitor and screen resolution of 1280×1024 are highly recommended.

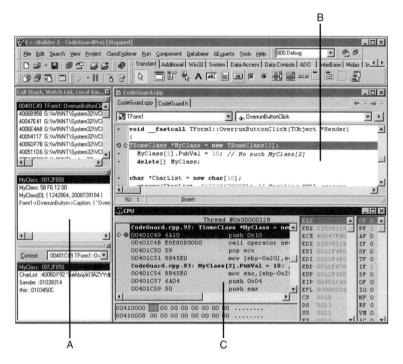

FIGURE 7.2

An example debugging window layout.

For the remainder of this section, it is assumed that you understand the basics of the debugger, such as using source breakpoints with expression and pass-count conditions, stepping over and into code, and using ToolTip expression evaluation (holding the mouse pointer over an expression while the application is paused in the debugger). We'll concentrate on several of the more advanced features.

Advanced Breakpoints

Apart from the standard source breakpoints that simply halt execution when the selected source or assembly line is reached, there are more advanced breakpoints that can be used in particular debugging cases. In the following section, we'll look at some of the new breakpoint features in C++Builder 5.

Module load breakpoints are particularly useful when debugging DLLs and packages. You can pause execution when a specified module is loaded, providing a perfect entry point into the DLL or package for debugging. To set a module load breakpoint, you have two options.

The first option applies when the application is already running within the IDE. First, display the Modules window by selecting View, Debug Windows, Modules. Next, in the modules list in the upper-left pane of the Modules window, locate the module for which you want to set the module load breakpoint. If the module is not in the modules list, then it has not yet been loaded by the application. In that case you will need to add the module to the modules list by selecting Add Module from the context menu, then name or browse to the module and select OK. Finally, select the module in the modules list and then select Break On Load from the context menu. This is shown in Figure 7.3. If the module has already been loaded by the application, then the breakpoint will work only when the module is loaded again, either after being dynamically unloaded or when the is restarted.

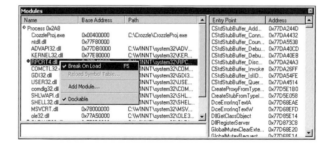

FIGURE 7.3

Setting a module load breakpoint from the Modules view.

The second option applies when the application is not yet running within the IDE. Select Run, Add Breakpoint, Module Load Breakpoint, then enter the module name or browse to it and select OK. Finally, run the application.

Address breakpoints and Data breakpoints provide a way to pause the application when a particular code address is reached or data at a particular address is modified. They can only be added when the application is running or paused.

Address breakpoints work in the same manner as source breakpoints, although instead of adding the breakpoint to a particular line of source code, you add the breakpoint to the memory address for a particular machine code instruction. When the machine code is executed, the breakpoint action is taken. If you set an address breakpoint for a machine code instruction that is related to a line of source code, the breakpoint is set as a normal source breakpoint on that line of source code. Address breakpoints are typically used when debugging external modules on a low level using the CPU view. The CPU view is explained in the section "The CPU View," later in this chapter.

We will now walk through a demonstration of how to set an address breakpoint. In the `Breakpoints` folder on the CD-ROM that accompanies this book, you will find the `BreakpointProj.bpr` project file. Load it with C++Builder, then compile and run the application by selecting Run, Run. When the form is displayed, pause the application by selecting Run, Program Pause from the C++Builder main menu. The CPU view, which we will use in a moment, will be displayed.

Next, select View, Units, then select `BreakpointForm` from the units list and select OK. The unit will be displayed in the Code Editor. Scroll down to the `AddressBreakpointButtonClick()` function. Right-click on the `Label2->Caption = "New Caption"` statement in the function and select Debug, View CPU from the context menu. The CPU view is again displayed, this time at the memory address where the machine code for the C++ statement is located.

In the upper-left pane in the CPU view, note the hexadecimal number on the far left of the line containing the machine code statement `lea eax,[ebp-0x04]`. On my system at present, this number is `004016ED`, but it is likely to be different on yours. This is the address at which we will set the address breakpoint.

To add an address breakpoint for this address, select Run, Add Breakpoint, Address Breakpoint, then, in the Address field, enter the address that you previously noted. Hexadecimal numbers, such as the address displayed in the CPU view that you noted, must be entered with a leading `0x`; in my case I would specify the address as `0x004016ED`.

To test the address breakpoint, continue the program by selecting Run, Run. Select the application from the Windows taskbar and click the Address Breakpoint button. The address breakpoint previously set will cause the application to pause. The CPU view will be displayed with the current execution point, marked by a green arrow, set on the address breakpoint line of machine code. You can continue the application by selecting Run, Run.

If, in the CPU view, you display the line of machine code at the address at which you wish to place an address breakpoint, you can set an address breakpoint simply by clicking in the gutter of the machine code line, as you would in source code for a source breakpoint. We could have done this in the previous example, but I want to demonstrate the overall principle of specifying the actual address.

Data breakpoints can be invaluable in helping to track bugs, by locating where in the code a particular variable or memory location is being set. As an example, load the

`BreakpointProj.bpr` project file from the previous demonstration. Run and then pause the application. Select Run, Add Breakpoint, Data Breakpoint. In the Address field, enter `Form1->FClickCount` and select OK. This private data member of the form counts the number of times that the form's `DataBreakpointButton` button is clicked. Setting this data breakpoint will cause the application to break whenever the count is modified.

As you can see, any valid data address expression can be entered, not just a memory address. Alternatively, to obtain the address, we can select Run, Inspect, enter `Form1->FClickCount` in the expression, and obtain the address from the top of the Debug Inspector window. This hexadecimal address could then be entered (with a leading `0x`) in the data breakpoint Address field.

To test the data breakpoint, continue the program by selecting Run, Run. Select the application from the Windows taskbar and click the Data Breakpoint button. The data breakpoint previously set will cause the application to pause at the location where the data was modified. If this is on a source line, the Code Editor will be displayed, otherwise the CPU view will be displayed. You can continue the application by selecting Run, Run.

TIP

Adding a data breakpoint for a property such as the `Caption` of a label or the `Text` of an edit box is much trickier. These properties are not direct memory locations that are written to when the property is modified. Instead, the properties use `Set` functions to change their values. To break when the property is changed, it is easiest to add an address breakpoint for the `Set` function of the property, rather than finding the memory address where the data is actually stored and adding a data breakpoint. I'll explain this method using the `Caption` property of `ClickCountLabel` on the form of the previous demonstration project.

With the application paused, select Run, Inspect. In the Expression field enter `Form1->ClickCountLabel`. Select the Properties tab in the Debug Inspector window and scroll down to the `Caption` property. The write method for this property is specified as `SetText`. Click on the Methods tab and scroll down to the `SetText` method. The address of this method will be displayed on the right. Select Run, Add Breakpoint, Address Breakpoint and enter the address of the `SetText` method, prefixing it with `0x` and leaving out the colon, then click on OK. Continue the application by selecting Run, Run. Now, whenever the label caption is modified, the breakpoint will pause the application.

For a standard `AnsiString` variable without a `Set` method to control its modification, such as the `FSomeString` private data member of the form in the demonstration project, you can set a data breakpoint on the `.Data` variable of the `AnsiString` class that contains the underlying string data. For the demonstration project, the data breakpoint would be set on `Form1->FSomeString.Data`.

When adding a data breakpoint, the Length field in the Add Data Breakpoint window should be specified for non-singular data types, such as structures or arrays. The breakpoint will pause the application when any memory location within this length from the data address is modified. Data breakpoints can also be added by selecting Break when Changed from the context menu in the View, Debug Windows, Watches view.

> **NOTE**
>
> Address and data breakpoints are valid only for the current application run. You must set them for each new run because the machine code instruction and data addresses can change each time.

New Breakpoint Features in C++Builder 5

Breakpoints can now be organized into groups and have actions. With breakpoint actions, you can enable and disable groups of actions, enable and disable exception handling, log a message to the event log, and log the evaluation of an expression to the event log.

Using these features, you can set up complex breakpoint interaction to break only in specific program circumstances. For example, you can cause a set of breakpoints to be enabled only when a specific section of code is executed.

By disabling and enabling exceptions, you can control error handling in known problem areas of code. Message logging helps automate variable inspection and execution tracing.

The new breakpoint action and group information are available in the breakpoint ToolTip in the Code Editor and in the breakpoint list window.

C++Builder Debugging Views

The debugger can be used to display many types of information that are helpful with debugging an application, such as local variables, a list of all breakpoints, the call stack, a list of the loaded modules, thread status, machine code, data and register status, an application event log, and more.

New to C++Builder 5 is the Floating-Point Unit (FPU) view, which shows the current state of the floating point and MMX registers. All debugging views are accessible from the View, Debug Windows menu option or by pressing the appropriate shortcut key. In the following sections we'll look at some of the advanced views and how you can use them in debugging your application.

The CPU View

The CPU view your application at the machine code level. The machine code and disassembled assembly code that make up your application are displayed along with the CPU registers and flags, the machine stack, and a memory dump. The CPU view has five panes, as depicted in Figure 7.4.

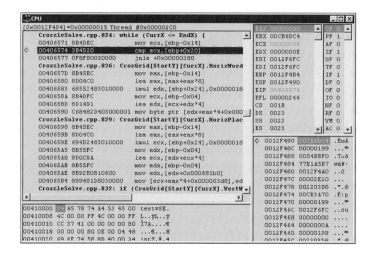

FIGURE 7.4

The CPU view.

The large pane on the left is the disassembly pane. It displays the disassembled machine code instructions, also known as assembly code, that make up your application. The instruction address is in the left column, followed by the machine code data and the equivalent assembly code. Above the disassembly pane, the effective address of the expression in the currently selected line of machine code, the value stored at that address, and the thread ID are displayed. In Figure 7.4 the effective address of [ebp+0x20] is 0x0012F4D4, the value stored at that location is 0x00000015, and the thread ID is 0x000002C0.

If you enabled the Debug Information option on the Compiler tab of the project options before compiling your application, the disassembly pane shows your C++ source code lines above the corresponding assembly code instructions. Some C++ source code lines can be seen in Figure 7.4.

In the disassembly pane, you can step through the machine code one instruction at a time, much like you step through one source code line at a time in the source code editor. The green arrow shows the current instruction that is about to be executed. You can set breakpoints and use other features similar to debugging in the source code editor. There are several options available in the context menu, such as changing threads, searching through memory for data, and changing the current execution point.

The CPU registers pane is to the right of the disassembly pane. It shows the current value of each of the CPU registers. When a register changes, it is shown in red. You can modify the value of the registers via the context menu.

On the far right is the CPU flags pane. This is an expanded view of the EFL (32-bit flags) register in the CPU register pane. You can toggle the value of a flag through the context menu. Consult the online help for a description of each of the flags.

Below the disassembly pane is the memory dump pane. It can be used to display the content of any memory location in your application's address space. On the left is the memory address, followed by a hexadecimal dump of the memory at that address and an ASCII view of the memory. You can change how this data is displayed from the context menu and also go to a specified address or search for particular data.

The final pane is the machine stack pane, located at the bottom right of the CPU window. It displays the content of the application's current stack, pointed to by the ESP (stack pointer) CPU register. It is similar to the memory dump pane and offers similar context menu options.

The CPU view is a good tool for getting to know how your application works at a very low level. If you come to understand your application at this level, then you will have a better understanding of pointers and arrays, you'll know more about execution speed (helpful when optimizing your application), and you'll find it easier to debug your application because you will know what's going on in the background.

The best reference for the x86 machine code instruction set and detailed information on the Pentium processor range is the Intel Architecture Software Developer's Manual. This three-volume set tells you just about everything you want to know about the Pentium processors. It is available for download from the Manuals section for the appropriate processor on Intel's Web site at `http://developer.intel.com/design/processor/`. More references and detail on assembly language programming can be found in Chapter 6.

Assembly language programming is a black art these days. It is extremely complex and is usually reserved only for writing small sections of very efficient, speed-critical code.

The Call Stack View

A call stack is the path of functions that lead directly to the current point of execution. Functions that have been previously called and returned are not in the call stack.

The Call Stack view displays the call stack with the most recently entered function first, at the top of the list. Used in conjunction with conditional breakpoints, the Call Stack view provides useful information as to how the function containing the breakpoint was reached. This is particularly useful if the function is called from many places throughout the application.

You can double-click a function listed in the Call Stack view to display it in the Code Editor. If there is no source code for the function—for example, if the function is located in an external module—then the disassembled machine code of the function is displayed in the CPU view. In either case, the next statement or instruction to be executed at that level in the call stack is selected.

A new feature in C++Builder 5 is the capability to bring up the Local Variables view for a particular function on the call stack by selecting View Locals from the context menu.

The Threads View

Debugging multiprocess and multithreaded applications can be very difficult. Threads in particular usually execute asynchronously. Often the threads in the application communicate with each other using the Win32 API `PostThreadMessage()` function or use a mutex object to gain access to a shared resource.

When debugging a multithreaded application, you can pause an individual thread. One thread may hit a breakpoint and another may not. The problems start occurring when another thread is still running and is relying on inter-thread communication, or the stopped thread has an open mutex that another thread is waiting for.

Even the fact that the application runs more slowly under the debugger can cause timing problems if the application is multithreaded. In general, it is bad programming practice not to allow for reasonable timing fluctuations, because you cannot control the environment in which the application is run.

The Threads view helps to alleviate some of these difficulties by giving you a snapshot of the current status of all processes and threads in the application. Each process has a main thread and may have additional threads. The Threads view displays the threads in a hierarchical way, such that all threads of a process are grouped together. The first process and the main thread are listed first. The process name and process ID are shown for each process, and the thread ID, state, status, and location are shown for each thread. Figure 7.5 shows an example of the Threads view.

FIGURE 7.5

The Threads view, showing a single process running four threads.

For secondary processes, the process state is Spawned, Attached, or Cross-Process Attach. The process state is Runnable, Stopped, Blocked, or None. The thread location is the current source position for the thread. If the source is not available, the current execution address is shown.

When debugging multiprocess or multithreaded applications, there is always a single current thread. The process that the thread belongs to is the current process. The current process and current thread are denoted in the Threads view by a green arrow, which can be seen in Figure 7.5. Most debugger views and actions relate to the current thread. The current process and current thread can be changed by selecting a process or thread in the Threads view and selecting Make Current from the context menu, from which you can also terminate a process. For information on additional settings and commands in the Threads view, see "Thread status box" in the Index of the C++Builder online help.

The Modules View

The Modules view lists all DLLs and packages that have been loaded with the currently running application or modules that have a module load breakpoint set when the application is not running. It is very useful when debugging DLLs and packages, as discussed in the "Advanced Breakpoints" section, earlier in this chapter. Figure 7.6 shows a typical Modules view.

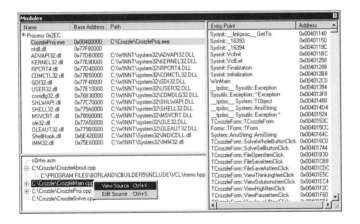

FIGURE 7.6

The Modules view, listing modules, source files, and entry points.

The Modules view has three panes. The upper-left pane contains the list of modules, their base addresses, and the full paths to their locations. Note that the base address is the address at which the module was actually loaded, not necessarily the base address specified on the Linker tab of the project options when developing the module. By selecting a module, you can set a module load breakpoint from the context menu.

The lower-left pane contains a tree view of the source files that were used to build the module. You can select a source file and view it in the Code Editor by selecting View Source from the context menu.

The right pane lists the entry points for the module and the addresses of the entry points. From the context menu, you can go to the entry point. If there is source available for the entry point, it will be displayed in the Code Editor. If there is no source, the entry point will be displayed in the CPU view.

The New FPU View

A new view in C++Builder 5 is the Floating-Point Unit (FPU) view. It enables you to view the state of the floating-point unit or MMX information when debugging your application. Figure 7.7 shows an example FPU view displaying the state of the floating-point unit.

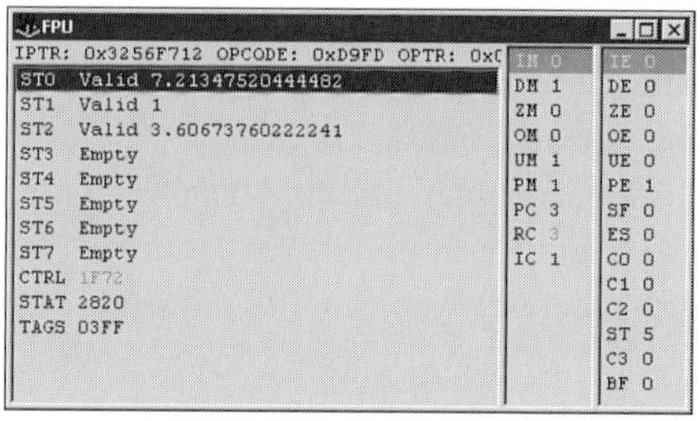

FIGURE 7.7

The new FPU view in C++Builder 5, displaying the state of the floating-point unit.

The FPU view has three panes. The left pane displays the floating-point register stack (ST0 to ST7 registers), the control word, status word, and tag words of the FPU. For the floating-point register stack, the register status and value are shown. The status is either Empty, Zero, Valid, or Spec. (special), depending on the register stack contents.

When a stack register's status is not Empty, its value is also displayed. You can toggle the formatting of the value from long double to words by selecting the appropriate option under Display As in the context menu. You can also zero, empty, or set a value for a particular stack register and zero or set a value for the control word, status word and tag word from the context menu.

The middle pane contains the FPU single and multi-bit control flags, which change as floating-point instructions are executed. Their values can be toggled or cycled via the context menu.

The right pane contains the FPU status flags. It is an expanded view of the status word in the FPU registers pane, listing each status flag individually. Their values can be toggled or cycled via the context menu.

When a value changes, it is displayed in red in all panes. You can see this effect best by performing single steps through floating-point instructions in the CPU view.

Watches, Evaluating, and Modifying

A watch is simply a means of viewing the content of an expression throughout the debugging process. An expression can be a simple variable name or a complex expression involving pointers, arrays, functions, values, and variables. The Watches view displays the expressions and their results in the watch list. You can display the Watches view by selecting View, Debug Windows, Watches. The Watches view is automatically displayed when a new watch expression is added.

You can add expressions to the watch list using one of three methods. The first method is from the Add Watch item of the context menu in the Watches view. The second method is by selecting Run, Add Watch, and the third method is by right-clicking on the appropriate expression in the Code Editor and selecting Debug, Add Watch at Cursor from the context menu. This last method automatically enters the expression for you.

Watches can be edited, disabled, or enabled via the context menu. Watches can be deleted by selecting the appropriate expression and pressing the Delete key or by selecting Delete Watch from the context menu. If the expression cannot be evaluated because one or more of the parts of the expression is not in scope, then an `undefined symbol` message appears instead of the evaluated result.

On the other hand, evaluating and modifying expressions allows you to more readily change the expression, view the subsequent result, and modify variables at runtime. With Evaluate/Modify, you can perform detailed live testing that is difficult to perform by other means.

To use Evaluate/Modify, your application must be paused. There are two ways to use it. One is to simply select Run, Evaluate/Modify and enter the expression to evaluate. Perhaps the easiest method is to invoke Evaluate/Modify from the Code Editor.

When the application is paused in the debugger, you can evaluate expressions in the source code simply by placing the mouse pointer over them. Evaluate/Modify allows you to change the expression at will. You can invoke it by right-clicking on the expression and selecting Debug, Evaluate/Modify. In the Evaluate/Modify window, you will see the expression and its result. The Modify field allows you to change the expression value if it is a simple data type. If you need to modify a structure or an array, you will have to modify each field or item individually.

Function calls can be included in the expression. Be aware, though, that evaluating an expression produces the same result as if your application executed that expression. If the expression contains side effects, they will be reflected in the running state of your application when you continue to step through or run.

Unlike the Watches view, the Evaluate/Modify dialog box doesn't update the result of the expression automatically when you step through your code. You must click the Evaluate button to see the current result. The expression result can also be formatted using a format modifier at the end of the expression. See the online help for more information.

Typical uses for Evaluate/Modify include testing error conditions and tracking down bugs. To test an error condition, simply set a breakpoint at or just before the error check or step through the code to reach it and then force an error by setting the appropriate error value using Modify. Use Single Step or Run to verify that the error is handled correctly.

If you suspect that a certain section of code contains a bug and sets incorrect data, set a breakpoint just after the suspected code, fix the data manually, and then continue execution to verify that the bad data is producing the bug's symptoms. Trace backward through code until you locate the bug, or use a data breakpoint to find when the data is modified.

The Debug Inspector

The Debug Inspector is like a runtime object inspector. It can be used to display the data, methods, and properties of classes, structures, arrays, functions, and simple data types at runtime, thus providing a convenient all-in-one watch/modifier.

With the application paused in the debugger, you can start the Debug Inspector by selecting Run, Inspect and entering the element to inspect as an expression, or by right-clicking on an element expression in the Code Editor and selecting Debug, Inspect from the context menu. The element expression in the second method is automatically entered into the inspector.

Figure 7.8 shows several data members of a form class in the Debug Inspector.

FIGURE 7.8

A form displayed in the Debug Inspector window.

The title of the Debug Inspector window contains the thread ID. In the top of the window are the name, type, and memory address of the element. There are up to three tabs, depending on the element type, that display the name and contents or address of each data member, method, or property. The Property tab is shown only for classes derived from the VCL. At the bottom of the window, the type of the currently selected item is shown.

The values of simple types can be modified. If the item can be modified, an ellipsis will be shown in the value cell. Click on the ellipsis and enter the new value.

The Debug Inspector can be used to walk down and back up the class and data hierarchy. To inspect one of the data members, methods, or properties in the current inspector window, simply select it and then choose Inspect from the context menu. You can also hide or show inherited items.

In C++Builder 5, there are three new Debug Inspector options that can be set from Tools, Debugger Options, in addition to the original Inspectors Stay On Top option. They are Show Inherited, Sort By Name, and Show Fully Qualified Names. Show Inherited switches the view in the Data, Methods, and Properties tabs between two modes, one that shows all intrinsic and inherited data members or properties of a class and one that shows only those declared in the class. Sort By Name switches between sorting the items listed by name or by declaration order. Show Fully Qualified Names shows inherited members using their fully qualified names and is displayed only if Show Inherited is also enabled. All three new options can be set via the context menu in the Debug Inspector.

The Debug Inspector is a commonly used tool during a debugging session because it displays so many items at once. It also allows you to walk down and up the class and data hierarchy.

CodeGuard

CodeGuard is new to C++Builder 5 Professional and Enterprise versions. It was previously seen in Borland C++ and has only now appeared in C++Builder. CodeGuard is a runtime checker for memory and resource use and function call validation.

Specifically, CodeGuard can detect the following types of runtime errors:

- Improper memory deallocation
- Invalid file streams or handles
- Invalid pointers
- Use of memory that has been deallocated
- Memory leaks
- Allocated memory that is not deallocated
- Incorrect arguments passed to Borland and Win32 API functions

- Borland and Win32 API functions that return an error value
- Invalid resource handles passed in Borland and Win32 API functions

An example of improper memory use is if your application attempts to free the same resource more than once or attempts to access memory that has already been freed. We'll look at many of the bugs that cause these errors later in this section.

CodeGuard outputs the errors that it finds in a log file that can be viewed within the C++Builder IDE. CodeGuard also can take you directly to the line of source code that caused the error.

Enabling and Configuring CodeGuard

To enable CodeGuard, you must compile it into your application. To do this, enable the CodeGuard Validation option on the CodeGuard tab of the project options for your application. To allow source line number identification for errors, you should also enable Debug Information and Line Number Information on the Compiler tab. Recompile the application with Build or Build All Projects.

Three other options are provided on the CodeGuard tab of the project options, as shown in Figure 7.9. The first allows CodeGuard to detect invalid pointers to local, global, and static variables and data overruns. The second allows CodeGuard to detect calls to methods of invalid or deleted objects. The third option allows CodeGuard to validate inline pointer accesses and will slow down program execution speed considerably. You will usually want to enable all three options. If you change any of these three options, you will need to recompile your application with Build or Build All Projects.

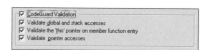

FIGURE 7.9
Enabling CodeGuard project options.

There are several CodeGuard options that can be configured via the CodeGuard configuration tool, accessible from Tools, CodeGuard Configuration, or the command-line tool CGCONFIG.EXE. The configuration options are grouped into four tabs.

The Preferences tab, shown in Figure 7.10, is used to set general CodeGuard preferences. The Enable option allows you to enable and disable CodeGuard without recompiling your application. It should be checked to turn on runtime error checking with CodeGuard. To fully disable CodeGuard, you should uncheck the CodeGuard Validation option on the CodeGuard tab of the project options and recompile your application with Build or Build All Projects. The stack fill frequency is a compromise between better error detection and execution speed for invalid access of the runtime stack. You should leave this at 2.

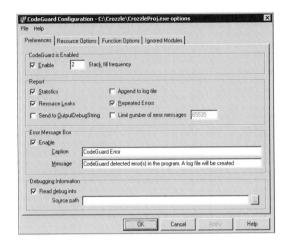

FIGURE 7.10
The Preferences page of the CodeGuard Configuration tool.

The CodeGuard Report and Error Message Box options define how CodeGuard reports errors. Under Report, the Statistics option will tell CodeGuard to output statistics on memory allocation and deallocation, selected Win32 API function calls, and resource usage, plus a module list at the end of the log file. The Resource Leaks option will report resource leaks detected, after the application terminates. Error Message Box will display a message box in applications run outside the IDE if CodeGuard detects an error. For information on other options on the Preferences tab, consult the C++Builder online help.

The Resource Options and Function Options tabs of the CodeGuard configuration allow you to set various tracking options for resources, file handles, and function calls. You should use the default settings unless you have a specific need to change them. One useful option on the Function Options tab is to log each call to specific functions.

The Ignored Modules tab allows you to tell CodeGuard to ignore specific modules (DLLs and packages) when detecting runtime errors. Use this option only if you have a specific need.

Using CodeGuard

Using CodeGuard is as simple as enabling and configuring it as detailed in the previous section and then running your application. CodeGuard will monitor the enabled and configured aspects of your application as it runs within or external to the C++Builder IDE. It will also report any errors to the CodeGuard log file with the name `<ProjectName>.cgl`. The CodeGuard log file is a text file that can be viewed and edited using any standard text editor; however, using the C++Builder IDE is the best way to access it.

The CodeGuard log can be viewed within the IDE by selecting View, Debug Windows, CodeGuard Log or by pressing Ctrl+Alt+O. C++Builder interprets the information in the CodeGuard log file and displays it in a more user-friendly way, with each error listed in a tree view. Each error can be expanded to list information specific to the error type. This information includes details such as where a resource was used, allocated, and freed; the call stack at the time of the error; and pointers to the source line(s) in the code that caused the error. Figure 7.11 shows an example CodeGuard Log window and information for an Access In Freed Memory error.

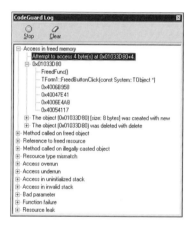

FIGURE 7.11

A CodeGuard Log window and freed memory access information.

There are two buttons on the CodeGuard Log window: Stop and Clear. When the Stop button is active, CodeGuard will stop the application when an error is encountered. If it is inactive, execution will continue and further errors can be logged in the same run. When the Clear button is enabled, the CodeGuard log is cleared each time the application is run.

Individual information nodes for the errors in the CodeGuard log can be double-clicked to jump to the source line in question if source is available, or the memory address in the CPU view if source is not available. You can also select View Source from the context menu. In Figure 7.11, double-clicking the selected Attempt to Access 4 Byte(s) line would jump to the source line where the freed memory was accessed. You can jump to the source line of error information that lists a call stack by double-clicking on the top function in the call stack.

Once CodeGuard has detected the error and you have jumped to the appropriate source line, it is only a matter of correcting the problem by using the correct memory/resource function or tracing the resource or function arguments forward or backward until the source of the problem is located. To simplify this process, you should use watches and data breakpoints.

Examining CodeGuard Errors and Their Causes

CodeGuard can detect many runtime errors. Here we will briefly see what most of the CodeGuard error messages mean and see an example of how they are caused. Usually the CodeGuard error is self-explanatory, easy to find in the source code, and easy to correct.

All of the following CodeGuard errors are demonstrated in an example application that is available in the CodeGuard folder on the CD-ROM that accompanies this book. The application is a simple form with buttons that cause the different runtime errors to occur. To use the application best, show the CodeGuard log before running the application and disable the Stop button.

For most errors, CodeGuard will report the call stack and list the applicable function at the top of the list, where the error occurred, and where the resource was allocated and deallocated if applicable. If a resource was involved, the number of bytes allocated and accessed is also reported where applicable.

Access In Freed Memory

An Access In Freed Memory error occurs when memory is accessed after it has been freed. Typically, the memory has been allocated with new or malloc and deallocated with delete or free. The following code shows an example of accessing freed memory:

```
#include <stdio.h>
#include <dir.h>

class TSomeClass {
    int FNumber;
public:
    int GetNumber() { return FNumber; }
    void SetNumber(int NewNumber) { FNumber = NewNumber; }
    int Double(int Val) { return Val*2; }
    int PubVal;
};

void MyFunc()
{
TSomeClass *MyClass = new TSomeClass;
    delete MyClass;
    MyClass->PubVal = 10;   // MyClass already freed.
}
```

CodeGuard will report where the freed memory was accessed, where the memory was originally allocated, and where the memory was freed.

All of the following CodeGuard errors replace the MyFunc() function in the previous example code to demonstrate other errors.

Method Called On Freed Object

The Method Called On Freed Object error is similar to the Access In Freed Memory error but is caused by a call to a method in a freed object rather than accessing memory as such.

```
void MyFunc()
{
TSomeClass *MyClass = new TSomeClass;
int Answer;
    delete MyClass;
    Answer = MyClass->Double(5);
}
```

CodeGuard will report where the method of the freed object was called, where the object was created, and where the object was freed.

Reference To Freed Resource

You will see the Reference To Freed Resource error if you attempt to free a resource twice. There are several ways to create this error; the following code demonstrates one, and you can find another in the ReferenceButtonClick() function in the example application on the CD-ROM.

```
void MyFunc()
{
TSomeClass *MyClass = new TSomeClass[10];
    delete[] MyClass;
    delete[] MyClass;
}
```

CodeGuard will report where the resource was freed the second time, causing the error. It will also report where the resource was allocated and where the resource was freed the first time.

Method Called On Illegally Casted Object

A call to a method outside the valid memory range will cause the Method Called On Illegally Casted Object error. The following example creates an array of two TSomeClass objects but attempts to call the method of the third object. Remember that arrays are zero based.

```
void MyFunc()
{
TSomeClass *MyClass = new TSomeClass[2];
```

```
int Answer;
    Answer = MyClass[2].Double(5); // No such MyClass[2]
    delete[] MyClass;
}
```

CodeGuard will report where the method of the bad object call is defined, where it was called, and where the object (memory) was allocated.

Resource Type Mismatch

The Resource Type Mismatch error is caused by freeing a resource in a manner not consistent with how the resource was allocated, such as using free on memory allocated with new. The memory should be freed with delete instead. There are several ways in which this error can occur. Two are listed here, and there are more in the source code on the CD.

```
void MyFunc()
{
TSomeClass *MyClass2 = new TSomeClass;
    delete[] MyClass2;
TSomeClass *MyClass3 = new TSomeClass[2];
    delete MyClass3;
}
```

CodeGuard will report where the resource was freed in an inconsistent manner and where the resource was originally allocated.

Access Overrun

An Access Overrun error occurs by accessing memory after the end of a region of memory, such as indexing the third array item in a list of two items or copying data past the end of a region of memory. Both of these are shown in the following example code.

```
void MyFunc()
{
TSomeClass *MyClass = new TSomeClass[2];
    MyClass[2].PubVal = 10; // No such MyClass[2]
    delete[] MyClass;

char *CharList = new char[10];
    strcpy(CharList, "1234567890"); // Trailing NULL overrun.
    delete[] CharList;
}
```

CodeGuard will report where the overrun occurred and where the resource was originally allocated.

Access Underrun

An Access Underrun error is similar to an Access Overrun, except that the invalid memory access is before the region of memory, not after it.

```
void MyFunc()
{
int *IntList = new int[2];
    IntList[-1] = 10;
    delete[] IntList;
}
```

CodeGuard will report where the underrun occurred and where the resource was originally allocated.

Access In Uninitialized Stack

Accessing an uninitialized area of the stack will cause this error. In the following example code, a pointer to a local variable on the stack is returned from a function. When the function returns, that part of the stack is no longer valid, and an error occurs when it is accessed.

```
void LocFunc(int **LocPtr)
{
int LocalVar;
    *LocPtr = &LocalVar;
}

void MyFunc()
{
int *LocPtr;
    LocFunc(&LocPtr);
    *LocPtr = 10;
}
```

CodeGuard will report where the uninitialized stack access occurred.

Access In Invalid Stack

An Access In Invalid Stack error occurs when an attempt is made to access memory below the bottom of the stack. In the following example code, access is attempted below the Name array stored on the bottom of the stack. It is different from an Access Underrun error in that the access is in the stack and in an allocated memory area.

```
void MyFunc()
{
char Name[20];
    strcpy(&Name[-1], "Someone");
}
```

CodeGuard will report where the invalid stack access occurred.

Bad Parameter

`Bad Parameter` errors usually occur when an invalid file or other resource handle is passed to one of the standard Borland or Win32 API functions. In the following example code, the file stream handle is invalid when `fclose` is called, because the file has not been opened.

```
void MyFunc()
{
FILE *Stream;
    fclose(Stream);
}
```

CodeGuard reports where the function was called with the bad parameter.

Function Failure

CodeGuard monitors the return value of many of the standard Borland and Win32 API functions. A return value of `-1` indicates that an error occurred when calling the function and will be logged by CodeGuard. The following example code calls the `chdir()` function with an invalid directory name, causing the `-1` error value to be returned.

```
void MyFunc()
{
    chdir("Z:\ZXCVBN");
}
```

CodeGuard reports where the function that returned the error value was called.

Resource Leak

A `Resource Leak` error occurs when a resource such as memory is allocated but not deallocated. For most of the objects in the VCL, the deallocation is handled automatically, so resource leak errors will most often occur when you allocate a custom area of memory or dynamically create a custom object. The second case is shown in the following example code: An object is created but not freed.

```
void MyFunc()
{
TSomeClass *MyClass = new TSomeClass;
}
```

CodeGuard will report where the resource was created.

There are additional CodeGuard errors not covered here. Those described are the most common that you will encounter. For additional errors and examples, see CodeGuard in the C++Builder online help.

Advanced Debugging

As mentioned previously, debugging is an advanced topic in itself. However, there are several specific issues and cases that are beyond the basic debugging techniques presented in the first section of this chapter.

For any serious application development and debugging, I thoroughly recommend that you use the Windows NT (WinNT) or Windows 2000 (Win2K, which is based on Windows NT) operating systems, and not the Windows 95 or Windows 98 (Win9x) operating systems. WinNT and Win2K provide a much more stable environment, particularly with buggy applications.

WinNT-based operating systems handle application stopping and crashes much better than Win9x. On a Win9x system, it is much easier to crash C++Builder or even the whole system when debugging or stopping an application midstream. Use Run, Program Reset sparingly, and stop the application through normal user means if possible.

When your application performs an illegal operation or access violation while running within the C++Builder IDE, an error occurs and you are presented with an error dialog box. On a Win9x system you should reset your application using Run, Program Reset before closing the dialog box. This usually recovers more reliably than when closing the dialog box first.

For really serious debugging, particularly of Windows system applications, you can obtain a debug version of the Windows operating system, called a "debug binary" for Win9x and "checked/debug build" for WinNT/2K. The checked build provides error checking, argument verification, and system debugging code for the Windows operating system code and Win32 API functions, mostly in the form of assertions, that are not present in the retail version. This checking imposes a performance penalty. Check builds of Windows operating systems are provided with some Microsoft Developer Network (MSDN) subscriptions.

Sometimes it is useful to know if your application is running in the context of the debugger. The Win32 API function `IsDebuggerPresent()` returns `true` if it is. You can use this fact to alter the behavior of the application at runtime, such as to output additional debug information to make the application easier to debug.

Now let's look at several advanced debugging issues.

Locating the Source of Access Violations

Earlier in this chapter we examined some basic techniques for locating bugs. Access violations (AVs) are sometimes more difficult to locate than general program bugs. There are other application errors that are similar to AVs, and the techniques described here apply to those also.

Access violations can be caused by access to memory that is not within the application's memory space. If at all possible, you should use CodeGuard to check your application at runtime.

CodeGuard can detect many errors that would normally result in an AV and pinpoint the exact line of source code that produced the error. If you can't use CodeGuard for your application or CodeGuard does not detect the error that caused the AV, there are other things you can do to track down the error.

When an AV occurs, a dialog box is presented with the message `Access violation at address YYYYYYYY. Read of address ZZZZZZZZ`. Application errors can present a different message, such as `The instruction at 0xYYYYYYYY referenced memory at 0xZZZZZZZZ`. In these cases, the YYYYYYYY address is the machine code that caused the error, and address ZZZZZZZZ is the invalid memory address that it attempted to access.

It is possible to locate where some access violations occurred by implementing a global exception handler. This was discussed earlier in this chapter. You can also use just-in-time (JIT) debugging, described later in this chapter, to bring the process into the debugger and go to the address YYYYYYYY. Alternatively, you can run your application within C++Builder and wait for the AV to occur.

If you can't reproduce the AV when running within C++Builder, simply pause your application using Run, Pause or by setting and hitting a breakpoint, then bring up the CPU view and select Goto Address from the context menu. This is not foolproof, but it often works. Enter the code address given in the AV dialog box in hexadecimal as 0xYYYYYYYY. The code around this address may give you some clue as to where in your source code the AV occurred, particularly if the application was compiled with debug information.

When the memory address ZZZZZZZZ is close to zero, for instance 00000089, the cause is often an uninitialized pointer that has been accessed. The following code would produce an AV with this memory address because the `MyButton` object was never created with `new`.

```
TButton *MyButton;
MyButton->Height = 10;
```

What is actually happening is that when `MyButton` is declared it is initialized with a value of zero. The address 00000089 is actually the address of the `Height` property within the `TButton` object if it were located at address zero.

As a general rule, you should explicitly initialize pointers to some recognizable value before the memory or object is allocated and back to that value once it has been freed. If you get an AV that lists this value, then you know an uninitialized pointer caused it.

Sometimes an AV can occur in a multithreaded application in which concurrent access to objects and data is not controlled. These can be very difficult to find. Use data breakpoints and the outputting debug information techniques described earlier in this chapter if you suspect concurrency problems.

Attaching to a Running Process

When a process is running outside the C++Builder IDE, you can still debug it using the integrated debugger by attaching to it while it is running. This feature can be handy during testing. When you detect the occurrence of a bug in the application, you can attach to the application process and track down the bug. The only drawback is that Windows does not provide a method for detaching from the process without terminating it.

To attach to a running process, select Run, Attach to Process. The Attach To Process window is displayed with a list of running processes on the local machine. Select the appropriate process from the list and click the Attach button. The C++Builder debugger will then attach to the process. The process will be paused, and the CPU view will be displayed at the current execution point. You can step through the code, set breakpoints, load the source code if available using View Source from the context menu, inspect values, and so on.

Attach To Process is even more handy with remote debugging. In the Attach To Process window, you can view and attach to processes on another machine that is running the remote debug server. This is covered in the "Using Remote Debugging" section, later in this chapter.

In the window you can also view system processes by checking Show System Processes.

You should be very careful about attaching to any old process; you can cause Windows to crash or hang by attaching to system processes. Stick to attaching to your own processes.

Using Just-In-Time Debugging

Just-in-time (JIT) debugging is a feature of the Windows NT and Windows 2000 operating systems that allows you to debug a process at the time that it fails, such as when an access violation is caused. JIT debugging is not available on Windows 9x machines.

If you've used Windows NT or Windows 2000 before, you've no doubt heard of Dr. Watson. This is a JIT debugging tool provided with Windows to help identify the cause of a program failure. The selected JIT debugging tool can be changed. The current JIT debugging tool is usually set via a Registry entry; however, new to C++Builder 5 is a feature that allows the Borland debugger launcher, BORDBG51.EXE, to be called instead of Dr. Watson. Then, with each JIT debugging instance, you can select which debugger to use from the debugger launcher, such as the C++Builder debugger, Delphi debugger, Dr. Watson, or even the Borland Turbo Debugger.

Prior to C++Builder 5, the call to Dr. Watson could be replaced with a call directly to the C++Builder debugger; no debugger selection was available. If only one debugger is configured in the list, it is automatically launched. See "Just in time debuggers" in the C++Builder online help for instructions on how to configure the JIT debuggers to list in the debugger launcher.

Once configured, JIT debugging is easy to use. When the application crashes, Windows will run the debugger launcher. Select the appropriate debugger from the list, BCB (C++Builder) in this case, and click OK. At this point, C++Builder will start if it is not already running, and the application will be paused as if it were attached to while running. You can then use any of the techniques described earlier in this chapter to locate the source of the bug.

Remote Debugging

Remote debugging is the capability to debug an application running on another machine using the C++Builder interactive debugger running on your local machine. It is beneficial for applications running on remote machines that would be inconvenient to access physically, and it does not require C++Builder to be installed on the remote machine.

Remote debugging is very useful for debugging distributed applications, such as those that use DCOM or CORBA. Debugging should be performed locally whenever possible due to the reduced performance when debugging across a network.

Remote debugging is supported for executables, DLLs, and packages. The application must have been compiled with debugging information, and the debugging symbol's .tds file must be available with the application on the remote machine. The easiest way to achieve this is to load the application's project into C++Builder on the local machine, specify the Final output path in the Directories/Conditionals tab of the project options to be the shared network folder on the remote machine where the application will run, and compile the application with debug information.

Remotely debugging an application is virtually seamless. Once the remote debug session is connected, you work just as you would when debugging a local application.

Configuring Remote Debugging

Remote debugging works by running the Borland debug server BORDBG51.EXE on the remote machine. You may notice that the Borland debug server is the same program as the Borland debug launcher, described previously in the "Using Remote Debugging" section. It can perform either of these functions depending on the command-line options used to start it. The debug server requires additional DLLs to be installed. The local C++Builder debugger communicates with the debug server.

On remote Windows NT and Windows 2000 machines, the debug server is usually installed as a service. It will show as Borland Remote Debugging Service in the Services applet of the Control Panel. The debug server service can be started or stopped from the applet and can be set to start automatically when the system boots. Use the -install and -remove command-line options to install and remove the service.

On remote Windows 9x machines, the debug server is a standalone process. This is also an option for WinNT/2K machines. In any case, the remote debug server must be running before remote debugging can commence.

You can install the debug server with associated DLLs required from the C++Builder installation CD using the standard install dialog or by running SETUP.EXE in the RDEBUG folder of the CD. Remote debugging uses TCP/IP for communication between the local C++Builder IDE and the remote debug server. You must have TCP/IP networking configured correctly on both machines.

To start the debug server manually, run BORDBG51.EXE -listen. You will need administration or debugging rights to run the debug server.

Using Remote Debugging

When the debug server has been installed on the remote machine and it is already running, you can start debugging remotely. From the local C++Builder IDE, open the project for the remote application that you will be debugging. Select Run, Parameters, click the Remote tab, and set Remote Path to the remote application's full path and application filename as you would use locally on that machine, such as C:\Temp\MyProj.exe. If you are debugging a DLL on the remote machine, enter the path and name of the remote application that will host the DLL. Enter any command-line parameters for the application in the Parameters field. Set Remote Host to the hostname or IP address of the remote machine.

To start debugging immediately, or when you don't have the application project loaded in C++Builder, just click the Load button. If you have the application project loaded, you can check Debug Project On Remote Machine and click OK. When you perform any debug command on the application within C++Builder, the debugging connection to the remote application will be established. You can then debug the application just as if it were running on the local machine.

If you get the error Unable to connect to remote host, check that the debug server service or process is running, Remote Host is set correctly, and you have connectivity to the remote host using ping.exe or another network tool. If you get the error Could not find program 'program', then check that Remote Path is correct and that the application is actually located there.

Another feature of remote debugging is an extension of Attach To Running Process. Select Run, Attach To Process, enter the name of the remote machine in the Remote Machine field, and press Enter. The processes on the remote machine are listed; select one and click Attach to debug it. To use remote process attachment, the remote machine must be running the debug server. Remember that when attaching to a running process, there is no way to detach without terminating it.

Debugging DLLs

Debugging a DLL is very similar to debugging any normal executable application except that a host application is required to load it. You can create the host application that uses the DLL, but in most cases you will be using an existing host, such as an application written in another language that uses the DLL that you have developed.

Load the DLL project into C++Builder and set any breakpoints in the DLL source code as necessary. Specify the host application that will load the DLL by entering the full path and name of the host application in the Host Application field on the Local tab from the Run, Parameters dialog. Enter any command-line parameters for the application in the Parameters field if necessary.

When the host application is specified, either select Load to run the host application and begin debugging or simply press OK and run the host application at a later time with Run, Run. You might do this after setting additional breakpoints or setting up watches, for example.

That's all there is to it. When the breakpoint in the DLL code is hit, you can step through the source code and use the Debug Inspector, watches, or any other technique during the debug process. You can use this technique for debugging COM objects and ActiveX components, though for separate processes you can do this only on Windows NT and Windows 2000 systems, which allow cross-process debugging.

Looking at Other Debugging Tools

A few other debugging tools are worth mentioning here to round out your toolset.

As stated earlier in this chapter, bugs are often introduced when changes are made to the code. I recommend that you use a version control system or some type of basic versioning, even if it means copying the project folder periodically. Most version control systems have a built-in `diff` function to compare two versions of the source code, which can be a great help in tracking down new bugs. There are freeware `diff` utilities also available. At one stage, the little-known `windiff.exe` shipped on some versions of the Windows installation CD. Visual Diff is a free tool from Starbase that can be downloaded from `http://www.starbase.com`.

TeamSource is a concurrent version control system frontend that is provided with C++Builder 5 Enterprise and can be purchased as an add-on to the Professional edition. With it you can compare two revisions of the same source file. TeamSource is covered in detail in Chapter 29, "Software Installation and Updates."

CodeSite from Raize Software, Inc. (`http://www.raize.com/`), is a fairly inexpensive but advanced debug output tool. It allows you to send information from your application to a central viewer that provides tools to help you analyze it. All kinds of data can be sent, including complete objects. Each output message is time stamped; in itself this is useful, but it can also be used for basic code timing. Overseer Debugger is similar in function to CodeSite. It is free and can be obtained from `http://delphree.clexpert.com/pages/projects/nexus/overseer_debugger.htm`.

GExperts includes the `dbugint` debugging interface to log debug output in a central place for later review using the `Gdebug.exe` tool. Your application can log different message types and has some extra control over the debug information logged. GExperts is free and is provided on the Companion Tools CD-ROM with C++Builder Professional and Enterprise. It can be downloaded from `http://www.gexperts.org/`.

ClassExplorer Pro from ToolsFactory (`http://www.toolsfactory.com`) is an integrated add-on for C++Builder and Delphi to assist with development and debugging. It greatly enhances class and file navigation and includes a context bar that displays the class and method of the current cursor position. It also provides a fully featured class designer including code generation templates and can create help file documentation of your classes and more. It is available free for non-commercial use.

Sleuth QA Suite from TurboPower Software Company (`http://www.turbopower.com`) contains two products: a runtime resource and API checking program called Sleuth CodeWatch, which is similar to CodeGuard, and a profiler called Sleuth StopWatch. Both are designed specifically for use with C++Builder and Delphi. CodeWatch can detect and filter out known VCL resource leaks to allow you to concentrate on your own bugs. Real-time graphs can alert you to slow memory leaks that occur over time. Sleuth StopWatch was briefly demonstrated in Chapter 6.

MemProof, provided on the Companion Tools CD-ROM with C++Builder Professional and Enterprise and also available at `http://www.totalqa.com/`, is another resource leak detection program. It is freeware and integrates with C++Builder. It can also track BDE and Interbase resource allocations, contains live counters, shows API function calls, and includes SQL tracing extension functions.

There are many third-party bug-tracking tools available. Here are just a few.

- PR-Tracker from Softwise Company. A relatively inexpensive solution to tracking problem reports, bugs, and defects (`http://www.prtracker.com/`).
- SWBTracker from Software With Brains. Also relatively inexpensive, this defect management software for developers is packed with features (`http://www.softwarewithbrains.com/`).
- TestTrack from Seapine Software Inc. (`http://www.seapine.com/`).

Doc-o-Matic from ToolsFactory is a documentation system. It generates HTML and help files from the source code comments in your application (`http://www.doc-o-matic.com`).

WinSight is provided with C++Builder 5 Professional and Enterprise. It provides class, window, and message debugging information at runtime. You can use it to see how your application creates its classes and windows and to monitor a window's messages.

OLE/COM Object Viewer, `OleView.exe`, is provided free in the Microsoft Platform SDK, available for download from the Microsoft Web site.

Many, many more tools exist for helping software developers in the area of debugging. If you find any gems, please let me know!

Testing

Testing is an extension to debugging. It is the detection and sometimes the location of errors. The two facets of software development sometimes overlap in the location of errors, when sufficient test output data can help pinpoint where the error is.

Testing is an essential part of the software development process. Without it, you're not very likely to produce a correctly working, let alone usable, application. The level of testing needed depends on the type of application you are developing, the importance of robustness and safety, and the resources that you have in the development time available (though if you're short on time you should cut features and not quality).

Testing is a massive subject in itself and many, many books have been devoted to it. Here we'll outline some of the general testing principles.

Testing Stages and Techniques

Many different stages of testing are carried out during the overall software development process. Some of the testing stages are described in the following list. Each stage is usually broken down into several smaller repetitive stages. The test stages are usually performed in the order listed:

- **Unit testing**   A *unit* is a small group of related functions or an object or objects. Unit testing and unit debugging often are performed together throughout the development process.

- **Code reviews**   This is a stage at which a programmer's code is checked by a second programmer, usually by eyeballing the source code and discussing it with the original developer.

- **Component testing**   A *component* is a group of units or objects or even a whole program that performs a specific set of functions. It is tested as a whole.

- **Integration testing**   This typically involves combining one or more components into a functional system and testing the interaction between those components and the rest of the system.

- **System testing**   This is testing the system as a whole and usually concentrates on certain aspects such as performance or robustness.

- **Acceptance testing**   This is usually just a milestone indicating that the system is ready for use by the customer by verifying that certain component and integration tests were successful.

- **Field testing**   Typically, field testing is performed by shipping alpha and beta test releases of the system to customers, who provide feedback on errors that are discovered.

- **Regression testing**   This is simply rerunning previous tests after changes are integrated with a working system to verify that the changes work correctly. They are usually performed after implementing a bug fix or adding a new feature.

In addition to these stages of testing, there are different testing techniques. The main two techniques are *whitebox* testing, also known as *glassbox* or *structural* testing, and *blackbox* testing, also known as *functional* testing.

Whitebox testing fully exposes the internals of the part of the system being tested. A number of test cases are used to check the execution path through every line of code. For each branch in the code, an additional test case is required. In some cases, changes to the source code are necessary to support the full range of whitebox testing. For small applications or specific parts of larger ones, you can use the interactive debugger.

Whitebox testing is usually performed at the unit and component testing stages.

> **TIP**
>
> When performing whitebox testing, use debug output, breakpoints, or a profiler that can report code coverage to check which parts of your code are and are not being tested in your test procedures. Formulate specific test cases to ensure that each part of the code is tested.

Blackbox testing is where the part of the system being tested is treated as a black box. This means that for testing purposes the internals of the system (how it works) are hidden; the only visible portion of the system is the interfaces. Data is fed in, and the output data is reviewed for correctness; the detail of what went on inside the box is hidden. Blackbox testing is usually performed at the component, integration, and system testing stages.

With blackbox testing, a wide range of inputs should be tested, including typical valid inputs, valid inputs that are not normally expected, and various invalid inputs. At the very minimum, all boundary conditions and a few middle points should be tested thoroughly.

The problem with blackbox testing is that you're not sure which parts of the code have been tested and which haven't, so by itself blackbox testing is often not enough. A combination of test methods generally produces the best results.

Both whitebox and blackbox testing methods are covered to death in textbooks dedicated to software testing.

Testing Tips

Always test your code! I don't know how many times in the past I've seen untested software, either mine or someone else's, come back to haunt the programmer. It is always better to have a smaller set of robust software than a large set of buggy software. Test your code even if the schedule will be delayed because of it, but inform your team leader or the project manager if you think that this will be so.

You should attempt to build tests into your application during development, not on top of it later. The best time to develop tests is when the code is fresh in your mind. If possible, develop automated tests.

When developing a replacement application, perform the data conversions early. This will not only ensure that you understand the existing system better, it will allow the development schedule to be estimated more accurately. Conversion tools, particularly if some detail of the existing data or system was missed, can take some time to develop.

Don't forget to test your tests! This particularly applies to built-in and automated testing. If the original tests don't test your application correctly or test insufficiently, then they give false hope.

The following are useful testing references:

- A good book that covers all aspects of software testing, applicable to programmers, testers, and project managers alike is *Testing Computer Software* by Kaner, Nguyen, and Falk. Publisher: John Wiley & Sons. ISBN 0-471-35846-0, 1999.

- Dr. Dobb's Journal (`http://www.ddj.com/`) from time to time contains articles on testing. You can purchase individual articles online, or you can buy a CD with over 11 years of issues for around US$80. In particular, the March 2000 issue contains several articles on testing and debugging.

Finally, tests are only as good as the application knowledge of the person analyzing the results. Know how the application should work and then verify that it does work.

Summary

Debugging is a very involved process of finding and fixing bugs. The breadth of issues could fill a book. I hope that this condensed version has shed some light on the subject in areas relevant to your development.

There are several new debugger enhancements in C++Builder 5 that haven't been covered here. Consult the online help for a complete list and their functions.

An excellent resource for help on locating and fixing bugs in general is the Borland newsgroups. They are listed in the "Newsgroups" section in Appendix A, "Information Sources." A good textbook on the subject is *Writing Solid Code* by Steve Maguire, published by Microsoft Press. ISBN 1-556-15551-4, 1993.

As your programming experience grows, try to learn and remember new debugging techniques. To save considerable development, support, and maintenance time, do everything you can to prevent them in the first place.

Using VCL Components

Malcolm Smith
Chris Winters
Damon Chandler
Jarrod Hollingworth
Khalid Almannai

IN THIS CHAPTER

- **VCL Overview**

- **The Streaming Mechanism**

- **Common Control Updates**

- **Miscellaneous VCL Enhancements**

- **Extending the VCL—More than Just a TStringList**

- **Advanced Custom Draw Events**

- **Control Panel Applet Wizard Components**

- **Making Use of Third-Party Components**

The complete text for this chapter appears on the CD-ROM.

Creating Custom Components

Malcolm Smith
Sean Rock
Jamie Allsop

IN THIS CHAPTER

- Why Create Custom Components
- Understanding Component Writing
- Writing Non-Visual Components
- Writing Visual Components
- Creating Custom Data-Aware Components
- Registering Components

The Visual Component Library (VCL) is an extremely powerful tool, and putting together an application is very easy, using the many stock components, classes, and methods that C++Builder provides. However, in some situations you may find that a component doesn't quite provide the capabilities you need. The capability to write and modify components gives you a distinct advantage over other programming languages and is one reason why C++Builder is the tool of choice for many programmers around the world. Creating custom components will give you an insight into how the VCL works and increase your productivity with C++Builder. Judging by the number of commercial component sites on the Internet, it can be a profitable exercise as well.

In this chapter, you will learn about creating properties, methods, and events; creating data-aware components; linking components together; component exceptions; modifying existing components; responding to messages sent to your component; and drawing your own components on the screen. You will also deal with some aspects of the Windows API, so you should review Chapter 24, "Using the Win32 API," if you are unfamiliar with API calls. You can also refer to the Win32 help files that ship with C++Builder for more information. Packages are mentioned in this chapter, so if this is a new concept for you, you should review "Understanding and Using Packages" in Chapter 2, "C++Builder Projects and More on the IDE," and "Using Packages Versus DLLs" in Chapter 15, "DLLs and Plug-Ins." You can also find more information under "PACKAGE macro" and "Creating packages and DLLs" in the C++Builder online help.

Why Create Custom Components

The task of creating components can be quite daunting at first. After reading several articles and tutorials on this topic, it is quite easy to find yourself wondering where to start. The easiest approach is to start with a component that already exists and build upon its features and capabilities.

As trivial as this may seem, you might just find yourself customizing or extending a number of the standard VCL components to suit the design and style of your real-world applications. While building a database application, you might drop a TDBGrid onto your form and change several properties to the same value. Similarly, while developing some in-house utilities, you always drop a TStatusBar onto your form, add some panels, and remove the size grip. Instead of doing this for every project, it would make sense to create your own custom component and have these properties set for you automatically. Not only does this make each new application faster to create, but I also have confidence that they are all bug free. Additionally, should I discover a new bug, all I have to do is correct the code in the component and recompile my projects. They will all inherit the changes without any additional reprogramming.

Understanding Component Writing

There are different types of components. Therefore, the ancestor of your own components will be determined by the very nature of that component.

Non-visual components are derived from `TComponent`. `TComponent` is the minimal descendant that can be used for the creation of a component, because it has the functionality for integration into the IDE and streaming of properties. For a more detailed explanation of streaming, refer to the section "The Streaming Mechanism" in Chapter 8, "Using VCL Components."

A non-visual component is one that is simply a wrapper for other complex code in which there is no visual representation provided to the user. An example is a component that receives error log information and automatically sends it to a linked edit control such as a `TMemo` or `TRichEdit` and appends it to a file on disk. The component itself is invisible to the user of the application, but it continues to function in the background, providing the functionality required by the application.

Windowed components are derived from `TWinControl`. These objects appear to the user at runtime and can be interacted with (such as selecting a file from a list). Although it is possible to create your own components from `TWinControl`, C++Builder provides the `TCustomControl` component to make this task easier.

Graphic components are similar to windowed components, with the main difference being that they don't have a window handle and therefore do not interact with the user. The absence of a handle also means fewer resources are being consumed. Although these components do not interact with the user, it is possible to have these components react to window messages such as those from mouse events. These components are derived from `TGraphicControl`.

Why Build Upon an Existing Component?

The biggest advantage you will find from building upon existing components is the reduced development time of projects. It is also worthwhile to know that all of your components used in your projects are bug free.

Take `TLabel` as an example, of which every project has more than one. If every project you created needed to maintain a particular design style, you could find yourself adding multiple label components and changing their properties to the same values for each new application. By creating a custom component descending from `TLabel`, you can add several of these new labels to a form and be left with only the task of setting their captions and positions.

To demonstrate how easy this can be, we can create a component in about a minute and having to type only three lines of code. From C++Builder's menu, choose Component, New Component. After the New Component dialog opens, select `TLabel` for the new component's

Ancestor Type, and for the Class Name, type in TStyleLabel. For a component that you will be installing into C++Builder's Component Palette and using in applications, you will probably want to choose a more descriptive class name. For this example, you could leave the other options with their default values and simply click the OK button. C++Builder will create the unit files for you; all that is needed is to add the lines of code that will set the label's properties. Once you've made the changes needed, save the file and from C++Builder's menu choose Component, Install Component. If you have the file open in C++Builder's IDE, the Unit File Name edit box will reflect the component's file. Click the OK button to install the component in the Component Palette. Listings 9.1 and 9.2 show the complete code.

LISTING 9.1 The TStyleLabel Header File, StyleLabel.h

```
//----------------------------------------------------------------------
#include <SysUtils.hpp>
#include <Controls.hpp>
#include <Classes.hpp>
#include <Forms.hpp>
#include <StdCtrls.hpp>
//----------------------------------------------------------------------
class PACKAGE TStyleLabel : public TLabel
{
private:
protected:
public:
    __fastcall TStyleLabel(TComponent* Owner);
__published:
};
//----------------------------------------------------------------------
#endif
```

LISTING 9.2 The TStyleLabel Code File, StyleLabel.cpp

```
//----------------------------------------------------------------------
#include <vcl.h>
#pragma hdrstop

#include "StyleLabel.h"
#pragma package(smart_init)
//----------------------------------------------------------------------
// ValidCtrCheck is used to assure that the components created do not have
// any pure virtual functions.
//

static inline void ValidCtrCheck(TStyleLabel *)
```

LISTING 9.2   Continued

```cpp
{
    new TStyleLabel(NULL);
}
//--------------------------------------------------------------------
__fastcall TStyleLabel::TStyleLabel(TComponent* Owner)
    : TLabel(Owner)
{
    Font->Name = "Verdana";
    Font->Size = 12;
    Font->Style = Font->Style << fsBold;
}
//--------------------------------------------------------------------
namespace Stylelabel
{
    void __fastcall PACKAGE Register()
    {
        TComponentClass classes[1] = {__classid(TStyleLabel)};
        RegisterComponents("TestPack", classes, 0);
    }
}
//--------------------------------------------------------------------
```

Another advantage to building upon existing components is the capability to create a base class with all the functionality it requires while leaving the properties unpublished. An example of this would be a specific TListBox type of component that doesn't have the Items property published to the user. By descending this component from TcustomListBox, it is possible to publish the properties you want the user to have access to (at designtime) while making the others available (such as the Items property) only at runtime.

Finally, the properties and events you add to an existing component means writing far less code than if you create the component from scratch.

Designing Custom Components

Although it might seem trivial, the same rules apply to component design as per-application development when creating a custom component from an existing one. It is important to think about the possible future direction your components might take. The previously mentioned components that provide a list of database information don't just descend from TListBox. Instead we decided to create a custom version of TCustomListBox that would contain the additional properties common to each descendant we wanted to create. Each new component was then built upon this custom version, eliminating the need for three different versions of the same code. The final version of each component contained nothing more than the code (properties, methods, and events) that made it unique compared to its relatives.

Using the VCL Chart

To gain an appreciation for C++Builder's VCL architecture, take some time to review the VCL chart that ships with the product. This resource gives you a quick visual overview of not only what components are available but also what they are derived from.

During your learning phase of component design and creation, you should endeavor to model your own components in this same object-oriented fashion, by creating strong, versatile base classes from which to create custom components. Although the source code for the C++Builder components are written in Pascal, it is a worthwhile exercise to look at each of the base classes for a particular component and see for yourself how they all come together. You will soon observe how components sharing the same properties are all derived from the same base class or a descendant of one.

Finally, the chart shows at a glance what base classes are available for your own custom component requirements. In combination with the VCL help files, you can quickly determine the most suitable class from which to derive your components. As mentioned previously, the minimum base class will be TComponent, TWinControl, or TGraphicControl, depending on the type of component you will be creating.

Writing Non-Visual Components

The world of components is built upon three main entities: properties, events, and methods. This section looks at each of these, with the aim of giving you a greater understanding of what makes up a component and how components work together to provide the building blocks of your C++Builder applications.

Properties

Properties come in two flavors: published and non-published. *Published* properties are available in the C++Builder Integrated Development Environment (IDE) at designtime (they are also available at runtime). *Non-published* properties are used at runtime by your application. We will look at non-published properties first.

Non-Published Properties

A component is a packaged class with some additional functionality. Take a look at the sample class in Listing 9.3.

LISTING 9.3   Getting and Setting Private Variables

```
class LengthClass
{
private:
```

LISTING 9.3 Continued

```
    int FLength;

public:
    LengthClass(void){}
    ~LengthClass(void){}
    int GetLength(void);
    void SetLength(int pLength);
    void LengthFunction (void);
}
```

Listing 9.3 shows a private variable used internally by the class and the methods used by the application to read and write its value. This can easily lead to messy code. Take a look at Listing 9.4 for another example.

LISTING 9.4 Using Set and Get Methods

```
LengthClass Rope;
Rope.SetLength(15);
// do something
int NewLength = Rope.GetLength();
```

The code in Listing 9.4 isn't complex by any means, but it can quickly become difficult to read in a complex application. Wouldn't it be better if we could refer to Length as a property of the class? This is what C++Builder allows us to do. In C++Builder, the class could be written as shown in Listing 9.5.

LISTING 9.5 Using a Property to Get and Set Private Variables

```
class LengthClass2
{
private:
    int FLength;

public:
    LengthClass2(void){}
    ~LengthClass2(void){}
    void LengthFunction(void);
    __property int Length = {read = FLength, write = FLength};
}
```

The sample code in Listing 9.4 would be as shown in Listing 9.6.

LISTING 9.6   Setting and Getting with a Property

```
LengthClass Rope;
Rope.Length = 15;
// do something
int NewLength = Rope.Length;
```

The class declaration has now been altered to use a __property (an extension to the C++ language in C++Builder). This property has read and write keywords defined. In Listing 9.6, when you read the Length property, you are returned the value of FLength; when you set the Length property, you are setting the value of FLength.

Why go to all this trouble when you could just make the FLength variable public? Properties allow you to do the following:

- You can make the Length property read-only by not using the write keyword.
- You can provide an application public access to private information of the class without affecting the implementation of the class. This is more relevant when the property value is derived or some action needs to be taken when the value of the property changes.

Listing 9.7 shows a slight variation.

LISTING 9.7   Combining Set and Get Methods with Properties

```
class LengthClass3
{
private:
    int FLength;
    int GetLength(void);
    void SetLength(int pLength);

public:
    LengthClass3(void){}
    ~LengthClass3(void){}
    void LengthFunction(void);
    __property int Length = {read = GetLength, write = SetLength};
}
```

The example in Listing 9.7 is starting to show how properties can become quite powerful. The property declaration shows that the value is returned by the GetLength() method when Length is read. When Length needs to be set, the SetLength() method is called.

The GetLength() method might perform some calculations based on other private members of the class. The SetLength() method might perform some validation and then continue to perform some additional tasks before finally setting the value of FLength.

In C++Builder, an example of this is the connection to a database source when the name of an alias is changed. As a developer, you change the name of the alias. In the background, the component is disconnecting from the current database (if there is one) before attempting to connect to the new source. The implementation is hidden from the user, but it is made available by the use of properties.

Types of Properties

Properties can be of any type, whether it is a simple data type such as int, bool, short, and so on or a custom class. When using custom classes as property types, there are two considerations. The first is that the class must be derived from TPersistent (at a minimum) if it is to be streamed to the form. The second is that, if you need to forward declare the class, you need to use the __declspec(delphiclass) keyword.

The code in Listing 9.8 will compile using typical forward declaration. Note that we haven't yet defined a property.

LISTING 9.8   Forward Declaration

```
class MyClass;
class PACKAGE MyComponent : public TComponent
{
private:
    MyClass *FMyClass;
// ...
};

class MyClass : public TPeristent
{
public:
      __fastcall MyClass (void){}
};
```

The PACKAGE keyword between the class name and class keyword is a macro that expands to code that allows the component to be exported from a package library (.BPL—Borland Package Library). A package library is a special kind of DLL that allows code to be shared between applications. For more information about package libraries and the PACKAGE macro, see "PACKAGE macro" and "Creating packages and DLLs" in the C++Builder online help.

But if we want to add a property of type MyClass, we need to modify the forward declaration as shown in Listing 9.9.

9

LISTING 9.9 Custom Class Property

```
class __declspec(delphiclass) MyClass;

class PACKAGE MyComponent : public TComponent
{
private:
    MyClass *FMyClass;
// ...

__published:
    __property MyClass *Class1 = {read = FMyClass, write = FMyClass};
};

class MyClass : public TPeristent
{
public:
    __fastcall MyClass (void){}
};
```

Published Properties

Publishing properties provides users with access to the properties of the component within the C++Builder IDE at designtime. The properties are displayed in the Object Inspector, allowing the user to see or change the current value of those properties. The properties are also available at runtime, but their main purpose is to provide the user a quick method of setting up the component settings without the need to write a single line of code. Additionally, published properties are streamed to the form, so their values become persistent. This means the values are restored each time the project is opened and when the executable is launched.

Published properties are defined the same as all other properties, but they are defined in the __published area of the class declaration. Listing 9.10 shows an example.

LISTING 9.10 Publishing a Property

```
class PACKAGE LengthClass : public TComponent
{
private:
    int FLength;
    int GetLength(void);
    void SetLength(int pLength);

public:
    __fastcall LengthClass(TObject *Owner) : TComponent(Owner) {}
    __fastcall ~LengthClass(void){}
```

LISTING 9.10   Continued

```
    void LengthFunction(void);

__published:
    __property int Length = {read = Getlength, write = Setlength};
}
```

The previous class is the same as in Listing 9.9 except that the Length property has been moved to the __published section. Published properties shown in the Object Inspector are readable and writeable, but it is possible to make a property read-only and still visible in the IDE by creating a dummy write method. If we were to add a published property in the above component that shows the current version of the component, it would be done as in Listing 9.11.

LISTING 9.11   A Version Property

```
const int MajorVersion = 1;
const int MinorVersion = 0;

class PACKAGE LengthClass : public TComponent
{
private:
    AnsiString FVersion;
    int FLength;
    int GetLength(void);
    void SetLength(int pLength);
    void SetVersion(AnsiString /* pVersion */ )
       {FVersion = AnsiString(MajorVersion) + "." +
       AnsiString(MinorVersion);}

public:
    __fastcall LengthClass(TObject *Owner) : TComponent(Owner)
          {SetVersion("");}
    __fastcall ~LengthClass(void){}
    void LengthFunction(void);

__published:
    __property int Length = {read = Getlength, write = Setlength};
    __property AnsiString Version = {read = FVersion, write = SetVersion};
}
```

We have defined a private variable FVersion, which has its value set in the class constructor. We have then added the Version property to the __published section and assigned the read and write keywords. The read keyword returns the value of Fversion, and the write method sets the value back to the original value. The variable name in the parameter list of

`SetVersion()` has been commented out to prevent compiler warnings that the variable is declared but not used. Because the property is of type `AnsiString`, the `SetVersion()` method by design must have an `AnsiString` parameter in the declaration.

Array Properties

Some properties are arrays, rather than simple data types such as `bool`, `int`, and `AnsiString`. This is not greatly documented for the user. An example of an array property is the `Lines` property of the `TMemo` component. This property allows the user to access the individual lines of the `Memo` component.

Array properties are declared the same as other properties, with two main differences: The declaration includes the appropriate indexes with required types, and these indexes are not limited to being integers. Listings 9.12 through 9.15 illustrate the use of two properties. One takes a string as an index, and the other takes an integer value as an index.

LISTING 9.12   Using a String as an Index

```
class PACKAGE TStringAliasComponent : public TComponent
{
private:
    TStringList RealList;
    TStringList AliasList;
    __AnsiString __fastcall GetStringAlias(AnsiString RawString);
    AnsiString __fastcall GetRealString(int Index);
    void __fastcall SetRealString(int Index, AnsiString Value);
public:
    __property AnsiString AliasString[AnsiString RawString] =
        {read = GetStringAlias};
    __property AnsiString RealString[int Index] = {read=GetRealString,
        write=SetRealString};
}
```

The previous example could be part of a component that internally stores a list of strings and another list of alias strings. The `AliasString` property takes the `RawString` value and returns the alias via the `GetStringAlias()` method. The one thing many component writers are confused about when they first start using array properties is that the declaration uses index notation (that is, `[]`), yet in code you use the same notation as calling another method. Look at the `RealString` property, and notice that not only does it have an `AnsiString` return type but it also takes an integer as an index. The `GetRealString()` method would be called when retrieving a particular string from the list based on the index, as in Listing 9.13.

LISTING 9.13   Array Property Read Method

```
AnsiString __fastcall TStringAliasComponent::GetRealString(int Index)
{
    if(Index > (RealList->Count -1))
        return "";
    return RealList->Strings[Index];
}
```

In code, the property would look like this:

```
AnsiString str = StringAlias1->RealString[0];
```

Now take a look at the `SetRealString()` method. If you are unfamiliar with using arrays as properties, this method declaration may look a bit odd. It takes as its first parameter an integer value as its index and an `AnsiString` value. The `RealList` `TStringList` variable will insert the `AnsiString` in the list at the position specified by the index parameter. Listing 9.14 shows the definition of the `SetRealString()` method.

LISTING 9.14   Array Property Write Method

```
void __fastcall TStringAliasComponent::SetRealString(int Index,
  AnsiString Value)
{
    if((RealList->Count - 1) < Index)
        RealList->Add(Value);
    else
        RealList->Insert(Index, Value);
}
```

In Listing 9.14, the value of the `Index` parameter is checked against the number of strings already in the list. If `Index` is greater, then the string specified by `Value` is simply added to the end of the list. Otherwise, the `Insert()` method of `TStringList` is called to insert the string at the position specified by `Index`. Now you can assign a string to the list like this:

```
StringAlias1->RealString[1] = "Some String";
```

Now here is the fun part. The `GetStringAlias()` method is the read method for the `AliasString` property, which takes a string as an index. You know that the string lists are arrays of strings, so every string has an index, or a position within the list. You can use the `IndexOf()` method of `TStringList` to compare the string passed as the index against the strings contained in the list. This method returns an integer value that is the index of the string within the list, or it returns -1 if the string is not present. Now all you have to do is return the string with the index returned from the call to `IndexOf()` from the list of aliases. This is demonstrated in Listing 9.15.

LISTING 9.15   The GetStringAlias() Method

```
AnsiString __fastcall TStringAliasComponent::GetStringAlias(
  AnsiString RawString)
{
    int Index;
    Index = RealList->IndexOf(RawString);
    if((Index == -1) || (Index > (AliasList->Count-1)))
        return RawString;

    return AliasList->Strings [Index];
}
```

To use the property, you would do something like this:

```
AnsiString MyAliasString = StringAlias1->AliasString("The Raw String");
```

Beyond Read and Write

The code examples in Listing 9.5 thru 9.15 have shown properties using read and write keywords as part of the declaration. C++Builder also provides three more options: default, nodefault, and stored.

The default keyword does not set the default value for the property. Instead, it tells C++Builder what default value will be assigned to this property (by the developer) in the component constructor. The IDE then uses this information to determine whether the value of the property needs to be streamed to the form. If the property is assigned a value equivalent to the default, then the value of this property will not be saved as part of the form. For example

```
__property int IntegerProperty = {read = Finteger, write = Finteger,
  default = 10};
```

The nodefault keyword tells the IDE that this property has no default value associated with it. When a property is declared for the first time, there is no need to include the nodefault keyword, because the absence of a default means there is no default. The nodefault keyword is mainly used when you need to change the definition of the inherited property. For example

```
__property int DescendantInteger = {read = Finteger, write = Finteger,
  nodefault};
```

Be aware that the value of a property with the nodefault keyword in its declaration will be streamed only if a value is assigned to the property or underlying member variable, either in one of its methods or via the Object Inspector.

The stored keyword is used to control the storing of properties. All published properties are stored by default. You can change this behavior by setting the stored keyword to true or false or by giving the name of a function that returns a Boolean result. The code in Listing 9.16 shows an example of the stored keyword in use.

LISTING 9.16   Using the stored Keyword

```
class PACKAGE LengthClass : public TComponent
{
protected:
    int FProp;
    bool StoreProperty(void);

__published:
    __property int AlwaysStore = {read = FProp, write = FProp, stored = true};
    __property int NeverStore = {read = FProp, write = FProp, stored = false};
    __property int SimetimesStore = {read = FProp, write = FProp,
      stored = StoreProperty};
}
```

Order of Creation

If your component has properties that depend on the values of other properties during the streaming phase, you can control the order in which they load (and hence initialize) by declaring them in the required order in the class header. For example, the code in Listing 9.17 loads the properties in the order PropA, PropB, PropC.

LISTING 9.17   Property Dependencies

```
class PACKAGE SampleComponent : public TComponent
{
private:
    int FPropA;
    bool FPropB;
    String FProC;
    void __fastcall SetPropB(bool pPropB);
    void __fastcall SetPropC(String pPropC);

public:
    __property int PropA = {read = FPropA, write = FPropA};
    __property bool PropB = {read = FPropB, write = SetPropB};
    __property String PropC = {read = FPropC, write = SetPropC};
}
```

If you have properties with dependencies and are having trouble getting them to initialize correctly, ensure that the order of the property declarations in the class is correct.

Events

An event in a component is the call of an optional method in response to another incident. The incident could be a hook for the user to perform a task before the component continues, the catching of an exception, or the trapping of a Windows message.

As a simple example, let's assume we have a component that traverses directories from a given root location. If this component were designed to notify the user when the current directory has changed, this would be referred to as an *event*. When the event occurs, the component determines if the user has provided an event handler (a method attached to the event) and calls the respective method. If this all sounds confusing, take a look at Listing 9.18.

LISTING 9.18   Declaring an Event Property

```
class PACKAGE TTraverseDir : public TComponent
{
private:
    AnsiString FCurrentDir;
    TNotifyEvent *FOnDirChanged;

public:
    __fastcall TTraverseDir(TObject *Owner) : TComponent(Owner){
      FOnDirChanged = 0;}
    __fastcall ~TTraverseDir(void){}
    __fastcall Execute();

__published:
    __property AnsiString CurrentDir = {read = FCurrentDir};
    __property TNotifyEvent OnDirChanged = {read = FOnDirChanged,
      write = FOnDirChanged};
}
```

Listing 9.18 shows the relevant sections of code to describe the declaration of a read-only property and a standard event. When this component is executed, there will be instances when the current directory is changed. Let's have a look at some example code:

```
void __fastcall TTraverseDir::Execute(void)
{
// perform the traversing of a directory

// This is where the directory has changed,
// call the DirChanged event if there is one.

if(FOnDirChanged)
```

```
    FOnDirChanged(this);

// remainder of component code here
}
```

The variable FOnDirChanged in the previous example is a pointer to a TNotifyEvent, which is declared as

```
typedef void __fastcall (__closure *TNotifyEvent)(System::TObject* Sender)
```

As you can see, the declaration indicates that a single parameter of type TObject* is expected. When the event is created (by double-clicking the event in the Object Inspector), the IDE creates the following code:

```
void __fastcall TTraverseDir::Traverse1DirChanged(TObject *Sender)
{
}
```

Within this code, the user can now add his own code to be performed when this event is called. In this case, the event is a standard event that simply passes a pointer of the object that generated the event. This pointer allows you to distinguish between multiple components of the same type within the project.

```
void __fastcall TTraverseDir::Traverse1DirChanged(TObject *Sender)
{
if(Sender == Traverse1)
    // perform this code for the component called Traverse1
else
    // handle the alternative here
}
```

How Do We Create an Event That Contains Additional Parameters?

You will recall that the standard event is defined as shown in the following code:

```
typedef void __fastcall (__closure *TNotifyEvent)(System::TObject* Sender)
```

The following code shows how to define a custom event:

```
typedef void __fastcall (__closure *TDirChangedEvent)(System::TObject* Sender,
bool &Abort)
```

In the previous code we have done two things:

- Created a unique typedef. TNotifyEvent is now TDirChangedEvent.
- Added the required parameters to the parameter list.

We can now modify our class declaration. The changes are shown in Listing 9.19.

LISTING 9.19   Custom Event Properties

```
typedef void __fastcall (__closure *TDirChangedEvent)(
  System::TObject* Sender, bool &Abort)

class PACKAGE TTraverseDir : public TComponent
{
private:
    TDirChangedEvent *FOnDirChanged;

__published:
    __property TDirChangedEvent OnDirChanged = {read = FOnDirChanged,
      write = FOnDirChanged};
}
```

Now when the user creates the event, the IDE will add the following code:

```
void __fastcall TTraverseDir::Traverse1DirChanged(TObject *Sender, bool &Abort)
{
}
```

There is only one more change to make, as shown in Listing 9.20: the source code that calls the event.

LISTING 9.20   Calling the Event

```
void __fastcall TTraverseDir::Execute(void)
{
// perform the traversing of a directory

bool &Abort = false;

// This is where the directory has changed,
// call the DirChanged event if there is one.

if(FOnDirChanged)
    FOnDirChanged(this, Abort);

if(Abort)
    // handle the abort process

// remainder of component code here
}
```

The component has been sufficiently modified to allow the user to abort the process if required.

Methods

Methods of a component are supporting routines developed to carry out the various tasks required. They are no different from the methods defined for a typical class. In writing components, the goal is to minimize the number of methods the application needs to call. There are some simple rules to follow when designing your components:

- The user must not be required to call any methods to make the component behave the way he expects. For example, the component must take care of all initializations.
- There must be no dependencies on the order in which given methods must be called. You must design your component to allow for any combination of events to take place. For example, if a user calls a routine that is state dependent (such as trying to query a database when there is no active connection), then the component must handle the situation. Whether the component should attempt to connect or should throw an exception is up to the developer, based on the component's function.
- The user must not be able to call a method that would change the state of a component while it is performing another task.

The best way to handle these situations is to write your methods so that they check the current component state. If all of the requirements are not valid, the component should attempt to correct the problem. Design your components to throw an exception if the component state cannot be corrected. If possible, create custom exceptions so that the user can check for these specific exception types. This is explained further in the next section.

Try to create properties rather than methods. Properties enable you to hide the implementation from the user and hence make the component more intuitive to use. As an example, a database component has a property called `Active` and equivalent `Open()` and `Close()` methods. The following two lines are equivalent:

```
Database1->Active = true
Database1->Open();
```

Likewise, so are these:

```
Database1->Active = false;
Database1->Close();
```

In my opinion, the `Active` property is what should be available to the user. It could be argued that `Open()` and `Close()` methods better describe what the component is doing, but I don't think there is a need for them when they can be represented by a single property, `Active`.

Methods you write for components will typically be public or protected. Private methods should only be written if they are very specific for that component, to the point that even derived components should not call them.

Public Methods

Public methods are those that the user needs to make the component perform as required. It is important to make sure that the methods are efficient, so that they don't tie up the operating system for too long. If this is unavoidable, consider creating an event (or a callback function) that can be used by the developer to inform the user of any processing activity taking place. Providing for the user to abort the processing (by either passing a reference to the event or using another property) is another possibility.

Imagine a component that searches a tree of directories for a given file. Depending on the system being searched, this could take a great deal of processing time. Rather than leaving the user wondering if the application has ceased functioning, it is better to create an event that is called within the method. This event can then provide feedback, such as the current directory being traversed.

Protected Methods

If your components have methods that must not be called by the application developer but need to be called from derived components, these methods are declared as *protected*. This ensures that the method is not called at the wrong time. It is safer to create public methods for the user that call protected methods when all requirements are established first.

When a method is created for the implementation of properties, it should be declared as a *virtual protected* method. This allows descendant components to enhance or replace the implementation used.

An example of a virtual protected method is the `Loaded()` method of components. When a component is completely loaded (streamed from the form), the `Loaded()` method is called.

In some cases, a descendant component needs to know when the component is loaded after all properties have been read, so that it can perform some additional tasks. An example is a component that performs validation in a property setter but cannot perform the validation until all properties have been read. In such a case, create a private variable called `IsLoaded` and set this to `false` in the constructor. (Although this would be done by default, doing it this way makes the code more readable.) Then overload the `Loaded()` method and set `IsLoaded` to `true`. This variable can then be used in the property-implementation methods to perform validation as required.

Listings 9.21 and 9.22 are from the custom `TAliasComboBox` component. `TAliasComboBox` is part of the free `MJFPack` package, which can be downloaded from `http://www.mjfreelancing.com`. The package contains other components that can be linked together in this fashion.

LISTING 9.21   The TAliasComboBox Header File

```
class PACKAGE TAliasComboBox : public TSmartComboBox
{
private:
    bool IsLoaded;

protected:
    virtual void __fastcall Loaded(void);
}
```

LISTING 9.22   The TAliasComboBox Source File

```
void __fastcall TAliasComboBox: :Loaded(void)
{
TComponent::Loaded();

if(!ComponentState.Contains(csDesigning))
    {
    IsLoaded = true;
    GetAliases();
    }
}
```

In this code, you can see that the Loaded() method has been overloaded in the class declaration. In the .CPP file, start by calling the ancestor Loaded() method and then your additional code. Listing 9.22 shows the component verifying that it is not in design mode before it retrieves available alias information. Because the state of certain properties may depend on other properties, additional methods for this component check the IsLoaded variable before performing any processing that may require the value of those properties to be set. Essentially, most of the processing by this component is performed only at runtime.

Creating Component Exceptions

Sometimes it is possible to rethrow an exception that you have caught in your component, which allows the user to deal with the situation. You have more than likely performed a number of steps in your component that need to be cleaned up when an exception occurs. After you have performed the cleanup process, you need to do one of two things.

First, you can rethrow the exception. This would be the standard approach for an error such as Divide By Zero. However, there are situations in which it would be better to convert the exception into an event. This provides very clean handling methods for your users. Don't make the mistake of converting all exceptions to events, because this can sometimes make it harder for your users to develop their applications.

An example might help to make this clearer. Imagine a component performing a number of sequential database queries. This component would be made up of a TStrings property that contains all the queries and an Execute() method that performs them. How does the user want to use this component? Something such as the following would be the most desirable.

```
MultiQuery->Queries->Assign(Memo1->Lines);
MultiQuery1->Execute();
```

This is very simple code for the user to implement, but what about a possible exception? Should the user be required to handle any exceptions himself? This might not be the best approach during one of the queries. A better approach would be to build an event that is called when an exception occurs. Within the event, the user should have the opportunity to abort the process.

Let's create a custom exception that will be called if the user attempts to execute an individual query when it is outside the available index range. For the moment, assume there is another method called ExecuteItem() that takes an index to the list of available queries.

First, we need to create the exception in the header file. This is as simple as creating a new exception class derived from the Exception class, as shown in Listing 9.23.

LISTING 9.23 A Custom Exception Class

```
class EMultiQueryIndexOutOfBounds : public Exception
{
public:
    __fastcall EMultiQueryIndexOutOfBounds(const AnsiString Msg) :
      Exception(Msg){}
};
```

That's it. Now if the user tries to execute a query (by index) and the index provided is outside the available range, we can throw our unique exception.

The code for throwing this exception would be that in Listing 9.24.

LISTING 9.24 Throwing the Custom Exception

```
void __fastcall TMultiQuery::ExecuteItem(int Index)
{
if(Index < 0 || Index > Queries->Count)
    throw EmultiQueryIndexOutOfBounds;
```

LISTING 9.24   Continued

```
// ... perform the query here
}
```

As you can see from Listings 9.23 and 9.24, a custom exception is very easy to create and implement. If this component is to perform the query at designtime, you need to provide the user with a message (rather than have an exception thrown within the IDE). You should modify the code as shown in Listing 9.25.

LISTING 9.25   Throwing an Exception at Designtime

```
void __fastcall TMultiQuery::ExecuteItem(int Index)
{
if(Index < 0 || Index > Queries->Count)
    {
    if(ComponentState.Contains(csDesigning))
        throw EmultiQueryIndexOutOfBounds("The Query index is out of range");
    else
        throw EmultiQueryIndexOutOfBounds;
    }

// ... perform the query here
}
```

The namespace

As you develop your components and name them, there might be other developers who by coincidence use the same names. This will cause conflicts when using both components in the same project. This is overcome with the namespace keyword.

When a component is created using the New Component Wizard, the IDE creates code similar to that shown in Listing 9.26.

LISTING 9.26   namespace Code

```
namespace Aliascombobox
{
    void __fastcall PACKAGE Register()
    {
        TComponentClass classes[1] = {__classid(TAliasComboBox)};
        RegisterComponents("MJF Pack", classes, 0);
    }
}
```

The namespace keyword ensures that the component is created in its own subsystem. Let's look at a case where namespace needs to be used even further within a package.

Suppose that two developers build a clock component and they both happen to create a const variable to indicate the default time mode. If both clocks are used in an application, the compiler will complain because of the duplication.

```
// From the first developer
const bool Mode12;    // 12 hour mode by default
class PACKAGE TClock1 : public TComponent
  {
  }
// From the second developer
const bool Mode12;    // 12 hour mode by default
class PACKAGE TClock2 : public TComponent
  {
  }
```

As you can see, it is important to develop your component packages with this possibility in mind. To get around this issue, use the namespace keyword. After all the #include statements in your header file, surround the code as shown in Listing 9.27.

LISTING 9.27   Surrounding Your Code

```
namespace NClock1
{
class PACKAGE TClock1 : public TComponent
  {
  }
}
```

Develop a convention for all your components. For example, you could start your namespace identifiers with a capital *N* followed by the component name. If it is possible that the same name already has been used, come up with something unique, such as prefixing with your company's initials. Using namespaces in this fashion ensures that your packages will integrate smoothly with others.

Responding to Messages

The VCL does a fantastic job of handling almost all of the window messages you will ever require. There are times, however, when there will be a need to respond to an additional message to further enhance your project.

An example of such a requirement is to support filename drag-and-drop from Windows Explorer onto a string Grid component. We can create such a component, called

TsuperStringGrid, that is nothing more than a descendant of TStringGrid with some additional functionality.

The drag-and-drop operation is handled by the API message WM_DROPFILES. The information needed to carry out the operation is stored in the TWMDropFiles structure.

The interception of window messages in components is the same as for other areas of your projects. The only difference is that we are working with a component and not with the form of a project. Hence, we set up a message map as shown in Listing 9.28.

LISTING 9.28   Trapping Messages

```
BEGIN_MESSAGE_MAP
    MESSAGE_HANDLER(WM_DROPFILES, TWMDropFiles, WmDropFiles)
END_MESSAGE_MAP(TStringGrid)
```

NOTE

There are no trailing semicolons used in declaring the message map. This is because BEGIN_MESSAGE_MAP, MESSAGE_HANDLER, and END_MESSAGE_MAP are macros that expand to code during compilation. The macros contain the necessary semicolons.

The code in Listing 9.28 creates a message map for the component (note TStringGrid in the END_MESSAGE_MAP macro). The message handler will pass all intercepts of the WM_DROPFILES messages to the WmDropFiles() method (which will be created shortly). The information is passed to this method in the TWMDropFiles structure as defined by Windows.

Now we need to create the method that will handle the message. In the protected section of the component we define the method as shown in the following code:

```
protected:
    void __fastcall WmDropFiles(TWMDropFiles &Message);
```

You'll notice we have provided a reference to the required structure as a parameter of the method.

Before this component will work, we need to register the component with Windows, telling it the string grid is allowed to accept the dropped filenames. This is performed when the component is loaded via the DragAcceptFiles() command.

```
DragAcceptFiles(Handle, FCanDropFiles);
```

In the previous code, the FCanDropFiles variable is used by the component to indicate whether it is allowed to accept the filenames as part of a drag-and-drop operation.

Now the method accepts the filenames when the component intercepts the Windows message. The code in Listing 9.29 is stripped slightly from the full version.

LISTING 9.29   Accepting Dropped Files

```
void __fastcall TSuperStringGrid::WmDropFiles(TWMDropFiles &Message)
{
char buff[MAX_PATH];
HDROP hDrop = (HDROP)Message.Drop;
POINT Point;
int NumFiles = DragQueryFile(hDrop, -1, NULL, NULL);
TStringList *DFiles = new TStringList;
DFiles->Clear();
DragQueryPoint(hDrop, &Point);
for(int i = 0; i < NumFiles; i++)
    {
    DragQueryFile(hDrop, i, buff, sizeof(buff));
    DFiles->Add(buff);
    }
DragFinish(hDrop);

// do what you want with the list of files now stored in DFiles

delete DFiles;
}
```

An explanation of this code is beyond the scope of this chapter. The help files supplied with C++Builder provide a good overview of what each function performs.

As you can see, intercepting messages is not hard once you understand how to set them up, although some understanding of the Windows API is required. Refer to the messages.hpp file for a list of the message structures available.

Designtime Versus Runtime

We've already made some references to the operation of a component at designtime compared to runtime. *Designtime* operation refers to how the component behaves while the user is creating the project in the IDE. *Runtime* operation refers to what the component does when the application is executed.

The TComponent object has a property (a Set) called ComponentState that is made up of the following constants: csAncestor, csDesigning, csDesignInstance, csDestroying, csFixups, csFreeNotification, csInline, csLoading, csReading, csWriting, and csUpdating. Table 9.1 lists these ComponentState flags and gives the purpose of each.

TABLE 9.1 The `ComponentState` Flags

Flag	Purpose
csAncestor	Indicates that the component was introduced in an ancestor form. Set only if `csDesigning` is also set. Set or cleared in the `TComponent::SetAncestor()` method.
csDesigning	Indicates that the component is being manipulated at designtime. Used to distinguish designtime and runtime manipulation. Set or cleared in the `TComponent::SetDesigning()` method.
csDesignInstance	Indicates that the component is the root object in a designer. For example, it is set for a frame when you are designing it, but not on a frame that acts like a component. This flag always appears with `csDesigning`. Set or cleared in the `TComponent::SetDesignInstance()` method. New in C++Builder 5.
csDestroying	Indicates that the component is being destroyed. Set in the `TComponent::Destroying()` method.
csFixups	Indicates that the component is linked to a component in another form that has not yet been loaded. This flag is cleared when all pending fixups are resolved. Cleared in the `GlobalFixupReferences()` global function.
csFreeNotification	Indicates that the component has sent a notification to other forms that it is being destroyed but has not yet been destroyed. Set in the `TComponent::FreeNotification()` method. New in C++Builder 5.
csInline	Indicates that the component is a top-level component that can be modified at designtime and also embedded in a form. This flag is used to identify nested frames while loading and saving. Set or cleared in the component's `SetInline()` method. Also set in the `TReader::ReadComponent()` method. New in C++Builder 5.
csLoading	Indicates that a filer object is currently loading the component. This flag is set when the component is first created and not cleared until the component and all its children are fully loaded (when the `Loaded()` method is called). Set in the `TReader::ReadComponent()` and `TReader::ReadRootComponent()` methods. Cleared in the `TComponent::Loaded()` method. (For more information on filer objects, see "TFiler" in the C++Builder online help index.)

TABLE 9.1 Continued

Flag	Purpose
csReading	Indicates that the component is reading its property values from a stream. Note that the csLoading flag is always set when csReading is set. That is, csReading is set for the period of time that a component is reading in property values when the component is loading. Set and cleared in the TReader::ReadComponent() and TReader::ReadRootComponent() methods.
csWriting	Indicates that the component is writing its property values to a stream. Set and cleared in the TWriter::WriteComponent() method.
csUpdating	Indicates that the component is being updated to reflect changes in an ancestor form. Set only if csAncestor is also set. Set in the TComponent::Updating() method and cleared in the TComponent::Updated() method.

The Set member we are most interested in is csDesigning. As long as the component exists in the IDE (as part of a developing project), the component will contain this constant as part of the Set to indicate that it is being used at designtime. To determine if a component is being used at designtime, use the following code:

```
if(ComponentState.Contains(csDesigning))
    // carry out the designtime code here
else
    // carry out the runtime code here
```

Why would you need to run certain code at runtime only? There are many instances when this is required, such as the following:

- To specifically validate a property that has dependencies available only at runtime
- To display a warning message to the user if he sets an inappropriate property value
- To display a selection dialog or a property editor if an invalid property value is given

Many component writers don't go to the trouble of providing the user with these types of warnings and dialogs. However, it is these extra features that make a component more intuitive and user friendly.

Linking Components

Linking components refers to giving a component the capability to reference or alter another component in the same project. An example in C++Builder is the TDriveComboBox component. This component has a property called DirList that allows the developer to select a

TDirectoryListBox component available on the same form. This type of link gives the developer a quick and easy method to update the directory listing automatically every time the selected drive is changed. Creating a project to display a list of directories and filenames doesn't get any easier than dropping three components (TDriveComboBox, TdirectoryListBox, and TFileListBox) onto a form and setting two properties. Of course, you still need to assign code to the event handlers to actually make the project perform something useful, but up to that point there isn't a single line of code to be written.

Providing a link to other components starts by creating a property of the required type. If you create a property of type TLabel, the Object Inspector will show all available components on the form that are of type TLabel. To show how this works for descendant components, we are going to create a simple component that can link to a TMemo or a TRichEdit component. To do this, you need to realize that both components descend from TCustomMemo.

Let's start by creating a component descending from TComponent that has a property called LinkedEdit (see Listing 9.30).

LISTING 9.30   Linked Components

```
class PACKAGE TMsgLog : public TComponent
{
private:
    TCustomMemo *FLinkedEdit;
➥// can be TMemo or TRichEdit or any other derived component

public:
    __fastcall TMsgLog(TComponent* Owner);
    __fastcall ~TMsgLog(void);

    void __fastcall OutputMsg(const AnsiString Message);

protected:
    virtual void __fastcall Notification(TComponent *AComponent,
      TOperation Operation);

__published:
    __property TCustomMemo *LinkedEdit = {read = FLinkedEdit,
      write = FLinkedEdit};
};
```

The code in Listing 9.30 creates the component with a single property, called LinkedEdit. There are two more things to take care of. First, we need to output the messages to the linked Memo or RichEdit component (if there is one). We also need to take care of the possibility that the user might delete the linked edit control. The OutputMsg() method is used to pass the text message to the linked edit control, and the Notification() method is used to detect if it has been deleted.

The following provides the output:

```
void __fastcall TMsgLog::OutputMsg(const AnsiString Message)
{
if(FLinkedEdit)
    FLinkedEdit->Lines->Add(Message);
}
```

Because both TMemo and TRichEdit components have a Lines property, there is no need to perform any casting. If you need to perform a task that is component specific (or handled differently), use the code shown in Listing 9.31.

LISTING 9.31   The OutputMsg() Method

```
void __fastcall TMsgLog::OutputMsg(const AnsiString Message)
{
TMemo *LinkedMemo = 0;
TRichEdit *LinkedRichEdit = 0;

LinkedMemo = dynamic_cast<TMemo *>(FLinkedEdit);
LinkedRichEdit = dynamic_cast<TRichEdit *>(FLinkedEdit);

if(FLinkedMemo)
    FLinkedMemo->Lines->Add(Message);
else
    {
    FLinkedRichEdit->Font->Color = clRed;
    FLinkedRichEdit->Lines->Add(Message);
    }
}
```

The final check is to detect the linked edit control being deleted. This is done by overloading the Notification() method of TComponent as shown in Listing 9.32.

LISTING 9.32   The Notification() Method

```
void __fastcall TMsgLog::Notification(TComponent *AComponent,
  TOperation Operation)
{
// We don't care about controls being added.
if(Operation != opRemove)
    return ;

// We have to check each one in case the user did something
```

LISTING 9.32 Continued

```
// like have the same label attached to multiple properties.
if(AComponent == FLinkedEdit)
    FLinkedEdit = 0;
}
```

The code in Listing 9.32 shows how to handle code resulting from another component being deleted. The first two lines are to show the purpose of the Operation parameter.

The most important code is the last two lines, which compare the pointer AComponent to the LinkedEdit property (a pointer to a component descending from TCustomMemo). If the pointers match, we NULL the LinkedEdit pointer. This removes the reference from the Object Inspector and ensures that our code is no longer pointing to a memory address that is about to be lost (when the edit component is actually deleted). Note that LinkedEdit = 0 is the same as LinkedEdit = NULL.

One final point is that if you link your component to another that has dependencies (such as TDBDataSet descendants that require a database connection), it is up to you to ensure that these dependencies are checked and handled appropriately. Good component design is recognized when the user has the least amount of work to do in order to get the component to behave as expected.

Linking Events Between Components

We've looked at how components can be linked together via properties. Our discussion so far has been of how a property of TMsgLog can be linked to another component so that messaging can be provided automatically without the user having to write the associated code.

What we are going to look at now is how to link events between components. Continuing with the previous examples, we're going to show how we intercept the OnExit event for the linked edit control (note that TMemo and TRichEdit both have an OnExit event and are of type TNotifyEvent) so that we can perform some additional processing after the user's code has executed. Let's assume the linked edit control is not read-only. This means the user could enter something into the log; this change needs to be recorded as a user-edited entry. We will demonstrate how to perform the intercept and leave the functionality up to you.

Component events can be implemented differently according to the nature of the event itself. If the component is looping through a process, then the code might simply have a call to execute the event handler if one exists. Take a look at the following example:

```
// start of loop
if(FOnExit)
    FOnExit(this);
endif;
// ...
// end of loop
```

Other events could result from a message. Listing 9.26 showed the message map macro for accepting files dropped onto a control from Windows Explorer as follows:

```
BEGIN_MESSAGE_MAP
    MESSAGE_HANDLER(WM_DROPFILES, TWMDropFiles, WmDropFiles)
END_MESSAGE_MAP(TStringGrid)
```

If our component has an OnDrop event, we can write our implementation as shown in the following code:

```
void __fastcall TSuperStringGrid::WmDropFiles(TWMDropFiles &Message)
{
if(FOnDrop)
    FOnDrop(this);
endif;

// ... remainder of code here
}
```

What you should have noticed by now is that the components maintain a pointer to the event handler, such as FOnExit and FOnDrop in the previous example. This makes it very easy to create our own pointer to note where the user's handler resides and then redirect the user's event so that it calls an internal method instead. This internal method will execute the user's original code, followed by the component's code (or vice versa).

The only other consideration to make is when you redirect the pointers. The logical place to do this is in the component's Loaded() method. This is called when the entire component is streamed from the form, and hence all of the user's event handlers have been assigned.

Define the Loaded() method and a pointer to a standard event in your class. (The event is the same type as the one we are going to intercept; in our case it is the OnExit event, which is of type TNotifyEvent.) We also need an internal method with the same declaration as the event we are intercepting. In our class we create a method called MsgLogOnExit. This is the method that will be called before the OnExit event of the linked edit control. In Listing 9.33, we include a typedef of type TComponent called Inherited. The reason will become obvious when we get to the source code.

LISTING 9.33   The TMsgLog Class Header File

```
class PACKAGE TMsgLog : public TComponent
{
typedef TComponent Inherited;

private:
    TNotifyEvent *FonUsersExit;
    void __fastcall MsgLogOnExit(TObject *Sender);
```

LISTING 9.33   Continued

```
protected:
    virtual void __fastcall Loaded(void);

// ... remainder of code not shown
}
```

In the source code, you might have something such as Listing 9.34.

LISTING 9.34   The TMsgLog Class Source File

```
void __fastcall TMsgLog::TMsgLog(TComponent *Owner)
{
FOnUsersExit = 0;
}

void __fastcall TMsgLog::Loaded(void)
{
Inherited::Loaded();

if(!ComponentState.Contains(csDesigning))
    {
    if(FlinkedEdit)
        {
        if(FlinkedEdit->OnExit)
            FOnUsersExit = FlinkedEdit->OnExit;

        FlinkedEdit->OnExit = MsgLogOnExit;
        }
    }
}

void __fastcall TMsgLog::MsgLogOnExit(TObject *Sender)
{
if(FOnUsersExit)
    FOnUsersExit(this);

// ... and now perform the additional code we want to do
}
```

When the component is first created, the constructor initializes FOnUsersExit to NULL. When the form is completely streamed, the component's OnLoaded event is called. This starts by calling the inherited method first (the typedef simply helps to make the code easy to read). Next we make sure the component is not in design mode. If the application is in runtime mode, we see if the component has a linked edit control. If so, we find out if the user has assigned a method to the `OnExit` event of that control. If these tests are `true`, we set our internal pointer `FOnUsersExit` to the address of the user's event handler. Finally, we reassign the edit control's event handler to our internal method `MsgLogOnExit()`. This results in the `MsgLogOnExit()` method being called every time the cursor exits the edit control, even if the user did not assign an event handler.

The `MsgLogOnExit()` method starts by determining if the user assigned an event handler; if so, it is executed. We then continue to perform the additional processing tasks we want to implement. The decision to call the user's event before or after our own code is executed depends on the nature of the event, such as data encryption or validation.

Writing Visual Components

As you've seen, components can be any part of a program that the developer can interact with. Components can be non-visual (`TOpenDialog` or `TTable`) or visual (`TListBox` or `TButton`). The most obvious difference between them is that visual components have the same visual characteristics during designtime as they do during runtime. As the properties of the component that determine its visual appearance are changed in the Object Inspector, the component must be redrawn or repainted to reflect those changes. Windowed controls are wrappers for Windows Common Controls, and Windows will take care of redrawing the control more often than not. In some situations, such as with a component that is not related to any existing control, redrawing the component is up to you. In either case, it is helpful to know some of the useful classes that C++Builder provides for drawing onscreen.

Where to Begin

One of the most important considerations when writing components is the parent class from which to inherit. You should review the help files and the VCL source code if you have it. This is time well spent; there is nothing more frustrating than having worked on a component for hours or days just to discover that it doesn't have the capabilities you need. If you are writing a windowed component (one that can receive input focus and has a window handle), derive it from `TCustomControl` or `TWinControl`. If your component is purely graphical, such as a `TSpeedButton`, then derive from `TGraphicControl`. There are very few if any limitations when it comes to writing visual components, and there is a wealth of freeware and shareware components and source code on the Internet from which to get ideas.

TCanvas

The `TCanvas` object is C++Builder's wrapper for the Device Context. It encapsulates various tools for drawing complex shapes and graphics onscreen. `TCanvas` can be accessed through the `Canvas` property of most components, although some windowed controls are drawn by

Windows and so do not provide a `Canvas` property. There are ways around this, and we'll discuss them shortly. `TCanvas` also provides several methods to draw lines, shapes, and complex graphics onscreen.

Listing 9.35 is an example of how to draw a line diagonally from the upper-left corner to the bottom-right corner of the canvas. The `LineTo()` method draws a line from the current pen position to the coordinates specified in the `X` and `Y` variables. First set the start position of the line by calling the `MoveTo()` method.

LISTING 9.35   Drawing a Line Using `MoveTo()`

```
Canvas->MoveTo(0, 0);
int X = ClientRect.Right;
int Y = ClientRect.Bottom;
Canvas->LineTo (X, Y);
```

Listing 9.36 uses the `Frame3D()` method to draw a frame around a canvas, giving the control a button appearance.

LISTING 9.36   Creating a Button Appearance

```
int PenWidth = 2;
TColor Top = clBtnHighlight;
TColor Bottom = clBtnShadow;
Frame3D(Canvas, ClientRect, Top, Bottom, PenWidth);
```

It is also very common to use API drawing routines with the `TCanvas` object to accomplish certain effects. Some API drawing methods use the DeviceContext of the control, although it isn't always necessary to get the `HDC` of the control to call an API that requires it. To get the `HDC` of a control, use the `GetDC()` API.

> **NOTE**
>
> `HDC` is the data type returned by the call to `GetDC()`. It is simply the handle of the DeviceContext and is synonymous with the `Handle` property of `TCanvas`.

```
HDC dc = GetDC(SomeComponent->Handle);
```

Listing 9.37 uses a form with `TPaintBox` (we'll use `TPaintBox` because its `Canvas` property is published) and calls the `RoundRect()` API to draw an ellipse within the `TPaintBox`. The `TPaintBox` can be placed anywhere on the form. The code would be placed in the `OnPaint` event handler for the `TPaintBox`. The full project can be found in the `PaintBox1` folder on the CD-ROM that accompanies this book. The project filename is `Project1.bpr`.

LISTING 9.37   Using API Drawing Methods

```
void __fastcall TForm1::PaintBox1Paint(TObject *Sender)
{
    // We'll use a TRect structure to save on typing
    TRect Rect;
    int nLeftRect, nTopRect, nRightRect, nBottomRect, nWidth, nHeight;

    Rect = PaintBox1->ClientRect;
    nLeftRect = Rect.Left;
    nTopRect = Rect.Top;
    nRightRect = Rect.Right;
    nBottomRect = Rect.Bottom;
    nWidth = Rect.Right - Rect.Left;
    nHeight = Rect.Bottom - Rect.Top;

    if(RoundRect(
        PaintBox1->Canvas->Handle, // handle of device context
        nLeftRect,  // x-coord. of bounding rect's upper-left       corner
        nTopRect,     // y-coord. of bounding rect's upper-left corner
        nRightRect,  // x-coord. of bounding rect's lower-right corner
        nBottomRect,  // y-coord. of bounding rect's lower-right corner
        nWidth,  // width of ellipse used to draw rounded corners
        nHeight  // height of ellipse used to draw rounded corners
        ) == 0)
        ShowMessage("RoundRect failed...");
}
```

Try changing the values of the `nWidth` and `nHeight` variables. Start with zero; the rectangle will have sharp corners. As you increase the value of these two variables, the corners of the rectangle will become more rounded. This method and other similar drawing routines can be used to create buttons or other controls that are rounded or elliptical. Some examples will be shown later. See "Painting and Drawing Functions" in the Win32 help files that ship with C++Builder for more information.

Using Graphics in Components

Graphics are becoming more commonplace in components. Some familiar examples are `TSpeedButton` and `TBitButton`, and there are several freeware, shareware, and commercial components available that use graphics of some sort. Graphics add more visual appeal to components and, fortunately, C++Builder provides several classes to handle bitmaps, icons, JPEGs, and GIFs. The norm for drawing components is to use an off-screen bitmap to do the drawing and then copy the bitmap to the onscreen canvas. This reduces screen flicker because the canvas is painted only once. This is very useful if the image you are working with contains complex shapes or images. The TBitmap class has a Canvas property, which is a TCanvas object and thus allows you to draw shapes and graphics off the screen.

The following example uses a form with a TPaintBox component. A TBitmap object is created and used to draw an image similar to a TSpeedButton with its Flat property set to true. The TBitmap is then copied to the screen in one action. In this example we add a TButton, which will change the appearance of the image from raised to lowered. The full project can be found in the PaintBox2 folder on the CD-ROM that accompanies this book. The project filename is Project1.bpr. First, take a look at the header file in Listing 9.38.

LISTING 9.38   Creating a Raised or Lowered Appearance

```
class TForm1 : public TForm
{
__published:    // IDE-managed Components
    TPaintBox *PaintBox1;
    TButton *Button1;
private:        // User declarations
    bool IsUp;
public:         // User declarations
    __fastcall TForm1(TComponent* Owner);
};
```

We declare a Boolean variable IsUp, which we'll use to swap the highlight and shadow colors and to change the caption of the button. If IsUp is true, the image is in its up state; if the value of IsUp is false, the image is in its down state. Because IsUp is a member variable, it will be initialized to false when the form is created. The Caption property of Button1 can be set to Up via the Object Inspector.

The OnClick event of the button is quite simple. It changes the value of the IsUp variable, changes the Caption property of the button based on the new value, and calls the TPaintBox's Repaint() method to redraw the image. This is shown Listing 9.39.

LISTING 9.39   The Button1Click() Method

```
void __fastcall TForm1::Button1Click(TObject *Sender)
{
    IsUp = !IsUp;
    Button1->Caption = (IsUp) ? "Down" : "Up";
    PaintBox1->Repaint ();
}
```

9

CREATING
CUSTOM
COMPONENTS

A private method, SwapColors(), is declared and will change the highlight and shadow colors based on the value of the IsUp variable. This is shown in Listing 9.40.

LISTING 9.40   The SwapColors() Method

```
void __fastcall TForm1::SwapColors(TColor &Top, TColor &Bottom)
{
    Top = (IsUp) ? clBtnHighlight : clBtnShadow;
    Bottom = (IsUp) ? clBtnShadow :  clBtnHighlight;
}
```

The final step is to create an event handler for the OnPaint event of the TPaintBox. This is shown in Listing 9.41.

LISTING 9.41   Painting the Button

```
void __fastcall TForm1::PaintBox1Paint(TObject *Sender)
{
    TColor TopColor, BottomColor;
    TRect Rect;

    Rect = PaintBox1->ClientRect;

    Graphics::TBitmap *bit = new Graphics::TBitmap;
    bit->Width = PaintBox1->Width;
    bit->Height = PaintBox1->Height;
    bit->Canvas->Brush->Color = clBtnFace;
    bit->Canvas->FillRect(Rect);
    SwapColors(TopColor, BottomColor);
    Frame3D(bit->Canvas, Rect, TopColor, BottomColor, 2);
    PaintBox1->Canvas->Draw(0, 0, bit);
    delete bit;
}
```

Listing 9.42 will go one step further and demonstrate how to use bitmap files as well as drawing lines on a canvas. Most button components, for example, contain not only lines and borders that give it shape, but also icons, bitmaps, and text. This can become a bit more complicated because it requires a second TBitmap to load the graphics file, the position of the graphic must be calculated and copied to the first bitmap, and the final result must be copied to the onscreen canvas. The full project can be found in the PaintBox3 folder on the CD-ROM that accompanies this book. The project filename is Project1.bpr.

Other mouse events such as OnMouseUp, OnMouseDown, and OnMouseOver are conveniently declared in the protected section of Tcontrol, so all that is necessary is to override the methods to which you want to respond. If you want derivatives of your component to have the capability to override these events, remember to declare them in the protected section of the component's header file. This is shown in Listing 9.45.

LISTING 9.45   Overriding TControl's Mouse Events

```
private:
    TMmouseEvent FOnMouseUp;
    TMouseEvent FOnMouseDown;
    TMouseMoveEvent FOnMouseMove;

protected:
    void __fastcall MouseDown(TMouseButton Button, TShiftState Shift, int X,
        int Y);
    void __fastcall MouseMove(TshiftState Shift, int X, int Y);
    void __fastcall MouseUp(TMouseButton Button, TShiftState Shift, int X,
        int Y);

__published:
    __property TMouseEvent OnMouseUp = {read=FOnMouseUp, write=FOnMouseUp};
    __property TMouseEvent OnMouseDown = {read=FOnMouseDown,
        write=FOnMouseDown};
    __property TMouseMoveEvent OnMouseMove = {read=FOnMouseMove,
        write=FOnMouseMove};
```

In the example projects shown previously, an event handler was created for the OnPaint() event of TPaintBox. This event is fired when the control receives the WM_PAINT message. TGraphicControl traps this message and provides a virtual Paint() method that can be overridden in descendant components to draw the control onscreen or, as TPaintBox does, provide an OnPaint() event.

These messages and others are defined in messages.hpp. If you have the VCL source code, take time to find out which messages or events are available and which methods can be overridden.

Putting It All Together

This section will cover putting all the above techniques into a basic component that you can expand and enhance. This component is not complete, although it could be installed onto C++Builder's Component Palette and used in an application. As a component writer, you should never leave things to chance; the easier your component is to use, the more likely it will be used. The example shown in Listings 9.46 and 9.47 will be a type of Button component that responds like a TSpeedButton and has a bitmap and text. The source code is shown in Listings 9.46 and 9.47, and then we'll look at some of the obvious enhancements that could be made. The source code is also provided in the ExampleButton folder on the CD-ROM that accompanies this book.

Listing 9.46   The TExampleButton Header File, ExampleButton.h

```
//----------------------------------------------------------------------------
#ifndef ExampleButtonH
#define ExampleButtonH
//----------------------------------------------------------------------------
#include <SysUtils.hpp>
#include <Controls.hpp>
#include <Classes.hpp>
#include <Forms.hpp>
//----------------------------------------------------------------------------

enum TExButtonState {esUp, esDown, esFlat, esDisabled};

class PACKAGE TExampleButton : public TGraphicControl
{
private:

    Graphics::TBitmap *FGlyph;
    AnsiString FCaption;
    TImageList *FImage;
    TExButtonState FState;
    bool FMouseInControl;
    TNotifyEvent FOnClick;
    void __fastcall SetGlyph(Graphics::TBitmap *Value);
    void __fastcall SetCaption(AnsiString Value);
    void __fastcall BeforeDestruction(void);
    void __fastcall SwapColors(TColor &Top, TColor &Bottom);
    void __fastcall CalcGlyphLayout(TRect &r);
    void __fastcall CalcTextLayout(TRect &r);
    MESSAGE void __fastcall CMMouseEnter(TMessage &Msg);
    MESSAGE void __fastcall CMMouseLeave(TMessage &Msg);
    MESSAGE void __fastcall CMEnabledChanged(TMessage &Msg);
protected:

    void __fastcall Paint(void);
    void __fastcall MouseDown(TMouseButton Button, TShiftState Shift,
                             int X, int Y);
    void __fastcall MouseUp(TMouseButton Button, TShiftState Shift,
                           int X, int Y);
```

LISTING 9.46   Continued

```
public:

    __fastcall TExampleButton(TComponent* Owner);

__published:

    __property AnsiString Caption = {read=FCaption, write=SetCaption};
    __property Graphics::TBitmap * Glyph = {read=FGlyph, write=SetGlyph};
    __property TNotifyEvent OnClick = {read=FOnClick, write=FOnClick};

BEGIN_MESSAGE_MAP
  MESSAGE_HANDLER(CM_MOUSEENTER, TMessage, CMMouseEnter)
  MESSAGE_HANDLER(CM_MOUSELEAVE, TMessage, CMMouseLeave)
  MESSAGE_HANDLER(CM_ENABLEDCHANGED, TMessage, CMEnabledChanged)
END_MESSAGE_MAP(TGraphicControl)
};
//--------------------------------------------------------------------------
#endif
```

LISTING 9.47   The TExampleButton Source File, ExampleButton.cpp

```
//--------------------------------------------------------------------------
#include <vcl.h>
#pragma hdrstop

#include "ExampleButton.h"
#pragma package(smart_init)
//--------------------------------------------------------------------------
// ValidCtrCheck is used to assure that the components created do not have
// any pure virtual functions.
//

static inline void ValidCtrCheck(TExampleButton *)
{
    new TExampleButton(NULL);
}
//--------------------------------------------------------------------------
__fastcall TExampleButton::TExampleButton(TComponent* Owner)
  : TGraphicControl(Owner)
{
    SetBounds(0,0,50,50);
    ControlStyle = ControlStyle << csReplicatable;
    FState = esFlat;
}
```

LISTING 9.47   Continued

```
//-------------------------------------------------------------------------

namespace Examplebutton
{
    void __fastcall PACKAGE Register()
    {
        TComponentClass classes[1] = {__classid(TExampleButton)};
        RegisterComponents("Samples", classes, 0);
    }
}
// -------------------------------------------------------------------------
void __fastcall TExampleButton::CMMouseEnter(TMessage &Msg)
{
    if(Enabled)
        {
        FState = esUp;
        FMouseInControl = true;
        Invalidate();
        }
}
// -------------------------------------------------------------------------
void __fastcall TExampleButton::CMMouseLeave(TMessage &Msg)
{
    if(Enabled)
        {
        FState = esFlat;
        FMouseInControl = false;
        Invalidate();
        }
}
// -------------------------------------------------------------------------
void __fastcall TExampleButton::CMEnabledChanged(TMessage &Msg)
{
    FState = (Enabled) ? esFlat : esDisabled;
    Invalidate();
}

// -------------------------------------------------------------------------
void __fastcall TExampleButton::MouseDown(TMouseButton Button, TShiftState
  Shift, int X, int Y)
{
    if(Button == mbLeft)
        {
        if(Enabled && FMouseInControl)
            {
```

LISTING 9.47 Continued

```cpp
            FState = esDown;
            Invalidate();
            }
        }
}
// --------------------------------------------------------------------------
void __fastcall TExampleButton::MouseUp(TMouseButton Button, TShiftState
  Shift, int X, int Y)
{
    if(Button == mbLeft)
        {
        if(Enabled && FMouseInControl)
            {
            FState = esUp;
            Invalidate();
            if(FOnClick)
                FOnClick(this);
            }
        }
}
// --------------------------------------------------------------------------
void __fastcall TExampleButton::SetGlyph(Graphics::TBitmap * Value)
{
    if(Value == NULL)
        return;

    if(!FGlyph)
        FGlyph = new Graphics::TBitmap;
    FGlyph->Assign(Value);
    Invalidate();
}

// --------------------------------------------------------------------------
void __fastcall TExampleButton::SetCaption(AnsiString Value)
{
    FCaption = Value;
    Invalidate();
}
// --------------------------------------------------------------------------
void __fastcall TExampleButton::SwapColors(TColor &Top, TColor &Bottom)
{
    if(ComponentState.Contains(csDesigning))
        {
        FState = esUp;
        }
```

9

CREATING
CUSTOM
COMPONENTS

LISTING 9.47 Continued

```cpp
    Top = (FState == esUp) ? clBtnHighlight : clBtnShadow;
    Bottom = (FState == esDown) ? clBtnHighlight : clBtnShadow;
}
// --------------------------------------------------------------------------
void __fastcall TExampleButton::BeforeDestruction(void)
{
    if(FImage)
        delete FImage;

    if(FGlyph)
        delete FGlyph;
}
// --------------------------------------------------------------------------
void __fastcall TExampleButton::Paint(void)
{
    TRect cRect, tRect, gRect;
    TColor TopColor, BottomColor;

    Canvas->Brush->Color = clBtnFace;
    Canvas->FillRect(ClientRect);
    cRect = ClientRect;
    Graphics::TBitmap *bit = new Graphics::TBitmap;
    bit->Width = ClientWidth;
    bit->Height = ClientHeight;
    bit->Canvas->Brush->Color = clBtnFace;
    bit->Canvas->FillRect(cRect);

    if(FGlyph)
        if(!FGlyph->Empty)
            {
            CalcGlyphLayout(gRect);
            bit->Canvas->BrushCopy(gRect, FGlyph,
                Rect(0,0,FGlyph->Width,FGlyph->Height),
                  FGlyph->TransparentColor);
            }
    if(!FCaption.IsEmpty())
        {
        CalcTextLayout(tRect);
        bit->Canvas->TextRect(tRect, tRect.Left,tRect.Top, FCaption);
        }

    if(FState == esUp || FState == esDown)
        {
        SwapColors(TopColor, BottomColor);
        Frame3D(bit->Canvas, cRect, TopColor, BottomColor, 1);
        }
```

Declare `read` and `write` Access

The access you allow your control is governed b
We are going to give our component full access.
cally take care of the read-only option, because t
that this will not stop the developer from writing
database via this control. If you require read-onl

The code in Listings 9.57 and 9.58 shows the de
sponding `read` and `write` implementation metho

LISTING 9.57   The `TDBMaskEdit` Class Declara

```
class PACKAGE TDBMaskEdit : public TMaskE
{
private:
    ...
    AnsiString __fastcall GetDataField(vc
    TDataSource* __fastcall GetDataSource
    void __fastcall SetDataField(AnsiStri
    void __fastcall SetDataSource(TDataSc
    ...
__published:
    __property AnsiString DataField = {re
        write = SetDataField, nodefault};
    __property TDataSource *DataSource =
        write = SetDataSource,  nodefault};
};
```

LISTING 9.58   The `TDBMaskEdit` Methods fro

```
AnsiString __fastcall TDBMaskEdit::GetDat
{
    return(FDataLink->FieldName);
}

TDataSource * __fastcall TDBMaskEdit::Get
{
    return(FDataLink->DataSource);
}

void __fastcall TDBMaskEdit::SetDataField
{
    FDataLink->FieldName = pDataField;
```

Creating Custom Data-Aware Components

Just as with any other custom component, it is important to decide from the start which ancestor will be used for the creation of a data-aware component. In this section we are going to look at extending the `TMaskEdit` edit component so that it will read data from a datasource and display it in the masked format provided. This type of control is known as a *data-browsing control*. We will then extend this control further to make it a data-aware control, meaning that changes to the field or database will be reflected in both directions.

Making the Control Read-Only

The control we are going to create already has `ReadOnly`, a read-only property, so we don't have to create it. If your component doesn't, create the property as you would for any other component.

If our component did not already have the `ReadOnly` property, we would create it as shown in Listing 9.56 (note that this code is not required for this component).

LISTING 9.56   Creating a Read-Only Property

```
class PACKAGE TDBMaskEdit : public TMaskEdit
{
private:
    bool FReadOnly;
protected:
public:
    __fastcall TDBMaskEdit(TComponent* Owner);
__published:
    __property ReadOnly = {read = FReadOnly, write = FReadOnly,
        default = true};
};
```

In the constructor we would set the default value of the property.

```
__fastcall TDBMaskEdit::TDBMaskEdit(TComponent* Owner)
  : TMaskEdit(Owner)
{
    FReadOnly = true;
}
```

Finally, we need to ensure that the component acts as a read-only control. You need to override the method normally associated with the user accessing the control. If we were creating a data-aware grid, it would be the `SelectCell()` method, in which you would check the value of the `ReadOnly` property and act accordingly. If the value of `ReadOnly` is `false`, you call the inherited method; otherwise, just return.

If the `TMaskEdit` control had a Se[...]

```
bool __fastcall TDBMaskEdit::
{
    if(FReadOnly)
        return(false);
    else
        return(TMaskEdit::Sele
}
```

In this case, we don't have to wor[...]

Establishing the Link

For our control to become data aw[...]
cate with a data member of a datal[...]

A data-aware control owns its data[...]
ize, and destroy the data link.

Establishing the link requires three[...]

1. Declare the data link class a[...]
2. Declare the read and write a[...]
3. Initialize the data link

Declare the Data Link

The data link is a class of type TF[...]
the header file.

```
#include <DBCtrls.hpp>

class PACKAGE TDBMaskEdit : p
{
private:
    TFieldDataLink *FDataLink
    ...
};
```

Our data-aware component now re[...]
other data-aware controls). These [...]
of the data link class. This enables[...]
and field.

We need to assign the `DataChange()` method to the `OnDataChange` event in the constructor. We also remove this assignment in the component destructor.

```
__fastcall TDBMaskEdit::TDBMaskEdit(TComponent* Owner)
  : TMaskEdit(Owner)
{
    FDataLink = new TFieldDataLink();
    FDataLink->Control = this;
    FDataLink->OnDataChange = DataChange;
}


__fastcall TDBMaskEdit::~TDBMaskEdit(void)
{
    if(FDataLink)
        {
        FDataLink->Control = 0;
        FDataLink->OnUpdateData = 0;
        FDataLink->OnDataChange = 0;
        delete FDataLink;
        }
}
```

Finally, define the `DataChange()` method as shown in the following code:

```
void __fastcall TDBMaskEdit::DataChange(TObject *Sender)
{
    if(!FDataLink->Field)
        {
        if(ComponentState.Contains(csDesigning))
            Text = Name;
        else
            Text = "";
        }
    else
        Text = FDataLink->Field->AsString;
}
```

The `DataChange()` method first checks to see if the data link is pointing to a datasource (and field). If there is no valid pointer, the `Text` property (a member of the inherited component) is set to an empty string (at runtime) or the control name (at designtime). If a valid field is set, the `Text` property is set to the value of the field's content via the `AsString` property of the `TField` object.

You now have a data-browsing control, so-called because it is capable only of displaying data changes in a datasource. It's now time to turn this component into a data-editing control.

Changing to a Data-Editing Control

Turning a data-browsing control into a data-editing control requires additional code to respond to key and mouse events. This enables any changes made to the control to be reflected in the underlying field of the linked database.

The `ReadOnly` Property

When a user places a data-editing control into his project, he expects the control NOT to be read-only. The default value for the `ReadOnly` property of `TMaskEdit` (the inherited class) is `false`, so we have nothing further to do. If you create a component that has a custom `ReadOnly` property added, be sure to set the default value to `false`.

Keyboard and Mouse Events

If you refer to the `controls.hpp` file, you will find protected methods of `TMaskEdit` called `KeyDown()` and `MouseDown()`. These methods respond to the corresponding window messages (`WM_KEYDOWN`, `WM_LBUTTONDOWN`, `WM_MBUTTONDOWN`, and `WM_RBUTTONDOWN`) and call the appropriate event if one is defined by the user.

To override these methods, add the `KeyDown()` and `MouseDown()` methods to the `TDBMaskEdit` class. Take the declarations from the `controls.hpp` file.

```
virtual void __fastcall MouseDown(TMouseButton, TShiftState Shift, int X,
  int Y);
virtual void __fastcall KeyDown(unsigned short &Key, TShiftState Shift);
```

Refer to the `controls.hpp` file (or the help file) to determine the original declaration.

Next we add the source code, shown in Listing 9.59.

LISTING 9.59   The `MouseDown()` and `KeyDown()` Methods

```
void __fastcall TDBMaskEdit::MouseDown(TMouseButton Button, TShiftState Shift,
  int X, int Y)
{
    if(!ReadOnly && FDataLink->Edit())
        TMaskEdit::MouseDown(Button, Shift, X, Y);
    else
        {
        if(OnMouseDown)
            OnMouseDown(this, Button, Shift, X , Y);
        }
}


void __fastcall TDBMaskEdit::KeyDown(unsigned short &Key, TShiftState Shift)
```

The other approach is to declare and initialize an array of TMetaClass* (or TComponentClass) by hand:

```
TMetaClass Components[3] = { __classid(TCustomComponent1),
                             __classid(TCustomComponent2),
                             __classid(TCustomComponent3) };
```

We then pass this to the RegisterComponents() function as before, but this time we must also pass the value of the last valid index for the array, in this case 2:

```
RegisterComponents("MyCustomComponents", Components, 2);
```

The final function call is simpler, but there is a greater chance of error in passing an incorrect value for the last parameter.

We can now see what a complete Register() function looks like:

```
namespace Thenameofthefilethisisin
{
    void __fastcall PACKAGE Register()
    {
        RegisterComponents("MyCustomComponents",
                    OPENARRAY( TMetaClass*,
                            ( __classid(TCustomComponent1),
                              __classid(TCustomComponent2),
                              __classid(TCustomComponent3) ) ) );
    }
}
```

Remember that you may have as many RegisterComponents() functions in the Register() function as required. You may also include other registrations such as those for property and component editors. This is the subject of the next chapter. You can place the component registration in the implementation file of the component, but typically the registration code should be isolated from the component implementation. For more details on this, refer to the "Component Distribution and Related Issues" section in Chapter 11, "More Custom Component Techniques."

Summary

This chapter covers a lot of ground. When creating custom components, review the VCL Chart and the VCL source code when deciding from which base class to derive your new component. You saw a simple example of how to enhance existing components with the TStyleLabel component and how to create non-visual components. You also saw examples of creating data-aware components and how they can be linked together, just like some of C++Builder's stock data-aware controls.

You will most likely find that creating your own custom visual components involves much more work than modifying an existing control. Start simple, and try to build classes to handle some of the more complicated stuff for you.

You saw how to trap messages sent to your component by Windows, modify the base class's default handler, create custom events, and call those events from within the component. Remember to make as many properties, methods, and events as is necessary so as not restrict the component user.

Whether you concentrate on writing applications, components, or both, creating custom components is almost another area of expertise with C++Builder. The more complicated your components become, the more your programming expertise will be tried. By creating custom components, you will not only increase your knowledge of the VCL architecture, you also will enhance your skills with C++Builder, as well as your C++ programming skills in general. This will give you complete control over the user interface of your applications and decreasing development time.

Creating Property and Component Editors

Jamie Allsop

IN THIS CHAPTER

- Creating Custom Property Editors
- Properties and Exceptions
- Registering Custom Property Editors
- Using Images in Property Editors
- Installing Editor-Only Packages
- Using Linked Image Lists in Property Editors
- Creating Custom Component Editors
- Registering Component Editors
- Using Predefined Images in Custom Property and Component Editors
- Registering Property Categories in Custom Components

As stated in Chapter 9, "Creating Custom Components," components are the building blocks of C++Builder. They are the essential elements of every C++Builder program. Developers spend much of their time working with components, learning about their features, and trying to make best use of the facilities that they offer. To that end, improving the designtime interface of a component is one of the single most powerful ways to improve a component's usefulness. Great effort is often spent by developers to improve the user interface for their customers. Component writers should also consider the interface that they present to their customers.

This chapter covers the techniques required to successfully implement property editors and component editors. Some of the biggest changes to C++Builder's IDE have been to allow improved property and component interfaces at designtime to help improve the productivity of developers. All of the new features added in C++Builder 5 are covered in depth, and definitive guidelines are presented as to their proper use.

This chapter aims to be a complete coverage of this often neglected area of component creation, and component developers should find it a useful reference. The chapter is divided into four main sections. The first section covers all aspects of property editors, including the new image capabilities. Component editors are then given a similar treatment. An effort has been made to present a logical approach to the development process for each. The third section covers the use of resources in editors. This is often mentioned, but actual guidelines are rarely given. Finally, the property categories are discussed, and details are given of how to register properties for specific categories, along with details on creating custom categories. Component writers should find this chapter informative.

All the code of the property editors and component editors discussed in this chapter is contained on the accompanying CD-ROM. By examining the source to these editors, it should be possible to develop a good understanding of the issues involved in creating custom editors for components. The code shown in the listings throughout the chapter is contained in two packages: the `EnhancedEditors` package (`EnhancedEditors.bpk`, a designtime-only package), and the `NewAdditionalComponents` designtime and runtime packages. The designtime package, called `NewAdditionalComponentsDTP.bpk`, contains property and component editor code as well as registration code. The runtime package, called `NewAdditionalComponentsRTP.bpk`, contains code for components.

It would probably be helpful to install these packages into your installation of C++Builder 5 before reading this chapter. That way you can see the effect that the property and component editors have while you are reading the chapter. Before you install either package, first copy the folder called `Chapter10Packages` to your hard drive. It contains the files you require. Feel free to give the folder a more imaginative name. Then copy both files in the `System` folder to a folder on the system path, for example `Windows\System` on Windows 9x machines or `WINNT\System32` on Windows NT and Windows 2000 machines. These files are runtime files required by the two designtime packages. Both of the designtime packages require the `TNonVCLTypeInfoPackage.bpl` runtime-only file (this file is discussed again shortly), and the `NewAdditionalComponentsDTP.bpl` designtime-only package also requires the `NewAdditionalComponentsRTP.bpl` runtime-only package.

To install the `EnhancedEditors` package, run C++Builder 5 and click on Install Packages on the Component menu. Click the Add button in the Design packages group and browse for the `EnhancedEditors.bpl` file. When you click Open, the Add Design Package dialog will close and the package will appear in the Design packages list as Enhanced Property and Component Editors. Click OK to finish. Table 10.1 lists the property and component editors contained in the `EnhancedEditors` package and indicates whether or not they are registered (in other words, installed) with the IDE when the package is installed.

TABLE 10.1 Property and Component Editors Registered by the `EnhancedEditors` Package

Editors	Registered
TShapeTypePropertyEditor	Yes
TImageListPropertyEditor	Yes
TImageIndexProperty	No—An Abstract Base Class
TPersistentDerivedImageIndexProperty	Yes
TComponentDerivedImageIndexProperty	Yes
TMenuItemImageIndexProperty	Yes
TTabSheetImageIndexProperty	Not required
TToolButtonImageIndexProperty	Yes
TCoolBandImageIndexProperty	Not required
TListColumnImageIndexProperty	Yes
TCustomActionImageIndexProperty	Not required
THeaderSectionImageIndexProperty	Not required
TDisplayCursorProperty	Yes
TDisplayFontNameProperty	Yes
TUnsignedProperty	Yes
TCharPropertyEditor	Yes
TSignedCharProperty	Yes
TUnsignedCharProperty	Yes
TImageComponentEditor	Yes

The method for installing the `NewAdditionalComponents` package is the same as for the `EnhancedEditors` package. Click on Install Packages on the Component menu. Click the Add button in the Design packages group and browse for the `NewAdditionalComponentsDTP.bpl` file. When you click Open, the Add Design Package dialog will close and the package will appear in the Design packages list as New Components for the Additional Palette Page. Click OK to finish. The following components are registered with the IDE by this package:

- `TEnhancedImage`
- `TFilterEdit`

The `TImageIndexPropertyEditor` property editor is also registered by this package. Additionally, the `TNonVCLTypeInfoPackage` runtime-only package (`TNonVCLTypeInfoPackage.bpl`) is included. This contains code referred to in Listings 10.7 and 10.8 in the section "Obtaining a `TTypeInfo*` (`PTypeInfo`) from an Existing Property and Class for a Non-VCL Type," later in this chapter. Both the `EnhancedEditors.bpk` and the `NewAdditionalComponentsDTP.bpk` package require this package for their registration code. Therefore, if you want to recompile either package, the header files (`*.h`) and import file (`.bpi`) of this package must be found by the IDE when it is compiling and linking the packages.

Creating Custom Property Editors

One of the best ways to improve a component's designtime interface is to ensure that property editors are easy to use and intuitive. This section looks at the main principles involved in creating your own property editors. All custom property editors descend ultimately from `TPropertyEditor`, which provides the basic functionality required for the editor to function within the IDE. Listing 10.1 shows the the class definition for `TPropertyEditor` (from `$(BCB)\Include\Vcl\DsgnIntf.hpp`, where `$(BCB)` is the C++Builder 5 installation directory).

LISTING 10.1   `TPropertyEditor` Class Definition

```
class DELPHICLASS TPropertyEditor;
typedef void __fastcall (__closure *TGetPropEditProc)(TPropertyEditor* Prop);

class PASCALIMPLEMENTATION TPropertyEditor : public System::TObject
{
    typedef System::TObject inherited;

private:
    _di_IFormDesigner FDesigner;
    TInstProp *FPropList;
    int FPropCount;
    AnsiString __fastcall GetPrivateDirectory();
```

LISTING 10.1   Continued

```
    void __fastcall SetPropEntry(int Index,
                                 Classes::TPersistent* AInstance,
                                 Typinfo::PPropInfo APropInfo);

protected:
    __fastcall virtual TPropertyEditor(const _di_IFormDesigner ADesigner,
                                       int APropCount);
    Typinfo::PPropInfo __fastcall GetPropInfo(void);
    Extended __fastcall GetFloatValue(void);
    Extended __fastcall GetFloatValueAt(int Index);
    __int64 __fastcall GetInt64Value(void);
    __int64 __fastcall GetInt64ValueAt(int Index);
    Sysutils::TMethod __fastcall GetMethodValue();
    Sysutils::TMethod __fastcall GetMethodValueAt(int Index);
    int __fastcall GetOrdValue(void);
    int __fastcall GetOrdValueAt(int Index);
    AnsiString __fastcall GetStrValue();
    AnsiString __fastcall GetStrValueAt(int Index);
    Variant __fastcall GetVarValue();
    Variant __fastcall GetVarValueAt(int Index);
    void __fastcall Modified(void);
    void __fastcall SetFloatValue(Extended Value);
    void __fastcall SetMethodValue(const Sysutils::TMethod &Value);
    void __fastcall SetInt64Value(__int64 Value);
    void __fastcall SetOrdValue(int Value);
    void __fastcall SetStrValue(const AnsiString Value);
    void __fastcall SetVarValue(const Variant &Value);

public:
    __fastcall virtual ~TPropertyEditor(void);

    virtual void __fastcall Activate(void);
    virtual bool __fastcall AllEqual(void);
    virtual bool __fastcall AutoFill(void);
    virtual void __fastcall Edit(void);
    virtual TPropertyAttributes __fastcall GetAttributes(void);
    Classes::TPersistent* __fastcall GetComponent(int Index);
    virtual int __fastcall GetEditLimit(void);
    virtual AnsiString __fastcall GetName();
    virtual void __fastcall GetProperties(TGetPropEditProc Proc);
    Typinfo::PTypeInfo __fastcall GetPropType(void);
    virtual AnsiString __fastcall GetValue();
    AnsiString __fastcall GetVisualValue();
    virtual void __fastcall GetValues(Classes::TGetStrProc Proc);
    virtual void __fastcall Initialize(void);
```

LISTING 10.1   Continued

```
    void __fastcall Revert(void);
    virtual void __fastcall SetValue(const AnsiString Value);
    bool __fastcall ValueAvailable(void);
    DYNAMIC void __fastcall ListMeasureWidth(const AnsiString Value,
                                             Graphics::TCanvas* ACanvas,
                                             int& AWidth);
    DYNAMIC void __fastcall ListMeasureHeight(const AnsiString Value,
                                              Graphics::TCanvas* ACanvas,
                                              int& AHeight);
    DYNAMIC void __fastcall ListDrawValue(const AnsiString Value,
                                          Graphics::TCanvas* ACanvas,
                                          const Windows::TRect& ARect,
                                          bool ASelected);
    DYNAMIC void __fastcall PropDrawName(Graphics::TCanvas* ACanvas,
                                         const Windows::TRect& ARect,
                                         bool ASelected);
    DYNAMIC void __fastcall PropDrawValue(Graphics::TCanvas* ACanvas,
                                          const Windows::TRect& ARect,
                                          bool ASelected);

    __property _di_IFormDesigner Designer = {read=FDesigner};
    __property AnsiString PrivateDirectory = {read=GetPrivateDirectory};
    __property int PropCount = {read=FPropCount, nodefault};
    __property AnsiString Value = {read=GetValue,  write=SetValue};
};
```

To customize the editor's behavior, one or more TPropertyEditor virtual (or DYNAMIC) functions must be overridden. You can save a lot of coding by deriving your custom property editor from the most appropriate property editor class. The hierarchy of TPropertyEditor descendants is shown in Figure 10.1. Descendants in shaded boxes are those that override the custom rendering functionality of TPropertyEditor. See the section "Using Images in Property Editors," later in this chapter, for more information.

The hierarchy shown in Figure 10.1 is useful when deciding which property editor to inherit from. The purpose of each property editor is fairly self-explanatory, with the exception of one or two of the more specialized. For your convenience, brief descriptions of the more commonly encountered property editors are given in Table 10.2.

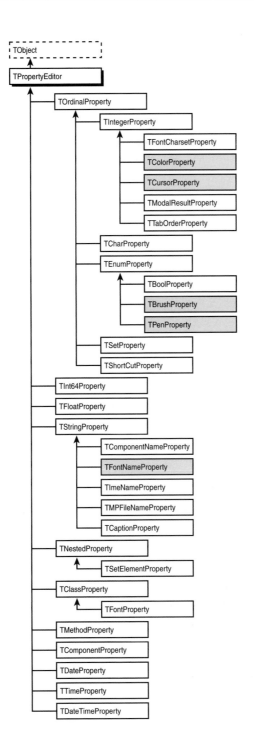

FIGURE 10.1

The TPropertyEditor *inheritance hierarchy.*

TABLE 10.2 Common Property Editor Classes and Their Use

Property Editor Class	Use
TCaptionProperty	The editor for all Caption and Text named AnsiString properties. The Caption property of TForm and the Text property of TEdit are examples. The difference between this property editor and the TStringProperty from which it derives is that the component being edited is continually updated as the property is edited. With TStringProperty the updating occurs after the edit has finished.
TCharProperty	The default editor for all char properties and sub-types of char. Displays either the character of the property's value or the value itself preceded by the # character. The PasswordChar (char) property of TMaskEdit is an example.
TClassProperty	The default editor for TPersistent-derived class properties. Published properties of the class are displayed as sub-properties when the + image before the property name is clicked. The Constraints (TSizeConstraints*) property of TForm is an example.
TColorProperty	The default editor for TColor type properties. Displays the color as a clXXX value if one exists, otherwise displays the value as hexadecimal (in BGR format; 0x00BBGGRR). The value can be entered as either a clXXX value or as a number. Also allows the clXXX value to be picked from a list. When the property is double-clicked, the Color dialog is displayed. The Color (TColor) property of TForm is an example.
TComponentProperty	The default editor for pointers to TComponent-derived objects. The editor displays a drop-down list of type-compatible objects that appear in the same form as the component being edited. The Images (TCustomImageList*) property of TToolBar is an example.
TCursorProperty	For TCursor properties. Allows a cursor to be selected from a list that gives each cursor's name and its corresponding image. The Cursor (TCursor) property of TForm is an example.
TEnumProperty	The default editor for all enum-based properties. A drop-down list displays the possible values the property can take. The Align (TAlign) and BorderStyle (TFormBorderStyle) properties of TForm are examples.
TFloatProperty	The default editor for all floating-point–based properties, namely double, long double, and float. The PrintLeftMargin (double) and PrintRightMargin (double) properties of TF1Book are examples.

TABLE 10.2 Continued

Property Editor Class	Use
TFontProperty	For TFont properties. The editor allows the font settings to be edited either through the Font dialog (by clicking the ellipses button) or by editing an expandable list of sub-properties. The Font (TFont) property of TForm is an example.
TIntegerProperty	The default editor for all int properties. The Height (int) and Width (int) properties of TForm are examples.
TMethodProperty	The default editor for pointer-to-method (member function) properties; that is, events. The editor displays a drop-down list of event handlers for the event type matching that of the property. The OnClick and OnClose events of TForm are examples.
TOrdinalProperty	All ordinal- (that is integral) based property editors ultimately descend from this class, such as TIntegerProperty, TCharProperty, TenumProperty, and TSetProperty.
TPropertyEditor	The class from which all property editors are descended.
TSetElementProperty	This editor is used to edit the individual elements of a Set. The property can be set to true to indicate that the element is contained in the Set and false to indicate that it is not.
TSetProperty	The default editor for all Set properties. Each element of the Set is displayed as a sub-property of the Set property allowing each element to be removed from or added to the Set as desired. The Anchors (TAnchors) and BorderIcons (TBorderIcons) properties of TForm are examples.
TStringProperty	The default editor for AnsiString properties. The Hint and Name properties of TForm are examples.

Choosing the right property editor to inherit from is linked inextricably with the requirements specification of the property editor. In fact, the hardest part of creating a custom property editor is deciding exactly what behavior is required. This is an issue that will come up later in this section.

The stages of developing a new property editor are summarized in the following list:

1. Decide exactly how you want the editor to behave. Property editors often are developed to offer a bounded choice that ensures proper component operation and an intuitive interface. The nature of bounding, such as to restrict the user to a choice of some discrete predefined values, must be decided.

2. Decide whether a custom property editor is even required. By slightly changing how a property is used, it may be that no custom property editor is necessary. To this end, it is

important to know which property editors are registered for which property types; Table 10.2 can be used as a guide. Because this section is about creating custom property editors, this thread will not be explored further. Needless to say, you cannot know too much about the existing property editors and how they work. A good source of information is the $(BCB)\Source\ToolsApi\DsgnIntf.pas file.

3. Choose carefully the property editor from which your custom property editor descends. A careful choice can save a lot of unnecessary coding.

4. Decide which property attributes are applicable to your property editor.

5. Determine which functions of the parent property editor need to be overridden and which do not.

6. Finally, write the necessary code and try it out.

Once it has been decided that a custom property editor is required and the parent property editor class has been chosen, the next step is to decide which property attributes are suitable. Every property editor has a method called GetAttributes() that returns a TPropertyAttributes Set. This tells the Object Inspector how the property is to be used. For example, if the property will display a drop-down list of values, you must ensure that paValueList is contained by the TPropertyAttributes Set returned by the property editor's GetAttributes() method. Unless the property attributes of the parent property editor class exactly match those required in the custom property editor, the GetAttributes() method must be overridden. Table 10.3 shows the different values that can be contained by the TPropertyAttributes Set. Methods that may require overriding as a result of the property editor having a particular attribute are also shown.

TABLE 10.3   TPropertyAttributes Set Values

Value	Purpose
paAutoUpdate	Properties whose editors have this attribute are updated automatically as they are changed in the Object Inspector, such as the Caption property of TLabel. Normally a property will not be updated until the Return key is pressed or focus leaves the property. SetValue() is called to convert the AnsiString representation to the proper format and ensure the value is valid. Overriding SetValue() is probably necessary.
	Override: SetValue(const AnsiString Value)
paDialog	Properties with this attribute display an ellipsis button (...) on the right side of the property value region. When clicked, this displays a form to allow the property to be edited. When the ellipses button is pressed, the Edit() method of the property editor is invoked. This must therefore be overridden for properties with this attribute.
	Override: Edit()

TABLE 10.3   Continued

Value	Purpose
paFullWidthName	Properties with this attribute do not display a value region in the Object Inspector. Rather, the property name extends to the full width of the Object Inspector.
paMultiSelect	Properties whose editors have this attribute may be edited when more than one component is selected on a form. For example, the property editor for the Caption property of TLabel and TButton has this attribute. When several TLabel and TButton components are placed on a form and selected, the Caption properties can be edited simultaneously. The Object Inspector displays all properties whose editors have the paMultiSelect attribute *and* whose property names and types are exactly the same.
paReadOnly	Properties whose editors have this attribute cannot be edited in the Object Inspector.
paRevertable	Properties whose editors have this attribute enable the Revert to Inherited menu item in the Object Inspector's context menu, allowing the property editor to revert the current property value to some default value.
paSortList	Properties with this attribute have their value lists sorted by the Object Inspector.
paSubProperties	Properties with this attribute tell the Object Inspector that the property editor has sub-properties that can be edited. A + symbol is placed in front of the property name. The TFont property editor is an example of this. In order to tell the Object Inspector which sub-properties to display, GetProperties() must be overridden. Override: GetProperties(TGetPropEditProc Proc)
paValueList	Properties whose editors have this attribute display a drop-down list of possible values that the property can take. A value may still be entered manually in the editable property value region. For example, TColor properties behave in this way. To provide a list of values for the Object Inspector to display, you must override the GetValues() method. Override: GetValues(Classes::TGetStrProc Proc)

Once the attributes of the property editor have been decided, it is easy to see which methods of the parent property editor must be overridden. Other methods may also require overriding; this will depend on the specifications of the property editor. Table 10.4 lists the virtual and DYNAMIC methods of TPropertyEditor. The methods are grouped and ordered according to their use and are not listed alphabetically.

TABLE 10.4 The virtual and DYNAMIC Methods of TPropertyEditor

Method	Declaration and Purpose
GetAttributes()	virtual TPropertyAttributes __fastcall GetAttributes(void); Returns a TPropertyAttributes Set. Invoked to set the property editor attributes.
GetValue()	virtual AnsiString __fastcall GetValue(); Returns an AnsiString that represents the property's value. By default (that is, in TPropertyEditor) it returns (unknown). Therefore, if you derive directly from TPropertyEditor, you *must* override this method to return the correct value.
SetValue()	virtual void __fastcall SetValue(const AnsiString Value); Called to set the value of a property. SetValue() must convert the AnsiString representation of the property's value to a suitable format. If an invalid value is entered, SetValue() should throw an exception that describes the error. Note that SetValue() takes a const AnsiString as its parameter and returns void. An exception therefore is the only appropriate method of dealing with invalid values.
Edit()	virtual void __fastcall Edit(void); Invoked when the ellipses button is pressed or the property is double-clicked (GetAttributes() should return paDialog). Normally used to display a form to allow more intuitive editing of the property value. Edit() can call GetValue() and SetValue(), or it can read and write the property value directly. If this is the case, then input validation should be carried out. If an invalid value is entered, an exception describing the error should be thrown.
GetValues()	virtual void __fastcall GetValues (Classes::TGetStrProcProc); Only called when paValueList is returned by GetAttributes(). The single parameter Proc is of type TGetStrProc, a __closure (pointer to an instance member function), declared in $(BCB)\Include\Vcl\Classes.hpp as: typedef void __fastcall (__closure *TGetStrProc) (const AnsiString S);

TABLE 10.4 Continued

Method	Declaration and Purpose

	The `Proc` parameter is in fact the address of a method with a `const AnsiString` called `S` as its single parameter, which adds the `AnsiString` passed to the property editor's drop-down list. Call `Proc(const AnsiString S)` once for every value that should be displayed in the property value's drop-down list, for example:
	`Proc(value1); //value1 is an AnsiString`
	`Proc(value2); //value2 is an AnsiString`
	and so on.

`Activate()`	`virtual void __fastcall Activate(void);` Invoked when the property is selected in the Object Inspector. Allows the property editor attributes to be determined only when the property becomes selected (with the exception of `paSubProperties` and `paMultiSelect`).
`AllEqual()`	`virtual bool __fastcall AllEqual(void);` Returns a `bool` value. Called only when `paMultiSelect` is one of the property editor's attributes (when it is returned by `GetAttributes()`). It determines if all properties of the same name and type for which that editor is registered are equal when more than one is selected at once (it returns `true`). If this is the case (they are equal), then `GetValue()` is called to display the value; otherwise the value region is blanked.
`AutoFill()`	`virtual bool __fastcall AutoFill(void);` Returns a `bool` value. Called only when `paValueList` is returned by `GetAttributes()`, it determines whether or not (returns `true` or `false`) the values returned by `GetValues()` can be selected incrementally in the Object Inspector. By default it returns `true`.
`GetEditLimit()`	`virtual int __fastcall GetEditLimit(void);` Returns an `int` representing the maximum number of input characters allowed in the Object Inspector for this property. Overriding this method allows this number to be changed. The default value for the Object Inspector is `255`.
`GetName()`	`virtual AnsiString __fastcall GetName();` Returns an `AnsiString` that is used by the Object Inspector to display the property name. This should be overridden only when the name determined from the property's type information is not the name that you want to appear in the Object Inspector.

TABLE 10.4   Continued

Method	Declaration and Purpose
GetProperties()	`virtual void __fastcall GetProperties(TGetPropEditProc Proc);` If it is required that subproperties be displayed, then you must override this method. The single parameter `Proc` is of type `TGetPropEditProc`, a `__closure` declared in `$(BCB)\Include\Vcl\DsgnIntf.hpp` as `typedef void __fastcall (__closure *TGetPropEditProc)(TPropertyEditor* Prop);` `Proc` is therefore the address of a method with a pointer to a `TPropertyEditor`-derived editor called `Prop` as its single parameter. Call `Proc(TPropertyEditor* Prop)` once for each subproperty, passing a pointer to a `TPropertyEditor`-derived editor as an argument. For example, `TSetProperty` overrides this method and passes a `TSetElementProperty` pointer for each element in its `Set`. `TClassProperty` also overrides the `GetProperties()` method, displaying a subproperty for each of the class's published properties.
Initialize()	`virtual void __fastcall Initialize(void);` This is invoked when the Object Inspector is going to use the property editor. `Initialize()` is called after the property editor has been constructed but before it is used. When several components are selected at once, property editors are constructed but are often then discarded because they will not be used. This method allows the possibility of postponing certain operations until it is certain that they will be required.
ListMeasureWidth()	`DYNAMIC void __fastcall ListMeasureWidth(const AnsiString Value, Graphics::TCanvas* ACanvas, int& AWidth);` This is called during the width calculation phase of the property's drop-down list. If images are to be placed alongside text in the drop-down list, this method should be overridden to ensure the list is wide enough.
ListMeasureHeight()	`DYNAMIC void __fastcall ListMeasureHeight(const AnsiString Value, Graphics::TCanvas* ACanvas, int& AHeight);` This is called during the height calculation phase of the property's drop-down list. If an image's height is greater than that of the property value text, this must be overridden to prevent clipping the image.

TABLE 10.4 Continued

Method	Declaration and Purpose
ListDrawValue()	DYNAMIC void __fastcall ListDrawValue(const AnsiString Value, Graphics::TCanvas* ACanvas, const Windows::TRect& ARect, bool ASelected); This is called to render the current list item in the property's drop-down list. If an image is to be rendered, this method must be overridden. The default behavior of this method is to render the text representing the current list value.
PropDrawValue()	DYNAMIC void __fastcall PropDrawValue(Graphics::TCanvas* ACanvas, const Windows::TRect& ARect, bool ASelected); This is called when the property value itself is to be rendered in the Object Inspector. If an image is to be rendered with the property value, this method must be overridden.
PropDrawName()	DYNAMIC void __fastcall PropDrawName(Graphics::TCanvas* ACanvas, const Windows::TRect &ARect, bool ASelected); This is called when the property name is to be rendered in the Object Inspector. If an image is to be rendered with the property name, this method must be overridden. However, this is rarely needed.

You now should have a reasonable idea of the capabilities that can be implemented for a custom property editor. The next few sections look at some of the most important methods and present basic coding guidelines for their proper use. The last five methods (ListMeasureWidth(), ListMeasureHeight(), ListDrawValue(), PropDrawValue(), and PropDrawName()) are concerned with rendering images in the Object Inspector and are looked at in the section "Using Images in Property Editors," later in this chapter.

The methods that are most often overridden by custom property editors are GetAttributes(), GetValue(), SetValue(), Edit(), and GetValues(), the first five methods in Table 10.4. Listing 10.2 shows a class definition for a custom property editor derived from TPropertyEditor.

10

TIP

A key point to note in Listing 10.2 is the use of the typedef:

    typedef TPropertyEditor inherited;

This allows inherited to be used as a namespace modifier in place of TPropertyEditor. This is commonly encountered in the VCL and makes it easy to call parent (in this case TPropertyEditor) methods explicitly while retaining code maintainability. If the name of the parent class changes, only this one occurrence needs to be updated.

For example, you can write code such as this in the property editor's GetAttributes() method:

```
    return inherited::GetAttributes() << paValueList >> paMultiSelect
```

This calls the property editor's base class GetAttributes() method, returning a TPropertyAttributes Set. paValueList is added to this Set, and paMultiSelect is removed from the Set. The final Set is returned.

Listing 10.2   Definition Code for a Custom Property Editor

```
class TCustomPropertyEditor : public TPropertyEditor
{
        typedef TPropertyEditor inherited;

public:
    virtual TPropertyAttributes __fastcall GetAttributes(void);
    virtual AnsiString __fastcall GetValue();
    virtual void __fastcall SetValue(const AnsiString Value);
    virtual void __fastcall Edit(void);
    virtual void __fastcall GetValues(Classes::TGetStrProc Proc);

protected:
    #pragma option push -w-inl
    inline __fastcall virtual
        TCustomPropertyEditor(const _di_IFormDesigner ADesigner,
                              int APropCount)
                            : TPropertyEditor(ADesigner, APropCount)
    { }
    #pragma option pop

public:
    #pragma option push -w-inl
    inline __fastcall virtual ~TCustomProperty(void) { }
    #pragma option pop
};
```

The `GetAttributes()` Method

The `GetAttributes()` method is very simple to implement. The only consideration is that you should change only the attributes that the parent class returns that have a direct effect on your code. Remaining attributes should be unchanged, so that you add only attributes that you definitely need and remove only attributes that you definitely don't want. Be sure to check the attributes of the parent class. You may not need to change them at all. For example, a property editor that derives directly from `TPropertyEditor` is required to display a drop-down list of values and should not be used when multiple components are selected. Suitable code for the `GetAttributes()` method is

```
TPropertyAttributes __fastcall TCustomPropertyEditor::GetAttributes(void)
{
    return inherited::GetAttributes() << paValueList >> paMultiSelect;
}
```

Since `TPropertyEditor::GetAttributes()` returns paRevertable, the following is the same:

```
TPropertyAttributes __fastcall TCustomPropertyEditor::GetAttributes(void)
{
  return TPropertyAttributes() << paValueList << paRevertable >> paMultiSelect;
}
```

The `GetValue()` Method

Use the `GetValue()` method to return an `AnsiString` representation of the value of the property being edited. To do this, use one of the `GetXxxValue()` methods from the `TPropertyEditor` class, where *Xxx* will be one of `Float`, `Int64`, `Method`, `Ord`, `Str`, or `Var`. These are listed in Table 10.5.

TABLE 10.5 `TPropertyEditor GetXxxValue()` Methods

Method	Description
GetFloatValue()	Returns an `Extended` value, in other words a `long double`. Used to retrieve floating-point property values, such as `float`, `double`, and `long double`.
GetInt64Value()	Returns an `__int64` value. Used to retrieve Int64 (`__int64`) property values.

GetMethodValue()	Returns a `TMethod` structure:
	`struct TMethod`
	`{`
	`    void *Code;`
	`    void *Data;`
	`};`
	Used to retrieve `Closure` property values, in other words, events.

10

TABLE 10.5   Continued

Method	Description
GetOrdValue()	Returns an int value. Used to retrieve Ordinal property values such as char, signed char, unsigned char, int, unsigned, short and long. Can also be used to retrieve a pointer value; the int must be cast to the appropriate pointer using reinterpret_cast.
GetStrValue()	Returns an AnsiString value. Used to retrieve string (AnsiString) property values.
GetVarValue()	Returns a Variant by value. Used to retrieve Variant property values. The Variant class models Object Pascal's intrinsic variant type. Refer to the online help for a description of Variants.

The following code shows an implementation of the GetValue() method to retrieve the value of a char-based property by calling the GetOrdValue() method.

```
AnsiString __fastcall TCustomPropertyEditor::GetValue()
{
    char ch = static_cast<char>(GetOrdValue());
    if(ch > 32 && ch < 128) return ch;
    else return AnsiString().sprintf("#%d", ch);

    // Note the '#' character is pre-pended to characters
    // that cannot be displayed directly. This is how the
    // VCL displays non-printable character values, for
    // example #8 is the backspace character (\b).
}
```

Notice the use of static_cast to cast the returned int value as a char. The casting operators are often used when overriding the GetValue() and SetValue() methods of TPropertyEditor. It is essential that their proper use be understood.

The SetValue() Method

Use the SetValue() method to set a property's actual value by converting the AnsiString representation to a suitable format. To do this, use one of the SetXxxValue() methods from TPropertyEditor, where Xxx will be one of Float, Int64, Method, Ord, Str, or Var. These are listed in Table 10.6.

TABLE 10.6   TPropertyEditor Set*Xxx*Value() Methods

Method	Sets
SetFloatValue()	Pass an Extended (long double) value as an argument. Used to set floating-point property values, namely float, double, long double.
SetInt64Value()	Pass an __int64 value as an argument. Used to set Int64 (__int64) property values.
SetMethodValue()	Pass a TMethod structure as an argument. Used to set Closure (event) property values.
SetOrdValue()	Pass an int value as an argument. Used to set Ordinal property values, namely char, signed char, unsigned char, int, unsigned, short, long. It can also be used to set pointer property values, though the pointer value must first be cast to an int using reinterpret_cast.
SetStrValue()	Pass an AnsiString as an argument. Used to set string (AnsiString) property values.
SetVarValue()	Pass a Variant as an argument. Used for variant (Variant) property values.

SetValue() should ensure that values passed to it are valid before calling one of the Set*Xxx*Value() methods, and it should raise an exception if this is not the case. The EPropertyError exception is sensible to use or serve as a base class from which to derive your own exception class. Sample code for an int property is shown in the following, where a value of less than zero is not allowed:

```
void __fastcall TCustomPropertyEditor::SetValue(const AnsiString Value)
{
    if(Value.ToInt() < 0)
    {
        throw EPropertyError("The value must be greater than 0");
    }
    else SetOrdValue(Value.ToInt());
}
```

The Edit() Method

The Edit() method is generally used to offer a better interface to the user. Often this is a form behaving as a dialog. The Edit() method can also call GetValue() and SetValue() or even call the Get*Xxx*Value() and Set*Xxx*Value() methods. It should be noted at this point that TPropertyEditor (and derived classes) has a property called Value whose read and write methods are GetValue() and SetValue(), respectively. Its declaration is

```
__property AnsiString Value = {read=GetValue, write=SetValue};
```

This can be used instead of calling `GetValue()` and `SetValue()` directly. Regardless of how `GetValue()` and `SetValue()` are called, the `Edit()` method should be able to display a suitable form to allow intuitive editing of the property's value.

There are two basic approaches that can be taken. The first is to allow the form to update the property's value while it is displayed. The second is to use the form as a dialog to retrieve the desired value or values from the user and then set the property's value when the form returns a modal result of `mrOK` upon closure. Which of the two approaches is taken affects the code that appears in the `Edit()` method.

Now we'll consider the first instance, in which the form will continually update the value of the property. There are two basic types of property value: one that represents a single entity, such as an `int`, and one that represents a collection of values, such as the class `TFont` (though the property editor for `TFont` behaves according to the second approach). The difference between the two is in how `Value` is used to update the property. In a class property, `Value` is a pointer. For the form to be able to update the property, it must have the address of `Value` or whatever `Value` points to. For a class property this is simple; the pointer to the class is read from `Value`, and the class's values are edited through that pointer. A convenient way to do this is to declare a property of the same type as the property to be edited. This can then be equated to `Value` before the form is shown, allowing initial values to be displayed and stored.

In a single entity, a reference to `Value` should be passed in the form's constructor. Using a reference to `Value` ensures that each time it is modified the `GetValue()` and `SetValue()` methods are called. The only other consideration for this approach is that it is probably a good idea to store the value or values that the property had when the form was originally shown. This allows the edit operation to be cancelled and any previous value or values restored. Suitable code for these situations is shown in Listing 10.3 and Listing 10.4, for a class property and a single entity property, respectively.

LISTING 10.3   Code for a Custom Form to Be Called from the `Edit()` Method for a Class Property

```
// First show important code for TMyPropertyForm

// IN THE HEADER FILE
//--------------------------------------------------------------------------//
#ifndef MyPropertyFormH
#define MyPropertyFormH
//--------------------------------------------------------------------------//
#include <Classes.hpp>
#include <Controls.hpp>
#include <StdCtrls.hpp>
```

LISTING 10.3   Continued

```cpp
#include <Forms.hpp>
#include "HeaderDeclaringTPropertyClass"
//---------------------------------------------------------------------------//
class TMyPropertyForm : public TForm
{
__published:      // IDE-managed Components
private:
   TPropertyClass* FPropertyClass;
   // Other declarations here for example restore values if 'Cancel'
   // is pressed

protected:
   void __fastcall SetPropertyClass(TPropertyClass* Pointer);
public:
   __fastcall TMyPropertyForm(TComponent* Owner);
   __property TPropertyClass* PropertyClass = {read=FPropertyClass,
                                    write=SetPropertyClass};

   // Other declarations here
};
//---------------------------------------------------------------------------//
#endif

// THE IMPLEMENTATION FILE
//---------------------------------------------------------------------------//
#include <vcl.h>
#pragma hdrstop

#include "MyPropertyForm.h"
//---------------------------------------------------------------------------//
#pragma package(smart_init)
#pragma resource "*.dfm"
//---------------------------------------------------------------------------//
__fastcall TMyPropertyForm::TMyPropertyForm(TComponent* Owner)
       : TForm(Owner)
{
}
//---------------------------------------------------------------------------//
void __fastcall TMyPropertyForm::SetPropertyClass(TPropertyClass* Pointer)
{
   FPropertyClass = Pointer;
   if(FPropertyClass != 0)
   {
      // Store current property values
   }
```

LISTING 10.3   Continued

```
}
//---------------------------------------------------------------//

// NOW SHOW THE Edit() METHOD

#include "MyPropertyForm.h" // Remember this

void __fastcall TCustomPropertyEditor::Edit(void)
{
   // Create the form
   std::auto_ptr<TMyPropertyForm*>
      MyPropertyForm(new TMyPropertyForm(0));
   // Link the property
   MyPropertyForm->PropertyClass
                 = reinterpret_cast<TPropertyClass*>(GetOrdValue());
   // Show the form. The form does all the work.
   MyPropertyForm->ShowModal();
}
//---------------------------------------------------------------//
```

Notice the use of reinterpret_cast to convert the ordinal (int) representation of the pointer to the class to an actual pointer to the class. Listing 10.4 is shorter than Listing 10.3 because only the different code is shown.

LISTING 10.4   Code for a Custom Form to Be Called from the Edit() Method for an int Property

```
// First show important code for TMyPropertyForm
//---------------------------------------------------------------//
// IN THE HEADER FILE CHANGE THE DEFINITION TO:

class TMyPropertyForm : public TForm
{
__published:    // IDE-managed Components
private:
  AnsiString& Value;
  int OldValue;
  // Other decalrations here

public:
  __fastcall TMyPropertyForm(TComponent* Owner,  AnsiString& PropertyValue);
  // Other declarations here
};
//---------------------------------------------------------------//
```

LISTING 10.4   Continued

```
#endif

//-------------------------------------------------------------------------//

// IN THE IMPLEMENTATION FILE MODIFY THE CONSTRUCTOR TO:

__fastcall TMyPropertyForm::TMyPropertyForm(TComponent* Owner,
                                            AnsiString& PropertyValue)
        : TForm(Owner),Value(PropertyValue)
{
   // Store the current property value. In this case it is an int
   // so code such as this is required
   OldValue = Value.ToInt();
}
//-------------------------------------------------------------------------//

// NOW SHOW THE Edit() METHOD, almost the same...

#include "MyPropertyForm.h" // Remember this

void __fastcall TCustomPropertyEditor::Edit(void)
{
   // Create the form as before, but pass the extra parameter!
   std::auto_ptr<TMyPropertyForm*>
     MyPropertyForm(new TMyPropertyForm(0, Value));
   // Show the form. The form does all the work.
   MyPropertyForm->ShowModal();
}
//-------------------------------------------------------------------------//
```

The difference between the second approach and the previous approach is that the value is modified after the modal form returns rather than continually modifying it while the form is displayed. This is the more common way to use a form to edit a property's value. Listing 10.5 shows the basic code required in the Edit() method.

LISTING 10.5   Code for a Custom Form to Be Called from the Edit() Method with No Updating Until Closing

```
#include "MyPropertyDialog.h" // Include the header for the Dialog!
                              // Dialog is TMyPropertyDialog

void __fastcall TCustomPropertyEditor::Edit(void)
{
   // Create the form
```

LISTING 10.5   Continued

```
std::auto_ptr<TMyPropertyDialog*>
   MyPropertyDialog(new TMyPropertyDialog(0));

// Set the current property values in the dialog
// MyPropertyDialog->value1 = GetValue();
// MyPropertyDialog->value2 = GetXxxValue();
// and so on...

// Show the form and see the result.
if(MyPropertyDialog->ShowModal() == IDOK)
{
   // Then set the new property value(s)
}
}
```

Note that `TMyPropertyDialog` might not be a dialog itself, but a wrapper for a dialog, similar to the standard dialog components. If this is the case, then the dialog would be shown by calling the wrapper's `Execute()` method. For more information on this method of displaying a dialog, refer to the C++Builder online help under "Making a Dialog Box a Component." In this case, such a dialog wrapper need only descend from `TObject`, not `TComponent`.

The `GetValues()` Method

The `GetValues()` method is used to populate the drop-down list of a property. This is done by successively calling `Proc()` and passing an `AnsiString` representation of the value. For example, if a series of values is desired that represents the transmission rate between a computer's communication port and an external modem, then assuming the property editor had `paValueList` as an attribute, the `GetValues()` method could be written as follows:

```
void __fastcall GetValues(Classes::TGetStrProc Proc)
{
   Proc("300");
   Proc("9600");
   Proc("57600");
   // and so on...
}
```

Using the `TPropertyEditor` Properties

`TPropertyEditor` has four properties that can be used when writing custom property editors. One of these, `Value`, we have already met in the previous two sections. The remaining three properties are not used very often. They are described in the following list:

- Designer   This property is read-only and returns a pointer to the IDE's IFormDesigner interface. This is used to inform the IDE when certain events occur or to request the IDE to perform certain actions. For example, if you write your own implementation for one of the SetXxxValue() methods, you must tell the IDE that you have modified the property. You do this by calling Designer->Modifed();. In fact, you would call TPropertyEditor's Modified() method, which calls the same code. TPropertyEditor's Revert() method also uses this property. You probably will not need to use this property. It is shown for completeness.

- PrivateDirectory   This property is a directory, represented as an AnsiString, as returned by GetPrivateDirectory(), which itself obtains the directory from Designer->GetPrivateDirectory(). Hence we can see that this directory is specified by the IDE. If your property editor requires a directory to store additional files, then it should be the directory specified by this property. This property is read-only.

- PropCount   This property is read-only and returns the number of properties being edited when more than one component is selected. It is only used when GetAttributes() returns paMultiSelect.

Considerations when Choosing a Suitable Property Editor

Consider a property in a component that wraps the Windows communication API and allows different baud rates to be set. The values that may be chosen are predetermined, though a user-defined baud rate may be specified. What is the best way to enter such values?

It would be nice to have a drop-down list of choices. It also would be nice if the values in the drop-down list were numbers, not enumerations. The first thought that springs to mind is a custom property editor that descends from TIntegerProperty but displays a drop-down list of the values that may be set. A user-defined value could be entered in the editing region of the property value in the Object Inspector. This is trivial to implement and will work fine.

Have we really thought about whether this is the best approach? Let's think again. All is well when a value from the drop-down list is chosen, but we must detect when a user-defined value is entered. This is relatively simple but requires that all values in the list be compared with the value returned by the property. If it is different, it is a user-defined baud rate. The component must then request a user-defined baud rate from the communication API equal to the value entered. Some values may be too big or too small. We must therefore perform bounds checking each time a value is entered. Our property editor is simple, but we have to write an increasing amount of maintenance code to support it. Not only that, but all these problems will be revisited by the runtime code.

We could restrict the values allowable to only those in the drop-down list by overriding the SetValue() method and then creating two separate properties: one to enter a user-defined baud rate and a Boolean property to indicate which we want to use.

It seems that we are doing an awful lot of code writing just to enter a simple integer. Let's go back to the start and look at our original requirements.

We want to be able to enter a value from a given list of possible values, and we want to be able to specify a user-defined value, which may not be acceptable. Our initial thought was probably to use an enumeration for the values, but the convenience of using actual integer values made that option seem more attractive. Let's look at the enumeration route. A set of values is easily generated; we can even ensure that they appear in numerical order in the drop-down list by using underscores between the enumeration initials and the value. For example, given an enum called `TBaudRate` with the initials `br`, the baud rates 9600 and 115200 could be represented as `br___9600` and `br_115200`, respectively.

We can even add a `brUserDefined` value to the enum. When `brUserDefined` is selected, an int `UserDefined` property can be read and the value tried. We therefore need this property as well. To do all this, we don't need to create a custom property editor at all since `TEnumProperty` is already defined as an editor for enum based properties. We have a problem though: Any time we want to set or get a value at runtime, we must use the enumeration, and this is often not convenient. We must make this enumeration available to the component user. In the interest of keeping the global namespace clean, we could wrap the enum in a namespace, but this will make the enum even more of a hassle to use, so we won't do that. In fact, most components don't do this either. That is why initials are used in the enum's values. For more information on naming enums, refer to the "Choosing Type Names" section in Chapter 3, "Programming in C++Builder."

So which is best? It all depends on *exactly* what is required of the property and the component as a whole. Since this is a hypothetical discussion, it is hard to choose which method is better. The one thing to remember is that you must make your components robust and easy to use. Overly complex code should be avoided especially, because it may hide some of the more subtle features of how your component works. The enumeration approach may be a bit of a hassle as you convert to and from int values, but everyone knows what you can and cannot do with them. The time you save on not having to write a custom property editor could be used elsewhere. Remember also that if you need to read a value, often you can simply create a read-only property so that, for example, the int value of the baud rate could be stored when it is successfully set by the enum property. This then could be read from an int-based read-only property.

Always think carefully when you are writing property editors and components in general. Consider the big picture and think ahead.

Properties and Exceptions

When a property value is to be changed and there is a possibility that the new value may not be valid, the function obtaining the value should detect the invalid value and throw an exception so that the user can enter a valid value. Where can the property value be changed? It can be requested to change from one of three places: from a property editor dialog, from a property editor, and from the property itself at runtime. The relationship between the three is shown in Figure 10.2. Note that the parameter to the SetValue() method is a const AnsiString even though it is pass-by-value (see Chapter 3 for a discussion of the const keyword). This only restricts Value from being modified within SetValue(). This is contrary to the normal use of const, where the main purpose of the keyword is to indicate that the argument passed to the function will not be modified. With pass-by-value, the argument is copied so it will not be modified in any way. If an error occurs, then throwing an exception is the only appropriate way of informing the user. The other set methods may also be written using this approach, that is, pass-by-value variables declared as const.

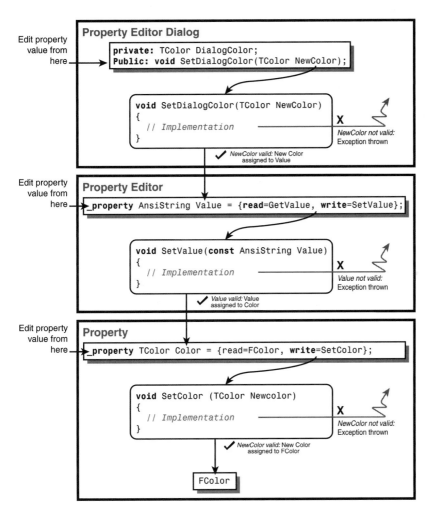

FIGURE 10.2

Exceptions thrown when editing a property.

From Figure 10.2 it can be seen that the set method for the property, in this case `SetColor()`, is ultimately called every time (unless an exception is thrown). It may then be tempting to detect only the validity of the property value at this stage and throw an exception from here. Remember that the purpose of throwing the exception is to detect the error and allow the user to enter a new value. By the time an exception is thrown from the property's set method, the user's edit operation is most likely finished. This may mean redisplaying a dialog or other inconveniences. You should throw an exception at the source of the error. Throwing an exception only from the property editor (or property editor dialog) is also no good, because the property editor will not be used at runtime, letting invalid values silently cause havoc.

The solution is to throw an exception from the point of error. It may not be the easiest solution to implement, but it is the most robust.

Registering Custom Property Editors

Registering property editors is almost straightforward. I say *almost* because even though `RegisterPropertyEditor()` is all that is required, the parameters that need to be passed are not always so trivial. As with other registration functions, the `RegisterPropertyEditor()` function must be placed inside the package's `Register()` function. The declaration for the `RegisterPropertyEditor()` function is

```
extern PACKAGE
    void __fastcall RegisterPropertyEditor(Typinfo::PTypeInfo PropertyType,
                                           TMetaClass* ComponentClass,
                                           const AnsiString PropertyName,
                                           TMetaClass* EditorClass);
```

Each parameter's purpose and an example of its use are shown in Table 10.7. The `PropertyType` and `PropertyName` parameters are used to specify criteria that must be matched by a property for it to be considered for use with the property editor.

TABLE 10.7   `RegisterPropertyEditor()` Parameters

Parameter Name	Purpose
`PropertyType`	This parameter expects a pointer to a `TTypeInfo` structure that contains type information for the property for which the editor is to be used. This parameter *must* be specified. If the property type is a VCL-derived class, the pointer can be obtained using the `__typeinfo` macro:
	`__typeinfo(TVCLClass)`
	Otherwise, it must be obtained either by examining the `typeinfo` of a similar existing property or by manually creating it. Both techniques are discussed in this section.

Table 10.7 Continued

Parameter Name	Purpose
ComponentClass	This parameter is used to specify whether or not the editor is to be used for all matching properties in all components or only matching properties in components of the type specified. To specify a particular component type, use the __classid operator (which returns TMetaClass* as required) with the component class name:
	__classid(TComponentClassName)
	Otherwise, specify all components by passing 0 as the parameter.
PropertyName	This parameter is used to specify a property name, in the form of an AnsiString, that a property must have (in addition to having the same type information). It is used to restrict the property specification. If all properties of matching type information are required, an empty AnsiString is passed (""). If ComponentClass is 0, this parameter is ignored.
EditorClass	This parameter must be specified. It tells the IDE which property editor you want to register. As in the ComponentClass parameter, a TMetaClass pointer is expected. The property editor class name is therefore passed wrapped in the __classid operator, such as
	__classid(TPropertyEditorClassName)

In Table 10.7 you can see that ComponentClass and PropertyName can both be given a value so that they do *not* restrict the property editor to a specific component class or property name, respectively. This is contrary to their normal use. The only parameter that requires any further comment is PropertyType. As was stated before, the __typeinfo macro can be used to retrieve this information if the property type is a VCL-based class (ultimately derived from TObject). The __typeinfo macro is defined in $(BCB)\Include\Vcl\Sysmac.h as

```
#define __typeinfo(type)  (PTypeInfo)TObject::ClassInfo(__classid(type))
```

If the property is not a VCL class, then information must be obtained through other means. There are two approaches to this: Either the appropriate PTypeInfo can be obtained from the property's name and the PTypeInfo of the class it belongs to or the PTypeInfo can be manually generated.

PTypeInfo is a pointer to a TTypeInfo structure:

```
typedef TTypeInfo* PTypeInfo;
```

TTypeInfo is declared in $(BCB)\Include\Vcl\Typinfo.hpp as

```
struct TTypeInfo
{
```

```
    TTypeKind Kind;
    System::ShortString Name;
};
```

TTypeKind, declared in the same file, is an enumeration of type kinds. It is declared as

```
enum TTypeKind { tkUnknown, tkInteger, tkChar,
                 tkEnumeration, tkFloat, tkString,
                 tkSet, tkClass, tkMethod,
                 tkWChar, tkLString, tkWString,
                 tkVariant, tkArray, tkRecord,
                 tkInterface, tkInt64, tkDynArray };
```

The Name variable is a string version of the actual type. For example, int is "int", and AnsiString is "AnsiString". The following two sections discuss how a TTypeInfo* pointer can be obtained for non-VCL property types.

Obtaining a TTypeInfo* (PTypeInfo) from an Existing Property and Class for a Non-VCL Type

This approach requires that a VCL class containing the property already be defined and accessible. Then a PTypeInfo for that property type can be obtained using the GetPropInfo() function declared in $(BCB)\Include\Vcl\Typinfo.hpp. PPropInfo is a typedef for a TPropInfo pointer, as in the following:

```
typedef TPropInfo* PPropInfo;
```

The GetPropInfo() function returns a pointer to a TPropInfo structure (PPropInfo) for a property within a particular class with a given property name, and optionally of a specific TTypeKind. It is available in one of four overloaded versions:

```
extern PACKAGE PPropInfo __fastcall GetPropInfo(PTypeInfo TypeInfo,
                                                const AnsiString PropName);

extern PACKAGE PPropInfo __fastcall GetPropInfo(PTypeInfo TypeInfo,
                                                const AnsiString PropName,
                                                TTypeKinds AKinds);

extern PACKAGE PPropInfo __fastcall GetPropInfo(TMetaClass* AClass,
                                                const AnsiString PropName,
                                                TTypeKinds AKinds);

extern PACKAGE PPropInfo __fastcall GetPropInfo(System::TObject* Instance,
                                                const AnsiString PropName,
                                                TTypeKinds AKinds);
```

These overloaded versions all ultimately call the first overloaded version of the method listed, namely

```
extern PACKAGE PPropInfo __fastcall GetPropInfo(PTypeInfo TypeInfo,
                                      const AnsiString PropName);
```

This is the version we are most interested in. The other versions also allow a Set of type TTypeKinds to be specified . This is a Set of the TTypeKind enumeration and is used to specify a TypeKind or TypeKinds that the property must also match. From the PPropInfo returned, we can obtain a pointer to an appropriate PTypeInfo for the property, which is the PropType field of the TPropInfo structure. TPropInfo is declared in $(BCB)\Include\Vcl\Typinfo.hpp as

```
struct TPropInfo
{
    PTypeInfo* PropType;
    void* GetProc;
    void* SetProc;
    void* StoredProc;
    int Index;
    int Default;
    short NameIndex;
    System::ShortString Name;
};
```

For example, the PTypeInfo for the Name property of TFont can be obtained by first obtaining a PPropInfo:

```
PPropInfo FontNamePropInfo = Typinfo::GetPropInfo(__typeinfo(TFont),
                                      "Name");
```

Then obtain the PTypeInfo for the required property:

```
PTypeInfo FontNameTypeInfo = *FontNamePropInfo->PropType;
```

This PTypeInfo value can now be passed to the RegisterPropertyEditor() function. What we have actually obtained from this is a pointer to the TTypeInfo for an AnsiString property. This PTypeInfo could therefore be obtained and used as the PTypeInfo parameter anytime the PTypeInfo for an AnsiString is required. Additionally, the PTypeInfo for a custom property for a custom component can be similarly obtained:

```
PPropInfo CustomPropInfo = Typinfo::GetPropInfo(__typeinfo(TCustomComponent),
                                      "CustomPropertyName");

PTypeInfo CustomTypeInfo = *CustomPropInfo->PropType;
```

Note that it is possibly more clear if TTypeInfo* and TPropInfo* are used instead of their respective typedefs (PTypeInfo and PPropInfo). The typedefs have been used here for easy comparison with the GetPropInfo() function declarations.

The intermediate steps shown to obtain the PTypeInfo can be ignored. For example, the following can be used as an argument to RegisterPropertyEditor() for the custom property of a custom component:

```
*(Typinfo::GetPropInfo(__typeinfo(TCustomComponent),
                    "CustomPropertyName"))->PropType
```

This method of obtaining a TTypeInfo* relies on there being a published property of the desired type already in use by the VCL. This may not always be the case. Also, sometimes it may appear that a type already in use matches a type you want to use, but in fact it does not. An example of this is the Interval property of the TTimer component. The type of the Interval property is Cardinal, which is typedefed to unsigned int in the file $(BCB)\Include\Vcl\Sysmac.h. It is reasonable then to believe that retrieving the TypeInfo* for this property would allow you to register property editors for unsigned int properties. This is not so. You must have a property whose type is unsigned int, and it must appear in a C++-implemented class. There is an important lesson here. The TTypeInfo* for a non-VCL class type is not necessarily the same if the property belongs to an Object Pascal–implemented class and not a C++-implemented class. There is a very simple and effective way around this problem, and that is to create a class containing published properties of the types we desire. We then use the techniques previously discussed to retrieve a suitable TTypeInfo*, which we then use to register our property editor. Listing 10.6 shows such a class.

LISTING 10.6   Non-VCL Property Types in a Single Class

```
class PACKAGE TNonVCLTypesClass : public TObject
{
public:
__published:

    // Fundamental Integer Types
    __property int IntProperty = {};
    __property unsigned int UnsignedIntProperty = {};

    __property short int ShortIntProperty = {};
    __property unsigned short int UnsignedShortIntProperty = {};

    __property long int LongIntProperty = {};
    __property unsigned long int UnsignedLongIntProperty = {};

    __property char CharProperty = {};
    __property unsigned char UnsignedCharProperty = {};
    __property signed char SignedCharProperty = {};

    // Fundamental Floating Point Types
```

LISTING **10.6**   Continued

```
    __property double DoubleProperty = {};
    __property long double LongDoubleProperty = {};
    __property float FloatProperty = {};

    // Fundamental Boolean type
    __property bool BoolProperty = {};

    // The AnsiString class
    __property AnsiString AnsiStringProperty = {};

private:
    // Private Constructor, class cannot be instantiated from
    inline __fastcall TNonVCLTypesClass() : TObject()
    { }


};
```

If you created a component called `TTestComponent` with an `unsigned int` property called `Size`, the following code would allow you to register a custom property editor:

```
RegisterPropertyEditor( *(Typinfo::GetPropInfo
                             (__typeinfo(TNonVCLTypesClass),
                              "UnsignedIntProperty")
                          )->PropType,
                         __classid(TTestComponent),
                         "Size",
                         __classid(TUnsignedProperty) );
```

The first parameter is a bit confusing. It is shown again for clarification:

```
*(Typinfo::GetPropInfo(__typeinfo(TNonVCLTypesClass),
                       "UnsignedIntProperty"))->PropType
```

This is the same as the code we saw earlier in this section. It's not very attractive to look at or easy to write. To help make it easier to use, you can create a class that contains `static` member functions that return the correct `TTypeInfo*` for each type. The definition for such a class is shown in Listing 10.7.

LISTING **10.7**   NonVCLTypeInfo.h

```
//--------------------------------------------------------------------//
#ifndef NonVCLTypeInfoH
#define NonVCLTypeInfoH
//--------------------------------------------------------------------//
#ifndef TypInfoHPP
```

LISTING 10.7 Continued

```cpp
#include <TypInfo.hpp>
#endif
//----------------------------------------------------------------//

class PACKAGE TNonVCLTypeInfo : public TObject
{
public:
    // Fundamental Integer Types
    static PTypeInfo __fastcall Int();
    static PTypeInfo __fastcall UnsignedInt();

    static PTypeInfo __fastcall ShortInt();
    static PTypeInfo __fastcall UnsignedShortInt();

    static PTypeInfo __fastcall LongInt();
    static PTypeInfo __fastcall UnsignedLongInt();

    static PTypeInfo __fastcall Char();
    static PTypeInfo __fastcall UnsignedChar();
    static PTypeInfo __fastcall SignedChar();

    // Fundamental Floating Point Types
    static PTypeInfo __fastcall Double();
    static PTypeInfo __fastcall LongDouble();
    static PTypeInfo __fastcall Float();

    // Fundamental Boolean type
    static PTypeInfo __fastcall Bool();

    // The AnsiString class
    static PTypeInfo __fastcall AnsiString();

private:
    // Private Constructor, class cannot be instantiated from
    inline __fastcall TNonVCLTypeInfo() : TObject()
    { }

};

// The definition for TNonVCLTypesClass goes here (Listing 10.6)

//----------------------------------------------------------------//
#endif
```

The implementation is shown in Listing 10.8.

LISTING 10.8 NonVCLTypeInfo.cpp

```cpp
#include <vcl.h>
#pragma hdrstop

#include "NonVCLTypeInfo.h"
//---------------------------------------------------------------------------//
#pragma package(smart_init)
//---------------------------------------------------------------------------//

PTypeInfo __fastcall TNonVCLTypeInfo::Int()
{
    return *(Typinfo::GetPropInfo(__typeinfo(TNonVCLTypesClass),
                            "IntProperty"))->PropType;
}

PTypeInfo __fastcall TNonVCLTypeInfo::UnsignedInt()
{
    return *(Typinfo::GetPropInfo(__typeinfo(TNonVCLTypesClass),
                            "UnsignedIntProperty"))->PropType;
}
//---------------------------------------------------------------------------//

PTypeInfo __fastcall TNonVCLTypeInfo::ShortInt()
{
    return *(Typinfo::GetPropInfo(__typeinfo(TNonVCLTypesClass),
                            "ShortIntProperty"))->PropType;
}

PTypeInfo __fastcall TNonVCLTypeInfo::UnsignedShortInt()
{
    return *(Typinfo::GetPropInfo(__typeinfo(TNonVCLTypesClass),
                            "UnsignedShortIntProperty"))->PropType;
}
//---------------------------------------------------------------------------//

PTypeInfo __fastcall TNonVCLTypeInfo::LongInt()
{
    return *(Typinfo::GetPropInfo(__typeinfo(TNonVCLTypesClass),
                            "LongIntProperty"))->PropType;
}

PTypeInfo __fastcall TNonVCLTypeInfo::UnsignedLongInt()
```

LISTING 10.8   Continued

```cpp
{
    return *(Typinfo::GetPropInfo(__typeinfo(TNonVCLTypesClass),
                            "UnsignedLongIntProperty"))->PropType;
}
//------------------------------------------------------------------------//

PTypeInfo __fastcall TNonVCLTypeInfo::Char()
{
    return *(Typinfo::GetPropInfo(__typeinfo(TNonVCLTypesClass),
                            "CharProperty"))->PropType;
}

PTypeInfo __fastcall TNonVCLTypeInfo::UnsignedChar()
{
    return *(Typinfo::GetPropInfo(__typeinfo(TNonVCLTypesClass),
                            "UnsignedCharProperty"))->PropType;
}

PTypeInfo __fastcall TNonVCLTypeInfo::SignedChar()
{
    return *(Typinfo::GetPropInfo(__typeinfo(TNonVCLTypesClass),
                            "SignedCharProperty"))->PropType;
}
//------------------------------------------------------------------------//

PTypeInfo __fastcall TNonVCLTypeInfo::Double()
{
    return *(Typinfo::GetPropInfo(__typeinfo(TNonVCLTypesClass),
                            "DoubleProperty"))->PropType;
}

PTypeInfo __fastcall TNonVCLTypeInfo::LongDouble()
{
    return *(Typinfo::GetPropInfo(__typeinfo(TNonVCLTypesClass),
                            "LongDoubleProperty"))->PropType;
}

PTypeInfo __fastcall TNonVCLTypeInfo::Float()
{
    return *(Typinfo::GetPropInfo(__typeinfo(TNonVCLTypesClass),
                            "FloatProperty"))->PropType;
}
//------------------------------------------------------------------------//

PTypeInfo __fastcall TNonVCLTypeInfo::Bool()
```

LISTING 10.8   Continued

```
{
   return *(Typinfo::GetPropInfo(__typeinfo(TNonVCLTypesClass),
                                 "BoolProperty"))->PropType;
}
//-------------------------------------------------------------------------//

PTypeInfo __fastcall TNonVCLTypeInfo::AnsiString()
{
   return *(Typinfo::GetPropInfo(__typeinfo(TNonVCLTypesClass),
                                 "AnsiStringProperty"))->PropType;
}
//-------------------------------------------------------------------------//
```

Using our previous example of registering a property editor for an unsigned int property
called Size in a component called TTestComponent, the registration function is

```
RegisterPropertyEditor(TNonVCLTypeInfo::UnsignedInt(),
                       __classid(TTestComponent),
                       "Size",
                       __classid(TUnsignedProperty));
```

The previous code is simple, easy to understand, and easy to write. This should be your preferred method of registering property editors for non-VCL based properties.

It was mentioned earlier that determining a TTypeInfo* for a non-VCL property implemented
in Object Pascal is not the same as one implemented in C++. An example of this is the
PasswordChar property of TMaskEdit. To register a new property editor for all char types
requires two registrations: one for Object Pascal–implemented properties and one for C++
implementations. The previous approach (a special class containing the appropriate non-VCL
type properties) works fine for C++ implementations, but in order to get the correct
TTypeInfo* for the Object Pascal implementations, the TTypeInfo* pointer must be determined directly from the VCL class, in this case from the PasswordChar property of TMaskEdit.
This was the very first way we used to obtain a TTypeInfo*. If we want to register a new char
property editor called TCharPropertyEditor for all components and all properties of type
char, the registrations required are

```
TPropInfo* VCLCharPropInfo = Typinfo::GetPropInfo(__typeinfo(TMaskEdit),
                                                  "PasswordChar");
// Register the property editor for native VCL (Object Pascal) components

RegisterPropertyEditor(*VCLCharPropInfo->PropType,
                       0,
                       "",
                       __classid(TCharPropertyEditor));
```

```
// Register the property editor for C++ implemented components

RegisterPropertyEditor(TNonVCLTypeInfo::Char(),
                       0,
                       "",
                       __classid(TCharPropertyEditor));
```

Obtaining a `TTypeInfo*` (`PTypeInfo`) for a Non-VCL Type by Manual Creation

Creating a `TTypeInfo*` manually is an alternative approach to obtaining a `TTypeInfo*` from a VCL class for a non-VCL type. It is shown largely for comparison purposes and also because it is a commonly used technique. However, it should generally be avoided in preference to the first method. Manually creating the required `PTypeInfo` pointer can be done in place before the call to `RegisterPropertyEditor()`, or the code can be placed in a function that will return the pointer.

There are two ways to write the code to do this. One is to declare a `static TTypeInfo` structure locally, assign the appropriate values to it, and use a reference to it as the `PTypeInfo` argument. The other is to allocate a `TTypeInfo` structure dynamically, assign the appropriate values, and then use the pointer as the `PTypeInfo` argument. Both methods for generating a suitable `PTypeInfo` for an `AnsiString` property are shown in Listing 10.9. Note that this code and other similar functions are found in the `GetTypeInfo` unit on the CD-ROM.

LISTING 10.9   Manually Creating a `TTypeInfo*`

```
// - - - - - - - - - - - - - - - - - - - - - - - - - - - - - - - - - - - - - - - - - - - //
//                            As Functions                                             //
// - - - - - - - - - - - - - - - - - - - - - - - - - - - - - - - - - - - - - - - - - - - //
TTypeInfo* AnsiStringTypeInfo(void)
{
   static TTypeInfo TypeInfo;
   TypeInfo.Name = "AnsiString";
   TypeInfo.Kind = tkLString;
   return &TypeInfo;
}

// OR

TTypeInfo* AnsiStringTypeInfo(void)
{
   TTypeInfo* TypeInfo = new TTypeInfo;
   TypeInfo->Name = "AnsiString";
   TypeInfo->Kind = tkLString;
```

LISTING 10.9 Continued

```
    return TypeInfo;
}

//-------------- In the Registration code simply write:------------------//

RegisterPropertyEditor(AnsiStringTypeInfo(),
                       0 ,
                       "" ,
                       __classid(TAnsiStringPropertyEditor));


//-----------------------------------------------------------------------//
//             In Place Before RegisterPropertyEditor()                  //
//-----------------------------------------------------------------------//

static TTypeInfo AnsiStringTypeInfo;
TypeInfo.Name = "AnsiString";
TypeInfo.Kind = tkLString;

RegisterPropertyEditor(&AnsiStringTypeInfo,
                       0 ,
                       "" ,
                       __classid(TAnsiStringPropertyEditor));

// OR

TTypeInfo* AnsiStringTypeInfo = new TTypeInfo;
TypeInfo->Name = "AnsiString";
TypeInfo->Kind = tkLString;

RegisterPropertyEditor(AnsiStringTypeInfo,
                       0 ,
                       "" ,
                       __classid(TAnsiStringPropertyEditor));
```

Notice that when the `TTypeInfo` structure is dynamically allocated (with `new`), it is not deleted after the call to `RegisterPropertyEditor()`. If this is done, the registration will fail. The reason for this is explained in the following section.

How to Obtain a `TTypeInfo*` for a Non-VCL Type

Which of the two approaches you use to obtain a `TTypeInfo*` for a non-VCL type—determine it from a VCL class or manually create it—is straightforward. Always use the first method when you can. In particular, you must use the first method if you are writing a property editor to override an existing property editor for which an editor has been specifically registered by the VCL (as opposed to being determined dynamically) or one that has been previously registered using the first approach. In general, the first approach is more robust, because you are using the VCL's representation of the `TTypeInfo*` for the given property. The need to use the first method to override a property editor registered using the first method should be noted. Creating a class with `static` member functions to return a suitable `TTypeInfo*` makes the first method just as easy as the manual creation method and should be considered the superior technique.

An important point about using the two approaches is that writing a function to a specific `PTypeInfo` (the second method) is *not* the same as obtaining the `PTypeInfo` from the VCL (the first method). The reason for this is that the implementation of `TPropertyClassRec`, used internally by the `RegisterPropertyEditor()` function, maintains only a `PTypeInfo` variable, not the actual values that it points to, namely the `Name` and `Kind` of the `TTypeInfo`. This is why a reference to a locally declared non-`static` `TTypeInfo` structure cannot be used and a dynamically allocated `TTypeInfo` structure must not be deleted (it is simply abandoned on free store).

Registering property editors is then relatively easy. However, care must be taken to ensure that the parameters passed are exact. Often it is possible to compile and install property editors that do not appear to function, only to find later that the registration code is not quite right (such as when the `PropertyName` parameter has been spelled incorrectly) and that the property editor worked all along.

Rules for Overriding Property Editors

With the knowledge of how to register custom property editors and the realization that it is possible to override any previously installed property editor, the question is this: What are the rules for overriding property editors? The following highlights the two main considerations:

- In general, property editors are used from newest to oldest. In other words, the most recently installed property editor for a given property will be used. The exception to this is noted in the next point.

- A newly registered property editor will override an existing property editor only if the specification used to register it is *at least as specific* as that used to register the existing editor. For example, if a property editor is registered specifically for the `Shape` property (of type `TShapeType`) in the `TShape` component, then installing a new editor for properties of type `TShapeType` for *all* components (`ComponentClass == 0`) will *not* override the property editor for the `Shape` property of `TShape`.

The only other consideration when overriding property editors is the method used to obtain the appropriate `PTypeInfo`, as previously discussed. Such property overriding can be seen in practice by examining the `EnhancedEditors` package on the accompanying CD-ROM.

Using Images in Property Editors

This section introduces the techniques required to render images in the Object Inspector for custom property editors. Some property editors already render images in the Object Inspector, and those were listed previously in Chapter 2, "C++Builder Projects and More on the IDE," in Table 2.4. Inheriting a property editor from one of the property editors listed in Table 2.4 or using a type that is registered for one of those property editors enables the use of the image rendering already coded for each. For example, a property of type TColor will appear automatically in the Object Inspector as other TColor properties do. However, there are many more types of properties that could benefit from the use of images when editing the property. To facilitate this, TPropertyEditor (the base class for all property editors) has six new methods, five of which can be overridden. The declarations for the five overridable functions are as follows:

```
DYNAMIC void __fastcall ListMeasureWidth(const AnsiString Value,
                                         Graphics::TCanvas* ACanvas,
                                         int& AWidth);

DYNAMIC void __fastcall ListMeasureHeight(const AnsiString Value,
                                          Graphics::TCanvas* ACanvas,
                                          int& AHeight);

DYNAMIC void __fastcall ListDrawValue(const AnsiString Value,
                                      Graphics::TCanvas* ACanvas,
                                      const Windows::TRect& ARect,
                                      bool ASelected);

DYNAMIC void __fastcall PropDrawValue(Graphics::TCanvas* ACanvas,
                                      const Windows::TRect& ARect,
                                      bool ASelected);

DYNAMIC void __fastcall PropDrawName(Graphics::TCanvas* ACanvas,
                                     const Windows::TRect& ARect,
                                     bool ASelected);
```

The remaining method, to be used in conjunction with the *Xxxx*DrawValue methods, is declared as

```
AnsiString __fastcall GetVisualValue();
```

These are listed in Table 10.8, along with a description of the purpose of each.

TABLE 10.8   New Methods for `TPropertyEditor` to Allow Custom Images

Method	*Purpose*
`ListMeasureWidth()`	This is used to allow the default width of an entry in the drop-down list to be modified. As the width of the overall drop-down list is set to that of the widest entry or greater, this is effectively the minimum width of the drop-down list.
`ListMeasureHeight()`	This is used to allow the default height of each list entry to be modified. Unless a large image is displayed (as is the case with `TCursor` properties), this method does not generally need to be overridden.
`ListDrawValue()`	This is called to render each property value in the drop-down list.
`PropDrawValue()`	This is called to render the selected property value for the property when it does not have focus. When the property has focus, the current property value is shown as an editable `AnsiString`.
`PropDrawName()`	This is called to render the property name in the Object Inspector. It is not required often.
`GetVisualValue()`	This is used to return the displayable value of the property. This method is used in conjunction with the `ListDrawValue()` and `PropDrawValue()` methods to render the `AnsiString` representation of the property value.

Where in the Object Inspector these methods are used is illustrated in Figure 10.3. You can see that the three most important methods to override are `ListMeasureWidth()`, `ListDrawValue()`, and `PropDrawValue()`.

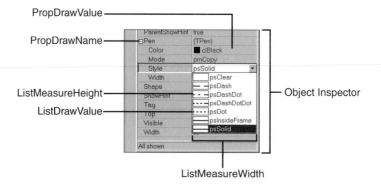

FIGURE 10.3

Areas in the Object Inspector that are affected by the new overridable `TPropertyEditor` *methods.*

To create your own custom images in the Object Inspector, you must derive a new property editor class from TPropertyEditor or from a class derived from TPropertyEditor. Which you do depends on the type of the property that the editor is for. For example, a property of type int would descend from TIntegerProperty. Refer to the section "Creating Custom Property Editors," earlier in this chapter, for more information. A new property editor class can then be defined according to the format in Listing 10.10. As an example, the editor is derived from TEnumProperty.

LISTING 10.10   Definition Code for a Property Editor That Renders Custom Images

```
#include "DsgnIntf.hpp"

class TCustomImagePropertyEditor : public TEnumProperty
{
   typedef TEnumProperty inherited;

public:
   DYNAMIC void __fastcall ListMeasureWidth(const AnsiString Value,
                                            Graphics::TCanvas* ACanvas,
                                            int& AWidth);

   DYNAMIC void __fastcall ListMeasureHeight(const AnsiString Value,
                                             Graphics::TCanvas* ACanvas,
                                             int& AHeight);

   DYNAMIC void __fastcall ListDrawValue(const AnsiString Value,
                                         Graphics::TCanvas* ACanvas,
                                         const Windows::TRect& ARect,
                                         bool ASelected);

   DYNAMIC void __fastcall PropDrawValue(Graphics::TCanvas* ACanvas,
                                         const Windows::TRect& ARect,
                                         bool ASelected);

   DYNAMIC void __fastcall PropDrawName(Graphics::TCanvas* ACanvas,
                                        const Windows::TRect& ARect,
                                        bool ASelected);

protected:
   #pragma option push -w-inl
   inline __fastcall virtual
      TCustomImagePropertyEditor(const _di_IFormDesigner ADesigner,
                                 int APropCount)
```

LISTING 10.10   Continued

```
                                    : TEnumProperty(ADesigner,
                                                    APropCount)
    { }
    #pragma option pop

public:
    #pragma option push -w-inl
    inline __fastcall virtual ~TCustomImagePropertyEditor(void)
    { }
    #pragma option pop

};
```

It is assumed that only the drawing behavior of the property editor is to be modified. The remainder of the class is not altered.

The implementation of each of the five DYNAMIC functions is discussed in the sections that follow. For each of the methods, comments will indicate the code that should be present in each method. This will be followed by the actual code used to produce the images shown in Figure 10.4, which shows a finished property editor in use.

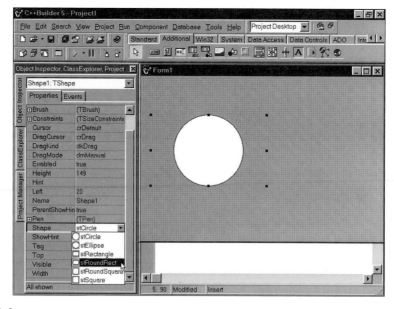

FIGURE 10.4

The TShapeTypePropertyEditor *in use.*

As an example, a property editor for the TShapeType enumeration from the TShape component will be developed. The class definition for such a property editor is exactly the same as that shown in Listing 10.10. However, the class is called TShapeTypePropertyEditor. The parameters used in the five image-rendering methods are detailed in Table 10.9, so that an overall picture of how they are used can be developed.

TABLE 10.9 Parameters for Custom Image-Rendering Methods

Method	Purpose
AWidth	This is the current width in pixels of the AnsiString representation of the value as it will be displayed in the Object Inspector, including leading and trailing space.
AHeight	This is the default height of the display area for the current item. Typically this is 2 pixels greater than the height of ACanvas->TextHeight("Ag"), where Ag is chosen simply to remind the reader that the actual font height of the current font is returned, that is the ascender height (from A) plus the descender height (from g). Adding 2 pixels allows a 1-pixel border. Remember that the ascender height also includes the internal leading height (used for accents, umlauts, and tildes in non-English character sets), typically 2 to 3 pixels. Refer to Figure 10.5 for clarification.
ACanvas	This encapsulates the device context for the current item in the Object Inspector.
ARect	This represents the client area of the region to be painted.
ASelected	This parameter is true when the list item is currently selected in the Object Inspector.

Figure 10.5 shows a diagram illustrating how the height of text is calculated.

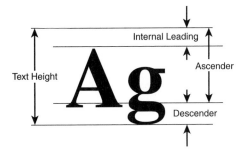

FIGURE 10.5

Calculating text height.

Figure 10.6 shows the relationship between the parameters in Table 10.9 and the actual render-ing of an image and text in the Object Inspector. This figure will be referred to throughout the discussion, and additional information is therefore shown.

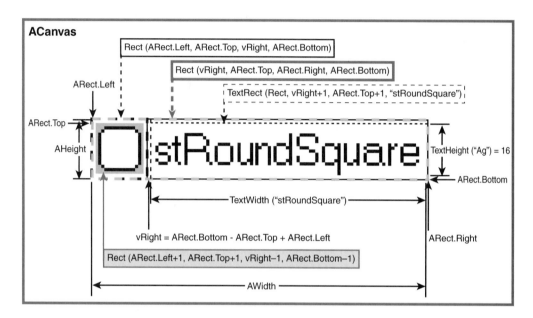

FIGURE 10.6

The relationship between image-rendering parameters and actual display.

The `ListMeasureWidth()` Method

Initially, `AWidth` is equal to the return value of `ACanvas->TextWidth(Value)`. However, if an image is added to the display, the width of the image must be added to `AWidth` to update it. This method, called during the width calculation phase of the drop-down list, allows you to do this. If a square image region is required, `AWidth` can simply be adjusted by adding `ACanvas->TextHeight("Ag")+2` to its current value. This is because this value will equal the default `AHeight` value, as previously mentioned in Table 10.9. (Also, see Figure 10.6, in which `ACanvas->TextHeight("Ag")+2` is 18 (16+2) pixels.) Remember that `Ag` could be replaced by any characters. If a larger image is required, a multiple of this value can be used or a constant can be added to the width. If the image width is known, then this can simply be added to the current `AWidth` value. The code is shown in Listing 10.11.

LISTING 10.11   Overriding the `ListMeasureWidth()` Method

```
void __fastcall
   TShapeTypePropertyEditor::ListMeasureWidth(const AnsiString Value,
                                              Graphics::TCanvas* ACanvas,
                                              int& AWidth)
{
   AWidth += (ACanvas->TextHeight("Ag")+2) + 0; // 0 can be replaced
                                                // by a constant
}
```

The `ListMeasureHeight()` Method

Unless an image is required that is larger then the default height, this method does not require overriding. However, if it does need modified, `AHeight` must not be given a value smaller than `ACanvas->TextHeight("Ag")+2`, because this would clip the text displayed. Therefore, two choices are available. A constant value can be added to the current `AHeight`, normally to maintain a constant ratio with the image width, or `AHeight` can be changed directly. If it is changed directly, the new value must be greater than `ACanvas->TextHeight("Ag")+2`; otherwise this value should be used. The code is shown in Listing 10.12.

LISTING 10.12   Overriding the `ListMeasureHeight()` Method

```
void __fastcall
   TShapeTypePropertyEditor::ListMeasureHeight(const AnsiString Value,
                                               Graphics::TCanvas* ACanvas,
                                               int& AHeight)
{
   AHeight += 0; // 0 could be replaced by a constant value
}
// OR :

void __fastcall
   TShapeTypePropertyEditor::ListMeasureHeight(const AnsiString Value,
                                               Graphics::TCanvas* ACanvas,
                                               int& AHeight)
{
   if( (ACanvas->TextHeight("Ag")+2) < ImageHeight )
   {
      AHeight = ImageHeight;
   }
}
```

The `ListDrawValue()` Method

This method does most of the hard work. It is this method that renders each item in the drop-down list by drawing directly onto the list item's canvas. To write well-behaved code, this method should have the layout in Listing 10.13. To get an appreciation of what the actual rendering code is doing, refer to Figure 10.6. For the big picture, refer to Figure 10.3.

LISTING 10.13   A Template for Overriding the `ListDrawValue()` Method

```
void __fastcall
    TCustomImagePropertyEditor::ListDrawValue(const AnsiString Value,
                                              Graphics::TCanvas* ACanvas,
                                              const Windows::TRect& ARect,
                                              bool ASelected)
{
    // Declare an int vRight to indicate the right most edge of the image.
    // The v prefix is used to indicate that it is a variable. This used
    // to follow the convention used in DsgnIntf.pas.

    try
    {
        // Step 1 - Save ACanvas properties that we are going to change.

        // Step 2 - Frame the area to be modified. This is required so that any
        //          previous rendering on the canvas is overwritten. For example
        //          when the IDE selection rendering is applied, i.e. the
        //          property value is surrounded by a dashed yellow and black
        //          line and the AnsiString representation is highlighted in
        //          clNavy, and focus then moves to another list value the
        //          modified parts of ACanvas are cleared, ready for the custom
        //          rendering. If the entire ACanvas is going to be changed then
        //          this operation is not required.

        // Step 3 - Perform any preparation required. For example paint a
        //          background color and place a highlight box around the image
        //          of the list value if ASelected is true.
        //
        //          To choose a color to match the current text used by windows
        //          select clWindowText, this is useful as an image border, hence
        //          this is often selected as a suitable ACanvas->Pen color.
        //
        //          To give the appearance of a clear background, clear border or
        //          both set the ACanvas->Brush and/or ACanvas->Pen color to
        //          clWindow.
        //
        //          To use a color the same as the Object Inspector choose
        //          clBtnFace.
```

LISTING 10.13   Continued

```
    // Step 4 - Determine the value of the current list item.

    // Step 5 - Draw the required image onto ACanvas.

    // Step 6 - Restore modified ACanvas properties to their original values.
  }
  __finally
  {
    // Perform the following operation to render the AnsiString
    // representation of the current item, i.e. Value, onto ACanvas.

    // 1. Either call the parents ListDrawValue method passing vRight as the
    //    l (left) parameter of the Rect variable, i.e.
    //
    //    TEnumProperty::ListDrawValue(Value,
    //                                 ACanvas,
    //                                 Rect(vRight,
    //                                      ARect.Top,
    //                                      ARect.Right,
    //                                      ARect.Bottom),
    //                                 ASelected);
    //    which becomes:
    //
    //    inherited::ListDrawValue(Value,
    //                             ACanvas,
    //                             Rect(vRight,
    //                                  ARect.Top,
    //                                  ARect.Right,
    //                                  ARect.Bottom),
    //                             ASelected);
    //
    //    using our typedef which is more maintainable.

    // 2. Or perform this operation directly by calling the TextRect() member
    //    function directly removing the need to call the parent version of
    //    this (ListDrawValue()) virtual function
    //    i.e.
    //    ACanvas->TextRect( Rect(vRight,
    //                            ARect.Top,
    //                            ARect.Right,
    //                            ARect.Bottom),
    //                       vRight+1,
    //                       ARect.Top+1,
    //                       Value );
  }
}
```

Actual code based on the template in Listing 10.13 is shown in Listing 10.14. The code renders each item in the drop-down list. Each item in the list consists of an image followed by text representing the enum value to which the item refers. Figure 10.4 shows an image of the rendered drop-down list.

LISTING 10.14   An Implementation of the `ListDrawValue()` Method

```
void __fastcall
   TShapeTypePropertyEditor::ListDrawValue(const AnsiString Value,
                                           Graphics::TCanvas* ACanvas,
                                           const Windows::TRect& ARect,
                                           bool ASelected)

{
   // Declare vRight ('v' stands for variable)
   int vRight = ARect.Bottom - ARect.Top + ARect.Left;

   try
   {
      // Step 1 - Save ACanvas properties that we are going to change

      TColor vOldPenColor = ACanvas->Pen->Color;
      TColor vOldBrushColor = ACanvas->Brush->Color;


      // Step 2 - Frame the area to be modified.

      ACanvas->Pen->Color = ACanvas->Brush->Color;
      ACanvas->Rectangle(ARect.Left, ARect.Top, vRight, ARect.Bottom);


      // Step 3 - Perform any preparation required.

      if(ASelected)                          // Choose a Pen color
      {                                      // depending on whether
         ACanvas->Pen->Color = clYellow;     // the list value is
      }                                      // selected or not
      else
      {
         ACanvas->Pen->Color = clBtnFace;
      }

      ACanvas->Brush->Color = clBtnFace;     // Choose a background color to
                                             // match the Object Inspector
```

LISTING 10.14 Continued

```
ACanvas->Rectangle( ARect.Left + 1,      // Draw the background onto
                    ARect.Top + 1,       // the Canvas using the
                    vRight - 1,          // current Pen and the
                    ARect.Bottom - 1 );  // current Brush :-)


// Step 4 - Determine the value of the current list item

TShapeType ShapeType = TShapeType(GetEnumValue(GetPropType(), Value));

// Step 5 - Draw the required image onto ACanvas

ACanvas->Pen->Color = clBlack;
ACanvas->Brush->Color = clWhite;

switch(ShapeType)
{
   case stRectangle   : ACanvas->Rectangle(ARect.Left+2,
                                           ARect.Top+4,
                                           vRight-2,
                                           ARect.Bottom-4);
                     break;
   case stSquare      : ACanvas->Rectangle(ARect.Left+2,
                                           ARect.Top+2,
                                           vRight-2,
                                           ARect.Bottom-2);
                     break;
   case stRoundRect   : ACanvas->RoundRect(ARect.Left+2,
                                           ARect.Top+4,
                                           vRight-2,
                                           ARect.Bottom-4,
                                           (ARect.Bottom-ARect.Top-6)/2,
                                           (ARect.Bottom-ARect.Top-6)/2);
                     break;
   case stRoundSquare : ACanvas->RoundRect(ARect.Left+2,
                                           ARect.Top+2,
                                           vRight-2,
                                           ARect.Bottom-2,
                                           (ARect.Bottom-ARect.Top)/3,
                                           (ARect.Bottom-ARect.Top)/3);
                     break;
   case stEllipse     : ACanvas->Ellipse(ARect.Left+1,
                                         ARect.Top+2,
                                         vRight-1,
                                         ARect.Bottom-2);
                     break;
```

10

**PROPERTY AND
COMPONENT
EDITORS**

LISTING 10.14   Continued

```
          case stCircle      : ACanvas->Ellipse(ARect.Left+1,
                                                ARect.Top+1,
                                                vRight-1,
                                                ARect.Bottom-1);
                               break;
          default : break;
        }

        // Step 6 - Restore modified ACanvas properties to their original values

        ACanvas->Pen->Color = vOldPenColor;
        ACanvas->Brush->Color = vOldBrushColor;

    }
    __finally
    {
        // Render the AnsiString representation onto ACanvas
        // Use method 1, call the parent method

        inherited::ListDrawValue(Value,
                                 ACanvas,
                                 Rect(vRight,
                                      ARect.Top,
                                      ARect.Right,
                                      ARect.Bottom),
                                 ASelected);
    }
}
```

Step 4 in Listing 10.14 is of crucial importance to the operation of `ListDrawValue()`. The value of the drop-down list item is determined here. This allows a decision to be made in Step 5 as to what should be rendered. For enumerations such as `TShapeType`, the `AnsiString` representation of the value must be converted to an actual value. The code that performs this is

```
TShapeType ShapeType = TShapeType(GetEnumValue(GetPropType(), Value));
```

`GetEnumValue()` is declared in `$(BCB)\Include\Vcl\TypInfo.hpp` and returns an `int` value. This `int` value is used to construct a new `TShapeType` variable called `ShapeType`. The function `GetPropType()` returns a pointer to a `TTypeInfo` structure containing the `TypeInfo` for the property type (in this case `TShapeType`). This could alternatively have been obtained using

```
*GetPropInfo()->PropType
```

This is similar to the approach used to obtain type information when registering property editors (see the section "Obtaining a `TTypeInfo*` (`PTypeInfo`) from an Existing Property and Class for a Non-VCL Type," earlier in this chapter, for more details) and can be used more generally. `Value` is the `AnsiString` representation of the current enumeration value. `GetPropType()` and `GetPropInfo()` are both member functions of `TPropertyEditor` and as such are declared in `$(BCB)\Include\Vcl\DsgnIntf.hpp`. Techniques such as these are indispensable to writing property editors, so it is important to be aware of them.

Each of the images is rendered according to the bounding `ARect` parameter. This means that the code does not need to be modified to enlarge or reduce the rendered images. To do this, simply change the values of `AWidth` and `AHeight`. Changing the constant `0` in the `ListMeasureWidth()` and `ListMeasureHeight()` methods to `10`, for example, will increase the rendered image size in the drop-down list by `10` pixels in each direction. Note that the image in the property value region will not be affected.

The `PropDrawValue()` Method

This method is responsible for rendering the current property value in the Object Inspector. The height of the area to be rendered is fixed (`ARect.Bottom` - `ARect.Top`) so there is less flexibility over the images that can be rendered compared with images rendered in the drop-down list. The code required for this operation is the same as that required to render the same value in the drop-down list. The only difference is the value of the `ARect` parameter. The rendering can therefore be carried out by the `ListDrawValue()` method, passing the `PropDrawValue()` parameters as arguments. The code for this member function is shown in Listing 10.15.

LISTING 10.15 An Implementation of the `PropDrawValue()` Method

```
void __fastcall
   TShapeTypePropertyEditor::PropDrawValue(Graphics::TCanvas* ACanvas,
                                           const Windows::TRect& ARect,
                                           bool ASelected)
{
   if( GetVisualValue() != "" )
   {
      ListDrawValue(GetVisualValue(), ACanvas, ARect, ASelected);
   }
   else
   {
      // As in the ListDrawValue method either the parent method can be called
      // or the code required to render the text called directly, i.e.
      //
```

LISTING 10.15   Continued

```
    // inherited::PropDrawValue(ACanvas, ARect, ASelected);
    //
    // or:
    //
    // ACanvas->TextRect( ARect,
    //                    ARect.Left+1,
    //                    ARect.Top+1,
    //                    GetVisualValue() );
    //
    // For comparison the text is rendered directly, i.e.

    ACanvas->TextRect( ARect,
                       ARect.Left+1,
                       ARect.Top+1,
                       GetVisualValue() );
  }
}
```

The `PropDrawName()` Method

This is the last of the overridable methods for custom rendering and the one least often required. It controls the rendering of the property Name (see Figure 10.3). As with the PropDrawValue() method, the height of the drawing region is fixed. This method has limited use, though it can be used to add symbols to properties that exhibit certain behavior, read-only properties for instance (such as About properties). Overuse should be avoided because it may confuse rather than help users.

Another possible use is to add an image to TComponent-derived properties to indicate the component required. This method is not used in the TShapeTypePropertyEditor example, but the required code, should it be needed, is shown in Listing 10.16.

LISTING 10.16   An Implementation of the `PropDrawName()` Method

```
void __fastcall
    TCustomImagePropertyEditor::PropDrawValue(Graphics::TCanvas* ACanvas,
                                              const Windows::TRect& ARect,
                                              bool ASelected)
{
    if( GetName() != "" )
    {
        // Write a function to render the desired image, similar to
        // the ListDrawValue() method, i.e.
        //
```

LISTING 10.16   Continued

```
        // PropDrawNameValue(GetName(), ACanvas, ARect, ASelected); // Must be
                                                                    // defined
    }
    else
    {
        // As in the PropDrawValue method either the parent method can be called
        // or the code required to render the text called directly, i.e.
        //
        // inherited::PropDrawName(ACanvas, ARect, ASelected);
        //
        // or:
        //
        // ACanvas->TextRect( ARect,
        //                    vRect.Left+1,
        //                    ARect.Top+1,
        //                    GetName() );
        //
        // For comparison the text is rendered directly, i.e.

        ACanvas->TextRect( ARect,
                           ARect.Left+1,
                           ARect.Top+1,
                           GetName() );
    }
}
```

The `TImageListPropertyEditor` from the `EnhancedEditors` package (see Table 10.1) does implement this method to display an icon representing a `TImageList` component for `TCustomImageList*` properties. Listing 10.17 shows its implementation of this method for comparison. Note that `ImageListPropertyImage` is a resource loaded in the property editor's constructor.

LISTING 10.17   An Alternative Implementation of the `PropDrawName()` Method

```
void __fastcall
    TImageListPropertyEditor::PropDrawName (Graphics::TCanvas* ACanvas,
                                            const Windows::TRect& ARect,
                                            bool ASelected)
{
    TRect ValueRect = ARect;

    try
    {
        // Clear the canvas using the current pen and brush
```

LISTING 10.17   Continued

```
      ACanvas->FillRect(ARect);

      if(GetName() != "")
      {
         if(Screen->PixelsPerInch > 96) // If Large fonts
         {
            ACanvas->Draw( ARect.Left + 1,
                           ARect.Top + 2,
                           ImageListPropertyImage );
         }
         else // Otherwise small fonts
         {
            ACanvas->Draw( ARect.Left + 1,
                           ARect.Top,
                           ImageListPropertyImage );
         }

         ValueRect = Rect( ARect.Left + 16 + 2,
                           ARect.Top,
                           ARect.Right,
                           ARect.Bottom );
      }
   }
   __finally
   {
      // Whether or not we successfully draw the image we must draw the text
      inherited::PropDrawName(ACanvas, ValueRect, ASelected);
   }
}
```

The code in Listing 10.17 is reasonably straightforward. Of note is the try/__finally block to ensure that the text is always rendered. The code inside the try block is similar to that in Listing 10.16; the only difference is that the ImageListPropertyImage resource is positioned differently, depending on whether the screen is using large or small fonts. Once the ImageListPropertyImage resource is rendered, the Rect for rendering the text is offset to allow for the width of the resource, in this case 16 pixels.

Installing Editor-Only Packages

In the previous section, an editor for properties of type TShapeType was developed, but there was no mention of its registration. This will now be discussed. In the earlier section "Registering Custom Property Editors," we saw that we must use the RegisterPropertyEditor() function to register the editor with the IDE. This will be discussed again shortly. The only other considerations are that this function *must* be called inside the `Register()` function and that this `Register()` function *must* be wrapped inside a namespace that is the same as the name of the file in which it is contained, with the restriction that the first letter of the namespace must be in uppercase and the remaining letters lowercase. You are not registering a component and will not have used the IDE Component Wizard to set up your basic code structure, so you must write this registration code yourself. Remembering this could save time, because not all coding mistakes give errors at compile time. The basic code structure required is shown in Listing 10.18.

LISTING 10.18   Registering Editor-Only Packages

```
#include <vcl.h>
#pragma hdrstop

#include "NameOfThisFile"    // Header empty except for include guards
#include "PropertyEditors.h" // Include the file that contains the Property
                             // Editor code
#include <TypInfo.hpp>       // Include for TPropInfo* and GetPropInfo()
//--------------------------------------------------------------------------//
#pragma package(smart_init)
//--------------------------------------------------------------------------//
namespace Nameofthisfile // First letter UPPERCASE, all other letters lowercase
{

    void __fastcall PACKAGE Register()
    {
        // Using the following Registration registers the 'TShapePropertyEditor'
        // for ALL properties of type 'TShapeType' for ALL components.

        TPropInfo* TShapeTypePropInfo = Typinfo::GetPropInfo(__typeinfo(TShape),
                                                             "Shape");

        RegisterPropertyEditor(*TShapeTypePropInfo->PropType,
                               0,
                               "",
                               __classid(TShapeTypePropertyEditor));
    }
}
```

10

Note that in Listing 10.18 the header file (`NameOfThisFile.h`) included for the registration code is empty and does not need to be included or present. In the package source file, the implementation file (`.cpp`) is included through the `USEUNIT()` macro, so the header is not needed.

Because the purpose of the package that contains this code is to register only editors (property or component), then the Designtime Only option in the Usage Options section on the Description page of the package's Options dialog should be selected.

Property and component editors are used from newest to oldest, provided their registration is at least as specific as that for the old editor. This allows editors currently registered to be overridden. This is the effect of the `EnhancedEditors` package (`EnhancedEditors.bpk`) accompanying this chapter on the CD-ROM. As can be seen from Listing 10.18, `TShapeTypePropertyEditor` is registered for ALL properties of type `TShapeType` for ALL components. Hence, the `Shape` property of `TShape` will now use this property editor. This opens up the possibility of separately customizing and updating the property and component editors of existing components. As was mentioned in the section "Images in Drop-Down Lists in the Object Inspector" in Chapter 2, "C++Builder Projects and More on the IDE," the `TFontNameProperty` editor is effectively disabled by default. To enable it requires the creation of an Expert using the Open Tools API. This is not easy. An alternative approach is to override the `TFontNameProperty` property editor to achieve the desired result. Such a property editor, called `TDisplayFontNameProperty`, has also been included in the `EnhancedEditors` package to enable the reader to examine how this is done.

Using Linked Image Lists in Property Editors

A common use of images in drop-down lists for property editors is to display images in an image index property that is linked to a component's `TCustomImageList*` property, or to display images contained in a component's parent's `TCustomImageList*` property. Linking an image index property to a `TCustomImageList*` in the same component will be shown as a general example. However, the only difference between linking to a `TCustomImageList*` on the same component and linking to a `TCustomImageList*` on a parent component is the method used to retrieve a copy of the pointer to the `TCustomImageList`, as we shall see. This will be highlighted in the "Linking to a Parent's `TCustomImageList`" and "A Generalized Solution for `ImageIndex` Properties" sections later in this chapter.

To illustrate how this is done, a `TEnhancedImage` component will be developed that has both an image index property and a `TCustomImageList*` property. Note that a `TCustomImageList` pointer is used to allow for other classes derived from this class; otherwise, `TImageList*` would be used. The purpose of this component is simple: to allow the `TEnhancedImage` component to be linked to a `TImageList` component if there is one placed on the same form. By changing the image index property of the `TEnhancedImage` component, the image displayed will match the image contained in the `TImageList` component at that index. It would also be preferable that this behavior be enabled only when required; otherwise, the component should behave as a normal `TImage` component. The definition for this component is shown in Listing 10.19.

LISTING 10.19 Definition of the `TEnhancedImage` Component

```cpp
//---------------------------------------------------------------------------//
#ifndef EnhancedImageH
#define EnhancedImageH
//---------------------------------------------------------------------------//
#include <SysUtils.hpp>
#include <Controls.hpp>
#include <Classes.hpp>
#include <Forms.hpp>
//---------------------------------------------------------------------------//

class PACKAGE TEnhancedImage : public TImage
{
        typedef TImage inherited;
private:
        Imglist::TCustomImageList* FImageList;
        int   FImageIndex;
        bool FUseImageList;

protected:
        virtual void __fastcall SetUseImageList(bool NewUseImageList);
        virtual void __fastcall SetImageIndex(int NewImageIndex);
        virtual void __fastcall SetImageList
                              (Imglist::TCustomImageList* NewImageList);
        virtual void __fastcall UpdatePicture(void);

        // Override Notification from TComponent
        virtual void __fastcall Notification(TComponent* AComponent,
                                             TOperation Operation);
public:
        __fastcall TEnhancedImage(TComponent* Owner);

__published:
        __property bool UseImageList = {read=FUseImageList,
                                       write=SetUseImageList,
                                       default=false};

        __property Imglist::TCustomImageList* ImageList = {read=FImageList,
                                                          write=SetImageList,
                                                          default=0};

        __property int ImageIndex = {read=FImageIndex,
                                     write=SetImageIndex,
                                     default=-1};
};

//---------------------------------------------------------------------------//
#endif
```

Because we want only to add extra functionality to the TImage component, we simply need to add our required additional properties to a class derived from TImage and then write any get and set functions necessary. Three properties are added: one for the TImageList, called ImageList, one for the image index, called ImageIndex, and one to decide whether to use the TImageList, called UseImageList. For each of these, we need a set method and an initialization in the class's constructor. We also override TComponent's Notification() method and have a function to update the picture if necessary each time one of these properties is changed. The implementation code is shown in Listing 10.20.

LISTING 10.20   Implementation for the TEnhancedImage Component Functions

```
//---------------------------------------------------------------------//
__fastcall TEnhancedImage::TEnhancedImage(TComponent* Owner)
        : TImage(Owner),
          FUseImageList(false),
          FImageIndex(-1),
          FImageList(0)
{
}
//---------------------------------------------------------------------//
void __fastcall TEnhancedImage::SetUseImageList(bool NewUseImageList)
{
   if(NewUseImageList != UseImageList)
   {
      FUseImageList = NewUseImageList;

      UpdatePicture();
   }
}
//---------------------------------------------------------------------//
void __fastcall TEnhancedImage::SetImageIndex (int NewImageIndex)
{
   if(NewImageIndex != FImageIndex)
   {
      FImageIndex = NewImageIndex;

      UpdatePicture();
   }
}
//---------------------------------------------------------------------//
void __fastcall
   TEnhancedImage::SetImageList(Imglist::TCustomImageList* NewImageList)
{
   if(NewImageList != FImageList)
   {
      FImageList = NewImageList;
```

LISTING 10.20   Continued

```
        if(ImageList == 0) ImageIndex =-1;
    }
}
//-------------------------------------------------------------------------//
void __fastcall TEnhancedImage::UpdatePicture(void)
{
    if( UseImageList
        && ImageList != 0
        && ImageIndex >= 0
        && ImageIndex < ImageList->Count )
    {
        std::auto_ptr<Graphics::TBitmap> Image(new Graphics::TBitmap());

        ImageList->GetBitmap(ImageIndex, Image.get());
        Picture->Assign(Image.get());
    }
}
//-------------------------------------------------------------------------//
void __fastcall TEnhancedImage::Notification(TComponent* AComponent,
                                             TOperation Operation)
{
    inherited::Notification(AComponent, Operation);

    if(Operation == opRemove)
    {
        if(AComponent == ImageList) ImageList = 0;
        // Can make more checks for other properties if needed
    }
}
//-------------------------------------------------------------------------//
```

The constructor holds no surprises; the data members for the class's properties are initialized in an initializer list. Looking now at SetUseImageList() and SetImageIndex(), we see that they both operate in the same way. If the new value requested does not equal the current value, then the current value is set to the new value. The UpdatePicture() method is then called. This looks at all the current property settings and adjusts the Picture property (inherited from TImage) as required. SetImageList() is similar; if the new value requested does not equal the current value, the current value is set to the new value. However, if the new value is 0 (that is, NULL: there is no TImageList), then ImageIndex is set to -1, the property's default value. Notice that after the initial assignment to FImageList, FImageList is not used in the following if statement; instead, the ImageList property is. This returns FImageList, so in this case it makes no difference which is used. However, if the property's internal representation may be different from that of the property itself (that is, a get function is required for the property), then it is better to read the property, not the data member. This also makes code more clear.

Similarly, ImageIndex, not FimageIndex, is updated to ensure that ImageIndex's set function is called. Attention should be paid to issues such as these when writing custom components.

The function that does most of the work is the UpdatePicture() function. It checks that there is a TImageList linked to the component, that we want to use the TImageList (UseImageList = true), and that the ImageIndex value is a valid index for the TImageList; in other words, it is zero or greater and less than the number of images in the list. If this is all true, the image is retrieved from the image list into the Graphics::TBitmap object (the Image variable) from which it is assigned to the Picture property. Notice that the Graphics::TBitmap object is declared using std::auto_ptr; this ensures that the object is deleted even if an exception is thrown. A common alternative is to use a try/__finally block. If this were the case, the code inside the if statement in UpdatePicture() would become

```
Graphics::TBitmap* Image = new Graphics::TBitmap();

try
{
   ImageList->GetBitmap(ImageIndex, Image);
   Picture->Assign(Image);
}
__finally
{
   delete Image;
}
```

Finally, the Notification() function derived from TComponent is overridden so that if a linked TImageList is deleted the component can reset the ImageList pointer to zero. Note that the inherited (that is, TImage) implementation is called first to ensure all notifications are handled. Again, ImageList is used instead of FImageList so that the set function for ImageList is automatically called. This is essential to the correct operation of the component; if it is not done, access violations are guaranteed.

We now have a component for which to write our image index property editor. The editor is for the ImageIndex property, an int property. Note that TImageIndex could be used instead, because this is simply a typedef for int (declared in $(BCB)\Include\Vcl\Imglist.hpp). The property editor is therefore derived from TIntegerProperty. Listing 10.21 shows the definition for our ImageIndex property editor. We call it TImageIndexPropertyEditor.

LISTING 10.21 TImageIndexPropertyEditor Definition

```
#include "DsgnIntf.hpp"

class TImageIndexPropertyEditor : public TIntegerProperty
{
   typedef TIntegerProperty inherited;
```

LISTING 10.21   Continued

```
private:
   static const int Border = 2;          // Border around image in Pixels
   static const int MaxImageWidth = 64;  // Max Width of image in Pixels
   static const int MaxImageHeight = 64; // Max Height of image in Pixels

protected:protected:
   virtual Imglist::TCustomImageList* __fastcall GetComponentImageList(void);

public:
   virtual TPropertyAttributes __fastcall GetAttributes(void);
   virtual void __fastcall GetValues(Classes::TGetStrProc Proc);

   DYNAMIC void __fastcall ListMeasureWidth(const AnsiString Value,
                                            Graphics::TCanvas* ACanvas,
                                            int& AWidth);

   DYNAMIC void __fastcall ListMeasureHeight(const AnsiString Value,
                                             Graphics::TCanvas* ACanvas,
                                             int& AHeight);

   DYNAMIC void __fastcall ListDrawValue(const AnsiString Value,
                                         Graphics::TCanvas* ACanvas,
                                         const Windows::TRect& ARect,
                                         bool ASelected);

   // This is a read-only property to be used as the
   // pointer to the component's image list
   __property Imglist::TCustomImageList* ComponentImageList
                                = {read=GetImageList};

protected:
   #pragma option push -w-inl
   inline __fastcall virtual
      TImageIndexPropertyEditor(const _di_IFormDesigner ADesigner,
                                int APropCount)
                                : TIntegerProperty(ADesigner,
                                                   APropCount)
      { }
   #pragma option pop

public:
   #pragma option push -w-inl
   inline __fastcall virtual ~TImageIndexPropertyEditor(void)
   { }
   #pragma option pop

};
```

The code in Listing 10.21 is similar to that previously shown for other property editors. However, a read-only `Imglist::TCustomImageList*` property has been added along with an appropriate get function:

```
virtual Imglist::TCustomImageList* __fastcall GetComponentImageList(void);
```

It is this get function that retrieves the pointer value of the component's `TCustomImageList*` property. This allows the images of the image list to be accessed. As in the previous section, we shall look at each of the methods of the `TImageIndexPropertyEditor` in turn to discuss any implementation issues.

The `GetAttributes()` Method

This is the method used to determine the atributes that the property editor should exhibit in the Object Inspector. We want to have a drop-down list of values (`paValueList`), and we do not want the property to be available for editing when more than one component is selected at once (`paMutliSelect`). The implementation required for this is

```
TPropertyAttributes __fastcall TImageIndexPropertyEditor::GetAttributes(void)
{
  return (inherited::GetAttributes()<< paValueList >> paMultiSelect);
}
```

The `GetComponentImageList()` Method

This is the key to the successful operation of this property editor. It is this method that makes the link between the component's `TCustomImageList*` and the image index property. It does this by retrieving a pointer to the component to which the property being edited belongs. It then uses this pointer to return the component's `TCustomImageList*`. The code required if the `TCustomImageList*` and image index property are in the same component is as follows:

```
Imglist::TCustomImageList* __fastcall
   TImageIndexPropertyEditor::GetComponentImageList(void)
{
   TEnhancedImage* Component = dynamic_cast<TEnhancedImage*>(GetComponent(0));

   if(Component)
   {
      return Component->ImageList;
   }
   else return 0;
}
```

Here we use `TPropertyEditor`'s `GetComponent()` method, declared as

```
Classes::TPersistent* __fastcall GetComponent(int Index);
```

This returns TPersistent* to the Index component being edited by this property editor. Because this editor does not have the paMultiSelect attribute, it can edit only one component at a time. As such, only a pointer to that single component (Index == 0) can be returned. This is then dynamic_casted to the component type that this editor is for. Once we have a correct pointer to our component, it is simple to return the pointer to the TCustomImageList property. If the dynamic_cast fails, 0 is returned.

The code required for an image index property whose component's parent contains the TCustomImageList is more complex. This is discussed in the section "Linking to a Parent's TCustomImageList," later in this chapter.

The GetValues() Method

This method is used to populate the property's drop-down list with appropriate values. In this case, the index of each image in the image list is appropriate. The code required is as follows:

```
void __fastcall TImageIndexPropertyEditor::GetValues(Classes::TGetStrProc Proc)
{
    TCustomImageList* ImageList = ComponentImageList;

    if(ImageList != 0)
    {
        for(int i = 0; i<ImageList->Count; ++i) Proc(IntToStr(i));
    }
}
```

The function simply returns the current image index as an AnsiString. Notice that the ComponentImageList property is not used directly. Its value is assigned to the TCustomImageList* ImageList local variable. This is because GetComponentImageList() is called every time ImageList is read. If ComponentImageList was used directly, there would be many unnecessary calls to GetComponentImageList(). It is better to read ComponentImageList once and copy it. This is done with all the methods that require the ComponentImageList pointer.

The ListMeasureWidth() and ListMeasureHeight() Methods

Of major concern to both these methods is the width and height of the images contained in the TImageList component. Because the size could be very large, upper limits on the displayable width and height should be specified. A sensible figure (and the one used by the VCL) is 64 pixels square. If the image width or height is greater than 64, then we will draw an image of only that width or height. The StretchDraw() method of TCanvas can be used to render a reasonable representation of a large image.

The choice of 64 as the maximum height and width of each image in the drop-down list is based on several criteria. First we must remember that we have a finite size with which to work, namely the resolution of the screen that displays the images. Also, we will most likely have multiple images. If we have five images, then we require 5×64 = 320 pixels in height to display the list. Even at higher resolutions, this will make the list quite large. A resolution of 64 is large enough to see detail on larger images but not too large as to make it impractical. It is also a power of 2, which most people who work with computers like. In the following code, the maximum allowed width and height have been replaced by the `static const` data members `MaxImageWidth` and `MaxImageHeight`, respectively. Also, a `static const` data member `Border` has been used to represent the desired border width around the image and is currently set to 2 pixels. The code for `ListMeasureWidth()` is

```
void __fastcall
   TImageIndexPropertyEditor::ListMeasureWidth(const AnsiString Value,
                                               Graphics::TCanvas* ACanvas,
                                               int& AWidth)
{
   TCustomImageList* ImageList = ComponentImageList;

   if(ImageList != 0)
   {
      if(ImageList->Width < MaxImageWidth)
      {
         AWidth += ImageList->Width + Border*2;
      }
      else AWidth += MaxImageWidth + Border*2;
   }
}
```

Note that an offset of 4 pixels (`Border*2`) is used to allow for some space between the images rendered and the text numbers representing the image index value. The code for `ListMeasureHeight()` is similar:

```
void __fastcall
   TImageIndexPropertyEditor::ListMeasureHeight(const AnsiString Value,
                                                Graphics::TCanvas* ACanvas,
                                                int& AHeight)
{
   TCustomImageList* ImageList = ComponentImageList;

   if(ImageList != 0)
   {
      if( ImageList->Height < MaxImageHeight && ImageList->Height > AHeight)
      {
         AHeight = ImageList->Height + Border*2;
```

```
   }
   else if(ImageList->Height > AHeight) AHeight = MaxImageHeight + Border*2;
}}
```

The code for the height appears slightly more complex because we need to consider the possibility that the image is less than the height required to render the text.

The `ListDrawValue()` Method

This is the most complex of the methods to implement. This is the method used to render the images from the `TImageList` component that the `TCustomImageList*` property points to. The code is shown in Listing 10.22.

LISTING 10.22   Implementing the `ListDrawValue()` Method

```
void __fastcall
   TImageIndexPropertyEditor::ListDrawValue(const AnsiString Value,
                                            Graphics::TCanvas* ACanvas,
                                            const Windows::TRect& ARect,
                                            bool ASelected)
{
   TRect ValueRect = ARect;

   try
   {
      TCustomImageList* ImageList = ComponentImageList;

      // Clear the canvas using the current pen and brush
      ACanvas->FillRect(ARect);

      if(ImageList != 0 && Value != "")
      {
         int ImageWidth = ImageList->Width;
         int ImageHeight = ImageList->Height;

         if(ImageWidth > MaxImageWidth || ImageHeight > MaxImageHeight)
         {
            std::auto_ptr<Graphics::TBitmap> Image(new Graphics::TBitmap());

            // Set the Bitmap's width and height to that of the image
            Image->Width  = ImageWidth;
            Image->Height = ImageHeight;

            // Draw the image from the ImageList onto the Bitmap's Canvas
            ImageList->Draw(Image->Canvas, 0, 0, StrToInt(Value), true);
```

LISTING 10.22   Continued

```
                if(ImageWidth > MaxImageWidth) ImageWidth  = MaxImageWidth;
                if(ImageHeight > MaxImageHeight) ImageHeight = MaxImageHeight;

                // Define the area to draw the image into
                TRect ImageRect = Rect( ARect.Left + Border,
                                        ARect.Top + Border,
                                        ARect.Left + Border + ImageWidth,
                                        ARect.Top + Border + ImageHeight );

                // Draw the image onto the canvas using StretchDraw
                ACanvas->StretchDraw(ImageRect, Image.get());
            }
            else
            {
                // Draw the image directly onto the canvas from the ImageList
                // leaving a 2 pixel border
                ImageList->Draw( ACanvas,
                                 ARect.Left + Border,
                                 ARect.Top + Border,
                                 StrToInt(Value),
                                 true );
            }

            ValueRect = Rect( ARect.Left + ImageWidth + Border*2,
                              ARect.Top,
                              ARect.Right,
                              ARect.Bottom );
        }
    }
    __finally
    {
        // Whether or not we successfully draw the image we must draw the text
        inherited::ListDrawValue(Value, ACanvas, ValueRect, ASelected);
    }
}
```

The essence of the code in Listing 10.22 is the determination of whether the size of the image means that it should be drawn using `ACanvas->StretchDraw()` or simply drawn as it stands. If the width or height of the image is larger than either the `MaxImageWidth` or `MaxImageHeight` static const data member, respectively, the image is first copied to a `Graphics::TBitmap` object before being `Stretchdrawn` onto the list's canvas. Otherwise, the image is drawn directly onto the list's canvas.

Notice the use of the `try/__finally` block to ensure that the inherited `ListDrawValue()` method is called to render the `Value` text, regardless of whether or not an exception occurs in the rest of the function, unless of course one is thrown on the first line outside the `try` block. This is intentional, because an exception thrown here would mean that `ValueRect` would not be valid, and the code in the `__finally` block could not be executed.

Aside from the elements of code just mentioned, the function is similar to that shown previously for the `ListDrawValue()` method, hence the canvas must be cleared so that previous rendering is removed. Be aware that this implementation of `ListDrawValue()` method fixes some dimension errors found in similar `ListDrawValue()` methods used in the VCL and also stretches the image when required. The VCL implementation fails to do this (at the time of writing of this book).

The `PropDrawValue()` Method

This method is overridden to display a small iconic version of the image. Its usefulness for this particular class is dubious, but the technique is shown for completeness. It is straightforward to remove the method if it is not required. The code is almost identical to that for the `ListDrawValue()` method, except that the `MaxImageWidth` and `MaxImageHeight` values are replaced by a `CurrentMaxSide` variable that is calculated from the height of the `ARect` parameter, allowing for a 1-pixel border around the image. Also, the inherited `PropDrawValue()` method is called instead of `ListDrawValue()`. The code is shown in Listing 10.23.

LISTING 10.23   Implementing the `PropDrawValue()` Method

```
void __fastcall
   TImageIndexPropertyEditor::PropDrawValue(Graphics::TCanvas* ACanvas,
                                            const Windows::TRect& ARect,
                                            bool ASelected)
{
   TRect ValueRect = ARect;

   try
   {
      TCustomImageList* ImageList = ComponentImageList;

      // Clear the canvas using the current pen and brush
      ACanvas->FillRect(ARect);

      if(ImageList != 0 && GetVisualValue() != "")
      {
         int ImageWidth = ImageList->Width;
```

10

LISTING 10.23   Continued

```cpp
        int ImageHeight = ImageList->Height;

        // Calculate the MaxSide as we want a square to display our image
        int CurrentMaxSide = ARect.Bottom - ARect.Top - 2;

        if(ImageWidth > CurrentMaxSide || ImageHeight > CurrentMaxSide)
        {
            std::auto_ptr<Graphics::TBitmap> Image(new Graphics::TBitmap());

            // Set the Bitmap's width and height to that of the image
            Image->Width  = ImageWidth;
            Image->Height = ImageHeight;

            // Draw the image from the ImageList onto the Bitmap's Canvas
            ImageList->Draw(Image->Canvas, 0, 0, StrToInt(Value), true);

            if(ImageWidth > CurrentMaxSide) ImageWidth  = CurrentMaxSide;
            if(ImageHeight > CurrentMaxSide) ImageHeight = CurrentMaxSide;

            // Define the area to draw the image into
            TRect ImageRect = Rect( ARect.Left + 2,
                                    ARect.Top + 1,
                                    ARect.Left + 2 + ImageWidth,
                                    ARect.Top + 1 + ImageHeight );

            // Draw the image onto the canvas using StretchDraw
            ACanvas->StretchDraw(ImageRect, Image);
        }
        else
        {
            // Draw the image directly onto the canvas from the ImageList
            // leaving a 1 pixel border
            ImageList->Draw( ACanvas,
                             ARect.Left + 2,
                             ARect.Top + 1,
                             StrToInt(Value),
                             true );
        }

        ValueRect = Rect( ARect.Left + ImageWidth + 2,
                          ARect.Top,
                          ARect.Right,
                          ARect.Bottom );
    }
}
```

LISTING 10.23   Continued

```
  __finally
  {
    // Whether or not we successfully draw the image we must draw the text
    inherited::PropDrawValue(ACanvas,  ValueRect, ASelected);
  }
}
```

Other Considerations when Rendering Images

The `TImageIndexPropertyEditor` property editor as it stands does everything that we want it to do except for one thing: When an image is larger than the allowable size and it is `Stretchdrawn()` onto the list's canvas, the aspect ratio of the image is not maintained. The code for this has not been included for this operation because it significantly complicates the code required for all four of the rendering methods. This would hide the main principles that should be understood when explaining the necessary steps to implement this property editor. However, this operation is probably the more correct way of implementing this property editor.

Linking to a Parent's `TCustomImageList`

An implementation of `TMenuItem`'s `ImageIndex` property will be presented to illustrate the code required to display an image in an image index property from a `TCustomImageList` descendant that is present in the component's parent class. Only the class definition and the `GetParentImageList()` method (the replacement for the `GetComponentImageList()` method) are shown, because the implementation for the other methods is essentially the same as that shown earlier for `TEnhancedImage`'s `ImageIndex` property.

We will call our property editor `TmenuItemImageIndexProperty`. Its class definition is shown in Listing 10.24.

LISTING 10.24   Definition Code for the `TMenuItemImageIndexProperty` Property Editor

```
#include "Dsgnintf.hpp"

class PACKAGE TMenuItemImageIndexProperty : public TIntegerProperty
{
    typedef TIntegerProperty inherited;

private:
    static const int Border = 2;
    static const int MaxImageWidth = 64;
    static const int MaxImageHeight = 64;
```

LISTING 10.24   Continued

```
protected:
    virtual Imglist::TCustomImageList* __fastcall GetParentImageList(void);

public:
    virtual TPropertyAttributes __fastcall GetAttributes(void);
    virtual void __fastcall GetValues(Classes::TGetStrProc Proc);

    DYNAMIC void __fastcall ListMeasureWidth(const AnsiString Value,
                                             Graphics::TCanvas* ACanvas,
                                             int& AWidth);

    DYNAMIC void __fastcall ListMeasureHeight(const AnsiString Value,
                                              Graphics::TCanvas* ACanvas,
                                              int& AHeight);

    DYNAMIC void __fastcall ListDrawValue(const AnsiString Value,
                                          Graphics::TCanvas* ACanvas,
                                          const Windows::TRect& ARect,
                                          bool ASelected);

    DYNAMIC void __fastcall PropDrawValue(Graphics::TCanvas* ACanvas,
                                          const Windows::TRect& ARect,
                                          bool ASelected);

    // This is a read-only property to be used as the pointer to the component's
    // image list
    __property Imglist::TCustomImageList* ParentImageList
                                       = {read=GetParentImageList};

protected:
    #pragma option push -w-inl
    inline __fastcall virtual
        TMenuItemImageIndexProperty(const _di_IFormDesigner ADesigner,
                                    int APropCount)
                                  : TIntegerProperty(ADesigner,
                                                     APropCount)
    { }
    #pragma option pop

public:
    #pragma option push -w-inl
    inline __fastcall virtual ~TMenuItemImageIndexProperty(void)
    { }
    #pragma option pop
};
```

The GetParentImageList() function can be implemented as shown in Listing 10.25.

LISTING 10.25   Implementation Code for the GetParentImageList()Method

```
Imglist::TCustomImageList* __fastcall
   TMenuItemImageIndexProperty::GetParentImageList(void)
{
   TMenuItem* Component = dynamic_cast<TMenuItem*>(GetComponent(0));

   if(Component)
   {
      TMenuItem* ParentMenuItem = Component->Parent;

      while(ParentMenuItem != 0 && ParentMenuItem->SubMenuImages == 0)
      {
         ParentMenuItem = ParentMenuItem->Parent;
      }

      if(ParentMenuItem != 0) return ParentMenuItem->SubMenuImages;
      else
      {
         TMenu* ParentMenu = Component->GetParentMenu();
         if(ParentMenu != 0) return ParentMenu->Images;
      }

   }

   return 0;
}
```

As always, the first and most important stage is to obtain a pointer to the component of the property being edited, in this case a pointer to a TMenuItem component. Once this is done, the parent of the TMenuItem can be obtained. In the case of a TMenuItem, the parent could either be another TMenuItem (in other words, the current TMenuItem is a sub-menu item) or a TMenu (or descendant such as TPopupMenu). If the TMenuItem is a sub-menu, then we must check to see if a SubMenuImages TCustomImageList* is available from the parent TMenuItem. The parent TMenuItem (if there is one) could also have a parent TMenuItem with available SubMenuImages, and so on. All possible parents are iterated through until none remain. If a parent TMenuItem is found with a non-zero SubMenuImages property, then the iteration stops and a pointer to the TCustomImageList is returned; otherwise, the Parent property will eventually point to zero. If this happens, the parent TMenu is obtained through the GetParentMenu() function. The TCustomImageList* of the TMenu's Images property is then returned. Most other ImageIndex property editors in components that refer to a parent's TCustomImageList are simpler to implement than this because normally there will be only one possible parent.

There is an easier way to implement this function (which the astute among you will have already thought of), and that is to use TMenuItem's GetImageList() function to return a suitable TCustomImageList pointer. The implementation of the GetParentImageList() function then becomes

```
Imglist::TCustomImageList* __fastcall
    TMenuItemImageIndexProperty::GetParentImageList(void)
{
    TMenuItem* Component = dynamic_cast<TMenuItem*>(GetComponent(0));

    if(Component)
    {
        return Component->GetImageList();
    }

    return 0;
}
```

The more complex method was shown to highlight the principles of obtaining a pointer to the component's parent.

We shall now advance our discussion further and consider an ImageIndex property editor for the THeaderSection class derived from TCollectionItem (and ultimately TPersistent) and used in the THeaderControl component. Our property editor will be called THeaderSectionIndexProperty. This will illustrate another useful technique when writing property editors and lead us to a more general solution for implementing and registering ImageIndex property editors for classes whose parent contains the TCustomImageList pointer.

Only the GetParentImageList() function will be shown (see Listing 10.26). As with the TMenuItemImageIndexProperty property editor, the primary concern is to obtain a pointer to the parent of the component that contains the ImageIndex property. If we examine the THeaderSection class, we see that it is a TCollectionItem-derived class and therefore has a corresponding TCollection-derived container class, in this case a THeaderSections class. A pointer to THeaderSection's container (a THeaderSections object) can be obtained from its Collection property. This returns a TCollection*, which must then be dynamic_casted to a THeaderSections pointer. Once we have a pointer to a collection items container, we need to determine the parent of the collection, which will contain the image list we require. The only method available for us to do this is the protected GetOwner() function. This returns a TPersistent*. Unfortunately, the function is protected so we have no way of getting at it directly. However, there is a method of calling this function.

To call a member of a class that is protected or private, you must do two things. First you must create a descendant of the class and promote the visibility of the required members (for example, functions or properties). In other words, you must redeclare as public those class members that you require access to. Such a class is called an *access* class. Once this is done, it is possible to access these class members by static_casting the class pointer to that of the access class. This technique is used in Listing 10.26.

LISTING 10.26 Code Required for the
`THeaderSectionIndexProperty::GetParentImageList()` Function

```
//--------------------------------------------------------------------------//
//                                                                          //
//                  THeaderSectionsAccessImageIndexProperty                 //
//                                                                          //
//--------------------------------------------------------------------------//

class THeaderSectionsAccess : public THeaderSections
{
public:
   DYNAMIC Classes::TPersistent* __fastcall GetOwner(void);
};

//--------------------------------------------------------------------------//
//                                                                          //
//                      THeaderSectionImageIndexProperty                    //
//                                                                          //
//--------------------------------------------------------------------------//

//--------------------------------------------------------------------------//

Imglist::TCustomImageList* __fastcall
   THeaderSectionImageIndexProperty::GetParentImageList(void)
{
   THeaderSection* Component = dynamic_cast<THeaderSection*>(GetComponent(0));

   if(Component)
   {
      THeaderSections* HeaderSections
                  = dynamic_cast<THeaderSections*>(Component->Collection);

      if(HeaderSections)
      {
         TPersistent* Owner
            = static_cast<THeaderSectionsAccess*>(HeaderSections)->GetOwner();

         THeaderControl* HeaderControl = dynamic_cast<THeaderControl*>(Owner);
```

LISTING 10.26   Continued

```
        if(HeaderControl)
        {
            return HeaderControl->Images;
        }
    }
}
return 0;
}
//-------------------------------------------------------------------------//
```

Once a pointer to the owner of the collection has been obtained, it can be dynamic_casted to the required type, in this case a pointer to a THeaderControl. We then return the pointer to the THeaderControl's TCustomImageList.

A Generalized Solution for ImageIndex Properties

The VCL contains several TPersistent- and TComponent-derived classes with ImageIndex properties. The previous section covered just two. Others are shown in Table 10.10.

TABLE 10.10   VCL Classes with ImageIndex Properties

Class	Derivation Hierarchy
TCoolBand	→ TCollectionItem → **TPersistent**
TCustomAction	→ **TComponent** → TPersistent
THeaderSection	→ TCollectionItem → **TPersistent**
TListColumn	→ TCollectionItem → **TPersistent**
TMenuItem	→ **TComponent** → TPersistent
TTabSheet	→ TWinControl → TControl → **TComponent** → TPersistent
TToolButton	→ TGraphicControl → TControl → **TComponent** → TPersistent

Note that Table 10.10 draws a distinction between those classes that descend from TComponent and those that descend only from TPersistent. Also, three of the classes, TListColumn, TMenuItem and TtoolButton, have special considerations when determining the parent TCustomImageList*. This will become clear later, when the implementations for generalized ImageIndex property editors are presented.

It would be possible and indeed perfectly proper to declare a property editor for the ImageIndex property of each of these classes. The code required for this is present on the accompanying CD-ROM in the PropertyEditors unit in the EnhancedEditors package.

However, it is also possible to write two more general property editors, one for TPersistent-derived classes and one for TComponent-derived classes. Regardless of what is done, it is appropriate to define a base class for any such property editors, allowing new property editors to be derived from the base class. Only the GetImageList() method will need to be overridden by derived classes. A suitable class definition is shown in Listing 10.27.

LISTING 10.27 Definition of the TImageIndexProperty Base Class

```
class PACKAGE TImageIndexProperty : public TIntegerProperty
{
    typedef TIntegerProperty inherited;

private:
    static const int Border = 2;
    static const int MaxImageWidth = 64;
    static const int MaxImageHeight = 64;

protected:
    virtual Imglist::TCustomImageList* __fastcall GetImageList(void) = 0;

public:
    virtual TPropertyAttributes __fastcall GetAttributes(void);
    virtual void __fastcall GetValues(Classes::TGetStrProc Proc);

    DYNAMIC void __fastcall ListMeasureWidth(const AnsiString Value,
                                             Graphics::TCanvas* ACanvas,
                                             int& AWidth);

    DYNAMIC void __fastcall ListMeasureHeight(const AnsiString Value,
                                              Graphics::TCanvas* ACanvas,
                                              int& AHeight);

    DYNAMIC void __fastcall ListDrawValue(const AnsiString Value,
                                          Graphics::TCanvas* ACanvas,
                                          const Windows::TRect& ARect,
                                          bool ASelected);

    DYNAMIC void __fastcall PropDrawValue(Graphics::TCanvas* ACanvas,
                                          const Windows::TRect& ARect,
                                          bool ASelected);

    // This is a read-only property to be used as the pointer to the component's
    // image list
    __property Imglist::TCustomImageList* RemoteImageList = {read=GetImageList};
```

LISTING **10.27**   Continued

```
protected:
    #pragma option push -w-inl
    inline __fastcall virtual
        TImageIndexProperty(const _di_IFormDesigner ADesigner,
                            int APropCount)
                        : TIntegerProperty(ADesigner,
                                           APropCount)
    { }
    #pragma option pop

public:
    #pragma option push -w-inl
    inline __fastcall virtual ~TImageIndexProperty(void)
    { }
    #pragma option pop
};
```

Note that TImageIndexProperty is an abstract base class because it contains a pure virtual function. This is the GetImageList() function that derived classes must implement. The implementation of TImageIndexProperty is similar to that shown previously.

By deriving our ImageIndex property editors from this class, we only need to write the GetImageList()method. Such a method for a TPersistentDerivedImageIndexProperty property editor is shown in Listing 10.28. Note that the variable FParentImageListName is a private AnsiString member initialized in the constructor as "Images".

LISTING **10.28**   Implementation of TPersistentDerivedImageIndexProperty

```
//----------------------------------------------------------------------------//
//                                                                            //
//                          TComponentAccess                                  //
//                                                                            //
//----------------------------------------------------------------------------//
class TComponentAccess : public TComponent
{
public:
    DYNAMIC Classes::TPersistent* __fastcall GetOwner(void);
};


//----------------------------------------------------------------------------//
//                                                                            //
//                  TPersistentDerivedImageIndexProperty                      //
//                                                                            //
//----------------------------------------------------------------------------//
```

LISTING 10.28   Continued

```
__fastcall
  TPersistentDerivedImageIndexProperty::TPersistentDerivedImageIndexProperty
                                      (const _di_IFormDesigner ADesigner,
                                       int APropCount)
                                     : TImageIndexProperty(ADesigner,
                                                           APropCount)
{
  FParentImageListName = "Images";
}
//--------------------------------------------------------------------------//


Imglist::TCustomImageList* __fastcall
  TPersistentDerivedImageIndexProperty::GetImageList(void)
{
  TPersistent* Parent
               = static_cast<TComponentAccess*>(GetComponent(0))->GetOwner();

  while( Parent != 0 && !dynamic_cast<TComponent*>(Parent) )
  {
    Parent = static_cast<TComponentAccess*>(Parent)->GetOwner();
  }

  if(Parent == 0) return 0;

  PPropInfo PropInfo
           = Typinfo::GetPropInfo(static_cast<PTypeInfo>(Parent->ClassInfo()),
                                  FParentImageListName);

  if(PropInfo == 0) return 0;

  return
  (
    reinterpret_cast<TCustomImageList*>(Typinfo::GetOrdProp(Parent, PropInfo))
  );
}
//--------------------------------------------------------------------------//
```

The code in Listing 10.28 is more straightforward than it first appears. As before, we use an access class to promote the visibility of, in this case, TComponent's protected GetOwner() method. Initially, the immediate parent of the component whose property is being edited is obtained by treating the component as a TComponent and calling the GetOwner() method. If there is a parent class and it is not a TComponent, then we check to see if the parent has a TComponent-derived parent. If it does have a TComponent-derived parent, we check to see if that parent has a TComponent-derived parent, and so on. When the while loop finishes, either

10

PROPERTY AND
COMPONENT
EDITORS

we have found a TComponent-derived parent or Parent is NULL. Providing there is a TComponent-derived parent, we can try to obtain a PPropInfo for a property that has the same name as that contained in the FParentImageListName AnsiString data member and belongs to Parent. This line is used to determine a PTypeInfo for Parent:

```
static_cast<PTypeInfo>(Parent->ClassInfo())
```

If a matching property exists, the GetOrdProp() function is used to obtain the TCustomImageList pointer. Because GetOrdProp() returns an int value, this must be cast to the correct pointer using reinterpret_cast.

This GetImageList()implementation can therefore be used for any TPersistent-derived classes with an ImageIndex property, so long as the parent's image list property is called "Images" (for example, TCoolBand and THeaderSection). If it is not, then a class must be derived from this one, and the AnsiString FParentImageListName must be changed. This is done with the TListColumn class, whose parent image list property is called "SmallImages".

Similarly, a property editor class for TComponent-derived classes, TComponentDerivedImageIndexProperty, can be written. The implementation of the GetImageList() method is shown in Listing 10.29.

LISTING 10.29   Implementation of TComponentDerivedImageIndexProperty::
GetImageList()

```
Imglist::TCustomImageList* __fastcall
   TComponentDerivedImageIndexProperty::GetImageList(void)
{
   TComponent* Parent
       = static_cast<TComponentAccess*>(GetComponent(0))->GetParentComponent();

   if(Parent == 0) return 0;

   PPropInfo PropInfo
           = Typinfo::GetPropInfo(static_cast<PTypeInfo>(Parent->ClassInfo()),
                               FParentImageListName);

   if(PropInfo == 0) return 0;

   return
   (
     reinterpret_cast<TCustomImageList*>(Typinfo::GetOrdProp(Parent, PropInfo))
   );
}
```

The code for the GetImageList() method of the TComponentDerivedImageIndexProperty property editor is almost identical to that of TPersistentDerivedImageIndexProperty. The only difference is that Parent is initially obtained as a TComponent-derived class, simplifying the code. This implementation can be used for TComponent-derived classes with an ImageIndex property, provided the parent's TCustomImageList property is called "Images" (for example, TTabSheet). This could also be used for TMenuItem and TToolButton, but in the case of TMenuItem we want to consider the SubMenuImages property also. The previous implementation for TMenuItem is better. For TToolButton, a better implementation is to use the ImageIndex property for the parent's Images property only when the button is enabled; otherwise, use the parent's DisabledImages property. The implementation for the GetImageList() method of a TToolButtonImageIndexProperty property editor is shown in Listing 10.30.

LISTING 10.30   Implementation of TToolButtonImageIndexProperty::GetImageList()

```
Imglist::TCustomImageList* __fastcall
   TToolButtonImageIndexProperty::GetImageList(void)
{
   TToolButton* Component = dynamic_cast<TToolButton*>(GetComponent(0));

   if(Component)
   {
      TToolBar* ParentToolBar = dynamic_cast<TToolBar*>(Component->Parent);

      if(ParentToolBar)
      {
         if(Component->Enabled) return ParentToolBar->Images;
         else return ParentToolBar->DisabledImages;
      }
   }
   return 0;
}
```

The code shown in Listing 10.29 is self-explanatory; if the TToolButton being edited is disabled (Enabled = false) then the DisabledImages image list in the parent TToolBar is used; otherwise, the normal Images image list is used.

The class hierarchy for this general solution to ImageIndex properties is shown in Figure 10.7.

From Table 10.10 we know that the TPersistentDerivedImageIndexProperty property editor will be used for the TCoolBand and THeaderSection components. The TComponentDerivedImageIndexProperty property editor will be used for the TCustomAction and the TTabSheet components.

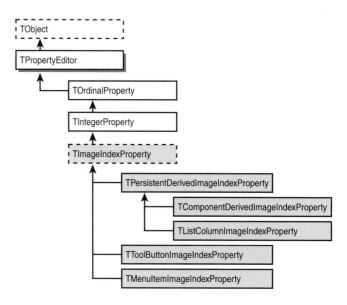

FIGURE 10.7

The TImageIndexProperty *inheritance hierarchy.*

Creating Custom Component Editors

The previous section discussed property editors for components as a method of allowing a more intuitive and robust interface at designtime. Component Editors take this further by allowing custom editors for the whole component to be created. Custom component editors also allow the context menu for each component (shown when the component is right-clicked) to be customized, along with specifying the behavior when a component is double-clicked on a form. This section, like the previous one, presents the background and principles required to create custom component editors. Component editors add the possibility of customizing the default behavior associated with editing a component and also allow additional behavior to be specified. There are two classes available for creating component editors: TComponentEditor and TDefaultEditor. The relationship between the two is shown in Figure 10.8.

Figure 10.8 shows additional information, namely the virtual functions that should be over-ridden in order to customize the component editor's behavior. This can be referred to when the virtual functions themselves are discussed later in this section, in Table 10.12 and in subsequent sections with the methods' names.

As was stated initially, creating a custom component editor allows the default behavior that occurs in response to the component being right-clicked or double-clicked in the IDE to be specified. Table 10.11 lists both mouse events and indicates which of the virtual functions are invoked. The default behavior of each of the classes is also stated.

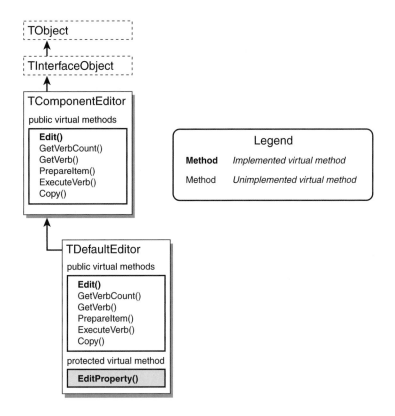

FIGURE 10.8
The TComponentEditor *inheritance hierarchy.*

TABLE 10.11 TComponentEditor and TDefaultEditor Mouse Responses

When the component is...	Default Action	virtual Functions Invoked
Right-Clicked	The component's context menu is displayed.	GetVerbCount() is invoked first. This is used to return the number of items to be added to the top of the default context menu.
		GetVerb() is called next. This allows an AnsiString representing each of the menu items to be returned.

TABLE 10.11 Continued

When the component is...	Default Action	virtual *Functions Invoked*
		`PrepareItem()` is called before the menu item is shown, allowing it to be customized.
		`ExecuteVerb()` is called only if one of the newly added menu items is clicked. Code to execute the desired behavior goes here.
Double-Clicked	The default action depends on the class from which the editor is derived. `TComponentEditor:` If items have been added to the context menu, the first item is executed. `TDefaultEditor:` An empty event handler is created for `OnChange`, `OnCreate`, or `OnClick`, whichever appears first in the component's list of event properties. If none of the above events exist for the component, a handler is created for the first event that appears. If the component has no events, then nothing happens.	`Edit()` is invoked. Code to perform the desired action is placed here.

In Figure 10.8 we can see that `TComponentEditor` and `TDefaultEditor` are essentially the same in that they offer similar functionality. Where they differ (as seen in Table 10.11) is in the implementation of the `Edit()` method. Choosing which of the two classes to derive your custom component editor from should be based on the following criteria.

If you want the component editor to generate an empty event handler for one of three default events or for a particular event, when the component is double-clicked, then you should derive it from `TDefaultEditor`; otherwise, derive it from `TComponentEditor`. If you do not create a custom component editor for a component, C++Builder uses `TDefaultEditor`.

Once the decision has been made as to which component editor class to derive from, the appropriate methods should be overridden. Table 10.12 lists the methods from both classes and details the purpose of each.

TABLE 10.12 `TComponentEditor` and `TDefaultEditor` virtual Functions

virtual *Function*	*Purpose*
`int GetVerbCount(void)`	Returns an `int` representing the number of menu items (verbs, as in *doing* words) that are going to be added.
`AnsiString GetVerb(int Index)`	Returns an `AnsiString` representing the menu item's name as it will appear in the context menu. The following conventions should be remembered:
	Use & to designate a hotkey.
	Append ... to an item that executes a dialog.
	Use a - to make the menu item a separator bar.
`void PrepareItem(int Index, const Menus::TMenuItem* AItem)`	`PrepareItem()` is called for each verb in the context menu, passing the `TMenuItem` that will be used to represent the verb in the context menu. This allows the menu item to be customized. It can also be used to hide an item by setting its `Visible` property to `false`.
`void ExecuteVerb(int Index)`	`ExecuteVerb()` is invoked when one of the custom menu items is selected. `Index` indicates which one.
`void Edit(void)`	`Edit()` is invoked when the component is double-clicked. What happens is user defined. The default behavior is listed in Table 10.11.
`void EditProperty(TPropertyEditor* PropertyEditor, bool& Continue, bool& FreeEditor)` (TDefaultEditor only)	Used to determine which event an empty handler is generated for when the component is double-clicked.
`void Copy(void)`	`Copy()` should be invoked when the component is copied to the Clipboard. This needs to be overridden only if a special format is needed to be copied to the Clipboard, such as an image from a graphical component.

Suitable class definitions for `TComponentEditor`- and `TDefaultComponent`-derived component editors are shown in Listing 10.31 and Listing 10.32, respectively.

LISTING 10.31   Definition Code for a Custom `TComponentEditor`-Derived Component Editor

```
#include "dsgnintf.hpp"

class TCustomComponentEditor : public TComponentEditor
{
    typedef TComponentEditor inherited;

public:
    // Double-Click
    virtual void __fastcall Edit(void);

    // Right-Click
    // CONTEXT MENU - Step 1
    virtual int __fastcall GetVerbCount(void);
    //              - Step 2
    virtual AnsiString __fastcall GetVerb(int Index);
    //              - Step 3 (OPTIONAL)
    virtual void __fastcall PrepareItem(int Index,
                                    const Menus::TMenuItem* AItem);
    //              - Step 4
    virtual void __fastcall ExecuteVerb(int Index);

    // Copy to Clipboard
    virtual void __fastcall Copy(void);

public:
    #pragma option push -w-inl
    inline __fastcall virtual
       TCustomComponentEditor(Classes::TComponent* AComponent,
                        _di_IFormDesigner ADesigner)
                           : TComponentEditor(AComponent, ADesigner)
    { }
    #pragma option pop
public:
    #pragma option push -w-inl
    inline __fastcall virtual ~TCustomComponentEditor(void) { }
    #pragma option pop
};
```

LISTING 10.32 Definition Code for a Custom `TDefaultEditor`-Derived Component Editor

```cpp
#include "dsgnintf.hpp"

class TCustomDefaultEditor : public TDefaultEditor
{
   typedef TDefaultEditor inherited;

protected:
   // Double-Click
   // CHOOSE EVENT
   virtual void __fastcall EditProperty(TPropertyEditor* PropertyEditor,
                                        bool& Continue,
                                        bool& FreeEditor);
public:
   // Right-Click
   // CONTEXT MENU - Step 1
   virtual int __fastcall GetVerbCount(void);
   //             - Step 2
   virtual AnsiString __fastcall GetVerb(int Index);
   //             - Step 3 (OPTIONAL)
   virtual void __fastcall PrepareItem(int Index,
                                       const Menus::TMenuItem* AItem);
   //             - Step 4
   virtual void __fastcall ExecuteVerb(int Index);

   // Copy to Clipboard
   virtual void __fastcall Copy(void);

public:
   #pragma option push -w-inl
   inline __fastcall virtual
      TCustomDefaultEditor(Classes::TComponent* AComponent,
                           _di_IFormDesigner ADesigner)
                        : TDefaultEditor(AComponent,  ADesigner)
   { }
   #pragma option pop
public:
   #pragma option push -w-inl
   inline __fastcall virtual ~TCustomDefaultEditor(void)  { }
   #pragma option pop
};
```

In Listing 10.31 and Listing 10.32, it can be seen that there is little difference between the definitions of the two kinds of component editor. In fact, the techniques for implementing context menu items are identical. The difference between the classes is that you override the `Edit()` method for a `TComponentEditor`-derived class's double-click behavior, whereas you override the `EditProperty()` method for a `TDefaultEditor` class's double-click behavior.

The following sections take each of the `virtual` methods in turn and discuss implementation issues. Information presented for the `Edit()` method is applicable only to `TComponentEditor`-derived classes, and information presented for the `EditProperty()` method is applicable only to `TDefaultEditor`-derived classes. Note that the example namespace modifiers used in the function implementation headers reflect this. `TCustomComponentEditor` is a hypothetical `TComponentEditor`-derived class, `TCustomDefaultEditor` is a hypothetical `TDefaultEditor`-derived class, and `TMyCustomEditor` is a class that could be derived from either.

The `Edit()` Method

The main purpose of overriding the `Edit()` method is to display a form to the user to allow easier editing of the component's values. A good example of this is the component editor for the `TChart` component on the Additional page of the Component Palette. To this end, the code required is similar to that presented for `TPropertyEditor`'s `Edit()` method in the "Creating Custom Property Editors" section, earlier in this chapter. As before, there are two approaches to implementing such a form. Either the form can update the component as the form itself is modified, or the component can be updated after the form is closed.

There is one extra and very important consideration that must be remembered: Each time the component is updated, the `Modified()` method of `TComponentEditor`'s `Designer` property *must* be called. This is so that the IDE knows that the component has been modified. Hence, the following is required after code that modifies the component:

```
if(Designer) Designer->Modified();
```

An `if` statement is used in the previous code to ensure that a non-zero value is returned from `Designer` before we try to call `Modified()`. If zero is returned, there is little we can do, because it means the IDE is not accessible. We know that, for the form to be able to change the component's properties, we must somehow link the form to the component, in a similar fashion as for property editors previously. This is reasonably straightforward and requires two things. The first is that a public property should be declared in the form's definition that is a pointer to the type of component the component editor is for. Secondly, this must be pointed to the actual instance of the component that is to be edited. The pointer to the current instance of the component is obtained by using `TComponentEditor`'s `Component` property, as follows:

```
TMyComponent* MyComponent = dynamic_cast<TMyComponent*>(Component);
```

The pointer obtained can be equated to the form's component pointer property. However, we must also make a reference to `Designer` available from within the form so that the IDE can be notified of changes that are made to the component. This can be passed as a parameter in the form's constructor. The component can then be modified directly through the property in the form. Suitable code for this approach is shown in Listing 10.33. Don't forget to call `Designer->Modified()` after the component is modified by the form.

LISTING 10.33   Code for a Custom Component Editor Form to Be Called from `Edit()`
That Allows Continual Updating

```
// First show important code for TComponentEditorForm

// IN THE HEADER FILE
//-------------------------------------------------------------------//
#ifndef MyComponentEditorFormH
#define MyComponentEditorFormH
//-------------------------------------------------------------------//
#include <Classes.hpp>
#include <Controls.hpp>
#include <StdCtrls.hpp>
#include <Forms.hpp>
#include "HeaderDeclaringTComponentClass"
//-------------------------------------------------------------------//
class TMyComponentEditorForm : public TForm
{
__published:    // IDE-managed Components
private:
  TComponentClass* FComponentClass;
  _di_IformDesigner& Designer;
  // Other declarations here for example restore values if 'Cancel'
  // is pressed

protected:
  void __fastcall SetComponentClass(TComponentClass* Pointer);
public:
    __fastcall TMyComponentEditorForm(TComponent* Owner,
                              _di_IformDesigner& EditorDesigner);

    __property TComponentClass* ComponentClass = {read=FComponentClass,
                                write=SetComponentClass};
  // Other declarations here
};
//-------------------------------------------------------------------//
#endif
```

LISTING 10.33   Continued

```cpp
// THE IMPLEMENTATION FILE
//-------------------------------------------------------------------------//
#include <vcl.h>
#pragma hdrstop

#include "MyComponentEditorForm.h"
//-------------------------------------------------------------------------//
#pragma package(smart_init)
#pragma resource "*.dfm"
//-------------------------------------------------------------------------//
__fastcall
TMyComponentEditorForm::
   TMyComponentEditorForm(TComponent* Owner,
                          _di_IformDesigner& EditorDesigner)
                        : TForm(Owner), Designer(EditorDesigner)
{
}
//-------------------------------------------------------------------------//
void __fastcall TMyPropertyForm::SetComponentClass(TComponentClass* Pointer)
{
   FComponentClass = Pointer;
   if(FComponentClass != 0)
   {
      // Store current component values and display them
   }
}
//-------------------------------------------------------------------------//

// NOW SHOW THE Edit() METHOD

#include "MyComponentEditorForm.h" // Remember this

void __fastcall TCustomComponentEditor::Edit(void)
{
   // Create the form
   std::auto_ptr<TMyComponentEditorForm*>
      MyComponentEditorForm(new TMyComponentEditorForm(0));

   // Link the component property
   MyComponentEditorForm->ComponentClass
                        = dynamic_cast<TComponentClass*>(Component);

   // Show the form. The form does all the work.
   MyPropertyForm->ShowModal();
}
```

As in the case of custom property editor forms, the component's current property values can be stored when the form's Component property is linked to the component. This allows the operation to be cancelled and the previous values restored. One thing to pay attention to is the possibility of a NULL pointer being returned from dynamic_cast; this should not occur, but if it does the form will not be able to modify any of the component's properties. An exception could be thrown to indicate this to the user.

The second approach to implementing the Edit() method is equally simple. A form is displayed as a dialog and, when it returns, the values entered are assigned to the component. A pointer to the current instance of the component being edited is obtained from TComponentEditor's Component property:

```
TMyComponent* MyComponent = dynamic_cast<TMyComponent*>(Component);
```

The code required in the Edit() method in this approach to its implementation is greater because the component property values must be assigned to the form after it is created but before it is shown. On closing, the form's values must be assigned to the requisite component properties. The code required for the Edit() method is shown in Listing 10.34.

LISTING 10.34   Code for a Custom Form to Be Called from the Edit() Method with No Updating Until Closing

```
#include "MyComponentEditorDialog.h" // Include the header for the Dialog!
                                      // Dialog is TMyComponentDialog

void __fastcall TCustomComponentEditor::Edit(void)
{
    TMyComponent* MyComponent = dynamic_cast<TMyComponent*>(Component);
    if(MyComponent != 0)
    {
        // Create the form
        std::auto_ptr<TMyComponentDialog*>
            MyComponentDialog(new TMyComponentDialog(0));

        // Set the current property values in the dialog
        // MyComponentDialog->value1 = MyComponent->value1;
        // MyComponentDialog->value2 = MyComponent->value2;
        // and so on...

        // Show the form and see the result.
        if(MyPropertyDialog->ShowModal() == IDOK)
        {
            // Then set the new property value(s)
            // MyComponent->value1 = MyComponentDialog->value1;
```

LISTING 10.34   Continued

```
        // MyComponent->value2 = MyComponentDialog->value2;
        // and so on...
        if(Designer) Designer->Modified(); // DON'T FORGET!
    }
  }
  else
  {
    throw EInvalidPointer
        ("Cannot Edit: A component pointer is not available!");
  }
}
```

In the second approach to implementing the `Edit()` method shown in Listing 10.34, implementation code for the dialog has not been shown. This is because there are no special considerations specific to this approach that need to be highlighted. Also be aware that a dialog
wrapper class could be used instead of calling the dialog directly, in which case the dialog's
`Execute()` method would be called to display the dialog.

The `EditProperty()` Method

The purpose of overriding the `EditProperty()` method is to specify a particular event or one
of a number of possible events that should have an empty event handler generated for it by the
IDE when the component is double-clicked. For example, consider a component for serial
communications. Typically, the most commonly used event would be one that signals when
data has been received and is available, perhaps named `OnDataReceived`. For this to be the
event for which a handler is generated, `EditProperty()` needs to be overridden as follows:

```
void __fastcall
    TCustomDefaultEditor::EditProperty(TPropertyEditor* PropertyEditor,
                                       bool& Continue,
                                       bool& FreeEditor)
{
    if( PropertyEditor->ClassNameIs("TMethodProperty") &&
        (CompareText(PropertyEditor->GetName(), "OnDataReceived") == 0) )
    {
        inherited::EditProperty(PropertyEditor, Continue, FreeEditor);
    }
}
```

The `if` statement checks two things. First it checks that the property editor is a
`TMethodProperty` class; in other words, it checks that the property editor is for an event. It
then checks to see if the property editor is called `OnDataReceived`. The `CompareText()` function is used for this. `CompareText()` returns `0` when the two `AnsiStrings` passed to it are

equal. Note that `CompareText()` is not case sensitive. If the property editor matches these criteria, then the parent `EditProperty()` method is called, in this case `TDefaultEditor`'s `EditProperty()`, which generates the empty event handler for this event. This is called by using the inherited `typedef` as a namespace modifier, so the previous code could be written as follows:

```
TDefaultEditor::EditProperty(PropertyEditor, Continue, FreeEditor);
```

The reason for using the `typedef` is that if the name of `TDefaultEditor` ever changed, the implementation code would not be affected. Only the class definition in the header file would need to be changed.

If a choice of events was to be specified, perhaps because the same component editor was to be registered for a variety of components, then the `if` statement would be replaced by `if-else-if` statements. For example:

```
if( PropertyEditor->ClassNameIs("TMethodProperty") &&
    (CompareText(PropertyEditor->GetName(), "OnEvent1") == 0) )
{
    inherited::EditProperty(PropertyEditor, Continue, FreeEditor);
}
else if( PropertyEditor->ClassNameIs("TMethodProperty") &&
        (CompareText(PropertyEditor->GetName(), "OnEvent2") == 0) )
{
    inherited::EditProperty(PropertyEditor, Continue, FreeEditor);
}
else if( PropertyEditor->ClassNameIs("TMethodProperty") &&
        (CompareText(PropertyEditor->GetName(), "OnEvent3") == 0) )
{
    inherited::EditProperty(PropertyEditor, Continue, FreeEditor);
}
```

It also could be replaced by a single `if` that ORs the possible event occurrences:

```
if( (PropertyEditor->ClassNameIs("TMethodProperty") &&
    (CompareText(PropertyEditor->GetName(), "OnEvent1") == 0)
    ||
    (PropertyEditor->ClassNameIs("TMethodProperty") &&
    (CompareText(PropertyEditor->GetName(), "OnEvent1") == 0)
    ||
    (PropertyEditor->ClassNameIs("TMethodProperty") &&
    (CompareText(PropertyEditor->GetName(), "OnEvent1") == 0) )
{
    inherited::EditProperty(PropertyEditor, Continue,  FreeEditor);
}
```

In either case, the first matching occurrence will be used.

The `GetVerbCount()` Method

Few methods are as easy to override as this. Simply return an integer that represents the number of additional menu items that you want to appear in the component's context menu. Don't forget that a separator bar constitutes a menu item. Sample code for three custom menu items would be as follows:

```
int __fastcall TMyCustomEditor::GetVerbCount(void)
{
    return 4;
}
```

The `GetVerb()` Method

Almost as straightforward as the `GetVerbCount()` method, this method requires that the `AnsiString` text for each menu item be returned. Remember that returning a - makes the menu item a separator bar. Sample code is

```
AnsiString __fastcall TMyCustomEditor::GetVerb(int Index)
{
    switch(Index)
    {
        case 0 : return "&Edit Component...";
        case 1 : return "© 2000 Me";
        case 2 : return "-";
        case 3 : return "Do Something Else";
        default : return "";
    }
}
```

If you do not specify an accelerator key (using the & symbol), then one is determined automatically by the IDE. In fact, all predefined context menu items' accelerator keys are determined by the IDE at runtime. This allows clashes with user-defined accelerator keys to be avoided. Accelerator key definitions for user-defined menu items take precedence over a predefined context menu item's accelerator key definitions. If a clash occurs, the predefined menu item's accelerator key is reassigned to a different letter. Finally, remember that a separator bar is automatically placed between the custom menu items and the predefined menu items, so it is not necessary to add one as the last item. However, doing so will not make any difference, because the context menu's `AutoLineReduction` property is set to `maAutomatic` (refer to the C++Builder online help for further details).

The `PrepareItem()` Method

This method, new to C++Builder 5, need not be implemented, and in fact it generally isn't. What it offers is the option to customize each menu item further. Most notably, it allows custom rendering of a menu item, the ability to disable the menu item (`Enable = false`), the ability to hide the menu item (`Visible = false`), and the ability to add sub-menu items. This is possible because `PrepareItem()` has two parameters. The first, `Index`, serves the same purpose as it does in the preceding context menu functions, namely to indicate which menu item the function call refers to. However, the second parameter is a pointer to the menu item (`TMenuItem`) that will be used to represent the menu item in the context menu. This gives you access to all the facilities that `TMenuItem` offers. There is a catch, however: The pointer is to `const TMenuItem`, so it is not possible to modify the menu item through the pointer passed. Instead, a non-`const` pointer of type `TMenuItem` should be pointed to the same menu item and the menu item modified through that pointer. For example, maintaining continuity with our previous examples, to custom render the second menu item (the copyright item), we would write the code in Listing 10.35.

LISTING 10.35 Basic Code for the `PrepareItem()` Method

```
void __fastcall TMyCustomEditor::PrepareItem(int Index, const Menus::TMenuItem*
AItem)
{
switch(Index)
    {
        case 0 : break;

        case 1 :
        {
            TMenuItem* MenuItem = const_cast<TMenuItem*>(AItem);

            // Now that we have a pointer we can do what we like
            // For example:
            // 1. To Disable the menu item write -
            // MenuItem->Enabled = false;
            // 2. To Hide the menu item write -
            // MenuItem->Visible = false;
            // 3. To add a bitmap to the menu item write -
            // MenuItem->Bitmap->LoadFromResourceName
            //                   (reinterpret_cast<int>(HInstance),
            //                    "BITMAPNAME");
            // or any other stuff, for example assign an event handler
            // or even add menu sub-items...
        }
                break;

        case 2 : break;
        case 3 : break;
        default : break;
    }
}
```

Pay particular attention to this line:

```
TMenuItem* MenuItem = const_cast<TMenuItem*>(AItem);
```

This is where we obtain the pointer with which we can edit the TMenuItem. Also note the third example of adding a bitmap to the menu item:

```
MenuItem->Bitmap->LoadFromResourceName(reinterpret_cast<int>(HInstance),
                                       "BITMAPNAME");
```

This assumes that a resource file has been imported into the package that contains an image called BITMAPNAME. Otherwise, MenuItem will be unable to load the image. Not being able to load the image is quite disastrous: The IDE will crash, so make sure your names are right. For more information on this, refer to the section "Using Predefined Images in Custom Property and Component Editors," later in this chapter, where this topic is covered in more detail. Note also that reinterpret_cast is used to cast HInstance of type void* to type int, as expected by the LoadFromResourceName member function.

Adding Custom Event Handlers to Context Menu Items

Adding custom event handlers to custom menu items involves a two-step process.

First, the required event handler must be written as a member function of the component editor class. Its signature must match exactly that of the event it is to handle. Second, when the PrepareItem() function is called and the non-const MenuItem pointer is obtained, the handler member function can be equated to the appropriate MenuItem event. For example, to create a custom event handler for the menu item's OnAdvancedDrawItem event, declare a function with a name such as AdvancedDrawMenuItem1() (because it refers to MenuItem 1) with the same parameters as OnAdvancedDrawItem in the component editor's class definition. You will probably want to make it protected and virtual, just in case you want to derive another class from this one. The code appearing in the class definition is as follows:

```
protected:
    virtual void __fastcall AdvancedDrawMenuItem1(System::TObject* Sender,
                                                  Graphics::TCanvas* ACanvas,
                                                  const Windows::TRect& ARect,
                                                  TOwnerDrawState State);
```

The empty implementation for this would be

```
virtual void __fastcall
    TMyCustomEditor::AdvancedDrawMenuItem1(System::TObject* Sender,
                                           Graphics::TCanvas* ACanvas,
                                           const Windows::TRect& ARect,
                                           TOwnerDrawState State)
{
    // Custom rendering code here
}
```

The second stage, to ensure that our event handler is called for this menu item, is to set `MenuItem`'s `OnAdvancedDrawItem` event to this one. Add the following line of code to that shown previously in Listing 10.35 (after `MenuItem` is obtained):

```
MenuItem->OnAdvancedDrawItem = AdvancedDrawMenuItem1;
```

Now, each time `OnAdvancedDrawItem()` is called, our custom rendering code will be executed. The remaining `TMenuItem` events can also be overridden: `OnMeasureItem`, `OnDrawItem`, and `OnClick`; removing the need for code in the `ExecuteVerb()` method for this item. However, this is not advised, because `ExecuteVerb()` conveniently centralizes the code associated with clicking on the context menu. That leaves only the `OnMeasureItem` and `OnDrawItem` events. Essentially, `OnDrawItem` is a simpler (and older) version of `OnAdvancedDrawItem`. It is called less often and contains less information. Use the `OnAdvancedDrawItem` instead. However, `OnMeasureItem` is a useful event that allows the size of the menu item as it appears in the context menu to be modified. The code required in the class definition for this event is as follows:

```
protected:
    virtual void __fastcall MeasureMenuItem1(System::TObject* Sender,
                                             Graphics::TCanvas* ACanvas,
                                             int& Width,
                                             int& Height);
```

A typical implementation for this would be

```
virtual void __fastcall
    TMyCustomEditor::MeasureMenuItem1(System::TObject* Sender,
                                      Graphics::TCanvas* ACanvas,
                                      int& Width,
                                      int& Height)
{
    Width = x - Height; // Where x is the required width subtracting Height
                        // allows for Flip Children's sub-menu arrow
    Height = y;         // Where y is the required height
}
```

Adding the line of code that follows to the `PrepareItem()` method in Listing 10.35 in the correct section for this item ensures the event will be called:

```
MenuItem->OnMeasureItem = MeasureMenuItem1;
```

One thing to remember is that modifying `Width` will have an effect on the size of the menu item only if it is bigger than the current context menu width, which is most likely controlled by other context menu items. In other words, the current context menu width will be equal to the width of the widest item. Notice that if a value is assigned to `Width`, perhaps because an image is going to be drawn inside the menu item, the value that should be assigned will be the desired width *minus* the default height. The reason for this is to allow for the sub-menu arrow symbol for the IDE's menu item `Flip Children`. See Figure 10.9.

10

PROPERTY AND COMPONENT EDITORS

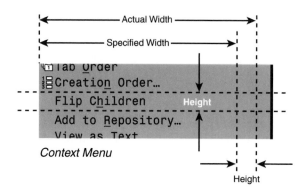

FIGURE 10.9

Cropped view of the `TImageComponentEditor` *context menu, showing height and width.*

The width required for the sub-menu arrow symbol is equal to the default `Height` of the Flip Children menu item. This value is added to any `Width` value that you specify, so in order to prevent having an unpainted strip down the right side of your context menu item, you must account for it by subtracting it from the width that you specify. Modifying the `Height` parameter will always have an effect on the height of the menu item, and setting it to `0` will make the item disappear.

The motivation behind defining your own custom event handlers for any of the menu items is so that the rendering of the item can be customized. There is increased scope for this with the new `OnAdvancedDrawItem` event. The `TOwnerDrawState Set` variable gives a lot of information about the current state of the item. For example, if the menu item is selected, `State` will contain `odSelected`, allowing code such as this to be placed in the event handler:

```
if(State.Contains(odSelected))
{
    // Draw the item with a clRed background
}
else
{
    // Draw the item with a clBtnFace background
}
```

Remember when you assign a handler to either `OnAdvancedDrawItem` or `OnDrawItem` that you are responsible for the entire rendering process, including displaying the text on the item's canvas. You will need to use the `TextRect` method of `TCanvas` to do so. For more information on this, refer to the "Using Images in Property Editors" section earlier in this chapter or to the C++Builder online help. An example custom component editor (`TImageComponentEditor`) that handles the `OnAdvancedDrawItem` and `OnMeasureItem` events for editing the `TImage` class is shown in Figure 10.10. The component editor also implements both Copy to Clipboard and Paste from Clipboard methods.

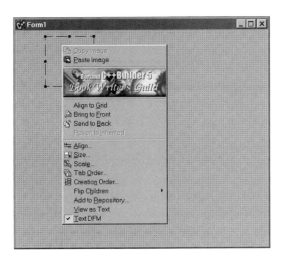

FIGURE 10.10

The context menu for `TImageComponentEditor`.

The possibilities offered by customizing the menu items using these events are endless. For example, it is possible to place your company logo as an image on one of the menu items or make all your custom menu items appear larger with a nicer background, making them stand out from the IDE-defined items. Incidentally, if you place menu items that perform no function, consider placing them *after* those that do. It can be very irritating after right-clicking on a component to have to study the menu for the item needed, especially if it is a common operation. Normally, items used most often should be placed first in the menu.

Adding Sub-Menu Items to Context Menu Items

Adding sub-menu items (which are `TMenuItems` themselves) to a custom context menu item requires that you create the sub-menu items that you want to add at runtime. The sub-menu items are then added to the appropriate menu item using the `Add()` method. Typically, more than one sub-menu will be added, and the `Add()` method is overloaded to accept an array of `TMenuItems` as well as single `TMenuItems`. Because the added sub-menu items are also of type `TMenuItem`, they have all the functionality of `MenuItem` and can be similarly customized. As an example, code to add sub-menu items to the second menu item will be shown (remember that the index is zero based). The number added is arbitrary; this could be made a `static const` value in the component editor class, for example. A symbolic name, `NoOfSubMenusForItem1`, is used in the code snippets for greater clarity.

First, the sub-menu items must be declared. If more than one sub-menu is required (as is the requirement here), it is simplest to declare an array of pointers to `TMenuItems`. We must be able to access the sub-menu items throughout our component editor class, so we shall declare the pointer array as a `private` variable in the class definition:

```
TMenuItem* SubMenuItemsFor1[NoOfSubMenusForItem1];
```

The sub-menu items must be constructed. A good place to do this is in the component editor's constructor. Currently, the constructor is empty and inline. It needs to be changed in both the class definition and the class implementation. The code required is

```
// In "MyCustomEditor.h" change the constructor declaration to
// the following and remove the surrounding #pragma option push
// and pop directives

__fastcall virtual TCustomComponentEditor(Classes::TComponent* AComponent,
                                _di_IFormDesigner ADesigner);

// The implementation for the constructor becomes:

__fastcall TCustomComponentEditor::
    TCustomComponentEditor(Classes::TComponent* AComponent,
                    _di_IFormDesigner ADesigner)
                    : TComponentEditor(AComponent, ADesigner)
{
    for(int i=0; i<NoOfSubMenusForItem1; ++i)
    {
        SubMenuItemsFor1[i] = new TMenuItem(Application);
        SubMenuItemsFor1[i]->Caption.sprintf("Sub-Menu %d", i);
        // Other Sub-Menu initialization
    }
    // Other Sub-Menu initialization
}
```

If the sub-menus are created in the component editor's constructor, then they should be deleted in the component editor's destructor. It is also currently empty and inline, so it must be changed as the constructor was. The code required is

```
// In "MyCustomEditor.h" change the destructor declaration to
// the following and remove the surrounding #pragma option push
// and pop directives

__fastcall virtual ~TCustomComponentEditor(void);

// The implementation for the destructor becomes:

__fastcall TCustomComponentEditor::~TCustomComponentEditor(void)
{
    for(int i=0; i<NoOfSubMenusForItem1; ++i)
```

```
    {
        delete SubMenuItemsFor1[i];
    }
}
```

With the code in place, it is trivial to add the sub-menus to menu item 1. Looking back to Listing 10.35, an implementation of the `PrepareItem()` method, we simply add the following line of code after the non-const pointer `MenuItem` is obtained:

```
MenuItem->Add(SubMenuItemsFor1, NoOfSubMenuItemsFor1-1);
```

From here the sub-menus can be used as any other menu items on the context menu.

> ## CAUTION
>
> Be careful not to assign code to a menu item with sub-menus in the `ExecuteVerb()` method. This can have unpredictable results.

The `ExecuteVerb()` Method

The `ExecuteVerb()` method is used to place the code that should be executed when one of the custom context menu items is clicked. The basic structure is the same as that for the `GetVerb()` method; that is, the code is wrapped inside a `switch` statement. Sample code is as follows:

```
void __fastcall TMyCustomEditor::ExecuteVerb(int Index)
{
    switch(Index)
    {
        case 0 : EditComponet();
                 break;
        case 1 : break; // Do nothing - copyright info
        case 2 : break; // Do nothing - Separator line
        case 3 : // Do something else ...
                 break;
        default : break;
    }
}
```

This shows the basic structure required to implement the `ExecuteVerb()` method. Typically, a menu item will show a dialog when it is clicked, unless the item is there as a line separator or to present textual or graphical information. To that end, the code that should be placed here depends very much on the features of the component being edited. In our example, clicking on the first menu item should invoke a form through which to edit the component. This is typical and the most useful for users. The code needed is identical to that shown previously for the

10

PROPERTY AND COMPONENT EDITORS

Edit() method. If the component editor is derived from TComponentEditor, and the Edit() method already contains the code required to show the component editor form, then it makes sense not to repeat that code. The best approach is to place the necessary code in a separate function, in this case EditComponent(), and call that function in both the ExecuteVerb() and Edit() methods. In fact, if the first menu item is used for this function, you need only ensure that the code is called from the ExecuteVerb() method. This is because TComponentEditor already implements the Edit() method to execute the code associated with the first menu item. Consequently, the Edit() method need not be overridden. Regardless of whether code is duplicated, if the code required to invoke a dialog is complex, it is better placed in a separate function.

All the necessary information regarding displaying forms has already been presented, and you are referred there for further information. The fourth method has been left undefined. Depending on the component, it could be anything. However, in all probability it will display a form to the user. The code presented previously for the Edit() method will also be applicable in this situation.

The Copy() Method

The Copy() method is used to copy *additional* Clipboard formats to the Clipboard, to allow additional functionality that users may expect or find especially useful. This might be something such as the capability to copy an image in a TImage component to the Clipboard so that it can be pasted into a graphics package. The code required to implement this method depends entirely on what data is to be copied, making the implementation of this method highly variable. Therefore, it will not be dwelled on. The principles are shown in the following sample code, which allows an image from a TImage component to be copied to the Clipboard.

```
#include "Clipbrd.hpp"

void __fastcall TImageComponentEditor::Copy(void)
{
    // Step 1 : Obtain a suitable pointer to the component
    TImage* Image = dynamic_cast<TImage*>(Component);

    // Step 2 : If successful then proceed
    if(Image)
    {
        // Step 3 : Obtain the required data in a format the
        //          clipboard will recognize

        WORD     AFormat;
        unsigned AData;
        HPALETTE APalette;
```

```
        Image->Picture->SaveToClipboardFormat(AFormat, AData, APalette);

        // Step 4 : Obtain a pointer to the global instance
        //          of the clipboard
        TClipboard* TheClipboard = Clipboard();

        // Step 5 : Copy the data to the clipboard
        TheClipboard->SetAsHandle(AFormat,  AData);
    }
}
```

The first stage is straightforward. A suitable pointer is obtained by dynamic_casting the TComponent pointer returned by TComponentEditor's Component property. If this doesn't work, then something is wrong. The second stage involves presenting the data in a way that the Clipboard will recognize. The data formats that the Clipboard supports are listed in the online help (it is also possible to register custom Clipboard formats; however, this is beyond the scope of this discussion). Once this is done, a pointer to the global instance of the Clipboard is obtained. Calling the global Clipboard() function returns this pointer. A new instance of TClipboard should *not* be created. Finally, the data can be copied to the Clipboard. A simpler implementation of the function is as follows:

```
void __fastcall TImageComponentEditor::Copy(void)
{
    TImage* Image = dynamic_cast<TImage*>(Component);

    if(Image)
    {
        Clipboard()->Assign(Image->Picture);
    }
}
```

The more complex approach was shown because it is more general, and the techniques are transferable to other copy operations.

It is important to note that this Copy() function does not interfere with the IDE's copying and pasting of components on forms using the normal menu and key shortcut methods. This function offers additional copying capabilities and must be invoked manually. It could therefore be placed as a menu item on the component's context menu. It is also perfectly conceivable that a Paste() method be defined and implemented. The definition for such a method would be

```
virtual void __fastcall Paste(void);
```

The corresponding implementation is

```
void __fastcall TImageComponentEditor::Paste(void)
{
    TImage* Image = dynamic_cast<TImage*>(Component);
```

10

PROPERTY AND COMPONENT EDITORS

```
  if(Image)
  {
    Image->Picture->Assign(Clipboard());
  }
}
```

Registering Component Editors

Registering component editors uses `RegisterComponentEditor()` and is straightforward. Its declaration is

```
extern PACKAGE void __fastcall
  RegisterComponentEditor(TMetaClass* ComponentClass,
                          TMetaClass* ComponentEditor);
```

This must be called inside the package's `Register()` function. Only two parameters are required. Both parameters will be `TObject` descendants, so the `__classid` operator can be used to obtain a `TMetaClass` pointer for each. The first parameter is the component class for which the component editor is to be registered. The second parameter is the component editor class itself. For example, to register a custom `TImage` component editor called `TImageComponentEditor`, you would write the following:

```
RegisterComponentEditor(__classid(TImage),
                        __classid(TImageComponentEditor));
```

Component editors are like property editors in that they are used from newest to oldest. As a result, it is possible to override existing component editors in preference to custom component editors offering greater capabilities.

Also as with property editors, it is possible to register component editor packages without components. This has been done with the `TImageComponentEditor` component editor discussed previously. It is included in the package containing the enhanced property editors developed in the "Using Images in Property Editors" section, earlier in this chapter.

Using Predefined Images in Custom Property and Component Editors

Much of the previous discussion centered around the graphical customization that could be performed. It was indicated that there was good scope for using predefined images to enhance the look and feel of the editors. However, little specific advice on this was given. The techniques presented in this section are guidelines that can be applied not just to custom editors (property or component) but to projects in general.

The first stage in using predefined images is to create them. This can be done using any graphics package, even C++Builder's Image Editor. The main concern is to ensure that the files for the images are in bitmap format (.bmp). You may also want to consider the color depth of the target platform. It may be that you can only use 8-bit color. You might create two sets of images at different color depths. With current systems, this is not as great a concern as it once was. Once the images are available, all that needs to be done is to incorporate them into your package.

You have a couple of choices on how to do this. One way is to use C++Builder's Image Editor tool to create a *compiled resource file* (.res file extension). You can then paste your images into bitmaps in the compiled resource file. Almost immediately you will probably notice that Image Editor is very limited and does not seem to understand the idea of palettes. However, you can easily create a compiled resource file using this method. Make a note of the *resource names* that you give to the bitmaps; these are the names that you will use when you want to load the resource in your code. It should be noted that Image Editor also allows you to create icons and cursors and add them to thecompiled resource file, which can be quite useful.

Another approach is to manually create a resource script file (.rc). To do this, create a new text file by selecting File, New and choosing Text from the New (default) page. Add a line in the following format:

ResourceID BITMAP *Filename*.bmp

Do this for each bitmap you want to add to the resource. *ResourceID* is the identifier for the resource and is how the code you write refers to the resource. *ResourceID* can be either an integer value or a unique identifier string. The identifier string is simply the string typed in place of *ResourceID*. If an integer value is required, a header file is normally created for the resource file and #define statements used to equate the string identifiers to numbers. This is resolved when the resource file is compiled. In the examples presented here, *ResourceID* will be an identifier string. BITMAP is a keyword telling the compiler that the resource is a bitmap, and *Filename* is the file containing the bitmap. This may or may not be enclosed in quotation marks—"*Filename*.bmp" is also valid. For example, the resource file for the EnhancedEditors package on the CD-ROM is

```
RESOURCE_CopyImage                  BITMAP  "CopyImage.bmp"
RESOURCE_PasteImage                 BITMAP  "PasteImage.bmp"
RESOURCE_GreyedPasteImage           BITMAP  "GrayedPasteImage.bmp"
RESOURCE_GreyedCopyImage            BITMAP  "GrayedCopyImage.bmp"
RESOURCE_ActiveWritersGuildLogo     BITMAP  "ActiveWritersGuildLogo.bmp"
RESOURCE_InActiveWritersGuildLogo BITMAP  "InActiveWritersGuildLogo.bmp"
```

RESOURCE_ is used as a tag to help occurrences of the resources stand out. Often all uppercase letters are used for resource names to make them stand out. However, all-uppercase words are difficult to read, so we will adopt the format shown in the previous code as an improvement to this practice. You may want to use RES_ for resources in compiled resource files (for example those created from the Image Editor) and RC_ for resources referenced in a resource script file. This allows a distinction to be made between the two in your code. To finish the resource script, simply save the file with the .rc extension. This is our resource file and all we need to add the specified images to our package (or project).

The manual method of creating a resource script file offers some advantages over using C++Builder's Image Editor. First, it allows individual images to be easily updated and edited using any graphics software tool. Also, it allows more than just bitmaps, icons, and cursors to be included. This allows a more centralized approach to be taken to resources based on their use, not their type. Image Editor is useful but lacks real power. Its inability to deal adequately with bitmap palettes makes it very frustrating. It's a shame that such a great visual RAD tool should come with such a woeful image resource editor and manager. Good editing is not so important, but the integrity of pasted images should be maintained, and the resource managing aspect should be improved. Perhaps a new version will appear in the next release.

Adding Resource Files to Packages

Once you have a saved .res containing the images that you want to use, or a .rc file referencing them, including it in your package is straightforward. From the Package Editor, click the Add to Package button. From the Add Unit page, browse to the .res or .rc file and click OK to include it. When this is done, a line similar to one of the following will be added between the #pragma hrdstop and #pragma package(smart_init) directives in the package's source file:

```
USERES("PathnameOfCompiledResource.res"); // for .res files
USERC("PathnameOfResource.rc");           // for .rc files
```

Normally you place the resource file in the same directory as the package, in which case only the filename of the resource is required. The difference between the use of a compiled resource and a resource script is that the compiled resource requires only linking to the package's .bpl file (or the project's .exe file); the resource script file is compiled when the package is compiled. Alternatively, compiled resource files can also be added to the package using the #pragma resource directive:

```
#pragma resource "PathnameOfCompiledResource.res"
```

Once the resources are added to the package, they can be accessed at will.

Using Resources in Property and Component Editors

In the previous sections on property editors and component editors, it was suggested that predefined images could be used, for example, in the drop-down list of a property value, as menu item images, or even as static logos in component editors. In fact, the possibilities are endless. In this section we will look at the key issues involved in using such images to accomplish this.

We have seen how to add resources to a package. With this done, it is reasonably simple to make use of those resources. When we want access to the resources, we typically load them into memory in a format that we can use. For single images, we should use `TBitmap`. (We also could use `TPicture`, which has a `TBitmap` property, or `TImage`, which has a `TPicture` property.) For multiple images of the same size, we should use `TImageList`. The methods offered by `TBitmap` for loading image resources are as follows:

```
void __fastcall LoadFromResourceName(int Instance,
                                     const AnsiString ResName);

void __fastcall LoadFromResourceID(int Instance,
                                   int ResID);
```

The first function, `LoadFromResourceName()`, is for use with resources with string name identifiers. The second is for use with resources with integer identifiers. In the examples that follow, `LoadFromResourceName()` will be used. The first parameter, `Instance`, expects the instance handle for the package that contains the resource. This is contained in the global `HInstance` variable, defined in `$(BCB)\Include\Vcl\Sysinit.hpp` as

```
extern PACKAGE HINSTANCE HInstance;
```

`HINSTANCE` is defined in `$(BCB)\Include\wtypes.h` as a `void*`. Hence `HInstance` must be cast to an `int` before use. Casting from a pointer to an `int` requires that we use `reinterpret_cast`:

```
reinterpret_cast<int>(HInstance)
```

`TImageList` offers the following methods for loading image resources (derived from `TCustomImageList`):

```
bool __fastcall ResourceLoad(TResType ResType,
                             AnsiString Name,
                             Graphics::TColor MaskColor);

bool __fastcall ResInstLoad(int Instance,
                            TResType ResType,
                            System::AnsiString Name,
                            Graphics::TColor MaskColor);
```

Only `ResInstLoad()` is usable inside a package, so it is the only one we will discuss, though the functions are the same, apart from the `Instance` variable. As before, the first variable required is `HInstance`. The second variable tells the image list what type the resource is: `rtBitmap` for a bitmap, `rtIcon` for an icon, and `rtCursor` for a cursor. A mask color can be specified in the last parameter, which is used only if `TImageList`'s `Mask` property is true.

Loading resources is reasonably trouble free. The main question is when to load the resources. Listing 10.36 shows a possible implementation of the OnAdvancedDrawItem event handler for the third custom context menu item in TImageComponentEditor.

LISTING 10.36   Loading and Displaying Image Resources

```
void __fastcall
    TImageComponentEditor::AdvancedDrawMenuItem3(System::TObject* Sender,
                                                 Graphics::TCanvas* ACanvas,
                                                 const Windows::TRect& ARect,
                                                 TOwnerDrawState State)
{
    std::auto_ptr<Graphics::TBitmap> Logo(new Graphics::TBitmap());

    if(State.Contains(odSelected))
    {
        Logo->LoadFromResourceName(reinterpret_cast<int>(HInstance),
                                "RESOURCE_ActiveWritersGuildLogo");
    }
    else
    {
        Logo->LoadFromResourceName(reinterpret_cast<int>(HInstance),
                                "RESOURCE_InActiveWritersGuildLogo");
    }
    // Draw Logo onto the Canvas
    ACanvas->Draw(ARect.Left, ARect.Top,  Logo);
}
```

Listing 10.36 requires little explanation. It simply checks the state of the menu item. It displays one image if it is selected and another if it is not. This works fine and is perfectly reasonable. However, it is inefficient. Logo is constructed every time the mouse moves over MenuItem3, the RESOURCE_ActiveWritersGuildLogo resource is loaded into it, and then Logo is destructed after the resource image is rendered. When the mouse moves off MenuItem3, this is repeated, except that the RESOURCE_InActiveWritersGuildLogo is loaded.

There is an alternative approach that is more efficient. It requires that the resources used by the component editor be loaded into TBitmap objects or TImageList objects when the component editor is constructed. In the present example function, this would require two TBitmap objects to be constructed in the TImageComponentEditor's constructor (and deleted in its destructor) and the necessary resources loaded into them. Pointers to the bitmaps would be private variables. Suitable code is shown in Listing 10.37.

LISTING 10.37   Improved Code-Handling Image Resources

```cpp
// FIRST THE CLASS DEFINITION

#include "dsgnintf.hpp"

class TImageComponentEditor : public TDefaultEditor
{
    typedef TComponentEditor inherited;

private:
    virtual void __fastcall AdvancedDrawMenuItem3(System::TObject* Sender,
                                                  Graphics::TCanvas* ACanvas,
                                                  const Windows::TRect& ARect,
                                                  TOwnerDrawState State);


    virtual void __fastcall MeasureMenuItem3(System::TObject* Sender,
                                             Graphics::TCanvas* ACanvas,
                                             int& Width,
                                             int& Height);

    // Private Data
    Graphics::TBitmap* ActiveWritersGuildLogo;
    Graphics::TBitmap* InActiveWritersGuildLogo;

public:
    // Right-Click
    // CONTEXT MENU - Step 1
    virtual int __fastcall GetVerbCount(void);
    //             - Step 2
    virtual AnsiString __fastcall GetVerb(int Index);
    //             - Step 3
    virtual void __fastcall PrepareItem(int Index,
                                        const Menus::TMenuItem* AItem);
    //             - Step 4
    virtual void __fastcall ExecuteVerb(int Index);

    // Copy image to Clipboard
    virtual void __fastcall Copy(void);

    // Paste image from Clipboard
    virtual void __fastcall Paste(void);

public:
    __fastcall virtual TImageComponentEditor(Classes::TComponent* AComponent,
```

LISTING 10.37   Continued

```cpp
                                          _di_IFormDesigner ADesigner);

public:
    __fastcall virtual ~TImageComponentEditor(void);
};

// NOW THE IMPLEMENTATION CODE

//--------------------------------------------------------------------------------//
//                              CONSTRUCTOR                                        //
//--------------------------------------------------------------------------------//
__fastcall TImageComponentEditor::TImageComponentEditor
                                (Classes::TComponent* AComponent,
                                 _di_IFormDesigner ADesigner)
            : TDefaultEditor(AComponent, ADesigner)
{
    ActiveWritersGuildLogo = new Graphics::TBitmap();
    InActiveWritersGuildLogo = new Graphics::TBitmap();

    ActiveWritersGuildLogo->LoadFromResourceName
                            (reinterpret_cast<int>(HInstance),
                             "RESOURCE_ActiveWritersGuildLogo");

    InActiveWritersGuildLogo->LoadFromResourceName
                            (reinterpret_cast<int>(HInstance),
                             "RESOURCE_InActiveWritersGuildLogo");
}
//--------------------------------------------------------------------------------//
//                              DESTRUCTOR                                         //
//--------------------------------------------------------------------------------//
__fastcall TImageComponentEditor::~TImageComponentEditor(void)
{
    delete ActiveWritersGuildLogo;
    delete InActiveWritersGuildLogo;
}
//--------------------------------------------------------------------------------//
void __fastcall
    TImageComponentEditor::AdvancedDrawMenuItem3(System::TObject* Sender,
                                                 Graphics::TCanvas* ACanvas,
                                                 const Windows::TRect& ARect,
                                                 TOwnerDrawState State)
{
    if(State.Contains(odSelected))
    {
        ACanvas->Draw(ARect.Left, ARect.Top, ActiveWritersGuildLogo);
```

LISTING 10.37   Continued

```
    }
    else
    {
       ACanvas->Draw(ARect.Left, ARect.Top, InActiveWritersGuildLogo);
    }
}
//--------------------------------------------------------------------//
```

In the new implementation of the `OnAdvancedDrawItem` event handler, you can see that it is much simpler and contains only code required to render the image, as it should be.

One final note: It is possible to load resources into a `TImageList` object using a loop. Simply name the set of related images to be loaded with a number as the last character or characters. For example, suppose we have 17 images that are suitable for placement in an image list. They are named RESOURCE_Image*XX*, where *XX* is a number ranging from 01 to 17. We would write

```
// In the class definition ----------------------------------------//
TImageList* ImageList;
//-----------------------------------------------------------------//
```

```
// In the Constructor ----------------------------------------------//
ImageList = new TImageList(this);
ImageList->Masked = false;

for(int i=0; i<17; ++i)
{
    ImageList->ResInstLoad(reinterpret_cast<int>(HInstance),
                    rtBitmap,
                    AnsiString("RESOURCE_Image").cat_sprintf("%.2d",i+1),
                    clWhite);
}
//-----------------------------------------------------------------//
```

```
// In the Destructor -----------------------------------------------//
delete ImageList;
//-----------------------------------------------------------------//
```

As you can see, working with resources is not difficult and can enable your editors and (perhaps even more) your projects to have a pleasing and professional interface.

Registering Property Categories in Custom Components

A category is a class that inherits ultimately from `TPropertyCategory`. This section looks at how you can use categories in custom components. There are essentially two issues that must be addressed. The first is to determine which categories are to be used by a component; if categories other than the 13 predefined categories are required (see Table 10.13), then such custom category classes must be created. The second is the registration of the appropriate properties (and events) in the appropriate categories. Each of these will be discussed in turn.

Understanding Categories and Category Creation

There are 13 predefined property categories in C++Builder. Their names and corresponding classes are shown in Table 10.13.

TABLE 10.13   Category Classes in C++Builder

Category Name	Category Class
Action	TActionCategory
Data	TDataCategory
Database	TDatabaseCategory
Drag, Drop and Docking	TDragNDropCategory
Help and Hints	THelpCategory
Input	TInputCategory
Layout	TLayoutCategory
Legacy	TLegacyCategory
Linkage	TLinkageCategory
Locale	TLocaleCategory
Localizable	TLocalizableCategory
Miscellaneous	TMiscellaneousCategory
Visual	TVisualCategory

For a brief description of each category, refer to the "Property Categories in the Object Inspector" section in Chapter 2. Declarations for the property categories listed in Table 10.13 can be found in the $(BCB)\Include\Vcl\DsgnIntf.hpp file.

Creating a new category requires that a new class be defined that inherits from TPropertyCategory or one of its descendants (for example, one of the 13 predefined categories). There is an additional stipulation that the Name and Description methods be overridden to suit the new category. Strictly speaking, overriding Description is not required, but it is trivial to accomplish and so should be done. Defining a new category requires the code in Listings 10.38 and 10.39 to be written with the appropriate customizations. *NameOfCategory* should be replaced with the actual name of the category, and the string values returned by Name and Description need to be suitable.

LISTING 10.38   Definition Code for a New Category

```
#include <Dsgnintf.hpp>

class PACKAGE TNameOfCategory : public TPropertyCategory
{
 typedef TPropertyCategory inherited;

 public:
        #pragma option push -w-inl
        virtual AnsiString __fastcall Name()
        {
          return Name(__classid(TNameOfCategory));
        }
        #pragma option pop

        static AnsiString __fastcall Name(System::TMetaClass* vmt);

        #pragma option push -w-inl
        virtual AnsiString __fastcall Description()
        {
          return Description(__classid(TNameOfCategory));
        }
        #pragma option pop

        static AnsiString __fastcall Description(System::TMetaClass* vmt);

        #pragma option push -w-inl
        // Constructor
        inline __fastcall TNameOfCategory (void) : TPropertyCategory() { }
        #pragma option pop

        #pragma option push -w-inl
        // Destructor
        inline __fastcall virtual ~TNameOfCategory (void) { }
        #pragma option pop
};
```

The two `static` member functions `Name` and `Description` must be overridden. Suitable implementation code for each is shown in Listing 10.39. An appropriate string is simply returned in each case. The string returned from `Name` is the string that is used in the Object Inspector. An alternative approach to implementing the `Name` and `Description` methods is to load a string from a resource so that different strings could be used for different locales.

10

LISTING 10.39   Implementation Code for a New Category

```
AnsiString __fastcall TNameOfCategory::Name(System::TMetaClass* vmt)
{
  return "Category Name";
}

AnsiString __fastcall TNameOfCategory::Description(System::TMetaClass* vmt)
{
  return "Category Name properties and/or events";
}
```

The definition code should be placed in the header file that contains your other registration-related definitions and the implementation code in the respective .cpp file. Once this is done, the new category is available for registering properties (and events). If your category does not derive directly from TPropertyCategory (for example you inherit from TInputCategory), then the typedef for inherited must be changed to reflect that, though there is no real benefit from such a derivation. It is best to inherit directly from TPropertyCategory.

Registering a Property or Properties in a Category

C++Builder provides two overloaded functions for registering a property or properties in a given category: RegisterPropertyInCategory() or RegisterPropertiesInCategory() (declared in $(BCB)\Include\Vcl\DsgnIntf.hpp). These registration functions are called in the package's Register() function. In effect, you are not registering a single property for a given category but rather a single property filter that may be applicable to more than one property. In this respect, the names chosen for the registration functions are misleading. For registering a single property filter in a category, you can use one of four overloaded functions:

```
extern PACKAGE TPropertyFilter* __fastcall
    RegisterPropertyInCategory(TMetaClass* ACategoryClass,
                               const AnsiString APropertyName);

extern PACKAGE TPropertyFilter* __fastcall
    RegisterPropertyInCategory(TMetaClass* ACategoryClass,
                               TMetaClass* AComponentClass,
                               const AnsiString APropertyName);

extern PACKAGE TPropertyFilter* __fastcall
    RegisterPropertyInCategory(TMetaClass* ACategoryClass,
                               Typinfo::PTypeInfo APropertyType,
                               const AnsiString APropertyName);

extern PACKAGE TPropertyFilter* __fastcall
    RegisterPropertyInCategory(TMetaClass* ACategoryClass,
                               Typinfo::PTypeInfo APropertyType);
```

Each of the previous functions uses a different method to specify which property filter you want to register in a given category. To register several property filters into a category at once, you can use one of the three overloaded versions of `RegisterPropertiesInCategory`:

```
extern PACKAGE TPropertyCategory* __fastcall
    RegisterPropertiesInCategory(TMetaClass* ACategoryClass,
                             const System::TVarRec* AFilters,
                             const int AFilters_Size);


extern PACKAGE TPropertyCategory* __fastcall
    RegisterPropertiesInCategory(TMetaClass* ACategoryClass,
                             TMetaClass* AComponentClass,
                             const AnsiString* AFilters,
                             const int AFilters_Size);


extern PACKAGE TPropertyCategory* __fastcall
    RegisterPropertiesInCategory(TMetaClass* ACategoryClass,
                             Typinfo::PTypeInfo APropertyType,
                             const AnsiString* AFilters,
                             const int AFilters_Size);
```

We see that there are seven functions from which you can register property filters for a specific category: four to register a single property filter and three to register multiple property filters. Based on the input parameters, the `RegisterPropertyInCategory()` function generates a single `TPropertyFilter`, and the `RegisterPropertiesInCategory()` function generates multiple `TPropertyFilters`. The IDE then uses a list of `TPropertyFilters` to determine which properties belong in which categories. Remember that a property can belong to more than one category. The definition for `TPropertyFilter`, found in the `$(BCB)\Include\Vcl\DsgnIntf.hpp` file, is shown in Listing 10.40.

LISTING 10.40   Definition of `TPropertyFilter`

```
class DELPHICLASS TPropertyFilter;
class PASCALIMPLEMENTATION TPropertyFilter : public System::TObject
{
    typedef System::TObject inherited;

private:
    Masks::TMask*       FMask;
    TMetaClass*         FComponentClass;
    Typinfo::TTypeInfo* FPropertyType;

    int FGroup;
```

10

LISTING 10.40   Continued

```
public:
    __fastcall TPropertyFilter(const AnsiString APropertyName,
                               TMetaClass* AComponentClass,
                               Typinfo::PTypeInfo APropertyType);

    __fastcall virtual ~TPropertyFilter(void);

    bool __fastcall Match(const AnsiString APropertyName,
                          TMetaClass* AComponentClass,
                          Typinfo::PTypeInfo APropertyType);

    __property TMetaClass* ComponentClass = {read=FComponentClass};
    __property Typinfo::PTypeInfo PropertyType = {read=FPropertyType};
};
```

Essentially, TPropertyFilter contains three important data members. These are shown in the following list:

- **Property Name Mask (FMask)**   If this is not an empty AnsiString, a TMask object (FMask) is created based on the AnsiString. This stores the property name mask that any property must match in order to satisfy this field of the filter. See Table 10.14 for a description of the special mask characters that can be used. Otherwise, any property name will do.

- **Component Class (FComponentClass)**   This is a TMetaClass* that indicates which component class a property must be part of to satisfy this field of the filter. If this is set to 0, any component class can be used.

- **Property Type (FPropertyType)**   This is a PTypeInfo (TTypeInfo*) that indicates what type the property must be to satisfy this field of the filter. If this is set to 0, the property type is irrelevant.

Table 10.14 shows the special characters that the property name argument can contain to generate a suitable property name mask.

TABLE 10.14   Special Mask Characters for the Property Name in a TPropertyFilter

Character	Purpose
*	Use as a wildcard character. Use the * character to signify any number of any character.
?	Use as a wildcard character. Use the ? character to signify a *single* wildcard character.

TABLE 10.14 Continued

Character	Purpose
[*SetorRangeorBoth*]	Use to specify a set or range (or both) of characters that a single character must match. For example, [AbcDE0-9] includes the characters AbcDE0123456789.
[!*SetorRangeorBoth*]	Use to specify a set or range (or both) of characters that a single character must *not* match. For example, [!AbcDEf-j] excludes the characters AbcDEfghij.

A *character* is any alphanumeric character. The mask is case-sensitive.

A *set* is a group of characters enclosed in brackets ([]). The characters are not separated by either commas or spaces—for example, [AbcDE].

A *range* is a range of characters; the first and last characters in a range are separated by a - character. Ranges are enclosed in brackets ([]). For example, [0-9] includes all the characters 0123456789.

Examples of using these registration functions are shown in Listing 10.40, earlier in this chapter. Table 10.15 lists the parameters to these functions and discusses the purpose of each. With the exception of ACategoryClass, all the parameters are used to specify the TPropertyFilter or TPropertyFilters relevant to a given property category, as defined by ACategoryClass.

TABLE 10.15 Parameters to the RegisterPropertyInCategory() and RegisterPropertiesInCategory() Functions

Parameter	Purpose
TMetaClass* ACategoryClass	Used to specify the category for which you want the property to be registered. Use the __classid operator to obtain the TMetaClass pointer for the given category class. Example: __classid(TMyCategory)
TMetaClass* AComponentClass	Used to generate the property filter. Use this parameter to specify a component to which the property must belong in order for it to be registered for the given category. Use the __classid operator to obtain the TMetaClass* for the required component class. Example: __classid(TMyComponent)

TABLE 10.15 Continued

Parameter	Purpose
`const AnsiString PropertyName`	Used to generate the property filter. Use this parameter to specify a property name mask that the property must match to be registered for the given category. For example, specify `"Shape"` to restrict the registration to those properties called `Shape`, or `"OnMouse*"` to restrict the registration to those properties (probably events) that begin `OnMouse`.
`Typinfo::PTypeInfo APropertyType`	Used to generate the property filter. Use this parameter to specify a `PTypeInfo` that the property must match in order to be registered for the given category. Effectively, this parameter allows you to restrict the properties to be registered to only those of a particular type. For example, you could restrict the registration to only those properties of type `int` by using the argument `&IntTypeInfo`, where `IntTypeInfo` is defined as `static TTypeInfo IntTypeInfo;` `IntTypeInfo.Name = "int";` `IntTypeInfo.Kind = tkInteger;` Refer to the "Registering Custom Property Editors" section for more details.
`const AnsiString* AFilters,` `const int AFilters_Size`	Used to generate the property filters and to specify an array of property name masks (by value) that must be matched by a property to be registered for the given category. Use the `OPENARRAY` macro to achieve this.
`const System::TVarRec*` `AFilters, const int` `AFilters_Size`	Used to generate the property filters and to specify an array of `TVarRec` values (by value) that must be matched by a property in order to be registered for the given category. Use the `ARRAYOFCONST` macro to achieve this. Values should be an `AnsiString` (to specify a property name mask), `TMetaClass*` (to specify a component class the property should belong to), or `PTypeInfo` (to specify a property type that the property must be).

From Table 10.15 we can see that the `RegisterPropertiesInCategory()` function requires either a const array of `TVarRec` (`$(BCB)\Include\Vcl\Systvar.h`) by value or a const array of `AnsiStrings` by value.

For a const array of `TVarRec` by value, the `ARRAYOFCONST(values)` macro is used (`$(BCB)\Include\Vcl\Sysopen.h`). The `ARRAYOFCONST(values)` macro equates to

```
OpenArray<TVarRec>values, OpenArrayCount<TVarRec>values.GetHigh()
```

This allows you to pass an array of `TVarRecs` by value to the registration functions and is why the array pointer parameter and the array size parameter are considered together. There is one problem with this, and that is that both `OpenArray<TVarRec>` and `OpenArrayCount<TVarRec>` are limited to 19 arguments. Therefore, if you need to register 20 or more properties or events to the same category, you must call the `RegisterPropertiesInCategory()` function more than once.

Similarly, for a const array of `AnsiStrings` by value, the `OPENARRAY(type,values)` macro can be used, which equates to

```
OpenArray<type>values, OpenArrayCount<type>values.GetHigh()
```

For an `OPENARRAY` of `AnsiStrings` we write the following:

```
OPENARRAY(AnsiString, "Value1", "Value2", "Value3");
```

Three example `AnsiStrings` are shown. As with the `ARRAYOFCONST` macro, you are limited to 19 arguments or fewer.

Table 10.16 shows the filters produced by each of the four overloaded versions of the `RegisterPropertyInCategory()` function.

TABLE 10.16   `TPropertyFilters` Generated by the `RegisterPropertyInCategory()` Function

Overloaded Function Parameter List	Property Filter(s) Generated: (Mask, Component, Type)
(TMetaClass* ACategoryClass, const AnsiString APropertyName)	(APropertyName, 0, 0)
(TMetaClass* ACategoryClass, TMetaClass* AComponentClass, const AnsiString APropertyName)	(APropertyName, AComponentClass, 0)
(TMetaClass* ACategoryClass, Typinfo::PTypeInfo APropertyType, const AnsiString APropertyName)	(APropertyName, 0, APropertyType)
(TMetaClass* ACategoryClass, Typinfo::PTypeInfo APropertyType)	("", 0, APropertyType)

Table 10.17 shows the filters produced by each of the three overloaded versions of the
`RegisterPropertiesInCategory()` function.

TABLE 10.17   `TPropertyFilters` Generated by the `RegisterPropertiesInCategory()`
Function

Overloaded Function Parameter List	Property Filter(s) Generated: (Mask, Component, Type)
(TMetaClass* ACategoryClass, const System::TVarRec* AFilters, const int AFilters_Size)	If AFilters[i] is an AnsiString: (AFilters[i], 0, 0) If AFilters[i] is a TMetaClass*: ("", AFilters[i], 0)
	If AFilters[i] is a PTypeInfo: ("", 0, AFilters[i])
(TMetaClass* ACategoryClass, TMetaClass* AComponentClass, const AnsiString* AFilters, const int AFilters_Size)	(AFilters[i], AComponentClass, 0)
(TMetaClass* ACategoryClass, Typinfo::PTypeInfo APropertyType, const AnsiString* AFilters, const int AFilters_Size)	(AFilters[i], 0, APropertyType)

Tables 10.16 and 10.17 should be used as a guide when choosing which of the seven over-loaded versions of the two registration functions to use when registering property filters. The property filters are described in terms of a property name mask (`Mask`), a component class that the property must belong to (`Component`), and a type the property must be (`Type`).

Of special note in Table 10.17 is the first `RegisterPropertiesInCategory()` overloaded function. The property filters produced from this depend on the argument types used in the `TVarRec` array. Note also that different types can be used in the same array, making this function very flexible. Listing 10.41 shows sample code using these registration functions. The code in Listing 10.41 assumes that the categories used have been previously defined and are available.

LISTING 10.41   Registering Properties in Categories in C++Builder

```
namespace Nameoffilecontainingthisregistration
{
    void __fastcall PACKAGE Register()
    {
        // 1 - Register a single property filter for TMouseCategory.
        //     The filter is ("OnMouse*", 0, 0), i.e. all properties
```

LISTING 10.41 Continued

```
//      (probably events) whose names begin "OnMouse"
// Use:
//      RegisterPropertyInCategory(TMetaClass* ACategoryClass,
//                                 const AnsiString APropertyName);

RegisterPropertyInCategory(__classid(TMouseCategory),
                           "OnMouse*");

// 2 - Register two property filters for TMouseCategory.
//     The first filter is ("", 0, CursoTypeInfo), i.e. for properties
//     of type TCursor.
//     The second filter is ("OnMouse*", 0, 0)
// Use:
//      RegisterPropertiesInCategory(TMetaClass* ACategoryClass,
//                                   const System::TVarRec* AFilters,
//                                   const int AFilters_Size);

PTypeInfo CursorTypeInfo
        = *Typinfo::GetPropInfo(__typeinfo(TForm),"Cursor")->PropType;

RegisterPropertiesInCategory(__classid(TMouseCategory),
                             ARRAYOFCONST(
                             ( CursorTypeInfo,
                               AnsiString("OnMouse*"),
                               AnsiString("EventName2") )) );

// 3 - Register two property filters for TMouseCategory.
//     The first filter is ("OnClick", 0, 0), i.e. for any property
//     (probably event) whose name is "OnClick".
//     The second filter is ("OnDblClick", 0, 0), i.e. for any property
//     (probably event) whose name is "OnDblClick".
// Use :
//      RegisterPropertiesInCategory(TMetaClass* ACategoryClass,
//                                   TMetaClass* AComponentClass,
//                                   const AnsiString* AFilters,
//                                   const int AFilters_Size)

TMetaClass* AnyComponent = 0;

RegisterPropertiesInCategory( __classid(TMouseCategory),
                              AnyComponent,
                              OPENARRAY( AnsiString,
                                         ("OnClick",
                                          "OnDblClick") ) );
  }
}
```

In Listing 10.41 not all possible uses and overloaded versions of the two category registration functions are shown. However, each of the possible parameters' uses is illustrated, so the correct method of calling each registration function should be easy to determine. Of all the parameters, `AComponentClass` is the least useful on its own, because the sub-properties of a class are unlikely to all belong in the same category unless the class is itself a property, in which case the sub-properties will fall under the same category as the class that contains them, by default.

Note that a `NULL TMetaClass*` is passed as an argument to the `AComponentClass` parameter in the third registration shown. This indicates that only the property name masks are part of the property filter. You cannot simply pass `0` because there will be an ambiguity over which version of `RegisterPropertiesInCategory()` you are calling. For example, a literal `0` could equally be a value for a `PTypeInfo` parameter. A similar technique can be used to pass a `NULL PTypeInfo`:

```
PTypeInfo AnyPropertyType = 0;
```

Summary

This chapter's aim was to cover the main concerns and techniques associated with the development of a component's designtime interface. To do this, a lot has been covered. The following highlights the main topics.

- The creation of custom property editors was discussed throughout the chapter. We saw that there are many different property editor classes already defined by the VCL and that correctly choosing the base class for our custom property editors can save a lot of unnecessary coding. Much of the information presented dealt with how to correctly override `TPropertyEditor`'s `virtual` (and `DYNAMIC`) methods. We paid particular attention to the new methods introduced in C++Builder 5, such as the five `DYNAMIC` methods used for rendering images in the Object Inspector. We also touched on the issue of throwing exceptions to indicate to the user when an invalid property value has been entered.

- A large portion of the chapter was devoted to the creation of custom component editors. We saw that, in contrast to creating custom property editors, there are only two classes from which we can derive our custom component editors: `TComponentEditor` and `TDefaultEditor`. Which one we choose depends on which double-click behavior we want: If we want our custom component editor to generate an event handler, we derive from `TDefaultEditor`; otherwise we use `TComponentEditor`. We also discussed how to correctly override `TComponentEditor`'s `virtual` methods. We paid particular attention to the `PrepareItem()` method, new to C++Builder 5, which allows users to fully customize the context menu that our custom component editor displays.

- For both property and component editors we saw that the `Edit()` virtual method can be used to display a form for editing a property or component. We saw that there were two approaches to this: Allow the form to modify the property or component while the form is being displayed or modify the property or component only after the form has returned.

- The use of image resources to improve the interface of an editor was discussed. Definite guidelines were given for this often-neglected topic. The material for this topic should prove useful for C++Builder projects in general.

- The correct techniques for registering property and component editors were detailed. In particular, the problem of determining type information for non-VCL types was examined and a robust solution presented.

- Property categories, new to C++Builder 5, were examined. We saw how to create our own custom proerty categories and also how to register property filters, which allow the IDE to determine which categories a property should appear in.

After reading this chapter, you should be able to tackle most of these issues. In particular, if time has been spent in some of the darker corners of the code, you should have developed a reasonable appreciation of how type information is dealt with by the VCL.

Creating property and component editors can be tricky, and many of the methods required can easily be misunderstood. Hopefully, much of the mystery that sometimes surrounds these topics has been removed.

More Custom Component Techniques

Jamie Allsop
Damon Chandler
Malcolm Smith

IN THIS CHAPTER

The complete text for this chapter appears on the CD-ROM.

Communications, Database, and Web Programming

PART

II

IN THIS PART

Communications Programming

Keith Turnbull II
Mark Davey

IN THIS CHAPTER

- **Serial Communication**
- **Internet Protocols—SMTP, FTP, HTTP, POP3**

No man is an island, and no program is an island either. Communication is the lifeblood of civilization and is an integral component of any computer program. Whether it's communicating with external peripherals via the serial port or connecting point to point via the Internet, programs need to have the capability to communicate with the world around them.

In this chapter, you will be introduced to the issues involved in serial port communications programming. You will also receive an introduction to the variety of network protocols that are available via the FastNet components included with C++Builder. After completing this chapter, you should have the necessary tools to communicate effectively with the world outside your program.

Serial Communication

Serial communication is a fundamental aspect of writing software to interface with external devices. In the world of systems programming, the computer is only a small component part of a wider system in which integration of those components is paramount. For most applications, use of the computer's serial port is more than adequate. In this short section, we shall examine some of the crucial design issues to ensure full advantage is taken of the available facilities.

> **NOTE**
>
> The related code example illustrates techniques related to communication problems that you may encounter in serial communications development. The code is intended for study rather than execution, because it is taken from a larger, complex system interfacing directly to a proprietary device. As such, practical means of opening serial ports, reading and writing data, and the problems of interpreting that data are presented with explanatory notes in the code. A short synopsis is provided at the end of this section for reference purposes.
>
> You will find that the Win32 API is replete with functions for serial communications. There is no good reason to want to control the low-level hardware, particularly if you want to provide compatible software across all Microsoft Windows–based operating systems. All functions are listed in the Win32 API Help under the section "About Communications."

You should already be aware of the importance of the Internet in recent times. The Internet exists primarily because the foundations it is built upon are solid, reliable, and widely documented. This fact is often misunderstood. The Internet is a system based on many protocols. A protocol is fundamental in good communication systems—open or proprietary. Users would find it very difficult to get anything done if no protocol existed in speech communication. The protocol of speech is a good basis on which to develop any other communication form.

The following are principle components to be considered when developing communications systems:

- Protocol
- State Machines
- Architecture
- Thread Synchronization Techniques
- Buffering

Protocol

A protocol is an agreement that defines behavior. You do not have to have a protocol in your serial implementation, but your application probably will not perform any useful task. What you require is a communications protocol stack.

A communications protocol stack provides a set of integrated protocols that work at levels (or *layers*, in communications parlance). Each layer will define how the parties communicate. You should conceive your design with three principle layers: Physical, Transport, and Application.

You can also think of a protocol stack as a class hierarchy. The base class is the lowest layer, providing the most basic functions (in this case, the physical hardware and how the bits are physically transmitted). The more specialized the descendant class, the higher the level of the protocol. At the bottom (your "concrete" class) is the application interface.

At the lowest layer (known as the Physical layer), you might specify RS-232, 8-bit, 1 stop bit, no parity. Simple and unambiguous. These are international standards that should be followed. The only problem is making sure the wires in the cable are correct.

Next is the Transport layer. The concern here is to get the data to the application. This layer will define the format of the data such that you know when a communication begins and ends. It defines how you distinguish between valid and corrupt data within that message and what to do if things are not quite the way they should be.

At the Application layer, we define what the transmitted data means. Is the message a command, data to be processed, or an error report? Given meaning, we infer purpose, and that is the job of the application.

The process of developing a protocol can be summed up in 10 steps:

1. Understand the requirements of the protocol
2. Understand the nature of potential errors
3. Determine the performance requirements if appropriate
4. Estimate the data flow in both directions
5. Determine common aspects in messages

6. Determine the appropriate architecture

7. Determine a testing method

8. Implement

9. Test

10. Repeat steps 8 and 9 until the protocol performs as required

Defining the Protocols

Defining protocols can be as simple or as complicated as you see fit. Having a clear under-standing of what you need to communicate, as well as what you want to communicate, will be a good start. From that point, you can consider application requirements as the goal to be achieved and the lower layers (Transport and Physical) to be how you intend to do it.

Protocols can be synchronous or asynchronous, ASCII or binary, and simple or complex. Whatever your decision, you will need to be able to test it and prove it works under as many conditions as possible. Here, ASCII-based protocols are good because it is possible to use tools such as HyperTerminal to validate your own application's results.

Clearly, ASCII-based communication would not be acceptable for more data-intensive or secure applications; in these instances, the use of binary protocols is essential. Binary protocols allow a much greater level of control over the data and, in some ways, simplify the processing requirement. The corollary is that they are much more difficult to debug.

Synchronous protocolsare important where continuous validation and presence detecting are important. They are generally simpler to implement because the sender cannot send again until a response has been received and validated. Asynchronous protocols are intended to provide performance advantages where data is independent of sequence—that is, when the command you send has no bearing on the next one sent.

The Application Protocol

The application protocol concerns itself with communicating information in support of func-tionality, that is, sending commands to a device or requests to a server. These requests mean something in the context of the application and the responses will be interpreted likewise.

The application protocol understands the contents of the message packet, and it is important to define how the application should do this. We may choose to interrogate a device to see if its memory is valid or to set its internal real-time clock. The application knows what commands the device understands and in what format it is expecting those commands.

We should list our command set and the data to be transmitted and received with all such rele-vant information (including word and byte formats). This forms the basis of the whole purpose of the protocol stack. The lower layers provide the means and mechanisms by which this infor-mation gets to the intended destination.

The application protocol yields the nature of possible errors, such as corrupted data, invalid responses, and timeouts. These errors may be dealt with at various layers. If they are considered at this layer, it may be easier to provide the lower-layer protocols to reduce their likelihood.

In addition, the amount of data to be transferred and the kinds of messages that will be required will soon become clear. This is important for determining implementation issues. In an object-oriented world, similar messages and their associated processing methods yield definite base and derived classes. Creating such a class hierarchy naturally yields safer, more reliable, and more maintainable code.

The Transport Protocol

Understanding the requirements of the application protocol provides ways of simplifying the implementation issues. The transport protocol's job is to package the application message and ensure it gets to the intended destination. We can now assume that the application has provided us with a message packet or data block for transmission.

A message generally consists of definite sections: a header, a data block, and a tail. Information such as the data block length and message ID should be included in the header. It is also a good idea in serial communications to signal that the block is about to begin. This allows the receiver to ignore data, if a break in communications occurs, until the designated character arrives. If this character arrives before the expected point, an error has occurred and the message can be abandoned.

In the application protocol we suggested listing the command set with all the relevant data fields. We can now extend this practical concept to include the transport protocol, which acts as a wrapper for the application protocol data.

A representation of this might be

```
<msgStartCharacter>;<msgLength>;<msgID>;<msgDataBlock>;<msgCheckSum>;
➡<msgEndCharacter>
```

where each bracketed element (<msgDataBlock>, for example) indicates a component of the message.

This format provides a useful basis for providing an interface. The receiver will look for a msgStartCharacter. When this is received, the receiver knows that this must be the start of the message. The next component is msgLength, the length (in bytes of the data block). Any msgStartCharacter received before msgLength data bytes should be interpreted as a valid component of the message. You read in that block, and you can then pass the msgID;msgDataBlock on to the higher-level application. However, you could also provide an error-detection protocol that says if you do not receive msgLength characters within your timeout period, you should ignore any that do arrive until you detect the next msgStartCharacter.

At this level, you may choose to implement a data-validation process whereby you encode a checksum within the message. <msgCheckSum> can be either a simple XOR (exclusive OR) of the total of the bytes in the data block or a complex CRC. You choose. The more complex the data validation, the more time it takes to create and validate. Your application will determine the likelihood of data errors (corruption in transmission, for example). If the environment is good and you have a short cable over RS232, an XOR checksum is fine. If you are going over unknown media (the Internet), a CRC is probably a far better choice.

If you have had a timeout or other error, the checksum will ensure that you are correct in ignoring the message. You may choose to implement a retry mechanism based on this feature.

An XOR checksum simply sums all the appropriate data bytes (those within the msgDataBlock component, for example) and XORs them with a known value. You can use 8-, 16- or 32-bit data formats. It is common to use unsigned values (simply ignore the sign bit and any bit carry values).

State Machines

To manage each protocol, the software must maintain information about what was sent so that it can properly determine how to respond. It needs to know what has been received in the past in case that affects the interpretation of the next input. It needs to know what to do when unexpected events occur during these sequences and what other vital pieces of data are required to deal properly with any request. As with all system software, you need a state machine.

State machines also enhance reliability. All related states can have appropriate messages to provide useful feedback to the application frontend.

Creating them is something you have probably done without realizing it. You probably have created buttons that are enabled or disabled according to the state of some other component on a form (OK and Cancel are prime candidates). This is a very simple state machine. A communications state machine is far more complex, but it has the same purpose.

Performance Versus Reliability

Your application will determine if you are interested in speed and efficiency or reliability and accuracy. Ideally, we want both, but this is tantamount to having your cake and eating it too. How do we achieve this? Is there a middle ground?

In serial terms, the faster you communicate, the better. However, the faster you go, the more error prone the communication is. Problems with cable length start to get significant over 50m with the standard PC COM Port RS-232. This problem is a result of the RS-232 port never having been intended to drive long cable runs, unlike the RS422 or R485 standard. You should be quite happy with a 4Km cable when using RS422.

Personally, I would rather have reliable data and go at the fastest possible rate, but this takes superior processing and equipment. If you are connecting to a local modem, you will be more concerned with the quality of the telephone line.

The data flow is important here. If you expect to receive lots of data in response to small transmissions, your receive side is far more important. If you intend to send large quantities and get small acknowledgements, your transmit side is king. In these cases, you can optimize your system to suit this requirement (buffer sizes, thread priority levels, and so on).

Errors

Errors will occur no matter how confident you are about your system and software. The nature of errors will also surprise you (it never ceases to amaze me).

Errors will occur in data, protocols, and interpretation—no matter how clear you think things are. Allowing for them at the outset is far better than trying to allow for them after you've written and devised your system.

You will get connection errors, synchronization errors, faulty message errors, data errors, and interpretation errors. Each has its own set of problems and resolutions. In this discussion, we allow for the basic ones (timeouts, data errors, and interpretation problems) as pointers to the importance of doing it right.

Architecture

Now you can consider the architecture of your serial input/output interface. Invariably, you will need to thread it on a computer. You will not get a responsive GUI if you do not. You should avoid threading if, and only if, you are toying with a very simple terminal-style system. Personally, I would still thread it.

Threading is imperative to making Windows work for you. The issue is what to thread and to what extent. If I thread, how do I control the processes?

This, in my opinion, is the most fascinating and probably the most fun part of making your system work. Multithreading is glorious when you get it right. You can achieve real performance and very impressive applications if you understand the concept, and achieving it is very satisfying.

If your protocol is purely asynchronous, you can send and receive completely independent messages and you will have to thread both the input and output. If you require a level of synchronicity (that is, you send a message and there will be a subsequent response), you may choose to have only one thread doing the reading and the writing.

In the main, I have both a "read" thread and a "write" thread. The advantages to me are that I can quickly respond to inbound data and also know efficiently when I have not received a response to a message I sent. Large amounts of data in or out generally pose no performance overhead on the system, and I am free to perform other application tasks concurrently.

Thread Synchronization Techniques

You must communicate with your threads. I use events to signal threads to do their work. Events are simple and effective. The thread awaits several events to be signaled. The write thread has an event that means "message ready, please send." Data to be sent is passed to the write thread by a public interface message (function call). This writes data via a critical section into the thread's private data space ready to be sent. At the same time, the write thread signals the read thread that data has been written, providing an efficient timeout validation system.

The read thread is awaiting the signal from the operating system to indicate data available. This causes the read thread to check to see how much data is available, read it into its internal buffer, and then signal the application via a `PostMessage()` call to start the protocol sequence.

I use windows messaging from the read thread to the application to indicate that data or a message has been received. This is reasonable given that if the write fails, the read thread timeout will occur and a failure message will arrive at the application via the read thread.

It is also a good idea to contain your threads within your protocol stack (or class)—or at least hide the application from direct interaction. This means that you can ensure your internal protocol state machine is not interfered with.

In this class, the received data is copied to an internal buffer. In so doing, you can allow for variable-length messages. If you have fixed-length messages, you can modify the read thread to read fixed-length blocks.

The protocol class is that which caused the message to be sent. It knows what to expect and normally how much data. This is not always possible. Some applications I have worked on have a protocol where the messages can be of variable lengths and the amount of response data is also not known. This is why taking into account the processing issues when planning your protocol is important.

The protocol class processes the input when it determines enough data has arrived to make a good analysis. The process does enable more data to arrive if the message is incomplete.

Finally, after the protocol class has processed the data, it sends a message to the application to say "received x msg and here is the data." If you create local data structures (or objects) within this class, remember to delete them in the application when you have finished with them.

Buffering

Buffering is a subject rarely mentioned, but one that will come back to bite you if you do not consider it early in your design process. Outbound data is best not buffered by your application unless you have lots to send. If you are a controller device sending "small" messages frequently to a slave, it is probably best not to buffer output at all. I even set the Windows Device Driver TX Buffer to 0 bytes as a matter of course. This ensures that I am not fooled into assuming data is transmitted because the `WriteFile()` command says so. I have a small receive buffer to provide a less bursty receive stream—although in applications with baudrates of up to 56Kbps, this is probably unnecessary, even on slow laptops.

What is necessary is to store the received data in a FIFO buffer. You get this free with the `AnsiString` class (I refer to it as `String`), adding new data to the end and removing processed data from the front. This is very effective and pretty quick. You can also use `String` for 8-bit binary data, and this is great to work with BlobStreams if you want to use a database to store your data.

If you are feeling particularly brave, the STL has good queue facilities that you might want to consider. The only issue to consider is performance. Using STL may make for more effective and flexible software, but the cost is usually in performance. When dealing with complex protocols, having control over data processing may be very important in debugging and testing.

Concluding Remarks on Serial Communications

The trick to serial communications is defining the protocol. From this, your specific (or general) thread architecture becomes clear. You can then determine how you want to perform interthread communications and how much buffering you want to do.

The protocol depends on your application and your considerations for error management, reliability, accuracy, performance, and maintainability. Many people forget that someone may have to maintain the code (including you) long after you write it. Having a clear idea of what you want to achieve and how you intend to do it is vital.

Learn about threading. You will find a rich set of operating system support for thread synchronization techniques including events, critical sections, and posting messages.

> **NOTE**
>
> In the `SerialIO` folder on the CD-ROM that accompanies this book, you will find an example project, `cd5Book.bpr`, for using serial communications. The project code provides examples of how you might structure your serial communications system. This code shows how to open, close, read, and write to the serial ports using Overlapped Input/Output, multithreading techniques, interthread communication techniques, and buffering.
>
> Due to space limitations, it is not possible to document the issues covered in more detail. Remember that this code is a fragment of a much larger system that performs proprietary operations, and as such is a vastly distilled variation.

Internet Protocols—SMTP, FTP, HTTP, POP3

With the expanding nature of the Internet and client/server programming, the need for rapid development of network-enabled applications is at a high level. The glue that holds client/server software together is the protocol that you use. A protocol is a code used by an application to transmit information in a standardized way to other applications. There will be times when it is beneficial to develop your own protocol for an application but, more often than not, you will use one of the many predefined protocols. In this section, we will explore the numerous components that C++Builder provides to allow for the rapid development of applications utilizing various protocols. Specifically, we will

- Tour the Internet and FastNet component tabs
- Examine example applications using HTTP, POP, SMTP, and TCP/IP.

Tour of Component Tabs

In C++Builder versions 3 and 4, all of the Internet programming components were included in a single tab, the Internet tab. For version 5 of C++Builder, Inprise has split the components into two sections. The first section is the Internet tab. This tab has the `TClientSocket` and `TServerSocket` components, as well as the various `PageProducer` components used to create Web server extension applications. A complete list of components can be found in Table 12.1. The second section is the FastNet tab; this tab has all of the FastNet ActiveX components that can be used to build a variety of network-enabled applications. A complete list of FastNet components can be found in Table 12.2.

TABLE 12.1 Internet Tab Components

Component	Use
TClientSocket	Encapsulates Winsock for use in client applications
TServerSocket	Encapsulates Winsock for use in server applications
TWebDispatcher	Allows a data module to be used as a Web server extension
TPageProducer	Used to convert an HTML template into an HTML document
TQueryTableProducer	Used to convert a TQuery into an HTML table
TDataSetTableProducer	Used to convert a TDataSet into an HTML table
TDataSetPageProducer	Used to apply the results of a TDataSet into an HTML document
TCppWebBrowser	Encapsulates the Internet Explorer Web browser for use in client applications

TABLE 12.2 FastNet Tab Components

Component	Use
TNMDayTime	Used for getting the date and time from Internet daytime servers
TNMMsg	Used for sending simple ASCII text messages across the Internet or an intranet using the TCP/IP protocol
TNMMsgServ	Used for creating a server to process TNMMsg messages
TNMEcho	Used for sending text to an Internet echo server and having that text echoed back to you
TNMFTP	Used to create an FTP client application
TNMHTTP	Used for conducting HTTP transfers across the World Wide Web
TNMNNTP	Used for the reading and posting of Internet news articles on Internet and intranet news servers
TNMStrm	Used for sending streams to a stream server across the Internet or an intranet
TNMStrmServ	Used for creating a stream server to receive streams across the Internet or an intranet
TNMPOP3	Used to create a client application to read email using the POP3 protocol
TNMSMTP	Used to create a client application to send email using the SMTP protocol
TNMTime	Used for getting the time from Internet time servers
TNUDP	Used for implementing the User Datagram Protocol (UDP) for sending datagram packets across the Internet or an intranet
TNMURL	Used to decode a URL into a user-readable string or to encode a readable string into a URL
TNMUUProcessor	Used to encode or decode MIME or uuencoded documents
Tpowersock	The base class for many of the FastNet socket components
TNMGeneralServer	The base class for developing multithreaded Internet servers
TNMFinger	Used for getting information about a user from an Internet finger server using the Finger protocol

An Example Chat Server

The first project that we will undertake is a client/server chat program. This program will allow users to connect to a central server and to send messages to other connected users. You can find the example chat server project, ChatServer.bpr, in the Chat\Server folder on the CD-ROM that accompanies this book.

Creating the Application

Create a new application by performing the following steps:

1. Select the File, New menu item. This will give you a form named Form1 and a .cpp file named Unit1.cpp.

2. Add a TMemo component to Form1 and assign LogMemo to its name property.

3. Add a TPanel component and assign alTop to its align property. Clear the Caption property of the panel.

4. Set the align property for LogMemo to alClient.

5. Add two TButton components to Panel1, one named StartButton and one named StopButton.

6. Add a TLabel component with the caption Port and a TEdit component with its name set to PortEdit.

7. Add a TServerSocket component from the Internet tab to the form and set its name to MyServer. You should arrange your components so that they resemble Figure 12.1.

8. Select the File, Save All menu item. This will bring up a Save dialog box. Place this project in its own directory; I recommend the folder name Server and the project name ChatServer.

FIGURE 12.1
The appropriate screen layout for the server.

Setting Up the User List

The next step is to create a TStringList to hold the currently connected users. To do this, first go to the Unit1.h file and add the line TStringList *ConnectedList; under the private: declaration.

Now go to the Unit1.cpp file and add to the form's OnCreate() method, as shown in the following:

```
void __fastcall TForm1::FormCreate(TObject *Sender)
{
    ConnectedList = new TStringList();
}
```

Starting and Stopping the Server

The third step in the project is to add code to the Start and Stop buttons. This will enable you to start and stop the server. In the OnClick() event of StartButton, add the following code:

```
void __fastcall TForm1::StartButtonClick(TObject *Sender)
{
    MyServer->Port = PortEdit->Text.ToIntDef(1971);
    Caption = MyServer->Port;
    MyServer->Active = true;
    StopButton->Enabled = true;
    StartButton->Enabled = false;
    PortEdit->Enabled = false;
}
```

The first line sets the port for your server. Because `PortEdit->Text` is an `AnsiString`, use the `ToIntDef()` method. This allows you to set a default value for the port in the event that the `PortEdit->Text` string is not a valid integer.

Next, add some code to the `OnClick()` event of the `StopButton` component as follows:

```
void __fastcall TForm1::StopButtonClick(TObject *Sender)
{
        MyServer->Active = false;
        StartButton->Enabled = true;
        StopButton->Enabled = false;
        PortEdit->Enabled = true;
}
```

You now have a program that allows you to set the port number that the chat server will use, as well as start and stop the server. Port numbers allow a single system, identified by the `Host` or `Address` property, to host multiple connections simultaneously. Some example default port numbers are 80 for Web servers and 23 for Telnet servers. The default server for the ChatServer is 1971. Port numbers can range from 1 to 9999.

Managing Connections

The next thing to do is manage the system when users log in and log off the server. First, you will add the following lines of code to the `OnClientConnect()` of `MyServer`:

```
void __fastcall TForm1::MyServerClientConnect(TObject *Sender,
     TCustomWinSocket *Socket)
{
    LogMemo->Lines->Add(Socket->RemoteAddress + " has connected.");
    ConnectedList->AddObject(Socket->RemoteAddress, Socket);
}
```

This adds a line to the `LogMemo`, telling you the address from which the client is connecting. Then you add the socket that the client is connecting with to the `ConnectedList` using the client address as your identifier string.

In the `OnClientDisconnect()` event for `MyServer`, you will want to add the following lines:

```
void __fastcall TForm1::MyServerClientDisconnect(TObject *Sender,
     TCustomWinSocket *Socket)
{
```

```
LogMemo->Lines->Add(Socket->RemoteAddress + " has disconnected.");
SendMessage(Format("%s has disconnected.",
    OPENARRAY(TVarRec,
        (ConnectedList->Strings[ConnectedList->IndexOfObject(Socket)]))),
        "Server");
ConnectedList->Delete(ConnectedList->IndexOfObject(Socket));
}
```

This adds a line to the LogMemo telling you that a client has disconnected. You then call the SendMessage() method, which will be added next, to inform all the currently connected users that a user has left.

Handling a Username and Sending Messages

The last thing you need to do for your server program is enable it to handle a username and to send messages to the users that are connected to the server. First, create a new method called SendMessage(). To do this, go into the Unit1.h file and add the following line under the public: declaration:

```
void __fastcall SendMessage(AnsiString aMessage, AnsiString aFrom);
```

In the Unit1.cpp, create a new method called SendMessage(), with two AnsiString parameters, aMessage and aFrom. Then add the following code to the end of your file:

```
void __fastcall TForm1::SendMessage(AnsiString aMessage, AnsiString aFrom)
{
    for(int i=0;i<MyServer->Socket->ActiveConnections;i++)
    {
        if(aFrom == "Server")
            MyServer->Socket->Connections[i]->SendText(
                Format("%s",OPENARRAY(TVarRec,(aMessage))));
        else
            MyServer->Socket->Connections[i]->SendText(
                Format("%s said: %s",OPENARRAY(TVarRec,(aFrom, aMessage))));
    }
}
```

This function cycles through all the connected sockets and sends a message formatted in the User said: text format (for example, if the user John types I am the walrus, the message sent to the connected sockets would be John said: I am the walrus). In the event that it is a message sent by the server, it sends only the message.

The last thing you need to do is handle messages sent from the client. This currently is broken into two categories: messages to be sent to other users and a special message to set the username of the user.

Add the code shown in Listing 12.1 to the OnClientRead() event of MyServer.

Adding Socket

In this step, you will
this component to My
Winsock connection
plug for your outlet.

Now you will arrange
achieved. Figure 12.2

FIGURE 12.2
A possible layout for the clie

It is now time to add fi
ConnectButton, add th

```
void __fastcall TFoi
{
    MySocket->Addres
    MySocket->Port =
    MySocket->Active

    ConnectButton->E
    DisconnectButtor
    MemoOut->Enabled
}
```

This function will set th
First, set the Address pr
method of AnsiString t
value in the PortEdit te
ting the Active property
connected, and enable th
ponent to allow the user

Now that you have provi
to stop it. In the OnClick
code:

```
void __fastcall TForm
{
    MySocket->Active

    ConnectButton->En
```

LISTING 12.1 OnClientRead Event

```
void __fastcall TForm1::MyServerClientRead(TObject *Sender,
    TCustomWinSocket *Socket)
{
    AnsiString TextIn, CurrentName;
    int iIndex;

    TextIn = Socket->ReceiveText();
    iIndex = ConnectedList->IndexOfObject(Socket);
    if(iIndex == -1)
        return;

    TStringList *UserName = new TStringList();

    if(TextIn.Pos("UserName=") == 1)
    {
        //Set User Name
        UserName->Text = TextIn;
        ConnectedList->Strings[iIndex] = UserName->Values["UserName"];
        SendMessage(Format("%s has connected.",
                        OPENARRAY(TVarRec,
                                (UserName->Values["UserName"]))),"Server");
    }
    else
    {
        //Send Message
        CurrentName = ConnectedList->Strings[iIndex];
        SendMessage(TextIn, CurrentName);
    }

    delete UserName;
}
```

The first thing you did in Listing 12.1 is set the ReceiveText of the socket to an AnsiString variable. Then you determined whether the socket was currently on your connected list; it should always be on the connected list, but better safe than sorry. You then checked to see if it is a UserName function. The text value of the UserName TStringList is set to the ReceiveText if it is a username. This allows the use of the Name=Value properties of the TStringList class. Next, you set the ConnectedList string to the UserName value. Finally, you send a message to all the users to let them know that a new user has connected and the name of that user. If it is not a UserName message, pass the ReceiveText and the user's name to the SendMessage() method.

You now have written a complete chat server. This will allow numerous clients to connect and exchange simple text messages. Later in the chapter, you will add HTTP capabilities to the server so that it can be started remotely via a Web browser and also allow you to view a list of

currentl
run the p

An E>

Now tha
commun
simple cl
send a m
might inc
example
accompar

Creatin

First, crea
This will
File, Save
Server.bj
by perforr

   1. Plac
     to Mr
     nam
   2. You
     set tr
   3. Set M
     you r
   4. Wher
     want
     conn
     of the
   5. Now

     a.

     b.

     c.

   6. The fi
     their c

Creating the Application

First you need to create a new application project by selecting the New Application option from the File menu. This will create a new application project with a form named Form1 and a unit file named Unit1.cpp. At this point you should select the File, Save All menu item. I recommend creating a new folder entitled Mail, and use the name Mail for the project. After you have the project started, you should set up the user interface by doing the following:

1. Place a TListView component from the Win32 tab on the form. Set the align property of the ListView to alBottom, and leave the name with the default ListView1.

2. Add two buttons to the form; name the first CheckMail with a caption of Check Mail, and name the second NewButton with a caption of New Mail.

3. Add three TEdit components named UserEdit, PasswordEdit, and HostEdit. Set the PasswordChar property of the PasswordEdit component to * or whatever character you want to show up in the edit box in place of the password the user enters. You may also want to assign a default mail server at this point. To do so, set the Text property of the HostEdit component to the default mail server (for example, mail.yourserver.com).

4. Add three TLabel components and set their caption properties as User Name, Password, and Server.

5. Now open the column editor by double-clicking the ListView1 component. Add two columns; the first will be called From and the second will be Subject.

6. Set the ViewStyle property of ListView1 to vsReport.

7. Add a TNMPOP3 component from the FastNet tab to your form. At this point, your application should look like Figure 12.3.

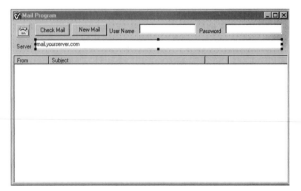

FIGURE 12.3

A possible layout for the Mail email window.

Adding POP Components and Getting Mail

Your first step here will be to go to the .h file for Unit1 and add a few public variables. In the public section, add the following line:

```
bool bConnected, bSummary
```

Then add the line

```
int myId
```

You are now ready to start adding some functionality to the application. The first thing you need to do is contact the POP server, authenticate yourself, and download a list of mail that is waiting to be read. In the OnClick event of the CheckMail component, add the code shown in Listing 12.2.

LISTING 12.2 CheckMail

```
void __fastcall TForm1::CheckMailClick(TObject *Sender)
{
    bConnected = false;
    NMPOP31->UserID = UserEdit->Text;
    NMPOP31->Password = PasswordEdit->Text;
    NMPOP31->Host = HostEdit->Text;
    NMPOP31->Connect();

    if(NMPOP31->Connected)
    {
        if(NMPOP31->MailCount > 0)
        {
            ListView1->Items->Clear();
            bSummary = true;
            for(int i = 0; i < NMPOP31->MailCount; i++)
            {
                myId = i + 1;
                NMPOP31->GetSummary(myId);
            }
        }
        else
            ShowMessage("No messages waiting");

        NMPOP31->Disconnect();
    }
}
```

The first thing in Listing 12.2 is to set the public variable bConnected to false and then set the properties in the NMPOP31 components. UserID is the name of the user on the POP server, and Password is that user's password. Host is the name of the POP server, for example mail.myserver.com.

After these properties are set, you connect to the server by calling the Connect() method. Following the connect attempt, check the Connected property of the TNMPOP3 component to determine if the connection was successful. If so, begin to process the list of messages waiting on the server. The first thing is to clear all the elements that were in ListView1. Then you set the bSummary variable to true to let the program know that you are getting summaries and not the whole message.

You then proceed to loop a number of times equal to the MailCount property of the TNMPOP3 component, which gives the number of messages waiting to be read on the server. The first thing you do in the loop is set the global variable myid equal to the loop value plus 1. Then you call the GetSummary() method of the TNMPOP3 component. This retrieves the summary for the message passed by the variable myId, and it also fires the RetrieveEnd event of the TNMPOP3 component. In the event that there is no mail waiting on the server, you will display the message No Messages Waiting to the user.

The final thing is to call the Disconnect() method of NMPOP31; this will disconnect you from the server. The last step in this section is to add code to the RetrieveEnd event of the NMPOP31 component, so add the following code to that event:

```
void __fastcall TForm1::NMPOP31RetrieveEnd(TObject *Sender)
{
    if(bSummary)
    {
        TListItem *Temp = ListView1->Items->Add();

        Temp->Caption = NMPOP31->Summary->From;
        Temp->SubItems->Add(NMPOP31->Summary->Subject);
        Temp->SubItems->Add(myId);
    }
}
```

There are two ways the RetrieveEnd event can be fired; the first is when a summary occurs, and the second is when a message is retrieved. To differentiate between the two, you need to add the global variable bSummary to the unit and set it to True when summarizing and False when retrieving a message. If you are summarizing, add a line to the ListView1 component. First, create a TListItem variable called Temp and set it equal to the ListView1->Items->Add return value. This gives the new ListView1 item. Next, you set the caption of the ListItem to the sender of the message. You obtain this from the From property of the Summary object found in NMPOP31. Then add the Subject as a subitem to the ListItem and the current ID (myId) as a second subitem. At this point, a line in the ListView1 should be present for each message waiting for the user on the mail server. Now that you can list the messages, you need to be able to read mail when you receive it.

Retrieving and Viewing Mail

The first thing to do in this step is create a new form that will be used to view a mail message. To do this, select the New Form option of the File menu. This will create a new form named Form2 and a new unit named Unit2. On this form, do the following:

1. Add a TPanel and set its align property to alTop and its caption to blank.

2. To Panel1, add four TLabel components called Label1, Label2, FromLabel, SubjectLabel.

3. Set Label1's caption to From and Label2's caption to Subject. At this point, leave the captions for FromLabel and SubjectLabel at their default values.

4. Add a TButton to the Panel and name it CloseButton.

5. Add the TMemo component to Form2 and set its align property to alClient.

6. Set the name property of the TMemo component to MailMemo. At this point, Form2 should look like Figure 12.4.

The only code for this form is to add the following line to the OnClick event of the CloseButton:

```
Close();
```

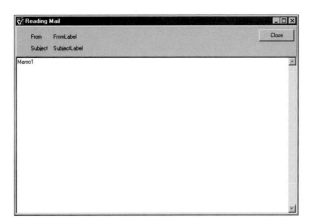

FIGURE 12.4

A possible layout for the mail reading form.

The next thing we need to do to retrieve and view mail is to include Unit2 in the main form (Form1). In Unit1.cpp, select the Include File Header option from the File menu and select Unit2. This will enable you to instantiate and manipulate copies of Form2 in Form1. The next thing to do is write code to start a copy of Form2 and fill it in with information when a user wants to read mail.

First, set the RowSelect property of ListView1 to True; this will allow a user to select an item in the ListView by clicking the entire row and not just the first element. Next, add code for when the user double-clicks an element in ListView1. In the ListView1 OnDblClick event, write the following code:

```
void __fastcall TForm1::ListView1DblClick(TObject *Sender)
{
    if(!NMPOP31->Connected)
        NMPOP31->Connect();
    if(ListView1->SelCount > 0)
    {
        bSummary = false;
        NMPOP31->GetMailMessage(
                    ListView1->Selected->SubItems->Strings[1].ToIntDef(0));
    }
    NMPOP31->Disconnect();
}
```

The first thing here is to determine if you have a connection to the server already and, if not, connect to the server by calling the Connect() method of NMPOP31. The next thing is to determine if there is an item selected in the ListView; this is done to prevent an error if a user double-clicks the ListView without actually selecting a mail message. After it is determined that there is a message to retrieve, set the global variable bSummary to False, because you are retrieving the entire message and not just the message summary. The next code line calls the GetMailMessage() method of NMPOP31 and passes the ID of the message you want to retrieve to this method. You obtain the ID of the message from the SubItems property of the selected item. You called the ToIntDef() method of AnsiString to ensure that you have a valid integer number.

Finally, disconnect from the server before leaving the subroutine. The GetMailMessage() method will cause an OnRetrieveEnd event to be fired, and this time you want to view the entire message, so you need to add some new code to the OnRetrieveEnd event of NMPOP31. Add the bold code from Listing 12.3 to the OnRetrieveEnd event.

LISTING 12.3   The OnRetrieveEnd Event

```
void __fastcall TForm1::NMPOP31RetrieveEnd(TObject *Sender)
{
    if(bSummary)
    {
        TListItem *Temp = ListView1->Items->Add();

        Temp->Caption = NMPOP31->Summary->From;
        Temp->SubItems->Add(NMPOP31->Summary->Subject);
        Temp->SubItems->Add(myId);
    }
    //New Code
```

LISTING 12.3   Continued

```
    else
    {
        TForm2 *Temp = new TForm2(NULL);
        Temp->MailMemo->Lines->Assign(NMPOP31->MailMessage->Body);
        Temp->FromLabel->Caption = NMPOP31->MailMessage->From;
        Temp->SubjectLabel->Caption = NMPOP31->MailMessage->Subject;
        Temp->Show();
    }
}
```

The first thing that occurs in Listing 12.3 is that you create a new instance of TForm2 and assign it to the variable Temp. Then you proceed to set the properties of Temp to represent the mail message that you are attempting to view. First, call the Assign() method of MailMemo's Lines, which is a TStringList object. This sets the MailMemo text to the body of the MailMessage object. Next, set the From label and the Subject label to Sender and Subject, respectively, as defined by the MailMessage object in NMPOP31. The last thing to do is call the Show() method of Temp.

At this point, you have a fully functioning mail reader program. However, reading mail is only half the battle, so we also need to develop a way to send mail in our email application.

Composing and Sending Mail

In this step, you will develop a form for composing email and add the code to use SMTP to send the mail to a mail server. The first thing is to add a new form to the project by selecting the New Form option in the File menu. This will add a form named Form3 and a unit named Unit3 to the project. Now add the user interface elements to Form3 by doing the following:

1. Add a TPanel to Form3 and set its align property to alTop. Set the caption property of Panel1 to blank.

2. Add a TMemo to Form3 and name this MessageMemo. Set the align property of MessageMemo to alClient.

3. Add five TEdit components to Panel1 named ToEdit, FromEdit, SubjectEdit, CCEdit, and BCCEdit. Clear the Text property of each TEdit.

4. Add five TLabel components to Panel1. Set the caption property of these as To, From, Subject, CC, and BCC.

5. Add a TNMSMTP component from the FastNet tab to the form. Leave the name property as the default, NMSMTP1.

6. Add two TButton components. Name one of these SendButton with a caption of Send, and name the other CancelButton with a caption of Cancel. At this point, your form should look like Figure 12.5.

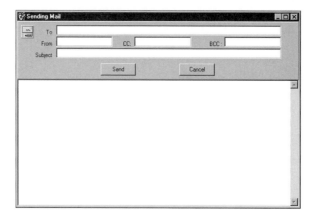

FIGURE 12.5

A possible layout for the email composing form.

Now that you have the user interface defined, all that remains is to include Unit1.h in the Unit3 file so, while in Unit3, select the Include Unit Header option from the File menu and select Unit1 from the resulting dialog box. Now you are ready to add SMTP support to the email program. In the OnClick event of SendButton, add the code shown in Listing 12.4.

LISTING 12.4   The OnClick Event of SendButton

```
void __fastcall TForm3::SendButtonClick(TObject *Sender)
{
    NMSMTP1->PostMessage->ToAddress->Clear();
    NMSMTP1->PostMessage->ToBlindCarbonCopy->Clear();
    NMSMTP1->PostMessage->ToCarbonCopy->Clear();

    NMSMTP1->PostMessage->ToAddress->CommaText = ToEdit->Text;
    NMSMTP1->PostMessage->FromAddress = FromEdit->Text;
    NMSMTP1->PostMessage->ReplyTo = FromEdit->Text;
    NMSMTP1->PostMessage->ToBlindCarbonCopy->CommaText = BCCEdit->Text;
    NMSMTP1->PostMessage->ToCarbonCopy->CommaText = CCEdit->Text;
    NMSMTP1->PostMessage->Body->Assign(MessageMemo->Lines);
    NMSMTP1->PostMessage->Subject = SubjectEdit->Text;


    NMSMTP1->PostMessage->LocalProgram = "My Emailer";

    if(NMSMTP1->Connected)
        NMSMTP1->Disconnect();

    NMSMTP1->UserID = Form1->UserEdit->Text;
    NMSMTP1->Host = Form1->HostEdit->Text;
    NMSMTP1->Connect();
```

Listing 12.4 Continued

```
    NMSMTP1->SendMail ();
}
```

The first thing is to clear out the information that is in the `NMSMTP1` component. The primary information object in `TNMSMTP` is `PostMessage`, which contains all the information relating to the message, including the body of the message and the Send To list.

Next, set the items to be sent. First, set the `ToAddress` property of `PostMessage`, which is a `TStringList` containing all the addresses to which to send the message. By using the `CommaText` property of `ToAddress`, you allow the user to have multiple recipients in the To field by separating them with a comma or a space. Then, set the `FromAddress` property according to the `FromEdit` text box. Set the `BlindCarbonCopy` property, which is similar to the `ToAddress` property; the difference is that `BlindCarbonCopy` is not included in the To and CC fields of the email. Then set the `ToCarbonCopy` property, which is identical to the `BlindCarbonCopy` property with the exception that those carbon copied are listed in the email header.

Next, assign the values of `MessageMemo` to the `Body` property of `PostMessage` (this is the actual text of the email message). Then set the `Subject` property, based on the `SubjectEdit` text box from the form. The last property you set is `LocalProgram`; this can be anything you want and is useful mainly if you are developing an integrated email sender/reader and need to know when your application has sent a message.

Now that the message is set, you need to set the properties for `NMSMTP1` and then send the message. First, check to ensure that the `NMSMTP1` component is not connected; if it is, you must first disconnect it. Then, set the `UserID` and `Host` properties of the component to the values that are defined in `Form1`, which is the main form of the email program. Finally, connect to the SMTP server and call the `SendMail()` function, which sends the mail.

All that is left on this form is to handle the success or failure of the mail message and to add `Close` code to the `OnClick` event of the `CancelButton`. The code for these events should be as follows:

```
void __fastcall TForm3::NMSMTP1Success(TObject *Sender)
{
    ShowMessage("Send Message Successful");
    Close();
}

void __fastcall TForm3::NMSMTP1Failure(TObject *Sender)
{
    ShowMessage("Send Message Failed");
}

void __fastcall TForm3::CancelButtonClick(TObject *Sender)
{
```

```
    Close();
}
```

Include Unit3 in the Unit1 code and add the code in the OnClick event of Form1's New Mail button to handle new mail. While in Unit1, select Include Unit Header and select Unit3. Then add the following code to the OnClick event of the NewMail component:

```
void __fastcall TForm1::NewButtonClick(TObject *Sender)
{
    TForm3 *OutMail = new TForm3(NULL);
    OutMail->ShowModal();
}
```

This will create an instance of Form3 and show it in a modal fashion. Finally, save this project and then run it. Congratulations: You have created an email client that is capable of sending and receiving mail.

In the demonstration version of the software, the mail is retained on the server when you read it. Most commercial software provides the user with the option to either save the mail on the server or delete it from the server when read or deleted, depending on the software. The TNMPOP3 component provides a DeleteMailMessage(int Number) method to allow for deleting messages from the server.

An Example HTTP Server

Perhaps the most widely used protocol in the world today is Hypertext Transfer Protocol (HTTP). Nearly every person who uses a computer has used a Web browser and visited a Web site. The browser is the HTTP client, and the site is the HTTP server. In this section, you will add some HTTP server functionality to your chat server. Specifically, you will learn how to do the following:

- View the status of the server remotely
- Start the server remotely
- View a list of the current users online

Adding the Web Server Socket

The first thing is to reopen the Chat Server application you developed earlier in this chapter. After you have the application open, add a second TServerSocket component from the Internet tab to the main form. This will be named HttpServer. You should then set the Port property of HttpServer to a port number of your choice. Port 80 is the standard port for HTML servers. If you are running a personal Web server or any other server on your chat server, you will need to select a port other than 80. For this example, I choose 8000. You will also need to determine what your IP address is. You can do this by running ipconfig.exe at a command prompt. Typically, a machine can use 127.0.0.1 to refer to itself as the localhost, but if you are behind a firewall or other such security, your IP address may be different. Next, set the Active property of HttpServer to True.

Adding Code to Handle the Server Requests

In a Web server, you typically would be expected to respond to a variety of request types and pass files and information back to the client. Because this example server is fairly basic and allows for only three functions, you have the advantage of hard coding all possible options for the server. The three functions that will be supported are Status, Start, and Users. You will treat each of these as a request for an HTML page. The request from your Web browser to activate the functions would be as follows (with your IP address in place of 127.0.0.1):

- http://127.0.0.1:8000/Status.htm
- http://127.0.0.1:8000/Start.htm
- http://127.0.0.1:8000/Users.htm

Add the code in Listing 12.5 to the OnClientConnect event of the HttpServer component.

LISTING 12.5 OnClientConnect Event

```
void __fastcall TForm1::HttpServerClientConnect(TObject *Sender,
    TCustomWinSocket *Socket)
{
    AnsiString aRequest, aResponse;

    aRequest = Socket->ReceiveText();

 if(aRequest.Pos("Status.htm") > 0)
    {
        aResponse = "<html><head><title>Status</title></head><body>Status :";
        aResponse += (MyServer->Active) ? "Running" : "Stopped";
        if(MyServer->Active)
        {
            aResponse += Format("<BR>Port: %d<BR>%d Users Connected",
                            OPENARRAY(TVarRec,(MyServer->Port,
                                MyServer->Socket->ActiveConnections)));
        }
        aResponse += "</body></html>";
    }
    else
    {
        if(aRequest.Pos("Start.htm") > 0)
        {
            if(!MyServer->Active)
                StartButton->Click();
            aResponse = "<html><head><title>Start</title></head>"
                        "<body>Started</body></html>";
        }
        else
        {
```

LISTING 12.5 Continued

```
            if(aRequest.Pos("Users.htm") > 0)
            {
                AnsiString aHead;

                aResponse = "";
                aHead = "<title>";
                for(int i=0; i< ConnectedList->Count; i++)
                {
                    aResponse += ConnectedList->Strings[i] + "<BR>";
                }
                aHead += ConnectedList->CommaText;
                aHead += "</title>";
                if(aResponse.Length() == 0)
                    aResponse = "No Users Connected";
                aResponse = "<html><head>" + aHead +
                            "</head><body>User List<br>" + aResponse +
                            "</body></html>";
            }
            else
            {
                aResponse = "<html><head><body>Invalid Request</body></html>";
            }
        }
    }

    Socket->SendText (aResponse);
    Socket->Close();
}
```

The first thing you do in this function is assign the browser's request to an `AnsiString` variable; this will allow for access to the request later in the function. Next, you determine the type of request it is. You do this by checking for the existence of one of the default pages in the request. When you find that you have a valid request, you process the request; otherwise, you proceed down the tree.

In the event that the request is a status request, you proceed to determine whether the server is started or not. If the server is started, you return a message of running and the port and number of users logged on. If the request is a start request, you determine if the server is running and, if it is not, you start the server and then return a message that the server is running. If the request is for the user list, you send a list of all the users defined by the `ConnectedList` property. Should it be an item that hasn't been defined, you return a standard error message.

After you have generated the response string, send that string to the Web browser via the socket's `SendText()` method. The last thing to do is call the `Close()` method on the socket;

this enables the Web browser to regain control of the client and render the HTML that you have returned to it.

There are many things you can do using this server as a base. You can increase the function available for complete remote administration of the chat server. You could allow the application to load pages from the server and display them to the browser, or even run CGI applications. This should provide you with the basics needed to start exploring HTTP server applications. At this point you should save the project and then run it.

Example FTP Client Software

With the advent of the World Wide Web and the spread of HTTP, File Transfer Protocol (FTP) seems to have diminished in popularity. Because most major Web browsers now have a form of FTP built into them, the demand for FTP clients has been shrinking. However, there are still plenty of legitimate uses for FTP, including auto-updating software and transferring files to and from a central facility.

To finish this examination of communication protocols, you will develop a simple FTP client using FastNet's TNMFTP component. You can find the example FTP client project, Ftp.bpr, in the Ftp folder on the CD-ROM that accompanies this book.

Creating the Application

As always, the first thing that you need to do is create a new application by choosing New Application from the File menu. Then do the following:

1. Place a TPanel on this new application, set the caption to blank, and set the align property to alTop.

2. Add a TListView component from the Win32 tab to the form; set its align property to alClient and its name property to MyTree.

3. Place three TLabel components on Panel1. Assign the caption property of these components the values User, Password, and Server.

4. Add three TEdit components and name them UserEdit, PasswordEdit, and ServerEdit. You can also set default values for all three, such as anonymous, mail@mail.com, and ftp.yourserver.com, respectively. Set the PasswordChar property of PasswordEdit to *.

5. Add three TButton components to Panel1 and name them StartButton, StopButton, and UploadButton. These buttons will have the captions Start, Stop, and Upload, respectively. Your user interface should now look similar to Figure 12.6.

Now that you have the user interface designed, you need to add some images to ImageList1. Double-click ImageList1 and then select act. I like to use the images from the Program Files\Common Files\Borland Shared\Images\Buttons directory and add fldropen.bmp and filenew.bmp. Because the bitmaps are 16×32 pixels and the Image component is set for

16×16, you will see a dialog box asking if you want to split the images. Select Yes and then delete the gray images from the component. You should now have two images—a folder image at index 0 and a file image at index 1.

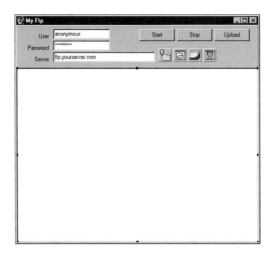

FIGURE 12.6
A possible user interface layout for the FTP program.

Connecting to the FTP Site

In this step, you will add functionality to the client that will allow access to a remote site. The first thing you need to do is add the following code to the OnClick event of the StartButton:

```
void __fastcall TForm1::StartButtonClick(TObject *Sender)
{
    MyFtp->Host = ServerEdit->Text;
    MyFtp->UserID = UserEdit->Text;
    MyFtp->Password = PasswordEdit->Text;
    MyFtp->Connect();
    StartButton->Enabled = false;
    StopButton->Enabled = true;
    MyTree->Items->Clear();
    DoList();
}
```

This is fairly straightforward code, similar to most of the other applications in this section. Start by setting the Host property of MyFtp to the server that the user has selected. Then set the user ID and password. For many sites, anonymous access is allowed. Anonymous access typically requires the user ID anonymous and an email address as the password. Then connect to the server, disable the Start button, and enable the Stop button. Next, clear all the items from the Items object of MyTree and call the DoList() function, which you will now add.

Listing Items from the Server

In this step, you will write a custom method to display the directory from the server. The first thing to do is set the `ParseList` property of `MyFtp` to `True`; this will store the information for the directory in the `TFTPDirectoryList` object, which is available through the runtime property `FTPDirectoryList` of `TNMFTP`. Next, add the following line to the public section of the file `Unit1.h`:

```
void __fastcall DoList();
```

Now you need to add the code shown in Listing 12.6 to `Unit1.cpp` at the bottom of the file.

LISTING 12.6   The `DoList()` Function

```cpp
void __fastcall TForm1::DoList()
{
    TTreeNode *Temp, *Root;
    int i;
    TCursor Save_Cursor = Screen->Cursor;

    Screen->Cursor = crHourGlass;     // Show hourglass cursor
    Root = MyTree->Selected;
    MyFtp->List();
    MyTree->Items->BeginUpdate();
    for(i=0;i<MyFtp->FTPDirectoryList->Attribute->Count;i++)
    {
        Temp = MyTree->Items->AddChild(
                        Root, MyFtp->FTPDirectoryList->name->Strings[i]);
        if((MyFtp->FTPDirectoryList->Attribute->Strings[i])[1] == 'd')
        {
            //Folder
            Temp->ImageIndex = 0;
            Temp->SelectedIndex = 0;
        }
        else
        {
            //File
            Temp->ImageIndex = 1;
            Temp->SelectedIndex = 1;
        }
    }
    MyTree->AlphaSort();
    MyTree->Items->EndUpdate();
    if(Root)
        Root->Expand(true);
    Screen->Cursor = Save_Cursor;
}
```

12

The first thing in Listing 12.6 is to save the current cursor so that you can restore the cursor at a later time. Then set the cursor to the hourglass, which is customary for an application that is processing. Next, set a TTreeNode object to the selected element MyTree; if no element is selected, this will be a NULL object, which is what you want in this case. Next you call the List() method of MyFtp. (There is a second listing method, Nlist(), that provides only the names of the elements, but that is not useful for this application.)

Call the BeginUpdate() method of the TTreeNodes object for MyTree; this will prevent the screen from updating until after you call the EndUpdate() method. This greatly increases the processing speed of the list display. You then cycle through the Attributes list of the TFTPDirectoryList element FTPDirectoryList. Because the Attributes list and the name list of FTPDirectoryList correspond to each other, you can use the same loop to process element type and name. While cycling through the Attributes list, first create a new TTreeNode as a child to the selected item, which if NULL is considered root. The caption for this is the element in the name list. Next, check the first character of the Attributes element; if it is a d, the object is a directory and you set the image and selected indexes to 0, which represents a directory image. Otherwise, set the indexes to 1 to represent a file.

Sort the tree and call the EndUpdate() method, which allows the screen to update. Next, check to see if there is a selected item and, if so, expand the elements under that item. Finally, set the screen cursor back to its original item.

Sorting the List and Handling Directory Changes and File Downloading

In this step, you'll sort the list first by type and then alphabetically within each type. Then you'll write a function that determines the full path of a selected node. Finally, you'll learn how to handle a double-click event in MyList to change directories or download a file.

The first thing to do is to set the SortType property of MyTree to stText and add the following code to the OnCompare event of MyTree:

```
void __fastcall TForm1::MyTreeCompare(TObject *Sender, TTreeNode *Node1,
     TTreeNode *Node2, int Data, int &Compare)
{
    if(Node1->ImageIndex > Node2->ImageIndex)
        Compare = 1;
    else
        if(Node1->ImageIndex == Node2->ImageIndex)
            Compare = CompareStr(Node1->Text, Node2->Text);
        else
            Compare = -1;
}
```

The first comparison is of ImageIndex. If the index of the first is greater, it is a file, and Compare is set to 1. If it is not greater, see if the indexes are the same, in which case both are files or both are directories. In that case, call the CompareStr() function, passing it the text from each node as an argument. If the index of the first is not greater and the indexes are not the same, set Compare to -1, because the first element is a directory and the second is a file.

When a user double-clicks an item in MyList, one of three things should occur:

- If it is a file, a download should begin.
- If it is an unloaded directory, it should list.
- If it is a loaded directory, it should expand.

The third option is the default option of TTreeView—it will expand automatically with no code necessary. To handle the other two possibilities, you need to add the code from Listing 12.7 to the OnDblClick event of MyTree.

LISTING 12.7   OnDblClick Event of MyTree

```
void __fastcall TForm1::MyTreeDblClick(TObject *Sender)
{
    if(MyTree->Selected->ImageIndex == 0)
    {
        if(MyTree->Selected->Count == 0)
        {
            MyFtp->ChangeDir(GetPath());
            DoList();
        }
    }
    else
    {
        AnsiString RemoteFile;

        RemoteFile = GetPath();
        SaveDialog1->FileName = MyTree->Selected->Text;
        if(SaveDialog1->Execute())
            MyFtp->Download(RemoteFile, SaveDialog1->FileName);
    }
}
```

First, determine if it is a directory or file that has been clicked. For a directory you have two choices: It is either a directory that has children and thus has been loaded already or it is a directory that has never been loaded and needs to be loaded. Check to see if the Count element of the Selected element is equal to 0. If so, it is an unloaded directory, so call the ChangeDir() method of MyFtp and pass the result of the GetPath() method as the directory argument. Then call the DoList() method to add the elements from the directory to the tree.

If it is a file you're dealing with, first set a local variable (RemoteFile) to the result of the GetPath() method. Next, set the FileName property of SaveDialog1 to the text of the selected node. Then call the `execute()` method of `SaveDialog1`. If the dialog ends with Cancel, do nothing; otherwise, call the `Download()` function of `MyFtp`, passing it the variable `RemoteFile` and the `FileName` property of `SaveDialog1`.

The `GetPath()` method is quite important to the download and directory portion of the application. Because a directory tree is inherent in the `MyList` item, use that to build a qualified pathname for directories or files. Add the following line to the public section of the `Unit1.h` file:

```
AnsiString __fastcall GetPath();
```

Next, add the code from Listing 12.8 to the end of the `Unit1.cpp` file.

LISTING 12.8   The `GetPath()` Function

```
AnsiString __fastcall TForm1::GetPath()
{
    TTreeNode *Base, *Temp;
    TStringList *TempList = new TStringList();
    int i;
    AnsiString ToReturn;

    Base = MyTree->Selected;
    TempList->Add(Base->Text);
    Temp = Base->Parent;
    while(Temp)
    {
        TempList->Add(Temp->Text);
        Temp = Temp->Parent;
    }
    for(i=TempList->Count-1;i>-1;i—)
    {
        ToReturn += "/" + TempList->Strings[i];
    }
    delete TempList;
    return ToReturn;
}
```

The first thing you do in Listing 12.8 is create a couple of holder `TTreeNode` variables and a new `TStringList`. Set the `Base` variable to the currently selected `TTreeNode` element of `MyList`. Then add the text of the node to `TempList` and set `Temp` equal to the parent element of the `Base` node. Next, loop as long as there is a parent node to the element you are working with, adding the text of each node in succession. What you have at the end is a list of each directory in reverse order to the file or directory that has been selected. All that remains is to step through the `TempList` backward and build a string with a slash and the directory name from the `TempList`. You can then delete the `TempList` and return the string that you have built.

Ending the Current Session and Uploading a File

To end the current session and enable the user to access a different FTP site, add the following code to the OnClick event of StopButton:

```
void __fastcall TForm1::StopButtonClick(TObject *Sender)
{
    MyFtp->Disconnect();
    StartButton->Enabled = true;
    StopButton->Enabled = false;
}
```

This calls the Disconnect() method of MyFtp and then enables the StartButton while disabling StopButton. This allows the user to change the server or user information and connect to the next site.

To upload a file, add the following to the OnClick event of UploadButton:

```
void __fastcall TForm1::UploadButtonClick(TObject *Sender)
{
    if(OpenDialog1->Execute())
    {
        MyFtp->Upload(OpenDialog1->FileName,
                    ExtractFileName(OpenDialog1->FileName));
    }
}
```

This fairly simple function calls the Execute method of OpenDialog1. If the function is run successfully, you then call the Upload method of MyFtp, passing as variables the filename (with the path) from the dialog box and the filename (without the path) as the second variable. At this point, save your file and then run the project.

You have now completed the section on communication protocols. With these examples, you should now have a grasp on the main protocols that make up the realm of network development today.

Summary

You now should have the skills and components necessary to expand your software from the boundaries of a single computer to the world around it. You have been equipped with a toolkit to create applications that use the serial port and an introduction to a wide variety of network protocols. Now that you have the building blocks to give your software the voice that it needs, you can allow your applications to stand up and be heard by the world around them.

12

COMMUNICATIONS
PROGRAMMING

Web Server Programming

Bob Swart
William Morrison

IN THIS CHAPTER

- Web Modules
- Web Server Application Wizard
- WebBroker Support Components
- Web Servers
- WebBroker Producing Components
- Web Application Wizards
- Maintaining State
- Web Security
- HTML and XML
- InternetExpress

This chapter covers Web server programming in C++Builder, which is supported by CGI/WinCGI and ISAPI/NSAPI techniques as provided by the WebBroker technology and InternetExpress features.

The C++Builder 5 WebBroker technology can be used to create Web server applications. It consists of a special data module, called the Web Module, two wizards, and a number of components. The most useful wizard is the Web Server Application Wizard. The other is the Database Web Application Wizard, which adds the capability to put a table on the Web Module.

The components can be divided into two groups: supporting components and classes, such as `TWebModule`, `TWebDispatcher`, `TWebRequest`, and `TWebResponse`, and producing components, such as `TPageProducer`, `TDataSetPageProducer`, `TDataSetTableProducer`, and `TQueryTableProducer`.

The WebBroker wizards and components are part of C++Builder 5 Professional. Additionally, C++Builder 5 Enterprise contains `TMidasPageProducer` and `TReconcilePageProducer` components, also known as part of the new InternetExpress feature.

> **NOTE**
>
> There are some files that must be manually prepared before the example projects provided for this chapter on the accompanying CD-ROM can be used. Please read and follow the instructions in the _README.TXT_ file provided in the _WebServer_ folder.

Web Modules

The terms *WebBroker* and *Web Module* are often used to refer to the same thing. The WebBroker can be seen as the part of the Web Module (the Action Dispatcher) that turns it from a data module into a Web Module. On the other hand, it can also be seen as the core feature that allows you to build ISAPI/NSAPI, CGI, or WinCGI Web server applications without having to worry about the differences between these protocols. Also, the Web Bridge allows developers to use a single API for both Microsoft ISAPI (all versions) and Netscape NSAPI (up to version 3.6), so again you don't have to concern yourself with the differences between these APIs. Moreover, Web server applications are non-visual applications (that is, they run on the Web server, but the user interface is represented by the client using a Web browser), and yet the Web Module wizards and components offer you design-time support, compared to writing other non-visual code using C++Builder.

Web Server Application Wizard

The standard Web Server Application Wizard can be found in the Repository (select File, New) in the first tab, named New. Once you start the Web Server Application Wizard, you need to select what kind of Web server application you want to create: ISAPI/NSAPI (the default choice), CGI, or WinCGI, shown in Figure 13.1.

FIGURE 13.1

The Web Server Application Wizard.

CGI

A common gateway interface (CGI) Web server application is a console application, loaded by the Web server for each request, and unloaded directly after completing the request. Client input is received on the standard input, and the resulting output (usually HTML) is sent to the standard output.

WinCGI

WinCGI is a Windows-specific implementation of the CGI protocol. Instead of standard input and standard output, an INI file is used to send information back and forth. The only programming difference with a standard (console) CGI application is that a WinCGI application is now a *GUI* application, albeit still a non-visible one, of course. In this chapter, I will use only standard CGI to demonstrate CGI/WinCGI features.

ISAPI/NSAPI

ISAPI (Microsoft IIS) or NSAPI (Netscape) Web server extension DLLs are just like WinCGI/CGI applications, with the important difference that the DLL stays loaded after the first request. This means that subsequent requests are executed faster (no loading/unloading).

Netscape will also support the ISAPI protocol in the future, and because you can use a "translation" DLL to map ISAPI calls to NSAPI (when using an older Netscape Web server), I'll use the term *ISAPI* in the remainder of this chapter when in fact I'm talking about both ISAPI and NSAPI.

CGI or ISAPI?

The source code generated for a CGI and for a WinCGI Web Module application is almost identical in both cases. Although an ISAPI/NSAPI DLL has a somewhat different main section (it is a DLL, not an executable), the Web Module itself is exactly the same for all three. Therefore, if you want to produce a CGI application, but you want to test it as an ISAPI DLL first (because you can debug ISAPI DLLs from within the C++Builder IDE itself), then you should just create two project targets (one for CGI and one for ISAPI) that share the same WebBroker unit. In order to archive this, you must create two projects (in a project group), delete the Web Module from the CGI executable, and add (share) the Web Module from the ISAPI DLL with the CGI executable. For the Web Module itself it doesn't really matter whether or not it is compiled as executable or DLL (it doesn't even know or need to know), but for us it is much more convenient to develop!

The main disadvantages are that CGI is much slower than ISAPI (the CGI application needs to be loaded and unloaded for every request) and the ISAPI DLL is harder to update (you must shut down the Web server) and less robust; a rogue DLL could potentially crash the entire Web server with it. Apart from that, a DLL that is loaded at all times does not mean that all your variables are cleared for every request, which means additional testing on your part. These are good reasons to make sure an ISAPI DLL is 100% error free before you deploy it. It is important to test and debug your Web server application before deployment—maybe even more important than your regular applications. More on this later.

WebBroker Support Components

After you make a choice in the New Web Server Application dialog (select CGI, or create both a CGI and ISAPI target as I explained earlier), C++Builder generates a new WebBroker project and an empty Web Module unit. Let's save this new project under the name WebShow and the generated unit under the name WebMod to be used for the entire chapter.

Before we continue, first go to the Project Options dialog, select the Linker page, and turn off the Use Dynamic RTL option. Switch to the Packages page and turn off the Build with Runtime Packages option. If you don't turn them off now, you will need to deploy them with your WebBroker application as well, which only adds dependencies that can go wrong. This is why I always deploy standalone executables of DLLs whenever possible (apart from some database drivers, of course). The Web server applications in this chapter will be similar ones; no dynamic RTL or runtime packages.

The Web Module is the place to drop the special WebBroker components, such as PageProducers and TableProducers. The WebBroker components can be found on the Internet tab of the C++Builder 5 Component Palette, shown in Figure 13.2. The InternetExpress-specific components can be found on the InternetExpress tab, as we'll see later in this chapter in the section "InternetExpress."

Displayed on the Component Palette, from left to right (in Figure 13.2), are the icons for TClientSocket and TServerSocket (not part of the WebBroker components), TCppWebBroker (useful for showing generated Web pages), TWebDispatcher, TPageProducer, TQueryTableProducer, TDataSetTableProducer, and TDataSetPageProducer. The TCppWebBroker ActiveX component is used to implement the IntraBob host application with which you can debug Web Module applications from within the C++Builder IDE itself (more on that later in this chapter).

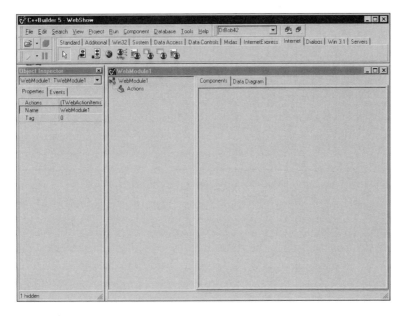

FIGURE 13.2
The Internet page of the C++Builder 5 Component Palette.

Apart from the components on the Component Palette, this chapter also covers the Web Module–supporting components such as TWebModule, TWebRequest, and TWebResponse.

TWebDispatcher

The TWebDispatcher component is built into the Web Module itself and is available to transform an existing data module into a Web Module (so TDataModule + TWebDispatcher = TWebModule). Only one TWebDispatcher is allowed per application, which means that an application can have at most one Web Module—or a data module with a TWebDispatcher component. Note that the only way to generate a Web Module is using the Web Server Application Wizard, which starts a new project—and hence still one Web Module per project. Considering this, it is rather unfortunate that C++Builder 5 does not give you a warning when you accidentally drop more than one TWebDispatcher on a data module (although it does complain if you try to drop one on a Web Module).

TWebDispatcher is responsible for patching through the incoming requests to a collection of Web action items.

TWebModule

A Web Module can be seen as a "Web-aware" data module. The most important property of the Web Module is the Actions property of type TWebActionItems. You can start the Action

Editor for these TWebActionItems in a number of ways. First, go to the Object Inspector and click on the ellipsis next to the (TWebActionItems) value of the Actions property. You can also right-click on the Web Module and select the Action Editor to specify the different requests that the Web Module will respond to. Finally, new in C++Builder 5, the Visual Data Module Designer shows all Action items as children of the Web Module, and you can right-click on Actions to add new ones.

A WebBroker Action is equivalent to a client request, and we can specify properties as well as an event for these specific actions. The Web server application—albeit only one application—can respond to each of the different actions implemented inside. The discriminating factor between these WebItemActions is their PathInfo property: the string immediately following the URL itself (but before any querystring values).

Using the Actions Editor, shown in Figure 13.3, you can define a number of Web action items. Each of these items can be distinguished from the others by the PathInfo property. PathInfo contains extra information added to the request, right before the Query fields. This means that a single Web server application can respond to different HTTP requests, each handled by a different Web action item.

For the examples used in this chapter, you must define nine different TWebActionItems that will be used to illustrate the different uses and capabilities of the Web Module components.

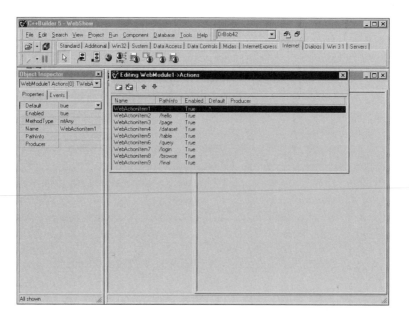

FIGURE 13.3

The Actions Editor.

Note that the first item has no `PathInfo` specified and is the only default Web action item. This means that it is the `TWebActionItem` that will be selected, both when `PathInfo` is not given and when no other `PathInfo` matches the given `PathInfo` (in other words, when the default action is needed). The other eight `PathInfo` values are `/hello`, `/page`, `/dataset`, `/table`, `/query`, `/login`, `/browse`, and `/final`, which will be used for feature demonstrations throughout this chapter.

In order to write an event handler for the default `TWebActionItem`, select `WebActionItem1` in the Actions Editor (refer to Figure 13.3), go to the Events tab of the Object Inspector, and double-click on the `OnAction` event. This will take you to the code editor in the following generated event handler code:

```
void __fastcall TWebModule1::WebModule1WebActionItem1Action(
     TObject *Sender, TWebRequest *Request, TWebResponse *Response,
     bool &Handled)
{

}
```

Before you write any event-handling code here, let's first examine the internals of the Web `Request` and `Response` parameters.

TWebResponse

The `Response` parameter (of type `TWebResponse`) has a number of properties to specify the generated output. The most important property is `Content`, a string in which you can put any HTML code that should be returned to the client. The following code will produce `Hello, world!`, for example:

```
void __fastcall TWebModule1::WebModule1WebActionItem1Action(
     TObject *Sender, TWebRequest *Request, TWebResponse *Response,
     bool &Handled)
{
   Response->Content = "<H1>Hello, world!</H1>";
}
```

Of course, you can assign anything to the `Response->Content` property. Usually, it will be of type `text/html`, which is the default value of the `Response->ContentType` property. In case you need to return anything else, you need to set the `Response->ContentType` to the correct type. Binary output (such as images) cannot be returned directly using `Response->Content`, but must be returned using the `Response->ContentStream` property, instead.

Other useful properties of the `Response` object include `ContentEncoding`, `Cookies` (to set cookie values), `StatusCode`, `ReasonString`, `WWWAuthenticate`, and `Realm` (see the section "Web Security," later in this chapter), `Date` and `Expires` (to manipulate the lifetime of the dynamically generated document), and `LogMessage` (to put a certain message in the Web server log file).

TWebRequest

The `Request` parameter (of type `TWebRequest`) contains a number of useful properties and methods that hold the input query. Based on the method used to send the query (`GET` or `POST`), the input data can be found in the `Query` and `QueryFields` or the `Content` and `ContentFields` properties. In code, you can determine this as follows:

```
void __fastcall TWebModule1::WebModule1WebActionItem1Action(
     TObject *Sender, TWebRequest *Request, TWebResponse *Response,
     bool &Handled)
{
  Response->Content = "<H1>Hello, world!</H1>";
  if (Request->Method == "GET")
    Response->Content = Response->Content + "<B>GET</B>" +
      "<BR>Query: " + Request->Query;
  else
    if (Request->Method == "POST")
      Response->Content = Response->Content + "<B>POST</B>" +
        "<BR>Content: " + Request->Content;
}
```

Other useful properties of the `Request` object include `CookieFields` (to read cookie values), `Authorization` (see the first part of the section "Web Security," later in this chapter), `Referrer`, `UserAgent`, and `Method` (to determine the `GET` or `POST` method protocol).

There are a number of important differences between the `GET` and `POST` protocols. When using the `GET` protocol, the query fields are passed on the URL. This is fast, but it limits the amount of data that can be sent (a few kilobytes at most, enough for most cases). A less-visible way to pass data is by using the `POST` protocol, in which content fields are passed using standard input/output techniques (or a Windows INI file for WinCGI). This is slower, but it is limited to the amount of free disk space. Besides, when using `POST`, you cannot see the data being sent on the URL itself, so there's no way of (accidentally) tampering with it and getting incorrect results.

Personally, I prefer to use the `POST` protocol (clean URLs, no limit on the amount of data, but slightly slower). I use the `GET` protocol only when I have a good reason.

Web Servers

It's time to test the first Web Module application. This requires a Web server, which can be a personal Web server (for Windows 95/98) or the Microsoft Internet Information Server (IIS) for Windows NT or Windows 2000. Chapter 30 of the *Borland C++Builder 5 Developer's Guide* that comes with C++Builder contains clear instructions on how to set up your (personal) Web server in order to be able to test and debug ISAPI DLLs or CGI applications. Note that this is not easy if you're using IIS version 4 or later (which comes with NT 4 Option Pack or Windows 2000), as described on page 30-26 of the Developer's Guide in detail.

Also note that a real Web server will not unload ISAPI DLLs once they are loaded for the first time. This means you have to manually stop the Web server (and the IIS admin service as well) before you can recompile your ISAPI DLL. Then you need to restart your Web server again (which automatically starts the IIS admin service) in order to reload and test the new version of your ISAPI DLL. Apart from that, a rogue ISAPI DLL could potentially crash the entire Web server—making it nonresponsive until you bring it down and up again. Recent versions of Internet Information Server have a Run in Separate Memory Space (Isolate Process) option, which helps to avoid this problem. Also, you can force IIS to unload ISAPI DLLs after each request, by unchecking the Cache ISAPI Applications option for the specific Web site in the Internet Service Manager dialog. This is quite useful, because it enables you to recompile an ISAPI DLL without having to unload the Web server itself. (If you do this in a production environment, you'll find that you lose all speed benefits of ISAPI DLLs, having them unloaded after each request.)

As an alternative to a "real" Web server, you can use the freeware IntraBob version 5.0, shown in Figure 13.4, which is my personal ISAPI debugger host for Delphi and C++Builder. It replaces the Web server and enables you to debug ISAPI DLLs while still on your local machine. Just put IntraBob.exe (available on the CD-ROM that accompanies this book or from my Web site at http://www.drbob42.com) in the same directory as your ISAPI project source code and enter the location of IntraBob as **Host Application** in the C++Builder 5 Run, Run Parameters dialog:

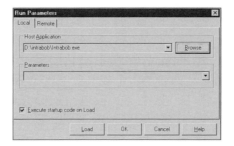

FIGURE 13.4
Using IntraBob as a Web Module host application.

When you run the ISAPI DLL, the host application IntraBob is executed. IntraBob shows a Web page that will trigger the actions of your Web server application. You can now use the C++Builder integrated debugger to set breakpoints in the source code. For example, set a breakpoint at the first line that checks Request->Method, and you see that the C++Builder IDE will break here as soon as you run the Web Module application.

To actually start the ISAPI DLL, you must first write a Web page containing an HTML form that will load the Web Module application. Using the current WebShow.bpr project, this means

13

WEB SERVER
PROGRAMMING

an action with value `http://localhost/scripts/WebShow.dll`; see the HTML code that follows:

```
<HTML>
<BODY>
<H1>WebBroker HTML Form</H1>
<HR>
<FORM ACTION="http://localhost/scripts/WebShow.dll" METHOD=POST>
Name: <INPUT TYPE=EDIT NAME=Name>
<P>
<INPUT TYPE=SUBMIT VALUE=Submit>
</FORM>
</BODY>
</HTML>
```

When you load this Web page in IntraBob, the WebBroker HTML Form Web page appears. You can fill in a value and click on the Submit button to load and start your first WebShow Web Module application.

IntraBob parses the HTML form and automatically fills in the Options tab, as shown in Figure 13.5, with the value of the remote CGI (or in this case ISAPI) application, the name of the local executable (or DLL), and `PathInfo`, if specified. Note that you can always turn to the Options tab and set these options manually (an easy way to request another `PathInfo` and fire a different `WebActionItem`):

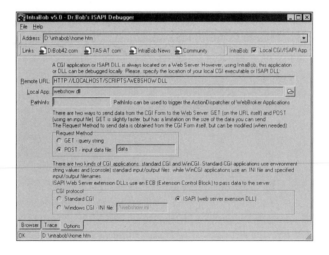

FIGURE 13.5

The IntraBob Options tab.

Remember the breakpoint you set on the first line, which checked the `Request->Method` value? As soon as you click on the Submit button, the default `WebActionItem` will be fired, meaning this breakpoint, shown in Figure 13.6, will be triggered, and you will end up in the C++Builder

Integrated Debugger. Here you can use ToolTip Expression Evaluation, for example, to check the value of Request->Method or Request->Content directly:

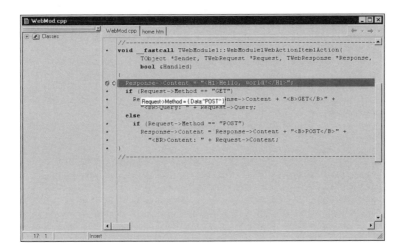

FIGURE 13.6

A Web Module breakpoint in the C++Builder IDE.

> **CAUTION**
>
> A "Delphi" exception is raised (a few times actually) with the following text:
>
> Project Intrabob.exe raised exception class Exception with message
> ➡"Only one data module per application". Process Stopped.
> ➡Use Step or Run to continue.
>
> This exception is raised of a bug in the way C++Builder loads and unloads ISAPI DLLs. We must manually fix the generated project source code for WebShow, which contains an unconditional CreateForm every time the DllEntryPoint is entered—for reason values Process Attach, Thread Attach, Process Detach, and Thread Detach—which should only be done for reason equals PROCESS ATTACH. I always change the CreateForm statement by inserting a single if statement, as follows:
>
> ```
> if (reason == DLL_PROCESS_ATTACH)
>   Application->CreateForm(__classid(TWebModule1), &WebModule1);
> ```
>
> This solves the problem nicely.

If you press F9 again, you see the final result in IntraBob, as seen in Figure 13.7.

FIGURE 13.7
Web Module output in IntraBob.

Voilà, you've just created an HTML form "spy," which will return the names and values of all input fields. This can be quite helpful when a certain WebActionItem doesn't seem to work, and you need to check if it indeed received the input data in good order. Note that spaces are replaced by plus signs (+). You'll find all special characters replaced by a % character, followed by the hexadecimal value of the character itself.

WebBroker Producing Components

It's now time to cover the WebBroker producing components. These are the WebBroker Internet components that we can find on the Internet tab of the Component Palette, such as TPageProducer, TDataSetPageProducer, TDataSetTableProducer, and TQueryTableProducer.

TPageProducer

You can put anything in the Response->Content string variable, even entire Web pages. Sometimes, however, you may want to return HTML strings based on a template, in which only certain fields need to be filled in (with a name and date or specific fields from a record in a table, for example). In those cases, you should use a TPageProducer component.

TPageProducer has two properties to specify predefined content. HTMLFile points to an external HTML file. This is most useful if you want to be able to change your Web page template without having to recompile the application itself (and have another team working on the HTML template while you're working on the application itself). The HTMLDoc property, on the other hand, is of type TStrings and contains the HTML text hardcoded in the DFM file. This is most useful when giving demonstrations or writing papers on WebBroker technology, but it is less flexible than the HTMLFile approach.

The predefined content of a TPageProducer component can contain any HTML code as well as special # tags. These # tags are "invalid" HTML tags, so they will be ignored by Web browsers but not by the OnHTMLTag event of TPageProducer. Inside this event, you can replace a TagString with ReplaceText. For more flexibility, # tags can also contain parameters, right after the name itself (for instance, Format=YY/MM/DD to specify the format to print the date). Check the online help for more information on the TagParams.

As an example of # tags, let's fill the HTMLDoc property with the following content:

```
<H1>TPageProducer</H1>
<HR>
<#Greeting> <#Name>,
<P>
It's now <#Time> and we're working with a PageProducer.
```

I've used three # tags that will fire the OnHTMLTag event of TPageProducer. To replace each of them with sensible text, see Listing 13.1 for the OnHTMLTag event.

LISTING 13.1   PageProducer First OnHTMLTag Event Handler

```
void __fastcall TWebModule1::PageProducer1HTMLTag(TObject *Sender,
     TTag Tag, const AnsiString TagString, TStrings *TagParams,
     AnsiString &ReplaceText)
{
  if (TagString == "Name")
    ReplaceText = "Bob"; // hardcoded name...
  else
  if (TagString == "Time")
    ReplaceText = DateTimeToStr(Now());
  else // TagString == "Greeting"
    if ((double)Time() < 0.5)
      ReplaceText = "Good Morning";
    else
      if ((double)Time() > 0.7)
        ReplaceText = "Good Evening";
      else
        ReplaceText = "Good Afternoon";
}
```

Note that I used an explicit (double) cast for the call to Time(), since it would otherwise introduce an ambiguity between the double and int results of TDateTime.

Using a ReplaceText with a fixed value of Bob feels a bit awkward, especially since the HTML form specifically asks the user to enter a name. Can't we just use that value here instead (by using QueryFields or ContentFields)? Yes, you can, because you can directly access the Request property of your TWebModule, which is always assigned to the Request property of the current action. The same holds for the Response property, by the way.

This effectively changes the code for the OnHTMLTag event, as follows (see Listing 13.2).

LISTING 13.2   PageProducer Second OnHTMLTag Event Handler

```
void __fastcall TWebModule1::PageProducer1HTMLTag(TObject *Sender,
      TTag Tag, const AnsiString TagString, TStrings *TagParams,
      AnsiString &ReplaceText)
{
  if (TagString == "Name")
  {
    if (Request->Method == "POST")
      ReplaceText = Request->ContentFields->Values["Name"];
    else
      ReplaceText = Request->QueryFields->Values["Name"];
  }
  else
  if (TagString == "Time")
    ReplaceText = DateTimeToStr(Now());
  else // TagString == "Greeting"
    if ((double)Time() < 0.5)
      ReplaceText = "Good Morning";
    else
      if ((double)Time() > 0.7)
        ReplaceText = "Good Evening";
      else
        ReplaceText = "Good Afternoon";
}
```

This will be the last time we explicitly check the Request->Method field to determine whether to use QueryFields (GET) or ContentFields (POST), by the way. From now on, unless specified otherwise, we'll assume a POST method (but you can still support GET as well as POST using this technique).

Before you can finally test this code, you need to connect an action item (the /hello action) to the page producer. There are two ways. New in C++Builder 5 is the Producer property of action items, which can be used to select PageProducer1 directly as the producer for WebActionItem2. The advantage is that it takes no code to write; the disadvantage is that it means you can't set a breakpoint, either. Of course, you can always write the event handler code for the /hello OnAction event:

```
void __fastcall TWebModule1::WebModule1WebActionItem2Action(
      TObject *Sender, TWebRequest *Request, TWebResponse *Response,
      bool &Handled)
{
```

```
Response->Content = PageProducer1->Content();
}
```

You can even use both techniques, in which case it is good to know that the Producer property value is executed first, followed by the event handler (in which case you may want to *add* something to Response->Content rather than duly overwriting it, of course).

In order to activate this specific WebActionItem, you need to be sure to pass the /hello PathInfo to the Web Module, either by specifying it in IntraBob's PathInfo edit box (refer to Figure 13.5) or by including the PathInfo string in the ACTION value of the home.htm starting Web page:

```
<FORM ACTION="http://localhost/scripts/WebShow.dll/hello" METHOD=POST>
```

If you load the HTML form in IntraBob, fill in the name **Bob Swart** again, and click on the Submit button, you get the output shown in Figure 13.8.

13

WEB SERVER PROGRAMMING

FIGURE 13.8
The output of TPageProducer.

A final word on the PageProducer component, especially for FrontPage users. Some Web page editors include the "feature" of inserting tag parameters in double quotes, so that when using such an editor, our <#Date Format> tag would become <#Date "Format">. The StripParamQuotes property—default set to true—makes sure that you can remove those unwanted quotes from your # tags. (If you don't have any problems, you can set StripParamQuotes to false, but beware of external templates pointed to by the HTMLFile property: One action of such a Web page editor may actually break your WebBroker application.)

TDataSetPageProducer

The TDataSetPageProducer component is derived from TPageProducer. Instead of just replacing # tags with a regular value, TDataSetPageProducer has a new DataSet property and will try to match the name of the # tag with a field name from the DataSet property. If one is found, TDataSetPageProducer will replace the # tag with the actual value of that field.

To illustrate the use of this component, drop a TDataSetPageProducer and a TTable component on the Web Module. Rename the TTable component TableBiolife, assign DatabaseName to BCDEMOS, TableName to biolife.db, and set the Active property to true (so you don't have to open the table yourself). Next, connect the DataSet property of the TDataSetPageProducer component to TableBiolife and put the following in the HTMLDoc property:

```
<H1>BIOLIFE Info</H1>
<HR>
<BR><B>Category:</B> <#Category>
<BR><B>Common_Name:</B> <#Common_Name>
<BR><B>Species Name:</B> <#Species Name>
<BR><B>Notes:</B> <#Notes>
```

These special HTML # tag codes indicate that you want to see four specific fields from the BIOLIFE table. TDataSetPageProducer will automatically replace the # tags with the actual value of these fields, so the only source code needed is for the TWebActionItem event handler (unless you want to use the Producer property, in which case no code is needed at all). Let's use the default TWebActionItem again, without a specific PathInfo. Start the Actions Editor, click on the fourth action item, go to the Events tab of the Object Inspector, and double-click the OnAction event to write the following code:

```
void __fastcall TWebModule1::WebModule1WebActionItem4Action(
    TObject *Sender, TWebRequest *Request, TWebResponse *Response,
    bool &Handled)
{
  Response->Content = DataSetPageProducer1->Content();
}
```

You also need to change the ACTION= value of the HTML form to start the /dataset TWebActionItem again, as follows:

```
<FORM ACTION="http://localhost/scripts/WebShow.dll/dataset" METHOD=POST>
```

The result of running the Web Module with this request is shown in Figure 13.9.

There are two things here that strike me as being not correct. First of all, you see (MEMO) instead of the actual content of the Notes field. Second, you don't get the value of the Species Name field.

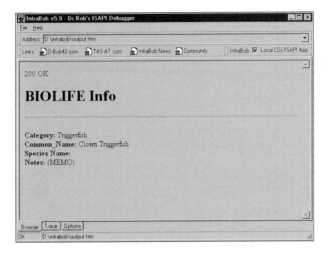

FIGURE 13.9

The output of TDataSetPageProducer.

You can solve the first problem by making use of the fact that the TDataSetPageProducer is derived from TPageProducer, so for every # tag, the OnHTMLTag event is still fired. Inside this event handler, you must check the value of the ReplaceText argument to see if it has been set to (MEMO), in which case you should change it to the real content. This can be done using the AsString property of the field:

```
void __fastcall TWebModule1::DataSetPageProducer1HTMLTag(TObject *Sender,
     TTag Tag, const AnsiString TagString, TStrings *TagParams,
     AnsiString &ReplaceText)
{
  if (ReplaceText == "(MEMO)")
    ReplaceText = TableBiolife->FieldByName(TagString)->AsString;
}
```

Sometimes you get (Memo) instead of (MEMO) as the value for TMemoFields. The difference is simple: (Memo) indicates an empty memo field, and (MEMO) indicates a memo field with some content—hence, some content that has to be processed by your OnHTMLTag event handler.

The second problem can be explained by the fact that the Species Name field contains a space, and spaces are used as terminators for the # tag names. As a result, TDataSetPageProducer would have been looking for a field named Species instead of Species Name.

Personally, I consider it bad database design if you specify fields with spaces in their names. Nevertheless, you may encounter this from time to time. I often add a new calculated field to the table, with a "correct" name (such as SpeciesName) that gets its value from the original field.

Another solution is to fall back to the OnHTMLTag event handler again, this time to replace the #Species TagString with the content of the actual field Species Name. In order to do so, you need to modify the OnHTMLTag event handler as follows:

```
void __fastcall TWebModule1::DataSetPageProducer1HTMLTag(TObject *Sender,
    TTag Tag, const AnsiString TagString, TStrings *TagParams,
    AnsiString &ReplaceText)
{
  if (TagString == "Species") // Species Name
    ReplaceText = TableBiolife->FieldByName("Species Name")->AsString;
  else
    if (ReplaceText == "(MEMO)") // Notes
      ReplaceText = TableBiolife->FieldByName(TagString)->AsString;
}
```

Using the above changes in the source code, the result is finally as expected, as shown in Figure 13.10.

FIGURE 13.10

The output of TDataSetPageProducer.

If you want to see more than one record, you can do two things: browse through the records or show more records at the same time. If you want to go from one record to the next (or the previous), you need to remember which record is the current one; that is, you need to *maintain state*. This is addressed in the section "Maintaining State," later in this chapter. The other solution is to show more than one record at a time, which can be implemented using another WebBroker component, namely TDataSetTableProducer.

TDataSetTableProducer

Like TDataSetPageProducer, TDataSetTableProducer also uses a DataSet property. This time, however, you get more than one record, and the output is formatted in a grid-like table.

Drop a second table on the Web Module, set its name to TableCustomer, set DatabaseName to BCDEMOS, TableName to customer.db, and Active to true. Now, drop a TDataSetTableProducer on the Web Module and set the DataSet property to TableCustomer. TDataSetTableProducer has a number of properties that are all used to control the HTML code being generated. First of all, you have the Header and Footer properties, which hold the lines of text that precede and follow the table output. Then you have the TableAttributes and RowAttributes properties, which can be used to define the layout (alignment, color, and so on) of the table itself and the rows.

A more visual approach to specifying what the table should look like can be experienced using the Column property and especially the Column property editor. From the Object Inspector, start the Columns property editor by clicking on the ellipsis next to the Columns property (THTMLTableColumns) value. This brings up the editor for DataSetTableProducer1->Columns (see Figure 13.11).

Because you open TableCustomer, you already see all fields in the editor. Initially, you cannot delete any fields from this view, nor can you move them. This may seem to be a problem, but it can be explained by the fact that you haven't explicitly specified which fields you would like to see in the output table. The reason you see *all* fields at this time is because that's the default behavior from any TDataSet-derived component: If you don't specify which fields you want, you get them all. However, to delete fields from the complete list or change the order in which the fields appear, you need to add a physical list of fields. Right-click with the mouse on the list of field names, and pick the Add All Fields option. You'll see no apparent change right now. However, the default list of all fields will become an actual list of all fields, and you can delete fields or move them around in the list.

You can also set the output table options, such as Border=1 to get a border, a value for the BgColor property to get a background color, and so forth. Note that individual fields (that is, columns) have to be set by selecting a field and going to the Object Inspector to set the BgColor, Align (left, center, right), and VAlign (top, middle, bottom, baseline) properties. To change the caption of the fields, you can modify the Title property (again in the Object Inspector). The Title property consists of properties such as Align (this time for the title only, not the entire column) and Caption. To change the title of a field, you need to change only the Title.Caption property of that field in the Object Inspector. These changes will automatically be reflected in the Columns editor, so after a bit of playing around with these properties, your output preview may look like Figure 13.11 (depending on your choice of colors, that is).

13

WEB SERVER PROGRAMMING

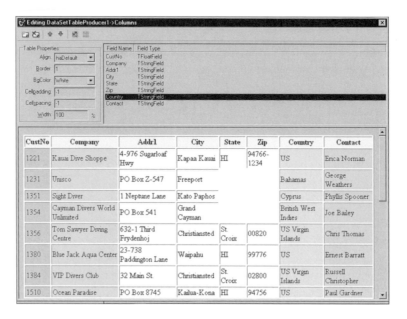

FIGURE 13.11
The editor for `TableProducer` columns.

That concludes the design-time tweaking of the `TDataSetTableProducer` output. Note that, for the `TDataSetTableProducer` example, you haven't written a single line of code yet. Of course, you need to hook it up to a `WebActionItem` `OnAction` event handler, which can be done using the `Producer` property or by writing the event handler for the `/table` `WebActionItem` as follows:

```
void __fastcall TWebModule1::WebModule1WebActionItem5Action(
    TObject *Sender, TWebRequest *Request, TWebResponse *Response,
    bool &Handled)
{
  Response->Content = DataSetTableProducer1->Content();
}
```

There are a few more ways we can tweak and customize the output a little further. First of all, we may want to "flag" certain customers with a special color. For example, all U.S.-based customers will be indicated with a red background, and all others will keep their original background colors (as specified at design time). Furthermore, if a cell is empty, I want to give it a gray (silver) background color. You can do all this and more using the `DataSetTableProducer` `OnFormatCell` event handler, which for the suggested changes is implemented as follows:

```
void __fastcall TWebModule1::DataSetTableProducer1FormatCell(
    TObject *Sender, int CellRow, int CellColumn, THTMLBgColor &BgColor,
    THTMLAlign &Align, THTMLVAlign &VAlign, AnsiString &CustomAttrs,
    AnsiString &CellData)
{
```

```
  if (CellData == "") BgColor = "Silver";
  else
    if ((CellColumn == 6) && (CellData.Pos("US") > 0))
      BgColor = "Red";
}
```

Executing this code produces the output shown in Figure 13.12. Although the figure is in black and white, if you compile and run the code, you will see the color results.

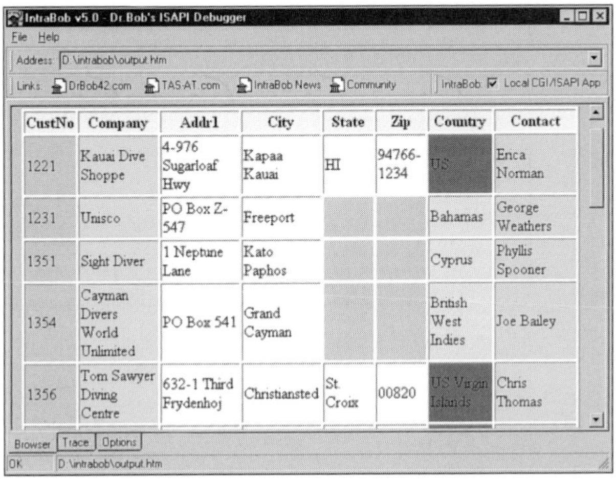

FIGURE 13.12
`TableProducer` *output in IntraBob.*

As a last enhancement, we may want to see the orders for a specific customer in a follow-up window. Orders are linked to the `CustNo` identifier, so we could change that one to a link that would start another Web Module request to dynamically generate HTML output with an overview of the orders for the given customer. Let's put that one on hold for now, since we can use the finalcomponent—`TQueryTableProducer`—to assist in solving this request.

TQueryTableProducer

The `TQueryTableProducer` produces output similar to the `TDataSetTableProducer`. The difference is not that we can connect a `TQuery` component only to the `TQueryTableProducer`. After all, we already can connect any `TDataSet` or derived component, including `TTables` and `TQuerys`, to the `TDataSetTableProducer`. The difference is that `TQueryTableProducer` has special support for filling in the parameters of a parameterized `TQuery`.

Drop a `TQueryTableProducer` component and a `TQuery` component on the Web Module. Set the `DatabaseName` (alias) of the `TQuery` component to `BCDEMOS`, rename it `QueryOrders`, and write the following code in the `SQL` property:

```
SELECT * FROM ORDERS.DB AS O
WHERE (O.CustNo = :CustNo)
```

This is an SQL query with one parameter. We now need to specify the type of the parameter in the `Parameter` Property Editor of the `TQuery` component. Click on the ellipsis next to the `Params` property in the Object Inspector. Select the `CustNo` parameter in the list and go to the Object Inspector to set `DataType` to `ftInteger`, `ParamTyp` to `ptInput`, and `Value` to a default value of `0` (so we can activate the query at design-time).

We can open the `TQuery` component (set `Active` to true) to see if we made any typing mistakes. Now, click on `TQueryTableProducer`, and assign the `Query` property to `QueryOrders`. Note that `TQueryTableProducer` contains the same properties to customize its output as `TDataSetTableProducer` (refer to the "TDataSetTableProducer" section, earlier in this chapter). In fact, `TQueryTableProducer` and `TDataSetTableProducer` are both derived from `TDSTableProducer`, and `TQueryTableProducer` adds only the query parameter handling to its special behavior. Before you continue, edit the `Columns` property and format the output at will.

`TQueryTableProducer` works by looking for the parameter name (`CustNo`, in this case) among the `ContentFields` (or `QueryFields`, if we're using the `GET` method) and filling in the value of the field as value for the parameter. In this case, it means we need a sample HTML startup file, defined as follows:

```
<HTML>
<BODY>
<H1>WebBroker HTML Form</H1>
<HR>
<FORM ACTION="http://localhost/scripts/WebShow.dll/query" METHOD=POST>
CustNo: <INPUT TYPE=EDIT NAME=CustNo>
<P>
<INPUT TYPE=SUBMIT>
</FORM>
</BODY>
</HTML>
```

Note that the name of the input field is `CustNo`, which is exactly the name of the `Query` parameter. If we fill in a value, such as `1221`, we should get all orders for that particular customer. As long as we set the `MaxRows` property to a high value (99,999,999 will do fine), we're pretty sure we will see all detail records. Note that setting the `MaxRows` property to a high value (especially for `TDataSetTableProducer`) results in more records being shown, but also results in bigger and certainly slower output. The latter is not only caused by the fact that the output is simply bigger and has to be transferred over the network, but also by the fact that an HTML table doesn't show itself until the closing `</TABLE>` tag is reached. This means that for a really big table with 99,999,999+ rows, we may actually see a blank browser window for a while, until the table is drawn.

To finish this example, we need only to write one line of code in the `OnAction` event handler for the `/query` `WebActionItem`:

```
void __fastcall TWebModule1::WebModule1WebActionItem6Action(
    TObject *Sender, TWebRequest *Request, TWebResponse *Response,
    bool &Handled)
{
  Response->Content = QueryTableProducer1->Content();
}
```

Running WebActionItem with the /query PathInfo and entering 1221 in the CustNo edit box, we get the result shown in Figure 13.13.

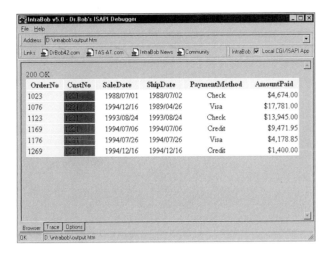

FIGURE 13.13

TQueryTableProducer *output in IntraBob.*

Now, this just screams to be used with the previous TDataSetTableProducer on the Customer table. In fact, we can do this by extending the OnFormatCell event handler from the TDataSetTableProducer to turn CustNo into a hyperlink request to the same Web server application with the /query PathInfo, followed by the CustNo field/value pair (which is then sent using the GET protocol). So, for the first column (where CellColumn has the value 0), we must change the actual CellData to a hyperlink to the /query WebActionItem with the current CellData (in other words, CustNo) as the value of a field named CustNo, all passed on the URL—thus using the GET protocol in a useful way again.

Alternately, we can change each CustNo value to a new form with the /query action and a hidden field with the CustNo name and specific CustNo value. Both options are implemented in the extended OnFormatCell event handler code shown in Listing 13.3. (You can switch by using #define LINK, which causes the LINK code to compile producing hyperlinks. Otherwise, without LINK defined, a button shows.)

LISTING 13.3 `DataSetTableProducer` `FormatCell` Event Handler

```
void __fastcall TWebModule1::DataSetTableProducer1FormatCell(
    TObject *Sender, int CellRow, int CellColumn, THTMLBgColor &BgColor,
    THTMLAlign &Align, THTMLVAlign &VAlign, AnsiString &CustomAttrs,
    AnsiString &CellData)
{
  if ((CellColumn == 0) && (CellRow > 0)) // first Column - CustNo
    CellData =
#ifdef LINK
      "<A HREF=\"http://localhost/scripts/WebShow.dll/query?CustNo=" +
        CellData + ">" + CellData + "</A>";
#else
      (AnsiString)"<FORM ACTION=\"WebShow.dll/query\" METHOD=POST>" +
      "<INPUT TYPE=HIDDEN NAME=CustNo VALUE=" + CellData + ">" +
      "<INPUT TYPE=SUBMIT VALUE=" + CellData + ">" +
      "</FORM>";
#endif
  else
  if (CellData == "") BgColor = "Silver";
  else
    if ((CellColumn == 6) && (CellData.Pos("US") > 0))
      BgColor = "Red";
};
```

To test the hyperlink option, you should use your real (personal) Web server. IntraBob can be used to test and debug ISAPI requests that are started by an HTML form. We can test the above Form option, which generates the output in Figure 13.14 for `TDataSetTableProducer` on the `Customer` table.

It should be clear from the figure what will happen when you click on one of these `CustNo` buttons. For example, if we click on the 1231 button to see which orders are placed for this company in the Bahamas (apart from a holiday for me and my family, that is), we get the output shown in Figure 13.15.

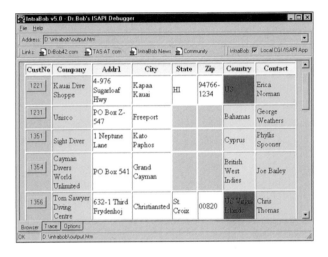

FIGURE 13.14

Master TableProducer *output in IntraBob.*

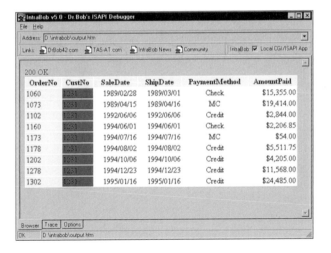

FIGURE 13.15

Detail QueryTableProducer *output in IntraBob.*

Web Application Wizards

Before we continue with the last component from the WebBroker toolset, let's first quickly
check out a wizard related to the TDataSetTableProducer. The Database Web Application

Wizard, found on the Business tab in the Object Repository, allows you to specify a database alias, a table name, some field names, and a few properties for TDataSetTableProducer. Then it generates a new Web Module application with a TWebModule, a TSession (AutoSessionName = true), a TTable, and a TDataSetTableProducer.

The one thing you could learn from this component is that you need a TSession component with AutoSessionName set to true to avoid BDE session conflicts, especially when writing ISAPI DLLs that use BDE tables. Other than that, what the Database Web Application Wizard does can easily be done by hand; personally, I never use this wizard.

As you may have noticed by now, the WebBroker technology is especially suited to produce HTML output, based on templates or at least a predefined set of properties. However, there is very little interaction. For truly state-of-the-art, dynamic Web pages, we can always extend WebBroker with InternetExpress (as will be done near the end of this chapter). First, it's about time to focus on state and security issues.

Maintaining State

Remember the DataSetPageProducer that we used on TableBiolife? Seeing a single record from a table in a Web browser is fine, but imagine that you want to jump to the next record, and the next, and the last, and back to the first again—but still see only one record at a time. In short, you want to be able to browse through the records in the table. We can do just that, using the TDataSetPageProducer and the code we've written so far, extending it just a bit to support browsing.

The main problem we have to solve when it comes to moving from one record to the next is maintaining state information: Which record (number) are we currently looking at? HTTP itself is a stateless protocol, so we must find a way to store this information ourselves.

Saving state information can be done in three different ways: using fat URLs, cookies, or hidden fields.

Fat URLs

A common way to retain state information is by adding Form variables with their values to the URL itself. We already did this in the /query?CustNo= example, where we added the CustNo key value to the URL. We can do something similar inside an HTML CGI form by modifying the ACTION part. For example, to state that we're currently looking at the first record, we could add RecNo=1 to the URL, resulting in

```
<FORM ACTION="http://localhost/scripts/WebShow.dll/dataset?RecNo=1"
➥METHOD=POST>
```

Note that the general METHOD to send Form variables is still POST, although the state (RecNo) variable is passed using the GET protocol. This means we'll see the RecNo and its value appear on the URL, which can be experienced with some search engines on the Web as well.

Personally, I believe that any information sent on the URL is prone to error, so I generally try to avoid it (although using the POST method to send regular form fields and the GET method to send state fields is actually a nice way to separate the two kinds of fields).

Cookies

Cookies are sent by the server to the browser. When you are using cookies, the initiative is with the Web server, but the client has the capability to deny or disable a cookie. Sometimes, servers even send cookies when you don't ask for them, which is a reason some people don't like cookies (like me, for example).

Cookies can be set as part of the Response, using the SetCookieField method. Like CGI values, a cookie is of the form NAME=VALUE, so we can insert RecNo=value as follows:

```
TStringList* Cookies = new TStringList();
Cookies->Add("RecNo="+IntToStr(Master->RecNo));
Response->SetCookieField(Cookies,NULL,NULL,Now()+1,false);
Cookies->Free();
```

Note that we're using a TStringList to set up a list of cookie values. Each list of cookies can have a domain and a path associated with it, to indicate which URL the cookie should be sent to. You can leave these blank. The fourth parameter specifies the expiration date of the cookie, which is set to Now+1 day, so the next time the user is back, the cookie should have expired. The final argument specifies if the cookie is used over a secure connection.

Assuming the user accepts the cookie, then having set the cookie is still only half the work. In a follow-up OnAction event, we need to read the value of the cookie, to determine how far to step with the Master table to be able to show the next record. In this case, cookies are part of the Request class, just like ContentFields, and they can be queried using the CookieFields property.

```
int RecNo = StrToInt(Request->CookieFields->Values["RecNo"]);
```

Other than that, cookies work just like any CGI content field. Just remember that, while a content field is part of your request (and is always current), a cookie may have been rejected, resulting in an older value (which was still on your disk), or no value at all, which will result in an exception thrown by StrToInt in the previous line of code.

Hidden Fields

Hidden fields are the third way, and in my book the most flexible, to maintain state information. To implement hidden fields, we first need to write an HTML form again (and place it in the HTMLDoc property), specifying the default WebActionItem, and using four different "submit" buttons (each with a different value as its caption). We also need to make sure the current record number is stored in the HTML form generated; we can do this by embedding a special # tag with the RecNo name inside. In the OnHTMLTag event handler, this tag will be replaced by the current record number of the table:

```
<FORM ACTION="http://localhost/scripts/WebShow.dll/dataset" METHOD=POST>
<H1>BIOLIFE Info</H1><HR>
<INPUT TYPE=SUBMIT NAME=SUBMIT VALUE="First">
<INPUT TYPE=SUBMIT NAME=SUBMIT VALUE="Prior">
<INPUT TYPE=SUBMIT NAME=SUBMIT VALUE="Next">
<INPUT TYPE=SUBMIT NAME=SUBMIT VALUE="Last">
<#RecNo>
<BR><B>Category:</B> <#Category>
<BR><B>Common_Name:</B> <#Common_Name>
<BR><B>Species Name:</B> <#Species Name>
<BR><B>Notes:</B> <#Notes>
</FORM>
```

In order to replace the #RecNo tag with the current record number, we use the HTML syntax for hidden fields, which is as follows:

```
<INPUT TYPE=HIDDEN NAME=RecNo VALUE=1>
```

This indicates that the hidden field named RecNo has a value of 1. Hidden fields are invisible to the end user, but the names and values are sent back to the Web server and Web Module application as soon as the user hits any of the four submit buttons. Apart from the hidden field, we can also display some visual information (as in Listing 13.4), such as the current record number and the total number of records in the table:

LISTING 13.4 DataSetPageProducer OnHTMLTag Event Handler

```
void __fastcall TWebModule1::DataSetPageProducer1HTMLTag(TObject *Sender,
    TTag Tag, const AnsiString TagString, TStrings *TagParams,
    AnsiString &ReplaceText)
{
  if (TagString == "RecNo")
    ReplaceText =
      "<INPUT TYPE=HIDDEN NAME=RecNo VALUE=" +
        IntToStr(TableBiolife->RecNo) + // current record number
      "> " + IntToStr(TableBiolife->RecNo) +"/"+
            IntToStr(TableBiolife->RecordCount) + "<P>";
  else
    if (TagString == "Species") // Species Name
      ReplaceText = TableBiolife->FieldByName("Species Name")->AsString;
    else
      if (ReplaceText == "(MEMO)") // Notes
        ReplaceText = TableBiolife->FieldByName(TagString)->AsString;
}
```

Now all we need to do is specify the action the WebActionItem has to perform for each of the submit buttons. We could have split this up into four different Web action items themselves, but then we'd have to use four forms, meaning four copies of the hidden field and any other information necessary. The default WebActionItem event handler shown in Listing 13.5 needs to obtain the value of the hidden `RecNo` field and the value of the submit button (with the specific action to be taken):

LISTING 13.5 `WebActionItem` Event Handler

```
void __fastcall TWebModule1::WebModule1WebActionItem4Action(
      TObject *Sender, TWebRequest *Request, TWebResponse *Response,
      bool &Handled)
{
  DataSetPageProducer1->DataSet->Open(); // In case it isn't open, yet!
  int RecNr = 0;
  AnsiString Str = Request->ContentFields->Values["RecNo"];
  if (Str != "") RecNr = StrToInt(Str);
  Str = Request->ContentFields->Values["SUBMIT"];
  if (Str == "First") RecNr = 1;
  else
    if (Str == "Prior") RecNr—;
    else
      if (Str == "Last") RecNr =
        DataSetPageProducer1->DataSet->RecordCount;
      else // if Str = 'Next' then { default }
        RecNr++;
  if (RecNr > DataSetPageProducer1->DataSet->RecordCount)
    RecNr = DataSetPageProducer1->DataSet->RecordCount;
  if (RecNr < 1) RecNr = 1;
  if (RecNr != DataSetPageProducer1->DataSet->RecNo)
    DataSetPageProducer1->DataSet->MoveBy(
      RecNr - DataSetPageProducer1->DataSet->RecNo);
  Response->Content = DataSetPageProducer1->Content();
}
```

The result is like the display we saw in Figure 13.10, but this time with four buttons that enable you to go to the first, prior, next, or last record of the BIOLIFE table, as in Figure 13.16 (note that in Figure 13.16, I've pressed the Next button three times already).

The techniques used here to keep state information and use it to browse through a table can be used in other places as well, of course. Note that, while we used the RecNo to retain the current record number, you could also pass the current (unique) key values and use them to search for the current record instead (especially when browsing a dynamic table to which lots of users are adding new records while you're browsing it).

If you want to perform more table browsing and interaction operations, then InternetExpress is the WebBroker extension you've been waiting for. But before we move to that last topic of this chapter, first we need to cover another important issue—security.

FIGURE 13.16
TDataSetPageProducer *and state information.*

Web Security

Web security is becoming more and more an issue these days, especially with e-commerce and e-business on one hand and hackers/crackers and Denial of Service and other attacks on the other hand. Even the simplest Web server application has to consider security in one way or another. Fortunately, there are tools and techniques to safeguard a Web server.

An important technique is to never place the database itself on the Web server. Place a firewall between the Web server and the Internet, and place another firewall between the Web server and the internal network—with your database server. This means your Web server is in a so-called "demilitarized zone" and has to go through proxies and firewalls to communicate with the outside as well as the inside world.

With the new TWebConnection component, C++Builder 5 includes support for proxies. This component is used in the client part of a MIDAS (Borland's Multi-tier Distributed Application Services Suite) multi-tier application, where it can connect to a remote database (another tier that is inside the network) through an HTTP proxy. A special ISAPI DLL httpsrvr.dll is used to make the connection with the database tier, and it must be installed and accessible by the Web server application. TWebConnection also has a Proxy property in which we can specify the IP address (or name) of the Proxy server. We also need to specify the UserName and Password properties to get through the proxy and access the database tier. Note that the TWebConnection component itself is not where the username and password are verified, but only the "router" to the proxy (as specified in the Proxy property).

If you don't use a proxy, then you can leave the `Proxy` property empty (as well as the `Username` and `Password` properties). However, in those cases you can also use a regular `TDCOMConnection` or high-end `TCORBAConnection` component, of course, and you don't need to connect over "plain" HTTP.

Secure Sockets Layer

Apart from securing your Web server and database servers with firewalls, you can also make sure incoming traffic (and data) is secured. This is especially important with sensitive input from the Web, like customer name and credit card information. For this purpose, the SSL (Secure Socket Layer) encryption protocol has been implemented to encrypt all data transmitted between a client and a server during the (secure) session. In a browser, you can notice this by the "lock," which is closed during a secure session. SSL uses Secure HTTP (also called S-HTTP) which translates into an `https://` prefix instead of `http://`. In order to use SSL, you should first obtain and install a public and private encryption key through a trusted source such as VeriSign. During the initial `https://` connection, the public key is sent from the server to the client, which then uses this public key to encrypt all data. When received by the server, the private key is used to decrypt the data again and work with it. As a consequence, apart from using the `https://` prefix, SSL can be relatively transparent for Web server application developers using WebBroker.

Authorization

Besides using SSL for incoming data protection, it is sometimes also a useful idea to have certain pages of your Web site available on a "members-only" basis. This means that you need some kind of basic authorization. Usually, this information is not considered mission critical, so the simple HTTP authorization built into the Web server can suffice in those cases—at least for the following example.

Using this authorization means that we need to verify the username and password and generate an answer in response to a correct username/password (the "members-only" information) or an incorrect combination (another try or error message). Although you can set permissions on directories using IIS, it is more fun—and more programming work—to use C++Builder and dynamically check the usernames and passwords.

HTTP Headers

The output of a CGI application or ISAPI DLL consists of an HTTP header followed by an empty line and the actual content. Inside the HTTP header, we specify the MIME-type of content (usually `text/html`, but it can also be `image/gif` or just about anything useful that can be imaged), so that the browser knows what to expect and can prepare itself. The Web server itself also adds a special first line to the HTTP header, which—in most cases—basically just says: `HTTP/1.0 200 OK`. This is the line that contains the result code of the dynamic Web page (everything is OK, so display the following content).

Suppose for a moment we could eliminate that first line and replace it with a special HTTP error code, namely 401, which means "unauthorized" and requests a user to log in first. We could produce the following HTTP header to force a user to log in to the realm /DrBob:

```
HTTP/1.0 401 Unauthorized
content-type: text/html
WWW-Authenticate: Basic realm="/DrBob"
```

Inside the OnAction event handler for WebActionItems, we can use the Request argument (of type TWebRequest), which has an Authorization property that holds the base 64–encoded HTTP authorization information.

Specifying custom HTTP headers also works the same way: You can return any HTTP response header using the Response->StatusCode and ReasonString properties. The type of authorization can be specified in the WWWAuthenticate property. I've only explored the basic type, and the realm can be set with the Realm property of the Response argument. Listing 13.6 illustrates this.

LISTING 13.6   Request Authorization

```
void __fastcall TWebModule1::WebModule1WebActionItem7Action(
      TObject *Sender, TWebRequest *Request, TWebResponse *Response,
      bool &Handled)
{
  AnsiString Auth = Request->Authorization;
  if (Auth.Pos("Basic ") == 1) Auth.Delete(1,6);
  if (Auth.Pos("bswart") == 0)
  {
    Response->StatusCode = 401;
    Response->ReasonString = "Unauthorized";
    Response->WWWAuthenticate = "Basic";
    Response->Realm = "/DrBob";
    Response->SendResponse();
  }
  else
    Response->Content = "Welcome:  ["+Request->Authorization+"]=["+Auth+"])";
}
```

Once I've finished generating the combined custom headers, I always call the Response.SendResponse method to avoid delays and send the HTTP headers directly to the client browser.

Note that the code in Listing 13.6 allows anything to enter. This isn't very practical; it is just an example to show how you can obtain and decode the Response.Authorization information inside a WebBroker or InternetExpress application.

If we develop a simple WebBroker CGI console application that outputs these few lines, we get an empty page. Nothing special happens. That's because the Web server still adds the special first line `HTTP/1.0 200 OK` to this page, and the second HTTP status code line is simply ignored. In order to tell the Web server *not* to add this special first line, we must rename the CGI executable or ISAPI DLL and give it an `NPH-` prefix (NPH stands for Non-Protocol Header), making it `NPH-WebShow.dll`.

Delphi VCL Problems

This code (Listing 13.6) works well with Netscape Navigator, but I found out that it doesn't quite work in Internet Explorer, due to password caching issues. If you return to a page that requires a username and password, IE5 will have remembered it for you—clearly a security breach if more than one person shares the machine.

Only one puzzle remains, and that is that neither Netscape Navigator nor Internet Explorer is able to show the name of the realm in the logon dialog, and we pass this information in the `Response.Realm` property. The only problem is that, for some reason, `SendResponse` doesn't use the `Realm` property. In fact, I found no place at all where this property is used, so we could have left that assignment out of the code.

Obviously, this is yet another bug in WebBroker. In this case, inside the `TISAPIResponse.SendResponse` and `TCGIResponse.SendResponse;` methods in resp. `IsapiApp.pas` and `CgiApp.pas`, we need to replace the single call to

```
AddHeaderItem(WWWAuthenticate, 'WWW-Authenticate: %s'#13#10);
```

with the following two lines (including a declaration of temporary variable `Tmp` of type `String` in the top of the procedure):

```
Tmp := Format('WWW-Authenticate: %s realm="%s"'#13#10, ['%s', Realm]);
AddHeaderItem(WWWAuthenticate, Tmp);
```

The first format replaces the realm string, and `AddHeaderItem` takes care of inserting the `WWWAuthenticate` string at the correct location.

This change to the `CGIApp.pas` and `ISAPIApp.pas` units resolves the unknown realm problem. Just put the modified Pascal unit in the same directory as your WebBroker project, add it to your C++Builder project, and build it so the new changes are included. This will overrule the buggy VCL library files with the updated Delphi source file. (And you learned another thing along the way: how to patch the Pascal VCL source files using C++Builder.)

Securing a Web Application

As has been illustrated, Web applications created with C++Builder offer tremendous flexibility in the presentation and gathering of data. They are the driving force behind today's e-commerce marketplace. Without them there would be no online stores with shopping carts to hold and process your purchases, or auction sites that track the bidding on a valuable trinket.

As in regular commerce, e-commerce generates, transfers, and stores huge amounts of sensitive and confidential data. As the Internet economy continues to grow, so will the amount of information collected.

C++Builder can be used to create different types of Web applications, and there are other tools that can also be used, such as ASP and Perl. Each tool has strengths and weaknesses, and choosing the right one for a particular application is an important decision. Choice of a development tool, however, is not the most important decision. That distinction lies with the often overlooked but extremely important choice of a method of securely storing the information gathered by a Web application.

As mentioned before, the Secure Socket Layer (SSL) helps guarantee the security of data during its transfer from the browser to the Web application. It is then the Web application's responsibility to ensure that it securely stores the information received. Unfortunately, this security concern is too often dealt with weakly or overlooked completely. The failure of developers to ensure that information is securely stored has resulted in the theft of vast amounts of personal and financial information from e-commerce sites. The theft of over 300,000 credit card numbers from the CD Universe Web site in 1999 illustrates the need for strong protection of stored information.

Issues to Consider

"Just because you aren't paranoid doesn't mean that they aren't out to get you." —Unknown

A Web application and the databases that it uses are in a rather unique predicament. Users must be able to access the Web server on which the Web application is running. This means that the Web server is exposed to attack from anyone on the Internet. Web server administrators attempt to keep their servers secure. However, hackers have been able to gain unauthorized access to them and have damaged or stolen the databases and applications on them. Internally generated problems such as poor password choice and password security (especially FTP passwords) greatly increase the potential for unauthorized access to the information stored on the system.

When considering security for Web applications, the only safe assumption to make is that a hacker will gain possession of your Web application, the application's databases, source code, passwords, and all other information stored on the server.

Figure 13.17 is a hexadecimal view of a WebBroker ISAPI that illustrates the ease with which usernames and passwords stored in a Web application can be extracted from the Web application. Information that has been hidden by dynamic password generation or concatenation can often be discovered through the use of a decompiler. Public domain utilities are also available that are designed to uncover a database's username and password.

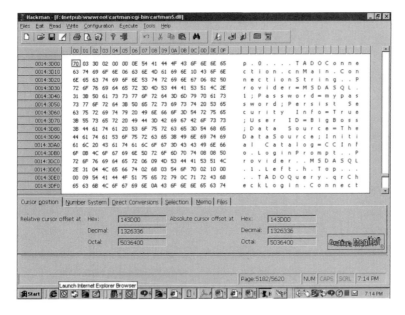

FIGURE 13.17

HackMan hexadecimal editor, copyright 1996-1999 by TechnoLogismiki.

Cryptography as the Answer

The purpose of this chapter is not to discuss cryptography as a science. Rather, the purpose is to discuss the effective use of cryptography in Web application development. The underlying math behind cryptographic algorithms is complicated, but using cryptography to secure information doesn't have to be.

Most Web applications that store sensitive information use cryptography, but the implementation is often weak or incorrect. Like a chain, cryptography is only as strong as its weakest link. It is the weak link that will be attacked and broken, exposing the stored information to the hacker.

Developers often choose a single strong cryptographic algorithm to install in a Web application, hoping that this "magic shield" will protect the sensitive information. This method fails to take into consideration the fact that the password used to encrypt the information is stored in the program or uses an easily predicted formula for generating passwords, such as concatenating the order ID and order date of a transaction, which will destroy the effectiveness of the cryptography. This can result in a Web application making the front page of a newspaper after a hacker has stolen several thousand passwords or credit card numbers from it.

Effective cryptography is a combination of algorithms and one-way hashes, acted upon by the steps dictated in a protocol. Only the proper implementation of a protocol will ensure that the information stored is secure. The following section presents a brief review of the basic components of cryptography, followed by a discussion of how a cryptographic protocol might be used to protect the sensitive information of a hypothetical online store.

> **CAUTION**
>
> No encrypted information can ever be considered completely secure. Breakthroughs in cracking encryption algorithms and brute force attacks (trying to decrypt by using every possible password) can expose protected information to a hacker.

Protocols, Algorithms, and One-Way Hashes

A protocol is a series of steps or procedures, some of which involve cryptography, that is used by a Web application to secure and retrieve information. A single weakness in a protocol can weaken or destroy the effectiveness of the most sophisticated algorithm.

An algorithm is a mathematical function used to perform the encryption and decryption of data. Algorithms can be either symmetric or asymmetric in nature. A symmetric algorithm uses the same key (password) for encryption and decryption. An asymmetric algorithm uses two keys: a public key for encryption and a private key for decryption. Examples of symmetric algorithms include DES, Blowfish, Twofish, and RC2. Examples of asymmetric algorithms include RSA, Rabin, and the Knapsack algorithms. Based on the amount of analysis to which these algorithms have been subjected, it is apparent that they are difficult to crack. A successful attack requires the exploitation of an implementation error or the use of time- and resource-consuming brute force. Errors that can be exploited by a hacker include failure to wipe the memory location where a key is stored, failure to overwrite or erase temporary files, and incorrect interpretation of an algorithm during coding.

Hash functions take a variable-length string as input and return a fixed-length string as the result (digest). In many hash functions, it is easy to predict a digest for a given input string or an input string for a given digest. One-way hash functions, however, are a special case. They are considered one-way because, while a digest can be predicted for any input string, it is virtually impossible to predict an input string given only the digest. An error of a single bit in duplicating an input string will cause a radical change in the resulting digest. One-way hashes have several uses in applied cryptography. We will use a one-way hash to generate a unique "session" key for a symmetric algorithm. Examples of one-way hashes include SHA, MD4, and MD5.

Securing an Online Store

For demonstration purposes, let's set up a simple online shopping cart Web application and try to store order information securely. To make the task more challenging, we will assume open access to the application's database, source code, and passwords. Although many issues will be discussed, this demonstration is not designed to be a comprehensive guide to securing a Web application.

Tools

To protect the information, we will use a hybrid cryptosystem that mixes the strength of a symmetric algorithm (fast encryption and decryption speeds) with the strength of an asymmetric algorithm (different encryption and decryption passwords). Blowfish will be the symmetric algorithm used; RSA will be the asymmetric algorithm. SHA will be the hash function used.

> **CAUTION**
>
> Some algorithms are patented. Depending on the patent holder, these algorithms may be freely used or may need to be licensed. It is also important to check import/export restrictions on algorithms being considered for use.

Step 1—Generating the Public and Private Keys

As discussed in the section "Protocols, Algorithms, and One-Way Hashes," earlier in this chapter, asymmetric algorithms have both a public key and a private key. Encryptions are generated using the public key; decryption is generated using the private key. The algorithm itself generates the public/private key set with a random seed value supplied by the user. Once the key set is generated, the public key can be stored in the database. The private key should be stored elsewhere, preferably on a system other than that used by the application. A key set can be used indefinitely; however, it should be replaced on a regular basis in order to limit the loss of information if a brute force attack on the key sets is attempted and is successful.

Step 2—Starting the Order

To accommodate the speed requirements of order processing, we will use the symmetric algorithm Blowfish to encrypt the data collected in the customer's order. However, we will first need to create a session key for Blowfish to use. We will use the SHA hash for this purpose. The strength of a hash is directly related to the degree of randomness of the information (variables) that is hashed. For example, if only the system time is hashed, a hacker can execute an attack using hashed dates from the previous month and attempt to decrypt the order using these hashes. A stronger hash would involve the system time, the tick count of the processor, the current memory usage of the system, and any other variables that are unique to the moment the hash is created.

Step 3—Encrypting the Order

Once the information is encrypted, consideration must be given to the manner in which it is stored. Some applications store the encrypted customer name in the Customer Name field, the address in the Address field, and so on. A serious weakness of this method is that it exposes plain text to the hacker. Having some of the plain text of the information that was encrypted can help a hacker break an encryption key. In the above example, although names and addresses are fairly random, credit card information and expiration dates are not; for example, all Discover cards start with 6011 or 1800. Armed with just this much plain text, a hacker may be able to break the key and retrieve the stored information.

The solution is to use Cipher Block Chaining (CBC) mode on a single string containing all of the information to be encrypted. CBC blends encrypted blocks as the algorithm cycles through the plain text. This results in the information being stored as one long encrypted string. A component descended from `TDataSetPageProducer` can be created that will separate the decrypted string into its proper fields.

A simple way to create the string that will be encrypted is to use a `TstringList` to store the field names and values and encrypt the `CommaText` property.

Step 4—Encrypting the Key

Once the order has been encrypted and stored, we must provide protection for the unique session key that was used in the encryption and will be needed for the decryption. We will use the asymmetric RSA algorithm to encrypt the session key. For encryption, RSA requires a pseudo-random seed value and the public key created in Step 1. Decryption of the session key will be accomplished using the private key created in Step 1, which has been safely stored on another computer.

To deny a hacker any kind of advantage, it is necessary to tidy up after completing a protocol. A protocol can create many temporary memory locations holding keys, variables, or even pieces of the unencrypted order. Inorder to cover these tracks, it is necessary to overwrite this information with junk data (Xs will suffice) and then delete it.

Retrieving the Order

Once the Web application is provided with the proper private key, it is a simple matter to decrypt the session key, which can then be used to decrypt the order itself. Back in plain text, the user can process the order as desired.

Attack!

It is axiomatic that any code that can be created can also be broken. The strength of a cryptographic protocol is not that it cannot be broken but the amount of time and resources required to break it. If the implementation of a protocol is strong, a hacker must rely on a brute force attack to retrieve the encrypted information. A brute force attack on a single encrypted order in a database can require months of processing. A brute force attack on a public and private key set will take the same processing time but will yield session keys used to encrypt order information. Key sets that are changed frequently limit the damage created by a successful brute force attack.

Returning to the chain analogy, let us examine the strength of the links in our protocol. The first link involves the generation of the public and private keys used in the RSA algorithm. The private key is secure if the user is diligent in hiding and storing it in a location away from the server. The second link in the chain involves the generation of the session key used by the Blowfish algorithm. Using several unique variables in the SHA hash formula will create a key that will be extremely difficult for a hacker to predict.

The Blowfish algorithm that uses the session key to encrypt the information in the order is the third link in the chain. This algorithm is currently accepted as one of the strongest available and is extremely difficult—if not impossible—to crack. Cipher Block Chaining (CBC)is the fourth link in the chain. By blending encrypted blocks into a single continuous string, CBC denies any advantage to the hacker that could be derived from plain text or the obvious field structure of a database. The fifth and final link is the RSA algorithm that encrypts the session key used by Blowfish in the encryption of the customer's order. RSA is also considered one of the strongest algorithms available. All in all, this simple protocol results in a chain of protection that is unlikely to be broken by any hacker.

Wrapping Up

In this section, we have established the need for strong Web application security and explored some practical ways in which cryptography can be used for protection against an assault by a hacker. The protocol used is not comprehensive protection against other types of attack, such as highjacking and replacing the public key in order to redirect future order information.

HTML and XML

One of the most hyped new features of C++Builder 5 Enterprise is its support of Extensible Markup Language (XML), which is most prominent in InternetExpress. In this section, I'll show you how to make use of InternetExpress and where XML is at its best—as a communication language between applications.

XML

XML is a subset of Standard Generalized Markup Language (SGML), and HTML is an application of SGML. The difference between XML and HTML is that syntax rules exist for HTML. An XML document needs to follow the general XML syntax rules, but the exact keywords (tags) that can be used in an XML document are up to the author of the document and are specified in something called the Document Type Definition (DTD). Together with a DTD, an XML document is said to be a self-describing document, and that's powerful indeed. An XML DTD for HTML documents probably exists as well. So an XML document is just an ASCII file and, although anyone and anything can read it, we should have access to the DTD file as well in order to understand it.

What is the advantage of XML? First, it's a simple file format that everyone and everything can read. Combined with the capability to define syntax rules in a DTD, we can put just about everything in XML, from books to Web pages to databases to customer order forms and invoices to entire operating or file systems. And when you can put anything in it, you can use it as a storage technique in a communication setup between two applications (or parts of an application).

I can see the sense of having an intermediate file format or language for data transfer (the Esperanto of computers), which XML and DTD can provide. XML support will be handy, especially with the open community on the Internet. On the other hand, I doubt if everything will become XML. One or two years from now, most tools and applications will have some kind of feature for importing and exporting to XML, just as most today have some sort of feature for exporting to HTML. But that doesn't mean that everything has gone to HTML, just as everything did not go to Java when this was predicted a few years ago (remember Corel's Java office suite?).

XML is a way to give structure to data and information that can be passed between one application to another, including between tiers, such as C++Builder 5 InternetExpress offers. We'll see this feature in the section "InternetExpress," later in this chapter. As such, it offers a standard format, independent of the communication protocol being used. This is also one of the reasons why XML will play an important role in Electronic Commerce EDI (Electronic Data Interchange) applications and situations. The fact that a DTD can be used to define (and check) the XML document itself means that—theoretically—everyone can talk to everyone and everything as long as the proper XML/DTD combination is used. Without a DTD, only applications that know the structure of the XML document itself—that is, those that have some knowledge built in—can truly interpret it.

Personally, I see XML as a portable file format, useful for communication between applications. Delphi 5 and C++Builder 5 InternetExpress makes use of XML to communicate between the MIDAS (Borland's Multi-tier Distributed Application Services suite) application server (`DataSetProvider`) and the client, which is a Web server in this case (`XMLProvider`, which talks only to a WebBroker `MidasPageProducer`). The XML that's being passed back and forth between the application server and the Web server actually contains MIDAS data packets. In previous versions of MIDAS, this data packet was in a propriety file format. Now it's in XML, which means it is more open. This is only in theory, though, because the MIDAS data packet does not come with a DTD. For now the only applications (or tiers) that have a good chance of understanding these XML packets are written in Delphi 5 or C++Builder 5.

In other words, although MIDAS clients and servers in C++Builder 5 can now send packets in XML, this is not really one of the core benefits of XML. I still can't connect a PowerBuilder client to a `DataSetProvider`, nor can Oracle8i produce XML capable of being used by an `XMLBroker` component. In fact, even within Delphi 5 applications, the XML produced by `DataSetProvider` seems to be usable only by an `XMLBroker` component, which in turn only talks to a `MidasPageProducer`. Between a `DataSetProvider` and a "regular" `ClientDataSet`, the data is still passed in the old proprietary (and undocumented) data format.

InternetExpress support of XML gives us a good headstart. We can create distributed applications in which the different tiers can communicate between each other by sending XML back and forth. We also can load and save MIDAS data packets in XML format. These are to be used by MIDAS-aware applications only, for now. But it's a start, and it's here.

InternetExpress

InternetExpress is based on MIDAS technology and WebBroker technology. MIDAS stands for MIddle-Tier Distributed Application Services (see Chapter 19, "Multi-Tier Distributed Applications with MIDAS 3") and is the Borland middleware technology to connect application servers to clients written in Delphi, C++Builder, and JBuilder. Apart from the integration of MIDAS with WebBroker, InternetExpress adds XML—a new and emerging Internet standard.

Customer Orders

The InternetExpress client gets its data from a MIDAS server, in this case from the MidasServer project that exports the customer and orders master/detail relation. That particular MIDAS server is implemented and explained in detail in Chapter 19, where it is also connected to a regular MIDAS client. InternetExpress can be seen as a special MIDAS client, so we won't concern ourselves with the MIDAS server, but just focus on the client side in the remainder of this chapter. You can read Chapter 19 first or just get the MidasServer project source code from the CD-ROM and make sure it is compiled and registered on your machine before continuing.

TMidasPageProducer

Assuming that the MidasServer is ready and available to connect to, it is time to turn the existing WebShow Web Module application into an InternetExpress MIDAS client. We still have two Web item actions left: /browse and /final. These will be used in this part of the chapter.

First, however, you must make a connection with the MIDAS application server and get the data we want to publish. Because we used a remote data module at the server side, we can use a DCOMConnection (from the MIDAS tab). Just drop one on the Web Module, and drop down the list of remote names. Somewhere among these names there must be the MidasServer.CustomerOrders server. The first part is the project name of the MIDAS server discussed in Chapter 19, and the second part of the name is the CoClass name of the remote data module from that project. This implies that a single MIDAS server can have more than one remote data module. Once we've selected the ServerName, we can toggle the Connected property. When it is set to true, the MIDAS server will be run and shown on your desktop. This proves that we can indeed find and connect to the MIDAS server. Now we still need to get the data from the server and turn it into a Web page. This is done by the two components from the InternetExpress tab: XMLBroker and MidasPageProducer. We need one of each, so drop them on your Web Module.

The XMLBroker component has a RemoteServer property, which must be set to the DCOMConnection component. Once this connection is in place, we can drop down the list of provider names to select the DataSetProviders from the remote server. In our case, we have only one—DataSetProviderCustomerOrders—but this implies that a given remote data module can have more than one DataSetProvider, as we stated earlier. Once ProviderName has been assigned, we're ready to proceed to the next step by actually designing the resulting Web page using MidasPageProducer.

Web Page Editor

If we right-click on MidasPageProducer, the Web page editor pops up. This is where we can visually design the resulting Web page. We have a Browser view (based on the Internet Explorer control), an HTML view (showing the resulting HTML source), and two panes on top. The left pane shows the components we create on MidasPageProducer, and the right pane shows the immediate children of a selected component.

Although we can create components here, there's no Component Palette. With another right-click of the mouse, we get the New Component dialog. This dialog shows the new components that we can create at this location (in the hierarchy of the left pane). When we start, for example, we can choose between a DataForm, a QueryForm, and a LayoutGroup. After we select a DataForm and right-click again, we can choose again between a DataGrid, a DataNavigator, a FieldGroup, and a LayoutGroup. The LayoutGroup, by the way, is nothing special, just a way to locate other components (such as a FieldGroup on the left of a DataGrid, for example). In practice, I've never used a LayoutGroup, although I used other techniques to lay out my Web page, which I'll share with you. For now, select a DataNavigator and a FieldGroup.

After we create these two components, the Browser page of the Web page editor will show two design-time warnings right above the navigator buttons. The DataNavigator has a warning stating that its XMLComponent is nil, and the FieldGroup has a warning stating that the XMLBroker is nil. The first warning is easy to fix: Just select the DataNavigator component and assign its XMLComponent to the FieldGroup (so this navigator will operate on the FieldGroup). Now, select the FieldGroup and assign the XMLBroker1 component (from our Web Module) to its XMLBroker component. This will get rid of the last warning and will also result in a list of all Customer fields in the browser window, including a special FieldStatus1 field. This last field contains a one-character status of the current record and indicates that a record is inserted, modified, or deleted. This is handy for a developer, but I'm not sure if I want my clients to see this field (nor do I expect them to care much about it). By default, all fields from the Customer (master) table will appear, but we can explicitly specify which fields we want to see by right-clicking on the FieldGroup and adding only those fields that are relevant, as shown in Figure 13.18.

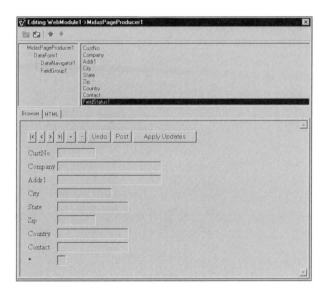

FIGURE 13.18
The Web page editor at design time.

Deployment

In order to deploy the InternetExpress client application, we must make sure we've done a couple of things. First of all, the resulting Web server application (in our case, WebShow.dll) must end up in a scripting directory on the Web server machine, just as with a regular WebBroker application. The easiest way to make sure the latest version is always in that location is to set the output directory of your project to the scripting directory on your local disk. IIS caches running ISAPI DLLs, and this doesn't always work, because the DLL on disk will be locked. That's another reason why I always use IntraBob to debug ISAPI DLLs.

Second, we should set the Producer property of the /browse WebActionItem to the MidasPageProducer component from our Web Module.

Last but not least, we need to make sure that the output generated can make use of a set of JavaScript files that are needed to parse the generated XML data packets (which will be embedded within the resulting HTML Web page). The JavaScript source files ship with your copy of C++Builder 5 Enterprise and can be found in the CBuilder5\Source\WebMidas directory. There are five files, and they total about 60KB of code. The easiest way to make sure that these JavaScript files can be found is by copying them to a location on the Web server and specifying that location in the IncludePathURL of the MidasPageProducer, which in my case is http://localhost/scripts—the same directory that holds the CGI executables and ISAPI DLLs themselves. If you're using IntraBob, you can simply specify ./ as IncludePathURL and copy the JavaScript files in the same directory where the ISAPI DLL and IntraBob.exe are located.

Once we make sure these last steps have been taken, we can rebuild the WebShow project one more time and execute the resulting ISAPI DLL inside IntraBob v5.0, Internet Explorer version 4+, or Netscape Communicator version 4+, the result of which is seen in Figure 13.19.

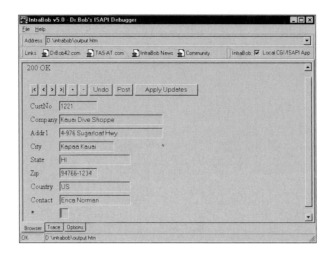

FIGURE 13.19

InternetExpress /browse *output in IntraBob.*

Final Master-Detail

The final example will include the full customer to orders master detail relationship in a single browser window, with full navigational support. Reopen the Web page editor (right-click on the MidasPageProducer) and add a DataGrid and another DataNavigator to the DataForm. Position the DataNavigator above the DataGrid, and make sure the DataGrid is the XMLComponent of the DataNavigator. You'll see one last design-time warning about the XMLBroker being nil for the DataGrid. To get rid of this last warning, you must assign the XMLBroker property of the DataGrid to the (only) available XMLBroker1 component again. This will remove the final warning, but the result is not as intended: The DataGrid will show the captions (field names) of the Customer (master) table and not of the Orders (detail) table. To take the last step, we must open up the XMLDataSetField property and specify TableOrders as a nested table field. This results in the DataGrid showing the right (detail) captions in the grid. Of course, we don't need to see every field, so add only the most important ones. This time, leave the StatusColumn1 field as well, so we can see when a detail record has been modified in the browser.

The widths of the columns in the DataGrid depend on the size of the table fields, which can be quite wide, as shown in Figure 13.20. To narrow the columns, just select some date fields and specify 12 as the value of the DisplayWidth properties. You can also change the name of some of the captions (for example, change PaymentMethod to Payment).

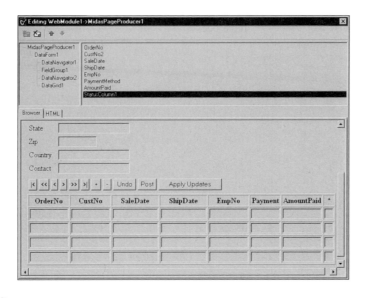

FIGURE 13.20
The Web page editor at design time for the master-detail output.

Although this is merely a functional Web page without any special design consideration (color scheme, graphics, fonts), it'll do for our final deployment and operational test. After all, you should make it work first, before you make it look good (or work fast, for that matter).

This time, we can use the /final WebActionItem to produce the MidasPageProducer output shown in Figure 13.21.

This single page contains it all. HTML with table and input definitions to create the look, XML that contains the master-detail table and field definitions along with the actual data, and JavaScript to parse the XML data and bind it to the input control that we see on the Web page. The good news is that it is all there. The bad news: It is all there!

Regarding the good news: When you browse through the data, you may note that the page doesn't flicker. The HTML stays put, and only the content (value) of the edit control changes. This is done by JavaScript code working with the XML data, and that's a pretty big "Oh, wow!" when you see it for the first time.

Regarding the bad news: When you browse through the data in this Web page, you may notice that all data is accounted for. The entire master-detail recordset has been sent over the wire. Now, consider a really larger customer-order relationship, where the master-detail "join" is several megabytes in size. It would take a lot of time—even with my cable modem—to send that over the wire. Ouch! Fortunately, we can limit the amount of data by modifying the MaxRecords property of XMLBroker and setting it to X to get only the first X records.

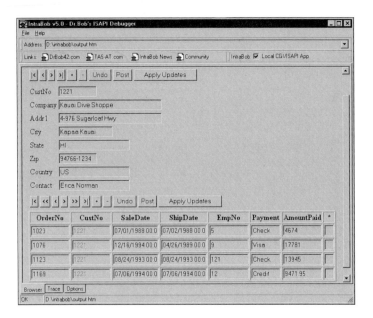

FIGURE 13.21

The InternetExpress /final *output in IntraBob.*

You may note that the CustNo fields inside the DataGrid look different than the other fields. That's because CustNo is a read-only field and should not be changed. The other fields are edit fields, and you can see some detail records that have been changed, causing the Status field to show the M for *modified*.

Note that the Status field is currently not visible because I've removed it from the list of fields that I want to see.

Note that any changes that we make inside the browser will remain there—inside the browser. In order to send our changes back to the MIDAS application server, we need to hit the Apply Updates button. This will send the updates in another XML packet back to the server, making any updates and reporting any reconcile errors that should occur. (For those of you who want to explore multiuser reconcile errors in more detail, check out the DEMOS\MIDAS\ INTERNETEXPRESS\INETXCUSTOM directory. It has two packages that contain—among others—a ReconcilePageProducer that you can connect to an XMLBroker component to take care of this for you. You also could read Chapter 19 for more details on MIDAS clients and servers.)

Web Page Design Issues

The resulting Web page looks a bit gray, like a programmer's Web page, and not at all something that people will want to look at for a long time. There are a number of ways to enhance the appearance of your output. First of all, we can edit the HTMLDoc property of the MidasPageProducer (just leave the # tags intact). For even more flexibility, we can use the

`HTMLFile` property, which points to an external file, overriding the `HTMLDoc` value. This results in template-based Web pages, and a third party can provide (and maintain) the external template for you.

In addition, you can manipulate each field in a `FieldGroup` or each cell in a `DataGrid` and specify the font, color, and so on (all using styles or plain HTML). A number of additional InternetExpress components can be found in the `Examples/MIDAS/InternetExpress` directories.

`Examples/MIDAS/InternetExpress/Inetxcustom/dclinetxcustom_bcb.bpk` is the package that needs to be built and is necessary to properly load the example project `Webshow.bpr` (which can be found on the CD-ROM). Load this package, compile it, and install it before you continue.

These packages include an `ImageNavigator` and more, which will be covered in detail in Chapter 19. The preparation for the final output of InternetExpress at design time can be seen in Figure 13.22.

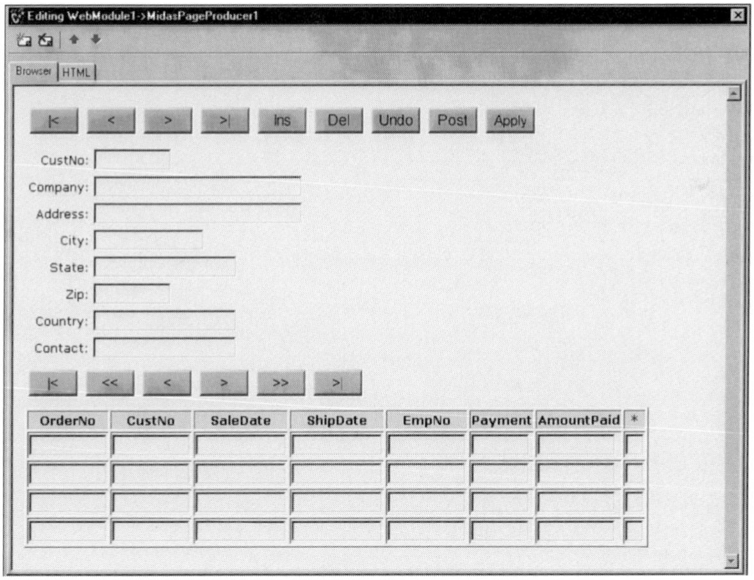

FIGURE 13.22

The InternetExpress /final *master-detail output in IntraBob.*

After you finished modifying the output settings (including modifications to the `HTMLDoc` property of `MidasPageProducer`), you can save the HTML in a file pointed to by `HTMLFile`. As long as you make sure that you include at least the five original # tags, you can add and modify anything in the HTML around it.

Summary

We've seen it all. Web Modules, Web action items, page producers, and table producers, for CGI and ISAPI. We've encountered problems and solved them or produced workarounds. And we've produced some pretty useful and powerful example programs along the way.

InternetExpress uses XML both for interapplication communication (between the MIDAS server and Web server applications) and for data packets inside the resulting Web page. Although some additional support is required for larger datasets, it is an excellent technique to quickly and interactively publish data on the Web in a truly thin-client way.

I hope this chapter has shown that the C++Builder 5 WebBroker and InternetExpress technologies are powerful tools for Internet server-side application development.

Database Programming

Mark Cashman
William Morrison
Stéphane Mahaux

IN THIS CHAPTER

- **Architecture Models for Database Applications**

- **Structured Query Language (SQL)**

- **ADO Express Components for C++Builder**

- **Data Acquisition Architectures**

- **Data Module Designer**

- **InterBase Express**

The complete text for this chapter appears on the CD-ROM.

Interfaces and Distributed Computing

IN THIS PART

DLLs and Plug-Ins

Joe Bonavita
Jean Pariseau

IN THIS CHAPTER

- **Using the DLL Wizard**
- **Writing and Using DLLs**
- **Using Packages Versus DLLs**
- **Using SDI Forms in a DLL**
- **Using MDI Child Forms in DLLs and Packages**
- **Using Microsoft Visual C++ DLLs with C++Builder**
- **Using C++Builder DLLs with Microsoft Visual C++**
- **Writing Plug-Ins**

Let's say you're asked to work on a project that processes data from a database and generates reports from that data. Now let's say you have to work on two projects that share the reports. The first thing that probably pops into your mind is to include the report in both projects and have each project call the report, given the data needed to print or display. That would be fine if the world never changed. Now suppose a customer calls up and say that he needs the report to display 1, 2, 3, or more fields. You're probably thinking, "That's happened to me before. I just change the report, rebuild the two projects that use the report, and ship it." It would be nice if you didn't have to touch the projects at all. If you had the report in a DLL, you would just add the fields to the report, rebuild the DLL, and ship that. There would be no need to rebuild the other projects at all.

Given the earlier example, this may or may not seem like it's really that big of a deal, but if you had say 3, 4, 5, or even 10 projects that share the same code, you would be thinking a lot differently about the way you would do this.

Throughout this chapter you are going to see how to build a DLL, export functions and classes, load the DLL dynamically and statically, place forms such as SDIs (single document interfaces) and MDIs (multiple document interfaces) in DLLs, and see some differences between packages and DLLs. We also will build a basic package, export its functions, and load and unload it. Finally, you'll see how to link statically to a DLL that was created in Visual C++ and use a DLL built in C++Builder with Visual C++.

Using the DLL Wizard

The simplest way to create a DLL is with the DLL Wizard. To bring up the DLL Wizard, select File, New, select the DLL Wizard from the New tab, and select OK. The DLL Wizard provides several options for you to choose from (see Figure 15.1).

The following options are presented on the DLL Wizard dialog.

C   You'll notice that the Use VCL option becomes disabled. That's because the VCL can only be included in a C++ project. A C project isn't going to know what classes are or how to compile them, so if you might be using any C++ code, don't choose this option.

C++   This option will give you access to the Use VCL, Multi Threaded, and VC++ Style DLL options. If this option is chosen, the compiler will use C++ to compile the code in the main module of the DLL, thus allowing you to use any C++ code in your DLL.

Use VCL   This option will create a DLL that can contain VCL components and classes. As mentioned previously, this option is available only when the C++ option also is chosen. This causes C++Builder to include the VCL.h file in your main module and changes the startup code and linker options for compatibility with VCL objects. You will also notice that the Multi Threaded option becomes disabled. The reason for this is because the VCL needs to have multithreading capabilities.

Multi Threaded   This option specifies that the DLL will have more than one thread of execution, so if you plan to have multiple threads in your DLL, it would be a good idea to choose this option. Remember that the VCL needs to have this capability, so if you try to add components into the DLL later on and didn't check this, you're going to run into a problem. To avoid this, always make sure that this option is checked any time the Use VCL option is checked, even if the option is grayed out.

VC++ Style DLL   This option specifies what type of entry point the DLL is going to have. If you want the DLL entry point to be `DLLMain()`, the Visual C++ style, check the VC++ style option; otherwise, `DLLEntryPoint()` is used for the entry point. We typically leave this option off even if we're going to use our DLL in Visual C++.

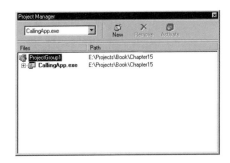

FIGURE 15.1
The DLL Wizard with its default options checked.

The majority of the time you will be using the defaults for the DLLs you are going to be creating. However, when the time comes for you to make these changes, you'll have a good idea as to what each option is going to do for you. For additional information, see the online help for C++Builder.

Writing and Using DLLs

A DLL (dynamic link library) is probably one of the most useful ways of modularizing a program there is. A DLL is a special kind of an executable that is loaded into memory by an application and can contain all the same code you would put into a normal executable. A DLL cannot be run on its own the way an executable can because it is not built the same, although once loaded it can load other DLLs or executables and perform the same as a standard executable.

A DLL can be loaded statically or dynamically. A statically linked DLL is linked to the executable when the executable is built and is loaded into memory when the executable is run. A dynamically linked DLL can be loaded and unloaded as needed, which can lessen the amount of resources the program needs to run. Another difference is that with static linking, a program will not run without the DLL, while a dynamically linked DLL doesn't have to be present as long as the program isn't calling for it.

There are different ways of loading DLLs, and there are also different kinds of DLLs. One of the two most common contains code and forms. The other might contain resources such as icons, bitmaps, forms, and so on. You can place bitmaps or icons in a DLL and load them from the DLL as needed. Another common type of DLL is one used for string tables. Using string tables in a DLL allows your programs to support different languages.

DLLs can be difficult to understand in the beginning, but once you get the hang of using them, you'll find that it's no different from using standard executables to carry out your functions.

The first thing you have to do is figure out what you want to be accessible from your DLL. Do you just want to export functions or maybe a class? This is entirely up to the people who are designing the DLL, but as a rule of thumb we like to export as many of the useful functions as we can, although you don't want to export everything. A major thing to remember when exporting a function or a class is whether that function can run without the need for other functions to be called or properties to be set first. You also don't want to export a function or a class that relies on another DLL unless you always plan to distribute both DLLs together.

Examples of the type of functionality you may want to put into a DLL include shell functions, network functions, and an OpenGL class. It also could include anycode that you feel may be useful at a later time.

Linking DLLs Statically

In the next three sections of this chapter, we will build an application that calls DLLs in three different ways. This is Calling Application, and the final version is located in the `CallingApp` folder on the CD-ROM that accompanies this book.

First we will build a statically linked DLL to call. It is located in the `SimpleDLL` folder on the CD-ROM. Then we will build a dynamically linked DLL. It is located in the `DynamicDLL` folder on the CD-ROM. Finally we will build a package for our Calling Application. It is located in the `Package` folder on the CD-ROM.

As we progress through these sections, we will build each piece and modify the Calling Application as we go, so that we can call each piece from the application. At the end of this section, we will present some additional notes on how to connect the pieces so that the application on the CD-ROM will work correctly. We'll start off by creating Calling Application, which will link statically to our DLL.

Create a new project and set the form's Caption property to Calling Application. Save the unit as CallingForm.cpp and save the project as CallingApp.bpr. The CallingApp project is going to be used over the next few sections. Therefore, the project on the CD-ROM contains all the code and modifications made throughout this section.

Now select View, Project Manager from the C++Builder main menu to display the Project Manager dialog, shown in Figure 15.2. Select the New button to display the Object Repository, then select DLL Wizard from the New tab and click OK. The DLL Wizard dialog is displayed.

FIGURE 15.2
The CallingApp project in the Project Manager.

Click OK to accept the default settings. Now select File, Save All from the C++Builder main menu, and save the unit and the project as SimpleDLL.cpp and SimpleDLL.bpr, respectively, and the project group as DLLProjectGroup.bpg. From the C++Builder main menu, select File, New. Select Unit from the New tab and click OK. Save this unit as DllFunctions.cpp. This is where the code will go inside the DLL itself. You should have noticed that we saved the project and the unit with the same name. Unlike when creating a new application, C++Builder doesn't create a project file or the main source file on its own with the same name as the project itself. This is because a DLL doesn't need any forms, so the DLL can use the file that contains the DllEntryPoint(). This is similar to WinMain() in a regular executable.

> **TIP**
>
> The Project Manager allows you to have multiple projects open at once and provides a nice graphical representation of the projects you have open. The Project Manager also shows all the files included in each project.

Add the following function to DllFunctions.cpp:

```
void Say(char *WhatToSay)
{
    ShowMessage("This is from within the DLL\n" + (String)WhatToSay);
}
```

and add this to `DllFunctions.h`:

```
extern "C" void __declspec(dllexport) Say(char *WhatToSay);
```

This tells C++Builder to export the function `Say()`. The `extern` keyword tells C++Builder to use the C calling convention, so that any compiler that supports C-type exports will be able to import this function. The `dllexport` storage class enables you to export functions and objects, and it is used for compatibility with Microsoft's C/C++ languages. Also, using `dllexport` eliminates the need for a definition file (`.def`). This will prevent you from needing a `.def` file for export definitions for this DLL. If you are using a DLL that was built from another compiler, then you may need one. Later on you will see that we will be using `dllimport`. This is used for the same reason as `dllexport`. It provides compatibility and enables you to import functions, data, and objects from a DLL. For more information on these, see the C++Builder online help.

Now save all the files and projects. After you've saved the project, you will need to build the DLL. You must make sure that `SimpleDLL` is the active project. The name of the active project will be displayed as the C++Builder main window caption. An example of what the caption might look like is `C++Builder 5 - SimpleDll`.

If this isn't the active project, you can change it in several ways. One way is by clicking View, Project Manager from the C++Builder main menu, and then double-clicking on the project that you want active or selecting the project and clicking the Activate button on the top right of the Project Manager. You can also right-click on the project and select Activate. Once you're certain that this is the active project, you can build it. C++Builder will generate a `.lib` file for the DLL and the DLL itself.

Return to the calling application and add a `TButton` to the `CallingForm` and set its caption to `Static`. In the button's `OnClick` event, add the following:

```
void __fastcall TForm1::Button1Click(TObject *Sender)
{
    // This will call the function in
    // the DLL.
    Say("Hello");
}
```

Finally, click on Project, Add to Project. Change Files of Type to Library File (`*.lib`) and choose the `SimpleDll.lib` file. This is what C++Builder will use to link to the functions in the DLL. Also, you must include the header file for the DLL.

Add this line to `CallingForm.cpp`:

```
#include "DllFunctions.h"
```

Now save the project and choose Project, Build All Projects. This will build both `CallingApp` and `SimpleDLL`. Make sure `CallingApp` is the active project, then run it and click the button. A message box will appear, as shown in Figure 15.3.

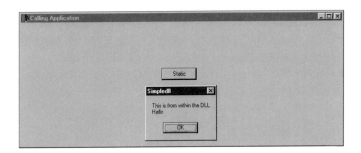

FIGURE 15.3
The `CallingApp` *project running with a message box from within the DLL.*

That's pretty much all there is to statically linking a DLL. As long as you include the proper header files to the `.cpp` files that will be using the functions or classes and include the `.lib` file in the project, everything else is the same as calling any other function.

Importing Functions from a Dynamically Linked DLL

There are a few basic steps that must be taken to dynamically link a DLL:

- Load the DLL and obtain a pointer to it.
- Get a pointer to the function you want to call.
- Call the function.
- Free the DLL.

There are also two different ways of importing functions from DLLs that are dynamically linked:

- Create a new `typedef` using the exported functions prototype.
- Cast each call to `GetProcAddress()` to the exported functions prototype.

To determine which one to use, you should first decide if you are going to be using any single function type or prototype of a function very often. This will help determine the way you want to cast your `GetProcAddress()` calls. The Windows API function `GetProcAddress()` will return a pointer to an exported function from a DLL, given a pointer to an instance of a DLL and the name of the exported function for which you want a pointer. For example, you might have a function being exported with a prototype such as int Add(int x, int y) and another that is int Subtract(int x, int y). You may want to use the same typecast for both.

```
typedef (int (__import *AddSubtract)(int, int))
AddSubtract *MyAdd, *MySubtract;
MyAdd    = (AddSubtract *)GetProcAddress(Dll, "_Add");
MySubtract = (AddSubtract *)GetProcAddress(Dll, "_Subtract");
```

Notice in the GetProcAddress() functions that there is a variable Dll. This variable is a pointer to the DLL that is loaded using the Windows API LoadLibrary() function. This will be explained in more depth in our first example of dynamically linking a DLL.

You may be wondering what the first line is doing. We are declaring a new type by using the typedef storage class specifier. AddSubtract will become a new type, a type of int (__import *)(int, int). It is actually a function that returns an int and takes two ints as parameters. The import keyword tells C++Builder that we are going to be importing this function from an external source. __import can also be replaced by __declspec(dllimport).

> **TIP**
>
> The preceding underscores for Add and Subtract in the GetProcAddress() functions are required because they are added by C++Builder to the beginning of the functions exported in the DLL.

The second line now declares two pointers of our new type, AddSubtract.

In the third and fourth lines, each of our pointers is getting the return value from the GetProcAddress() functions. Also notice that the GetProcAddress() return values are being cast to our new type AddSubtract. This way you don't need to do a long typecast such as this in the header:

```
int(__import *MyAdd)(int x, int y);
int(__import *MySubtract)(int x, int y);
```

or such as this in source:

```
MyAdd = (int(__import *)(int, int))GetProcAddress(Dll, "_Add");
MySubtract = (int(__import *)(int, int))GetProcAddress(Dll, "_Subtract");
```

The first way is much neater and can help keep things more organized, but you do have to remember that you have now created a new typedef AddSubtract that may or may not be useful elsewhere throughout your program. The second way is usually all right when a call appears only once and you're not too concerned with how the pointer is declared or how the returned pointer from GetProcAddress() is typecast.

For the most part, importing a function is a really personal preference. I prefer the first way, but others may prefer the second way. After importing functions enough, you'll gain your own style. Maybe you'll be using #define instead and creating a macro to do the work. For the importing examples, we're going to be using the typedef technique.

Now let's create the dynamic DLL. Click File, New and from the New tab choose DLL Wizard. Accept the defaults and save the unit and project as DynamicDll.cpp and DynamicDll.bpr, respectively. Next click File, New and from the New tab choose Unit. Save the unit as DynamicFunctions.cpp.

CAUTION

You can save this project either in the same folder as the SimpleDLL project or in a separate folder. If you save it in its own folder, when you load the DLL later, you will have to specify its full path.

Go to DynamicFunctions.cpp and add the following:

```
void DynamicSay(char *WhatToSay)
{
    ShowMessage("This is from within the Dynamic DLL\n" + (String)WhatToSay);
}
```

In the header, add the following:

```
extern "C" void __declspec(dllexport) Say(char *WhatToSay);
```

Now save the project and build it.

Now reopen the CallingApp we created previously and add a second TButton to it. Set the Caption property to Dynamic as shown in Figure 15.4.

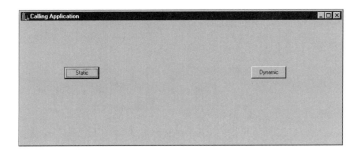

FIGURE 15.4

CallingApp's main window, now showing two buttons.

15

DLLS AND
PLUG-INS

In `CallingForm.h` we'll add a `typedef` defining what the exported function looks like. We'll also add a pointer of the new `typedef` type.

```
private:
    typedef void __declspec(dllimport) SayType (char *);
    SayType *LoadSayFunction;
```

Next add an `OnClick` event for the new `TButton` and insert the code from Listing 15.1.

LISTING 15.1   The `Button2Click` Event

```
void __fastcall TForm1::Button2Click(TObject *Sender)
{
    // First we need to load the Dll.
    HINSTANCE Dll = LoadLibrary("Dynamic.dll");

    // Check and make sure the Dll loaded
    if (Dll)
    {
        // Get the address of the function.
        LoadSayFunction = (SayType *)GetProcAddress(Dll, "_Say");
        if (LoadSayFunction)
            LoadSayFunction("Dynamic Hello");
        else
            ShowMessage(SysErrorMessage(GetLastError()));

        // After we're done with the Dll we have to free it.
        FreeLibrary(Dll);
    }
    else
    {
        ShowMessage(SysErrorMessage(GetLastError()));
        ShowMessage("Unable to load the DLL");
    }
}
```

This code needs some explanation.

Notice the first line:

```
HINSTANCE Dll = LoadLibrary("Dynamic.dll");
```

The `HINSTANCE` is the type returned by the `LoadLibrary()` function. This is a Win32 API function (for more information on this, see the Win32 SDK Reference). It attempts to load the DLL using the given name. You can include a full path here. If just the name is provided, then Windows will use the search paths to try and load it. If the DLL cannot be loaded, `LoadLibrary()` will return NULL. This explains why the `DLL` variable is checked on the next line:

```
If (Dll)
```

We don't want to try to use a library that wasn't loaded. If the DLL didn't load, we have an else:

```
else
{
    ShowMessage(SysErrorMessage(GetLastError()));
    ShowMessage("Unable to load the DLL");
}
```

This will show a message telling us what the error was that caused the DLL not to load.

Next we have to get the address to the exported function. The Win32 API function GetProcAddress() takes two parameters. The first is the instance of the DLL that was loaded, and the second is the name of the function we want a pointer to. GetProcAddress() returns a FARPROC, so it can be cast to whatever type we need. In this case we cast it to our new type SayType.

```
LoadSayFunction = (SayType *)GetProcAddress(Dll, "_Say");
```

Here is where we get a pointer to the exported function _Say(). Notice that we are casting the returned pointer to our defined typedef SayType.

> ## TIP
>
> C++Builder by default adds an underscore to the beginning of the functions it exports. There is an option under Project, Options on the Advanced Compiler tab called Generate Underscores. If you uncheck this option, the function will export without the underscore, as shown in Figure 15.5.

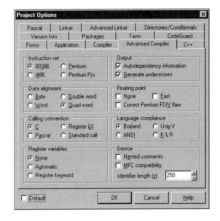

FIGURE 15.5
The Project Options, Advanced Compiler tab.

15

DLLs AND
PLUG-INS

Check again and make sure that the function succeeded before using the pointer. Trying to use this pointer if it did not load will result in an access violation.

Once you have a valid pointer, you can use it just like you would any other function:

```
LoadSayFunction("Dynamic Hello");
```

After we're done using this DLL, we want to free it. DLLs can be freed using the Win32 API function `FreeLibrary()`, which takes one parameter, the `HINSTANCE` Dll we got from `LoadLibrary()`.

Because we added all the functionality needed to load our DLL dynamically and call our function, you can save, build, and run the project. Click on the Dynamic button that we added earlier and you'll see a new message box come up with our message from the DLL (see Figure 15.6).

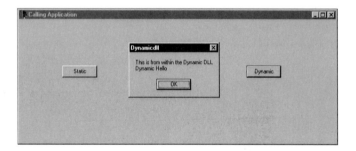

FIGURE 15.6

`CallingApp`'s *main window, now showing a message box from the dynamic DLL.*

That's it for loading a dynamic DLL. You may be thinking that the static DLL is much easier to use, which is true, but remember that the static DLL loads when your program starts and stays around until your program closes. Also, if the static DLL is missing for some reason, your program won't run at all.

Exporting Classes

Now that you know how to export simple functions, let's see how to export entire classes.

Reopen the `SimpleDll` project and add a new unit to it. Save this unit as `StaticClass.cpp`. Go to the header. Here we're going to add a class. We'll call it `TStaticClass`. Our class will have one variable, `m_AlreadySaidHi`, one property, `TimesCalled`, and one method, `SayHi()`.

```
__declspec(dllexport) class TStaticClass
{
private:
    int FTimesCalled;
```

```
public:
    __fastcall TStaticClass ();
    __fastcall ~ TStaticClass ();
      bool m_AlreadySaidHi;
      void __fastcall SayHi(void);
    __property int TimesCalled = {read = FTimesCalled};
};
```

Notice that we're using the same export technique used to export the functions earlier, except we're not using the extern C. Also notice how our class looks like any other class you would have in a standard executable.

Next go to .cpp and add the constructor and destructor. Give our two variables default values.

```
__fastcall TStaticClass:: TStaticClass ()
{
    FTimesCalled   = 0;
    m_AlreadySaidHi = false;
}
//-------------------------------------------------------------------------
__fastcall TStaticClass::~ TStaticClass ()
{
}
```

Now we need to add our method with its functionality:

```
void __fastcall TStaticClass::SayHi(void)
{
    ShowMessage("Hello! From our DLL Class");
    FTimesCalled++;
    m_AlreadySaidHi = true;
}
```

Once this is done and saved, build the DLL.

Reopen the CallingApp.bpr project and add the following to CallingApp.h:

```
#include "StaticClass.h"
...
private:
TStaticClass *StaticClass;
```

Go to .cpp and add another TButton. Set its caption to Static Class. Add an OnClick event to the button and place the following code there:

```
void __fastcall TForm1::Button3Click(TObject *Sender)
{
    if (!StaticClass->m_AlreadySaidHi)
        StaticClass->SayHi();
```

```
    else
    {
        ShowMessage("You've already called this function " +
                    (AnsiString)StaticClass->TimesCalled + " times.");
        StaticClass->SayHi();
    }
}
```

Now we'll create the `StaticClass` class. Add the following code in the form's constructor:

```
__fastcall TForm1::TForm1(TComponent* Owner)
    : TForm(Owner)
{
    StaticClass = new TStaticClass;
}
```

We're going to want to destroy the class, so we'll add a destructor to the form and place the `delete` there.

```
__fastcall TForm1::~TForm1()
{
    delete StaticClass;
}
```

Remember also to add this to the header:

```
public:
__fastcall TForm1::~TForm1();
```

Now you can save, build, and run the `CallingApp` project and click on the Static Class button. You will see a message box that says `Hello! From our DLL Class` (see Figure 15.7). Click it again and you will see a message box that tells you how many times you've clicked this button.

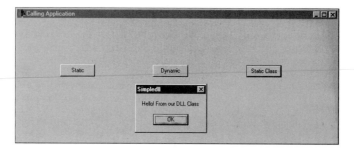

FIGURE 15.7

A message box from a class contained in our DLL.

Notice that we used a variable, a property, and a method from our class, just as we would use them from any other class. Once you understand how to go about exporting methods and classes from DLLs, there's not too much you can't do with them.

Using Packages Versus DLLs

Packages are DLLs with specific VCL extensions. Using packages will provide you with better compatibility with the calling application because the calling application was written in C++Builder and uses the VCL. There are a few differences between using a package and using a DLL. For example, you would use LoadPackage() instead of LoadLibrary() and FreePackage() instead of FreeLibrary().

A package uses the same instance of the VCL that your project is using and can share its global memory. This gives your package more knowledge about the calling application itself and also makes the calling application more aware of what's in the package. A major benefit to using a package is when you have an MDI child form in your package. When the child is being created, it will be able to find its parent form. In a DLL, you have to trick the DLL to think it is in the same application as the parent form. A disadvantage is that other development tools cannot use the package because it is specific to C++Builder. If you're thinking of using a package or a DLL with Visual C++, then you're going to have to use a DLL.

We'll create a small package to use for our example. Click File, New and choose Package (see Figure 15.8). Next we'll add a new unit. Click File, New and choose Unit. Save the package as ThePackage.bpk and the unit as PackageFunctions.cpp. This is going to be pretty much the same as the DLLs we created earlier.

FIGURE 15.8
The New Items dialog box.

Let's once again add a function called Say(). Go to the header for the PackageFunctions.cpp unit and add the following:

```
extern "C" void __declspec(dllexport)PackageSay(char *WhatToSay);
```

Now go to the .cpp and add

```
void PackageSay(char *WhatToSay)
{
    ShowMessage(WhatToSay);
}
```

Build the package, and a .bpl file will be created. This is the package itself. By default, all packages go to the Projects\Bpl folder under the C++Builder folder. You can change this by going to Project, Options and clicking on the Directories/Conditionals tab. The last edit field under directories says BPI/LIB Output. Here you can specify where you would like the package to go (see Figure 15.9).

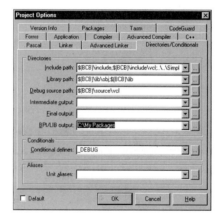

FIGURE 15.9
The Projects Options screen.

Copy the .bpl file that we just built from its original location to the folder where you saved the CallingApp project.

Now open the CallingApp project once again. Add another TButton, set its caption to Package, and add an OnClick event for it. Then add the code from Listing 15.2.

LISTING 15.2   The `Button4Click` Event

```
void __fastcall TForm1::Button4Click(TObject *Sender)
{
    // First we need to load the Package.
    Windows::HINST Package = LoadPackage("ThePackage.bpl");

    // Check and make sure the Package loaded
    if (Package)
    {
        // Get the address of the function.
        SayFromPackage = (SayType *)GetProcAddress((HINSTANCE)Package,
                                                  "_PackageSay");
        // Make sure we have the address then call the function.
        if (SayFromPackage)
            SayFromPackage("Package Hello");
        else
            ShowMessage(SysErrorMessage(GetLastError()));

        // After we're done with the Package we have to free it.
        UnloadPackage(Package);
    }
    else
    {
        ShowMessage(SysErrorMessage(GetLastError()));
        ShowMessage("Unable to load the Package");
    }
}
```

Now add the following to the header:

```
private:
SayType *SayFromPackage;
```

Notice that we're using the same type we created earlier for the dynamic DLL.

In this code you'll see that the only difference between loading a DLL and a package is the `LoadPackage()` and `UnloadPackage()` functions. You still use `GetProcAddress()` to get a pointer to the function you want.

Once again save, build, and run the `CallingApp` project. Click on the Package button, and again another message box will come up, as shown in Figure 15.10.

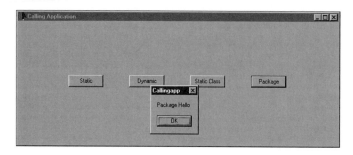

FIGURE 15.10

CallingApp *displaying the message box from our package.*

Using SDI Forms in a DLL

There will be times when you will want to put forms into your DLLs. This can really help make a project more modular and also allow for using plug-ins. The technique is the same as putting any other function in a DLL.

We're not going to list all the code necessary to place a form in the DLL, but we'll list the basic code that you need. I will include this in the sample project MDIChildDLL.bpr that you will find in the MDIDLL folder on the CD-ROM that accompanies this book.

1. Add a form to the DLL.

2. Export a function called ShowMyForm() like this:

   ```
   extern "C" void __declspec(dllexport)ShowMyForm(void);
   ```

3. Add this function to the .cpp.

4. Create the form and then show it:

   ```
   TForm *MyForm = new Tform(NULL);
   MyForm->ShowModal();
   delete MyForm;
   ```

That's all there is to it. Call this function the same way you did any of the others. I'll be putting this code in the dynamic DLL if you would like to see it. Figure 15.11 shows an example of this.

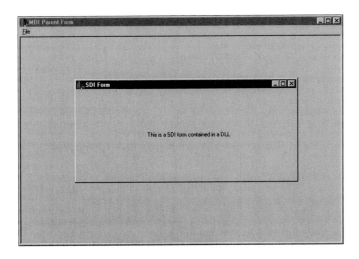

FIGURE 15.11
The MDI parent form displaying a SDI form.

Using MDI Child Forms in DLLs and Packages

One question asked more than any about DLLs is "How do I use a MDI child form in a DLL?" The problem with putting MDI children in DLLs is that the child can't find its parent. Therefore, you must trick the DLL into thinking it is part of the application that contains the parent.

Using MDI Child Forms in DLLs

Start off by creating a DLL, and save the project and `.cpp` as `MDIChildDLL.bpr` and `MDIChildDLL.cpp`. Now add a new form to it and set the following properties:

- `Name = Child`
- `FormStyle = fsMDIChild`
- `Caption = MDI Child`
- `Height = 200`
- `Width = 400`

Create an `OnClose` event for the form and enter `Action = caFree;`. Next, place a label on the form and set its caption to `I'm a MDI Child in a DLL!`. Now save the form as `MDIChild.cpp`.

Next we're going to need an exported method to call this form. Go to the project's main source unit `MDIChildDLL.cpp` and add the following code:

```
#include "MDIChild.h"
TApplication *ThisApp = NULL;
```

15

We're going to add the prototype to the source unit right above the function because we really don't need a header for this unit. This DLL is going to be dynamically linked.

```
extern "C" void
    __declspec(dllexport)ShowMDIChildForm(TApplication *CallingApp);


void ShowMDIChildForm(TApplication *CallingApp)
{
    if (!ThisApp)
    {
        ThisApp = Application;
        Application = CallingApp;
    }
    Child = new TChild(Application);
    Child->Show();
}
```

In this code, you'll notice that our function takes one parameter, a TApplication. The reason for this is that we are going to switch the Application instance for the DLL to the Application instance of the calling application itself. This will make the MDI child fully aware of its parent form.

Next we're going to have to make sure that we switch the Application instance back to what it was when the DLL first loaded. Let's use DllEntryPoint() for this. Add the following to the DllEntryPoint() function so that it looks like the following:

```
int WINAPI DllEntryPoint(HINSTANCE hinst, unsigned long reason,
                         void* lpReserved)
{
    // If the DLL is being unloaded then we need to reset its
    // Application instance to what it originally was.
    if ( (reason == DLL_PROCESS_DETACH) && (ThisApp) )
        Application = ThisApp;
    return 1;
}
```

The DllEntryPoint() has a parameter called reason that will tell you what the calling process wants to do. These are the four possible reasons:

- DLL_PROCESS_ATTACH

- DLL_THREAD_ATTACH

- DLL_THREAD_DETACH

- DLL_PROCESS_DETACH

In our case, we're only concerned with DLL_PROCESS_DETACH. If this is the reason, then we want to reset the application's instance. (For more information on this topic see the WIN32 SDK Reference.)

Before you save and build the DLL, there's one more thing you must do. You must build the DLL using the dynamic RTL and Runtime packages. Swapping the application instance for the DLL will allow the DLL to see the MDI parent form, but it won't allow the parent form to know about the MDI child forms. To change these options, click on Project, Options and go to the Packages tab. On the bottom, check the Build with Runtime Packages box. Next click on the Linker tab and make sure the Use Dynamic RTL box is checked. Once this is done, you can save and build the DLL (see Figures 15.12 and 15.13).

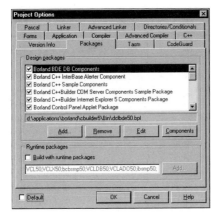

FIGURE 15.12
The Packages tab of the Project Options dialog.

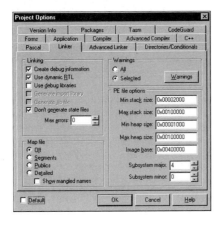

FIGURE 15.13
The Linker tab of the Project Options dialog.

Next we have to create the calling application with the MDI parent form.

Create a new project and set the following properties for the main form:

- Name = Parent
- Caption = MDI Parent Form
- FormStyle = fsMDIForm

Add a TMainMenu component with its Caption property set as &File. Then add two items below File. Set the first one's caption to &New and the second one's caption to E&xit.

Now save the unit as ParentForm.cpp and the project as MDIParent.bpr. Create an OnClick event for the &New menu item and add the code from Listing 15.3.

LISTING 15.3   The New1Click Event

```cpp
void __fastcall TParent::New1Click(TObject *Sender)
{
    typedef void __declspec(dllimport)ShowChildType(TApplication *);
    ShowChildType *ShowMDIChild;

     // See if the DLL is loaded already.
    if (!Dll)
        Dll = LoadLibrary("MDIChildDLL.dll");
    // Check and make sure the Dll loaded
    if (Dll)
    {
        // Get the address of the function.
        ShowMDIChild = (ShowChildType *)GetProcAddress(Dll,
                                            "_ShowMDIChildForm");
        // Make sure we have the address then call the function.
        if (ShowMDIChild)
            ShowMDIChild(Application);
        else
        {
            ShowMessage(SysErrorMessage(GetLastError()));
            // If we couldn't get the address of the function
            // we want to free the Dll.
            FreeLibrary(Dll);
        }

    }
    else
    {
        ShowMessage(SysErrorMessage(GetLastError()));
        ShowMessage("Unable to load the DLL");
    }
}
```

This looks familiar, doesn't it? It's pretty much the same code we used in the DynamicDLL project earlier, except this time our HINSTANCE Dll is being declared in the header, and we load the DLL only once. If you don't check to see if the DLL is already loaded and call LoadLibrary() anyway, it will increment the usage count on the DLL. It doesn't load another instance of it. This can be useful if you have multiple functions that require the use of a function contained in the DLL. If this is the case, then each time you call LoadLibrary(), you should also call FreeLibrary(). If you called LoadLibrary() twice and FreeLibrary() once, the reference count will be decremented, and the DLL will not be freed until FreeLibrary() is called again. This way, the DLL can be freed when you're done with your program.

In the header, add the following:

```
private:
    HINSTANCE Dll;
```

Now go back to the .cpp and in the constructor place the following:

```
__fastcall TParent::TParent(TComponent* Owner)
    : TForm(Owner)
{
    Dll = NULL;
}
```

One of the last things you need to do is make sure that any MDI children are freed before closing. Add an OnClose event for the parent form with the following code:

```
void __fastcall TParent::FormClose(TObject *Sender, TCloseAction &Action)
{
    //Make sure all the children forms are closed
    while (MDIChildCount)
        MDIChildren[0]->Free();

    FreeLibrary(Dll);
}
```

This will ensure that all the MDI children are closed. You may be wondering what is going on here. The while(MDIChildCount) is saying to continue looping until MDIChildCount = 0. MDIChidren[0]->Free(), which is being executed each time through the loop, is saying to free the first MDI child. The MDI children are reordered after an MDI child is freed.

Normally you wouldn't have to worry about this if the MDI children were actually contained in the same application as the parent. However, C++Builder has a limitation as to what it's going to know about and what it isn't.

You will also need to build this using the dynamic RTL and Runtime packages. (See the explanation of how to set this in the section "Using MDI Child Forms in DLLs," earlier in this chapter.)

Save, build, and run the program now. You can click on File, New as many times as you want, and each time another form will be created. You can either close individual child forms in any order or just close the application with the forms open. See Figure 15.14 for the final results.

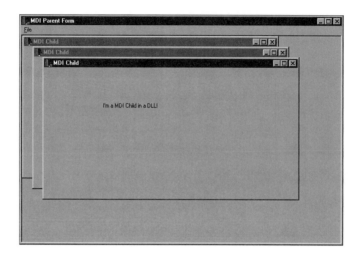

FIGURE 15.14

The MDI parent form with three MDI child forms open within it.

Using MDI Child Forms in Packages

There is a big advantage to using MDI child forms in packages rather then in DLLs. Though the process is pretty much the same, the final outcome is more stable. The DLL and the calling application are both fully aware of each other, meaning that the MDI children will be able to see the MDI parent and the parent will be able to see the children. This is because they both can share their global resources.

For our example we are going to create a new package but use the same calling application as with the MDIChildDll project. You can find the code for the new package, MDIChildPackage.bpk, in the MDIPackage folder on the CD-ROM that accompanies this book.

Click on File, New and choose the Package tab as we did earlier. Add a new form to the package; save the form as MDIChildPkForm.cpp and the package as MDIChildPackage.bpk.

Now set the following properties as we did for the DLL:

- Name = Child
- FormStyle = fsMDIChild
- Caption = MDI Package Child

- Height = 200
- Width = 400

Create an `OnClose` event for the form and enter `Action = caFree;`. Include the header for the child in the source file (`MDIChildPackage.cpp`) for the DLL.

```
#include "MDIChildPkForm.h"
```

Add the following code to the `MDIChildPackage.cpp` unit. This is similar to the exported function of the DLL, except this function doesn't take a parameter and doesn't need to switch its application instance. Also, we don't need a header file here because we don't plan to link this package statically to our calling application. However, if you want to statically link the DLL, you can create a header file and put the prototype of the function there, then include the header in `MDIChildPackage.cpp`.

```
extern "C" void __declspec(dllexport)ShowMDIChildPkForm(void);

void ShowMDIChildPkForm(void)
{
    Child = new TChild(Application);
    Child->Show();
}
```

Now you can save and build the package. Remember that the package is going to be placed in the C++Builder `Projects\Bpl` folder. Copy the package from this location to the location of the `MDIParent` application.

Reopen the `MDIParent` application and add another item to the `TMainMenu` component we used earlier. Place the item directly under the `&New` item and set its `Caption` property to `New &Package`. Create an `OnClick` event for this item and modify it as shown in Listing 15.4.

LISTING 15.4   The `NewPackage1Click` Event

```
void __fastcall TParent::NewPackage1Click(TObject *Sender)
{
    typedef void __declspec(dllimport)ShowChildPkType(void);
    ShowChildPkType *ShowPackageChild;
    if (!Package)
        Package = LoadPackage("MDIChildPackage.bpl");
    // Check and make sure the Package loaded
    if (Package)
    {
        // Get the address of the function.
        ShowPackageChild =
            (ShowChildPkType *)GetProcAddress((HINSTANCE)Package,
```

15

LISTING 15.4   Continued

```
                                          "_ShowMDIChildPkForm");
        // Make sure we have the address then call the function.
        if (ShowPackageChild)
            ShowPackageChild();
        else
        {
            ShowMessage(SysErrorMessage(GetLastError()));
            // If we couldn't get the address of the function
            // we want to free the Package.
            UnloadPackage(Package);
        }

    }
    else
    {
        ShowMessage(SysErrorMessage(GetLastError()));
        ShowMessage("Unable to load the Package");
    }
}
```

The previous code is almost identical to the code for calling the MDI child contained in the DLL. The differences are that we're using `LoadPackage()` and the exported function that we want doesn't take a parameter.

The last thing we have left to do to make sure the package works is to modify the `OnClose` event for the parent form. Change the event to look like the following:

```
void __fastcall TParent::FormClose(TObject *Sender, TCloseAction &Action)
{
    //Make sure all the children forms are closed
    while (MDIChildCount)
        MDIChildren[0]->Free();

    if (Dll)
        FreeLibrary(Dll);
    if (Package)
        UnloadPackage(Package);
}
```

If you look at the `OnClose` event now, you'll see that we still use the `while` statement to close all the MDI child forms, plus we added an `if` statement to `FreeLibrary()` and a separate `if` statement for the `UnloadPackage()` function.

Basic Plug-In Architecture

Since plug-ins are just specialized DLLs or packages, the access methods will be very similar. The only difference is in where and how we define the interface between the calling program and the library. As discussed earlier in this chapter, a standard DLL is accessed through a few Windows API commands. Those commands are LoadLibrary(), GetProcAddress(), and FreeLibrary(). As a brief refresher, we'll give a quick example of these commands in Listing 15.5.

LISTING 15.5   Simple DLL Access

```
typedef double (__stdcall *ADDFUNCTIONPTR)(double,double);
HINSTANCE dllInstance;
ADDFUNTIONPTR dllAddFunctionAddress;
DllInstance = ::LoadLibrary("MyDll.dll");
DllAddFunctionAddress = (ADDFUNCTIONPTR) ::GetProcAddress(dllInstance, "Add");
FreeLibrary (dllInstnce);
```

The code snippet in Listing 15.5 demonstrates a simple routine that loads a DLL named MyDLL.dll and finds a function called Add() that takes two doubles as parameters and returns a double. Let's walk through it.

The first line defines a function pointer that we'll use to hold the address of the function we want in the DLL. Don't forget that we can do only two things with a function: call it or take its address. The layout of a function pointer is

```
<return type of funtion>(*<name of function pointer>)(arg1, arg2, ... , argn);
```

Working with function pointers can be awkward if we have to keep typing out the whole thing, so we define our function pointer type to be named ADDFUNCTIONPTR. Now that we have defined a new type of pointer, we create an instance of it and name it dllAddFunctionAddress. Next we load the DLL and get its instance handle. After loading the library, we call the Windows API command GetProcAddress() with the instance of the DLL we want to look in and the function we want to find.

In Listing 15.5 you'll find a declaration of __stdcall. Without this directive, we would have to append an underscore to every label exported from the DLL. The appended underscore is largely a C++ practice, but it can cause your program to not be able to find the function it seeks. After finding the function, GetProcAddress() returns its address to dllAddFunctionAddress. Since this is only an example, we just free the library without doing anything else.

A Simple Plug-In Design

Now we are finally going to do some plug-in development. Probably the simplest style of plug-in is that of a library that contains not much more than a bunch of functions that will be exported from the DLL. For example, suppose that we have the need to develop a library that contains the name of a geometric shape, such as a triangle. We're going to throw in a twist; we want to reserve the capability to swap different types of these shapes in and out of the application. In the second DLL we will hold a circle. A natural response for object-oriented programmers would be to use a base class for shapes that defines how to hold the shape name and display it. The actual triangle and circle shapes would be derived from the base shape class. Listing 15.6 has the definition of the base class, and Listings 15.7 and 15.8 describe the triangle and circle classes, respectively.

LISTING 15.6 Definition of the Base Class, BaseShape

```
class BaseShape
{
public:
    BaseShape(){};
    ~BaseShape(){}
    virtual char* GetShapeType() = 0;
};
```

LISTING 15.7 The TriangleShape Class Definition

```
class TriangleShape :  public BaseShape
{
public:
    TriangleShape() : BaseShape() {};
    ~TriangleShape();
    virtual char* GetShapeType();
};
TriangleShape::GetShapeType()
{
    return "Triangle";
}
```

LISTING 15.8 The CircleShape Class Definition

```
class CircleShape
{
public:
    CircleShape() : BaseShape(){};
    ~CircleShape();
    vritual char* GetShapeType();
};
CircleShape::GetShapeType()
{
        return "Circle";
}
```

In a program, we would just create an instance of each class and access its respective `GetShapeType()` method. For a plug-in, we have to rearrange things slightly. All plug-ins are similar in one way: Each is designed with a predetermined interface. In other words, the developer of the application that will access our plug-in lays down the law by telling us that the calling application will be looking for a specifically named function or functions that will return a certain type. In our case, the application will be looking for a function that will take no parameters and return a pointer to `char`. To turn this system into a plug-in, we would move the base class definition into the application by including the header of the base object. Since the base object has methods declared as pure virtual functions, we have to override the virtual methods from a base class. The caller doesn't have any idea what the shapes could be that it is calling, so we have to find a way to call all types of shapes. The easiest way would be to declare a derived class within the caller that can get the name of any type of shape. This is accomplished by a class that we will call `GenericShape`:

```
class GenericShape : public BaseShape
{
    GenericShape() : BaseShape(){};
    ~GenericShape(){};
    virtual char* GetShapeName();
}
```

One problem, though, is that we still need a way to call the plug-in and get the name of the shape in it. Earlier in this chapter, we discussed the `GetProcAddress()` method. This would be perfect for our needs. Since we have a class that will be a generic shape container, we just need to add a method to look into the plug-in and get the shape name. Listing 15.9 contains only the header for the `GenericShape` class, so now it's time to add the method that will get the shape name. The work we are doing here all belongs in the application, because we are designing a way to access the plug-in and get the data we want. First let's see what the actual plug-in will look like. Since our plug-in needs to return only a shape name, we'll use a single function. We won't list the whole DLL, since a vanilla DLL sample can be found just by creating a new DLL with the DLL Wizard. Let's add one function:

```
extern "C" char* __declspec(dllexport) __stdcall GetShapeName()
{
    // If this was the triangle plugin, we would return
    // triangle
return "Circle";
}
```

That's it for the plug-in. We have a simple exported function that takes no parameters and returns a `char*`. See Listing 15.9.

LISTING 15.9   The `GetShapeName()` Function

```
char* GenericShape::GetShapeName()
{
    typedef char* (__stdcall *SHAPENAMEADDR)();
    HISTANCE plugin;
    SHAPENAMEADDR shapeNameFunc;
    plugin = ::LoadLibrary("ShapePlugin.dll");
    if (plugin)
    {
        shapeNameFunc =  (SHAPENAMEADDR)GetProcAddress(plugin,"GetShapeName");
        if (shapeNameFunc)
            char* tempName = shapeNameFunc();
        FreeLibrary(plugin);
        return tempName;
    }
    ShowMessage("Error! Couldn't load library");
    return 0;
}
```

Listing 15.9 requires slightly more explanation.

This method will look for a DLL named `ShapePlugin`. After trying to load the library, we test to make sure everything worked out. If the DLL can't be found, we notify the caller and return a `0`. If we found the DLL, our function looks in the library for a function named `GetShapeName()` that matches our parameter and return type needs and returns the address of the function. Next we test that we have a valid address and, if we do, we call the address `shapeNameFunc`, which is the returned function pointer. The name of the shape is returned from the DLL, and we pass it back to the caller.

With this style plug-in, the definition or interface to the code is moved to within the application, and only the implementation of the code resides in the DLL. Because a DLL is nothing more than executable binary code, we can swap different methods of the code in and out while the definition and pointers to the code still reside inside the application. Therefore, the application knows only the type of instructions it wants to call and where they are in the memory. The DLL or plug-in then tells the application, "If you supply me with a name for a type of function and its parameters, I'll execute it for you and return the result."

Rather an elegant solution, don't you think? There is one major flaw here: The method of plug-in access is very tedious. Having to access explicitly the methods to load the plug-in and work with it would start to get very old very fast. In the next chapter, which discusses COM, we'll discuss how Microsoft takes the modular programming strategy to the next level in offering a much more robust and flexible method of design, but at the cost of the needed support code becoming much more complicated. Microsoft wasn't after ease of use but a very strong, robust, and well-defined system. COM's most important defining feature is that of the interface. This whole interface business will help isolate us from the low-level DLL access methods that we have used so far. Being able to define and access an interface is the most important thing to remember when designing plug-ins, so we start off discussing the layout of our plug-in interface.

`TIBCB5PlugInBase` Class

Now that we have an idea of how we can design and use simple plug-ins, it's time to present a much more mature and capable system. Believe it or not, C++Builder has a wonderful implementation of plug-ins. If you are fortunate enough to have access to either the Professional or Enterprise version, look in the source for the Open Tools API. The classes in the Open Tools API encapsulate methods that we can use to access and work with the IDE. Whether building project wizards or debugging add-ons, this is where you would work. Incidentally, this collection of classes represents an excellent source of information regarding the implementation of plug-ins.

All of the classes in the Open Tools API derive from one central base class, `TInterface`. It's not this class that we are interested in but the one that is used in every wizard or IDE add-in, `TIExpert`. Like all other VCL classes, the names of the Open Tools classes start with a `T`, which in Borland parlance equates to mean *type*. There is one aberration in all of the Open Tools classes that isn't found in many other VCL classes, and that is the `I` between the `T` and the first letter of the VCL class names. This `I` stands for *interface* and denotes a singular idea in the world of programming. An interface defines the manner in which all derived classes can work. In C++, an interface is defined as having method definitions without implementations. To denote this in code, each function is declared as being "pure virtual" and can be represented with the `virtual` modifier and a trailing `= 0` after each defined class method. The pure virtual idea states that a class with methods defined as being pure virtual can't be instantiated itself but has to be instantiated by a derived class that overrides each pure virtual method. Let's take a look at `TIExpert` in Listing 15.10.

LISTING 15.10   `TIExpert`, Delphi Version

```
TIExpert = class(TInterface)
  public
    { Expert UI strings }
    function GetName: string; virtual; stdcall; abstract;
    function GetAuthor: string; virtual; stdcall; abstract;
    function GetComment: string; virtual; stdcall; abstract;
    function GetPage: string; virtual; stdcall; abstract;
    function GetGlyph: HICON; virtual; stdcall; abstract;
    function GetStyle: TExpertStyle; virtual; stdcall; abstract;
```

LISTING 15.10   Continued

```
      function GetState: TExpertState; virtual; stdcall; abstract;
      function GetIDString: string; virtual; stdcall; abstract;
      function GetMenuText: string; virtual; stdcall; abstract;

      { Launch the Expert }
      procedure Execute; virtual; stdcall; abstract;
    end;
```

This class doesn't look like your standard C++ class, and that's for a very good reason: It's Object Pascal, not C++. Except for a few syntactic differences, they are essentially the same. A C++ version can be found in Listing 15.11. As you can see, they aren't very different from one another. This is how we will model our plug-in interface. There is one problem with the code in Listing 15.11, though: There is no constructor present. This issue has to be addressed in the derived class or the correct linkage won't happen, so keep this in mind.

LISTING 15.11   TIExpert, C++Builder Version

```
class TIExpert : public TInterface
public:
    virtual String __stdcall GetName(void) = 0;
    virtual String __stdcall GetAuthor(void) =0 ;
    virtual String __stdcall GetComment(void) =0;
    virtual String __stdcall GetPage(void) = 0;
    virtual HICON __stdcall GetGlyph(void) = 0;
    virtual TExpertStyle __stdcall GetStyle(void) =0;
    virtual TExpertState __stdcall GetState(void) =0;
    virtual String __stdcall GetIDString(void) =0;
    virtual String __stdcall GetMenuText(void) = 0;
    virtual void __stdcall Execute(void) = 0;
};
```

For our base class, TIBCB5PluginBase, we can make a few changes. We aren't really interested in plug-in state or style within the framework that we will be designing, but feel free to try to implement anything from the Open Tools API that you find interesting. There are many good examples of design and implementation strategy to be found there.

The layout form TIBCB5PluginBase can be found in Listing 15.12. The specification for the following classes is located in the header file IBCB5PluginBase.h in the TBCB5PluginComponents folder on the CD-ROM that accompanies this book.

LISTING 15.12 The `TIBCB5PluginBase` Class Specification

```
class TIBCB5PluginBase
{
public:
    // The plugin name will double as an ID. You want
    // to make sure that it is a unique name.
    virtual char* __stdcall GetPluginName(void) = 0;
    virtual char* __stdcall GetPluginAuthor(void) = 0;
    virtual char* __stdcall GetMenuText(void) = 0;
    virtual HICON __stdcall GetPluginGlyph(void) = 0;
    virtual char* __stdcall GetPluginVersion(void) = 0;
    virtual bool __stdcall Execute() = 0;
    virtual char* __stdcall GetPluginCopyright(void) = 0;
    virtual void __stdcall DoneExpert(void) = 0;
};
```

Let's examine the `TIBCB5PluginBase` class, which will be the base class for all of our plug-ins. As shown with `TIExpert`, all of the members are declared as pure virtual, so we need to override each of these members in our derived class. We'll place our derived plug-in class within a DLL, so fire up C++Builder and launch the DLL Wizard. This can be found by selecting the New menu item and DLL Wizard from the New indexed page. Choose the default and press OK. Before saving the DLL, use the Project Options dialog to set the extension to `plg`, which we'll consider to be short for "plug-in." Save the project. Select New from the menu and add a new header file to the directory that you set up for the project. Add the class definition from Listing 15.12 to the header file and save it.

On to the good stuff. Open the DLL project again and add the code from Listing 15.13. Let's explore `TDemoPlugin`, which by the way is the name of our plug-in.

LISTING 15.13 The `TDemoPlugin` Class Definition

```
class TDemoPlugin : public TIBCB5PluginBase
{
private:
    HWND FParentApp;

public:

    TDemoPlugin(HWND ParentApp);
    ~TDemoPlugin();
    virtual char* __stdcall GetPluginName(void);
    virtual char* __stdcall GetPluginAuthor(void);
    virtual char* __stdcall GetMenuText(void);
```

15

**DLLs AND
PLUG-INS**

LISTING **15.13**   Continued

```
    virtual HICON __stdcall GetPluginGlyph(void);
    virtual char* __stdcall GetPluginVersion(void);
    virtual TBCB5PluginType __stdcall GetPluginType(void);
    virtual char* __stdcall GetPluginCopyright(void);
    virtual bool __stdcall Execute();
    virtual void __stdcall DonePlugin(void);
};
```

For those of you who learned C++ with C++Builder, you'll notice immediately that there aren't any AnsiString types in our class. This is to avoid the need to include any of the Borland memory management DLLs. Another plus of using these NULL-terminated char* strings is that you can develop the plug-ins for your application with another compiler, such as Microsoft's Visual C++. Please note that if you decide later to export a VCL class or a function that either returns an AnsiString or takes an AnsiString as a parameter from the plug-in, or any other DLL, you'll have to include the Borland memory management DLLs.

Even though all of the methods here are pretty much self-explanatory, there are a couple that need explanation. Here comes that bit about the constructor/destructor that we talked about earlier. The definition for TIExpert had no Object Pascal constructor or destructor. The C++ version also had neither of them. What we didn't see was that these constructors are required in the derived classes, so here they are in TDemoPlugin. Added to the constructor is a HWND parameter. This feature will allow us to pass in the handle of the calling application in the event that you add parent-dependent classes to the DLL, such as child MDI windows, C++Builder forms, and so on.

Also added to the class is a method called DoneExpert(), which will be called from the parent application and will notify us of the impending destruction of the object. If you would rather use Windows messaging to accomplish this, an invisible window could be added so that these messages could be received. The GetMenuText() and GetGlyph() methods will allow us to supply information to the calling application concerning how the DLL will be represented in either a menu or toolbar of the calling application. There are two other methods that we explore here: Execute() and DonePlugin(). The rest of the methods can be found in the TBCB5PluginComponents folder on the CD-ROM that accompanies this book. In Listing 15.14 you'll find the code for our Execute() and DonePlugin()methods.

LISTING **15.14**   The Execute() and DonePlugin() Methods

```
bool __stdcall TDemoPlugin::Execute()
{
    ShowMessage("Plugin Activated!");
    return true;
}
```

LISTING 15.14   Continued

```
//-------------------------------------------------------------------
void __stdcall TDemoPlugin::DonePlugin(void)
{
    if (this)
        delete this;
}
```

Since we really don't have room for an intensive plug-in here, Execute() is rather limited in its functionality. All it does is show a message that the plug-in is activated. Here is where you can do anything you like with the plug-in. The DonePlugin() method is called by the parent application. It first checks to see that it really exists and, if it does, it calls delete, which tells the system to call the plug-in's destructor.

Finally, we need a method to act as the setup instrument for our plug-in. The calling application will acquire the address of this function through the Windows API call GetProcAddress() that we discussed earlier in this chapter. This is our doorway to the outside world and can be found in Listing 15.15. We want to return a pointer to our plug-in to the calling application. This is how the application will actually call the methods of our class. Since the only thing the application will know about our plug-in is the base class, we'll cast the pointer to this within the application. Therefore, we need to return the TDemoPlugin pointer through a void pointer. That's it for the plug-in. Just compile it and you're done here.

LISTING 15.15   The RegisterPlugin() Function That Can Be Called to Create the Plug-In

```
extern "C" __declspec(dllexport)
void* __stdcall RegisterPlugin(HWND ParentApp)
{
    // instantiate the plugin class
    thisPlugin = new TDemoPlugin(ParentApp);
    return thisPlugin;
}
```

TBCB5PluginManager

C++Builder offers what is arguably the best and easiest environment for C++ development. This is due chiefly to the fact that C++Builder uses Borland's powerful and easy VCL framework of plug-and-play components. These components offer a great alternative to the usual typing, typing, and more typing that plagues all of the other C++ compilers and environments. Therefore, a drop on the form of a component and setting a few properties would make plug-in management a breeze, hence the TBCB5PluginManager. We won't analyze every detail of the plug-in manager because this is a chapter on plug-ins and not component development.

It would make our lives easier to give the manager a plug-in to load, access methods that would spare us from all the dreadful Windows API work that we used earlier, and a common place to control our plug-in operations. A quick summary of some of the manager's features can be found in Tables 15.1, 15.2, and 15.3.

TABLE 15.1   Properties of the Plug-In Manager

Property	Description
PluginExtension	File extension of plug-ins to load
PluginFolder	Folder in which to look for plug-ins
Version	Version of the plug-in manager
PluginCount	Number of loaded plug-ins

TABLE 15.2   Plug-In Manager Methods

Method	Description
LoadPlugin()	Load a single plug-in
LoadPlugins()	Automatically load all plug-ins in plug-in folder
UnLoadPlugin()	Unload a specified plug-in
GetLoadedPlugins()	Return a list of loaded plug-ins

TABLE 15.3   Plug-In Manager Events

Event	Description
OnStartLoading	Allows the user to allow/disallow loading of plug-in
OnFinishedLoading	Notifies the user of the name of the plug-in just loaded

The code for the TBCB5PluginManager can be found in the TBCB5PluginComponents folder on the CD-ROM that accompanies this book, under the name TBCB5PluginTools.bpk. The code is rather easy to follow, but there is quite a bit of it, so we won't go into detail. Here are a few helpful hints concerning the plug-in manager. If you want to guarantee that each plug-in is loaded only once, use the FileName value of the OnStartLoad event. You'll have to use the GetLoadedPlugins() method to return a list of strings and iterate through the list for a match.

If there is a match, you can set the CanLoad value of the OnStartLoad event to false, which won't allow the plug-in to be loaded. To add menu text or a toolbar glyph, use the OnFinishedLoading event and use either the FileName or Glyph field to retrieve the needed items.

Wrapping Up Plug-Ins

That's it for plug-ins. There is so much more to this subject that could be covered. The plug-in manager needs some major work to be a truly useful component, but the difficult areas are done. You just need to supply your own features. There are a few things that you should try to remember:

- Always use the __stdcall modifier in all methods to be accessed that are in the DLL.
- Take care that you carefully map out the plug-in interface, because it is your application's gateway to the world.
- Try to keep each plug-in as development tool–neutral as possible so that users can use other development environments to create plug-ins that can be used by your applications.

Summary

In this chapter you have seen how to build a basic statically linked DLL and export functions, load a dynamic DLL and get the address of its exported functions, export classes, use SDI and MDI forms, and create a basic package. Next time you work on a project that looks like it could be modularized, there's a good chance you can do using DLLs or packages. Another thing to keep in mind is the reusability of your code. You know how much well-designed C++ code can be reused, so put that code in a DLL and reuse it whenever you can.

One thing we didn't mention about DLLs is that they can be called dynamically from other tools besides Visual C++. A good example is for your installation program. We've written many DLLs that perform a task such as validating a serial number. We use this DLL with InstallShield Professional to validate a serial number to allow for the installation of the software and also use it in the software to validate user licenses. We've done the same thing with database work such as updating during installation or after installation.

There is much more that can be done with DLLs, such as for plug-ins, but trying to cover everything in one chapter is an impossible task. To find out more about DLLs and packages, see the C++Builder online help and the Win32 Programmer's Reference for DLLs.

COM Programming

Ionel Munoz

IN THIS CHAPTER

- **Understanding COM Servers and Clients**
- **Outgoing Interfaces and Event Sinks Revisited**
- **Writing the COM Server**
- **Writing the Proxy/Stub DLL**
- **Writing the COM Client**
- **Recommended Readings**

The Component Object Model (COM) is the Microsoft technological proposal for developing component-based software ("componentware"). It is so overfilled with documentation that nothing we could add here would significantly increase the body of information already available.

For that reason, in this chapter you won't be introduced to COM. A basic understanding is assumed, although some concepts will be explained. If you feel you are a COM novice, please close this book and go, for example, to Chapter 13 of *C++Builder 4 Unleashed* (written by Kent Reisdorph and published by Sams Publishing) before coming back.

With all the bells and whistles around Kylix and Linux, you may also wonder why we programmers are still interested in COM. I am not a Windows evangelist, but you can bet that Windows will stay in our PCs for a long while. Desktop computing throughout the world is based mostly on Windows, and Windows versions are more COM-oriented each time. You have no choice: COM first, then DCOM, and COM+ later is the right path to follow to being a good Windows developer. And being a good Windows developer will open a bunch of possibilities to you.

COM provides a basis for building on your applications as a cooperative set of independent binary units. The most important benefits of COM are

- It specifies a standard at binary level, for developing and using components in any language or development tool.
- It provides transparency. The user of a component does not have to know where the component actually resides. Even if the component is in a remote server, the client uses it as a local component.

C++Builder 5, like any first-class Windows development tool, is very well suited for COM development. This chapter's objective is to provide information you won't find easily in other sources and to give you a picture of C++Builder 5 from a COM programmer's perspective.

Understanding COM Servers and Clients

In one of my favorite movies, a very tough guy comes out of the movie screen into the real world. He tries to break the glass window of a car with his hand, and he finds that it hurts. He then realizes that things are very different in the real world.

C++Builder is made for the real world. You won't be hurt, because C++Builder protects you with an iron glove.

With the introduction of ATL 3.0 in C++Builder 5, the power of writing COM clients and servers is boosted. There are always some poorly documented points, however. For example, how to develop dispinterface-based event sinks with C++Builder is a constant subject in

Borland newsgroups (see `nntp://forums.inprise.com/borland.public.cppbuilder.`
`activex`). Version 5 not only supports this, but also documents it very well in its help files.

> **NOTE**
>
> If you don't know what a dispinterface is, surely you didn't follow the recommendation at the beginning of this chapter. Please, go to an introductory text about COM and then come back.
>
> It should be clear, however, that dispinterfaces are not real COM interfaces but command interfaces for accessibility from scripting languages. They are implemented through the standard `IDispatch` interface.

For the other type of events, meaning those that are fired from custom interfaces, we have news that is not so good. At the server side, C++Builder wizards offer nothing yet; we have to spend time making that work by our own programming skills. Furthermore, at the client side you also are responsible for writing all the code.

In this chapter you will learn how to fire both types of events from a COM server object and how to catch them and respond properly on the client side. You will also see how to write the proxy/stub DLL for custom interfaces, which is rather poorly documented in C++Builder.

Outgoing Interfaces and Event Sinks Revisited

A COM object may implement several interfaces for playing different roles in various contexts. Clients call methods on these interfaces, and servers react according to their respective implementations.

Normally, a COM object also wants to be able to notify its clients that something interesting has happened, such as that a lengthy operation is finished. This enables the client to take the results without having to poll the server periodically.

The way COM objects communicate with their clients is by using outgoing interfaces, which clients should implement for the server to call when needed. A client connects its interfaces to a server by using connection points.

> **NOTE**
>
> If you want to learn more about COM, go to the MSDN site at
> `http://msdn.microsoft.com/`.

> Connection points–based events are highly coupled. You will see a newer event model in COM+. Even so, the new model doesn't exclude the use of old connection points for many purposes, mostly when you care about speed.

For connecting to a server object that exposes an outgoing interface, the client will need an object that implements the interface. Such an object is called an *event sink*.

In short, an event sink is a COM object on the client side that implements one interface, which is defined as an outgoing interface in a COM object on the server side. The client can then connect the event sink to the server through a connection point and start receiving events. The server calls the methods of the sink object interface. Figure 16.1 illustrates how it works.

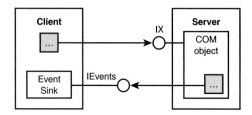

FIGURE 16.1
Event sinks and connection point–based events.

Now let's get our hands dirty by writing both a COM server and a client from scratch in C++Builder. This should form the basis for a good COM start.

Writing the COM Server

Because defining a problem is 50% of its solution, first let's briefly define what our server will do.

It will be a zodiac server, for those who are interested in the horoscope and in the mysteries of astrology. We programmers are occupied in less ethereal issues, so our task is only to make it work for the benefit of others.

The server will provide two services:

- It will retrieve a string containing the zodiac sign of any client program's user, given his birthday. This information should be available to every kind of client, even crippled ones like Visual Basic programs.

- It will give extended information based on the client's birthday, such as advice, typical personality, the sign's element (earth, fire, water, air), regent planet, and so on. A structure should be filled with this information, which will be available only for more advanced clients, meaning those that are developed in C++ or Delphi.

Knowing this, we will implement only one single COM object in our server. The object will have two interfaces: the simpler one, derived from IDispatch (dual), for making it available from VB; and the more complex one, a custom interface for powerful clients to retrieve extended information.

> **NOTE**
>
> Dual interfaces are actually a patch to improve performance when using the server from strongly typed client languages, while maintaining compliance with Visual Basic and scripting languages.
>
> It is a good practice to keep away from dual interfaces when possible, because of their "patch" nature. In spite of that, C++Builder implicitly encourages the use of dual interfaces (at least its wizards are very oriented to them). The reason behind this is probably that many organizations still need to maintain Visual Basic backward compatibility.

The object will also raise events for those clients that prefer to receive the information asynchronously because they are too busy doing other tasks. We will have two outgoing interfaces in our COM object: a dispinterface and a custom interface for providing simple and extended zodiac information, respectively.

Choosing the Server Type

We can refer to COM servers as binaries that contain the implementation of at least one COM component. Depending on where the server resides, it can be classified as inproc, outproc, or remote.

An inproc (in-process) server is always a DLL (OCX files, where ActiveX controls usually reside, are actually DLLs). This kind of server makes its components reside in the client's address space. The main advantage is speed. The main disadvantage is that if the server crashes, the client will probably crash too, because they are not isolated.

An outproc (out-of-process) server is an executable. Its advantages and disadvantages are mainly the negation of those for inproc servers.

A `remote` server resides in a different machine than the client. It can be implemented as a DLL (using a `surrogate` process that wraps the DLL) or an EXE file.

COM+/MTS –compatible objects must be developed in DLLs to take full advantage of these technologies. Therefore, they tend to be the choice when there is no reason to prefer an EXE file. Thus, our server will be an `inproc` server, because its use is promoted by Microsoft.

Choosing a Threading Model

Although there are several threading models shown in C++Builder's COM wizards, there are basically two types of threads. According to the new COM terminology, they are apartment threads and free threads.

Briefly, a COM apartment is a logical scope opened in a thread by a call to `CoInitialize()` (or `CoInitializeEx()`) and closed by `CoUninitialize()`. The main purpose of apartments is to define boundaries for synchronization. For each thread in which COM objects are going to be used, an apartment should be created. Sometimes the COM Library does it for you, sometimes not. There are many details involved in this process that are beyond the scope of this book.

Apartment threads have a Windows message loop associated with them and are conceived for user interface components. All calls to the component's methods are done by the apartment's thread; therefore, they are synchronized for you. ActiveX controls are forced to reside in apartment threads.

A free thread may not have a message loop. Calls from any thread are allowed, so it is the component's obligation to provide the mechanism of synchronizing the calls it receives.

C++Builder follows the old COM lingo. The types of threading models C++Builder offers are

- **Single**   The server provides no multithreading support. The COM Library serializes all calls in the main thread of the client, attaching the component to one big single apartment. This implies a serious performance hit. Never, ever use this model.

- **Apartment (Single-Threaded Apartment, or STA)**   Each method is executed in the thread that is associated with the component. Calls are then serialized in the component's thread using the apartment's Windows message loop. Each component is able to reside in its own apartment, eliminating the main thread affinity present in the old Single model. This is the more scalable model.

- **Free (Multi-Threaded Apartment, or MTA)**   As stated before, any thread can call any method at any time. You are responsible for protecting the internal state of your component from concurrency conflicts.

- **Both**   The component claims to be compliant with both models. COM will make the component reside in the same type of apartment as its client, if possible. This is a very flexible solution, because it avoids many marshaling issues.

- **Neutral**   This is a new threading model available only in COM+. Multiple threads can call the object at the same time, but synchronization is provided by COM+. In COM this model maps to STA.

The threading model of a COM object is statically declared, and it is the component's responsibility to behave in a way consistent with the threading model it claims to support. Saying that a component supports a given threading model means that it is compliant with a particular thread synchronization policy.

We would like to choose the STA model, because it is the preferred one in almost any situation. Nevertheless, we will choose MTA, because we want to cover some marshaling issues in this chapter, and because it is the recommended choice for developing certain types of high-performance servers (such as for accessing hardware devices).

Creating the Server

To start creating our simple COM server in C++Builder

1. Launch C++ Builder.
2. Select File, New from the main menu. The New Items dialog appears.
3. Select the ActiveX tab and double-click the ActiveX Library icon, seen in Figure 16.2.

FIGURE 16.2
The New Items dialog with the ActiveX Library icon selected.

4. Save the project with the name `ZodiacServer`.

At this point, you have an empty `inproc` COM server.

> **NOTE**
>
> If you want to create an empty `outproc` server, just create a new application.

Adding a COM Object

Now let's add a COM object implementation:

1. Select File, New. The New Items dialog appears.
2. Select the ActiveX tab. Because we want an object with a dual interface (so it will be accessible from scripting languages), double-click on the Automation Object icon. The New Automation Object dialog appears.

> **NOTE**
>
> Selecting the COM Object icon will give us a COM object with a default custom interface instead of dual. You can try the example using this feature if you like, but keep in mind that in that case your COM object won't be accessible from any scripting language. Also, some descriptions we give here obviously won't apply.

3. Name your object `Zodiac` and enter a description if you want.
4. Check the Generate Event Support Code option, in order to automatically create all the ATL code involved in raising events through an outgoing dispinterface.
5. Because our object is going to be a free-threaded object, select the Free threading model. Figure 16.3 shows the final state of the dialog.

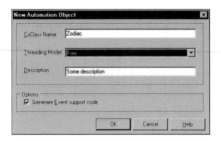

FIGURE 16.3
The New Automation Object dialog, with all the desired options set.

The Type Library Editor (TLE) is now in front of you. If not, click the View, Type Library menu item in the IDE. You will see something such as what is seen in Figure 16.4.

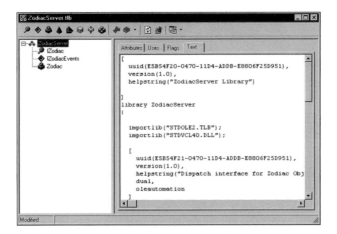

FIGURE 16.4
The TLE window, showing the newly created COM object.

In the left pane of this window are the coclass Zodiac and two interfaces: IZodiac, which is a dual interface and the default interface of your server object, and the IZodiacEvents dispinterface, which is the outgoing interface that represents the events your object will fire.

NOTE

Just as in C++, there are classes in COM. They are called *coclasses*. A coclass is an entity that claims to implement one or more interfaces. Thus, a coclass can be seen in IDL as the declaration of a COM object class. Every coclass has a very important attribute called the *class id* (see the uuid attribute in the IDL declaration below). This attribute uniquely identifies the coclass:

```
[
    uuid(4992BB45-FCA6-11D3-ADDB-BCAF427C7F50),
    version(1.0),
    helpstring("Zodiac Object")
]
coclass Zodiac
{
  [default] interface IZodiac;
  [default, source] dispinterface IZodiacEvents;
};
```

In a coclass declaration, all the implemented interfaces are listed. An interface marked as source is an outgoing interface; therefore, that interface is not actually implemented by the coclass, but by its connection point.

Pressing the Text tab, you can see what you have so far in IDL: the source text of your Type Library.

NOTE

A Type Library contains data describing what a COM server has inside. It is a way of binary-documenting every COM component, such as the interfaces it implements and their signatures. Type Libraries are normally generated (compiled) from IDL sources, although there are tools, like C++Builder itself, that seem to work directly on the binary.

Type Libraries can be distributed linked to the server as a resource or separately as a TLB file. You always have the choice of not distributing your Type Libraries, and certain organizations promote that practice as a matter of security. There are special types of servers that are forced to distribute their Type Libraries, such as automation servers and ActiveX controls.

Developing COM components with C++Builder is very Type Library–centric. C++Builder also promotes binding the Type Library to your server. In addition, the Type Library Editor (TLE) is the main tool you have in C++Builder for implementing the features your COM server exposes.

To provide the functionality we want, add one method to the IZodiac interface:

1. Right-click over IZodiac in the left pane of the Type Library Editor. In the pop-up menu, select New, Method.

2. Rename the new method from Method1 to GetZodiacSign.

3. In the left pane, select the method name; click on the Parameters tab in the right pane.

4. Add the long input (in) parameters Day and Month, which represent the client's birthday. Also add the output (out, retval) BSTR* parameter Sign, for returning the zodiac sign name. In Figure 16.5, the mouse pointer is over the ellipsis button in the Modifier field of the Sign parameter. By pressing the button, you can set the modifiers for the parameter.

NOTE

Parameters can be basically in, out, or in-out. These are marshaling-related modifiers for stating if a parameter's value travels from the client to the server, from the server to the client, or both.

There are some rules: For out parameters the server allocates the memory, and the client is responsible for freeing it. For in parameters the client has all the control; it allocates and it frees the memory. For in-out parameters, the memory can be reallocated by the server, but the client still is responsible for freeing the memory.

The retval modifier means *return value*. It makes sense for tools that generate wrappers at the client side. We will see its use when implementing the client.

There are many other parameter attributes and related issues, but we won't cover them in this book.

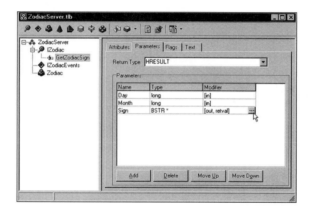

FIGURE 16.5
Adding parameters to a method using the TLE.

The GetZodiacSign() method, as you should guess, will return the zodiac sign name when we give the day and the month of the user's birthday.

Following the same process, add the method for getting the zodiac sign asynchronously. Its signature is

```
HRESULT _stdcall GetZodiacSignAsync([in] long Day, [in] long Month );
```

See that GetZodiacSignAsync() has no Sign output parameter. Thus, for getting the sign we will define an event that returns the zodiac sign name. It will be fired when the operation started by GetZodiacSignAsync() finishes.

Click on the `IZodiacEvents` dispinterface and add the `OnZodiacSignReady()` method (using the same steps as for adding methods to `IZodiac`). The `OnZodiacSignReady()` signature is

```
HRESULT OnZodiacSignReady([in] BSTR Sign );
```

Don't miss that the parameter `Sign` is `in` for this method. This is because this method will be called by the server on a client's event sink. From the client perspective, the parameter comes from the server, and it is then an input parameter.

The current state of the TLE is shown in Figure 16.6.

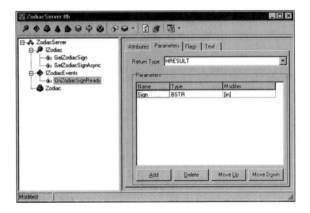

FIGURE 16.6
The TLE showing the `Zodiac` *coclass and all the interfaces it claims to implement so far.*

To this point it seems we have the first part of what we want, declared at interface level. What it is not said yet is that all the boilerplate code is also generated by C++Builder! We must implement the functionality now, but you will see that this is as easy as filling some methods' bodies that are already in your source files.

Before going on, press the Refresh Implementation button, the third from the right in the TLE (you can save your work as well). Your project is now composed of four files: `ZodiacServer.cpp`, `ZodiacImpl.cpp`, `ZodiacServer_TLB.cpp`, and `ZodiacServer_ATL.cpp`.

Dissecting the Generated Code

Instead of rushing to write the working code, it is useful to understand first what C++Builder generated for you.

> **NOTE**
>
> In C++Builder, ATL 3 is used to write COM servers. ATL stands for the *ActiveX Template Library*, which makes extensive use of templates. It is the Microsoft framework for writing COM code.

ZodiacServer_TLB.hcontains the C++ translation of every type contained in ZodiacServer's Type Library (including interfaces) that we declared using the TLE. This is a mapping from IDL to C++. ZodiacServer_TLB.h is included at the very beginning of ZodiacImpl.h, which is the header file of the Zodiac coclass implementation:

```
#include "ZodiacServer_TLB.h"
```

> **NOTE**
>
> The ZodiacServer_TLB.h file will be revisited when developing the client. ZodiacServer_ATL.h and ZodiacServer_ATL.cpp contain the declaration and implementation, respectively, of the _Module object (an instance of CComModule), which ATL uses to represent the server itself and all its global data.
>
> ZodiacServer.cpp contains the DLL entry point and the COM registering/unregistering server global functions. It also contains the Object Map, by which the coclasses of your server are mapped to their respective class factories.

To see the class that implements our COM object, open the ZodiacImpl.h file:

```
class ATL_NO_VTABLE TZodiacImpl :
  public CComObjectRootEx<CComMultiThreadModel>,
  public CComCoClass<TZodiacImpl, &CLSID_Zodiac>,
  public IConnectionPointContainerImpl<TZodiacImpl>,
  public TEvents_Zodiac<TZodiacImpl>,
  public IDispatchImpl<IZodiac, &IID_IZodiac, &LIBID_ZodiacServer>
```

The C++ class TZodiacImpl is the C++ counterpart of the COM coclass Zodiac. It inherits from the ATL template CComObjectRootEx, which implements all the reference counting and interface-querying mechanisms of IUnknown and some of the synchronization, depending on the chosen threading model. Because we chose MTA, our class inherits from CComObjectRootEx<CComMultiThreadModel>.

CComCoClass, also a template class from ATL, provides the default class factory for the object, defines the aggregation model, and deals with some COM error information issues, as we will see later. Note that by inheriting from `CComCoClass<TZodiacImpl, &CLSID_Zodiac>` explicitly suggests that the CLSID of your object is mapped to the object's class. This association is completed in the Object Map declared in `ZodiacServer.cpp`:

```
BEGIN_OBJECT_MAP(ObjectMap)
  OBJECT_ENTRY(CLSID_Zodiac, TZodiacImpl)
END_OBJECT_MAP()
```

Hence, the relationship between the declared COM coclass and its implementation in your server is established at code level.

`IDispatchImpl` is another template, used for implementing `IDispatch`-derived (dual) interfaces. This class deals with the intricate details of implementing an `Invoke()` method capable of forwarding automation calls to your specific COM interface. Also, all the other `IDispatch` services are already written there. `IDispatchImpl` is declared in `atlcom.h` in this way:

```
template <class T, const IID* piid,
          const GUID* plibid = &CComModule::m_libid, WORD wMajor = 1,
          WORD wMinor = 0, class tihclass = CComTypeInfoHolder>
class ATL_NO_VTABLE IDispatchImpl : public T
{
  (snip.)
};
```

Notice that `IDispatchImpl` derives from the template parameter T, which is evaluated to `IZodiac` in our case. Thus, `IDispatchImpl<IZodiac, &IID_IZodiac, &LIBID_ZodiacServer>`, as a template instantiation, not only implements the basic `IDispatch` interface mechanisms specifically for our dual interface `IZodiac`, it also makes our class derive indirectly from `IZodiac`. Using inheritance is the main way we have in C++ to indicate that a class implements a given interface, and this is a good example of that.

NOTE

Aggregation is another way of implementing a COM interface, but it won't be covered in this book.

The `IConnectionPointContainerImpl` class, also a template from ATL, makes our COM object a connection point container, therefore preparing it for firing events. `IConnectionPointContainerImpl` manages a collection of `IConnectionPointImpl` objects, one for each outgoing interface our object supports.

So far so good; all of this basic ATL code does most of the heavy and repetitive work needed for implementing a COM server.

> **NOTE**
>
> You don't have to worry about the ATL implementation details for writing your COM servers. An overview is given here to help you to understand the basics. If you want to go deeper on ATL 3 issues, the book *ATL Internals* (Chris Sells et al., ISBN: 0201695898, Addison-Wesley Publishing) is the best I can recommend.

Let's continue our dissection. The template class TEvents_Zodiac in ZodiacServer_TLB.h was generated by the TLE. It deserves special attention because it implements the code responsible for actually firing our events. Take a look at the method Fire_OnZodiacSignReady():

```
template <class T> HRESULT
TEvents_Zodiac<T>::Fire_OnZodiacSignReady(BSTR Sign)
{
  T * pT = (T*)this;
  pT->Lock();
  IUnknown ** pp = m_vec.begin();
  while (pp < m_vec.end())
  {
    if (*pp != NULL)
    {
      m_EventIntfObj.Attach(*pp);
      m_EventIntfObj.OnZodiacSignReady(Sign);
      m_EventIntfObj.Attach(0);
    }
    pp++;
  }
  pT->Unlock();
}
```

In this method, iteration is done through an array of our server-connected clients. Each of them is informed that the operation was finished by calling the OnZodiacSignReady() method of m_EventIntfObj.

The member m_EventIntfObj is an instance of IZodiacEventsDisp. This class is declared in ZodiacZerver_TLB.h as shown in Listing 16.1.

LISTING 16.1   ZodiacZerver_TLB.h: The Declaration of IZodiacEventsDisp

```
template <class T>
class IZodiacEventsDispT : public TAutoDriver<IZodiacEvents>
{
```

LISTING 16.1   Continued

```
public:
  IZodiacEventsDispT(){}

  void Attach(LPUNKNOWN punk)
  { m_Dispatch = static_cast<T*>(punk); }

  HRESULT          __fastcall OnZodiacSignReady(BSTR Sign/*[in]*/);

};
typedef IZodiacEventsDispT<IZodiacEvents> IZodiacEventsDisp;
```

As you can see, IZodiacEventsDisp is a class instance of the template class
IZodiacEventsDispT, which derives from TAutoDriver<IZodiacEvents>. TAutoDriver is a
template wrapper around any automation object. TAutoDriver is responsible for internally calling into its OleFunction() method the Invoke() method of the IDispatch interface of the
inner automation object. TAutoDriver doesn't come from ATL, but it is a C++Builder class
declared in utilcls.h.

Because TZodiacImpl derives also from TEvents_Zodiac, we are now able to call the
Fire_OnZodiacSignReady() method wherever we want to fire the corresponding event. ATL
and EZ-COM (something I think Borland has not defined very well) took care once more of all
the boilerplate code.

This strange and large declaration in ZodiacImpl.h, which is shown in Listing 16.2, is completed with some macros and one static function.

LISTING 16.2   ZodiacImpl.h: Declaring the Class Attributes for Registration

```
// Data used when registering Object
//
DECLARE_THREADING_MODEL(otFree);
DECLARE_PROGID("ZodiacServer.Zodiac");
DECLARE_DESCRIPTION("Some description");

// Function invoked to (un)register object
//
static HRESULT WINAPI UpdateRegistry(BOOL bRegister)
{
  TTypedComServerRegistrarT<TZodiacImpl>
  regObj(GetObjectCLSID(), GetProgID(), GetDescription());
  return regObj.UpdateRegistry(bRegister);
}
```

The macros shown in Listing 16.2 are for specifying information that will be recorded in the Windows Registry: the threading model, the program ID, and the description of our coclass. The `UpdateRegistry()` static function is used to register that information, plus the COM object class. This function is invoked when the COM server is about to be registered.

> **NOTE**
>
> The C++Builder registering process implementation differs from that provided by Visual C++, which is based on script files instead (.rgs). This is the main point on which ATL programming in both tools differs.

More macro-based code is used to declare the COM map, which makes our class respond affirmatively when a call to `QueryInterface()` is received that asks for IZodiac, Idispatch, or IConnectionPointContainer:

```
BEGIN_COM_MAP(TZodiacImpl)
  COM_INTERFACE_ENTRY(IZodiac)
  COM_INTERFACE_ENTRY2(IDispatch, IZodiac)
  COM_INTERFACE_ENTRY_IMPL(IConnectionPointContainer)
END_COM_MAP()
```

Note in this code that the map is filled using different macros, depending on the case. The most frequently used of all of them is COM_INTERFACE_ENTRY, whose purpose is to insert one interface in the map. It must be combined with deriving from that interface. As we will see later, implementing its methods is also mandatory.

The connection point map, which gives shape to the entries in the connection point array, is written as follows:

```
BEGIN_CONNECTION_POINT_MAP(TZodiacImpl)
  CONNECTION_POINT_ENTRY(DIID_IZodiacEvents)
END_CONNECTION_POINT_MAP()
```

The connection point map is used to create a collection of the interface identifiers of each supported outgoing interface. Because the dispinterface IZodiacEvents is outgoing, an entry with its identifier was added. Some code in IConnectionPointContainerImpl searches this collection to see if a given connection point is implemented. Don't forget that the outgoing interface itself is not implemented, its connection point is.

Writing Method Bodies

Now we are ready to provide our own functionality. Open the file ZodiacImpl.cpp and you will see this:

```
/////////////////////////////////////////////////////////////////////////
// TZodiacImpl
STDMETHODIMP TZodiacImpl::GetZodiacSign(long Day, long Month, BSTR* Sign)
{
}

STDMETHODIMP TZodiacImpl::GetZodiacSignAsync(long Day, long Month)
{
}
```

As you can guess, the only thing you have to do now is write some code in the method bodies.

First, let's implement `GetZodiacSign()`. We only have to obtain the `Sign` string, given the `Day` and `Month` parameters. To implement this, a database query is used, but you are free to choose your own implementation. A first version of the method could be as follows:

```
static TCOMCriticalSection CS;

STDMETHODIMP TZodiacImpl::GetZodiacSign(long Day, long Month, BSTR* Sign)
{
  TCOMCriticalSection::Lock Lock(CS);

  ::GetZodiacSign(Day, Month, *Sign);

  return S_OK;
}
```

> **NOTE**
>
> The details of the implementation are hidden by the function `::GetZodiacSign()`, which accesses a parameterized query in a DataModule to obtain the sign from a table. You can see the entire code in the companion CD, although we will explain some issues here.

Because our object is MTA, we used a `TCOMCriticalSection` object (declared in `utilcls.h`) for blocking concurrent access to the shared resources, in this case the database query. One instance of the `TCOMCriticalSection::Lock` nested class takes the ownership of the critical section when constructed and releases it when destroyed. This is the synchronization we are providing, because, as you know, COM won't do it for us in this case.

We implemented `::GetZodiacSign()` in the outer scope as seen in Listing 16.3.

LISTING 16.3 `ZodiacImpl.cpp`: Implementation of the `GetZodiacSign()` Function

```cpp
void GetZodiacSign(long Day, long Month, BSTR& Sign)
{
  // Parameterize the Query object, passing the Day and Month,
  // activate the Query, etc.:
  (snip.)
  .

  .
  // Get the sign name from the database:
  ZodiacDataModule->QZodiac->First();
  WideString wstrSign =
    ZodiacDataModule->QZodiac->FieldByName(_T("Name"))->AsString.c_str();
  Sign = wstrSign.Detach();
}
```

The `WideString` object is a `BSTR` wrapper. It takes the ownership of the contained string, but because the `Sign` parameter is an `out`, we have to allocate the string on our side and give its ownership to the client. Thus, we detach the `BSTR` from the `WideString` object.

It is not difficult, as you see, but we left out a very important detail: error handling.

Adding Better Error Support

Many programmers tend to underestimate the importance of proper error handling and support. In COM, error handling becomes vital, because the high level of isolation among components (which can exist even in different machines) could make us ignore detailing errors when they occur.

In addition, there are no exception classes in COM, such as those CORBA provides. For that reason, the first thing a C++Builder COM programmer must do is wrap all the interface method bodies with `try/catch` blocks. C++Builder sometimes generates these blocks for you, but it should always be done, even when C++Builder believes not. Of course, trivial methods in which exceptions are very improbable may ignore this rule. The reason is that C++ exceptions cannot go beyond the interface method boundaries. Imagine what kind of crash would occur if a C++ exception were propagated to a Visual Basic client.

We swallow all exceptions in the scopes of our methods. How then can we provide richer error information to our clients, if we only have the possibility of returning `HRESULT` codes? The `ISupportErrorInfo` interface was designed to provide a workaround to this COM drawback:

```cpp
interface ISupportErrorInfo : IUnknown
{
  HRESULT InterfaceSupportsErrorInfo([in] REFIID riid);
};
```

A server object takes advantage of this interface by implementing it and by writing code to enrich the error information it wants to publish to the client. This code must do the following: When an exception is caught, you call the COM function `CreateErrorInfo()` to create an error object. This function returns an `ICreateErrorInfo` interface, which has several methods for filling the error object with your custom information, such as the description and the `IID` of the offending interface.

After giving that information, you can query the `IErrorInfo` interface to the error object, which does the opposite by providing methods for exposing the error details you set before. Then call the COM function `SetErrorInfo()` to associate the error info object with the current thread of execution, and that's it.

> **NOTE**
>
> For a client it is very easy when an error code is returned from an interface method to call the function `GetErrorInfo()` to obtain extended information on the error represented by the simple `HRESULT` value. `GetErrorInfo()` returns the `IErrorInfo` interface of the last `ErrorInfo` object associated with the caller's logical thread of execution. See the SDK help on `GetErrorInfo()` to learn more about this.

Fortunately, ATL encapsulates all the dirty work your server object must do in one method call: `Error()`, defined in `CComCoClass`. Now our method body can be written as shown in Listing 16.4.

LISTING 16.4 `ZodiacImpl.cpp`: The Implementation of the `TZodiacImpl::GetZodiacSign()` Method

```
STDMETHODIMP TZodiacImpl::GetZodiacSign(long Day, long Month, BSTR* Sign)
{
  HRESULT hResult = S_OK;

  try
  {
    TCOMCriticalSection::Lock Lock(CS);

    ::GetZodiacSign(Day, Month, *Sign);
  }
  catch(Exception& e)
  {
    hResult = Error(e.Message.c_str(), IID_IZodiac, E_FAIL);
  }
  catch(...)
  {
    hResult = Error(_T("Catastrophic error: internal crash"),
```

LISTING 16.4 Continued

```
                    IID_IZodiac, E_UNEXPECTED);
    }

    return hResult;
}
```

The Error() function will create and fill the error info object associated with the interface IZodiac, using the message provided by the catch exception and the error code passed to it. This error code is returned and assigned to the result we will give to the client.

Everything is now fine, but we forgot to implement ISupportErrorInfo! At this point you should know how to do it.

1. Make TZodiacImpl inherit from ISupportErrorInfo in ZodiacImpl.h:

```
class ATL_NO_VTABLE TZodiacImpl :
    public CComObjectRootEx<CComMultiThreadModel>,
    public CComCoClass<TZodiacImpl, &CLSID_Zodiac>,
    public IConnectionPointContainerImpl<TZodiacImpl>,
    public TEvents_Zodiac<TZodiacImpl>,
    public IDispatchImpl<IZodiac, &IID_IZodiac, &LIBID_ZodiacServer>,
    public ISupportErrorInfo
```

2. Add an entry in the COM map for ISupportErrorInfo:

```
BEGIN_COM_MAP(TZodiacImpl)
    COM_INTERFACE_ENTRY(IZodiac)
    COM_INTERFACE_ENTRY2(IDispatch, IZodiac)
    COM_INTERFACE_ENTRY_IMPL(IConnectionPointContainer)
    COM_INTERFACE_ENTRY(ISupportErrorInfo)
END_COM_MAP()
```

3. Declare the ISupportErrorInfo methods in the class:

```
class TZodiacImpl :
    (snip.)
{
    (snip.)
    public:
    STDMETHOD(InterfaceSupportsErrorInfo)(REFIID riid);
};
```

4. Implement the InterfaceSupportErrorInfo() method in ZodiacImpl.cpp in this way:

```
STDMETHODIMP TZodiacImpl::InterfaceSupportsErrorInfo(REFIID riid)
{
    static const IID* arr[] =
    {
        &IID_IZodiac
```

```
    };
    for (int i=0; i < (sizeof(arr) / sizeof(arr[0])); i++)
    {
      if (InlineIsEqualGUID(*arr[i],riid))
        return S_OK;
    }
    return S_FALSE;
  }
```

> **NOTE**
>
> We left open the `InterfaceSupportsErrorInfo` implementation to add more inter-
> faces later if needed.

Implementing a Method That Fires an Event

Listing 16.5 is the implementation of the method that must asynchronously notify the same
results as the one we implemented in the previous section.

LISTING 16.5   `ZodiacImpl.cpp`: The Implementation of the
`TZodiacImpl::GetZodiacSignAsync()` Method

```cpp
STDMETHODIMP TZodiacImpl::GetZodiacSignAsync(long Day, long Month)
{
  try
  {
    TCOMCriticalSection::Lock Lock(CS);

    BSTR Sign = NULL;
    ::GetZodiacSign(Day, Month, Sign);
    Fire_OnZodiacSignReady(Sign);
    SysFreeString(Sign);
  }
  catch(Exception &e)
  {
    return Error(e.Message.c_str(), IID_IZodiac, E_FAIL);
  }
  catch(...)
  {
    return Error(_T("Catastrophic error: internal crash"),
                 IID_IZodiac, E_UNEXPECTED);
  }
  return S_OK;
};
```

Everything should be familiar to you in this code. We already saw that
`Fire_OnZodiacSignReady()` is responsible for firing the event from the server object by calling the proper method in the client sink.

Even so, note the subtle memory management issue: The server allocates the `Sign` string, but this time the server also is responsible for freeing it because, from the client's point of view, `Sign` is an `in` parameter. We have to be very careful to avoid leaks when programming COM.

Now our COM object is capable of receiving automation calls and firing dispinterface-based events. We also want a custom interface to provide extended zodiac information, and we want events to be fired from a custom outgoing interface. We will write these features in the coming section.

Implementing a Custom Interface

Be prepared to deal directly with your IDL and C++ code when implementing custom interfaces. The TLE is still an immature feature of C++Builder, in spite of its age. It doesn't behave very well when dealing with non-dual interfaces, and it has some bugs that can make you crazy. Before rushing to define more interfaces and methods, sit back and think about the custom types you will use as arguments, and start by defining them first.

We are going to define the structured type we will use as a parameter type for some of the custom interface methods. The IDL declaration of it will look like this:

```
typedef struct tagTDetailedZodiacSign
{
  BSTR Sign;
  long House;
  BSTR Element;
  BSTR Planet;
  BSTR Details;
  BSTR Advice;
} TDetailedZodiacSign;
```

To add the new type, follow these steps:

1. Press the New Record button on the TLE (the fifth from the left in the TLE toolbar).

2. Rename the record `TDetailedZodiacSign`.

3. Add all the fields defined in the `struct` declaration. Select the structure name in the left pane and press the New Field button on the TLE toolbar, indicated by the cursor in Figure 16.7. The type of each field can be set in the right pane.

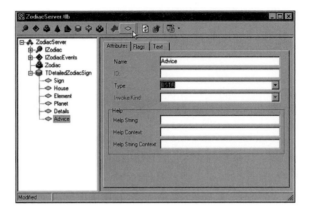

FIGURE 16.7

Inserting a new record in the TLE and adding some record fields.

To add a new interface, follow these steps:

1. Launch the TLE (View, Type Library).

2. Press the New Interface button (first from the left in the TLE toolbar).

3. Rename the new interface to IDetailedZodiac.

4. Select the interface in the left pane. In the right pane, select the Attributes tab and ensure that IDetailedZodiac inherits from IUnknown instead of IDispatch (see Figure 16.8).

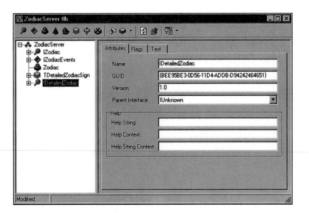

FIGURE 16.8

The IDetailedZodiac interface in the TLE.

5. In the Indicators page of the interface, uncheck the Dual and Ole Automation check boxes. If you find these check boxes grayed, press the Text tab and erase the attributes oleautomation and dual.

We are ready now to add the following two methods:

```
HRESULT _stdcall GetDetailedZodiacSign([in] long Day, [in] long Month,
                        [out] TDetailedZodiacSign * DetailedSign );

HRESULT _stdcall GetDetailedZodiacSignAsync([in] long Day, [in] long Month );
```

The process is the same as when we added methods to the IZodiac dual interface. Don't forget that the third parameter's GetDetailedZodiacSign() type is a pointer to a custom structure. Figure 16.9 illustrates how to select the parameter type.

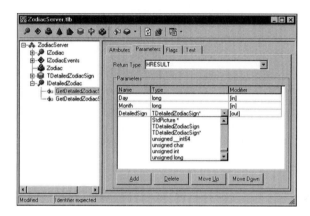

FIGURE 16.9
Selecting a custom type for a parameter.

Now that the interface is declared, we should use the TLE to state that the Zodiac coclass implements it:

1. In the left pane, select the Zodiac coclass.

2. Select the Implements tab in the right pane. You will see a list of all the interfaces the Zodiac coclass claims to implement.

3. Right-click on the pane and a pop-up menu will appear. Click the Insert Interface menu item. The Insert Interface dialog appears (see Figure 16.10).

4. Select the IDetailedZodiac interface in the dialog and press OK. You will notice that now the IDetailedZodiac interface was added to the list of implemented interfaces.

5. Save your work.

Figure 16.10

The Insert Interface dialog, with the interface IDetailedZodiac *selected.*

After saving your work, open the ZodiacImpl.h file and see what is new. The first thing we notice is that TZodiacImpl now inherits from a strange new macro:

```
class ATL_NO_VTABLE TZodiacImpl :
  public CComObjectRootEx<CComMultiThreadModel>,
  public CComCoClass<TZodiacImpl, &CLSID_Zodiac>,
  public IConnectionPointContainerImpl<TZodiacImpl>,
  public TEvents_Zodiac<TZodiacImpl>,
  public IDispatchImpl<IZodiac, &IID_IZodiac, &LIBID_ZodiacServer>,
  DUALINTERFACE_IMPL(Zodiac, IDetailedZodiac)
{
(snip.)
};
```

That macro seems to say that TZodiacImpl implements the dual interface IDetailedZodiac. But IDetailedZodiac is not dual! The TLE introduced wrong code, so it must be changed by inheriting directly from IDetailedZodiac. The following is the correct version that the TLE should have generated:

```
class ATL_NO_VTABLE TZodiacImpl :
  public CComObjectRootEx<CComMultiThreadModel>,
  public CComCoClass<TZodiacImpl, &CLSID_Zodiac>,
  public IConnectionPointContainerImpl<TZodiacImpl>,
  public TEvents_Zodiac<TZodiacImpl>,
  public IDispatchImpl<IZodiac, &IID_IZodiac, &LIBID_ZodiacServer>,
  public IDetailedZodiac
{
(snip.)
};
```

In the COM map, the TLE introduced the same error:

```
BEGIN_COM_MAP(TZodiacImpl)
  COM_INTERFACE_ENTRY(IZodiac)
  COM_INTERFACE_ENTRY2(IDispatch, IZodiac)
  COM_INTERFACE_ENTRY_IMPL(IConnectionPointContainer)
  DUALINTERFACE_ENTRY(IDetailedZodiac)
END_COM_MAP()
```

Substitute the `DUALINTERFACE_ENTRY` macro for `COM_INTERFACE_ENTRY`. The fixed COM map is now

```
BEGIN_COM_MAP(TZodiacImpl)
  COM_INTERFACE_ENTRY(IZodiac)
  COM_INTERFACE_ENTRY2(IDispatch, IZodiac)
  COM_INTERFACE_ENTRY_IMPL(IConnectionPointContainer)
  COM_INTERFACE_ENTRY(IDetailedZodiac)
END_COM_MAP()
```

All is done, except the implementation of the `IDetailedZodiac` methods in `ZodiacImpl.cpp`.

Since it doesn't introduce anything new to you, the implementation of the method `GetDetailedZodiacSign()` won't be explained here. You can always go to the companion CD to see what it contains.

The `GetDetailedZodiacSignAsync()` method, however, is very similar to `GetZodiacSignAsync()`, but it should fire a custom event that we have not defined yet.

Firing Custom Events

Why would you care about firing custom events? The answer is simple: performance. When calling methods through a dispinterface, there is always one additional level of indirection: You must get the dispatch ID of the method and call the `Invoke()` function of the `IDispatch` interface of your object. When the `Invoke()` method is called, a lot of parameters are passed. Among them are the dispatch ID, the type of the invocation, and the actual parameters of the call, which are forced to be `VARIANT`. Development tools such as C++Builder hide this process (at least partially), but the overhead is there. If you care about speed, use custom events instead.

On the other hand, the advantage of using dispinterface-based events has to do with the late binding nature of `IDispatch` interface invocations. Events of this kind, though slower, can be used in scripting languages such as JavaScript or VBScript.

Now you know the reasons for writing custom events support. The IDL declaration of the custom outgoing interface we want to implement would be as follows:

```
[
  uuid(4992BB4F-FCA6-11D3-ADDB-BCAF427C7F50),
  version(1.0)
]
 interface IDetailedZodiacEvents: IUnknown
{
  HRESULT _stdcall OnDetailedZodiacSignReady(
                      [in] TDetailedZodiacSign * DetailedSign );
}
```

As you can see, OnDetailedZodiacSignReady() is almost the same as the
OnZodiacSignReady() method, ignoring the trivial differences.

To start coding IDetailedZodiacEvents, launch the TLE again (View, Type Library) and follow the same steps as when adding the IDetailedZodiac custom interface and its methods.
The state of the TLE after inserting the IDetailedZodiacEvents interface is shown in Figure 16.11.

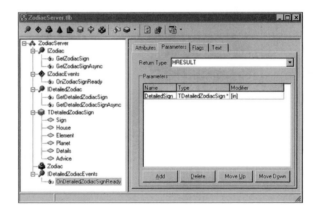

FIGURE 16.11

The TLE state, after inserting the custom interface IDetailedZodiacEvents.

Now the interface is declared in the TLE, but no interface is exactly outgoing. An interface is
outgoing or ingoing relative to a coclass.

To state that the Zodiac coclass implements IDetailedZodiacEvents as an outgoing interface,
follow these steps:

1. Click the Zodiac coclass in the left pane of the TLE.

2. Select the Implements tab, and right-click over the grid of interfaces that appears there.

3. In the pop-up menu that appears, select Insert Interface, as you did before. The Insert
   Interface dialog box appears.

4. Select the `IDetailedZodiacEvents` interface in the dialog and press OK.

5. Right-click over the `IDetailedZodiacEvents` interface name, and check Source in the pop-up menu that appears, as seen in Figure 16.12.

6. Save your work.

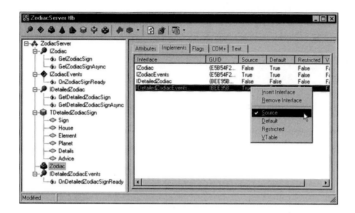

FIGURE 16.12

Using the TLE to indicate that `IDetailedZodiacEvents` *is a custom outgoing interface of the* `Zodiac` *coclass.*

The declaration is now complete: The Type Library of our server now says that instances of the `Zodiac` coclass fire those events declared as methods in the `IDetailedZodiacEvents` interface.

Now if you open `ZodiacImpl.h`, you will find... nothing new! C++Builder didn't generate the custom event support. Therefore, we must write the boilerplate code on our own, because the TLE didn't help us in doing so.

If you read carefully the implementation of `TEvents_Zodiac` in `Zodiac_TLB.h`, writing the equivalent code for firing our custom events won't be too hard. Listing 16.6 shows one possible solution.

LISTING 16.6 `ZodiacImpl.h`: The `TEvents_DetailedZodiac` Template Implementation

```
template <class T>
class TEvents_DetailedZodiac :
   public IConnectionPointImpl<T,
          &IID_IDetailedZodiacEvents,
          CComDynamicUnkArray>
{
   public:
   HRESULT Fire_OnDetailedZodiacSignReady(TDetailedZodiacSign* DetailedSign)
```

LISTING 16.6   Continued

```
{
    T * pT = (T*)this;
    pT->Lock();
    IUnknown ** pp = m_vec.begin();
    while (pp < m_vec.end())
    {
        if (*pp != NULL)
        {
            CComQIPtr<IDetailedZodiacEvents,
                    &IID_IDetailedZodiacEvents> ptrEvents = *pp;
            if (ptrEvents != NULL)
                ptrEvents->OnDetailedZodiacSignReady(DetailedSign);
        }
        pp++;
    }
    pT->Unlock();

    return S_OK;
}
};
```

The main difference we introduced is that there is no use of any m_EventIntfObj wrapper member. Now the call is made directly to the interface IDetailedZodiacEvents, with the subsequent gain in performance.

The use of CComQIPtr<IDetailedZodiacEvents, &IID_IDetailedZodiacEvents> is to query the IDetailedZodiacEvents interface from the connected IUnknown client interface. The query is done automatically in the implementation of the CComQIPtr constructor, which is an ATL class. The CComQIPtr, when destroyed, automatically releases the wrapped interface reference.

> **NOTE**
>
> The TEvents_DetailedZodiac template class can be used as a starting point for supporting any other custom events, by making only minor adjustments to its code.

It's time to join this final piece to the entire puzzle. To modify the code of TZodiacImpl (in ZodiacImpl.h), follow these steps:

1. Modify the `TZodiacImpl` class so that it inherits from `TEvents_DetailedZodiac <TZodiacImpl>`:

```
class ATL_NO_VTABLE TZodiacImpl :
  public CComObjectRootEx<CComMultiThreadModel>,
  public CComCoClass<TZodiacImpl, &CLSID_Zodiac>,
  public IConnectionPointContainerImpl<TZodiacImpl>,
  public TEvents_Zodiac<TZodiacImpl>,
  public IDispatchImpl<IZodiac, &IID_IZodiac, &LIBID_ZodiacServer>,
  public IDetailedZodiac,
  public TEvents_DetailedZodiac <TZodiacImpl>
{
// snip
};
```

2. Modify the connection point map to support a new entry. The line that was added is marked with **bold** typeface:

```
BEGIN_CONNECTION_POINT_MAP(TZodiacImpl)
  CONNECTION_POINT_ENTRY(DIID_IZodiacEvents)
  CONNECTION_POINT_ENTRY(IID IDetailedZodiacEvents)
END_CONNECTION_POINT_MAP()
```

The object is now ready to raise the custom events declared in `IDetailedZodiacEvents` from any place in its code.

In the implementation of `GetDetailedZodiacSignAsync()`, add a call to `Fire_OnDetailedZodiacSignReady()`. This notifies your clients that the asynchronous operation was concluded, but now using a custom interface instead of a dispinterface. This is shown in Listing 16.7.

LISTING 16.7   ZodiacImpl.cpp: The Implementation of the `TZodiacImpl::GetDetailedZodiacSignAsync()` Method

```
struct TDetailedZodiacSignImpl : public TDetailedZodiacSign
{
   TDetailedZodiacSignImpl()
   {
     Sign = NULL;
     Element = NULL;
     Element = NULL;
     Planet = NULL;
     Details = NULL;
     Details = NULL;
     Advice = NULL;
   }
```

LISTING 16.7   Continued

```
    ~TDetailedZodiacSignImpl()
    {
        if (Sign != NULL)
          SysFreeString(Sign);
        if (Element != NULL)
          SysFreeString(Element);
        if (Planet != NULL)
          SysFreeString(Planet);
        if (Details != NULL)
          SysFreeString(Details);
        if (Advice != NULL)
          SysFreeString(Advice);
    }
};

STDMETHODIMP TZodiacImpl::GetDetailedZodiacSignAsync(long Day, long Month)
{
  try
  {
    TCOMCriticalSection::Lock Lock(CS);

    TDetailedZodiacSignImpl DetailedSign;
    ::GetDetailedZodiacSign(Day, Month, DetailedSign);
    Fire_OnDetailedZodiacSignReady(&DetailedSign);
  }
  catch(Exception &e)
  {
    return Error(e.Message.c_str(), IID_IDetailedZodiac, E_FAIL);
  }
  return S_OK;
};
```

The outer scope function `::GetDetailedZodiacSign()` allocates and sets values to the strings fields of `TDetailedZodiacSign`. Note that the wrapper `TDetailedZodiacSignImpl`, written to free the allocated memory, is used here because the server (which is now the client of the actual client) is responsible for freeing any memory it passes to the client sink via an `in` parameter. This is very important, and for that reason we again insist on it.

At this point, we have a COM server object that fires events when it finishes operations called by clients. It is time to compile and register the server by clicking on the Run, Register ActiveX Server menu item of the C++Builder IDE. If everything went all right, a message box stating `Successfully registered ActiveX Server C:\Your Path\ZodiacServer.dll` will appear. Easy enough?

The only thing we have to do now is write the proxy/stub DLL for those non-automation-compatible custom interfaces our server exposes. We are almost finished building the server with C++.

Writing the Proxy/Stub DLL

When the client and the server reside in different apartments or in different processes or computers, a process named *marshaling* does its work. It involves two main entities: the proxy and the stub.

The proxy is always in the same address space as the client. It is responsible for properly packaging the parameters passed to a method to forward them to the server in a suitable way (over a network, using interprocess communication, or crossing apartment boundaries).

The stub lives in the address space of the server. It does the opposite: It unpacks the parameters received from clients to invoke directly the server methods. This is often referred to as *unmarshaling*. Figure 16.13 shows how the entire process works.

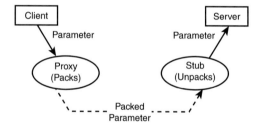

FIGURE 16.13

The marshaling mechanism: proxy/stubs DLLs in action.

> **NOTE**
>
> There are three types of marshaling: Type Library Marshaling is provided automatically by COM for dispinterfaces and oleautomation custom interfaces via `oleaut32.dll`. Standard Marshaling is implemented by developing your own proxy/stub DLLs for non-oleautomation custom interfaces; this is what we are going to develop here. Custom Marshaling is for those objects that implement the `IMarshall` interface.

LISTING 16.8   Continued

```
[(snip.)]
interface IDetailedZodiac: IUnknown
{
  [id(0x00000001)] HRESULT _stdcall GetDetailedZodiacSign([in] long Day,
            [in] long Month, [out] TDetailedZodiacSign * DetailedSign );
  [id(0x00000002)] HRESULT _stdcall GetDetailedZodiacSignAsync([in] long Day,
            [in] long Month );
};

[(snip.)]
interface IDetailedZodiacEvents: IUnknown
{
  [id(0x00000001)] HRESULT _stdcall OnDetailedZodiacSignReady(
                            [in] TDetailedZodiacSign * DetailedSign );
};
};
```

We have to edit this file to prepare it for generating the proxy/stub code. To edit the file, follow these steps:

1. Open the file in your preferred text editor.

2. Take out of the library section all the custom interfaces that are not marked as automation compatible and erase everything else.

NOTE

This is necessary because the Microsoft IDL compiler (MIDL) generates proxy/stub code only for those interfaces that are defined outside the library section of an IDL source file. Note that a dual interface, which is by definition oleautomation compatible, doesn't need to be there, because its marshaling is done automatically by COM via Type Library Marshaling.

3. Import the `objidl.idl` file in the beginning of the IDL file, to include standard OLE type declarations (see Listing 16.9).

The modified version of `ZodiacServer.idl` will be as in Listing 16.9.

LISTING 16.9 The Modified `ZodiacServer.idl`, Ready to Be Compiled by the MIDL Compiler

```
// Standard COM definitions:
import "objidl.idl";

  [(snip.) ]
  typedef struct tagTDetailedZodiacSign
  {
    BSTR Sign;
    long House;
    BSTR Element;
    BSTR Planet;
    BSTR Details;
    BSTR Advice;
  } TDetailedZodiacSign;

  [(snip.) ]
  interface IDetailedZodiac: IUnknown
  {
    [id(0x00000001)] HRESULT _stdcall GetDetailedZodiacSign([in] long Day,
                [in] long Month, [out] TDetailedZodiacSign * DetailedSign );
    [id(0x00000002)] HRESULT _stdcall GetDetailedZodiacSignAsync(
                [in] long Day, [in] long Month );
  };

  [(snip. )]
  interface IDetailedZodiacEvents: IUnknown
  {
    [id(0x00000002)] HRESULT _stdcall OnDetailedZodiacSignReady(
                          [in] TDetailedZodiacSign * DetailedSign );
  };
```

The IDL is ready to be compiled with the MIDL command-line compiler. It will generate several source files for creating the proxy/stub DLL, as we will see later.

The MIDL compiler is located in your C++Builder `Bin` folder. It is a good idea to use a batch file to specify its location, the include paths, and the MIDL options. Batch files run a set of commands and have a `.bat` filename extension. The commented source code of an example batch file is shown in Listing 16.10.

LISTING 16.10   A Batch File for Compiling IDL Files with the MIDL Compiler

```
rem  All paths here defined are the paths in my PC. You must use yours:

@echo off
rem Include path for any idl files you use:
set INCPATH=c:\progra~1\borland\cbuild~1\include\;
➡c:\progra~1\borland\cbuild~1\include\idl

rem Borland C++ Builder preprocessor path:
set CPPPATH=c:\progra~1\borland\cbuild~1\bin

rem MIDL path:
set MIDLPATH=c:\progra~1\borland\cbuild~1\bin

rem Invoke MIDL:
@echo on

%MIDLPATH%\midl -ms_ext -I%INCPATH% -cpp_cmd%CPPPATH%\CPP32  -cpp_opt "-P-
➡ -oCON -DREGISTER_PROXY_DLL -I%INCPATH%" %1
```

> **NOTE**
>
> C++Builder's help explains very well the options we set for the preprocessor compiler
> in this batch file. For information on other MIDL switches, go to MSDN at
> http://msdn.microsoft.com/.

Save this batch file as makeIDL.bat. Now we can use it in this way:

makeIDL ZodiacServer.idl

Once terminated, the MIDL compiler will give you the following output files, resulting from
the compiling process:

- ZodiacServer.h
- ZodiacServer_i.c
- ZodiacServer_p.c
- dlldata.c

You must not forget to create a .def file to allow the proxy/stub DLL to be registered or unregistered. That .def file can be saved as ZodiacServerPS.def and will be as follows:

LIBRARY   ZODIACSERVERPS

  DESCRIPTION 'Zodiac Proxy/Stub DLL'

```
EXPORTS
   DllGetClassObject PRIVATE
   DllCanUnloadNow PRIVATE
   DllRegisterServer PRIVATE
   DllUnregisterServer PRIVATE
   GetProxyDllInfo PRIVATE
```

It is not so important to understand what is in each of the files MIDL generated. The one thing you need to know is that you must create a DLL project using all these files (there are five, including ZodiacServerPS.def and ZodiacServer.h).

Now let's create the DLL project with C++Builder. All the isolated pieces should be joined to solve the puzzle.

To create the DLL project, follow these steps:

1. Launch C++Builder.
2. Press File, New in the main menu of the IDE. The New Items dialog appears.
3. Press the DLL Wizard icon under the New tab in the dialog. The DLL Wizard dialog appears.
4. Set Source Type to C, as seen in Figure 16.15, and press OK.

FIGURE 16.15
The DLL Wizard dialog box, with C selected as the source style.

5. Delete from your project the Unit1.c file that was added to your project automatically by C++Builder.
6. Add to your project the MIDL generated .c files and the .def we saw before.
7. Click on Project, Options. The Project Options dialog appears.
8. Click the Conditional/Defines tab and define

        WIN32;_WINDOWS;_MBCS;_USRDLL;REGISTER_PROXY_DLL;_WIN32_WINNT=0x0400

    or

        WIN32;_WINDOWS;_MBCS;_USRDLL;REGISTER_PROXY_DLL;_WIN32_DCOM

    if you want your proxy to be compliant with Windows 9x.

9. Press OK.
10. Save the project as ZodiacServerPS.bpr.

11. Compile the project. You will obtain the proxy/stub DLL binary.

12. Register it as a COM server by typing in the command prompt (use the Windows taskbar Start, Run): `regsvr32 c:\your path\ZodiacServerPS.dll`.

Voilà! Your custom interfaces now have a marshaling DLL. You are ready to use your server with any client.

What comes next? We want to demonstrate what happens on the client side. We are going to create the COM client that uses our server capabilities, to see how to write event sinks in C++Builder and how the server and the client relate to each other.

Writing the COM Client

To create a simple COM client that uses the server we developed, launch C++Builder and create a new, empty application. The client must have a user interface for providing the user's birthday. It must have some way to request the zodiac information from the server—simple or detailed, synchronously or asynchronously—and show the response to the user.

The client's main form is presented in Figure 16.16.

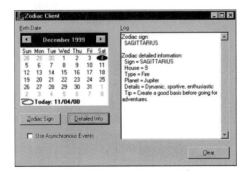

FIGURE 16.16
The user interface of the COM client program.

The Log panel at right shows the information received from the server. When checked, the Use Asynchronous Events check box at bottom left causes the client to call the asynchronous methods instead of the synchronous ones.

You probably are able to create this user interface by yourself, adding the needed event handlers and so on. In the companion CD are the source files of the client project, as well. For that reason, let's assume that the user interface is already created, and that you saved your work as `ZodiacClient`. The main form of the client application is named `MainForm`, and its unit is `Main`. We can now concentrate in the COM-related details.

Importing the Type Library

For a client to know the types your server exposes (including classes and interfaces), it is necessary to import the server's Type Library in the client.

To import the Type Library of the server, follow these steps:

1. Click on Project, Import Type Library in the BCB IDE. The Import Type Library dialog appears (see Figure 16.17).

2. Uncheck the Generate Component Wrapper check box. That indicates that you want only the C++ translation of the Type Library, not VCL component wrappers installed in the Component Palette.

3. In the list box, select the name of the Type Library of your server. In our example it is ZodiacServer Library (Version 1.0). Press the Create Unit button. The file `ZodiacServer_TLB.cpp` will be added to your project.

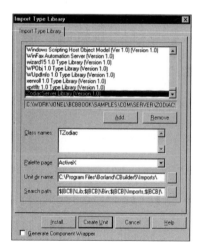

FIGURE 16.17
Importing the zodiac server Type Library.

NOTE

We imported the server's Type Library on purpose. If you compare the server sources `ZodiacServer_TLB.cpp` and `ZodiacServer_TLB.h` with these, you will notice that they are the same! But because COM is a binary standard, you won't very often have the

source code of a server. Also, remember that a server can be written in any programming language.

The main advantage of distributing the Type Library is that it can be used to generate
specific language declarations of all the components and types it describes. That will
guarantee that your components are capable of describing themselves so as to be
operational in any development platform.

Looking at the Generated C++ Constructions

The interfaces and coclasses that were defined in the server are declared in
`ZodiacServer_TLB.h`. There are also several wrapper classes, which are part of C++Builder
EZ-COM (meaning Easy COM, but it is not so easy).

Take a look at the `IZodiac` and `IDetailedZodiac` interfaces in Listing 16.11.

LISTING 16.11   `ZodiacServer_TLB.h`: The Declarations of the `IZodiac` and
`IDetailedZodiac` Interfaces

```
interface IZodiac : public IDispatch
{
public:
  virtual HRESULT STDMETHODCALLTYPE GetZodiacSign(
                  long Day/*[in]*/, long Month/*[in]*/,
                  BSTR* Sign/*[out,retval]*/) = 0; // [1]
  virtual HRESULT STDMETHODCALLTYPE GetZodiacSignAsync(long Day/*[in]*/,
                  long Month/*[in]*/) = 0; // [2]

#if !defined(__TLB_NO_INTERFACE_WRAPPERS)
  BSTR __fastcall GetZodiacSign(long Day/*[in]*/, long Month/*[in]*/)
  {
    BSTR Sign = 0;
    OLECHECK(this->GetZodiacSign(Day, Month, (BSTR*)&Sign));
    return Sign;
  }
#endif //   __TLB_NO_INTERFACE_WRAPPERS
};

(snip.)

interface IDetailedZodiac  : public IUnknown
{
public:
```

LISTING 16.11 Continued

```
virtual HRESULT STDMETHODCALLTYPE GetDetailedZodiacSign(
            long Day/*[in]*/, long Month/*[in]*/,
Zodiacserver_tlb::TDetailedZodiacSign* DetailedSign/*[out]*/) = 0; // [1]
   virtual HRESULT STDMETHODCALLTYPE GetDetailedZodiacSignAsync(
            long Day/*[in]*/, long Month/*[in]*/) = 0; // [2]
};
```

As you can see, IZodiac inherits from IDispatch, and IDetailedZodiac inherits from IUnknown. Remember that they are dual and custom, respectively.

In IZodiac we also have a second version of the GetZodiacSign() method, which is an overloading of the interface method of the same name. This function was generated because we declared the parameter Sign as retval, for return value.

This GetZodiacSign() wrapper returns the string instead of an HRESULT. This is cleaner when calling the function. Internally, GetZodiacSign() calls the original method, passing its result to the OLECHECK macro, which raises an exception if the call fails.

> **NOTE**
>
> Sadly, the OLECHECK macro implementation merges assertion issues with error handling ones and doesn't use the IErrorInfo capabilities your server may implement (as ZodiacServer does). For that reason, the message that goes with the fired exception is unusable, except for debugging purposes. You can play with some preprocessor definitions (such as NO_PROMPT_ON_HRCHECK_FAILURE), but the results won't cover the error handling needs you may have as a COM professional developer.
>
> On the companion CD, a file named ComThrow.h provides several macros to be used in COM development error/exception handling. Brief documentation is included in the header file itself, as are examples of how to use those macros in clients and servers.
>
> It is recommended to substitute the OLECHECK macro, wherever it is, for one of the macros declared in ComThrow.h, depending on your specific needs, and taking the corresponding actions in your sources. This will create more robust and user-friendly COM code.

Now we know how interfaces are defined in _TLB.h files. However, C++Builder clients will normally use several template class instances instead of raw interfaces. These are called *smart interfaces*. The class TCOMIZodiac is a smart interface. Listing 16.12 shows how it looks.

LISTING 16.12   `ZodiacServer_TLB.h`: The Declaration of the `TCOMIZodiac` Smart Interface

```
template <class T /* IZodiac */ >
class TCOMIZodiacT : public TComInterface<IZodiac>,
                     public TComInterfaceBase<IUnknown>
{
public:
  TCOMIZodiacT() {}
  TCOMIZodiacT(IZodiac *intf, bool addRef = false) :
    TComInterface<IZodiac>(intf, addRef) {}
  TCOMIZodiacT(const TCOMIZodiacT& src) : TComInterface<IZodiac>(src) {}
  TCOMIZodiacT& operator=(const TCOMIZodiacT& src)
    { Bind(src, true); return *this;}

  HRESULT          __fastcall GetZodiacSign(long Day/*[in]*/,
                                            long Month/*[in]*/,
                                            BSTR* Sign/*[out,retval]*/);
  BSTR             __fastcall GetZodiacSign(long Day/*[in]*/,
                                            long Month/*[in]*/);
  HRESULT          __fastcall GetZodiacSignAsync(long Day/*[in]*/,
                                                 long Month/*[in]*/);
};
typedef TCOMIZodiacT<IZodiac> TCOMIZodiac;
```

`TCOMIZodiac` is an instantiation of the template `TCOMIZodiacT`. Using `TCOMIZodiac`, you will work with your server seamlessly, because this will be just another C++ class for you. The smart interface has several methods (including initializers and operators) that will make your life easier.

Some of the most important operators are inherited from the `TComInterface` template, whose `TComInterface<IZodiac>` class instance is one of the `TCOMIZodiacT` ancestors. `TComInterface` implements the `*` and `->` indirection operators to return the raw COM interface. Additionally, `TComInterface` implements an assignment operator, which releases the currently enclosed interface before assigning a new one to it.

Smart interfaces are initialized using a template specialization of `TCoClassCreatorT`, which provides an easy way to instantiate COM objects. This creator template is defined in `utilcls.h` as shown in Listing 16.13.

LISTING 16.13   `Utilcls.h`: The `TCoClassCreatorT` Template Class

```
template <class TOBJ, class INTF, const CLSID* clsid, const IID* iid>
class TCoClassCreatorT : public CoClassCreator
{
public:
  static TOBJ    Create();
```

LISTING 16.13   Continued

```
static HRESULT Create(TOBJ& intfObj);
static HRESULT Create(INTF** ppintf);

static TOBJ    CreateRemote(LPCWSTR machineName);
static HRESULT CreateRemote(LPCWSTR machineName, TOBJ& intfObj);
static HRESULT CreateRemote(LPCWSTR machineName,  INTF** ppIntf);
};
```

C++Builder's help states that TCoClassCreatorT is designed to create objects implementing dual interfaces, but it also works well with objects exposing only custom interfaces.

> **NOTE**
>
> Smart interfaces and creators, although template based, are not from ATL, but from C++Builder itself.

The most important method of TCoClassCreatorT is the static method Create(), which internally calls ::CoCreateInstance() to instantiate the COM coclass it wraps. It also returns a smart interface object that encloses the coclass's default raw interface.

> **NOTE**
>
> The CreateRemote() method in TCoClassCreatorT is for bringing DCOM capabilities into play, but its use is discouraged because specifying machine names doesn't scale well. To do remote instantiations, use DCOM administration tools instead (dcomcnfg). Transparency is one of the COM goals, so avoid using CreateRemote().

The class CoZodiac is the creator template instance we will use. It is declared in ZodiacServer_TLB.h as follows:

```
typedef TCoClassCreatorT<TCOMIZodiac, IZodiac,
                         &CLSID_Zodiac,  &IID_IZodiac> CoZodiac;
```

Creating and Using the COM Server Object

For instantiating the server object in your client, declare a member of type TCOMIZodiac in the main form:

```
class TMainForm : public TForm
{
  TMonthCalendar *FCalendar;
  TButton *btnZodiac;
```

```
 TButton *btnDetailedZodiac;
 TCheckBox *chkAsync;
 TMemo *memLog;
 (snip.)
private:  // User declarations
 TCOMIZodiac FZodiac;
};
```

Notice that we included the declaration of the user interface components. This lets us refer to them freely in the rest of this section.

Now write the following in the FormCreate() event handler:

```
FZodiac = CoZodiac::Create();
```

If you run your client program, it will instantiate the COM server object without any problem. You don't even have to worry about calling CoInitialize(), because internally the creator ensures that it is called! Also, when your client is terminated, the destructor of TCOMIZodiac will release the server interface it holds.

We can now invoke any method of IZodiac on the FZodiac instance. In the Click event handler of the Zodiac Sign button, write the code in Listing 16.14 (our Zodiac Sign button is bound to the member btnZodiac).

LISTING 16.14   Main.cpp: The Click Event Handler of the Zodiac Sign Button

```
void __fastcall TMainForm::btnZodiacClick(TObject *Sender)
{
  TDateTime TheDate(FCalendar->Date);
  unsigned short year = 0;
  unsigned short month = 0;
  unsigned short day = 0;
  TheDate.DecodeDate(&year, &month, &day);
  if (!chkAsync->Checked)
  {
    BSTR bstrSign = FZodiac.GetZodiacSign(day, month); // Wrapper used!
    WideString wstrSign = bstrSign;

    memLog->Lines->Add(_T("Zodiac sign:"));
    memLog->Lines->Add(_T("  ") + wstrSign);
    memLog->Lines->Add(_T(""));
  }
  else
  {
    OLECHECK(
      FZodiac.GetZodiacSignAsync(day,  month));
  }
}
```

NOTE

Here we always use early binding, as any C++ client normally does.

If the Use Asynchronous Event check box (chkAsync) is unchecked, this code logs the zodiac sign in a memo when the synchronous method is received. If the chkAsync check box is checked, it will call the asynchronous service. An event handler should trap the event fired by the server. For that reason, now we are going to write the dispinterface-based event sink.

Catching Dispinterface-Based Events

All we need is a COM instance in the client that implements the dispinterface declared in the server coclass as outgoing. Since C++Builder 4, patch 1, the template class TEventDispatcher is in utilcls.h to help us to write IDispatch-based event sinks. It implements the IDispatch interface for servers to call when firing events. Its InvokeEvent() method is used to forward the server calls to their corresponding event handlers. InvokeEvent() looks like this:

```
// To be overriden in derived class to dispatch events
  virtual HRESULT InvokeEvent(DISPID id, TVariant* params = 0) = 0;
```

TEventDispatcher also exposes some methods for connecting the sink to and disconnecting it from a server: ConnectEvents() and DisconnectEvents(), respectively.

In our case, we will use the TEventDispatcher template for creating a class that will delegate the processing of the COM event to a C++Builder VCL event handler (see Listing 16.15). We declared this in ZodiacSink.h.

LISTING 16.15 ZodiacSink.h: Implementation of the Event Sink for the IZodiacEvents Dispatch Interface

```
// The C++Builder VCL event handler declaration:
typedef void __fastcall (__closure * TZodiacSignReadyEvent)(BSTR Sign);
//--------------------------------------------------------------------
// Create a class that handle IZodiacEvents
class TZodiacSink :
    public TEventDispatcher<TZodiacSink, &DIID_IZodiacEvents>
{
protected:
  // Event field
  TZodiacSignReadyEvent FOnZodiacSignReady;

  // Event dispatcher:
```

LISTING 16.15 Continued

```
HRESULT InvokeEvent(DISPID id, TVariant* params)
{
    // Forwarding to the VCL event property if assigned:
    if ((id == 1) && (FOnZodiacSignReady != NULL)) // OnZodiacSignReady
      FOnZodiacSignReady(params[0]);
    return S_OK;
}

// Reference to the event sender (ATL smart pointer used)
CComPtr<IUnknown> m_pSender;

public:
    __property TZodiacSignReadyEvent OnZodiacSignReady =
      { read = FOnZodiacSignReady, write = FOnZodiacSignReady };

public:
  TZodiacSink() :
      m_pSender(NULL),
      FOnZodiacSignReady(NULL)  {  }

  // When destroyed it will disconnect automatically:
  virtual ~TZodiacSink()    { Disconnect(); }

  // Connect to server
  void Connect(IUnknown* pSender)
  {
      if (pSender != m_pSender)
        m_pSender = pSender;
      if (NULL != m_pSender)
        ConnectEvents(m_pSender);
  }

  // Disconnect from server
  void Disconnect()
  {
    if (NULL != m_pSender)
    {
      DisconnectEvents(m_pSender);
      m_pSender = NULL;
    }
  }
};
```

LISTING 16.16   Continued

```
  (snip.)
  memLog->Lines->Add(_T("  Tip = ")
}
else
{
  OLECHECK(
    DetailedZodiac->GetDetailedZodia
}
}
```

This method is almost the same thing as the b
most important lines are highlighted in **bold** t
method by yourself, so let's write the custom
code.

Writing the Custom Interfac

Once again, a COM object in the client is need
interface: IDetailedZodiacEvents. This job h
we will use ATL, and we previously saw most

In CustomEvents.h we wrote a custom event s
Listing 16.17.

LISTING 16.17   CustomEvents.h: The TCust
Event Sinks

```
template <class Base, class Interface, c
class TCustomSink : public Base
{
private:
  CComPtr<IUnknown> m_ptrSender; // Even
  DWORD m_dwCookie;              // Conn

public:
  TCustomSink() :
    m_dwCookie(0) { }

  virtual ~TCustomSink()  { Disconnect();

  // IUnknown implementation:
  STDMETHOD_(ULONG, AddRef)() { return 1;
  STDMETHOD_(ULONG, Release)() { return 1
  STDMETHOD(QueryInterface)(REFIID iid, v
```

Don't miss that in InvokeEvent() we check the value of the dispatch ID sent from the server (which is 1), to then forward the call to the proprietary method. That is the logic of dispinterfaces: detect the dispatch ID and then delegate the event processing to the corresponding handler.

To use our class, create a member of its type in TMainForm:

```
TZodiacSink FZodiacSink;
```

Also add to the form a VCL event handler of the type TZodiacSignReadyEvent. Its implementation will be as follows:

```
void __fastcall TMainForm::OnZodiacSignReady(BSTR Sign)
{
    WideString wstrSign = Sign;
    memLog->Lines->Add(_T("Zodiac sign (ASYNCHRONOUS):"));
    memLog->Lines->Add(_T("  ") + wstrSign);
    memLog->Lines->Add(_T(""));
    wstrSign.Detach();
}
```

We log the zodiac sign in the memo text when the event is received. Note that WideString wstrSign detaches the wrapper BSTR at the very end, because if not we will crash. Because Sign is an in parameter, the server is solely responsible for freeing it. The WideString wrapper was used here only for our comfort, because it overloads the + operator.

At this point, we are ready to add the following lines of code to the FormCreate() event handler implementation. This code is for connecting to the server and being ready to receive events:

```
// Set the VCL event handler property to the
// form's TZodiacSignReadyEvent handler:
FZodiacSink.OnZodiacSignReady = OnZodiacSignReady;
// Connect to the server:
FZodiacSink.Connect(FZodiac);
```

All the connection point mechanisms are prepared to work, although the dirtiest code was hidden from the mundane programmer! Compile and test, and you will see the results.

> **NOTE**
>
> Before running the example, use the BDE to create the database alias ZODIAC, making it point to the server\data subfolder in the example's directory. See the BDE documentation on how to do this.

Querying for the C[

We are ready to learn how to u[
IDetailedZodiac. Several sma[
one for each interface the serve[

```
typedef TComInterface<IZod[
typedef TComInterface<IZod[
typedef TComInterface<IDet[
                    &IID_[
typedef TComInterface<IDet[
                    &IID_[
```

Notice that the types are templa[
we already saw.

TComInterface is so smart that, [
type it wraps, it makes a call to [
interface is as simple as writing [

```
// Doing implicit QueryIn[
IDetailedZodiacPtr Detail[
```

That simple code line makes an i[
we are able to call the IDetailed[
(btnDetailedZodiac), double-cl[
Listing 16.16 in the generated me[

LISTING 16.16 Main.cpp: The [

```
void __fastcall TMainForm::b[
{
  TDateTime TheDate(FCalenda[
  unsigned short year = 0;
  unsigned short month = 0;
  unsigned short day = 0;
  TheDate.DecodeDate(&year, [
  // Doing implicit QueryInt[
  IDetailedZodiacPtr Detaile[
  if (!chkAsync->Checked)
  {
    TDetailedZodiacSignImpl [
    OLECHECK(
      DetailedZodiac->GetDeta[

    memLog->Lines->Add(_T("Zo[
    memLog->Lines->Add(_T("[
```

LISTING 16.17 Continued

```
    { return _InternalQueryInterface(iid, ppvObject); }

public:
  // Methods for connecting/disconnecting from the event sender
  HRESULT __fastcall Connect(IUnknown* pSender)
  {
    HRESULT hr = S_FALSE;

    if (pSender != m_ptrSender)
    {
      m_ptrSender = pSender;
      if (m_ptrSender != NULL)
      {
        CComPtr<IUnknown> ptrUnk;
        QueryInterface(IID_IUnknown, reinterpret_cast<LPVOID*>(&ptrUnk));
        hr = AtlAdvise(m_ptrSender, ptrUnk, *piid, &m_dwCookie);
      }
    }

    return hr;
  }


  HRESULT __fastcall Disconnect()
  {
    HRESULT hr = S_FALSE;

    if ( (m_ptrSender != NULL) &&
         (0 != m_dwCookie) )
    {
      hr = AtlUnadvise(m_ptrSender, *piid, m_dwCookie);
      m_dwCookie = 0;
      m_ptrSender = NULL;
    }

    return hr;
  }
};
```

As you can see, the template class implements the IUnknown interface. TCustomSink must be used with CComObjectRoot to take advantage of the QueryInterface() mechanism that is already provided by ATL, via CComObjectRoot::InternalQueryInterface() and interface maps. The Base template argument in the TCustomSink declaration is the user's class that derives from CComObjectRoot.

Another interesting thing is that we used the ATL functions `AtlAdvise()` and `AtlUnadvise()` (see the `Connect()` and `Disconnect()` methods in Listing 16.17). These functions do all the work needed to connect to (or disconnect from) a server using connection points.

To reuse this class to create your own custom event sinks, follow these steps:

1. Define a COM object based on ATL that derives from `CComObjectRootEx` (or `CComObjectRoot`) and from `CComCoClass`.

2. The object should implement the event's custom interface by inheriting from it and writing its methods' bodies.

3. Declare the creatable sink, meaning the actual class of your sink object, as follows:

   `typedef TCustomSink<CMySink, &IID_IMyEvents> TMyCreatableSink;`

   `CMySink` in this case must implement the custom interface `IMyEvents`.

Listing 16.18 is the full listing of the file `ZodiacCustomSink.h`, which implements the COM object and custom event sink for the `IDetailedZodiacEvents`.

LISTING 16.18   `ZodiacCustomSink.h`: The `TDetailedZodiacSinkImpl` Class, Which Implements the Event Sink for `IDetailedZodiacEvents` Custom Events

```
#if !defined(ZODIACCUSTOMSINK_H__)
#define ZODIACCUSTOMSINK_H__

#include <atlvcl.h>
#include <atlbase.h>
#include <atlcom.h>
#include <ComObj.HPP>
#include <utilcls.h>
#include "CustomSinks.h"
#include "ZodiacServer_TLB.h"

// The C++Builder VCL event handler declaration:
typedef void __fastcall (__closure * TDetailedZodiacSignReadyEvent)
    (TDetailedZodiacSign& DetailedSign);

//-----------------------------------------------------------------------
// Create a class that receive IDetailedZodiacEvents
class ATL_NO_VTABLE TDetailedZodiacSinkImpl :
  public CComObjectRootEx<CComSingleThreadModel>,
  public CComCoClass<TDetailedZodiacSinkImpl, &CLSID_NULL>,
  public IDetailedZodiacEvents
{
public:
```

LISTING 16.18   Continued

```
  TDetailedZodiacSinkImpl() :
    FOnDetailedZodiacSign(NULL)
  {
  }

  DECLARE_THREADING_MODEL(otApartment);

BEGIN_COM_MAP(TDetailedZodiacSinkImpl)
  COM_INTERFACE_ENTRY(IDetailedZodiacEvents)
END_COM_MAP()

protected:
  // Event field
  TDetailedZodiacSignReadyEvent FOnDetailedZodiacSign;

public:
  __property TDetailedZodiacSignReadyEvent OnDetailedZodiacSign =
    { read = FOnDetailedZodiacSign, write = FOnDetailedZodiacSign };

// IDetailedZodiacEvents
public:
  STDMETHOD(OnDetailedZodiacSignReady(TDetailedZodiacSign* DetailedSign))
  {
    if (FOnDetailedZodiacSign != NULL)
      FOnDetailedZodiacSign(*DetailedSign);
    return S_OK;
  }
};

typedef TCustomSink<TDetailedZodiacSinkImpl, IDetailedZodiacEvents,
                    &IID_IDetailedZodiacEvents>      TZodiacCustomSink;

#endif //ZODIACCUSTOMSINK_H__
```

Notice the use of those ATL classes and macros we saw when developing our server. The difference here is that there is no need for any object map in the server, because the object is not creatable from any client. Also for that reason, the class ID does not matter, so we used CLSID_NULL. TDetailedZodiacSinkImpl implements only the interface the server needs to raise events, and it delegates event processing to a VCL event handler of type TDetailedZodiacSignReadyEvent, in the same way we saw in the TZodiacSink class in the previous section.

The class `TZodiacCustomSink` is the final sink object class, as declared in the following typedef, which was seen in Listing 16.18:

```
typedef TCustomSink<TDetailedZodiacSinkImpl, IDetailedZodiacEvents,
                    &IID_IDetailedZodiacEvents>
        TZodiacCustomSink;
```

It uses the `TCustomSink` template wrapping around `TDetailedZodiacSinkImpl`. In this stage, the custom event sink type is ready to be used.

To start writing the code that takes advantage of our new custom event sink class, declare a member of type `TZodiacCustomSink` in the main form:

```
TZodiacCustomSink FZodiacCustomSink;
```

Add to the main form the VCL event handler whose implementation is partially presented here:

```
void __fastcall TMainForm::OnDetailedZodiacSignReady(
                    TDetailedZodiacSign& DetailedSign)
{
    memLog->Lines->Add(_T("Zodiac detailed information (ASYNCHRONOUS):"));
    memLog->Lines->Add(_T("  Sign = ") + AnsiString(DetailedSign.Sign));
    (snip.)
    memLog->Lines->Add(_T("  Tip = ") + AnsiString(DetailedSign.Advice));
    memLog->Lines->Add(_T(""));
}
```

Finally, following the pattern we used to connect to dispinterface-based event sinks (see the previous section), append the following lines of code to the end of the `FormCreate()` event handler:

```
// Set the VCL event handler property to the
// form's TDetailedZodiacSignReadyEvent handler:
FZodiacCustomSink.OnDetailedZodiacSign = OnDetailedZodiacSignReady;
// Connect to the server:
FZodiacCustomSink.Connect(FZodiac);
```

Now the entire mechanism is assembled. Our work is finished: We have a client that uses all the capabilities of the `ZodiacServer`. Compile and test once more, then go for a beer!

Recommended Readings

For more information on C++Builder programming

- *C++Builder 4 Unleashed*, Kent Reisdorph et al.; 1999, Sams Publishing; ISBN 0-672-31510-6

To learn more about COM/COM+

- *Inside COM*, Dale Rogerson; 1997, Microsoft Press; ISBN 1-57231-349-8
- *Inside Distributed COM*, Guy Eddon, Henry Eddon; 1998, Microsoft Press; ISBN 1-57231-849-X
- *Understanding COM+*, David S. Platt; 1999, Microsoft Press; ISBN 0-7356-0666-8
- *Mastering COM and COM+*, Ash Rofail, Yasser Shohoud; 1999, Sybex, Inc.; ISBN 0-7821-2384-8

For really learning ATL

- *ATL Internals*, Brent Rector, Chris Sells; 1999, Addison Wesley; ISBN 0-201-69589-8

Other interesting related readings

- *Delphi COM Programming*, Eric Harmon; 2000, Macmillan Technical Publishing; ISBN 1-57870-221-6

Internet resources

- `nntp://forums.inprise.com/borland.public.cppbuilder.activex`
- `http://community.borland.com/cpp/`
- `http://www.cetus-links.org/oo_ole.html`
- `http://www.techvanguards.com/`
- `http://msdn.microsoft.com/`

Summary

A technology like COM is nothing by itself. Developing COM components for real world uses, such as accessing large databases, interacting with hardware devices, or whatever, will be almost effortless once you master C++Builder as a whole, not only its COM features.

This chapter helped you in your first COM-oriented steps with C++Builder. You saw how to create a COM server, how to implement dual and custom interfaces, and how to fire events from a COM object. We also wrote a proxy/stub DLL for the custom interfaces exposed by a COM server object. Finally, a COM client that implements event sinks was explained. DCOM issues are going to be covered in the next chapter, where you will learn to scale up your COM servers and clients to a networking configuration.

Now that you know how to start developing your own COM clients and servers, go ahead and try it. COM is a complex technology, but you will become a fluent developer in less time than you can imagine!

Going Distributed: DCOM

Eduardo Bezerra

CHAPTER

17

IN THIS CHAPTER

- **What Is DCOM?**
- **The DCOMCnfg Utility Tool**
- **Field Testing DCOM**
- **Programming Security**

In the previous chapter, you learned what COM is and how to use it. This knowledge is paramount to the contemporary programmer targeting the Windows platform because COM objects are an intrinsic part of the operating system today.

More and more of the operating system services are being exposed in the form of COM objects, taking the place of traditional Application Programming Interfaces (APIs).

Until recently, those COM objects suffered from one big weakness—they could only be used from within the confines of a single computer. It was impossible to move the components to different machines on the network to create a distributed system.

To address this problem, Microsoft created DCOM. DCOM extends COM providing the ability to activate COM objects remotely. But DCOM introduces security and programming issues that we're going to explore in this chapter.

What Is DCOM?

Distributed COM is Microsoft's solution allowing COM objects to work on different machines across the network. It extends COM by allowing objects to be accessed remotely.

You can view DCOM as the wire specification of COM. If you take a COM object and distribute it across the network, you get a DCOM object. DCOM is just plain COM with security added to it. Technically speaking, DCOM was made possible by the extension of Remote Procedure Calls (RPCs) to Object RPC, and it first appeared when Microsoft released Windows NT 4.0.

DCOM has been ported to some UNIX flavors and can now be used as a cross-platform solution for distributed systems.

Despite other great competing technologies, DCOM is gradually becoming mainstream. This is due to the growing acceptance of the Windows NT operating system family on the corporate market.

DCOM uses the concept of Location Transparency, which means that you can run a COM server on a different machine on the network without requiring code modification. Neither the server nor the client needs to be concerned about where the other is running. They can be on the same machine, on a local area network, or in a wide area network, such as the Internet. For the client, the location of the server is a Registry setting that can be easily modified.

All this simplicity comes with a price, though. DCOM is governed by the security inherent to the Microsoft network Domain Model.

DCOM clients and servers must abide by the rules of authentication and authorization. This implies that clients must perform some sort of log in to access the machine where the server lives. Servers must authenticate the client, verifying whether he is really who he says he is, and authorize access by checking whether the user has the necessary privileges.

DCOM applications can rely on security settings stored in the Registry or can change their security settings through code. These two kinds of security are known as *declarative security* and *programmatic security*, respectively.

To successfully use DCOM, you must learn how to deal with its security aspects. In this chapter, you'll learn about the basics of DCOM security and see how C++Builder 5 handles programmatic security and activation of remote objects.

Windows OS Family and DCOM

DCOM comes standard with Windows 98, Windows NT 4.0, and Windows 2000, but you have to add it to Windows 95. You can download DCOM95 from Microsoft's Web site at `http://www.microsoft.com/com` or you can do a full install of Internet Explorer 4/5 in Windows 95 to get DCOM95 installed.

> **NOTE**
>
> If your network has a Domain Controller, you should configure your Windows 95 and 98 machines to use user-level security; otherwise, you won't be able to perform authenticated DCOM calls.

Windows 95 and 98 are best suited for use as DCOM clients because they can't dynamically launch and execute DCOM servers and don't have native security.

The DCOMCnfg Utility Tool

The DCOM Configuration Utility (DCOMCnfg.exe) is the tool that you use to modify DCOM settings that are specific to a server or that apply system wide acting on all registered servers on a given machine.

When you run the DCOMCnfg utility tool, you're presented with a dialog-based screen (see Figure 17.1), which exhibits the following tabs: Applications, Default Properties, Default Security, and Default Protocols.

> **NOTE**
>
> All relevant discussion of DCOMCnfg.exe in this chapter is based on the version that comes with Windows NT 4.0 with Service Pack 4 or later and Windows 2000. Windows 9X presents a slightly modified version of this configuration tool.

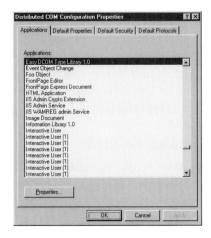

FIGURE 17.1
The DCOMCnfg configuration utility tool.

Global Security Settings

The Applications tab shows a list of all the servers containing the AppID Registry key that are registered on the machine. You can select any server and click the Properties button to have access to its settings.

The Default Properties tab (see Figure 17.2) is the place where you can completely enable or disable DCOM on the computer and configure system-wide default levels of authentication and impersonation.

On this tab, you also have the option to enable or disable COM Internet Services (CIS). CIS introduces new features to the DCOM model that allow clients and servers to communicate in the presence of proxy servers and firewalls. You can learn more about CIS on the Microsoft MSDN Web site at `http://msdn.microsoft.com/library/backgrnd/html/cis.htm`.

Authentication can be configured for when a client first connects, when a method call is made, or on every network packet passed between the client and server.

You can turn off authentication by selecting None at the Default Authentication Level combo box. Although risky, this would allow users without valid security credentials to have access to your server. Users coming from the Internet, for example, could benefit from this option.

The Default Impersonation Level combo box controls whether the server can determine the identity of the connected client and, if it can, use this identity to access system resources acting like the client itself. You can choose from the following:

- Anonymous—The client identity is unavailable.
- Identity—The server can impersonate the client only to obtain its identity.

- Impersonate—The server can impersonate the client to access local system resources on the client's behalf.

- Delegate—The server can impersonate the client to access local and remote resources on the client's behalf. Requires Windows 2000 running Kerberos as the Security Service Provider (SSP).

In the Default Security tab (see Figure 17.3), you can configure system-wide defaults for access, launch, and configuration permissions.

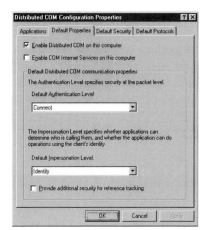

FIGURE 17.2
The Default Properties tab.

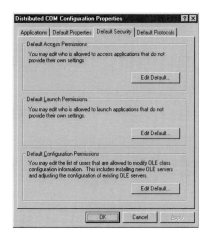

FIGURE 17.3
The Default Security tab.

Default Access Permissions relates to who is allowed or denied access to servers registered on the machine. If you want to let any user access your server, you can allow access permission to the built-in account Everyone.

Default Launch Permissions relates to who is authorized to load and run a server process. If you want to let any user execute your server, you can allow launch permission to the built-in Everyone account. Note that this option cannot be set programmatically.

Default Configuration Permissions states the precise type of access (Read, Full Control, or Special Access) you can set under HKEY_CLASSES_ROOT Registry key. This effectively controls user access rights to Registry entries related to DCOM setting.

The Default Protocols tab (see Figure 17.4) is used to arrange the ordering and availability of network protocols used by DCOM. You can configure DCOM for access over firewalls by selecting the desired network protocol and clicking the Properties button. Unless you have a good understanding of network protocols and operating system administration, you should leave these options unchanged.

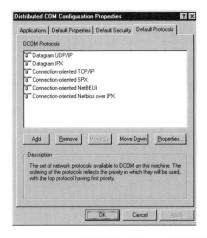

FIGURE 17.4
The Default Protocols tab.

Bear in mind that all options in the Default Properties tab and Default Security tab operate system wide. Modifying those options are likely to break some server installed on the system. The best course of action is to only change the settings for an explicit server component.

Per-Server Security Settings

Selecting a server from the Applications tab and clicking the Properties button gives you access to the security options related to that specific server.

The General tab (see Figure 17.5) on the Easy DCOM Type Library 1.0 Properties dialog shows the server's registered name, its type, local path, and authentication level. You can use the Authentication Level combo box to modify the authentication level of the server.

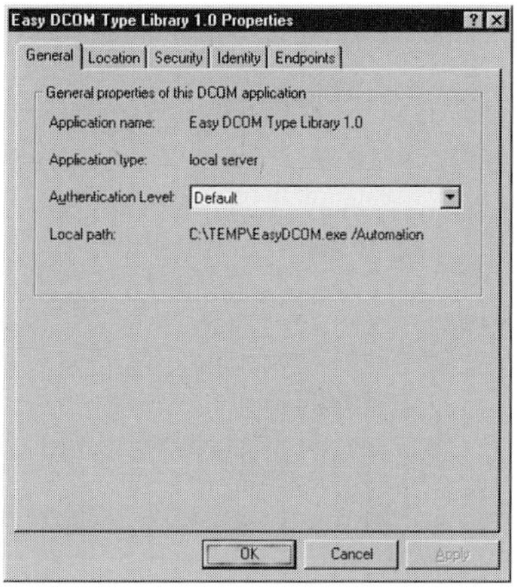

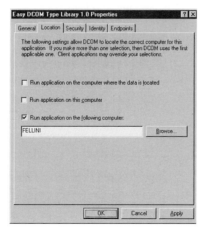

FIGURE 17.5
The General tab.

From the Location tab (see Figure 17.6), you can select from where the server will be executed. For example, by checking the Run Application on Following Computer option and entering the name of the computer, you can change the location from where the server will be activated.

FIGURE 17.6
The Location tab.

17

GOING
DISTRIBUTED:
DCOM

The Security tab (see Figure 17.7) lets you choose between using the system-wide default security settings or using custom security settings. All custom options work the same as the options showed for the Default Security tab (refer to Figure 17.3).

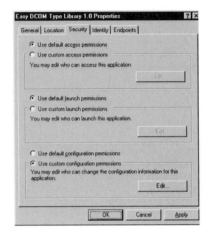

FIGURE 17.7

The Security tab.

The Identity tab (see Figure 17.8) is where you configure the account under which the server will run. The options are

- The Interactive User—Uses the account of the user who happens to be logged on at the server's machine. When there is no one logged on the system, the activation request will fail. This option is useful for debugging purposes because the server may have access to the desktop of the logged user.

- The Launching User—Uses the account of the user that requested the server object. A new copy of the server process will be created for every distinct client. This is the default option and must be avoided because it is not good for distributed applications.

- This User—Uses a specific account that can be a local or domain account. You can elect to use an already defined account or create a new one to suit your needs. Most of the time, this is the preferred option to choose from because you know beforehand the privileges your server will have when it's running.

DCOM will use the default global settings stored in the Registry on behalf of every server that has not been customized through the use of the DCOMCnfg utility tool. If you do customize the settings of a server, those settings will take precedence over the global ones. Nevertheless, programmatic security will always take precedence over declarative security.

You should always remember to configure Launch Permissions setting the users or group of users authorized to launch your server. Forgetting to do so may make your server unavailable for remote client access.

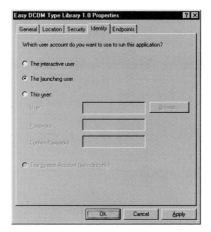

FIGURE 17.8
The Identity tab.

We are not going to cover the Endpoints tab in this chapter. Please refer to the DCOMCnfg documentation for further information.

Field Testing DCOM

We're going to create a very simple COM server and client to experiment with DCOM. This server will be able to return the name of the remote host computer and its current date/time.

The server will be packaged as an EXE binary. We won't use a DLL packaged server because it requires a surrogate to work out-of-process. It will use type library marshaling to avoid the registration of a proxy/stub marshaling DLL. You can refer to Chapter 16, "COM Programming," for a better understanding of COM marshaling.

Creating the Server Application

You're free to create whatever directory structure you want, but I choose to use a main folder with two subfolders named Server and Client for this project.

You can find the code for the example server application in the EasyDCOM\Server folder on the CD-ROM that accompanies this book.

To create the server application, do the following:

1. Launch C++Builder 5.
2. Select File, New, Application from the main IDE menu.
3. Save the project in the Server folder as EasyDCOM.bpr renaming Unit1.cpp to MainUnit.cpp.
4. Switch to the main project's form.

5. Press F11 to activate the Object Inspector.

6. Type frmMain at the Name Property.

7. Design your project's main form to look like the screen in Figure 17.9.

FIGURE 17.9
The EasyDCOM main form.

8. Select File, New from the main menu.

9. Switch to the ActiveX tab.

10. Double-click Automation Object. The New Automation Object dialog will appear.

11. Type HostInfo in the CoClass Name field.

12. Enter Easy DCOM Type Library 1.0 in the Description field and click OK.

13. Select View, Type Library to bring the Type Library Editor (TLE) to the front.

14. On the left pane, select the IHostInfo interface.

15. From the TLE toolbar, click the New, Property button down arrow and select Read Only from its pop-up menu.

16. Rename Property1 to Info.

17. On the right pane, select the Parameters tab and change Parameters type to BSTR* (see Figure 17.10).

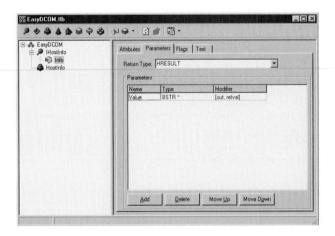

FIGURE 17.10
The TLE editor showing the read-only property info.

18. Press the Refresh button in the TLE editor to update the source files.

19. Switch to the `HostImpl.cpp` file and add the following code to the `get_Info()` method:

```
STDMETHODIMP THostInfoImpl::get_Info(BSTR* Value)
{
    try {
        char lpBuffer[MAX_COMPUTERNAME_LENGTH + 1];
        unsigned long nSize = sizeof(lpBuffer);

        if (GetComputerName(lpBuffer, &nSize) == 0)
            return HRESULT_FROM_WIN32(GetLastError());

        WideString strVal = AnsiString().
            sprintf("Date and time at %s is: %s",
            lpBuffer, DateTimeToStr(Now()));

        *Value = strVal.Detach();
    }
    catch(Exception &e) {
        return Error(e.Message.c_str(), IID_IHostInfo);
    }
    return S_OK;
};
```

20. Press F9 to compile and run the server.

Let's understand the code for the `Info` property of our EasyDCOM server.

We started by calling the Win32 API function `GetComputerName()` to store the computer name in the `lpBuffer` variable returning the appropriate `HRESULT` on error.

We then instantiated a `WideString` object based on the computer name and its current date and time.

We invoked the `Detach()` method of the `WideString` object to release ownership from the underlying `BSTR` because COM states that an out parameter has to be allocated by the server and released by the client.

Creating the Client Application

You can find the code for the example client application in the `EasyDCOM\Client` folder on the CD-ROM that accompanies this book.

To create the client application, do the following:

1. Start a new application and save the project in the `Client` folder as `EasyDCOMClient.bpr`, renaming `Unit1.cpp` to `MainUnit.cpp`.

2. Design your project's main form, adding the necessary components to look like the screen in Figure 17.11. When done, rename your components as follows:

Original Name	New Name
Form1	frmMain
GroupBox1	gbxLocal
GroupBox2	gbxRemote
Edit1	txtLocal
Edit2	txtRemote
Button1	cmdInfo
Button2	cmdFinish

FIGURE 17.11

The EasyDCOMClient *main form and its components.*

3. Open EasyDCOMClient.cpp and add the following:

```
USEUNIT("..\Server\EasyDCOM_TLB.cpp");
```

4. Open MainUnit.h and add the following:

```
#include "..\Server\EasyDCOM_TLB.h"
```

5. We're going to take advantage of C++Builder 5 EzCOM technology by declaring a smart interface variable to our EasyDCOM server.

Add the following code under TfrmMain class private section:

```
TCOMIHostInfo m_objHost;
```

6. Double-click the project's main form and add the following code to its OnCreate event:

```
char lpBuffer[MAX_COMPUTERNAME_LENGTH + 1];
unsigned long nSize = sizeof(lpBuffer);

GetComputerName(lpBuffer, &nSize);

txtLocal->Text = AnsiString().sprintf("Date and time at %s is: %s",
                                      lpBuffer, DateTimeToStr(Now()));
```

7. EzCOM also provides us with a creator class that has static methods for creating local and remote instances of our object.

Double-click the cmdInfo button and add the following code to its OnClick event:

```
if (!m_objHost.IsBound()) {
    AnsiString strHost;
```

```
if (InputQuery("Create Server", "Enter computer name:",
    strHost)) {

    if (strHost.IsEmpty())
        OleCheck(CoHostInfo::Create(m_objHost));
    else
        OleCheck(CoHostInfo::CreateRemote(WideString(strHost),
                                    m_objHost));

    WideString strValue;
    OleCheck(m_objHost.get_Info(&strValue));

    txtRemote->Text = strValue;
    }
}
```

8. Double-click the cmdFinish button and add the following code to its OnClick event:

    `Close();`

9. Click the project's main form, press F11 to activate the Object Inspector, and switch to its Events tab. Double-click the OnClose event and write the following code:

    `m_objHost.Unbind();`

10. Press F9 to compile and run the client. Click the Go Get button to display the Create Server dialog. When asked for the machine name, leave it blank and click OK to create the server locally.

Let's review the code for the client application.

The OnCreate event code for the main form retrieves and shows the name of the local computer and its date and time.

The handler code for the cmdInfo button calls the IsBound() method on the smart interface object verifying whether the server object is already instantiated and proceeds accordingly.

The InputQuery() function receives the NETBIOS name, DNS name, or IP address of the remote machine and stores it in the strHost variable.

If strHost returns empty, the server is locally instantiated using the Create method; otherwise, the CreateRemote() method accepts the machine name or IP address stored in strHost and tries to instantiate the server at the specified machine. OleCheck() is used to verify the returned HRESULT, throwing an exception on fail.

The get_Info() method is invoked passing the address of a WideString variable. This variable is then filled with information returned from the hosting machine and its value is shown in the txtRemote edit control.

Before closing the form, the Unbind() method of the smart interface object is invoked to release the server.

Now it's time to move our EasyDCOM sample to another machine on the network. Copy EasyDCOM.exe to a local drive on the remote machine and run it once to perform self-registration.

> **NOTE**
>
> If you choose a Windows 9X box, it won't be able to automatically launch the server; you'll have launch it manually.

Configuring Launch and Access Permissions

Let's assume, for the sake of our discussion, that the remote and client machines participate in a Microsoft network domain.

We're going to grant launch permission to anyone participating on the network, so proceed as follows:

1. Run DCOMCnfg.exe and double-click Easy DCOM Type Library 1.0 from the Applications tab list box.

2. Go to the Security tab and select Use Custom Launch Permissions. Click the Edit button and then the Add button. Double-click the built-in account Everyone and then click OK (see Figure 17.12). We're explicitly saying that anyone on the network can now load and run the server, but we still need to grant access to its services.

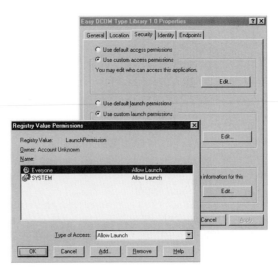

FIGURE 17.12
Granting Launch Permission to the Everyone *account.*

3. From the Security tab, select Use Custom Access Permissions. Click the Edit button and then the Add button. Select the local or domain account to which you want to grant access permission and then click OK (see Figure 17.13).

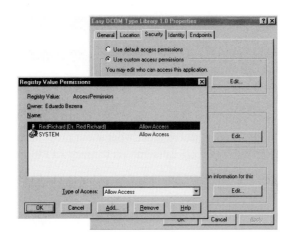

FIGURE 17.13

Granting access permission to a selected account.

Configuring Identity

We're going to choose which account the server will use when running. The best option, as already mentioned, is to select This User and enter an account that gives the server all the necessary privileges it needs when running.

Go to the Identity tab (refer to Figure 17.8). Select This User and enter or browse for the username. Enter the password, confirm it, and click OK.

Running the Example

What have we accomplished in terms of DCOM security for our sample application?

First, we stated that anyone could launch our server. Next, we selected the user or group of users that have clearance to access our server. Last, we solved the identity problem of our server by specifying the account it would use when running.

We're now ready to go.

Start `EasyDCOMClient.exe` on the client machine, click the Go Get button and enter the remote machine name or IP address when asked. You should see something like the screen in Figure 17.14.

FIGURE 17.14

EasyDCOMClient *talking to its server on a remote machine.*

Programming Security

So far, we have looked at declarative security, but what about programmatic security? Well, as matter of fact, COM is implicitly making calls into its security API for us.

What happens is that under the hood, COM reads the settings stored in the registry and calls the CoInitializeSecurity() function.

CoInitializeSecurity() is called exactly once for each process that uses COM, establishing process-wide security settings. It configures the security packages that will be used by COM, the authentication level for each process, and which users will be allowed access to the object.

CoInitializeSecurity Function Parameters

CoInitializeSecurity() is, by far, the most important COM security API function and has the following parameters:

```
PSECURITY_DESCRIPTOR pVoid,     //Points to security descriptor
LONG cAuthSvc,                  //Count of entries in asAuthSvc
SOLE_AUTHENTICATION_SERVICE * asAuthSvc,
                    //Array of names to register
void * pReserved1,    //Reserved for future use
DWORD dwAuthnLevel,   //Default authentication level
DWORD dwImpLevel,     //Default impersonation level
SOLE_AUTHENTICATION_LIST * pAuthList,
                    //Authentication information for
                    // each authentication service
DWORD dwCapabilities, //Additional client and/or
                    // server-side capabilities
void * pReserved3     //Reserved for future use
```

Some parameters apply to both servers and clients, while others apply solely to clients or to servers exclusively.

The first parameter, pVoid, applies only when the process acts like a server. It's used to control access permissions, and its value can be a pointer to an AppID GUID, a SECURITY_DESCRIPTOR, or an IAccessControl interface.

If a NULL pointer value is passed on pVoid, COM will grant access to anyone. This achieves the same functionality as using DCOMCnfg to grant access permission to the built-in Everyone account. If a valid pointer is passed on pVoid, the dwAuthnLevel (fifth parameter) cannot be set to RPC_C_AUTH_LEVEL_NONE.

The second and third parameters, cAuthSvc and asAuthSvc, are also used for servers. They are used for registering the authentication packages with COM and refer to an array of SOLE_AUTHENTICATION_SERVICE structures.

The SOLE_AUTHENTICATION_SERVICE structure has the following members:

```
typedef struct tagSOLE_AUTHENTICATION_SERVICE {
        DWORD           dwAuthnSvc;
        DWORD           dwAuthzSvc;
        OLECHAR*        pPrincipalName;
        HRESULT         hr;
} SOLE_AUTHENTICATION_SERVICE;
```

You can pass -1 (cAuthSvc) and NULL (asAuthSvc) to use the default security packages available on the system. NTLM (NT Lan Manager) is the only authentication service available on Windows NT 4.0, but you can use Kerberos with Windows 2000.

The fifth parameter, dwAuthnLevel, is used for setting the authentication level and applies to both clients and servers. It is equivalent as setting per-server authentication level (refer to Figure 17.5) through the use of DCOMCnfg. For this parameter, the value specified by the server is the minimum allowed. The actual value used will be the higher of the client and server values. If the client calls in with a lower value, the call fails.

The sixth parameter, dwImpLevel, applies only to clients. It sets the impersonation level the client has toward the server. It is equivalent to setting the global impersonation level (refer to Figure 17.2) through the use of DCOMCnfg. The clear advantage here is that you're no longer dependent on system-wide settings; you're now in control of the impersonation level, and this per-client setting cannot be achieved by the use of DCOMCnfg.

You can choose from one of the following impersonation levels:

```
RPC_C_IMP_LEVEL_DEFAULT
RPC_C_IMP_LEVEL_ANONYMOUS
RPC_C_IMP_LEVEL_IDENTIFY
RPC_C_IMP_LEVEL_IMPERSONATE
RPC_C_IMP_LEVEL_DELEGATE
```

As you might have guessed, they're equivalent to their DCOMCnfg counterparts (refer to Figure 17.2).

The eighth parameter, dwCapabilitiesis used for both clients and servers to describe additional capabilities they might have. The value for this parameter can be one or more of the following bitmasks:

- EOAC_NONE—Indicates that no capability flags are set.
- EOAC_MUTUAL_AUTH—Not used. Mutual authentication is automatically provided by some authentication services.
- EOAC_SECURE_REFS—Determines that reference-counting calls must be authenticated to avoid malicious releases. Refer to Figure 17.2 for the equivalent option using DCOMCnfg.
- EOAC_ACCESS_CONTROL—Must be used when passing an IAccessControl interface pointer as an argument to the parameter pVoid of CoInitializeSecurity().
- EOAC_APPID—Indicates that the pVoid parameter to CoInitializeSecurity() is a pointer to an AppID GUID. CoInitializeSecurity() searches the AppID in the Registry and reads the security settings from there.

Using CoInitializeSecurity

We're going to modify our sample application to completely turn off DCOM security by using CoInitializeSecurity(). This modification will make our sample application suitable for Internet access.

To accomplish this, we must allow access to anonymous users, disable authentication, and disable impersonation. It turns out that this is very simple to implement using CoInitializeSecurity().

As stated earlier, CoInitializeSecurity() must be called only once per process just before any significant COM calls. You must make the call on both the client and server sides just after calling CoInitialize().

To turn off security in our EasyDCOM sample, do the following:

1. Open EasyDCOM.cpp.
2. Add the following code just below the line containing the try block inside WinMain:
   ```
   CoInitialize(NULL);
   ```

   ```
   CoInitializeSecurity(NULL,
       -1,
       NULL,
       NULL,
       RPC_C_AUTHN_LEVEL_NONE,
       RPC_C_IMP_LEVEL_ANONYMOUS,
       NULL,
       EOAC_NONE,
       NULL);
   ```
3. Add the following code above the line containing the return statement at the end of WinMain:
   ```
   CoUninitialize();
   ```

4. Open `EasyDCOMClient.cpp`, repeat steps 2 and 3 and add the following line below the include for `vcl.h`:

```
#include <objbase.h>
```

Let's see what we have done.

We started by calling `CoInitialize()` saying that we wanted to join the main STA (refer to Chapter 16 for more information about threads and apartments). Next `CoInitializeSecurity()` is called with the appropriate parameters to solve our problem.

For the `pVoid` parameter of `CoInitializeSecurity()`, we passed `NULL`, telling COM that anyone is welcome to access our server.

For the `cAuthSvc` and `asAuthSvc` parameters, we stuck with the defaults of `-1` and `NULL`, respectively, letting COM use the available security packages on the system.

Because we're not interested in authenticating any user calling into our object, we used `RPC_C_AUTH_LEVEL_NONE` for the `dwAuthnLevel` parameter.

For the `dwImpLevel` parameter, we use `RPC_C_IMP_LEVEL_ANONYMOUS` because we're not going to impersonate the client to discover its credentials or act on its behalf. Remember, we actually don't know who the client is.

For the `dwCapabilities` parameter, we just pass `EOAC_NONE`.

That's all; we completely turned off security for our sample application. From now on, any anonymous user will be able to make calls into our server.

17

GOING
DISTRIBUTED:
DCOM

> **NOTE**
>
> Servers using connection points over DCOM could also make use of this technique to turn off DCOM security because they will want to access the sink object (see the event sink example in Chapter 16) implemented at the client side.
>
> If you try to use the event sink sample application from Chapter 16 over a DCOM connection, it will fail with an Access Denied error. This is because the client, now acting as a server, will verify if the caller has the necessary credentials to access its sink object. The client will try to ensure that the server account is allowed access to its sink object.
>
> You can work around this problem by making the server account the same as the client account. In other words, the client on the client machine and the identity of the server on the server machine must use a login account with the same name and password.
>
> The problem with this approach is that you must know beforehand what account the client will be using.

Understanding DLL Clients and Security

What if we need to implement the client for our remote server as an ActiveX control to be used inside some container, such as Internet Explorer or IIS and Active Server Pages? Well, that is trouble.

An in-proc-server (DLL) is loaded into the address space of a container process and, when this happens, COM has already called `CoInitializeSecurity()`, explicitly or implicitly.

It doesn't matter if the container application issued the call or if COM did it based on Registry settings. Even if you call `CoInitializeSecurity()` in your code, it will be too late; by that time, all COM security settings are already in place.

One possible solution for this case could be the creation of an intermediary out-of-proc server (EXE) that would take care of security issues and make calls into the remote server on behalf of the ActiveX client. To the ActiveX client, this intermediary server would look like the remote server.

The bottom line is that you can't control security through the use of `CoInitializeSecurity()`from inside a DLL. You should keep that in mind when writing DLL clients for your remote servers.

Implementing Programmatic Access Control

You can indicate which individual users or group of users are allowed or denied access to your server by using the `pVoid` parameter of `CoInitializeSecurity()`. When providing a valid argument for this parameter, the authentication level must be at least `RPC_C_AUTH_LEVEL_CON-NECT`; otherwise; `CoInitializeSecurity()` will fail.

We're going to show you how you can use a `SECURITY_DESCRIPTOR`, instead of an `AppID GUID` or `IAccessControl` interface, to supply security information using the `pVoid` parameter in a call to `CoInitializeSecurity()`.

The `SECURITY_DESCRIPTOR` structure has the following members:

```
typedef struct _SECURITY_DESCRIPTOR {
    BYTE   Revision;
    BYTE   Sbz1;
    SECURITY_DESCRIPTOR_CONTROL Control;
    PSID Owner;
    PSID Group;
    PACL Sacl;
    PACL Dacl;
} SECURITY_DESCRIPTOR;
```

Creating a security descriptor with the outdated Win32 Security API is, to say the least, arcane. C++Builder 5 and its ATL support greatly simplify this job with a class called `CSecurityDescriptor`.

> **NOTE**
>
> Programmatic modification of access control lists (ACLs) via the Win32 Security API is a very complex procedure that requires careful coding and testing.
>
> Beginning in Windows NT 4.0 with Service Pack 2, COM provides the IAccessControl interface. This interface, which is implemented in CLSID_DCOMAccessControl system object, is also considered an easy alternative to programming ACLs other than using the raw security API.

CSecurityDescriptor can be used anywhere a SECURITY_DESCRIPTOR structure is required, thanks to its conversion operators. You can use its methods to initialize a new security descriptor to allow or deny access to particular accounts.

The built-in account SYSTEM must always be included in the access control list because the system's Service Control Manager (SCM) needs this account to manage COM servers.

For demonstration purposes, we're going to change our server to only accept requests from clients using the Guest account. This account is disabled by default when the operating system is first installed.

Let's keep modifying our EasyDCOM sample application by doing the following:

1. Open EasyDCOM.cpp and add the following code below the line containing the include for atlmod.h:

```
#include <atl\atlcom.h>
```

2. Add the following code above the line containing the call to CoInitialize():

```
CSecurityDescriptor sd;
sd.InitializeFromProcessToken();
sd.Allow("Guest", COM_RIGHTS_EXECUTE);
sd.Allow("NT_AUTHORITY\\SYSTEM", COM_RIGHTS_EXECUTE);
```

3. Replace the call to CoInitializeSecurity() with the following:

```
CoInitializeSecurity(sd, -1, NULL, NULL, RPC_C_AUTHN_LEVEL_CONNECT,
    RPC_C_IMP_LEVEL_IDENTIFY, NULL, EOAC_NONE, NULL);
```

4. Open EasyDCOMClient.cpp and delete the lines containing CoInitialize(), CoInitializeSecurity(), and CoUninitialize().

To experiment with the sample, you will need to enable the Guest account and give it the same password on both the client and server machines. As an alternative you can log on as Guest on the machine hosting the server and run the client application from there.

You can replace the Guest account with the name of a valid local or domain account. You must use the format DOMAIN\UserOrGroup or MACHINE\UserOrGroup when passing the account name to the `Allow` method of `CSecurityDescriptor`. If you suppress the `DOMAIN` or `MACHINE` from the account name, the current machine name is assumed.

If you try to run the sample without being logged as `Guest`, you will receive an `Access Denied` error coming from the server. This is because only the `Guest` account is granted access to the server now.

> **TIP**
>
> Windows 2000 comes with a new command-line utility called RunAs. This utility allows an application to be run under the credentials of a supplied account. RunAs is an excellent tool for testing COM servers under the credentials of different client principals.

Let's examine the code.

A `CSecurityDescriptor` object, represented by the variable `sd`, is instantiated and, encapsulated inside it, a new security descriptor is created.

Next, we called the `InitializeFromProcessToken()` method to take care of all subtle details regarding the internals of the security descriptor.

The call to `Allow` passed `Guest` as the account name and the value `COM_RIGHTS_EXECUTE` to grant access rights to the `Guest` account. We did the same to grant access to built-in `System` account, this time using `NT_AUTHORITY\SYSTEM` as the account name.

Last, `CoInitializeSecurity()` is called passing the `sd` object as an argument for its first parameter. We use `RPC_C_AUTHN_LEVEL_CONNECT` as the authentication value, `RPC_C_IMP_LEVEL_IDENTIFY` as the identity value, and the default values for all other parameters.

Implementing Interface-Wide Security

Up to this point, we have centered our discussion on process-wide security settings that can be configured using `CoInitializeSecurity()`. But what if we need to control security only during method calls, for example, to make a specific call encrypted instead of encrypting the entire process?

`IClientSecurity` Interface

COM helps us with this scenario by providing a finer control of security at the interface level for both clients and servers. At client-side, the underlying remoting layer, represented by the Proxy Manager, implements the `IClientSecurity` interface. At server-side, the Stub Manager implements the `IServerSecurity` interface.

The methods of the IClientSecurity interface are QueryBlanket(), SetBlanket(), and CopyProxy().

QueryBlanket() retrieves the authentication information used by the interface proxy. This information is the security information passed to CoInitializeSecurity() during process initialization. You call QueryBlanket() using NULL on all parameters that you don't want to retrieve information.

SetBlanket()sets the authentication information to be used by a particular interface proxy. Its use affects all clients of the proxy.

CopyProxy() makes a private copy of the interface proxy that you can use later with SetBlanket(). This method allows multiple clients to independently change their interface security settings.

The parameters for QueryBlanket() and SetBlanket() correspond to the parameters of CoInitializeSecurity() with one notable exception, the seventh parameter—pAuthInfo. This parameter is dependent of the security package in use. It points to a COAUTHIDENTITY structure when the NTLM security package is being used.

The COAUTHIDENTITY structure has the following members:

```
typedef struct _COAUTHIDENTITY
{
    USHORT *User;
    ULONG UserLength;
    USHORT *Domain;
    ULONG DomainLength;
    USHORT *Password;
    ULONG PasswordLength;
    ULONG Flags;
} COAUTHIDENTITY;
```

You can make calls using the credentials of an arbitrary user if you pass the pAuthInfo parameter a COAUTHIDENTITY structure pointer filled with username, password, and domain information. When you pass NULL to this parameter, each COM method call is made using the credentials of the client process.

To use IClientSecurity, you must use QueryInterface() on the Proxy Manager for IID_IClientSecurity, call one of its methods, and then release the interface. COM makes our life easier by providing wrappers that encapsulate this sequence.

The COM wrapper functions for the methods of the IClientSecurity interface are CoQueryProxyBlanket(), CoSetProxyBlanket(), and CoCopyProxy().

IServerSecurity Interface

At the server-side, the IServerSecurity interface can be used to identify and impersonate the client. You can call CoGetCallContext() from within a method call to obtain an interface

pointer to this interface. IS\erverSecurity has the methods QueryBlanket(),
ImpersonateClient(), RevertToSelf(), and IsImpersonating().

QueryBlanket() is analogous to its sibling in IClientSecurity interface; it returns the security settings in use. For example, you could use QueryBlanket() to determine whether the
client is using encryption or to discover the client identity.

During a method call, you can use ImpersonateClient() to let the server use the security credentials of the client. The impersonation level used by the client determines if the server can
actually access system objects acting as the client itself, or if the server can only use the
client's credentials to perform access checks.

RevertToSelf() restores the security credentials of the server and stops the server from impersonating the client. COM will automatically restore the server's security credentials prior to
leaving a method call, even if you forget to call RevertToSelf() explicitly.

IsImpersonating() is used to check whether the server is currently impersonating the client.

COM offers the following functions as wrappers for the methods of the IS\erverSecurity
interface: CoQueryClientBlanket(), CoImpersonateClient(), and CoRevertToSelf().

Using the Blanket

To demonstrate the use of the IS\erverSecurity and IClientSecurity interfaces, we're going
to create a brand new example. This example will let the client change its identity and interrogate the server to discover the current identity in use. It will also let the server create a local
file using the credentials of the client. Later, through the use of Windows Explorer, you will be
able to access the properties of the file object and see its owner to confirm whether the file was
created using the identity you supplied.

To conduct this experiment, I created two local accounts named CommonUser and ExtraUser,
members of the User group, on both the client and server machines, and logged on the client
machine using the ExtraUser account.

I used DCOMCnfg to configure the server to allow access and launch permissions to everyone,
and set the identity of the server (refer to Figure 17.8) to use the Administrator account.

The example server application that we will create in the following section is provided in the
Blanket\Server folder on the CD-ROM that accompanies this book.

> **NOTE**
>
> In the absence of an NT Server domain, the workstation machine is, in effect, the only
> member of its own domain.

Create our new sample server as follows:

1. Start by creating an EXE server called `Blanket` with an Automation Object that has a CoClass name of `ObjBlanket`. Next use the TLE editor to add the following two methods:

```
[id(1)] HRESULT _stdcall BlanketInfo([out, retval] BSTR * Value);
[id(2)] HRESULT _stdcall CreateFile([in] BSTR Value);
```

2. Now you need to implement the methods. Open `ObjBlanketImpl.cpp` and add the following code to the `BlanketInfo` method:

```
try {
    *Value = NULL;
    LPWSTR pPrivs;

    OleCheck(CoQueryClientBlanket(NULL, NULL, NULL, NULL, NULL,
                                  (LPVOID*)&pPrivs, NULL));

    WideString strInfo = pPrivs;
    *Value = strInfo.Detach();
}
catch(Exception &e) {
    return Error(e.Message.c_str(), IID_IObjBlanket);
}
return S_OK;
```

This method makes use of the `CoQueryClientBlanket()` to retrieve the name of the client principal and return it to caller. It performs this operation by passing `NULL` to all parameters except the sixth, `pPrivs`. This tells `CoQueryClientBlanket()` that we're only interested in information regarding the identity of the client.

3. Add the following code to the `CreateFile()` method:

```
try {
    OleCheck(CoImpersonateClient());

    HANDLE hFile = ::CreateFile(AnsiString(Value).c_str(),
                                GENERIC_WRITE,
                                FILE_SHARE_WRITE,
                                NULL,
                                CREATE_ALWAYS,
                                FILE_ATTRIBUTE_NORMAL,
                                NULL);

    if (INVALID_HANDLE_VALUE == hFile)
        return HRESULT_FROM_WIN32(GetLastError());

    CloseHandle(hFile);
    OleCheck(CoRevertToSelf());
}
```

17

GOING
DISTRIBUTED:
DCOM

```
catch(Exception &e) {
    return Error(e.Message.c_str(),IID_IObjBlanket);
}
return S_OK;
```

Here, we started by calling `CoImpersonateClient()` to begin impersonating the client. We made this call because we wanted to create a local file using the identity supplied by the client instead of the identity currently in use by the server process.

Remember that we manually set the server's identity to use the credentials of the `Administrator` account. So if the call to `CoImpersonateClient()` succeeds, we will be able to see a different owner for the created file.

Before leaving the method, we closed the file handle and called `CoRevertToSelf()` to tell the server to stop impersonating the client and revert to its own identity.

You can now build the project. When done, copy the server to the remote machine and run it once to perform self-registration.

You can find the code for the example client application in the `Blanket\Client` folder on the CD-ROM that accompanies this book.

The client will also be an EXE application. To create the client application do the following:

1. Start a new project and save it as `BlanketClient` renaming `Unit1` to `MainUnit`.

2. Design its main form to look like Figure 17.15, and rename its components as follows:

Original Name	New Name
Form1	frmMain
RadioButton1	rdoLoged
RadioButton2	rdoIdnty
GroupBox1	gbxIdn
GroupBox1	gbxInfo
Label1	lblUser
Label2	lblDomain
Label3	lblPwrd
Edit1	txtUser
Edit2	txtDomain
Edit3	txtPwrd
Edit4	txtInfo
Button1	cmdCallServer
Button2	cmdSetIdentity
Button3	cmdGetInfo

Going Distributed: DCOM

CHAPTER 17

743

17

GOING
DISTRIBUTED:
DCOM

| Button4 | cmdCreateFile |
| Button5 | cmdFinish |

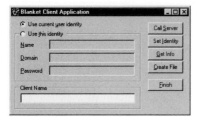

FIGURE 17.15

The BlanketClient *main form and its components.*

3. Open MainUnit.h and add the following header file to its list of header files:

   ```
   #include "..\Server\Blanket_TLB.h"
   ```

4. Declare two private data members in the TfrmMain derived class as the following:

   ```
   TCOMIObjBlanket m_objBlanket;
   SEC_WINNT_AUTH_IDENTITY m_pAuthInfo;
   ```

5. Add the following two private member functions to the TfrmMain class:

   ```
   void GetAuthInfo();
   void SetAuthInfo();
   ```

You will find the code for MainUnit.cpp in Listing 17.1.

LISTING 17.1 The Code for MainUnit.cpp, Main Form of the BlanketClient Project

```
#include <vcl.h>
#pragma hdrstop
#include "MainUnit.h"

#pragma package(smart_init)
#pragma resource "*.dfm"

TfrmMain *frmMain;

__fastcall TfrmMain::TfrmMain(TComponent* Owner) : TForm(Owner)
{
    m_AuthInfo.Flags    = SEC_WINNT_AUTH_IDENTITY_ANSI;
    m_AuthInfo.User     = NULL;
    m_AuthInfo.Domain   = NULL;
    m_AuthInfo.Password = NULL;
}
```

LISTING 17.1   Continued

```cpp
void __fastcall TfrmMain::FrmMain_Close(TObject *Sender, TCloseAction &Action)
{
    m_objBlanket.Unbind();

    delete[] m_AuthInfo.User;
    delete[] m_AuthInfo.Domain;
    delete[] m_AuthInfo.Password;
}

void __fastcall TfrmMain::CmdCallServer_Click(TObject *Sender)
{
    if (!m_objBlanket.IsBound()) {
        AnsiString strHost;

        if (InputQuery("Create Server", "Enter computer name:", strHost)) {
            if (strHost.IsEmpty())
                OleCheck(CoObjBlanket::Create(m_objBlanket));
            else
                OleCheck(CoObjBlanket::CreateRemote(WideString(strHost),
                                                    m_objBlanket));
            ShowMessage("Server created");
        }
    }
}

void __fastcall TfrmMain::CmdCreateFile_Click(TObject *Sender)
{
    if (m_objBlanket.IsBound()) {
        AnsiString strFile;

        if (InputQuery("Create File", "Enter path and file name:", strFile)) {
            OleCheck(m_objBlanket.CreateFile(WideString(strFile)));
            ShowMessage("File created");
        }
    }
}

void __fastcall TfrmMain::CmdFinish_Click(TObject *Sender)
{
    Close();
}

void __fastcall TfrmMain::CmdGetInfo_Click(TObject *Sender)
{
    if (m_objBlanket.IsBound())
        GetAuthInfo();
}
```

LISTING 17.1 Continued

```cpp
void __fastcall TfrmMain::CmdIdentity_Click(TObject *Sender)
{
    gbxIdn->Enabled = rdoIdnty->Checked ? true : false;

    txtDomain->Color = rdoIdnty->Checked ? clWindow : clBtnFace;
    txtPwrd  ->Color = rdoIdnty->Checked ? clWindow : clBtnFace;
    txtUser  ->Color = rdoIdnty->Checked ? clWindow : clBtnFace;
}

void __fastcall TfrmMain::CmdSetIdentity_Click(TObject *Sender)
{
    if (m_objBlanket.IsBound()) {
        if (rdoIdnty->Checked)
            SetAuthInfo();

        OleCheck(CoSetProxyBlanket(m_objBlanket,
                                   RPC_C_AUTHN_WINNT,
                                   RPC_C_AUTHZ_NONE,
                                   NULL,
                                   RPC_C_AUTHN_LEVEL_CONNECT,
                                   RPC_C_IMP_LEVEL_IMPERSONATE,
                                   rdoIdnty->Checked ? &m_AuthInfo : NULL,
                                   EOAC_NONE));
    }
}

void TfrmMain::GetAuthInfo()
{
    WideString strInfo;
    OleCheck(m_objBlanket.BlanketInfo (&strInfo));
    txtInfo->Text = strInfo;
}

void TfrmMain::SetAuthInfo()
{
    delete[] m_AuthInfo.User;
    delete[] m_AuthInfo.Domain;
    delete[] m_AuthInfo.Password;

    m_AuthInfo.UserLength     = txtUser  ->Text.Length();
    m_AuthInfo.DomainLength   = txtDomain->Text.Length();
    m_AuthInfo.PasswordLength = txtPwrd  ->Text.Length();

    m_AuthInfo.User     = (PUCHAR)new TCHAR[txtUser  ->Text.Length()+1];
    m_AuthInfo.Domain   = (PUCHAR)new TCHAR[txtDomain->Text.Length()+1];
    m_AuthInfo.Password = (PUCHAR)new TCHAR[txtPwrd  ->Text.Length()+1];
```

17

GOING
DISTRIBUTED:
DCOM

LISTING **17.1**   Continued

```
        lstrcpy((LPTSTR)m_AuthInfo.User    , (LPCTSTR)txtUser  ->Text.c_str());
        lstrcpy((LPTSTR)m_AuthInfo.Domain  , (LPCTSTR)txtDomain->Text.c_str());
        lstrcpy((LPTSTR)m_AuthInfo.Password, (LPCTSTR)txtPwrd  ->Text.c_str());
}
```

You can see from Listing 17.1 that we initialized some of the members of m_AuthInfo in the constructor of TfrmMain. According to the OLE Programmer's Reference help file that comes with C++Builder 5, COM will keep a pointer to the identity information contained in this structure until a new value is used, or until COM itself is uninitialized.

The SetAuthInfo() private member function acts like a helper method for dealing with the SEC_WINNT_AUTH_IDENTITY structure. It avoids memory leaks and correctly assigns identity information to its members.

The Set Identity button handles client identity change. It performs its action by calling CoSetProxyBlanket() to adjust the interface security settings telling the Proxy Manager to use identity information contained in the m_AuthInfo member variable.

Identity information is toggled between the current logged user identity (process token credentials) and the supplied identity through the use of a NULL argument in the pAuthInfo parameter of the CoSetProxyBlanket() function.

CoSetProxyBlanket() is called with a RPC_C_IMP_LEVEL_IMPERSONATE level of impersonation to let the server effectively behave as the client using the credentials supplied in the pAuthInfo parameter.

The event handler for the Get Info button calls the server's BlanketInfo() method to retrieve the current user identity name and place the result in the txtInfo edit box.

The Create File button handles file creation at the remote machine, asking for a path and a filename and executing the server's CreateFile() method. The remote file is then created using the identity currently in use.

Let's try our sample and proceed as follows:

1. Start BlanketClient.exe and click the Call Server button. Enter the name of the host machine to instantiate the Blanket server.

2. Click the Get Info button and you should see something like the screen in Figure 17.16. This is the result of pressing the Get Info button while BlanketClient is using the credentials of the current logged user, ExtraUser.

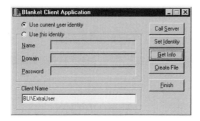

Figure 17.16

BlanketClient *running under the current logged user account.*

3. Click the Create File button and enter C:\RemFile1.Txt to create a remote file named RemFile1.Txt on the root of the host's drive C.

   Figure 17.17 shows the file properties. You can confirm that the remote file was created under credentials of the ExtraUser account.

Figure 17.17

RemFile1.Txt *properties shows* ExtraUser *as its owner.*

4. Fill the identity fields with information from the CommonUser account and click the Set Identity button to change the client identity. Figure 17.18 shows the result of clicking the Get Info button after performing this operation.

5. Click the Create File button again. This time, give the remote file the name RemFile2.Txt.

   Figure 17.19 now shows that the remote file was created under credentials of the CommonUser account.

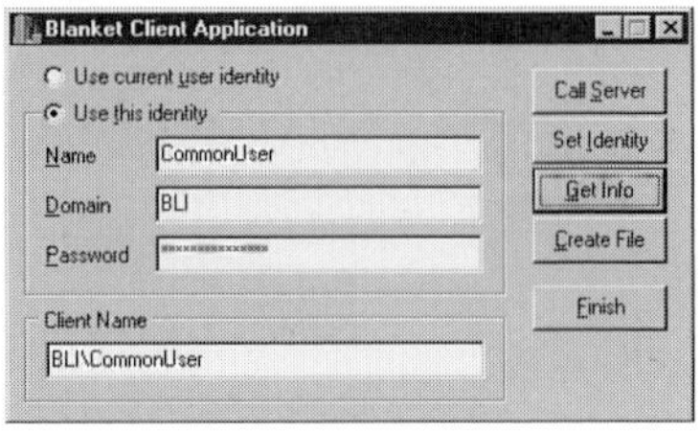

FIGURE 17.18
BlanketClient *using the credentials of the* CommonUser *account.*

FIGURE 17.19
RemFile2.Txt *properties shows* CommonUser *as its owner.*

Summary

DCOM is a very big subject that deserves an entire book by itself. It's a huge technology that has many subtle aspects. In this chapter, we tried to address its most important features.

You were introduced to DCOM and learned that it brings remote capabilities to COM objects, and that it introduces important issues like security as well.

You learned how to use the DCOMCnfg configuration tool to control DCOM settings stored in the Registry for specific components and for all components in the system.

You also saw how to use CoInitializeSecurity() to programmatically control security at server- and client-sides, and you learned how to control security at the interface level through the use of IClientSecurity and IServerSecurity interfaces implemented by the Proxy and Stub managers.

If you're serious about developing distributed systems, you must definitely read Chapter 19, "Multi-Tier Distributed Applications with MIDAS 3," and take a look at MIDAS and InternetExpress. These technologies come with the Enterprise version of C++Builder 5 and provide an excellent alternative to the use of DCOM.

One Step Ahead: COM+

Ionel Munoz

IN THIS CHAPTER

- Introducing COM+
- Using COM+ Services
- Developing and Using COM+ Events
- Developing and Using COM+ Transactional Objects

The complete text for this chapter appears on the CD-ROM.

Multi-Tier Distributed Applications with MIDAS 3

Bob Swart

IN THIS CHAPTER

- **Introduction to MIDAS**
- **MIDAS Clients and Servers**
- **MIDAS 3 Enhancements**

In this chapter, you will learn about multi-tier database computing as implemented in a C++Builder-hosted technology called Multi-Tier Distributed Application Services (MIDAS).

Using a multi-tier database architecture, you can partition applications so that you can access data on a second machine (a database server) without having a full set of database tools on your local machine. It also allows you to centralize business rules and processes and distribute the processing load throughout the network.

The examples in this chapter use MIDAS version 3, which means that you must have a copy of the Enterprise edition of C++Builder 5 to run the programs in this chapter. In fact, MIDAS itself is available only in the Enterprise edition of C++Builder, so you might as well skip this chapter if you do not have C++Builder 5 Enterprise (or at least a trial edition).

Note that in order to use the example projects provided on the CD-ROM that accompanies this book, you should read and follow the instructions in the README.TXT file provided in the MIDAS folder.

Introduction to MIDAS

MIDAS supports a three-tier technology, which in its classic form consists of the following:

- A database server on one (server) machine
- An application server on a second (middle-tier) machine
- A thin client on a third (client) machine

The server should be a tool such as InterBase, Oracle, MS SQL server, and so on. The application server and the thin client should be built in C++Builder. The application server will contain the business rules and the tools for manipulating the data. The client will do nothing more than present the data to the user for viewing and editing.

In some situations, more than one tier can exist on the same machine (like the database server and the application server). However, as long as they are separate executables, they can still be considered separate tiers. *N-tier computing* refers to the fact that all these tiers can be spread out across multiple machines. For instance, you might have the employee server on one machine and the payroll server on another machine. One of these application servers might access Oracle data from a third machine, and the other server might access InterBase data from a fourth. Hence, you have not three tiers, but *n* tiers.

> **NOTE**
>
> The term n-tier can be a bit misleading, at least from some perspectives. No matter how you break up your database servers, application servers, and clients, you still end

up with a maximum of three tiers of computing. Just because you have the middle tier spread out over 10 machines doesn't really change the fact that all 10 machines are involved in middle-tier computing. The three tiers are shown in Figure 19.1.

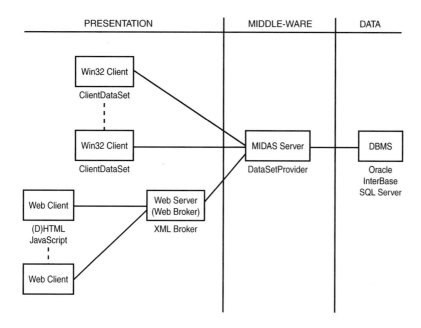

FIGURE 19.1

The three tiers of multi-tier architecture.

MIDAS is based on technology that allows you to package datasets and send them across the network as parameters to remote method calls. It includes technology for converting a dataset into a Variant or XML package on the server side and then unbundling the dataset on the client and displaying it to the user in a grid. This last is done with the aid of the TClientDataSet or TMidasPageProducer component.

Seen from a slightly different angle, MIDAS is a technology for moving a dataset from a TTable or TQuery object on a server to a TClientDataSet object on a client. TClientDataSet looks, acts, and feels exactly like a TTable or TQuery component, except that it doesn't have to be attached to the BDE or any other database driver for that matter—apart from the MIDAS middleware DLL itself. In this particular case, TClientDataSet gets its data from unpacking the variant that it retrieves from the server.

MIDAS allows you to use all the standard C++Builder components, including database tools, in your client-side applications, but the client side is a true thin client: It does not have to include or link any database drivers apart from the `MIDAS.DLL` itself (but at least you're relieved from BDE or ODBC installation scenarios). Installing `MIDAS.DLL` on the client is sometimes referred to as a zero-configuration thin client. And while it's not exactly zero-configuration, it's indeed very simple to set up a MIDAS client, as this chapter will show.

> **NOTE**
>
> Borland has always used names from Greek mythology, such as Delphi, Kylix, and now MIDAS. Midas was a mythical king of Greece who received from Dionysus a gift enabling him to turn all he touched into gold. After his food and members of his family were turned into gold, Midas grew weary of the gift and was released from it by washing his hands in a river. The sands of that river were then turned to a golden color, a fact to which contemporary visitors to Greece can still attest today.

The two different layers of the MIDAS technology are as follows:

- The components found on the Component Palette and built in the VCL (`TDataSetProvider`, `TClientDataSet`, and `TXMLBroker`). The first two are found on the Midas tab of the Component Palette, the last one on the InternetExpress tab.

- The protocol used to send messages over the Internet. This layer might be DCOM, HTTP, or just plain old TCP/IP (sockets). Different connection components can be found on the Midas tab of the Component Palette.

The built-in C++Builder components enable you to easily connect two machines and pass datasets back and forth between them. In the simplest scenarios, they make it possible for you to build middle-tier and client applications with just a few clicks of the mouse.

MIDAS gives you the ability to actually split the application in two parts, where one end implements the presentation layer (GUI) and the other the database layer (including business rules). In a regular client/server approach, the client—implemented in C++Builder Professional for example—would be a fat client, needing database connectivity code to talk to the server (usually a DBMS). In the n-tier approach, the client is a true thin client, with no need for any database connectivy at all. This is all taken care of by the `MIDAS.DLL` which is the local "mini DBMS." The MIDAS server does need actual database connectivity, since this layer communicates with the real DMBS (just like the client in the client/server approach would). As a direct consequence, MIDAS (thin) clients are sometimes also called *zero-configuration* clients.

MIDAS Clients and Servers

The best way to understand what MIDAS is and how it works is to actually build an application, consisting of a client and a server. Usually, I start with the MIDAS server to encapsulate and export the datasets. Then the next step is to build a MIDAS client that connects to this server and displays the data in some way.

Creating a Simple MIDAS Server

We will now show you how to build your first MIDAS server. The code demonstrated in this section is provided in the project `SimpleMidasServer.bpr`, in the `MIDAS\simple` folder on the CD-ROM that accompanies this book.

To build your first MIDAS server, select File, New Application to open a new empty application. The fact that the main form of this application is shown ensures that the MIDAS server will remain loaded (the message loop of the main form keeps the MIDAS server alive). The `Caption` property of the main form is set to `C++Builder 5 Developer's Guide`. However, to be able to easily identify the MIDAS server, I always drop a `TLabel` on the main form, set its `Font` property to something that's big and readable (like Comic Sans MS 24pt.), and set the `Caption` property of the `TLabel` component to the name of the MIDAS server (`My First MIDAS Server` in this case). Resizing the main form and giving it a noticeable background color in the `Color` property helps to identify it among your other applications, as shown in Figure 19.2.

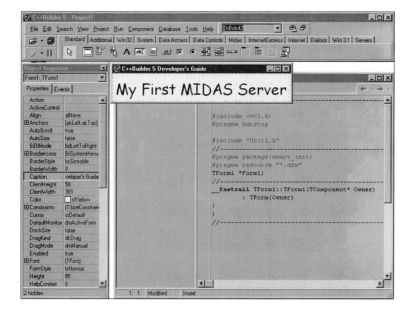

FIGURE 19.2

The `My First MIDAS Server` *main form.*

To turn a regular application into a middleware database server, you have to add a remote data module to it. This special data module can be found on the Multi-Tier tab of the Object Repository (see Figure 19.3), so select File, New and go to the Multi-Tier tab.

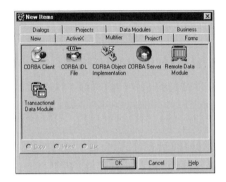

FIGURE 19.3

The Remote Data Module icon inside the Object Repository.

The Multi-Tier tab shows several CORBA wizards (see Chapter 20, "Distributed Applications with CORBA," for more about those), a remote data module, and a Transactional Data Module. The Transactional Data Module can be used with Microsoft Transaction Server (MTS) prior to Windows 2000 or COM+ in Windows 2000 and later; it won't be covered here. It's the normal remote data module that you need to select to create your first simple MIDAS server.

When you select the Remote Data Module icon and click on the OK button, the New Remote Data Module Object dialog, which is shown in Figure 19.4, opens.

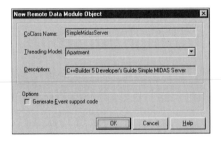

FIGURE 19.4

The New Remote Data Module Object dialog.

There are a few options you must specify. CoClass Name is the name of the internal class. This must be a name that you can remember, so use SimpleMidasServer at this time (one word, because no spaces are allowed). Threading Model is the second option you can set. By default, it is set to Apartment, which is almost always the correct choice. Alternative choices are Single, Free, Both, and Neutral. Although you almost never need to change this option, it's important to know what they all mean.

The Single threading model setting supports only one client request at a time. If more than one client wants to make a request, they must all wait in line. Only one client request is executed and in a single thread. This avoids all possible multithreading issues, but it can kill your performance (unless you never expect more than one client to make a request at the same time).

The Apartment threading model setting assumes that more than one client can make a request at roughly the same time, meaning that more than one request may need to be handled simultaneously. Using the Apartment threading model means that each instance of the remote data module handles one client request at a time. In order to handle more client requests, a separate thread is created for each request. As a consequence, each request runs in its own separate little "apartment" (hence the name) and, while instance data is safe, you must be aware of threading issues with global variables. This model can be used with regular BDE datasets, in which you need a TSession component with AutoSessionName set to True to make sure each thread (that is, each request) gets its own unique BDE session.

The Free threading model means that each thread can handle more than one client request at the same time. This approach gets harder, since you must guard against not only global variable threading issues, but also against instance data. This threading model can be selected when you're using ADO datasets.

The Both threading model is a variation on the Free threading model, with serialized callbacks to client interfaces. This will not be covered in this chapter.

The final model is the Neutral threading model. This is a new model that's available only under COM+ (in Windows 2000) and will otherwise map to the Apartment threading model.

See the "Choosing a Threading Model" section of Chapter 16, "COM Programming," for more information about the different threading models and their consequences.

After the Threading Model option, you can enter a description. What you enter here will end up in the Registry for the ProgID of the application server interface. It is also the help string for the interface in the type library. You can enter anything you want, but I've entered C++Builder 5 Developer's Guide Simple MIDAS Server, as you can see in Figure 19.4.

Finally, you may want to let the wizard generate a separate interface for managing events with the Generate Event Support Code option. Managing events in automation objects is not a topic of this chapter, so leave this option unchecked.

After you've completed all options inside the New Remote Data Module Object dialog, press OK to generate the remote data module. The result is a remote data module that looks very

19

MULTI-TIER
DISTRIBUTED
APPLICATIONS

much like a regular data module. Visually, there's no difference, and you can treat it like a regular data module by dropping a TSession component (from the Data Access tab) on it and setting the AutoSessionName property of the TSession component to True. (Remember that you need to do this when using BDE and the Apartment threading model, as discussed earlier.)

Once you have a TSession component, you can add other components from the Data Access tab of the Component Palette. For example, you can drop a TTable component and set its name to TableCustomer. Set its DatabaseName property to BCDEMOS and open the drop-down combo box for the TableName property to select the customer.db table.

Now it's time to work on the so-called "remote" aspects of this data module. Go to the Midas tab of the Component Palette. Here you'll find a TDataSetProvider component. This component is the key to exporting datasets from a remote data module to the outside world (more specifically: to MIDAS client applications). Drop the TDataSetProvider component on the remote data module and assign its DataSet property to TableCustomer. This means that the TDataSetProvider will "provide" or export TableCustomer to a MIDAS client application that connects to it (one that you will build in the following section). The RemoteDataModule of SimpleMidasServer should now look similar to Figure 19.5.

> **NOTE**
>
> Later in this chapter, we'll examine the TDataSetProvider component in more detail. For now, the most important property is the Exported property, which is set to true to indicate that TableCustomer is exported (by default). You can set this property to false to hide the fact that TableCustomer is exported from the remote data module, so clients cannot connect to it. This can be useful for example in a 24×7–running middleware data base server where you need to make a backup of certain tables and must ensure that nobody is working on them during the backup. With the Exported property set to false, no one can make a connection to them (until you set it to true again, of course).

Basically, this is all it takes to create a simple MIDAS server. The only things that's left for you is to save the project (for example using a Save All). I've put the main form in file ServerMainForm.cpp, the remote data module will be placed in file SimpleMidasServerImpl.cpp, and I've put the project itself in SimpleMidasServer.bpr. After the project is saved, you need to compile and run it. Running the MIDAS server—which shows only the main form, of course—will register it (inside the Windows Registry), so any MIDAS client can find and connect to it. If you ever want to move the MIDAS server to another directory (on the same machine), you only need to move it and immediately run it again, so it re-registers itself for that new location. This is a very convenient way of managing MIDAS server applications.

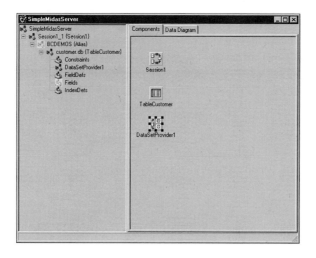

FIGURE 19.5
The SimpleMidasServer *remote data module.*

Later in this chapter, we'll see how to deploy a MIDAS server on another machine (in case you're wondering at this time).

Examining MIDAS Server Registration

Let's examine this MIDAS server application registration process in a little more detail. Open the header file for the source unit SimpleMidasServerImpl. Inside SimpleMidasServerImpl.h, you'll see a function definition for UpdateRegistry(), which is repeated in Listing 19.1 for your convenience.

LISTING 19.1   The UpdateRegistry Function

```
// Function invoked to (un)register object
//
static HRESULT WINAPI UpdateRegistry(BOOL bRegister)
{
  TRemoteDataModuleRegistrar regObj(GetObjectCLSID(), GetProgID(),
        GetDescription());
  // Disable these flags in order to disable use by socket or Web connections.
  // Also set other flags to configure the behavior of your application server.
  // For more information, see atlmod.h and atlvcl.cpp.
  regObj.Singleton = false;
  regObj.EnableWeb = true;
  regObj.EnableSocket = true;
  return regObj.UpdateRegistry (bRegister);
}
```

The `UpdateRegistry()` function ensures that the MIDAS 3 remote data module is registered (or unregistered) automatically when you want to use the middleware application server as an automation server. Note that the `UpdateRegistry()` method enables both socket and Web connections (using HTTP). If for some reason you want to disable one of these protocols, you simply have to assign `false` to the `EnableWeb` or `EnableSocket` field of the `regObj` variable.

The C++Builder 5 documentation even treats this as a security feature: If your MIDAS server is not registered to support the socket or Web connection, then it won't be visible to a socket or Web connection component at all. C++Builder 4 MIDAS servers never had any of this and, as a result you could basically run any automation object on the server using the socket connection component. To prevent that, the C++Builder 5 Socket (and Web) connection components will now show only MIDAS servers that are registered properly.

So far, you haven't written a single line of C++ code for the simple MIDAS server. Let's see what it takes to write a MIDAS client to connect to it.

Creating a MIDAS Client

There are a number of different MIDAS clients that you can develop. These include regular Windows (GUI) applications, ActiveForms, and even Web server applications (using Web Broker or InternetExpress). In fact, just about everything can act as a MIDAS client, as you'll see in a moment. For now, you'll create a simple regular Windows application that will act as the first simple MIDAS client to connect to the simple MIDAS server of the previous section. At this stage, you should not be trying to run the client and the server on separate machines. Instead, get everything up and running on one machine, and then later you can distribute the application on the network. The code demonstrated in this section is provided in the project `SimpleMidasClient.bpr`, in the `MIDAS\simple` folder on the CD-ROM that accompanies this book.

Select File, New Application to start a new C++Builder application.

> ### NOTE
>
> At this time, you may decide to add a data module to it (using File, New and selecting a data module from the New tab of the Object Repository). In order to avoid unnecessary screenshots in this book, I skip the data module and use the main form to drop my non-visual (MIDAS) components as well as my normal visual components.
>
> I repeat, just to put everything together on one place, I am NOT using a data module in this MIDAS client. Instead, I'm just placing my data access components on the main form of the MIDAS client.

Of course, if you want to use your own data module to separate data access from presentation (user interface), then by all means go ahead.

A project that demonstrates the use of a DataModule can be found in the MIDAS\simple2 folder on the CD-ROM that accompanies this book. The project filename is also SimpleMidasClient.bpr.

Before anything else, your MIDAS client must make a connection with the MIDAS server application. This connection can be made using a number of different protocols, such as (D)COM, TCP/IP (sockets), and HTTP. The components that implement these connection protocols are TDCOMConnection, TSocketConnection, and TWebConnection, respectively. For the first SimpleMidasClient, you'll use the TDCOMConnection component, so drop one from the MIDAS tab onto the main form of your MIDAS client.

The TDCOMConnection component has a property called ServerName, which holds the name of the MIDAS server you want to connect to. In fact, if you open the drop-down combo box for the ServerName property in the Object Inspector, you'll see a list of all registered MIDAS 3 servers on your local machine. In your case, this list might include only one item (SimpleMidasServer.SimpleMidasServer), but all MIDAS 3 servers that are registered will end up in this list eventually. The names consist of two parts: The part before the dot denotes the application name, and the part after the dot denotes the remote data module name. In the current case, select the SimpleMidasServer remote data module of the SimpleMidasServer application. Once you've selected this ServerName, you'll notice that the ServerGUID property of the TDCOMConnection component also gets a value, as found in the Registry. Developers with a good memory are free to type in the ServerGUID property here in order to automatically get the corresponding ServerName name.

The fun really starts when you double-click on the Connected property of the TDCOM Connection component, which will toggle this property value from false to true. To actually make the connection, the MIDAS server will be executed (automatically). This results in the automatic execution and opening of the main form of the SimpleMidasServer that you created in the previous section. See Figure 19.6 for the resulting SimpleMidasServer at runtime.

FIGURE 19.6

The SimpleMidasServer *at runtime.*

19

**MULTI-TIER
DISTRIBUTED
APPLICATIONS**

> **NOTE**
>
> It may appear now that there are two ways to close the MIDAS server: either by assigning false to the Connected property of the TDCOMConnection component or by simply closing down the SimpleMidasServer (by clicking on the close button of its main form). The former will work, but the latter is not a good idea, as a COM Server Warning will try to tell you (see Figure 19.7).
>
> If you still decide to close the MIDAS server this way, then the TDCOMConnection component on the MIDAS client main form will still think it's connected. In a real-world situation where a MIDAS server (or a connection to it) is terminated, the same thing will happen: The MIDAS client still thinks it has a connection, but in fact the connection is gone. In the "Implementing Error Handling" section, later in this chapter, we'll cover the error checking that you must include in order to be able to survive such circumstances without too many problems.

FIGURE 19.7

COM Server Warning when closing SimpleMidasServer *the wrong way.*

Double-click again on the Connected property of the TDCOMConnection component to close down the MIDAS server. Now that you've seen you can connect to it, it's time to import some of the datasets that are exported by the remote data module, or rather by the TDataSetProvider component on the remote data module. Drop a TClientDataSet component on the main form, and connect its RemoteServer property to the TDCOMConnection component. The TClientDataSet component will obtain its data from the MIDAS server. You now need to specify which provider to use—in other words, from which TDataSetProvider you want to import the dataset into the TClientDataSet component. This can be done with the ProviderName property of the TClientDataSet component. Just open the drop-down combo box and you'll see a list of all available provider names, those that have their Exported property set to true. In this case, there is only one—the only TDataSetProvider component that you used on the SimpleMidasServer in the previous section—so select that one.

NOTE

Before you picked a value for the `ProviderName` property, you closed down the `SimpleMidasServer`. However, when you opened up the drop-down combo box to list all available `TDataSetProvider` components on the remote data module that currently have their `Exported` property set to `true`, there is only one way (for C++Builder and the Object Inspector) to know exactly which of these providers are available—by asking the `SimpleMidasServer` (more specifically, by actively looking at the remote data module and finding out which of the available `TDataSetProvider` components have their `Exported` property set to `true`). And since the `SimpleMidasServer` was down, it has to be started again in order to present this list to you in the Object Inspector. As a result, the moment you drop-down the combo box of the `ProviderName` property, the `SimpleMidasServer` will be started again.

Once you've selected the `RemoteServer` and `ProviderName`, it's time to open (or activate) the `TClientDataSet`. You can do this by setting the `Active` property of the `TClientDataSet` component to `true`. At that time, the `SimpleMidasServer` is feeding data from the `TableCustomer` table via the `TDataSetProvider` component and a COM connection to the `TDCOMConnection` component, which routes it to the `TClientDataSet` component on your simple MIDAS client.

Now you can drop a `TDataSource` component and move to the Data Controls tab of the Component Palette and drop one or more data-aware controls. To keep the example simple, just drop a `TDBGrid` component. Connect the `DataSet` property of the `TDataSource` component to the `TClientDataSet`, and connect the `DataSource` property of the `TDBGrid` component to the `TDataSource`. Since the `TClientDataSet` component was just activated, you should immediately see live data at designtime, provided by the `SimpleMidasServer`.

In Figure 19.8 you'll see the `SimpleMidasClient` main form so far. Note that I've enabled Component Captions, an option found in the Preferences page of the Tools, Environment Options dialog.

You are almost ready. First give the `Caption` property of the main form a useful name (like `SimpleMidasClient`). Then save your work. Put the main form in the `ClientMainForm.cpp` file and call the project `SimpleMidasClient`. Now you're ready to compile and run the MIDAS client. Again, you haven't written a single line of C++ code, but rest assured—that will change soon enough in the upcoming sections.

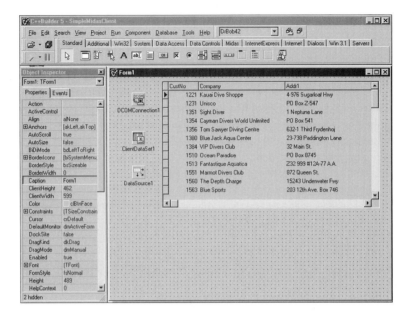

FIGURE 19.8

SimpleMidasClient *at designtime.*

Using the Briefcase Model

When you run the SimpleMidasClient, you see the entire CustomerTable data inside the grid.
You can browse through it, change field values, even enter new records or delete records.
However, once you close the application, all changes are gone, and you're back at the original
dataset inside the C++Builder IDE again. No matter how hard you try, the changes that you
make to the visual data seem to affect the data inside the (local) TClientDataSet only, and not
the (remote) actual TableCustomer.

What you experience here is actually a feature of the so-called *briefcase model*. Using this
model, you can disconnect the client from the network and still access the data. To do so, save
a remote dataset to disk, shut down your machine, and disconnect from the network. You can
then boot up again and edit your (local) data without connecting to the network.

When you get back to the network, you can reconnect and update the database. A special
mechanism notifies you of database errors and any conflicts that need to be resolved. For
instance, if two people edited the same record, you will be notified and given options to
resolve any problem.

You don't actually have to be able to reach the server at all times to be able to work with your data. This capability is ideal for laptop users or for sites that want to keep database traffic to a minimum.

You've already experienced that (apparently) your SimpleMidasClient works on the local data inside your TClientDataSet component only. It appears you can even save the data to a local file and load it again. To save the current content of a TClientDataSet, you need to drop a TButton on the main form, set the Name property to ButtonSave, set Caption to Save, and write the following C++ code for the OnClick event handler:

```
void __fastcall TForm1::ButtonSaveClick(TObject *Sender)
{
  ClientDataSet1->SaveToFile("customer.cds",dfBinary);
}
```

This saves all records from the TClientDataSet in a file called customer.cds in the current directory. cds stands for ClientDataSet, but you can use your own file and extension names, of course. Note the dfBinary flag that is passed as the second argument to the SaveToFile method of TClientDataSet. This value indicates that I want to save the data in binary— Inprise/Borland propriety—format. Alternately, I could specify to save the data in XML format, passing the dfXML value. An XML file will be much larger (14,108 versus 7,493 bytes for the entire TableCustomer data), but it has the advantage that it can be used by other applications as well. You won't be doing so in this chapter, so I'll stick to the smaller (and more efficient) binary format.

Similarly, to enable the functionality to load the customer.cds file again into your TClientDataSet component, you need to drop another TButton component, set its Name property to ButtonLoad, set Caption to Load, and write the following C++ code for the OnClick event handler:

```
void __fastcall TForm1::ButtonLoadClick(TObject *Sender)
{
  ClientDataSet1->LoadFromFile("customer.cds");
}
```

Note that the LoadFromFile method of the TClientDataSet component does not need a second argument; it's obviously smart enough to determine whether it's reading a binary or an XML file. And while the binary file can probably be generated only by another TClientDataSet component, the XML file could actually have been produced by a different application.

Armed with these two buttons, you can now (locally) save the changes to your data and even reload those changes—even if you stop and start the simple MIDAS client application again.

To control whether the TClientDataSet component is connected to the MIDAS server live, you can drop a third TButton component on the form that toggles the Active property of the

19

MULTI-TIER
DISTRIBUTED
APPLICATIONS

TClientDataSet component. Set the Name property of this TButton to ButtonConnect and give the Caption property the value Connect. Now, write the following code for the OnClick event handler, as can be seen in Listing 19.2.

LISTING 19.2   ButtonConnect OnClick Event Handler

```
void __fastcall TForm1::ButtonConnectClick(TObject *Sender)
{
  if (ClientDataSet1->Active) // close and disconnect
  {
    ClientDataSet1->Close();
    DCOMConnection1->Close();
  }
  else // open (will automatically connect)
  {
//  DCOMConnection1->Open();
    ClientDataSet1->Open();
  }
}
```

> **NOTE**
>
> Note that to close the connection, you actually have to close the TClientDataSet component and close the TDCOMConnection as well. To open the connection, you need only to open the TClientDataSet component, which will implicitly open the TDCOMConnection as well.

Finally, there's one more thing you really need to do: Make sure the TDCOMConnection and TClientDataSet components are *not* connected to the SimpleMidasServer at designtime. Otherwise, whenever you open your SimpleMidasClient project in the C++Builder IDE again, it will need to make a connection to the SimpleMidasServer—loading that MIDAS server. And when—for one reason or another—SimpleMidasServer is not found on your machine, you will have a hard time loading the SimpleMidasClient project. So I always make sure they are not connected at designtime. In order to do so, you have to assign false to the Connected property of the TDCOMConnection component (which will unload the main form of the SimpleMidasServer) and false to the Active property of the TClientDataSet component (which means you won't see any data at designtime anymore).

If you try to talk to a DCOM server but can't reach it, the system will not immediately give up the search. Instead, it can keep trying for a set period of time that rarely exceeds two minutes. During those two minutes, however, the application will be busy and will appear to be locked up. If the application is loaded into the IDE, then all of C++Builder will appear to be locked up. You can have this problem when you do nothing more than attempt to set the Connected property of the TDCOMConnection component to true.

Note that there is no solution to this problem. This is simply a warning NOT to leave the Connected property of a TDOMConnection set to true, because it can cause your IDE (and machine) to appear hung when you next open the project.

Now, when you recompile and run your SimpleMidasClient, it will show up with no data inside the TDBGrid component (see Figure 19.9). This is the time to click on the Connect button to connect to the SimpleMidasServer and obtain all records (from the database server). However, there are times (for example, when you are on the road or not connected to the machine that runs the SimpleMidasServer), when you cannot connect to the SimpleMidasServer. In those cases, you can click on the Load button instead and work on the local copy of the records. Note that this local copy is the one that you last saved, and it is updated only when you click on the Save button to write the entire contents of the TClientDataSet component to disk.

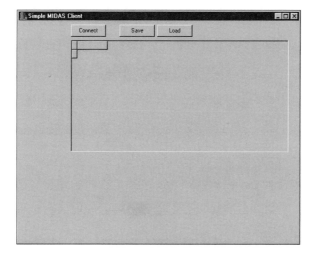

FIGURE 19.9

SimpleMidasClient *at runtime (without* SimpleMidasServer *running).*

At this time you may want to write some additional code that disables the Save button until some data is present inside the TClientDataSet component. Otherwise, clicking on the Save button will produce a zero-byte customer.cds file. When you try to load that file, for some reason the TClientDataSet will make a connection to the SimpleMidasServer anyway (probably because it is active but still contains no records). Surely, this is not the way it was intended.

Using ApplyUpdates

It's nice to be able to connect or load a local dataset and save it to disk again. But how do you ever apply your updates to the actual (remote) database again? This can be done using the ApplyUpdates method of the TClientDataSet component.

Drop a fourth button on the SimpleMidasClient main form, set its Name property to ButtonApplyUpdates and the Caption property to Apply Updates. Like the Save button, this button should be enabled only when the TClientDataSet component actually contains some data. (I leave that as an exercise. Check the project on the accompanying CD-ROM for a full implementation.)

The OnClick event handler of the Apply button should get the following code:

```
void __fastcall TForm1::ButtonApplyUpdatesClick(TObject *Sender)
{
  ClientDataSet1->ApplyUpdates(0);
}
```

The ApplyUpdates method of the TClientDataSet component has one argument: the maximum number of errors that it will allow before it stops applying updates. With a single SimpleMidasClient connected to the SimpleMidasServer, you will never encounter any problems, so feel free to run your SimpleMidasClient now. Click on the Connect button to connect to (and load) the SimpleMidasServer, and use the Save and Load buttons to store and read the contents of the TClientDataSet component to and from disk. You can even remove your machine from the network and work on your local data for a significant amount of time, which is exactly the idea behind the briefcase model (your laptop being the briefcase). Any changes you make to your local copy will remain visible, and you can apply the changes to the remote database with a click on the Apply Updates button—once you'vet reconnected to the network with the SimpleMidasServer.

Implementing Error Handling

What if two clients, botht using the briefcase model, connect to the SimpleMidasServer, obtain the entire TableCustomer, and make changes to the first record? According to what you've built so far, both clients could then send the updated record back to the MIDAS server using the ApplyUpdates method of the TClientDataSet component. If both pass zero as value for the MaxErrors argument of ApplyUpdates, the second one to attempt the update will be stopped. The second client could pass a numerical value bigger than zero to indicate a fixed number of errors or conflicts allowed before the update is stopped. However, even if the second client passed -1 as its argument (to indicate that it should continue updating no matter how many errors occur), it will never update the records that have been changed by the previous client. You need reconcile actions to handle updates on already-updated records and fields.

Fortunately, C++Builder contains a very useful dialog especially written for this purpose. Whenever you need to do error reconciliation, you should consider adding this dialog to your MIDAS client application (or write one yourself, but at least do something about it). To use the one available in C++Builder, just select File, New, go to the Dialogs tab of the Object Repository, and select the Reconcile Error Dialog icon, which can be seen in Figure 19.10.

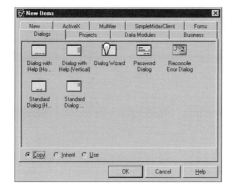

FIGURE 19.10
The Reconcile Error Dialog icon inside the Object Repository.

Once you select this icon and click OK, a new unit is added to your SimpleMidasClient project. This unit contains the definition and implementation of the Update Error dialog that can be used to resolve database update errors (see Figure 19.11).

Once this unit is added to your SimpleMidasProject, there is something very important you have to check. First save your work (put the new unit in file ErrorDialog.cpp). Now, unless you've already unchecked the option to auto-create forms inside the Preferences tab of the Tools, Environment Options dialog, you need to make sure that TReconcileErrorForm is not auto-created by your application. In the Forms tab of the Project, Options dialog, you'll find a list of auto-create forms and a list of available forms. ReconcileErrorForm should not be on the auto-create list. An instance of ReconcileErrorForm will be created dynamically, on-the-fly, when it is needed.

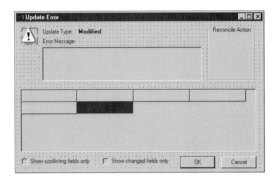

FIGURE 19.11
Update (Reconcile) Error dialog at designtime.

When or how do you use this special `ReconcileErrorForm`? It's actually very simple. For every record for which the update did not succeed (for whatever reason), the `OnReconcileError` event handler of the `TClientDataSet` component is called. This event handler of `TClientDataSet` is defined as follows:

```
void __fastcall TForm1::ClientDataSet1ReconcileError(
    TClientDataSet *DataSet, EReconcileError *E, TUpdateKind UpdateKind,
    TReconcileAction &Action)
{

}
```

This event handler has four arguments: the `TClientDataSet` component that raised the error, a specific `ReconcileError` that contains a message about the cause of the error condition, the `UpdateKind` that generated the error (insert, delete, or modify), and the `Action` that should be taken. `Action` can return the following enum values (the order is based on their actual enum values):

- `raSkip`—Do not update this record, but leave the unapplied changes in the change log. Be ready to try again next time.
- `raAbort`—Abort the entire reconcile handling; no more records will be passed to the `OnReconcileError` event handler.
- `raMerge`—Merge the updated record with the current record in the (remote) database, only changing (remote) field values if they changed on your side.
- `raCorrect`—Replace the updated record with a corrected value of the record that you made in the event handler (or inside `ReconcileErrorDialog`). This is the option in which user intervention is required.

- raCancel—Undo all changes inside this record, turning it back into the original (local) record.

- raRefresh—Undo all changes inside this record, but reload the record values from the current (remote) database, not from the original local record you had.

The good thing about ReconcileErrorForm is that you don't really need to concern yourself with all this. You only need to pass the arguments from the OnReconcileError event handler in the TClientDataSet component to the HandleReconcileError function from the ErrorDialog.

This can be done in two steps. First, you need to include the ErrorDialog unit header inside the SimpleMidasClient main form definition (or the data module, if you decided to use one). Click on the ClientMainForm and select File, Include Unit Hdr to get the Use Unit dialog (see Figure 19.12).

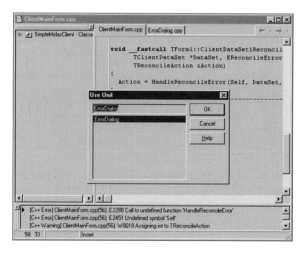

FIGURE 19.12

Add the ErrorDialog *unit header to the* ClientMainForm *unit.*

With the ClientMainForm as your current unit, the Use Unit dialog will list the only other available unit, which is the ErrorDialog. Just select it and click OK.

The second thing you need to do is to write one line of code in the OnReconcileError event handler of the TClientDataSet component to call the HandleReconcileError() function from the ErrorDialog unit (that you just added to your ClientMainForm import list). The HandleReconcileError() function has the same four arguments as the OnReconcileError event handler (not a real coincidence, of course), so it's a matter of passing arguments from one to another, nothing more and nothing less. The `OnReconcileError` event handler of the `TClientDataSet` component can be coded similar to Listing 19.3.

LISTING 19.3   Completed `OnReconcileError` Event Handler

```
void __fastcall TForm1::ClientDataSet1ReconcileError(
    TClientDataSet *DataSet, EReconcileError *E, TUpdateKind UpdateKind,
    TReconcileAction &Action)
{
  Action = HandleReconcileError(this, DataSet,  UpdateKind, E);
}
```

Demonstrating Reconcile Errors

How does all this work in practice? In order to test it, you obviously need two (or more) `SimpleMidasClient` applications running simultaneously. For a complete test using the current `SimpleMidasClient` and `SimpleMidasServer` applications, you need to perform the following steps:

1. Start the first `SimpleMidasClient` and click on the Connect button (the `SimpleMidasServer` will now be loaded as well).

2. Start the second `SimpleMidasClient` and click on the Connect button. Data will be obtained from the `SimpleMidasServer` that's already running.

3. Using the first `SimpleMidasClient`, change the Company field for the first record.

4. Using the second `SimpleMidasClient`, also change the Company field for the first record (make sure you don't change it to the same value as in the previous step).

5. Click on the Apply Updates button of the first `SimpleMidasClient`. All updates will be applied without any problems.

6. Click on the Apply Updates button of the second `SimpleMidasClient`. This time, one or more errors will occur, because the first record had its Company field value changed (by the first `SimpleMidasClient`). The `OnReconcileError` event handler is called.

7. Inside the Update Error dialog (see Figure 19.13), you can now experiment with the Reconcile Actions (Abort, Skip, Cancel, Correct, Refresh, and Merge) to get a feel for what they do. Pay special attention to the differences between Skip and Cancel and those between Correct, Refresh, and Merge.

Skip moves on to the next record, skipping the requested update (for the time being). The unapplied change will remain in the change log. Cancel also skips the requested update, but it cancels all further updates (in the same update packet). The current update request is skipped in both cases, but Skip continues with other update requests, and Cancel cancels the entire `ApplyUpdate` request.

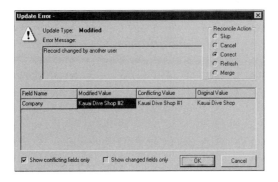

FIGURE 19.13

The Reconcile Error dialog in action.

Refresh just forgets all updates you made to the record and refreshes the record with the current value from the server database. Merge tries to merge the update record with the record on the server, placing your changes inside the server record. Refresh and Merge will not process the change request any further, so the records are synchronized after Refresh and Merge (while the change request can still be redone after a Skip or Cancel).

Correct, the most powerful option, actually gives you the option of customizing the update record *inside* the event handler. For this you need to write some code or enter the values in the dialog yourself.

Accessing the Server Remotely

At this stage, you should have a pretty good feel for how the `SimpleMidasServer` and its client work. The final stage is to make the connection not just locally, but also remotely.

When setting up DCOM, it is best to set up the server half of the DCOM program on a machine that's running as a Windows NT domain server. In particular, you don't want to run the server on a Windows 95 or Windows 98 machine, and it is best if the server machine is a domain server and the client machines are all part of this domain. If you don't have an NT domain server available, then you probably should set up your client and server machines to have the same logon and the same password, at least during the initial stages of testing. Windows 98 ships with DCOM as part of the system, whereas Windows 95 machines need to have DCOM added to the system. You can download the DLLs necessary to implement DCOM on a Windows 95 machine from the Microsoft Web site.

You must have the server registered on both the client and the server. The client program could still locate and launch the server if you failed to register it, but COM could not marshal data back and forth if the type library for the server is not registered on the client machine. You can do so by running the server once on both machines, or by running it once on the server and then registering the TLB file on the client using `TRegSvr.exe` (in the `CBuilder\bin` directory). In this case, the TLB file is called `SimpleMidasServer.tlb`. This file was generated automatically when you created the server.

When you access this server remotely from a client machine, you need to copy the single C++Builder client executable to the client side only. No database tools are needed, other than the `MIDAS.DLL` file.

Creating a MIDAS Master-Detail Server

Time to start a second, more complex example of a MIDAS server. The code demonstrated in this section is provided in the project `MidasServer.bpr`, in the `MIDAS` folder on the CD-ROM that accompanies this book.

Make sure you start to work in a new empty directory (to avoid overwriting files from the previous example by accident). I've listed the steps you need to perform to create the server yourself, to make it a bit easier.

- First, start a new project using File, New Application. Save the main form in `MainForm.cpp` and the project in `MidasServer.bpr`.
- Like the first `SimpleMidasServer` example, make sure the main form can be identified as your (second) MIDAS server application (see Figure 19.14). This means just adding a label, an image, or anything that will help identify this main form, so you'll know immediately when it (and hence your second MIDAS server) is running.

FIGURE 19.14
Master-detail MIDAS server main form.

- Next, start the Remote Data Module Wizard from the Multi-Tier tab of the Object Repository, as you've done before. This time, specify `CustomerOrders` as CoClass Name, and use the default values for all other options. This will result in a middleware database server with the name `MidasServer.CustomerOrders`, as you'll see when you start to build the `MidasClient` for this server.
- Once you have a new remote data module, drop two `TTable` components. Set the `Name` property of one to `TableCustomer` and the other to `TableOrders`.
- For each of these `TTable` components, set the `DatabaseName` property to `BCDEMOS`.

- Click on `TableCustomer` and select `customer.db` as the value for the `TableName` property. Click on `TableOrders` and select `orders.db` as the value for the `TableName` property.

You're now ready to define the master-detail relationship between `TableCustomer` and `TableOrders`.

Click on the Data Diagram tab (new in C++Builder 5) of the `CustomerOrders` remote data module. Here, you can visually define the master-detail relationship, which will only take you a few simple steps.

- First you need to drag both `customer.db` and `orders.db` from the left pane (the ClassExplorer) to the right pane (the Data Diagram). That will show both `TableCustomer` and `TableOrders` in the Data Diagram.

- Unfortunately, these two tables will not show any of their fields. You need to select the tables in the left pane again, open the `customer.db` and `orders.db` nodes, select the `Fields` node for each table, and right-click with the mouse. From the pop-up menu that follows, pick the Add All Fields entry. Do this for both the `customer.db` and `orders.db` tables until you have something that resembles Figure 19.15.

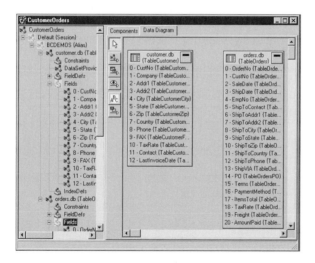

FIGURE 19.15

The Data Diagram, showing all fields of `TableCustomer` *and* `TableOrders`.

- Once all fields are added to both tables, you can create a master-detail relationship between the two tables by creating a link between two fields. Inside the Data Diagram, click on the third button from the top (the one with the fly-over hint Master Detail). Then

click on the Master table (`TableCustomer`) and then drag to the Detail table
(`TableOrders`). When you let go of the mouse button, the Field Link Designer dialog
will pop up to let you specify the fields from the Detail and Master tables that you want
to link together. In this case, select the `CustNo` index first, and then select the `CustNo`
field in both the Detail Fields and Master Fields list boxes. A click on the Add button
will prepare the link between the two `CustNo` fields, as can be seen in Figure 19.16.

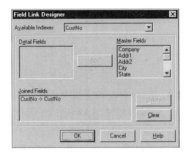

FIGURE 19.16
The Field Link Designer dialog, working on a `CustNo->CustNo` *link.*

Clicking on the OK button will create the `CustNo` link between `TableCustomer` and
`TableOrders`. The Data Diagram will show this to you, as can be seen in Figure 19.17.

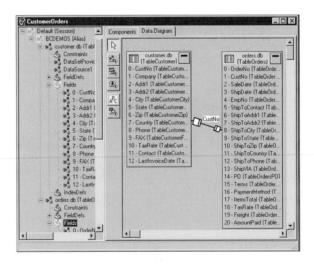

FIGURE 19.17
The Data Diagram, showing the `CustNo` *master-detail relationship.*

Now that you have created the master-detail relationship, you must return to the Components tab of the `CustomerOrders` remote data module. It's time to export the tables to the outside world.

> **NOTE**
>
> When you return to the Components tab, you'll see a `TDataSource` component that wasn't there a moment ago. This component was created dynamically by C++Builder when you created the master-detail relationship. The `DataSet` property of the `TDataSource` component points to `TableCustomer`, the `MasterSource` property of `TableOrders` points to the `TDataSource` component, and the `MasterFields` and `IndexName` properties of `TableOrders` both point to the `CustNo` field. This produces the current `CustNo` master-detail relationship. Of course, you could have done this all by hand yourself, but it's really much easier to use the C++Builder IDE.

Exporting Master-Detail DataSets

In the `SimpleMidasServer` example, you used a single `TDataSetProvider` component to export `TableCustomer` from the remote data module. This time, you might feel the urge to use two `TDataSetProvider` components: one to export `TableCustomer` and one to export `TableOrders` from the remote data module. That would export the two tables all right, but not their master-detail relationship. In fact, you would have to redefine the master-detail relationship at the client side again. For a normal application, this may work (defining the master-detail relationship at the client side). However, for a multi-tier application in which the data for the tables is provided by a database server, this situation has at least two real problems.

First of all, the detail `TClientDataSet` component on the `MidasClient` will have to fetch and store all detail records from the database server, even if only a few of the detail records are actually needed at the client side (after the master-detail relationship has been established). A potentially large number of records are sent over for nothing, wasting precious bandwidth. Of course, this problem can be overcome by using parameters, sent from the client to the server, but this involves more work and could introduce bugs that are hard to trace.

The second problem in defining the master-detail relationship on the client side has to do with the fact that it's more difficult to apply updates using two separate client datasets. This is caused by the fact that the `TClientData` component doesn't apply updates for multiple tables in a single transaction, but on a dataset-by-dataset basis (that is, you must make a separate call to `ApplyUpdates` for each table).

As a result, you should try not to export master-detail datasets as separate entities. Fortunately, `TDataSetProvider` is able to export two (or more) tables having a master-detail relationship as a single entity—provided you connect the `TDataSetProvider` component to the master `TTable`, being the `TableCustomer` of your MIDAS server. The trick is that the master table will automatically include a `DataSetField` for the detail records, and only for those detail records that are relevant to the current master record, sending only those records over the wire that are needed!

You need only to drop a single `TDataSetProvider` component (which can be found on the Midas tab) on the Components tab of the remote data module and connect its `DataSet` property to `TableCustomer`. This will export both `TableCustomer` and `TableOrders` (as a nested field) from the remote data module.

Save your work again (the assigned name is `CustomerOrdersImpl.cpp`). Note again that you didn't have to write a single line of C++ code for the MIDAS server application. Compile the `MidasServer` project and run it to register it on your machine. Now it's time to start working on the MIDAS client application that retrieves this master-detail data.

Creating a MIDAS Master-Detail Client

The new MIDAS server needs a new MIDAS client as well. The code demonstrated in this section is provided in the project `MidasClient.bpr`, in the `MIDAS` folder on the CD-ROM that accompanies this book.

Start another new application (using File, New Application). Save the main form as `ClientMainForm.cpp` again and save the project as `MidasClient.bpr`. Drop a `TDCOMConnection` component (from the Midas tab) on the main form. Once you open up the drop-down combo box for the `ServerName` property of the `TDCOMConnection` component, you should see both `SimpleMidasServer.SimpleMidasServer` (the first example) and `MidasServer.CustomerOrders` (the second example). Obviously, you want to select the `MidasServer.CustomerOrders` as the value for the `ServerName` property. You can set the `Connected` property of the `TDCOMConnection` component to `true` to test if the `MidasServer` actually gets loaded correctly.

Now, drop a `TClientDataSet` component (which can be found on the Midas tab as well) in order to retrieve the data via the `TDCOMConnection` component from the remote data module. Connect the `RemoteServer` property of the `TClientDataSet` component to the `TDCOMConnection` component, which is named DCOMConnection1 by default. Next, you need to select the right provider that's exported from the remote data module. In this case, there is still only one provider (you exported only the `TableCustomer` using `DataSetProvider1`), so select the only choice you have as the value for the `ProviderName` property of the `TClientDataSet` component, which should be DataSetProvider1 by default.

Now, go to the Data Access tab of the Component Palette and drop a TDataSource component right next to the TClientDataSet component (so you know that they'll belong together). Connect the DataSet property of the TDataSource component to the TClientDataSet component. Move over to the Data Controls tab of the Component Palette to drop a TDBGrid component on the form. Connect the DataSource property of the TDBGrid component to the TDataSource component.

In order to see live data at designtime again, you only have to set the Active property of the TClientDataSet component to true and presto! See Figure 19.18 for remote customer data in the C++Builder IDE at designtime.

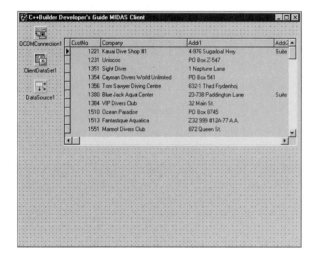

FIGURE 19.18

The MIDAS client main form showing customer data at designtime.

Using Nested Tables

You may have noticed (from Figure 19.18 for example) that the TDBGrid appears to show data only from TableCustomers. If you scroll all the way to the right of the TDBGrid component, you'll notice one last field called TableOrders. The TDBGrid component apparently cannot show the actual contents of this field, because it only displays (DATASET). Actually, that particular last field named TableOrders is a TDataSetField.

It gets even better when you run the MidasClient application and click on the TableOrders field inside the DBGrid. This will show an ellipsis, and when you click on that ellipsis (or double-click on the DATASET field itself), a new pop-up window will appear (see Figure 19.19), showing the detail records belonging to the master record that you just clicked on.

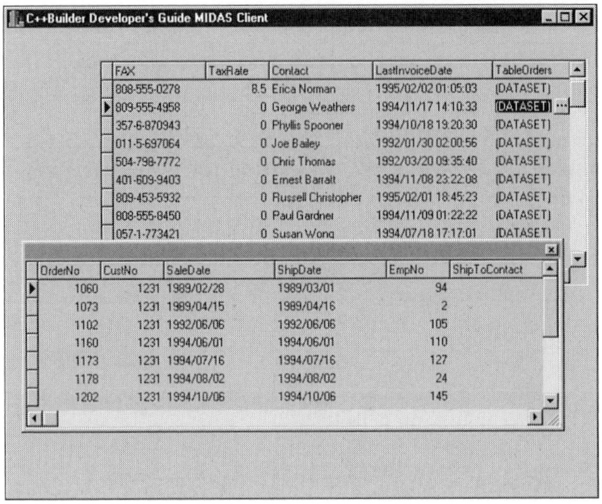

FIGURE 19.19

MIDAS client showing customer data and client detail.

I have to admit that—at first—it looks nice to have a new pop-up window show the detail records of the particular master record (that you used to double-click on the DATASET column). However, after a few minutes the excitement disappears, and I wonder about my clients. Would they like this interface? Wouldn't it be better to display the detail records in another TDBGrid component right under the first one? Your taste may differ, but at least it's possible, like almost anything in C++Builder.

Close the MidasClient application if it's still running and return to the C++Builder IDE. Drop another TClientDataSet component on the main form (which will be called ClientDataSet2 by default). This time, you need to look at the DataSetField property of ClientDataSet2; the second TClientDataSet component. Somehow, you have to connect this property with the persistent TableOrders field of type TDataSetField. The only problem—which becomes apparent once you drop down the list of available DataSetFields—is that there are no persistent fields, yet.

To use the nested dataset (the detail records), you must create a persistent DataSet field for the nested data. This sounds more difficult than it is, because the easy way is just to double-click on the first TClientDataSet component (ClientDataSet1) to start the Fields Editor (at design-time), right-click in the Fields Editor, and select Add All Fields. This will create persistent fields for every field, including a DataSetField for the nested detail table. Note that if you double-click on ClientDataSet2, you get a ClientDataSet2: Missing data provider or data packet error, which is caused by the fact that ClientDataSet2 is (still) not connected to a provider or DataSetField.

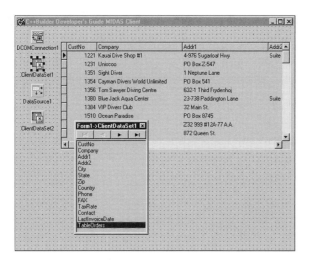

FIGURE 19.20
The Fields Editor showing TableCustomer *fields.*

Once TableOrders has been turned into a persistent field, you can drop down the combo box for the DataSetField property of the second TClientDataSet component. The combo box will show the ClientDataSet1.TableOrders as the only possible dataset field to select, so pick it. Note that this ClientDataSet is not connected directly to a remote server, but indirectly, since it gets its data from the nested dataset that the first TClientDataSet component received from the remote data server.

You can now drop a second TDataSource component (from the Data Access tab) and a second TDBGrid component (from the Data Controls tab). Connect the second TDataSource (DataSource2) to the second TClientDataSet (ClientDataSet2) and the second TDBGrid (DBGrid) to this second TDataSource (DataSource2). This will show live detail data at designtime.

This is a good solution for both displaying and updating master-detail relationships. Sometimes displaying the detail in a pop-up window may be what you need, and sometimes my solution using a second TClientDataSet component is more suited.

The problem of updating the master-detail relationship is solved by the fact that you now have only one call to ApplyUpdates to make (from the first TClientDataSet component—the one directly connected to the remote server). This automatically updates the entire nested table.

Understanding MIDAS Bandwidth Bottlenecks

While even the `SimpleMidasServer` example has some potential (bandwidth) bottlenecks, they will become more noticeable when looking at the master-detail MidasServer and MidasClient pair.

When a `TClientDataSet` is set to `Active`, it makes a request to the `TDataSetProvider` component on the remote data module to send data over the wire. How much data depends on both the size of the individual records and, of course, the number of records. The latter is determined by the value of the `PacketRecords` property of the `TClientDataSet` component. By default, this property is set to `-1`, meaning `TClientDataSet` just says "send me all available records."

For a relative small `BCDEMOS` example using `customers.db` (only 55 records) and `orders.db` (only 205 records), this is hardly a problem. But imagine a real-world customers table. Surely it would hold more than 55 customers. Even a small table of customers could easily hold a thousand or more records. And what about the orders? A few thousand perhaps? At a hundred bytes or more for each table, that could lead to a few hundred kilobytes to send over the wire as soon as the MidasClient connects to the MidasServer (and requests all data to be sent). And that's in a small shop, not an airline reservation desk or an online bookstore. I'm sure you understand why this has the potential of being a serious performance bottleneck if not a show stopper, especially with multiple MidasClients all talking to the same MidasServer over the same wire.

Minimizing Bottlenecks Using `PacketRecords`

There are a few ways to minimize the impact of this bottleneck. First and most obvious is to change the `PacketRecords` property to a value other than `-1`. Depending on the number of records you want to display at the same time, you may want to set `PacketRecords` of the first `TClientDataSet` to `20` or so. This will make sure that only the first 20 records are transferred when the first connection is made. As soon as you start to browse through the `TDBGrid` component and reach for the twenty-first record, the `TClientDataSet` will perform another request to the `TDataSetProvider` component on the remote data module, to obtain the next set of 20 records. Thus, after two requests, the client shows 40 records inside the `TDBGrid`. This continues until all records have been moved from the remote data module to the `TClientDataSet` component inside the MidasClient application.

> **NOTE**
>
> You don't need to modify `PacketRecords` of the second detail `TClientDataSet`. The nested dataset is already at the client side, contained as `DataSetField` within the master record itself.

LISTING 19.4   Continued

```
  {
    void* Current = Master->GetBookmark();
    try
    {
      Master->Last();
      OwnerData = Master->FieldByName("CustNo")->AsString;
      Master->GotoBookmark(Current);
    }
    __finally
    {
      Master->FreeBookmark(Current);
    }
  }
}
```

The `Master->Last()` statement is the one that will generate a stack overflow if the
`FetchOnDemand` property of the `TClientDataSet` component is set to `true`. In that case, moving to the last record will actually trigger the `TClientDataSet` component to fetch (on demand)
all records, which will fire this `OnBeforeGetRecords` event handler again, and so on until you
finally get a stack error.

Anyway, just before the `TDataSetProvider` component on the remote data module from the
MidasServer sends the requested records, the `BeforeGetRecords` event handler is called,
including the `OwnerData` value as you passed on the `ClientDataSet` side (see Listing 19.5).

LISTING 19.5   Server `DataSetProvider` `OnBeforeGetRecords` Event Handler

```
void __fastcall TCustomerOrders::DataSetProvider1BeforeGetRecords(
      TObject *Sender, OleVariant &OwnerData)
{
  TVariant Variant = OwnerData;
  if (!VarIsEmpty(Variant))
  {
    TLocateOptions LocateOptions;
    TDataSet* DataSet = ((TDataSetProvider*) Sender)->DataSet;
    if (DataSet->Locate("CustNo", Variant, LocateOptions))
      DataSet->Next();
  }
}
```

Now that both `BeforeGetRecords` event handlers have fired, it's time to actually send the
records from the MidasServer remote data module to the MidasClient.

After the records are sent, the TDataSetProvider component is able to send some information back to the TClientDataSet (like the number of actual records in the entire dataset on the server side), which could be started using the AfterGetRecords event handler of the TDataSetProvider component as can be seen in Listing 19.6.

LISTING 19.6   Server DataSetProvider OnAfterGetRecords Event Handler

```
void __fastcall TCustomerOrders::DataSetProvider1AfterGetRecords(
    TObject *Sender, OleVariant &OwnerData)
{
  TDataSet* DataSet = ((TDataSetProvider*) Sender)->DataSet;
  if (DataSet->Active)
    OwnerData = IntToStr(DataSet->RecordCount);
  else
    OwnerData = AnsiString("n/a");
}
```

Note that you again pass an AnsiString value in the OwnerData parameter (which is of type OleVariant). Passing AnsiString values always seems to work for me, whereas a direct assignment of DataSet->RecordCount to OwnerData doesn't compile.

Now, the value of OwnerData as passed by the OnAfterGetRecords event handler of the TDataSetProvider component will be picked up at the client side by the OnAfterGetRecords event handler of the TClientDataSet component. Storing the value somewhere is a different matter, so I've just used a ShowMessage dialog to display the number of records at the server side, as you can see in Listing 19.7.

LISTING 19.7   ClientDataSet OnAfterGetRecords Event Handler

```
void __fastcall TForm1::ClientDataSet1AfterGetRecords(TObject *Sender,
    OleVariant &OwnerData)
{
  ShowMessage("Number of records at server: " + WideString(OwnerData));
}
```

Using the implementations of the OnBeforeGetRecords and OnAfterGetRecords event handlers for both the TClientDataSet (on the client) and the TDataSetProvider (on the server), you can compile the MidasServer and MidasClient projects and test them. This is your last chance to set the FetchOnDemand property of the TClientDataSet component to false to prevent a stack error, by the way (as I mentioned at the beginning of this section).

In order to test them, you need to run the MidasClient project, which will load the MidasServer when connecting to it. As soon as a connection to the MidasServer is made, the

TClientDataSet makes its first request for data (calling the GetNextPacket method), which results in a call to the OnBeforeGetRecords() from the TClientDataSet, passing nothing, since the Active property is still false at that time. So, the OnBeforeGetRecords method of the TDataSetProvider will be called, but with an empty OwnerData argument, which means no further actions are taken. Then, the first 20 (value of PacketRecords) records are sent by the TDataSetProvider component to the TClientDataSet component. After this, the OnAfterGetRecords event handler of the TDataSetProvider is called, in which it collects the number of records of its DataSet component (the TableCustomer, which has 55 records). The value 55 is passed in OwnerData and is received at the client side when the OnAfterGetRecords event handler of the TClientDataSet is called. This results in a message dialog, seen in Figure 19.22, that shows Number of records at server: 55, just as expected.

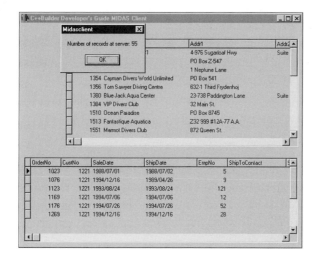

FIGURE 19.22
Result of manually sending OwnerData *between client and server.*

The MidasClient will now show up with only the first 20 records inside the DBGrid. When you browse through these records until number 20 and you want the next one, you won't get it. Similarly, when you press Ctrl+End, no additional records are fetched. You see only 20 records at the client (the value of PacketRecords), and you know that 55 exist at the server. Of course, the reason you don't get any more records at this time is because you've set the FetchOnDemand property to false. In order to get more packets with records, you now have to call the GetNextPacket method manually. This can be done by adding a TButton component to the client main form (name it ButtonFetch and set Caption to Fetch, as shown in Figure 19.23) with the following code for the OnClick event handler:

```
void __fastcall TForm1::ButtonFetchClick(TObject *Sender)
{
  ClientDataSet1->GetNextPacket();
}
```

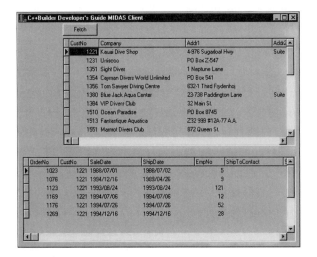

FIGURE 19.23

Manually fetching packets with records from server to client.

If you click on the Fetch button, the next packet of 20 records is retrieved, resulting in a total of 40 records in the client. Clicking on Fetch one more time will retrieve the final 15 records. At that time, the DataSet at the MidasServer will no longer be active, so you cannot obtain the RecordCount anymore (which is why I had to add the else clause in the OnAfterGetRecords event for the TDataSetProvider).

In short, the MIDAS 3 server doesn't know anything; it has to be told the complete state by the clients, and both clients and server can communicate using the OwnerData parameter of some helpful Before and After event handlers. Note that the OwnerData parameter that is used to pass data is of type OleVariant. You can put just about anything in it, but it helps if you know beforehand what to expect (on the other side), which is why I usually try to pass an AnsiString just to be sure.

Apart from the Before and After events, TClientDataSet has two additional events for Post and Scroll, with no direct counterpart on the TDataSetProvider side. Obviously, these routines have only a DataSet as an argument and no OwnerData.

A final word on this: Assigning true to the FetchOnDemand property of the TClientDataSet will ensure that the relevant state information is automatically sent from the client to the server.

However, there are situations in which you might want to be in control, in which case you need to rely on the techniques I showed you in this section. It's also important to be able to manage state by yourself (at the client side) when working with stateless protocols such as MTS, CORBA, or HTTP.

InternetExpress Applications

So far you've seen a single MidasClient using the `TClientDataSet` component to load and store packets of records. This `TClientDataSet` component can be used in regular Win32 applications (as you've seen so far) or in ActiveForm applications (see Chapter 22, "Using ActiveX Techniques," for an example thin-client ActiveForm that connects to the MidasServer from this chapter).

Apart from `TClientDataSet`, C++Builder contains another component that can be used to manage packets of records, namely the `TXMLBroker` component (also available only in the Enterprise edition of C++Builder 5). This one is especially happy with packets in XML format, as I also mentioned earlier. Just like a `TClientDataSet` component, the `XMLBroker` component connects to a connection component like `TDCOMConnection` (but you also have `TWebConnection` and `TSocketConnection`—see upcoming sections of this chapter), and it also uses a `ProviderName` to get the data from a specific `TDataSetProvider`. In fact, the only visible difference between a `TXMLBroker` component and a `TClientDataSet` component is the fact that the former uses XML and the latter uses the binary format to receive and send data packets.

Where or when should you use `TXMLBroker` then? The `TXMLBroker` component is actually part of a special feature set called InternetExpress, which can be seen as the marriage of the WebBroker technology (see Chapter 13, "Web Server Programming") with MIDAS, as you've seen so far. In fact, in the "InternetExpress" section of Chapter 13, you built a simple InternetExpress application that acts both as a MIDAS client and as a Web server (Web module) application. I refer to that chapter to let you build the basic InternetExpress application, so please make sure you've read that one and have run through the InternetExpress example application.

XMLBroker->MaxRecords

In this section, I'll cover some MIDAS-specific features of the InternetExpress client application that you need to know. First of all, let's concern ourselves with bandwidth bottlenecks. Using `TClientDataSet`, you could specify the number of records that were sent in each packet from the server (`TDataSetProvider`) to the client (`TClientDataSet`) using the `PacketRecords` property. As you can read in Chapter 13, the `XMLBroker` has no such property. However, it does have a `MaxRecords` property that limits the number of records that are sent from the `TDataSetProvider` to the TXMLBroker component. Unfortunately, this is a one-time limit, as only one packet with records (in XML format) is sent from the TDataSetProvider component to the TXMLBroker component. There is no way you can ask for a second packet of records. Actually, there is a way, but even if you call the GetNextPacket method manually (as you did using the TClientDataSet earlier in this chapter), the DataSet property of the TDataSetProvider component will still be reset to its first record right after the OnBeforeGetRecords event and just before the actual sending of records from the TDataSetProvider to the TXMLBroker component. This is caused by the fact that the TXMLBroker component specifies the grReset flag in its GetXMLRecords method, which means no matter how you try to position the dataset at the server side, whenever you actually get the records, a reset (of the dataset cursor and hence the first record position) is performed. The only workaround I could think of is to derive a new component called TBDataSetProvider, which does not set the grReset flag inside the GetXMLRecords method.

Fortunately, the other optimization technique (minimizing the number of fields that you want to pass from the MIDAS server to the client) still works as planned. This is especially useful for InternetExpress components, because XML data is taking up more space (and hence bandwidth) than data in binary format. As an example, the CustomerOrders master-detail relationship, even at 55 master records and just over 200 detail records, is taking up more than 72KB. And that's not counting the 60KB of additional JavaScript files you need to download just to connect the XML data to the HTML controls.

XMLBroker->MaxErrors

Another useful property of the TXMLBroker component is MaxErrors. Like the MaxErrors parameter of the TClientDataSet method ApplyUpdates, this property specifies when applying updates should be stopped. An Apply Updates button using InternetExpress is present inside the Web browser, and this button will execute another action of the WebBroker application that results in the TXMLBroker sending the updates inside an XML packet back to the TDataSetProvider component—again, very similar to what the TClientDataSet component does. The only difference is that the data is now in XML format instead of binary, and you cannot show the ReconcileError dialog inside a Web browser. Or can you? Yes, you can actually.

In the CBuilder5/Examples/MIDAS/InternetExpress/Inetxcustom directory you'll find a special designtime package dclinetxcustom_bcb.bpk that is necessary in order to properly load the example project Webshow.bpr and needs to be built and installed. It contains a special PageProducer-derived component called TReconcilePageProducer (which can be found on the InternetExpress tab after you've installed this package). Note that you should also add the source path $(BCB)\examples\midas\internetexpress\inetxcustom to the Include path of the Directories/Conditionals tab of your Project Options dialog. This makes sure that you can compile the applications that use the `TReconcilePageProducer`.

Now, load the ShowWeb project from Chapter 13 into the C++Builder 5 IDE, and drop a `TReconcilePageProducer` on the Web module (this component is available on the InternetExpress tab of the Component Palette after you've installed the `dclinetxcustom_bcb.bpk` package). You can play a little bit with the properties of this `PageProducer`, but the most important thing you need to do is to assign it to the `ReconcileProducer` property of the `TXMLBroker` component.

Now, whenever a reconcile error occurs inside the MidasServer, and it sends the error back to the `TXMLBroker` component, the `ReconcilePageProducer` will be used to produce dynamic HTML output that clearly shows what the problem is.

WebConnection Component

Apart from using DCOM as a communication protocol, as implemented using the `TDCOMConnection` component, MIDAS supports two other protocols as well: TCP/IP (sockets) and HTTP. The latter is called `TWebConnection` and is especially useful in situations where you need to go through a proxy or firewall, which can be quite a problem (or at least quite a task) using the regular `TDCOMConnection` component.

`TWebConnection` is found on the Midas tab of the Component Palette. It is perfect to use for stateless HTTP communication connecting to a MIDAS 3 server (which is also stateless, as you've seen).

For the remainder of this section, you should probably copy the MidasClient project from its original directory to a new directory, where you can experiment on it using the `TWebConnection` component. Note that this precaution is only necessary with the MidasClient project; we won't be modifying the MidasServer at all.

Using the MidasClient project, you can replace the current `TDCOMConnection` component with a `TWebConnection` component. Now the `TWebConnection` component has to connect to the MidasServer you created in this chapter. The `TWebConnection` component makes this connection by using the HTTP protocol. However, in order to use a `WebConnection`, you must make sure that `WININET.DLL` is installed on the client system (which is available if you have Internet Explorer version 3 or higher installed), the server must have Internet Information Server version 4 or higher or Netscape Enterprise version 3.6 or higher, and finally you must install a special Inprise/Borland-made `ISAPI DLL` called `HTTPSRVR.DLL` (found in the `CBUILDER5\BIN` directory) in a `cgi-bin` or `scripts` directory on the Web server that the `TWebConnection` component uses to connect to. `HTTPSRVR` is responsible for launching the MidasServer on the Web server and will marshal all requests from the client to the application server interface, sending packets of records back.

For more information on Web servers, ISAPI DLLs, and general Web server programming, see Chapter 13.

As a direct consequence, the URL property of the WebConnection component must point to http://localhost/cgi-bin/httpsrvr.dll (which points to the scripts directory on my local machine—I could also have used http://192.168.92.201/cgi-bin/httpsrvr.dll). Next, you can click on the ServerName property, open up the list of available MIDAS servers, and select the MidasServer.CustomerOrders MIDAS server. You can make sure that the connection actually works by double-clicking on the Connected property of the TWebConnection component. If the value turns to true, you're OK.

> **NOTE**
>
> Note that you don't actually see the MIDAS server running. That's because HTTPSRVR (started by the Web server) is activated by another user (the default Internet user), and as a result you don't see any visual representation of the middleware server at this time (as you did when using a DCOM or the upcoming Sockets middleware server).

To make sure the server is actually running, you can always take a look at the Task Manager, of course. Inside the Task Manager, you'll see the MidasServer running, while (not so) surprisingly, no indication of that is seen at the desktop.

Other than this, the TWebConnection component works exactly the same as the TDCOMConnection component, with one difference: security. The TWebConnection component allows you to take advantage of SSL security and to communicate with a MidasServer application that is protected behind a firewall. For all this, the TWebConnection component has a number of helpful properties, such as Proxy, ProxyByPass, UserName, and Password. The UserName and Password properties of TWebConnection can be used to go through a proxy or if the Web server requires authorization or authentication.

Object Pooling

Finally, a Web connection can use object pooling. This feature allows the server to create a pool of multiple server instances for client requests. This way, the MidasServer doesn't use the resource for the remote data module and database connection unless it's actually needed.

Object pooling gives you the capability to set a maximum for the number of instances of the remote data module inside the MIDAS server application. Whenever a client request is received, the MIDAS server checks to see if a free remote data module exists in the pool. If not, it creates a remote data module instance (but never more than the specified maximum number of remote data module instances) or raises an exception with the message Server too busy. The remote data module, in its turn, services the client requests and duly waits for the next one. After a certain period of time without client requests, the remote data module is freed automatically (by the object pooling mechanism).

In previous versions of MIDAS, this feature would not have been possible, since we now have instances of a remote data module that service more than one client. As a result, the server cannot rely on state information—this has to be maintained by the client. As indicated previously, MIDAS 3 is indeed stateless.

The big question should now be: How do we enable object pooling for HTTP connections? We must get inside the UpdateRegistry() method again—found in the header file of your remote data module. Inside the UpdateRegistry() method, an object regObj is used to configure the behavior of the application server. With object pooling, we must set three additional property values.

First, regObj.MaxObjects specifies the maximum number of instances. If a client request is received by the MIDAS server and no remote data modules are available, then an exception with message Server too busy is raised.

Second, regObj.Timeout specifies the number of minutes the remote data module can wait idle in the pool of remote data modules. After spending the specified amount of time without a single client request, the remote data module will be freed automatically by the MIDAS server. According to the documentation, the MIDAS server checks every 6 minutes to see if any remote data module should be freed. Specifying a timeout value of 0 means that the remote data module will never time out, so in that case the only useful feature you're using is the limit on the amount of remote data module instances.

After these two property settings, the regObj.RegisterPooled must be set to true to indicate that you want to use object pooling.

In practice, there's a fourth property value you can set: regObj.Singleton specifies whether or not the remote data module should be a singleton (but we already set that to false). If you set it to true, the number of instances and timeout arguments will be ignored, and only a single remote data module (which must be free threaded) will be created to handle all client requests.

An example modified UpdateRegistry for a remote data module with up to 10 instances that time out after 42 minutes of inactivity can be seen in Listing 19.8.

LISTING 19.8   UpdateRegistry to Enable Connection Pooling

```
// Function invoked to (un)register object
//
static HRESULT WINAPI UpdateRegistry(BOOL bRegister)
{
  TRemoteDataModuleRegistrar regObj(GetObjectCLSID(),
                                    GetProgID(), GetDescription());
  // Disable these flags in order to disable use by socket or Web connections.
  // Also set other flags to configure the behavior of your application server.
  // For more information, see atlmod.h and atlvcl.cpp.
  regObj.Singleton = false;
  regObj.MaxObjects = 10;
  regObj.Timeout = 42;
  regObj.RegisterPooled = true;   regObj.EnableWeb = true;
  regObj.EnableSocket = true;
  return regObj.UpdateRegistry(bRegister);
}
```

Note that I've used hard-coded magic numbers 10 and 42 here. This is not a good idea in real life, especially since it means that you need to recompile the MIDAS server whenever you want to make some changes (for example, if you add new memory to the server, which can then handle more than 10 instances). That's not even considering that the same MIDAS server could be placed on multiple machines, each of a different configuration (see the section "Object Broker," at the end of this chapter). I always recommend using an external configuration file where you can specify—for each machine, and for every time you first start the MIDAS server application—the number of instances and timeout minutes. This adds flexibility to the power already present in object pooling.

Socket Server

So far, you've mainly worked with the TDCOMConnection component and the TWebConnection component. However, MIDAS 3 can also employ a third protocol: TCP/IP (plain sockets). This is done by using the TSocketConnection component (the third of the three Connection components available on the Midas tab of the Component Palette from C++Builder 5 Enterprise).

If you don't have an NT domain server available on your network, then you should probably not try to use DCOM at all and instead should use plain TCP/IP. A socket connection will work even if no NT server is in the equation, and it is usually much easier to set up than a DCOM connection. However, security is much more difficult to enforce on a socket connection (unlike the TWebConnection component, for example).

You can easily convert either SimpleMidasClient or MidasClient into a TCP/IP application. You don't even need to make any changes to your MIDAS servers to make it work. To get started building your sockets-based MIDAS program, run the ScktSrvr.exe program found in the CBuilder5/Bin directory on the server machine. This program must be running on the server, or this system will not work. Note that ScktSrvr.exe can either be run as a normal application or be used as an NT service (using the -install and -uninstall command-line parameters).

Drop a TSocketConnection component from the Midas page of the Component Palette on the main form of the MidasClient application. Set its Address property to the IP address of the machine where the MidasServer application resides. This can be a remote machine or your current machine (such as localhost). Fill in the ServerName property, just as you did in the DCOM example earlier in this chapter, by dropping down the ServerName combo box and selecting the MidasServer.CustomerOrders MIDAS server. You should now be able to test your connection by setting the Connected property of the TSocketConnection component to true. As I explained earlier, you should not leave the Connected property set to true at designtime.

Assuming you have dropped down a TSocketConnection component on the form and set its ServerName property correctly, then you can drop a new TButton component, set its Name property to ButtonSocket, Caption to Socket, and write the event handler code as seen in Listing 19.9.

LISTING 19.9   SocketConnection to Remote Machine

```
void __fastcall TForm1::ConnectTCPIP1Click(TObject *Sender)
{
  AnsiString S;
  if (InputQuery("Enter Machine Name or IP-Address:",
                 "Machine Name/IP-Address", S))
  {
    SocketConnection1->Address = S;
    ClientDataSet1->RemoteServer = SocketConnection1;
    ClientDataSet1->Active = true;
  }
}
```

When the user clicks on the Socket button, he is prompted for the IP address of the machine where the server resides. Assuming your system is set up correctly, you can also pass in the human-readable equivalent of that IP address, like localhost or—in my case—DrBob42.

The code sets the Address property of the TSocketConnection component to the address supplied by the user. It then changes the RemoteServer property of the TClientDataSet so that it no longer points at the TDCOMConnection component but at that TSocketConnection component. Finally, it sets the Active property of the TClientDataSet to true. Setting the Active

19

MULTI-TIER
DISTRIBUTED
APPLICATIONS

property to `true` will automatically cause the `TSocketConnection.Connected` property to be set to `true` as well, as you've seen earlier.

At this stage, you should be fully connected to your server and viewing your data. This approach will work equally well whether the server is on the same machine or on a remote machine. Furthermore, you don't need an NT domain server or even an NT server, though I always recommend that you use one when working with MIDAS.

Note that the MIDAS server does not have to be changed to connect to a client using DCOM or sockets (TCP/IP). In fact, once you have a working MIDAS server, you only need to run it to allow it to register itself (so you can locate it and connect to it from a MIDAS client). This COM-specific Registry is done by the inherited `UpdateRegistry` call, and is performed by all versions of MIDAS. It's actually quite convenient, because if you want to move the server application to another location (on the same machine), you only need to re-run it to re-register itself and allow clients to connect to it.

Usually, I write MIDAS applications that communicate using DCOM. However, in some cases you may want to use plain sockets instead. A regular remote data module can communicate using sockets, provided you've left that particular communication protocol enabled in the `UpdateRegistry` method. Clients need to connect to the remote data module using the `SocketConnection` component. However, in order for a connection to be made to the MIDAS application server, you also need to run the socket server on the server machine. Using C++Builder 4, you had two socket server applications: `ScktSrvr.exe` (the socket server) or `ScktSrvc.exe` (the NT service edition of the socket server). In C++Builder 5, these two are combined in a single `ScktSrvr.exe` that can either be run as a normal application or be used as an NT service (using the `-install` and `-uninstall` command-line parameters).

As I mentioned before, the C++Builder 5 `ScktSrvr` checks the Registry to see if a MIDAS server has enabled the socket communication protocol (that is, whether or not the `EnableSocket` field of the `regObj` has been assigned to `true` inside the `UpdateRegistry()` function). For C++Builder 4 MIDAS servers, this isn't present, which means that if you upgrade a C++Builder 4 MIDAS server to C++Builder 5, you must not forget to include a new `UpdateRegistry` method. If, for any reason, the new MIDAS server doesn't register itself as using the socket communication protocol, then you can always use the C++Builder 5 socket server (and not the C++Builder 4 socket server) and in the Connections menu specify that you don't want `Registered Object Only` (you want to see unregistered objects as well).

This change will not take affect until the socket server is restarted, but then you can see C++Builder 5 MIDAS servers using the `TSocketConnection` component—registered or not.

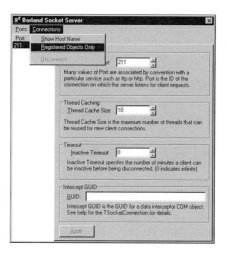

FIGURE 19.24
Borland socket server looking at all objects.

A final new feature regarding the TSocketConnection component has to do with callbacks. TDCOMConnection components always support callbacks, and TWebConnection components never support callbacks. With a TSocketConnection component you can specify using the SupportCallbacks property, whether or not the TSocketConnection component will marshal calls from the MidasServer to the MidasClient over an interface supplied as a callback. If you don't want to do that, then you can set SupportCallbacks to false (it's true by default). Setting it to false has the advantage that you then need only Winsock 1 support to deploy your MidasClient, whereas otherwise (with SupportCallbacks set to true) you need Winsock 2 or higher. Since Win95 doesn't include Winsock 2 by default, this means one less deployment problem.

Object Broker

You've now seen three possible connection components that exist in C++Builder 5 Enterprise: TDCOMConnection, TWebConnection, and TSocketConnection, all connecting to a single MIDAS server application. However, sometimes you don't have a single MIDAS server to connect to, but multiple MIDAS servers. Reasons for having multiple MIDAS servers can be diverse, but most often this is done for load balancing and failover. If one server goes down, others can take over, and having 10 servers all over the world usually results in fewer bottlenecks than having one big server.

Imagine having to determine at the client side which of these MIDAS servers to connect to. You'd need to know exactly which servers are available (or you might miss one—maybe the last one that's available at the time) and how to connect to them. In an ideal world, you wouldn't want all your clients to know about this. Fortunately, MIDAS 3 offers a helpful hand in this case, by means of the concept called Object Brokering.

With Object Brokering, you make a connection from the client to a server without knowing which server you'll end up with. Each of the three connection components has a property called `ObjectBroker`. This property can be used to connect to a component derived from `TCustomObjectBroker`. It will then be responsible for telling the connection component which server to use (by specifying the `ServerName` or `ServerGUID`). Note that when you actually use an `ObjectBroker`, the local values specified for the `ServerName` and `ServerGUID` properties will be ignored as far as your application is concerned; `ObjectBroker` will supply you with dynamic values at runtime.

As an example of how to implement your own Object Brokering techniques, C++Builder 5 Enterprise comes with a `TSimpleObjectBroker` component (found on the MIDAS tab of the Component Palette).

`TSimpleObjectBroker` itself contains two interesting properties. `Servers` contains a list of available servers, for each of which you can specify the `ComputerName`, the `Port` (211 by default), and `Enabled`. Note that you as a developer must make sure that this list is filled and maintained properly. If you add a new server or a server goes down, you must update the list.

The second property is `LoadBalanced`. As the name indicates, this property tries to ensure that the servers are load balanced, or at least that a request is balanced among the servers. The technique used here is based on a random generator. When `LoadBalanced` is set to `true`, each connection component will be connected to a random server from the list. When `LoadBalanced` is set to `false` (the default), each connection component on the client application will be connected to the first server on the list.

The `TSimpleObjectBroker` component is implemented in unit `ObjBrkr` (found in the `$(BCB)\Source\Vcl` directory) and contains a fairly simple algorithm. Picking a random server isn't such a bad idea, but obviously it's not really intelligent, either. If you ever need to write your own Object Broker algorithm, then `TSimpleObjectBroker` might be a good place to start.

One final word on Object Brokering: Once a connection component is connected to a MIDAS server, it will remain connected to that particular server until the `Connected` property is set to `false` again. When you reconnect (set `Connected` back to `true`), you may end up with a different server.

Deployment

Deploying MIDAS is fairly easy. You have to find the correct set of DLLs and packages for your client application and include MIDAS 3 itself (which consists of only `MIDAS.DLL` for

MIDAS 3 and `DBCLIENT.DLL` for MIDAS 2). There are no database drivers and no additional setup, only your client and `MIDAS.DLL`. You might need to register the server on your client machine as well, or at least the type library for the server—see the "Accessing the Server Remotely" section, earlier in this chapter.

You also need to purchase an official license. A MIDAS 2 license was pretty expensive at US$5,000.00 per hardware server. You are allowed to run as many MIDAS 2 servers on a machine as you want and can. MIDAS 3 now has a new lower-than-ever deployment license model, which incidentally has no effect on the MIDAS 2 licensing model (another reason to upgrade your MIDAS 2 applications to MIDAS 3). A MIDAS 3 license for an unlimited server is now only US$299.95. As a result of this much lower price, Borland no longer offers a per-seat client license, making the licensing scheme not only much cheaper, but easier as well.

When do you need to purchase a MIDAS license? That depends on the MIDAS data packet (sent from the provider to the `ClientDataSet` or `XMLBroker` and back). In his MIDAS 3 licensing article on the Borland Community site, John Kaster (Borland Developer Relations) has formulated two rules:

1. If the MIDAS data packet goes from one machine to another by any means, a license is required.

2. If the MIDAS data packet always stays on the same machine, you do not need a license.

Note that "by any means" includes copying to a floppy disk, using email, copying from one hard disk to another, backing up from one machine and restoring on another then resolving the data, and so on. Basically, this means any method of transferring the data packet from one machine to another (including retyping or a WAP connection).

This greatly reduced license fee is a tremendous opportunity for C++Builder 5 developers who need to develop *n*-tier solutions. Previously, clients had serious problems with the MIDAS 2 license fees (especially if you had to prove all benefits first), but now I have little reluctance suggesting a multi-tier MIDAS 3 approach.

Summary

In this chapter, you looked at Borland's multi-tier technology called MIDAS. In particular, you saw how to create servers and clients and how to use DCOM, sockets, and HTTP to connect to a remote server.

This technology is important for several reasons:

- It provides a means of creating thin clients that make few demands on the client system.
- It simplifies—in fact, nearly eliminates—the need to configure the client machine.

- It allows you to partition applications in logical compartments. If you want, each of these compartments can be run on a separate machine, thereby distributing the load of the application.

- It provides a means for distributing a load over several server machines or for routing the load to a specific machine with the power to handle heavy demands.

- It provides a robust architecture for handling and reporting (reconciliation) errors, particularly in a multiuser environment.

- It allows you to use a briefcase technology that stores files locally and allows you to reload them when it is time to update the server. This capability is ideal for laptop users who spend a lot of time on the road.

For many users, this technology is so compelling that it entirely replaces the standard client/server database architectures. These users are attracted to the capability to partition an application into logical pieces, even if the entire application is being run on a single machine. However, the biggest benefits achieved by this architecture become apparent when you bring multiple machines and servers into play.

This chapter should get you started using some of the more sophisticated aspects of this technology. There will come a time when nearly every computer in the world will be continually connected to nearly every other computer. When that occurs, distributed computing will become one of the most essential fields of study in computer programming. MIDAS 3 is a very helpful piece of technology in this respect.

Distributed Applications with CORBA

Ruurd F. Pels

IN THIS CHAPTER

The goal of the Common Object Request Broker Architecture (CORBA) is to provide an object-oriented architecture that is distributed, cross-platform, and scalable. It is created and maintained by the Object Management Group (OMG). This chapter deals with CORBA and C++Builder. CORBA support is available only in the Enterprise edition of C++Builder. The same holds for JBuilder and Delphi. But do not despair: For the less wealthy or pampered, I'll have a little surprise.

We will discuss what CORBA is and why we should use it, how it works, and what the main components are of the Visibroker CORBA implementation that comes with C++Builder. We will also look at the Interface Definition Language that is used to specify interfaces between subsytems and what is new with C++Builder 5.

Then we will move on to the more practical issues of how to operate the wizards and other functionalities of C++Builder that deal with CORBA. Following that, we will discuss the implementation models we can use when implementing distributed applications with CORBA.

If you're disappointed at not having the Enterprise version of C++Builder, then I will explain how to use CORBA without all the nifty C++Builder support at all. In fact, the whole story takes a surprising turn in the end.

Introduction to CORBA

One factor in software engineering is the size of systems. System sizes are growing very rapidly. We are (more or less) able to build systems that consist of 10 to 30 million lines of code. Ten years ago we could manage systems of about 1 million lines of code. Extrapolating, in the year 2010 we might be building systems that consist of a whopping 100 million lines of code.

The danger lies in the fact that the chance of successfully implementing, testing, and deploying such systems is inversely proportional to the size of such systems. Therefore, critical success factors in being able to deliver such systems will be the flexibility with which we can divide such systems and the uniformity of the way we can specify interfaces between subsystems. These things will become very important in the not-so-distant future.

One way of creating such systems is using CORBA. At the time this book is being written, the CORBA standard is at version 2.3. If you want information about the standard, visit http://www.omg.org. However, the OMG is only an institution that stipulates the standard. Several companies provide implementations. There is a large number of implementations for a large variety of operating systems and hardware. In addition, CORBA is integrated in systems such as databases (Oracle 8i), document retrieval systems (Lotus Domino), and X Windows window managers (Gnome). One of the major advantages of CORBA over the Component Object Model (COM) in all its forms is that so many large companies contribute to OMG. CORBA is an *open standard*, and anyone can implement the standard on his favorite computer architecture. Besides Visigenic, a subsidiary of Inprise, there is a large number of others that implement the standard. There are even open source implementations.

Borland C++Builder integrates with the Visigenic implementation in two flavors—a real CORBA integration and a method to create a CORBA interface that is a look-alike of a COM interface. In this chapter, we will discuss only the first one.

How CORBA Works

Most if not all CORBA implementations work over TCP/IP. The programmer designs an interface in Interface Definition Language (IDL). The CORBA implementation tools take that interface definition and turn it into stub code. Then it leaves the programmer with the task of filling in the blanks. The generated stub code is very portable. Most CORBA implementations do not generate C++ code that adheres strictly to the latest standards, for the sole reason that not all C++ compilers are able to compile such code.

The stubs take care of flattening the arguments passed to it into a form that can be transported and interpreted in a platform-independent manner. This is called *marshaling*. On the receiving end, the stubs take care of re-creating the argument and subsequently calling the method in your implementation. This is called *unmarshaling*. Then the whole mechanism of marshaling on the server end and unmarshaling on the client end is used again to transport the result back to the client. This means, for example, that a program running on an Intel-based machine can call a method in a program running on a totally different architecture. The stub code and the supporting CORBA and network layers will take care of the necessary translations for you.

CORBA is basically a standard in synchronous communication. This means that if you call a method in a remote object, you have to wait until your humble servant is done processing. However, there are a number of provisions in the standard for different means of communications, such as one-way calls and events.

Static and Dynamic

Because of the fact that the CORBA layer flattens a method call into a message, it is relatively easy to add functionality to construct CORBA method invocations from scratch. This is called *dynamic invocation*. What happens is that you bypass stub code and control the assembly of a message from your own code. It is readily apparent that this is helpful, but using it will lead you into difficulties. If you use it, you are responsible for assembling the message that goes from client to server and disassembling the answer. If the interface definition changes, you must change the code. Static invocation is more flexible and has the added benefit that you can use your compiler to check on the number and types of arguments.

Always or On-Demand

Most CORBA implementations provide you with two different methods of starting the server. The simple one is to start the server and let it provide the services you implemented. The other method makes use of an *activation daemon*. This is a server that interprets a client request and goes looking for a server process that can handle it. The daemon needs to know what interface is provided by your server and where the server executable is stored. If it knows that, it will start the server if necessary.

Flat or Hierarchical

Included in the CORBA standard is the naming service, which allows you to categorize your services in a tree-like manner. If you must implement a large number of services, you must definitely look into the naming services of CORBA. The naming services make it possible to bind a logical name to a service you implement at runtime. Giving it another name does not require you to recompile your code. The naming service also makes it possible to bind more than one name to the same service. It is more difficult to handle, but it makes using the services you have implemented easier in the production stage.

Consider, for example, an inventory tracking application for a company that has multiple production facilities. Using the naming services, I could run the same service under different names, one for each production facility the company owns. For example, the service named NewYork/Inventory/Tracking would refer to the inventory tracking application in New York, and Seattle/Inventory/Tracking would refer to the same application for the Seattle production facility. The implementation even can resideon different computers acting on different databases.

Who Is the Server and Who Is the Client

CORBA does not make a distinction between clients and servers. Any process can be either or both. This means that you can write a client process that at the same time acts like a server process.

Consider an application in which the client needs to be notified if a certain event occurs during its use. The server then needs to notify only those clients that requested to be notified. One way of ensuring that the server process notifies the right clients is to pass the server a reference to an object in the client. This means that the implementation of the notification object resides in the client part and not the server part of the application.

The Object Request Broker

The Object Request Broker (ORB) flattens object method invocations into messages and back and sends them to the proper server. In Visibroker, they are implemented as DLLs. This means that every machine that is running a CORBA client or server has to be provided with the ORB executables.

The Basic Object Adapter

The Basic Object Adapter (BOA) serves as a registry for the services provided by a server. The BOA makes it possible for the server to announce its services and for the ORB to find services requested by clients.

The Portable Object Adapter

In the newest CORBA standard you will find the Portable Object Adapter (POA). In earlier CORBA standards, the BOA could not be implemented in a portable manner. Since then, the standard has changed so that it can be. However, using a POA is a whole different ballgame, and the C++Builder IDE has not yet caught up. It still uses the BOA instead of the POA.

CORBA Versus COM

There are a number of advantages and disadvantages to using COM over CORBA. The advantages of COM are

- It's free.
- It is ubiquitous.

The disadvantages of COM are

- It supports a smaller number of platforms.
- It is not an open standard.
- DCOM clients need the server executable to make Registry entries that allow it to call the server.
- The documentation that comes with COM is hard to understand.

If you're dealing with an infrastructure that consists mainly of WinTel architecture, then use COM, DCOM, or COM+. It works fine. But if you are dealing with a wide variety of hardware and operating system combinations, COM and its variants are not going to help you. Even worse, in the development environments provided by Microsoft, no support whatsoever is given to enable you to use CORBA. You must follow the Poor Man's CORBA approach outlined later in this chapter. However, you are on your own.

Visibroker Components

In addition to the tools to generate stubs for C++, Delphi CORBA clients, and Java, the Visibroker implementation consists of three main components. These are not the only ones, but we need only these three for a CORBA-based system:

- The Smart Agent
- The Object Activation Daemon
- The Console

The Smart Agent

The osagent executable is referred to as the *smart agent*. The smart agent is not part of the CORBA specification, but it serves an important role as a kind of phone book. As soon as a CORBA server is started, it contacts the smart agent and asks it to register the details about the interfaces provided by the CORBA server to any interested parties. A CORBA client program in turn contacts the same smart agent to find out if a certain interface is available. It asks the smart agent to set up a connection from the client to the server. In that respect, it is truly an agent. It acts on behalf of both CORBA server and CORBA client. Once a connection is made, the smart agent does not play a further role in the dealings between server and client.

The Object Activation Daemon

The smart agent is also a bit dumb in some respects. It assumes that the server process is running if an interface is available. The Object Activation Daemon (OAD) is a trick to fool the smart agent into believing that a server process is running when it is not. You provide the Object Activation Daemon with enough information to start the server process after the smart agent requests a connection to the server process. The information you provide is stored in an interface repository, which stores the interface itself as well as the name of the server process and any arguments and environment variables needed by the server process. To register that information in an interface repository, use an oadutil tool. To use it effectively, you will want to write batch files. C++Builder can actually execute batchfiles after a server build is done.

The Console

The console is a goodie that is new. It comes with Visibroker 4 and was not contained in the previous versions. This tool lets you browse the available CORBA services that are running.

The Interface Definition Language

To specify how an interface between systems looks, we use CORBA's Interface Definition Language (IDL). COM uses the same term and, in fact, it is referred to as Microsoft IDL, and the program that converts it into code is called MIDL. MIDL uses the .idl extension to identify a COM interface, and both languages look a lot alike.

IDL enables you to specify an interface but not to specify the implementation of such an interface. You have to provide that in the language you are generating from your IDL specification: C++, Java, or any other language that has a mapping. You use IDL to define types, constants, and interfaces. An IDL identifier can contain letters, digits, and the underscore character, but it cannot begin with an underscore. In fact, you might want to avoid using the underscore at all, because some languages do not support it in identifier names. Furthermore, since IDL files are preprocessed before they are passed to the IDL compiler, the IDL compiler understands preprocessor directives.

IDL supports the use of `typedef` to assign a name to a type definition. It supports the types `float`, `double`, `long`, `short`, `unsigned long`, `unsigned short`, `char`, `boolean`, `octet`, `Any`, and `NamedValue`. The `Any` type is an arbitrary IDL type that is similar to `Variant` in COM. `NamedValue` is a pair consisting of a name (a string) and a value of type `Any`. IDL also supports multidimensional arrays with predefined dimensions. It provides two template types: `sequence` and `string`. A `sequence` is a one-dimensional array of a certain type, either bounded (`typedef sequence<octet,6> SixBytesMax`) or unbounded (`typedef sequence<any> ABunchOfAnyes`). A `string` is a sequence of `char`. When using a bounded string, keep in mind that the terminating null is not considered to be part of the length of the string; that is, `typedef string<15>` is a string that contains 15 characters. String types are mapped to the C++ type `char*`. You must use `CORBA::string_alloc(CORBA::Ulong)` and `CORBA::string_free(char*)` for dynamically allocating and destroying strings.

Furthermore, IDL supports the constructed types `struct`, `union`, and `enum`. The `struct` and `enum` constructed types look exactly like their C++ counterparts in terms of syntax, and the `union` looks entirely different. It needs a tag field to specify which `union` member is currently assigned.

```
union ExampleUnion switch(long)
{
  case 1: long x;
  case 2: string y;
};
```

Constants are also supported. Their syntax looks exactly like that of C++ for defining constants. For example

```
const long Foo = 42;
```

IDL does not support constants of the `octet` type.

The `interface` Keyword

An interface is declared with the keyword `interface`. An interface is the definition of what services a server object provides to its clients. An interface does not have a notion of access control. This means that everything you specify is public. Interfaces are mapped to a class in C++, and the generated classes are all derived from `CORBA::Object`. You can use forward declarations of interfaces to reference those not yet defined or to let the interface currently being defined reference itself.

The name of the keyword stresses that classes generated by the IDL compiler should be regarded as interfaces, not C++ classes in their regular meaning. This means that the recommended way to use CORBA is to let a CORBA-generated interface class act as an interface to "real" objects in the server implementation.

20

DISTRIBUTED APPLICATIONS WITH CORBA

The `attribute` Keyword

Attributes are like properties in Delphi or C++Builder. If you want a client to prevent writing to an attribute, prefix the attribute with the `readonly` keyword, for example

```
interface ReadWrite {
  attribute long CanBeWritten;
  readonly attribute string ReadOnly;
}
```

In the generated C++ stubs, an attribute is implemented using a getter function and, if you did not specify `readonly`, a setter function that uses the name of the attribute.

Methods

Methods are like regular function members in C++. You *must* specify the return type, however. Also, every parameter must be provided with the direction in which it is passed to the server using the keywords `in` (to the server), `out` (from the server), or `inout` (to and from the server). If you choose not to wait for the result of a call to a method, you may specify the return type as `void` and prepend the `oneway` keyword. Overloading names is not allowed because some languages that have an IDL mapping do not support it.

Type Definitions

An interface can contain type definitions. Because an interface provides a name scope, referencing such types from outside an interface requires the use of the scope operator, such as `MyInterface::MyTypeDefinition`.

Exceptions

An interface can contain exception types. In the C++ implementation, these exceptions are all derived from `CORBA::UserException`, which in turn is derived from `CORBA::Exception`. Exception types can be used in method specifications to specify which ones can be raised when calling a method:

```
interface Pitcher {
  exception NoBallAvailable {
  };
  void Throw() raises (NoBallAvailable);
};
```

Throwing an exception in the C++ implementation of a CORBA object is as easy as using the C++ `throw` keyword with an object of the proper type:

```
void PitcherImpl::Throw() {
  if (IcannotFindABall() == true) {
    throw Pitcher::NoBallAvailable;
  }
};
```

Catching exceptions also works just like non-CORBA exceptions:

```
void PitcherClient::Throw() {
  try {
    pitcher.Throw();
  }
  catch (Pitcher::NoBallAvailable& pitcherx) {
    // catch the Pitcher::NoBallAvailable exception
    ...
  }
  catch (CORBA::UserException& userx) {
    // catch all other CORBA user exceptions
    ...
  }
}
```

Inheritance

CORBA supports inheritance, even multiple inheritance. However, it supports multiple inheritance only if there are no definitions that have the same name in one of the ancestor interfaces. You do not need to redefine methods in a descendant interface if you derive it from an ancestor interface.

All interfaces are implicitly derived from the CORBA::Object interface. This means that if you pass a parameter of type CORBA::Object, you may actually pass any interface object.

Modules

A module groups interfaces and is somewhat equivalent to a C++ namespace. In fact, given the correct switch, the IDL compiler produces code that maps a module to a namespace. A module defines a name scope. To specify a name in a module from outside the module, you must use the scope operator, such as MyModule::MyInterface.

Those who combine Java and C++ implementations should be aware of the package switch in the idl2java compiler. That switch lets you prepend a package name to the Java stub classes generated. The alternative would be to add a number of nested modules to adhere to the Java naming standard for packages, such as what follows:

```
module com {
  module company {
    module packagename {
      module ModuleOne {
        interface InterfaceOne {
          ...
} } } } }
```

However, this would lead to C++ classes representing the interface that must be referenced as com::company::mainpackagename::ModuleOne::InterfaceOne. This would safely be regarded as suboptimal. In that case, you want to pass `com.company.mainpackagename` as the value for the package switch and reference the C++ stub class as `ModuleOne::InterfaceOne`.

What's New in C++Builder 5

Actually, there is quite a bit that is new. If you look at the C++Builder side of things, it looks as if nothing much has changed. The C++Builder wizards work with an older CORBA standard as provided by Visibroker 4.

If you're looking at the Visibroker side of things, almost everything has changed. For example, the following is how a CORBA server was started previously:

```
CORBA::ORB_var orb = CORBA::ORB_init(argc, argv);
CORBA::BOA_var boa = orb->BOA_init(argc, argv);
BarImpl bar_BarObject("BarObject");
boa->obj_is_ready(&bar_BarObject);
boa->impl_is_ready();
```

And this is how we do it according to the new CORBA specification:

```
CORBA::ORB_var orb = CORBA::ORB_init(argc, argv);
CORBA::Object_var obj =
  orb->resolve_initial_references("RootPOA");
PortableServer::POA_var rootPOA =
  PortableServer::POA::_narrow(obj);
CORBA::PolicyList policies;
policies.length(1);
policies[(CORBA::ULong)0] =
  rootPOA->create_lifespan_policy(PortableServer::PERSISTENT);
PortableServer::POAManager_var poa_mgr =
  rootPOA->the_POAManager();
PortableServer::POA_var myPOA =
  rootPOA->create_POA("bar_poa", poa_mgr, policies);
BarImpl barServant;
PortableServer::ObjectId_var barId =
  PortableServer::string_to_ObjectId("Bar");
myPOA->activate_object_with_id(barId, &barServant);
poa_mgr->activate();
orb->run();
```

Now, would that qualify as different? It would. The problem was that OMG had a very under-specified standard for the BOA. In the 2.3 standard, the OMG made a good specification that can be followed. In fact, if you look at the documentation provided with Visibroker, you will see that it is very much extended in functionality, compared to the version that came with C++Builder 4.

There is too much to go into, but there are a few things you should be aware of. One is the addition of a number of IDL keywords. Another is that the IDL keywords are no longer case sensitive. This means that you can no longer use names that are spelled the same as keywords but with different capitalization. As a temporary measure, you still can escape the name and end up with the same class names, like so:

```
interface _Interface {...};
```

Also, there have been a number of little changes in the validity of names. Refer to the release notes that come with Visibroker 4.

Totally gone is the use of the `ptie` model. Since the architecture of the ORB has changed dramatically, it is no longer supported.

C++Builder Support for CORBA

Let's get down to the nitty gritty of programming CORBA with C++Builder. We will go through all elements in the C++Builder IDE that relate to CORBA and explain what they do.

Environment Options

The environment options for CORBA will be displayed if you select Tools, Environment Options and click the CORBA tab. There are two options, as shown in Figure 20.1.

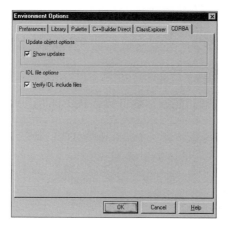

FIGURE 20.1

The Environment Options dialog, showing the CORBA tab.

C++Builder can update your implementation if the underlying IDL is changed. The Show Updates option tells C++Builder whether you want to see the Project Updates dialog when you refresh your implementation classes to reflect changes made in your IDL files. You can update manually through the Project Updates dialog or automatically by unchecking the option.

If you check the Verify IDL Include Files option, C++Builder will check for included IDL files that are not included in the project. If the files are not included, they will not be taken into account when you make or build a project. If implicitly included IDL files are present, that might lead to surprises. If you check the option, and there are any implicitly included IDL files, C++Builder will offer to add them to the project through the Add Included IDL Files dialog.

Debugger Options

The debugger options related to CORBA will be displayed if you select Tools, Debugger Options and click the Language Exceptions tab. In the Language Exceptions tab, shown in Figure 20.2, you can toggle three exception types that have to do with CORBA.

FIGURE 20.2
The Debugger Options dialog, showing the Language Exceptions tab.

The exception types related to CORBA are Visibroker Internal Exceptions, CORBA System Exceptions, and CORBA User Exceptions. You also will see VCL EAbort Exceptions and Microsoft DAO Exceptions, but those two exception types do not relate to CORBA.

In this dialog, you can specify exception types by name and have them ignored by the debugger.

Project Options

The project options related to CORBA will be displayed if you select Project, Options and click the CORBA tab. Several groups of options are available, shown in Figure 20.3. These options deal with the way IDL is translated into stub code by the IDL compiler and what C++Builder should do with the result of the translations.

The Code Generation group of options deals with what type of code you want to generate. We'll discuss the Tie and Virtual Impl. Inheritance options in the "Implementation Models" section, later in this chapter. The Object Wrapper option generates code that acts as a wrapper around the client and server stubs. On the client side, wrapper methods are called before calling the stub and after the stub returns. On the server side, the wrapper methods are called before calling the object implementation and after the object implementation returns. Possible uses for object wrappers are caching results, debugging, and timing operations. Refer to the Visibroker documentation for more details. The Typecode Information option generates code that is needed for clients that use the Dynamic Invocation Interface. If you uncheck this option, you must register a server with the Interface Repository in the OAD yourself. Refer to the Visibroker documentation for more details.

Figure 20.3
The Project Options dialog, showing the CORBA tab.

Next we see a File Extensions group of options, where we can modify the extension of the headers generated by the IDL compiler. There is an Additional IDL option in which you can specify any additional flag for the IDL compiler. Don't remove the -boa switch here; it is used to enable the idl2cpp compiler to generate backward-compatible class names. If you remove the switch, the wizards will not work. Then there is a group of options named IDL Compilation, where you can specify what C++Builder is going to do with the results of the IDL compilation. Finally, there is the Corba.h Options group, where you can specify what extra support you need in the resulting stub code. If you check the Include IR check box, the IDL compiler will add the necessary code that will allow you to use the Interface Repository. If you check the Include DSI check box, the IDL compiler will add code that will allow you to use the Dynamic Skeleton Interface. Refer to the Visibroker documentation for details.

The CORBA Server Wizard

The CORBA Server Wizard is located on the Multitier tab of the New Items dialog, which is displayed by selecting File, New. This is a fairly simple wizard (see Figure 20.4). It lets you specify if the CORBA server process is a Windows application or a console application.

FIGURE 20.4

The CORBA Server Wizard.

In a console application you have the option to add VCL support. The bottom half of the dialog shows a list of IDL files you added. Optionally, the wizard can create a new IDL for you. The result of the wizard is a new project. If you generate a console application, you will notice the reference to a variable called Cerr, with an uppercase *C*. It is defined in one of the Visibroker includes to make their CORBA implementation portable between different compilers. Here is what they did:

```
#if defined(_VIS_STD) && !defined(BUILD_ORBDLL) && !defined(_VIS_STD_NO_DEF)
#define Cout    std::cout
#define Cerr    std::cerr
#define Clog    std::clog
#define Endl    std::endl
#else
#define Cout    cout
#define Cerr    cerr
#define Clog    clog
#define Endl    endl
#endif
```

Exactly. The Visibroker developers are using preprocessor commands to accommodate compilers that do not yet know namespaces as well as compilers that *do* understand them.

The CORBA Client Wizard

This wizard, also on the Multitier tab of the New Items dialog shown in Figure 20.5, looks almost exactly like the previous one.

The exceptions are that you can choose to initialize the BOA, but you cannot create a new IDL file. You can only add them to the project. Again, the result is a new project.

CORBA IDL File Wizard

This wizard, also on the Multitier tab of the New Items dialog, is exactly the same as a lot of others that create files for you. It creates a new file with an .idl extension. That's it.

FIGURE 20.5
The CORBA Client Wizard.

CORBA Object Implementation Wizard

If you do not have an IDL file in your project, this wizard will fail silently. You must have a proper CLASSPATH environment variable for the IDL compiler to work. Make sure that it points to the proper runtime JAR file. Troubleshooting is possible by invoking idl2cpp from the bin directory inside the vbroker directory, where all Visibroker executables are stored.

If you invoke this wizard from the Multitier tab of the New Items dialog, you will see that it first runs the IDL compiler, which can take a while. It probably does that to be able to determine the proper choices in the wizard itself. Then, C++Builder opens the CORBA Object Implementation Wizard dialog, shown in Figure 20.6.

FIGURE 20.6
The CORBA Object Implementation Wizard.

20

In the IDL Interface panel, first pick the name of one of the IDL files in the project. Next, specify the name of the interface for which to make an implementation class. The unit name and the class name are filled in the Implementation Class panel. If we create a server application with VCL enabled and choose Delegation (Tie), we can create a data module in which to place components used in the code to implement the CORBA object.

In the Instantiation panel, we can influence the instantiation of the CORBA object. If we choose to instantiate the object in WinMain, or if we create a console application in `main()`, we can also specify one or more names for the CORBA object. If we specify more than one name, more than one CORBA object of the class we write will be instantiated.

Finally, if we check Show Updates, we continue with the Project Updates dialog.

The Project Updates Dialog

In the Project Updates dialog, shown in Figure 20.7, we see two panels.

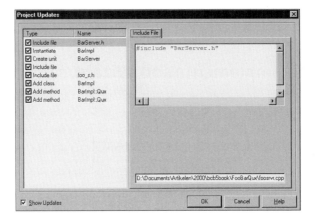

FIGURE 20.7

The Project Updates dialog.

The left panel contains the list of changes, and the right panel contains the details. If you do not want to apply one or more of the proposed changes, you can turn any of them off by unchecking it in the left panel. The label of the Details pane shows what component the detail concerns. Sometimes it is a unit, an include file, or a block of code, and sometimes it shows a definition tab and an implementation tab. This depends on the type of change C++Builder prepared for you. You also can edit the details. Under the Details panel, the filename in which the proposed changes are made is shown. You cannot edit that filename. Clicking OK applies the proposed changes you select in the left panel.

> **NOTE**
>
> If you uncheck the Show Updates box in the wizard, the Project Updates dialog will not reappear. If you want to see it again, you have to re-enable it in the CORBA tab of the Environment Options dialog.

The Use CORBA Object Wizard

We can access this wizard in two ways. The first way is by selecting Edit, Use CORBA Object. Alternatively, we can enable the CORBA toolbar by checking View, Toolbars, CORBA. Then we see an extra toolbar containing three buttons. The leftmost invokes the CORBA Object Implementation Wizard, the center one propagates changes in IDL to your code, optionally showing the Project Updates dialog, and the rightmost one invokes the Use CORBA Object Wizard, shown in Figure 20.8.

This wizard can write the code you need to use a CORBA object from a client. The CORBA Object options lets you select the IDL file in which the interface of the object you want to use is defined. Next you select an interface and specify an object name. That object name is one of the names you used when instantiating the CORBA object while using the CORBA Object Implementation Wizard. It should be one of the names you provided in the list, or it should be one of the CORBA objects you instantiated.

Under the CORBA Object options, there is a set of tabbed options. With them you can select how to use the CORBA object. The first tab is Use in Form.

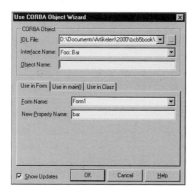

FIGURE 20.8

The Use CORBA Object Wizard, showing the Use in Form tab.

Here you can specify a form name and a property name. C++Builder creates a property and some property code through which you can access the CORBA object. It takes care of binding to the remote CORBA object for you when you use the property for the first time.

The second tab is Use in main(), shown in Figure 20.9. This means that a variable is created for you in main() through which you can access the remote object.

The last tab is Use in Class, shown in Figure 20.10. This makes it possible to wrap access to the remote CORBA object in a class. That is a good thing, because it enables you to glue access to a remote CORBA object to the rest of your code and hide the conversion details in a separate class.

FIGURE 20.9

The Use CORBA Object Wizard, showing the Use in main() tab.

FIGURE 20.10

The Use CORBA Object Wizard, showing the Use in Class tab.

Differences Between C++Builder 4 and C++Builder 5

From the IDE point of view, there is not much difference between C++Builder versions 4 and 5. The layout and functionality of some of the dialogs have changed, but basically it is the same. C++Builder still uses classes for scoping as opposed to namespaces, but that might be a good thing from the standpoint of portability. However, as you might have noticed, the Visibroker components are version 4.0, quite different from the Visibroker version that comes with Delphi 5 and JBuilder 3. Actually, you might get into trouble if you also use JBuilder 3 or Delphi 5 and installed C++Builder 5 most recently. It will replace the Visibroker components and render JBuilder 3 and Delphi 5 CORBA support useless. If you can, upgrade to JBuilder 3.5. It uses the same Visibroker version as C++Builder 5. Delphi 5 users are not yet so lucky. To make Delphi 5 work, again you must have orb_br.dll of the Visibroker version that comes with Delphi 5, rename it orbpbr.dll, and then hexedit orbpas50.dll to point to orbpbr.dll instead of orb_br.dll.

Implementation Models

In C++, there are a number of choices to make for the implementation model, shown in Figure 20.11. Let's assume that our interface has the name Bar and that it lives in the module Foo. If you are browsing through the inheritance interface, you will notice that it hangs together from a number of classes. At a certain point you will find that the skeleton class is derived from three other classes. This is what happens if you specify the boa switch to the idl2cpp compiler. It adds the heavy lined parts in Figure 20.11 to make it backward compatible.

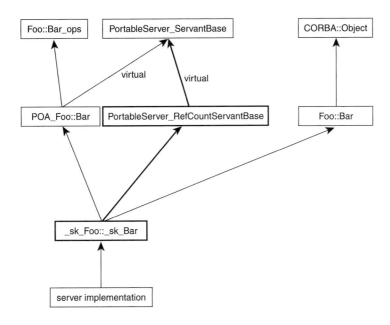

FIGURE 20.11
The object model used to create backward compatibility.

If you remove the switch, you will see that a server object must be inherited from POA_Foo::Bar, and the class you use in the CORBA client still is Foo::Bar. The inheritance diagram shown in Figure 20.12 is much simpler.

Alas, the wizards will not work with this kind of implementation.

What you can see here is that in the new CORBA standard the server implementation class is not derived from CORBA::Object. It is derived from PortableServer_ServantBase. What we see in the ancestor relationships of POA_Foo::Bar is that the PortableServer_ServantBase class is virtually inherited by POA_Foo::Bar. This is what we call a mix-in class. POA_Foo::Bar inherits the methods to implement from Foo::Bar_ops and the CORBA methods from PortableServer_ServantBase.

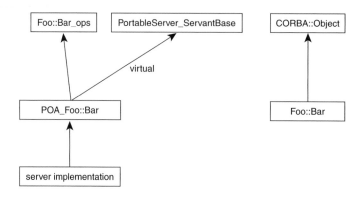

FIGURE 20.12
The object model according to the new CORBA standard.

Inheritance

The inheritance model is the simplest model there is. You must derive your implementation class from the `_sk_Foo::_sk_Bar` class, where the `_sk_` prefix stands for skeleton. The skeleton class itself is derived from the interface class we will use on the client side of the story. That class in turn is publicly derived from `CORBA::Object`. In the new CORBA standard, you derive from `POA_Foo::Bar` directly. In both cases, you must fill in the getter and setter methods of attributes you specified in the interface.

Virtual Implementation Inheritance

In this case, the only difference is that the `Foo::Bar` class is virtually inherited from `CORBA::Object`. This can be useful if you want to mix a CORBA interface into another inheritance hierarchy on the client side. There is at least one other example of using virtual inheritance from `CORBA::Object`. Because the `Foo::Bar` class is the specification of an interface on the client side, you might consider using those classes as interfaces in the Java sense of the word. You might conceive of a client object that needs two or more CORBA client interfaces to be added to its functionality. You derive that class from `Foo::Bar` and `Foo:Fiz`. Now you must use virtual inheritance to refer to the same `CORBA::Object` object in the top of the inheritance tree. Let's say that a client object needs two CORBA objects to operate: `Foo::Bar` and `Foo::Fiz`. If you do not use virtual inheritance, `Foo::Bar` and `Foo::Fiz` refer to two different `CORBA::Object` objects. Using virtual inheritance, you will end up with the famous square inheritance diagram, referencing one `CORBA::Object` object.

Delegation Model (Tie)

If you choose Delegation Model (Tie), you will use the delegation model on the server side. This means that the CORBA side is self contained, and you provide the functionality in a class that can have nothing to do with CORBA. You will be provided with a template class that contains a pointer to the `template` argument. Any operation is forwarded through the pointer to your implementation class. Your implementation class should provide all operations defined in the IDL interface you specified. When instantiating the server object, you must provide the `template` class with a pointer to the class that really implements the getter and setter methods in the IDL interface.

This implementation model is the most elegant model to retrofit a CORBA interface onto an existing class you already have. You might want to consider using it all the time, because the delegation model lets you split the CORBA server implementation into a separate CORBA part and an implementation part. Any changes in the CORBA implementation besides a change in the interface will not affect your implementation at all.

Poor Man's CORBA

If you do not own the Enterprise version of C++Builder, JBuilder, or Delphi, you might conclude that CORBA is not for you. Actually, you still can use CORBA. What you lack is the support for CORBA in the IDE. But you still can get a developer license of Visibroker 4, which is fully functional. If you specify the right switches, you will be able to generate the necessary stub classes and build CORBA clients and servers from there. Then again, it is possible to add batch files to your project group that let you automate that particular part of building servers and clients.

In fact, if you want to use the much simpler inheritance graph of the new CORBA standard and the new way of registering and binding to CORBA objects, even owners of the Enterprise version end up using the poor man's CORBA approach.

Summary

We went into C++Builder support quite well, but we barely scratched the surface of CORBA. For example, I did not discuss naming services, event services, gatekeepers, IIOP, activators…. There is a lot more to know about CORBA than the things I told you here. You might be tempted to look into those things. You might try downloading a documentation set from the Borland Web site. It is dry reading, but I can assure you that you will find out a lot about CORBA.

Microsoft Office Integration

Jay Banks

IN THIS CHAPTER

- **Overview of Integration with Microsoft Office**
- **How to Integrate**
- **Integrating with Word**
- **Integrating with Excel**
- **Using C++Builder 5's Server Components**
- **Going Further**

The integration of Microsoft Office with C++Builder offers a number of possibilities for useful applications, from simple utilities to assist day-to-day work in the office to large program suites that simply employ Microsoft Office as a collection of useful word processing and spreadsheet components. This chapter outlines some of the reasons to integrate with Microsoft Office and how to do so and offers some suggestions of applications that could be developed by integrating with Microsoft Office.

Overview of Integration with Microsoft Office

One of the big benefits in using an office-type package is the amount of effort it saves. I for one would like to have even a tiny percentage of the money saved through cut and paste alone.

With Microsoft Office, it is possible to make things even easier for the user by using Office's built-in programming language—Visual Basic for Applications—to create shortcuts and automate common tasks. The cut-and-paste of today can be the automatic paragraph swap of tomorrow.

Besides the option to improve Microsoft Office to suit your own needs, things get even more interesting when we add the fact that Office is also an automation server. Those nice people at Microsoft left all the hooks and eyes in place for us to take control of Office and make it do what we want from within our own programs.

This means that if we need to provide our programs with word processing power, it's not a problem. We just use the Office programs that the user already has installed. We can launch Office for them (or at least something that looks like it), or we can quietly take hold of it and use it in the background. If you ever thought that you'd like to be able to get your program reports in a standard format, you can. Word may not beat TQuickRep for ease of programming, but you can send a Word document via email with much more confidence that the recipient will be able to read it.

By integrating our own applications with Microsoft Office, we gain three major benefits:

1. Access to established programs and interfaces to enhance the features of our own programs.

    If you need to give your users a word processor or spreadsheet as part of your own program, you no longer need to write your own or obtain a third-party component. Your users get to work with programs they're already used to, and they'll appreciate the convenience this offers them.

2. Access to common documents and document formats.

    Throw away those file format documents. Instead of trying to locate the relevant information on how to read and write from common files, you can make use of the expert code already written to do it by making use of the application itself.

3. Task automation.

If you've ever needed to perform the same operation on a number of documents, you know how much effort is involved in performing the task, opening the next file, repeating the task, opening the next file, and so on. With automation, we can prepare the operation we're going to carry out, choose the files we're going to work with, and then set it running.

How to Integrate

Now that we know why we might want to integrate with Office, we need to come to grips with the question of how to do so. Fortunately, Microsoft Office publishes a number of interfaces to itself, either as OLE automation servers or as COM objects. C++Builder gives us two ways to get to these services quickly and relatively painlessly—the `TOleContainer` component and automation objects.

The choice of which method to use depends entirely on what you need Office to do. `TOleContainer` is the best choice for when you need to actually embed the Office application into your own so that it appears as part of your application. On the other hand, if you want to take more control, use `OleVariant` to obtain automation objects implemented in Office.

Using `TOleContainer`

`TOleContainer` is the easiest way to integrate Office into your own applications. Create a new application and place a copy of `TOleContainer` in the middle of the form. Resize it so that there is a border of about 50 pixels on all four sides of the control.

Now double-click on `OleContainer`. This will launch the Insert Object dialog, which should look something like that shown in Figure 21.1. In this instance, I've scrolled down until the Microsoft Office objects are shown.

Select the Microsoft Word document from the dialog box and click OK.

Now that we've finished preparing, build and run the program. You should see a plain form with an empty panel in its center. Double-click on the panel, and after a brief interlude your form should be transformed. The Word menus appear at the top of the form, and the panel changes into a Word document. When you're finished experimenting, close the program and return to C++Builder.

Right-click on the `OleContainer` and select the Delete Object menu item. This will unlink your application from Word. Beneath the `OleContainer`, add three buttons named `Button_Word`, `Button_Excel`, and `Button_PPoint` and labeled `Word`, `Excel`, and `PowerPoint`, respectively.

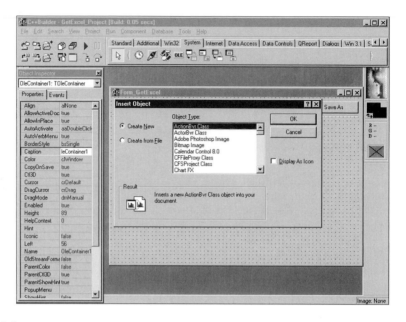

FIGURE 21.1

C++Builder's Insert Object dialog.

Add the code in Listing 21.1 to their OnClick methods. In the TOleContainer folder on the CD-ROM that accompanies this book, you will find a sample project TOleContainer_Demo.bpr that provides the code used in this example.

LISTING 21.1   Word, Excel, and PowerPoint Code

```
//-- Code for the "Word" Button
void __fastcall TForm_OleContainer::Button_WordClick(TObject *Sender)
{
    OleContainer1->CreateObject("Word.Document",false);
    OleContainer1->DoVerb(ovShow);
}

//-- Code for the "Excel" Button
void __fastcall TForm_OleContainer::Button_ExcelClick(TObject *Sender)
{
    OleContainer1->CreateObject("Excel.sheet",false);
    OleContainer1->DoVerb(ovShow);
}

//-- Code for the "PowerPoint" Button
void __fastcall TForm_OleContainer::Button_PPointClick(TObject *Sender)
```

Microsoft Office Integration

CHAPTER 21

831

21

MICROSOFT
OFFICE
INTEGRATION

LISTING 21.1   Continued

```
{
    OleContainer1->CreateObject("Powerpoint.show",false);
    OleContainer1->DoVerb (ovShow);
}
```

Once you've added the code, build and run the program. This time if you double-click on the panel, it throws an exception with the message `Operation not allowed on an empty OLE container`. Select OK to resume.

Instead of clicking on the panel, click one of the three buttons below it. With Excel and Word, the panel becomes an appropriate document and the form gains the application's menu bar as shown in Figure 21.2.

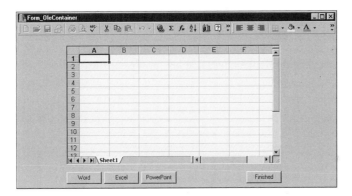

FIGURE 21.2
The OleContainer program, demonstrating Excel.

Clicking the PowerPoint button changes the panel to an empty slide but doesn't update the menus. Why? Microsoft implemented PowerPoint differently from Word and Excel. This is just one of those things you need to be aware of.

Using Automation

Using automation objects is a more powerful method for integration than `TOleContainer`. You gain a great deal more control over each object and its properties. The only drawback is that with increased control the objects are more complex to use and program for.

Each automation object has a number of properties and methods that it makes available. Once you have created an automation object, you then have access to its properties and methods, much in the same way that you have access to a control's properties and methods once you have a pointer to it.

C++Builder provides two main ways for using automation: type libraries and OLE automation objects. Type libraries are library files that contain descriptions of the interfaces that an application makes available and any types, structures, and classes that are used to exploit them. Type libraries give you the benefit of type checking, but you need to either create a new type library using the Import Type Library menu or obtain them from another source before using them and be prepared for a performance hit when you're compiling.

OLE automation objects rely on the developer knowing the names of the various interfaces and the properties and methods they make available. OLE automation objects don't have the benefit of type checking and rely on you having some form of documentation for the application you're automating. However, they are much faster to compile because they are not using the additional source and library files needed by type libraries.

For simplicity, we're going to use OLE automation for most of this chapter. We'll also look at the facilities offered by C++Builder for using type libraries. This means that you'll need a good source of documentation. Fortunately, Office comes with its own built-in documentation.

Launch Word, and launch the Visual Basic editor (press Alt+F11 or use the Tools, Macro, Visual Basic Editor menu item). This will display the Visual Basic editor, which contains the help files for Word's Visual Basic interface, providing you've installed the option. If you haven't, now would be a good time. Type Application into the index, and locate the description of the Word Application object. You should get something that looks like Figure 21.3.

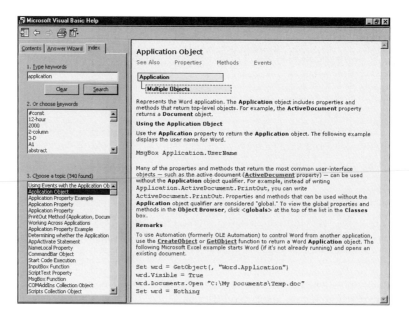

FIGURE 21.3

An example from the Microsoft Office help file.

Microsoft Office Integration

CHAPTER 21

833

21

MICROSOFT
OFFICE
INTEGRATION

You can use this to obtain the properties, methods, and events for the object you're examining, as well as the usual useful information. What's helpful is that this works for all of the Microsoft Office applications, so when you need information about objects for Office, you can get it here.

Using Variants and Automation Objects

In C++Builder, variants make using automation very simple. Not only can they contain automation objects, variants also have a number of routines to make using an automation object easy.

The methods most useful in obtaining and manipulating automation objects are

- `CreateObject()`
- `GetActiveObject()`
- `OleFunction()`
- `OleProcedure()`
- `OlePropertyGet()`
- `OlePropertySet()`

`CreateObject()` and `GetActiveObject()` are used to create and obtain an active automation object, respectively. The remaining functions essentially do what they say they will. It is also worth pointing out that `OleFunction()`, `OleProcedure()`, `OlePropertyGet()`, and `OlePropertySet()` are essentially wrappers for the `Exec()` method.

`Exec()` is used by C++Builder to execute a procedure or function or to retrieve or set a property value. To do this, it relies on four classes to access the desired automation feature:

- `Function()`
- `Procedure()`
- `PropertyGet()`
- `PropertySet()`

The `Function()` class is used to define functions, `PropertyGet()` to obtain property values, and so on. These classes are defined in advance of their use by `Exec()` and must be cleared using their `ClearArgs()` method before they can be reused. Let's take a brief look at this in use, before moving on to looking at some applications in more detail.

Create a new application, place a button on the form, name it `Button_LaunchWord`, and label it Launch Word. Add the code in Listing 21.2 to the button's `OnClick` method. This example is provided on the accompanying CD-ROM. The project, `automation_objects.bpr`, can be found in the `AutomationObj` folder.

LISTING 21.2   Launching Word

```
void __fastcall TForm_Automation::Button_LaunchWordClick(TObject *Sender)
{
    Variant word_app;
    Variant word_docs;
    Variant word_this_document;
    Variant word_range;

    word_app = Variant::CreateObject("word.application");
    word_docs = word_app.OlePropertyGet("documents");

    word_docs.OleProcedure("Add");

    word_app.OlePropertySet("Visible", (Variant)true);
}
```

The same code built using `Exec()` would look like the contents of Listing 21.3. Create a new button named `Button_LaunchWordExec`, and label it Launch with Exec, and then add the code in Listing 21.3 to its `OnClick` method.

LISTING 21.3   Launching Word Using `Exec()`

```
void __fastcall TForm_Automation::Button_LaunchWordExecClick(TObject *Sender)
{
    Variant word_app;
    Variant word_docs;
    Variant word_this_document;
    Variant word_range;

    Function Documents("Documents"); //-- Define the Documents function
    Function AddDocument("Add");      //-- Define the add documents function
    PropertySet Visibility("Visible"); //-- Define the visibility property

    word_app = Variant::CreateObject("word.application");
    word_docs = word_app.Exec(Documents);

    word_docs.Exec(AddDocument);

    Visibility << True;
    word_app.Exec (Visibility);
}
```

Figure 21.4 shows the `LaunchWord` program in action.

Microsoft Office Integration

CHAPTER 21

835

21

MICROSOFT
OFFICE
INTEGRATION

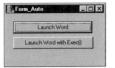

FIGURE 21.4

The LaunchWord *program in action.*

One of the remaining things is to ensure that the utilcls.h library is included in your code. Using variants for automation employs TAutoArgs, which is defined in utilcls.h, and as long as you have the following line as one of your includes, then there shouldn't be any problem.

```
#include <utilcls.h>
```

Build and run the program, and when the form appears, press the Launch Word button. This will start a new copy of Word (whether you're currently already running Word or not) with a blank document.

Guarding Against Macro Viruses with Automation

One of the strengths of automation is that it allows the developer a great deal of flexibility and eliminates the need to distract the user by requiring him to respond a lot. The downside of this is that if you open an Office document that contains a macro virus, then the office application assumes you know what you're doing and doesn't ask to make sure you want to open the document.

If you're planning to use automation to open documents, then contamination from macro viruses is a real risk. Make sure you've got an up-to-date antivirus program. Office will let you open an infected file, but a good antivirus program will prevent your program from opening the document and can save you from a great deal of embarrassment and expense.

Using Word Basic

When Microsoft originally released Word 97, they included the facility to write simple programs to extend its functionality through a new language—Word Basic. While this has been replaced in Word 98 onward by Visual Basic for Applications, Microsoft has left a working interface to Word Basic in the later editions of Word.

This interface is available through the word.basic automation object, and while it does not offer the same range of functions as VBA, there are occasions when it is worthwhile, particularly if you're concerned about the version of Office that your target audience will be using.

If you think your users may be using Office 97, you may be better off using Word Basic over VBA for compatibility. Your more up-to-date users will still be able to use your software, and there's no disadvantage for users of the older software.

Integrating with Word

Microsoft Office is a large and complex piece of software that allows developers access to some of its internal interfaces. This section presents an overview of how to use some of those interfaces to perform simple tasks such as loading, saving, and creating Word documents.

Collections

As the name suggests, a collection is used to store groups of objects in Word. Each collection will have two key resources that make it useful: the count property and the item method. The count property tells you how many objects are in the collection, and the item method is used to fetch references to a required item, either by number or by name (if the object has one). Several collections have other properties and methods that provide additional and frequently useful tools. An excellent example is the documents collection and its add method that creates a new document.

The Application Object

The application object is the nerve center for Microsoft Word and is the starting point for any program that needs to use Word. After you create or obtain the application object, it is possible to obtain references to the collections or properties needed to make Word perform as required.

There are two ways to obtain an application object for Word. Either create a new instance or obtain a reference to an existing one. Variant objects provide two methods for obtaining an application: CreateObject() and GetActiveObject(). CreateObject() is used to create new instances of automation objects, and GetActiveObject() attempts to obtain the reference to an existing automation object. If either call fails, it raises an EoleSysError exception.

To obtain a Word automation object, use the program ID word.application. When you are first trying to obtain an application object, it is often desirable to use an existing (open) copy when possible. This avoids having several copies of the same application open one after the other, and it can speed up your application because you're not waiting for part of Office to load.

Create a new application and add a button to it named Button_LaunchWord, with the label Launch Word. Add the code in Listing 21.4 to the OnClick method of the button.

The source code for this example is provided in the project example3.bpr, which can be found in the LaunchWord folder on the accompanying CD-ROM.

LISTING 21.4 A System-Friendly LaunchWord

```
void __fastcall TForm1::Button_LaunchWordClick(TObject *Sender)
{
try
    {
        my_word = Variant::GetActiveObject("word.application");
    }
    catch (...)
    {
        //-- We've failed in our attempt to get a current copy of word.
        //-- Create a new one!
        try
        {
            my_word = Variant::CreateObject("word.application");
        }
        catch (...)
        {
            //-- We've not been able to create a new word object
            Application->MessageBox("Unable to obtain Word
automation object","Error:",MB_OK|MB_ICONERROR);
        }
    }
    my_word.OlePropertySet("Visible", (Variant)True);
}
```

Also, add a variable to the form's class:

```
Variant  my_word;
```

Build and run the program, and when the form appears, press the Launch Word button. If you already have Word open, nothing will appear to happen (we haven't done anything with the automation object yet). However, if Word isn't open, then when the exception is thrown, C++Builder will come to a halt to tell you about it. This doesn't happen when you run the program as a standalone.

Working with Documents

Now that we've opened a copy of Word, we need to be able to do something useful with it. Naturally enough, we'll look at working with documents.

Once you've obtained an interface to Word, you now have access to its documents collection. This is an object in its own right and contains properties and methods for listing the open documents, opening and creating documents, and so on.

The `documents` collection can be obtained from the application object as follows:

```
my_documents = my_word.OlePropertyGet("Documents");
```

We'll add this to our application in a moment.

Creating a New Document

The `Add` method is used to create new documents in Word. This method has a number of optional parameters that can be used to enhance the way it behaves.

To create a normal blank document, the `Add()` method is all that is required. To create a new document using a template, simply provide the name of the template to be used. Add a new button to the application and name it `Button_CreateDocument`, set its label to Create Document, then add the code in Listing 21.5 to its `OnClick` method.

LISTING 21.5   Creating a Document

```
void __fastcall TForm1::Button_CreateDocumentClick(TObject *Sender)
{
    Variant  this_doc;
    long  doc_count;


    my_docs  = my_word.OlePropertyGet("Documents");
    this_doc  = my_docs.OleFunction("Add");

    doc_count  = my_docs.OlePropertyGet("Count");
    ShowMessage((AnsiString)"there are " + doc_count + " document(s) ");
}
```

While we're making changes, add the following variable to the form's class:

```
Variant  my_docs;
```

Rebuild and run the application. The result should look like Figure 21.5. Click the Create Document button; this should now throw an exception with the message `Variant does not reference an automation object`. Before we can attempt to do anything with Word, we must make sure that we've actually obtained a reference to it. Allow the application to continue, and this time press the Launch Word button. Then press the Create Document button. A new document is added in Word and you are told how many documents you currently have open, frequently a useful piece of information.

Microsoft Office Integration

CHAPTER 21

839

21

MICROSOFT
OFFICE
INTEGRATION

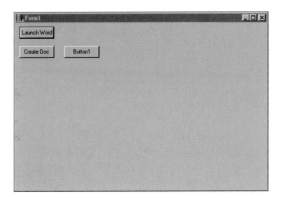

FIGURE 21.5
The program so far.

Using the Save Method for Documents

Now that we've created a document, the next thing to do is to save it. There are several ways to do this, with one of the save methods, or using the document's own SaveAs method.

There are three possible ways to use the save method: to save an individual document, to save all current documents, or to save a version of a document. This depends on which object actually uses the method. A document or version object saves a copy of itself, and a documents collection saves all open documents.

We'll demonstrate using the save function by adding a new Button_QuickSave button labeled Quick Save to our form and placing the code in Listing 21.6 in its OnClick method.

LISTING 21.6   Saving a Document

```
void __fastcall Tform1::Button_QuickSaveClick(TObject *Sender)
{
    Variant  this_doc;

    this_doc  = my_word.OlePropertyGet("ActiveDocument");
    this_doc.OleProcedure ("Save");
}
```

Build and run the application, and then run through the cycle of launching Word and creating a new document. Then press the Quick Save button. Word should show its Save As dialog, because the document doesn't have a name yet. Close the application and return to C++Builder.

Add a button named `Button_QuickSaveAs` with the label Quick Save As, and place the code in Listing 21.7 in its `OnClick` event.

LISTING 21.7   Saving a Document "As"

```
void __fastcall TForm1::Button_QuickSaveAsClick(TObject *Sender)
{
    Variant  this_doc;

    this_doc  = my_word.OlePropertyGet("ActiveDocument");
    this_doc.OleProcedure("SaveAs",(Variant)"c:\\saved_as. doc");
}
```

Build the application and execute it. This time, when you've launched Word and created a new document, if you click the Quick Save As button, Word will save the document using the filename we provided in the `SaveAs` command.

The `SaveAs` method has more parameters than just the filename, so if you want to use all of them, you may want to consider using the `Exec()` method directly (`OleProcedure()` is a wrapper for the `Exec()` method).

Opening a Document

Now that we can create and save documents, we will want to be able to retrieve them later. This can be done with the `documents` collection and its `Open` method.

Once the name of a document is known, it can be loaded using the open method. Add a new button named `Button_QuickOpen` to your application, and set its label to `Quick Open`. Now we'll try to reload the document we created earlier.

Add the code in Listing 21.8 to the button, then build and execute the program. After you've started Word, click the Quick Open button. Word will load the document you saved earlier.

LISTING 21.8   Loading a Document

```
void __fastcall Tform1::Button_QuickOpen(TObject *Sender)
{
    Variant    this_doc;
    my_docs    = my_word.OlePropertyGet("Documents");

    this_doc= my_docs.OleFunction("Open",(Variant)"c:\\saved_as.doc");
}
```

Getting Text from Word

So far, we've looked at the basic operations of Word: creating, saving, and opening documents. It's now time to start looking at something more useful and see how to extract information from Word. We're going to create an application that will open a document, extract a list of words from it, and create a new document containing a sorted list of words.

The keys to extracting words are the `range` object and the `words` collection. The `range` object specifies which portion of the document is to be used (in our case, all of it). When this has been set, we can obtain the collection of words it holds.

A `range` object works by setting the start and end character positions of the text it covers, but if you don't specify the start and end, the entire document will be selected. When you need to select a specific part of a document, you can provide the start and end points yourself (for example, to select the first 20 characters of a document), or you can use the fact that many objects possess `range` objects themselves. Listing 21.9 shows some code snippets that are included only to demonstrate the different ways to select a range.

LISTING 21.9   Selecting a Range Versus a Paragraph

```
//-- Obtain entire document range
my_range = my_docs.OleFunction("Range");

//-- Obtain first 33 characters
my_range = my_docs.OleFunction("Range",(Variant) 0, Variant(33));

//-- Obtain 2nd Paragraph
my_paras = my_docs.OlePropertyGet("Paragraphs");
my_para  = my_paras.OleFunction("Item",(Variant) 2);
p_range  = my_para.OlePropertyGet("Range");
my_range = my_docs.OleFunction("Range", p_range.OlePropertyGet("Start"),
                                        p_range.OlePropertyGet("End"));
```

Once we've selected a range within our document, the next step is to obtain its `words` collection. This is simply a matter of getting the `words` property from the range.

As soon as we have a `words` collection, we can obtain a list of the words held in a document. We'll do that now by creating a program to obtain an interface to Word's active document. Create a new application with a list box (leaving the default name) and a button named `Button_LoadWords` with the label Load Words, and add the code in Listing 21.10 to the button's `OnClick` method.

This example can be found in the `example_4.bpr` project, which can be found in the `LoadWords` folder on the accompanying CD-ROM.

LISTING 21.10   LoadWords Code

```
void __fastcall Tform1::Button_LoadWords(TObject *Sender)
{
    Variant  my_doc;
    Variant  my_word;
    long  word_count;
long  index;

    try
{
    my_word = Variant::GetActiveObject("word.application");
}
catch (...)
{
    //-- Word must not be open - show a message and quit!
    ShowMessage("Please open word and load a document and retry");
    return;
}

//-- Obtain the current document in word
    my_doc     = my_word.OlePropertyGet("ActiveDocument");

    //-- Skip over the 'range' business as we're getting all of the
    //-- words in the document…
    my_words   = my_doc.OlePropertyGet("Words");

    //-- Get the number of words in the document
    word_count = my_words.OlePropertyGet("Count");

    //-- And copy them all into our list box
    for (index=1;index<word_count;index++)
    {
        ListBox1->Items->Append(my_words.OleFunction("Item",
                          (Variant)index));


    }
}
```

Build and execute the application, then launch Word. Type a few random words into the document and then click the Load Words button on the application. The list box should fill with the words you've typed in.

You'll notice that besides the words themselves, you've also picked up punctuation and some control characters. Word likes to treat these items as though they were actual words, which can be be useful or not, depending on what you're trying to do.

Microsoft Office Integration

CHAPTER 21

843

21

MICROSOFT
OFFICE
INTEGRATION

If you try to use the program on a large document, you'll also notice that it takes a long time to get all of the words. This is an unfortunate side effect of the method we're using. It isn't really surprising that when you ask for words one at a time, getting them takes a while.

Fortunately, Word itself gives us all of the facilities we need to avoid stepping through entire documents word by word to find paragraphs or other markers. With a `selection` object, we can access the entire body of the text as a single item and copy it into a standard C++Builder control, such as the `RichEdit` control as shown in Figure 21.6.

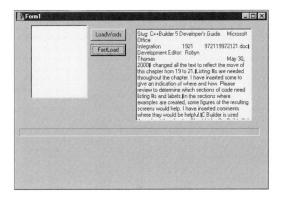

FIGURE 21.6

The display shows the contents of the `RichEdit` *control with the document holding this chapter.*

Return to the application, and add a new button named `Button_FastLoad` with the label Fast Load, and a `RichEdit` control to the form. Add the code shown in Listing 21.11 to the button's `OnClick` method. When you next run the program, click on the Fast Load button. In a very short time you'll see the contents of your Word document appear in the `RichEdit` box. Once you have the text in C++Builder, it is much easier and faster to extract all of the words from the document by stepping through each word manually.

LISTING 21.11 `FastLoad` Code

```
void __fastcall TForm1::Button_FastLoadClick(TObject *Sender)
{
    Variant     my_doc;
    Variant     my_word_app;
    Variant     my_words;
    Variant     my_selection;

    try
    {
```

LISTING 21.11   Continued

```
    my_word_app = Variant::GetActiveObject("word.application");
}
catch (...)
{
    //-- Word must not be open - show a message and quit!
    ShowMessage("Please open word and load a document and retry");
    return;
}

//-- Obtain the current document in word
my_doc    = my_word_app.OlePropertyGet("ActiveDocument");

//-- Select all of the text in the document
my_doc.OleProcedure("Select");
my_selection = my_word_app.OlePropertyGet("Selection");

RichEdit1->Clear();
RichEdit1->Text = my_selection.OlePropertyGet("Text");
}
```

Putting Objects into Word Documents

We've now covered the basic process of extracting text from Word, so one of the next tasks is to begin putting text back into Word. Now that we've obtained a list of words, we'll create a new program that creates a new document and puts the words back in alphabetical order. We're going to do this by sticking with our good friend, the range object.

Inserting Text into Word

There are two main ways to add text to a Word document: the InsertBefore and InsertAfter methods, which add text to the beginning or end of the current range as their respective names indicate. They also stretch the range to include the new text. This means that you need to be aware of how you want to add the lines to the text and select the right method.

Inserting Objects into Word

It is also possible to insert items such as new paragraphs, page breaks, and other formatting information. Other methods exist for adding tables, images, and so on. We'll explore adding tables and text to documents.

We've briefly mentioned that adding text to Word makes use of ranges, and adding other items to Word is very similar. The only differences are that instead of using the range object, we use the collection that the new item will eventually belong to, and the Add method will replace the current range unless it has been collapsed. Collapsing a range just means that start and end points are consolidated at either the start or end of the range, which prevents accidents when removing text you'd rather hang on to.

Code to create a new table at the end of a document is seen in Listing 21.12.

LISTING 21.12   Creating a New Table

```
Long    num_rows = 5;
long    num_columns   = 3;

//-- Get the range
my_doc    = my_word.OlePropertyGet("ActiveDocument");
my_range  = my_doc.OleFunction("Range");

//-- Collapse the range
my_range.OleProcedure("Collapse",(Variant)0);

//-- Insert the table
my_tables   = my_range.OlePropertyGet("Tables");
my_table    = my_tables.OleFunction("Add",my_range,(Variant)num_rows,
➥(Variant)num_columns);
```

This code grabs the range for the active document and collapses it so that the insert point becomes the end of the range. Either omit the zero or replace it with 1 (one) to change the insert point to the start of the range. It also adds a new `table` object to the `tables` collection. Note that the range is used as a parameter within the `Add` function. We're telling the `Add` method where to place the table, not directly adding to the range itself.

Creating the Vocabulary Program

Earlier we mentioned that we'd be looking at a program to get words from a document and put them back in a new document. This is the Vocabulary program, shown in Figure 21.7. The Vocabulary program can be found in the `VocabA` folder on the accompanying CD-ROM. The project filename is `vocab_proj.bpr`.

This program loads a Word document, grabs its entire contents into an `AnsiString`, and then extracts the words by looking for spaces and other word breaks. Once it has the words, it relies on a sorted list box to remove any duplicates (duplicate words should clump together in the list), and then it builds a table to export the words. This is the part of the program we're really interested in (see Listing 21.13).

One of the other things that the program does is format the table so that there is a heading column with the name of the file that the words were taken from. This makes use of the `cells` collection that belongs to the table. Each cell can be accessed from the table using its row and column number (starting at 1, not 0). The cell object has a merge method, which it uses to merge from a start cell (the calling cell) to a destination cell. In this case, we merge the top four cells into one to create a header.

FIGURE 21.7

The Vocabulary program.

Each cell has its own range, and this range can be used just like any other range. You want recursive table inserts, where the top-left cell of each table contains a new 2×2 table? Not a problem. The only problem with this setup is that to enter text into a cell, you need to obtain a reference to it and get its range. This is more of a slight annoyance than a problem, but lots of them together could stack up.

LISTING 21.13   Inserting Words into a Table

```
void __fastcall TVocabForm::ReportWordsFromList(Variant doc,TListBox *lb)
{
    Variant    my_tables;
    Variant    this_range;
    Variant    this_table;
    Variant    start_cell;
    Variant    end_cell;
    Variant    cell_range;

    long    num_columns = 4;
    long    num_rows = (lb->Items->Count+num_columns-1)/num_columns;
    long    words;
    long    this_column;
    long    this_row;
```

Microsoft Office Integration

CHAPTER 21

847

21

MICROSOFT
OFFICE
INTEGRATION

LISTING 21.13   Continued

```
    Procedure InsertAfter("InsertAfter");    //-- Exec Procedure - InsertAfter

    //-- Set the range of the object
    this_range = doc.OleFunction("Range");

//-- Obtain the tables collection for the selected range
    my_tables = this_range.OlePropertyGet("Tables");

    //-- Create a new table to contain a header line + all words...
    this_table    = my_tables.OleFunction("Add",this_range,
                                    (Variant)(num_rows+1),
                                    (Variant)(num_columns));
    start_cell    = this_table.OleFunction("Cell",(Variant)1,(Variant)1);
    end_cell    = this_table.OleFunction("Cell",(Variant)1,
                                    (Variant)num_columns);
    start_cell.OleProcedure("Merge",end_cell);

    //-- Set the title
    cell_range    = start_cell.OlePropertyGet("Range");

    cell_range.Exec(InsertAfter << "Words from '" + OpenDialog1->FileName +
➡"'");

    this_column    = 1;
    this_row    = 2;

    //-- Now copy in the words...
    for (words=0;words<lb->Items->Count;words++)
    {
        start_cell    = this_table.OleFunction("Cell",(Variant)this_row,
                                        (Variant)this_column);
        cell_range    = start_cell.OlePropertyGet("Range");

        InsertAfter.ClearArgs();
        cell_range.Exec(InsertAfter << lb->Items->Strings[words]);

        this_column++;
        if (this_column>num_columns)
        {
            this_row++;
            this_column=1;
        }
    }
}
```

Integrating with Excel

Now it's time to move to one of the other applications in Microsoft Office—Excel. Like Word, Excel exposes most of its internal workings as automation objects, and like Word, it makes use of collections to store sections of its documents.

You know from experience that Word and Excel are two very different programs to use and are also very different to program for. Fortunately, many of the processes used in programming for Word can be used with Excel and, even when a comparable process does not exist, Excel is still relatively friendly to use.

Obtaining the Application Object

Obtaining Excel's application object uses an identical process to that for getting Word's application object. The only difference is the name of the automation object we're requesting.

For Excel, we need to obtain `excel.application` instead of `word.application`. To do so, use the following command:

```
Variant my_excel = Variant::CreateObject("excel.application");
```

Working with Workbooks

In Word, the largest collection is the document, which holds all of the text, tables, images, and so on. Excel treats things slightly differently and allows you to use workbooks, which are made up of a number of worksheets. Worksheets hold all of the text, formulae, and so on for Excel.

Workbooks can be obtained in one of two ways. We can ask the application object for the `workbooks` collection or the `activeworkbook` property. The collection will give you the whole range of workbook functionality (add, open, close, and so on), and `activeworkbook` gets you only the access to the current workbook.

Creating New Workbooks

Creating a new workbook relies as always on the `Add` method in the `workbooks` collection. You can rely on the default document template or, if you have something more exotic in mind, you can give the `Add` method the name of a template to use when you're creating the workbook. As each workbook is created, Excel assigns it a name, usually along the lines of Book 1, Book 2, and so on. This is useful when saving the document later.

The new workbook will be created with a number of blank worksheets, according to the current value of the `SheetsInNewWorkbook` property of the application object. This is demonstrated in Listing 21.14. The source code for this example can be found in the `GetExcel` folder on the accompanying CD-ROM, in the `GetExcel_Project.bpr` project.

Microsoft Office Integration

CHAPTER 21

849

21

MICROSOFT
OFFICE
INTEGRATION

LISTING 21.14   Creating an Excel Workbook

```
void __fastcall TForm_GetExcel::Button_NewWorkbookClick(TObject *Sender)
{
    Variant     all_workbooks;
    Variant     my_workbook;

    //-- Get workbooks collection
    all_workbooks    = my_excel.OlePropertyGet("Workbooks");

    //-- Set number of worksheets to 1
    my_excel.OlePropertySet("SheetsInNewWorkbook",(Variant)1);

    //-- Create a new workbook
    my_workbook        = all_workbooks.OleFunction("Add");
}
```

Saving Workbooks

A workbook can be saved in a number of ways, the most common being the Save and SaveAs methods. These methods behave in a similar way to their counterparts in Word, but with a subtle difference. Because Excel workbooks are created with names, they can be saved without asking the user to provide a filename. The save functions don't ask the user to provide a filename. They make do with whatever has been provided. The Save function is demonstrated in Listing 21.15.

LISTING 21.15   Saving the Active Workbook

```
void __fastcall TForm_GetExcel::Button_SaveClick(TObject *Sender)
{
    Variant  my_workbook = my_excel.OlePropertyGet("ActiveWorkbook");

    my_workbook.OleProcedure ("Save");
}
```

The SaveAs function behaves similarly to the Save function. In fact, if you use SaveAs without providing any parameters, it behaves just like the Save method. However, you can provide parameters to control how and where the document is saved. In its simplest form, the SaveAs method allows you to save a document using a filename you want, rather than the current or default document name. The SaveAs function is shown in Listing 21.16.

LISTING 21.16   SaveAs for Workbooks

```
void __fastcall TForm_GetExcel::Button_SaveAsClick(TObject *Sender)
{
    Procedure SaveAs("SaveAs");
    Variant  my_workbook = my_excel.OlePropertyGet("ActiveWorkbook");

    my_workbook.Exec(SaveAs << "C:\\my_file.xls");
}
```

Opening a Workbook

Being able to create new documents and save them leads naturally to the question of how to re-open workbooks and retrieve your work. This is also similar to the Word method and uses the open method of the workbooks collection. Once you know the name of the document, it is simply a question of passing the filename to the method (see Listing 21.17).

LISTING 21.17   Opening a Workbook

```
void __fastcall TForm_GetExcel::Button_OpenClick(TObject *Sender)
{
    Variant    all_workbooks = my_excel.OlePropertyGet("workbooks");
    Procedure Open("Open");

    if (OpenDialog1->Execute())
    {

        all_workbooks.Exec(Open << OpenDialog1->FileName);
    }
}
```

Just as in Word, the open method can be used as an import tool, because it will read any file into Excel that Excel would normally be able to read. If you're planning to work with a large number of text files, it will probably be worth considering the OpenText method. This method loads a text file into Excel and attempts to parcel it into cells ready for use. While similar to the regular open method, OpenText is for importing text files and has a number of optional parameters for that task. Check your help files for details.

Using the Active (Current) Workbook

The application object keeps track of which workbook is currently being used by Excel and makes it available as the activeworkbook property. Once you have a workbook, the next thing is to select a worksheet from either the worksheets collection or the activesheet property. If you're not using the currently active worksheet, you need to call its activate method to ensure that the worksheet you want to use becomes the active one.

21

Then we can begin to extract information from Excel. To do this, we use the range object. The range object remains highly versatile and can be used to represent a collection of cells from an entire worksheet down to a single cell. range is demonstrated in Listing 21.18.

> **NOTE**
>
> One thing to be careful with is the way that Microsoft has named its different properties and objects. You will find that many objects are obtained by asking for a property of the same name. For example, a range object is obtained by requesting a range property. This isn't really a big problem, but you do need to be clear which of these you're considering when designing and writing integration applications.

LISTING 21.18   Demonstrating the range Property

```
//-- Obtain reference to all cells in the worksheet
my_range = my_worksheet.OlePropertyGet("Range");

//-- Obtain reference to the cells between A1 and E7
my_range = my_worksheet.OlePropertyGet("Range",(Variant)"A1:E7");

//-- Obtain reference to a single cell
my_range = my_worksheet.OlePropertyGet ("Range",(Variant)"C4");
```

Putting Cells into Excel Worksheets

Each range has properties that allow you to enter data and formulae into Excel, the value and formula properties in particular. These properties can work across several cells at the same time and are very similar. Consider the OnClick event shown in Listing 21.19 from the GetExcel program in Figure 21.8.

LISTING 21.19   Setting Cell Contents

```
void __fastcall TForm_GetExcel::Button_WorkbookClick(TObject *Sender)
{

    Variant     my_workbook;
    Variant     my_worksheet;
    Variant     my_range;

    PropertyGet     Range("Range");
    PropertySet     SetValue("Value");
```

LISTING 21.19   Continued

```
PropertySet     SetFormula("Formula");
PropertyGet     GetValue("Value");
PropertyGet     GetFormula("Formula");

my_workbook  = my_excel.OlePropertyGet("ActiveWorkbook");
my_worksheet = my_workbook.OlePropertyGet("ActiveSheet");

Range.ClearArgs();
SetValue.ClearArgs();
my_range     = my_worksheet.Exec(Range << "A1");
my_range.Exec(SetValue << "My Excel Worksheet");

Range.ClearArgs();
my_range     = my_worksheet.Exec(Range << "B1:B5");
my_range.Exec(SetFormula << "=rand()");

Range.ClearArgs();
SetFormula.ClearArgs();
my_range     = my_worksheet.Exec(Range << "A2");
my_range.Exec(SetFormula << "=sum(b1:b5)");

ShowMessage(my_range.OlePropertyGet("Value"));
ShowMessage(my_range.OlePropertyGet ("Formula"));
}
```

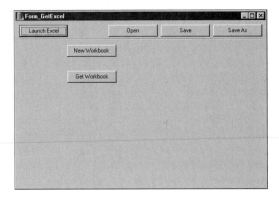

FIGURE 21.8

The GetExcel program.

Microsoft Office Integration

CHAPTER 21

853

21

MICROSOFT
OFFICE
INTEGRATION

The main difference between the two properties is the format in which the values are assigned to the cells. The `value` property accepts the value that is assigned, but the `formula` property needs to be formatted in the same way as when creating a formula in a spreadsheet.

There are other ways to enter information into spreadsheets, such as the `text` property, which is very similar to the `value` property except that it automatically formats all values entered into it or read from it as strings. While you can get away with using just the `value` property in most instances, it is probably best to get into the habit of using the `text` property whenever you want the inserted value to be considered as only text. If you enter `12345` using the `value` property, it will be entered into the cell as the number 12345, whether you wanted it to be a string or not.

Each `range` possesses a number of properties and methods for altering the appearance of the cells it contains. This can be as simple as altering the font used to display the cells or as involved as drawing borders around clusters of cells.

For example, the `font` property of a `range` returns a `font` object, which in turn has properties for color (`color`), style (`bold`, `italic`, `shadow`, and so on), and size.

Other useful properties for formatting cells are the `borders` collection, `height` and `width` properties, and the `interior` collection, which set the borders surrounding cells, their dimensions, and the color and pattern of the cells, respectively.

Getting Cells from Excel

Let us briefly reexamine the last line of code from Listing 21.19. This particular line does not insert any information into Excel and, instead of setting the property, uses `OlePropertyGet` to read the value from the cell.

```
ShowMessage(my_range.OlePropertyGet("Value"));
```

This works not only for the value of a cell, but also for its formula, so you can query cells to find out how they're formed.

Using C++Builder 5's Server Components

Besides the OleAutomation features we've been using for most of this chapter, C++Builder 5 also offers the capability to employ ATL (ActiveX Template Library) and makes this feature available through the `OleServer` component and its derivatives. On the Servers tab of the Component Palette, you will see a number of components for connecting to Word and Excel, as shown in Figure 21.9.

Figure 21.9

The Servers tab Component Palette.

These components allow you to add Office integration to your programs rapidly by dropping them into your applications and supplying the code to begin controlling Word through them. As a demonstration of this, we'll look at converting the Vocabulary program so that it uses the OleServer components.

Before we start on the new program, we'll examine some of the Server components we're going to be using. Make sure that the Code Completion option in the Environment Options dialog is active and create a new application, then drag WordApplication and WordDocument components onto the main form. Create a new button as well, and then double-click on the button to edit its code.

Once you have the code displayed, enter the following text and wait for the Code Completion feature to kick in.

```
WordApplication1->
```

After a pause, C++Builder should display a list of the available functions and properties (see Figure 21.10).

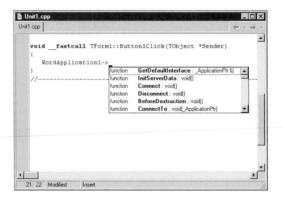

Figure 21.10

WordApplication*'s functions and properties.*

Microsoft Office Integration

Chapter 21

855

21

MICROSOFT
OFFICE
INTEGRATION

If you scroll through the list displayed by C++Builder, you'll notice that many of the functions and properties we've been using through OleAutomation are still available. While this will work to our advantage when we start programming using these components, we need to be careful not to assume too much about them. Some of the functions and properties behave in slightly different ways, have changed names, or have even gained or lost parameters.

The `WordApplication` and `WordDocument` Components

The `WordApplication` component represents the core Word application, much like the application object we have been using throughout this chapter. `WordApplication` offers tighter integration with Word, at the cost of increased complexity. Your programs will gain more access to the features of Word, will gain easier access to features of Word reducing the number of intermediary steps, and will be checked more stringently at compile time. The business end of OleAutomation is really checked only when you run your integrated application.

However, your programs will also be larger and take longer to compile than applications built using OleAutomation, because they place more demands on C++Builder and your program than on the application with which you are integrating. Just as `WordApplication` is equivalent to Word's `application` object, the `WordDocument` component represents the ATL version of Word's `document` object, and offers the same advantages and disadvantages as the `WordApplication` component.

With that caution, let's proceed to the main event and look at the new code for the Vocabulary program.

Vocabulary Revisited

Rather than rewrite the entire vocabulary program, it makes more sense to simply update those parts of the program that deal with Microsoft Word. We'll begin with the code to launch Word and then look at the process of extracting text from documents, creating new documents, and inserting text into them. We will use the `WordApplication` and `WordDocument` components to connect to and control Word.

The project for this example is `vocab_proj.bpr`, and can be found in the `VocabB` folder on the accompanying CD-ROM.

Getting Started

The first thing we need to do is to connect to and gain control of Microsoft Word. In the past, this involved checking to see if an existing copy of Word was open and, if not, creating a new one. This time we can employ the `connect()` method and cut out a few steps. Listing 21.20 contains the new code for launching and displaying the Word interface.

LISTING 21.20 Launching Word

```
/*
||
|| PrepareWord
||
*/
void __fastcall TVocabForm::PrepareWord(void)
{
    try
    {
        WordApplication1->Connect();
    }
    catch(...)
    {
        ShowMessage("Unable to load Word");
    }
    WordApplication1->Visible = True;
}
```

As you can see, the code is similar to that in the original Vocabulary program but is much simpler and more streamlined. In fact, if you were to strip out the error checking (not something we recommend), you would be left with only two lines of code.

It was mentioned that this code uses the `Connect()` method to gain control of Word. This is one of the basic methods available to OleServer and its derivatives. It simply looks for a copy of the appropriate Ole Automation server and either gains access to an existing server or creates a new instance of one.

This makes use of the `Visible` property to ensure that Word is actually displayed. You'll notice that, unlike the Ole Automation version of this code, you can access the property directly without having to employ an intermediary function such as `OlePropertySet()`.

Fetching Text from Word

Now that we've successfully opened our interface to Word, we need to be able to open a document and extract text from it. This means that we'll need to use the `WordApplication` component to open a document and connect the `WordDocument` component to it so that we can gain access to the document we've just loaded.

Opening a document in Word is simply a case of using the `Open()` method of the `documents` collection, and this hasn't changed in the move from Ole Automation.

Listing 21.21 shows the new version of the code needed to open a Word document and extract its contents.

LISTING 21.21   Extracting Text from Word

```
/*
||
|| Get the document's vocabulary
||
*/
void __fastcall TVocabForm::Button_VocabClick(TObject *Sender)
{
    OleVariant FileName;
    wchar_t *doc_contents;
    RangePtr my_range;

    PrepareWord();

    if (OpenDialog1->Execute())
    {
        FileName = OpenDialog1->FileName;

        //-- We've got a file name - Open the document
        WordDocument1->ConnectTo(WordApplication1->Documents->Open(FileName));
        WordDocument1->Select();

        //-- Now get the words from the document
        my_range = WordDocument1->Range(EmptyParam,EmptyParam);
        doc_contents = my_range->get_Text();

        //-- Now translate the words into the list
        //-- Make the list run as fast as possible
        //-- by unsorting it & hiding it
        ListBox_Words->Sorted  = false;
        ListBox_Words->Visible = false;
        ListBox_Words->Clear();

        TransferWordsToList(doc_contents,ListBox_Words);

        //-- Now remove duplicate words
        RemoveDuplicateWordsFromList(ListBox_Words);

        //-- Show the word list again
        ListBox_Words->Visible = true;

        //-- Create a new document
        WordDocument1->ConnectTo(WordApplication1->Documents->Add());

        //-- Create "Word Report" in the document
        ReportWordsFromList(ListBox_Words);
    }
}
```

At first glance, this code is again similar to that contained in the original version of Vocabulary. However, the main changes are that we no longer need as many intermediary steps. Instead of using several OleVariants to hold the numerous temporary variables and objects that we needed previously, we are using only three.

We've also cleaned up the process for extracting the text from Word. In fact, most of this listing is taken up by code for manipulating the word lists, whereas most of the previous code was needed to manipulate Word.

We can see that the process of loading a Word document is now condensed into a single line of code:

```
WordDocument1->ConnectTo(WordApplication1->Documents->Open(FileName));
```

Although this code performs a number of steps, it is still remarkably simple. We obtain the documents collection property directly from the WordApplication component and in turn use its Open() method to load the file. Once we've loaded the file, we immediately pass the results into the WordDocument component's ConnectTo() method so that we can access the contents of the document directly.

We could break this line into different steps. The Code Completion feature gives us the names of the different structures and types being used to pass information into and out of the various methods. This is not as simple as the Ole Automation method, which does have the benefit of being typeless, but it does ensure that you can gain easier access to the various methods and data types more directly.

Having opened a document, we select its content and copy it into a text buffer. As before, we still need to employ the range object to select the entire contents of the document.

```
my_range = WordDocument1->Range(EmptyParam,EmptyParam);
```

EmptyParam is the equivalent of passing a Null into the function. In this case it is used to ensure that we acquire the whole document in a single range.

Once we have the range, we need to use the get_Text() method to get the text itself. You'll notice that this is one of those occasions when we use a name that differs slightly from the Ole Automation name, although we could have used the property directly.

```
doc_contents = my_range->get_Text();
```

This is one area in which we need to take extra care. The get_Text() method doesn't return a value in a normal type, but instead uses wide characters. This isn't really a problem, but it is worth pointing out. If you start getting strange contents from your documents, this is worth checking.

Microsoft Office Integration

CHAPTER 21

859

21

MICROSOFT
OFFICE
INTEGRATION

As you can see, we don't actually perform any conversions on wide text. We simply dump it straight into `TransferWordsToList()`, which expects an `AnsiString`, and let C++Builder sort things out for us.

Putting Text Back

We've demonstrated that it is simple enough to load documents and extract text from them. You'll be pleased to know that it's equally simple to create new documents and insert text back again.

Listing 21.21 contains part of the code needed to do this. It creates a new document prior to calling `ReportWordsFromList()` to insert the words we've gathered into a document.

The code to create a new document in this instance looks like this:

```
WordDocument1->ConnectTo(WordApplication1->Documents->Add());
```

Once more, we're using the `WordApplication` component to obtain the `documents` collection, and then we're using a `Documents` method, the `Add()` method in this case. This code simply creates a new document using the default template and returns a handle to the document.

Instead of maintaining a reference to the document, we're simply connecting to it immediately with the `WordDocument`. Once the document has been created, `ReportWordsFromList()`, shown in Listing 21.22, is called to insert the words we've collected into a document.

LISTING 21.22   Inserting Text into Word

```
/*
||
|| Report all words from a list into a report
||
*/
void __fastcall TVocabForm::ReportWordsFromList(TListBox *lb)
{
    long words;

    WordDocument1->Range(EmptyParam,EmptyParam)->InsertAfter(
        StringToOleStr("Words from '" + OpenDialog1->FileName + "'\n\n"));

    for (words=0;words<lb->Items->Count;words++)
    {
        WordDocument1->Range(EmptyParam,EmptyParam)->InsertAfter(
            StringToOleStr(lb->Items->Strings[words]+"\n"));
    }
}
```

Inserting text into the document is done by obtaining a range (with hopefully no surprises there!), and inserting the text into or around the range.

```
WordDocument1->Range(EmptyParam,EmptyParam)->InsertAfter(
StringToOleStr(lb->Items->Strings[words]+"\n"));
```

As you can see, this isn't at all complex. What is worth mentioning is the need for an end-of-line character. The first time this program was run, the end-of-line was omitted and the program displayed a jumbled page of words.

By now you'll have noticed that the table functions have been left out in this version of the code. There are a number of reasons for this omission, one of which is to demonstrate how simple the code for inserting text actually is now that we have discarded Ole Automation. Another is that the code to place tables in documents using the WordDocument component isn't anywhere as pleasant to write, read, or use as it is for Ole Automation.

The WordDocument component doesn't expose the functionality that would have made it easy to convert the code. This is one of the persistent downsides to using the ATL, in that if it hasn't been deliberately made available by the original developers, you're pretty much stuck.

Final Thoughts About ATL and OleServers

Like any tool available to developers, there are both benefits and disadvantages to using OleServers or ATL directly. Because you are creating closer links to the program you are integrating with, you gain some features you wouldn't have had access to previously, and your code will execute faster because you are moving through fewer layers to gain access to the hosting application.

However, you are placing additional loads onto C++Builder in terms of compilation and size of your application, and occasionally tighter links mean that you have less flexibility. When first installing a copy of C++Builder 5, it asked if it would be going to use the OleServers for Office 97 or 2000. While it is possible that the WordDocument component we have been using throughout this section is equally at home with either version of Microsoft Office, it is a certainty that the more loosely bound Ole Automation method is not at all concerned about the version of Office it is connecting to, as long as it is one of these.

Learn your tools so that you know which is best for your application. Ole Automation is better for some applications, but you will find occasions when using ATL gives you that extra something that you just can't do without.

Going Further

So far we've looked at some of the ways of using two of the applications within Microsoft Office. This leaves plenty to explore in Office.

Microsoft Office Integration

CHAPTER 21

861

21

MICROSOFT
OFFICE
INTEGRATION

Word

The following are some example projects to extend your use of Word:

- A Document Manager Database

  This program is used to import all of the words in documents, remove the most common words (such as *and*, *the*, *on*) from the word list, and place the rest in a database so that documents can be found quickly according to the words they contain.

  You could even extend this idea so that the program searches network folders and updates documents automatically. This could be shared between users so that they can find documents quickly.

- A Report Library

  Create a library of routines for creating reports using Word. Instead of using QReport for reports, you can insert Word and have your reports in an easily distributable format.

  Because you'd be using Word, you not only get the benefit of distribution, you also gain a lot of control over the formatting and layout of the document. You could even provide options to save as HTML for updating Web sites.

- A Correspondence Program

  While mail merge is a common feature of word processors, it is not always compatible with the datasources you want to employ, and it doesn't always contain the features you want to use. By taking direct control of Word, it is possible to search a document for fields and populate them automatically. It is also possible to keep copies of merged documents for each person you send the document to and even to keep track of which documents were sent where, when, and to whom.

Excel

To extend our examination of Excel, you could insert charts and databases into cells and use them to present or capture information.

Example projects could be as follows:

- A Web Site Log Analysis

  Import logs from your Web site and use them to update columns in a spreadsheet, so that you can analyze the traffic visiting your Web site. This would work well as a workbook, with one sheet kept for raw data, another for summary information, and others for charts and reports.

- A Data-Capture Questionnaire

  If you need to capture a large amount of information, you may want to consider providing those questioned with a spreadsheet (a Word document works well here, too) into which to enter their answers, and then write a program that imports completed question-naires and processes them into a summary.

- A To-Do List

  If you find yourself in need of to-do lists, one way to maintain them is to use Excel. Each row in a worksheet becomes a task, with its status (complete, unfinished, in progress) and the date it needs to be finished. You can write a program to maintain the list and remind you of tasks in a timely fashion. You can print the task list out in a sensible format, too.

Other Office Applications

One of the best things about Microsoft Office is that, in addition to Word and Excel, there are other programs you can use. Some of these are just as controllable through automation as Word and Excel.

Outlook

Besides it's use as an email program, Outlook is also useful as a scheduler, task list, reminder system, and all-round personal information manager. Its application object is available at outlook.application.

Unlike Word and Excel, Outlook does not usually obtain collections or objects but instead uses methods to generate references to objects. For example, the code in Listing 21.23 creates a new mail message using Outlook.

LISTING 21.23   Creating a New Outlook Mail Message

```
Variant my_outlook = Variant::CreateObject("outlook.application");
Variant my_message = my_outlook.OleFunction("CreateItem",(Variant) 0);
    //-- 0 - New Mail Item
my_message.OleProcedure ("Display");
```

Access

Access may not seem like the most likely candidate with which to integrate. C++Builder has better database support and, while Access is ideal for creating small database applications quickly, it isn't particularly scaleable or robust. It's also not the most commonly used part of Office, other than in the Professional and Small Business editions.

Even so, C++Builder is an ideal tool for migrating applications from Access and into other databases. The application object for Access can be obtained using access.application. Application ideas include the following:

Microsoft Office Integration

CHAPTER 21

863

21

MICROSOFT
OFFICE
INTEGRATION

- A Database Mapping Application

  While Access is a useful tool for developing prototype applications, it is frequently helpful to be able to obtain a complete description of all of the tables and queries. Access makes this information available, but you'll need to select each table individually and inspect them one by one. A database mapping tool would be far more helpful, to open an Access database and produce a report based on the tables and queries it contains.

- A Marionette Application

  If your users are already used to Access databases and you don't want to change, an alternative would be to create an application that maintains Access as a front end and uses C++Builder to manipulate data in the background.

- A Data-Capture Tool

  Access is a good candidate for use as a data-capture tool. Sometimes it is even better than Excel if the data you're looking for is complex. C++Builder is an ideal tool for interrogating the Access database and collating all of the data from several copies of the database.

Project

Microsoft Project isn't really part of Office, but it does exhibit the same features for integration. By creating an instance of the application object using `msproject.application`, you can obtain collections of projects, resources, tasks, and so on, all of which are ideal for linking to other systems via C++Builder.

Suggestions for applications could be as follows:

- A Team Task Manager

  Each member of a project team can have a program that tells him what tasks he is currently supposed to be carrying out. The program can log the date and time when the team member signs out a task and when he signs it back in.

  This has the added advantage of making it possible to query a project to see which tasks are currently being performed, who is performing the tasks, and which tasks are in danger of slipping.

- An Animated Project Display

  C++Builder could be used to extract data from a project and maintain it in a database of versions. Then it could replay the development of the project by playing back versions of the project over time.

- A Billing System

  Project already has the capability to track the costs attached to a resource's use. This could be used to link with an accounting system to produce invoices and other documents.

Still More Applications

Applications supporting OLE Automation are increasingly common. The methods used to integrate with Office are equally useful for integrating with other programs.

Some of the applications that support integration are

- FrontPage (`frontpage.application`)
- Visio (`Visio.Application`)
- Internet Explorer (`InternetExplorer.Application`)
- Adobe Photoshop (`Photoshop.Application`)
- Fusion (`fusion.application`)

Other Methods of Integration

We have looked at only two of the ways in which C++Builder can gain control of Microsoft Office. As C++Builder has evolved from its earliest incarnations, it has gained the capability to employ type libraries. Version 5 adds a number of common Ole Servers as components, the Servers components tab, and the capability to create more by creating subclasses of the `TOleServer` class.

Summary

In this chapter we've looked at the ways in which Microsoft Office can be integrated with C++Builder. In particular, we've touched on the main ways of controlling Office using C++Builder and some of the things that can be done through integration.

While we have concentrated on Word and Excel, the techniques used here can be applied with most Office applications and several other programs that allow use of their facilities through Ole Automation. Besides the methods for integrating covered in this chapter, it is also possible to employ alternative automation techniques to drive the coding of the methods we've covered here.

Creating and manipulating documents is useful, but it is the capability to create and extract content that makes integration such a powerful tool. There is a lot involved in integrating applications with Microsoft Office, but this is not to say that integration is difficult. This is a large topic, because Office is a large collection of complex tools. Starting an application and making it perform basic tasks can be achieved quickly and simply, and there is a lot to learn about how to make Office perform in exciting and unexpected ways.

Keep your help files handy, and experiment with everything. If you're not sure about a command, try it out. Office will tell you soon enough if it doesn't appreciate what you're trying to do.

Using ActiveX Techniques

Bob Swart
Damon Chandler

IN THIS CHAPTER

The complete text for this chapter appears on the CD-ROM.

Advanced Topics

PART
IV

IN THIS PART

Data Presentation with C++Builder

Jeppe Cramon
Stéphane Mahaux
Dan Butterfield

IN THIS CHAPTER

- **Presenting Data in Reports**
- **Printing Text and Graphics**
- **Using Advanced Printing Techniques**
- **Creating Charts with the** TChart **Component**

Areas where Windows has distinct advantages over the old DOS system, at least as far as the average user is concerned, are printing, printer management, and data presentation in the form of reporting and charting. The vastly improved printing system means no more choosing a port and driver to use—just pick a printer and print to it—while enhanced graphics, combined with better screen and printer resolutions, provide much more scope for high-quality data presentation.

The relatively easy-to-use Windows printing system puts more of an onus on the programmer, however, and even with the help of API and VCL provided functions, adding professional printing and data presentation capabilities to applications can be a difficult task. In this chapter we will take a look at basic and advanced printing techniques using the API and VCL, reporting using QBS Software's QuickReport components, and charting using Steema SL's TeeChart components. Both QuickReport and TeeChart are bundled with C++Builder.

Presenting Data in Reports

This section presents how to get more value from reports. While the design of the report itself is certainly very important, so is the ability to view it without printing it and to save and share it.

Understanding the Value of a Report

When you are talking database application, you are usually also talking reports. Creating a sophisticated report—one with more than a basic one- or two-table dump—has always been a time-consuming endeavor. But it is worthwhile because well-designed reports are great at summarizing and interpreting the data. This is very important because it is rarely the data itself, but rather its interpretation, that is valuable.

Unfortunately, reports are too often regarded as simply a means of printing the content of a database table. So much for using the power of the computer, and so much for the paperless office. Reports can add value by providing a different and hopefully more complete view of the data. A report could be used to get a list of your customers alphabetically, but what if it could also provide a snapshot of their spending habits and group that by field office? Now the user has useful information! Now the user is empowered by more knowledge. And the report doesn't even have to be printed to achieve this; simply viewing it on the screen does the trick.

Furthermore, generated reports can be saved to disk. That may seem trivial, but it has a big implication: The whole application is no longer required—just a viewer. This means it could easily be shared over a network, distributed by email, or archived without wasting room or paper. Now we are productive!

Using QuickReport to Produce Reports

C++Builder is bundled with QuickReport, from QBS Software Ltd. (www.qbss.com)—formerly QuSoft Ltd. These reports are created using the RAD model and are linked directly into the program. They can be very complex and can include C++ code for absolute flexibility. The Professional version includes an editor so that report layouts can be saved in a separate file and customized by the user. This editor is fairly basic, so users will not have difficulty creating their own reports. The flip side of the coin is that complex ones will have to be created in the IDE and linked into the program or created with another tool.

Apart from being viewed and printed, a generated report can be saved to disk. The importance of this feature was discussed earlier. QuickReport's native file format is a special kind of metafile. In other words, it is an image. It will be viewed exactly as it was intended. It contains all the formatting and allows zooming. On the other hand, reports saved in this format can be viewed only through an application that uses the component provided in the package.

If reports need to be shared with people who won't be using your application, you will be happy to hear that QuickReport provides filters, so reports can be saved in many formats. The standard version of QuickReport, bundled with C++Builder, includes filters for the text-only, comma-delimited, and HTML formats. The Professional version, which must be purchased separately, includes additional filters for Microsoft Excel, rich text/Microsoft Word, and Windows metafile. These are all popular formats, and some are even platform independent.

Understanding the Philosophy of the Custom Viewer

A user may want to view a report without printing it. This is especially important if the generated reports add value by providing a different or more complete view of the data. Furthermore, viewing saved reports also provides many important benefits.

23

DATA PRESENTATION
WITH C++BUILDER

> **TIP**
>
> To fully understand how the custom viewer is built requires a basic understanding of QuickReport, such as how to create a report derived from the TQuickRep component. A basic understanding of the TQRPreview component would also be beneficial.
>
> Please refer to the QuickReport documentation for more information about these components.

Included on the companion CD-ROM is a QuickReport viewing class built around the TQRPreview component. It is called TQuickReportViewer and is designed with three major goals in mind:

- To provide excellent integration with the calling application. This is accomplished by providing two methods to show the report viewer: in its own form, or imbedded inside another form's windowed control (such as a panel or a tab sheet).

- To allow dynamic viewing of generated reports (derived from TQuickRep). This is often referred to as *previewing*; however, I find that term inappropriate because it infers that printing is the ultimate goal.

- To allow loading and viewing of saved report images (QRP files).

The first and third goals are demonstrated in the example project called QRViewer. It is a QRP file viewer. It highlights how easily the TQuickReportViewer class can be integrated in an application by embedding the complete viewer inside a TTabSheet control. This is shown in Figure 23.1.

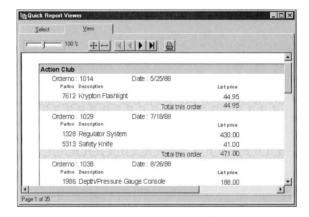

FIGURE 23.1

The QRViewer *project shows how the* TQuickReportViewer *class can be embedded inside another form.*

NOTE

The companion CD-ROM contains an executable called QRViewer.exe built from the QRViewer project. It could be put inside a shared folder containing saved QRP reports to provide easy viewing. It does not use packages or dynamic RTL, so it is completely standalone. It is also compressed (by about 50%) to make it easier to send electronically along with a saved report.

The second goal is demonstrated in the project called QRPreviewer. A dummy report (which doesn't contain any data, just a title) is generated and viewed. Here, the viewer is displayed in its own form and is very similar to the default previewer. However, a project could derive from the TQuickReportViewer class to provide additional customization and features. Also, the class provides an easy API for viewing and saving QR reports. QRPreviewer is shown in Figure 23.2.

FIGURE 23.2

The QRPreviewer *project shows the* TQuickReportViewer *class in its own form.*

The important point is that the TQuickReportViewer class is used in both projects and integrates seamlessly into the programs.

Custom Viewer Source Code

Let's have a look at the custom viewer's source code. Groups of related methods will be listed together, preceded by their detailed analysis. Some less-important methods are omitted; for the complete source, please refer to the ReportViewer.cpp file found on the companion CD-ROM.

Although Preview() and ClosePreview() are the only methods required to view a generated report, the whole class will be discussed.

Most of the initialization is accomplished in the Init() method, which can be called easily from the three overloaded constructors for the class. Only one constructor is included in Listing 23.1.

LISTING 23.1   Initializing the Class

```
__fastcall TQuickReportViewer::TQuickReportViewer( TComponent* Owner )
    : TForm(Owner),
      newQRPrinter_M(    NULL )
{
    Init( Owner, false ) ;
}//Constructor


void __fastcall TQuickReportViewer::Init( TComponent* Owner,
                                          const bool showForm )
{
    // Transfer the contents of the form ?
    // ie: The owning windowed control is also the new parent.
    // Note: If the owner is another form,
    //        it just means that they should be destroyed together.
    TWinControl* ownerAndParent = dynamic_cast<TWinControl*>( Owner ) ;
    if( ownerAndParent && (! dynamic_cast<TForm*>(ownerAndParent)) )
        Client_Panel->Parent  = ownerAndParent ;
    else
    {
        Visible              = showForm ;
        Exit->Visible        = true ;
        ToolButton4->Visible = true ;
    }//else this form is used alone

    // Register Filter components
    SaveDialog->Filter = QRExportFilterLibrary->SaveDialogFilterString ;

    // Set default view
    FitClick( NULL ) ;
}//Init()
```

All of the viewer's controls are actually children of Client_Panel. It sits unnoticed on the form because it is aligned to alCLient and has no borders or other visible properties. If this form should be embedded inside another form or windowed control, the form's owner will also be assigned as the parent of Client_Panel. As a result, Client_Panel and all its child controls will be redisplayed inside control ownerAndParent. This is a great trick; controls don't have to be displayed inside the form that owns them. Put another way, Client_Panel is owned by the QuickReportViewer class and will be destroyed with it; however, it is displayed on another form.

When the export filter components were dropped on the viewer, they automatically registered themselves with QuickReport. As a result, it is child's play to assign them to the `SaveDialog->Filter` property.

Displaying the page number is simple, as shown in Listing 23.2. It is worth including it because it also displays the total page count of the report. The total count cannot be known until the report is fully generated. This makes sense because the number of pages used will increase throughout the report-generation process. That is fine in most situations; the page count displayed will simply increase as the report is being generated. Remember that QuickReport will display the first page as soon as it is generated, even before continuing with the others.

However, sometimes the total number of pages used by the report must be known before the report is ever displayed. In that case, the report must be completely generated before being displayed. This is accomplished by calling the report's `Prepare()` method.

LISTING 23.2 Displaying the Page Number

```
void __fastcall TQuickReportViewer::DisplayPageNumber(
    const int pageNumber ) const
{
    // Update status bar
    String page( "Page " ) ;
    page += pageNumber ;

    int pageCount = QRPreview->QRPrinter->PageCount ;
    if( pageCount < 1 )
        pageCount = 1 ;
    page += " of " ;
    page += pageCount ;

    StatusBar->SimpleText = page ;

    // Update buttons
    if( pageNumber <= 1 )
    {
        First->Enabled    = false ;
        Previous->Enabled = false ;
    }//if beginning
    else
    {
        First->Enabled    = true ;
        Previous->Enabled = true ;
    }//else not beginning
```

LISTING 23.2   Continued

```
    if( pageNumber >= pageCount )
    {
        Next->Enabled = false ;
        Last->Enabled = false ;
    }//if end
    else
    {
        Next->Enabled = true ;
        Last->Enabled = true ;
    }//else not end
}//DisplayPageNumber()
```

Preview() and ClosePreview()are the only methods required to view a generated report. At the beginning of Preview(), the passed report class is assigned an OnPreview() handler. It tells QuickReport to use this form to display the generated report by having the viewer share the report's canvas. The source code in Listing 23.3 shows exactly how to proceed.

LISTING 23.3   Viewing a Generated Report

```
void __fastcall TQuickReportViewer::Preview( TQuickRep* report )
// DESC: This is the only method which needs to be called to view
//       a generated report.
//
// WARNING: The source code after a call to this function will
//          NOT_ be executed until after a call to ClosePreview(),
//          unless THREADSAFE_DBENGINE is defined.
//
// WARNING: It assumed that all the datasets are already active.
{
    assert( report ) ;

    // A new QRPrinter canvas is always created
    // by Preview()/PreviewModeless().
    ClosePreview() ;

    // Assign event-handler so this class can see the report.
    report->OnPreview = PrepareViewer ;

    // Form may have been closed (hidden)
    if( Client_Panel->Parent == this )
        Visible = true ;

    // Preview the report
    #ifdef THREADSAFE_DBENGINE
```

LISTING 23.3   Continued

```cpp
        TCursor Save_Cursor = Screen->Cursor;
        Screen->Cursor = crHourGlass;
        try
        {
            // NOTE: PreviewModeless() returns after the report is generated.
            report->PreviewModeless();

            DisplayPageNumber( QRPreview->PageNumber ) ;
        }//try
        __finally
        {
            Screen->Cursor = Save_Cursor ;
        }//finally
    #else
        // NOTE: Preview() does NOT return until ClosePreview() is called.
        //       So ALL code after the call to Preview() will _NOT_ be
        //       executed until after the previewer is closed.
        //       For this reason, I can't change the cursor to an hourglass
        //       (it would not be reset even after its generation).
        report->Preview();
    #endif

    // Remove event handler because this instance of the class
    // is not guaranteed to exist the next time the report is previewed.
    // NOTE: This code is not time-sensitive.
    report->OnPreview = NULL ;
}//Preview()

void __fastcall TQuickReportViewer::PrepareViewer( TObject *sender )
{
    // Warning: There is a bug when loading compressed reports;
    //          however, the button can't be disabled because
    //          it is used for exporting as well.
    DefaultQRViewer_G->SaveReport->Enabled = true ;
    DefaultQRViewer_G->FitWidth->Down    = true ;

    // Share the report's canvas with the previewer .
    TQRPrinter* qrPrinter = dynamic_cast<TQRPrinter*>( sender ) ;
    assert( qrPrinter ) ;

    QRPreview->QRPrinter = qrPrinter ;
}//PrepareViewer()

void __fastcall TQuickReportViewer::ClosePreview( void )
// Free the report's canvas
// Call this method when the report is no longer needed.
```

23

DATA PRESENTATION
WITH C++BUILDER

LISTING 23.3   Continued

```
// NOTE: See Preview() for other effects of this method.
{
    if( QRPreview->QRPrinter )
    {
        QRPreview->QRPrinter->ClosePreview( QRPreview ) ;
        QRPreview->QRPrinter = NULL ;
    }//if

    SaveReport->Enabled  = false ;
}//ClosePreview()
```

Next, Preview() generates and displays the report. The preferred method is to define the THREADSAFE_DBENGINE macro because the report class is then modeless. Unfortunately, this option is only available if the database engine used is guaranteed to be threadsafe. Otherwise, the report class behaves like a modal form. That is, it does not return control to the caller until the report is closed by the normal call to ClosePreview(). To use the THREADSAFE_DBENGINE macro, simply uncomment its definition at the top of ReportViewer.cpp.

Notice that the code at the end of the Preview() method is not time sensitive.

Two methods allow the report to be saved, either using a dialog box or without user interaction. As far as the calling application is concerned, saving a report is quite easy. True, the Save() method (shown in Listing 23.4) is a little long; however, the program needs to call it with only two simple parameters. Besides, most of it is error checking and allowing the report to be exported to different file formats.

The method is really split into two sections. If using the QuickReport file format, it simply calls the printer canvas's own Save() method. If exporting, then it retrieves information about the requested type from the export filter library, dynamically creates an appropriate filter class, and uses the latter to generate the report file.

LISTING 23.4   Saving a Generated Report

```
void __fastcall TQuickReportViewer::SaveReportClick( TObject *Sender )
// Save or export the report showing.
// Note: If this function is called from another unit,
//       Have it look at SaveDialog->FileName
//       to see if the report was saved (not canceled).
{
    SaveDialog->FileName = "" ;

    if( SaveDialog->Execute() )
        Save( SaveDialog->FileName, SaveDialog->FilterIndex - 1 ) ;
```

LISTING 23.4   Continued

```
    else
        SaveDialog->FileName = "" ;
}//SaveReportClick()



void __fastcall TQuickReportViewer::Save( String fileName, int filterIndex )
// 'fileName' must include the correct file extension.
//      The dialog will add one if none is given.
// 'filterIndex' indicates the file format to use.
//      A value of 0 will use the QuickReport native format (QRP).
//      Any other value is used as an index into the filter library.
//      This library is populated from filter components dropped onto the form
//      (using their creation order).
{
    if( ! QRPreview->QRPrinter )
        Beep() ;

    else
    {
        assert( ! fileName.IsEmpty() ) ;

        // Get the file's extension.
        int    len = fileName.Length() ;
        int    pos = fileName.Pos(".") ;
        String fileExt( fileName.SubString( pos + 1,
                                            len - pos ).UpperCase() ) ;

        // Save (in native format)
        if( filterIndex == 0 )
        {
            // Verify that the extension matches the filter chosen.
            if( fileExt != "QRP" )
                Application->MessageBox("The file extension given does not "
                                        "match the format selected.",
                                        "Wrong file extension", MB_OK ) ;
            else
                QRPreview->QRPrinter->Save( fileName ) ;
        }//if save

        // Export
        else
        {
            // Get filter details
            // Note: Subtract 1 from filterIndex because
            //       the filter library uses a 0-based index.
```

LISTING 23.4 Continued

```
                --filterIndex ;
                assert( (filterIndex >= 0) &&
                        (filterIndex < QRExportFilterLibrary->Filters->Count) ) ;
                TQRExportFilterLibraryEntry* filterEntry(
                        static_cast<TQRExportFilterLibraryEntry*>
                        ( QRExportFilterLibrary->Filters->Items[filterIndex] ) ) ;

                // Verify that the extension matches the filter chosen.
                if( fileExt != filterEntry->Extension )
                    Application->MessageBox("The file extension given does not "
                                            "match the format selected.",
                                            "Wrong file extension", MB_OK ) ;
                else
                {
                    TQRExportFilter* exportFilter = NULL ;

                    if( fileExt == "TXT" )
                        exportFilter = new TQRAsciiExportFilter( fileName ) ;
                    else if( fileExt == "HTM" )
                        exportFilter = new TQRHTMLDocumentFilter( fileName ) ;
                    else
                        exportFilter = new TQRCommaSeparatedFilter( fileName ) ;

                    try
                    {
                        assert( exportFilter ) ;
                        QRPreview->QRPrinter->ExportToFilter( exportFilter ) ;
                    }//try
                    __finally
                    {
                        delete exportFilter ;
                    }//__finally
                }//else file extension is valid
            }//else export
    }//else there is a report to save
}//Save()
```

Again, two methods allow the report to be loaded, either using a dialog box or without user interaction. Most of the work is preparing the form. The actual loading is done by the TQRPrinter class. Please see Listing 23.5.

While the viewer allows both saving and exporting, only native QuickReport (.qrp) files may be loaded. For the other file formats, their related applications must be used. Also note that .qrp files are saved, populated report images, not report editor forms.

LISTING 23.5   Loading a Previously Saved QuickReport

```cpp
void __fastcall TQuickReportViewer::LoadReportClick( TObject *Sender )
// Open a QRP file.
// Note: If this function is called from another unit,
//        Have it look at OpenDialog->FileName
//        to see if a report was opened (not canceled).
{
    OpenDialog->FileName = "" ;

    if( OpenDialog->Execute() )
        Load( OpenDialog->FileName ) ;
    else
        OpenDialog->FileName = "" ;
}//LoadReportClick()



void __fastcall TQuickReportViewer::Load( String fileName )
// Open a QRP file.
// Note: QRP Files are saved, populated report images; not report editor forms.
{
    TCursor Save_Cursor = Screen->Cursor;
    Screen->Cursor = crHourGlass;
    try
    {
        // Assign a new QRPrinter canvas if necessary
        if( newQRPrinter_M == NULL )
            newQRPrinter_M = new TQRPrinter ;
        QRPreview->QRPrinter = newQRPrinter_M ;

        // Load the requested file
        QRPreview->QRPrinter->Load( fileName ) ;
        QRPreview->PageNumber = 1 ;
        QRPreview->PreviewImage->PageNumber = 1 ;

        SaveReport->Enabled  = false ;
        DisplayPageNumber( QRPreview->PageNumber ) ;
        FitClick( FitWidth ) ;

        // Form may have been closed (hidden)
        if( Client_Panel->Parent == this )
            Visible = true ;
    }//try
    __finally
    {
```

LISTING 23.5   Continued

```
        Screen->Cursor = Save_Cursor ;
    }//finally
}//Load()
```

QuickReport Custom Viewer Summary

That's it. We saw how the constructor can imbed the previewer inside another form, how QuickReport can be directed to use a custom previewer, how to save and export the generated report, and how to load a saved report. Not surprisingly, that corresponds exactly to the public interface of the TQuickReportViewer class.

The purpose of using a custom QuickReport viewer is to improve integration in the application. The class presented here can be used either in its own form or embedded into another form or windowed control.

This viewer can be used to display generated reports. These can be saved in many popular file formats. This allows them to be easily shared or archived. The same viewer can then be used to display reports saved in the QuickReport native format.

Reports are often an important part of database applications. That is why adequate integration is so important.

Printing Text and Graphics

This section will deal with the various techniques that can be applied for printing text and graphics on your printer. I will be covering techniques for writing data and text directly to the printer, without having to go through VCL's encapsulation of the GDI (Graphics Device Interface), as well as techniques for printing text and graphics to the printer using the VCL.

It's expected that you have the basic knowledge about how the TPrinter class works. If you haven't worked with the TPrinter class before, I recommend having a look at the Printing example, which can be found in the Examples\Apps\Printing directory under your C++Builder directory.

Printing Text

This section will explain the various aspects of printing text, a task that can range from printing raw text directly to the printer while surpassing the printing system (notably GDI) to printing beautifully formatted text with various fonts and sizes. I will concentrate mostly on the direct printing features and how to use the text printing features of the printers TCanvas. Changing font sizes and otherwise formatting the printed text is merely a matter of extending the functionality described in this section.

Printing Text and Data Directly to the Printer

First I will be covering how to write text and data directly to the printer without having to use a TCanvas, which is VCL's encapsulation of the GDI.

The simplest way and often the way that seems to trouble the most users is sending text or data directly to the printer. With the use of a few simple Win32 API functions, we can be up and running in no time.

Under Windows 3.x, you could use functions like Escape() or EscapeEx() to handle the job, but under Win32, these API functions have been made obsolete and will therefore not be covered here, as better alternatives exist.

The best way to write directly to the printer under Win32 is to use the WritePrinter() function. This function instructs the print spooler that we're writing directly to the printer, specified in the function call. Listing 23.6 is an example of how to set up a printer to use WritePrinter(). The keywords are OpenPrinter(), WritePrinter(), ClosePrinter(), StartDocPrinter(), StartPagePrinter(), EndPagePrinter(), EndDocPrinter(), DOC_INFO_1, PRINTER_DEFAULTS, and HANDLE.

LISTING 23.6   Write Directly to the Printer Using WritePrinter()

```
// -- See PrintSample1 for the complete source code
void __fastcall TMainForm::Print(char *szPrinterName)
{
    HANDLE hPrinter;        // Printer handle
    PRINTER_DEFAULTS pd;    // Printer access rights for
                            // WinNT/Win2K only, ignored by Win9x

    // Init the printer defaults
    ZeroMemory(&pd, sizeof(pd));
    // NT access rights
    pd.DesiredAccess = PRINTER_ACCESS_USE;

    // Open printer and get a handle to it (which is saved in
    // hPrinter)
    if(OpenPrinter(szPrinterName, &hPrinter, &pd))
    {
        // Doc info
        DOC_INFO_1 docInfo1;
        // Init the DocInfo1 structure
        ZeroMemory(&docInfo1, sizeof(docInfo1));

        // --- Setup the Doc1 information ---
        // Name of the Doc (which is shown in the Print Manager)
```

LISTING 23.6   Continued

```
docInfo1.pDocName        = "Print Sample 1";

// Port/File (not used here)
docInfo1.pOutputFile     = 0;

// Data are sent in RAW format (RAW and EMF are supported
// by both Win9x and Win NT). Win NT also supports TEXT.
docInfo1.pDatatype       = "RAW";


// --- Start doc (Notice second parameter specifies the
// Doc Info type) ---
if(!StartDocPrinter(hPrinter, 1,  (LPBYTE)&docInfo1))
{
    // Something went wrong (use GetLastError() to find
    // out what went wrong)
    return;
}

// --- Tell the printer we want to print
if (!StartPagePrinter(hPrinter))
{
    // Something went wrong (use GetLastError() to find
    // out what went wrong
    return;
}


// ---------------------------------
// --- Start of WritePrinter Code ---
// ---------------------------------
DWORD dwWritten;       // Length of data actually sent
AnsiString asBuffer; // Buffer to hold data/text to be
                       // sent

// Write "Hello World!" to the Printer  (including carriage
// return and line feed (New Line))
asBuffer = "Hello World!\r\n";
if(!WritePrinter(hPrinter, (LPVOID)asBuffer.c_str(),
                asBuffer.Length(), &dwWritten))
{
    // An error happened while sending data to the
    // printer.
    // Use LastError to figure out what went wrong.
    return;
```

LISTING 23.6 Continued

```
        }

        // Write a Form Feed (also called New Page) to the Printer
        asBuffer = "\f";
        if(!WritePrinter(hPrinter, (LPVOID)asBuffer.c_str(),
                        asBuffer.Length(), &dwWritten))
        {
            // An error happened while sending data to the
            // printer.
            // Use LastError to figure out what went wrong.
            return;
        }

        // -------------------------------
        // --- End of WritePrinter Code ---
        // -------------------------------

        // Tell the printer we're done printing
        if (!EndPagePrinter(hPrinter))
            return;

        // End the document
        if(!EndDocPrinter(hPrinter))
            return;

        // Close the printer
        ClosePrinter(hPrinter);
    }
}
```

Even though we only use a few functions, there's still quite some code to set up to print just a few lines of text. To make this task a little easier, I've created a small class called TPrintRaw, which encapsulates the printer API in a few easy methods. Listing 23.7 is a sample of how to use the TPrintRaw class, which does the same as the example in Listing 23.6. You can find the source code for TPrintRaw on the CD-ROM.

LISTING 23.7 Write Directly to the Printer Using TPrintRaw

```
// -- See PrintSample2 for the complete source code
void __fastcall TMainForm::Print(char *szPrinterName)
{
    // Create a new instance of TPrintRaw class
    TPrintRaw *pPrintRaw = new TPrintRaw();
```

23

DATA PRESENTATION
WITH C++BUILDER

LISTING 23.7   Continued

```
// Set title of print job in the print manager
pPrintRaw->Title = "Print Sample 2";

// Set the name of the Printer we wish to print to
pPrintRaw->PrinterName = szPrinterName;

// Prepare to print
pPrintRaw->BeginDoc();

// Print raw (return code 0 is success)
// Write "Hello World!" to the printer (including a New Line)
AnsiString asBuffer = "Hello World!";
if (pPrintRaw->WriteLine(asBuffer))
    Application->MessageBox("An error occurred while sending"
                            " data to the printer",
                            "Printer Sample 2", MB_OK |
                            MB_ICONERROR);

// Write a Form Feed (also known as New Page) to the printer
// Note: This makes the printer eject the paper
pPrintRaw->NewPage();

// Done Printing
pPrintRaw->EndDoc();

// Clean up
delete pPrintRaw;
}
```

As you can see, the normal flow of a print job using VCL is first to call `BeginDoc()` and then perform the various printing tasks—calling `WriteLine()` and so on. When you're done with everything, you finish it off by calling `EndDoc()`.

Table 23.1 shows a list of methods and properties available in `TPrintRaw`.

TABLE 23.1   TPrintRaw Methods and Properties

Name	Type	Description
BeginDoc()	Method	Instructs the print spooler to start printing a new document.
EndDoc()	Method	Instructs the print spooler that we are done printing the document.

TABLE 23.1   Continued

Name	Type	Description
NewLine()	Method	Inserts a new line (line feed) in the document.
NewPage()	Method	Inserts a new page (form feed) in the document. Remember to call this when you're done printing the last page, to have the printer eject the paper.
Write()	Method	Writes a string to the document.
WriteBuffer()	Method	Writes data or text to the document.
WriteLine()	Method	Write a string to the document and inserts a new line at the end of the written text.
WriteFile()	Method	Writes the contents of a file (binary or ASCII) to the printer.
PrinterName	Property	Gets or sets the name of the printer to print to.
Printing	Property	Returns true if currently printing; otherwise returns false.
Title	Property	Gets or sets the title of the document shown in the Print Manager.

Printing Text to the Printer Using the VCL

The VCL provides an encapsulation of the Win32 GDI called TCanvas, which is available through the Printer() object. TCanvas contains several methods for controlling and writing text, such as the following:

- TextExtent() returns the space (width and height) a string written with the current font of the canvas will occupy as a TSize. TextExtent() is a test function that doesn't write any text to the canvas and doesn't update the PenPos property. The same goes for TextHeight() and TextWidth().

- TextHeight() returns the same as Printer()->Canvas->TextExtent("Hello World!").cy.

- TextWidth() returns the same as Printer()->Canvas->TextExtent("Hello World!").cx.

- TextOut() writes a string to the canvas starting at point (x,y) and updates the PenPos property to the end of the string.

- TextRect() writes a string to the canvas at point (x,y) inside a clipping rectangle. A clipping rectangle limits the size of the text displayed. Any portion of the text that falls out of the rectangle is clipped and isn't displayed. The point (x,y) is the top left corner for displayed text.

Press F1 to see the parameters for the TCanvas methods.

To control the drawing and printing position (the pen position) on the canvas, use the property PenPos.

CAUTION

Every measure is in pixels, and the top left corner of the paper is (0,0).

Here's a small example of how to use TextRect():

```
TRect rect;
rect.Top = 30;
rect.Left = 30;
rect.Bottom = 110;
rect.Right = 110;
Canvas->TextRect(rect, 35, 35, "Hello World");
```

This will display text that falls inside the rectangle with the upper-left corner (30,30) and the bottom-right corner (110,110). The text is displayed at point (35,35), which is inside the clipping rectangle where all or some of the text, depending on the extent of the text, will be displayed.

Two general notes should be made:

- It's possible to access the TPrinter's Canvas property only after BeginDoc() has been called on the Printer() object. This also means that calls to Win32 functions that requires handles, like GetDeviceCaps(), should use Printer()->Handle before BeginDoc() is called and Printer()->Canvas->Handle after BeginDoc() has been called.

- Do not instantiate separate TPrinter objects by calling the TPrinter constructor. Instead, use the global instance of TPrinter, which is returned by the Printer() method. To use TPrinter, you must include its header file called printers.hpp.

Listing 23.8 is a sample of how to use the VCL to make a line printer with word wrap functionality.

LISTING 23.8   Example Line Printer

```
// --- See PrintSample3 for the complete source code
// Print the contents of Memo to the selected Printer.
// The methods can print in two ways: With or without Word wrap
```

LISTING 23.8 Continued

```cpp
// which can be set by the TCheckBox named WordWrapCheckBox.
void __fastcall TMainForm::Print()
{
    // --- Local variables --- //
    int iLineNumber=1;                         // Line number being
                                               // printer on the
                                               // current page

    AnsiString asCurrentLine;                  // Text of the current
                                               // line being printed
    int iStartX = 0, iStartY = 0;              // Start (X,Y) point
                                               // to print from.


    // Set the printing title
    Printer()->Title = "Print Sample 3";

    // Start the printing job
    Printer()->BeginDoc();

    // Make sure the printer and the memo has the same font
    Printer()->Canvas->Font->Assign(Memo->Font);

    // Height of the line (calculated just once)
    int iLineHeight = Printer()->Canvas->TextHeight(" ");

    // --- Start writing one line at a time --- //
    for(int iLine=0; iLine < Memo->Lines->Count; iLine++)
    {
        // Get the current line to be printed
        asCurrentLine = Memo->Lines->Strings[iLine];

        // Check if the line to be printed exceeds the width of
        // the page. If it does any the user have chosen print
        // with word wrap the word wrap routine will be run,
        // else the general print routine without word wrap
        // will be run.
        bool bExceedsWidth;
        bExceedsWidth = Printer()->Canvas->TextWidth(asCurrentLine)
                        +iStartX >= Printer()->PageWidth;

        // Word Wrap?
        if (WordWrapCheckBox->Checked && bExceedsWidth)
        {
            // -------------------------- //
            // --- Print with WordWrap --- //
            // -------------------------- //
```

LISTING 23.8   Continued

```
// Temporary variable
int iCount=1;

// Start copying one char at a time from the current
// line to be printed to the temporary string until
// we exceed the width
Printer()->Canvas->PenPos = TPoint(iStartX,
                        Printer()->Canvas->PenPos.y);

while(iCount <= asCurrentLine.Length())
{
    // Print one char at a time to the printer
    Printer()->Canvas->TextOut
            (
            Printer()->Canvas->PenPos.x,
            iStartY+iLineHeight*iLineNumber-1,
            asCurrentLine[iCount]
            );

    // If it's not the very last char, check if we
    // will exceed the width of the page next
    // time we print a char
    if (iCount != asCurrentLine.Length())
    {
        if (Printer()->Canvas->PenPos.x +
            Printer()->Canvas->TextWidth
                    (
                    asCurrentLine[iCount+1]) >
                    Printer()->PageWidth
                    )
        {
            // New line
            iLineNumber++;
            Printer()->Canvas->PenPos = TPoint
                        (
                        iStartX,
                        Printer()->Canvas->PenPos.y+
                        iLineHeight
                        );
        }
    }

    // New page?
```

LISTING 23.8 Continued

```
            if (Printer()->Canvas->PenPos.y+iLineHeight >=
                Printer()->PageHeight)
            {
                // Start a new page
                Printer()->NewPage();
                iLineNumber = 1;
                Printer()->Canvas->PenPos = TPoint
                                    (
                                    iStartX,
                                    Printer()->Canvas->PenPos.y
                                    );
            }

            // Next char
            iCount++;
        } // ! while

        // --- After having finished a Word wrapped line we
        //      need to insert a new line as usual and we
        //      need to check if a New Page is required
        //      as well ---

        // New line
        iLineNumber++;
        Printer()->Canvas->PenPos = TPoint
                            (
                            iStartX,
                            Printer()->Canvas->PenPos.y+
                            iLineHeight
                            );
        // New page?
        if (Printer()->Canvas->PenPos.y+iLineHeight >=
            Printer()->PageHeight)
        {
            // Start a new page
            Printer()->NewPage();
            iLineNumber = 1;
            Printer()->Canvas->PenPos = TPoint
                                (
                                iStartX,
                                Printer()->Canvas->PenPos.y
                                );
        }
    }
    else
    {
```

LISTING 23.8   Continued

```
                // -------------------------- //
                // --- Print without WordWrap --- //
                // -------------------------- //

                // -1 is used since iLineNumber is 1 based (start
                // value is 1 instead of 0) else we would get
                // an off-by-one error.
                Printer()->Canvas->TextOut
                                (
                                iStartX,
                                iStartY+iLineHeight*iLineNumber-1,
                                asCurrentLine
                                );

                // Check PenPos to see if we're going to extend the
                // height of the page next time we write a line.
                // If we do, then insert a new page!
                // NB: times 2 is because the PenPos.y hasn't been
                // updated to point at the next line.

                // New Page?
                if (Printer()->Canvas->PenPos.y+2*iLineHeight >=
                    Printer()->PageHeight)
                {
                    // Start a new page
                    Printer()->NewPage();
                    iLineNumber = 1;
                }
                else
                {
                    iLineNumber++;           // Ready for next line
                }
            } // ! if (wordwrap)
        } // ! for (all lines)

    // Update the caption with the number of pages printed
    Caption = Application->Title + " - " + Printer()->PageNumber +
            " Page(s) Printed";

    // End the printing job
    Printer()->EndDoc();
}
```

Printing Graphics

In this section we will give examples of how to properly print bitmaps and other image types to the printer. There's a lot of misunderstanding on how this should be accomplished, and we will try to explain how printing normally is performed and what's wrong with the current method.

Printing Bitmaps Using the VCL

The TCanvas class provides two functions for blitting (*blitting* is the operation of copying the bits of an image from one device context to another) bitmaps on canvases: Draw() and StretchDraw(). However, neither is very appropriate for blitting to a printer canvas, for several reasons. As mentioned earlier, TCanvas is an encapsulation of the Windows GDI, which is a series of routines that perform operations on a Device Context (DC). The Device Context is a structure that defines a set of graphic objects, their associated attributes, and the graphic modes that affect the output. The graphic objects can be pens for line drawing, brushes for painting and filling, bitmaps for copying or scrolling parts on the screen, palettes for defining sets of available colors, regions for clipping and other operations, plus a path for painting and drawing operations.

The problem with Draw() and StretchDraw() is that they work on standard bitmaps of the type device dependent bitmap (DDB), which are device driver and driver version dependent. This means that a DDB for a screen is different than the same DDB for a printer. This creates problems when blitting, because the DDB doesn't contain header information necessary for proper translation when passed between the different devices. For more information about blitting, read the article "Blitting Between DCs for Different Devices Is Unsupported" at http://support.microsoft.com/support/kb/articles/q195/8/30.asp. The Article ID is Q195830.

Many use DDBs because they require less memory and are faster than device independent bitmaps (DIBs). Some printer drivers detect DDB blitting and correct the problems that can arise, but not all printer drivers implement this and, of those that do, not all of them handle it equally well. It's therefore a good rule of thumb not to use Draw() or StretchDraw() on a printer canvas.

To solve this problem, Microsoft has provided GDI functions for converting a DDB to a DIB: GetDIBits() and StretchDIBits(). Reportedly, there are problems with these functions. The problem is that when calling GetDIBits(), in order to get the image bits, the palette is often neglected in the process. The best thing to do is to manufacture a really good DIB header and color table. If the image is coming from a .res file, disk file, or other reliable DIB source, the job is easy, providing you do not mind retrieving the DIB directly from the source, with no VCL code between you and the image. Note that building a good bitmap reader is not exactly

easy (as evidenced in the VCL). Getting a good color table from a screen image is more difficult, because you must take into account the correct palette, should the device be a palette
device. That includes 1-, 4-, and 8-bit images, all of which have color tables. Finally, should
the printer be a palette device (which is rare), you must make a palette available to the printer.
Under NT, just about every printer has at least a palette structure under the hood (even if it is
internally bypassed), not that this is really valuable here.

Luckily for us, the VCL provides wrappers for `GetDIBits()`, called `GetDIBSizes()` and
`GetDIB()`, which contain palette handling. Listing 23.9 is a sample of how to use these wrappers.

LISTING 23.9 Printing Using `StretchDIBits()`

```
// --- See StretchBltBitmap.cpp in the PrintTools directory
//     for the complete source code ---
// pCanvas -> Destination canvas
// ix, iY, iWidth and iHeight -> Defines the rectangle on the
//                               canvas to blit the DDB
//                               (Device Dependent Bitmap)
// pBitmap -> The bitmap to blit
void __fastcall StretchBltBitmap(TCanvas *pCanvas, int iX, int iY,
                                 int iWidth, int iHeight,
                                 Graphics::TBitmap *pBitmap)
{
    // --- Local variables --- //
    unsigned int iInfoHeaderSize=0;  // Size of Bitmap info
                                     // header
    unsigned int iImageSize=0;       // Size of Bitmap image
    BITMAPINFO *pBitmapInfoHeader;   // Pointer to Bitmap info
                                     // header
    unsigned char *pBitmapImageBits; // Pointer to Bitmap Image
                                     // Bits

    // First we call GetDIBSizes() to determine the amount of
    // memory that must be allocated before calling GetDIB()
    // NB: GetDIBSizes() is a part of the VCL.
    GetDIBSizes(pBitmap->Handle,    // Bitmap handle
                iInfoHeaderSize,    // Bitmap info header size
                                    // (data size)
                iImageSize);        // Bitmap bits size

    // Next we allocate memory according to the information
    // returned by GetDIBSizes()
    pBitmapInfoHeader = new BITMAPINFO[iInfoHeaderSize];
    pBitmapImageBits  = new unsigned char[iImageSize];
```

LISTING 23.9   Continued

```
    // Call GetDIB() to convert a device dependent bitmap into a
    // Device Independent Bitmap (a DIB).
    // NB: GetDIB() is a part of the VCL.
    GetDIB(pBitmap->Handle,      // Bitmap handle
           pBitmap->Palette,     // Bitmap palette
           pBitmapInfoHeader,    // Bitmap info header (data)
           pBitmapImageBits);    // Bitmap bits


    // Last we'll copy the color data for a rectangle of pixels
    // in the DIB to the specified destination rectangle.
    // NB: StrecthDIBits() is supplied by the Win32 API.
    StretchDIBits(pCanvas->Handle,    // Destination Canvas
                  iX,                 // Destination upper X coord
                  iY,                 // Destination upper Y coord
                  iWidth,             // Destination Width
                  iHeight,            // Destination Height
                  0,                  // Source upper X coord
                  0,                  // Source upper Y coord
                  pBitmap->Width,     // Source Width
                  pBitmap->Height,    // Source Height
                  pBitmapImageBits,   // Image Bits
                  pBitmapInfoHeader,  // Image Data (Info Header)
                  DIB_RGB_COLORS,     // Usage: The color table
                                      // contains literal RGB
                                      // values.
                  SRCCOPY);           // Raster operation code:
                                      // Copies the source
                                      // rectangle directly to
                                      // the destination rectangle

    // Clean up. Release allocated memory.
    delete []pBitmapInfoHeader;
    delete []pBitmapImageBits;
}
```

Listing 23.10 is an example from `PrintSample4`, which you can find on the CD-ROM, on how to call this function. You must install the `TPrintDIB` component in C++Builder before trying to open the `PrintSample4` project.

LISTING 23.10   Printing Using `StretchBltBitmap`

```
// See PrintSample4 for the complete source code.
void __fastcall TMainForm::PrintBmpVCLButtonClick(TObject *Sender)
```

LISTING 23.10   Continued

```cpp
{
    // Set orientation to Portrait
    Printer()->Orientation = poPortrait;

    // Set a title for the print job
    Printer()->Title = "Print Sample 4 (VCL)";

    // Start printing
    Printer()->BeginDoc();

    // Find the correct scaling (only works correctly for images
    // smaller than the paper. It doesn't scale in that sense!)
    float fPrinterVert = (float)GetDeviceCaps
                                (
                                Printer()->Canvas->Handle,
                                LOGPIXELSY
                                );
    float fPrinterHorz = (float)GetDeviceCaps
                                (
                                Printer()->Canvas->Handle,
                                LOGPIXELSX
                                );
    float fScreenVert  = (float)GetDeviceCaps
                                (
                                this->Canvas->Handle,
                                LOGPIXELSY
                                );
    float fScreenHorz  = (float)GetDeviceCaps
                                (
                                this->Canvas->Handle,
                                LOGPIXELSX
                                );
    int iHeight = (int) ((float)Image->Picture->Bitmap->Height *
                                (fPrinterVert / fScreenVert));
    int iWidth  = (int) ((float)Image->Picture->Bitmap->Width *
                                (fPrinterHorz / fScreenHorz));

    // Print bitmap (VCL version)
    StretchBltBitmap(Printer()->Canvas, 0, 0, iWidth, iHeight,
                    Image->Picture->Bitmap);

    // Done printing
    Printer()->EndDoc();
}
```

Joe C. Hecht has posted a Delphi sample code to Deja.com on how to handle the palette conversion yourself instead of depending on Microsoft or Borland functions. The C++Builder component, called `TPrintDIB`, is included on the accompanying CD-ROM in the `TPrintDIB` subdirectory under this chapter. This C++Builder version of Joe C. Hecht's Delphi code is done by Damon Chandler and Dave Richard. The component should provide even better palette handling than Borland's implementation, though I haven't been able to find any differences in my test prints. Joe C. Hecht also has an improved version of this called `TExcellentImagePrinter` that is shareware. You can find it at `http://www.code4sale.com/joehecht`. The following is an extract from `PrintSample4` on how to use the `TPrintDIB` component. The scale code has been left out, because it's the same as in Listing 23.10. You must install `TPrintDIB` in C++Builder before trying to open the `PrintSample4` project.

```
// Print bitmap (TPrintDIB version)
PrintDIB->StretchDrawDIB(Printer()->Canvas->Handle, 0, 0,
                         iWidth, iHeight,  Image->Picture->Bitmap);
```

Printing Other Types of Graphics Using the VCL

A simple way of printing images other than bitmaps is to load the image into an instance of the `TPicture` class. This can be done either through a `TImage` component or a dynamically created instance of `TPicture`, and then copy the image's content to a `TBitmap` and print this bitmap using the `StretchBltBitmap()` function listed earlier or `TPrintDIB`. Listing 23.11 is an example of printing a picture loaded into a `TImage` object called `Image1`:

LISTING 23.11 Printing Pictures Other than Bitmaps

```
// TBitmap instance which will contain the converted picture
Graphics::TBitmap *pBitmap = new Graphics::TBitmap();

try
{
    // Prepare the bitmap
    pBitmap->Width  = Image1->Picture->Width;
    pBitmap->Height = Image1->Picture->Height;
    pBitmap->PixelFormat = pf24bit;

    // Convert the picture to a bitmap
    pBitmap->Canvas->Draw(0,0, Image1->Picture->Graphic);

    // Print the image
    Printer()->BeginDoc();
    StretchBltBitmap(Printer()->Canvas, 0, 0, 3000, 3000,
                     pBitmap);
```

LISTING 23.11   Continued

```
      Printer()->EndDoc();
   }
   catch(...) {}

   // Clean up
   delete pBitmap;
```

Using Advanced Printing Techniques

Included on the accompanying CD-ROM in the section for this chapter is a tool called Device Info, which can be helpful when you need to get an overview of device-specific information. The program uses the Win32 API function GetDeviceCaps(), which is covered in the next section.

Determining Printer Resolution

The printer resolution (also known as Print Quality) is measured in pixels per inch (ppi). There are two ways to access this information:

- Use GetDeviceCaps() with parameters LOGPIXELSX and LOGPIXELSY to get both the horizontal and vertical resolutions.

  ```
  int iLogPixelsX = GetDeviceCaps(Printer()->Handle, LOGPIXELSX);
  int iLogPixelsY = GetDeviceCaps(Printer()->Handle, LOGPIXELSY);
  ```

- Use the TFont's PixelsPerInch property. Notice that the information returned from PixelsPerInch is valid only when the vertical and horizontal resolutions are the same (some Inkjet printers have different vertical and horizontal resolutions), because PixelsPerInch is the same as GetDeviceCaps() with LOGPIXELSY. Remember that the printer must be printing, and BeginDoc() must have been called on the Printer() object before trying to access the printer's Canvas property.

  ```
  int iPixelsPerInch = Printer()->Canvas->Font->PixelsPerInch;
  ```

Determining the Printable Paper Size

You can get information about the current paper size in both pixels and millimeters. You can't print on all of the paper, so knowing the size of the printable and non-printable areas can be very useful.

Pixels Method

The following functions return the sizes in pixels:

- Use `GetDeviceCaps()` with parameters `HORZRES` and `VERTRES` to get the number of pixels vertically and horizontally.

```
int iHorzRes = GetDeviceCaps(Printer()->Handle, HORZRES);
int iVertRes = GetDeviceCaps(Printer()->Handle, VERTRES);
```

- Use the `TPrinter`'s `PageWidth` and `PageHeight` properties, which actually are the `TPrinter`'s encapsulation of the two calls made in the first method.

```
int iHorzRes = Printer()->PageWidth;
int iVertRes = Printer()->PageHeight;
NB: There's an error in the Borland Help example for using PageWidth and
➥PageHeight.
The line: TPrinter Prntr = Printer();should be changed to: TPrinter *Prntr
➥= Printer();
```

Millimeters Method

To get the size of the paper in millimeters, repeat the calls made in the first method in the previous section with the parameters `HORZSIZE` and `VERTSIZE` instead of `HORZRES` and `VERTRES`.

Determining the Physical Sizes

There are two kinds of physical paper information that can be useful. One is the actual size of the paper, which is almost always greater than the printable size, the other is the physical offset. The physical offset is the length from the left side and the top of the paper to the start of the printable area. The results are returned in device units (pixels).

Physical Paper Size

Call `GetDeviceCaps()` with the parameters `PHYSICALWIDTH` and `PHYSICALHEIGHT` to get the physical size of the paper.

Physical Offset

There are two kinds of offsets:

- The distance from the left edge of the paper to the left edge of the printable area. To get this information, use `GetDeviceCaps()` with parameter `PHYSICALOFFSETX`.
- The distance from the top edge of the paper to the top edge of the printable area. To get this information, use `GetDeviceCaps()` with parameter `PHYSICALOFFSETY`.

Determining Printer Drawing Capabilities

To determine what the printer supports in terms of GDI drawing features, we can once again use the GetDeviceCaps() function. This information can be useful if your application requires a printer to support various GDI functions in order to print properly. Actually, the fact that your printer doesn't fully support all features doesn't mean you can't use them. The GDI will emulate them for you. One exception is that GDI can't emulate BitBlt(), StretchBlt(), or DIBStretchBlt() on a printer that doesn't support raster scanline pixels, such as a pen plotter.

There are five main categories from which to gather information:

- RASTERCAPS   Contains information about what bitmap functions the printer supports, such as StretchDIBits:

```
if (GetDeviceCaps(Printer()->Handle, RASTERCAPS) & RC_STRETCHDIB)
    // The printer supports StretchDIBits
else
    // The printer doesn't support StretchDIBits
```

- CURVECAPS   Contains information about what curve-drawing functions the printer supports, such as circles:

```
if (GetDeviceCaps(Printer()->Handle, CURVECAPS) & CC_CIRCLES)
    // The printer supports drawing of Circles
else
    // The printer doesn't support drawing of Circles
```

- LINECAPS   Contains information about what line drawing functions the printer supports, such as whether the printer supports polylines:

```
if (GetDeviceCaps(Printer()->Handle, LINECAPS) & LC_POLYLINE)
    // The printer supports drawing of PolyLines
else
    // The printer doesn't support drawing of PolyLines
```

- POLYGONALCAPS   Contains information about what polygonal drawing functions the printer supports, such as rectangles:

```
if (GetDeviceCaps(Printer()->Handle, POLYGONALCAPS) & PC_RECTANGLE)
    // The printer supports drawing of Rectangles
else
    // The printer doesn't support drawing of Rectangles
```

- TEXTCAPS   Contains information about what text-drawing functions the printer supports, such as italics:

```
if (GetDeviceCaps(Printer()->Handle, TEXTCAPS) & TC_IA_ABLE)
    // The printer supports drawing of Italics.
else
    // The printer doesn't support drawing of Italics
```

How to Print with a Rotated Font

Assuming that your printer supports rotated characters and the font is a TrueType font, the sample in Listing 23.12 demonstrates how printing with rotated fonts can be achieved.

LISTING 23.12   Printing with a Rotated Font

```
// --- See PrintSample5 for the complete source code ---
void __fastcall TMainForm::PrintWithRotatedFont()
{
    // --- Local variables --- //
    TLogFont logFont;                 // A VCL encapsulation of the
                                      // WIN32 LOGFONT.
                                      // The LOGFONT structure defines
                                      // the attributes of a font.
    HFONT hOldFont;                   // Handle to the font (before
                                      // the logfont attributes
                                      // were applied)
    HFONT hNewFont;                   // Handle to the font (after
                                      // the logfont attributes
                                      // are applied)

    // Start the printing procedure
    Printer()->BeginDoc();
    Printer()->Canvas->Font->Name = "Arial";
    Printer()->Canvas->Font->Size = 24;

    // Create an instance of TLogFont from the Printer canvas'
    // current font.
    GetObject(Printer()->Canvas->Font->Handle,
              sizeof(logFont),
              &logFont);
    // Set it rotate 45 degrees counter clockwise
    logFont.lfEscapement = 450;
    logFont.lfOrientation = 450;

    // Apply the logfont attributes to the current font and save
    // the handle to it in hNewFont
    hNewFont = CreateFontIndirect(&logFont);
    // Save a handle to the old font (the printers canvas'
    // current font) and set the printers canvas' font to the new
    // font
    hOldFont = SelectObject(Printer()->Canvas->Handle, hNewFont);

    // Print text to the printer using the rotated font
    Printer()->Canvas->TextOut(
```

LISTING 23.12   Continued

```
            // 2.5" to the right and 3.0" down
            int(2.5*GetDeviceCaps(Printer()->Canvas->Handle,
                                LOGPIXELSY)),
            int(3.0*GetDeviceCaps(Printer()->Canvas->Handle,
                                LOGPIXELSY)),
            "Rotated Text!");

    // Restore the old font, so it's now the printers canvas'
    // current font
    SelectObject(Printer()->Canvas->Handle, hOldFont);
    // Delete our instance of the new font
    DeleteObject(hNewFont);

    // Done printing
    Printer()->EndDoc();
}
```

Getting Access to Printer Settings and Setup

The key to accessing printer settings information is the Win32 DEVMODE structure. This structure contains information about device setup, the data that can be changed from printout to printout, the number of copies to be printed, and so on. You can access and use the DEVMODE using various functions. Win32's DocumentProperties(), GetPrinter(), SetPrinter(), and DeviceCapabilities() will be covered here, as will TPrinter's GetPrinter() and SetPrinter(). The Win32 GetPrinter() and SetPrinter() functions open up even more detailed data that is hidden in the various PRINTER_INFO structures. To gain access to the read-only data (such as paper bin names, paper names, paper sizes), use DeviceCapabilities().

The following is a short overview of what the different functions can do:

- DeviceCapabilities()   This function retrieves the capabilities of a printer device driver.
- DocumentProperties()   This function retrieves or modifies printer initialization information or displays a printer-configuration property sheet for the specified printer.
- TPrinter's GetPrinter() and SetPrinter()   These are TPrinter's encapsulation of DocumentProperties(). VCL also contains an encapsulation for the Print Setup dialog that DocumentProperties() can display, called TPrinterSetupDialog. If you want to use TPrinter's methods during printing, such as the TCanvas methods, you need to use GetPrinter() instead of DocumentProperties() to set up the printing, because the DocumentProperties() function requires you perform an OpenPrinter() call first to get

a printer handle. It can't use TPrinter's Handle property, which keeps you from using TPrinter, because you're working with two different handles that can't work together. Use Get/SetPrinter() if you need to get or set the DEVMODE for a printer. SetPrinter() is used only to update the Capabilities property of TPrinter. SetPrinter() doesn't change any default values. To change default values, use Win32's SetPrinter() and PRINTER_INFO_2. More about that later.

- Win32's GetPrinter()   This function retrieves information about a specified printer. The information is returned at different levels, specified by the level variable in the call. Win 95/98 supports levels 1, 2, and 5, and Windows NT/2000 supports levels 1–9. The result is returned in a level structure, such as a PRINTER_INFO_2 structure for level 2.

- Win32's SetPrinter()   This function sets the data for a specified printer or sets the state of the specified printer by pausing printing, resuming printing, or clearing all print jobs. Win 95/98 supports levels 0, 2, and 5, and Windows NT/2000 supports levels 0, 2–5, and 7–9.

CAUTION

TPrinter's GetPrinter() and SetPrinter() functions shouldn't be confused with Win32's GetPrinter() and SetPrinter() functions.

In general you should consult the Win32 Reference for details about the contents of the DEVMODE and the PRINTER_INFO structures. The functions and methods mentioned earlier will be covered later in this section, together with some less common API functions.

How to Get the Default Printer Name

TPrinter supplies a good encapsulation for getting the default printer name. To read the default printer name, set the PrinterIndex property to -1 and call TPrinter's GetPrinter() to get the name of the printer (device).

```
char szDeviceName[CCHDEVICENAME], // Printer Name
     szDriverName[MAX_PATH],       // Dummy variable
     szPortName[MAX_PATH];         // Dummy variable
THandle hPrnDevMode;              // Dummy variable

// Select the default printer
Printer()->PrinterIndex = -1;

// Get the name of the default printer (szDeviceName now
// contains the default printers name)
```

```
Printer()->GetPrinter(szDeviceName, szDriverName, szPortName,
                      hPrnDevMode);
```

The name of the printer can also be read directly from the `Printers` property:

```
Printer()->Printers->Strings[Printer()->PrinterIndex];
```

This requires that `PrinterIndex` has been set to `-1` prior to calling this property.

How to Set the Default Printer

There are three ways to do this, and they are discussed and demonstrated in the following text and in Listings 23.13, 23.14, and 23.15. You can find the full source code in the `Samples` subdirectory for this chapter under `SetDefaultPrinter`.

As mentioned earlier, the `PRINTER_INFO` structures are used to get and set information about a given printer. Get the information with Win32's `GetPrinter()` function, and set it with Win32's `SetPrinter()` function.

The first method is to write the information in the `WIN.INI` file. This works under all versions of Windows. Even though `WIN.INI` is a leftover from the Win 3.x days, it's still used for a few purposes under the new versions of Windows. One of them is reading and setting the default printer. The `Profile` string, from the `PrinterPorts` section in the INI file, looks like this under Windows 9x:

```
HP LaserJet 4P,HPPCL5MS,LPT1:
```

and like this under Windows NT/2000:

```
HP LaserJet 4P,winspool,LPT1:
```

You don't need to remember all of this, because you can gain access to this information using `TPrinter`'s `GetPrinter()`. However, for some reason, `GetPrinter()` returns different results under Win9x and Windows NT/2000, and neither of the results is complete. Often either the driver name or the port name is empty. This is why I've added code to the sample in Listing 23.13 that retrieves all of the information from the INI file itself before setting the default printer.

LISTING 23.13   Set Default Printer Using INI Files

```
void __fastcall TMainForm::SetDefaultPrinterINI()
{
    char szDeviceName[CCHDEVICENAME], // Printer Name
         szDriverName[MAX_PATH],       // Name of driver
         szPortName[MAX_PATH];         // PortName/File/UNC Path
    THandle hPrnDevMode;               // Handle to the memory area
```

LISTING 23.13   Continued

```
                                    // containing the DEVMODE
                                    // structure

// Get Printer Info (this way we avoid having to remove any
// eventual "On LPT1:" strings (which also can be translated
// on other systems)
// Get Name
Printer()->GetPrinter(szDeviceName, szDriverName,
                      szPortName, hPrnDevMode);
if (!strlen(szPortName) || !strlen(szDriverName))
{
    // --- szPortName or szDriverName was empty, fill them ---
    char szTemp[MAX_PATH];
    GetProfileString("Devices", szDeviceName, "",
                     szTemp, MAX_PATH);

    // Find the index of the next comma
    char *pszPos = StrPos(szTemp, ",");
    if (pszPos)
    {
        // Get Driver Name
        int iLength = strlen(szTemp)-strlen(pszPos);
        strncpy(szDriverName, szTemp, iLength);
        // Terminate string
        szDriverName[iLength] = '\0';
        // Get Port Name
        strcpy(szPortName,  ++pszPos);
    } // ! if
} // ! if

// Create the profile string for the new default printer
AnsiString asProfileString = AnsiString(szDeviceName)+","+
                             szDriverName+","+szPortName;

// To help the user, show the Profile string in the caption
Caption = Application->Title + " [ProfileString: \"" +
          asProfileString + "\"]";

// Write the profile string to WIN.INI (set the new
// default printer)
WriteProfileString(TEXT("Windows"),TEXT("Device"),
                   asProfileString.c_str() );

// Depending on the OS send out the correct BROADCAST message
if (IsNT())
{
```

LISTING 23.13   Continued

```
        // New message type for NT/W2k
        SendMessageTimeout(HWND_BROADCAST, WM_WININICHANGE, 0L,
                           0L, SMTO_NORMAL, 1000, NULL);
    }
    else
    {
        // Old message type for windows 9x
        SendMessageTimeout(HWND_BROADCAST, WM_WININICHANGE, 0L,
                           (LPARAM)(LPCTSTR)"windows", SMTO_NORMAL,
                           1000, NULL);
    }
}
```

The second method is to use Win32's SetPrinter() on a PRINTER_INFO_5 structure. This
works only under Windows 95/98. First we call GetPrinter() to calculate the amount of
memory that's needed to fill the PRINTER_INFO_5 structure. (The PRINTER_INFO_2 structure
also could have been used here, but the PRINTER_INFO_5 structure is smaller and we don't need
all the extra information PRINTER_INFO_2 contains.) Then we allocate that memory and call
GetPrinter() to fill the PRINTER_INFO_5 structure. Then we set its attribute to the default
printer and save this change with a call to SetPrinter(). This is shown in Listing 23.14.

LISTING 23.14   Setting the Default Printer Using SetPrinter() and PRINTER_INFO_5

```
bool __fastcall TMainForm::SetDefaultPrinter9x
                             (char *pszPrinterName)
{
    HANDLE hPrinter;          // Printer handle
    BOOL   bSucces = TRUE;    // Success flag

    // --- Open printer and get a handle to it ---
    if(OpenPrinter(pszPrinterName, &hPrinter, NULL))
    {
        // Printer info (note: PRINTER_INFO_2 could also
        // have been used but the PRINTER_INFO_5
        // struct is smaller)
        LPPRINTER_INFO_5 printerInfo;
        DWORD dwBytesNeeded = 0;

        // Get bytes needed
        GetPrinter(hPrinter, 5, NULL, 0, &dwBytesNeeded);
        if (dwBytesNeeded &&
            (printerInfo = (LPPRINTER_INFO_5)
                        malloc(dwBytesNeeded)) != NULL)
```

LISTING 23.14   Continued

```
    {
        // --- Set the struct to the contents of the
        // printers old settings ---
        if (GetPrinter(hPrinter, 5, (LPBYTE) printerInfo,
                        dwBytesNeeded, &dwBytesNeeded))
        {
            // Set the default attribute
            printerInfo->Attributes |=
                                    PRINTER_ATTRIBUTE_DEFAULT;

            // Update printer settings
            if (SetPrinter(hPrinter, 5,
                            (LPBYTE) printerInfo, 0))
            {
                bSucces = TRUE;
            }
            else
            {
                bSucces = FALSE;
            } // ! if SetPrinter()
        }
        else
        {
            bSucces = FALSE;
        } // ! if GetPrinter()

        // Deallocate memory
        free(printerInfo);
    }
    else
    {
        bSucces = FALSE;
    } // ! if malloc()

    // Close the printer
    ClosePrinter(hPrinter);
    return bSucces;
}
else
{
    return FALSE;
} // ! if OpenPrinter()
}
```

The third method is to use Win32's `SetDefaultPrinter()`, which is available only in Windows 2000.

```
bool __fastcall TMainForm::SetDefaultPrinter2K(char *pszPrinterName)
{
    // Windows 2000 only (requires BCB5 or the Windows 2000 SDK
    // to be installed)
    return SetDefaultPrinter (pszPrinterName)
}
```

Resetting `TPrinter`

Sometimes the `Printer()` object needs to be forced to load the `DEVMODE` for the selected printer internally. We can do this by calling `SetPrinter()` with the `THandle` parameter set to zero.

```
void ResetTPrinter()
{
    char szDeviceName[CCHDEVICENAME], // Dummy variable (Device Name)
         szDriverName[MAX_PATH],      // Dummy variable (Driver Name)
         szPortName[MAX_PATH];        // Dummy variable (Port Name)
    THandle hPrnDevMode;              // Dummy variable (DEVMODE)

    Printer()->GetPrinter(szDeviceName, szDriverName, szPortName, hPrnDevMode);
    Printer()->SetPrinter(szDeviceName, szDriverName,  szPortName, 0);
}
```

General Information About Accessing `DEVMODE` Using `TPrinter`

Before we proceed with the more advanced topics, we should discuss how to access the `DEVMODE` (or `TDevMode`, as the VCL encapsulation is called) for a printer. To obtain a pointer to the `DEVMODE` structure for a printer, you must first call `TPrinter`'s `GetPrinter()` method to obtain a pointer to the memory object that contains this structure. Next you call Win32's `GlobalLock()` function to obtain a pointer to the first byte of the memory object, which is the `DEVMODE` structure as shown in Listing 23.15.

LISTING 23.15   An Example of Using `DEVMODE` and `TPrinter`'s `GetPrinter()` Function

```
    char szDeviceName[CCHDEVICENAME], // Printer Name
         szDriverName[MAX_PATH],      // Dummy variable
         szPortName[MAX_PATH];        // Dummy variable
    THandle hPrnDevMode;              // Dummy variable
    PDEVMODE pDevMode;                // DeviceMode pointer

    // Get the name of the default printer (szDeviceName now
```

LISTING 23.15 Continued

```
// contains the default printers name)
Printer()->GetPrinter(szDeviceName, szDriverName,
                       szPortName, hPrnDevMode);

if (hPrnDevMode!=0)
{
    // Obtain the pointer to the DEVMODE
    pDevMode =  (PDEVMODE) GlobalLock((HANDLE)hPrnDevMode);
    if (pDevMode == NULL)
        throw Exception("Couldn't get pointer "
                        "to DEVMODE struct");

    // Here comes your code for working with the
    //DEVMODE structure

    //...
    //...
    // Eg. set the printer bin to the manual bin
    pDevMode->dmFields |= DMBIN_MANUAL;
    pDevMode->dmDefaultSource = DMBIN_MANUAL;

    // Finally we need to release the DEVMODE structure
    GlobalUnlock((HANDLE)hPrnDevMode);

    // Do the printing with the new settings
    Printer()->BeginDoc();
    Printer()->Canvas->TextOut(0,0,"Hello World!");
    Printer()->EndDoc();
}
else
    throw Exception("Couldn't obtain printer handle!");
```

This changes only the settings for the current printer and only as long as you don't change the PrinterIndex property. It doesn't change the system's default setting, not even if you call TPrinter's SetPrinter() function after changing the DEVMODE structure. SetPrinter() is used only to update TPrinter's Capability property. To change the default settings, you need to work on the DEVMODE pointer, which you can access through the PRINTER_INFO_2 structure for the printer for which you want to set the settings.

Using PRINTER_INFO_2

Besides the DEVMODE structure, the other structure that contains valuable information about a printer is PRINTER_INFO_2. Here you can find information about the name of the server the printer is attached to (if any), the real name of the printer (not always the same as the pDeviceName in DEVMODE), the number of jobs that are queued for the printer, the printer's status, and so on. A listing of the complete PRINTER_INFO_2 structure follows:

```
typedef struct _PRINTER_INFO_2 {
    LPTSTR    pServerName;
    LPTSTR    pPrinterName;
    LPTSTR    pShareName;
    LPTSTR    pPortName;
    LPTSTR    pDriverName;
    LPTSTR    pComment;
    LPTSTR    pLocation;
    LPDEVMODE pDevMode;
    LPTSTR    pSepFile;
    LPTSTR    pPrintProcessor;
    LPTSTR    pDatatype;
    LPTSTR    pParameters;
    PSECURITY_DESCRIPTOR pSecurityDescriptor;
    DWORD     Attributes;
    DWORD     Priority;
    DWORD     DefaultPriority;
    DWORD     StartTime;
    DWORD     UntilTime;
    DWORD     Status;
    DWORD     cJobs;
    DWORD     AveragePPM;
} PRINTER_INFO_2, *PPRINTER_INFO_2;
```

As you can see, it contains helpful information about a printer. Listing 23.16 is a sample of how to read and set comments for a printer. The approach for working with the structure is similar for the rest of the PRINTER_INFO structures.

Listing 23.16   Example of Getting and Setting Printer Comments

```
AnsiString __fastcall TMainForm::GetComment(char *szPrinterName)
{
    HANDLE            hPrinter;    // Handle to the printer
    PRINTER_DEFAULTS  pd;          // (Only used under Windows
                                   // NT/2000, ignored by
                                   // Windows 9x)
    DWORD             dwNeeded;    // Size of PRINTER_INFO_2
                                   // structure in bytes
    PRINTER_INFO_2    *pPrtInfo2;  // Pointer to the
                                   // PRINTER_INFO_2 struct.
    AnsiString        asComment;   // Comment collected from
                                   // PRINTER_INFO_2
```

LISTING 23.16 Continued

```cpp
// Init the Printer defaults structs
ZeroMemory(&pd, sizeof(PRINTER_DEFAULTS));
// Get full access
pd.DesiredAccess = PRINTER_ALL_ACCESS;

// Open printer
if(!OpenPrinter(szPrinterName, &hPrinter, &pd))
{
   // OpenPrinter() has failed
   throw Exception("Call to OpenPrinter() failed");
}

// Get the size of the PRINTER_INFO_2 structure
// (2 indicates the level)
if(!GetPrinter(hPrinter, 2, NULL, 0, &dwNeeded))
{
    // If it's anything else but
    // ERROR_INSUFFICIENT_BUFFER we bail out
    if(GetLastError() != ERROR_INSUFFICIENT_BUFFER)
    {
       ClosePrinter(hPrinter);
       throw Exception("1st call to GetPrinter() failed");
    }
}

// Allocate enough memory for the PRINTER_INFO_2 structure
pPrtInfo2 = (PRINTER_INFO_2*) malloc(dwNeeded);
if(pPrtInfo2 == NULL)
{
   // malloc() failed
   ClosePrinter(hPrinter);
   throw Exception("Call to malloc() failed");
}

// Fill the PRINTER_INFO_2 structure with information
if(!GetPrinter(hPrinter, 2, (LPBYTE)pPrtInfo2,
               dwNeeded, &dwNeeded))
{
   // Second call to GetPrinter() failed
   free(pPrtInfo2);
   ClosePrinter(hPrinter);
   throw Exception("2nd call to GetPrinter() failed");
}

// Get the comment
asComment = pPrtInfo2->pComment;
```

LISTING 23.16   Continued

```cpp
    // Clean up.
    free(pPrtInfo2);
    ClosePrinter(hPrinter);

    // return comment
    return asComment;
}
//----------------------------------------------------------------
void __fastcall TMainForm::SetComment(char *szPrinterName,
                                       AnsiString &asComment)
{
    HANDLE              hPrinter;   // Handle to the printer
    PRINTER_DEFAULTS    pd;         // (Only used under Windows
                                    // NT/2000, ignored by
                                    // Windows 9x)
    DWORD               dwNeeded;   // Size of PRINTER_INFO_2
                                    // structure in bytes
    PRINTER_INFO_2      *pPrtInfo2; // Pointer to the
                                    // PRINTER_INFO_2 struct.

    // Init the Printer defaults structs
    ZeroMemory(&pd, sizeof(PRINTER_DEFAULTS));
    // Get full access
    pd.DesiredAccess = PRINTER_ALL_ACCESS;

    // Open printer
    if(!OpenPrinter(szPrinterName, &hPrinter, &pd))
    {
        // OpenPrinter() has failed
        throw Exception("Call to OpenPrinter() failed");
    }

    // Get the size of the PRINTER_INFO_2 structure
    // (2 indicates the level)
    if(!GetPrinter(hPrinter, 2, NULL, 0, &dwNeeded))
    {
        // If it's anything else but
        // ERROR_INSUFFICIENT_BUFFER we bail out
        if(GetLastError() != ERROR_INSUFFICIENT_BUFFER)
        {
            ClosePrinter(hPrinter);
            throw Exception("1st call to GetPrinter() failed");
        }
```

LISTING 23.16   Continued

```
    }

    // Allocate enough memory for the PRINTER_INFO_2 structure
    pPrtInfo2 = (PRINTER_INFO_2*) malloc(dwNeeded);
    if(pPrtInfo2 == NULL)
    {
        // malloc() failed
        ClosePrinter(hPrinter);
        throw Exception("Call to malloc() failed");
    }

    // Fill the PRINTER_INFO_2 structure with information
    if(!GetPrinter(hPrinter, 2, (LPBYTE)pPrtInfo2,
                   dwNeeded, &dwNeeded))
    {
        // Second call to GetPrinter() failed
        free(pPrtInfo2);
        ClosePrinter(hPrinter);
        throw Exception("2nd call to GetPrinter() failed");
    }

    // Set the comment
    pPrtInfo2->pComment = asComment.c_str();

    // Update the Printer with the new information
    if(!SetPrinter(hPrinter, 2, (LPBYTE)pPrtInfo2, 0))
    {
        // SetPrinter() has failed
        free(pPrtInfo2);
        ClosePrinter(hPrinter);
        throw Exception("Call to SetPrinter() failed");
    }

    // Clean up.
    free(pPrtInfo2);
    ClosePrinter(hPrinter);
}
```

As mentioned earlier, the TPrinter's GetPrinter() isn't capable of setting the system defaults. To do so, such as to change the default paper bin, you need to use the PRINTER_INFO_2 structure shown in Listing 23.17.

LISTING 23.17   Setting the Printer's Paper Source to the Manual Feeder

```
void SetDefaultPaperSourceToManualFeed(char *szPrinterName)
{
    HANDLE            hPrinter;        // Handle to the printer
    PRINTER_DEFAULTS  pd;              // (Only used under
                                       // Windows NT/2000,
                                       // ignored by Windows 9x)
    DWORD             dwNeeded;        // Size of PRINTER_INFO_2
                                       // structure in bytes
    PRINTER_INFO_2    *pPrtInfo2;      // Pointer to the
                                       // PRINTER_INFO_2 struct.

    // Init the Printer defaults structs
    ZeroMemory(&pd, sizeof(PRINTER_DEFAULTS));
    // Get full access
    pd.DesiredAccess = PRINTER_ALL_ACCESS;

    // Open printer
    if(!OpenPrinter(szPrinterName, &hPrinter, &pd))
    {
        // OpenPrinter() has failed
        throw Exception("Call to OpenPrinter() failed");
    }

    // Get the size of the PRINTER_INFO_2 structure
    // (2 indicates the level)
    if(!GetPrinter(hPrinter, 2, NULL, 0, &dwNeeded))
    {
        // If it's anything else but
        // ERROR_INSUFFICIENT_BUFFER we bail out
        if(GetLastError() != ERROR_INSUFFICIENT_BUFFER)
        {
            ClosePrinter(hPrinter);
            throw Exception("1st call to GetPrinter() failed");
        }
    }

    // Allocate enough memory for the PRINTER_INFO_2 structure
    pPrtInfo2 = (PRINTER_INFO_2*) malloc(dwNeeded);
    if(pPrtInfo2 == NULL)
    {
        // malloc() failed
        ClosePrinter(hPrinter);
        throw Exception("Call to malloc() failed");
    }
```

LISTING 23.17 Continued

```
    // Fill the PRINTER_INFO_2 structure with information
    if(!GetPrinter(hPrinter, 2, (LPBYTE)pPrtInfo2,
                   dwNeeded, &dwNeeded))
    {
        // Second call to GetPrinter() failed
        free(pPrtInfo2);
        ClosePrinter(hPrinter);
        throw Exception("2nd call to GetPrinter() failed");
    }

    // Set papersource to DMBIN_MANUAL
    pPrtInfo2->pDevMode->dmFields |= DMBIN_MANUAL;
    pPrtInfo2->pDevMode->dmDefaultSource = DMBIN_MANUAL;

    // Update the Printer with the new information
    if(!SetPrinter(hPrinter, 2, (LPBYTE)pPrtInfo2, 0))
    {
        // SetPrinter() has failed
        free(pPrtInfo2);
        ClosePrinter(hPrinter);
        throw Exception("Call to SetPrinter() failed");
    }

    // Clean up.
    free(pPrtInfo2);
    ClosePrinter (hPrinter);
}
```

Other Paper-Related Functions

The approach for getting and setting the DEVMODE structure is the same for all of the various
types listed in the next section, which is why I've only included one example. Access to the
DEVMODE structure was covered in the previous sections.

Setting the Paper Type

Windows has a long list of predefined paper types that you can use to print your application on
a specific type of paper. The list in Table 23.2 is only a few of them. The full list of paper
types can be found in the documentation for the DEVMODE structure in the Win32 Reference.

TABLE 23.2 Selected Windows Paper Types

Value	Meaning
DMPAPER_LETTER	Letter, 8 1/2×11 inches
DMPAPER_LEGAL	Legal, 8 1/2×14 inches
DMPAPER_10X14	10×14 inches
DMPAPER_11X17	11×17 inches
DMPAPER_12X11	Windows 98, Windows NT 4.0, and later: 12×11 inches
DMPAPER_A3	A3 sheet, 297×420 millimeters
DMPAPER_A3_ROTATED	Windows 98, Windows NT 4.0, and later: A3 rotated sheet, 420–297 millimeters
DMPAPER_A4	210–297 millimeters
DMPAPER_A4_ROTATED	Windows 98, Windows NT 4.0 and later: A4 rotated sheet, 297–210 millimeters
DMPAPER_A4SMALL	A4 small sheet, 210–297 millimeters
DMPAPER_A5	A5 sheet, 148–210 millimeters

You can set the paper size for the printer using the predefined types in Table 23.2 and the following code:

```
// Set the paper size to A4
pDevMode->dmFields |= DM_PAPERSIZE;
pDevMode->dmPaperSize = DMPAPER_A4;
```

Set the bit flag of the dmField field to inform the printer which fields have been changed and change the specified field to the new setting. This code should be put into Listing 23.17 where specified to change the setting.

> **NOTE**
>
> The dmPaperSize member can be set to zero if the dmPaperWidth and dmPaperHeight members specify the paper size.

To set a custom paper size for the printer, use the following code:

```
// Set the paper size to a custom length and width
pDevMode->dmFields |= DM_PAPERLENGTH;
pDevMode->dmPaperLength= 1000;          // In Tenths Of A Millimeter
pDevMode->dmFields |= DM_PAPERWIDTH;
pDevMode->dmPaperWidth= 1000;          // In Tenths Of A Millimeter
```

> **NOTE**
>
> This works only under Windows 9x. Under Windows NT/2000, you need to make a custom form of structure `FORM_INFO_1` type and add to the printer using the `AddForm()` function. Then select the form using `PRINTER_INFO_2`. You can find more information about the `FORM_INFO` structure in the Win32 Reference.
>
> ```
> strcpy(pPrtInfo2->pDevMode->dmFormName, "My Form Name");
> pPrtInfo2->pDevMode->dmFields |= DM_FORMNAME;
> pPrtInfo2->pDevMode->dmFields &= !(DM_PAPERSIZE | DM_PAPERLENGTH |
> ➡DM_PAPERWIDTH);
> ```

How to Get a List of Supported Paper Types and Paper Bins

In the `Samples` directory on the CD-ROM is a project called `PaperAndBin`. This project contains a complete sample of how to get access information about the supported paper and bin types/names for a printer. Listing 23.18 shows some of the source code from this sample.

LISTING 23.18 Fill Three String Variables with the Correct Printer Information (Name, Port, and Driver)

```
void __fastcall TMainForm::FillPrinterNames()
{
    // szDeviceName, szDriverName and szPortName as declared
    // as private variables in the Form's class
    //(in the Form's headerfile)
    THandle hPrnDevMode;      // Handle to the memory area
                              // containing the DEVMODE structure

    // Get Printer Info (this way we avoid having to remove any
    // eventual "On LPT1:" strings (which can be translated on
    // other systems)

    // Update selected printer (from selection in ComboBox)
    Printer()->PrinterIndex = PrinterComboBox->ItemIndex;

    // Get Name
    Printer()->GetPrinter(szDeviceName, szDriverName,
                    szPortName, hPrnDevMode);
    // Check if either the port name or driver name is empty
    if (!strlen(szPortName) || !strlen(szDriverName))
    {
        // --- szPortName or szDriverName was empty, fill them ---
        char szTemp[MAX_PATH];
```

LISTING 23.18   Continued

```
        GetProfileString("Devices", szDeviceName, "",
                         szTemp, MAX_PATH);
        // Find the index of the next comma
        char *pszPos = StrPos(szTemp, ",");
        if (pszPos)
        {
            int iLength = strlen(szTemp)-strlen(pszPos);
            // Get the driver name
            strncpy(szDriverName, szTemp, iLength);
            szDriverName[iLength] = '\0'; // Terminate string
            // Get the port name
            strcpy(szPortName, ++pszPos);
        } // ! if
    } // ! if
}
```

The project contains `FillPrinterNames()`, an encapsulation of the call to `TPrinter`'s `GetPrinter()`. It fills `szDriverName` and `szPortName` correctly. This function is called before each call to the `FillPaperInfo()` and `FillBinInfo()` functions, so the necessary information is available. Every time a new printer is selected in the `PrinterComboBox`, the `TListBoxs` on the screen are cleared and `FillPrinterNames()`, `FillPaperInfo()`, and `FillBinInfo()` are called to fill them again. Figure 23.3 shows the user interface for the `PrinterAndBin` sample project.

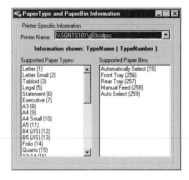

FIGURE 23.3

`PrinterAndBin` in action.

How to Get the Paper Types and Names

The FillPaperInfo() function collects the paper types and names. At the end of the function it fills a TListBox called PaperListBox with the information it has gathered as shown in Listing 23.19.

LISTING 23.19   Getting Paper Types and Names and Inserting Them into PaperListBox

```
void __fastcall TMainForm::FillPaperInfo()
{
    // Notice: In the project header file I've created a const
    // names CCHPAPERNAME with the value 64. This should have
    // been  done by Microsoft, but they didn't do it, so we have
    // to do it ourselves ;)

    // Note: szDeviceName, szDriverName and szPortName are
    // declared as private variables Form's class
    //(in the Form's headerfile) and are already filled with
    // the information we need.

    // Get the number of papers
    int iNumOfPapers = DeviceCapabilities(szDeviceName,
                                          szPortName,
                                          DC_PAPERS,
                                          NULL,
                                          NULL);

    // Allocate memory to contain the list of paper type-numbers
    WORD *pwPaperTypes = new WORD[iNumOfPapers];
    // Get the list of types
    DeviceCapabilities(szDeviceName,
                       szPortName,
                       DC_PAPERS,
                       (LPTSTR)pwPaperTypes,
                       NULL);

    // Allocate memory to contain all paper names
    char *pszPaperNames = new char[iNumOfPapers*CCHPAPERNAME];

    // Get list of paper names
    DeviceCapabilities(szDeviceName,
                       szPortName,
                       DC_PAPERNAMES,
                       pszPaperNames,
                       NULL);
```

LISTING 23.19   Continued

```
    // Fill the ListBox with the information
    char *pszName;
    for (int iLoop=0; iLoop < iNumOfPapers; iLoop++)
    {
        pszName = &pszPaperNames[iLoop*CCHPAPERNAME];
        PaperListBox->Items->Add(AnsiString(pszName)+
                        " ("+IntToStr(pwPaperTypes[iLoop])+")");
    }
}
```

How to Get the Paper Bin Types and Names

The FillBinInfo() function collects the paper bin types and names. At the end of the function it fills a TListBox called BinListBox with the information it has gathered, as shown in Listing 23.20.

LISTING 23.20   Getting Paper Bin Types and Names and Inserting Them into BinListBox

```
void __fastcall TMainForm::FillBinInfo()
{
    // Notice: In the project header file I've created a const
    // names CCHBINNAME with the value 24. This should have been
    // done by Microsoft, but they didn't do it, so we have to
    // do it ourselves ;)

    // Note: szDeviceName, szDriverName and szPortName are
    // declared as private variables Form's class (in the Form's
    // headerfile) and are already filled with the information
    // we need.

    // Get the number of bins
    int iNumOfBins = DeviceCapabilities(szDeviceName,
                                        szPortName,
                                        DC_BINS,
                                        NULL,
                                        NULL);

    // Allocate memory to contain the list of bin type-numbers
    WORD *pwBinTypes = new WORD[iNumOfBins];
    // Get the list of types
    DeviceCapabilities(szDeviceName,
                       szPortName,
```

LISTING 23.20 Continued

```
                    DC_BINS,
                    (LPTSTR)pwBinTypes,
                    NULL);

// Allocate memory to contain all bin names
char *pszBinNames = new char[iNumOfBins*CCHBINNAME];

// Get list of paper names
DeviceCapabilities(szDeviceName,
                   szPortName,
                   DC_BINNAMES,
                   pszBinNames,
                   NULL);


// Fill the ListBox with the information
char *pszName;
for (int iLoop=0; iLoop < iNumOfBins; iLoop++)
{
    pszName = &pszBinNames[iLoop*CCHBINNAME];
    BinListBox->Items->Add(AnsiString(pszName)
            +" ("+IntToStr(pwBinTypes[iLoop])+")");
}
}
```

Setting the Printer Bin

Sometimes you will need to choose the paper bin your program should print from, because many companies use different paper types and sizes, each of which has its own paper bin in the printer. For your application to support this type of printing, you must support more than the default paper bin that is set up using the printer driver. The following is a list of common bin values that you can use to do this. In case of a driver-specific bin, the value will be greater than or equal to DMBIN_USER.

- DMBIN_ONLYONE
- DMBIN_LOWER
- DMBIN_MIDDLE
- DMBIN_MANUAL
- DMBIN_ENVELOPE
- DMBIN_ENVMANUAL
- DMBIN_AUTO
- DMBIN_TRACTOR

Setting Collate Mode

Collate Mode specifies whether collation should be used when printing multiple copies. The dmCollate field is ignored unless the printer driver indicates support for collation by setting the dmFields member to DM_COLLATE. DMCOLLATE_TRUE provides a faster and more efficient output for collation, because the data is sent to the device driver only once, no matter how many copies are required. The printer is simply instructed to print the page again.

```
pDevMode->dmFields |= DM_COLLATE;
pDevMode->dmCollate = DMCOLLATE_TRUE; // Other possible value: DMCOLLATE_FALSE
```

Getting Printer Resolutions

Call DeviceCapabilities() with the parameter DC_ENUMRESOLUTIONS to get a list of the resolution the printer supports. Calling and collecting this information is similar to the method for paper names and paper bin methods, which were covered earlier.

Getting Printer Status

To read the status of a printer, you can use the Status field of the PRINTER_INFO_2 structure. Status includes Paper Jam, Paper Out, Busy, and so on. Listing 23.13 shows how to gather this information from a PRINTER_INFO_2 structure. For a detailed example of how to get the status for a printer and a printer job, read "HOWTO: Get the Status of a Printer and a Print Job" with ID Q160129, which is available on MSDN (http://msdn.microsoft.com).

This is just a small subset of the information that can be read and set using DEVMODE, DeviceCapabilities, and PRINTER_INFO_2. If you're looking for something that isn't covered here, have a look in the Win32 Reference under DEVMODE, DeviceCapabilities, and PRINTER_INFO. The methods for reading and setting the data have been covered previously, so it's just a matter of reusing the methods on the new problem.

Working with Jobs

A full discussion on printer jobs would exceed the scope of this chapter. We will cover this subject briefly to give you a start on this area of printing. Where possible we will refer to related articles on this subject that are available on the Internet.

To get a list of printer jobs for a given printer, you can use two different calls: the Win32 GetPrinter() function with a PRINTER_INFO_2 structure or EnumJobs() with either a JOB_INFO_1 or a JOB_INFO_2 structure. PRINTER_INFO_2 gives only the number of jobs queued on the printer, which is why it's not often used. JOB_INFO_2 gives more information than JOB_INFO_1, but both give much more information about the print jobs than PRINTER_INFO_2. By using EnumJobs() and a JOB_INFO structure, you can get information about the job ID, document name, status of the job, position in queue, total number of pages in the job, pages printed, and much more. For an introduction on how to call EnumJobs() properly, read

"HOWTO: How to Call Win32 Spooler Enumeration APIs Properly" with ID Q158828. This can be found on MSDN (`http://msdn.microsoft.com/support/kb/articles/Q158/8/28.asp`).

The Win32 API also supplies functions for working with print jobs, such as `AddJob()`, `GetJob()`, `SetJob()`, and `ScheduleJob()`. For notification about changes in the print queue, Win32 offers two possibilities. A Windows message named `WM_SPOOLERSTATUS` ought to work under Windows 9x/NT/2000, but I've been successful only in getting it to work under Windows 9x. A set of functions named `FindFirstPrinterChangeNotification()`, `FindNextPrinterChangeNotification()`, and `FindClosePrinterChangeNotification()` work only under Windows NT/2000. For an example of how to create a print queue monitor (using these APIs and `EnumJobs()`), read "SAMPLE: PrintMon.exe Demonstrates the Win32 Spooler API" with ID Q196805, which is available on MSDN.

An example of how to catch the `WM_SPOOLERSTATUS` message under C++Builder is in Listing 23.21. To keep it as simple as possible, we'll make a message map that catches the `WM_SPOOLERSTATUS` message and calls a class method with the message using the VCL wrapper for `WM_SPOOLERSTATUS` called `TWMSpoolerStatus`.

Add the code in Listing 23.21 to the form's (here called `TMainForm`) header file:

LISTING 23.21   Catching the `WM_SPOOLERSTATUS` Message

```
class TMainForm : public TForm
{
__published:    // IDE-managed Components
    TLabel *JobsLabel;
    TStatusBar *StatusBar;
private:        // User declarations
    void __fastcall WMSpoolerStatus(TWMSpoolerStatus &message);
public:         // User declarations
    __fastcall TMainForm(TComponent* Owner);

BEGIN_MESSAGE_MAP
    MESSAGE_HANDLER(WM_SPOOLERSTATUS,
                    TWMSpoolerStatus,
                    WMSpoolerStatus)
END_MESSAGE_MAP(TForm)
};
```

The `WMSpoolerStatus()` method should look like Listing 23.22 in your source file.

LISTING 23.22   The WM_SPOOLERSTATUS Message Handler

```
void __fastcall TMainForm::WMSpoolerStatus(TWMSpoolerStatus &msg)
{
    // Get data from the message
    int iStatus     = msg.JobStatus;
    int iNumOfJobs  = msg.JobsLeft;

    // Write the number of jobs in label names JobsLabel
    JobsLabel->Caption = "Jobs left in queue: "+
                         IntToStr(iNumOfJobs);

    // Update text in Status bar to show that we received
    // a message
    StatusBar->SimpleText = "Message Received...";

    // Pass the message on (so others may receive it too)
    msg.Result = false;
}
```

If you're interested in catching printer jobs and working on their data content, the best way to go about it is to write a custom print processor based on the sample code available in the Windows 9x/NT/2000 Device Driver Kits (DDKs). Unfortunately, you need to write a print processor for each version of Windows. That means you need to make one for Windows 95/98/98 Second Edition, one for Windows NT 4, and one for Windows 2000. The Win32 API supplies the following functions for installing, deleting, and setting up print processors.

- Installing GetPrintProcessorDirectory() returns the Windows directory where the print processor should be installed. AddPrintProcessor() installs the print processor.

- Deleting DeletePrintProcessor() uninstalls a print processor from the system.

- Setting Up   Use the pPrintProcessor field in PRINTER_INFO_2 to specify the name of the print processor a given printer should use. Use the pDataType to specify the data type the printer should write in. The most common are: RAW, EMF, and TEXT. Use EnumPrintProcessors() to get a list of print processors in the system.

How to Catch the Pressing of the Print Screen Button

There are two ways to catch the pressing of the Print Screen button:

The first method is to make a message-handling method that uses GetAsyncKeyState() to catch the VK_SNAPSHOT message; set the TApplication OnIdle() event to call this method. The following code is from the sample CatchPrintScreen_1 that can be found on the CD-ROM.

Add the following declaration to your form's class (in the header file):

```
void __fastcall AppIdle(TObject *Sender, bool &Done);
```

Add the following to the form's OnCreate() event (in the source file):

```
void __fastcall TMainForm::FormCreate(TObject *Sender)
{
    Application->OnIdle = AppIdle;
}
```

Then implement AppIdle:

```
void __fastcall TMainForm::AppIdle(TObject *Sender, bool &Done)
{
    if (GetAsyncKeyState(VK_SNAPSHOT) != 0)
        Application->MessageBox("Got it!", "Print Screen Caught",
                            MB_OK | MB_ICONINFORMATION);
    Done = True;
}
```

The second method is to create a message map to catch the WM_HOTKEY message (the VCL encapsulation is called TWMHotKey) as in the WM_SPOOLERSTATUS sample in Listing 23.21. Finally, register the hotkey using RegisterHotKey() in the form's OnCreate() event and unregister again using UnregisterHotKey() in the form's OnDestroy() event. Your form's header file should look something like this, from the sample CatchPrintScreen_2 that can be found on the CD-ROM:

```
const int ID_SNAPSHOT = 1000;

class TMainForm : public TForm
{
__published:    // IDE-managed Components
    void __fastcall FormCreate(TObject *Sender);
    void __fastcall FormDestroy(TObject *Sender);
private:        // User declarations
    void __fastcall WMHotKey(TWMHotKey &msg);
public:         // User declarations
    __fastcall TMainForm(TComponent* Owner);

BEGIN_MESSAGE_MAP
    MESSAGE_HANDLER(WM_HOTKEY,TWMHotKey,WMHotKey)
END_MESSAGE_MAP(TForm)
};
```

Your source file should include the following code:

```
void __fastcall TMainForm::FormCreate(TObject *Sender)
```

23

```
{
    // ID_SNAPSHOT is declared as a const in the header
    // file for the form
    RegisterHotKey(Handle, ID_SNAPSHOT, 0, VK_SNAPSHOT);
}
//---------------------------------------------------------------
void __fastcall TMainForm::FormDestroy(TObject *Sender)
{
    UnregisterHotKey(Handle, ID_SNAPSHOT);
}
//---------------------------------------------------------------
void __fastcall TMainForm::WMHotKey(TWMHotKey &msg)
{
    if (msg.HotKey == ID_SNAPSHOT)
    {
        Application->MessageBox("Got it!", "Print Screen Caught",
                                MB_OK | MB_ICONINFORMATION);
        // Pass on the message so others can receive it
        msg.Result = false;
    }
}
```

Printing a Form

The VCL class TForm has a Print() method, which prints the visible parts of the window to the default printer. The scaling of the print depends on the form's PrintScale property, which can have the values poNone, poProportional, and poPrintToFit. Using the form's Print() function has many drawbacks; for example, only the visible parts of the form are printed. A better way to print forms is to use TExcellentFormPrinter, which is shareware and can be downloaded from http://www.code4sale.com/joehecht.

Creating a Print Preview

It would require an entire chapter to fully explain how to make your own print preview component. However, the following example should give you an idea of how to approach this subject. The example is far from production code, but it gives some hints on how to use SetWindowExtEx() and SetViewportExtEx() to achieve the proper conversion between screen coordinates and printer coordinates. The print preview data source is implemented as a TBitmap, which is something you should avoid doing in a real Print Preview component, as it has too many limitations. A better solution would be to use a TMetaFile. The sample is called PrintPreview and can be found on the CD-ROM.

Using Printer-Related Conversion Routines

In combination with text and bitmap printing, the following functions can help you work with real-world units of measure such as millimeters or inches. The routines shown in Listing 23.23 use a property named MeasureUnit (of the type TMeasureUnit, which can be either Millimeters or Inches) to control the conversion between pixels and measuring units. iDefaultDPI is an integer constant with the value 300, which is used in cases where a call to GetDeviceCaps() fails. This helps us to get safely out of a failed conversion.

LISTING 23.23 Printer Measure Conversion Routines

```
enum TMeasureUnit { Inches, Millimeters };

float __fastcall PixelsToMeasureUnitHorz(unsigned int Pixels)
{
    // Local variable
    float fTmp;

    try
    {
        // GetDeviceCaps returns pixels per inch
        fTmp = (float)Pixels/GetDeviceCaps(Printer()->Handle,
                                LOGPIXELSX);
    }
    catch(...)
    {
        // Set a value measured from our default resolution (300)
        fTmp = (float)Pixels/iDefaultDPI;
    }

    // Convert it to millimeters or just return it as inches
    if (MeasureUnit == Millimeters)
        // Convert from inches to mm's
        return fTmp*25.4;
    else
        return fTmp;

}
//--------------------------------------------------------------
float __fastcall PixelsToMeasureUnitVert (unsigned int Pixels)
{
    // Local variable
    float fTmp;

    try
```

LISTING 23.23   Continued

```
    {
        // GetDeviceCaps returns pixels per inch
        fTmp = (float)Pixels/GetDeviceCaps(Printer()->Handle,
                                    LOGPIXELSY);
    }
    catch(...)
    {
        // Set a value measured from our default resolution (300)
        fTmp = (float)Pixels/iDefaultDPI;
    }

    // Convert it to millimeters or just return it as inches
    if (MeasureUnit == Millimeters)
        // Convert from inches to mm's
        return fTmp*25.4;
    else
        return fTmp;


}
//---------------------------------------------------------------
unsigned int __fastcall MeasureUnitToPixelsHorz(float Measure)
{
    // Local variable
    float fTmp;

    try
    {
        // GetDeviceCaps returns pixels per inch
        fTmp = (float)Measure * GetDeviceCaps(Printer()->Handle,
                                        LOGPIXELSX);
    }
    catch(...)
    {
        // Set a value measured from our default resolution (300)
        fTmp = (float)Measure * iDefaultDPI;
    }

    // Are we converting from millimeters or inches to pixels?
    if (MeasureUnit == Millimeters)
        // Convert from inches to mm's
        return (int)fTmp/25.4;
    else
        return (int)fTmp;
}
```

LISTING 23.23 Continued

```
//-------------------------------------------------------------
unsigned int __fastcall MeasureUnitToPixelsVert(float Measure)
{
    // Local variable
    float fTmp;

    try
    {
        // GetDeviceCaps returns pixels per inch
        fTmp = (float)Measure * GetDeviceCaps(Printer()->Handle,
                                        LOGPIXELSY);
    }
    catch(...)
    {
        // Set a value measured from our default resolution (300)
        fTmp = (float)Measure * iDefaultDPI;
    }

    // Are we converting from millimeters or inches to pixels?
    if (MeasureUnit == Millimeters)
        // Convert from inches to mm's
        return (int)fTmp/25.4;
    else
        return (int)fTmp;
}
```

Other Printer-Related Information

The following is a list of some common questions about printing and their answers. If you're looking for an answer to something that isn't covered, search DejaNews (www.deja.com) or MSDN (http://msdn.microsoft.com) for the answer.

How Can I Show the Printer Setup Dialog?

Call OpenPrinter() to get a handle to the printer for which you want to show the Printer Setup dialog. Then call PrinterProperties() with your form's handle and the printer handle you just got from OpenPrinter(). Finally, remember to perform a ClosePrinter() on the printer handle.

How Can I Add New Printers to the System?

Use AddPrinter() and specify its settings by passing along a pre-setup PRINTER_INFO_2 structure. For AddPrinter() to work, you must be sure that the given printer's driver is installed. Use EnumPrinterDrivers() to get a list of all installed printer drivers. DeletePrinter() is the counterpart to AddPrinter().

How Can I Install a New Printer Driver?

Use `AddPrinterDriver()` to install the printer driver. Use
`GetPrinterDriverDirectory()` to get the directory where the driver should be placed
before it's installed. `DeletePrinterDriver()` is the counterpart to `AddPrinterDriver()`.

How Can I Create a Printer Connection?

Use `AddPrinterConnection()` to create a printer connection or call
`ConnectToPrinterDlg()` to show the dialog box that lets users browse and connect to
printers on a network. `DeletePrinterConnection()` is the counterpart to
`AddPrinterConnection()`.

Creating Charts with the TChart Component

The `TChart` charting component from Steema Software SL has been supplied with both Delphi
and C++Builder since version 3. It is a very powerful library of charting routines written
entirely using VCL and is provided in three flavors:

- A regular version—`TChart`, found on the Additional tab of the Component Palette
- A data-aware version—`TDBChart`, found on the Data Controls tab of the Component
  Palette
- A QuickReport version—`TQRChart`, found on the QReport tab of the Component Palette

We'll stay with the regular version.

The main features of the standard version of `TChart` are that it has 11 series types, 7 statistical
functions, and designtime chart and series editing. It contains a vast array of objects, objects in
this case being distinct parts of a chart: axes, series, titles, legends, and so on.

The version included with the C++Builder distribution has many example applications and reasonable documentation, but example code in the help pages is in Delphi rather than
C++Builder. This makes it trickier to come to grips with the more advanced charting techniques, so an introduction to some of these techniques is presented here. The `TChart` Web site
at www.steema.com has a good selection of FAQs and tips for both C++Builder and Delphi.

Getting Started with TeeChart

Adding a chart to an application couldn't be simpler. All that's required is to drop a `TChart`
component on a form and resize the skeleton chart as necessary. The `TChart` component is
derived from `TPanel` and thus inherits `TPanel` properties.

> **NOTE**
>
> It's also possible to add a chart using the New Application dialog. Choose File, New and double-click the TeeChart Wizard icon on the Business tab.

To add one or more series to the chart and to alter a vast array of chart and series properties, simply double-click the chart to start the designtime chart editor.

Designtime Chart Editing

The designtime chart and series editor gives access to most chart and series properties in a more intuitive manner than the Object Inspector. The editor has two main tabs: the Chart tab, which gives access to chart properties and facilitates the addition of a series to the chart, and the Series tab, which allows alteration of series-related properties.

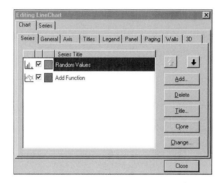

FIGURE 23.4
The TChart designtime chart and series editor.

Adding a new series to a chart automatically fills the series with random data (designtime only), enabling chart and series property changes to be observed immediately.

Adding Data to Charts

Adding data to chart is easy; just use the series Add() method. This adds one value to a series at a time, so generally it should be inside a loop to add an array of values:

```
for (int i=0; i<TotalPointCount; i++)
{
    Series1->Add(SomeData[i], (String) (i+1), clTeeColor);
}
```

The Add() method has three arguments. The first is the value to be added (in this case an array element); the second is a label for the point; the third is the point color, where clTeeColor assigns a default color to the point.

Obviously, each point in a chart has an x value (the position of the point on the "x" or horizontal axis) and a y value (the position of the point on the "y" or vertical axis). The Add() method will automatically assign series x values, so each consecutive value in the y array (this is the array SomeData in the example) will get a consecutive x value. Therefore, the y value at array index 0 will be given an x value of 0, the y value at array index 1 will be given an x value of 1, and so on.

To specify an x value for each y value and hence create true scatter plots, use the AddXY() method instead. This function has the same form as the Add() method but accepts an additional argument, which is an array of x values:

```
for (int i=0; i<TotalPointCount; i++)
{
    Series1->AddXY(XData[i], YData[i], (String) (i+1), clTeeColor);
}
```

It is possible to assign an array of values directly to a chart series without the need to add values one at a time. A very good example and detailed explanation of this technique is available on the TeeChart Web site, and so it will not be covered here.

Altering Chart Appearance at Runtime

Chart appearance set at designtime using the chart and series property editor is often adequate for very simple charting applications. The capability to change chart and series properties at runtime, however, makes charts more interesting for the user and aids data visualization.

The sample TChart project Chart.bpr, supplied on the CD-ROM that accompanies this book, demonstrates some useful TChart techniques. These are described in detail in the following sections.

Making Simple Property Changes

Not surprisingly, all published chart and series properties may be changed at runtime. This is extremely easy to do and so doesn't warrant much coverage. The sample chart application allows the user to switch between a 2D and a 3D view of the charts by use of a check box. The code to alter this property of the charts is placed in the check box's OnClick event handler:

```
LineChart->View3D = ViewCheck->Checked;
```

TChart charts are updated (redrawn) automatically whenever a property changes, so no further action is necessary.

Using the `OnGetBarStyle` Event

Most chart objects also respond to events. These events are generally available via the C++Builder Object Inspector as expected, but some aren't published and hence have little or no documentation. Perhaps the most useful of these is the `OnGetBarStyle` event, which is fired every time an individual bar in a bar series is drawn. An obvious use of this is to change the style or color of a bar based on its index, as demonstrated in the example chart application.

The first task is to assign the event handler to the bar series. In the example program, the bar chart series is called `Series1`, and the event handler is assigned in the form's constructor:

```
Series1->OnGetBarStyle = this->GetBarStyle;
```

The event handler function may then be defined as shown. The arguments are `Sender`, a pointer to the bar series that fired the event (of type `TCustomBarSeries`), `ValueIndex`, which is the index of the bar about to be drawn, and `BarStyle`, a reference to a `TBarStyle` type. This last argument allows the style of the bar to be altered.

```
void __fastcall TChartForm::GetBarStyle(TCustomBarSeries *Sender,
        int ValueIndex, TBarStyle &BarStyle)
{
    TBarStyle Style[6] = {bsArrow,
    bsCilinder,
    bsEllipse,
    bsInvPyramid,
    bsPyramid,
    bsRectangle};

    BarStyle = Style[(ValueIndex + 1) % 6];
}
```

> **NOTE**
>
> Watch out for the peculiar spelling of one of the `TBarStyle` values, `bsCilinder`. This is not a printing error!

The example function simply assigns a style to each bar based on the bar's position in the series and also alters the bar color (not shown).

Interacting with Charts

Moving beyond designtime chart design and runtime appearance changes, the `TChart` component provides mechanisms by which the user may interact with charts at runtime. This is achieved through provision of chart object event handlers and functions. This opens up a world of possibilities for dynamic charting so that, for example, a user may retrieve bar chart y-values, change point colors, alter axis scaling, and add or remove series points.

Getting Chart Values

Using the `OnClickSeries` event, it's simple to retrieve the value of a bar in a bar chart. This event has the arguments `Sender` (of type `TCustomChart`), which identifies the chart that fired the event, `Series` (of type `TChartSeries`), which identifies the series the event has been fired for, and `ValueIndex`, which provides the index of the point that's been clicked and the usual mouse-related arguments:

```
void __fastcall TChartForm::LineChartClickSeries(TCustomChart *Sender,
TChartSeries *Series, int ValueIndex, TMouseButton Button,
TShiftState Shift, int X, int Y)
{
}
```

Each `TChartSeries` object contains a list of series values, accessed via the `YValues->Value` property:

```
YValue->Caption = Series->YValueToText(Value);
```

The example program converts this value to text and displays it on the main application form as a label.

Converting Screen Coordinates to Chart Coordinates

In a similar vein, it's a relatively simple matter to convert screen coordinates to chart coordinates. This makes it possible to write functions that, for example, allow the user to draw a selection box around various points on a chart and perform some predefined action on them.

The example program uses this technique to display chart x and y coordinates in the form's caption whenever the mouse is hovering over a chart. Using the chart `OnMouseMove` event (remember `TChart` is derived from `TPanel`), we must first get the screen coordinates of the chart bounding box:

```
TChart *TheChart = dynamic_cast<TChart>(Sender);
TRect TheChartRect = TheChart->ChartRect;
```

It's possible to convert screen coordinates to chart coordinates only when the mouse is hovering over the chart area (inside the axes), so check that the mouse is inside this area:

```
if ((X > TheChartRect.Left && X < TheChartRect.Right)
&& (Y > TheChartRect.Top && Y < TheChartRect.Bottom))
{
}
```

Where X and Y are the mouse screen coordinates as passed to the `OnMouseMove` event handler.

The `CalcPosPoint()` function is provided to convert screen coordinates to chart coordinates. It's a member of the `TChartAxis` component, and any particular chart will probably have at least two of these objects associated with it: one for the bottom or x-axis and one for the left or y-axis. Therefore, to convert the mouse y position to the chart y coordinate:

```
double YValue = TheChart->LeftAxis->CalcPosPoint(Y);
```

There are many useful functions and properties associated with the `TChartAxis` component to make axis management and custom chart drawing possible.

Creating Charts Dynamically

Previous sections have dealt with designtime and runtime manipulation of charts created at designtime. This section will present the technique for creating charts at runtime, used in the example program to draw 20 pie charts on a scroll box.

The first task, as multiple charts are to be created, is to declare an array of charts and chart series. In the example program this is done in the form's constructor:

```
PieCharts = new TChart *[PieChartCount];
PieSeries = new TPieSeries *[PieChartCount];
```

Make sure, of course, that the array pointers (`PieCharts` and `PieSeries` in this example) have been declared as the correct type in the form header file. Because we are creating an array of VCL objects, these must be declared as pointers to pointers:

```
TChart **PieCharts;
TPieSeries **PieSeries;
```

Then assign each chart and chart series to the form and make the scroll box its parent:

```
PieCharts[i] = new TChart(this);
PieSeries[i] = new TPieSeries(this);
PieCharts[i]->Parent = PieChartScrollBox;
```

Each series must then be assigned to a chart, as a chart object does not automatically have a series type associated with it. It should now be obvious how to assign more than one series, perhaps of more than one type, to any particular chart:

```
PieCharts[i]->AddSeries(PieSeries[i]);
```

All that's left is altering any properties of the charts and assigning data as described in an earlier section.

Printing Charts

There are several ways to print charts. The easiest is to use the `Print()` method of the form containing the chart, which is great for test prints. However, the quality is not really good enough for charts.

Happily, the `TChart` component provides several of its own printing methods that generate charts of a far better quality than the form printing method. The simplest of these is the chart `Print()` method:

```
LineChart->Print();
```

This will print the chart using the full print page width and height at screen resolution by default. Printing at screen resolution is often unsuitable for charting applications (after all, printer resolutions are much greater than screen), but it's possible to change the resolution, and therefore the quality, of printed charts. Each `TChart` has a runtime property called `PrintResolution` that may be set to an integer value in the range -100 to 0, where -100 means the chart is printed at maximum printer resolution, and 0 means the chart is printed at screen resolution.

```
LineChart->PrintResolution = PrintResScroll->Position;
```

> **NOTE**
>
> The `TChart` help file entry for the `PrintResolution` property states that it's a read-only property. This is incorrect!

It's also possible to specify a rectangle for a chart to be scaled to on the printed page, using the `PrintPartial` and `PrintRect` methods.

Using the `PrintPartialCanvas` Method

Multiple charts may be printed on a page using the `TChart PrintPartialCanvas` method. This allows one or more charts to be drawn directly onto the printer canvas and, unlike previously described printing methods, does not automatically start a print job or eject the page when completed.

To set up several charts for printing to one page, first define a `TRect` for each chart, in which the rectangle describes the position of the chart on the page. For example, the following describes an area that's the top third of the printed page's full width:

```
PrintRect[0].Left = 0;
PrintRect[0].Right = (Printer()->PageWidth - 1);
PrintRect[0].Top = 0;
```

```
PrintRect[0].Bottom = (Printer()->PageHeight - 1) / 3;
```

Next, start the print job, but make sure the print resolution is set for each chart first.

```
Printer()->BeginDoc();
```

CAUTION

Always set the resolution for all the charts to be printed on one page before opening the printer page with `Printer()->BeginDoc()`.

Then, for each chart to be printed on a page (for which a rectangle has already been defined), call the `PrintPartialCanvas()` method. This method accepts a `TCanvas` item and a `TRect` item as arguments. The `TCanvas` item is the printer canvas, and the `TRect` item is the rectangle defined for the chart currently being drawn.

```
LineChart->PrintPartialCanvas(Printer()->Canvas, PrintRect[0]);
```

Once the `PrintPartialCanvas` method has been called for every chart to be printed, print the page:

```
Printer()->EndDoc();
```

There's a minor intermittent problem associated with printing this way. Occasionally the scaling of text and graphics to the printed page will go astray and must be reset manually. If this problem occurs with chart printing in an application, get the original mapping mode of the printer device context before doing any printing:

```
int MapMode = GetMapMode(Printer()->Handle);
```

Then after each item is sent to the printer canvas, reset the mapping mode:

```
SetMapMode(Printer()->Handle, MapMode);
```

This should resolve any printer scaling issues.

Upgrading to TeeChart Pro

The standard version of TeeChart that is supplied with C++Builder and Delphi is obviously rich in features and quite adequate for occasional charting. For more regular chart use, however, it's worthwhile upgrading to TeeChart Pro. The Pro version contains all the functionality of the standard version, plus the following:

- 100% source code
- Nine extra series types

- Six sample custom series types
- Nine extra statistical functions
- OpenGL 3D
- Runtime access to the chart and series editor

One of the extra series types, combined with OpenGL 3D, allows for true 3D surface charts (that's three axes—x, y, and z). Perhaps the most useful addition, however, is runtime access to the chart editor. This allows the user to tailor charts at runtime, and it's even possible to add extra functionality to the editor, for example by adding custom buttons.

There is also an ActiveX version of TeeChart, making it possible to serve real-time charts to the Internet.

Summary

In this chapter we saw how to create a QuickReport viewer to view a report without printing it, and we investigated techniques for saving and loading QuickReports for report sharing. We took an in-depth look at both basic and advanced techniques for all aspects of printing text and graphics, using both API and VCL functions. Techniques presented include printing text directly to the printer, printing bitmaps, getting and setting printer properties, and scaling issues.

Finally, we've had a brief introduction to the TChart component's advanced charting capabilities, including creating charts dynamically and TChart printing issues.

Using the Win32 API

Paul Gustavson
Chris Winters

IN THIS CHAPTER

Borland C++Builder is a development environment designed to support the creation of 32-bit Windows applications. The operative word is Windows. This includes Microsoft Windows 9x, Millennium (Me), NT, and 2000. In time, Borland's Kylix will support the creation of 32-bit Linux applications, but for now, the focus for C++Builder is primarily Windows. C++Builder makes the job of creating 32-bit Windows applications faster and easier using the C++ language. To help facilitate the development of Windows applications, C++Builder allows the developer to access and use the Windows 32-bit (Win32) Application Programming Interface (API), either directly or indirectly through middleware components. This chapter examines the Win32 API and highlights cases and example usage of the Win32 API.

Win32 API Versus Win32 Middleware

There are several resource frameworks supported by Borland that facilitate Windows development and help reduce the development effort. Within the context of software development, a resource framework provides a structure, interface, and often a building block that can be used by a developer during the construction of his software program. The most noteworthy framework familiar to Borland developers is the Visual Component Library (VCL). VCLs are described in detail in Chapter 8, "Using VCL Components," and Chapter 9, "Creating Custom Components." VCL is considered to be the key ingredient to Borland's Rapid Application Development (RAD) environments of Delphi and C++Builder—VCL makes RAD a reality. Prior to VCL, Borland provided the Object Windows Library (OWL), a C++ application framework for earlier versions of Windows. Borland also supports the Microsoft Foundation Class (MFC) Library, arguably the most popular C++ windows application framework. Whether it is VCL, OWL, or MFC, middleware components and frameworks are designed to ease the burden of development by encapsulating many of the Windows 32-bit (Win32) Application Programming Interface (API) calls into reusable objects and methods.

In most cases, it is a good idea to at least consider using Win32 middleware in the development of a Windows application. After all, middleware reduces the time and effort to write Windows code. Furthermore, middleware components and frameworks, such as VCL, OWL, and MFC, provide an object-oriented interface and wrapper to a more structure-based Win32 API. Despite these advantages, there are several instances when the raw Win32 API routines should be examined, understood, and possibly used directly within a program. For one thing, the Win32 API allows for faster code execution and less memory use than middleware calls. Because middleware, in essence, is an abstract interface and wrapper of the Win32 API, performance can sometimes be a bit sluggish due to the myriad of parametric conditions that it must support. Furthermore, developers who use Win32 API calls tend to have a better understanding of how their applications interact with the operating system, other applications, and peripherals. By design, middleware tends to mask the relationship between the application and the operating system (OS). Fortunately, the source code for many of the VCL components are provided with the Professional and Enterprise versions of C++Builder and by a majority of third-party VCL vendors. Examination of the code can help a developer understand the intricate elements of the Win32 API calls contained within a component class or foundation class.

Perhaps the most compelling reason for C++Builder developers to use raw Win32 calls directly with an application is when a desired capability is not provided by the VCL. Experienced programmers frequently encounter situations when the VCL falls short of the need. The Win32 API often fills the gap for many programmers by providing the required functionality and flexibility. Because of the object-based interface and reusability of VCL, it's highly encouraged that if a VCL component provides a needed capability, it should be used and reused as often as necessary. However, if there's no VCL that can help perform task, the Win32 API should be applied.

Brief History of Windows and the API

To fully comprehend the broad capability of the Win32 API, it's beneficial to look back at the history of Windows and the development of the Windows API. In the early 1980s, Microsoft began the development of a product called the Interface Manager that later became known as Windows. Supposedly Microsoft, as well as Apple, leveraged designs from the work pioneered by the Xerox Palo Alto Research Center (PARC). Xerox PARC introduced the concept of a graphical windowing environment better known today as the Graphical User Interface (GUI). Microsoft's objective was and has been to provide an easy-to-use GUI with device-independent graphics and multitasking support. Interestingly enough, Apple had been working on a similar concept known as *Lisa*, but it wasn't until the release of Apple's Macintosh that the world had a true taste of the potential of the modern GUI environment.

In 1985, Microsoft released Windows 1.0 to the general public. It was intended to extend DOS by providing a more graphical interface for applications, although it was still very "DOS-ish" in appearance. Applications could be tiled with no overlapping capability. Multiple applications could cooperatively run within the same memory space. Other products in the PC marketplace also provided these types of capabilities, including Quarterdeck's DESQview, IBM's TopView, and Digital Research's GEM. The unique aspect of each of these environments was that a user could launch more than one application and, based on user intervention (such as keystrokes), the underlying environment could "task switch" between the applications. Task switching allowed not only for the one application to be activated, but for applications to perform what appeared to be concurrent processing.

In Windows 1.0, task switching between applications was accomplished through the `GetMessage()` API routine. The `GlobalAlloc()` API routine was used frequently to support memory allocation for an application within the confines of the available memory space. Both these API routines are still available today, although they have been modified and improved. However, they are seldom used for today's windows development.

In 1987, Windows 2.0 was released and provided the familiar look of icons and overlapping windows. The Win API provided greater support for dialog box creation and processing. DOS applications could be launched within Windows via PIF files. Eventually Windows 2.0 broke the 1MB memory barrier hindered by earlier versions of DOS. Windows 2.0 was updated to version 2.1, but due to the advent of the Intel 80386 chip, the next version of Windows was revamped to support some of the newer features of Intel's architecture and released as Win/386. Subsequently, Windows 2.1 was re-released as Win/286 in order to align the two products with Intel's current architectures. Specifically, Win/386 took advantage of Intel's new processor by providing a non-preemptive multitasking capability improving significantly on the honor-system approach of the cooperative multitasking schema of version 1.0, which required the `GetMessage()` routine. By allocating a slice of CPU time for each application, task switching between applications could be accomplished somewhat autonomously.

In 1990, Windows 3.0 was released, and the world slowly began to take notice. Win 3.0 provided support for up to 16MB of RAM with the 386 enhanced mode. The API provided better graphical support and better memory management support. `GlobalAlloc()` could now be used to support allocation of larger heap regions and allowed offset addressing of application memory based on segmented memory. Utility applications began to be shipped with Windows, such as Program Manager and File Manager. Add-on OS extensions and support libraries were introduced, such as the multimedia extensions still supported today by Windows Multimedia System (MMSYSTEM) dynamic link library (DLL).

Windows 3.1 was released in April 1992 and provided support for TrueType fonts, object linking and embedding (OLE), in addition to the multimedia capabilities, such as `PlaySound()`. Common dialog boxes were provided that simplified programmer development for common tasks such as printing, saving, and opening files and color selection. A majority of PC vendors began to ship systems bundled with Windows 3.1. At this point, Windows provided support only for 16-bit segmented memory address space and 16-bit integers, despite the fact that Intel's 386 and 486 CPUs provided a 32-bit architecture. In early 1994, Microsoft released Windows for Workgroups (WFW) version 3.11. WFW provided a poor man's network operating system and became commonplace on corporate America's desktops. It was also designed to integrate with Windows New Technology (NT) OS–based systems (described below). The API available for Win 3.x (which includes WFW) embodied the final and complete set of functions, structures, and callback messages known today as the Win16 API.

In 1993, just prior to the WFW release, Microsoft released Windows New Technology (NT) version 3.1 with very little fanfare, even though NT provided Microsoft's first true 32-bit API architecture Windows framework. The kernel took advantage of Intel's 486 32-bit architecture by providing true preemptive multitasking and supported a 32-bit flat address space and 32-bit integers. Shortly after the NT release, the Win32s API was released, which made it possible for developers to create 32-bit applications for Windows 3.x. 32-bit support was accomplished by providing a dynamic link library (DLL) within Windows 3.x that acted as a proxy by converting the 32-bit calls to the 16-bit calls required by the kernel. Thus, the OS was still rooted in a 16-bit segmented address space and limited to 16-bit integer support. However, Win32s provided the opportunity for programmers to begin the design and development of applications for 32-bit Windows, such as NT and the forthcoming Windows 95.

In August 1995, Windows 95 was released with a great deal of fanfare. The user interface was completely revamped and improved, and the OS provided a variant of the Win32 API used by NT 3.51. Like NT, Windows 95 provided support for concurrent processes, independent threads of execution, and a flat (linear) 32-bit address model, but lacked many of the security and server capabilities provided by NT. It was also still tied to the Disk Operation System (DOS), although that was masked. The biggest benefit, however, was that a majority of Win 3.x applications developed using the Win16 API and Win32s API could run flawlessly under Windows 95. This was extremely appealing to consumers.

The criticism with NT was that the majority of existing Win 3.x applications were simply incompatible with NT, and NT lacked a significant repertoire of Win32 applications. Case in point, at the Borland Developer's Conference in Orlando in June 1994, a year prior to the Windows 95 release, a survey was taken of the audience in the Borland C++ Product Address to determine the number of programmers developing applications for various operating environments. A majority of the audience, several hundred, indicated by the raising of hands that they were developing applications for Win 3.x. Twenty or so developers indicated that they were developing applications for IBM's OS/2. However, only two developers out of a crowd of several hundred indicated that they were developing applications for NT. The reason was that there wasn't as much as a demand for NT platform applications. Because Windows 95 supported Win32 development and leveraged legacy Win16 applications, it was only then that applications began to migrate to Win32 and NT platform. In fact, it is common belief that Win95 was originally created as a temporal vehicle to encourage 32-bit Windows application development and to transition consumers completely over to NT. Win95 was intended to live a short life and eventually be replaced by a consumer version of NT. The first step in making this happen occurred when Microsoft updated NT to provide the same look and feel as Windows 95. NT version 4.0 was released in August 1996 and was largely embraced by corporate America. However, it lacked the multimedia support home consumers desired (video games, for example).

Eventually Microsoft updated Windows 95 to support the Universal Serial Bus and a 32-bit File Allocation Table (FAT) with Windows 95 OEM (Original Equipment Manufacturer) Service Release 2 (OSR2) in 1997. Win95 OSR2 exposed additional routines in the Win32 API, including browser-specific elements used by Internet Explorer version 3.0, new and

24

updated graphics and multimedia support provided through DirectX 2, Open GL 1.1, and ActiveMovie, and other items, such as the Cryptographic API and the new `GetDiskFreeSpaceEx()` routine, that provide support for larger hard drives. When Windows 98 was released in June 1998, it contained nearly 10,000 API routines. Needless to say, Microsoft continually adds API routines to Windows through updates and new versions.

Since Windows 98, Microsoft has released Windows 98 Second Edition (SE) in May 1999, Windows 2000 in February 2000, and Windows Millenium (Me) in September 2000. Windows 2000 replaced the NT 4.0 product line, but has not yet supplanted Win 9x. Windows Me provided an update to the 98 product line, which included the removal of the DOS boot screen, and new multimedia features and application tools for users, but is still based on the Win 9x architecture. Both Windows 98/Me and Windows 2000 are foundationally different at the kernel level, but the most current version of the Win32 API supports Win 9x, Me, NT, and 2000. As a result, applications developed for Windows 98/Me will often run smoothly under Windows 2000. Reciprocally, with few exceptions, Windows 2000 applications also run under Windows 98/Me. What hasn't changed drastically but does continue to be improved and expanded is the Win API. Since the mid-80s, when the first Win API was introduced for Windows 1.0, the Win API has grown quite significantly, and yet today's API retains many of the original calls and callbacks. As new technologies continue to be influenced by the computing industry and introduced by Microsoft, the API will certainly undergo revisions and updates. Even so, a majority of the current structures and routines within the API will continue to be supported by forthcoming versions of Windows. Certainly, over time, more and more undocumented/unpublished Win32 API calls will be revealed and used. The success of Windows has been and will be dependent on the availability of the Win32 API. Access and knowledge of the Win32 API allows developers to create quality applications and components, resulting in greater choice and satisfaction for Windows users.

Win32 API Functional Areas

This short history lesson provides some insight into the Windows API and what it was intended to support. The Win32 API provides function calls, callbacks, and structures required to support the integration, management, and operation of an application within a Windows operating environment. API calls often perform various services for a Windows application, such as providing a common dialog box for opening and saving files or sending a document to the printer. There are many other tasks that the Win32 API provides as well. There are allegedly over 10,000 API elements available within Windows 98, Me, and Windows 2000. The Windows core system libraries, typically found in the `Windows/System` directory, contain a majority of these Win32 API routines. The key libraries include the Windows kernel library (`kernel32.dll`), user library (`user32.dll`), and the graphical device interface (GDI) library (`gdi32.dll`).

Also important are some of the extensions and support libraries that have been introduced by Microsoft (and other vendors) over the evolution of Windows. For example, when Windows 3.x and Windows 95 emerged as the operating environment of the modern era, Microsoft never imagined how much the World Wide Web would influence the evolution and role of Windows. Netscape's Web browser war with Microsoft heavily influenced the Win32 API extensions and support libraries that came from Microsoft.

Extensions and support libraries include the SHELL library and MMSYSTEM library, Windows Sockets (WinSock), DirectX, and the Windows Internet Extensions (WinInet) API. Extensions and support libraries are not necessarily required for Windows to work, but provide feature sets for developer's that make programs more robust and powerful. To discover the full list of the available functions and services supported by any of the Win32 libraries, simply use Borland's `impdef` command-line tool to create an interface definition (`.def`) file of the DLL, as shown in the following example:

```
impdef -a user32.def user32.dll
```

The `.def` file, which can be viewed by any text editor, will contain a list of available functions that can be used by application developers. Browsing the `windows/system` directory will reveal almost an infinite number of DLLs, yet only a small percentage of those are true Win32 API DLLs. Typically, a Win32 DLL contains a `32` embedded within the filename. The Properties feature (see Figure 24.1) within Windows Explorer can be used to reveal more information about the DLL. If it says *Microsoft* and says *API*, most likely it's a Win32 API.

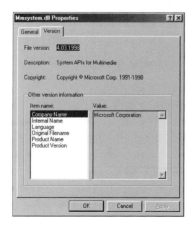

FIGURE 24.1
The DLL Properties dialog.

24

USING THE
WIN32 API

Trying to understand each and every API element is a daunting task that few individuals can master, especially because each update to Windows or Internet Explorer potentially introduces new API routines, many of which are undocumented. However, the basic functional areas of Windows, as identified in Figure 24.2, provides the necessary insight regarding the composition of the API and the capabilities the API provides for developers.

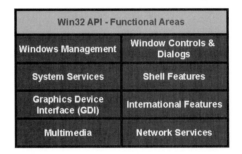

FIGURE 24.2
Functional area block diagram.

The Win32 API can be grouped into eight functional areas:

- Windows Management
- System Services
- Graphical Device Interface
- Multimedia Services
- Common Controls and Dialogs
- Shell Features
- International Features
- Network Services

Let's explore each of these areas.

Windows Management

Windows applications are created and managed through the functions supported by the user library (`user32.dll`). The user library interface includes services for window and menu management, dialogs, message boxes, mouse and keyboard access, and other built-in controls.

It's important to understand a concept of a window. A window acts as the interface between the user and the application. At least one window, called the main window, is created by a Windows application. Applications can create additional windows as well. A window's primary purpose is to display information and receive input from a user. Windows Management functions are used to control the aspect of the windows created and used by an application. Mouse and keyboard input is received by the main window through messages that are passed on by the system through Windows Management support. Windows Management functions also provide the capability for an application to display icons, menus, and dialog boxes that receive and display additional user information.

The functions in Table 24.1 provide a sampling of some of the more popular Windows Management API routines used to create and manage windows. These routines are accessed simply by including the windows.h header file or Borland's vcl.h header file within your application's source file.

TABLE 24.1 Common Windows Management Functions

Windows Management Common Functions	Description
CascadeWindows()	Cascades the specified windows or the child windows of the specified parent window.
CloseWindow()	Minimizes but does not destroy a specified window.
CreateWindow()	Creates an overlapped, pop-up, or child window.
DestroyWindow()	Destroys a window. The system responds by sending a WM_DESTROY message to a specified window.
EnableWindow()	Enables or disables mouse and keyboard input to a specified window or control.
EnumWindows()	Enumerates by looping through each top-level window on the display and passing the handle of each window individually to an application-defined callback function.
EnumWindowsProc()	Used by the EnumWindows() function. This is the application-defined callback function that EnumWindows() uses to pass the handles of top-level windows.
FindWindow()	Retrieves the handle to the top-level window in which the class name and window name match the specified strings.
FindWindowEx()	Retreives the handles of available active windows. Similar to FindWindow(), but also provides support for locating child windows.
GetWindowRect()	Retrieves the screen coordinates of the specified window.
GetWindowText()	Retrieves the title bar caption of the specified window.
MoveWindow()	Moves the location and size of a specified window.

24

USING THE
WIN32 API

TABLE 24.1 Continued

Windows Management Common Functions	Description
SetWindowText()	Modifies the text of the title bar for the specified window.
ShowWindow()	Sets the show state of the specified window. Show states include hiding, maximizing, minimizing, restoring, and activating a window.
TileWindows()	Tiles the specified windows or the child windows of the specified parent window.
WinMain()	Called by the system as the initial entry point for a Win32-based application.

There are many other Windows Management routines that have not been described. In fact there is a total of 648 routines available in version 4.10.2222 of the user32.dll. Use Borland's impdef command-line tool, described earlier, to view the full list of the available Windows Management functions.

System Services

System service functions allow an application to manage and monitor resources, provide access to files, folders, and input and output devices, and allows an application to log events and handle errors and exceptions. Furthermore, system services functions provide features that can be used to create other types of applications, such as console applications and driver services.

The Windows kernel library (kernel32.dll) provides a majority of the low-level system service support for the operating environment. This includes file access, memory and resource management, and multitasking and multithreading support. All Windows applications use the Windows kernel to operate. For instance, when an application needs memory (both at startup and during execution), it requires the Windows kernel to allocate the necessary memory.

These key aspects of the system services are described in Table 24.2.

TABLE 24.2 Key System Services

Feature	Description
Atoms	Support for sharing strings with applications through 16-bit integer identifiers.
Communication	Support for communication resources, such as serial ports, parallel ports, and modems.

TABLE 24.2 Continued

Feature	Description
Console Support	Support of input/output management for character-mode (non-GUI) applications.
Debugging	Provides "event-driven" support for application debugging.
Device I/O	Support for device driver communication within an application.
Dynamic Data Exchange (DDE)	Support for transferring data between applications. DDE functions are actually supported by the user library (user32.dll) and the Dynamic Data Exchange Management Library (DDEML).
Dynamic Link Library (DLL)	Support for creating and managing libraries that can be loaded by an application at runtime.
Error Message	Support for handling messages, such as MessageBeep() and FlashWindow().
Event Logging	Support for recording application events into a log.
File Mapping	Support for mapping a file's contents to a virtual address location.
Files	Support for file input and output of storage media.
Handles and Objects	Support for creating and managing handles and objects that provide an abstract and secure access to Windows system resources.
Help Support	Support routines used in conjunction with the Windows Help application. Help support is actually provided by the user library (user32.dll), but Microsoft considers help support to be a facet of system services.
Interprocess Communication (IPC)	Support mechanisms for facilitating communication and data sharing between applications. Mechanisms include file mapping, shared memory, anonymous and named pipes, mailslots, and the Clipboard.
Large Integer Operations	Support for 64-bit integer operations.
Mailslots	Support for creating and managing one-way IPC (mailslots).
Memory Management	Support for allocating and using memory.
Pipes	Support for creating, managing, and using pipes. Pipes are IPC communication conduits that allow one process to communicate with another process.
Portable Execution File Manipulation	Support for manipulating or accessing a portable executable (PE) image through routines provided by the IMAGEHLP DLL.
Power Management	Provides functions and messages that reveal the system power status and notify of power management events.

24

USING THE
WIN32 API

TABLE 24.2   Continued

Feature	Description
Process and Thread	Support for multitasking, scheduling, Management and creating and managing multiple threads and child processes within an application.
Registry	Support for storing, accessing, and managing the Windows system-defined database with application and system component configuration data.
Security	Support for granting or denying application and user access to an object. Many of the security routines are provided by the Advanced API library (`advapi32.dll`).
Services	Support for automated services in which an application (or driver) can operate without user intervention (or user knowledge). Support for these types of applications is controlled by the Service Control Manager (SCM). Many of the service routines are provided by the Advanced API library (`advapi32.dll`).
String Manipulation	Support for copying, comparing, sorting, formatting, and converting character strings and determining character types.
Structured Exception Handling	Provides compiler support for exception handling and termination.
Synchronization	Provides mechanisms that threads can use to synchronize access to a resource.
System Information	Support for determining and retrieving system information, such as computer name, user name, environment variables settings, processor type, and system color information.
System Messages	Support for notifying applications and drivers of device change events.
System Shutdown	Support for logging off the current user or shutting down the system.
Tape Backup	Support for allowing backup applications to perform tape read/write and initialization and retrieving tape and drive information.
Time	Support for retrieving and setting the date and the time for the system, files, and the local time zone.
Windows Stations and Desktop	Support for Win32 services to call USER32 and GDI32 functions, regardless of the logon account in which the service is running.

There is a total of 745 system service kernel library routines (kernel32.dll) available in current versions of Windows that support the features previously described. Use Borland's impdef command-line tool, described earlier, to view the full list of the available system service functions supported by the kernel library. Also, keep in mind that the user library and several other ancillary libraries, such as the imagehlp.dll and advapi32.dll, provide additional system service support.

Graphical Device Interface

The graphical device interface (GDI), supported by the gdi32.dll dynamic link library, provides the capability for a window to draw and to print. This includes drawing lines, text, font service, and color management.

One of the key elements to the GDI is the device context. A *device context* (DC) represents a data structure defining a set of graphic objects, attributes, and output modes. DCs are created using the CreateDC() and GetDC() functions. There is a myriad of other DC functions that are commonly used as well. There are seven types of GDI objects that can be selected into a device context (see Table 24.3).

TABLE 24.3 The Seven Types of GDI Object

Feature	Description
Bitmap	Used for copying or scrolling parts of the screen
Brush	Used for painting and filling the interior of polygons, ellipses, and paths
Font	Used for identifying type, size, and style of a type font
Palette	Used for defining the set of available colors
Path	Used for painting and drawing operations
Pen	Used for line drawing
Region	Used for clipping and other operations

There is a total of 334 GDI routines available in current versions of Windows. Use Borland's impdef command-line tool, described earlier, to determine the full list of the available Windows GDI functions supported by the gdi32.dll.

The Windows GDI can be extremely useful for providing 2D graphic rendering and visualization for business applications. Borland's VCL wraps much of the GDI functionality within the TImage and TCanvas classes. Because the VCL provides a solid encapsulation of the GDI, the benefit of using the raw Win32 GDI is not all that substantial for the C++Builder developer.

24

USING THE
WIN32 API

The biggest debilitating factor with the GDI, whether used directly or through the VCL, is that its performance is marginal at best. Using the GDI to display real-time, fast-paced graphic images often provides a lesson in frustration for both developers and users. In regards to frames per second, it's slow, even with the best hardware. Fortunately, the DirectDraw API, which is part of Microsoft's DirectX Game SDK, provides a much-improved library alternative for 2D graphics display. For those requiring high-performance 2D rendering, DirectDraw is the answer. Although DirectX is considered an extension of the Win32 API because it is supported by both Windows 9x and NT 2000, it is not within the scope of this chapter. For more information on DirectX, see Chapter 26, "Advanced Graphics with DirectX and OpenGL."

Multimedia Services

A growing number of applications today incorporate multimedia elements, such as sound and video, to enrich the experience of the user. Some of the extension libraries Microsoft has provided for Windows include the Multimedia System Library (MMSYSTEM.DLL), the Microsoft Video for Windows Library (MSVFW32.DLL), and the Microsoft Audio Compression Manager Library (MSACM32.DLL). Originally, multimedia features were not part of the Windows API. However, the Windows operating system has evolved to support and promote multimedia. In fact, the modern Windows platform is, for all practical purposes, a multimedia appliance, similar to a TV or stereo. Multimedia devices and data formats, such as MIDI, waveform audio, and video, are supported by Windows. The MMSYSTEM.DLL, MSVFW32.DLL, and MSACM32.DLL provide a majority of the basic multimedia capabilities. Microsoft has also introduced a multimedia API known as DirectX to better support games, music, and video. However, this section primarily focuses on the capabilities provided by MMSYSTEM.DLL, MSVFW32.DLL, and MSACM32.DLL. The multimedia headers files for these DLLs are DIGITALV.H, MCIAVI.H, MMSYSTEM.H, MSACM.H, VCR.H, and VFW.H.

Table 24.4 describes the various multimedia services provided by these libraries.

TABLE 24.4 Multimedia Services

Feature	Description
Audio Compression Manager (ACM)	Provides system-level support for audio compression, decompression, filtering, and conversion (uses MSACM32.DLL).
Audio Mixers	Provides services to control the routing of audio lines to a destination device for playing or recording. Also provides support for manipulating volume and other effects (uses MMSYSTEM.DLL).
AVICap	Provides video capture capabilities including interface support for acquiring video and waveform-audio hardware and support for controlling streaming video capturing to disk (uses MSVFW32.DLL).

TABLE 24.4   Continued

Feature	Description
AVIFile	Provides functions and macros for accessing audio-video interleaved (AVI) files (uses `MSVFW32.DLL`).
DrawDib	Provide GDI-independent functions used to transfer device independent bitmaps (DIBs) to video memory (uses `MSVFW32.DLL`).
Joysticks	Provides support for managing joysticks and other ancillary input devices that track positions within an absolute coordinate system (touch screen, digitizing tablet, and light pen) (uses `MMSYSTEM.DLL`).
MCIWnd Window Class	Provides a window class for controlling multimedia devices. Provides support for easily adding multimedia playback or recording capabilities to an application (uses `MSVFW32.DLL`).
Media Control Interface (MCI)	Provides device-independent support for playing multimedia devices (waveform audio devices, CD player, MIDI sequencers, and digital-video devices) and recording multimedia resource files (uses `MMSYSTEM.DLL`).
Multimedia File I/O	Provides buffered and unbuffered file I/O service and support for Resource Interchange File Format (RIFF) files, such as wave files and video files (uses `MMSYSTEM.DLL`).
Multimedia Timers	Provides support for scheduling periodic, high-resolution timer events (uses `MMSYSTEM.DLL`).
Music Instrument Digital Interface (MIDI)	Provides the MIDI Mapper to translate and redirect the incoming MIDI messages and other various MIDI services, such as querying for devices and managing, streaming, and recording MIDI message data. (Note: MCI services, which provide a MIDI sequencer, can be used in conjunction with the MIDI services.) (Uses `MMSYSTEM.DLL`.)
Video Compression Manager (VCM)	Provides video data compression and decompression support (uses `MSVFW32.DLL`).
Waveform-Audio	Provides utilities for adding (playing and recording) waveform-audio sounds (uses `MMSYSTEM.DLL`).

24

USING THE
WIN32 API

Among the three DLLs mentioned in Table 24.4, there are more than 240 functions that support the multimedia services. Use Borland's `impdef` command-line tool, described earlier, to determine the full list of the available multimedia functions (contained in `MMSYSTEM.DLL`, `MSVFW32.DLL`, and `MSACM32.DLL`). The import libraries for these DLLs are `WINMM.LIB`, `VFW32.LIB`, and `MSACM32.LIB`, respectively.

Common Controls and Dialogs

A collection of predefined, common window controls is provided within Windows through the common control library (`COMCTL32.DLL`). In addition to controls, a collection of common window dialogs are provided through the common dialog library (`COMDLG32.DLL`). The idea behind providing common controls and dialogs is to allow developers to quickly utilize common interface elements within a program rather than spending lengthy time and effort writing custom window interfaces. For the most part, Borland C++Builder provides a palette full of common controls and dialogs through the Visual Component Library (VCL). However, it's important that developers be aware of the Win32 API common controls and dialogs that are available.

There are reportedly 22 common controls for Windows in version 4.71 of `COMCTL32.DLL`, which came with Internet Explorer version 4.0. Examination of the `commctrl.h` file provided with C++Builder reveals the Win32 elements available with the common control library. These controls are described in Table 24.5.

TABLE 24.5 Common Controls

Common Control	Description	Borland VCL Equivalent
Animation Control	Plays simple AVI (video) clips without sound	`TAnimate`
ComboBoxEx*	Provides support for item images within a combo box	None
Date and Time Picker	Provides an interface for exchanging date and time information with the user	`TDateTimePicker`
Drag List Box	Provides a list box that allows items to be dragged from one position to another	None
Flat Scroll Bar*	Provides a unique three-dimensional scrollbar, created using the `InitializeFlatSB()` routine	None

TABLE 24.5 Continued

Common Control	Description	Borland VCL Equivalent
Header Controls	Used to place resizable headers above columns of text or numbers	`THeaderControl`
Hot-Key Controls	Allows entry of hotkey keystroke combinations	`THotKey`
Image List	Provides a collection of equal size images referenced by an index, created using the `ImageListCreate()` routine	`TImageList`
IP Address*	Allows an IP address to be entered in an easily understood format	None
List View	Displays a collection of items as large icons, small icons, detailed list, or report view within a window control	`TListView`
Monthly Calendar	Provides a graphical calendar interface for viewing and selecting dates	`TMonthCalendar`
Page Scroller*	Provides a scrollable window containing a child window (such as a control) that is too large to be seen entirely	`TPageScroller`
Progress Bars	Used to provide graphical status feedback for lengthy operations	`TProgressBar`
Property Sheets	Presents viewable and editable properties of an item in a tabbed page form	`TPageControl`
Rebar (Coolbar)	Used to contain one or more bands composed of any combination of a gripper bar, bitmap, text label, and a child window	`TCoolBar`

TABLE 24.5 Continued

Common Control	Description	Borland VCL Equivalent
Status Bar	Provides a panel control used to display text and graphical information	TStatusBar
Tab Controls	Defines multiple pages within the area of a window (similar to dividers in a notebook)	TTabControl
Toolbars	Contains one or more selectable buttons within a panel bar	TToolBar
Tooltip Controls	Used to display a small pop-up window displaying a text description	THintWindow
Trackbars	Provides a slide indicator with optional tick marks used for adjusting an integer value within a specified range	TTrackBar
Tree View Controls	Displays a hierarchical list of items and subitems within a window frame consisting of a label and an optional bitmapped image	TTreeView
Up-Down Controls	Provides an edit control consistingof a pair of arrow buttons used to increase or decrease a value	TUpDown

* Introduced in Internet Explorer 4.0.

Unless otherwise noted, these controls are created by using either the `InitCommonControlsEx()` routine or the `CreateWindowEx()` routine, by selecting the proper flags associated with each feature. A majority of these features are supported by Borland's VCL. There are 82 available routines within the common control library (`comctl32.dll`) that support these and possibly other common controls. Use Borland's `impdef` command-line tool, described earlier, to determine the full list of the available common control functions supported by the Win32 API.

In addition to common controls, Microsoft provides common dialogs. There are presently eight common dialogs contained in version 4.00.950 of COMDLG32.DLL. C++Builder, however, provides VCL wrappers for each of these dialogs, as shown in Table 24.6.

TABLE 24.6 VCL Equivalents for Microsoft API Common Dialog Functions

Common Dialog	Microsoft API Call	VCL Equivalent
Choose Color	ChooseColor()	TColorDialog
Choose Font	ChooseFont()	TFontDialog
Find Text	FindText()	TFindDialog
Open File	GetOpenNameFile()	TOpenDialog
Save File	GetSaveFileName()	TSaveDialog
Print Setup	PageSetupDlg()	TPrinterSetupDialog
Print	PrintDlg()	TPrintDialog
Replace Text	ReplaceText()	TReplaceDialog

Examination of the commdlg.h file provided with C++Builder reveals the Win32 elements available with the common dialog library. Creating the .def file for the commdlg.dll will further reveal the available API routines.

Shell Features

The term *Shell* is used within Windows to describe an application that enables a user to group, start, and control other applications. Shell features include drag-and-drop file support, file association support for starting and finding other applications, and the capability to extract icons from other files. The Shell aspect of the Win32 API is a very powerful feature set and is contained within the Shell32.dll. The principle header file included within the source code of an application that provides the Shell features is the SHELLAPI.H. The basic features of the Shell API are described in Table 24.7.

TABLE 24.7 Basic Features of the Shell API

Shell Feature	Description
Drag-and-Drop	Allows a user to select one or more files in Windows Explorer (or even the old File Explorer provided with Win 3.x) that can be dragged and dropped into an open application that has previously used the DragAcceptFiles Shell function. A WM_DROPFILES message is received by the open application, which is used to retrieve the filenames and display the position at which the files were dropped. This is accomplished using the DragQueryFile and DragQueryPoint Shell functions.

TABLE 24.7 Continued

Shell Feature	Description
File Association Support for Starting and/or Finding Other Applications	Back in the Win 3.x days, Microsoft provided the Associate dialog box within File Explorer. This allowed a user to associate a filename extension with a particular application. Since Windows 95, a more detailed Associate dialog box is provided within Windows Explorer called the Open With dialog. The Registry provides an automated association of filename extensions and applications. Within Windows Explorer, a file that is double-clicked and has an association with a specific application will cause the application to load and open the selected file. The `FindExecute` and `ShellExecute` routines contained within the Shell API make use of this file association. The `FindExecutable()` function is used to retrieve the name and handle to the application associate with a specified file. `ShellExecute` and `ShellExecuteEx` are used to open or print a specified file. The application required to open a file is launched based on the file association.
Extracting Icons	Applications, dynamic link libraries, and icon files are typically represented by one or more icons. The handle of an icon can be retrieved easily by using the `ExtractIcon` Shell routine.

There is a total of 120 Shell routines available in current versions of Windows, many of which are undocumented. Use Borland's `impdef` command-line tool, described earlier, to view the full list of the available Shell library functions. Some of the undocumented and little-known Shell routines are described later in the chapter.

International Features

The Win32 API provides support for non-English development and deployment to international markets. For example, languages other than English and technical symbols are best represented using the 16-bit Unicode character set that is supported by Windows. National Language Support (NLS) functions help target an application for specific international markets. The various internal features are described in Table 24.8.

TABLE 24.8 National Language Support Functions

International Feature	Description
End-User-Defined Characters (EUDC)	Provides support for customized characters that are not available in standard screen or printer fonts. EUDC includes Far Eastern language syntax, such as Japanese and Chinese.

TABLE 24.8 Continued

International Feature	Description
Input Method Editor (IME)	Provides a collection of functions, messages, and structures used to support Unicode and double-byte character sets. IME functionality is provided by `imm32.dll`.
National Language Support	Provides support for adapting and transitioning applications to various language-specific and location-specific environments.
Unicode and Character Sets	Provides support for character encoding, including the Unicode standard. Character encoding, such as Unicode, allows applications to support multilingual text processing.

Network Services

Network services allow communication between applications on different computers on a network. The network functions are used to create and manage connections to shared resources, such as directories and network printers, on computers in the network. The Win32 network interfaces include Windows Networking, Windows Sockets, NetBIOS, RAS, SNMP, and Network DDE and are described in Table 24.9.

TABLE 24.9 The Win32 Network Interfaces

Network Interface	Description
Windows Networking (WNet)	Provides a set of network-independent functions for implementing networking capabilities within an application. Functionality is provided by the Win32 Network Interface DLL (`mpr.dll`). All network functions are prefixed by `WNet`.
Ported LAN Manager Functions	Provides functionality for a network operating system and was originally designed for OS/2-based servers. Now it is no longer considered to be part of the Win32 API. However, much of the functionality is still provided by Windows through the `netapi32.dll`.
NetBIOS Interface	Used to communicate via a network with applications on other computers. The Network Basic Input/Output System (NetBIOS) functionality is provided by the `netapi32.dll`.
Network Dynamic Data Exchange	Allows DDE to work over a network. Functionality is provided by the WFW DDE Share Interface (`nddeapi.dll`). All network DDE functions are prefixed by `NDde`.

Table 24.9   Continued

Network Interface	Description
Remote Access Service (RAS)	Allows users at remote locations to connect directly to a computer network, accessing one or more RAS servers. Supports dial-up networking. RAS functionality is provided by the `rasapi32.dll`. All RAS functions are prefixed by RAS.
Simple Network Management Protocol (SNMP)	Used for exchanging network management information through the SNMP Internet standard protocol. See Windows Help for more information.
Windows Sockets (WinSock)	Used for TCP and UDP network data exchange. WinSock is based on the Berkeley Software Distribution (BSD) UNIX sockets paradigm. Windows Socket functionality is provided by `wsock32.dll` (WinSock version 1.1) or by `ws2_32.dll` (WinSock version 2.0).

Anatomy and Operation of a Windows Program

The functional areas of the Win32 API described earlier provide an initial foundation for understanding the composition and capabilities of the API. Before diving into real-world examples, however, there are fundamental rules of operation that occur between the Windows operating environment and a Win32 application that developers should first grasp. This section examines the basic anatomy and operation of a Windows program.

WinMain()

`WinMain()`, supported by the Windows Management area, is the most essential Win32 function of an application. Those who have been around C++Builder long enough have probably noticed the `WinMain()` function located within the itty-bitty C++ file known as the Project Source File. `WinMain()` is the entry point for all Windows applications; it must be there. It is a Win32 API function contained within your program that is called when an application is launched. `WinMain()` replaces the ANSI standard `main()` declaration required for C++ console applications. Borland C++Builder automatically generates the `WinMain()` file, and, for the most part, developer's need not bother with the composition of this function because C++Builder does this job for you. However, there are some instances when it's useful to tweak and add additional capabilities within the `WinMain()` function block. Some of these cases will be examined later.

Understanding the composition of a `WinMain()` function provides a good place to begin to learn about how Windows operates. The following declaration is used by all Windows applications, regardless of the development environment it was created under:

```
WINAPI WinMain(HINSTANCE, HINSTANCE, LPSTR, int)
```

The first parameter identifies the module handle for the application that has been invoked. A call to the `GetModuleHandle()` Windows routine will obtain the application handle. A handle is a very important element to the Win32 API. In a short while, we will take a take a deeper look into the various types of handles Windows uses to effectively manage applications and processes.

The second parameter is a remnant from the Win16 API and exists within the Win32 API, most likely for the sake of portability of a 16-bit legacy application to the Win32 environment. In Win16, the parameter is used to identify a previous instance of an application if one existed; in Win32, the second parameter is always `NULL`. Because each process runs in a unique protected address space, each program is an independent process in Win32. There is no second instance that can occur within the same address space. However, this doesn't preclude an application from being launched multiple times. Multiple invocations of an application within Win32 will create multiple independent processes. To determine if another copy of the application has already been invoked, it is recommended that a mutex object be created within the `WinMain()` function using the `CreateMutex()` function call described later in the chapter.

The third parameter within `WinMain()` provides a pointer to the command-line string. The command line can be used to provide runtime arguments for an application. There are several ways to retrieve the collection of parameters within the command line. One way is to use the Win32 `GetCommandLine()` call and to dissect the returned string to determine the number of parameters and associated values. C++Builder provides a simpler method to receive command-line arguments through the combination of the `ParamCount()` and `ParamStr()` routines provided by Borland (independent of Win32). `ParamCount()` and `ParamStr()` mimic the functionality that the `argv` and `argc` parameters provided with the standard `main()` function used by console applications.

Finally, the fourth parameter of `WinMain()` identifies the start state of how the window should be initially displayed. The parameter can be any one of the values in Table 24.10 as described in the Windows Help.

24

TABLE 24.10   `WinMain()` Message Constants

Value	Meaning
SW_HIDE	Hides the window and activates another window.
SW_MINIMIZE	Minimizes the specified window and activates the top-level window in the system's list.

TABLE 24.10   Continued

Value	Meaning
SW_RESTORE	Activates and displays a window. If the window is minimized or maximized, Windows restores it to its original size and position (same as SW_SHOWNORMAL).
SW_SHOW	Activates a window and displays it in its current size and position.
SW_SHOWMAXIMIZED	Activates a window and displays it as a maximized window.
SW_SHOWMINIMIZED	Activates a window and displays it as an icon.
SW_SHOWMINNOACTIVE	Displays a window as an icon. The active window remains active.
SW_SHOWNA	Displays a window in its current state. The active window remains active.
SW_SHOWNOACTIVATE	Displays a window in its most recent size and position. The active window remains active.
SW_SHOWNORMAL	Activates and displays a window. If the window is minimized or maximized, Windows restores it to its original size and position (same as SW_RESTORE).

Window Handles

The WinMain() discussion introduced the notion of handles. Handles are an extremely important aspect of the Win32 API because all window resources are identified by some type of handle. Examples of entities with handles include modules, processes, threads, frame windows, menus, bitmaps, icons, cursors, and color space. A handle is always represented by a 32-bit unsigned value. Handles provide the means and mechanism to control and manipulate objects, such as a window and children process, and provides the ability to pass input to other applications through message callbacks. Many of the examples described in this chapter will make use of handles.

Windows Messages

Windows messages provide the interaction mechanism used to pass input to various objects represented by a handle. There are many types of predefined Windows messages that both the Windows system and applications can dispatch. For instance, when a user clicks the mouse, moves a mouse, or resizes the active screen, the system generates a message to the appropriate application indicating the action that occurred. Messages are used to signify input, system changes, or direct information passed from one application to another. The key to making messaging work is knowing the handle for which the message is to be delivered.

SendMessage()/PostMessage()

Delivery of messages are performed several different ways. The two most popular ways to dispatch Windows messages within an application is through the SendMessage() and PostMessage(). The SendMessage() function transmits a specific message to either a single window handle or to all top-level windows. The application that called SendMessage() then waits until the message has been processed by the targeted window. Similarly, PostMessage() performs the same action, but does not bother to wait for the message to be processed and returns immediately.

Both SendMessage() and PostMessage() require four elements: a window handle indicating the target window, a message identifier that describes the purpose of the message, and two 32-bit message parameters. The message parameters can be used to pass value information or address information to the destination handle. The LRESULT value returned by the SendMessage() or PostMessage() function specifies the result of the message processing. For instance, a return value of nonzero indicates success for PostMessage(). See Windows Help for more information.

```
LRESULT SendMessage(
    HWND hWnd,      // handle of destination window
    UINT Msg,       // message to send
    WPARAM wParam,  // first message parameter
    LPARAM lParam   // second message parameter
);
```

Message Identifiers

There are well over 200 predefined constants known as Windows Message Identifiers. Windows Message Identifiers are used frequently to perform interrupt handling between applications and the operating system. In addition to predefined Windows messages, custom Windows messages can be defined. It is recommended that the RegisterWindowMessage() function from the Windows Management functional area be used to define a custom window message to guarantee that it is unique throughout the system.

A majority of the predefined Windows Message Identifiers all begin with the WM_ prefix. The following are several of the more popular messages:

- WM_PAINT   Message to repaint window.
- WM_QUIT   Message queue to quit application.
- WM_LBUTTONDBLCLK   The left mouse button was double-clicked.
- WM_LBUTTONDOWN   The left mouse button was pressed.
- WM_LBUTTONUP   The left mouse button was released.

- `WM_MBUTTONDBLCLK`   The middle mouse button was double-clicked.
- `WM_MBUTTONDOWN`   The middle mouse button was pressed.
- `WM_MBUTTONUP`   The middle mouse button was released.
- `WM_RBUTTONDBLCLK`   The right mouse button was double-clicked.
- `WM_RBUTTONDOWN`   The right mouse button was pressed.
- `WM_RBUTTONUP`   The right mouse button was released.
- `WM_NCHITTEST`   Mouse event just occurred.
- `WM_KEYDOWN`   Non-system key is pressed.
- `WM_TIMER`   Timer event message.

Responding to Windows Messages

To respond to messages sent either by the `SendMessage()` or `PostMessage()` routines, an application needs to have some type of event response table. There are several ways to set up an event response table. The most popular way within C++Builder is to declare callback routines and a message map within the protected area of the main form's class declaration. An example is as follows:

```
protected:      // User declarations
// Engine Callback Messages.
    void __fastcall Process_wmPaint(TMessage &);
    void __fastcall Process_wmQuit(TMessage &);
    void __fastcall Process_wmXYZ(TMessage &);
    BEGIN_MESSAGE_MAP
       MESSAGE_HANDLER(WM_PAINT,TMessage,Process_wmPaint);
       MESSAGE_HANDLER(WM_QUIT,TMessage,Process_wmQuit);
       MESSAGE_HANDLER(WM_XYZ,TMessage,Process_wmXYZ);
    END_MESSAGE_MAP(TForm);
```

Within the source code for an application, the callback routine would look something like the following:

```
void __fastcall Tform1::Process_wmXYZ(TMessage Msg)
{
    int fromhandle = LOBYTE(LOWORD(Msg.WParam));
    int infoid = Msg.LParam;
    AnsiString StatusText =
    " Application sent message XYZ\nApplication Handle = " +
➥IntToStr(fromhandle) +
    "\nInfo = " + IntToStr(infoid);

    MessageBox(Handle,StatusText,"Received Message Callback",MB_OK);
}
```

Borland's `TMessage`, defined in the following code, provides the structure for the Windows message:

```
struct TMessage
{
    Cardinal Msg;
    union
    {
        struct
        {
            Word WParamLo;
            Word WParamHi;
            Word LParamLo;
            Word LParamHi;
            Word ResultLo;
            Word ResultHi;
        };
        struct
        {
            int WParam;
            int LParam;
            int Result;
        };

    };
} ;
```

Typically, a message passed by `SendMessage()` or `PostMessage()` will contain information within the `WParam` and `LParam`. A callback routine will most likely examine and decipher the 32-bit values. It's important to note that either one of these 32-bit values could potentially represent a pointer to an accessible address location if the caller resides within the same process as the recipient (in Win16, address space was accessible across multiple processes; Win32 is more protected). If a pointer is passed, more data than just a 32-bit item can be shared with other objects.

Real-World Examples Using the API

The best way to understand how to use the Win32 API during C++Builder development is to look at some real-world examples. The examples in the following section highlight some of the key and common routines used by developers to create and manage robust Windows applications. Some of the undocumented and API routines introduced in Windows 2000 are explored as well.

24

USING THE
WIN32 API

`InternalHigh` is reserved for operating system use. This member, which specifies the length of the data transferred, is valid when the `GetOverlappedResult()` function returns `TRUE`.

`Offset` specifies a file position at which to start the transfer. The file position is a byte offset from the start of the file. The calling process sets this member before calling the `ReadFile()` or `WriteFile()` function. This member is ignored when reading from or writing to named pipes and communications devices.

`OffsetHigh` specifies the high word of the byte offset at which to start the transfer. This member is ignored when reading from or writing to named pipes and communications devices.

`HEvent` identifies an event set to the signaled state when the transfer has been completed. The calling process sets this member before calling the `ReadFile()`, `WriteFile()`, `ConnectNamedPipe()`, or `TransactNamedPipe()` function.

If `ReadFile()` was successful, it will return `TRUE`; if not, it will return `FALSE`.

WriteFile()

`WriteFile()` writes data to disk. The data is written to disk provided by the file pointer position. After completion, the file pointer is adjusted by the number of bytes written. Just like `ReadFile()`, if the file is opened by the `FILE_FLAG_OVERLAPPED` option, the file pointer has to be adjusted by the application. For this reference and example, we will not use this option.

`WriteFile()`'s parameters are as follows:

```
BOOL WriteFile(
    HANDLE hFile,      // handle to file to write to
    LPCVOID lpBuffer,      // pointer to data to write to file
    DWORD nNumberOfBytesToWrite,      // number of bytes to write
    LPDWORD lpNumberOfBytesWritten,      // pointer to number of bytes written
    LPOVERLAPPED lpOverlapped // pointer to structure needed for overlapped I/O
    );
```

`hFile` is the handle of the file.

`lpBuffer` is the buffer containing the data to be sent to disk.

`nNumberOfBytesToWrite` is the number of bytes to be written to disk.

`lpNumberOfBytesWritten` is the number of bytes written to disk.

`lpOverlapped` is a pointer to an overlapped structure that is required if the handle to the file was opened with the `FILE_FLAG_OVERLAPPED` flag.

`WriteFile()` returns `TRUE` if the function is successful; otherwise, it returns `FALSE`.

Let's look at an example on how to write and read to a file. Start by loading in C++Builder and creating a new application.

Place the components shown in Table 24.16 on a form.

TABLE 24.16 A List of Components to Place in the `WriteFile()` Component

Component	Property
Form1	Left = 235
	Top = 184
Label1	Left = 9
	Top = 9
	Width = 124
	Caption = Enter a filename to create:
Label2	Left = 8
	Top = 130
	Width = 262
	Caption = When you click CREATE, a buffer will be written and displayed in the caption below. Clicking READ will read it back and display it.
	WordWrap = True
Label5	Name = BufferLabel1
	Left = 8
	Top = 205
	Caption = Buffer
Label3	Left = 6
	Top = 186
	Caption = Stuff in buffer---
Label4	Left = 10
	Top = 56
	Caption = Enter some text here for test buffer.
Edit1	Left = 7
	Top = 25
	Width = 265
	Height = 21
	Text = c:\test.txt
Button1	Left = 13
	Top = 98
	Width = 75
	Height = 25
	Caption = &Create

24

TABLE 24.16 Continued

Value	Meaning
Button2	Left = 200
	Top = 98
	Width = 75
	Height = 25
	Caption = &Read
Edit2	Left = 8
	Top = 72
	MaxLength = 255
	Text = This is example text that will be written to a file.

Save the project as readwrite. Save the unit as mainform.cpp. Insert the code from Listing 24.4.

LISTING 24.4 ReadFile(), WriteFile(), and CreateFile() Function Examples

```cpp
//--------------------------------------------------------------------
#include <vcl\vcl.h>
#pragma hdrstop
#include "mainform.h"
//--------------------------------------------------------------------
#pragma resource "*.dfm"
TForm1 *Form1;
   HANDLE hSrc;      //Create a handle to a file to read and write
//--------------------------------------------------------------------
__fastcall TForm1::TForm1(TComponent* Owner): TForm(Owner)
{
}
//--------------------------------------------------------------------
void __fastcall TForm1::Button1Click(TObject *Sender)
{
   char buffer[255];        //Buffer to hold data
   DWORD bytes_written;     //Amount of bytes to be written

   /*Prepare to open the file for write access. the CREATE_ALWAYS
     flag means to create the file always, re-writing over the old.
     We will open the file for random access.
   */
   hSrc = CreateFile(Edit1->Text.c_str(), GENERIC_WRITE, 0, NULL,
          CREATE_ALWAYS, FILE_FLAG_RANDOM_ACCESS, 0);
```

LISTING 24.4   Continued

```
  //If the handle to the file is invalid, then generate an error
  if(hSrc == INVALID_HANDLE_VALUE)
    {
     Application->MessageBoxA("Error In Opening File", NULL, NULL); return;
    }

  //Copy the contents of the EditBox into the buffer
  strcpy(buffer, Edit2->Text.c_str());

  //Now perform the write....
  WriteFile(hSrc, buffer, sizeof(buffer), &bytes_written, NULL);
  //CLOSE the file after writing...
  CloseHandle(hSrc);

  //Put buffer into the label caption
  BufferLabel->Caption = buffer;
}
//-------------------------------------------------------------------------
void __fastcall TForm1::Button2Click(TObject *Sender)
{
   BufferLabel->Caption = "";

   //Declare buffer to recieve data
   char Buffer[255];
   DWORD dwRead;

  //Open the file for read access, with no attributes, and if the file exists...
   hSrc = CreateFile(Edit1->Text.c_str(), GENERIC_READ, 0, NULL,
           OPEN_EXISTING, FILE_ATTRIBUTE_NORMAL, 0);

  if(hSrc == INVALID_HANDLE_VALUE)
    {
     Application->MessageBoxA("Error In Opening File", NULL, NULL); return;
    }

  if(ReadFile(hSrc , Buffer, sizeof(Buffer), &dwRead, NULL) )
    {
      BufferLabel->Caption =Buffer;
      ShowMessage("Read OK");
    }
    else
    { ShowMessage("Nope, not read");  }
    CloseHandle (hSrc);
}
```

In the Listing 24.4, make sure you enter the HANDLE hSrc; to create the handle to the file. Note that there are button events in the code to do all the work. You can create the events automatically by double-clicking on the button. C++Builder automatically generates the code in the header and main source file.

If you haven't already, go ahead and compile and run this program. As you will see, it's quite easy to read and write to a file.

There are more I/O functions in the Win32 API that can be used for file manipulation, such as MoveFile(), DeleteFile(), and several new SHx functions. The SHx functions are the newer Shell functions provided in Windows 95 and Windows NT 4. Let us first explore some of the older file manipulation functions and then examine some of the newer Shell functions that can be used to accomplish similar feats.

MoveFile()

The MoveFile() function is used to move an existing file or directory from one location to another location on a similar drive or tape volume. However, it cannot move files or directories from one drive or tape volume to another storage media. MoveFile() will fail if the target destination is a different media from the source location. This is because the directory locations are actually renamed on the same media and not actually moved.

MoveFile() takes on the following parameters:

```
Bool MoveFile(LPCTSTR lpszExisting  , LPCTSTR lpszNew);
```

lpszExisting is the pointer to a null terminated string that contains the name of an existing file or directory.

lpszNew is the pointer to a null terminated string of the new location. The name of the destination must not exist.

It returns TRUE if successful; otherwise, it returns FALSE.

```
MoveFile("C:\\Winters\\Lauren\\Pics" , "c:\\Sexton\\Family\\Pics\\Backup);
```

DeleteFile()

DeleteFile() works just like the ANSI C/C++ standard unlink() function. It removes a file from the media. If it cannot delete an existing file or the file is currently opened or does not exist, the function will return FALSE (will fail).

DeleteFile() has the following parameter:

```
bool DeleteFile(LPCSTR lpszFileName)
```

lpszFileName is the pointer to a null-terminated string of the name of the file.

```
DeleteFile("c:\\Collin\\TextFiles\\music.txt");
```

CopyFile()

CopyFile() copies files to another location on the media. The attributes are copied along with the file, but not the security attributes.

CopyFile() has the following parameters:

```
bool LPCSTR lpszExistingfile , LPCSTR lpsz NewFile, BOOL FailIfExisting)
```

lpszExsistingFile is the name of the existing file desired to copy.

lpszNewFile is the pointer to a null terminated string of the destination file.

failIfExisting takes action on existing file. If TRUE, the function fails, meaning that the file will not be overwritten. If FALSE, the file can be overwritten.

```
CopyFile("file.txt" , "file.txt" , true);
```

CreateDirectory()

CreateDirectory() will create a directory on the storage media. If an OS supports security, CreateDirectory() applies a security descriptor to the new directory. Windows 9x does not support security on its system, but NT does.

CreateDirectory() has the following parameters:

```
bool CreateDirectory(LPCSTR lpszPath,LPSECURITYATTRIBUTES lpSecurityAttributes)
```

lpszPath is the pointer to a null terminated string for the new directory.

lpSecurityAttributes is a pointer to a structure that specifies the security attributes for the directory. The file system must support security.

```
CreateDirectory("C:\\Wratchford\\Files" , NULL);
```

Using the Magic of Shell

Shell functions are a big thing in Windows 98/2000 programming. Newer Shell functions are best known as SHx functions because many of them have the SH prefix. A few common ones and new ones supported in Windows 2000 are described in the following sections. Several newer Shell functions have replaced the older Win32 API routines because they are more versatile. Although the older API routines can still be used for simple transfers or manipulation, the new API routines are quicker yet sometimes very hard to use. Well, no one ever said that Windows programming is easy—just fun!

Interfacing with a Browser

With much of today's data available via the World Wide Web, it is often necessary for an application to interface with the platform's default Web browser. The Win32 API Shell extensions make it possible to provide this type of interface. The following example demonstrates a customized wrapper routine that uses the ShellExecute() function to open a browser with a specified address (URL). ShellExecute() is a scaled-down version of the ShellExecuteEx() function described earlier.

```
int  RunBrowser (char* URL)
{
    if (! ShellExecute(NULL, "open", URL, NULL, NULL, SW_SHOW))
    {
        char data[100];
        sprintf(data,"Could not run browser with URL '%s'",URL);
        MessageBox(NULL,data,"Operation Error!",MB_OK);
        return -1;
    }
    return 0;
}
```

The second parameter indicates a desire to "open" a file. The third parameter provides information about where that file is. The Shell library deciphers URL descriptors and will use the registered browser that supports URLs.

Steroid File Operation Support

SHFileOperation() is a versatile file operation function that is often hard to tackle for the beginner but is often asked about regarding its capability to support multiple directory transfers. The SHFileOperation() is significantly more powerful than the MoveFile() because it can transfer files and directories over to a new volume. It can also transfer children files within a directory. The SHFileOperation() is widely used in Windows 95 and later. It is quite powerful and flexible and is often seen in action when directories are being moved or the Recycle Bin is being emptied.

The example code, shown in Listing 24.5 and provided on the CD-ROM included with this book, demonstrates how to copy files and subdirectories all at once from one location to another.

LISTING 24.5   Using the SHFileOperation()

```
//Declare the SHFILEOPSTRUCT structure to fill in information for use
//of SHFileOperation function.
SHFILEOPSTRUCT op;

//Clear out any thing within the structure for safe keeping
  ZeroMemory(&op, sizeof(op));

  String RestoreDir, RestoreToDir;
```

LISTING 24.5   Continued

```
/*We are going to assign a directory to this string. RestoreDir will
now hold the SOURCE directory. */

    RestoreDir = "C:\\MYFILES\\";

//Set length of string and add 1
    RestoreDir.SetLength(RestoreDir.Length() + 1);

//Add a NULL
    RestoreDir[RestoreDir.Length()] = '\0';
//Do it again. Increment the string and then add another.
    RestoreDir.SetLength(RestoreDir.Length() + 1);
    RestoreDir[RestoreDir.Length()] = '\0';

//RestoreToDir will hold the destination directory. The files
//will be copied there.
   RestoreToDir = "C:\\TEMP"

//Add a path mark and to NULLs
      RestoreToDir  = RestoreToDir +"\\";
      RestoreToDir.SetLength(RestoreToDir.Length()+NULL+NULL);

op.hwnd = 0;     //This is a handle to the main window, used 0 for ours

op.wFunc= FO_COPY;    //Tell SHFileOperation to COPY files

op.pFrom = RestoreDir.c_str();  //Source directory

op.pTo =  RestoreToDir.c_str();   //Destination directory

op.fFlags=FOF_FILESONLY;   //Tells to copy files only, even if used the *.*

/* Here, we assign an integer to the literal 'copy_done'. Since
   SHFileOperation returns a value, you can capture the value for
error handling. In this part, we'll use Labels.
For example purposes, we'll just throw in a label. */

//Execute SHFileOperation and capture value.
    int copy_done = SHFileOperation(&op);

    if (copy_done == 0)
    {
      if (op.fAnyOperationsAborted)
      {
```

LISTING 24.5   Continued

```
        Label1->Caption = "Copy process halted!";
      }
    else
      {
        Label1->Caption = "Restore operation successful!";
      }
  }
else
  {
    Label1->Caption = "Copy process unsuccessful.";
  }
```

When this example is executed, all files and subdirectories under the MYFILES directory will be copied over to the \TEMP directory.

As illustrated in the following code snippet, it is required by the function that the string RestoreDir be double NULL terminated. Not knowing to do this is a frequent problem.

```
//Add a NULL
    RestoreDir[RestoreDir.Length()] = '\0';
//Do it again. Increment the string and then add another.
    RestoreDir.SetLength(RestoreDir.Length() + 1);
    RestoreDir[RestoreDir.Length()] = '\0';
```

Also illustrated in Listing 24.5, the structure SHFILEOPSTRUCT, defined by op, must first be initialized for the SHFileOperation() function to respond properly. The structure SHFILEOP-STRUCT contains many items and has the following format:

```
typedef struct _SHFILEOPSTRUCT { // shfos
    HWND           hwnd;
    UINT           wFunc;
    LPCSTR         pFrom;
    LPCSTR         pTo;
    FILEOP_FLAGS   fFlags;
    BOOL           fAnyOperationsAborted;
    LPVOID         hNameMappings;
    LPCSTR         lpszProgressTitle;
} SHFILEOPSTRUCT, FAR *LPSHFILEOPSTRUCT;
```

At first appearance, there seems to be many items to fill out. The parameters and explanations follow.

hwnd is the handle of the dialog box to use to display information about the status of the operation. At this point, you should be familiar with this important attribute.

wFunc indicates the operation to perform. This member can be one of the values shown in Table 24.17.

TABLE 24.17   Possible Operations

Member	Value
FO_COPY	Copies the files specified by pFrom to the location specified by pTo. You can copy files from one location to another location even across volumes.
FO_DELETE	Deletes the files specified by pFrom. The pTo is ignored because we are just deleting the files. See flags under this parameter for Recycle Bin operations.
FO_MOVE	Moves the files specified by pFrom to the location specified by pTo. This will actually take the source files and physically move them to another location. It does support over-the-volume transfers.
FO_RENAME	Renames the files specified by pFrom.

pFrom represents a pointer to a buffer specifying one or more source filenames. Multiple names must be null-separated. The list of names must be double–null-terminated. As previously listed, you must follow this rule. For example, if you have many files in a list, you could use a regular \0, which is the separator for those files. At the end of the list, use double-null termination.

pTo represents a pointer to a buffer that contains the name of the destination file or directory. The buffer can contain mutiple destination filenames if the fFlags member specifies FOF_MULTIDESTFILES. Multiple names must be null-separated. The list of names must be double–null-terminated.

fFlags indicates the flags that control the file operation. This member can be a combination of the values shown in Table 24.18.

TABLE 24.18   File Operation Flags

Flag	Value
FOF_ALLOWUNDO	Preserves undo information, if possible.
FOF_CONFIRMMOUSE	Not implemented.
FOF_FILESONLY	Performs the operation only on files if a wildcard filename (*.*) is specified.
FOF_MULTIDESTFILES	Indicates that the pTo member specifies multiple destination files (one for each source file) rather than one directory where all source files are to be deposited.

TABLE 24.18   Continued

Flag	Value
FOF_NOCONFIRMATION	Responds with Yes to All for any dialog box that is displayed.
FOF_NOCONFIRMMKDIR	Does not confirm the creation of a new directory if the operation requires one to be created.
FOF_RENAMEONCOLLISION	Gives the file being operated on a new name (such as Copy #1 of...) in a move, copy, or rename operation, if a file of the target name already exists.
FOF_SILENT	Does not display a progress dialog box. Nothing will appear while this function is in operation.
FOF_SIMPLEPROGRESS	Displays a progress dialog box, but does not show the filenames.
FOF_WANTMAPPINGHANDLE	Fills in the hNameMappings member. The handle must be freed by using the SHFreeNameMappings() function.

fAnyOperationsAborted is used to indicate the status result of the operation. TRUE is received if the user aborted any file operations before they were completed; otherwise, FALSE is received for a successful operation.

hNameMappings identifies a handle of a filename-mapping object containing an array of SHNAMEMAPPING structures. Each structure element within the array contains the old and new pathnames for each file that was moved, copied, or renamed. This member is used only if fFlags includes FOF_WANTMAPPINGHANDLE.

lpszProgressTitle represents a pointer to a string to customize the title of a dialog box. This member is used only if fFlags includes FOF_SIMPLEPROGRESS. The dialog caption of this function can be customized for your application. Instead of text such as Deleting or Copying Files... appearing in the caption, you can set your own. You could put something more elaborate, such as Deletion of Mr. Burfict's files in progress....

In Listing 24.5, a SHFILEOPSTRUCT record variable op is declared first. After declaring the SHFILEOPSTRUCT record variable op, it's best to always clear it out using the function ZeroMemory(). This will NULL out the structure information so that you can start using it. There are a wide variety of things to choose from when initializing the SHFILEOPSTRUCT record variable that will affect the operation of the SHFileOperation() function.

Two of the important items of the SHFILEOPSTRUCT record are pTo and pFrom. When filling out this information, keep in mind to double–null-terminate the string for its operation. Having only one null termination will cause SHFileOperation() to think that the list of files provided contains only one item and will only perform operation for that one particular item. Of course, you can put a list of items in, and `SHFileOperation()` will act upon it, provided it is double–null-terminated. However, to enable a list of files, it is important to include the `FOF_MULTIDESTFILES` flag for it to work properly. Otherwise, it's bound to produce an error.

After declaring the structure, clearing it out, and filling in the members of the `SHFILEOPSTRUCT` record, the `SHFileOperation()` function can then be called.

Listing 24.5 provides a clear idea on how `SHFileOperation()` works. `SHFileOperation()` is supported only in Windows 95/98/Millennium (Me) and NT 2000.

One novel way of using the `SHFileOperation()` function is to delete files and place them in the Recycle Bin. The following is an example of a `DirectoryListBox`. Within the `DirectoryListBox`, a user is provided the ability to select a directory and delete it. The code snippet in Listing 24.6 illustrates how to perform a directory deletion.

LISTING 24.6 Deleting All Files in a Directory

```
  SHFILEOPSTRUCT op;   //Declare structure variable

//Clear out memory
  ZeroMemory(&op, sizeof(op));
  String DelDir;     //Our directory handle

  //Get the CURRENTLY selected item in the list...
  DelDir = DirectoryListBox2->Items->Strings[DirectoryListBox2->ItemIndex];

      DelDir.SetLength(DelDir.Length() + 1);
          DelDir[DelDir.Length()] = '\0';
      DelDir.SetLength(DelDir.Length() + 1);
          DelDir[DelDir.Length()] = '\0';

  String BS;
  BS =  "You are going to BLOW AWAY " + DelDir + "!!! Are you sure?";
  int theanswer = Application->MessageBox(BS.c_str(), "WARNING!", MB_YESNO);

  switch(theanswer)
   {
    case ID_NO:
                if(NoNag==0)
                 {ShowMessage("Yeah! Think again!");} return;
   }
   //Set up structure for SHFIleOperation for source and destination...
   op.hwnd = 0;
   op.wFunc= FO_DELETE;     //Delete files flag
   op.pFrom = DelDir.c_str();
```

LISTING 24.6   Continued

```
    op.fFlags=FOF_ALLOWUNDO;
//Flag to send to Recycle Bin (must have FO_DELETE flag set)

    int copy_done = SHFileOperation(&op);

    if (copy_done == 0)
    {
      if (op.fAnyOperationsAborted)
        {
         ShowMessage("You have halted the directory removal. Some files may be
                      contained in the Recycle Bin. Simply go there if you need
                      to restore those files.");
        }
      else
        {
         ShowMessage("Remove directory successful!");
        }
    }
    else
    {
        ShowMessage("Directory removal process unsuccessful.");
    } //Whew! A lot of work!

//Since we deleted the directory in the DirectoryListBox, we must go
//back one because we'll get an error if one did not exist!
 DirectoryListBox2->Items->Strings[DirectoryListBox2->ItemIndex-1];
//Go back one since the old is gone
//Update DirectoryListbox
 DirectoryListBox2->Update();
```

When this code runs, it will go through the parent directory selected by the user and delete all files and children files within that directory. All the files are transferred to the Recycle Bin. To tell SHFileOperation() that you want the files to go there, it's important to use the FOF_ALLOWUNDO flag for the fFlags attribute in combination with FO_DELETE flag for the wFunc attribute.

The two examples provided thus far have demonstrated how powerful the SH*x* functions can be. There are other SH*x* functions that are useful as well.

Recycle Bin Operations

The Shell provides the capability to perform queries and actions on the Recycle Bin, such as determining how many files are in it, the size in bytes, and even emptying the bin without user interaction. SHEmptyRecycleBin() and SHQueryRecycleBin() are new functions supported by the Shell DLL (Windows 98/2000). These are powerful functions used for Recycle Bin manipulation. For example, the following code snippet will query the number of items in the Recycle Bin and empty it. The user does not have to go into the Recycle Bin at all. This functionality could be used in a system utility clean-up program and for other purposes.

```
//Declare structure variable
SHQUERYRBINFO RCinfo;
 RCinfo.cbSize = sizeof(shqbi);
 //Total size of objects in Recycle Bin expressed in bytes
//We'll set it to Zero for now…
 RCinfo.i64Size = 0;
//Total count of items in the Recycle Bin
 RCinfo.i64NumItems  = 0;


// Ask the Recycle Bin how many items and put the value into the structure.
  if(S_OK !=SHQueryRecycleBin("C:\\", &shqbi) )
   {
    Label1->Caption = "Error!";
     return;
   }

   int one = RCinfo.i64NumItems;
   int two = RCinfo.i64Size;

//Now, delete all entries in Recycle Bin. Confirm user too!
 SHEmptyRecycleBin(0,0,SHERB_NOPROGRESSUI);
   Label1->Caption = one;
   Label2->Caption = two;
```

This function is also supported on Windows 95, but you must have Shell32.dll version 4.00.

The SHQUERYRBINFO structure is quite small. The format is as follows:

```
typedef struct _SHQUERYRBINFO {
    DWORD cbSize;
    __int64 i64Size;
    __int64 i64NumItems;
} SHQUERYRBINFO, *LPSHQUERYRBINFO;
```

cbSize is the total size of the structure.

i64Size is the total size of all the objects in the specified Recycle Bin, in bytes.

i64NumItems is the total number of items in Recycle Bin.

The two new APIs, SHEmptyRecycleBin() and SHQueryRecycleBin(), have small parameters also. The parameters are described in the following sections.

SHQueryRecycleBin()

SHQueryRecycleBin() function queries the Recycle Bin. It can return the items inside it and their number and size.

```
HRESULT SHQueryRecycleBin (
    LPCTSTR pszRootPAth,
    LPSHQUERYRBINFO pSHQueryRBInfo
);
```

The function only returns one successful value, S_OK, if successful; otherwise, it may return an OLE type error if it fails.

The first parameter, pszRootPath, identifies a pointer to a null-terminated string that contains the path of the Recycle Bin. pszRootPath must contain the drive and the path mark. You can also specify folders (or directories) as well, for example, (c:\\Leroy Burfict PC\\MyFiles\\Work). If you specify NULL or a 0, it will get information on all drives and all Recycle Bins.

The second parameter, pSHQueryRBInfo, identifies an address of the SHQUERYRBINFO structure that receives Recycle Bin information. The cbSize must be set prior to calling this function.

SHEmptyRecycleBin()

SHEmptyRecycleBin() is used to empty the Recycle Bin.

```
HRESULT SHEmptyRecycleBin (
    HWND hwnd,
    LPCTSTR pszRootPAth,
    DWORD dwFlags
);
```

The function only returns one successful value, S_OK, if successful or it may return an OLE type error if it fails. The return value is the same value as SHQueryRecycleBin().

The first parameter, hwnd, identifies a handle to the parent window of the dialog box or window that might be displayed during the operation to be provided. If a dialog or window won't be displayed, this parameter can be NULL.

The second parameter, pszRootPath, is the same as described previously for the SHQueryRecycleBin() function. It identifies a pointer to a null terminated string that contains the path of the Recycle Bin. It must contain the drive specifier and the path separator. You can also specify folders (or directories) as well. For example (c:\\Will Carter PC\\Pics\\Pub). If you specify NULL or a 0, then it will get information on all drives and all Recycle Bins.

The third parameter, dwFlags, is used to identify one or more of the values shown in Table 24.19.

TABLE 24.19   SHEmptyRecycleBin Flags

Flag	Value
SHERB_NOCONFIRMATION	No dialog confirming the deletion of the objects will be displayed.
SHERB_NOPROGRESSUI	No dialog indicating the progress will be displayed.
SHERB_NOSOUND	No sound will be played when the operation is complete.

Folder Browsing

Another Shell function that has captured programmers' attention is the SHBrowseForFolder() function. This function can browse through folders and lets the user choose which folder to pick for locations. You've probably seen this function at work when you've installed drivers and Windows queries for a folder location.

Providing the capability for a user to select a folder location can be extremely useful. To understand how to use the SHBrowseForFolder() function, let us create an example that will allow a user to select an existing folder. The folder location will then placed into a label field that can be used to deposit files and subfolders.

Browsing for a Folder

Start C++Builder and drop a button and a label on the form. It makes no difference where the button or label is placed.

Insert the following header file declaration and string variable declaration at the top of the Unit1.cpp code:

```
#define NO_WIN32_LEAN_AND_MEAN
#include <shlobj.h>
String Directory;
```

Using Borland's Object Inspector, create an OnClick event for the button that was placed on the form. Insert the following code within this event method. Compile and run the application.

```
BROWSEINFO BrowsingInfo;
char FolderName[MAX_PATH];
LPITEMIDLIST ItemID;

memset(&BrowsingInfo, 0, sizeof(BROWSEINFO));
BrowsingInfo.hwndOwner      = Handle;
BrowsingInfo.pszDisplayName = FolderName;
BrowsingInfo.lpszTitle      = "Choose your folder:";
ItemID = SHBrowseForFolder(&BrowsingInfo);
```

```
    if(ItemID) {
        char DirPath[MAX_PATH]="";
        SHGetPathFromIDList(ItemID, DirPath);
        /* path is now in DirPath */
    Directory = DirPath;
    }

    Label1->Caption = Directory;
```

When you run the example, you should be able to pick a folder (or directory). The label will then contain the location you picked.

SHBrowseForFolder() only has one parameter:

```
WINSHELLAPI LPITEMIDLIST WINAPI SHBrowseForFolder(
    LPBROWSEINFO lpbi
    );
```

The parameter represents a structure defined by LPBROWSEINFO. The function will return a pointer to an item identifier in the list. If the user picks Cancel in the dialog, it returns NULL.

lpbi is a pointer to the structure LPBROWSEINFO.

The structure has items that need to be filled out:

```
typedef struct _browseinfo {
    HWND hwndOwner;
    LPCITEMIDLIST pidlRoot;
    LPSTR pszDisplayName;
    LPCSTR lpszTitle;          ow
    UINT ulFlags;
    BFFCALLBACK lpfn;
    LPARAM lParam;             ow
    int iImage;
} BROWSEINFO, *PBROWSEINFO, *LPBROWSEINFO;
```

hwndOwner identifies the handle of the owner window for the dialog box.

pidlRoot represents a pointer to an item identifier list (an ITEMIDLIST structure) specifying the location of the root folder from which to browse. Only the specified folder and its subfolders appear in the dialog box. This member can be NULL; in that case, the namespace root (the desktop folder) is used.

The ITEMIDLIST structure is defined as follows:

```
typedef struct _ITEMIDLIST { // idl
    SHITEMID mkid;  // list of item identifers
} ITEMIDLIST, * LPITEMIDLIST;
typedef const ITEMIDLIST * LPCITEMIDLIST;
```

pszDisplayName represents a pointer to a buffer that receives the display name of the folder selected by the user. The size of this buffer is assumed to be MAX_PATH bytes.

lpszTitle represents a pointer to a null-terminated string that is displayed above the tree view control in the dialog box. This string can be used to specify instructions to the user.

ulFlags identifies a value specifying the types of folders to be listed in the dialog box and other options. This member can include zero or more of the values shown in Table 24.20.

TABLE 24.20   Types of Folders to Be Listed

Flag	Value
BIF_BROWSEFORCOMPUTER	Only returns computers. If the user selects anything other than a computer, the OK button is grayed.
BIF_BROWSEFORPRINTER	Only returns printers. If the user selects anything other than a printer, the OK button is grayed.
BIF_DONTGOBELOWDOMAIN	Does not include network folders below the domain level in the tree view control.
BIF_RETURNFSANCESTORS	Only returns file system ancestors. If the user selects anything other than a file system ancestor, the OK button is grayed.
BIF_RETURNONLYFSDIRS	Only returns file system directories. If the user selects folders that are not part of the file system, the OK button is grayed.
BIF_STATUSTEXT	Includes a status area in the dialog box. The callback function can set the status text by sending messages to the dialog box.

lpfn identifies an address to an application-defined function that the dialog box calls when events occur. This member can be NULL. For more information, see the description of the BrowseCallbackProc() function within the Win32 API Help documentation.

lParam represents an application-defined value that the dialog box passes to the callback function (if one is specified).

iImage identifies a variable that receives the image associated with the selected folder. The image is specified as an index to the system image list.

As you can see, the standard Shell and SHx functions we've described are quite powerful and flexible. It could take a whole book to cover Shell programming. It's recommended that you refer to C++Builder's Win32 API Reference Guide for more information and experiment with some of the undocumented Shell features contained in the SHELL32.DLL, but, of course, use extreme caution. The magic of the Shell is not to be treated lightly.

24

USING THE WIN32 API

Implementing Multimedia Services

As described earlier, Win32 provides quite a number of multimedia services. Playback of media data and accurate timers are two useful capabilities.

Multimedia File Playback

Borland provides a VCL component known as TMediaPlayer that can be used to manipulate and play multimedia clips. TMediaPlayer provides a wrapper to the MCIWnd routines supported by the VFW32.DLL. Although TMediaPlayer is extremely useful, leveraging the MCIWnd routines directly can provide a bit more flexibility and is really not that difficult to use. For example, MCIWndCreate() provides a fairly simple routine that can be used to play CD music, waveform-audio (wave) files, MIDI files, or video clips (see Figure 24.3). The complete source code example described in this section is provided in the MMedia folder on the CD-ROM that accompanies this book.

The following code snippet shows how the multimedia features provided by the Win32 API can be used to play back a video clip:

```
void __fastcall TForm1::SpeedButtonPlayMMFileUsingWin32Click(TObject *Sender)
{
  OpenDialog1->DefaultExt = "AVI";
  OpenDialog1->FileName = "*.avi";
  if (OpenDialog1->Execute())
    MCIWndCreate(Handle,                          // application window handle
        NULL,                                     // instance handle
        WS_VISIBLE | WS_CHILD | MCIWNDF_SHOWALL,  // window styles
        OpenDialog1->FileName.c_str());           // filename
}
```

MCIWndCreate() actually creates a VCR-like window (using the MCIWND_WINDOW_CLASS) containing a play/stop control button, a trackbar, and a panel for displaying the video if it is a video clip.

A less expensive way to play wave files, though, is to use the PlaySound() function as follows:

```
void __fastcall TForm1::SpeedButtonPlayWaveUsingWin32Click(TObject *Sender)
{
  OpenDialog1->DefaultExt = "WAV";
  OpenDialog1->FileName = "*.wav";
  if (OpenDialog1->Execute())
    PlaySound(OpenDialog->FileName.c_str(), NULL, SND_ASYNC);
}
```

FIGURE 24.3

The multimedia player program.

PlaySound() is an extremely useful routine provided by the MMSYSTEM.DLL. Often, sound files need to be played in the background of an application, to produce a sound effect, for example. PlaySound does not provide the VCR-like controls or a trackbar as MCIWndCreate() does. Furthermore, sounds are played instantaneously when the PlaySound() function is called. The DirectSound features supported by DirectX provide additional capabilities for sound manipulation and management allowing multiple sounds to be played simultaneously. Discussion of DirectSound, however, is not within the scope of this chapter.

Swiss Watch Accuracy with the Multimedia Timer

Borland provides a very simple and easy-to-use VCL timer component known as TTimer. TTimer encapsulates the Win32 API Timer functions. It uses the SetTimer() function to enable timer events, provides an event handler OnTimer to respond to WM_TIMER message notifications, and uses the KillTimer() function to disable timer events. When the SetTimer() routine is called, an application requests the Windows System to notify the process (the application) of continual updates until the timer is disabled via the KillTimer() routine. The frequency of these updates is based on the interval provided within the SetTimer() interval timeout parameter (also known as the Interval property value within TTimer). Although the interval frequency can be identified in milliseconds, timers are not always that accurate. WM_TIMER message notifications may occur more frequently than expected or, if other processes are tying up the system, less frequently than expected. It's never a sure bet. However, there is one way to receive more accurate updates by using the multimedia timers. The multimedia timer is an extension of the original Win32 API and provides better resolution than the standard Windows timer.

Examination of the MMSYSTEM.H file provided by Microsoft and Borland reveals the functions that are available.

Computer Name

The following custom wrapper is used to retrieve the computer label name identified within the Registry. GetComputerName() is the Win32 API function used to obtain the information. The name buffer and pointer to the size of the name buffer are passed as parameters. This custom function can be found in the win32_util.cpp source file, located in the Win32Code folder on the accompanying CD-ROM.

```
AnsiString ComputerName()
{
    AnsiString Name;
    DWORD size = MAX_COMPUTERNAME_LENGTH + 1;
    char name[MAX_COMPUTERNAME_LENGTH + 1];
    name[0] = '\0';  // initialize

    GetComputerName(name, &size);

    Name = AnsiString (name);
    return Name;
}
```

Available Memory

The following custom wrapper is used to determine the available free memory. GlobalMemoryStatus() is the Win32 API function used to obtain the information. After the memory information is received, the wrapper function calculates the kilobyte size and returns this information as an AnsiString value. This custom function can be found in the win32_util.cpp source file, located in the Win32Code folder on the accompanying CD-ROM.

```
AnsiString MemFree()
{
  AnsiString FreeMem;
  MEMORYSTATUS memory ;

  memory.dwLength = sizeof (memory) ;
  GlobalMemoryStatus (&memory) ;

  unsigned int value2 = 0;
  unsigned int value1 = memory.dwAvailPhys / 1024;

  if (value1 >= 1000)
  {
     value2 = value1 / 1000;
     value1 = (value1 - (value2 * 1000.0));
     FreeMem = AnsiString(value2) + "," + AnsiString(value1) + " KB";
  }
  else
```

```
        FreeMem = AnsiString(value1)  + " KB";
    return FreeMem;
}
```

Temporary File Location

Sometimes it is useful to store data in a temporary file location, such as the Windows `Temp` directory. The location of the `Temp` directory, however, may vary on different computers. Fortunately, `GetTempPath()` is a Win32 API function that obtains the path for the `Temp` folder. The following custom wrapper function provides an example of how to use `GetTempPath()`:

```
void _fastcall TempFileLocation(AnsiString& filelocation, AnsiString extension)
{
    AnsiString TempDir;
    UINT BufferSize = GetTempPath(0,NULL);
    TempDir.SetLength(BufferSize+1);
    GetTempPath(BufferSize+1,TempDir.c_str());
    unsigned int id = GetNewID();
    AnsiString temp = UINT_To_Ansi(id);
    AnsiString TempFile = AnsiString("temp") + UINT_To_Ansi(id) + "."
➡ + extension;
    char * tempfile = new char[TempDir.Length() + TempFile.Length()];
    sprintf(tempfile,"%s%s",TempDir.c_str(),TempFile.c_str());
    filelocation = AnsiString(tempfile);
    delete[] tempfile;
}
```

This technique is used to generate those directory names you often see in the `Temp` directory from time to time (especially after an aborted install). The example actually uses a wrapper function defined earlier called `GetNewId()` (see the section "Using Globally Unique Identifiers (GUIDs)"). `GetNewID()` is used to retrieve a unique 32-bit value that's used as part of the filename generated for the `tempfile`. These custom functions can be found in the `win32_util.cpp` source file, located in the `Win32Code` folder on the accompanying CD-ROM.

File Size

Have you ever wanted to get the size of a file quickly and efficiently? Well, with a little help of the `CreateFile()`, you can. Let's start with an example, and the explanation will follow.

Start a new project application with the latest and greatest C++Builder. The File Size code is provided in the project `FSize.bpr` in the `FSize` folder on the CD-ROM that accompanies this book.

Using the following chart, insert the components onto `Form1`. Edit the properties as listed in Table 24.21. The `FileListBox` and the `DirectoryListBox` are located on the Win3.1 tab on the Component Palette.

24

TABLE 24.21   Components to Insert

Component	Property
Form1	Height = 355
	Width = 480
DirectoryListBox1	Height = 150
	Left = 8
	Width = 190
	Top = 8
	FileList = FileListBox1
FileListBox1	Height = 150
	Left = 200
	Width = 190
	Top = 8
	Mask = *.*
Label	Name = Label1
	Caption = File Size
	Left = 8
	Top = 175
Label	Name = Label2
	Caption = 0000
	Left = 55
	Top = 175

Add the code in Listing 24.8. Note the include for itoa().

LISTING 24.8   Determining the File Size of a File

```
//------------------------------------------------------------------------
#include <vcl.h>
#include <stdlib.h>   //For itoa -DON'T forget this!
#pragma hdrstop

#include "Unit1.h"
//------------------------------------------------------------------------
#pragma package(smart_init)
#pragma resource "*.dfm"
TForm1 *Form1;
//------------------------------------------------------------------------
__fastcall TForm1::TForm1(TComponent* Owner)
        : TForm(Owner)
{
```

LISTING 24.8   Continued

```c
}
//------------------------------------------------------------------------
char* CommaAdd(int nValue);
//------------------------------------------------------------------------
char* CommaAdd(int nValue)
 {
  size_t i, j=0;
  char buff1[20];
  static char buff2[25];
//convert the value to ASCII
   itoa(nValue , buff1, 10);

   int MEG;    //MEG -if size is < 999,999 then it's a MB, else k size....
    if(nValue > 999999)
    MEG = 1;
     else
      MEG = 0;

   //insert 'da commas
   for(i=0; i <strlen(buff1); i++)
    {
     if(i && ((strlen(buff1) -i) %3) == 0)
       { buff2[i+j] = ','; j++;   }
       buff2[i+j] = buff1[i];
    }
    buff2[i+j] = buff1[i];
    if(MEG == 1)
     strcat(buff2 , " M");
     else
      strcat(buff2 , " K");
    return buff2;
 }
//------------------------------------------------------------------------
```

In the FileListBox's OnClick event, insert this code in:

```c
//------------------------------------------------------------------------
void __fastcall TForm1::FileListBox1Click(TObject *Sender)
{
  HANDLE file;
    int size;
        AnsiString str;
 file = CreateFile(FileListBox1->FileName.c_str(),
                   GENERIC_READ,FILE_SHARE_READ,
                   NULL, OPEN_EXISTING, NULL, NULL);
```

24

LISTING 24.8 Continued

```
if(file == INVALID_HANDLE_VALUE)
  ShowMessage("Invalid handle!");
   else
      {
        size = GetFileSize(file, NULL);   str.SetLength(size);
        str = size;
              char *GetFileSizeInfo;
              GetFileSizeInfo = CommaAdd(size);
              lb_Size->Caption = GetFileSizeInfo;
      }
}
```

The custom function CommaAdd() takes an integer as a value and converts it to a character string buffer. Within that buffer, it inserts commas in the proper location based on size quantities, determines if the size is a MB or a KB size value, and then returns the buffer.

The OnClick event, on the other hand, makes use of another Win32 API commonly used, called CreateFile(). This function does more than just create files; it can work with practically any input/output stream. For example, the GENERIC_READ flag passed as a parameter into CreateFile() function allows a file opened up for read access.

In this example, we simply want to access the file that is identified within the FileListBox. The CreateFile() function passes FileListBox1->FileName.c_str() as the first parameter. This is the filename inside the list box. Notice the .c_str() at the end of the line. This converts an AnsiString to a regular char *. The second parameter that CreateFile() contains is GENERIC_READ, indicating the type of access it should use. GENERIC_READ access flag is simply Read Only mode.

Because the return handle does not rely on inherited child processes or security on a directory, we set the fourth parameter to NULL. The OPEN_EXISTING flag in the fifth parameter indicates that if the file does not exist, the function will fail. Finally there are NULLs in the sixth and seventh parameter. The sixth parameter specified file attributes. Because we are not working with them, this value is set to NULL. The seventh parameter is set to NULL because we are not creating any template files. In Windows 9x, this should always be set to NULL.

If all goes well, CreateFile() successfully returns a handle to the file. If CreateFile() was not successful, it returns an INVALID_HANDLE_VALUE. We created a message to show that the file could possibly be in use. However, we could have gotten more information with the GetError() Win32 API function. CreateFile() is discussed in detail in the section "Fundamental File I/O," earlier in this chapter.

The `ShowMessage()` function is presented in this example. This is a nice C++Builder function used to quickly create a message box for the user.

After success, `GetFileSize()` is called and returns file size as an integer. `GetFileSize()` is declared as follows:

```
DWORD GetFileSize(
  HANDLE hFile,           // handle to file
  LPDWORD lpFileSizeHigh  // high-order word of file size
);
```

`GetFileSize()` takes in a handle to a file; in this case, it is the handle returned from `CreateFile()`.

The second parameter is not important in the example because we want the true size or the low size of the file. If you wanted a high size of the file, you could insert a parameter that points a long pointer to a `DWORD` (doubleword) to obtain one. For an example of the low and high size of a file, simply right-click a filename in Explorer and choose Properties. This will show you two sizes, the low and the high size of the file.

Next, the `char * GetSizeInfo` variable is declared and the custom `CommaAdd()` function described earlier is used to fill the `GetSizeInfo` value. An example of the functionality provided by `GetSizeInfo` is shown in Figure 24.5.

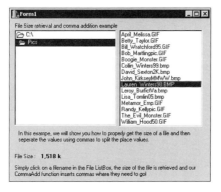

FIGURE 24.5
Showing the file size and displaying commas in the appropriate places.

Free Disk Space and Serial Number

Now that we know how to determine the size of a file, let's look into determining the free disk space available on a drive. It's often useful to get the drive space and serial number of a drive. `GetDiskFreeSpace()`, used earlier, does not determine the serial number, but the `GetVolumeInformation()` API function does. In fact, this function can retrieve all types of information about a drive—volume names, file system types, and more. In the following example, we are only interested in getting a volume name and serial number. We want to use both these functions in conjunction with each other because they work quite well. It would be particularly useful if these two API functions were combined. Fortunately, C++Builder makes it easy to integrate the two.

The GetDiskFreeSpace() function has the following parameters:

```
BOOL GetDiskFreeSpace(

    LPCTSTR lpRootPathName,      // address of root path
    LPDWORD lpSectorsPerCluster,    // address of sectors per cluster
    LPDWORD lpBytesPerSector,     // address of bytes per sector
    LPDWORD lpNumberOfFreeClusters,    // address of number of free clusters
    LPDWORD lpTotalNumberOfClusters     // address of total number of clusters
    );
```

The lpRootPathName points to a string of the drive and path. The rest of the parameters of the drive are passed to gain information.

- pSectorsPerCluster points to a variable for the number of sectors per cluster.

- lpBytesPerSector points to a variable for the number of bytes per sector.

- lpNumberOfFreeClusters points to a variable for the total number of free clusters on the disk.

- lpTotalNumberOfClusters points to a variable for the total number of clusters on the disk.

In the following example we are also going to use the CommaAdd() function built in the example above. Again, it is used to format a number with appropriate commas in the right positions. Our goal is to create a custom function called GetDriveInfo().

Start C++Builder. Place six caption labels and a button on a blank form. Neither the button nor the labels have to be named. Next, create a custom declaration in the source header file under the public section of the class as seen in Listing 24.9.

LISTING 24.9   GetDriveInfo() Example—Header File

```
//--------------------------------------------------------------------------
#ifndef Unit1H
#define Unit1H
//--------------------------------------------------------------------------
#include <Classes.hpp>
#include <Controls.hpp>
#include <StdCtrls.hpp>
#include <Forms.hpp>
```

LISTING 24.9 Continued

```
//-------------------------------------------------------------
class TForm1 : public TForm
{
__published: // IDE-managed Components
        TButton *Button1;
        TLabel *Label1;
        TLabel *Label2;
        TLabel *Label3;
        TLabel *Label4;
        TLabel *Label5;
        TLabel *Label6;
        void __fastcall Button1Click(TObject *Sender);
private: // User declarations
public:      // User declarations
        __fastcall TForm1(TComponent* Owner);
        void __fastcall TForm1::GetDriveInfo (String &drive);

};
//-------------------------------------------------------------
extern PACKAGE TForm1 *Form1;
//-------------------------------------------------------------
#endif
```

The custom function GetDriveInfo() is now declared in the header file. Insert the following code block within the source (.cpp) file to properly define the function.

```
void __fastcall TForm1::GetDriveInfo (String &drive)
{
  //Caption = String ("Details of drives on this system- ") + drive ;

  String YourDrive = drive;
  String volumeinfo;
  volumeinfo.SetLength (255);
//Set a length so we put  a length spec in GetVolumeInformation()
  DWORD serialnumber ;

  if (GetVolumeInformation (YourDrive.c_str (), volumeinfo.c_str(),
                            volumeinfo.Length(), &serialnumber,
                            NULL, NULL, NULL,NULL))
  {
    Label1->Caption = volumeinfo ;

    //Translate integer to chars for serial number
    char STRING[35];
    ltoa (serialnumber , STRING, 16);
```

24

```
    Label2->Caption = STRING;

    DWORD spc;      //Sectors per cluster
    DWORD bps;      //Bytes per cluster
    DWORD cluster;    //clusters
    DWORD freeclust;    //freeclusters

    GetDiskFreeSpace (YourDrive.c_str (),&spc,&bps,&freeclust,&cluster) ;
    Label3->Caption = CommaAdd(spc);
    Label4->Caption = CommaAdd(bps);
    Label5->Caption = CommaAdd(cluster);

    int free_bytes = freeclust * spc * bps;
    Label6->Caption = CommaAdd (free_bytes);
  }
  else
  {
    ShowMessage ("Problem reading drive information.");
  }
}
```

This custom function merges the GetDiskFreeSpace() and GetVolumeInformation() Win32
API calls. These two functions are the key points of the code. Notice that the information in
the variable integer serialnumber is converted to a string for proper reading. The reason for
this is because the function returns a DWORD, and it's best if it's converted to an ASCII string.
We created this wrapper function in case you need it in other applications. It uses the
CommaAdd() function and the Win32 API and dumps the information into labels we have
placed. This concept can be useful for About boxes or some other type function. Next, use
Borland's Object Inspector to create an OnClick event handler for the button. Insert the following code within this method:

```
void __fastcall TForm1::Button1Click(TObject *Sender)
{
  GetDriveInfo("C:\\");
}
```

The header file for the program should resemble Listing 24.9.

The .cpp file for the program should be changed to resemble Listing 24.10.

LISTING 24.10   GetDriveInfo() Example—.ccp File

```
//-------------------------------------------------------------------
#include <vcl.h>
#include <stdlib.h>       //NOTE! Do not forget this header, it's for itoa()
#pragma hdrstop
```

LISTING 24.10 Continued

```cpp
#include "Unit1.h"
//---------------------------------------------------------------------------
#pragma package(smart_init)
#pragma resource "*.dfm"
TForm1 *Form1;
char* CommaAdd(int nValue);
//---------------------------------------------------------------------------
__fastcall TForm1::TForm1(TComponent* Owner)
        : TForm(Owner)
{
}
//---------------------------------------------------------------------------
char* CommaAdd(int nValue)
 {
    size_t i, j=0;
  char buff1[20];
  static char buff2[25];
    //convert the value to ASCII
   itoa(nValue , buff1, 10);

   //insert 'da commas
   for(i=0; i <strlen(buff1); i++)
    {
     if(i && ((strlen(buff1) -i) %3) == 0)
       { buff2[i+j] = ',';  j++;   }
       buff2[i+j] = buff1[i];
    }
    buff2[i+j] = buff1[i];
    return buff2;

 }
//---------------------------------------------------------------------------
void __fastcall TForm1::GetDriveInfo (String &drive)
{
  //Caption = String ("Details of drives on this system- ") + drive ;

  String YourDrive = drive;
  String volumeinfo;
  volumeinfo.SetLength (255);
//Set a length so we put  a length spec in GetVolumeInformation()
  DWORD serialnumber ;

  if (GetVolumeInformation (YourDrive.c_str (), volumeinfo.c_str(),
                            volumeinfo.Length(), &serialnumber,
```

LISTING 24.10   Continued

```
                              NULL, NULL, NULL,NULL))
  {
    Label1->Caption = volumeinfo ;

    //Translate integer to chars for serial number
    char STRING[35];
    ltoa (serialnumber , STRING, 16);
    Label2->Caption = STRING;

    DWORD spc;      //Sectors per cluster
    DWORD bps;      //Bytes per cluster
    DWORD cluster;    //clusters
    DWORD freeclust;   //freeclusters

    GetDiskFreeSpace (YourDrive.c_str (),&spc,&bps,&freeclust,&cluster) ;
    Label3->Caption = CommaAdd(spc);
    Label4->Caption = CommaAdd(bps);
    Label5->Caption = CommaAdd(cluster);

    int free_bytes = freeclust * spc * bps;
    Label6->Caption = CommaAdd (free_bytes);
  }
  else
  {
    ShowMessage ("Problem reading drive information.");
  }
}

void __fastcall TForm1::Button1Click(TObject *Sender)
{
  GetDriveInfo("C:\\");
}
```

When you compile and run the example application, the information about the drive will appear when the button is pressed. If you want to use drives other than C:, replace C:\\ with another drive.

As you can see, the GetDiskFreeSpace() and GetVolumeInformation() functions are the key points of the code. Notice that we took the information in the variable serialnumber and converted it to a string for proper reading. The reason is because the function returns a DWORD, and it's best if it's converted to an ASCII string.

Flashing a Notification

The question often arises in newsgroups about finding a certain window or setting the text of a window. FlashWindowEx(), FindWindow(), and SetWindowText() are quite popular functions used to support this capability. In this section, we will examine these functions and explain how they can be used to support developer needs.

FlashWindowEx()

FlashWindowEx() is a NEW Win32 API supported by Windows 98 and Windows 2000. It can be used as a replacement for the not-so-old FlashWindow() function. FlashWindow() simply flashes a window to alert the user that something in that particular program either occurred and is in need of the user's attention, or a response to let the user know that that window is ready to receive focus. These great additional functions to the operating system are located in the WINUSER.H header file.

FlashWindow() can simply flash a window by itself, but it cannot continuously flash a window unless you apply a timer. FlashWindowEx(), however, provides a built-in timer capability and is more robust. The FlashWindowEx() timer can be set in milliseconds, the number of times to flash can be set, and flash stop flags can be set.

You may have noticed the use of this new feature when using Windows 98. Well-known programs, such as America Online's Instant Messenger, Yahoo Pager, and ICQ, use this feature.

The declaration for this function is as follows:

```
BOOL FlashWindowEx {
  PFLASHWINFO pfwi  // Pointer to a structure for flash status information
);
```

FlashWindowEx() takes on a pointer to a structure that holds information about the way it is going to perform. The return value is the Window's state before the call to FlashWindowEx(). If the window was active before the call, the function will return a nonzero; otherwise, the return will be zero. FlashWindowEx() requires a pointer to a structure containing the flash information. The structure provides the main ingredients to get FlashWindowEx() to work. The FlashWindow() function is certainly easier to use, but the examples described later will show the simplicity and power the FlashWindowEx() function provides.

The FLASHINFO structure is as follows:

```
typedef struct {
  UINT   cbSize;
  HWND   hwnd;
  DWORD  dwFlags;
  UINT   uCount;
  DWORD  dwTimeout;
} FLASHWINFO, *PFLASHWINFO;
```

When this structure is filled out and passed as a parameter to the `FlashWindowEx()` function, it controls the way the `FlashWindowEx()` function is going to execute. `dwFlags` is the real workhorse in determining how the flashes are going to be carried out. Table 24.22 shows the different flags.

TABLE 24.22   `FlashWindowEx()` Flags

Flag	Meaning
FLASHW_STOP	Stop flashing. The system restores the window to its original state.
FLASHW_CAPTION	Flash the window caption.
FLASHW_TRAY	Flash the taskbar button.
FLASHW_ALL	Flash both the window caption and taskbar button. This is equivalent to setting the `FLASHW_CAPTION` and `FLASHW_TRAY` flags.
FLASHW_TIMER	Flash continuously until the `FLASHW_STOP` flag is set.
FLASHW_TIMERNOFG	Flash continuously until the window comes to the foreground.

The table shows how to use and control `FlashWindowEx()` to flash a specified destination window.

FindWindow()

If you needed to find a certain window, you can do it easily with the Win32 API function `FindWindow()`. This function will find the top-level window based on its title and classname and returns a handle for it. However, `FindWindow()` does not perform any child searches or searches for windows that are below the top-level window. The function `FindWindowEx()` can be used for that.

The `FindWindow()` is in the following format:

```
HWND FindWindow(
  LPCTSTR lpClassName,   // class name
  LPCTSTR lpWindowName   // window name
);
```

The parameters for `FindWindow()`, `lpClassName` and `lpWindowName` are pointers to a null-terminated string. The `lpClassName` parameters can accept the classname of a window, and `lpWindowName` can accept a window's title name.

The return for `FindWindow()` is the handle of the window if it was found.

SetWindowText()

`SetWindowText()` will change the window's title bar if it has one. If the window is a control, such as a button, only the text of the button is changed. However, you cannot change the text in another control in another application.

```
BOOL SetWindowText(
  HWND hWnd,          // handle to window or control
  LPCTSTR lpString    // title or text
);
```

The SetWindowText() is pretty easy to use. The parameter hWnd is a handle to the window in which you want to make a change. The parameter lpString is the pointer to a null-terminated string to change the window's title bar text.

Putting It All Together

In the example illustrated in Listing 24.11, we will write a program containing a button. In this button's click event handler, a message will be sent out to Notepad. If Notepad is launched, it will change the title of Notepad and then will flash.

1. To start, launch C++Builder and the IDE will be ready to go.

2. Drop a button on the form.

3. Double-click the button to create an OnClick event and type in the code in Listing 24.11.

LISTING 24.11   Using FlashWindow() to Send a Notification to the User

```
void __fastcall TForm1::Button1Click(TObject *Sender)
{

 HWND hHandle = FindWindow (NULL,"Untitled - Notepad");

  FLASHWINFO pf;
  pf.cbSize = sizeof(FLASHWINFO);
  pf.hwnd = hHandle;
  pf.dwFlags = FLASHW_TIMER|FLASHW_ALL;
  pf.uCount = 8;
  pf.dwTimeout  = 75;

  FlashWindowEx(&pf);

  if(hHandle)
    SetWindowText(hHandle, "Notepad");
}
```

4. Run the program by pressing F9 on the keyboard or clicking the Run button (depicted by a green arrow that resembles a VCR Play button).

5. When C++Builder launches the program, minimize C++Builder so that the program is out of the way.

6. Launch Notepad.

7. Minimize Notepad.

Click the button in your program and you will see Notepad change from `untitled - Notepad` to Notepad. It will also flash very quickly. Now let's explain this code in greater detail.

```
HWND hHandle = FindWindow (NULL,"Untitled - Notepad");
```

This line retrieves the handle to the main window of Notepad. When you launched Notepad and clicked the button, the program found Notepad by its window title name and returned a handle to a window. The window title name for Notepad is shown, and the handle is assigned to the `hHandle` variable.

For example, if you saved a text file under the name `test1`, Notepad will be called `test1`. The window title/name will take the place of the new name.

Not all windows are like that. For example, if you launched another application, you will see that its name is quite different.

So, how does this help me? Simple! If you were developing an application and you knew the window name of another already, you can implement this. If you did not know the name of a window, simply use the wrapper functions described earlier to get the handle to the window, or enumerate through the windows and put the name in a list.

Let us examine the structure required by the `FlashWindowEx()` function:

```
FLASHWINFO pf;
pf.cbSize = sizeof(FLASHWINFO);
pf.hwnd = hHandle;
pf.dwFlags = FLASHW_TIMER|FLASHW_ALL;
pf.uCount = 8;
pf.dwTimeout  = 75;


 FlashWindowEx(&pf);
```

The `FLASHWINFO` contains all the information the `FlashWindowEx()` function needs to perform its job. A new structure variable called `pf` is declared based on this structure type. It is then initialized and passed as a parameter into `FlashWindowEx()`. Let's examine the types within the structure.

`cbSize` is simply used to identify the size of the `FLASHWINFO` structure.

`hwnd` provides the handle to the destination window. In the previous example, a handle to Notepad was obtained as follows:

```
HWND hHandle = FindWindow (NULL,"Untitled - Notepad");
```

`dwFlags` are the flags for `FlashWindowEx()`. Instead of flashing both the caption and the caption in the task bar, you could use the `FLASHW_TRAY` to flash in the taskbar tray only. In the example, both the tray and caption are flashed. The `FLASHW_TIMER` flag indicates that the `FLASHW_STOP` flag is set.

The uCount parameter is the number of times you want the window to flash. In the example, eight counts were identified. After eight counts, the FlashWindowEx() function knows when to quit and set the FLASHW_STOP flag.

The dwTimeout parameter contains the number of milliseconds the window is to flash. In the example, the flashing is pretty quick, but you are encouraged to change the setting and see the differences for yourself.

As demonstrated, FlashWindowEx() can notify the user that an error occurred or that some type of event has occurred without message boxes. It's a notification procedure to let the user know that the application's window does not have any focus. It is particularly useful when you don't want the operation of a user's program to be interrupted with message boxes. The FlashWindowEx() will notify the user by a flash instead of a message box (see Figure 24.6). The message box, on the other hand, requires that a user perform the extra step of closing it.

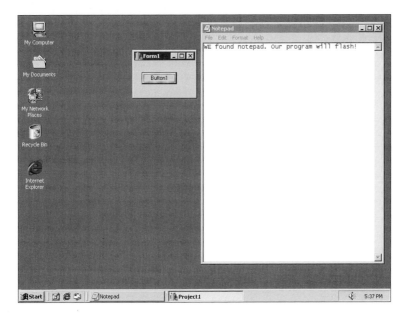

Figure 24.6
Running the example program will cause Notepad to flash after it finds it.

Adding System Support

It's sometimes useful to add system-support capabilities to an application, such as the capability to quickly lock an NT workstation, disable Ctrl+Alt+Delete, or shut down (and reboot) a machine. The Win32 API provides many useful routines to help perform these types of tasks. However, it's important to note the danger of providing these types of capabilities. If you're going to implement these types of functionality (and debugging in the process), be sure to save early and often, or you might just wish you had selected another hobby or profession.

Locking an NT Workstation

It's time to introduce you to another new Win32 API named `LockWorkStation()`, which is used to automatically lock an NT system. `LockWorkStation()` takes no parameters, and it's automatic. Locking workstations or servers couldn't be easier. The function mimics the well-known Ctrl+Alt+Delete keys and selects `Lock Workstation`. The system is then locked until later use. This function is in the `WINUSER.H` header file.

With the following one line of code, you can automate what used to be a manual operation under NT. Unfortunately, this function is not supported by Windows 9x:

```
LockWorkStation();
```

System Shutdown

A lot of beginners often ask how to automate the shutdown of a Windows PC. By using the `ExitWindowsEx()` or `ExitWindows()` function, you can properly shut down the system. The following code demonstrates how to use the `ExitWindowsEx()` API function:

```
ExitWindowsEx(EWX_SHUTDOWN,0);
```

This routine is not new like the `LockWorkStation()` function, but it sure has a lot of power in manipulating your system—by turning it off. If your PC has power conservation methods in the BIOS, `ExitWindowEx()` will automatically shut down your PC's power, too.

`ExitWindowsEx()` is an easy way to shut down Windows, but you can do a lot more than just shut down Windows. The `ExitWindowEx()` function has more flags with which to work. The format is as follows:

```
BOOL ExitWindowsEx(
    UINT uFlags,     // shutdown operation
    DWORD dwReserved    // reserved
    );
```

`uFlags` are flags to specify which shutdown type you wish to perform. Table 24.23 shows the values.

TABLE 24.23 System Shutdown Function Flags

Flags	Value
EWX_FORCE	Forces processes to terminate. When this flag is set, Windows does not send the messages WM_QUERYENDSESSION and WM_ENDSESSION to the applications currently running in the system. This can cause the applications to lose data, so you should use this flag only in an emergency.
EWX_LOGOFF	Shuts down all processes running in the security context of the process that called the ExitWindowsEx() function. Then it logs the user off.
EWX_POWEROFF	Shuts down the system and turns off the power. The system must support the power-off feature. Windows NT: The calling process must have the SE_SHUTDOWN_NAME privilege. Windows 95: Security privileges are not supported or required.
EWX_REBOOT	Shuts down and then restarts the system. Windows NT: The calling process must have the SE_SHUTDOWN_NAME privilege.
EWX_SHUTDOWN	Shuts down the system to a point at which it is safe to turn off the power. All file buffers have been flushed to disk, and all running processes have stopped. Windows NT: The calling process must have the SE_SHUTDOWN_NAME privilege.

The dwReserved parameter is currently not used.

Animating Effects

A new windows common control introduced to Windows 98 and Windows 2000 enables window animation effects that will dazzle your users. The new API, AnimateWindows(), is a common control function that shows animation for your forms. You have probably seen this using Windows 98. It is also anticipated that more and more programs will begin using these types of window effects in the future. This new API has several features, and they are a nice jawdropper when you use them correctly and wisely. If the coding is right, you can have some fancy form effects or component effects too.

AnimateWindow()

AnimateWindow() looks quite easy, but if you don't use it correctly, you won't get good results. It has the following parameters:

```
BOOL AnimateWindow(
  HWND hwnd,      // handle to window
  DWORD dwTime,   // duration of animation
```

```
    DWORD dwFlags  // animation type
);
```

hwnd is a handle to the window in which you want to animate.

dwTime is the time in milliseconds to perform the animation.

dwFlags represent different flags and types of animation you can perform. Listed in Table 24.24 are the flags from which to choose.

TABLE 24.24   AnimateWindow() Flags

Flag	Value
AW_SLIDE	Uses slide animation. By default, roll animation is used. This flag is ignored when used with AW_CENTER.
AW_ACTIVATE	Activates the window. Do not use this value with AW_HIDE.
AW_BLEND	Uses a fade effect. This flag can be used only if hwnd is a top-level window.
AW_HIDE	Hides the window. By default, the window is shown.
AW_CENTER	Makes the window appear to collapse inward if AW_HIDE is used. If AW_HIDE is not used, the window appears to expand outward.
AW_HOR_POSITIVE	Animates the window from left to right. This flag can be used with roll or slide animation. It is ignored when used with AW_CENTER or AW_BLEND.
AW_HOR_NEGATIVE	Animates the window from right to left. This flag can be used with roll or slide animation. It is ignored when used with AW_CENTER or AW_BLEND.
AW_VER_POSITIVE	Animates the window from top to bottom. This flag can be used with roll or slide animation. It is ignored when used with AW_CENTER or AW_BLEND.
AW_VER_NEGATIVE	Animates the window from bottom to top. This flag can be used with roll or slide animation. It is ignored when used with AW_CENTER or AW_BLEND.

The return values are a zero or a value greater than zero. The function will fail if the window uses the window region, when you are trying to show the window when it is already visible, and when you hide the window when it is already hidden.

The window procedures for the window and its child windows may need to handle any WM_PRINT or WM_PRINTCLIENT messages. Dialog boxes, controls, and common controls already handle WM_PRINTCLIENT. The default window procedure already handles WM_PRINT.

Let's try it out.

1. Start C++Builder and create a new application.

2. In the form's `FormShow` and `FormClose` event handlers, add the following code:

```
void __fastcall TForm1::FormShow(TObject *Sender)
{
  AnimateWindow(Form1->Handle, 2000, AW_BLEND | AW_HOR_POSITIVE);
}
//------------------------------------------------------------------

void __fastcall TForm1::FormClose(TObject *Sender, TCloseAction &Action)
{
  AnimateWindow(Form1->Handle, 1000, AW_HIDE | AW_BLEND |
➥AW_VER_POSITIVE);
}
```

3. Compile this code, run it, and enjoy the show.

Notice how the application form appeared slowly (two seconds), and note that the form faded when the program closed.

Instead of popping an application onscreen, you can add dimension to your programs.

NOTE

Using `AnimateWindow()` may not work for all users, because the Animate Windows feature can be disabled within the Windows Control Panel.

Using the `AW_HIDE` in the `FormClose` event tells `AnimateWindow()` to hide the application and internally does this, using the effect.

Want to see something even better? Replace the `FormClose` event with the following code:

```
AnimateWindow(Form1->Handle, 1000, AW_HIDE | AW_SLIDE | AW_HOR_POSITIVE |
➥AW_VER_NEGATIVE);
```

This effect makes the window animate diagonally. You can combine `AW_HOR_POSITIVE` or `AW_HOR_NEGATIVE` with `AW_VER_POSITIVE` or `AW_VER_NEGATIVE` to animate a window in different diagonal positions.

How about this one? Replace the same code in the `FormClose` event with the following:

```
AnimateWindow(Form1->Handle, 1000, AW_HIDE | AW_SLIDE | AW_VER_POSITIVE);
```

This effect makes the window sink to the bottom and then disappear.

24

USING THE
WIN32 API

You're encouraged to try playing with the timing values, too. Instead of 1,000 milliseconds, try 2,500. For an interesting fade, try using AW_BLEND. The form will look like rolling movie credits.

As you can see, Microsoft has spent a lot of time on the GUI interface and has put some interesting features into windows that can really spice up things.

Shaping Your Applications

Systems programming is fun. Manipulating forms and making them do cool and interesting things can create jawdropper reactions. In this section, we will explore the concept of regions and cover a handful of related functions such as CombinRgn(), CreateEllipticRgn(), GetClientRect(). These functions can control how windows look. Instead of the same old rectangle window look, the look of a window can be changed by using regions. C++Builder makes combining the Win32 API functions to create regions on your system very easy. These and other APIs are located in the WINGDI.H header file.

What's a region? A *region* is an area that bounds the window. Anything outside the region is not considered part of the window. The window clips anything else outside the region, giving the window a different look.

CreateRoundRectRgn()

Let's start with the CreateRoundRectRgn() function. This function will create a rectangular window with rounded edges.

The CreateRoundRectRgn() function has the following parameters:

HRGN CreateRoundRectRgn(

```
    int nLeftRect, // x-coordinate of the region's  upper-left corner
    int nTopRect, // y-coordinate of the region's upper-left corner
    int nRightRect, // x-coordinate of the region's lower-right corner
    int nBottomRect, // y-coordinate of the region's lower-right corner
    int nWidthEllipse,    // height of ellipse for rounded corners
    int nHeightEllipse // width of ellipse for rounded corners
    );
```

nLeftRect specifies the x coordinate of the upper-left corner of the region.

nTopRect specifies the y coordinate of the upper-left corner of the region.

nRightRect specifies the x coordinate of the lower-right corner of the region.

nBottomRect specifies the y coordinate of the lower-right corner of the region.

nWidthEllipse specifies the width of the ellipse used to create the rounded corners.

nHeightEllipse specifies the height of the ellipse used to create the rounded corners.

The following example is provided to show you how to create a round-edged window:

```
RECT R  = GetClientRect();
HRGN MyRegion = CreateRoundRectRgn(0,0,150,110,15,10);
SetWindowRgn(Handle , MyRegion , true);
```

This is easy to do. The only thing difficult to do is determining the coordinates. It's often necessary to play with them a bit to make the windows look the way you want, but that is the only drawback.

Let's create a program that will have scrollbars to size up all the locations for us, display the coordinates, and change the look of our window while we are doing it.

Start C++Builder. Place the components in Table 24.25 on the form.

TABLE 24.25   Components to Add to Our Example Form

Component	Property
Form1	Width = 369
	Height = 416
Label1	Left = 16
	Top = 53
Label2	Left = 16
	Top = 120
Label3	Left = 16
	Top = 37
	Caption = x-coordinate of the region's
	lower-right corner
Label4	Left = 16
	Top = 104
	Caption = y-coordinate of the region's
	lower-right corner
Label5	Left = 16
	Top = 176
	Caption = x-coordinate of the region's
	upper-left corner
Label6	Left = 16
	Top = 192
Label7	Left = 16
	Top = 248
	Caption = y-coordinate of the region's
	upper-left corner

TABLE 24.25   Continued

Component	Property
Label8	Left = 16 Top = 264
Label9	Left = 16 Top = 312 Caption = height of ellipse for rounded corners
Label10	Left = 16 Top = 312
Label11	Left = 16 Top = 368 Caption = width of ellipse for rounded corners
Label12	Left = 16 Top = 368
TrackBar	Name = Track1 Left = 8 Top = 144 Width = 297 Height = 27 Frequency = 1
TrackBar	Name = Track2 Left = 8 Top = 216 Width = 305 Height = 27
TrackBar	Name = Track3 Left = 8 Top = 8 Width = 297 Height = 27 Max = 230 Min = 70 Frequency = 5 Position = 190

TABLE 24.25   Continued

Component	Property
TrackBar	Name = Track4
	Left = 8
	Top = 72
	Width = 297
	Height = 27
	Max = 100
	Frequency = 5
TrackBar	Name = Track5
	Left = 8
	Top = 280
	Width = 233
	Height = 27
TrackBar	Name = Track6
	Left = 8
	Top = 336
	Width = 233
	Height = 27

The only code you have to put in is in the form's source and the `TrackBar3`'s `OnChange` event. Set every other `TrackBar` to the `TrackBar3`'s `OnChange` event in the Object Inspector. You can find the `Trackbar` on the Win32 Tab of the Component Palette.

The code is shown in Listing 24.12.

LISTING 24.12   Create an Irregular Form with `CreateRoundRectRgn()`

```
//--------------------------------------------------------------
#include <vcl\vcl.h>
#pragma hdrstop

#include "Unit1.h"
//--------------------------------------------------------------
#pragma resource "*.dfm"
TForm1 *Form1;
//--------------------------------------------------------------
__fastcall TForm1::TForm1(TComponent* Owner)
    : TForm(Owner)
{
```

24

USING THE
WIN32 API

LISTING 24.12   Continued

```
  Form1->Height = 416;
  Form1->Width  = 369;

 Track3->Max = Form1->Width+10;
 Track3->Min = 70;
 Track3->Position = Form1->Width;   //Start off with full size form

 Track4->Max = Form1->Height+10;
 Track4->Min = 195;
 Track4->Position = Form1->Height;   //Start off with full size form

 Track1->Max = 20; //Let's not go farther than the position on the bar
 Track1->Min = 0;
 Track1->Position = 0;

 Track2->Max = 230;
 Track2->Min = 0;
 Track2->Position = 0;

 Track5->Max = 500;
 Track5->Min = 0;
 Track5->Position = 31;

 Track6->Max = 500;
 Track6->Min = 0;
 Track6->Position = 31;
}
//------------------------------------------------------------------------
void __fastcall TForm1::Track3Change(TObject *Sender)
{
 //Create the handle to the region and get handle from the CreateRoundRgn
function if valid
 //THe trackbars are going to be the positions within the function
 HRGN MyRegion = CreateRoundRectRgn(Track1->Position,Track2->Position,Track3->
➥Position,Track4->Position,Track5->Position,Track6->Position);

 //Set the Window's region by this function
 //Parameters: SetWindowRgn(Handle to a window, Handle to the region HRGN,
redraw after setting region)
 SetWindowRgn(Handle , MyRegion , true);

 //Labels will keep track of all positions
 Label1->Caption = Track3->Position;
 Label2->Caption = Track4->Position;
```

LISTING 24.12   Continued

```
Label6->Caption = Track1->Position;
Label8->Caption = Track2->Position;
Label10->Caption = Track5->Position;
Label12->Caption = Track6->Position;
Form1->Update ();
}
```

Remember to set all of the other TrackBar's events to match TrackBar3's OnChange event. Compile and run the program.

In this example, TrackBars are being used to change the position of the window. The window's region is modified using CreateRoundRectRgn(). The labels embedded in the form capture and display the window's region positions. When you use this Win32 API, you can rely on this example to place your coordinates instead of second guessing them or using graph paper to plot out the regions.

CreateEllipticRgn()

What if we wanted an even different look? There's another function called CreateEllipticRgn() that gives your window an oval-shaped appearance. It will actually make a window round or oval, depending on the parameters to the function. CreateEllipticRgn() has the following parameters:

```
HRGN CreateEllipticRgn(

    int nLeftRect,
// x-coordinate of the upper-left corner of the bounding rectangle
    int nTopRect,
// y-coordinate of the upper-left corner of the bounding rectangle
    int nRightRect,
// x-coordinate of the lower-right corner of the bounding rectangle
    int nBottomRect
// y-coordinate of the lower-right corner of the bounding rectangle
    );
```

nLeftRect specifies the x coordinate of the upper-left corner of the bounding rectangle of the ellipse.

nTopRect specifies the y coordinate of the upper-left corner of the bounding rectangle of the ellipse.

nRightRect specifies the x coordinate of the lower-right corner of the bounding rectangle of the ellipse.

24

USING THE
WIN32 API

nBottomRect specifies the y coordinate of the lower-right corner of the bounding rectangle of the ellipse.

The parameters are somewhat similar to the CreateRoundRectRgn() function, except that you only specify the whole width of the circle. The following example uses the CreateEllipticRgn() function:

```
HRGN HRegion
HRegion = CreateEllipticRgn(0,0,Form1->Width, Form1->Height);
SetWindowRgn(Handle , hRgn1 , true);
```

This example code changes your form to a semi-round circle (an oval). We started at Left(0) Top(0) and worked our way to the form's width and height, yielding a result that looks like an oval.

CombineRgn()

CombineRgn() function is a powerful function. CombinRgn() can actually take the regions that you specify and merge them together. A lot of programs these days that have the irregular window shapes usually use the CombineRgn() function. Along with the CreateEllipticRgn(), CreateRoundRect(), and CreatePolygonRgn() functions, you can specify regions to make your windows look even glamorous.

CombineRgn() has the following parameters:

```
int CombineRgn(
    HRGN hrgnDest,      // handle to destination region
    HRGN hrgn1,      // handle to source region
    HRGN hrgn2,      // handle to source region
    int fnCombineMode      // region combining mode
    );
```

hrgnDest identifies a new region with dimensions defined by combining two other regions. (This region must exist before CombineRgn()is called.)

hrgn1 identifies the first of two regions to be combined.

hHrgn2 identifies the second of two regions to be combined.

fnCombineMode specifies a mode indicating how the two regions will be combined. This parameter can be one of the values in Table 24.26.

TABLE 24.26   CombineRgn() Flags

Flags	Values
RGN_AND	Creates the intersection of the two combined regions
RGN_COPY	Creates a copy of the region identified by hrgnSrc1

TABLE 24.26   Continued

Flags	Values
RGN_DIFF	Combines the parts of hrgnSrc1 that are not part of hrgnSrc2
RGN_OR	Creates the union of two combined regions
RGN_XOR	Creates the union of two combined regions except for any overlapping areas

The return value specifies the type of the resulting region. It can be one of the values shown in Table 24.27.

TABLE 24.27   CombineRgn() Return Values

Return Value	Description
NULLREGION	The region is empty.
SIMPLEREGION	The region is a single rectangle.
COMPLEXREGION	The region is more than a single rectangle.
ERROR	No region is created.

Interesting enough, the regions do not need to be distinct. For example, if you pass three regions (Region1, Region1, and Region2) as the parameters, you can see that Region1, the original region already passed, will be destined to hold the final region. This is completely okay. However, if you do pass another region separate from the other declared regions, you must pass an already declared region before calling this API.

The following is an example of using CombineRgn() function. Hopefully, the example will clarify any issues you may have and give you a better understanding of how to use the function.

```
HRGN Region1, Region2;
Region1 = CreateRectRgn(0, 0, 100, 100);
Region2 = CreateRectRgn(50, 50, 150, 150);
CombineRgn(Region1, Region1, Region2, RGN_XOR);
SetWindowRgn(Handle , hRgn1 , true);
```

Using this example, you will see your form turn into two boxes with a box hole in the middle of it. The hole is there because the RGN_XOR flag was used. The two regions overlap, but do not combine with the intersecting regions. If we use the RGN_OR flag, you will see they now intersect and combine.

Also, we used Region1 as the destination and a created region. Why did we do this? Well, remember that we need a destination region, and Region1 will be overwritten by Region1 and Region2 combined. Because we passed the parameter, the function knows the coordinates and sends them to the Region1 destination.

But let's not stop here. Earlier, we mentioned something about the CreatePolygonRgn() function. Let's go over that because it's another region function that's quite interesting.

CreatePolygonRgn() function has the following parameters:

```
HRGN CreatePolygonRgn(

    CONST POINT *lppt,    // pointer to array of points
    int cPoints,     // number of points in array
    int fnPolyFillMode    // polygon-filling mode
    );
```

lppt points to an array of POINT structures that define the vertices of the polygon. The polygon is presumed closed. Each vertex can be specified only once.

CPoints specifies the number of points in the array.

fnPolyFillMode specifies the fill mode used to determine which pixels are in the region. This parameter can be one of the values shown in Table 24.28.

TABLE 24.28   Possible fnPolyFillMode Modes

Parameter	Value
ALTERNATE	Selects alternate mode (fills area between odd-numbered and even-numbered polygon sides on each scan line)
WINDING	Selects winding mode (fills any region with a nonzero winding value)

To pass the proper parameters to the CreatePolygonRgn() function, we can both use the Win32 API and C++Builder's POINT structure. This function relies on point pixel locations to create a region. This is similar to connect the dots, where the function will create the region based on these dots.

The POINT structure is a structure that defines the x and y coordinates of an object. You simply fill it in. To create a multiple-point coordinate, simply declare a POINT structure variable with an array.

Let's create an example. The following code is an example of how to utilize the CreatePolygonRgn() function. Forgive me on the points to create a Stop sign, but for the record and example, it's good enough to see. If you take note, we use another great Win32 API called GetClientRect(). This function gets the client's rectangular coordinates and returns the values to the RECT structure. The RECT structure is the structure that has the upper-left and lower-right coordinates of an object. GetClientRect() is part of the C++Builder VCL; so is RECT.

1. Start C++Builder and create a new application.

2. On the application's main form, Form1, change the color to clRed and place a button on the form.

3. Insert the following code on the OnClick event:

```
void __fastcall TForm1::BitBtn1Click(TObject *Sender)
{
 Close();
}
Then, in the Form's source code insert the following code:
__fastcall TForm1::TForm1(TComponent* Owner)
        : TForm(Owner)
{

 RECT R;
   R = GetClientRect();
   POINT p[8];
   p[0].x =87; p[0].y =0;
   p[1].x =25; p[1].y =59;
   p[2].x =24; p[2].y =123;
   p[3].x =79; p[3].y =176;
   p[4].x =171; p[4].y =173;
  p[5].x =207; p[5].y =123;
   p[6].x =208; p[6].y =59;
   p[7].x =156; p[7].y =0;

   HRGN MyRegion;

   MyRegion =  CreatePolygonRgn(p, 8, ALTERNATE);

   SetWindowRgn(Handle, MyRegion, true);
}
```

In the code in step 3, we declared the RECT structured variable called R. The GetClientRect() function returned the forms client's coordinates, which were assigned to R.

Then we declared POINT p. This is an array of points to create our stop sign (see Figure 24.7).

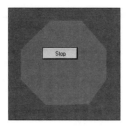

FIGURE 24.7
This is how we declared the points—by tracing or connecting the dots.

After declaring all of our array of points, we create a handle named MyRegion. We call CreatePolygonRgn() function and, if it is successful, it will return a handle to the MyRegion.

Notice the parameters inside the CreatePolygonRgn() function. We passed the POINT structure variable p. It takes the structure address as the first parameter. Then, we must pass how many points inside the structure. If we had passed the number 4, we would get a really funky form. After that, we used ALTERNATE fill mode.

After being successful, we change the way our window looks by calling the SetWindowRgn() function, which changes the window's region.

When you run the example application, you should see a somewhat red stop sign with a button on the form waiting for you to close it out.

We've only covered the basics of regions here to give you a better understanding of how regions work with C++Builder. If you want to learn more about creating windows with regions, visit Microsoft's MSDN Web site at http://www.microsoft.com/msdn. Perform a search for window regions or irregular windows.

Writing Control Panel Applets the Old-Fashioned Way

Control Panel applets are small programs that can configure the environment of Windows, another application, or some type of hardware. Control Panel applets, better known as applets, are actually dynamic link libraries (DLL). However, these specific DLLs are actually renamed to an extension .cpl. This signifies a Control Panel applet and lets the user or developer differentiate between normal DLLs and Control Panel applets.

This section provides a discussion of Control Panel applets. We will explain the ins and outs, write a small utility, and turn it into a Control Panel applet. C++Builder 5 already has a Control Panel Applet Wizard with which you can quickly write an applet, but we want to show you the Win32 way, which is quite easy, and give you a behind-the-scenes look at the Win32 API combined with C++Builder.

Understanding Control Panel Applets

The primary purpose of a Control Panel applet is to allow the user to interact with the configuration of the system or application. The applet responds to a mouse double-click within the Control Panel to activate it. Typically, Control Panel applets are used to configure an environment of a large program or Windows itself. For example, you may have written a large program and, instead of loading that program and making the user wait until it loads just to configure it, you can create a utility to configure it and store the parameters in the Registry. Control Panel applets are distinguished by icons and small captions below them. They also contain additional text in the Control Panel status bar briefly describing their operation.

Control Panel applets are very easy to write, it just looks hard. First let's get a behind-the-scenes look at how they work.

Control Panel applets are a compiled as a special Dynamic Linked Library and export the standard entry-point function, CPLApplet(). This function performs requests in the form of Control Panel messages and executes the requested jobs, such as initialization of the application, obtaining the icons, displaying and managing the internal dialogs boxes, and simply closing the process.

When the Control Panel loads, it always retrieves various information on each applet. Control Panel is the controlling application that manages every aspect of the Control Panel applets. Of course, you could write your own, as long it can send messages and process the return information in the way Control Panel does.

As soon as you select Start, Settings, Control Panel, Control Panel reads all the applets (or .CPLs) inside the \Windows\System or \Winnt\System32 directory. It then queries against the icons, figures out how many dialogs are in an applet, and gathers other important data about each applet. That's why it takes about two to three seconds to load.

When the Control Panel loads, or the controlling program that calls on the Control Panel applets loads, the address of the CPLApplet() function is used to passes the applet messages. The format of CPLApplet() function is as follows:

```
LONG APIENTRY CPlApplet(
    HWND hwndCPl,     // handle to Control Panel window
    UINT uMsg,     // message
    LONG lParam1,     // first message parameter
    LONG lParam2     // second message parameter
);
```

hwndCPl identifies the main window of the controlling application.

uMsg specifies the message being sent to the Control Panel application.

lParam1 specifies additional message-specific information.

lParam2 specifies additional message-specific information.

The return value on the CPLApplet() depends on the message. We will examine those shortly. Also note that the hwndCP1 parameter for dialog boxes or other windows requires a handle to a parent window.

The CPLApplet() function is called many times when Control Panel or the controlling application loads. The return values depend on the parameters passed. The values depend especially on the uMsg parameter. You must write applets in a certain way because the messages sent to the CPLApplet() are in a certain order.

Table 24.29 shows you the order of messages and values.

TABLE 24.29 Message Order

Message	Order	Operation
CPL_INIT (#define constant value = 1)	The first calling. Immediate callout after the .CPL containing the applet is loaded.	Sent to indicate CPLApplet() was found. *lParam1* and *lParam2* are not used. Returns TRUE or FALSE indicating whether the Control Panel should proceed. If it fails, it releases control of the applet and ceases all communication of the .CPL.
CPL_GETCOUNT (#define constant value = 2)	Called after the CPL_INIT. It returns a non-zero value.	Sent to determine the number of applets to be displayed. It returns a non-zero value. Return the number of applets you want to display in the Control Panel window. *lParam1* and *lParam2* are not used yet.

TABLE 24.29 Continued

Message	Order	Operation
CPL_INQUIRE (#define constant value = 3)	Called after the CPL_GETCOUNT. Return value is greater than or equal to 1. The CPLApplet() function will be called once for each dialog box, specifying which dialog box is using a zero-based indexed value. The value is placed in lParam1.	Sent for information about each applet. The CPLApplet() provides information on a dialog box. The lParam1 parameter points to the loading dialog. The lParam2 parameter points to the structure CPLINFO. From this structure, CPLApplet() gets information such as name, icon, and so on.
CPL_ NEWINQUIRE (#define constant value = 8)	If CPL_INQUIRE is not used, you can use this. This has the same order and effect of CPL_INQUIRE.	Same operation as CPL_ENQUIRE, only lParam2 points to a structure named NEWCPLINFO, signifying new data for the .CPL itself. For performance, Win95-NT uses the CPL_INQUIRE.
CPL_DBLCLK (#define constant value = 5)	Called after the user has double-clicked the applet's icon.	Sent when the applet's icon has been double-clicked. lParam1 is the applet number that was selected. lParam2 is the applet's lData value. This message should initiate the applet's dialog box. This will actually show the form you designed for the applet.

TABLE 24.29   Continued

Message	Order	Operation
CPL_STOP (#define constant value = 6)	Called once for each dialog box right before the application closes. It is specified by the *lParam1* parameter on its zero-based value.	The CPLApplet() should attempt to free any resources allocated for the dialog box. Sent for each applet when the control panel is exiting. *lParam1* is the applet number. *lParam2* is the applet's index lData value. Do all applet-specific cleaning up here.
CPL_EXIT (#define constant value = 7)	Sent once. This message is sent after the last CPL_STOP message is sent from the indexed dialogs. It is called immediately before the controlling application uses the FreeLibrary() to free the .CPL containing the applet.	Sent just before the Control Panel calls FreeLibrary(). *lParam1* and *lParam2* are not used. Do non-applet–specific cleaning up here—freeing resources, memory de-allocation, and so on.

Going by the order, the CPLApplet() function received the CPL_INIT message when loading the Control Panel applet by the controlling application (Control Panel). The function initializes, allocates memory, and should return a non-zero value. If the CPLApplet() fails, it returns zero (or FALSE) and tells the controlling application to cease communication with the Control Panel applet.

Next, if the CPL_INIT was a success, the controlling application sends a CPL_GETCOUNT message. The function returns a number of dialog boxes that are supported by the Control Panel applet. For example, if you supported three dialog boxes, the CPLApplet() function returns 3.

CPLApplet() then receives a CPL_INQUIRE message and one CPL_NEWINQUIRE message for each dialog box that is supported by the Control Panel applet. The function fills in a CPLINFO or a NEWCPLINFO structure containing information about each dialog supported. This information contains the name, icon, and a description of the applet. Fill in CPLINFO's idIcon, idName, idInfo, and lData fields with the resource ID for an icon to display, name and description string IDs, and a long data item associated with applet #*lParam1*. This information can be cached by the caller at runtime and across sessions.

Usually under Windows 95 and NT, you should utilize the CPL_INQUIRE message and ignore the CPL_NEWINQUIRE message, for performance sake. The CPL_INQUIRE contains information about the dialog boxes information returned from the CPLINFO structure that can be cached. CPL_NEWINQUIRE cannot be cached, so it can bring performance down. Sometimes, when you see the Control Panel loading slowly, it may be because other applets send the CPL_NEWINQUIRE message because of compatibility. The CPL_NEWINQUIRE message is the same as CPL_INQUIRE except *lParam2* is a pointer to a NEWCPLINFO struct. This message is useful only if you need to change your applet's icon or display information based on the state of your system.

However, a Control Panel applet should handle both CPL_INQUIRE and CPL_NEWINQUIRE messages, but CPL_NEWINQUIRE can be ignored. The developer must not make any assumptions about the order or dependence of CPL inquiries. *lParam1* is the applet number to register, a value from 0 to (CPL_GETCOUNT - 1). *lParam2* is a pointer to a CPLINFO structure.

The CPLApplet() function then receives the CPL_DBCLK message indicating that the user has activated the Control Panel applet. The message contains the dialog box identifier and the value is sent to the lData parameter. When the controlling application sends the CPL_DBLCLK and CPL_STOP messages, it passes this value back to your application.

After the last CPL_STOP message, the CPL_EXIT is received by CPLApplet() function. The function should free any and all memory allocated and unregister the applet. Immediately after this process is finished, a call to FreeLibrary() function is called.

Creating the Control Panel Applet

Let's begin creating an applet. First, there are a few general rules to keep in mind during and after creating a Control Panel applet:

- The applet must be copied to the \windows\system or \winnt\system32 directory for use. All Control Panel applets are stored there.

- You can register the Control Panel applet in the Registry. You can store it in the MMCPL key under HKEY_CURRENT_USER\Control Panel key.

- Make sure the compiled DLL is renamed to a .CPL before copying to the specified destination directory. You can set the default extension directory in C++Builder by selecting Project, Options. Choose the Application tab from the Project Options dialog. In the Output Settings, you can change the Target Extension to CPL. When C++Builder compiles, it should return the compiled program with the extension .CPL.

24

USING THE
WIN32 API

- The order in which the applet DLLs are loaded by CONTROL.EXE is not guaranteed. Control Panels can be sorted for display and so on. Sometimes, yours might load in alphabetical order, but this is all determined by the controlling application or Control Panel itself.

With these basic rules established, you're ready to build an applet.

1. Open C++Builder.

2. Close all windows and do not save any projects, forms, and so on. Make sure C++Builder does not have any projects loaded.

3. Choose File, Close All for this option. What we want to do is create two forms with some components. It will be a skeletal program for our Control Panel applet.

4. Choose File, New Form from C++Builder's File menu.

5. A form will appear. Place a label and a button on it. Set the properties shown in Table 24.30.

TABLE 24.30 Properties to Set in Our Example Applet

Component	Property
Label1	Caption = This is Dialog 1 in my applet!
Button1	Caption = Close

6. Type the following in the OnClick event of the button:
```
void __fastcall TForm1::Button1Click(TObject *Sender)
{
 Close();
}
```

7. Save the form as Form1.

8. Choose File, New Form and place the same components on the form.

9. Add an OnClick event to Button1 and place the same code within the event handler as described in step 6.

10. Change the name of the form to Form2 within the Object Inspector, and save the form as Form2.

11. You now should have two separate forms. Choose File, Close All from C++Builder's File menu.

Now we have to create a resource file for our icons used by the applet. It is not mandatory to create two icons, but Windows will set a default icon if one is not present. Both parts of the applet will get the same icon if none was presented. Because we want the applet to stand out a bit, it's a good idea to create and use something other than the default.

To do this, minimize C++Builder and open up Image Editor. Create a new resource. You can do this by selecting File, New and choosing Resource File. After that, a dialog will appear. Inside the dialog, right-click with your mouse and choose New, Icon. Select 32×32, 16 colors, and press OK. Right-click that new icon and rename it ICON1.

Then select the CONTENTS parent tree, right-click, and choose New, Icon. Select 32×32, 16 colors, and press OK. Right-click that new icon and rename it ICON2. You should now have two icons named ICON1 and ICON2.

Save the resource file as MyCPL.RES.

Now go into ICON1 and ICON2 and create pictures for them. You can go into them by double-clicking the icons' caption. You can draw anything you like. In this example, the text i1 and i2 was used for each icon, respectively. You can choose to create any icon you want.

After drawing your art in the icons, choose File, Save. Close out the Image editor. Keep in mind where you saved the resource file.

So far, we have created the two dialog boxes that will appear in the applet and icons to go with our dialog boxes, but we haven't created the applet itself. To do this, maximize C++Builder and close everything in its environment (if anything is open). Then choose File, New. A New Items dialog will appear. This is the Object Repository and it will contain items to choose. Select the DLL Wizard icon within the New Page view. The DLL Wizard dialog should appear, requesting the type of DLL to be created. The default values are appropriate, so click OK to select the default settings. After a few seconds, C++Builder will generate the necessary code for creating a DLL; it should be similar to the following code:

```
//--------------------------------------------------------------------------

#include <vcl.h>
#include <windows.h>
#pragma hdrstop
#pragma argsused
int WINAPI DllEntryPoint(HINSTANCE hinst, unsigned long reason, void*
➡lpReserved)
{
        return 1;
}
```

C++Builder auto-generates this, and we are now ready to create an applet.

Before you get ahead of yourself, be sure to save your work. Choose File, Save Project As and save Unit1.cpp as Main. Save the project itself as MyCPL, preferably in the same directory where you saved your newly created forms. You will now return to C++Builder.

Choose Project, Add to Project, and select Form1 from the file list box. Do the same to add Form2 form.

If you did this properly, you should now have both forms appear and both forms added to the project. You can verify by choosing View, Project Manager. Form1 and Form2 should be in the list.

Now we need to add the resource file that contains the icons to the project. Choose Project, Add to Project. A file list box will appear. Under the File Type drop-down menu, instead of type .cpp, choose .RES for resource files. MyCPL.RES should then appear in the file list box. Choose that file. The resource file is now added to our project.

Before we proceed, let's make sure our compiled DLL will end up having an extension of .CPL. Choose Projects, Options, Application Page. Within the Output File Settings edit control, change the DLL extension to .CPL. When C++Builder compiles the DLL, it will create the resulting file as a .CPL Control Panel applet file type.

The next step is to implement the CPLApplet() function within the .cpp source file, as shown in the following. Be sure not to forget to include the CPL.H file.

```
CPlApplet(HWND HwControlPanel, int Msg, int LParam1, int LParam2)
{
  switch(Msg)
   {
    case CPL_INIT:
      //Return successful inits... Is it live, or is it an Applet?
      MyProgInstance = GetModuleHandle("MyCPL.cpl");
      return true;

    case CPL_GETCOUNT:
      //How many icons are going to be displayed in our Applet?
      return 2;

    case CPL_NEWINQUIRE:
      {
         //Control Panel asks for display information...
         //This information is read while CP loads...

         switch (LParam1)
         {
          case 0:
            {
               NEWCPLINFO *Info = (NEWCPLINFO *)LParam2;
               ZeroMemory(Info, sizeof(NEWCPLINFO));
               Info->dwSize = sizeof(NEWCPLINFO);
               Info->hIcon = LoadIcon(HInstance, "ICON1");
```

```
            strcpy(Info->szName, "The Applet #1");
            strcpy(Info->szInfo, "This is Applet #1");
             return 0;
          }
      case 1:
        {
            NEWCPLINFO *Info2 = (NEWCPLINFO *)LParam2;
            ZeroMemory(Info2, sizeof(NEWCPLINFO));
            Info2->dwSize = sizeof(NEWCPLINFO);
            Info2->hIcon = LoadIcon(HInstance, "ICON2");
            strcpy(Info2->szName, "The Applet #2");
            strcpy(Info2->szInfo, "This is Applet #2");
             return 0;
        }
      }

      //More applets if needed...

    }

case CPL_DBLCLK:
 //Since they double clicked on the displayed icon, show form!
    try
    {      //Hey! -Up 'dere!

      if(LParam1==0)
        {
         Application->Initialize();
         Application->CreateForm(__classid(TForm1), &Form1);
         Application->Run();
        }
      else
        {
         Application->Initialize();
         Application->CreateForm(__classid(TForm2), &Form2);
         Application->Run();
        }
    }
    catch (Exception &exception)
    {
      Application->ShowException(&exception);
    }
    return 0;

case CPL_STOP: break;
case CPL_EXIT: break;
```

```
  }//End of switch
}
```

The code within your example program should resemble the code in Listing 24.13.

LISTING 24.13   Creating the Heart of the Control Panel Applet Code

```
//-----------------------------------------------------------------------
#include <vcl.h>
#include <cpl.h>          //Don't forget to include this header for the CPLs!

#include <windows.h>
#pragma hdrstop
#pragma argsused

// Tell C++Builder to use all of these resources, reguardless...
USEFORM("Form1.cpp", Form1);
USEFORM("Form2.cpp", Form2);
USERES("MyCpl.res");

//Declare a handle to our Applet
HINSTANCE MyProgInstance =NULL;

//The DLLEntryPoint. The start of a DLL....
int WINAPI DllEntryPoint(HINSTANCE hinst, unsigned long reason, void*
►lpReserved)
{
  if (reason==DLL_PROCESS_ATTACH)
      MyProgInstance=hinst;
         return 1;
}
//-----------------------------------------------------------------------


//The Control Panel will do all the calling, inquiring, through this function
//As you can see, the WINMAIN is now replaced....
extern "C" int __stdcall __declspec(dllexport)

CPlApplet(HWND HwControlPanel, int Msg, int LParam1, int LParam2)
{
  switch(Msg)
   {
    case CPL_INIT:
      //Return successful inits... Is it live, or is it an Applet?
       MyProgInstance = GetModuleHandle("MyCPL.cpl");
```

LISTING 24.13   Continued

```
       return true;

 case CPL_GETCOUNT:
    //How many icons are going to be displayed in our Applet?
    return 2;

 case CPL_NEWINQUIRE:
    {
       //Control Panel asks for display information...
       //This information is read while CP loads...

       switch (LParam1)
       {
        case 0:
          {
             NEWCPLINFO *Info = (NEWCPLINFO *)LParam2;
             ZeroMemory(Info, sizeof(NEWCPLINFO));
             Info->dwSize = sizeof(NEWCPLINFO);
             Info->hIcon = LoadIcon(HInstance, "ICON1");
             strcpy(Info->szName, "The Applet #1");
             strcpy(Info->szInfo, "This is Applet #1");
              return 0;
          }
        case 1:
          {
             NEWCPLINFO *Info2 = (NEWCPLINFO *)LParam2;
             ZeroMemory(Info2, sizeof(NEWCPLINFO));
             Info2->dwSize = sizeof(NEWCPLINFO);
             Info2->hIcon = LoadIcon(HInstance, "ICON2");
             strcpy(Info2->szName, "The Applet #2");
             strcpy(Info2->szInfo, "This is Applet #2");
              return 0;
          }
       }

       //More applets if needed...

    }

 case CPL_DBLCLK:
    //Since they double clicked on the displayed icon, show form!
    try
    {      //Hey! -Up 'dere!

       if(LParam1==0)
```

LISTING 24.13   Continued

```
              {
               Application->Initialize();
               Application->CreateForm(__classid(TForm1), &Form1);
               Application->Run();
              }
              else
              {
               Application->Initialize();
               Application->CreateForm(__classid(TForm2), &Form2);
               Application->Run();
              }
          }
          catch (Exception &exception)
          {
            Application->ShowException(&exception);
          }
          return 0;

      case CPL_STOP: break;
      case CPL_EXIT: break;

    }//End of switch
}
```

Believe it or not, the coding is done! If you haven't yet, go ahead and save your work and compile and link the project. After completion, move MyCPL.CPL into the \windows\system or \windows\system32 directory. Open up Control Panel and you should see the newly created applet.

To quickly run our Control Panel applet without Control Panel interfering, we could issue the following command at the Start, Run menu:

```
rundll32 shell32.dll,Control_RunDLL mycpl.cpl @0
```

where @ describes which applet dialog you want to fire off at a zero-based value. For example, this code line will fire off the first applet dialog.

The following will fire off the second dialog we have:

```
rundll32 shell32.dll,Control_RunDLL mycpl.cpl @1
```

RunDLL32.EXE calls on Shell32.DLL. Inside, the Shell32.DLL contains a special function to call on different applets and parameters.

You may have noticed the use of `CPL_NEWINQUIRE` in the example code and maybe are asking why the `CPL_NEWINQUIRE` message was included instead of the `CPL_INQUIRE` message. This was chosen to keep the example short, clean, and easy to describe. The `CPL_NEWINQUIRE` and `CPL_INQUIRE` structures are quite different. If the `CPL_INQUIRE` is used, the icons and a strings for the applet names must be contained inside a resource script (`.rc`). The `.rc` file can be compiled with C++Builder's `BRCC32.EXE` resource compiler, which will turn it into a Resource (`.RES`) file. Make sure there is a header file to define the values of the constants of the text.

An example of creating a string list is as follows:

```
STRINGTABLE
 BEGIN
ID_ICONTEXT1 "This is Applet 1";
ID_ICONTEXT2 "Applet #2";
 END
```

Using `CPL_INQUIRE` requires that the `LoadString()` function be used within the application to pull out the string list and then assign that to the structure. This allows the applet to utilize the string list and resources from the icons. However, this is a little more work than using the `CPL_NEWINQUIRE` structure. Because it's a simple example program, there's not much performance decrease in using the `CPL_NEWINQUIRE structure`. However, if you made a fairly large program, you should consider using `CPL_INQUIRE`. As we've demonstrated, creating small, simple, clear applications that run under Control Panel is fairly easy and effective.

Summary

Within this chapter, we've looked at many of the elements and aspects of the Win32 API. By programming using the Win32 API, developers can begin to understand the low-level intricate elements of Windows. Understanding the Win32 API provides a distinct advantage for the Windows developer.

Applying the Win32 API within your application can be quite challenging, but it's also fun. It's like putting the pieces of a puzzle together; if you connect and use the right pieces, you end up with a good, solid, creative application. One of the keys to effective C++Builder development is knowing when to make use of the Win32 API. For example, when there are no VCLs available that perform a required task, the Win32 API should be explored. Also, if Win32 API calls can significantly improve on an application's performance and capability, the calls should be applied.

This chapter has provided several examples that showed how and when to use Win32 API calls, callbacks, and structures. It has armed you with the essentials, but it has only scratched the surface of what the API can provide. Keep in mind that within Borland C++Builder, the opportunity exists to create new VCLs as well as great applications based on some of the common and unique Win32 API routines available. As a developer, you should consider utilizing the Win32 API, applying it, and possibly using it the next time you develop a Windows application. You just might find that your best ideas can be realized through the Win32 API!

Now, go out and Win the world!

Multimedia Techniques

Damon Chandler
Siu-Fan Wu
Rob Allen

IN THIS CHAPTER

- **The Graphical Device Interface (GDI)**
- **Image Support**
- **Image Processing**
- **Audio Files, Video Files, and CD Music**

Many applications require some type of multimedia support. Oftentimes, multimedia technologies are used simply to enhance an application's user interface. Other applications rely heavily on multimedia-based techniques for the exchange of information with the user. Indeed, some applications are designed specifically for creating, managing, displaying, or playing multimedia files.

In this chapter, we will discuss several techniques for supporting multimedia in an application. The degree of support is based solely on the specific needs of the application itself. As we will discover, Windows presents several interfaces that provide a common means by which an application can communicate with the target device driver.

Support for the display of still images is accomplished through the use of the Windows Graphics Device Interface (GDI). An application indirectly communicates with the display driver through functions presented by the GDI. We will examine the GDI and its corresponding VCL classes. Specifically, we will discuss the use of the TCanvas, TBrush, TPen, and TFont classes, and how these objects can be used to render graphical output to the display monitor and printer. Next, we will examine the TBitmap and TJPEGImage VCL classes and how they are used to support bitmap and JPEG images, respectively. We will also discuss the basis of other image file formats and some techniques for supporting these types of images in a VCL application.

We will then give an introduction to image processing, demonstrating several techniques for manipulating images. The techniques covered include accessing and modifying pixel values, thresholding, color and grayscale image inversion, contrast adjustment using histograms, zooming using geometrical transformations, and smoothing and edge detection using spatial operations.

Audio and video support is typically accomplished via the Media Control Interface (MCI). Here, an application indirectly communicates with the audio and video playback device drivers through the functions presented by the MCI. Windows also presents more specialized interfaces for use with specific media formats. We will demonstrate the use of the MCI for support of audio and video playback, along with the use of the Waveform-Audio Interface for playback of signal-processed waveform-audio files.

The Graphical Device Interface (GDI)

The majority of the visible portion of a Windows GUI program written in C++Builder is built using forms and controls. However, some of the GUI will consist of graphics and pictures. This is where the GDI subsection of Windows comes into play. The GDI is one of the core parts of the Windows operating system and is housed in GDI.DLL and GDI32.DLL. It encompasses hundreds of functions (on my Windows NT system there are 401 exports in GDI32.DLL). Everything that draws in Windows uses the GDI, including Windows itself.

The GDI exists for one main reason: device independence. When you draw using GDI functions, you do not need to know the specifics of programming every video card and printer on the market today and tomorrow. The GDI provides a layer of abstraction between your application code and the hardware.

There is not enough space here to cover all the features available within the GDI; see the VCL help starting at TCanvas. In addition, there is a lot of information in the Microsoft help, available from the Help, Windows SDK menu item.

The Windows API and the Device Context

As with just about every other part of Windows programming, you need a handle to interface with the GDI. The handle is known as the *Device Context* (DC); in the standard Windows API, you get it using the following:

```
HDC hDC = GetDC(hWindow);
```

The DC returned is attached to a specific window, and you cannot draw outside of the client area of that window. To draw anywhere on the desktop, you would supply pass NULL as the hWindow argument to GetDC(). As you would expect in Windows API programming, the DC is passed as a parameter into every GDI drawing function. When you have finished drawing, you should release the DC using the following call:

```
ReleaseDC(hD);
```

Understanding TCanvas: The C++Builder Interface

When programming using C++Builder, we know that, to improve efficiency, it is preferable to use components over raw API code. Drawing lines and filled areas is no different, and we use the TCanvas component. TCanvas is a wrapper around the GDI functionality and is available as a property on the TForm and TPrinter components and on most common control components. You access it as a property of the component. For example, to draw a rectangle on the form, you would use the following:

```
Canvas->Rectangle(10, 10, 100, 100);
```

What Does It Do?

TCanvas provides an object-oriented approach to programming the Windows API. The biggest advantage is that it handles resources for you. There are some fairly complex rules concerning how to manage GDI resources when using the raw API; TCanvas handles these rules for you seamlessly. Also, TCanvas provides the standard VCL property system for getting and setting many of the attributes of the underlying Device Context that simplify your code and make it much easier to read and understand.

Key Methods

TCanvas has several key properties you should know about:

- TPen Pen—The currently selected pen for drawing
- TBrush Brush—The currently selected brush
- TFont Font—The currently selected font
- TPoint PenPos—Positions the pen ready for drawing

It is important to note that the canvas will use the current pen, brush, font, and position as appropriate when drawing. These must be changed before the drawing function is called.

What Does It Leave Out?

TCanvas and its associated classes are coded in the file graphics.pas, but they do not cover all of the GDI functions. Borland has implemented only the most commonly used functions. Also, some of the helper classes such as TRect and TPoint do not provide much more functionality than their underlying Windows API counterparts and could be a lot more helpful.

But all is not lost. As with all C++Builder programming, the Windows API is just a function call away, and TCanvas provides a Handle property to allow access to any of the GDI function calls. Going back to our original rectangle, this could be called as follows:

```
Rectangle(Canvas->Handle, 10, 10, 100, 100);
```

This would achieve exactly the same results.

NOTE

Some of the VCL classes used to wrap around the common GDI structures do not add nearly as much value as they could. Good examples are TRect, TPoint, and TSize, which are very thin wrappers. Borland's engineers could have taken the opportunity to provide more comprehensive functionality for these helper classes.

For example, TRect is an encapsulation of a rectangle. It contains four useful functions: operator==(), operator!=(), Height(), and Width(). With a little bit of imagination, the class could have been made really useful. For instance, functions could provide the capability to see if another point or rectangle is contained within or touches the TRect. Also, functions to scale the rectangle or move it would be useful.

Is it difficult to provide your own? Of course not, but it would have been neater to have just written

```
If( myRect->Contains(myPoint){ // do something... }
```

Using TCanvas

It is normal to draw only to the canvas within the TForm's OnPaint event handler. This ensures that the display is kept current. It is also normal to create a hidden canvas using a TImage that is exactly the same size as the form and draw to the hidden canvas and then copy it to the form canvas in OnPaint. This has the advantage of speeding up the display.

As an example, consider the implementation of an analog clock. If there is no second hand, the display needs to be updated only once per minute. The drawing code will have to calculate the angle at which to draw the hands and so will take a short time. Whenever the window is obscured and then uncovered, the OnPaint function will be called. To optimize the redrawing speed, a second hidden canvas is used.

The OnPaint event handler would then look something like this:

```
void __fastcall TForm1::FormPaint(TObject *Sender)
{
    // copy the information on the hidden canvas onto the form's canvas.
    Canvas->CopyRect(ClientRect, HiddenImage->Canvas, HiddenImage->ClientRect);
}
```

This is illustrated in an example later in this section.

Drawing Lines and Curves

Drawing lines and curves is easy with a TCanvas: Just set up the relevant pen and then call the appropriate function. There are many functions in TCanvas for line drawing that are readily available in the C++Builder documentation. A simple line is drawn using two commands:

```
Canvas->PenPos = TPoint(1, 1);
Canvas->LineTo(9, 1);
```

Note that all the *XxxTo()* functions start from the current pen position and, as with most GDI drawing functions, draw *up to but not including* the last point specified. That means that when you draw a rectangle from (1,1) to (10,10), the pixel at (10,10) is not drawn. Figure 25.1 shows how a line drawn from (1,1) to (9,1) does not fill the last pixel. This also includes functions like Ellipse() in which you provide a bounding box.

Drawing Filled Areas

Filled images use both a pen and a brush. The pen is used for the outline, and the brush is used to fill in the interior. For example, a rectangle would be drawn using the following:

```
TRect MyRect(10, 10, 100, 300);
Canvas->Rectange(myRect)
```

Ellipses are slightly different in that you provide the bounding rectangle. Then the system draws the ellipse so that it just touches the rectangle.

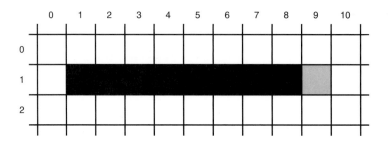

FIGURE 25.1

`LineTo(9,1)` *does not fill in the last pixel.*

Drawing Text

There is more than one way to draw text. The easiest is to use `TextOut()`, which starts at a specified (x,y). This function repositions the `PenPos` to the end of the drawn text, allowing for easy continuation. `TextRect()` will draw the text within a rectangle and clip any text that does not fit.

The size of the text depends on the font. For a fixed-pitch font, such as Courier, each letter takes up the same amount of space, whether it is an *i* or a *w*. With a variable-pitch font, each letter is a different width, so that the *i* takes up less space than the *w*. To calculate the width and height a given string will take up, `TCanvas` provides the function `TextExtent()`, which returns a `TSize` that can be used for positioning the text as appropriate.

As an example, in the analog clock example code, the text is drawn using the following:

```
AnsiString text = "Right Click for Menu...";
TSize textSize = HiddenImage->Canvas->TextExtent(text);
int x = (HiddenImage->Width - textSize.cx) / 2;
int y = HiddenImage->Height - textSize.cy - 2;
HiddenImage->Canvas->TextOut(x, y, text);
```

This ensures that the text is centered at the bottom of `HiddenImage`.

Customizing a Drawing

Lines and text don't make a very interesting display unless we can customize the drawing. The most obvious things to customize are the color and thickness of the line and the font characteristics of text. C++Builder provides a number of helper classes to `TCanvas` that enable easy customization.

> **NOTE**
>
> To customize a particular drawing operation, it is important that the change (for example, the color) is made *before* calling the drawing function.

TColor

The color of a graphics object in the VCL is set using the TColor property. TColor is a VCL mapping of the Windows API COLORREF value, which uses a 32-bit number to specify the color. The color is divided into the constituent components Red, Green, and Blue, so Red is (255,0,0), and White is (255,255,255). This is how a standard color monitor displays colors; if you look very closely at the screen with a magnifying glass, you will see three separate pixels (one red, one green, and one blue) for each pixel that your eye can see from further away.

Simple arithmetic shows that using this system the maximum number of colors is 255×255×255 = 16,581,375, or approximately 16 million. Not all displays attached to a Windows computer are capable of displaying this many colors at any given resolution, so the number of colors that can be displayed might be 16, 256, 65536, or 16 million. The number of colors available is also known as the *color depth*. Table 25.1 lists the possible colors and a description.

TABLE 25.1 Representation of Colors at Different Color Depths

Number of Colors	Description
16 colors	With a 16-color VGA display, the colors are fixed and are listed in the help for TColor.
256 colors	A 256-color display is palette based. This means that only 256 colors can be displayed at one time, but the choice of which colors can be set from the full range of colors.
65,536 colors	The Red, Green, Blue (RGB) values are stored in a 16-bit value. When you choose a color, Windows applies the value closest to the one selected.
16 million colors	All colors are available for display.

There is not enough space in this section to cover palette management for 256-color displays. Look at a good Windows API reference text such as Petzold's *Programming Windows*, Microsoft Press, ISBN: 157231995X. To determine the number of colors available, use the GetDeviceCaps() Windows API function to find the number of planes and the number of bits per pixel. This code snippet will calculate the number of colors:

```
int BitsPerPixel = GetDeviceCaps(Canvas->Handle, BITSPIXEL);
int NumberOfPlanes = GetDeviceCaps(Canvas->Handle, PLANES);

int NumberofColours = 1 << (NumberOfPlanes * BitsPerPixel);
```

TPen

When you draw a line or a lined object such as an empty circle, the current pen is used to define the color, thickness mode, and style. The style determines how the line is drawn: solid, dotted, dashed, and so on. If the width is greater than 1, the line will be solid, so if you need a thick dotted line, you have to draw multiple lines next to each other.

TPen has a mode that defines how the pen's color is affected by the underlying color already on the canvas. Of particular interest is the pmNotXor mode, which will perform a "not xor" of the pen's color with the underlying canvas color. This is particularly useful for drawing temporary lines over an image when the line will be erased shortly afterward. The line can then be erased by redrawing the line over the first line as the pmNotXor mode will cancel out the two lines, leaving the original image displayed. This can be used, for example, to select the zooming region within a graphics program. As the mouse moves, the rectangle making up the zoom area changes, and the original picture is still displayed.

TBrush

The current brush is used to determine how to fill in an object. TBrush has the properties Color and Style. Style determines whether to fill in the object or use a pattern of lines to shade the area. The Style property takes the values bsSolid, bsCross, bsClear, bsDiagCross, bsBDiagonal, bsHorizontal, bsFDiagonal, and bsVertical. These should be self explanatory. The effect of these styles can be seen in the analog clock program example.

TFont

The current font is used in text functions such as TextOut(). This has all the attributes that you would expect, such as color, name, height, and style. The size of the font can be set in two ways: Height in pixels or Size in points. If you set one, then the other is automatically calculated. This is useful because most users will want to set the font size in points, not in pixels.

An Analogue Clock Example

To demonstrate these ideas, an analog clock project, clock.bpr, is provided in the GDI folder on the CD-ROM that accompanies this book. This clock is based on an old Borland C++ OWL example aclock and shows a simple clock with hour and minute hands. This is shown in Figure 25.2.

Figure 25.2

The analogue clock example program.

Note

This example program is intended to show the use of the Canvas for drawing. The important functions are the form's `InitialiseImage()`, `DrawClockToHiddenImage()`, and `FormPaint()`. Because it is an example, there is no error checking, and the supporting code is not necessarily a shining example of software engineering.

All drawing is done to the canvas of a hidden `TImage` that is copied onto the form's `Canvas` in the `OnPaint()` event handler. The example shows the use of the `Font`, `Brush`, and `Pen` properties of the canvas, along with the drawing of lines for the hands and an ellipse for the clock face. Using the context menu, the brush style of the clock face can be changed to show the different effects, along with the style of the hands.

Image Support

The Windows GDI provides native support for the bitmap file format and presents many GDI functions that are specifically designed for use with bitmap objects. However, if you are interested in displaying other image formats, you will need to use other measures. Specifically, you'll have to provide a conversion routine such that you can construct a bitmap object from the information contained in the file itself.

It is not our intention here to go into the specifics of each image file format. Indeed, such a topic is worthy of a text on its own. Instead, we'll provide a general overview of the most common file formats. We'll first concentrate on the bitmap object, its complementary GDI functions and structures, and the VCL `TBitmap` class. Later, we'll discuss other image file formats and where you can obtain more information on each. We will also mention some third-party libraries that can be used to convert to and from a bitmap.

The Windows Bitmap Object

The GDI presents two types of bitmaps: device-dependent bitmaps (DDBs) and device-independent bitmaps (DIBs). The former is a type of GDI graphic object, defined by the `BITMAP` structure, which can be used in much the same way as most other graphic objects. Namely, you can select a DDB into a memory device context and use any of the applicable GDI functions to perform rendering. Unfortunately, the GDI does not provide a direct means by which the bits of a DDB can be accessed. In contrast, a DIB is defined by the information contained in a `BITMAPINFO` structure and an array of pixels. In this way, you always have direct access to the bits of a DIB. There is a catch, however: DIBs cannot be selected into a memory device context, so rendering a DIB is generally slower than rendering a DDB.

To overcome the limitations imposed by DDBs and DIBs, Microsoft engineers developed the hybrid *DIB section bitmap*. This is simply a composite of the former two types, defined by the `DIBSECTION` structure.

```
typedef struct tagDIBSECTION {
    BITMAP            dsBm;
    BITMAPINFOHEADER  dsBmih;
    DWORD             dsBitfields[3];
    HANDLE            dshSection;
    DWORD             dsOffset;
} DIBSECTION;
```

Unlike a true DDB, the bits of a DIB section bitmap are readily accessible. Unlike a true DIB, DIB section bitmaps can be selected into a memory device context. These two complementary aspects are particularly important when both efficient pixel manipulation and efficient rendering are required. In fact, the VCL `TBitmap` class is based on the DIB section bitmap.

The `TBitmap` Class

The `TBitmap` class is the VCL's encapsulation of the Windows bitmap object. The class descends from the abstract `TGraphic` base class, and it dynamically adapts to use either a DDB or a DIB section bitmap. This functionality is presented by the internal VCL `CopyBitmap()` function. It is from within this function that either a DDB is created via the GDI functions `CreateBitmap()` (for monochrome bitmaps) and `CreateCompatibleBitmap()` or else a DIB section bitmap is created via the `CreateDIBSection()` GDI function. While it is beyond the scope of this text to discuss the specifics of the `CopyBitmap()` VCL function, let's examine those properties and member functions of the `TBitmap` class that provide support for other image types.

The `TBitmap` class relies heavily on the `TBitmapCanvas` and `TBitmapImage` classes. The former, a descendant of the `TCanvas` class, expands its parent class to encapsulate the GDI memory device context. The latter, a descendant of the `TSharedImage` class, handles the resource counting and destruction of the DDB or DIB section bitmap. This latter task is accomplished via the `DeleteObject()` GDI function.

For image rendering support, the `TBitmapCanvas` class inherits the `Draw()`, `StretchDraw()`, and `CopyRect()` member functions from its parent class. The `TBitmapCanvas::CreateHandle()` function performs the task of selecting the bitmap (and palette, when appropriate) into the underlying memory device context. Thus, when the `Draw()`, `StretchDraw()`, or `CopyRect()` member function is used, the `TCanvas` class can rely solely on the `StretchBlt()` or `TransparentStretchBlt()` GDI function.

Aside from the rendering member functions presented by the `TCanvas` class, the `TBitmap` class provides the `ScanLine` property. This property uses the internal `TBitmap::GetScanLine()` member function, which simply returns an offset pointer to the bits of the DIB section bitmap. When you convert from other formats, you'll need access to these bits so that you can directly manipulate the pixels of the image. In this way, the `ScanLine` property significantly eases the task of pixel manipulation.

JPEG Images

JPEG (pronounced "jaypeg") is not a file format; it is an image compression protocol developed by the Joint Photographic Experts Group. JPEG images are compressed in a lossy fashion, meaning that some information is discarded during compression. While the decompressed image is not identical to the original, for most natural images there is little or no degradation in visual quality. Moreover, the degree of compression can be adjusted, allowing for decompressed images of varying quality.

The JPEG compression process consists of three stages: reduction of pixel redundancy via a Discrete Cosine Transform (DCT), quantization of transform data (DCT coefficients), and reduction of data redundancy. It is in the second stage (quantization) that information is discarded. Typically, this is where human visual system (HVS) characteristics are taken into account, although there is no strict specification for the type of quantization that should be performed. For more information on the JPEG image format specifics, refer to `http://www.jpeg.org/`.

The VCL provides support for JPEG images through the `TJPEGImage` class. The main compression and decompression routines are handled via the JPEG image compression library of the Independent JPEG Group (IJG). Like the `TBitmap` class, `TJPEGImage` is a descendant of the `TGraphic` class.

The `TJPEGImage` class implements the `TPersistent::Assign()` and `AssignTo()` member functions so that you can easily convert between instances of `TJPEGImage` and `TBitmap`. Moreover, because the `TJPEGImage` class is designed for use with the Windows GDI and the rest of the

25

VCL, the class maintains an internal bitmap representation of the underlying image such that rendering via the GDI is possible. The JPEG data itself is maintained via the `TJPEGData` class.

The `TJPEGImage` class provides several properties designed to manage the underlying JPEG data. For example, the `CompressionQuality` property can be used to adjust the amount of degradation incurred during compression. The `Performance` property can be used to manipulate the amount of time necessary to decompress the JPEG data. The `Scale` property determines the resolution of the resulting bitmap during decompression. The `ProgressiveDisplay` and `ProgressiveEncoding` properties allow for support of progressive decompression, where the currently decompressed portion of the image can be viewed before the entire image is decompressed. These properties, along with the `Smoothing` property, are ideal for situations in which a progressive transmission scheme is employed.

Support for file, stream, and Clipboard operations is provided via the `LoadFromClipboardFormat()`, `LoadFromStream()`, `LoadFromFile()`, `SaveToClipboardFormat()`, `SaveToStream()`, and `SaveToFile()` member functions. These are inherited from the `TGraphic` class, and their use is entirely straightforward. Note that for Clipboard operations, the `TJPEGImage` class uses internal bitmap representation.

GIF Images

The Graphics Interchange Format (GIF, pronounced "jiff") was created in 1987 by CompuServe Corporation. Unlike JPEG images, GIF images are compressed in a lossless fashion, meaning no information is lost during compression. That is, the decompressed image is identical to the original. GIF images also support progressive display (interlacing), multiple images (animated GIF), and transparency as of the latest format revision (GIF89a). More information on GIF can be found at `http://www.geocities.co.jp/SiliconValley/3453/gif_info/`.

Many developers are reluctant to support the GIF format, the use of which has been shrouded by licensing issues. In fact, it is not the format itself that is in question; rather it is the specification for the use of the LZW (Lempel-Ziv-Welch) compression algorithm. This modification of the Lempel-Ziv 78 (LZ78) compression algorithm is patented by Unisys Corporation. CompuServe has publicly granted a royalty-free license to use the GIF format, but Unisys requires that developers purchase a license.

The VCL does not provide native support for the GIF format. To display GIF images, you'll need to convert the (decompressed) data to the bitmap format. While this can be done manually through the `ScanLine` property, there is still the issue of decompressing the data and reading or writing the data to or from a file. There are several third-party libraries available to handle this task. Of particular interest is the free `TGIFImage` VCL component from Anders Melanders that can be found at `http://www.melander.dk/delphi/gifimage/`.

PNG Images

The Portable Network Graphics (PNG, pronounced "ping") format was designed to expand upon and relieve the patent hassle of the GIF format. Like its predecessor, a PNG image is compressed in a lossless manner. Unlike the GIF format, PNG does not rely on the LZW algorithm. Instead, a variation of the Lempel-Ziv 77 (LZ77) compression algorithm is employed. This is the same compression algorithm used by the major file compression applications.

Like the GIF format, the PNG format allows for transparent pixels. However, through the use of an Alpha channel, PNG images may also contain pixels of variable transparency (alpha blending). Moreover, in contrast to the GIF format, PNG images are not limited to 256 colors. To compensate for display monitor variations, the PNG specification allows for encoded gamma information. There is also support for progressive display, accomplished via a two-dimensional interlacing scheme. Unfortunately, the PNG format does not allow for multiple images (animation).

To provide support for display of PNG images, you'll need a means by which to convert the PNG format to a DIB. As always, you can perform this conversion manually; in that case, the latest PNG format specifications are needed. You can find them at http://www.libpng.org/pub/png/spec/PNG-Contents.html. As with many image formats, there are several third-party libraries that can perform this conversion for you. For example, the free PNGDIB conversion library by Jason Summers, found at http://home.mieweb.com/jason/imaging/pngdib/, provides the read_png_to_dib() function that can read a PNG image file and yield a DIB (BITMAPINFO, color table, and bits). It also presents the write_dib_to_png() function for writing a PNG file from a DIB.

Using this library, to initialize a TBitmap object with information contained in a PNG file, you first call the read_png_to_dib() function to create a DIB from the PNG, and then use the SetDIBits() GDI function (or the ScanLine property) to fill the TBitmap object. This is demonstrated in Listing 25.1.

LISTING 25.1   Converting a PNG Format Image to a TBitmap

```
if (OpenDialog1->Execute())
{
   TCHAR filename[MAX_PATH];
   lstrcpyn(filename, OpenDialog1->FileName.c_str(), MAX_PATH);

   // declare and clear the PNGD_P2DINFO structure
   PNGD_P2DINFO png2dib;
   memset(&png2dib, 0, sizeof(PNGD_P2DINFO));
```

LISTING 25.1   Continued

```cpp
// initialize the structure size and filename
png2dib.structsize = sizeof(PNGD_P2DINFO);
png2dib.pngfn = filename;

// convert from PNG to DIB
if (read_png_to_dib(&png2dib) == PNGD_E_SUCCESS)
{
    Graphics::TBitmap* Bitmap = Image1->Picture->Bitmap;
    Bitmap->Width = png2dib.lpdib->biWidth;
    Bitmap->Height = png2dib.lpdib->biHeight;

    HBITMAP hBmp = Bitmap->ReleaseHandle();
    HDC hDC = Canvas->Handle;
    try
    {
        //
        // TODO: add palette support...
        //

        // convert from DIB to TBitmap
        SetDIBits(
            hDC, hBmp, 0,
            png2dib.lpdib->biHeight, png2dib.bits,
            reinterpret_cast<LPBITMAPINFO>(png2dib.lpdib),
            DIB_RGB_COLORS
            );
    }
    catch (...)
    {
        Bitmap->Handle = hBmp;
        GlobalFree(png2dib.lpdib);
    }
    Bitmap->Handle = hBmp;
    GlobalFree(png2dib.lpdib);
}
}
```

Similarly, to create a PNG file from information contained in a TBitmap object, you first construct a DIB from the TBitmap via the GetDIBSizes() and GetDIB() VCL utility functions (from graphics.pas), and then use the write_dib_to_png() function to write the PNG file. This is demonstrated in Listing 25.2.

LISTING 25.2   Converting a `TBitmap` Image to PNG Format

```cpp
if (SaveDialog1->Execute())
{
    TCHAR filename[MAX_PATH];
    lstrcpyn(filename, SaveDialog1->FileName.c_str(), MAX_PATH);

    BITMAPINFO bmi;
    Graphics::TBitmap* Bitmap = Image1->Picture->Bitmap;

    //
    // determine the size of the DIB info
    // (BITMAPINFOHEADER + color table) and the
    // size of the bits (pixels)
    //
    unsigned int info_size = 0, bits_size = 0;
    GetDIBSizes(Bitmap->Handle, info_size, bits_size);

    // allocate memory for the bits
    unsigned char *bits = new unsigned char[bits_size];
    try
    {
        // get the BITMAPINFOHEADER + color table and the bits
        if (GetDIB(Bitmap->Handle, Bitmap->Palette, &bmi, bits))
        {
            // declare and clear the PNGD_D2PINFO structure
            PNGD_D2PINFO dib2png;
            memset(&dib2png, 0, sizeof(PNGD_D2PINFO));

            // initialize the structure
            dib2png.structsize = sizeof(PNGD_D2PINFO);
            dib2png.flags = PNGD_INTERLACED;
            dib2png.pngfn = filename;
            dib2png.lpdib = &bmi.bmiHeader;
            dib2png.lpbits = bits;

            // convert the DIB to PNG, then save to file
            if (write_dib_to_png(&dib2png) != PNGD_E_SUCCESS)
            {
                throw EInvalidGraphic("Error Saving PNG!");
            }
        }
    }
    catch (...)
    {
        delete [] bits;
    }
    delete [] bits;
}
```

Included on the companion CD-ROM is a project (PROJ_PNGDIBDEMO.CPP in the PNGDemo folder) that demonstrates the use of the PNGDIB library.

Image Processing

Image processing commonly refers to the manipulation and analysis of pictorial information by digital computers. Applications of image processing range from high-end military systems to a small digital camera.

An image is stored in a computer in a 2D array of numbers for easy manipulation. Each picture element is called a *pixel*. The number of pixels used to store an image is called the *resolution*. The higher the number of pixels, the higher the resolution. We'll work with several images in this section, in either 256×256 or 512×512 resolution.

The number of bytes required to represent a pixel depends on the number of gray shades that the pixel can display. In the case of a black-and-white image, one bit per pixel is enough. For grayscale images, it is normally accepted that the human visual system cannot distinguish more than 256 levels of shade. Therefore, one byte per pixel is sufficient. In the case of true color images, each pixel is represented by a triplet of red, green, and blue, with each represented by one byte—a total of three bytes per pixel. A simple calculation tells us that to store a 512×512 image in true color, you need 512×512×3 bytes = 768KB of information. The large amount of memory required to store and manipulate images is why image processing has been restricted to high-end systems until recently. Consider that the Apple II computer (in use when I started programming) had only 48KB of RAM available!

Image data is seldom stored in raw form. Many different image formats are available for different applications. The native image format in the Windows environment is the Windows Bitmap (BMP), which will be used throughout this chapter. Other commonly used formats include TIFF and PCX.

It is not the intention here to go into detailed mathematical descriptions of the techniques used in image processing. However, some basic techniques will be explained, using examples constructed with C++Builder. The image-processing code demonstrated in this section is built into the IPro.bpr sample image-processing application project, available in the ImageProcessing folder on the CD-ROM that accompanies this book. Figure 25.3 shows what the image-processing application looks like in action, displaying the peppers.bmp image on the CD-ROM.

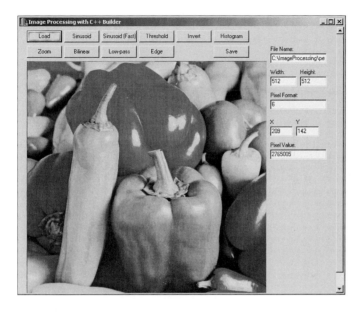

FIGURE 25.3

A simple image-processing application.

Displaying and Obtaining Image Information

The first thing you may want to do with an image is to display it and extract information such as resolution and color depth from the file. The easiest way is to use the TImage component, which can be found under the Additional tab of the Component Palette. After dropping it onto a form, you may want to set the AutoSize property to true so that it can automatically adjust itself for different image sizes. The code in Listing 25.3 loads an image selected from an Open dialog box into the image component when a particular button is clicked. It then displays basic information about the image to the user in a series of edit boxes. Within the project, the default values are used for the components' names.

LISTING 25.3   Loading and Obtaining Image Information

```
void __fastcall TForm1::Button1Click(TObject *Sender)
{
    OpenDialog1->Filter = "Bmp files (*.bmp)|*.BMP";
    if (OpenDialog1->Execute())
    {
        Image1->Picture->Bitmap->LoadFromFile(OpenDialog1->FileName);
        Edit1->Text = OpenDialog1->FileName;
```

25

LISTING 25.3   Continued

```
        Edit2->Text = Image1->Width;
        Edit3->Text = Image1->Height;
        Edit4->Text = Image1->Picture->Bitmap->PixelFormat;
    }
}
```

The first statement displays an Open dialog box, OpenDialog1 of type TOpenDialog, with a filter for BMP files. If the dialog box returns true, this means the user has selected a file, which is then loaded into the Image1 bitmap. Obtaining the image information can be easily done by accessing the properties of Image1. In particular, PixelFormat is an enum type defined in the C++Builder graphics.hpp header file as follows:

```
enum TPixelFormat {pfDevice, pf1bit, pf4bit, pf8bit, pf15bit, pf16bit,
                   pf24bit, pf32bit, pfCustom};
```

Therefore, a 24-bit true color image will give a numeric value of 6 for PixelFormat. An 8-bit grayscale image has a PixelFormat of 3. It should be noted that although the Load() function of the sample application can handle BMP files of all sizes and color depths, most other functions assume a size of 256×256 and an 8-bit grayscale, for the sake of simplicity.

Figure 25.3, previously, shows the image information that we obtained in the top four edit boxes to the right of the image.

Accessing Individual Pixel Values Using TCanvas->Pixels

Before you can perform any image-processing operations, you must have access to the individual pixel values of the image. The easiest way to obtain individual pixel value is to use the Pixels property of TCanvas. You can use it as a 2D array with coordinate (x,y) measured from the top-left corner of the image. Listing 25.4 shows how the mouse position and pixel value can be accessed and displayed to the user when the mouse is moved across the image. You can see this information in the bottom three edit boxes in Figure 25.3.

LISTING 25.4   Accessing Pixel Value when Moving the Mouse

```
void __fastcall TForm1::Image1MouseMove(TObject *Sender, TShiftState Shift,
                                        int X, int Y)
{
    Edit5->Text = X;
    Edit6->Text = Y;
    Edit7->Text = Image1->Canvas->Pixels[X][Y];
}
```

The current coordinate of the mouse is passed into the event handler as X and Y. The pixel value is a TColor, and its interpretation depends on PixelFormat. For grayscale images, the gray level is given by the lowest-order byte of the pixel value. For 24-bit color images, the lower three bytes represent RGB color intensities for blue, green, and red, respectively. The value $00FF0000 represents pure blue, $0000FF00 is pure green, and $000000FF is pure red.

You can also set a pixel value using `TCanvas->Pixels[][]`. For example, adding the following line to the `Image1MouseMove()` event handler will draw a line on the image while the mouse is moving:

```
Image1->Canvas->Pixels[X][Y] = clWhite;
```

Using `Canvas->Pixels[X][Y]` is straightforward but extremely slow. Therefore, it should be used only for infrequent or causal access to pixel values. The most efficient way to access image data is to use `ScanLine`, which will be explained in the section "Fast Access to Pixel Value Using `ScanLine`," later in this chapter.

Image Generation

Very often, image processing professionals have to create test images to work with, such as an image with known image statistics. We will create a test image that provides some insight into the properties of the human visual system. The image is a sinusoidal variation of gray level in the horizontal direction. The frequency of the variation, called spatial frequency, is increasing with x. The amplitude of the sine wave decreases linearly with increasing y. The code to create the image is shown in Listing 25.5. It should be noted that the following code makes use of the standard math function `sqrt()`, so the `math.h` header file must be included in the unit. You can refer to the actual project (`IPro.bpr`) on the CD-ROM.

LISTING 25.5   Creating a Sinusoidal Image Using `TCanvas->Pixels`

```
void __fastcall TForm1::Button2Click(TObject *Sender)
{
    int x, y;
    int Amplitude, Gray;
    float Period;
    TColor RGB;

    Image1->Picture->Bitmap = new Graphics::TBitmap;
    Image1->Picture->Bitmap->PixelFormat = pf24bit;
    Image1->Picture->Bitmap->Width = 256;
    Image1->Picture->Bitmap->Height = 256;
    for (y=0; y<=255; y++)
        for (x=0; x<=255; x++)
        {
            Amplitude = 64*(255-y)/255;
            Period = 100*sqrt(1/(1+(exp(0.013*x)*exp(0.027*x)/400)));
```

LISTING 25.5   Continued

```
          Gray = Amplitude*sin(2*M_PI/Period*x)+128;
          RGB = (Gray << 16) | (Gray << 8) | Gray;
          Image1->Canvas->Pixels[x][y] = RGB;
      }
}
```

First a TBitmap is created for us to draw on. Next, the PixelFormat, Width, and Height of the image are set. Inside the nested for loop, the pixel value of each pixel is calculated. The details of the mathematics involved are beyond the scope of this book. Finally, we draw the pixel by setting the Image1->Canvas->Pixels values. The image created is shown in Figure 25.4.

FIGURE 25.4

A varying sinusoid.

NOTE

It is obvious from Figure 25.4 that the sensitivity of the visual system to contrast varies with the spatial frequency, reaching a maximum at intermediate frequencies while falling off for very low or very high frequencies. This kind of information about our visual system is useful in applications such as image transmission and compression, because it helps us to determine how to allocate bandwidth or storage space to information contained in an image. Less important information (that which cannot be seen very well anyway) should receive less bandwidth or storage space.

Finally, you may want to save the image for future use. This can be done using the SaveToFile() function when a button is clicked, demonstrated in the following code:

```
void __fastcall TForm1::Button5Click(TObject *Sender)
{
        Image1->Picture->Bitmap->SaveToFile("test.bmp");
}
```

You could use a TSaveDialog to allow the user to specify the filename instead of test.bmp.

Fast Access to Pixel Value Using ScanLine

Even on a Pentium III 500MHz PC, the previous example for creating a 256×256 image will take a second or two to run. This is because TCanvas->Pixels has a very high overhead. It is better to perform image-processing operations in a 2D array and then copy the result to the image's TBitmap using ScanLine. Listing 25.6 is another version of the last example, using ScanLine instead of Pixels.

LISTING 25.6 Creating a Sinusoidal Image Using ScanLine

```
void __fastcall TForm1::Button3Click(TObject *Sender)
{
    int x, y;
    int Amplitude;
    float Period;
    BYTE ImageData[256][256], *LinePtr;

    Image1->Picture->Bitmap = new Graphics::TBitmap;
    Image1->Picture->Bitmap->PixelFormat = pf24bit;
    Image1->Picture->Bitmap->Width = 256;
    Image1->Picture->Bitmap->Height = 256;
    for (y=0; y<=255; y++)
        for (x=0; x<=255; x++)
        {
            Amplitude = 64*(255-y)/255;
            Period = 100*sqrt(1/(1+(exp(0.013*x)*exp(0.027*x)/400)));
            ImageData[x][y] = Amplitude*sin(2*M_PI/Period*x)+128;
        }
    // Copy the image data to bitmap
    for (y=0; y<=255; y++)
    {
        LinePtr = (BYTE *) Image1->Picture->Bitmap->ScanLine[y];
        for (x=0; x<=255; x++)
        {
            LinePtr[x*3]   = ImageData[x][y];       // Red
            LinePtr[x*3+1] = ImageData[x][y];       // Green
            LinePtr[x*3+2] = ImageData[x][y];       // Blue
        }
    }
    Image1->Refresh();
}
```

A 2D byte array `ImageData` is used to store the image data calculated. After the whole image is computed, the image data is copied to the bitmap line-by-line. `LinePtr` is used to store the pointer to the first pixel of a line, returned by the property `ScanLine` of `TCanvas`. Each pixel value has to be copied three times for the three color components. Using this version, the image appears almost instantaneously when executed.

Point Operations: Thresholding and Color/Grayscale Inversion

Point operations are processes that alter the gray levels of an image on a pixel-by-pixel basis. Point operations can be dependent on pixel position or pixel value. In the latter case, it is sometimes called *grayscale transformation*. The use of position-dependent transformation is usually for correction of camera defects or uneven illumination. Grayscale transformation is normally used to enhance low-quality images. A sample image to be used to demonstrate point operations, `splash.bmp` on the CD-ROM, is shown in Figure 25.5.

FIGURE 25.5
The original image for point operations.

Thresholding is the simplest form of grayscale transformation. A pixel value is converted according to the equation in Figure 25.6. The grayscale value of the pixel is set to 0 (zero—black) if its original value is less than a given threshold (value), and set to 255 (white) if the original value is greater than or equal to the threshold. This simply turns the grayscale image to black-and-white (no shades of gray).

$$
\begin{cases}
=0 & <threshold \\
=255 & \geq threshold
\end{cases}
$$

FIGURE 25.6
Image thresholding.

The threshold can be a fixed value or dynamically determined by some other means. A typical example is to convert a grayscale image to a black-and-white image, which is called *binarization*.

In Listing 25.7, each pixel value is compared with the threshold of 128. If it is higher than the threshold, the pixel is converted to white; otherwise it is converted to black. The result of applying thresholding to Figure 25.5 is shown in Figure 25.7.

LISTING 25.7   Image Thresholding

```
void __fastcall TForm1::Button11Click(TObject *Sender)
{
    int x, y;
    BYTE* LinePtr;

    // image thresholding
    for (y=0; y<=255; y++)
    {
        LinePtr=(BYTE*)Image1->Picture->Bitmap->ScanLine[y];
        for (x=0; x<=255; x++)
            if (LinePtr[x] > 128)
                LinePtr[x] = 255;
            else
                LinePtr[x] = 0;
    }
    Image1->Refresh ();
}
```

FIGURE 25.7
A result of applying thresholding.

Determining the threshold can be a difficult task, often involving prior knowledge about the image. Alternatively, the threshold can be calculated from image statistics such as average and standard deviation, but the implementation is beyond the scope of this book.

25

MULTIMEDIA
TECHNIQUES

Another example of point operations is grayscale inversion, with which we can obtain the negative of an image by performing a subtraction operation, as shown in Listing 25.8.

LISTING 25.8   Image Inversion

```
void __fastcall TForm1::Button4Click(TObject *Sender)
{
    int x, y;
    BYTE* LinePtr;

    // image inverting
    for (y=0; y<=255; y++)
    {
        LinePtr=(BYTE*)Image1->Picture->Bitmap->ScanLine[y];
        for (x=0; x<=255; x++)
            LinePtr[x] = 255 - LinePtr[x];
    }
    Image1->Refresh ();
}
```

The result of inverting the original image in Figure 25.5 is shown in Figure 25.8, which looks like the negative of a photograph.

FIGURE 25.8
The result of inverting an image.

Global Operation: Histogram Equalization

Global operation refers to processing based on global image properties. The word *global* means that the properties have to be derived from the whole image. A typical example is histogram equalization. Depending on the lighting, an image captured may not make full use of the dynamic range. In that case, the image will have low contrast. An example is shown in Figure 25.9 (`couple.bmp` from the CD-ROM).

FIGURE 25.9

A low-contrast image.

The histogram of the image in Figure 25.9 is shown in Figure 25.10. A histogram is the plotting of the number of occurrences for each gray level in an image. The gray level from 0 to 255 is displayed horizontally from left to right. The more times a gray level occurs, the higher the line at that position in the histogram. If we examine the histogram of the pixel values of the image, we can see that it is skewed toward the left, which means that most of the pixels are quite dark.

FIGURE 25.10

A histogram of a low-contrast image.

The first step in histogram equalization is to obtain a histogram of the grayscale distribution of the image. In the remainder of this section, we will look at code from the `TForm1::Button10Click()` function in the example application.

In Listing 25.9, `Histogram` is declared as an array of size 256—the number of different gray levels for an 8-bit image. `Histogram` is first initialized to `0` (zero); then, for the pixel value of each pixel in the image, the corresponding *bin* (counter for each gray value) of the histogram is incremented.

LISTING 25.9 Computation of a Pixel Value Histogram

```
// initialize the histogram
for (i=0; i<=255; i++)
    Histogram[i] = 0;
// Construct the histogram
for (y=0; y<=255; y++)
    for (x=0; x<=255; x++)
        Histogram[ImageData[x][y]]++;
```

The equations to calculate the new position of a pixel during zoom-in are shown in Figure 25.15.

$$x' = a(x-x_0) + x_0$$
$$y' = a(y-y_0) + y_0$$

FIGURE 25.15

Forward calculation of pixel position.

Where (x',y') is the new position for the pixel (x,y), a is the zooming factor, and (x_0,y_0) is the zooming center. However, because the calculated new positions generally do not fall into an integer position, it is normal practice to apply the previous equations in reverse. For each pixel in the new output image, the original position of the pixel is calculated using the equation in Figure 25.16.

$$x = \frac{x' + (a-1)\, x_0}{a}$$
$$y = \frac{y' + (a-1)\, y_0}{a}$$

FIGURE 25.16

Backward calculation of pixel position.

From Figure 25.17, it is obvious that the calculated position will generally land on a non-integer position, but this time the neighboring pixels can be used to obtain the pixel value.

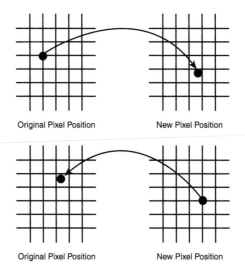

Original Pixel Position   New Pixel Position

Original Pixel Position   New Pixel Position

FIGURE 25.17

Forward and backward calculation of pixel position.

The simplest method is to take the nearest neighbor's pixel value. This is demonstrated in Listing 25.12, and the complete function is available in the `TForm1::Button6Click()` function in the example application.

LISTING 25.12   Image Zooming Using the Nearest Neighbor Method

```
// Calculate the output image
for (y=0; y<=255; y++)
    for (x=0; x<=255; x++)
    {
        // nearest neighbour
        i = INT((x+(zoom-1)*x0) / zoom ); // x0 = 127, y0 = 127
        j = INT((y+(zoom-1)*y0) / zoom ); // zoom = 4
        Output[x][y] = ImageData[i][j];   // store the calculated value
    }
```

It should be noted that the newly calculated image should be stored in another array. It is a common mistake to write the calculated value in the original image array, producing unpredictable results.

It can be seen from the resultant image that the "blocky" effect is quite visible. It can be improved by using bilinear interpolation instead of the nearest neighbor approach. Bilinear interpolation makes use of the four nearest neighbors of the calculated position to obtain a weighted average using the formula, which can be visualized in Figure 25.18.

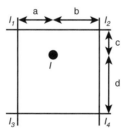

FIGURE 25.18

Bilinear interpolation of pixel value.

The code implementing bilinear interpolation is shown in Listing 25.13. This is performed in the `Bilinear()` function. Only the section of the `TForm1::Button7Click()` function that calls `Bilinear()` is shown here.

LISTING 25.13   Image Zooming Using the Bilinear Interpolation Method

```
int Bilinear(BYTE Image[][256], float i, float j)
{
    int x1, y1, x2, y2;
    float Gray;

    x1 = (int)floor(i);
    x2 = x1+1;
    y1 = (int)floor(j);
    y2 = y1+1;
    Gray = (y2-j)*(x2-i)*Image[x1][y1] + (y2-j)*(i-x1)*Image[x2][y1]
            + (j-y1)*(x2-i)*Image[x1][y2] + (j-y1)*(i-x1)*Image[x2][y2];
    return INT(Gray);
}

void __fastcall TForm1::Button7Click(TObject *Sender)
{
    // Initialization code not shown.

    // Calculate the output image
    for (y=0; y<=255; y++)
        for (x=0; x<=255; x++)
        {
            i = (x+(zoom-1)*x0) / zoom; // calculate original position
            j = (y+(zoom-1)*y0) / zoom;
            Output[x][y] = Bilinear(ImageData, i, j);
        }

    // Copy back to the image not shown.
}
```

From the resultant images, shown in Figure 25.19 and Figure 25.20, you can see that the image obtained with bilinear interpolation is smoother and more appealing. To get even better results, higher orders of interpolation can be used that are more mathematically complicated, such as cubic.

FIGURE 25.19

The image magnified four times using the nearest neighbor method.

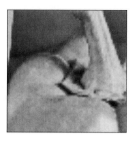

FIGURE 25.20
The image magnified four times using the bilinear interpolation method.

Spatial Operation: Smoothing and Edge Detection

Spatial operation refers to the processing techniques that work on groups of pixels rather than on a single pixel. A wide range of techniques falls into this category, and the purposes of applying spatial operations can be varied, as will be seen.

In spatial operations, a mask is used to define the region of interest and the contribution of each pixel. Based on the mask, a newly calculated value is then assigned to the pixel in the center. For practical reasons, the mask is usually square, with sizes such as 3×3 and 5×5. However, sometimes the size of a mask can be as large as 17×17, as in the case of a Mexican-Hat function, which has some properties similar to those of the human eye's retina and is therefore often used in computer vision systems.

The simplest spatial filtering is a smoothing filter that has a 3×3 mask, as follows:

```
1/9  1/9  1/9
1/9  1/9  1/9
1/9  1/9  1/9
```

Effectively, a pixel value is replaced by the averaged pixel value of a 3×3 neighborhood. Technically, it is called a low-pass filter because it has the effect of attenuating high-frequency components of an image. This technique is shown in the Lowpass() function and called from the TForm1::Button8Click() function in Listing 25.14.

LISTING 25.14   Image Smoothing with a 3×3 Mask

```
int Lowpass(BYTE Image[][256], int x, int y)
{
    int Mask[3][3] = {{1, 1, 1,}, {1, 1, 1}, {1, 1, 1}};
    int i, j, sum=0;

    for (j=-1; j<=1; j++)
```

LISTING 25.14 Continued

```
        for (i=-1; i<=1; i++)
            sum += Image[x+i][y+j]*Mask[i+1][j+1];
    return INT(sum/9.0);
}

void __fastcall TForm1::Button8Click(TObject *Sender)
{
    // Initialization code not shown.

    // Calculate the low-pass image
    for (y=1; y<=254; y++)
        for (x=1; x<=254; x++)
            Output[x][y] = Lowpass(ImageData, x, y);

    // Copy back to the image not shown.
}
```

The effect of smoothing is quite evident in the image. The result after applying the mask to the image in Figure 25.14 is shown in Figure 20.21. If a larger mask is used, the effect of smoothing is enhanced.

FIGURE 25.21
Low-pass filtered image with a 3×3 mask.

For high-pass filtering, a commonly used mask is

```
-1/9 -1/9 -1/9
-1/9  1   -1/9
-1/9 -1/9 -1/9
```

The negative values in the mask simply say that if a pixel has a value higher than its neighbors, it should be enhanced. Edge detection is a form of high-pass filtering because edges in an image are associated with high spatial frequencies, that is, areas with fast-changing content. Edge detection is an important pre-processing technique often employed in a computer vision system because it helps to define the boundary of an object—the first step to object recognition. The result of applying the previous mask to Figure 25.14 is shown in Figure 25.22.

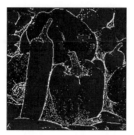

FIGURE 25.22
High-pass filtered image with a 3×3 mask.

There is an implementation complication that needs attention. When applying the mask to pixels at the edges of an image, the mask may extend beyond the image. To avoid this problem, the simplest solution is to leave the pixels on the edges initially and then copy the next available pixel value to it after processing. Interpolation can be employed for a better result.

Audio Files, Video Files, and CD Music

The Windows multimedia system provides a standard means by which multimedia devices can be controlled. This system simply delegates the communication between an application and a particular device driver. The Media Control Interface (MCI) adds even more flexibility by providing a common means by which applications can communicate with all supported audio and video devices. From the developer's point of view, the specifics of the device are irrelevant; oftentimes, even the type of device is of no concern.

In this section, we'll first discuss the use of the MCI for creating general-purpose audio and video applications. As you will soon discover, the MCI is perhaps the easiest multimedia interface to work with. Next, we'll examine the use of the waveform-audio interface and how it can be used for increased audio-based functionality. Finally, we'll tackle the issue of audio streams, and examine how to read and write waveform-audio files.

The Media Control Interface

In the same way that the GDI offers a generic means by which you can communicate with graphics-based devices, the Windows MCI allows you to program multimedia devices in a device-independent manner. Before the advent of the MCI, developers were required to write code that targeted specific devices. Often this process involved using procedures specific to a particular device driver. It's not hard to imagine the hassle that such a scheme would present, where the consumer base would be limited to a specific range of device types. For example, many of the early DOS-based games required that the sound card be compatible with the Sound Blaster standard.

Using Command Messages and Strings

Applications communicate with the MCI via a set of predefined messages and string constants. In much the same way that window messages are used with the user interface services, the MCI provides a set of command messages and strings that can be used to manipulate MCI devices. Many of these messages offer corresponding command strings that can be used for a more intuitive (and readable) approach. Here, we will limit our discussion to the MCI command messages; the message constants are defined in the mmsystem.h header file available with C++Builder.

Similar to the SendMessage() API function that is used to send messages to windows, the mciSendCommand() function is used to send command messages to MCI devices.

```
MCIERROR mciSendCommand(
    MCIDEVICEID IDDevice,
    UINT uMsg,
    DWORD fdwCommand,
    DWORD dwParam
    );
```

When using the mciSendCommand() function, oftentimes a device identifier is specified as the IDDevice parameter. This serves the same purpose as the hWnd parameter of the SendMessage() function. Namely, the function needs to know to which MCI device to send the message. A device identifier is returned when a device is opened via the MCI_OPEN message.

Decoding Error Constants

The mciSendCommand() function returns a 32-bit value indicating the success or failure of the operation. If successful, this value is set to MMSYSERR_NOERROR, defined in the mmsystem.h header file as identically zero. If an error does occur, the return value is set to one of the predefined error constants. Because these values have little meaning to the user (or the developer), the MCI presents the mciGetErrorString() function, which can be used to translate these error codes into meaningful messages (compared with FormatMessage). Listing 25.15 demonstrates the use of this function.

LISTING 25.15   Decoding MCI-Related Errors Via the mciGetErrorString() Function

```
bool mciCheck(DWORD AErrorNum, bool AReport = true)
{
    if (AErrorNum == MMSYSERR_NOERROR) return true;
    if (AReport)
    {
```

LISTING 25.15   Continued

```
        char buffer[MAXERRORLENGTH];
        mciGetErrorString(AErrorNum, buffer, MAXERRORLENGTH);
        MessageBox(NULL, buffer,  "MCI Error", MB_OK);
    }
    return false;
}
```

Working with MCI Devices

The first step to working with an MCI device is to open or initialize the device; as previously stated, you accomplish this task via the MCI_OPEN message. Because you are interested in retrieving a device identifier, you send this message with a NULL IDDevice parameter. If successful, the identifier of the opened device is returned in the wDeviceID data member of corresponding MCI_OPEN_PARMS structure; this is the MCI_OPEN_PARMS that was specified as the dwParam argument.

```
typedef struct tagMCI_OPEN_PARMS {
    DWORD        dwCallback;
    MCIDEVICEID wDeviceID;
    LPCSTR       lpstrDeviceType;
    LPCSTR       lpstrElementName;
    LPCSTR       lpstrAlias;
} MCI_OPEN_PARMS, *PMCI_OPEN_PARMS, *LPMCI_OPEN_PARMS;
```

Typically, the lpstrDeviceType data member is set to NULL, and the lpstrElementName data member is assigned a filename. This is the most robust approach because it allows the MCI to perform automatic type selection. That is, the appropriate device will be selected according to the type of file specified. In cases where the lpstrDeviceType data member is explicitly specified, it is oftentimes assigned a string value corresponding to the type of device requested. For example, to open the CD audio device, you can specify it as cdaudio. Other string identifiers include avivideo, dat, digitalvideo, mmmovie, other, overlay, scanner, sequencer, vcr, videodisc, and waveaudio. However, it should be stressed that unless support for a specific device is intended, it is best to let the MCI perform automatic type selection. This is especially important when a new technology is presented that has no predefined type identifier (for example, the MP3 format). Listing 25.16 demonstrates the use of the MCI_OPEN message via a simple wrapper function.

LISTING 25.16   Using the MCI_OPEN Command Message

```
bool mciOpen(MCIDEVICEID& ADevID, const char* AFileName,
    const char* ADevType = NULL)
{
    MCI_OPEN_PARMS mop;
```

LISTING 25.16   Continued

```
    memset(&mop, 0, sizeof(MCI_OPEN_PARMS));
    mop.lpstrElementName = const_cast<char*>(AFileName);
    mop.lpstrDeviceType = const_cast<char*>(ADevType);

    DWORD flags = 0;
    if (AFileName) flags = flags | MCI_OPEN_ELEMENT;
    if (ADevType) flags = flags | MCI_OPEN_TYPE;
    if (mciCheck(mciSendCommand(NULL, MCI_OPEN, flags,
                                reinterpret_cast<DWORD>(&mop))))
    {
        ADevID = mop.wDeviceID;
        return true;
    }
    return false;
}
```

Once the MCI device is open and an identifier is retrieved, your next task is to set the time format of the device. This aspect of the MCI is rather specific to the device type, as certain types of devices can support only certain time formats. For example, specifying a track number is valid for CD audio devices, but it is clearly invalid for wave form audio devices.

You can set the time format for a device via the MCI_SET command message. Whenever applicable, it is best to use the MCI_FORMAT_MILLISECONDS format, which is supported by all devices. An example wrapper function that uses the MCI_SET message is provided in Listing 25.17.

LISTING 25.17   Using the MCI_SET Command Message

```
bool mciSetTimeFormat(MCIDEVICEID ADeviceID, DWORD ATimeFormat)
{
    MCI_SET_PARMS msp;
    memset(&msp, 0, sizeof(MCI_SET_PARMS));
    msp.dwTimeFormat = ATimeFormat;

    return mciCheck(mciSendCommand(ADeviceID, MCI_SET,
                    MCI_SET_TIME_FORMAT, reinterpret_cast<DWORD>(&msp)));
}
```

After the time format is set correctly, you're free to work with the device in much the same way as you would its physical counterpart. For example, to play the device, you use the MCI_PLAY message. To rewind or fast-forward the device, you use the MCI_SEEK message. To pause the device, you use the MCI_PAUSE message. Similarly, the MCI_STOP message is used to stop the device, while the MCI_CLOSE message closes the device. For a complete list of messages, refer to http://msdn.microsoft.com/library/psdk/multimed/mci_7vvt.htm. The wrapper functions presented in Listing 25.18 demonstrate the use of these messages. Included on the companion CD-ROM is a sample project that better demonstrates their use. See the Proj_mp3Demo.bpr project in the MP3Demo folder, and specifically the MCIManip.cpp source file.

LISTING 25.18 Use of the MCI_PLAY, MCI_SEEK, MCI_PAUSE, MCI_STOP, and MCI_CLOSE Command Messages

```
bool mciPlay(MCIDEVICEID ADeviceID, DWORD AStart, DWORD AStop)
{
    MCI_PLAY_PARMS mpp;
    memset(&mpp, 0, sizeof(MCI_PLAY_PARMS));
    mpp.dwFrom = AStart;
    mpp.dwTo = AStop;

    DWORD flags = 0;
    if (static_cast<int>(AStart) >= 0 && static_cast<int>(AStop) >= 0)
        flags = MCI_FROM | MCI_TO;

    return mciCheck(mciSendCommand(ADeviceID, MCI_PLAY | flags,
                    NULL, reinterpret_cast<DWORD>(&mpp)));
}

bool mciSeek(MCIDEVICEID ADeviceID, DWORD APos)
{
    MCI_SEEK_PARMS msp;
    memset(&msp, 0, sizeof(MCI_SEEK_PARMS));
    msp.dwTo = APos;

    return mciCheck(mciSendCommand(ADeviceID, MCI_SEEK, MCI_TO,
                    reinterpret_cast<DWORD>(&msp)));
}

bool mciPause(MCIDEVICEID ADeviceID)
{
    return mciCheck(mciSendCommand(ADeviceID, MCI_PAUSE, 0, 0));
}

bool mciStop(MCIDEVICEID ADeviceID)
{
    return mciCheck(mciSendCommand(ADeviceID, MCI_STOP, 0, 0));
}

void mciClose(MCIDEVICEID ADeviceID)
{
    mciCheck(mciSendCommand(ADeviceID, MCI_CLOSE, 0, NULL));
}
```

25

Retrieving the Status of a Device

Often it is necessary to provide feedback to the user about the status of a device. For example, if you want to create a CD player, you'll most likely want to inform the user of the current track, the track length, and the current position within the track. More generally, you need to indicate the operating mode of the device (playing, paused, stopped, and so on) to inform the user as to what functionality is available. This information is retrieved via the MCI_STATUS message, as demonstrated in Listing 25.19.

LISTING 25.19   Use of the MCI_STATUS Command Message

```
bool mciStatus(MCIDEVICEID ADeviceID, DWORD AQueryGroup, DWORD AQueryItem,
    DWORD AQueryTrack, DWORD& AResult)
{
    MCI_STATUS_PARMS msp;
    memset(&msp, 0, sizeof(MCI_STATUS_PARMS));
    msp.dwItem = AQueryItem;
    msp.dwTrack = AQueryTrack;

    if (mciCheck(mciSendCommand(ADeviceID, MCI_STATUS, AQueryGroup,
                reinterpret_cast<DWORD>(&msp))))
    {
        AResult = msp.dwReturn;
        return true;
    }
    return false;
}
```

The project Proj_CDDemo.bpr in the CDDemo folder on the CD-ROM that accompanies this book is a sample CD player that demonstrates all of the techniques shown in these sections.

There is a wide variety of constants that can be specified as the AQueryGroup parameter, each with a corresponding set of constants that can be assigned to the AQueryItem and AQueryTrack arguments. For example, to retrieve the total number of tracks present on the media of a CD audio device, you specify MCI_STATUS_ITEM as the AQueryGroup parameter and MCI_STATUS_NUMBER_OF_TRACKS as the AQueryItem parameter. To determine the current track number, you set the AQueryGroup parameter to MCI_STATUS_ITEM and the AQueryItem parameter to MCI_STATUS_CURRENT_TRACK. Also, note that when retrieving length, position, track, or frame information, the format of the returned data depends on the device's current time format. For a complete listing of status flags, refer to http://msdn.microsoft.com/library/psdk/multimed/mci_7vvt.htm.

Polling a Device and MCI Notifications

While you now have a means of retrieving information about a device, you still need to know when to perform this interrogation. Unfortunately, the MCI presents a limited notification scheme in which only two notification messages, MM_MCINOTIFY and MM_MCISIGNAL, are defined. The latter is useful only for digital video devices. While the former message sounds promising, it is posted only after a command operation has completed. For example, if you use the mciPlay() wrapper function (of Listing 25.18) to begin the playback of a waveform audio file, the MM_MCINOTIFY message will be posted only when the file has finished playing or playback has otherwise been manipulated. Specifically, this message is posted to the window whose handle is specified via the dwCallback data member of the structure specified as the dwParam argument of the mciSendCommand() function. As such, you need to modify the wrapper functions to accept an hWnd parameter. The sample project Proj_mp3Demo.bpr, in the MP3Demo folder on the CD-ROM that accompanies this book, demonstrates handling the MM_MCINOTIFY message.

In most cases, receipt of the MM_MCINOTIFY message is a sufficient indication of when to determine the status of the operating mode. For example, you can provide a handler for the MM_MCINOTIFY message in which you update the enabled state of your play, pause, and stop buttons. Yet, when retrieving information about a frequently updated attribute such as current position, the MM_MCINOTIFY message is not suitable. Instead, you need to poll the device at a regular interval. This task is typically performed in response to timer messages. In some cases, it is sufficient to use system timer messages; in others it is recommended to use the multimedia timer services. See http://msdn.microsoft.com/library/psdk/multimed/mmtime_4msz.htm for more information.

Concluding Remarks About the MCI

Just what types of files does the MCI support? This depends on the audio/video codecs that are installed on the target platform. Many of these codecs are installed when a newer version of Microsoft Media Player is installed. A good rule of thumb is that if Media Player can support a specific file format, so can the MCI. In fact, Media Player itself relies heavily on the MCI.

Included on the companion CD-ROM are two MCI-related demonstration projects: Proj_MP3Demo.bpr in the MP3Demo folder and Proj_VideoDemo.bpr in the VideoDemo folder. The former is a simple MP3 audio player, which can actually support waveform audio (RIFF-based) files as well. The latter demonstrates the use of the MCI for displaying video files (AVI, MPEG). Again, the actual supported file formats of both of these demonstration projects are limited by the currently installed codecs. Refer to the comments included at the beginning of the source code for more information.

While the MCI is perhaps the easiest of all multimedia interfaces to work with, it is quite limited in the functionality that it presents. For example, when playing a media file through the

MCI, you are never given access to the file's associated data stream. This is especially detrimental if your application is to perform any type of signal processing or format conversion. In this case, you need to go beyond the MCI and work with other multimedia interfaces. For extended audio functionality, this is typically accomplished via the Waveform-Audio Interface.

The Waveform Audio Interface

The Windows multimedia service provides the Waveform Audio Interface (waveform API) to allow applications to control the input and output of waveform audio. This interface gives an application direct access to the sound buffer, so in cases where other audio formats must be supported, a simple conversion is all that is necessary. For example, many of the commercial applications that provide support for the MP3 format do so through the waveform API. Moreover, in situations where signal processing is due, direct access to the sound buffer is crucial. For example, if you're interested in creating an audio player with graphic equalization capabilities, you'll need to process the sound buffer before sending it to the output device.

Recall that the `lpstrElementName` data member of the `MCI_OPEN_PARMS` structure is typically assigned the name of a media file that is to be played. In this case, the MCI automatically handles the task of opening and loading the file. However, the waveform API does not present such a structure, and thus you're forced to use other measures for file I/O. For example, one potential solution is to open the file manually using the `TFileStream` VCL class. In this case, you'd need to be sufficiently versed with the waveform audio file format specification (RIFF). An alternative approach is to use the multimedia file I/O services, which is indeed completely valid for many situations. However, because these services are so generalized, working with waveform audio files proves nearly as difficult as the manual solution. Fortunately, Windows provides the AVIFile services, a set of functions and macros specifically designed for use with waveform audio and AVI files. As such, let's now digress from the waveform API and examine the AVIFile services.

Opening and Closing Waveform Audio Files

A waveform audio file is a type of RIFF (Resource Interchange File Format) file that contains time-based audio content. In fact, that's really all you need to know. As mentioned, you do not need to concern yourself with the specifics of the file format itself; instead, you can use the `AVIFile` functions and macros. These functions and macros, presented in the `VFW.H` header file and the `AVIFIL32.DLL` dynamic link library, provide a convenient means of working with waveform audio files and streams.

Before you can use the AVIFile services, you need to initialize the `AVIFIL32.DLL` library via the `AVIFileInit()` function. Similarly, when you're finished with the library, you release it via the `AVIFileExit()` function.

The AVIFile functions rely on OLE for handling file and stream-based operations, so you need to provide a means of error checking. For those functions that return the standard STDAPI type, you can use the SUCCEEDED macro as in the following wrapper function:

```
bool wavCheck(HRESULT AErrorCode)
{
    return SUCCEEDED(AerrorCode);
}
```

Let's begin our examination of the AVIFile services by performing the simplest of tasks, that of opening a waveform audio file. This is accomplished via the AVIFileOpen() function:

```
bool wavOpenFile(PAVIFILE& ApFile, const char* AFileName,
    unsigned int AMode)
{
    return wavCheck(AVIFileOpen(&ApFile, AFileName, AMode, NULL));
}
```

The AMode parameter specifies the access mode and can be assigned the same access-related constants that are used with the OpenFile() API function (OF_READ, for example). The ApFile argument receives a pointer to an AVIFILE structure that simply holds the address of the file-handler interface. Because this filehandler interface is released only when its reference count drops to zero, it is important that you decrement its reference count when the interface is no longer needed. This is accomplished via the AVIFileClose() function:

```
void wavCloseFile(PAVIFILE& ApFile)
{
    AVIFileClose(ApFile);
    ApFile = NULL;
}
```

Working with Audio Streams

While opening and closing a waveform audio file is rather trivial, you'll need to work with the stream handler interface to obtain any useful information. This task proves slightly more complicated. Recall that the PAVIFILE type holds a pointer to the filehandler interface. Similarly, a pointer to the stream handler interface is stored in a variable of type PAVISTREAM. You can retrieve a pointer to this latter interface via the AVIFileGetStream() function. You release the interface via the AVIStreamRelease() function. The wrapper functions presented in Listing 25.20 demonstrate the use of these AVIFile functions.

LISTING 25.20   Using the `AVIFileGetStream` and `AVIStreamRelease` Functions

```
bool wavOpenStream(PAVISTREAM& ApStream, PAVIFILE ApFile)
{
    return wavCheck(AVIFileGetStream(ApFile, &ApStream, streamtypeAUDIO, 0));
}

void wavCloseStream(PAVISTREAM& ApStream)
{
    AVIStreamRelease(ApStream);
    ApStream = NULL;
}
```

Working with the stream handler interface is not unlike working with the `TMemoryStream` class or one of the `basic_streambuf` descendant classes. However, you have at your disposal several functions specifically designed for use with waveform audio and AVI files. For example, the `AVIStreamInfo()` function can be used to retrieve information about the content of the stream. This function fills an `AVISTREAMINFO` structure with information specific to its media content:

```
bool wavGetStreamInfo(PAVISTREAM ApStream, AVISTREAMINFO& AStreamInfo)
{
    return wavCheck(AVIStreamInfo(ApStream, &AStreamInfo,
                    sizeof(AVISTREAMINFO)));
}
```

When working with an audio stream, you'll need to know the format of the data itself. For waveform audio files, this information is conveyed via the data members of a `WAVEFORMATEX` structure. This structure is simply used to describe how audio samples are stored in the corresponding waveform audio data. As such, a particularly useful function when working with waveform audio streams is the `AVIStreamReadFormat()` function. It is the role of this function to fill the data members of the `WAVEFORMATEX` structure based on information in the stream. The `AVIStreamFormatSize()` macro complements this function by reporting the size of the contained structure. Listing 25.21 demonstrates the use of the `AVIStreamReadFormat()` function and the `AVIStreamFormatSize()` macro.

LISTING 25.21   Using the `AVIStreamReadFormat()` Function and the `AVIStreamFormatSize()` Macro

```
long wavCalcFormatStructSize(PAVISTREAM ApStream)
{
    long required_bytes = 0;
    AVIStreamFormatSize(ApStream, 0, &required_bytes);
    return required_bytes;
}
```

LISTING 25.21   Continued

```
bool wavReadFormatStruct(PAVISTREAM ApStream, WAVEFORMATEX& ApFormatStruct)
{
    memset(&ApFormatStruct, 0, sizeof(WAVEFORMATEX));
    long size = wavCalcFormatStructSize(ApStream);
    return wavCheck(
        AVIStreamReadFormat(ApStream, 0, &ApFormatStruct,  &size)
        );
}
```

Like the `TMemoryStream::Read()` or the `basic_ifstream::read()` member function, the
AVIFile services provide a means by which an application can read media content from a
stream. This is the audio data buffer that you're interested in and, as you will see later, access
to this buffer is essential to producing audio output via the waveform API. The
`AVIStreamRead()` function is used to read media content from a stream into an application-
defined buffer. Similarly, the `AVIStreamWrite()` function is used to write data from a buffer
into a stream. Listing 25.22 demonstrates the use of these functions.

LISTING 25.22   Reading and Writing Audio Data to and from a Stream

```
long wavCalcBufferSize(PAVISTREAM ApStream)
{
    long required_bytes = 0;

    AVISTREAMINFO StreamInfo;
    if (wavGetStreamInfo(ApStream, StreamInfo))
    {
        required_bytes = StreamInfo.dwLength * StreamInfo.dwScale;
    }
    return required_bytes;
}

long wavReadStream(PAVISTREAM ApStream, long AStart, long ANumBytes,
    char* ABuffer)
{
    long bytes_read = 0;

    AVISTREAMINFO StreamInfo;
    if (wavGetStreamInfo(ApStream,  StreamInfo))
    {
        long num_samples = static_cast<float>(ANumBytes) /
                        static_cast<float>(StreamInfo.dwScale);
        AVIStreamRead(ApStream, AStart, num_samples, ABuffer, ANumBytes,
                    &bytes_read, NULL);
```

25

MULTIMEDIA
TECHNIQUES

LISTING 25.22   Continued

```
    }
    return bytes_read;
}


long wavWriteStream(PAVISTREAM ApStream, long AStart, long ANumBytes,
    char* ABuffer)
{
    long bytes_written = 0;

    AVISTREAMINFO StreamInfo;
    if (wavGetStreamInfo(ApStream, StreamInfo))
    {
        long num_samples = static_cast<float>(ANumBytes) /
                           static_cast<float>(StreamInfo.dwScale);
        AVIStreamWrite(ApStream, AStart, num_samples, ABuffer, ANumBytes,
                       AVIIF_KEYFRAME, NULL, &bytes_written);
    }
    return bytes_written;
}
```

The `wavCalculateBufferSize()` wrapper function is comparable to the `TMemoryStream::Size` property. It uses the `wavGetStreamInfo()` wrapper function to calculate the size of the audio buffer. Also note that, as the stream handler interface is intrinsically linked to the filehandler interface, any data that you write to the stream will automatically be written to the file once the stream is closed. As such, if you're interested in manipulating only the content of the stream, you'll need to create a secondary stream that is not associated with a particular file. For more information on this task, see `http://msdn.microsoft.com/library/psdk/multimed/avifile_4alv.htm`.

Now that you have a framework by which you can manipulate waveform audio files, let's return to our examination of the waveform API and investigate the means by which you can output waveform audio sound. As with the MCI, the functions and structures of the waveform API are declared and defined, respectively, in the `MMSYSTEM.H` header file.

Opening and Closing Waveform Audio Devices

The waveform API provides the `waveOutOpen()` function for use in opening a waveform audio output device. This function requires an initialized `WAVEFORMATEX` structure and, if successful, assigns an `HWAVEOUT` variable the handle to the open device. Similarly, the `waveOutClose()` function is used to close the waveform audio device. The wrapper functions of Listing 25.23 demonstrate the use of these functions.

LISTING 25.23 Opening and Closing a Waveform Audio Device

```
bool wavPlayOpen(HWAVEOUT& AHWavOut, long ACallback, DWORD ANotifyInstance,
    DWORD AOpenFlags, WAVEFORMATEX& AFormatStruct)
{
    return wavCheck(
        waveOutOpen(&AHWavOut, WAVE_MAPPER, &AFormatStruct, ACallback,
                    ANotifyInstance, AOpenFlags)
        );
}

void wavPlayClose(HWAVEOUT AHWavOut)
{
    waveOutReset(AHWavOut);
    waveOutClose (AHWavOut);
}
```

The `ACallback`, `ANotifyInstance`, and `AOpenFlags` parameters can be used to specify a means of notification; we will return to this issue shortly. For the `AFormatStruct` parameter, you can use the `wavReadFormatStruct()` wrapper function of Listing 25.21.

Once an output device is open, you use the `waveOutWrite()` function to initiate playback. Specifically, you pass this function a pointer to a buffer of audio data that the function will send to the opened output device driver. However, the audio output device must know the size of the audio block that it's going to receive. For this reason, the `waveOutWrite()` function cannot accept a plain data buffer; instead, the function requires the address of a `WAVEHDR` structure.

Among other things, a `WAVEHDR` structure stores a pointer to the audio data buffer in its `lpData` data member and the length of this buffer in its `dwBufferLength` data member. To ensure compatibility with the output device, you must allow the driver to prepare your `WAVEHDR` structure before you can pass it to the `waveOutWrite()` function. This task is accomplished via the `waveOutPrepareHeader()` function. Similarly, after the device driver has finished playing the audio block, you must unprepare the header using the `waveOutUnprepareHeader()` function before you can free the associated memory. Listing 25.24 demonstrates the use of these functions.

LISTING 25.24 Initiating an Ending Waveform Audio Playback

```
bool wavPlayBegin(HWAVEOUT AHWavOut, WAVEHDR& AWavHdr)
{
    if (wavCheck(waveOutPrepareHeader(AHWavOut, &AWavHdr, sizeof(WAVEHDR))))
    {
        return wavCheck(
```

Listing 25.24   Continued

```
            waveOutWrite(AHWavOut, &AWavHdr, sizeof(WAVEHDR))
            );
    }
    return false;
}

void wavPlayEnd(HWAVEOUT AHWavOut, WAVEHDR& AWavHdr)
{
    waveOutReset(AHWavOut);
    waveOutUnprepareHeader(AHWavOut, &AWavHdr, sizeof(WAVEHDR));
}
```

Let's solidify these concepts with a simple example that demonstrates how to play a waveform audio file. Recall that, because the waveform API presents no native means of loading the audio data from disk, we will first need to use our AVIFile wrapper functions. Once we read the audio data block from the stream into our buffer, we can then use our waveform API wrapper functions to control playback. The code for this example is presented in Listing 25.25. An example project, Proj_DSPDemo.bpr, can be found on the companion CD-ROM in the DSPDemo folder.

Listing 25.25   Playing a Quantized Waveform Audio File

```
const long MAX_BLOCK_SIZE = 6000 * 1024;

if (!OpenDialog1->Execute()) return;
const char* filename = OpenDialog1->FileName.c_str();

PAVIFILE pFile = NULL;
if (wavOpenFile(pFile, filename, OF_READ))
{
    PAVISTREAM pStream = NULL;
    if (wavOpenStream(pStream, pFile))
    {
        long block_size = wavCalcBufferSize(pStream);
        if (block_size < MAX_BLOCK_SIZE)
        {
            char* buffer = new char[block_size];
            if (wavReadStream(pStream, 0, block_size, buffer)
                == block_size)
            {
                QuantizeBuffer(buffer, block_size);

                WAVEFORMATEX FormatStruct;
```

LISTING 25.25   Continued

```
            if (wavReadFormatStruct(pStream, FormatStruct))
            {
                HWAVEOUT HWavOut;
                if (wavPlayOpen(HWavOut, NULL, NULL, NULL,
                                FormatStruct))
                {
                    WAVEHDR WavHdr;
                    memset(&WavHdr, 0, sizeof(WAVEHDR));
                    WavHdr.lpData = buffer;
                    WavHdr.dwBufferLength = block_size;

                    if (wavPlayBegin(HWavOut, WavHdr))
                    {
                        ShowMessage("Playing: " +
                                    AnsiString(filename));
                        wavPlayEnd(HWavOut, WavHdr);
                    }
                    wavPlayClose(HWavOut);
                }
            }
        }
        delete [] buffer;
    }
    wavCloseStream(pStream);
    }
    wavCloseFile(pFile);
}

void QuantizeBuffer(char* ABuffer, long ABufferLength)
{
    short int min_val = 0, max_val = 0;
    for (int index = 0; index < ABufferLength; ++index)
    {
        if (ABuffer[index] < min_val) min_val = ABuffer[index];
        if (ABuffer[index] > max_val) max_val = ABuffer[index];
    }

    for (int index = 0; index < ABufferLength; ++index)
    {
        if (ABuffer[index] < 0) ABuffer[index] = min_val;
        if (ABuffer[index] > 0) ABuffer[index] = max_val;
    }
}
```

25

Notice in Listing 25.25 that we placed a limit on the size of the audio data block. Indeed, we would not want to load too large of a file such that we deplete system resources. When working with large audio data blocks, small segments of the media content are read from the stream then sent to the driver in an iterative fashion. That is, once the driver has finished with the current buffer, we continually supply it with new information. However, for such a method to be successful, we will need a means by which we can determine when the driver has finished with the buffer. That is, the `waveOutWrite()` function returns immediately, so we have no way of knowing when the driver has completed playback. This is where the `ACallback` parameter of our `wavPlayOpen()` wrapper function comes in. Specifically, we can assign this argument the handle of a window or an event, an identifier of a thread, or even the address of a specific callback function. In this way, we can establish a crucial means of notification. See `http://msdn.microsoft.com/library/psdk/multimed/mmmsg_6g2t.htm` for information on the `MM_MON_DONE` message.

Concluding Remarks on the Waveform Audio Interface

We have covered a wide variety of multimedia functions, structures, messages, and macros, but there are still more to explore. For example, the Windows multimedia system also provides specific interfaces for controlling MIDI and AVI playback. Moreover, each of these interfaces, including the Waveform Audio Interface and the MCI, provides services for sound input as well as output. There is even an interface for working with audio mixer devices. See `http://msdn.microsoft.com/library/psdk/multimed/mixer_10xf.htm` for more information. This latter area is particularly opportune when the volume of specific audio channels needs to be controlled.

Summary

In this chapter, we have examined several methods by which an application can provide multimedia support. First, we examined the fundamentals of the Windows GDI and how many aspects of this interface are abstracted by the VCL. We looked at the `TCanvas`, `TBrush`, `TPen`, and `TFont` classes and their use in rendering graphical output. We also examined several image file formats and discussed the use of the `TBitmap` and `TJPEGImage` classes.

We then looked at image processing, which is a very broad subject in itself. We provided an overview of several fundamental image-processing techniques and how to employ them using C++Builder. With this material as an introduction, you should be able to expand on it and develop your own image-processing applications.

Finally, we investigated how audio and video files are supported through use of the MCI. We examined the various MCI-related command messages and discussed their generic use in controlling multimedia devices. We also looked at the AVIFile services and Waveform Audio Interface and how these interfaces are used to manage and effect playback of waveform audio files.

Advanced Graphics with DirectX and OpenGL

William Woodbury

IN THIS CHAPTER

One of the problems programmers (especially game programmers) had when they moved from DOS to graphical operating systems (such as Microsoft Windows) was the performance they seemed to lose in their real-time applications. This occurred as a result of the overhead associated with multitasking and the high-resolution interactive graphics used in the user interface. This performance loss has been tackled with the introduction of high-speed multimedia APIs such as OpenGL and Microsoft's DirectX APIs.

OpenGL is a high-level interface into graphics hardware, with software emulation of all its functions (for computers without the hardware). DirectX is a set of APIs that allows programmers to access the lower-level hardware on a computer running a Microsoft Windows operating system. This chapter covers the use of OpenGL and the DirectDraw and DirectSound DirectX APIs with Borland C++Builder 5 at an introductory level.

High-performance graphics are a must for a lot of modern software. It isn't as hard as it looks. This chapter covers all the main requirements for displaying quality 3D graphics and animation.

Introduction to OpenGL

This section gives a general introduction to what OpenGL is and what it can be used for. OpenGL is a 3D graphics API. This means it is a library of routines that simplify the creation of complex real-time 3D graphics.

OpenGL in itself is just a specification for the routines. The actual implementation may vary. The main ones are the Silicon Graphics, Inc. (SGI) and Microsoft (MS) implementations. The actual specification was created and is maintained by the OpenGL Architecture Review Board (ARB), an independent body formed solely for that purpose.

OpenGL is generally platform independent. If the programmer sticks to the ARB-approved functions, the code can be ported to any platform that has an OpenGL implementation.

OpenGL implementations will use graphics hardware if it is present. This is extremely useful, because most modern home and office computers have some form of hardware 3D acceleration. Even if the hardware is not present, the software implementations are very highly optimized, hence very fast.

OpenGL is becoming the world standard in real-time graphics. Every self-respecting 3D modeling package uses OpenGL for its real-time display. Most new games also rely on the standard.

OpenGL code is aesthetically pleasing. The function and variable names use naming standards that are easy to understand and follow.

Advanced Graphics with DirectX and OpenGL

CHAPTER 26

1097

26
ADVANCED
GRAPHICS WITH
DIRECTX AND
OPENGL

OpenGL Versus Direct3D

Direct3D is Microsoft's answer to OpenGL. It is a 3D graphics API that can interface into hardware. If you try using Direct3D, bear in mind that it isn't portable, and there is only one implementation, the Microsoft one.

> **NOTE**
>
> Do NOT mix OpenGL with either DirectDraw or Direct3D. This is because some OpenGL drivers use these APIs to simulate OpenGL calls on computers without OpenGL cards. If DirectDraw or Direct3D is used in the same program, they may clash with OpenGL, producing unpredictable results.

The OpenGL Command Structure

OpenGL follows a common command structure for the construction of any primitive (object) in a 3D scene.

Most OpenGL commands are completely primitive independent. This means that they can be issued for any OpenGL primitive and have the same effect. An example of this would be the `glColor3f()` command; it can be issued for any OpenGL primitive and have the same effect of setting the color of the primitive.

The type of primitive that is drawn is determined by the parameters of a function called `glBegin()`. All actual drawing (specification of points) in OpenGL goes on between `glBegin()` and `glEnd()` statements.

Drawing Loops in C++Builder Using `OnIdle()`

When a scene is drawn, it is usually done in an update loop. This means that a loop constantly runs in which the scene is drawn using OpenGL, and then all the dynamic parts are updated (for example, the objects are moved). This is how animation effects are produced.

There are a couple of ways in which a programmer can achieve this:

- Using a thread: This is a fairly good method, but multithreading has overhead.
- Using `OnIdle()`: This is the preferred method. `OnIdle()` is a virtual function that is called when the system is idle, when no other commands or messages are being processed or issued.

The function you want `OnIdle()` to point to should be defined as follows, replacing *IdleFunction()* with an appropriate name:

```
void __fastcall TForm1::IdleFunction( TObject* Sender, bool &done )
{
```

The first line in the function should be

```
    done = false;
```

This will request more idle time from the system. The rest of the function can be anything. Usually it is just drawing code followed by a page flip, if double buffering is being used.

The `OnIdle()` function is set as follows:

```
    Application->OnIdle = IdleFunction;
```

This can be set at any time to any correctly defined function. It is advisable not to set `OnIdle()` until after OpenGL has been initialized. If the handler contains OpenGL code, then the code will not execute correctly, and the results may be unpredictable.

Using OpenGL

Most OpenGL programs have the same general structure, usually broken down into the following stages:

1. Setup and initialization: This is where the rendering and device contexts are created, in other words, where OpenGL is initialized.

2. Setup of rendering environment: This is where the conditions in the virtual environment are set up, such as lights, fog, and the shading model.

3. Transformation of primitives: This is where the position, orientation, and scale of the points to be drawn are defined. See the section "Stage 3: 3D Transformations," later in this chapter.

4. Drawing of primitives: This is where the actual points and the primitives that they represent are defined. Material specification and texturing also are done here.

5. Flip surfaces: This is specific to double-buffered drawing.

Stages 2 to 5 are usually in a drawing loop, as described in the section "Drawing Loops in C++Builder Using `OnIdle()`," earlier in this chapter.

Stage 1: OpenGL Initialization

Before graphics can begin, some initialization needs to be performed to prepare the operating system for OpenGL display. For OpenGL to function it needs something called a rendering

Advanced Graphics with DirectX and OpenGL

Chapter 26

1099

26

ADVANCED
GRAPHICS WITH
DIRECTX AND
OPENGL

context. You can think of this as an OpenGL version of a device context. OpenGL uses this to store information, such as its current state.

> **NOTE**
>
> Windows-compatible implementations of OpenGL have an extra set of commands specifically for interaction with the operating system. These are called the *Wiggle functions*, due to the fact that all the function names have the letters wgl prefixed. This stands for Win32 GL.

OpenGL can create a rendering context from a device context via the function wglCreateContext(). Listing 26.1 creates an OpenGL rendering context.

LISTING 26.1 OpenGL Initialization: OpenGLInit()

```
// globals (either in the TForm1 class or global)
HDC hDC;
HGLRC hRC;

bool TForm1::OpenGLInit( void )
{
// This will get a device context from the main window (TForm1)
    hDC = GetDC( Handle );

    // If an error occurred in GetDC then NULL will have been returned
    if( hDC == NULL )
        return( false );

    // This function will be explained shortly
    SetGLPixelFormat( hDC );

    // This will use the device context to create a rendering context
    hRC = wglCreateContext( hDC );

    // If an error occurred in wglCreateContext then
    // NULL will have been returned
    if( hRC == NULL )
        return( false );
```

Once device and rendering contexts have been created, they next have to be set as the ones that OpenGL and Windows are to use. Another wgl function comes to the rescue in the form of wglMakeCurrent(), used as follows:

```
    wglMakeCurrent( hDC, hRC );
    return( true );
}
```

You may have noticed the SetGLPixelFormat() function in the previous segment of code. This is an important stage; it is where the OpenGL-specific bits of the device context are set, so that OpenGL can communicate properly with Windows.

This requires the setting of a structure named PIXELFORMATDESCRIPTOR. The SetGLPixelFormat() function looks generally like Listing 26.2.

LISTING 26.2   Setting OpenGL Pixel Format: SetGLPixelFormat()

```
void SetGLPixelFormat( HDC hdc )
{
    int PixelFormatIndex;
    PIXELFORMATDESCRIPTOR PixelFormat=
    {
        sizeof( PIXELFORMATDESCRIPTOR ), // the size of the structure
               1,                        // structure version
        PFD_DRAW_TO_WINDOW |             // draw direct to window
                                         // (not to an off screen bitmap)
        PFD_SUPPORT_OPENGL |             // allow DC to support OpenGL calls
                                         // (may be useful!)
        PFD_DOUBLEBUFFER,                // use a double buffer
        PFD_TYPE_RGBA,                   // use RGBA color mode
        24,                              // use 24 bit color
        0, 0, 0, 0, 0, 0, 0, 0, 0, 0, 0, 0, 0,  // unused
        32,                              // use a 32 bit z buffer
        0, 0,                            // unused
        PFD_MAIN_PLANE,                  // draw to main plane
        0, 0, 0, 0                       // unused
    };

    // This will select an appropriate pixel
    // format index for the above format
    PixelFormatIndex=ChoosePixelFormat( hdc, &PixelFormat );

    // Set the pixel format and leave function
    SetPixelFormat( hdc, PixelFormatIndex, &PixelFormat );
}
```

How Rendering Works in OpenGL

Displaying 3D graphics can involve a complex group of processes. The OpenGL API tries to make this as painless as possible by encapsulating complicated concepts in easy-to-use functions.

The Viewport

The viewport is what the programmer uses to define the window in which OpenGL is displayed. This is simply a 2D area of the screen into which OpenGL plots the virtual 3D world.

The view that OpenGL projects into the viewport is always from the origin of the 3D world (that is, from coordinate 0,0,0), along the z-axis.

NOTE

> Lack of space prohibits going into detailed 3D theory or terminology. Most mathematics or 3D graphics textbooks will adequately explain 3D coordinates.

When using OpenGL to display 3D graphics, the programmer first converts the local coordinate system to transformed world coordinates, and then converts these to viewer-relative coordinates. *Transformed world coordinates* means points in space that have had transformation matrices applied to them and have changed from being relative to the object space they were created in to being relative to world space. For more information, see the "Stage 3: 3D Transformations" section, later in this chapter, or a good 3D mathematics or graphics textbook.

The local coordinate system is the original untransformed points in 3D space. Various transformations (which will be covered later) are then applied to these points to shift them into the world or global coordinate system. The local coordinate systems of the point groups (objects) should then be correctly positioned relative to each other.

The coordinates must then be transformed so that they appear correct relative to the position and orientation of the viewer. This is done by applying the reverse of the transformations used to position the viewer to every object in the scene. This effectively moves the viewer back to the origin, while keeping all the other objects relative to him. Therefore, when the *scene* (the collective term for all the 3D objects and artifacts in the virtual world) is drawn into the viewport, it appears relative to the viewer. Figure 26.1 shows the way the viewer is oriented to the global coordinate system.

Viewer coordinates and direction

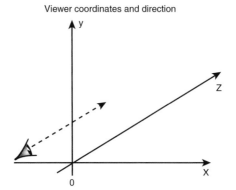

FIGURE 26.1

How the viewer is oriented to the global coordinate system.

This may be a bit hard to digest for those who are new to 3D graphics. Don't worry; it will make more sense in later examples. The main faculty, which makes creating 3D graphics easier, is visualization. This is the ability to see, in your mind's eye, what effect specific transformations are having on 3D points. This skill can be developed, but some people find it comes naturally to them. This is very useful. To those of you who find visualization hard: don't panic. If you write your code well, you will see the results on your screen.

Setting Up a Viewport

There are two important functions that the programmer uses to define his viewport. One of these sets the actual viewport (the window into the virtual world), and the other sets how 3D data is displayed in this viewport. The two main display methods are *perspective* and *orthographic*. Perspective display multiplies all the 3D coordinates by a matrix, which produces the impression of perspective (objects get smaller the farther away from the camera they are). Orthographic display plots points onto the screen in a linear fashion, without respect to distance. This produces flat-looking images, which are less realistic. It is useful for technical programs such as CAD packages where the data needs to be displayed directly.

Listing 26.3 shows a simple function that will set either a perspective or an orthographic viewport.

LISTING 26.3 Setting Up a Viewport: `SetViewport()`

```
void TForm1::SetViewport( bool Perspective )
{
    float w, h, Aspect;

    w=Width;
```

LISTING 26.3   Continued

```
    h=Height;

    // we don't want any divisions by zero
    if(h==0)
        h=1;

    // set the actual viewing area to the whole
    // client area
    glViewport(0, 0, w, h);

    // set the matrix mode to projection
    // (i.e. we want operations from here onward
    // to affect the projection matrix only)
    glMatrixMode(GL_PROJECTION);
    // load an identity matrix (that is the matrix
    // equivalent of zero)
    glLoadIdentity();

        // if the user is trying to create a perspective viewport then...
    if(Perspective)
    {
        // ...set one
        Aspect=(GLfloat)w/(GLfloat)h;
        gluPerspective(60.0f, Aspect, 1.0f, 1000.0f);
    }
    // otherwise the user is trying to create an orthographic
    // viewport so...
    else
    {
        // ...set one
        if(w<=h)
            glOrtho(-250.0f, 250.0f, -250.0f*h/w, 250.0f*h/w, 1.0f, 1000.0f);
        else
            glOrtho(-250.0f*w/h, 250.0f*w/h, -250.0f, 250.0f, 1.0f, 1000.0f);
    }

    // return to the modelview matrix (this is the
    // transformation matrix, see the transformations
    // section)
    glMatrixMode(GL_MODELVIEW);
    glLoadIdentity();
}
```

In the code comments, you'll notice references to the *matrix*. The matrix is a mathematical device that can be used to perform operations on vectors or other matrices. These operations, with respect to 3D graphics, can be projection (as used in Listing 26.3, the projection matrix) or transformation. A transformation is an operation on 3D coordinates, such as moving them (translation), rotating them, or scaling them. Transformation is covered in a later section of this chapter.

glViewport() is the function that sets the actual viewing window in client coordinates (in a window). This is the port through which a 3D scene is viewed. The parameters of this function are

```
glViewport( int x, int y, int x2, int y2 )
```

x,y is the bottom-left corner of the window, and x2,y2 is the top right.

glOrtho() requests that an orthographic projection matrix be used and sets the way the matrix affects data.

```
glOrtho( int x, int y, int x2, int y2, float near, float far )
```

x,y is the bottom-left corner of the viewing volume, and x2,y2 is the top right of the viewing volume. The data inside this viewing volume is squashed into the defined viewport. near is the shortest distance to the viewer at which 3D data is visible, and far is the longest.

gluPerspective() requests that a perspective projection matrix be used and sets the way the matrix affects data. The parameters of this function are as follows:

```
gluPerspective( float fov, float aspect, float near, float far )
```

fov is the field of view in which data is visible. It is the "viewing cone" of visibility. aspect is the width to height display aspect ratio. near and far are the same parameters as in glOrtho().

> **TIP**
>
> The glu prefix on gluPerspective() indicates that this function belongs to the OpenGL utilities suite of functions.

The OpenGL State Machine

The user controls the way OpenGL renders by changing entities called *states*. A state, in the terms of OpenGL, is an internal variable that allows the user to control various aspects of the rendering process. Most of these states are Boolean (either on or off, true or false), but some are float and vector values (such as light position and color).

Setting and Unsetting States

The main functions for controlling Boolean state are `glEnable()` and `glDisable()`. To enable 2D texture mapping, you would code the following:

```
glEnable( GL_TEXTURE_2D );
```

To disable it, you would code the following:

```
glDisable( GL_TEXTURE_2D );
```

Getting a State

To find out whether a Boolean state is set or not, the `glIsEnabled()` function can be used, as follows:

```
if( glIsEnabled( GL_TEXTURE_2D ) ) ...
```

Stage 2: Setting Up a Rendering Environment with Lighting and Shading

Without light and dark, everything in a scene would look flat. OpenGL allows you to light your scene easily using a few simple commands. The next section describes how light affects a scene and the model that is used to simulate lighting and shading.

Lighting and Shading Models

Dynamic shading updates in real-time to reflect changes in virtual lighting conditions. It is very important in creating a realistic environment. Dynamic shading is achieved in OpenGL by using virtual lights, which can be set to produce different lighting effects.

Shading on any particular polygon (a flat surface composed of three or more 3D points) is dependent on three different types of light: ambient, diffuse, and specular.

Ambient light is the light level that is normally present in an environment. It is composed of light that has been reflected so many times that its source is indeterminate.

Diffuse and specular light are both reflected directly off the polygon from the light source. Diffuse light is reflected in random directions; as a result, it is visible from any point at which the lighted side of the polygon is visible. Specular light is reflected such that the angle of reflection (incidence) is equal to the angle at which the light hits the polygon. This is shown in Figure 26.2.

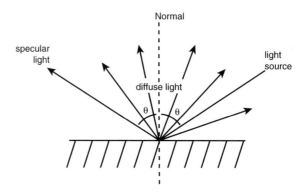

FIGURE 26.2
How light interacts with a flat surface.

OpenGL's Shading Models

There are two shading models that OpenGL uses, commonly called the *flat model* and the *smooth model*. Both are optimized for maximum speed and therefore do not apply the lighting equation to every pixel drawn.

In the smooth model, the equation is applied to all the points that make up the polygon (three points for a triangle, four for a quad). These values are then interpolated to get the lighting values for each point on the polygon. This method works extremely well in almost every case.

In the flat model, the equation is applied once to the polygon as a whole, so it is all shaded the same color. This works fine as long as the polygon is fairly small.

The smooth model is slightly slower than the flat model but produces much better results, especially when the model contains few polygons (in which case the flat model looks very artificial).

Setting Up Lights for Dynamic Shading

Lights are set up using the glLight() set of functions.

> **TIP**
>
> Most functions in OpenGL are named using the following convention:
>
>   gl<*FunctionName*>[n][t](...)
>
> <*FunctionName*> is a basic description of what the function applies to (for example, Vertex, Light, Normal).
>
> [n] is the number of parameters that the function takes.
>
> [t] is the type of parameter that the function takes (for example, f for floats, d for doubles, i for integers). If v is appended to [t], then the function receives [n] parameters in an array instead of as separate arguments.
>
> Examples of OpenGL functions following this convention are glLightfv(...), glVertex3f(...), and glNormal4fv(...).

The actual lighting parameters of the light are set up in Listing 26.4.

LISTING 26.4   Setting Up Lighting Parameters

```
// set the lights ambient component to a dark gray
float AmbientColor[4]={0.2f, 0.2f, 0.2f, 1.0f};
glLightfv(GL_LIGHT0, GL_AMBIENT, AmbientColor);

// set the lights diffuse component to a lighter gray
float DiffuseColor[4]={0.8f, 0.8f, 0.8f, 1.0f};
glLightfv(GL_LIGHT0, GL_DIFFUSE, DiffuseColor);

// set the lights specular component to bright white
float SpecularColor[4]={1.0f, 1.0f, 1.0f, 1.0f};
glLightfv(GL_LIGHT0, GL_SPECULAR, SpecularColor);
```

Next, set the position of the light in your scene:

```
// set the lights position to the origin
float LightPosition[4]={0.0f, 0.0f, 0.0f, 0.0f};
glLightfv(GL_LIGHT0, GL_POSITION, LightPosition);
```

Notice that the parameters for the light's color components are passed as float arrays of four elements. These elements correspond to the red, green, blue, and alpha components. The alpha component is irrelevant when setting lights, so just set it to 1.0f. The values are clamped to between 0.0f, no brightness, and 1.0f, full brightness. If the user provides a value outside this range, it is set to `0.0f` if it is lower or `1.0f` if it is higher. This allows OpenGL to remain device independent, because it works out the actual color values internally, dependent on the device and rendering contexts.

The elements in the `LightPosition` array are x, y, z, and w coordinates. The w coordinate can be left set to `0.0f` (its use is too advanced to go into in this chapter).

What we have described is a simple overview of lighting. There are different types of light, and the method previously described will create the standard type: an omnidirectional light. Spotlights can also be created in OpenGL with lighting cones and directionality. See the "OpenGL References" section later in this chapter for some useful references.

Stage 3: 3D Transformations

A static scene is all very well, but movement and animation are where 3D graphics can really be applied to great effect. A transformation, in geometric terms, is any operation performed on points that alters the points' relationship to each other. Generally these include scaling, rotation, and translation.

The Transformation Pipeline (from 3D Coordinates to Pixels)

In OpenGL (as in most, if not all, 3D APIs) the data goes through three stages. It starts off as points in a local coordinate system. A local coordinate system describes untransformed points relative to a fixed origin in a solid object or mesh. Each mesh therefore has its own local coordinate system. These points are then transformed into the world coordinate system using matrix operations. The world coordinate system describes every point to be drawn in a scene (virtual world) relative to a fixed origin. The transformed points are not displayable until they have been projected into two dimensions (because computer screens are flat). OpenGL does this automatically as long as viewport and projection matrixes are defined. The last stage is the display, which is also done automatically by OpenGL using the device and rendering contexts specified.

Therefore, all the programmer has to worry about is setting up the viewport (see the "How Rendering Works in OpenGL" section earlier in this chapter), providing the points (this is done using the `glVertex()` set of functions) and transforming them. This section discusses the basics of the latter.

The Three Transformations

There are three main transformations that are applied to points in OpenGL: translation, scaling, and rotation. The transformations themselves are applied to the points you provide internally; therefore, you always give points in local coordinates.

Translation

Figure 26.3 shows the effect of translation.

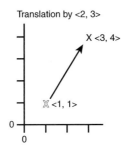

Translation by <2, 3>

X <3, 4>

X <1, 1>

FIGURE 26.3

The effect of translating a point.

Translation means to move your points around. It is very simple to apply using the glTranslatef() method and giving an x, y, and z translation to it. All points are moved along the transformed axes by these amounts. For example

```
glTranslatef(100.0f, 200.0f, 300.0f);
```

Scaling

This multiplies the coordinates of the points by the given amounts in x, y, and z. For example, if a coordinate is -5,-2,4 and is multiplied by 2,-1,3, the result will be -10,2,12. The following is an example:

```
glScalef(2.0f, 2.0f, 1.0f);
```

Rotation

The effect of rotation is shown in Figure 26.4.

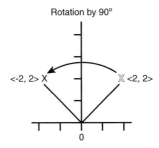

Rotation by 90°

<-2, 2> X

X <2, 2>

0

FIGURE 26.4

The effects of rotation on a point.

This rotates points around an axis you define relative to their transformed local coordinate axis. You define this axis as a vector from the origin out a distance of one unit in x, y, and z space. For example 1,0,0 is the positive x-axis. Use glRotatef() as shown here:

```
glRotatef(45.0f, 1.0f, 0.0f, 0.0f);
glRotatef(180.0f, 0.0f, 1.0f, 0.0f);
glRotatef(23.5f, 0.0f, 0.0f, 1.0f);
```

This rotation sequence will rotate 45.0 degrees around the positive x-axis, 180.0 degrees around the positive y-axis, and 23.5 degrees around the positive z-axis.

Order of Transformation

The order in which transformations are applied is crucial to the desired results. It is important to note, for instance, that a translation followed by a rotation will not produce the same result as a rotation followed by a translation. Translation always occurs along the local axis, and if these have been rotated, then the effect of translation will be altered.

Stage 4: Drawing Primitives

Drawing primitives involves specifying the material to use for the primitive and defining all the points in space that determine its shape. These allow complex and realistic objects to be created.

Setting Material Properties

A *material*, in OpenGL, is a set of properties that is used to determine how primitives are drawn. The main functions for handling and setting material properties are in the glMaterial() set. Its use is shown in Listing 26.5.

LISTING 26.5 Setting Material Properties

```
// these colors will produce a polished red material
float AmbientColor[4]={0.1f, 0.0f, 0.0f, 1.0f},
      DiffuseColor[4]={0.8f, 0.0f, 0.0f, 1.0f}
      SpecularColor[4]={1.0f, 1.0f, 1.0f, 1.0f};
// set the materials ambient color
glMaterialfv(GL_FRONT_AND_BACK, GL_AMBIENT, AmbientColor);
// set the materials diffuse color
glMaterialfv(GL_FRONT_AND_BACK, GL_DIFFUSE, DiffuseColor);
// set the materials specular color
glMaterialfv(GL_FRONT_AND_BACK, GL_SPECULAR, SpecularColor);
```

Note the use of the GL_FRONT_AND_BACK constant: GL_FRONT or GL_BACK can also be used in place of it, allowing different materials to be defined for the front and back sides of primitives.

Advanced Graphics with DirectX and OpenGL

CHAPTER 26

1111

26

ADVANCED
GRAPHICS WITH
DIRECTX AND
OPENGL

Also, the ambient and diffuse properties can be set to the same values at the same time, using GL_AMBIENT_AND_DIFFUSE as the second parameter.

There is another way of setting materials for primitives that is easier but less flexible than the previous method. This is the use of glColorMaterial(). The command causes OpenGL to allow materials from the command on to be defined by calls to glColor(). This means the material colors will follow the pixel colors. glColorMaterial() is used as follows:

```
glColorMaterial(GL_FRONT, GL_AMBIENT_AND_DIFFUSE);
// from now on the ambient and diffuse material
// properties for the front of primitives will be
// defined by glColor()
```

After glColorMaterial() has been called, glColor() can be used to define material properties, as shown in Listing 26.6.

LISTING 26.6 Setting Material Properties Using glColorMaterial() and glColor()

```
float ColorArray[4]={1.0f, 1.0f, 0.2f, 1.0f};

// set current color using separate values
glColor4f( 1.0f, 0.5f, 0.2f, 1.0f );
// from now on the front of any primitives drawn will have a
// material whose ambient any diffuse properties are the same
// as the color elements used above

// set the current color using an array of values
glColor4fv( ColorArray );
// from now on the front of any primitives drawn will have a
// material whose ambient any diffuse properties are the same
// as the color array used above
```

You may be wondering how OpenGL knows which is the front and which is the back of a primitive. This is decided by the order of the points that define the primitive (specifically a polygon). The points are defined either in clockwise order or in counterclockwise order. You can set OpenGL to recognize either of these as the front face, using the glFrontFace() command:

```
// to define a clockwise point order as the front face:
glFrontFace( GL_CW );
// to define a counterclockwise point order as the front face
➡(this is the default):
glFrontFace ( GL_CCW );
```

TIP

Every OpenGL state has a default value that is set by OpenGL during initialization. You need to set new states only if you want something other than OpenGL's default behavior. In practice, however, it makes code clearer if you set all the states you need, regardless of the default value. This makes it easier to understand and follow.

Setting Lighting Normals

In mathematical terms, a normal is a line that is exactly perpendicular to a plane. In OpenGL, *normal* has a slightly more flexible meaning. It is still linked to geometric primitives, but it does not need to be at exactly 90° to them. In OpenGL, normals are used for lighting purposes alone. If you remember the lighting diagram in the "Lighting and Shading Models" section, earlier in this chapter, then you will remember that the normal line is what defines how the light reflects. Diffuse light reflects at all angles, with intensity dependent on the light source's angle. Specular light reflects only at the angle of reflection around the normal. Therefore, if you alter the theoretical normal in the model without altering the actual plane, the lighting conditions will change.

Now imagine defining different normals for different points on a single flat plane. This would produce the appearance of a non-flat surface. This is how OpenGL allows the use of normals. The user can define different normals for each point on a polygon, and OpenGL then interpolates the lighting model between them. This can be used to create smooth surface effects in low polygon models (a model that doesn't contain many polygons).

Normals are defined in OpenGL using the glNormal() set of commands, as in Listing 26.7.

LISTING 26.7   Setting a Normal Using glNormal()

```
// an array along the negative z axis
float NormalArray[3]={0.0f, 0.0f, -1.0f};

// set a normal along the positive x axis
// using separate values
glNormal3f( 1.0f, 0.0f, 0.0f );

// set a normal using an array of values
glNormal3fv( NormalArray );
```

Of course, in practice, this code is fairly useless, and your normals are very unlikely to be that easy to define. It would be much easier to use a function to work out the normal to a plane

Advanced Graphics with DirectX and OpenGL

CHAPTER 26

1113

26

ADVANCED
GRAPHICS WITH
DIRECTX AND
OPENGL

from three of its points. This is fairly easy, using a vector method known as the cross product. What a cross product actually calculates can be seen in Figure 26.5.

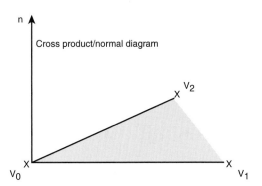

FIGURE 26.5
n is the result of a cross product between vectors (v1-v0) and (v2-v0).

A function to work out the normal to a plane could look like Listing 26.8.

LISTING 26.8   Calculating a Normal Using a Cross Product

```
#define X        0
#define Y        1
#define Z        2

void WorkOutNormal( float PlanePoint0[3], float PlanePoint1[3],
                    float PlanePoint2[3], float NormalOut[3] )
{
    float VectorA[3], VectorB[3];
    double Length, OneOverLength;

    // this works out the to vectors along the plane from a
    // single point
    VectorA[X] = PlanePoint1[X] - PlanePoint0[X];
    VectorA[Y] = PlanePoint1[Y] - PlanePoint0[Y];
    VectorA[Z] = PlanePoint1[Z] - PlanePoint0[Z];
    VectorB[X] = PlanePoint2[X] - PlanePoint0[X];
    VectorB[Y] = PlanePoint2[Y] - PlanePoint0[Y];
    VectorB[Z] = PlanePoint2[Z] - PlanePoint0[Z];

    // calculate the actual cross product
    NormalOut[X] = VectorA[Y] * VectorB[Z] - VectorA[Z] * VectorB[Y];
```

LISTING 26.8   Continued

```
        NormalOut[X] = VectorA[Z] * VectorB[X] – VectorA[X] * VectorB[Z];
        NormalOut[X] = VectorA[X] * VectorB[Y] – VectorA[Y] * VectorB[X];

        // reduce the normal to a unit vector
        Length = NormalOut[X] * NormalOut[X] + NormalOut[Y] * NormalOut[Y] +
                NormalOut[Z] * NormalOut[Z];
        // make sure a square root is legal
        if( Length > 0 )
            OneOverLength = 1/sqrt( Length );
        else
            OneOverLength = (1/0.0001);

        NormalOut[X] *= OneOverLength;
        NormalOut[Y] *= OneOverLength;
        NormalOut[Z] *= OneOverLength;
}
```

The use of the function in Listing 26.8 is shown in Listing 26.9.

LISTING 26.9   Creating and Using a Normal with `WorkOutNormal()`

```
float Vertex0[3]={-1.0f, -1.0f, 0.0f},
Vertex1[3]={0.0f, 1.0f, 0.0f},
Vertex2[3]={1.0f, -1.0f, 0.0f};
float Normal[3];

WorkOutNormal(Vertex0, Vertex1, Vertex2, Normal);
// Normal now contains the mathematical normal to the plane
// defined by Vertex0, Vertex1 and Vertex2
glNormal3fv(Normal);
// do drawing stuff . . .
```

Of course the `WorkOutNormal()` function works out only the mathematically exact normal to a plane. This does not take advantage of OpenGL's capability to use arbitrary normals. There are a few methods that can be used to create normals to simulate smooth surfaces. Most of them involve averaging the normals of surrounding polygons in a mesh, but there isn't enough room to cover these methods here.

The Drawing Pipeline

The following sections describe the low-level details of actual scene specification. This includes specifying the type of primitive to draw and how to draw it. A primitive is any basic shape that can be drawn, such as points, lines, and filled triangles.

In OpenGL, drawing commands are not executed as soon as they are issued. Instead, they are put in a drawing queue that is processed either when OpenGL gets time or when `glFlush()` is called. This (as the name would suggest) flushes the drawing queue.

> **TIP**
>
> The order of commands is always kept the same inside the queue.

Specifying Primitives

All the primitives in OpenGL (points, lines, polygons, and various strips) are defined using points. A point is a position in 3D space, usually defined by three numbers: the x, y, and z coordinates. These are given to OpenGL via the `glVertex()` set of commands. It has many varieties, all handling different types of data. Some of these varieties take only two parameters. These are for drawing pseudo-2D primitives, where the z coordinate is taken to be 0.

The type of primitive that the vertices (3D or 2D points) are to describe is determined by the parameter given to `glBegin()`. The actual points are specified using `glVertex()` between calls to `glBegin()` and `glEnd()`:

```
// Draw a triangle
glBegin( GL_TRIANGLES );
    glVertex3f( -10.0f, -10.0f, 0.0f );
    glVertex3f( 0.0f, 10.0f, 0.0f );
    glVertex3f( 10.0f, -10.0f, 0.0f );
glEnd();
```

The `glBegin()` and `glEnd()` commands can be issued at any point in a program as long as

- The calls are not nested (for example, a `glBegin()`/`glEnd()` pair isn't called inside another `glBegin()`/`glEnd()` pair).
- OpenGL has been initialized, both rendering and device contexts.
- Each `glBegin()` has a corresponding `glEnd()`.

Polys, Points, and Lines

A polygon (or poly) is any primitive defined by more than two points (any finite plane). It has surface area. A point is any position in 3D space. It has no surface area. A line is a connection between two points. It also has no surface area. These primitives as well as other OpenGL primitives are listed in Table 26.1 along with their constants.

TABLE 26.1   OpenGL Primitives and Their Defined Constants

Constant	Primitive
GL_POINT	A point or dot
GL_LINE	A line
GL_TRIANGLE	A three-sided polygon defined by three points
GL_QUAD	A four-sided polygon defined by four points
GL_POLYGON glBegin() and glEnd()	An n-sided polygon defined by n points between
GL_TRIANGLE_STRIP	n triangles in a strip, defined by $n+2$ points
GL_QUAD_STRIP	n quads in a strip, defined by $2n+2$ points

How to Draw OpenGL Primitives

Primitives are very easy to draw using OpenGL. They are always defined with respect to the local coordinate system. (Coordinate systems will be explained later in this chapter.) Some basic code to draw a red cube with normals for lighting could look like Listing 26.10.

LISTING 26.10   Drawing an Object with Color and Normals

```
// Note: remember to setup OpenGL contexts and material properties
// before beginning to draw

// set the vertex color to pure red
glColor3f( 1.0f, 0.0f, 0.0f );

// remember to tell OpenGL what primitive type you are defining
// we are drawing in Quads (four sided polygons)
glBegin( GL_QUADS );
// front
glNormalf( 0.0f, 0.0f, 1.0f );
glVertex3f( -1.0f, 1.0f, -1.0f );
glVertex3f( 1.0f, 1.0f, -1.0f );
glVertex3f( 1.0f, -1.0f, -1.0f );
glVertex3f( -1.0f, -1.0f, -1.0f );
// back
glNormalf( 0.0f, 0.0f, -1.0f );
glVertex3f( 1.0f, 1.0f, 1.0f );
glVertex3f( -1.0f, 1.0f, 1.0f );
glVertex3f( -1.0f, -1.0f, 1.0f );
glVertex3f( 1.0f, -1.0f, 1.0f );
// right
glNormalf( 1.0f, 0.0f, 0.0f );
```

Advanced Graphics with DirectX and OpenGL

CHAPTER 26

1117

26

ADVANCED
GRAPHICS WITH
DIRECTX AND
OPENGL

LISTING 26.10   Continued

```
glVertex3f( 1.0f, 1.0f, -1.0f );
glVertex3f( 1.0f, 1.0f, 1.0f );
glVertex3f( 1.0f, -1.0f, 1.0f );
glVertex3f( 1.0f, -1.0f, -1.0f );
// left
glNormalf( -1.0f, 0.0f, 0.0f );
glVertex3f( -1.0f, 1.0f, -1.0f )
glVertex3f( -1.0f, 1.0f, 1.0f );
glVertex3f( -1.0f, -1.0f, 1.0f );
glVertex3f( -1.0f, -1.0f, -1.0f );
// top
glNormalf( 0.0f, 1.0f, 0.0f );
glVertex3f( -1.0f, 1.0f, 1.0f );
glVertex3f( 1.0f, 1.0f, 1.0f );
glVertex3f( 1.0f, 1.0f, -1.0f );
glVertex3f( -1.0f, 1.0f, -1.0f );
// bottom
glNormalf( 0.0f, -1.0f, 0.0f );
glVertex3f( -1.0f, -1.0f,  -1.0f );
glVertex3f( 1.0f, -1.0f, -1.0f );
glVertex3f( 1.0f, -1.0f, 1.0f );
glVertex3f( -1.0f, -1.0f, 1.0f );
glEnd();
// force the draw queue to be executed
glFlush();
```

You may notice that many of the vertex definitions are repeated. This is inefficient, and OpenGL has its own methods for dealing with this (`glVertexArrays()` and so forth), but these methods are more advanced than will be covered here. The other method for dealing with this is to store your vertex, primitive, and normal definitions in arrays. This is another way the cube could be drawn. This is shown in Listing 26.11.

LISTING 26.11   Drawing an Object with Vertex and Polygon Arrays

```
// firstly define the arrays:
// the vertex array
float Verts[8][3]=
{
    {-1.0f, 1.0f, -1.0f},
    {1.0f, 1.0f, -1.0f},
    {1.0f, -1.0f, -1.0f},
    {-1.0f, -1.0f, -1.0f},
    {1.0f, 1.0f, 1.0f},
    {-1.0f, 1.0f, 1.0f},
    {-1.0f, -1.0f, 1.0f},
```

LISTING 26.11   Continued

```
        {1.0f, -1.0f, 1.0f}
};
// the primitive array
// this contains the indices into the Verts array which
// define the quads
int Polys[6][3]=
{
    {0, 1, 2, 3},
    {4, 5, 7, 6},
    {1, 4, 7, 2},
    {5, 0, 3, 6},
    {5, 4, 1, 0},
    {3, 2, 7, 6}
};
// and finally the normals for the above quads
float Normals[6][3]=
{
    {0.0f, 0.0f, -1.0f},
    {0.0f, 0.0f, 1.0f}
    {1.0f, 0.0f, 0.0f},
    {-1.0f, 0.0f, 0.0f},
    {1.0f, 0.0f, 0.0f},
    {-1.0f, 0.0f, 0.0f}
};

// the cube can now be drawn in a loop like so:
int i;

glColor3f(1.0f, 0.0f,  0.0f);
glBegin(GL_QUADS);
    for(i=0; i<6; i++)
    {
        glNormalfv(Normals[i]);
        glVertex3fv(Verts[Polys[i][0]]);
        glVertex3fv(Verts[Polys[i][1]]);
        glVertex3fv(Verts[Polys[i][2]]);
    }
glEnd();
// force the draw queue to be executed
glFlush();
```

This is a much more efficient way of drawing meshes, from the standpoint of coding. A mesh is any object constructed from vertices and primitive definitions, such as the method just discussed. Unfortunately, it isn't any more efficient from the standpoint of processing. This method comes into its own when drawing multiple meshes. The same drawing code can be used for each mesh.

Display Lists—A More Efficient Way to Draw Primitives

OpenGL allows a more code space–friendly approach to scene specification and manipulation than the methods described in the previous section. Display lists are basically drawing macros. They store a list of OpenGL commands that the programmer specifies. This list can then be executed at any point during the program with a single command.

The advantages of using display lists include the fact that they are generally more efficient than the commands would be if executed separately (inline). They also make coding more concise.

Each list you create in OpenGL is referred to using an ID number. This can be provided by you or requested from OpenGL. The latter method is preferable, because it relieves the programmer from keeping track of which IDs are free. The first stage to creating a display list is to request a free ID using glGenLists(). This function is called with an int parameter that specifies the number of free list IDs to allocate. It returns the first ID allocated. The rest of the IDs are sequentially above that (first ID, first ID+1, first ID+2, and so on).

The next stage is to begin recording the list using the glNewList() command. The first parameter of glNewList() is the ID number of the list. The second is a constant that tells OpenGL whether to record the list for later use or to record it and execute the commands as well. The two constants are GL_COMPILE and GL_COMPILE_AND_EXECUTE.

Any OpenGL command (with a few obscure exceptions; see the OpenGL specifications) executed between glNewList() and glEndList() will be compiled into the list.

To execute a list, simply call glCallList(ID). Listing 26.12 is a quick example.

LISTING 26.12   Creating a Display List

```
int ListID;

// get a free list ID
ListID = glGenLists( 1 );

// start compiling the list
glNewList( ListID, GL_COMPILE );

// do some OpenGL stuff

// stop compiling the list
glEndList();
```

LISTING 26.12   Continued

```
// do some other stuff

// call the list
glCallList( ListID );
```

Stage 5: Flipping Surfaces

Stage 5 consists of calling one function, SwapBuffers(). This is demonstrated in the UpdateOpenGLScene() function of the example OpenGL program outlined in the following section.

An Example OpenGL Program

An example program that demonstrates most of the OpenGL principles previously discussed can be found in the OpenGL folder on the CD-ROM that accompanies this book. The project file is named OpenGLExample.bpr. The program itself is a solar system simulator. The solar system model is built up hierarchically from the center star outward to each planet orbiting it and each moon orbiting each planet (the hierarchy can theoretically go to an infinite depth of orbital systems). Each satellite (as the orbiting bodies are called) has these parameters associated with it:

- Orbital velocity, in degrees per time unit
- Current orbit position, in degrees
- Orbital distance from the object it is orbiting, in distance units
- Radius of the actual satellite, in distance units
- Color of the satellite, in red, green, blue, and alpha components
- Quadric Object, which is used by OpenGL to draw the satellite
- Moons orbiting the satellite, which are the next step in the hierarchy

The program is very simple in its methods. It sets up OpenGL device and rendering contexts. Then it sets up a light at the origin to create the effect of a star. Next the solar system model is initialized. I've left it up to you to add moons. The model isn't correctly proportioned, but if you want a sense of the overwhelming distances between our planets, try changing DISTANCE_DIV, SUN_RADIUS_DIV, and RADIUS_DIV all to 500000.0f and recompiling.

All drawing goes on in the OnIdle() event handler, which is set to point at UpdateOpenGLScene(). All UpdateOpenGLScene() does is

Advanced Graphics with DirectX and OpenGL

CHAPTER 26

1121

26

ADVANCED
GRAPHICS WITH
DIRECTX AND
OPENGL

- Clear the screen
- Clear the transformation matrix
- Transform out to the viewer distance and rotation
- Call the star draw function
- Clear the depth buffer (so all drawing goes over the stars)
- Call the solar system draw function (only need to call the function for the sun; all the others are called hierarchically from it)
- Call the solar system draw orbit function
- Flush the OpenGL draw pipeline
- Flip the double buffer

The timer is set up to update the positions of the satellites, based on time. It will only do this if the animation is set to play, which is controlled by the Play button. The speed slider controls the speed of the animation. The comments in the source code explain what exactly is going on at each stage.

This program was designed and written for a 24-bit color graphics mode. This is the ideal setup for running it. The OpenGL graphics will not display correctly in any 256 indexed color graphics mode.

The project must also contain two libraries called OpenGL32.lib and Glu32.lib. These should be located in the standard C++Builder LIB\PSDK folder.

When the program is running, the left mouse button can be used to rotate the view (hold down and draw), the right mouse button to zoom in and out from the camera target, and both mouse buttons to pan the view.

OpenGL Conclusion

Programming using the OpenGL API is a huge subject, and many books have used hundreds of pages to explore it. In this chapter I have tried to cover what I feel are the most basic and important aspects of it, to start the reader on the road to high quality real-time 3D graphics. Obviously major portions of the API have been completely skipped (texture mapping for example, which I dropped in favor of an example program), but this should provide a framework for you to develop applications using OpenGL.

OpenGL References

If you're interested in learning more about OpenGL and 3D graphics programming in general, then you should have a look at these resources:

- The OpenGL Web site at `http://www.opengl.org`:

  Excellent OpenGL resource link, full of the latest in technology, tutorials, and other links.

- The OpenGL mailing list (send an email to `ListGuru@fatcity.com` with the subject line `SUBSCRIBE OPENGL-GAMEDEV-L`):

  This is where I go if I have a question, whether it's technical or not, and I always get quick answers.

- *OpenGL Programming Guide* (The Red Book) Second Edition, by the OpenGL Architecture Review Board (Mason Woo, Jackie Neider, and Tom Davis), ISBN 0-201-46138-2, published by Addison-Wesley:

  This is the definitive guide to OpenGL, written by the people who designed it. It is a bit daunting for the beginner, but it's the most comprehensive book I've read on the subject.

- *OpenGL SuperBible* (The Blue Book), Richard S. Wright Jr., Michael Sweet, ISBN 1-57169-073-5, published by Waite Group Press:

  This is a friendlier book than the *OpenGL Programming Guide* and is written specifically about the Microsoft implementation of OpenGL. It is Windows specific and comes with a nice example CD.

Introduction to DirectX

DirectX is Microsoft's high-performance interface into multimedia hardware. It is called Direct because it gives the programmer an API that provides direct interaction with low-level drivers. The API is designed mainly with games programming in mind, but many application programmers use it for any animation and audio that require high performance. DirectX is designed to run only on Microsoft operating systems (specifically Windows 9x, 2000, and NT).

COM Basis of the DirectX API

DirectX architecture relies quite heavily on Microsoft's Component Object Model. COM is a programming method that allows applications to use a COM object (similar to a C++ class) that can be used by other applications concurrently. All COM objects are based on the same class, called `IUnknown`. This class has three functions:

- `AddRef()`, which increments the object's internal reference count (how many other programs are using the object)

- `Release()`, which decrements the reference count

- `QueryInterface()`, which is used to obtain an interface to the object, to allow it to be used

Advanced Graphics with DirectX and OpenGL

CHAPTER 26

1123

26

ADVANCED
GRAPHICS WITH
DIRECTX AND
OPENGL

> **NOTE**
>
> For more detail on the Component Object Model, see Chapter 16, "COM Programming."

In DirectX you don't need to worry about the workings of COM, because the APIs are about as simple as COM objects can be.

Non-Object DirectX Functions

DirectX has a few functions that are not part of any of the actual APIs or objects. These are mainly initialization functions, although there are others. You will also need to use some COM-specific functions. These are

- `CoInitialize()`, which prepares the program for using a COM object
- `CoCreateInstance()`, which creates an instance of a particular COM object

Both functions are shown in Listing 26.14.

Using DirectDraw

DirectDraw is DirectX's 2D raster graphics API. It is much faster and more powerful than the Windows GDI. This section provides an introduction to its most useful functions.

Initialization of a DirectDraw Object

DirectDraw objects are created using the `DirectDrawCreate()` function. Into this function are passed a device GUID and a pointer to the DirectDraw object. The device GUID is a number that indicates the hardware device you want to draw with. To select the primary device (usually the main graphics adapter), you can pass `NULL` for this parameter. It is also possible to find out which hardware devices are present and registered on the computer. This is called *enumeration* and can be done using `DirectDrawCreate()`. There is not room here to describe this method, but it is fairly simple, and it is well documented in other literature and the help files.

To create a DirectDraw object safely, you can do as shown in Listing 26.13.

LISTING 26.13   Creating a DirectDraw Object

```
// The standard return type for DirectX functions is HRESULT.
// It either contains DD_OK if the function was successful or an error code
HRESULT DDError;
// This is a pointer to the actual DirectDraw object
```

LISTING 26.13   Continued

```
LPDIRECTDRAW tempDD;

// Try to get a DD (DirectDraw) object
DDError=DirectDrawCreate(NULL, &tempDD, NULL);
// If there was an error (check using the FAILED macro)
if(FAILED(DDError))
{
    // Return error
    return ( false );
}
```

This is all that is needed to create a standard DirectDraw interface. No COM was required. The COM becomes useful when you want to get an interface to a more current version of DirectDraw. The latest version at the time this is being written is 7.0, with 8.0 well on its way. Using the methods we have presented will return only a basic DirectDraw object. To get a different version, do as shown in Listing 26.14, after creating the DirectDraw object as in Listing 26.13.

LISTING 26.14   Getting a Different DirectDraw Interface Version

```
// The interface into DirectDraw2
LPDIRECTDRAW2 DirectDraw2Interface;

// Check for DirectDraw2 on the system
DDError=tempDD->QueryInterface(IID_IDirectDraw2,
                               (LPVOID *)&DirectDraw2Interface);

// If we can't find it then return error
if(FAILED(DDError))
{
    return ( false );
}
// Prepare for COM
CoInitialize(NULL);

// Try to create the DD2 interface
DDError=CoCreateInstance(CLSID_DirectDraw, NULL, CLSCTX_ALL,
                         IID_IDirectDraw2, (LPVOID *)&DirectDraw2Interface);

// If we failed the return error
if(FAILED(DDError))
{
    return ( false );
```

Advanced Graphics with DirectX and OpenGL

CHAPTER 26

1125

26

ADVANCED
GRAPHICS WITH
DIRECTX AND
OPENGL

LISTING 26.14 Continued

```
}
// next we try to initialize the DirectDraw object with
// the default device (NULL)
DDError=DirectDraw2Interface->Initialize(NULL);
if(FAILED(DDError))
{
    return ( false );
}
// We can switch off the COM initialization now
CoUninitialize();

// Return success
return  ( true );
```

This will try for a DirectDraw 2 interface and return an error if it can't find one. A better thing to do would be to make use of the best interface you can get and adjust your program to take this into account. All the functionality covered in this chapter is basic and is included with every version of DirectX, so don't worry about trying to get the latest version (although, in practice, it is usually a good idea).

Adjusting Display Settings for DirectDraw

DirectDraw allows the programmer to completely leave the restrictions of the desktop behind and do his own thing. It does this by allowing the user to change the display mode the graphics card is running in and going full screen. This means that the desktop disappears, and the programmer has a blank screen to mess around with.

Before changing the resolution of the screen (its width and height dimensions in pixels), you need to set something called the cooperative level. This defines how Windows regards the application. If the cooperative level includes the DDSCL_EXCLUSIVE flag, then Windows gives the application full control over the display area. This flag is used in conjunction with DDSCL_FULLSCREEN to achieve full-screen mode for the application. If you use DDSCL_NORMAL, then the application will run in a window. You cannot use this flag with the DDSCL_EXCLUSIVE flag. There are other flags as well, but these are the most important.

The example in Listing 26.15 shows how to go to full-screen exclusive mode.

LISTING 26.15 Setting Full Screen Exclusive Mode

```
bool SetExclusiveMode( HWND Window )
{
    HRESULT DDError;
```

LISTING 26.15   Continued

```
if(DirectDraw2Interface==NULL)
    return(false);
// try to set full-screen excluseive mode
DDError = DirectDraw2Interface->SetCooperativeLevel( Window,
                                        DDSCL_ALLOWREBOOT |
                                        DDSCL_EXCLUSIVE |
                                        DDSCL_FULLSCREEN );

// if an error occured
if(DDError!=DD_OK)
{
    return(false);
}
return(true);
}
```

> **NOTE**
>
> The DDSCL_ALLOWREBOOT flag in SetCooperativeLevel() allows the user to reboot the machine using Alt+Ctrl+Del.

It is also possible, using a DirectDraw interface, to change the resolution of the display device (video monitor and card). This can be done using the SetDisplayMode() function of the DirectDraw interface:

```
DirectDraw2Interface->SetDisplayMode( Width, Height,
                            BitsPerPixel, RefreshRate, Flags);
```

The parameters and their meanings are shown in Table 26.2.

TABLE 26.2   Table of Parameters for SetDisplayMode()

Parameter Name	Description	Units
Width	The desired display width	Pixels
Height	The desired display height	Pixels
BitsPerPixel	The desired bit depth of the pixels	Bits Per Pixel
RefreshRate	The speed at which you want the monitor to refresh; use 0 if you don't care	Hertz (refreshes a second)
Flags	Extra info	N/A

Advanced Graphics with DirectX and OpenGL

CHAPTER 26

1127

26

ADVANCED
GRAPHICS WITH
DIRECTX AND
OPENGL

To set a display mode with 640×480 resolution and 16-bit color, use `SetDisplayMode()`:

```
DirectDraw2Interface->SetDisplayMode(640, 480, 16, 0, 0);
```

Most, if not all, modern graphics cards are capable of this display mode. It is a standard resolution for high-performance computer games. When your application exits, the previously set display mode will automatically be restored, so you don't need to worry about it.

> **NOTE**
>
> Using DirectDraw it is possible to find out all the display modes a graphics card is capable of before you set one. If you do this and use a mode only from the compiled list, then the change of display mode has more chance of success. Unfortunately, the methods used to acquire the list are beyond the scope of this chapter.

Drawing Surfaces

A DirectDraw object is only really useful for the methods previously described, getting the computer and video card ready for high-speed graphics. To actually draw on the screen, you need to use something called a *surface*. The programmer uses a class called `IDirectDrawSurface` to create and manipulate these objects. A surface is an off-screen drawing canvas, just like the screen, but contained in memory. It is similar to a `TCanvas` but about 1000 times faster (a rough guesstimate!).

You create surfaces using the DirectDraw object you already initialized. The first surface you need to create is called the *primary surface*. This is the main drawing surface, the one that will eventually end up on the screen. This surface can be either double or single buffered.

> **NOTE**
>
> Double-buffering means that you actually use two surfaces for display. One is currently onscreen, and the other is the one being altered. Once it has been altered, it is swapped with the one currently being displayed. This method has the benefit that the user cannot see the display being updated. He sees it only one frame at a time. Single buffering is when all display altering is done straight to the visible buffer. This does not look pleasing, especially if the alteration contains a clear screen.

Listing 26.16 is a code snippet demonstrating how to use the double buffered animation method to create a primary buffer.

LISTING 26.16   Creating a Primary DirectDraw Buffer

```
// declared globally or in class
LPDIRECTDRAWSURFACE3 pPrimarySurface, pBackBuffer;

bool CreateSurfaces( void )
{
    HRESULT DDError;
    // these are what you use to describe the type of surface you would
    // like to create
    DDSURFACEDESC SurfaceDescription;
    DDSCAPS BackBufferCaps;

    if(DirectDraw2Interface==NULL)
        return(false);

    // set the description to all 0s
    ZeroMemory(&SurfaceDescription, sizeof(DDSURFACEDESC));
    // always need to set the dwSize member of DirectX structures to the
    // size of the structure
    SurfaceDescription.dwSize = sizeof(DDSURFACEDESC);
    // tell the creation proc what fields in the description are valid
    SurfaceDescription.dwFlags = DDSD_CAPS | DDSD_BACKBUFFERCOUNT;
    // set the capabilities we would like to get

    SurfaceDescription.ddsCaps.dwCaps =
        // primary surface, always display
        DDSCAPS_PRIMARYSURFACE |
        // it will be double buffered
        DDSCAPS_FLIP |
        // it has more surfaces associated with it (i.e. the other buffer
        // which it double buffers with)
        DDSCAPS_COMPLEX;
    // we want 1 buffer to be associated with the primary (the double buffer)
    SurfaceDescription.dwBackBufferCount = 1;

    //Try to create the surface
    DDError = DirectDraw2Interface->CreateSurface(&SurfaceDescription,
                                        (LPDIRECTDRAWSURFACE *)
                                        &pPrimarySurface, NULL);
    // if we failed...
    if(FAILED(DDError))
    {
```

LISTING 26.16   Continued

```
        // ...then return error
        return(false);
    }
    // set the back buffer description to all zeros
    ZeroMemory(&BackBufferCaps, sizeof(DDSCAPS));
    // ask to create a backbuffer
    BackBufferCaps.dwCaps = DDSCAPS_BACKBUFFER;
    // try to get it from the primary surface
    DDError = pPrimarySurface->GetAttachedSurface(&BackBufferCaps,
                                                  &pBackBuffer);
    // If we couldn't create, then return error after freeing primary surface
    if(FAILED(DDError))
    {
        // call the release function to delete the primary surface
        pPrimarySurface ->Release();
        return(false);
    }
    return (true);
}
```

Using the GDI on DirectDraw Surfaces

To do simple graphics easily on a DirectDraw surface, you can use the Windows GDI (graphics device interface). All you need to do is get a device context for the surface, do the drawing, and then release it.

To get a device context, you can use the GetDC() function of IDirectDrawSurface. You can then use the standard GDI functions on the device context. Then you must always call ReleaseDC() to free the device context.

Listing 26.17 will write text onto a surface using the GDI.

LISTING 26.17   Writing Text to a Surface Using the GDI

```
// declared globally or in class
LPDIRECTDRAWSURFACE3 pPrimarySurface, pBackBuffer;

bool TextOutDD( int x, int y, char *szText, COLORREF color,
                COLORREF backcolor)
{
    // the device context
    HDC hDeviceContext;
    // this will hold the error value (if any)
    HRESULT DDError;
```

LISTING 26.17 Continued

```
    if(pBackBuffer==NULL)
        return(false);
    // try and get the device context to the backbuffer
    DDError = pBackBuffer->GetDC(&hDeviceContext);

    // if we failed...
    if( FAILED( DDError ) )
    {
        // ...then return error
        return( false );
    }

    // set the background color for the text
    SetBkColor(hDeviceContext, backcolor);
    // set the foreground color for the text
    SetTextColor(hDeviceContext, color);

    // out put the text
    ::TextOut(hDeviceContext, x, y, szText, lstrlen(szText));

    // release the device context back to the surface
    pBackBuffer->ReleaseDC(hDeviceContext);
    // return no error
    return( true );
}
```

In Listing 26.17, the drawing goes on in the back buffer (pBackBuffer). This is all very well, but it won't show up on the screen. To make the buffers swap, you use the Flip() function of IDirectDrawSurface. Sometimes a buffer can be lost. This is indicated by an error value return from Flip(). This error can be easily caught and corrected by reinitializing the surfaces. The function shown in Listing 26.18 will do a safe flip with error checking.

LISTING 26.18 Flipping Double-Buffered Primary Surfaces

```
// declared globally or in class
LPDIRECTDRAWSURFACE3 pPrimarySurface, pBackBuffer;

void FlipSurfaces( void )
{
    HRESULT DDError;

    // loop until there is no error returned, or DirectDraw says
    // that it is still drawing
```

Advanced Graphics with DirectX and OpenGL

CHAPTER 26

1131

26

ADVANCED
GRAPHICS WITH
DIRECTX AND
OPENGL

LISTING 26.18   Continued

```
while( true )
{
    // Try to flip the surfaces
    DDError = pPrimarySurface->Flip(NULL, 0);
    // if we were successful then leave
    if( !FAILED( DDError ) )
    {
        break;
    }
    // otherwise lets see whats wrong
    else if( DDError == DDERR_SURFACELOST )
    {
        // the surfaces have been lost, so lets reinitalise them
        CreateSurfaces();
        // call the restore function to get back our graphics
        DDError = pPrimarySurface->Restore();
        // if that failed then we better leave, because something
        // is seriously awry
        if( FAILED(DDError) )
            break;
    }
    // if DirectDraw was still drawing when we tried to flip then we
    // should carry on trying to flip, until it isn't.  Otherwise...
    else if( DDError != DDERR_WASSTILLDRAWING )
    {
        // ...we'll leave, and flip again soon
        break;
    }
}
}
```

Loading Bitmaps into a Surface

Being able to draw text and lines on surfaces is all very well, but what would be better is being able to draw bitmaps. This can be done easily using the TBitmap component. First you need to load your bitmap. This will usually be a BMP file. Listing 26.19 is a code snippet showing how to load your bitmap file into a TBitmap.

LISTING 26.19   Loading a Windows BMP into a TBitmap

```
bool LoadBitmapIntoTBitmap( Graphics::TBitmap *&NewBitmap,
                            AnsiString FileName )
{
```

LISTING 26.19   Continued

```
    // assign NULL to the TBitmap so that we can tell if it has been
    // allocated successfully
    NewBitmap = NULL;
    // try and allocate some memory
    NewBitmap = new Graphics::TBitmap();
    // try and load the bitmap file
    NewBitmap->LoadFromFile( FileName );

    if(NewBitmap==NULL)
        return( false );
    // return no error
    return(true);
}
```

As you can see, the TBitmap should be passed to the LoadBitmapIntoTBitmap() function unallocated. If the function returns true then it was successful and the bitmap is contained within the Canvas property of the TBitmap. The function can easily be modified to load the bitmap from a resource ID in the file's executable. Change AnsiString FileName to int ResourceID and NewBitmap->LoadFromFile(FileName); to NewBitmap->LoadFromResourceID(HInstance, ResourceID);.

The next stage is to create a new IDirectDrawSurface3 to hold the bitmap. The code in Listing 26.20 does just this.

LISTING 26.20   Creating a DirectDraw Surface from a TBitmap

```
bool CreateSurfaceFromTBitmap( LPDIRECTDRAWSURFACE3 *pSurface,
                               Graphics::TBitmap *Bitmap )
{
    // this will point at the new surface
    TCanvas *SurfaceCanvas;
    // this will describe the new surface
    DDSURFACEDESC SurfaceDescription;
    HRESULT DDError;
    HDC hDeviceContext;

    // zero the memory of the surface description
    ZeroMemory(&SurfaceDescription, sizeof( DDSURFACEDESC ));

    // set the size member
    SurfaceDescription.dwSize = sizeof( DDSURFACEDESC );

    // set the flags to indicate that the capabilities, width and
```

Advanced Graphics with DirectX and OpenGL

CHAPTER 26

1133

26

ADVANCED
GRAPHICS WITH
DIRECTX AND
OPENGL

LISTING 26.20 Continued

```
// height fields are valid
SurfaceDescription.dwFlags = DDSD_CAPS | DDSD_WIDTH | DDSD_HEIGHT;

// set the capabilities to create a plain off-screen surface
SurfaceDescription.ddsCaps.dwCaps = DDSCAPS_OFFSCREENPLAIN;

// set the width and height to the same as the Bitmap
SurfaceDescription.dwWidth = Bitmap->Width;
SurfaceDescription.dwHeight = Bitmap->Height;

//Try to create the surface
DDError = DirectDraw2Interface->CreateSurface( &SurfaceDescription,
                                               (LPDIRECTDRAWSURFACE *)
                                               pSurface, NULL );

// if we failed...
if(FAILED( DDError ))
{
    // ...then return error
    return( false );
}

// otherwise lets copy the Bitmap to the surface
// get a device context for the surface
DDError = (*pSurface)->GetDC( &hDeviceContext );
 // if we failed...
if(FAILED( DDError ))
{
    // ...then return error
    return( false );
}

// create a new canvas to access the surface
SurfaceCanvas = new TCanvas();

// point the new canvas at the surface's device context
SurfaceCanvas->Handle = hDeviceContext;

// draw the Bitmap onto the surface canvas
SurfaceCanvas->Draw( 0, 0, Bitmap );

// release the device context back to the surface
(*pSurface)->ReleaseDC( hDeviceContext );

// free the TCanvas
```

LISTING 26.20   Continued

```
    delete SurfaceCanvas;

    // return success
    return( true );
}
```

> **NOTE**
>
> Of course, pSurface must be passed to the function unallocated.

You now have three surfaces: a primary display surface that the user can see, a back buffer surface for drawing to, and a bitmap surface (or more than one) that contains a sprite you want to
display. Now you need to put them together. Listing 26.21 will draw a bitmap 1000 times onto
the back buffer.

LISTING 26.21   The Bitmap Demo Procedure

```
// global or in the main class, this must have been initalised when
// BitmapDemo is called:
LPDIRECTDRAWSURFACE3 pBitmapSurface;
LPDIRECTDRAWSURFACE3 pPrimarySurface, pBackBuffer;


bool TForm1::BitmapDemo( void )
{
    // a general loop counter
    int i;
    // the x and y coordinates to draw at
    int x, y;
    // the maximum x and y cords possible keeping the bitmap
    // on the back buffer
    int maxX, maxY;
    // structures to hold information about the surfaces being used
    DDSURFACEDESC BackBufferDesc, BitmapDesc;
    // holds error value
    HRESULT DDError;

    // zero the memory, like always
    ZeroMemory(&BackBufferDesc, sizeof(DDSURFACEDESC));
    // set the size member, like always
    BackBufferDesc.dwSize=sizeof(DDSURFACEDESC);
```

Advanced Graphics with DirectX and OpenGL   1135

CHAPTER 26

26
ADVANCED
GRAPHICS WITH
DIRECTX AND
OPENGL

LISTING 26.21 Continued

```
    // get the surface description of the back buffer (we want to know
    // its width and height)

    DDError = pBackBuffer->GetSurfaceDesc(&BackBufferDesc);

    // if we failed then return error
    if(FAILED( DDError ))
        return( false );

    // we also want to know the width and height of the bitmap surface:
    ZeroMemory(&BitmapDesc, sizeof(DDSURFACEDESC));
    BitmapDesc.dwSize=sizeof(DDSURFACEDESC);
    DDError = pBitmapSurface->GetSurfaceDesc(&BitmapDesc);

    // if we failed then return error
    if(FAILED( DDError ))
        return( false );

    // calculate the maximum possible x and y coordinates while keeping the
    // whole bitmap inside the back buffer
    maxX=BackBufferDesc.dwWidth-BitmapDesc.dwWidth;
    maxY=BackBufferDesc.dwHeight-BitmapDesc.dwHeight;

    // loop for 1000 times
    for(i=0; i<1000; i++)
    {
        // get a random coordinate
        x=random( maxX );
        y=random( maxY );
        // blit the bitmap onto the back buffer
        pBackBuffer->BltFast(x, y, pBitmapSurface, NULL,
                        DDBLTFAST_NOCOLORKEY);
    }
    return( true );
}
```

If you study the code in Listing 26.21, you'll see a IDirectDrawSurface2 member function named BltFast() being used (see Table 26.3 for a list of BltFast() parameters). This function basically copies a rectangle of pixels from one surface to another. It is mind-numbingly fast and fairly flexible.

```
HRESULT IDirectDrawSurface2::BltFast( DWORD x, DWORD y,
                        LPDIRECTDRAWSURFACE3 SourceSurface,
                        LPRECT SourceRect, DWORD Flags );
```

TABLE 26.3   Table of Parameters for BltFast()

Parameter Name	Description
x	The x coordinate at which to blit
y	The y coordinate at which to blit
SourceSurface	A pointer to the DirectDrawSurface to copy from
SourceRect	The rectangle of pixels to copy (give NULL for the whole surface)
Flags	The Flags parameter of BltFast() allows you to specify the way the bitmap is copied. The possible Flags are
	DDBLTFAST_DESTCOLORKEY: Use the color key of the destination DirectDrawSurface.
	DDBLTFAST_SRCCOLORKEY: Use the color key of the source DirectDrawSurface.
	DDBLTFAST_NOCOLORKEY: Use no color key.
	DDBLTFAST_WAIT: Don't return until the bitmap has been blitted or an error occurs.

The color key (in this context) means a color that isn't copied. This is used so that a sprite that isn't rectangular can be blitted if it has a specific color in it that represents transparent (for example, black) and the color key is set to that. It is possible to set a range of values for the color key (for instance, black to pure blue, as in the following example). You can set the color key for a surface as shown in Listing 26.22.

LISTING 26.22   Setting the Color Key for a Surface

```
// holds the color key information
DDCOLORKEY ColorKey;

// zero its memory
ZeroMemory( &ColorKey, sizeof( DDCOLORKEY ) );
// set the lowest value for the color key (dark blue)
ColorKey.dwColorSpaceLowValue = RGB(0, 0, 0);
ColorKey.dwColorSpaceHighValue = RGB(0, 0, 255);
// set the color key for the surface
DDError = Surface->SetColorKey(DDCKEY_COLORSPACE | DDCKEY_SRCBLT, &ColorKey);
// DDCKEY_COLORSPACE tells SetColorKey that we are providing a range of colors
// DDCKEY_SRCBLT tells it that we are providing the source color key
```

A DirectDraw Example Program

An example DirectDraw program, with the project filename DirectDraw.bpr, is located in the DirectDraw folder on the CD-ROM that accompanies this book. It is very simple, but it demonstrates all the techniques outlined in this section.

First it initializes DirectDraw and sets an appropriate cooperative level and screen resolution. Then it loads a bitmap into a DirectDraw Surface. Next it draws this bitmap on to the Primary Buffer 1000 times. It displays some text and then flips the surfaces. The user can then press any key to exit.

If you select the Directories/Conditionals tab of Project, Options, you will notice that I have added $(BCB)\lib\PSDK to the library path. The project uses the ddraw.lib library file provided with C++Builder, as can be seen in the DirectDraw.cpp project source file and DirectDraw.bpr project options files. This library path simply allows us to avoid specifying the absolute path to it.

In your own DirectDraw applications, you can simply select Project, Add to Project from the main menu. In the Files of Type combo box, select Library File (*.lib) and browse to the ddraw.lib file in the \Lib\PSDK folder where C++Builder was installed.

DirectDraw Conclusion

That is pretty much it for this introduction. I'll leave it up to you to implement something useful using the techniques we have looked at.

The OnIdle() event handler of your application can be used for updating frames, as described in the "Drawing Loops in C++Builder Using OnIdle()" section, earlier in this chapter. You should be able to implement fast-action arcade games using the routines that we have outlined. As far as DirectDraw in a window is concerned, the techniques are slightly different but not difficult.

Using DirectSound

DirectSound is the audio equivalent of DirectDraw. It is a direct route to the audio hardware on any system with DirectX installed. It is very fast and hence low latency (sound events occur when you trigger them, not when the system gets around to it).

There are a few parallels between DirectDraw and DirectSound:

- Both are based on the COM architecture.
- Each has a main interface and a main sub-interface: IDirectDraw and IDirectDrawSurface, respectively, for DirectDraw; IDirectSound and IDirectSoundBuffer, respectively, for DirectSound.

- Both can have a cooperative level set to gain different levels of control over the hardware.

Without further discussion, let's initialize DirectSound.

Initializing a DirectSound Object

To create a DirectSound object, we use the helper function `DirectSoundCreate()`. To this function you pass a pointer to an interface object and a GUID for the device you want. As in `DirectDrawCreate()`, you can pass NULL for the GUID if you want the default device. After creating the interface you can set the cooperative level. You'll usually want to set this to `DSSCL_NORMAL` if you are writing a windowed application. This allows other programs to use the same device to output sound. If you are writing a full-screen application or game, you'll probably want to use `DSSCL_EXCLUSIVE` so that other applications are muted.

Listing 26.23 is a short code sample illustrating the creation of an `IDirectSound` object and the setting of the cooperative level.

LISTING 26.23   Initializing a DirectSound Object

```
// declared globally or in the class
LPDIRECTSOUND DirectSoundInterface;

// need to pass HWND handle of main application Window.
// note:
//     If using DirectDraw as well then you must pass
//     the same Window handle.
//
bool InitializeDirectSound( HWND WindowHandle )
{
    // to hold any error result
    HRESULT DError;

    // lets try and grab the default sound device
    DError = DirectSoundCreate( NULL, &DirectSoundInterface, NULL );

    // if we got an error
    if( FAILED(DError) )
    {
        // return error
        return( false );
    }

    // lets try and set the cooperative level to normal
    DError = DirectSoundInterface->SetCooperativeLevel(WindowHandle,
                                        DSSCL_NORMAL);
```

Advanced Graphics with DirectX and OpenGL

CHAPTER 26

1139

26

ADVANCED
GRAPHICS WITH
DIRECTX AND
OPENGL

LISTING 26.23 Continued

```
    // if we failed then...
    if( FAILED(DError) )
    {
        // release the IDirectSound object
        DirectSoundInterface->Release();
        // return error
        return( false );
    }

    // otherwise return success
    return( true );
}
```

An IDirectSound object has another object that is associated with it. This is called the primary buffer and is automatically created and maintained by DirectX. Its purpose is the output of wave data. The programmer tells DirectSound what to put into this buffer and how to mix it. Objects called secondary buffers are used to store sound samples and send them to DirectSound's primary buffer when they are to be played. It is possible to change the wave format (the sample rate, number of channels, and bits per sample) of the primary buffer once the IDirectSound object has been created. Unfortunately, there isn't room to go into that process here (even though it is fairly simple). See the DirectX documentation.

Creating a Secondary Buffer

There are three stages to creating a secondary sound buffer:

- Load the wave data into a flat array. This data can be loaded from a file or from a resource.
- Create a sound buffer using the IDirectSound object.
- Parse the wave data into the sound buffer.

We will cover each stage and provide a source sample demonstrating how to complete the process.

Stage 1: Loading Wave Data

We will cover loading wave data from a WAV file. All that is required is to copy the contents of the file into an array. This is then used in Stage 3 (parsing the wave data into the sound buffer). Listing 26.24 is a simple piece of code that will load the file.

LISTING 26.24 Loading a WAV File to Memory

```
bool LoadWAVFromFile( char *&Data, int &Size, char *FileName )
{
    // the file pointer
    FILE *fp;
    // will hold the length of the file
    fpos_t EndOfFilePos;

    // lets try and open the file for reading in binary
    fp = fopen(FileName, "rb");
    // if we failed then return error
    if( fp == NULL )
    {
        return( false );
    }
    // find end of file
    fseek(fp, 0, SEEK_END);
    // get position at end of file (i.e. file length)
    fgetpos(fp, &EndOfFilePos);
    // find the beginning of the file again
    fseek(fp, 0, SEEK_SET);

    // set the size
    Size=(int)EndOfFilePos;

    // allocate the buffer for the size of the file
    Data = new char[(long)EndOfFilePos];
    // if there wasn't enough memory ...
    if( Data == NULL )
    {
        // ... then close the file and ...
        fclose(fp);
        // ... return error
        return( false );
    }
    // read the data
    if( (signed)fread( Data, 1, EndOfFilePos, fp ) != EndOfFilePos )
    {
        // if we didn't read the right amount of data then close the file ...
        fclose(fp);
        // ...free the buffer...
        delete []Data;
        // ...and return error
        return( false );
    }
```

LISTING 26.24 Continued

```
    // close the file and return success
    fclose(fp);
    return( true );
}
```

We now have a flat array of chars that contains all the data in the WAV file, including header and actual wave information.

Stage 2: Creating a Secondary Buffer

This stage is simple enough. The IDirectSound object is used to create a pointer to a IDirectSoundBuffer interface. This is shown in Listing 26.25.

LISTING 26.25 Creating a Secondary DirectSound Buffer

```
// declared globally or in the class
LPDIRECTSOUND DirectSoundInterface;

bool CreateSecondaryBuffer( LPDIRECTSOUNDBUFFER *DirectSoundBuffer,
                            DSBUFFERDESC &DSBufferDescription )
{
    // holds any error
    HRESULT DSError;

    // set the size member
    DSBufferDescription.dwSize = sizeof(DSBUFFERDESC);
    // set the flags member
    DSBufferDescription.dwFlags = DSBCAPS_STATIC | DSBCAPS_GLOBALFOCUS;
    // try and create the sound buffer.
    DSError = DirectSoundInterface->CreateSoundBuffer(&DSBufferDescription,
                                                      DirectSoundBuffer,
                                                      NULL);
    // if we failed then return error
    if( FAILED( DSError ) )
    {
        return( false );
    }
    return ( true );
}
```

You will notice that the dwFlags member of DSBUFFERDESC is set to DSBCAPS_STATIC | DSBCAPS_GLOBALFOCUS. The first flag indicates to DirectSound that the buffer is to be statically loaded into memory. The second flag indicates that the sound can be played when the application is running in the background.

Stage 3: Parsing the Wave Data into the Direct Buffer

This is the most complex stage, but the code provided will parse a standard WAV file. First it checks that the file (which is actually a buffer in memory) is the correct format. Then it reads the buffer and extracts the format and wave data. This is shown in Listing 26.26.

LISTING 26.26   Parsing the Wave Buffer into the Header and Data

```
bool ParseWavBuffer( char *&pBuffer, WAVEFORMATEX **ppWaveHeader,
                     unsigned char **ppbWaveData, DWORD *&pdwWaveSize )
{
    // this is a DWORD pointer to the current position in the buffer
    DWORD *pdw;
    // this is a DWORD pointer to the end of the buffer
    DWORD *pdwEnd;
    // this holds a riff code
    DWORD dwRiff;
    // this holds the file type riff code
    DWORD dwType;
    // this hold the length of data
    DWORD dwLength;

    if(pBuffer==NULL)
        return(false);
    // check to make sure pointers are set to NULL
    if(ppWaveHeader!=NULL)
        *ppWaveHeader=NULL;
    if(ppbWaveData!=NULL)
        *ppbWaveData=NULL;
    if(pdwWaveSize)
        *pdwWaveSize=0;

    // set the DWORD pointer to the buffer
    pdw=(DWORD *)pBuffer;
    // get the riff file format riff
    dwRiff=*pdw++;
    // get the data length
    dwLength=*pdw++;
    // get the riff file type ID
    dwType=*pdw++;

    // check we are a riff file
    if(dwRiff!=mmioFOURCC('R', 'I', 'F', 'F'))
    {
        return(false);
    }
```

Advanced Graphics with DirectX and OpenGL

CHAPTER 26

1143

26

ADVANCED
GRAPHICS WITH
DIRECTX AND
OPENGL

LISTING 26.26   Continued

```
// check we are a WAVE file
if(dwType!=mmioFOURCC('W', 'A', 'V', 'E'))
{
    return(false);
}
// get a pointer to the end of the data
pdwEnd=(DWORD *)((unsigned char *)pdw+dwLength-4);

// loop while we haven't reached the end of the data
while(pdw<pdwEnd)
{
    // get the section type
    dwType=*pdw++;
    // get the section length
    dwLength=*pdw++;

    switch(dwType)
    {
    // if this section is format info ...
    case mmioFOURCC('f', 'm', 't', ' '):
        // if we haven't yet got format info
        if(ppWaveHeader && !*ppWaveHeader)
        {
            // if the format isn't as long as it should be...
            if(dwLength<sizeof(WAVEFORMAT))
            {
                // ... then return error
                return(false);
            }
            // set the wave header to point as this part of the data
            *ppWaveHeader=(WAVEFORMATEX *)pdw;
            // if we have data and header then return
            if((!ppbWaveData||*ppbWaveData) &&
                (!pdwWaveSize ||* pdwWaveSize))
                return(true);
        }
        break;
    // if this section is data
    case mmioFOURCC('d', 'a', 't', 'a'):
        // if we haven't got data yet
        if((ppbWaveData && !*ppbWaveData) ||
           (pdwWaveSize && !* pdwWaveSize))
        {
            // get the data pointer
            if(ppbWaveData)
```

LISTING 26.26   Continued

```
                        *ppbWaveData=(unsigned char *)pdw;
                    // get the data length
                    if(pdwWaveSize)
                        * pdwWaveSize =dwLength;
                    // if we have everything then return
                    if(!ppWaveHeader || *ppWaveHeader)
                        return(true);
                }
                break;
            }
            // go to the next word alignment
            pdw=(DWORD *)((unsigned char *)pdw+((dwLength+1)&~1));
        }
        // we shouldn't have gotten this far, so return error
        return(false);
}
```

Bringing Together the WAV Loader Functions

Now all we need is a function to bring all these together. First we need to load the WAV file into buffers: one for the wave data, and one for the header. Next we need to create the IDirectSoundBuffer. Then we need to lock the IDirectSoundBuffer, load the data into it, and then unlock it. The code shown in Listing 26.27 does these things.

LISTING 26.27   Loading a WAV File into a DirectSound Buffer

```
bool BCBDirectSound::LoadWAVIntoDirectSoundBuffer( LPDIRECTSOUNDBUFFER
                                                    *DSBuffer, char *FileName )
{
    // will hold the loaded WAV file
    char *WAVFile;
    // the loaded WAV file's size
    int WAVFileSize;
    // the new DirectSoundBuffer description
    DSBUFFERDESC NewSoundBufferDescription;
    // the actual wave data parsed from the file
    unsigned char *WaveData;
    // pointers to the locked DirectSoundBuffer
    LPVOID pMem1, pMem2;
    // the sizes of the locked pointers
    DWORD dwSize1, dwSize2;
    // to hold errors
    HRESULT DSError;
```

Advanced Graphics with DirectX and OpenGL

CHAPTER 26

1145

26

ADVANCED
GRAPHICS WITH
DIRECTX AND
OPENGL

LISTING 26.27 Continued

```
// initialize WAVFile
WAVFile=NULL;

// zero the sound buffer description
ZeroMemory(&NewSoundBufferDescription, sizeof(DSBUFFERDESC));

// if we can't load the wav file then return error
if(!LoadWAVFromFile( WAVFile, WAVFileSize, FileName ))
    return( false );
// if we can't parse the wav file then return error
if(!ParseWavBuffer( WAVFile, &NewSoundBufferDescription.lpwfxFormat,
                    &WaveData, &NewSoundBufferDescription.dwBufferBytes ))
{
    delete WAVFile;
    return( false );
}
// if we can't create the DirectSoundBuffer then return error
if(!CreateSecondaryBuffer( DSBuffer, NewSoundBufferDescription ))
{
    delete WAVFile;
    return( false );
}
// try to lock off the DirectSoundBuffers memory
DSError = (*DSBuffer)->Lock(0, NewSoundBufferDescription.dwBufferBytes,
                            &pMem1, &dwSize1, &pMem2, &dwSize2, 0);
// if we failed then return error
if(FAILED(DSError))
{
    delete WAVFile;
    return( false );
}
// copy the first piece of locked memory
memcpy(pMem1, WaveData, dwSize1);
// if the second piece of memory needed to be locked then copy that to
if(dwSize2!=0)
    memcpy(pMem2, WaveData+dwSize1, dwSize2);
// unlock the memory again
(*DSBuffer)->Unlock(pMem1, dwSize1, pMem2, dwSize2);

// free the memory
delete WAVFile;

// return no error
return ( true );
}
```

We now have a perfectly functional `IDirectSoundBuffer`. The rest is extremely simple. To play the buffer you can call

```
DSError = DSBuffer->Play(res1, res2, how);
```

The first two parameters are reserved and must be 0 (zero). The last one specifies how you would like to play the buffer: either 0 to play it once and then stop or `DSBPLAY_LOOPING` to play it in a loop forever. The return value is of the type `HRESULT`. You can use the `FAILED()` macro to determine if the `Play()` command succeeded.

One problem with the above is that if the sound is already playing, instead of playing again over the top of the already playing version, it just carries on playing. This is all right for sounds that can occur only once (such as speech or a button click). However, you may want to play some sounds over other copies of themselves. The `IDirectSound` interface provides a function to copy `IDirectSoundBuffers` and achieve this.

A DirectSound Example Program—A Multiple Sound Player

In the `DirectSound` folder on the CD-ROM that accompanies this book, you will find an example program that demonstrates all of the DirectSound techniques discussed in this chapter. It includes the code for a sound engine, included in the `BCBDirectSound` unit.

First it initializes DirectSound. Then it sets the application's `OnIdle()` handler to point at one that is user defined and that constantly calls a function called `UpdatePlayingSounds()`. This function searches through the stack of playing sounds and removes any that have finished. The user can load WAV files using the File menu and play them by double-clicking on them.

Similar to the DirectDraw example program, `$(BCB)\lib\PSDK` has been added to the library path for the project. The project uses the `dsound.lib` library file provided with C++Builder.

In your own DirectSound applications, you can simply select Project, Add to Project from the main menu, then in the Files of Type combo box select Library File (`*.lib`) and browse to the `dsound.lib` file in the `\Lib\PSDK` folder where C++Builder was installed.

Taking DirectX Further

In addition to DirectDraw and DirectSound, which are the easiest APIs to use, DirectX includes other interfaces for using a variety of devices and multimedia formats. The following list shows other APIs included in DirectX:

- DirectInput is the DirectX API designed for low-latency user input, using keyboard, mouse, or joystick.

- DirectPlay is a network gaming API. It is designed to make connecting across the Internet, a LAN, or a serial cable much easier.
- Direct3D is the DirectX answer to high-speed (hardware-accelerated) 3D real-time graphics. It is designed for game programming.

DirectX References

This is a large subject, and you're bound to need additional information on DirectX programming. There are several places that you can look, including books written specifically on the subject and resources provided by Microsoft. Some useful resources are provided in the following list:

- *Inside DirectX*, Bradley Bargen and Peter Donnelly, ISBN 1-57231-696-9, published by Microsoft Press

  This is the most comprehensive guide to DirectDraw, DirectSound, DirectPlay, and DirectInput.
- The MSDN SDK Help

  This is provided with any subscription to MSDN and covers every aspect of DirectX.
- The DirectX Developers mailing list at `DIRECTXDEV@discuss.microsoft.com`

  Here are people who know what they are talking about: top DirectX developers and members of the teams that wrote DirectX.
- The MSDN DirectX Developer Center at `http://msdn.microsoft.com/DirectX`

  This is the main Internet resource for DirectX developers.

Summary

Within the space of this chapter, most of the basic functionality of the OpenGL, DirectDraw, and DirectSound APIs has been discussed. Of course, entire books have been devoted to the subject, so if you want to know more, have a look at the books, Web sites, and mailing lists mentioned.

Using the knowledge you have gained, you should be able to integrate high-performance graphics and sound into any Borland C++Builder 5 application. Something to remember about the DirectX API's in particular is that the computer your program is designed to run on must have drivers of the appropriate version installed, or the commands will fail. Always check the return values of any DirectX commands that have a reasonable chance of failing (initialization, creation of interfaces, and such). OpenGL will not bring your application down if a call fails, but the displayed results may be unpredictable or nonexistent.

C++Builder Application Deployment

PART V

IN THIS PART

Creating Help Files and Documentation

Drew Avis

IN THIS CHAPTER

- Technical Writing 101—Ten Quick Steps to Better Writing
- Types of Documentation
- Strategies for Online Documentation
- Help Formats
- WinHelp Format Help Files: The Windows Standard
- Microsoft HTML Help Files
- Help Properties and Methods in the VCL
- Resources for the Help Author

We've all had the experience before: searching first the online help and then the manual for a simple piece of information. You could be looking for a procedure for completing a task or a reference for an error message. But it's not there or, even worse, it's there but it's wrong. The documentation you provide is the only thing standing between your application and your users, and it can have a profound effect on their satisfaction with and perception of your product. Good documentation is so important to software users that it is increasingly an important consideration when users decide to purchase software, and is often part of product reviews in the media.

There is a story about the Microsoft team working on Word 97 that demonstrates this. While talking to users of the previous version (Word 95) to discover what new features users would value, the team discovered that 80% of desired features were already in the older product. This emphasized two things: Features can be buried in a poorly planned user interface, and bad documentation can keep them buried.

Regardless of the size of your application, it needs help (and I don't mean debugging). This chapter will outline the various documentation formats you can provide to your users and the different approaches you can take to documenting your applications.

> **NOTE**
>
> If you work for a medium to large organization, you can probably skip this chapter because you're lucky enough to have access to professional technical writers, folks who have developed special skills in writing documentation. If you don't have access to a writing group—if you are working for yourself, are a contractor responsible for the entire project, or work for a small organization—take this advice: Consider hiring a professional technical communicator to do your documentation for you. Various organizations (such as the Society for Technical Communication or the IEEE Technical Communication SIG) have local chapters in many cities and can easily provide you with a list of contract technical writers.
>
> On the other hand, if you're the type who is your own marketer, sales rep, customer support tech, and chief financial officer, read on, because you're going to be your own technical writer, too.

Technical Writing 101—Ten Quick Steps to Better Writing

Before we delve into the nuts and bolts of help systems and manual suites, let's take a quick look at what makes good technical writing.

- *Know your audience*—This is the most fundamental step to creating good documentation. Who exactly are your users? What are their needs when they turn to your documentation?

- *Remember the three Cs of technical writing*—Make it concise, complete, and correct.

- *Style counts*—In technical communication circles, style is a codeword for "consistency." For example, do you use bold for emphasis in one chapter and italics in another? Invest in a decent style guide. Microsoft Press publishes a guide specifically for software documentation. *The Chicago Manual of Style* is a good general-purpose style guide.

- *Plan your documentation from the beginning*—Remember that writing documentation will take time and may affect your development time line.

- *Always proofread your writing, and always have someone else proofread it as well*—Preferably someone who didn't fail English class in grade 8.

- *A picture can be worth a thousand words, but occasionally a picture is more like a thousand kicks to the head*—If a graphic provides additional information not already in the text or substantially reduces the amount of text, use it. If it merely looks good, cut it. If it merely looks good and weighs 500KB, cut it fast!

- *Work through all your procedures at least once*—Be sure that you're not missing a crucial step or adding unnecessary steps.

- *Always tell a user what to expect when he follows a procedure*—Don't just tell the user to click OK; tell him what will happen next.

- *Always tell a user if there is a danger of causing data loss or damage to the system*—This is important information that should be placed before a dangerous or risky procedure.

- *Treat your documentation as a fundamentally important feature of your application*—It's the only thing standing between your user and the interface.

Types of Documentation

Back in the good old days, there was one kind of documentation software developers provided with their products—a manual. In those days, the manual was often an unorganized, poorly written jumble of instructions for various commands and references for assorted errors, but rarely all the errors the user was likely to encounter. As the industry matured, its technical documentation matured with it, and today we see an array of performance support tools that accompany software. The following is a brief list of common documentation types, divided along the lines of media (paper or electronic):

Paper

- Manual
- Troubleshooting
- Reference
- Quick Start
- Keyboard Shortcuts
- Quick Reference

Electronic

- Help System
- Context-Sensitive Help
- Wizards
- Tutorials
- Daily Tips
- ToolTips
- What's This?
- Readme/Release Notes
- Web Site
- Knowledge Base

As the cost of printing and the power of online help systems have increased, software vendors have been moving away from the traditional paper manual. Instead, developers have been providing most documentation electronically, and the trend is to provide only online documentation and forego printed matter altogether. Microsoft followed this trend with the release of Windows 95, which had no printed documentation other than a thin installation manual. Unfortunately, Windows 95 also has fairly poor online (electronic) documentation and is not the best model to follow.

Strategies for Online Documentation

Before you begin documenting your application, you should sketch out a documentation plan—an overview of the types of help a user might need and how you are going to deliver that help. The exercise often begins with the question *Who will use this application?*—audience analysis. At the very least, most users will require procedures for accomplishing major tasks (or procedural information—see the "Procedural Help" section, later in this chapter).

Next, what sort of reference and conceptual information will users need? Will these sections be added to the main help file (as a glossary, for example) or in a separate help file (as a syntax reference)? How will you link procedural information to reference information and vice versa? Finally, decide if you will provide instructional help or tutorials with examples that will assist users in learning your application.

While the principles of good writing carry over from printed documentation to online documentation, there are some differences that will affect how you organize online help.

Approaches to Help

There are several broad categories of help that serve different information needs of end users (Hackos & Stevens). Consider the following categories of information:

- Procedural
- Reference
- Conceptual
- Instructional

Procedural Help

Procedural help is the most common type of help provided for end users (see Figure 27.1), probably because it is task-based and meets the immediate need to accomplish something. Good procedures start at a common point (the main screen, for example) and take the user step-by-step through a task. They indicate where to exercise caution and tell the user what to expect after each step ("The File Manager Window Appears").

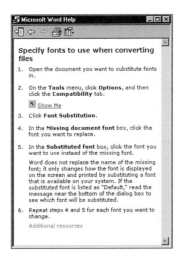

FIGURE 27.1

Example of procedural help from Microsoft Word.

However, good procedures are hard to write. How do you know what steps to include? How much can you assume the user knows? For example, should you tell the user to click the Close button to close a window? There are no easy answers to these questions. One approach is to write novice and expert procedures and label them as such; another is to write expert procedures and place novice information in expandable text or pop-ups, where the novice user can access them if needed.

Two basic types of information that are procedural are feature/tasks and troubleshooting. While good feature/task procedures will help a user through features and tasks in the application, troubleshooting procedures are invaluable for helping users solve problems when something goes wrong.

The following are some tips for writing procedures:

- Include a simple purpose statement at the beginning of the procedure. For example, "This procedure is used to add a new customer in the customer database."

- Provide the big picture. If the user must first create a customer profile before the customer can be added to a database, say so, and create a link to that topic.

- Tell the user what to expect when he completes a step. If a step is dangerous and may cause data loss or software failure, point this out before the step, not after.

- Provide just enough information to complete the task.

Reference Help

Any information that is not meant to be learned or memorized should be placed in reference help where it can be looked up whenever needed (see Figure 27.2). For this reason, strong organization principles must be applied to a reference section, and it must be very easy to search and navigate. Reference information is seldom task-based. Good reference help is exhaustive; it must contain every conceivable topic within its scope to be effective. If your reference is a glossary of terms used in your software, every single term should be included. Examples of reference information are: formulas used in the software, data tables used in the software, background reading (collected articles), and programming language syntax.

Conceptual Help

Conceptual information covers the "why" of what your application does. This information is not usually needed to perform individual tasks, but it may be very helpful to long-term maintenance or use of the software (see Figure 27.3). Conceptual help should assist users in making decisions and link to procedures to follow when those decisions have been made. This type of help does not need to be exhaustive—you do not need to include every bit of information about the application's background—but you should provide enough information for users to gain a reasonable understanding of why they need to perform certain tasks.

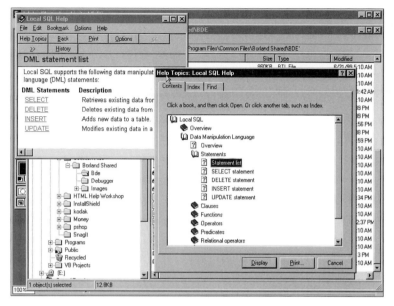

FIGURE 27.2

Example of reference help from Local SQL Server help, including contents.

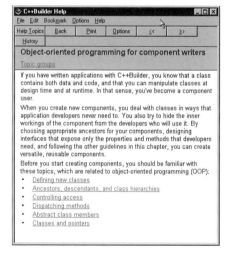

FIGURE 27.3

Example of conceptual help from C++Builder.

Instructional Help

Instructional information is designed to teach users how to use your software. For this reason, instructional information will often explain why a user must perform a certain step and will explain terms in detail (see Figure 27.4). Sections of instructional information should include a learning statement telling the user what he will learn by reading the section. Good instructional information also contains highly detailed examples and often steps the user through these examples with commentary at each step. The more relevant the example is to a user's situation, the more the user will learn. In contrast to generic procedural help, instructional help should be verbose and specific.

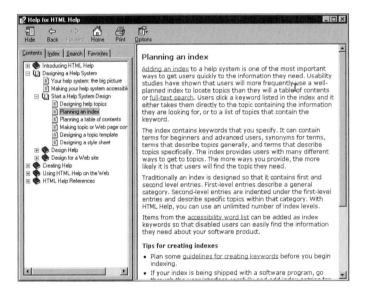

FIGURE 27.4
Example of instructional help from HTML Help Workshop.

Help Formats

Help or a *help system* has come to mean product documentation formatted to be used onscreen. Table 27.1 provides a list of current help formats.

TABLE 27.1   Help Formats

Name	Description	Comments
WinHelp, Windows Help	Compiled help format developed by Microsoft, current version is 4, supported on Windows 95/98.	The original and still most popular Windows help system, version 4 supports 256-color graphics, table of contents, index, full text search, pop-ups, keywords, related keywords, and hypertext links. No new releases planned (dead technology) but third parties support enhancements (background graphics, Web links, advanced search). Compiled from `.rtf` source to `.hlp` format.
HTML Help	Compiled help format developed by Microsoft, supported in Windows 98, 2000. Current version is 1.3.	Currently supported help system, is not yet as fully featured or mature as WinHelp. Native browser shipped with Windows 98, 2000, NT5; viewable on Windows 95 and and NT4 using Internet Explorer (at least version 4). Compiled from `.html` source into `.chm` format.
NetHelp	Native HTML Help format developed by Netscape. Current version: 2.	Net Help has never really caught on as a help system format, but it is used in Navigator. NetHelp 2 requires Netscape Navigator 4 or later. Supports some basic context sensitivity.
Independent Native HTML Help Formats	Native HTML Help formats, developed by third-party help-authoring tool developers.	Typically, these formats use JavaScript and Java to simulate HTML Help features but are usually platform and browser independent. Examples are WebHelp (developed by RoboHelp) and InterHelp (developed by ForeHelp).
Java Help	HTML/XML help format, developed by Sun Microsystems.	Requires JVM and Java Help browser. Best suited to Java applications. Runs on any platform.

There is a myriad of other help formats that are not directly applicable to C++Builder applications (such as Windows CE Help, Oracle Help, and help variants available for Linux and UNIX).

27

CREATING HELP
FILES AND
DOCUMENTATION

WinHelp Format Help Files: The Windows Standard

Although there are many help formats available, standard WinHelp is the best choice for the majority of C++Builder projects because of its richness of features and ease of deployment. It will run on all Windows systems (the 16-bit version 3 is compatible back to Windows 3.1), and there are a large number of free and commercial tools that produce this format. The next most popular choice would be HTML Help, which is standard for Windows 98, 2000, and NT5. It also shows up in MS Office 2000. The most recent release of HTML Help (1.3, released with Windows 2000) has more features, but it is more difficult to install if you are not targeting a single OS (Windows 2000). For example, HTML Help requires at least Internet Explorer (IE) 4.

The most important difference between WinHelp and HTML Help is the degree to which the former is supported in C++Builder. All of C++Builder's help properties and methods are geared toward WinHelp and require little or no extra coding to provide context sensitivity. On the other hand, HTML Help is not well supported in C++Builder, but it can be implemented with some extra effort.

Let's take a look at the standard WinHelp features (see Figure 27.5) and some of the tools available to author it.

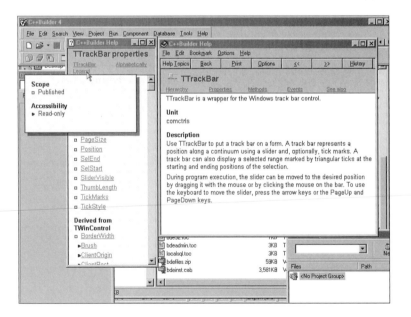

FIGURE 27.5

Example of a standard WinHelp system from C++Builder, showing a main window, a secondary window, and a pop-up window.

The following are the basic building units of WinHelp:

- *Topics*—A *topic* is a section of text covering a single theme. Topics have titles and appear in windows (windows can have scrolling and non-scrolling regions—the title often appears in a non-scrolling region at the top of the window).

- *Links*—Also called *jumps*, these are hypertext links that jump to another topic. In WinHelp, these are always single-underlined and in green. Pop-up links display a pop-up topic in another window that disappears as soon as the mouse is clicked. Pop-up links are always dashed-underlined and in green.

- *Table of Contents (TOC)*—A list of major topics in the help file, the TOC is arranged in an explorer tree-view with books containing one or more topics or sub-books. A TOC can contain entries across help files and can link related help topics.

- *Index*—A list of keywords that link to their related topics.

- *Search*—WinHelp supports a full-text search. The search index is dynamically generated the first time a help file is used (in an `.fts` file).

Help-Authoring Tools

The professional help-authoring field is dominated by a few players. Table 27.2 lists the most popular commercial products.

TABLE 27.2   Help-Authoring Tools

Product	Vendor	Comments
RoboHelp	Bluesky	Complete authoring tool, available in a number of "suites." Relies on MS Word. Produces HTML Help, WinHelp, and several other formats.
ForeHelp	ForeHelp	Complete authoring tool. Available in HTML and WinHelp versions. Self-contained editor.
Doc-To-Help	WexTech	Complete authoring tool. Relies on MS Word.
WebWorks Publisher	Quadralay	Expensive and complete authoring tool. Relies on Adobe FrameMaker. Produces WinHelp, HTML, and a number of other formats.

Context-Sensitive Help

Context-sensitive refers to help that is aware of the active control or form. That is, when the user is viewing a dialog, the cursor is in a text box, or the mouse is hovering over a button, help specific to that item appears. There are generally four types of context-sensitive help:

- ToolTips
- What's This? or pop-up help
- Standard WinHelp
- Embedded help

ToolTips

ToolTips appear when the mouse pauses over a control for a few seconds. The text is usually very simple and describes or names the control.

What's This? or Pop-Up Help

This type of help appears when a user right-clicks an item or selects the What's This? button and clicks a control (see the example in Figure 27.6). It appears as a pop-up window. The text usually describes the item and may provide some brief procedural or task-based information.

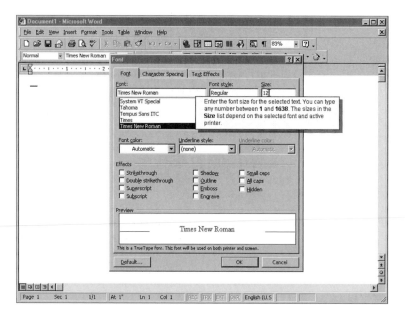

FIGURE 27.6

Example of "What's This?" help.

Standard WinHelp

When a user presses F1, C++Builder will open the application's help file. If a context ID is attached to the form or active control when the user presses F1, the topic indicated by that context ID will appear. This is an excellent way to provide an overview of the tasks that can be performed on a form or with a control.

Embedded Help

This refers to the most often overlooked form of help provided to users—text that appears in dialog boxes, in error messages, over buttons and other controls, and any help information that is hard coded into the application.

The MS Help Workshop

C++Builder comes with the Microsoft WinHelp compiler Help Workshop. It is in the C++Builder directory under /help/tools/ as hcw.exe. You can write simple help files in WinHelp format using nothing more than a text editor that can save a file in rich text (.rtf) format and hcw. However, this approach is not recommended for larger help systems or systems that implement many of WinHelp 4's features. This approach is akin to coding a large Web site by hand in raw HTML; it's possible but tedious and prone to error. You are better off using one of the many freeware, shareware, or commercial help-authoring products available (see "Help-Authoring Tools Available on the Internet" at the end of this chapter). After completing the following tutorial, you will see how simple it would be to automate the process with a small number of macros in a scriptable text editor (such as Word), which is the approach of many commercial and non-commercial authoring packages. In fact, most help-authoring systems use hcw.exe as their compiler; they just manage topic codes, index entries, and so on, and save a precompile version of the help system in .rtf format that gets compiled by hcw.

What follows is a short tutorial to get you started on MS Help Workshop. You can also view the HCW help for more information on WinHelp API calls and compiler options. Sample files based on this tutorial are on the CD-ROM that accompanies this book, in the folder HelpExample. The rich text file is called help_ex.rtf, the map file is help_ex.map, the project file is help_ex.hpj, and the compiled file is help1.hlp. A C++Builder project that calls the help file is also included.

WinHelp is compiled from rich text source, but it relies on tags to create separate help topics, topic IDs, links between the topics, index entries, and a browse sequence. Tags are inserted as footnotes on the first line of the topic. Technically, WinHelp only requires topic IDs to compile. In reality, a usable help system requires at least a browse sequence, topic titles, and links.

This tutorial will take you through the steps necessary to create a simple help system for your C++Builder project.

1. Create a topics file. (In this example, I will use MS Word, but you can use any text editor that handles generic rich text format.)

   Open a new file. Write a list of topics that follow, each on its own line between topics. Under each topic title, write a few sentences of help. The first topic should be Overview or Contents because this simple help file will not have a standard Topics tab.

   Overview

   Edit Box

   Check Box

   Glossary

   Figure 27.7 shows this file in Microsoft Word after the footnote codes have been added.

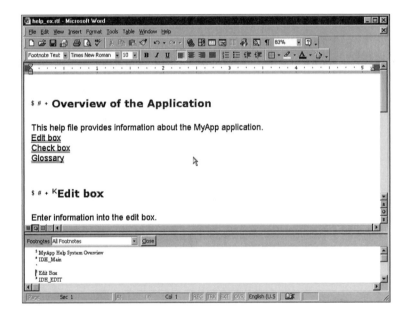

FIGURE 27.7

Example of editing a topics file in Microsoft Word.

2. Each topic requires tags to indicate its ID, title, and so on. Enter the tag by placing the cursor before the topic header text and inserting a footnote. For the footnote's symbol, use the tag symbol in the table. In the footnote itself, enter the ID, title, keywords, or browse sequence text. Table 27.3 lists the tags to enter for each topic.

TABLE 27.3   Topic Tags

Tag Type	Symbol	Purpose	Notes
ID	#	Each topic needs a unique identifier. Used as destination name for links.	Do not use these characters: # = + @ * % !. Use no more than 255 characters. Should start with IDH_ if the topic will be called from within a C++ application (context sensitive).
Title	$	Title of the topic as it will appear on the Contents tab and in Find windows.	Up to 255 characters (spaces count).
Keyword	K	List of keywords used to create the help file's index.	Keywords should be separated by a semicolon. Do not use spaces before or after keywords. Do not use carriage returns. 255 characters max per keyword.
A Keyword	A	List of keywords used to associate a topic with other topics. (Used primarily for See Also buttons.)	Keywords should be separated by a semicolon. Do not use spaces before or after keywords. Do not use carriage returns. 255 characters max per keyword.
Browse Sequence	+	Used to determine the order of topics when the user clicks Browse buttons (<< and >>). Most systems use a single browse sequence.	Do not use these characters: # = + @ * % !Do not use spaces. Max of 50 characters. To use browse sequences, you must also activate the Browse buttons in the project file. The easiest way to activate an automatic browse sequence is to add the + tag to each topic but leave it blank. HCW will put topics in the order they are in the source rich text file; to change the order, just change the order of topics in the .rtf.

27

CREATING HELP FILES AND DOCUMENTATION

TABLE 27.3 Continued

Tag Type	Symbol	Purpose	Notes
Window	>	Used to determine in what type of window the topic will appear. Standard systems use three types of windows: main topics, procedure topics, and pop-up (or What's This?) help.	Use the same name as a window defined in the help project file (see step 7). The default is the main window. You do not need to enter this tag for topics appearing in the main window.

3. Define formatting for the help project. Settings such as font, color, and size of text will carry over to the help system. When formatting text, do not use fonts that may not be installed on the user's system (in other words, do not use anything other than standard Windows fonts). Tables do not translate well into WinHelp; tables do not reflow, and settings, such as borders and shading, do not carry over. If you must use a table, make it as narrow as possible and use a simple border. Alternately, to preserve shading or special formatting, save the table as a .bmp graphic and display it that way.

4. Create topic jumps.

   Perform the following steps to create hypertext jumps from one topic to another within the help system.

   a. Find the text (or graphic) you would like to tag as a help jump.

      Example: For more information, refer to Writing Online Help.

   b. Enter the ID for the topic jumped to after the link text (adding no extra space).

      Example (if the topic ID is IDH_WRITING_HELP): For more information, refer to Writing Online Help IDH_WRITING_HELP.

   c. Select the jump text and format it as double underlined (see Figure 27.8). (Format the text as single underlined to create a pop-up topic.)

   d. Select the topic ID and format it as hidden text.

      Example: For more information, refer to Writing Online Help.

5. Save the Word file in rich text format (.rtf).

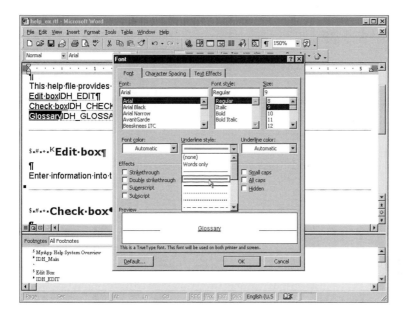

27

CREATING HELP
FILES AND
DOCUMENTATION

FIGURE 27.8
Setting double underline format in Word.

6. Create a MAP file that links help topics to C++Builder Help IDs. You can create this file in Word or any other text editor because it is a simple text file.

You can link help topics to a form or VCL component's `HelpContext` property. The easiest way to assign help topics to different components is to set each component's `HelpContext` property at designtime and then associate the `HelpContext` property to topic IDs in a map file.

There are other ways to call specific help topics from within C++Builder—see the section "Adding What's This? Help to C++Builder," later in this chapter.

You can skip creating a separate map file if you want to add Topic ID/Context ID pairs manually in the help project. This is probably okay for smaller projects, but it is easier to manage larger projects with a single or multiple map files. For example, developers could create separate map files for each form. In updates, only files associated with changed forms would have to be edited.

Map files are ASCII text files, each line having the following format:

```
#define TOPIC_ID HelpContextNumber
```

where `TOPIC_ID` is a topic's ID, and `HelpContextNumber` is the `HelpContext` property of a VCL control. C and C++ style comments are valid in map files. An example map file is shown in the following code segment:

```
/* MyAppHelp.MAP
   The following topics are used on the main form
*/

#define IDH_ OVERVIEW 10 // overview topic
#define IDH_FORM1 20 // form 1 default topic
#define IDH_EDIT1 30 // edit 1 topic
#define IDH_CHECK1 40 // Checkbox1 topic
#define IDH_FORM2 50 // form 2 default topic
#define IDH_EDIT2 60 // edit 2 topic
```

Save the map file as a text file. Give it a .map extension.

7. Create a help project file, and compile the help file.

Start Help Workshop (see Figure 27.9).

FIGURE 27.9

Microsoft Help Workshop main screen.

Add the .rtf source file to the project by clicking Files. The Topic Files dialog appears. Click Add, and select the .rtf.

To add Browse buttons, add a help window and add buttons. Click Windows, and enter a name for the main window (usually MAIN). Add a second window type for pop-up (What's This? help)—base this window on "error message." Set various properties, such as title bar text, position (use auto-sizer to make things easy), color, and buttons. On the Buttons tab, check Browse.

Add the map file to the project. Click Map, Include, and add the `.map` file. Note that the topic ID and context numbers can be added manually by clicking Add. This is an alternative to creating a MAP file (in step 5).

Click Save and Compile to save the project and compile the help file.

8. Link the help file to your C++Builder project.

   In your C++Builder project, set the compiled help file as the application's help file under Project, Options, Application, Help file, or set the help file at runtime with the following code:

   ```
   Application->HelpFile = "MyApp.hlp";
   ```

   Next, set each component's `HelpContext` property to the number used in the help file. For example, set Form1's `HelpContext` to `10`. Components with a `HelpContext` of `0` inherit their parent's `HelpContext` number.

   You can now compile and test your application's help file. Press F1 when any component has the focus to view the associated help topic.

Adding What's This? Help to C++Builder

What's This? help is a form of help especially suited to dialog boxes that allow a user to accomplish a specific task, and on which the user may require help for each control. It is typically accessed through a help button (?) on the window's title bar. When a user clicks the help button, the cursor changes to `TCursorType crHelp (-20)`; then, when the user clicks a control, a pop-up window appears with the help topic associated with that control's `HelpContext` number. Authoring What's This? help is the same as authoring standard help; keep in mind the following tips:

- What's This? help topics should not have a non-scrolling region. If they do, only the text in the non-scrolling region will appear. Non-scrolling regions of a help window are defined with the "keep with next" paragraph tag. All text at the beginning of a topic with this tag applied will appear in the non-scrolling region, while the rest of the text will appear in the help window proper.

- In C++Builder, set the form for which you would like to provide What's This? help with the following properties:

  - `BorderStyle` should be `bsDialog`. `bsDialog` makes the form a standard dialog with borders that are not resizable.

  - `BorderIcons` should be `biSystemMenu = true`, `biMinimize` and `biMaximize = false`, `biHelp = true`.

Forms with these settings will have the What's This? help button, and help will appear in a pop-up window at the cursor position. The dialog on the right in Figure 27.10 illustrates these settings. The dialog is from the sample help project on the CD-ROM.

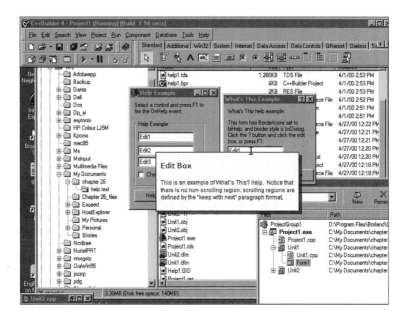

FIGURE 27.10

What's This? help in a C++Builder form.

> **CAUTION**
>
> One caveat: Even pressing F1 will display help in a pop-up; to display help in the standard WinHelp window in these dialogs, use the `Application->HelpJump()` or `Application->HelpContext()` methods in the `OnHelp` event.

Expanding Your Help Project Using Advanced Features

WinHelp supports many other features that you can use to enhance your help.

- *Macros*—WinHelp supports a large number of macros that add functionality to the help system. For example, to add a link to topics related to printing, type the text for the link, and then an exclamation mark and the KLink macro: `related topics!KLink(printing, print, printer)`. Apply the link formatting (double underline) to the link text and

He

C++B
lows ¿

Hel

TWin

The H€
focus ¿
appear
way, a
More t

TApp

This p
through
erty at
guage,

TCust

Use thi
conveni
topics f
property

Help

TAppli

This me
of WinH
HELP_CO

bool

Example

Applicat

hidden character formatting to the macro text (including the exclamation mark). The Microsoft Help Workshop contains a complete reference of WinHelp macros.

- *Build Tag*—You can specify a build tag for topics and then indicate which build tags to include or exclude from a help file in the help project file. This allows you to create a single help source file for different versions of your application. For example, you might give the build tag pro to certain topics that only apply to the professional version of your application. Exclude the pro build tag when compiling the help for a basic version, and these topics will not be included in the final file.

- *Window Type*—WinHelp allows you to define several different window types. Typically, a standard topic window contains a non-scrolling title area and a scrolling region containing topic text. You may want to define a second window for procedures and another window for pop-up help. For example, What's This? help cannot contain a non-scrolling region.

Microsoft HTML Help Files

Unlike Help Workshop (which ships with C++Builder), you need to download the most current version of Microsoft's HTML Help Workshop, shown in Figure 27.11, from their Web site at `http://msdn.microsoft.com/workshop/author/htmlhelp/`.

HTML Help is limited in that it requires Internet Explorer (at least version 4) on Windows 95 or NT4. The HTML Help viewer/Internet Explorer is distributed with Windows 98, 2000, and NT5.

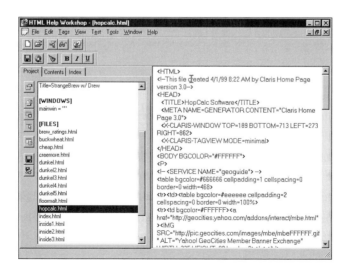

FIGURE 27.11

Microsoft HTML Help Workshop.

TABLE 27.4   WinHelp API Command Methods

Int Command	Action	Int Data
HELP_COMMAND	Runs a Help macro or macro string.	Address of a string that specifies the name of the Help macro(s) to run. If the string specifies multiple macro names, the names must be separated by colons or semicolons. You must use the short form of the macro name for some macros because WinHelp does not support the long name.
HELP_CONTENTS	Displays the topic specified by the Contents option in the OPTIONS section of the .HPJ file. This command is for backward compatibility. New programs should provide a .CNT file and use the HELP_FINDER command.	Ignored; set to 0.
HELP_CONTEXT	Displays the topic identified by the specified context identifier defined in the MAP section of the .HPJ file.	Unsigned long integer containing the context topic identifier.
HELP_CONTEXTMENU	Displays the Help menu for the selected window, and then displays (in a pop-up window) the topic for the selected control.	Address of an array of double word pairs. The first word in each pair is an identifier, and the second a context number for a topic.
HELP_CONTEXTPOPUP	Displays in a pop-up window the topic identified by the specified context identifier defined in the MAP section of the .HPJ file.	Unsigned long integer containing the context identifier for a topic.
HELP_FINDER	Displays the Help Topics dialog box.	Ignored; set to 0.

TABLE 27.4 Continued

Int Command	Action	Int Data
HELP_FORCEFILE	Ensures that WinHelp is displaying the correct Help file. If the incorrect Help file is being displayed, WinHelp opens the correct one; otherwise, there is no action.	Ignored; set to 0.
HELP_HELPONHELP	Displays Help on how to use WinHelp, if the WINHLP32.HLP file is available.	Ignored; set to 0.
HELP_INDEX	Displays the topic specified by the CONTENTS option in the OPTIONS section of the .HPJ file. This command is for backward compatibility. New programs should provide a .CNT file and use the HELP_FINDER command.	Ignored; set to 0.
HELP_KEY	Displays the topic in the keyword table that matches the specified keyword, if there is an exact match. If there is more than one match, this command displays the Topics Found list box.	Address of a keyword string. Multiple keywords must be separated by semicolons.
HELP_MULTIKEY	Displays the topic specified by a keyword in an alternative keyword table.	Address of a MULTIKEYHELP structure that specifies a table footnote character and a keyword.
HELP_PARTIALKEY	Displays the topic in the keyword table that matches the specified keyword if there is an exact match. If there is more than one match, this command displays the Topics Found dialog box. To display the Index without passing a keyword, you should use a pointer to an empty string.	Address of a keyword string. Multiple keywords must be separated by semicolons.

- Name: SOS Help! Info-Author

  Cost: 30-day commercial demo

  System requires: Win 95

  Web site: `http://www.lamaura.com/`

  Output: Windows 3.x, Windows 95

- Name: Visual Help Pro

  Cost: 30-day commercial demo

  System requires: Win 95

  Web site: `http://www.winwareinc.com/`

  Output: Windows 3.1, Windows 95, HTML Help

- Name: Windows Help Designer

  Cost: Shareware ($49 to $79)

  System requires: Win 95/NT

  Web site: `http://www.visagesoft.com/`

  Output: Windows 95, HTML Help

Summary

No application should be delivered to end users without some form of help. However, the only thing worse than no help is bad help. As this chapter has shown, help can come in many forms and file formats. The format that is still the most popular in the Windows world is WinHelp, despite Microsoft's emphasis on the newer HTML Help format. For C++Builder, WinHelp is a natural choice because it is supported transparently through the VCL, and C++Builder ships with the Microsoft Help Workshop.

The true challenge of writing help, however, is not selecting the right delivery format, but writing concise and truly useful information. It is useful to plan your help files carefully, deciding what information is procedural, reference, conceptual, and instructional. During this stage, it is also important to discover what information your users actually need. After you have a good idea of what your users' needs are, you are on your way to writing high-quality online help.

Software Distribution

Simon Rutley-Frayne
Phillip H. Blanton II
Khalid Almannai

IN THIS CHAPTER

- **Language Internationalization and Localization**
- **Resource DLL Wizard**
- **Other Files and Programs to Ship**
- **Copyrighting and Software Licensing**
- **Software Protection**
- **Shareware**
- **Distribution and Marketing Via the Internet**

The complete text for this chapter appears on the CD-ROM.

Software Installation and Updates

Simon Rutley-Frayne
J. Alan Brogan
Yoto Yotov

IN THIS CHAPTER

- **Install and Uninstall**
- **CAB and INF Files**
- **Versions, Updates, and Patches**
- **Version Control and TeamSource**
- **Using InstallShield Express**

We've already taken a look at software distribution issues, including shareware methods and marketing in Chapter 28, "Software Distribution." In this chapter, we shall discover methods for trouble-free installation and maintenance of your software, be it a shareware or commercial application.

Here, we shall investigate the use of ClickTeam's InstallMaker, cabinet (.CAB) and info (.INF) files, and InstallShield Express (ISX, bundled with C++Builder) for software installation. We'll also discuss software maintenance with advice on creating and distributing software updates and patches, and we'll introduce you to TeamSource, the new version control system.

Install and Uninstall

After you have created your application, you need to have a way that your end users can install it—and all the associated files—easily, so that it will run correctly.

Creating an installation program will allow you to control which files should be installed to where, and will do it in such a way that even a novice user can install your application and run it.

There are quite a few installation creator programs on the market, some freeware and some shareware or full commercial versions. I will list a few Web sites at the end of this section so you can have a look at each of them for yourself.

Installation Program Creators

An installation program that the end user will use works in much the same way that C++Builder does. You tell it what you want it to do in the way of creating a script, compiling it, including and compressing the application files, and creating the user interface. This is then put into a series of installation files that you distribute.

How They Work

Some installation creator programs use a wizard-type method of getting the script created; you simply fill in the blanks with items such as the application files to be included, the default destination directory, and Readme and Licensing information.

This information is converted into the script that the program reads at build time to create the actual installation files.

These files come in two different types: a single installation file or a multiple file installation. Both have the same result, but the advantages and disadvantages of each are discussed in the next sections.

Single File Installation

The advantage of this file type is that all of your installation is contained in one file, which can be easily placed on a CD-ROM.

The disadvantage is that it is virtually impossible to distribute your application via a floppy disk set because the single installation file is normally larger than 1.44MB.

Multiple File Installation

The advantage of this type of installation is that you can distribute these installation files on floppy disks.

The disadvantage is that there are more files to become corrupted. I have had this problem before and the most annoying thing was it was a file only 2Kb in size and the installation program would not work without it.

Install Maker

Install Maker from ClickTeam comes in two versions, a commercial version for which you have to pay for the license, and a freeware version that shows a screen message to the end user about how the installation file has been created by Install Maker from ClickTeam.

For more information on the licensing of Install Maker, go to http://www.clickteam.com.

How to Create an Installation Program with Install Maker

You can download this installation program from the ClickTeam Web site or from the CD-ROM that accompanies this book.

Install Maker is perfect for standalone applications that have no complicated features that need to be added, such as Registry entries and database capabilities. For those features, you are better off using Installshield.

Install Maker creates a relatively small installation program with good compression rates for included files. We will step you through the processes of the wizard that are shown when you create an installation program.

1. Navigating the Welcome Screen

   After you have Install Maker installed, run it and you will be presented with the Installation Wizard. At this stage, you have the option to carry on using the Wizard or to use the main user interface to create your installation program.

   If this is your first time using this application, I would advise that you use the wizard until you know your way around the program better.

2. Designating the Source and Destination Directories

   Now you can select the folder where all of your files should be stored. It's a good idea to have all of your files in one separate folder for this type of installation. You can also have subfolders, for example

   ```
   MyApplcationFolder - MySubfolder
   ```

   Install Maker can then collect all of these files in the main folder and subfolders (installed with the same name) and install them in the desired directory on the end user's computer. To enable this feature, select the Include Sub-Directories check box (set as active by default).

3. Specifying the Program Title

   Next, specify the language of the install application, either English or French. Install Maker developers are French, hence the language choice.

   Now enter a relevant name for your installation application. This will be shown to end users when they run this file.

   We should point out that at any time during the wizard setup, you can press the Preview button to see what the current screen will look like when an end user runs the installation application at that point.

4. Creating the Shell

   On this screen, find the main executable file that you want to create an icon for and give an appropriate name. You also have the option of putting that icon on the desktop screen; we would advise against this because too many icons on the end users desktop makes the desktop confusing.

5. Inserting Additional Information

   On this screen, you have the option of entering some additional text, a Readme file or licensing information for example. This section does not have an open file button, but will allow you to enter some text in the provided field via the copy and paste method. After you have added your additional information, we suggest you look at all of the text to make sure the formatting of the text is correct; click the Preview button for a true representation.

6. Setting the Installation Window

   You can now choose the size of installation screen you want and the name you want shown to end users when they run the installation program.

7. Specifying Bitmap Images for the Installation

   This next part of the wizard allows you to place two bitmap images in your installation program. One word of caution though: Any extra files you add to this program will make the overall size of the installation program larger. This is not a real consideration when you are going to distribute your application via a CD-ROM, but if you are thinking of distributing your application on the Internet or floppy disk(s), think hard about making the overall file as small as possible, to make it more attractive to potential customers.

The first image you can select will need to be a certain size, 128 pixels wide by 280 pixels high and of no more than 256 colors. This image will be shown on the main introduction screen and to the left of the text in the main text box. If you are unsure, just select an image and click the Preview button.

The second image will be tiled all over the background of the main screen and should be no more than 256 colors. Again, if you are unsure, click the Preview button.

8. Specifying the Default Installation Directory

The next screen allows you to enter the default directory in which you want your application and associated files installed on your end user's computer. For instance

```
"C:\Program Files\MyCompany\MyApplcation"
```

The idea of this is that if the end user is a novice computer user, all he has to do is click Next during the installation process to successfully install your application.

The default directory can be any valid drive and directory; you should not even consider a different drive for obvious reasons.

This wizard also gives you the option of retrieving the installation directory from an `*.ini` file of a Registry entry.

9. Setting the End Page Options

In this section of the wizard, you can provide a Readme file or a license agreement that will be available for the end user to read when the installation program finishes.

You can also choose to have an application file run when the installation program finishes.

10. Creating an Uninstall Program

The next screen only has one option available for you to select and that is to create an uninstall program. This should always be checked (set as checked by default) unless there are some exceptional circumstances because the end user should always have an easy way to uninstall your application if needed.

With this option checked, the installation program will create a small `.exe` file that can be run by the end user should he want to remove your application. This can be done by the short cut icon automatically created at install time or via the Control Panel, Add/Remove Programs option.

11. Completing the Wizard

This brings us to the last screen of the wizard, and it gives you the option of building the installation program or not. If you are happy that you have set all the options correctly,

29

go ahead and click the Finish button and build your installation program. On the other hand, if you are not sure you have set all the options correctly, just click the Back button to check the check box and look at the program's settings.

12. Building the Installation Program

After you have chosen to build your installation program, the wizard will ask where to build the .exe file and what to call it. This is obviously up to you, but don't put it in the same directory or subdirectory of your main application files; otherwise, this file will be added to your installation program if you have to remake it.

When the file has been built, you can save the project files in a safe place ready for future updates or corrections as and when they are needed.

You can also test your newly created installation program. The best way to do so is to open Windows Explorer and run the file the same way that an end user would. When you are happy with the installation program and have made all the changes you want, it is always best to run the installation program on a different computer to verify that the application is being installed correctly and that all of the application works.

Don't worry if you don't get it right the first time; just go back and make the changes to your project files and then build the installation program again and test it again. Make sure you uninstall the current version of your application first.

13. Creating Extra Icons for Extra Files

You can make an extra icon for your application in the main user interface after you have finished with the Wizard setup process, and you may also want an extra icon for your help file or Readme.txt file if you have either of those.

To do this, select the Files tab and then select the file for which you want to create an icon. There are two fields on the right side of the screen called Folder and Name. Simply name the folder where you want to install the icon, name the icon something relevant, and that is it—a new icon to install with your application.

> **NOTE**
>
> To install the new icon to the same folder as the auto-generated icons, use the same folder name as your main .exe file.

Uninstalling

The next thing that installation programs have is a method for your end users to uninstall your application. Most installation programs have this feature already built in and set automatically, like Install Maker, so you don't have to worry about including or adding the function.

Unfortunately, end users who install your application may not want to keep it, for whatever reason. Therefore, you should make sure that they can uninstall it easily and, if at all possible, completely.

It is a well-known fact that many of the applications you install do not uninstall themselves completely—hence, the need for Windows Cleaner programs. As developers, it is up to us to make sure that our applications don't leave redundant files or Registry entries on the end users' hard drives.

The obvious way to do this is to note all of the files you need to make your application work on another computer, and then be sure they have been removed.

To do this, run your installation program and, when it has finished, run the uninstall method to see if the files have been removed. The only way that files can be left behind is if the end user adds the files either on his own or as part of your program or if you have not set the automatic uninstall option.

This is very difficult if not impossible for you to do by setting the auto uninstall feature of an installation creator program. The reason is that this type of feature will only uninstall the files and Registry entries it installed in the first place. This feature cannot remove anything that was created during the runtime of your application.

You may have come across this with other applications that you have uninstalled yourself. When the uninstall program has run, it may give an error message to say that folder *xx* could not be removed. When you look at why the error was generated, the reason will be that there were foreign files in that folder that were created at runtime by the application and were not there when the application was initially installed, so the folder could not be deleted.

Sometimes, there are files that will need to be left on the end user's computer. For example, your application may use certain DLL files that are needed by the Windows system to continue running. When this happens, the end user sees a message that says the file is a system file and asks if he wants to remove it.

The following are some Internet links for other installation creator programs:

Setup Factory: `http://www.indigorose.com/`

Inno Setup: `http://www.jordanr.dhs.org/`

Soysal Setup: `http://www.soysal.com/ssetup`

Wise Setup: `http://www.wisesolutions.com/imakfeat.htm`

CAB and INF Files

Cabinet and information files are an effective way of distributing and reducing the download time of your software and Internet applications. Their seamless integration with the Microsoft Internet Explorer Web browser allows automatic file installation and version management. In the following pages, you'll learn how to create your own CAB and INF files.

About CAB Files

When it comes to storing or transferring files, no one wants to deal with large amounts of data. A solution to this problem is so-called file compression. File compression programs take advantage of the fact that there are often patterns in the sequences of ones and zeroes. They assign specific codes to these patterns, thus transforming large files into smaller ones.

Microsoft's way of compressing files is the CAB format (short for Cabinet) based on the Lempel-Ziv compression. In fact, both Microsoft Windows and Microsoft Office are distributed using CAB installation packages, as shown in Figure 29.1. Of course, a relevant question would be why you as a developer would want to use this format.

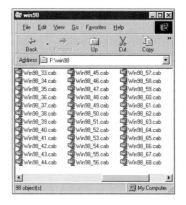

FIGURE 29.1
Microsoft Windows installation using CAB packages.

In addition to reducing download time, which should be the obvious intent of all compression products, CAB files are currently the easiest way of compressing and distributing ActiveX controls and Java classes over the Internet. Microsoft also provides developers with the necessary tools and components to utilize this technology in its Cabinet Software Development Kit (SDK).

> **CAUTION**
>
> You'll find the CABARC utility that is part of the Cabinet SDK in the C++Builder BIN folder. Unfortunately, other useful programs that I'll describe later in this chapter are not distributed with C++Builder. Therefore, before continuing, you should download the latest version of the Cabinet SDK from http://msdn.microsoft.com/workshop/management/cab/cabdl.asp.

Creating and Extracting CAB Files

The Cabinet SDK comes with the following three utilities found in the CABINET SDK\BIN directory:

- EXTRACT.EXE   Simple extract utility.
- CABARC.EXE   Basic create/extract/view utility.
- MAKECAB.EXE   Powerful setup/manage/create/extract/view utility. Uses directive files.

As you can see, multiple possibilities are offered to you. For demonstration purposes, I'll use the CABARC utility because it easily accomplishes all we need (not to mention that it's used by the C++Builder IDE).

To learn the command options offered by this utility, simply type CABARC from the command prompt. Listing 29.1 contains the output.

LISTING 29.1   CABARC Command Options

```
Microsoft (R) Cabinet Tool - Version 1.00.0601 (03/18/97)
Copyright (c) Microsoft Corp 1996-1997. All rights reserved.

Usage: CABARC [options] command cabfile [@list] [files] [dest_dir]

Commands:
   L   List contents of cabinet (e.g. cabarc l test.cab)
   N   Create new cabinet (e.g. cabarc n test.cab *.c app.mak *.h)
   X   Extract file(s) from cabinet (e.g. cabarc x test.cab foo*.c)

Options:
  -c   Confirm files to be operated on
  -o   When extracting, overwrite without asking for confirmation
  -m   Set compression type [LZX:<15..21>|MSZIP|NONE], (default is MSZIP)
  -p   Preserve path names (absolute paths not allowed)
```

LISTING 29.1   Continued

```
-P  Strip specified prefix from files when added
-r  Recurse into subdirectories when adding files (see -p also)
-s  Reserve space in cabinet for signing (e.g. -s 6144 reserves 6K byte
-i  Set cabinet set ID when creating cabinets (default is 0)

Notes
-----
When creating a cabinet, the plus sign (+) may be used as a filename
to force a folder boundary; e.g. cabarc n test.cab *.c test.h + *.bmp

When extracting files to disk, the <dest_dir>, if provided, must end in
a backslash; e.g. cabarc x test.cab bar*.cpp *.h d:\test\

The -P (strip prefix) option can be used to strip out path information
e.g. cabarc -r -p -P myproj\ a test.cab myproj\balloon\*.*
The -P option can be used multiple times to strip out multiple paths
```

> **TIP**
>
> Another efficient way to master the Cabinet SDK utilities is to read their online documentation found in the \DOCS folder, which will provide you with examples and further explanations.

Basically, compressing and uncompressing is a matter of using the appropriate command options. For example, to create a CAB file containing all DLLs in the current directory, enter the following:

```
cabarc n newcab.cab *.dll
```

To extract these DLLs to another directory, enter the following:

```
cabarc x newcab.cab *.dll c:\windows\desktop\
```

> **CAUTION**
>
> When uncompressing CAB files, do not forget to put a backslash at the end of the destination directory. In the previous example, the command `cabarc x newcab.cab *.dll c:\windows\desktop` would have extracted all DLLs to the current directory.

Creating Self-Extracting CAB Files

As we saw, creating and extracting CAB files is quite easy when you have the right tools. But imagine the following scenario: You have a small CAB file that you want to distribute over the Internet. Unfortunately, you don't want to push your users to download and learn any third-party software. Wouldn't it be great to create a single .exe file that will extract its contents to the current directory?

Well, it's possible and extremely easy to do. Simply execute the following:

```
copy /b extract.exe+newcab.cab newcab.exe
```

If you run newcab.exe now, it will self-extract without any additional effort.

About INF Files

Information (INF) files are plain text files providing setup instructions for device drivers, software applications, or Internet components. Of course, not all INF files contain such complex install instructions—some of them simply modify the Registry.

INF files are organized in sections. Each section contains specific entries and directives used to copy files, install drivers, or perform any other appropriate tasks. In the following pages, I'll try to describe the INF file architecture and its most common directives.

CAUTION

Do not confuse INF files and INI files. They both have a similar syntax, but INI (initialization) files are only used to store configuration information.

INF Sections and Directives

Windows Setup searches sections by name. Therefore, the section order is not important. All section names must be enclosed in brackets ([ ]) and should not exceed 28 characters, as shown in the following:

```
[Strings]
Msg="Welcome"
```

NOTE

Section names, entries, and directives are not case-sensitive. If an information file contains two sections with the same name, Setup will merge their contents into one single section.

29

SOFTWARE
INSTALLATION
AND UPDATES

Tables 29.1 and 29.2 describe the most common INF sections and directives.

TABLE 29.1   INF Sections

Section	Description
ClassInstall32	Initializes and installs device setup classes
ControlFlags	Specifies whether the model/device is displayed in the Add New Hardware Wizard
DestinationDirs	Specifies the destination directory of copy, delete, or rename file operations
InterfaceInstall32	Initializes and installs device interface classes
Manufacturer	Identifies the manufacturer of the devices
SourceDisksFiles	Specifies the locations of files to be installed
SourceDisksNames	Specifies the distribution/CD-ROM disks for the installation
Strings	Defines all strkey tokens used in the INF file

TABLE 29.2   INF Directives

Directive	Description
AddInterface	Installs support for device interfaces
AddReg	Adds/modifies Registry subkeys and value entries
AddService	Installs the services of a device driver
BitReg	Sets bits within REG_BINARY Registry value entries
CopyFiles	Transfers files from the distribution disks to the destination directory
DelFiles	Deletes files from the destination directory
DelReg	Removes Registry subkeys and value entries
DelService	Deletes existing services
Ini2Reg	Moves lines from existing INI files into the Registry
LogConfig	References a set of hardware configuration resources
RenFiles	Renames files in the destination directory
UpdateIniFields	References sections in which modifications are made to existing INI files
UpdateInis	Reads/writes lines in existing INI files

We've only provided a general summary of common INF sections and directions in these two tables. More thorough descriptions can be found in the Windows Driver Development Kit (DDK) documentation, available online at `http://www.microsoft.com/ddk/`.

> **TIP**
>
> INF files include support for comments. Characters following a semicolon (;) on the same line are considered as comments (unless enclosed in quotes).

Creating INF Files

We're now ready to create a sample INF file. The file that we will create in the following steps, `Sample.inf`, is provided in the `INF Files` folder on the CD-ROM that accompanies this book.

As previously mentioned, information scripts are plain text files. You're free to use the word processor of your choice—I personally prefer C++Builder. From the C++Builder menu, select File, New and click on the Text object. Save the new file as `Sample.inf`.

Your installation script should accomplish the following tasks:

- Copy all program files (in this case `PROGRAM.EXE` and `PROGRAM.TXT`) to the `Windows` directory.

- Modify the registry so that `PROGRAM.EXE` automatically runs at Windows start-up.

You've guessed right! The first step uses the `CopyFiles` directive to transfer files to the destination directory. Its syntax is as follows:

```
Copyfiles=@filename | file-list-section[, file-list-section]...
```

To copy a single file, specify its name preceded by an @. To copy a list of files, create a new section and specify the section name. Your code may look like the following:

```
CopyFiles=Sample.Copy

[Sample.Copy]
Program.exe
Program.txt
```

Unfortunately, some crucial information is missing—the source and destination directories. As you saw in Table 29.1, the `DestinationDirs`, `SourceDisksNames`, and `SourceDisksFiles` sections provide this information:

```
[DestinationDirs]
Sample.Copy=10
```

```
[SourceDisksNames]
1="Drive D:"

[SourceDisksFiles]
Program.exe=1
Program. txt=1
```

> **NOTE**
>
> When specifying the target directory, you can use predefined values, such as 24 (Applications directory), 11 (System directory), 30 (Root directory of boot drive), and so on. In the previous example, 10 points to the Windows directory. (As previously mentioned, the description of each number value can be found in the DDK online documentation.)
>
> If you want to create a new destination folder, then simply combine those predefined values with your own string value. For instance, to create a MyProgram folder on the user's boot drive, enter
>
> ```
> Sample.Copy=30,"MyProgram"
> ```

You can now move to the next step—autorun `Program.exe` at Windows startup. This is done by adding your program's path to the `HKEY_LOCAL_MACHINE\SOFTWARE\Microsoft\Windows\CurrentVersion\Run` Registry key. The `AddReg` directive will help us:

```
AddReg=add-registry-section[, add-registry-section] ...

[add-registry-section]
reg-root, [subkey], [value-entry-name], [flags], [value]
```

Table 29.3 contains the possible values of `reg-root`.

TABLE 29.3   Registry Root Values

Value	Description
HKCR	Abbreviation for HKEY_CLASSES_ROOT
HKCU	Abbreviation for HKEY_CURRENT_USER
HKLM	Abbreviation for HKEY_LOCAL_MACHINE
HKU	Abbreviation for HKEY_USERS

The `subkey` and `value` parameters specify what Registry keys or values should be created. For example,

```
AddReg=Sample.Reg

[Sample.Reg]
HKLM,"Software\Microsoft\Windows\CurrentVersion\Run","SampleProgram",,
➡"%10%\Program.exe "
```

Notice how predefined values enclosed in percent signs (%) are expanded to a string value (in this case, the Windows directory).

You're almost there—two sections are missing. The first—Version—specifies the signature. By default, this signature is $CHICAGO$, Chicago being the beta name of Windows 95. (This does not mean that your scripts are not compatible with Windows NT or in fact, any 32-bit version of Windows.) The second and most important one—DefaultInstall—is the portion of code that will be executed when you install the INF file. Listing 29.2 contains the final version of Sample.inf.

LISTING 29.2   The Complete Sample.inf File

```
[Version]
Signature="$CHICAGO$"

[DefaultInstall]
AddReg=Sample.Reg
CopyFiles=Sample.Copy

[Sample.Copy]
Program.exe
Program.txt

[DestinationDirs]
Sample.Copy=10

[SourceDisksNames]
1="Drive D:",,,

[SourceDisksFiles]
Program.exe=1
Program.txt=1

[Sample.Reg]
HKLM,"Software\Microsoft\Windows\CurrentVersion\Run","SampleProgram",,
➡"%10%\Program.exe"
```

29

To test your script, copy `Sample.inf`, `PROGRAM.EXE`, and `PROGRAM.TXT` to a floppy disk or to the root directory of your hard drive (in my case, drive D:), right-click the `Sample.inf` icon, and choose Install. Figure 29.2 shows that a new value has been added to the Registry.

FIGURE 29.2

New Registry value added by the installation script.

About Internet Packages

Suppose you've created an ActiveX control or an ActiveX executable, and you want to make it available for download. How can you allow your users to install your Internet application directly from a Web site?

Microsoft has provided a simple solution—a combination of the power of INF and CAB files called Internet packages. The OCX control and all required files are compressed in one or more CAB packages. Then, the INF file directs your browser where to find these packages and how to install them.

> **CAUTION**
>
> At the time this book is being written, Microsoft Internet Explorer (version 3.x or later) is the only Web browser that supports CAB-based Internet packages.

Understanding Internet Packages

In Chapter 22, "Using ActiveX Techniques," you learned how to deploy ActiveX controls and forms using the C++Builder Web deployment options. You've now become familiar with INF and CAB files, and a quick look back at these deployment tools will help you understand how Internet packages work.

For demonstration purposes, I created and deployed a small ActiveForm project (see Figure 29.3). Let's first consider how packaged ActiveX controls are embedded in a Web page. Listing 29.3 contains the HTML source code of the Web page generated by C++Builder.

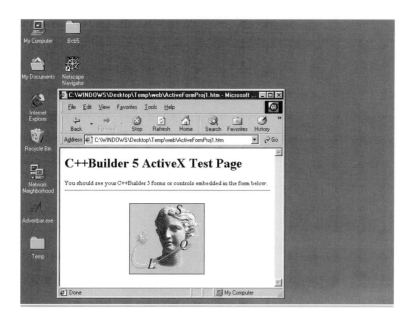

FIGURE 29.3

ActiveFormProject1 *displayed in Internet Explorer.*

LISTING 29.3   ACTIVEFORMPROJ1.HTM

```
<HTML>
<H1> C++Builder 5 ActiveX Test Page </H1><p>
You should see your C++Builder 5 forms or controls embedded in the form below.
<HR><center><P>
<OBJECT
     classid="clsid:FE0A6145-3478-11D4-B120-0080C8DF95D0"
     codebase="C:\WINDOWS\Desktop\Temp\web\ActiveFormProj1.inf"
     width=160
     height=148
     align=center
     hspace=0
     vspace=0
>
</OBJECT>
</HTML>
```

29

SOFTWARE
INSTALLATION
AND UPDATES

Obviously, ActiveX forms are embedded in Web pages using the OBJECT tag. In addition to the dimensions and alignment of the control, this tag contains two important attributes—CLASSID and CODEBASE. CLASSID specifies the unique class identifier under which your object has been registered in the Windows Registry. CODEBASE indicates the location and, optionally, the version of the file containing your object.

As shown in Listing 29.3, CODEBASE points to an INF file. However, other file types are also supported. For example, if you have a single ActiveX control that does not require any supporting DLLs, you can point CODEBASE directly to an OCX file:

```
codebase="C:\WINDOWS\Desktop\Temp\web\ActiveFormProj1.ocx#version=1,0,0,0"
```

Another, even better, solution is to specify the location of a Cabinet file. This CAB package should contain your INF, OCX, and, if necessary, DLL files:

```
codebase="C:\WINDOWS\Desktop\Temp\web\ActiveFormProj1.cab#version=1,0,0,0"
```

Now, take a look at the heart of your Internet package—the information file (see Listing 29.4).

LISTING 29.4   ACTIVEFORMPROJ1.INF

```
;C++Builder-generated INF file for ActiveFormProj1.ocx
[Add.Code]
ActiveFormProj1.ocx=ActiveFormProj1.ocx
VCL50.bpl=VCL50.bpl

[ActiveFormProj1.ocx]
file=C:\WINDOWS\Desktop\Temp\web\ActiveFormProj1.cab
clsid={FE0A6145-3478-11D4-B120-0080C8DF95D0}
RegisterServer=yes
FileVersion=1,0,0,0

[VCL50.bpl]
file=
FileVersion=5,0,6, 18
DestDir=11
```

Actually simpler than you thought, isn't it? The INF file contains the list of files to be installed. Each file is described in its own section. In each section, you'll find the location of the CAB package, the file version, and the destination directory. For example, the target directory of VCL50.BPL is 11. Remember the predefined values previously described? Indeed, 11 represents the Windows System directory.

Versions, Updates, and Patches

In this section we will look into version control and how to implement patches and updates. Patches and updates are the logical advancement of your application, and these methods make an easy way for your end users to keep up to date on the latest developments of your application.

Versions

Versions of software are very important; they make end users aware of the version they are using and if there is a newer version available for them to use. It also allows you to give more accurate technical support. For example, a function in version 1.1 may not be available in version 1.0, or a bug may not have been fixed.

How to Use Versions

You can implement your own form of version control by adding a version number in the AboutBox of your application, or you can allow C++Builder to do it for you by selecting Project, Options, and then the Version Info tab. Here you set the option of allowing C++Builder to add the version information into the application you are creating. This includes Major Number, Minor Number, Release Number, and Build Number.

You can set C++Builder to autoincrement your version information so that the build number is incremented by one every time you build your application.

The Version Info tab also allows you to enter some information about the file you are creating, such as your company information, file description, and copyright notices.

All of this information will be shown to the end users if they right-click your file to look at its properties.

Alternatively, you can use a third-party component to store the version information and then allow your end users to see this information in the application.

Ideally, you don't want to burden your end users with having to open Windows Explorer and then right-click the file (once they have found it). To simply find out the version information of the application, the easiest way is to have a simple line in the AboutBox of the application so that end users can see easily what version of the application they are running. Something similar to the following would do:

```
MyApplication
Version 1.1
```

Then, when you update the file you can increment the version number to 1.2 and so on. we have chosen to add a slightly longer version number to your applications so that we can add updates without changing the main version number of the application. For example,

```
MyApplcation
Version 1.1.0.0
```

When we do an update, such as fix a bug, we just increment the last digit.

```
MyApplication
Version 1.1.0.1
```

This way, all the main documentation and program names will stay the same, which can save a lot of time when making Web pages and so on, and end users still know that they have the latest version.

Another important item to have as part of your version control is an update record. A simple text file will do, located in the same folder as your project files.

The information contained in the document should be the version number and the updates made to the file in that build. For example,

```
1.1.0.0 First public release.
------
1.1.0.1 Fixed Font formatting bug.
--------
Change Main screen bitmap.
```

This way, you can keep track of all the changes you make to your application, and if you get a technical support question about your application, you can see if the bug has been fixed in the version the end user has.

Updates for Application Improvements

Updates are the inevitable advancement of your application. What is best to implement updates, and what is the best way of doing it? We are going to offer some methods so that you can make up your own mind.

Application Advancement

When you change anything in your application, it qualifies as an update of your application. You must then decide if it is worth making this update available to your end users, or if it's better to wait for some more improvements before you release the next version. Obviously, we can't tell you when you should release your updates because it will be determined by many factors. A major bug fix should be released immediately so that other end users don't have the same problem(s). The next issue to consider is how you are going to let your end users know that you're releasing an updated version.

Update Notification Methods

If you have a shareware application, the update notification of your customers will not be a problem because you will have all of your customer records on your computer from their registration details. You could create an application with all of the customer email addresses in it and send notifications that way or via your default email program informing them of the available update.

The first method is the easiest method. A simple database with an email component as part of the application will make sending mass emails easy.

For your shareware applications, you can have a database with all of your customer records on one tab, and on another tab have the applications they are registering along with purchasing information, such as dates purchased and any unlock codes generated. You can then have a TMemo component for writing the email you want to send to every customer and a TEmail component for sending the email from your registration application to your default email program, ready for sending.

I use an emailing component from AHM Triton Tools (www.tritontools.com) for sending the emails from my registration application, but there are many freeware components for sending mails via MAPI or SMTP email programs. TEmail from http://www.econos.de/ is such a component, although at the time of writing it is not available for C++Builder 5.

In your registration application, just ask the application to step through each customer record, use the email address from the records database and the message from the TMemo, and then send each email in turn. This way, you don't have to write hundreds of individual emails or add every customers' address to the CC field of the original email.

Another way of informing your customers that an update is available is to put the update information in a prominent place on your Web page, if you have one. The only disadvantage is that you are relying on the customer to come back to your Web site for update information.

Another method is Listbot (see http://www.listbot.com), which has a free email service that your customers can join. This will send an email to every customer who has joined this service. This is a good idea but, again, you are relying on your customers to join the service. If they don't, they could miss out on the update information.

The only guaranteed way of letting your customers know about the update is to send them a personal email.

Implementing Your Updates

After you have your updated application complete and ready to send out to your end users (or have it ready for them to download), you have to decide how you should make the update available to them. Do you create a patch program, or simply have the whole application wrapped in its installation program?

When to Provide a New Download

Sometimes, it is just as easy to provide the end user with a new installation file, making sure that the installation program is set to overwrite or update current files.

The end user will already have used your installation program to initially install your application, so the end user shouldn't be worried by new programs that they may know nothing about.

One of the downfalls of developers is that they tend to forget that Mr. and Mrs. J. Doe don't know as much about computers as they do. Developers tend to take their advanced knowledge of computers for granted. As a developer, you really need to take a few steps back and see your application and installation program from novice users' eyes.

Patches

Patches are another method of updating. They allow you to keep the original application file and then edit it programmatically to the new updated version.

To create a patch, you must find a way to scan the original application file and then find the differences in the ANSI code between that file and the new updated one. Then, the patch can write an editing script to update the original file to the updated version.

A good program to do this for you is Patch Maker from Click Team. Patch Maker is available in a freeware and commercial version, and you can download it from `http://www.` `clickteam.com` or from the CD-ROM that accompanies this book.

Providing a Patch

If you decide to provide your end users with a patch program, you first have to create that patch. The freeware version of Patch Maker from Click Team does this job very well. Patch Maker is covered in the following section.

Patches simply look at the current version of the application file and then, if it is the correct one, it updates it by editing the application file to the updated version.

It is very important to keep track of the versions that have been made, because a patch program will patch only the correct version. For example

First Release Version	1.0
Bug Fixed Version	1.1
Upgrade Version	1.2

If you create a patch from version 1.1 to version 1.2, you could not run the same patch on version 1.0 to try and update it to version 1.2. The patch program would return an error to the end user.

Patch Maker

After you have installed Patch Maker, you will need to do some preparation work before you can use it successfully.

First, you need to have a directory with your original application file in it and nothing else. You then need another directory with the new update application file in it and nothing else. The reason for this is that Patch Maker will ask you for the directories during the wizard setup of the patch you are trying to create.

While Patch Maker can create a patch for multiple files, we will concentrate on the single file patch because it is most likely that you will only update one file at a time. There is no reason why you can't experiment for yourself and create a patch for multiple files.

After you have created your updated file, start Patch Maker. You are now presented with the Patch Wizard, ready to begin the creation of your application's patch.

1. Navigating the Welcome Screen

   On this screen, you have the option to continue using the wizard or to use the main user interface to create your installation program.

   If this is your first time using this application, I would advise that you use the wizard until you know your way around the program.

2. Designating the Source and Destination Directories

   This screen of the wizard asks you for two directories:

   • The directory where the old version of your file is—the file that is to be updated

   • The directory that contains your new updated file

   This is where you can experiment with multiple files because this application asks you for directories as opposed to one file at a time.

   Because we are only going to create a single file patch, you can uncheck the Include Sub-Directories check box.

3. Setting Your Program's Title

   Here you can set the language for your patch program, either French or English.

   You can also set the name for your patch program. This name will be shown to the end user in the main text area (not the title) when he runs this patch program. Therefore, the name chosen should be the title of the application to be updated and perhaps the new version number.

   If you are unsure about what the patch program will look like when the end user runs it, you can select the Preview button to see the screen you are working on as the end user will see it.

4. Inserting Additional Information

   This screen gives you the option of entering some additional text, a Readme file about the updates that have been made, for example. This section does not have an open file button, but will allow you to enter some text in the provided field by the copy and paste method. After you have added your additional information, I suggest you look at all of the text to make sure that the formatting of the text is correct. Select the Preview button for a true representation.

5. Setting the Patch Window

   You can now choose the size of installation screen you want and the main title you want shown to the end user when he runs the installation program.

6. Defining and Using Bitmaps for the Patch Maker

   This part of the wizard setup allows you to place two bitmap images in your installation program. Just remember that any extra files you add to this program will make the overall size of the patch bigger.

   The first image you can select should be a certain size—128 pixels wide by 280 pixels high with 256 colors. This image will be shown on the main introduction screen and to the left of the text in the main text box. If you are unsure, just select an image and click the Preview button.

   The second image will be tiled all over the background of the main screen and should be no more than 256 colors. Again, if you are unsure, click the Preview button.

7. Setting the Default Installation Directory

   This screen allows you to enter the default directory into which you want your application and associated files installed. For example,

   ```
   "C:\Program Files\MyCompany\MyApplcation"
   ```

   The default directory should be the same as your installation program. If you do not run the patch in the correct directory, the patch will not work and will return an error message of "Nothing to do" to the end user who is trying to implement the patch. Your end users should also be made aware of this information. If end users don't run the patch in the same directory where they installed your application, the patch will be unsuccessful.

   This section of the Wizard also gives you the option of retrieving the installation directory from an `*.ini` file that is currently on the destination computer or a Registry entry that is on the destination computer.

   If you click on the Registry base button, you are prompted for three values: Root Key, Key, and Sub Key. These values will be set by you at design time.

8. Using the End Screen

   On the last screen of the wizard, Patch Maker gives you the option of building the update program or not. If you are satisfied that you have set all the options correctly, go ahead and click the Finish button and build your patch program. If, on the other hand, you are not sure you have set all the options correctly, just click the Back button to check the check box and look at the program's settings.

9. Building the Patch Program

After you have chosen to build your patch program, you will be asked where to build the `.exe` file and what to call it. This is obviously up to you, but don't put it in the same directory or subdirectory of your main application files.

When the file has been built, you can save the project files in a safe place, ready for future updates or corrections as and when they are needed.

You can also test your newly created patch program. The best way is to open Windows Explorer and run the file the same way that an end user would.

Just make sure that you currently have installed the application file that is to be updated in the default directory. Run the patch program, and then open the application file to make sure the changes have been made. If it is a bug that has been fixed and not a visible change, the best method of checking that the patch has been successful it to check the version number of the application file.

Some Tips on Updates and Patches

Use these tips to help decide when and how you should update your application:

- When an update becomes available, inform your end users in as many places as possible—via email and your Web page.
- Do not bombard users with update information because too many emails from you will be classed as junk mail.
- Fix bugs in your applications and make the update available as soon as possible.
- Never send an update or patch by direct email unless the customer gives you permission first.
- If there are small changes made to your application, consider releasing the next update when more changes have been made.

Version Control and TeamSource

Transactions destroy old data.

A version of data can be thought of as a snapshot of the data at a particular point in time. Simply put, version control involves the keeping of backup copies of these snapshots. In version control jargon, taking such a snapshot is known as "checking in" the data to the "archive."

The most valuable data programmers have is source code, and we are continually changing it. That change sometimes adds more code, but more often it involves changing existing code.

Every time a line is changed, the old version of that line is lost. Use of version control software, such as TeamSource, allows us to keep backup copies of the older versions of the code.

TeamSource is a separate program bundled with the Enterprise Edition of C++Builder and Delphi. It is also available as a standalone product. TeamSource is used to keep track of, and control, the changes that source code undergoes in the evolution of a project.

TeamSource is particularly useful when used in conjunction with C++Builder (or Delphi) projects, but it is not limited to only those projects. It is useful with any project that involves many files that are maintained in one folder (and possibly subfolders). If there are significant text files in the project, TeamSource can provide extra functionality in handling those files, but it can as easily provide version control for a set of specifications (maintained as Word documents) or a set of Web pages (maintained as HTML and image files), and so on.

Who Should Use TeamSource?

TeamSource was designed for use by teams of developers (hence the name), but is also useful to those who are developing alone.

Why Should TeamSource Be Used?

At its simplest, TeamSource allows a single developer to maintain a history of the path along which a project has changed. When hindsight shows that a wrong turn has been taken on that path, TeamSource allows you to move back along the path. It also allows you to move forward more confidently, because you know such wrong turns can be corrected.

You might want to move back because a recent innovation has proved unworkable to such a degree that it must be abandoned, so you want to "go back and start again." However, a more common reason for having access to older versions of the code is because you want to be able to easily access the source code as it was when the project was released to customers. While the code has changed since that release, users may still bring up issues with that release.

TeamSource can also involve management of multiple simultaneous versions of a project. A team might develop one project in different directions. For example, a simple employee database application may have to be updated to move to a client/server model and to add extra tables. Without TeamSource, it might be better to handle these changes after each other. With TeamSource, it is easier to allow parallel development of the two strands, merging them together at a later stage when they have stabilized.

A software project is a complex object and can be made up of various parts, each of which might be subject to separate version control—more stable libraries that change less often, and code for the particular project that may change daily.

When Should TeamSource Be Used?

Use of TeamSource should be based on a considered strategy. The simplest strategy is that files should be checked in at the end of every day. The addition of a new feature takes a number of days, and the check-ins at the start and end of that time are noted so that you can roll back to those milestones (bookmarks) as required.

A more sensible strategy would be to check in for each transaction. In developing code, a transaction is all the changes involved in adding or changing a feature of the code. What counts as a "feature" is a variable quantity, and any significant feature can often be broken into tasks, sub-tasks, sub-sub-tasks, and so on. However, features are usually already closely defined in most software teams. Indeed, the tasks and sub-tasks are often clearly defined as well.

Where Can TeamSource Be Used?

TeamSource can be used on a LAN or a standalone machine. Version control software, such as TeamSource, is an extra form of source code backup. Hence, archives should be kept on a separate device from the working project, and that device should be as separate as reasonable from the original. TeamSource allows this.

If a reasonable strategy is used to determine when check-ins are done, TeamSource can be a better form of backup than the nightly backup of files. When disaster occurs, it is more likely that you will want to get back to "before we added that form," rather than simply "where we were last Tuesday."

Of course, catastrophes happen too, and then we want to get back to "as much as we can get, from as recently as possible," so TeamSource is an enhancement of backup, not a replacement.

How Is TeamSource Used?

TeamSource, like C++Builder, is based on the idea of projects, and projects are based on folders.

TeamSource is more tightly bound to folders than C++Builder. As far as TeamSource is concerned, a project consists of all files in a folder and its subfolders, and no other files. This does not reflect the flexibility available within C++Builder. In C++Builder, one might include within a project files that are shared with another project and are in a separate folder. Because TeamSource is less flexible in this regard, it can often be helpful to reorganize folders before starting to use TeamSource.

New Projects

A TeamSource project requires more effort in its setup than it does in its normal use. Spending a little extra effort in setting it up correctly can ensure that normal use is very easy; this will help ensure that it will be used regularly.

When you use TeamSource for the first time, you are asked for your name and email address, and then you must create a new project before it can be used further. To do this, go to the File menu and choose New Project. This gives a dialog that gives you a choice between importing an existing project or creating a new project from scratch.

Importing a New Project

A sole developer usually will create projects from scratch. In a team setting, one member will create a project, and other members will later import it. Importing a project is straightforward; you simply use a standard Open dialog to find the project file created earlier, and specify a folder where that project is to be stored on the local machine (see "Specifying the Local Directory," later in this chapter). All files of the project are then copied to that folder, and the project will be updated with newer versions found in the local directory.

Setting Up a New Project from Scratch

There are a number of steps in setting up a new project:

- You must create a project.
- You can specify a local directory.
- You can specify project options.
- You can get other users to import the project.

Creating a Project

Creating a project from scratch is Wizard based—you must step through seven dialogs that require you to specify details of the project. (Don't be put off by the length of this list—the default values that TeamSource supplies are usually enough for many of these.)

1. The Project You Are Creating —There are three general details required for the project:

   1.1   The project name—Use a descriptive natural language name (spaces allowed).

   1.2   The name of the project file—This defaults to the same as the project name with spaces removed. You can shorten this name as required. Do not include any path information as part of this filename; the path will be given later.

   1.3   The version controller to be used—This defaults to Borland's Zlib, although others can be used.

2. The Project Folder—This is the folder path where the TeamSource project files are to be stored. You specify the path by typing it directly or by browsing to a folder by using the … button. Normally this folder would be on a separate machine (or at least a separate disk) from your C++Builder project. When sharing TeamSource projects among users over a LAN, it would be common to specify a folder on a file server.

> **CAUTION**
>
> You must ensure that all who are to use the project have sufficient access rights to the project folder.

3. The Project Subfolders—TeamSource maintains an `Archive` folder (the record of versions of code that it will maintain), a `History` folder (which contains a list of check-ins to the project), and one for lock files (which allow one user to write to the project while preventing others from doing so). These three folders default to subfolders of the main project folder, but you can change them if you want.

4. The Mirror Tree—TeamSource can, if you want, maintain a mirror of the project (a copy of the current state of all files in the project). If you want such a mirror, you must turn this option on (check the Enable Mirror Tree box) and specify a folder where it is stored. Again, this will default to a subfolder of the project folder, but you may want to specify a separate machine or disk to serve as a backup.

5. Publishing—You can specify a summary file that will contain the comments made when developers check in a group of files. You can also specify a log file that includes more information from check-ins, such as who checked in the files, when they were checked in, which files were involved, as well as summary and file comments. You can also specify an SMTP server to allow TeamSource to send notifications of check-ins by email.

6. Email Addresses—If you gave an SMTP server in the previous step, you can now specify the email addresses of those who are to be notified of changes to the project. After each check-in, a notification will be sent to each email address containing details of either

   • The summary file (see previous step)
   • The log (see previous step)
   • The list of files that were changed

7. Confirmation—The last step displays all the information you have entered, allowing you to make sure that it is all correct and to return to earlier steps to change details if necessary.

Of all these steps the most significant items are

   • Project name
   • Project folder
   • SMTP server
   • Email addresses for notifications

29

SOFTWARE INSTALLATION AND UPDATES

If you supply these four, you often can simply keep clicking the Next button and let TeamSource fill in the rest. For a single developer, it can be enough to only supply the first two—a name and a folder for the project.

Specifying the Local Directory

When you have created the project, TeamSource will prompt you to choose a local directory— this is the folder where your C++Builder project is stored.

You might answer No to this dialog because, perhaps, the C++Builder project is not on this machine (see "Handling Local Directories," later in this chapter) or for other reasons, but usually you will answer Yes.

TeamSource then offers you a dialog allowing you to add local folders. Type in the path to the local folder, or browse from the ... button. You can add more than one folder, and the full archive will be stored in each.

Next, TeamSource will offer to run the Content Wizard on the local directories. Again, you may want to defer this until later, but usually you would answer Yes. This Wizard will examine the contents of the local directories and then show you a dialog with these directories and any subfolders. You can click on each folder in turn and you will be shown a list of file types in that folder.

TeamSource will maintain versions of all the file types listed. You will probably want to edit these lists, especially to remove intermediate (`*.obj`, `*.il*`) files, backup files (`*.~cpp`), and the other flotsam that tends to collect in such folders (`*.tmp`, `*.cgl`, and so on).

When the project has been set up locally and remotely, you are brought back to TeamSource's main screen, which shows you summary information about the project.

Project Options

The user who created the project has Administrator access to the project. Before the project is fully used, it is worthwhile for this user to go through the options that govern how it can be used. This is helpful for a single user; for a team, it is mandatory: One option that needs to be set is which users can access the project.

To set such options, you should obtain an Administrator Lock (see "Requesting a Lock," later in this chapter) and then choose Options from the Project menu. This will bring up a four-part dialog—General, Directories, Users, and Publishing.

General

The General tab of the Project Options dialog allows you to do the following:

- Change the name of the version info file—TeamSource can maintain a file that contains the current version number of the project. This file will be stored in the root directory of the archive.

- Detect new local directories—When this is checked, TeamSource will find new subfolders on the local machine. If you have such folders that are relevant to the C++Builder project, but you do not want TeamSource to maintain versions of them, uncheck this box.

- Decide what level of comments is required when files are checked in—You can require Summary Comments (one comment for a group of files or File Comments (individual comments for each file of a group). If you check these boxes, developers will not be able to check in files without such comments.

- Tell TeamSource the initial version number of the project—This will be especially useful if you are creating a new TeamSource archive for an old C++Builder project for which C++Builder already maintains a version number. The version number format is the same for both programs (1.3.23.8, for example, where 1 is the major version number, 3 is the minor version number, 23 is the milestone, and 8 is the build number).

Directories

The Directories tab allows you to change the folders in which TeamSource stores the archive. These folders are the same as for creating a project (see steps 3 and 4 of "Creating a Project," earlier in this chapter).

Users

You can indicate on the Users tab which users have what access to the project. You can add as many users as you want, granting each of them one of three levels of access:

- Read-Only—Such a user can copy files from the archive, but cannot change the archive. In particular, they will not be able to check in files.

- Read-Write—Such a user can check files into the archive.

- Administrator—If you grant a user Read-Write access, you can go further and grant him Administrator access as well. This allows them to check in files and to change the project's options (they can use this tab of the dialog to add more users, for example).

After users have been added, they can be deleted or edited. Editing a user allows changing his username or granting him a different level of access. You cannot edit your own details.

TIP

A user's name within TeamSource is the same as his login name for Windows.

At the bottom of this dialog, there is also a check box to Allow Guest Access to This Project. If you check this box, any user can access the project, and their access will be limited to Read-Only.

29

SOFTWARE
INSTALLATION
AND UPDATES

If you are using Windows 9x and not using a login name, you will be listed with the username "Guest". In this case, Guest will have full Administrator access rights to the project.

Publishing

The Publishing tab allows you to change how users are notified by email of check-ins to the archive. The details here are the same as for creating a project (see steps 5 and 6 of "Creating a Project," earlier in this chapter).

Handling Local Directories

What TeamSource names the "local directory" may be thought of as simply the folder where your C++Builder project is stored. In less simple cases, this might not be a local folder because either it is not on your machine or it is not just one folder.

The local folder might not be on your machine because you are simply setting up a TeamSource project that other developers will use. Such a situation might arise where a team leader sets up the archive so that he can retain Administrator access to it, and other developers maintain the C++Builder projects on other machines that are to be checked in.

In such a case, the team leader may not want to have a copy of the C++Builder project on his own machine and would not specify a local machine.

The local folder might not be just one folder because it can be many. TeamSource can handle such a situation gracefully if all the folders have a common root. For example, if a C++Builder project contains the files `D:\programming\projects\mailApp\form1.cpp` and `D:\programming\libraries\internet\my-email.cpp`, it would be prudent to set `D:\programming\` as the local folder.

In such a scenario, there are likely to be other subfolders of `D:\programming\`, and these should be pruned from the directory tree of the archive. There are also likely to be other files in `D:\programming\libraries\internet\` that are not relevant to the `mailApp` archive. All files in that folder must initially be included and later some can be excluded individually.

An alternative strategy for this example might be to maintain two separate archives, one for the `mailApp` project and another for the `library\internet` project. This would make it easier to set up the archives but harder to maintain them. After working on the `mailApp` project, a developer will easily remember to update the `mailApp` archive. If such work showed up a small bug in `my-email.cpp` that was corrected, the fact that a separate archive needed updating can be forgotten.

TeamSource Windows

There are three different ways of looking at the files in an archive, and TeamSource provides a different window for each. TeamSource refers to them as "Views," and so there are windows called Remote View, Local View, and History View.

Remote View shows the files as they appear in the central archive. Local view shows the changes that need to be made to files on the local machine in order to synchronize them with the central archive. History View shows a log of changes made to the archive.

Remote View

You can press F7, click the Remote icon on the left, or choose View, Remote Project from the menus in the main TeamSource window to bring up a view of the remote folder(s) of the archive. This is a two-paned view, showing an Explorer-like tree of folders on the left and a list view of file versions on the right.

Remote Directories' Properties

Right-clicking any of the remote directories gives a menu with options allowing you to view their Properties. If you obtain an Administrator lock before right-clicking, you can also Add or Delete subdirectories and edit the Properties. The Properties of directories include which version controller it uses, which files it includes, which it excludes, and its production rules. A production rule is, for example .cpp -> .obj (it informs TeamSource that .obj files are produced from .cpp files of the same name). Therefore, TeamSource need not store a version of a .obj file, as long as it has a .cpp file of the same name.

Unfortunately, such rules must be set individually for each folder within each project. It is not possible to set general production rules for all projects.

Remote Files' Actions

Right-clicking a remote file will bring up a menu with a number of available actions. Of these actions, Compare Revisions would be commonly used, and the others are used less often.

- View Tip Revision—This shows the most recent version of the file.
- View Any Revision—Pick a version of the file, and then view it.

- Save Revision As—Pick a version of the file, and then save it to disk.

- Delete from Project—You must lock the project before removing all of a file's versions from the project.

- View Archive Report—See when each version was checked in, by whom, and so on.

- Compare Revisions—This brings up a dialog that allows you to specify two versions of the file. TeamSource will then show a visual comparison of the two versions, highlighting the lines that have been added to and subtracted from one revision to produce the other. Differences between the files that are only spaces are ignored in such a comparison, if you specify that in Options, Preferences.

Local View

You can press F8, click on the Local icon on the left, or choose View, Local Project from the menus in the main TeamSource window to bring up a Local view of the archive. This is a two-paned view, showing what TeamSource thinks you should change locally on the left, and what you should change remotely on the right.

Because this view shows the archive from the perspective of the local machine, it is the view most often used by developers. Files that have been changed by the developer are on the local machine, and so will be checked in using the Local view. Files added by other members of the team are missing from the local machine and can be copied to the local machine using the Local view.

For each file shown in Local view, TeamSource will recommend an action for that file to keep the archive up to date. For example, if a developer has changed a file on the local machine, then that file will be shown in the Local view with a recommendation that it should be checked in.

Using Local View to Check in Files

In normal day-by-day usage of TeamSource, the most common activity will be checking in files. Unlike other version controllers, files do not need to be locked and checked out before being worked on. Instead, developers can change their local copies and later check in the changed files.

Usually, a developer will switch to Local view and see a list of files in the right pane that need to be checked in. The developer should obtain a lock, select the files, and click the Do It! button, and those files will be checked in. If the project requires a summary comment, this can be entered by clicking the Comment button before clicking Do It!.

Recommended Actions for the Files Shown in Local View

TeamSource may make a number of different recommendations for changes to the remote or local files so that the archive is kept current. If an action is recommended for the local version of a file, then that file will be listed in the right pane. If an action is recommended for the remote version of a file, then that file will be listed in the left pane. If no action is needed for a file, then that file will not be shown in Local view.

In the left and right panes, these recommendations are listed in the Action column and denoted by the small icons beside the files' names. These recommended actions are based on comparisons between timestamps and the local, remote, and base versions of files.

Local versions are the files stored on the local machine, and remote versions are those stored in the TeamSource archive. Base versions are those at the time you synchronized local and remote files (last check in, last pull, and so on). When you check in a file, TeamSource writes the filename, version number, and timestamp to a file called `something.tsl` (if the project is called `something`) to the local directory.

Depending on the differences between these versions, TeamSource may recommend some of the following actions:

- Copy—The remote version is newer, and you should update your own version of the file by copying the file from the remote to the local machine. If you choose this action, TeamSource will ask for confirmation before overwriting the local file.

- Merge—The remote version is newer than your last check-in, and you have also changed the local file since the last check-in. The normal version controller used with TeamSource (Borland's ZLib) does not support automatic merging, so you will have to do the merge by hand. If you use another controller that does support automatic merging (PVCS, for example), this can be done.

- Merge by Hand—Automatic merging could not be performed, so it must be done manually.

- Correct by Hand—Something has gone wrong. TeamSource can determine what should be done to a file by comparing local, remote, and base versions in most normal cases, but it will not always be able to recommend the correct action. For example, if the local file date is Tuesday and both base and remote versions are dated Thursday, TeamSource will not be able to recommend an action because the local file is earlier than it was when last checked in.

  When TeamSource's recommended action is to correct by hand, I suggest that the first thing you do is right-click the file and choose View File Info. This will show the local, remote, and base times as TeamSource knows them, and that may help you track the source of the problem.

  Correct by Hand errors are usually due to factors outside TeamSource (for example, the previous example could be caused by moving an old copy of the file to the local directory). Another factor to consider, especially if you get a lot of such errors, is how time is handled by machines on your LAN. A colleague with whom I was sharing a TeamSource project saw most files as Correct by Hand, whereas I saw few such files. However, the mistake was on my machine, whose time zone was set to Eastern Standard Time, whereas the other machines were correctly set to GMT.

- Delete—The file has been removed from the project, so you should remove it from the local machine.
- Remove—The file has been removed locally, so you should also remove it from the project.
- Touch—The local file's date has changed, but its contents are unchanged. Choosing this action synchronizes the versions' dates.

Using Local View for Other Actions

By using the context menu or hot keys within the Local view, you can use the listed files in a number of ways:

- View Local Changes—Shows changes between the local file and the most recent version you got from the archive (the base version).
- View All Changes—Shows changes between the local file and the latest version in the project (the remote version).
- View Remote Changes—Shows changes between remote and base versions.
- View File Info—Shows dates of local, base, and remote versions.
- Revert—Copies the remote file over the local file.
- Change the Comments for the Selected File—Allows you to review, and change, any comments added to that file.
- Change the Recommended Action for the File— Allows you to choose a different action for the file. Commonly this will be used to change the recommended action from Merge by Hand to either Copy or Check-In.
- Move Files from One Pane to the Other—Some actions are only possible in one pane, so you may have to move the file to take that action.

History View

This view is also two paned. The list of check-ins is shown on the left, when they happened, and who performed them. Details of the selected check-in are shown on the right, the summary comment, and the list of files.

Version Controllers

TeamSource uses Borland's ZLib version controller by default, and also provides support for Merant's PVCS controller, although potentially it can support any controller. Which controller is used can be changed by choosing Controllers from the project menu.

If you want to use another version controller, you must provide a TeamSource extension (a
.tsx file). A .tsx file is a DLL that provides the extra functionality you require (or simply
interfaces to another controller) to TeamSource by implementing its required interfaces.

Bookmarks

You can set bookmarks in the history of the versions checked in by TeamSource. A *bookmark*
is a stage you can return to easily because the version of all files in the project that are present
when the bookmark is created can later be brought back together.

Bookmarks can be particularly useful when matched with released versions of software.
Consider a user who is using a version released many months or years ago who discovers an
issue that needs to be addressed. If a bookmark was created when that version was released,
you can quickly return to that version and address the issue.

To set up a bookmark, you should choose Bookmarks from the Project menu. This will lead to
a dialog box that allows you to add, edit, and delete bookmarks. When you choose to add a
bookmark, you will need to give it a name and decide whether it is local or global. A local
bookmark is available only to the user who created it. A global bookmark is available to all
users but can be created only by a user with Administrator access to the project.

Pulling Projects

In the normal course of events, the local project is likely to be more up to date than the archive
stored on a remote machine because changes are made on the local machine and are later
checked in to the remote machine.

However, if more than one developer is working on a project or if there are losses from the
local machine (in case of corruption) or for other reasons, the remote archive's files may be
more recent. In this case, you may want to "pull" the project—copy all files from the remote
archive to the local machine.

This can be done by choosing Pull To from the Project menu. You will have the option of a
Fast Pull, which will only pull those files that are more recent on the remote machine. If you
do not do a fast pull, all files will be copied from remote to local.

A further option when pulling is that you can pull files from a previously created bookmark.
This might overwrite files on the local machine with older files from the remote archive, so
you may want to back up local files first (by checking them in).

Locks

Locks are required when one user wants to change the archive in some way. The most common
reason for this will be when checking files in. When a project is being set up, it will also be
common to require a lock so that project options can be changed.

29

Locking with TeamSource is unlike some other version control systems in that you can only lock the whole archive, rather than locking individual files. Furthermore, with TeamSource you only need to lock on check-in, unlike other version control systems that can require you to check out a file, which locks it, then keep the lock while changes are made, and then check the file back in, which releases the lock.

Requesting a Lock

You can request a lock from the Project menu or by pressing F4. In either case, you will be asked how long you want to keep the lock, which defaults to five minutes. At the end of this period, you will not lose the lock, but other users can then challenge the lock. If you have Administrator access to a project, you can also request an Administrator lock, which cannot be challenged and can be retained even after TeamSource is closed.

You can also add a comment for the lock to explain to other users why you have locked the project.

Challenging Locks

A list of locks on the current project appears at the bottom of the main TeamSource window. This shows current locks that have been granted, those that are requested, and those that are being confirmed.

Right-clicking an item list provides a menu that allows you to release a lock, change its comment, or extend it. You can also use this menu to yield a lock to another user in the queue. This menu has a further option called Verify Current Lock. Choosing this challenges the current lock.

When you challenge a lock within the time requested for it, you will be told how much of this time remains. If that time has elapsed, the user who acquired the lock will be notified of the challenge. The user is shown a dialog that he can use to release the lock or to extend the time for which he will keep it. If the user does not respond to this dialog within about two minutes, the lock is automatically released.

Using InstallShield Express

Here we will look at how to use the version of InstallShield that is shipped with C++Builder 5. We will talk you through how to make your own installation program for your finished application. We won't be able to cover every scenario for creating installation programs for every type of application, but we will give you a solid foundation on which to build. InstallShield comes with many features that you as a developer can make use of; the basics are the same for every application you develop, but the extras are there for you if you need them.

Installing InstallShield

InstallShield comes free with C++Builder and has since Version 1 of C++Builder. Most of you have at least looked at InstallShield, even if you've not taken a stab at making an installation program yourself for your new application.

If you haven't already installed InstallShield, put your C++Builder 5 CD-ROM in your CD-ROM drive and it should autostart. If it doesn't, browse to the folder called `Isxpress` on your CD-ROM drive and double-click the `Setupex.exe` file. This will start the installation program for InstallShield Express.

The version of InstallShield that comes with C++Builder is not the full retail version; it is a special version made for C++Builder, and some of the extra features of the full retail version are not available in this copy. Having said that, there is everything here that any developer could ever need to distribute their applications to the real world.

Getting Started in InstallShield

Now that you have installed InstallShield Express, you are ready to think a little bit about the type of installation you need for your application. For example, when you compiled your application in C++Builder, did you set the Linker options to Use Dynamic RTL? If so, you will have to include additional `.dll` files with your application. Additionally, if you selected Build with Runtime Packages on the Packages tab, you will also need to add additional files to your installation program; otherwise, it will not run on another computer. It is sometimes a tough call when choosing these options. The main advantage/disadvantage is that when these settings are unchecked, it will make your application bigger in size, by which I mean the `*.exe` or `*.dll` file that you are working on. Obviously the opposite applies when they are checked. But you will need to include extra files so that your program will work on another computer.

When you have finished developing your application, think about all of the files you need to make your application work on another computer. Extra files could be help files, Readme files, DLLs to which you have linked, and data files that you may need (database files, example files). When you have identified all the files you need, it might be a good idea to put them in a separate folder so that you know which files you need for your application.

The first time you use InstallShield, you will be asked which type of installation project you want to create. Click Create a New Setup Project in the screen. Next, give your setup project a meaningful name and choose to create this project in a new directory. This keeps your installation files and project files in one, easy-to-find place.

You are now presented with the main screen of InstallShield. You will see that it has a lot of options to make the installation program you need. These are arranged as a list and will be checked off as you complete them, so they are called the Setup Checklist by InstallShield.

The Setup Checklist (see Figure 29.4) is the part of the program that is presented to you after you have chosen to create a new project in InstallShield.

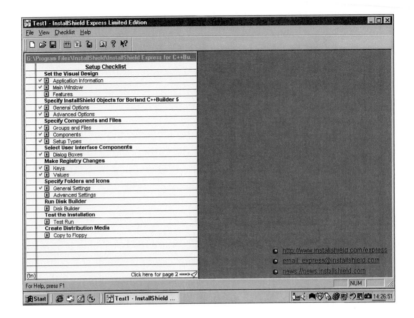

FIGURE 29.4

The main selection screen of InstallShield Express with all the options available to you.

Set the Visual Design

On the main screen, start by opening Application Information, and then type the name of the program that you want to appear in the Add/Remove Programs dialog.

If you choose your application executable, InstallShield will automatically add the specified executable file to the Program Files group in the Groups and Files dialog and create an icon for the executable file in the General Icon Settings dialog, as long as there is not already an entry in either dialog.

The version information should be set based on the version of your application. If you have set it in C++Builder, it will automatically be placed in this box for you. This version number is used by InstallShield to keep older application versions from overwriting new versions.

The company name should also be set appropriately. Your application will be set automatically in the Registry this way, and all installation paths and start menu entries will also have this name by default.

Check the destination directory. You may feel that there is a more appropriate location than the one InstallShield has chosen for you. The <Program Files> macro should be left at the start of the path. This location can vary on different machines because not everyone has his copy of Windows installed to C:\, and end users will be given the choice on where they want to install your application.

On the Main Window page, set the text and graphics to what you want to appear in the background while your application is installing. The image will have to be a bitmap and should be only 16 colors. You can use 256 colors, but you will get an error message from InstallShield. It is quite safe to ignore this and carry on with your project, as long as you are sure that all of your end users will have a screen color rate of 256 colors or greater. Otherwise the image will look distorted).

In the Features section, it is advisable that you leave Automatic Uninstaller turned on. The explanation of this feature is beyond the scope of this chapter.

Specify InstallShield Options for Borland C++Builder 5

In this section, select all of the items that apply to your application on the General page. You will know if you need any of these settings by determining the extra files you will need to add to your application to get it to work on another computer.

If you choose BDE or SQL-Links, you should also include BDE Control Panel File. If you used runtime packages, select all of those from the list that need to be included by your application.

If you choose the BDE Object, then it is a good idea to use a full BDE install. Otherwise, there will be problems with other BDE applications that use different database engines, and you may have difficulty upgrading. In this case, click the Settings button and go through the following steps of the BDE Setup Wizard to set up the BDE alias(es) that your application will need.

1. Click Next and add a new alias. Type the name of the alias exactly as it is on your PC.

2. Set the path, type, and necessary configuration parameters for each alias as you include them. It is usually best to put your database files in a directory under the installation target directory. Indicate this by preceding the path with <INSTALLDIR>. For example, if I were installing my database files into the directory data underneath my installation directory, I would enter <INSTALLDIR>\databases.

3. Click Finish at the end of the wizard, and this will make the necessary Registry settings to be configured on the target machine and ensure that necessary files are included.

To see all of the files that you have included, you can look under the Advanced tab.

Specify Components and Files

InstallShield collects files together into logical groups. You can call the groups anything you like, bearing in mind you should keep the names relevant for easy use. You may remember what group B1 means now, but will you remember in a few weeks time when you need to update your application? The file groups are not seen by the end user.

All files in the same group will be installed to the same directory by your end user when he installs your application. You will normally leave the File Update Method, found in the Properties section, set at its default value. There should be a group for your application files. There can be additional groups for components you checked in the previous step. If you use the BDE, you will need to create a file group for your database. The destination should be the same as you entered in the BDE Setup Wizard.

If you have any Windows system files, such as DLLs and OCXs, you should give them a destination of <WINSYSDIR>. Don't forget any .dll libraries that you imported into your project.

To get files into the relevant sections, you can open Explorer and drag and drop the files into the groups; it really is as simple as that.

To start Explorer, if it isn't already, click the Launch Explorer button on the Groups tab of the Specify Components and Files dialog (see Figure 29.5). Resize Explorer so that you can drag your files across. Then simply drop them in the relevant group.

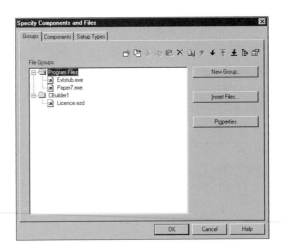

FIGURE 29.5
The Groups tab of the Specify Components and Files dialog of InstallShield Express showing two files in the Program Files group and one in the CBuilder1 group.

To make a new group, click New Group, type the name of the new group, and then select the new installation directory, if different from the default.

Select User Interface Components

The Components dialog allows you to create and modify your components (the building blocks of a custom setup) and write a description of each to help the user. We won't go into that in this section, though, because it gets very involved.

This is the fun part of InstallShield. In this section, you choose how you want your installation program to be presented to the end user; you have many features from which to choose.

It's a good idea to make sure that the dialogs you include are appropriate to the application that is going to be installed. The default settings are not always the ones you want.

A welcome bitmap always looks professional but, again, we have the trade-off in size. Adding a bitmap to your installation program will inevitably make it bigger, and if you are going to distribute it on the Internet, this has to be a considered factor. However, if it will be distributed via CD-ROM, bitmap away because size becomes irrelevant.

You also have a space for your software license and Readme documents. Many Internet shareware/freeware vendors advise that you put such information in your installation program as well as in the main Zip file of your application. While it is true that many end users never read the information contained in the software license and Readme files, if you have given them every chance of reading it, they can't complain.

Remember that when including text in these options, you must edit the text files so that they are at most 65 columns wide; otherwise, it won't be formatted in the same way you typed it. I use good old Notepad to do this and make sure word-wrap is turned off.

You also have the option to use Setup Type and Custom Setup dialogs. You should not use these unless you have included multiple application setup components.

If at anytime you are unsure what a particular setup option looks like to the user, you can click the Preview button to see what the style of dialog looks like. It won't be exactly the same as the one you are creating, but it will give you an idea what it looks like.

In almost all applications, you will want to have a Program Folder dialog. This is the folder that will hold the icons of your application. The user can change the name of this if he wants.

Normally, you will want to include the Start Copy and Progress dialogs in your installation program. This will assure your end users that the installation has not frozen, but is, in fact, installing your application.

Billboards are a good way to educate your customers about features of your product and other products that you or your company makes. The billboards are bitmaps with a similar name followed by a number. They will appear as the installation proceeds, but bear in mind two things:

- We have the issue about space again; the more bitmaps you include, the bigger your installation program becomes.

- How long will it take your application to install? There is no point in having billboards if your application is only going to take a few seconds to install; the end user won't have enough time to read them.

The Setup Complete dialog is only used to its full advantage if you include .dlls, .ocxs, or any runtime packages. This way, if a .dll or .ocx could not be updated at the time of installation, the user can be prompted to reboot the computer before using the application.

Make Registry Changes

In this section, you can set Registry information that your application needs—for example, default values that are stored in the Registry by your application and are needed when starting your application for the first time, or any other information that you need to store in the Registry.

To use this section, just choose the key section you use in your application (you should know this already, along with the necessary values needed). The following is the method for adding the key to your installation program. See Figure 29.6 for what the finished key layout looks like.

```
HKEY_CURRENT_USER\CBUILDER\TEST\INSTALL
```

You simply click the HKEY_CURRENT_USER key already available to you and then select Add Key. Then type the first part of the new key **CBUILDER** and so on until you have all the Registry paths needed to add your values.

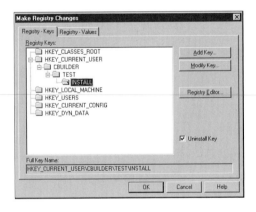

FIGURE 29.6

Set default keys and values in the Registry options.

If you make a mistake, you can either use the modify key button to change the text or just select the key you have made the mistake in and delete it.

If you want the Registry entries you have added to be removed by the uninstall feature of InstallShield, simply check the Uninstall Key check box.

To add a value to the Registry setting, first make sure you have selected the Registry key to which you want to add the value, click the Values tab, and add your value name and a default value. You also have to select the type of value you are using (String, Binary, DWORD He). In most cases, it will be String, but if it is different, you will know this at development time.

Specify Folders and Icons

This dialog allows you to specify the icons and folders that your program will use in the Windows Start Menu after installation. If you selected an executable in the Visual Design screen, it will appear here automatically. Any icons you want to add, as well as the default, must be added manually; otherwise, they will not appear when the end user installs your application.

To do this, click Run Command and, from the list shown in Figure 29.7, select the file for which you want to create an icon, enter any run parameters if needed, add a description that will be shown under the icon, and click Add Icon. Do this for all of the icons your application needs. Most files have default icons associated with them, such as Help files and Readme files.

FIGURE 29.7

Add icons to your application and documentation.

29

The Advanced tab allows you to choose where your icons will be placed. The Program Menu is the normal place to put an application. Choosing the Start menu will place your icons on the menu you see immediately after clicking the Start button in Windows. The Desktop option should be used with caution, but might be appropriate if your end users are not familiar with computers, or the application will be in constant use. But too many icons on the desktop will make it cluttered. The Startup option will cause your program to run after anybody logs in or boots the computer. Send To will put your application on the Send To menu that many applications use.

Run Disk Builder

Now for the bones of InstallShield. This is where all of your project files come together and become an installation program—much like a project in C++Builder.

First choose your desired media type. If you choose 1.44MB type, InstallShield will break down your installation program into 1.44MB disk size folders ready for you to copy to floppy disk(s). Later in this program you can get InstallShield to do the actual breakdown for you.

If you want to make a single file installation, CD-ROM media type is the best choice for you. When you have chosen your desired media type, click the Build button and the installation program will be created for you. If you receive errors while the building is taking place, correct them and click Build again. The project can be saved, so you can change the project as much as you like—add files, remove files, or make whatever changes you need to. When you are satisfied, come back to this section, select the media type, and click Build—perfect for future updates and most of the hard work has been done.

Create Distribution Media

If you are distributing on floppy disk(s), you can use this dialog to make the actual disk copies for you. The options are pretty straightforward. Select the directory or drive you want the disks copied to and then click Copy All Disk Images.

I should point out that you don't need to do this part of InstallShield if you don't want to because your disk images have already been created in the Build process and have been saved in the folder specified by you when setting up the installation project. All you have to do is copy the contents of each folder, marked Disk1 for Disk 1 and so on, to your floppy drive. Make sure you have enough floppies formatted with appropriate labels on them first.

The version of InstallShield Express that comes with C++Builder 5 does not include an option for making a single-file executable. You can purchase Package for the Web from InstallShield corporation (http://www.InstallShield.com) to do this for you. You can also use a package, such as WinZip or PK-Zip. Commercial versions of both of these programs allow you to create self-extracting executable programs and run a program from the archive after extraction. This method is almost essential if you are going to distribute your application on the Internet because the smaller your application's total size, the more likely it will be downloaded.

Testing

When you have created your installation program, you will need to find a PC on which to test it. I always test the installation program on the same computer as the installation project first, just to make sure I'm satisfied with the user interface (bitmaps, Readme file layout, and so on). Then, if I need to make any changes, I can do so easily, rebuild the project, and test again until I am happy—making sure that I have uninstalled the prior installation first.

When you are satisfied with the layout of the installation program, you can then go to another computer to test the actual installation of your application. Ideally, it would be best to install on a clean version of Windows each time. Unfortunately, we don't live in an ideal world, so make do as best you can.

Don't worry if your installation doesn't work the first time; see what is wrong and then go back to your computer that has the project files on it, make the necessary adjustments, rebuild, and try again until you get it right.

After you have successfully installed your application, it is well worth the time to make sure that all of the aspects of your application work correctly and that all components/files have been installed correctly. Ideally, try installing to different disks, different directories, and with different component options (if you have set them). This can take a long time, but is well worth the effort. There is nothing worse than an irate end user who can't get your application installed after downloading it from the Internet.

There you have it, a look into InstallShield Express. As with all programs, it's a good idea to use it before you really have to. That way, you can make as many mistakes as you like without the stress of a deadline to meet.

Summary

This chapter, combined with Chapter 28, "Software Distribution," should give you a good insight into the installation, marketing, distribution, and maintenance of software. Although all of these techniques have been discussed with reference to C++Builder, they are applicable to software developed with any compiler/RAD tool. The use of these methods can greatly enhance your software and your users' opinion of it.

We looked at methods for installation and maintenance of your software, using ClickTeam's Install Maker, Cabinet and info files, and InstallShield Express. We also discussed software maintenance, focusing on creating and distributing software updates and patches, and finally we looked at source code control using TeamSource, the new version control system included with C++Builder 5 Enterprise.

29

SOFTWARE INSTALLATION AND UPDATES

Knowledge Base

PART

VI

IN THIS PART

Tips, Tricks, and How Tos

Pete Pedersen
Khalid Almannai
Paul Gustavson
Phillip H. Blanton II
John MacSween

CHAPTER

30

IN THIS CHAPTER

- **Making the Enter Key Simulate the Tab Key**
- **Determining the OS Version**
- **Programming Using Floating-Point Numbers**
- **Implementing Splash Screens**
- **Preventing More than One Instance of an Application from Running**
- **Working with Drag-and-Drop**
- **Capturing the Screen**
- **Implementing a** `TJoyStick` **Component**
- **Creating a Windows System Monitor-Like Application**
- **Examining a Soundex Application**
- **Using Tree View Components**
- **Implementing an Icon Extraction Utility**
- **Creating a Windows Explorer-Like Application**
- **Working with NT Services**
- **Using Cryptography**
- **Creating a World Daylight Clock**

The complete text for this chapter appears on the CD-ROM.

A Real-World Example

John MacSween

IN THIS CHAPTER

- Examining a World Wave Statistics Program
- Examining the Source Code
- Examining the Code for `TMainUnit`
- Making Some Improvements

The complete text for this chapter appears on the CD-ROM.

Appendix

IN THIS PART

Information Sources

Dan Butterfield
Jarrod Hollingworth

IN THIS APPENDIX

- **Borland Web Sites**
- **CodeCentral**
- **Discussion Lists and Forums**
- **Newsgroups**
- **Web Sites**
- **Books and Magazines**
- **Conferences and User Groups**

This appendix lists many useful resources for C++Builder developers, whether they be printed magazines and books or online component library, articles, or magazine Web sites. A complete and up-to-date list of online references, containing links to more than 70 Web sites at the time of the writing of this book, is available on the "Resources" page of this book's Web site at `http://www.bcb5book.force9.co.uk/`.

By using the wealth of information available in the resources listed here and elsewhere, you will surely be able to find the answer to any C++Builder-related question that you ask.

Borland Web Sites

The Borland Web sites hold some of the best information for C++Builder developers anywhere on the Internet, as you might expect. In a great move, Borland has developed its community Web site, a place to be frequented by all Windows developers, C++Builder, and other Borland product developers in particular.

Borland Community Web Site

The Borland Community Web site can be found at `http://community.borland.com` and is perhaps the most important Web site for C++Builder developers on the entire Internet. With regular articles from Borland staff and others on everything including how-tos, technical articles, industry news, reviews, and the latest information on recent and upcoming products, it's more than worthy to be your default browser home page.

Figure A.1 shows the main community page. From it you can drill down to particular articles of interest, first by product area (C++, Delphi, Java, Linux), and then by neighborhood (components, database, distributed computing, multimedia/graphics, and so on). and topic. There are also sections on news, street talk, TIPs (Technical Information Papers), FAQs (Frequently Asked Questions), white papers, articles, and more.

You must sign up as a Borland Community member to access the Downloads page, get involved in the online chats, access CodeCentral (covered later in the "CodeCentral" section), and participate in the surveys.

TIP

One of the great opportunities to learn about some of the advanced features of C++Builder is to fire questions at the Borland R&D team through the regular live chats that are held on specific topics. The schedule of upcoming live chats is available from the Chat page. Some previous topics include the C++Builder compiler, libraries, debugger, and ActiveX. Transcripts of past chats are available.

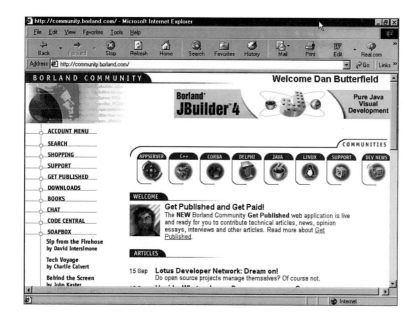

FIGURE A.1

The main page of the Borland Community Web site at http://community.borland.com.

From the C++Builder area, you can access a large list of C++Builder FAQs and TIPs. Check these before searching for solutions to your problems in other areas.

Due to the similarities between C++Builder and Delphi, you should also look at the Delphi articles and information on the Borland Web sites. The "Migration from Delphi" section in Chapter 1, "Introduction to C++Builder," can help you understand Delphi code by providing comparisons between C++ and Object Pascal (Delphi code).

At the time of the writing of this book, Borland is offering to pay $100 U.S. for articles published. If you feel that you have something to contribute to this area, please do! For full details, see http://community.borland.com/getpublished.

Borland Main Web Site

The main Borland Web site can be found at http://www.borland.com and offers a wealth of product-related information. You can get to the C++Builder page from the C++Builder link or by going directly to http://www.borland.com/bcppbuilder, where you'll find a list of links to C++Builder product and support information, additional resources, and news and press articles. Some of the links point to articles in the Borland Community Web site and vice versa.

From the Tools & Components link in the Additional Resources section on the C++Builder main page, you'll find a list of hundreds of third-party tool providers. These providers produce components and other software to assist you in the development of your application.

The Quickstart and Developer's Guide manuals that ship with C++Builder are available from the Borland Web site. This allows you to view them wherever you are. You can find them by clicking the Documentation link from the main C++Builder page.

The latest updates and patches for C++Builder are available for download from the Downloads page. From the List Servers/Mailing Lists link, you can sign up to receive the latest information on technical issues via email and to be notified when updates and patches are released.

In summary, be sure to check the Borland Community Web site regularly and use the resources available in both Borland Web sites to your advantage.

CodeCentral

CodeCentral is a Web-based repository for code samples related to all Borland products. The idea is that anyone who has discovered a solution to a technical/programming problem with a Borland product can post example code along with an explanation. Anyone can post code on any Borland tool-related subject, and a few searches of the archive will reveal contributions from several of the authors of this book.

This obviously has great potential as a resource, so we'll take a brief tour of the CodeCentral Web site. The main page of the site can be accessed from the Borland Community Web site (see the "Borland Web Sites" section earlier in this appendix) and is shown in Figure A.2 (titles and banners not shown). Note that you must be a member of the Borland Community site (membership is free) to use this service.

The first thing to note is the link to a license agreement. This essentially states that you use code from CodeCentral at your own risk and explains copyright issues.

Further down the page is a table showing the number of articles/examples available for each Borland product, in several categories. The product and category headings are hyperlinked, so it's possible to list articles in three ways: by one category for all products, by one product for all categories, or by one category for one product, as demonstrated in Figure A.2.

The hyperlinks immediately above this table allow you to find out who is the most popular author, view latest submissions, see the most popular downloads, and display usage statistics for the CodeCentral site.

Finally, there are two icons between the license agreement link and the article links mentioned previously. These icons, a magnifying glass over a document and a pen and notebook, are links to a search page (CodeCentral: Finder) and submission page, respectively. The main part of the search page is shown in Figure A.3.

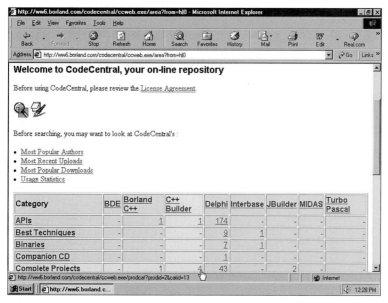

FIGURE A.2

The main page of Borland's CodeCentral Web site.

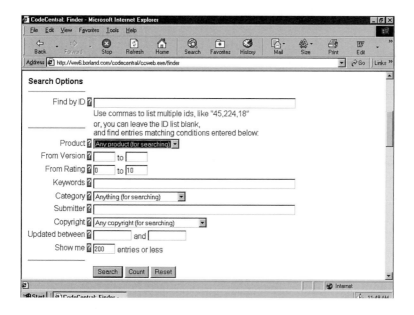

FIGURE A.3

The Finder page of Borland's CodeCentral Web site.

The CodeCentral Finder allows you to perform very detailed searches to find articles relevant to your particular Borland product problem. The search options are explained very well at the bottom of the search page, so we won't describe them here.

Discussion Lists and Forums

Along with newsgroups (see the section "Newsgroups," later in this appendix, for newsgroups relevant to C++Builder), email discussion lists and Web-based forums are extremely useful resources for solving any C++Builder problems you may encounter. Good explanations of problems posted to active discussion lists will generally generate an expert solution within hours. Even if some threads don't appear to be particularly interesting, it's often possible to find a solution to a problem you didn't know you had.

Web-Based Forums

There are several Web-based forums available, though these are mostly general C++ forums. Forums are very similar to newsgroups in that whole message threads can be viewed, and it's easy to "pop in" to ask a question. The advantages of Web-based forums are that they can be used from anywhere with Internet access (newsgroup availability depends on the particular newsfeed used) and message archives are readily available at the site.

Several good C++-oriented forums with brief descriptions are provided in the following list.

- *Delphi Forums C/C++ Forum* —This is an active C/C++ forum with at least one new post per day, and it is hosted by Delphi Forums. There are four main areas: beginner C/C++, advanced C/C++, jobs, and book/product/site reviews. `http://forums.delphi.com/ab_cplus/start`
- *Dr. Dobb's Journal C/C++ Discussion Forum*—This site has reasonable activity, with roughly one message posted per day. `http://www.ddj.com/topics/cpp`

Some other forums with low activity are included in the following list.

- `http://pa.pulze.com/cppdir/wwwboard`   This is the "Programmer's Archive C++ Discussion Board." It has very low activity, having only 5 messages posted in 6 months.
- `http://www.projectperl.com/service/boards/c/`   This C++ forum is one of several hosted by "ProjectPerl." It has low activity, with only 11 messages in a year.
- `http://www.programmerspractice.com/cpp/cpp_toc.htm`   A very low activity C++ forum.

- *PrestoNet C/C++ Discussion Group*   This site hosts several forums, one of which is C++Builder specific. It is apparently still active, but there have been no new messages since March 1999.

Email Discussion Lists

Email discussion lists are an old concept but are still very popular. The advantage they have is that questions and answers are emailed to subscribers directly, so you don't have to check a newsgroup or Web site for an answer to your question. Because it's necessary to subscribe to email discussion lists, there is often a strong sense of community amongst list members that generally isn't seen on newsgroups or Web-based forums. A big disadvantage, of course, is that you receive a lot of unwanted/irrelevant email when you're subscribed to an active list.

There is really only one C++Builder discussion list worth subscribing to, and that is the list administered by Jon Jenkinson of "The Bits" C++Builder Web site. This list is extremely active, with 10–50 messages per day, and it is particularly notable as the place where initial discussions were held on the creation of this book.

To subscribe to this list, which is hosted by Topica, point your browser to `http://www.top-ica.com/lists/cbuilder/subscribe`. Alternatively, you can send an email message to `cbuilder-subscribe@topica.com`.

There are some additional email discussion lists noted on the Borland Web site (see `http://www.borland.com/contact/listserv.html` and `http://www.borland.com/contact/otherlst.html`), but these have very low activity.

Newsgroups

Borland hosts a large set of newsgroups, covering just about every aspect of all their products. These newsgroups can be accessed via `forums.inprise.com`—Borland's own news server.

Table A.1 contains an alphabetical list of newsgroups most relevant to C++Builder users, along with message post counts and averages as an indication of activity.

More information on these sites may be found on the Borland Web site at `http://www.inprise.com/newsgroups`, including general newsgroup etiquette and advice (`http://www.inprise.com/newsgroups/guide.html`), a description of topics discussed on each newsgroup (`http://www.inprise.com/newsgroups/cppbnewsdesc.html`), and where to look for searchable archives (`http://www.inprise.com/newsgroups/ngsearch.html`).

TABLE A.1   Relevant Borland Newsgroup Activity for September 2000

Newsgroup	Total posts	Average posts/day
borland.public.codecentral	119	4
borland.public.community	151	5
borland.public.cppbuilder.activex	341	11
borland.public.cppbuilder.announce	5	<1
borland.public.cppbuilder.commandlinetools	320	11
borland.public.cppbuilder.database	47	2
borland.public.cppbuilder.database.ado	112	4
borland.public.cppbuilder.database.desktop	396	13
borland.public.cppbuilder.database.interbaseexpress	116	4
borland.public.cppbuilder.database.multi-tier	38	1
borland.public.cppbuilder.database.sqlservers	123	4
borland.public.cppbuilder.graphics	332	11
borland.public.cppbuilder.ide	861	29
borland.public.cppbuilder.internationalization	7	<1
borland.public.cppbuilder.internet	491	16
borland.public.cppbuilder.language	1955	65
borland.public.cppbuilder.ms_compatibility	108	4
borland.public.cppbuilder.multimedia	22	<1
borland.public.cppbuilder.non-technical	865	29
borland.public.cppbuilder.oodesign	19	<1
borland.public.cppbuilder.thirdpartytools	225	8
borland.public.cppbuilder.upgrade	61	2
borland.public.cppbuilder.vcl.components	47	2
borland.public.cppbuilder.vcl.components.using	1348	45
borland.public.cppbuilder.vcl.components.writing	303	10
borland.public.cppbuilder.winapi	1189	40
borland.public.install.cppbuilder	101	3
borland.public.interbase	504	17
borland.public.kylix.non-technical	960	32
borland.public.midas	526	18
borland.public.tasm	94	3

TABLE A.1   Continued

Newsgroup	Total posts	Average posts/day
borland.public.teamsource	64	2
borland.public.xml	53	2
inprise.public.corba.cppbuilder	155	5
inprise.public.midas	6	<1
interbase.public.interbaseexpress	13	<1

There are also several C++-related newsgroups that are available from most news servers. These are listed in Table A.2.

TABLE A.2   Relevant C++ Newsgroup Activity for September 2000

Newsgroup	Total posts	Average posts/day
comp.lang.c++	2135	71
comp.lang.c++.moderated	642	21
comp.std.c++	268	9

Web Sites

Perhaps one of the best resources for information on programming with C++Builder is the multitude of Web sites containing technical articles, how-tos, answers to frequently asked questions, reusable components, and third-party tools.

There are a few C++Builder-related Web rings. Web rings allow you to navigate among a list of Web sites dedicated to a particular subject. The sites that are part of the Web ring contain Web ring navigation links, usually at the bottom of the Web page, so that you can easily jump to other Web sites in the ring. The C++Builder-related Web rings are shown in the following list.

- *Borland C++Builder Webring*—Over 40 Web sites
- *The C++Builder Programmer's Ring*—Over 20 Web sites
- *The Delphi Corner*—Over 70 Web sites
- *Delphi Developers Webring*—Over 10 Web sites

These Web rings can be found by searching for Borland at http://webring.yahoo.com/.

How-Tos and Technical Articles

Along with the many component repository sites, there are a large number of C++Builder Web sites containing how-tos, technical articles, and answers to frequently asked questions. Some of the best Web sites are provided in the following list.

- Dr.Bob's C++Builder Gate —`http://www.drbob42.com/cbuilder`   Bob Swart and Ruurd Pels, who both are authors of this book, run the C++Builder Gate Web site. It is perhaps one of the best-known independent C++Builder Web sites and is regularly updated with useful articles.

- The Bits C++Builder Information and Tutorials Site—`http://www.thebits.org`   This is perhaps one of the best sites for tutorials on various C++Builder topics.

- BCBDEV.COM—`http://www.bcbdev.com`   This site contains many great articles and answers to frequently asked questions.

- Bytamin-C The C++ Developers Site!—`http://www.bytamin-c.com`   Bytamin-C contains some good articles, how-tos, tips and tricks, reviews, and components. A good all-around site.

- BCB–CAQ—`http://bcbcaq.freeservers.com`   The BCB CAQ (Commonly Asked Questions) site contains information about various C++Builder components and other related programming issues. It is maintained by Damon Chandler, one of the authors of this book.

- Just Another Web Site about C++ Builder—`http://www.leunen.com/cbuilder`   This site contains a few useful tips and articles.

Component Repositories

There are many component repository Web sites that contain very useful components that you can use in your applications, saving you time (and money) by not having to develop the functionality yourself that they provide. Some components are free, and others are sold as shareware or commercial products.

Because C++Builder can compile and use Delphi code, C++Builder developers have an abundance of third-party components from which to choose. The following Web sites are just a few of the many that contain components and tools that you can use.

- Codecorner—`http://www.codecorner.com`   CodeCorner lists over 240 components in well-organized categories.

- ComponentSource—`http://www.componentsource.com`   ComponentSource contains thousands of components for all development environments, including Delphi and C++Builder and ActiveX components.

- Delphi Pages—http://www.delphipages.com Comprehensive component and resource site for C++Builder and Delphi, listing over 1,500 components in various categories.

- DelphiSource—http://www.delphisource.com DelphiSource contains a large archive of components for C++Builder and Delphi in many categories.

- Delphi Super Page—http://delphi.icm.edu.pl/ This is probably *the* component resource for all versions of C++Builder and Delphi. It contains over 5,500 files to download and attracts some 30,000+ visitors per week.

- Indy (formerly known as Winshoes) Free Internet Components— http://www.nevrona.com/Indy Indy is a set of free Internet components and comes with full source.

- Internet Component Suite—http://users.swing.be/francois.piette/indexuk.htm Internet Component Suite is a freeware set of components for adding HTTP, FTP, NMTP, and other Internet protocol communication to your application.

- Raize Software Solutions, Inc.—http://www.raize.com Home of the Raize Components native VCL component suite, containing over 90 visual components, and the CodeSite debugging tool.

- RX Library—http://www.rxlib.com Home of the RxLib component set, which contains a large number of visual and data-aware components and objects and routines with full source.

- TurboPower Software Company—http://www.turbopower.com TurboPower is renowned for its award-winning component suites and tools. Some of its products include Abbrevia, a set of data compression components; AsyncProfessional for serial, FTP, Fax, and paging communications; Internet Professional for Internet communications; LockBox for data encryption; Orpheus, a collection of over 100 specialized components; and SysTools.

- VCL Crawler—http://www.vclcrawler.com This site is a relative newcomer. At the time of the writing of this book, it has over 100 components for download.

- Woll2Woll—http://www.woll2woll.com Woll2Woll produces several award-winning component suites for C++Builder and Delphi, including InfoPower, a set of greatly enhanced data-aware components including grid and combo-lookup controls, and many other components.

A

INFORMATION SOURCES

Books and Magazines

Perhaps the most popular source of information on software development is found in books and magazines. Books tend to contain a large amount of relevant information, and magazines provide a constant stream of regular articles. Both cover a wide variety of topics.

In the following sections, we will look at several books and magazines related to C++Builder. Detailed information on books, online purchasing, and reader reviews can be found at reputable online book stores, such as Amazon.com (`http://www.amazon.com`), FatBrain (`http://www.fatbrain.com`), or Barnes and Noble (`http://www.bn.com/`).

> **Tip**
>
> Excerpts from many books published by Macmillan USA imprints (Sams, Que, and so on) can be found at InformIT. The excerpts include selected chapters and, in some cases, the entire book! Join for free and read at `http://www.informit.com`.

C++Builder Books

To date, there have been about a dozen books written about C++Builder. The driving force behind this book was to create a new type of C++Builder reference book, containing material not found anywhere else, to add to the relatively short list of printed reference material already available.

The three best C++Builder books available are listed here with brief descriptions of contents and focus.

- *Borland C++Builder 4 Unleashed*, Reisdorph, K. (1999), Sams, pp. 1248, ISBN 0672315106—This book covers many topics, from beginner to advanced experience levels, with the focus on intermediate level. It covers databases and distributed programming quite well, which account for almost 30 percent of the content. *Borland C++Builder 4 Unleashed* is a perfect companion to *C++Builder 5 Developer's Guide*.

- *C++Builder How-To: The Definitive C++Builder Problem Solver*, Miano, J., Cabanski, T. and Howe, H. (1997), Waite Group, pp. 822, ISBN 157169109X—Somewhat dated, this book still contains many useful how-tos and techniques for C++Builder programmers. When it was first published, it was *the* C++Builder book to own. Unfortunately, it only covers features of Borland C++Builder 3, many of which have changed in versions 4 and 5.

- *Sams Teach Yourself Borland C++Builder 4 in 24 Hours*, Reisdorph, K. & Gill, B. (1999), Sams, pp. 451, ISBN 0672316269—Aimed at beginner-intermediate programmers, this book is all about learning how to program with C++Builder. It provides a general overview to the most common programming tasks and techniques.

Due to the similarities between C++Builder and Delphi, books written on Delphi are also very relevant. The only real difference between C++Builder and Delphi is the programming language itself. If you are versed in C++, it is not too difficult to understand Delphi's Object

Pascal. The "Migration from Delphi" section in Chapter 1, "Introduction to C++Builder," will assist in understanding the differences between C++ and Object Pascal.

For details on the other C++Builder related books available, search for *C++ Builder*, *C++Builder*, and *Delphi* on the online bookstores previously mentioned. The full copy of the original *Charlie Calvert's Borland C++Builder Unleashed* book, *Sams Teach Yourself Delphi 4 in 21 Days*, and excerpts from *Sams Teach Yourself Borland C++Builder 4 in 24 Hours* is available at InformIt.

General C++ Books

There are huge numbers of C++ books available. The most popular (and arguably the best) are listed here with brief comments.

- *Thinking in C++, Vol. 1* (Second Edition), Eckel, B. (2000), Prentice-Hall, pp. 720, ISBN 0139798099—In this, the second edition of his *Thinking in C++* tutorial, Bruce Eckel explains the ins and outs of the C++ programming language in a clear and concise manner that has proved invaluable to novices and experts alike. It is provided for free on the companion CD-ROM that ships with *C++Builder Professional and Enterprise*, and it is also available online from `http://www.mindview.net/ThinkingInCPP2e.html`.

- *Effective C++ (2nd Ed.)*, Meyers, S. (1997) Addison-Wesley, pp. 304, ISBN 0201924889—This is also a must-have book for C++ developers. It isn't designed to teach the C++ language but, with great use of examples, it gives tips on improving your C++ programming techniques, particularly class design.

- *The C++ Programming Language* (Third Edition), Stroustrup, B. (1997), Addison-Wesley, pp. 928, ISBN 0201889544—The creator of C++, Bjarne Stroustrup, presents the full specification of the language and standard template library. This is not really a book for the beginner, but it is the ultimate C++ reference and is essential for everyone who is serious about programming with C++.

For details on other C++-related books, search for *C++* on the online bookstores previously mentioned. The full copy of *Sams Teach Yourself C++ in 21 Days,* Second Edition and various excerpts from other C++ books are available at InformIt.

Magazines

There are several magazines relevant to C++Builder. Some are devoted entirely to C++Builder, while others contain articles on C++ in general. There are also several Delphi magazines. Some of the most relevant magazines are described in the following list.

- *CbuilderZine*—A good-looking online magazine devoted to C++Builder, with regular tutorial articles, recent Borland news, new product and book reviews, and a component

A

download area. `http://www.cbuilderzine.com`. Additionally, there is also a DelphiZine, which can be found at `http://www.delphizine.com`.

- *C++Builder Developer's Journal*—Managed by Kent Reisdorph, author of several C++Builder books, this journal contains many high-quality articles from prominent developers each month. It is available in print via subscription. Registered customers can access back issues online. For a list of back issues, subscription, and more information, see `http://www.reisdorph.com`.

- *C/C++ Users Journal*—This monthly magazine is available in print, and several articles each month are made available online. `http://www.cuj.com`

Conferences and User Groups

Around the world, several Borland conferences (typically known as BorCon) are held every year. The largest of these is held in the U.S. The eleventh annual conference was held in July 2000 and attracted over 2,200 attendees. Conferences are also held in Australia, France, Germany, and the UK.

These conferences are feature packed. Over several days, dozens of tutorials and technical sessions are presented on all Borland products—including C++Builder—by Borland and independent experts from around the world. Often, the hardest part is deciding which of the great sessions to attend! Apart from the tutorials and technical sessions, there are opening and closing keynotes, product addresses, exhibitors sessions, informal "birds of a feather" sessions, special (not to be missed) events, and a computer lab that's provided for the convenience of the attendees.

The conferences are one of the best places to get intense training on a variety of topics and talk to Borland staff, C++Builder developers, authors, and speakers in the flesh. For information on the upcoming conferences, see `http://www.borland.com/events/`.

If you can't get to a conference, attending a C++Builder, Delphi, or Borland user group is a great alternative. I'd recommend joining one, in any case. There are many such groups in the U.S. and around the world. For what is typically a small membership fee, the user group holds regular meetings at which tutorials and technical sessions are given by group members, and informal discussions take place. This is a great way to learn and build on your experience. For a list of user groups, see `http://www.borland.com/programs/usergroups/uglist.html`.

INDEX

SPECIAL NOTE TO READERS

Chapters 2, 4, 8, 11, 14, 18, 22, 28, 30, and 31 are located only on the CD accompanying this book. Please note that in the back-of-the-book index where you're now located, the pages for information found in these chapters are marked by CD:. For example, if you see a page number like this—CD:1771—you will go to page 1771 on the CD. CD: is not included on the page numbers located on the CD. Instead, the page numbers appear as usual.

SYMBOLS